DICTIONARY OF QUOTATIONS AND PROVERBS

THE EVERYMAN EDITION

DICTIONARY OF QUOTATIONS AND PROVERBS

THE EVERYMAN EDITION

COMPILED BY
D. C. BROWNING
MA (GLASGOW), BA, B LITT (OXON)

CHANCELLOR
PRESS

The Everyman Dictionary of Quotations and Proverbs was
first published in Great Britain in 1951

This volume first published in Great Britain in 1982 by
Octopus Books Limited

under license from

J. M. Dent & Sons Limited
Aldine House
33 Welbeck Street
London W1

This edition published in 1988 by
Chancellor Press
59 Grosvenor Street
London W1

ISBN 1 85152 074 0

Printed in Austria

CONTENTS

INTRODUCTION

CONTAINING just over 10,000 quotations and proverbs, this dictionary is to all intents and purposes an entirely new compilation. That, of course, is not to deny its debt to other dictionaries, including its predecessor in Everyman's Library. But fashions change in quotation as in everything else, and by modern standards the dictionaries of a past generation seem ill-proportioned. For example, the previous *Everyman's Dictionary of Quotations* allotted over 200 entries to Byron, and over 70 to Young (of *Night Thoughts* fame), while Browning had only seven, and Kipling only ten.

It has been the editor's aim to readjust the balance by giving less space to old-fashioned authors and more to those now popular. The net has also been cast wider, for extracts are given from nearly a thousand authors — about double the number that appeared in this volume's predecessor. The newcomers are by no means all modern, for they include — to take a few names at random — Aubrey, Jane Austen, Bismarck, Beau Brummell, Catullus, Clough, De Quincey, Evelyn, Kenneth Grahame, Hogg, Lang, Lear, Luther, Maeterlinck, Marryat, Nelson, Patmore, Sallust, Spooner, Traherne, Queen Victoria, Artemus Ward, Xenophon, and Zola.

VARIETY OF CONTENTS.
The quotations are of the most varied kind. There are famous sayings, from Lord Acton's 'Power tends to corrupt, and absolute power corrupts absolutely' to Zamoyski's 'The king reigns, but does not govern'; the greatest lines and passages of the best-known poems are quoted, from *Paradise Lost* (which provides 121 extracts) to *Mary had a little Lamb*, and including such old forgotten favourites as *Somebody's Darling* and 'I have no pain, dear mother, now'; solitary tags like 'The villain still pursued her' or 'It's a long time between drinks' are given a local habitation and a name; and for the more frivolous there is a small but select collection of limericks in the Anonymous section.

Among the newcomers, perhaps the most interesting are the extracts from Mr. Churchill's war speeches, where the most famous of his phrases are given with context and date—'I have nothing to offer but blood, toil, tears, and sweat'; 'Never in the field of human conflict was so much owed by so many to so few'; 'Give us the tools and we will finish the job'; 'Some chicken; some neck.' Readers who have a weakness for detective fiction may find the Holmesiana worthy of study—'You see, but you do not observe'; 'The curious incident of the dog'; 'You know my methods'; '"Elementary," said he.'

TWO INNOVATIONS.
In the setting-out of the quotations there are two innovations which it is hoped will add to the usefulness of the volume. The first is the indication of the calling and nationality of each author. In most dictionaries of quotations the only clue to an author's identity is the date, and even well-informed readers may be at a loss with some of the less-known British or American names.

The second innovation is the giving of day and month, as well as year, of each author's birth and death. This, it is hoped, will be helpful to journalists and others who want the exact date for centenary celebrations and similar purposes. All dates have been checked and rechecked, and if they are found at variance with those of any other work of reference, it should be remembered that dates are sometimes in dispute.

ORDER AND ARRANGEMENT.

The arrangement of the authors is alphabetical, as before, a single list being used and foreign authors put in their place among English ones. The name under which each is listed is the one most commonly used. For instance, quotations from *Alice in Wonderland* are give under 'Lewis Carroll,' to which there is a cross-reference from the author's real name, C. L. Dodgson. Similarly, Latin authors are given under their familiar anglicised names, with the Latin form in brackets, e.g. 'Horace (Quintus Horatius Flaccus).' Quotations of doubtful authorship are placed at the end and grouped according to literary forms.

Within each author, the arrangement of the quotations is as far as possible chronological. The works of Shakespeare, however, appear in alphabetical order. In the case of the Bible the usual order of the books has been followed.

ALLOTMENT OF SPACE.

In allotting space among the different authors, the editor has tried to hold a just balance and to avoid favouritism of any kind. It is instructive to see how the numbers work out, though it must always be borne in mind that the 'quotability' of an author is not a reliable index of his greatness, and that it is not necessarily the finest passages that have become the most familiar. Shakespeare, of course, has the lion's share, with nearly 1,300 entries; indeed, the play of *Hamlet* alone, with 180 entries, supplies more quotations than any other single author except Milton, who has just over 250, though the Bible exceeds this with 567.

Pope comes third of the authors, with over 150 entries, and Tennyson fourth, a little behind him. Then there is a big gap till we come to Browning and Wordsworth, both about 90. Johnson, Byron, and Kipling have just over 80, and Burns just under. Dickens has 70 and Walter Scott 60, with Dryden in between. Coleridge, Cowper, Gilbert, and Goldsmith are all in the fifties. Shelley, Keats, and Lewis Carroll have a little over 40 each, Gray and Stevenson a little under. Among foreign writers Horace and Virgil easily top the list with 25 each.

PROVERBS.

Like the quotations, the proverbs are an entirely fresh selection, in which quality rather than quantity has been aimed at. It would have been quite easy to have increased the number ten times over, but the list would have lost instead of gaining in usefulness. There has been ample space for including all that are well-known or of special interest, and the opportunity has been taken of indicating the earliest appearance of each and also explaining obscure points. It is often the pithiest proverbs whose meaning is not at once apparent. For example, 'Back may trust, but belly won't,' 'Let alone makes many a loon,' 'No money, no Swiss,' all call for explanatory comment.

Annotation is particularly necessary in the case of Scottish proverbs. For instance, the familiar 'Jouk and let the jaw gae by' was given in the previous volume as 'Joke and let the jaw gae o'er,' apparently under the impression that the 'jaw' was a 'telling-off' instead of a pailful of slops. Foreign proverbs have, of course, been provided with a translation.

INDEX.

It is hoped that the value of the index has been increased by incorporating the proverbs with the quotations. This enables the proverbs to be much more fully and clearly indexed.

Every effort has been made to choose the right key-words, that is, those that form the salient point in each quotation, and are the most memorable part of it. Generally speaking, nouns have been preferred to verbs or adjectives for reference words, but when the noun is quite colourless, like 'man' or 'thing' there did not seem much point in indexing all its occurences. Foreign and Old English words are inserted alphabetically with the rest, Greek letters being identified with their nearest English equivalents. On an average there are three index references per quotation, but, of course, the number varies with the size of the quotation; Hamlet's 'To be or not to be' speech requires 48.

USES OF THE DICTIONARY.

It will be observed that the index takes up a very large proportion of the total space. This is necessary if the reader is to depend upon it for two of his main objectives—selecting suitable quotations for special occasions and obeying the time-honoured admonition, 'Always verify your references.' A further use of the dictionary is that it forms a series of samples giving an idea of what each author is like. It is difficult to run over, for example, the list of extracts from Dickens or Johnson without wanting to read the books they are taken from; and there is no one so widely read but that he may make pleasant discoveries among authors that are new to him.

1950   D.C.B.

For the fifth reprint the whole volume has been carefully gone over and one or two errors and misprints corrected. A few dates of early authors have been newly inserted or adjusted in conformity with the latest researches, and dates have also been filled in of those moderns who have died since the work was first published.

1965   D.C.B.

QUOTATIONS

QUOTATIONS

ABRANTES, DUC D', see Junot, Andoche

ACCIUS, LUCIUS, Roman dramatist, 170–86? B.C.

1 Oderint dum metuant. – Let them hate as long as they fear. *Atreus.*

ACTON, JOHN EMERICH EDWARD DALBERG ACTON, 1st BARON, English historian, 10 Jan. 1834–19 June, 1902

2 Power tends to corrupt, and absolute power corrupts absolutely.
Great men are almost always bad men.
 Historical Essays and Studies, appendix.

ADAMS, CHARLES FOLLEN, US poet, 21 April, 1842–8 March, 1918

3 I haf von funny leedly poy
Vot gomes schust to mine knee:
Der queerest schap, der createst rogue
As efer you dit see. *Yawcob Strauss.*

ADAMS, FRANKLIN PIERCE, US journalist, 15 Nov. 1881–23 March, 1960

4 Go, lovely Rose that lives its little hour!
Go, little booke! and let who will be clever!
Roll on! From yonder ivy-mantled tower
The moon and I could keep this up for ever.
 Lines on and from "Bartlett's Familiar Quotations."

ADAMS, JOHN QUINCY, US President, 11 July, 1767–23 Feb. 1848

5 Think of your forefathers! Think of your posterity!
 Speech at Plymouth, Massachusetts, 22 Dec. 1802.

ADAMS, SARAH FLOWER, English poetess, 22 Feb. 1805–14 Aug. 1848

6 Nearer, my God, to Thee,
Nearer to Thee!
E'en though it be a cross
That raiseth me.
 Nearer, my God, to Thee.

ADDISON, JOSEPH, English author, 1 May, 1672–17 June, 1719

7 And, pleased the Almighty's orders to perform,
Rides in the whirlwind and directs the storm. *The Campaign, 291.*

8 The spacious firmament on high,
With all the blue ethereal sky,
And spangled heavens, a shining frame,
Their great Original proclaim. *Ode.*

9 Soon as the evening shades prevail,
The moon takes up the wondrous tale,
And nightly to the listening earth
Repeats the story of her birth. *Ibid.*

10 Poetic fields encompass me around,
And still I seem to tread on classic ground. *A Letter from Italy.*

11 'Tis not in mortals to command success,
But we'll do more, Sempronius; we'll deserve it. *Cato, I. ii.*

12 Blesses his stars and thinks it luxury.
 Ibid, iv.

13 The woman that deliberates is lost.
 Ibid., IV. i.

14 It must be so – Plato, thou reason'st well! –

Else whence this pleasing hope, this
   fond desire,
This longing after immortality?
Or Whence this secret dread and inward
   horror
Of falling into naught? Why shrinks the
   soul
Back on herself and startles at
   destruction?
'Tis the Divinity that stirs within us,
'Tis Heaven itself that points out an
   hereafter,
And intimates Eternity to man.
Eternity! – thou pleasing-dreadful
   thought!   *Ibid, V. i.*

1   The soul, secured in her existence,
      smiles
    At the drawn dagger and defies its point.
    The stars shall fade away, the sun
       himself
    Grow dim with age, and nature sink in
       years;
    But thou shalt flourish in immortal
       youth,
    Unhurt amidst the war of elements,
    The wrecks of matter, and the crush of
       worlds.   *Ibid.*

2   Sir Roger told them, with the air of a
    man who would not give his judgment
    rashly, that much might be said on both
    sides.   *The Spectator, 122.*

3   I have often thought, says Sir Roger, it
    happens very well that Christmas
    should fall out in the middle of Winter.
                                   Ibid, 269.

4   A woman seldom asks advice before she
    has bought her wedding clothes.
                                   Ibid, 475.

5   I have but ninepence in ready money,
    but I can draw for a thousand pounds.
    (Contrasting his powers in conversation
    and in writing.)
        Boswell, Life of Johnson, an. 1773.

6   See in what peace a Christian can die.
                                Dying words.

**ADELER, MAX (CHARLES
HEBER CLARK), US author, 11
July, 1847–10 Aug. 1915**

7   Oh no more he'll shoot his sister with
    his little wooden gun;
    And no more he'll twist the pussy's tail
    and make her yowl for fun.
    The pussy's tail now stands out straight;
    the gun is laid aside;
    The monkey doesn't jump around since
    little Willie died.   *In Memoriam.*

8   We have lost our little Hanner in a very
    painful manner.   *Little Hanner.*

**ADY, THOMAS, English author,
17th century**

9   Matthew, Mark, Luke, and John,
    The bed be blest that I lie on.
    Four angels to my bed,
    Four angels round my head,
    One to watch, one one to pray,
    And two to bear my soul away.
                       A Candle in the Dark.

**Æ (GEORGE WILLIAM
RUSSELL), Irish poet, 10 April,
1867–17 July, 1935**

10 The blue dusk ran between the streets:
    my love was winged within my mind,
    It left to-day and yesterday and thrice a
    thousand years behind.
    To-day was past and dead for me, for
    from to-day my feet had run
    Through thrice a thousand years to walk
    the ways of ancient Babylon.
                                   Babylon.

**AESCHYLUS, Greek dramatist,
525–456 B.C.**

11 Οὐ γὰρ δοκεῖν ἄριστος, ἀλλ' εἶναι θέλει
    – He wishes not to seem, but to be, the
    best.   *Seven against Thebes, 588.*

12 Ποντίων τε κυμάτων
    Ἀνήριθμου γέλασμα.
    – And sea waves' unnumbered laughter.
                        Prometheus Bound, 89.

13 Τὸ δ' εὖ νικάτω.
    – But let the good prevail.
                           Agememnon, 121.

À KEMPIS, THOMAS, see Kempis, Thomas à

AKENSIDE, MARK, English doctor and poet, 9 Nov. 1721–23 June, 1770

14 Such and so various are the tastes of men.
The Pleasures of the Imagination, III. 567.

AKERS, ELIZABETH CHASE, US authoress, 9 Oct. 1832–7 Aug. 1911

15 Backward, turn backward, O Time, in your flight,
Make me a child again just for to-night!
Rock me to Sleep.

ALDRICH, HENRY, Dean of Christ Church, Oxford, 1647–14 Dec. 1710

16 If all be true that I do think,
There are five reasons we should drink:
Good wine – a friend – or being dry –
Or lest we should be by and by –
Or any other reason why.
Reasons for Drinking.

ALDRICH, JAMES, US poet, 1810–Oct. 1856

17 Her suffering ended with the day,
Yet lived she at its close,
And breathed the long, long night away
In statue-like repose.

But when the sun in all his state
Illumed the eastern skies,
She passed through Glory's morning gate
And walked in Paradise.   *A Death Bed.*

ALEXANDER, CECIL FRANCES, English poetess, 1818–12 Oct. 1895

18 All things bright and beautiful,
All creatures great and small,
All things wise and wonderful,
The Lord God made them all.
All Things Bright and Beautiful.

19 Do no sinful action,
Speak no angry word;
Ye belong to Jesus,
Children of the Lord.
Do no Sinful Action.

20 There is a green hill far away,
Without a city wall,
Where the dear Lord was crucified,
Who died to save us all.
There is a Green Hill.

21 By Nebo's lonely mountain,
On this side Jordan's wave,
In a vale in the land of Moab,
There lies a lonely grave.
The Burial of Moses.

ALEXANDER, SIR WILLIAM, EARL OF STIRLING, Scottish poet and statesman, 1567?–12 Sept. 1640

22 The weaker sex, to piety more prone.
Doomsday. Hour V. 55.

23 Those golden palaces, those gorgeous halls,
With furniture superfluously fair;
Those stately courts, those sky-encount'ring walls
Evanish all like vapours in the air.
The Tragedy of Darius, IV. iii.

ALFORD, HENRY, Dean of Canterbury, 10 Oct. 1810–12 Jan. 1871

24 Ten thousand times ten thousand,
In sparkling raiment bright,
The armies of the ransomed saints
Throng up the steeps of light.
Ten Thousand Times Ten Thousand.

ALLAINVAL, LÉONOR JEAN CHRISTINE SOULAS D', abbé, French author, 1700?–2 May, 1753

25 L'embarras des richesses. – The embarrassment of riches.
Title of play.

ALLEN, ELIZABETH AKERS, see Akers, Elizabeth Chase

ALLINGHAM, WILLIAM, Irish poet, 19 March, 1824–18 Nov. 1889

1 Up the airy mountain,
Down the rushy glen,
We daren't go a-hunting
For fear of little men. *The Fairies.*

2 Four ducks on a pond,
A grass-bank beyond,
A blue sky of spring,
White clouds on the wing:
What a little thing
To remember for years –
To remember with tears! *A Memory.*

ANSTEY, CHRISTOPHER, English poet, 31 Oct. 1724–3 Aug. 1805

3 If ever I ate a good supper at night,
I dream'd of the devil, and wak'd in a fright.
The New Bath Guide, iv. A Consultation of the Physicians.

APPLETON, THOMAS GOLD, US author, 31 March, 1812–17 April, 1884

4 Good Americans, when they die, go to Paris.
O. W. Holmes, Autocrat of the Breakfast Table, vi.

ARCHIMEDES, Greek scientist, 287?–212? B.C.

5 Ευρηκα. – I have found it. (Eureka!)
On making a discovery.

6 Δός μοι πoῦ στῶ, καὶ κινῶ τὴν γῆν. –
Give me somewhere to stand, and I will move the earth.
In reference to the lever.

ARIOSTO, LUDOVICO, Italian poet, 8 Sept. 1474–6 July, 1533

7 Natura il fece, e poi ruppe la stampa. –
Nature made him, and then broke the mould. *Orlando Furioso, x. 84.*

ARISTOPHANES, Greek dramatist, 448?–380? B.C.

8 Νεφελοκοκκυγία. – Cloudcuckooboroug
(The city built by the birds.)
The Birds, 821.

ARISTOTLE Greek philosopher and scientist, 264–322 B.C.

9 Ανθρωπος φυσει πολιτικὸν ὦον.
– Man is by nature a civic animal.
Politics, I. ii.

10 Προαιρεῖσθαι τε δεῖ ἀδύνατα εικότα μᾶλλον η δυνατὰ απίθανα.
– Plausible impossibilities should be preferred to unconvincing possibilities.
Poetics, xxiv.

ARMSTRONG, NEIL, US astronaut, 5 Aug. 1930 –

11 That's one small step for a man, one giant leap for mankind.
On setting foot on the moon, 3.56 a.m. BST, 21 July, 1969.

ARNOLD, SIR EDWIN, English poet, 10 June–24 March, 1904

12 Shall any gazer see with mortal eyes,
Or any searcher know by mortal mind?
Veil after veil will lift – but there must be
Veil upon veil behind.
The Light of Asia, VIII.

ARNOLD, GEORGE, US poet, 24 June, 1834–9 Nov. 1865

13 The living need charity more than the dead. *The Jolly Old Pedagogue.*

ARNOLD, MATTHEW, English poet and critic, 24 Dec. 1822–15 April, 1888

14   Be his
My special thanks, whose even-balanc'd soul,
From first youth tested up to extreme old age,
Business could not make dull, nor passion wild:
Who saw life steadily, and saw it whole:

The mellow glory of the Attic stage;
Singer of sweet Colonus, and its child.
(Sophocles.) *To a Friend.*

15 Others abide our question. Thou art free.
We ask and ask: Thou smilest and art still,
Out-topping knowledge. *Shakespeare.*

16 And thou, who didst the stars and sunbeams know,
Self-school'd, self-scann'd, self-honour'd, self-secure,
Didst walk on earth unguess'd at. Better so!
All pains the immortal spirit must endure,
All weakness that impairs, all griefs that bow,
Find their sole voice in that victorious brow. *Ibid.*

17 Now the great winds shoreward blow;
Now the salt tides seaward flow;
Now the wild white horses play,
Champ and chafe and toss in the spray.
The Forsaken Merman, 4.

18 Children dear, was it yesterday
(Call yet once) that she went away?
Ibid., 48.

19 'Tis Apollo comes leading
His choir, the Nine.
The leader is fairest,
But all are divine.
Empedocles on Etna, II.

20 Too fast we lived, too much are tried,
Too harass'd, to attain
Wordsworth's sweet calm, or Goethe's wide
And luminous view to gain.
Obermann, 77.

21 We cannot kindle when we will
The fire that in the heart resides,
The spirit bloweth and is still,
In mystery our soul abides:
But tasks in hours of insight will'd
Can be through hours of gloom fulfill'd.
Morality.

22 Truth sits upon the lips of dying men.
Sohrab and Rustum, 656.

23 But the majestic River floated on.
Out of the mist and hum of that low land,
Into the frosty starlight, and there mov'd,
Rejoicing, through the hush'd Chorasmian waste,
Under the solitary moon: he flow'd
Right for the Polar Star, past Orgunjè,
Brimming, and bright, and large: then sands begin
To hem his watery march, and dam his streams,
And split his currents; that for many a league
The shorn and parcell'd Oxus strains along
Through beds of sand and matted rushy isles—
Oxus, forgetting the bright speed he had
In his high mountain cradle in Pamere,
A foil'd circuitous wanderer – till at last
The long'd-for dash of waves is heard, and wide
His luminous home of waters opens, bright
And tranquil, from whose floor the new-bath'd stars
Emerge, and shine upon the Aral Sea.
Ibid, 875.

24 Strew on the roses, roses,
And never a spray of yew.
In quiet she reposes:
Ah! would that I did too. *Requiescat.*

25 To-night it doth inherit
The vasty Hall of Death. *Ibid.*

26 Crossing the stripling Thames at Bablock-hithe.
The Scholar Gipsy, 74.

27 Still nursing the unconquerable hope,
Still clutching the inviolable shade.
Ibid, 211.

28 And that sweet city with her dreaming spires. *Thyrsis, 20.*

29 So have I heard the cuckoo's parting cry,
From the wet field, through the vext garden-trees,
Come with the volleying rain and tossing breeze. *Ibid, 57.*

1 The foot less prompt to meet the
morning dew,
The heart less bounding at emotion
new,
And hope, once crush'd, less quick to
spring again.   *Ibid, 138.*

2 Hath man no second life? – Pitch this
one high!
Sits there no judge in heaven, our sins to
see? –
More strictly, then, the inward judge
obey!
Was Christ a man like us? – Ah! let us
try
If we then, too, can be such men as he!
                    Anti-desperation.

3 Whispering from her towers the last
enchantments of the Middle Age . . .
Home of lost causes, and forsaken
beliefs, and unpopular names, and
impossible loyalties! (Oxford.)
        Essays in Criticism, 1st series, preface.

4 I am bound by my own definition of
criticism: a disinterested endeavour to
learn and propagate the best that is
known and thought in the world.
        *Ibid, Functions of Criticism at the Present
                                        Time.*

5 Poetry is simply the most beautiful,
impressive and widely effective mode of
saying things, and hence its importance.
                    Ibid, Heinrich Heine

6 In poetry, no less than in life, he is 'a
beautiful and ineffectual angel, beating
in the void his luminous wings in
vain.'
        *(Quoting from his own essay on Byron.)
                    Ibid, 2nd series. Shelley.*

7 The pursuit of perfection, then, is the
pursuit of sweetness and light.
                    Culture and Anarchy.

8 The word which our Bibles translate by
'gentleness' means more properly
'reasonableness with sweetness,' 'sweet
reasonableness.'
        St. Paul and Protestantism, preface.

9 Culture, the acquainting ourselves with

the best that has been known and said
in the world, and thus with the history
of the human spirit.
                    Literature and Dogma, preface.

**ARNOLD, SAMUEL JAMES,
English dramatist, 1774–1852.**

10 For England, home, and beauty.
                    The Death of Nelson.

**ARNOLD, THOMAS, Headmaster
of Rugby, 13 June, 1795–12 June,
1842**

11 What we must look for here is, first,
religious and moral principles;
secondly, gentlemanly conduct;
thirdly, intellectual ability.
                    Address to his scholars.

**ASQUITH, HERBERT, HENRY,
EARL OF OXFORD AND
ASQUITH, English Prime
Minister, 12 Sept. 1852–15 Feb. 1928.**

12 Wait and see.   *Various Speeches, 1910.*

**AUBREY, JOHN, English
antiquary, born 12 March, 1626,
buried 7 June, 1697.**

13 *Anno* 1670, not far from Cirencester,
was an apparition: being demanded,
whether a good spirit, or a bad?
returned no answer, but disappeared
with a curious perfume and most
melodious twang. Mr. W. Lilly
believes it was a fairy.
                    Miscellanies. Apparitions.

14 He was a handsome, well-shaped man:
very good company, and of a very ready
and pleasant smooth wit.
                    Brief Lives. William Shakespeare

**AUCHINLECK, ALEXANDER
BOSWELL, LORD, Scottish
Judge, 1706–31 Aug. 1782**

15 He gart kings ken that they had a *lith* in
their neck. (Of Cromwell.
Lith=joint.)
        *Boswell, Journal of a Tour to the Hebrides,
                        6 Nov. 1773, note.*

AUGIER, GUILLAUME VICTOR ÉMILE, French dramatist, 17 Sept. 1820–25 Oct. 1889.

16 La nostalgie de la boue. – Home-sickness for the gutter.
Le mariage d'Olympe – The Marriage of Olympe, I. i.

AUGUSTINE (AURELIUS AUGUSTINUS), SAINT, Bishop of Hippo, 13 Nov. 354–28 Aug. 430 A.D.

17 Da mihi castitatem et continentiam, sed noli modo. – Give me chastity and continence, but not now.
Confessions, VIII. vii.

18 Securus judicat orbis terrarum. – The verdict of the world is final.
Contra Epistolam Parmeniani, iii. 24.

AUGUSTUS (GAIUS JULIUS CAESAR OCTAVIANUS, formerly GAIUS OCTAVIUS), Roman Emperor, 23 Sept. 63 B.C.–19 Aug. A.D. 14.

19 Quintili Vare, legiones redde. – Quintilius Varus, give me back my legions.
When three legions were annihilated by the Germans, A.D. 9.

20 Ad kalendas Graecas. – On the Greek calends. (I.e. never.)
Suetonius, Divus Augustus, lxxxvii.

AURELIUS, MARCUS (MARCUS AURELIUS ANTONINUS), Roman Emperor, April, 121–17 March, 180.

21 Ἐκεῖνος μέν φησιν· 'πόλι φίλη Κέκροπος', σὺ δὲ οὐκ ἐρεῖς· πόλ φίλ. The poet says 'Dear city of Cecrops'; and wilt not thou say 'O dear city of God'?
Meditations, IV. xxiii.

AUSTEN, JANE, English novelist, 16 Dec. 1775–18 July, 1817

22 But are they all horrid, are you sure they are all horrid? (Catherine Morland, of a list of novels.) *Northanger Abbey, vi.*

23 It is a truth universally acknowledged, that a single man in possession of a good fortune must be in want of a wife. *Pride and Prejudice, i.*

24 How can you contrive to write so even? (Miss Bingley) *Ibid, x.*

25 It is happy for you that you possess the talent of flattering with delicacy. May I ask whether these pleasing attentions proceed from the impulse of the moment, or are the result of previous study? (Mr. Bennet.) *Ibid, xiv*

26 Nobody is on my side, nobody takes part with me; I am cruelly used, nobody feels for my poor nerves. (Mrs. Bennet.) *Ibid, xx.*

27 You ought certainly to forgive them as a Christian, but never to admit them in your sight, or allow their names to be mentioned in your hearing. (Mr. Collins.) *Ibid, lvii.*

28 A basin of nice smooth gruel, thin, but not too thin. *Emma, xii.*

29 All the privilege I claim for my own sex . . . is that of loving longest, when existence or when hope is gone. (Anne Elliot.) *Persuasion, xxiii.*

30 What dreadful hot weather we have! It keeps me in a continual state of inelegance. *Letters, 18 Sept 1796.*

31 Miss Blachford is agreeable enough. I do not want people to be very agreeable, as it saves me the trouble of liking them a great deal. *Ibid, 24 Dec 1798.*

32 The little bit (two inches wide) of ivory on which I work with so fine a brush as produces little effect after much labour. *Ibid, 16 Dec. 1816.*

AUSTIN, ALFRED, English Poet Laureate, 30 May, 1835–2 June, 1913

33 An earl by right, by courtesy a man. *The Season.*

AYTOUN, WILLIAM EDMONSTOUNE, Scottish poet, 21 June, 1813–4 Aug. 1865

1 News of battle! – news of battle!
Hark! 'tis ringing down the street:
And the archways and the pavement
Bear the clang of hurrying feet.
Edinburgh after Flodden, I.

2 Come hither, Evan Cameron!
Come, stand beside my knee.
The Execution of Montrose, I.

3 Do not lift him from the bracken,
Leave him lying where he fell –
Better bier ye cannot fashion:
None beseems him half so well.
The Widow of Glencoe, I.

4 Take away that star and garter –
Hide them from my aching sight!
Neither king nor prince shall tempt me
From my lonely room this night.
Charles Edward at Versailles on the Anniversary of Culloden, I.

5 Fhairshon swore a feud
Against the clan McTavish;
Marched into their land
To murder and to rafish.
The Massacre of the Macpherson, I.

BACON, FRANCIS, VISCOUNT ST. ALBANS, English Lord Chancellor, 22 Jan. 1561–9 April, 1626

6 Come home to men's business and bosoms. *Essays, dedication.*

7 What is truth? said jesting Pilate, and would not stay for an answer.
Ibid, i. Of Truth.

8 Men fear death as children fear to go in the dark; and as that natural fear in children is increased with tales, so is the other. *Ibid, ii. Of Death.*

9 It is as natural to die as to be born; and to a little infant perhaps the one is as painful as the other. *Ibid.*

10 Revenge is a kind of wild justice.
Ibid, iv, Of Revenge.

11 He that hath wife and children hath given hostages to fortune; for they are impediments to great enterprises, either of virtue or mischief.
Ibid, viii, Of Marriage and Single Life.

12 The remedy is worse than the disease.
Ibid, xv, Of Seditions and Troubles.

13 A little philosophy inclineth man's mind to atheism, but depth in philosophy bringeth men's minds about to religion.
Ibid, xvi, Of Atheism.

14 God Almighty first planted a garden; and, indeed, it is the purest of human pleasures. *Ibid, xlvi, Of Gardens.*

15 Studies serve for delight, for ornament, and for ability. *Ibid, l, Of Studies.*

16 Some books are to be tasted, others to be swallowed, and some few to be chewed and digested. *Ibid.*

17 Reading maketh a full man, conference a ready man, and writing an exact man.
Ibid.

18 Histories make men wise; poets, witty; the mathematics, subtile; natural philosophy, deep; moral, grave; logic and rhetoric, able to contend. *Ibid.*

19 If a man will begin with certainties, he shall end in doubts; but if he will be content to begin with doubts, he shall end in certainties.
Advancement of Learning, I. V. 8.

20 I have taken all knowledge to be my province.
Letter to Lord Burleigh, 1592.

21 Nam et ipsa scientia potestas est. – For knowledge itself is power.
Meditationes Sacrae. De Haeresibus. – Religious Meditations. Of Heresies.

22 The world's a bubble; and the life of man
Less than a span. *The World.*

23 Who then to frail mortality shall trust,
But limns the water, or but writes in dust. *Ibid.*

BAILEY, PHILIP JAMES, English poet, 22 April, 1816–6 Sept. 1902

24 We live in deeds, not years; in thoughts, not breaths;
In feelings, not in figures on a dial.
We should count time by heart-throbs.
He most lives
Who thinks most – feels the noblest –
acts the best. *Festus, V.*

BAILLIE, LADY GRISELL or GRIZEL, Scottish poetess, 25 Dec. 1665–6 Dec. 1746

25 And werena my heart licht I wad dee.
Werena my Heart Licht.

BAILLIE, JOANNA, Scottish dramatist, 11 Sept. 1762–23 Feb. 1851

26 The wild-fire dances on the fen
The red star sheds its ray;
Uprouse ye then, my merrie men!
It is our op'ning day. *Orra, III. i.*

BAIRNSFATHER, BRUCE, English artist, July, 1888–29 Sept. 1959.

27 Well, if you knows of a better 'ole, go to it. *Caption of war cartoon, 1915.*

BALFOUR, ARTHUR JAMES BALFOUR, 1ST EARL OF, 25 July, 1848–19 March, 1930

28 The energies of our system will decay, the glory of the sun will be dimmed, and the earth, tideless and inert, will no longer tolerate the race which has for a moment disturbed its solitude. Man will go down into the pit, and all his thoughts will perish.
The Foundations of Belief, I. i.

29 A frigid and calculated lie.
Speech, Constitutional Club, 26 Oct. 1909.

BALL, JOHN, English priest, died 15 July, 1381

30 When Adam dolve and Eve span,
Who was then the gentleman?
Attributed.

BALZAC, HONORÉ DE, French novelist, 20 May, 1799–17 Aug. 1850

31 Elles doivent avoir les défauts de leur qualités. – They are bound to have the defects of their qualities.
Le Lys dans la vallée. – The Lily in the Valley, 369.

BAMPFYLDE, JOHN CODRINGTON, English poet, 27 Aug. 1754–1796?

32 Rugged the breast that beauty cannot tame. *Sonnet in Praise of Delia.*

BANKS, GEORGE LINNAEUS, English author, 2 March, 1821–3 May, 1881

33 For the cause that lacks assistance,
For the wrong that needs resistance,
For the future in the distance,
And the good that I can do.
What I Live for.

BANVILLE, THÉODORE FAULLAIN DE, French poet, 14 March, 1823–15 March, 1891

34 Nous n'irons plus aux bois, les lauriers sont coupés. – We'll go no more to the woods, the laurel trees are cut. (*Taken from a folk song.*) *Les Stalactites, iii.*

BARBAULD, ANNA LETITIA, English authoress, 20 June, 1743–9 March, 1825

35 Life! we've been long together
Through pleasant and through cloudy weather;
'Tis hard to part when friends are dear;
Perhaps 'twill cost a sigh, a tear;
Then steal away, give little warning,
Choose thine own time;
Say not 'Good night,' but in some brighter clime
Bid me 'Good morning.' *Life.*

BARBOUR, JOHN, Scottish poet, 1316?–13 March, 1395

36 A! fredome is a nobill thing!
Fredome mayss man to haiff liking!

Fredome all solace to man giffis:
He levys at ese that frely levys.
The Bruce, I. 225.

BARÈRE DE VIEUZAC, BERTRAND, French revolutionary, 10 Sept. 1755–13 Jan. 1841

1 L'arbre de la liberté ne croît qu'arrosé par le sang des tyrans. – The tree of Liberty only grows when watered by the blood of tyrants.
Speech, National Convention, 1792.

BARHAM, RICHARD HARRIS, English clergyman, 6 Dec. 1788–17 June, 1845

2 You intoxified brute! – you insensible block! –
Look at the clock! – Do! – Look at the clock!
The Ingoldsby Legends. Patty Morgan, i.

3 And, talking of epitaphs – much I admire his,
'Circumspice, si monumentum requiris';
Which an erudite verger translated to me,
'If you ask for his monument, Sir-come-spy-see!'
Ibid, The Cynotaph.

4 The Jackdaw sat on the Cardinal's chair!
Bishop, and abbot, and prior were there;
Many a monk, and many a friar,
Many a knight, and many a squire.
Ibid, The Jackdaw of Rheims.

5 Never was heard such a terrible curse!
But what gave rise
To no little surprise,
Nobody seemed one penny the worse!
Ibid.

6 Heedless of grammar, they all cried,
'That's him!'
Ibid.

7 She drank prussic acid without any water,
And died like a Duke-and-a-Duchess's daughter.
Ibid, The Tragedy.

8 She help'd him to lean, and she help'd him to fat,
And it look'd like hare – but it might have been cat.
Ibid, The Bagman's Dog.

9 The sacristan, he says no word that indicates a doubt,
But he puts his thumb unto his nose, and spreads his fingers out!
Ibid, Nell Cook.

10 'Twas in Margate last July, I walk'd upon the pier,
I saw a little vulgar boy – I said, 'What make you here?'
Ibid, Misadventures at Margate.

11 What Horace says is,
Eheu fugaces
Anni labuntur, Postume, Postume!
Years glide away, and are lost to me, lost to me!
Ibid, Epigram: Eheu Fugaces.

BARING, MAURICE, English author, 27 April, 1874–15 Dec. 1945.

12 Because of you we will be glad and gay,
Remembering you, we will be brave and strong;
And hail the advent of each dangerous day,
And meet the great adventure with a song.
Julian Grenfell (1888–1915).

BARING-GOULD, SABINE, English clergyman and author, 28 Jan. 1834–2 Jan. 1924

13 Onward, Christian soldiers,
Marching as to war,
With the Cross of Jesus
Going on before.
Onward Christian Soldiers.

14 Hell's foundations quiver
At the shout of praise.
Ibid.

15 Now the day is over,
Night is drawing nigh,
Shadows of the evening
Steal across the sky.
Now the Day is over.

BARNARD, LADY ANNE,
Scottish poetess, 8 Dec. 1750–6
May, 1825

16 When the sheep are in the fauld, when
the kye's a' at hame,
And a' the weary warld to rest are gane.
Auld Robin Gray.

17 My father urged me sair – my mother
didna speak,
But she looket in my face till my heart
was like to break;
They gied him my hand – my heart was
in the sea –
And so Robin Gray was gudeman to
me. *Ibid.*

BARNERS *or* BERNES *or*
BARNES, JULIANA, English
authoress, born 1388?

18 Of the offspring of the gentilman Jafeth
come Habraham, Moyses, Aron, and
the profettys; also the Kyng of the
right lyne of Mary, of whom that
gentilman Jhesus was borne.
Blasyng of Armys.

BARNFIELD, RICHARD, English
poet, baptised 13 June, 1574, buried
6 March, 1627

19 As it fell upon a day
In the merry month of May. *An Ode.*

20 King Pandion, he is dead,
All thy friends are lapp'd in lead. *Ibid.*

BARNUM, PHINEAS TAYLOR,
US showman, 5 July, 1810–7 April,
1891

21 You can fool some of the people all the
time, and all of the people some of the
time; but you can't fool all of the
people all the time. *Attributed.*

BARRETT, EATON STANNARD,
Irish author, 1786–20 March, 1820

22 Not she with trait'rous kiss her Saviour
stung,
Not she denied Him with unholy
tongue;

She, while apostles shrank, could danger
brave,
Last at His cross, and earliest at His
grave. *Woman, I. 143.*

BARRIE, SIR JAMES MATTHEW,
Scottish author, 9 May, 1860–20
June, 1937

23 I do loathe explanations.
My Lady Nicotine, xvi.

24 If it's heaven for climate, it's hell for
company. *The Little Minister, iii.*

25 It's a weary warld, and nobody bides
in't. *Ibid, iv.*

26 You canna expect to be baith grand and
comfortable. *Ibid, x.*

27 Let no one who loves be called
altogether unhappy. Even love
unreturned has its rainbow.
Ibid, xxiv.

28 When the first baby laughed for the first
time, the laugh broke into a thousand
pieces and they all went skipping
about, and that was the beginning of
the fairies. *Peter Pan, I.*

29 To die will be an awfully big adventure.
Ibid, III.

30 It's a sort of bloom on a woman. If you
have it, you don't need to have
anything else; and if you don't have it,
it doesn't much matter what else you
have. (Of charm.)
What every Woman knows, I.

31 A young Scotsman of your ability let
loose upon the world with £300, what
could he not do? It's almost appalling
to think of; especially if he went among
the English. *Ibid.*

32 You've forgotten the grandest moral
attribute of a Scotsman, Maggie, that
he'll do nothing which might damage
his career. *Ibid, II.*

BARTHÉLEMY, AUGUSTE MARSEILLE, French poet, 1796–23 Aug. 1867

1 L'homme absurde est celui qui ne change jamais. – The absurd man is the one who never changes.
Ma justification – My Justification.

BASHFORD, SIR HENRY HOWARTH, English doctor, 1880–15 Aug. 1961

2 As I came down the Highgate Hill
I met the sun's bravado,
And saw below me, fold on fold,
Grey to pearl and pearl to gold,
London like a land of old,
The land of Eldorado. *Romance.*

BASSE *or* BAS, WILLIAM, English poet, died 1653?

3 Renowned Spenser, lie a thought more nigh
To learned Chaucer, and rare Beaumont lie
A little nearer Spenser, to make room
For Shakespeare in your threefold, fourfold tomb. *On Shakespeare.*

BATES, KATHERINE LEE, US poetess, 29 Aug. 1859–28 March, 1929

4 America! America!
God shed His grace on thee
And crown thy good with brotherhood
From sea to shining sea!
America the Beautiful.

BAXTER, RICHARD, English clergyman, 12 Nov. 1615–8 Dec. 1691

5 I preached as never sure to preach again,
And as a dying man to dying men.
Love breathing Thanks and Praise, II.

BAYLY, THOMAS HAYNES, English author, 13 Oct. 1797–22 April, 1839

6 I'd be a butterfly; living a rover,
Dying when fair things are fading away.
I'd be a Butterfly.

7 Oh! no! we never mention her,
Her name is never heard;
My lips are now forbid to speak
That once familiar word.
Oh! no! we never mention her. Song.

8 We met – 'twas in a crowd. *Song.*

9 Why don't the men propose, mamma,
Why don't the men propose?
Why don't the Men propose?

10 She wore a wreath of roses,
The night that first we met.
She wore a Wreath of Roses.

11 O pilot! 'tis a fearful night,
There's danger on the deep. *The Pilot.*

12 Absence makes the heart grow fonder.
Isle of Beauty.

13 Gaily the Troubadour
Touched his guitar. *Welcome me Home.*

14 I'm saddest when I sing. *Song.*

15 The mistletoe hung in the castle hall,
The holly branch shone on the old oak wall. *The Mistletoe Bough.*

BEATTIE, JAMES, Scottish poet, 25 Oct. 1735–18 Aug. 1803

16 Mine be the breezy hill that skirts the down,
Where a green grassy turf is all I crave,
With here and there a violet bestrewn,
Fast by a brook or fountain's murmuring wave;
And many an evening sun shine sweetly on my grave! *The Minstrel, II. 17.*

17 At the close of the day, when the hamlet is still,
And mortals the sweets of forgetfulness prove,
When naught but the torrent is heard on the hill,
And naught but the nightingale's song in the grove. *The Hermit.*

18 He thought as a sage, though he felt as a man. *Ibid.*

BEAUMONT, FRANCIS, English dramatist, 1584–6 March, 1616

19   What things have we seen
Done at the Mermaid! heard words that
   have been
So nimble and so full of subtile flame
As if that every one from whence they
   came
Had meant to put his whole wit in a jest,
And had resolved to live a fool the rest
Of his dull life.   *Letter to Ben Jonson.*

20 Mortality, behold and fear!
What a change of flesh is here!
      On the Tombs in Westminster Abbey.

21 Here are sands, ignoble things,
Dropt from the ruin'd sides of kings.
                          Ibid.

BEDDOES, THOMAS LOVELL, English poet, 20 July, 1803–26 Jan. 1849.

22 If there were dreams to sell,
What would you buy?
Some cost a passing-bell,
Some a light sigh.   *Dream-Pedlary.*

BEERS, ETHEL LYNN, US poetess, 13 Jan. 1827–11 Oct. 1879

23 All quiet along the Potomac to-night,
No sound save the rush of the river,
While soft falls the dew on the face of
   the dead –
The picket's off duty forever.
                    The Picket Guard.

BEITH, JOHN HAY, see Hay, Ian

BELL, HENRY GLASSFORD, Scottish author, 8 Nov. 1803–7 Jan. 1874

24 I looked far back into other years, and
   lo! in bright array
I saw, as in a dream, the forms of ages
   passed away.
It was a stately convent, with is old and
   lofty walls,
And gardens with their broad, green
   walks, where soft the footstep falls.
                    Mary Queen of Scots.

25 The scene was changed. It was the court
– the gay court of Bourbon;
And 'neath a thousand silver lamps a
   thousand courtiers throng.   *Ibid.*

BELLOC, JOSEPH HILAIRE PIERRE, English author, 27 July, 1870–16 July, 1953

26 Child, do not throw this book about;
Refrain from the unholy pleasure
Of cutting all the pictures out!
Preserve it as your chiefest treasure.
      The Bad Child's Book of Beasts,
                          dedication.

27 When I am living in the Midlands,
That are sodden and unkind,
I light my lamp in the evening:
My work is left behind;
And the great hills of the South Country
Come back into my mind.
                 The South Country.

28 I will hold my house in the high wood,
Within a walk of the sea,
And the men that were boys when I was
   a boy
Shall sit and drink with me.   *Ibid.*

29 Balliol made me, Balliol fed me,
Whatever I had she gave me again;
And the best of Balliol loved and led me,
God be with you, Balliol men.
      To the Balliol Men still in Africa.

30 There's nothing worth the wear of
   winning
But laughter and the love of friends.
                 Dedicatory Ode.

31 Remote and ineffectual Don
That dared attack my Chesterton.
                 Lines to a Don.

32 He does not die that can bequeath
Some influence to the land he knows,
Or dares, persistent, interwreath
Love permanent with the wild
   hedgerows;
He does not die, but still remains
Substantiate with his darling plains.
                    Duncton Hill.

33 His sins were scarlet, but his books were
   read.   *Epigrams. On his Books.*

1 The chief defect of Henry King
Was chewing little bits of string.
*Cautionary Tales for Children. Henry
King.*

BENNETT, ENOCH ARNOLD, English novelist, 27 May, 1867–27 March, 1931

2 There was no influenza in my young
days. We called a cold a cold.
The Card, viii.

3 There was a young man of Montrose,
Who had pockets in none of his clothes.
When asked by his lass
Where he carried his brass,
He said, 'Darling, I pay through the
nose.' *Limerick.*

BENSON, ARTHUR CHRISTOPHER, Master of Magdalene College, Cambridge, 24 April, 1862–17 June, 1925

4 By feathers green, across Casbeen
The pilgrims track the Phoenix flown,
By gems he strew'd in waste and wood,
And jewell'd plumes at random thrown.
The Phoenix.

5 Land of Hope and Glory, Mother of the
Free,
How shall we extol thee, who are born
of thee?
Wider still and wider shall thy bounds
be set;
God, who made thee mighty, make thee
mightier yet. *Land of Hope and Glory.*

BENTHAM, JEREMY, English jurist, 15 Feb. 1748–6 June, 1832

6 All punishment is mischief; all
punishment in itself is evil.
Principles of Morals and Legislation, xiii.

BENTLEY, EDMUND CLERIHEW, English author, 10 July, 1875–30 March, 1956

7 Geography is about maps,
But biography is about chaps.
Biography for Beginners.

8 What I like about Clive
Is that he's no longer alive. *Ibid, Clive.*

9 George the Third
Ought never to have occurred.
Ibid, George III.

10 They say, 'Shall these things perish
utterly,
These that were England through the
glorious years –
Faith and green fields and honour and
the sea?'
I simply wag my great, long, furry ears.
Ballade of Plain Common Sense.

BENTLEY, RICHARD, English classical scholar, 27 Jan. 1662–14 July, 1742

11 It is a maxim with me that no man was
ever written out of reputation but by
himself. *Monk's Life of Bentley, 90.*

12 A very pretty poem, Mr. Pope, but it's
not Homer. (Of Pope's translation of
the Iliad.) *Attributed.*

BERKELEY, GEORGE, BISHOP OF CLOYNE, Irish philosopher, 12 March, 1685–14 Jan, 1753

13 Westward the course of empire takes its
way;
The four first acts already past,
A fifth shall close the drama with the
day:
Time's noblest offspring is the last.
*On the Prospect of Planting Arts and
Learning in America.*

BERNES, *see* Barners, Juliana

BETHMANN HOLLWEG, THEOBALD VON, German Chancellor, 29 Nov. 1856–1 Jan. 1921

14 Just for a scrap of paper, Great Britain is
going to make war on a kindred nation
who desires nothing better than to be
friends with her.
To the British Ambassador, 4 Aug. 1914.

BICKERSTAFFE, ISAAC, Irish dramatist, 1735?–1812?

15 There was a jolly miller once,
Lived on the river Dee;
He worked and sung from morn till night
No lark more blithe than he.
And this the burthen of his song
For ever used to be –
I care for nobody, no, not I,
If no one cares for me.
Love in a Village, I. iii.

BICKERSTETH, EDWARD HENRY, BISHOP OF EXETER, 25 Jan. 1825–16 May, 1906

16 Peace, perfect peace? in this dark world of sin!
The blood of Jesus whispers peace within. *Peace, Perfect Peace.*

BIERCE, AMBROSE, US author, 24 June, 1842–1914?

17 Woman would be more charming if one could fall into her arms without falling into her hands. *Epigrams.*

BINYON, ROBERT LAURENCE, English poet, 10 Aug. 1869–10 March, 1943

18 With proud thankgiving, a mother for her children,
England mourns for her dead across the sea. *For the Fallen.*

19 They shall grow not old, as we that are left grow old:
Age shall not weary them, nor the years condemn.
At the going down of the sun and in the morning
We will remember them. *Ibid.*

BIRKENHEAD, FREDERICK EDWIN SMITH, 1ST EARL OF, English Lord Chancellor, 12 July, 1872–30 Sept. 1930

20 The world continues to offer glittering prizes to those who have stout hearts and sharp swords.
Rectorial Address, Glasgow University, 7 Nov. 1923.

BIRRELL, AUGUSTINE, English MP and author, 19 Jan. 1850–21 Nov. 1933

21 That great dust-heap called 'history.'
Obiter Dicta, 1st series. Carlyle.

22 Libraries are not made; they grow.
Ibid, 2nd series. Book-Buying.

BISMARCK, OTTO EDUARD LEOPOLD, PRINCE VON, German Chancellor, 1 April, 1815–28 July, 1898

23 Blut und Eisen. – Blood and iron.
Speech, Prussian House of Deputies, 28 Jan. 1886.

BLACKSTONE, SIR WILLIAM, English jurist, 10 July, 1723–14 Feb. 1780

24 The royal navy of England hath ever been its greatest defence and ornament;
it is its ancient and natural strength – the floating bulwark of the island.
Commentaries, I. xiii.

25 Time whereof the memory of man runneth not to the contrary. *Ibid, xviii.*

26 That the king can do no wrong, is a necessary and fundamental principle of the English constitution. *Ibid, III. xvii.*

BLAIR, ROBERT, Scottish minister, 1699–4 Feb. 1746

27 The schoolboy, with his satchel in his hand,
Whistling aloud to bear his courage up.
The Grave, 58.

28 Its visits
Like those of angels, short and far between. *Ibid, 588.*

BLAKE, JAMES, US song-writer, 1862–1935

29 East Side, West Side, all around the town,
The tots sang 'Ring-a-rosie,' 'London Bridge is falling down';

Boys and girls together, me and Mamie
Rorke,
Tripped the light fantastic on the
sidewalks of New York.
The Sidewalks of New York.

**BLAKE, WILLIAM, English poet
and artist, 28 Nov. 1757–12 Aug.
1827**

1   How have you left the ancient love
That bards of old enjoy'd in you!
The languid strings do scarcely move!
The sound is forc'd, the notes are few!
To the Muses.

2   Piping down the valleys wild,
Piping songs of pleasant glee,
On a cloud I saw a child.
Songs of Innocence, introduction.

3   My mother bore me in the southern
wild,
And I am black, but O my soul is white.
Ibid, The Little Black Boy.

4   When the voices of children are heard on
the green,
And laughing is heard on the hill.
Ibid, Nurse's Song.

5   Tiger! Tiger! burning bright
In the forests of the night,
What immortal hand or eye
Could frame thy fearful symmetry?
Songs of Experience. The Tiger.

6   Never seek to tell thy love,
Love that never told can be;
For the gentle wind does move
Silently, invisibly.   *Love's Secret.*

7   Mock on, mock on, Voltaire, Rousseau;
Mock on, mock on, 'tis all in vain!
You throw the sand against the wind,
And the wind blows it back again.
Mock on, mock on, Voltaire.

8   To see a World in a grain of sand,
And Heaven in a wild flower,
Hold Infinity in the palm of your hand,
And Eternity in an hour.
Auguries of Innocence.

9   A robin redbreast in a cage
Puts all Heaven in a rage.   *Ibid.*

10   He who bends to himself a Joy
Doth the winged life destroy;
But he who kisses the Joy as it flies
Lives in Eternity's sunrise.
Gnomic Verses, xvii, I.

11   A petty sneaking knave I knew –
O! Mr. Cr(omek), how do ye do?
On Friends and Foes, xxi.

12   I will not cease from mental fight,
Nor shall my sword sleep in my hand,
Till we have built Jerusalem
In England's green and pleasant land.
Milton, preface.

13   A fool sees not the same tree that a wise
man sees.
Marriage of Heaven and Hell. Proverbs of Hell.

14   Damn braces. Bless relaxes.   *Ibid.*

**BLAMIRE, SUSANNA (THE
'MUSE OF CUMBERLAND'),
English poetess, 12 Jan. 1747–5
April, 1794**

15   And ye sall walk in silk attire,
And siller hae to spare.
The Siller Crown.

**BLANCHET, PIERRE, French
dramatist, 1459?–1519**

16   Revenons à nos moutons. – Let us get
back to our sheep (= to our subject).
Patelin, 1191

**BLAND, MRS. HUBERT, see
Nesbit, Edith**

**BLISS, PHILIP, US evangelist, 9
July, 1838–29 Dec. 1876**

17   Hold the fort, for I am coming.
Ho, my Comrades, see the Signal.

**BLOOMFIELD, ROBERT, English
poet, 3 Dec. 1766–19 Aug. 1823**

18   Strange to the world, he wore a bashful
look,
The fields his study, Nature was his
book.   *The Farmer's Boy. Spring, 31.*

BLUNT, WILFRID SCAWEN,
English poet, 17 Aug. 1840–10 Sept.
1922

19 He who has once been happy is for aye
Out of desctruction's reach.   *Esther, 1.*

20 I like the hunting of the hare
Better than that of the fox.
                    The Old Squire.

BOBART, JACOB, English
botanist, 2 Aug. 1641–28 Dec. 1719

21 Think that day lost whose (low)
descending sun
Views from thy hand no noble action
done.   *Virtus sua Gloria.*

BOETHIUS or BOETIUS, ANICIUS
MANLIUS SEVERINUS, Roman
philosopher, 480?–524?

22 In omni adversitate fortunae
infelicissimum est genus infortunii fuisse
felicem. – In every adversity of fortune
the most unhappy kind of misfortune is
to have been happy.
Consolatio Philosophiae – Consolation of
Philosophy, II, iv.

BOLINGBROKE, HENRY ST.
JOHN, VISCOUNT, statesman, 1
Oct. 1678–12 Dec. 1751

23 Nations, like men, have their infancy.
On the Study and Use of History, letter iv.

24 The dignity of history.   *Ibid, letter v.*

25 All our wants, beyond those which a
very moderate income will supply, are
purely imaginary.
        Letter to Swift, 17 March, 1719.

BONAR, HORATIUS, Scottish
minister, 19 Dec. 1808–31 July, 1889

26 A few more years shall roll,
A few more seasons come,
And we shall be with those that rest
Asleep within the tomb.   *Hymn.*

BONE, JAMES Scottish journalist,
1872–23 Nov. 1962

27 The City of Dreadful Height.
            Description of New York.

BOOTH, BARTON, English actor,
1681–10 May, 1733

28 True as the needle to the pole,
Or as the dial to the sun.   *Song.*

BORROW, GEORGE HENRY,
English author, 5 July, 1803–26 July,
1881

29 There's night and day, brother, both
sweet things; sun, moon, and stars,
brother, all sweet things; there's
likewise a wind on the heath. Life is very
sweet, brother; who would wish to die?
            Lavengro, xxv..

BOSQUET, PIERRE FRANÇOIS
JOSEPH, French Marshal, 8 Nov.
1810–5 Feb. 1861

30 C'est magnifique, mais ce n'est pas la
guerre. – It is magnificent, but it is not
war.
    On the charge of the Light Brigade at
            Balaclava, 25 Oct. 1854.

BOSSIDY, JOHN COLLINS, US
doctor, 17 June, 1860–1928

31 And this is good old Boston,
The home of the bean and the cod,
Where the Lowells talk only to Cabots
And the Cabots talk only to God.
        On the Aristocracy of Harvard

BOSWELL, ALEXANDER, see
Auchinleck, Lord

BOSWELL, JAMES, Scottish
biographer, 29 Oct. 1740–19 May,
1795

32 Yes, Sir; you tossed and gored several
person. (When Johnson said 'We had a
good talk.')   *Life of Johnson, an. 1769.*

33 He (Dr. Johnson) has no formal
preparation, no flourishing with his

sword; he is through your body in an
instant.   *Ibid, an. 1775.*

BOTTOMLEY, GORDON, English author, 20 Feb. 1874–25 Aug. 1948

1   When you destroy a blade of grass
    You poison England at her roots.
                        To Ironfounders and others.

2   Your worship is your furnaces,
    Which, like old idols, lost obscenes,
    Have molten bowels; your vision is
    Machines for making more machines.
                        Ibid.

BOULTON, SIR HAROLD EDWIN, 2ND BARONET, English poet, 7 Aug. 1859–1 June, 1935

3   Speed, bonny boat, like a bird on the
    wing;
    'Onward!' the sailors cry;
    Carry the lad that's born to be king
    Over the sea to Skye.   *Skye Boat Song.*

4   When Adam and Eve were dispossessed
    Of the garden hard by Heaven,
    They planted another one down in the
    west,
    'Twas Devon, glorious Devon!
                        Glorious Devon.

BOURDILLON, FRANCIS WILLIAM, English author, 22 March, 1852–13 Jan. 1921

5   The night has a thousand eyes,
    And the day but one;
    Yet the light of the bright world dies
    With the dying sun.   *Light.*

BOWEN OF COLWOOD, CHARLES SYNGE CHRISTOPHER BOWEN, BARON, English judge, 1 Jan. 1835–10 April, 1894

6   The rain it raineth on the just
    And also on the unjust fella:
    But chiefly on the just, because
    The unjust steals the just's umbrella.
                        Sichel, Sands of Time.

BOWEN, EDWARD ERNEST, English schoolmaster, 30 March, 1836–8 April, 1901

7   Forty years on, growing older and
    older,
    Shorter in wind, as in memory long,
    Feeble of foot, and rheumatic of
    shoulder,
    What will it help you that once you were
    strong?
                        Forty Years On. Harrow School Song.

BRADFORD, JOHN, English Protestant martyr, 1510?–1 July, 1555

8   But for the grace of God there goes John
    Bradford.
    On seeing some criminals taken to execution.

BRADLEY, FRANCIS HERBERT, English philosopher, 30 Jan. 1846–18 Sept. 1924

9   Metaphysics is the finding of bad
    reasons for what we believe upon
    instinct.
                        Appearance and Reality, preface.

BRAMSTON, JAMES, English poet, 1694?–16 March, 1744

10 What's not destroy'd by Time's
    devouring hand?
    Where's Troy, and where's the Maypole
    in the Strand?   *Art of Politics, 71.*

BRATHWAITE, RICHARD, English poet, 1588?–4 May, 1673

11 Hanging of his cat on Monday
    For killing of a mouse on Sunday.
                        Barnabee's Journal, i.

BRERETON, JANE, English poetess, 1685–7 Aug. 1740

12 The picture, plac'd the busts between,
    Adds to the thought much strength;
    Wisdom and Wit are little seen,
    But Folly's at full length.
                        *On Mr. Nash's Picture at Full Length
                        between the Busts of Sir Isaac Newton
                        and Mr. Pope.*
    (Also attributed to Lord Chesterfield.)

BRETON, NICHOLAS, English poet, 1545?–1626?

13 Much ado there was, God wot;
   He would love, and she would not.
   Phillida and Coridon.

14 I wish my deadly foe no worse
   Than want of friends, and empty purse.
   A Farewell to Town.

15 A mad world, my masters.
   Title of dialogue.

BRIDGES, ROBERT SEYMOUR, English Poet Laureate, 23 Oct. 1844–21 April, 1930

16 I heard a linnet courting
   His lady in the spring.
   I heard a Linnet courting.

17 Whither, O splendid ship, thy white
      sails crowding,
   Leaning across the bosom of the urgent
      West,
   That fearest nor sea rising, nor sky
      clouding,
   Whither away, fair rover, and what thy
      quest?   *A Passer-by.*

18 Perfect little body, without fault or stain
      on thee,
   With promise of strength and manhood
      full and fair!   *On a Dead Child.*

19 Spring goeth all in white,
   Crowned with milk-white may:
   In fleecy flocks of light
   O'er heaven the white clouds stray.
   Spring goeth all in White.

20 So sweet love seemed that April morn.
   When first we kissed beside the thorn,
   So strangely sweet, it was not strange
   We thought that love could never
      change.   *So Sweet Loved seemed.*

21 I never shall love the snow again
   Since Maurice died.
   I never shall love the Snow again.

22 My delight and thy delight
   Walking, like two angels white,
   In the gardens of the night.
   My Delight and thy Delight.

BRIGHT, JOHN, English statesman, 16 Nov. 1811–27 March, 1889

23 The Angel of Death has been abroad
   throughout the land; you may almost
   hear the beating of his wings.
   Speech, House of Commons, 23 Feb. 1855.

24 I am for "Peace, retrenchment and
   reform," the watchword of the great
   Liberal party thirty years ago.
   Ibid, Birmingham, 28 April, 1859.

25 England is the mother of Parliaments.
   Ibid, 18 Jan. 1865.

26 The right honourable gentleman . . .
   has retired into what may be called his
   political Cave of Adullam.
   Ibid, House of Commons, 13 March, 1866.

BROMLEY, ISAAC HILL, US journalist, 6 March, 1833–11 Aug. 1898

27 John A. Logan is the Head Centre, the
   Hub, the King Pin, the Main Sprin,
   Mogul and Mugwump of the final plot
   by which partisanship was installed in
   the Commission.
   Editorial, New York Tribune, 16 Feb. 1877.

BRONTË, EMILY JANE, English authoress, 30 July, 1818–19 Dec. 1848

28 Riches I hold in light esteem
   And love I laugh to scorn;
   And lust of fame was but a dream,
   That vanished with the morn.
   The Old Stoic.

29 No coward soul is mine,
   No trembler in the world's storm-
      troubled sphere:
   I see Heaven's glories shine,
   And faith shines equal, arming me from
      fear.   *Last Lines.*

30 Though earth and man were gone,
   And suns and universes ceased to be,
   And Thou wert left alone,
   Every existence would exist in Thee.
   Ibid.

BROOKE, RUPERT CHAWNER, English poet, 3 Aug. 1887–23 April, 1915

1 Breathless, we flung us on the windy hill,
Laughed in the sun, and kissed the lovely grass.   *The Hill.*

2 Unkempt about those hedges blows
An English unofficial rose.
                    The Old Vicarage, Grantchester.

3 Curates, long dust, will come and go
On lissom, clerical, printless toe;
And oft between the boughs is seen
The sly shade of a Rural Dean.   *Ibid.*

4 For England's the one land, I know,
Where men with Splendid Hearts may go.   *Ibid.*

5 And in that Heaven of all their wish,
There shall be no more land, say fish.
                                      Heaven.

6   Live hair that is
Shining and free; blue-massing clouds;
the keen
Unpassioned beauty of a great machine;
The benison of hot water; furs to touch;
The good smell of old clothes.
                            The Great Lover.

7 Blow out, you bugles, over the rich
Dead.   *The Dead.*

8 If I should die, think only this of me:
That there's some corner of a foreign field
That is for ever England.   *The Soldier.*

BROOKS, NOAH, US author, 24 Oct. 1830–16 Aug. 1903

9 Punch, brothers, punch with care,
Punch in the presence of the passenjare.
    *Inspired by a notice to conductors of
    New York horse-cars.*

(This has been claimed for Mark Twain, probably because he used it without acknowledgment, and for Isaac Hill Bromley.)

BROOKS, PHILLIPS, Bishop of Massachusetts, 13 Dec. 1835–23 Jan. 1893

10 O little town of Bethlehem,
How still we see thee lie;
Above thy deep and dreamless sleep
The silent stars go by.
        O Little Town of Bethlehem.

BROUGH, ROBERT BARNABAS, English author, 10 April, 1828–26 June, 1860

11 My Lord Tomnoddy is thirty-four;
The Earl can last but a few years more.
My Lord in the Peers will take his place:
Her Majesty's councils his words will grace.
Office he'll hold and patronage sway;
Fortunes and lives he will vote away;
And what are his qualifications? – ONE!
He's the Earl of Fitzdotterel's eldest son.
                    My Lord Tomnoddy.

BROUGHAM AND VAUX, HENRY PETER BROUGHAM, BARON, English Lord Chancellor, 19 Sept. 1778–7 May, 1868

12 The schoolmaster is abroad, and I trust to him, armed with his primer, against the soldier in full military array.
Speech, House of Commons, 29 Jan. 1828.

13 In my mind, he was guilt of no error, he was chargeable with no exaggeration, he was betrayed by his fancy into no metaphor, who once said, that all we see about us, Kings, Lords, and Commons, the whole machinery of the State, all the apparatus of the system, and its varied workings, end in simply bringing twelve good men into a box.
        *Speech on the Present State of the Law,
                        7 Feb. 1828.*

14 The great Unwashed.   *Attributed.*

BROWN, JOHN, English clergyman and author, 5 Nov. 1715–23 Sept. 1766

15 Truth's sacred fort th' exploded laugh shall win;

And coxcombs vanquish Berkeley by a grin.
An Essay on Satire, occasioned by the Death of Mr. Pope, II. 223.

BROWN, THOMAS, English author, 1663–16 June, 1704

16 I do not love thee, Doctor Fell,
The reason why I cannot tell;
But this alone I know full well,
I do not love thee, Doctor Fell.
Translation of Martial, Epigrams, I xxxii.
(No. 158:5 infra.)
(A slightly different version is given in Brown's Works.)

BROWN, THOMAS EDWARD, Manx poet, 5 May, 1830–30 Oct. 1897

17 O blackbird, what a boy you are!
How you do go it. *The Blackbird.*

18 A garden is a lovesome thing, God wot.
My Garden.

BROWNE, CHARLES FARRAR, see Ward, Artemus

BROWNE, SIR THOMAS, English doctor and author, 19 Oct. 1605–19 Oct. 1682

19 At my devotion I love to use the civility of my knee, my hat, and hand.
Religio Medici, part 1. 3.

20 I love to lose myself in a mystery, to pursue my Reason to an O *altitudo!*
Ibid, 9.

21 We carry within us the wonders we seek without us. There is all Africa and her prodigies in us. *Ibid, 15*

22 All things are artificial, for nature is the art of God. *Ibid, 16.*

23 It is the common wonder of all men, how among so many millions of faces there should be none alike.
Ibid, part II. 2.

24 What song the Syrens sang, or what name Achilles assumed when he hid himself among women, though puzzling questions, are not beyond all conjecture. *Hydriotaphia, v.*

25 But the inequity of oblivion blindly scattereth her poppy, and deals with the memory of men without distinction to merit of perpetuity. *Ibid.*

26 Man is a noble animal, splendid in ashes and pompous in the grave. *Ibid.*

27 Sleep is a death, O make me try
By sleeping, what it is to die,
And as gently lay my head
On my grave, as now my bed.
Religio Medici, part II. 12.

BROWNE, WILLIAM, English poet, 1590?–1645?

28 Underneath this sable hearse
Lies the subject of all verse,
Sidney's sister, Pembroke's mother,
Death! ere thou hast slain another
Learn'd and fair and good as she,
Time shall throw a dart at thee.
Epitaph on the Countess of Pembroke.
(This was formerly attributed to Ben Jonson.)

BROWNE, SIR WILLIAM, English doctor, 1692–10 March, 1774

29 The King to Oxford sent a troop of horse,
For Tories own no argument but force:
With equal care to Cambridge books he sent,
For Whigs allow no force but argument.
Epigram in reply to Trapp's.
(No. 302:9 infra.)

BROWNING, ELIZABETH BARRETT, English poetess, 6 March, 1806–30 June, 1861

30 Or from Browning some
'Pomegranate,' which, if cut deep down the middle,
Shows a heart within blood-tinctured, of a veined humanity.
Lady Geraldine's Courtship, 41.

1 Do you hear the children weeping, O
  my brothers,
  Ere the sorrow comes with years?
  The Cry of the Children, 1.

2 But the child's sob in the silence curses
  deeper
  Than the strong man in his wrath.
  Ibid, 13.

3 And kings crept out again to feel the
  sun. *Crowned and Buried, 11.*

4 In the pleasant orchard closes,
  'God bless all our gains,' say we;
  But 'May God bless all our losses'
  Better suits with our degree.
  The Lost Bower, 1.

5 Our Euripides, the human,
  With his droppings of warm tears.
  Wine of Cyprus, 12.

6 'Yes,' I answered you last night;
  'No,' this morning, sir, I say.
  Colours seen by candle-light
  Will not look the same by day.
  The Lady's 'Yes.'

7 Unless you can muse in a crowd all day
  On the absent face that fixed you;
  Unless you can love, as the angels may,
  With the breadth of heaven betwixt you;
  Unless you can dream that his faith is
  fast,
  Through behoving and unbehoving;
  Unless you can die when the dream is
  past –
  Oh, never call it loving!
  A Woman's Shortcomings.

8 'Guess now who holds thee?' – 'Death,'
  I said. But, there,
  The silver answer rang, . . . 'Not
  Death, but Love.'
  Sonnets from the Portuguese, i.

9 How do I love thee? Let me count the
  ways.
  I love thee to the depth and breadth and
  height
  My soul can reach, when feeling out of
  sight
  For the ends of Being and ideal Grace.
  I love thee to the level of every day's

Most quiet need, by sun and candle-
  light.
  I love thee freely, as men strive for
  Right;
  I love thee purely, as they turn from
  Praise.
  I love thee with the passion put to use
  In my old griefs, and with my
  childhood's faith.
  I love thee with a love I seemed to lose
  With my lost saints, – I love thee with
  the breath,
  Smiles, tears, of all my life! – and, if God
  choose,
  I shall but love thee better after death.
  Ibid. xliii.

10 Since when was genius found
  respectable? *Aurora Leigh, VI.*

11 What was he doing, the great god Pan,
  Down in the reeds by the river?
  Spreading ruin and scattering ban,
  Splashing and paddling with hoofs of a
  goat,
  And breaking the golden lilies afloat
  With the dragon-fly on the river.
  A Musical Instrument.

**BROWNING, ROBERT, English
poet, 7 May, 1812–12 Dec. 1889**

12 Sun-treader, life and light be thine for
  ever. (Shelley.) *Pauline, 148.*

13 Over the sea our galleys went,
  With cleaving prows in order brave.
  Paracelsus, iv.

14 Who will, may hear Sordello's story
  told. *Sordello, I. I.*

15 And still more labyrinthine buds the
  rose. *Ibid. 476.*

16   Any nose
  May ravage with impunity a rose.
  Ibid. VI. 877.

17 O'er night's brim, day boils at last.
  Pippa Passes, introduction.

18 Say not 'a small event!' Why 'small'?
  Costs it more pain that this, ye call
  A 'great event,' should come to pass,

Than that? Untwine me from the mass
Of deeds which make up life, one deed
Power shall fall short in or exceed!
Ibid.

19 The year's at the spring
And day's at the morn;
Morning's at seven;
The hill-side's dew-pearled;
The lark's on the wing;
The snail's on the thorn:
God's in his heaven –
All's right with the world!
Ibid. 1. Morning.

20 Some unsuspected isle in far-off seas.
Ibid. 2. Noon.

21 You'll love me yet! – and I can tarry
Your love's protracted growing:
June reared that bunch of flowers you
carry,
From seeds of April's sowing.
Ibid. 3. Evening.

22 All service ranks the same with God –
With God, whose puppets, best and
worst,
Are we: there is no last nor first.
Ibid. IV. Night.

23 Marching along, fifty-score strong,
Great-hearted gentlemen, singing this
song.
Cavalier Tunes. Marching Along.

24 Boot, saddle, to horse, and away!
Ibid. Boot and Saddle.

25 Just for a handful of silver he left us,
Just for a riband to stick in his coat.
The Lost Leader.

26 We shall march prospering, – not thro'
his presence;
Songs may inspirit us, – not from his
lyre;
Deeds will be done, – while he boasts his
quiescence,
Still bidding crouch whom the rest bade
aspire.
Ibid.

27 Never glad confident morning again.
Ibid.

28 I sprang to the stirrup, and Joris, and he;
I galloped, Dirck galloped, we galloped
all three.
*'How they brought the Good News from
Ghent to Aix,' 1.*

29 Where I find her not, beauties vanish;
Whither I follow her, beauties flee;
Is there no method to tell her in Spanish
June's twice June since she breathed it
with me?
Garden Fancies. The Flower's Name, 6.

30 Gr-r-r – there go, my heart's
abhorrence!
Water your damned flower-pots, do!
Soliloquy of the Spanish Cloister, 1.

31 There's a great text in Galatians,
Once you trip on it, entails
Twenty-nine distinct damnations,
One sure, if another fails.
Ibid. 7.

32 'St, there's Vespers! *Plena gratiâ
Ave, Virgo!* Gr-r-r – you swine!
Ibid. 9.

33 There are flashes struck from midnights,
There are fire-flames noondays kindle,
Whereby piled-up honours perish,
Whereby swollen ambitions dwindle,
While just this or that poor impulse,
Which for once had play unstifled,
Seems the sole work of a lifetime
That away the rest have trifled.
Christina, 4.

34 Round the cape of a sudden came the
sea,
And the sun looked over the mountain's
rim:
And straight was a path of gold for him,
And the need of a world of men for me.
Parting at Morning.

35 Nay but you, who do not love her,
Is she not pure gold, my mistress?
Song.

36 Beautiful Evelyn Hope is dead.
Evelyn Hope, 1.

37 Something to see, by Bacchus,
something to hear, at least!
Up at a Villa – Down in the City, 2.

1 Your ghost will walk, you lover of
   trees,
   (If our loves remain)
   In an English lane,
   By a cornfield-side a-flutter with
   poppies.   *'De Gustibus –'*

2 A castle, precipice-encurled,
   In a gash of the wind-grieved Apennine.
                                    Ibid.

3 Open my heart and you will see
   Graved inside of it, 'Italy.'   *Ibid.*

4 Oh, to be in England
   Now that April's there.
                  Home Thoughts, from Abroad.

5 That's the wise thrush; he sings each
   song twice over,
   Lest you should think he never could
   recapture
   The first fine careless rapture!   *Ibid.*

6 Nobly, nobly Cape St. Vincent to the
   North-west died away;
   Sunset ran, one glorious blood-red,
   reeking into Cadiz Bay.
                  Home-Thoughts, from the Sea.

7 'Tis not what man Does which exalts
   him, but what man Would do!
                                    Saul, 18.

8 Oh, the little more, and how much it is!
   And the little less, and what worlds
   away!   *By the Fire-Side, 39.*

9   Only I discern –
   Infinite passion, and the pain
   Of finite hearts that yearn.
                       Two in the Campagna, 12.

10 This is a spray the Bird clung to,
   Making it blossom with pleasure.
                                Misconceptions.

11 Lose who may – I still can say,
   Those who win heaven, blest are they!
                              One Way of Love.

12 It is but to keep the nerves at a strain,
   To dry one's eyes and laugh at a fall,
   And, baffled, get up and begin again.
                               Life in a Love.

13 Better sin the whole sin, sure that God
   observes;
   Then go live his life out! Life will try his
   nerves,
   When the sky, which noticed all, makes
   no disclosure,
   And the earth keeps up her terrible
   composure.   *Before, 4.*

14 Ah, did you once see Shelley plain,
   And did he stop and speak to you
   And did you speak to him again?
   How strange it seems and new!
                                Memorabilia.

15 Hobbs hints blue, – straight he turtle
   eats:
   Nobbs prints blue, – claret crowns his
   cup:
   Nokes outdares Stokes in azure feats, –
   Both gorge. Who fished the murex up?
   What porridge had John Keats?
                               Popularity, 13.

16 There's a woman like a dewdrop, she's
   so purer than the purest.
                  A Blot in the 'Scutcheon, I. iii.

17 It was roses, roses, all the way.
                                The Patriot.

18 The air broke into a mist with bells.
                                    Ibid.

19 That's my last Duchess painted on the
   wall,
   Looking as if she were alive.
                              My Last Duchess.

20 'For I' – so I spoke – 'am a poet:
   Human nature, – behoves that I know
   it!'   *The Glove.*

21 There may be heaven; there must be
   hell;
   Meantime, there is our earth here – well!
                               Time's Revenges.

22 'Tis an awkward thing to play with
   souls,
   And matter enough to save one's own.
                            A Light Woman, 12.

23 Who knows but the world may end to-
   night?   *The Last Ride Together, 2.*

24 Sing, riding's a joy! For me, I ride.
Ibid, 7.

25 And you, great sculptor – so, you gave
A score of years to Art, her slave,
And that's your Venus, whence we turn
To yonder girl that fords the burn!
Ibid, 8.

26 So munch on, crunch on, take your
nuncheon,
Breakfast, supper, dinner, luncheon!
The Pied Piper of Hamelin, 7.

27 A thousand guilders! Come, take fifty!
Ibid, 9.

28 He said, 'What's time? Leave Now for
dogs and apes!
Man has Forever.'
A Grammarian's Funeral.

29 That low man seeks a little thing to do,
Sees it and does it:
This high man, with a great thing to
pursue,
Dies ere he knows it.
That low man goes on adding one to
one,
His hundred's soon hit;
This high man, aiming at a million,
Misses an unit. *Ibid.*

30 He settled *Hoti's* business – let it be! –
Properly based *Oun* –
Gave us the doctrine of the enclitic *De*,
Dead from the waist down. *Ibid.*

31 Here's the top-peak; the multitude
below
Live, for they can, there:
This man decided not to Live but
Know –
Bury this man there? *Ibid.*

32 And the sin I impute to each frustrate
ghost
Is – the unlit lamp and the ungirt loin.
The Statue and the Bust.

33 You should not take a fellow eight years
old
And make him swear to never kiss the
girls. *Fra Lippo Lippi, 224.*

34 Ah, but a man's reach should exceed his
grasp,
Or what's a heaven for?
Andrea del Sarto, 97.

35 And have I not Saint Praxed's ear to
pray
Horses for ye, and brown Greek
manuscripts,
And mistresses with great smooth
marbly limbs?
*The Bishop orders his Tomb at Saint
Praxed's Church, 73.*

36 Aha, ELUCESCEBAT quoth our
friend?
No Tully, said I, Ulpian at the best!
Ibid, 99.

37 Just when we are safest, there's a sunset-
touch,
A fancy from a flower-bell, someone's
death,
A chorus-ending from Euripides, –
And that's enough for fifty hopes and
fears
As old and new at once as nature's self.
Bishop Blougram's Apology, 182.

38 No, when the fight begins within
himself,
A man's worth something. *Ibid, 693.*

39 God be thanked, the meanest of his
creatures
Boasts two soul-sides, one to face the
world with,
One to show a woman when he loves
her. *One Word more, 17.*

40 Oh, good gigantic smile o' the brown
old earth.
James Lee's Wife, vii. Among the Rocks.

41 On earth the broken arcs; in heaven, a
perfect round. *Abt Vogler, 9.*

42 Grow old along with me!
The best is yet to be.
Rabbi Ben Ezra, 1.

43 Then, welcome each rebuff
That turns earth's smoothness rough,
Each sting that bids nor sit nor stand but
go!

Be our joys three-parts pain!
Strive, and hold cheap the strain;
Learn, nor account the pang; dare, never
    grudge the throe.   *Ibid, 6.*

1   Setebos, Setebos, and Setebos!
    'Thinketh, He dwelleth i' the cold o' the
        moon.   *Caliban upon Setebos, 24.*

2   What is he buzzing in my ears?
    'Now that I come to die,
    Do I view the world as a vale of tears?'
    Ah, reverend sir, not I!   *Confessions, 1.*

3   How sad and bad and mad it was –
    But then, how it was sweet!   *Ibid, 9.*

4   Fear death? – to feel the fog in my
        throat,
    The mist in my face.   *Prospice.*

5   I was ever a fighter, so – one fight more,
    The best and the last!   *Ibid.*

6   No! let me taste the whole of it, fare like
        my peers
    The heroes of old,
    Bear the brunt, in a minute pay glad
        life's arrears
    Of pain, darkness and cold.   *Ibid.*

7   Each life unfulfilled, you see;
    It hangs still, patchy and scrappy:
    We have not sighed deep, laughed free,
    Starved, feasted, despaired, – been
        happy.   *Youth and Art, 16.*

8   It's wiser being good than bad;
    It's safer being meek than fierce;
    It's fitter being sane than mad.
        Apparent Failure, 7.

9   O lyric Love, half angel and half bird
    And all a wonder and a wild desire.
        The Ring and the Book, I. 1391.

10   What I call God
    And fools call Nature.
        Ibid, X. The Pope, 1073.

11 Why comes temptation but for man to
        meet
    And master and make crouch beneath
        his foot,
    And so be pedestalled in triumph?
        Ibid, 1185.

12 Abate, – Cardinal, – Christ, – Maria, –
        God, . . .
    Pompilia, will you let them murder me?
        Ibid, XI. Guido, 2426.

13   'With this same key
    Shakespeare unlocked his heart,' once
        more!
    Did Shakespeare? If so, the less
    Shakespeare he!   *House, 10.*

14 I want to know a butcher paints,
    A baker rhymes for his pursuit,
    Candlestick-maker much acquaints
    His soul with song, or, haply mute,
    Blows out his brains upon the flute!
        Shop, 21.

15 Good, to forgive;
    Best, to forget!
    Living, we fret;
    Dying, we live.
        La Saisiaz, introduction.

16 Such a starved bank of moss
    Till that May-morn,
    Blue ran the flash across:
    Violets were born!
        The Two Poets of Croisic, introduction.

17 Sky – what a scowl of cloud
    Till, near and far,
    Ray on ray split the shroud
    Splendid, a star!   *Ibid.*

18 Never the time and the place
    And the loved one all together!
        Never the Time and the Place.

19 Truth, that's brighter than gem,
    Trust, that's purer than pearl, –
    Brightest truth, purest trust in the
        universe – all were for me
    In the kiss of one girl.
        Asolando. Summum Bonum.

20 One who never turned his back but
        marched breast forward,
    Never doubted clouds would break,
    Never dreamed, though right were
        worsted, wrong would triumph,
    Held we fall to rise, are baffled to fight
        better,
    Sleep to wake.   *Ibid, epilogue.*

21 No, at noonday in the bustle of man's
worktime
Greet the unseen with a cheer!   *Ibid.*

BRUCE, MICHAEL, Scottish poet, 27 March, 1746–5 July, 1767

22 Sweet bird! thy bow'r is ever green,
Thy sky is ever clear;
Thou hast no sorrow in thy song,
No winter in thy year.
Ode to the Cuckoo.

BRUMMELL, GEORGE BRYAN ('BEAU BRUMMELL'), English dandy, 7 June, 1778–30 March, 1840

23 Who's your fat friend?
Of the Prince of Wales.

BRYAN, WILLIAM JENNINGS, US statesman, 19 March, 1860–26 July, 1925

24 The humblest citizen of all the land,
when clad in the armour of a righteous
cause, is stronger than all the hosts of
Error.
*Speech, National Democratic Convention,
Chicago, 10 July, 1896.*

25 We will answer their demand for a gold
standard by saying to them: You shall
not press down upon the brow of labour
this crown of thorn. You shall not
crucify mankind upon a cross of gold.
Ibid.

BRYANT, WILLIAM CULLEN, US poet and journalist, 3 Nov. 1794–12 June, 1878

26 So live, that when thy summons comes
to join
The innumerable caravan which moves
To that mysterious realm, where each
shall take
His chamber in the silent halls of death,
Thou go not, like the quarry-slave at
night,
Scourged to his dungeon, but, sustained
and soothed
By an unfaltering trust, approach thy
grave,

Like one that wraps the drapery of his
couch
About him, and lies down to pleasant
dreams.   *Thanatopsis, 73.*

27 The visions of my youth are past –
Too bright, too beautiful to last.
The Rivulet.

BRYDGES, SIR SAMUEL EGERTON, English genealogist, 30 Nov. 1762–8 Sept. 1837

28 The glory dies not, and the grief is past.
Sonnet on the Death of Sir Walter Scott.

BUCHANAN, ROBERT WILLIAMS, Scottish author, 18 Aug. 1841–10 June, 1901

29   She just wore
Enough for modesty – no more.
White Rose and Red, part 1. V. 60.

30 The Fleshly School of Poetry.
*Article in Contemporary Review,
Oct. 1871.*

BUCKINGHAM, GEORGE VILLIERS, 2ND DUKE OF, 20 Jan. 1628–16 April, 1687

31 What the devil does the plot signify,
except to bring in fine things?
The Rehearsal, III. i.

BUCKINGHAM AND NORMANBY, JOHN SHEFFIELD, 1ST DUKE OF, 7 April, 1648–24 Feb. 1721

32 Read Homer once, and you can read no
more,
For all books else appear so mean, so
poor,
Verse will seem prose; but still persist to
read,
And Homer will be all the books you
need.   *Essay on Poetry, 322.*

BUCKSTONE, JOHN BALDWIN, English actor and dramatist, 14 Sept. 1802–31 Oct. 1879

33 On such an occasion as this,
All time and nonsense scorning,

Nothing shall come amiss,
And we won't go home till morning.
Billy Taylor, I. ii.

BUFFON, GOERGES LOUIS LECLERC, COMTE DE, French scientist, 7 Sept. 1707–16 April, 1788

1 Le style est l'homme même. – The style is the man himself.
Discours sur le style – Discourse on Style.

2 La génie n'est autre chose qu'une grande aptitude à la patience – Genius is nothing else but a great aptitude for patience.
Attributed.

BUNN, ALFRED, English theatre manager, 1796?–20 Dec. 1860

3 I dreamt that I dwelt in marble halls,
With vassals and serfs at my side.
The Bohemian Girl, II.

4 The heart bow'd down by weight of woe
To weakest hopes will cling. *Ibid.*

5 When other lips and other hearts
Their tales of love shall tell. *Ibid, III.*

BUNNER, HENRY CUYLER, US author, 3 Aug. 1855–11 May, 1896

6 Love must kiss that mortal's eyes
Who hopes to see fair Arcady.
No gold can buy you entrance there;
But beggared Love may go all bare –
No wisdom won with weariness;
But Love goes in with Folly's dress –
No fame that wit could ever win;
But only Love may lead Love in
To Arcady, to Arcady.
The Way to Arcady.

BUNYAN, JOHN, English author, baptised 30 Nov. 1628, died 31 Aug. 1688

7 The name of the slough was Despond.
Pilgrim's Progress, part 1.

8 Set down my name, Sir. *Ibid.*

9 Then Apollyon straddled quite over the whole breadth of the way. *Ibid.*

10 It beareth the name of Vanity Fair,
because the town where 'tis kept is
lighter than vanity. *Ibid.*

11 So soon as the man overtook me, he was but a word and a blow. *Ibid.*

12 A castle called Doubting Castle, the owner whereof was Giant Despair.
Ibid.

13 So he passed over, and all the trumpets sounded for him on the other side.
Ibid, part II.

14 Some said 'John, print it'; others said, 'Not so.'
Some said, 'It might do good'; other said, 'No.' *Ibid, Apology for his Book.*

15 He that is down need fear no fall,
He that is low, no pride.
Ibid, Shepherd boy's song in the Valley of Humiliation.

BURCHARD, SAMUEL DICKINSON, US clergyman, 6 Sept. 1812–25 Sept. 1891

16 We are Republicans, and don't propose to leave our party and identify ourselves with the party whose antecedents have been Rum, Romanism, and Rebellion.
Speaking for a deputation of clergymen, New York, 29 Oct. 1884.

BURDETTE, ROBERT JONES, US clergyman, 30 July, 1844–19 Nov. 1914

17 Yet though I'm full of music
As choirs of singing birds,
'I cannot sing the old songs' –
I do not know the words.
Songs without Words.

BURGESS, FRANK GELETT, US humorist, 30 Jan. 1866–18 Sept. 1951

18 I never saw a Purple Cow
I never hope to see one;
But I can tell you, anyhow,
I'd rather see than be one.
The Purple Cow.

19 Ah, yes, I wrote the 'Purple Cow' –
I'm sorry, now, I wrote it!
But I can tell you, anyhow,
I'll kill you if you quote it!
Cinq Ans Après.

**BURGON, JOHN WILLIAM,
English clergyman, 21 Aug. 1813–4
Aug. 1888**

20 Match me such marvel save in Eastern
clime,
A rose-red city half as old as Time.
Petra, 132.

**BURGOYNE, JOHN, English
General and dramatist, 24 Feb.
1722–4 June, 1792**

21 You have only, when before your glass,
to keep pronouncing to yourself nimini-
pimini – the lips cannot fail of taking
their plie.   *The Heiress, III. ii.*

**BURKE, EDMUND, Irish
statesman, 12 Jan. 1729–9 July, 1797**

22 I am convinced that we have a degree of
delight, and that no small one, in the real
misfortunes and pains of others.
On the Sublime and Beautiful, part I. 14.

23 There is, however, a limit at which
forbearance ceases to be a virtue.
*Observations on a Publication,
'The Present State of the Nation.'*

24 When bad men combine, the good must
associate; else they will fall, one by one,
an unpitied sacrifice in a contemptible
struggle.   *Thoughts on the Cause of the
Present Discontents.*

25 The cant of *Not men, but measures. Ibid.*

26 A wise and salutary neglect.
Speech on Conciliation with America.

27 The worthy gentleman who has been
snatched from us at the moment of the
election, and in the middle of the
contest, whilst his desires were as warm,
and his hopes as eager as ours, has
feelingly told us what shadows we are,
and what shadows we pursue.
*Speech at Bristol on Declining the Poll,
1780*

28 It is now sixteen or seventeen years since
I saw the Queen of France, then the
Dauphiness, at Versailles; and surely
never lighted on this orb, which she
hardly seemed to touch, a more
delightful vision. I saw her just above
the horizon, decorating and cheering the
elevated sphere she just began to move
in, – glittering like the morning star, full
of life, and splendour, and joy . . . Little
did I dream that I should have lived to
see such disasters fallen upon her in a
nation of gallant men, in a nation of men
of honour and of cavaliers. I thought ten
thousand swords must have leaped from
their scabbards to avenge even a look
that threatened her with insult. But the
age of chivalry is gone. That of
sophisters, economists, and calculators,
has succeeded; and the glory of Europe
is extinguished for ever.
Reflections on the Revolution in France.

29 That chastity of honour which felt a
stain like a wound.   *Ibid.*

30 Vice itself lost half its evil, by losing all
its grossness.   *Ibid.*

31 Kings will be tyrants from policy, when
subjects are rebels from principle. *Ibid.*

32 Learning will be cast into the mire and
trodden down under the hoofs of a
swinish multitude.   *Ibid.*

33 The men of England, the men, I mean,
of light and leading in England. *Ibid.*

34 And having looked to government for
bread, on the very first scarcity they will
turn and bite the hand that fed them.
Thoughts and Details on Scarcity.

35 He was not merely a chip of the old
block, but the old block itself.
Of Pitt's first speech, 26 Feb. 1781.

36 It is not a good imitation of Johnson; it
has all his pomp, without his force; it
has all the nodosities of the oak without
its strength; it has all the contortions of
the Sybil without the inspiration. (On
Croft's life of Dr. Young.)
Boswell, Life of Johnson, an. 1781.

BURNEY, FRANCES or FANNY (MME. D'ARBLAY), English novelist, 13 June, 1752–6 Jan. 1840

1 'True, very true, ma'am,' said he (Mr. Meadowes), yawning, 'one really lives nowhere; one does but vegetate, and wish it all at an end.' *Cecilia, VII. v.*

BURNS, ROBERT, Scottish poet, 25 Jan. 1759–21 July, 1796

2 Tho' this was fair, and that was braw,
And yon the toast of a' the town,
I sigh'd, and said among them a',
'Ye are na Mary Morison.'
Mary Morison.

3 Auld Nature swears, the lovely dears
Her noblest work she classes, O;
Her prentice han' she tried on man,
And then she made the lasses, O!
Green grow the Rashes.

4   Nature's law
That man was made to mourn.
Man was made to mourn.

5 Man's inhumanity to man
Makes countless thousands mourn!
Ibid.

6 The heart aye's the part aye
That makes us right or wrang.
Epistle to Davie, a Brother Poet.

7 O Thou, who in the heavens does dwell,
Who, as it pleases best Thysel',
Sends ane to heaven, and ten to hell,
A' for Thy glory,
And no for ony gude or ill
They've done afore Thee!
Holy Willie's Prayer.

8 I was na fou, but just had plenty.
Death and Doctor Hornbook.

9 Some wee short hour ayont the twal'
Ibid.

10 There's some are fou o' love divine,
There's some are fou o' brandy.
The Holy Fair, 27.

11 Wee sleekit, cowrin, tim'rous beastie,

O, what a panic's in thy breastie!
To a Mouse.

12 The best-laid schemes o' mice and men
Gang aft a-gley.
Ibid.

13 The mother, wi' her needle and her shears,
Gars auld claes look amaist as weel's the new. *The Cotter's Saturday Night, 5.*

14 The halesome parritch, chief of Scotia's food.
Ibid, 11.

15 He wales a portion with judicious care,
And 'Let us worship God!' he says with solemn air.
Ibid, 12.

16 From scenes like these old Scotia's grandeur springs,
That make her lov'd at home, rever'd abroad:
Princes and lords are but the breath of kings,
'An honest man's the noblest work of God.'
Ibid, 19.

17 O thou! whatever title suit thee –
Auld Hornie, Satan, Nick, or Clootie.
Address to the Devil.

18 But fare-you-weel, auld Nickie-ben!
O wad ye tak a thought an' men'!
Ye aiblins might—I dinna ken—
Still hae a stake:
I'm wae to think upo' yon den,
Ev'n for your sake!
Ibid.

19 His locked, letter'd, braw brass collar,
Show'd him the gentleman and scholar.
The Twa Dogs, 13.

20 Freedom and whisky gang thegither!
The Author's Earnest Cry and Prayer, postscript, 7.

21 Then gently scan your brother man,
Still gentler sister woman;
Though they may gang a kennin wrang,
To step aside is human.
Address to the unco Guid.

22 What's done we partly may compute,
But know not what's resisted. *Ibid.*

23 O wad some Power the giftie gie us
To see oursels as ithers see us!
It wad frae mony a blunder free us,
And foolish notion.   *To a Louse.*

24 Wee, modest, crimson-tippèd flow'r.
                    To a Mountain Daisy.

25 I waive the quantum o' the sin,
The hazard of concealing;
But och! it hardens a' within,
And petrifies the feeling.
              Epistle to a Young Friend.

26 To catch dame Fortune's golden smile,
Assiduous wait upon her;
And gather gear by ev'ry wile
That's justified by honour;
Not for to hide it in a hedge,
Nor for a train attendant;
But for the glorious privilege
Of being independent.   *Ibid.*

27 But facts are chiels that winna ding,
An' downa be disputed.   *A Dream*

28 The poor inhabitants below
Was quick to learn and wise to know,
And keenly felt the friendly glow,
And softer flame;
But thoughtless follies laid him low,
And stain'd his name. *A Bard's Epitaph.*

29 Your poor, narrow foot-path of a street,
Where twa wheel-barrows tremble
    when they meet.   *The Brigs of Ayr*

30 Great chieftain o' the pudding-race.
                    Address to a Haggis.

31 Here lie Willie Miche's banes,
O Satan, when ye tak him,
Gie him the schulin o' your weans,
For clever deils he'll mak them!
              Epitaph for a Schoolmaster.

32 Whoe'er he be that sojourns here,
I pity much his case,
Unless he come to wait upon
The Lord their God,—His Grace.

33 There's naething here but Highland
    pride,
And Highland scab and hunger:
If Providence has sent me here,

'Twas surely in an anger.
                    The Bard at Inveraray.

34 Up in the morning's no for me,
Up in the morning early.
                    Up in the Morning.

35 Of a' the airts the wind can blaw,
I dearly like the west,
For there the bonnie lassie lives,
The lassie I lo'e best.   *Of a' the Airts.*

36 Aye waukin', O!
Waukin' still and wearie:
Sleep I can get nane
For thinking on my dearie.
              Simmer's a Pleasant Time.

37 Should auld acquaintance be forgot,
And never brought to mind?
Should auld acquaintance be forgot,
And auld lang syne!   *Auld Lang Syne*

38 We'll tak a cup o' kindness yet,
For auld lang syne.   *Ibid.*

39 We twa hae run about the braes,
And pu'd the gowans fine;
But we've wander'd mony a weary fit,
Sin' auld lang syne.   *Ibid.*

40 And there's a hand, my trusty fere,
And gie's a hand o' thine!
And we'll tak a right gude-willie
    waught,
For auld lang syne.   *Ibid.*

41 Go, fetch to me a pint o' wine,
And fill it in a silver tassie;
That I may drink before I go.
A service to my bonnie lassie.
                    My Bonnie Mary.

42 John Anderson my jo, John,
When we were first acquent,
Your locks were like the raven,
Your bonnie brow was brent;
But now your brow is beld, John,
Your locks are like the snow;
But blessings on your frosty pow,
John Anderson, my jo.
                    John Anderson my Jo.

43 My love she's but a lassie yet.   *Title.*

1 Whistle o'er the lave o't.   *Title*

2 Hear, Land o' Cakes, and brither Scots,
Frae Maidenkirk to Johnny Groat's;—
If there's a hole in a' your coats,
I rede you tent it:
A chiel's amang you takin' notes,
And, faith, he'll prent it!
*On the late Captain Grose's Peregrinations
thro' Scotland.*

3˙ My heart's in the Highlands, my heart is
not here,
My heart's in the Highlands, a-chasing
the deer;
A-chasing the wild deer, and following
the roe,
My heart's in the Highlands wherever I
go.
(Traditional.)   *My Heart's in the
Highlands.*

4 To make a happy fireside clime
To weans and wife,
That's the true pathos and sublime
Of human life.   *Epistle to Dr. Blacklock.*

5 Where sits our sulky sullen dame,
Gathering her brows like gathering
storm,
Nursing her wrath to keep it warm.
Tam o' Shanter, 10.

6 Auld Ayr, wham ne'er a town surpasses
For honest men and bonnie lasses.
Ibid., 15.

7 Ah, gentle dames! it gars me greet
To think how mony counsels sweet,
How mony lengthen'd, sage advices
The husband frae the wife despises!
Ibid., 33.

8 His ancient, trusty, drouthy crony:
Tam lo'ed him like a very brither;
They had been fou for weeks thegither.
Ibid., 43.

9 Kings may be blest, but Tam was
glorious,
O'er a' the ills o' life victorious.
Ibid., 57.

10 But pleasures are like poppies spread,
You seize the flow'r, its bloom is shed;
Or like the snow falls in the river,

A moment white—then melts for ever;
Or like the Borealis race,
That flit ere you can point their place;
Or like the rainbow's lovely form
Evanishing amid the storm.   *Ibid., 59.*

11 Ah, Tam! ah, Tam! thou'll get thy
fairin!
In hell they'll roast thee like a herrin!
Ibid., 201.

12 Ye banks and braes o' bonnie Doon,
How can ye bloom sae fresh and fair?
How can ye chant, ye little birds,
And I sae weary fu' o' care?
The Banks o' Doon.

13 What can a young lassie do wi' an auld
man?   *Title.*

14 Critics!—appall'd I venture on the
name,
Those cut-throat bandits in the paths of
fame.
Second Epistle to Robert Graham of Fintry.

15 Ae fond kiss and then we sever.
Ae Fond Kiss.

16 But to see her was to love her,
Love but her, and love for ever.   *Ibid.*

17 Had we never lov'd sae kindly,
Had we never lov'd sae blindly,
Never met—or never parted,
We had ne'er been broken-hearted.   *Ibid.*

18 The deil's awa wi' the Exciseman.   *Title.*

19 O saw ye bonnie Lesley
As she gaed o'er the Border?
She's gane, like Alexander,
To spread her conquests farther.
To see her is to love her,
And love but her for ever;
For Nature made her what she is,
And never made anither!   *Bonnie Lesley.*

20 Here awa, there awa, wandering Willie.
Wandering Willie.

21 Whistle, and I'll come to ye, my land.
Title.

22 Scots, wha hae wi' Wallace bled,
Scots, wham Bruce has aften led,

Welcome to your gory bed,
Or to victory. *Bannockburn.*

23 Now's the day, and now's the hour;
See the front o' battle lour;
See approach proud Edward's power—
Chains and slavery! *Ibid.*

24 Liberty's in every blow!—
Let us do or die! *Ibid.*

25 O my luve's like a red, red rose,
That's newly sprung in June:
O my luve's like the melody
That's sweetly play'd in tune.
A Red, Red Rose.

26 And I will luve thee still, my dear,
Till a' the seas gang dry. *Ibid.*

27 He turn'd him right and round about
Upon the Irish shore;
And gae his bridle-reins a shake,
With adieu for evermore, my dear;
With adieu for evermore.
(Found in a ballad.)
It was a' for our Rightfu' King.

28 Contented wi' little, and cantie wi' mair.
Contented wi' Little.

29 When I think on the happy days
I spent wi' you, my dearie;
And now what lands between us lie,
How can I be but eerie?

30 How slow ye move, ye heavy hours,
As ye were wae and wear!
It wasna sae ye glinted by,
When I was wi' my dearie.
How Long and Dreary is the Night.

31 The rank is but the guinea's stamp;
The man's the gowd for a' that.
A Man's a Man for a' That.

32 A king can mak a belted knight,
A marquis, duke, and a' that;
But an honest man's aboon his might,
Guide faith, he mauna fa' that. *Ibid.*

33 For a' that, and a' that,
It's coming yet for a' that,
That man to man, the warld o'er,
Shall brothers be for a' that. *Ibid.*

34 O wert thou in the cauld blast. *Title.*

35 Gin a body meet a body
Coming through the rye;
Gin a body kiss a body,
Need a body cry?
(Old song rewritten.)
Coming through the Rye.

36 Some hae meat, and canna eat,
And some wad eat that want it;
But we hae meat, and we can eat,
And saw the Lord be thankit.
(Authorship doubtful.)
The Selkirk Grace.

**BURTON, ROBERT, English
clergyman and author, 8 Feb.
1577—25 Jan. 1640**

37 Naught so sweet as melancholy.
*Anatomy of Melancholy. The Author's
Abstract.*

38 They lard their lean books with the fat
of others' works.
Ibid., Democritus to the Reader.

39 We can say nothing but what hath been
said . . . . Our poets steal from Homer
. . . . He that comes last is commonly
best. *Ibid.*

40 One was never married, and that's his
hell; another is, and that's his plague.
Ibid., part I. ii. iv. 7.

41 Tobacco, divine, rare, superexcellent
tobacco, which goes far beyond all their
panaceas, potable gold, and
philosopher's stones, a sovereign
remedy to all diseases.
Ibid., part II. iv. ii. 1.

42 But, as it is commonly abused by most
men, which take it as tinkers do ale, 'tis
a plague, and mischief, a violent purger
of goods, lands, health, hellish, devilish,
and damned tobacco, the ruin and
overthrow of body and soul. *Ibid.*

**BUTLER, JOSEPH, BISHOP OF
DURHAM, 18 May, 1692—16 June,
1752**

43 Things and actions are what they are,
and the consequences of them will be

what they will be: why then should we desire to be deceived?

Fifteen Sermons, vii. 16.

BUTLER, NICHOLAS MURRAY, President of Columbia University, New York, 2 April, 1862–7 Dec. 1947

1 An expert is one who knows more and more about less and less.

Commencement Address.

BUTLER, SAMUEL, English poet, baptised 8 Feb. 1612, died 25 Sept. 1680

2 And pulpit, drum ecclesiastic,
Was beat with fist instead of a stick.

Hudibras, I. i. II.

3 Beside, 'tis known he could speak Greek
As naturally as pigs squeak;
That Latin was no more difficile
Than to a blackbird 'tis to whistle.

Ibid, 51.

4 He was in logic a great critic,
Profoundly skill'd in analytic.
He could distinguish and divide
A hair 'twixt south and south-west side.
On either which he would dispute,
Confute, change hands, and still confute.

Ibid, 65.

5 For rhetoric, he could not ope
His mouth, but out there flew a trope.

Ibid, 81.

6 For he by geometric scale
Could take the size of pots of ale.

Ibid, 121.

7 And wisely tell what hour o' th' day
The clock does strike, by algebra.

Ibid, 125.

8 For every why he had a wherefore.

Ibid, 132.

9 He knew what's what, and that's as high
As metaphysic wit can fly.   *Ibid, 149.*

10 Such as take lodgings in a head
That's to be let unfurnished.   *Ibid, 161.*

11 'Twas Presbyterian true blue.

Ibid, 191.

12 Such as do build their faith upon
The holy text of pike and gun.

Ibid, 195.

13 And prove their doctrine orthodox
By apostolic blows and knocks.

Ibid, 199.

14 Compound for sins they are inclin'd to
By damning those they have no mind to.   *Ibid, 215.*

15 The trenchant blade, Toledo trusty,
For want of fighting was grown rusty,
And eat into itself, for lack
Of some body to hew and hack.

Ibid, 359.

16 For rhyme the rudder is of verses,
With which, like ships, they steer their courses.   *Ibid, 463.*

17 With many a stiff thwack, many a bang,
Hard crab-tree and old iron rang,

Ibid, ii. 831.

18 Ay me! what perils do environ
The man that meddles with cold iron.

Ibid, iii. I.

19 If he that in the field is slain
Be in the bed of honour lain,
He that is beaten may be said
To lie in honour's truckle-bed.

Ibid, 1047.

20 But those that write in rhyme still make
The one verse for the other's sake;
For one for sense, and one for rhyme,
I think's sufficient at one time.

Ibid, II. i. 27.

21 Not by your individual whiskers,
But by your dialect and discourse.

Ibid, 155.

22 Some have been beaten till they know
What wood a cudgel's of by th' blow;
Some kicked until they can feel whether
A shoe be Spanish or neat's leather.

Ibid, 221.

23 The sun had long since in the lap
Of Thetis taken out his nap,
And, like a lobster boiled, the morn
From black to red began to turn.
Ibid, ii. 29.

24 Have always been at daggers-drawing,
And one another clapper-clawing.
Ibid, 79.

25 What makes all doctrines plain and
clear?
About two hundred pounds a year.
And that which was proved true before,
Prove false again? Two hundred more.
Ibid, III. i. 1277.

26 He that complies against his will
Is of his own opinion still.
Ibid, iii. 547.

**BUTLER, SAMUEL, English
author, 4 Dec. 1835–18 June, 1902**

27 Life is one long process of getting tired.
Note Books. Lord, What is Man? Life.

28 Life is the art of drawing sufficient
conclusions from insufficient premises.
Ibid.

29 The phrase 'unconscious humour' is the
one contribution I have made to the
current literature of the day.
Ibid, The Position of a Homo unius Libri.

30 I keep my books at the British Museum
and at Mudie's.
*The Humour of Homer. Ramblings
in Cheapside.*

31 Stowed away in a Montreal lumber
room
The Discobulus standeth and turneth his
face to the wall;
Dusty, cobweb-covered, maimed and
set at naught,
Beauty crieth in an attic and no man
regardeth.
O God! O Montreal!
A Psalm of Montreal.

**BUTLER, WILLIAM, English
doctor, 1535–29 Jan. 1618**

32 Doubtless God could have made a better

berry, but doubtless God never did. (Of
the Strawberry.)
Walton, Compleat Angler, I. v.

**BYROM, JOHN, English poet, 29
Feb. 1692–26 Sept. 1763**

33 God bless the King! – I mean the Faith's
Defender;
God bless (no harm in blessing) the
Pretender!
But who Pretender is, or who is King, –
God bless us all! – that's quite another
thing. *To an Officer of the Army.*

34 Some say, compar'd to Bononcini,
That Mynheer Handel's but a ninny;
Other aver that he to Handel
Is scarcely fit to hold a candle.
Strange all this difference should be
'Twixt Tweedledum and Tweedledee.
*On the Feuds between Handel
and Bononcini.*

35 Christians awake! Salute the happy
morn,
Whereon the Saviour of the World was
born! *Hymn for Christmas Day.*

**BYRON, GEORGE GORDON
NOEL BYRON, 6TH LORD, 22
Jan. 1788–19 April, 1824**

36 When we two parted
In silence and tears,
Half broken-hearted
To sever for years. *When we two parted.*

37 If I should meet thee
After long years,
How should I greet thee? –
With silence and tears. *Ibid.*

38 Fools are my theme, let satire be my
song.
English Bards and Scotch Reviewers, 6.

39 'Tis pleasant, sure, to see one's name in
print;
A book's a book, although there's
nothing in 't. *Ibid, 51.*

40 With just enough of learning to
misquote. *Ibid, 66.*

1   As soon
Seek roses in December – ice in June;
Hope constancy in wind, or corn in
chaff;
Believe a woman or an epitaph,
Or any other thing that's false, before
You trust in critics who themselves are
sore.   *Ibid, 75.*

2 Better to err with Pope, that shine with
Pye.   *Ibid, 102.*

3 Oh, Amos Cottle! Phoebus! what a
name!   *Ibid, 399.*

4 So the struck eagle, stretch'd upon the
plain,
No more through rolling clouds to soar
again,
View'd his own feather on the fatal dart,
And wing'd the shaft that quiver'd in his
heart;
Keen were his pangs, but keener far to
feel
He nursed the pinion which impell'd the
steel.   *Ibid, 841.*

5 Maid of Athens, ere we part,
Give, oh give me back my heart!
                                   Maid of Athens.

6 Maidens, like moths, are ever caught by
glare.   *Childe Harold's Pilgrimage, I. 9.*

7 Adieu, adieu! my native shore
Fades o'er the waters blue.   *Ibid, 13.*

8 My native land – good night!   *Ibid.*

9 Once more upon the waters! yet once
more!
And the waves bound beneath me as a
steed
That knows his rider.   *Ibid, iii. 2.*

10 Stop! – for thy tread is on an Empire's
dust!
An earthquake's spoil is sepulchred
below!   *Ibid, 17.*

11 There was a sound of revelry by night,
And Belgium's capital had gather'd then
Her beauty and her chivalry, and bright
The lamps sone o'er fair women and
brave men;

A thousand hearts beat happily; and
when
Music arose with its voluptuous swell,
Soft eyes look'd love to eyes which
spake again,
And all went merry as a marriage bell;
But hush! hark! a deep sound strikes like
a rising knell!   *Ibid, 21.*

12 Did ye not hear it? – No; 'twas but the
wind,
Or the car rattling o'er the stony street;
On with the dance! let joy be
unconfined;
No sleep till morn, when Youth and
Pleasure meet
To chase the glowing Hours with flying
feet.   *Ibid, 22.*

13 Arm! Arm! it is – it is – the cannon's
opening roar!   *Ibid.*

14 He rush'd into the field, and, foremost
fighting, fell.   *Ibid, 23.*

15 And there was mounting in hot haste.
                                   Ibid, 25.

16 Rider and horse, – friend, foe, – in one
red burial blent.   *Ibid, 27.*

17 The castled crag of Drachenfels
Frowns o'er the wide and winding
Rhine.   *Ibid, 55.*

18 By the blue rushing of the arrowy
Rhone.   *Ibid, 71.*

19 Sapping a solemn creed with solemn
sneer.   *Ibid, 107.*

20 I have not loved the world, nor the
world me;
I have not flatter'd its rank breath, nor
bow'd
To its idolatries a patient knee.
                                   Ibid, 113.

21 I stood in Venice, on the Bridge of
Sighs;
A palace and a prison on each hand.
                                   Ibid, iv. I.

22 Where Venice sate in state, throned on
her hundred isles.   *Ibid.*

23 Then farewell, Horace; whom I hated
  so,
  Not for thy faults, but mine.   *Ibid, 77.*

24 Yet, Freedom! yet thy banner, torn, but
  flying,
  Streams like the thunder-storm *against*
  the wind.   *Ibid, 98.*

25 He reck'd not of the life he lost nor
  prize,
  But where his rude hut by the Danube
  lay,
  There were his young barbarians all at
  play,
  There was their Dacian mother – he,
  their sire,
  Butcher'd to make a Roman holiday.
    Ibid, 141.

26 While stands the Coliseum, Rome shall
  stand;
  When falls the Coliseum, Rome shall
  fall;
  And when Rome falls – the World.
    Ibid, 145.
  (Saying of the ancient pilgrims, quoted
  from Bede by Gibbon, *Decline and Fall
  of the Roman Empire,* lxxi.)

27 There is a pleasure in the pathless
  woods,
  There is a rapture on the lonely shore,
  There is society, where none intrudes,
  By the deep sea, and music in its roar:
  I love not Man the less, but Nature
  more,
  From these our interviews, in which I
  steal
  From all I may be, or have been before,
  To mingle with the Universe, and feel
  What I can ne'er express, yet cannot all
  conceal.   *Ibid, 178.*

28 Roll on, thou deep and dark blue Ocean
  – roll!
  Ten thousand fleets sweep over thee in
  vain;
  Man marks the earth with ruin – his
  control
  Stops with the shore.   *Ibid, 179.*

29 He sinks into thy depths with bubbling
  groan,
  Without a grave, unknell'd,
  unconffin'd, and unknown.   *Ibid.*

30 Time writes no wrinkle on thine azure
  brow:
  Such as creation's dawn beheld, thou
  rollest now.   *Ibid, 182.*

31 Muse of the many-twinkling feet!
    The Waltz.

32 Know ye the land where the cypress and
  myrtle
  Are emblems of deeds that are done in
  their clime?
  Where the rage of the vulture, the love
  of the turtle,
  Now melt into sorrow, now madden to
  crime.   *The Bride of Abydos, i. I.*

33 The blind old man of Scio's rocky isle.
    Ibid, ii. 2.

34 Hark! to the hurried question of
  Despair:
  'Where is my child?' – an echo answers,
  'Where?'   *Ibid, 27.*

35 O'er the glad waters of the dark blue
  sea,
  Our thoughts as boundless, and our
  souls as free,
  Far as the breeze can bear, the billows
  foam,
  Survey our empire, and behold our
  home!   *The Corsair, i. I.*

36 She walks in beauty, like the night
  Of cloudless climes and starry skies;
  And all that's best of dark and bright
  Meet in her aspect and her eyes:
  Thus mellow'd to that tender light
  Which heaven to gaudy day denies.
    She walks in Beauty.

37 Oh! snatch'd away in beauty's bloom,
  On thee shall press no ponderous tomb.
    Oh! snatch'd away in Beauty's Bloom.

38 The Assyrian came down like the wolf
  on the fold,
  And his cohorts were gleaming in
  purple and gold;
  And the sheen of their spears was like
  stars on the sea,
  When the blue wave rolls nightly on
  deep Galilee.
    The Destruction of Sennacherib.

1 There be none of Beauty's daughters
With a magic like thee;
And like music on the waters
Is thy sweet voice to me.
Stanzas for Music.

2 Then the few whose spirits float above
the wreck of happiness
Are driven o'er the shoals of guilt or
ocean of excess;
The magnet of their course is gone, or
only points in vain
The shore to which their shiver'd sail
shall never stretch again.
Stanzas for Music.

3 Eternal Spirit of the chainless Mind.
Sonnet on Chillon.

4 My hair is grey, but not with years.
The Prisoner of Chillon, 1.

5 Fare thee well! and if for ever,
Still for ever, fare thee well.
Fare thee well.

6 And both were young, and one was
beautiful. *The Dream, 2.*

7 A change came o'er the spirit of my
dream. *Ibid, 3.*

8 So we'll go no more a-roving
So late into the night.
So we'll go no more a-roving.

9 My boat is on the shore,
And my bark is on the sea
To Thomas More.

10 Here's a sigh to those who love me,
And a smile to those who hate;
And, whatever sky's above me,
Here's a heart for every fate. *Ibid.*

11 The nursery still lisps out in all they
utter –
Besides, they always smell of bread and
butter. *Beppo, 39.*

12 In virtues nothing earthly could surpass
her,
Save thine 'incomparable oil', Macassar!
Don Juan, i. 17.

13 But – Oh! ye lords of ladies intellectual,
Inform us truly, have they not hen-
peck'd you all? *Ibid, 22.*

14 A little while she strove, and much
repented,
And whispering 'I will ne'er consent' –
consented. *Ibid, 117.*

15 'Tis sweet to hear the watch-dog's
honest bark
Bay deep-mouth'd welcome as we draw
near home;
'Tis sweet to know there is an eye will
mark
Our coming, and look brighter when
we come. *Ibid, 123.*

16 Sweet is revenge – especially to women.
Ibid, 124.

17 Man's love is of man's life a thing apart,
'Tis woman's whole existence.
Ibid, 194.

18 A solitary shriek, the bubbling cry
Of some strong swimmer in his agony.
Ibid, ii. 53.

19 The best of life is but intoxication.
Ibid, 179.

20 Alas! the love of women! it is known
To be a lovely and a fearful thing.
Ibid, 199.

21 In her first passion woman loves her
lover,
In all the others all she loves is love.
Ibid, iii. 3.

22 He was the mildest manner'd man
That ever scuttled ship or cut a throat.
Ibid, 41.

23 The isles of Greece, the isles of Greece!
Where burning Sappho loved and sung.
Ibid, 86.

24 The mountains look on Marathon –
And Marathon looks on the sea;
And musing there an hour alone,
I dream'd that Greece might still be free.
Ibid.

25 Place me on Sunium's marbled steep,
Where nothing, save the waves and I,
May hear our mutual murmurs sweep;
There, swan-like, let me sing and die.
Ibid.

26 And if I laugh at any mortal thing,
'Tis that I may not weep. *Ibid, iv. 4.*

27 The tocsin of the soul – the dinner-
bell. *Ibid, 49.*

28 When Bishop Berkeley said 'there was
no matter,'
And proved it – 'twas no matter what he
said. *Ibid, xi. I.*

29 But Tom's no more – and so no more of
Tom. *Ibid, 20.*

30 'Tis strange the mind, that very fiery
particle,
Should let itself be snuff'd out by an
article. *Ibid, 60.*
(Of Keats's death.)

31 The English winter – ending in July,
To recommence in August.
Ibid, xiii. 42.

32 Society is now one polish'd horde,
Form'd of two mighty tribes, the *Bores*
and *Bored*. *Ibid, 95.*

33 The world is a bundle of hay,
Mankind are the asses who pull;
Each tugs in a different way,
And the greatest of all is John Bull.
Epigram.

34 Who kill'd John Keat?
'I,' says the Quarterly,
So savage and Tartarly;
''Twas one of my feats.' *John Keats.*

35 Oh, talk not to me of a name great in
story;
The days of our youth are the days of
our glory;
And the myrtle and ivy of sweet two-
and-twenty
Are worth all your laurels, though never
so plenty.
*Stanzas written on the Road between
Florence and Pisa.*

36 My days are in the yellow leaf;
The flowers and fruits of love are gone;
The worm, the canker, and the grief
Are mine alone.
*On this Day I complete my
thirty-sixth Year.*

37 Seek out – less often sought than found –
A soldier's grave, for thee the best;
Then look around, and choose thy
ground,
And take thy rest. *Ibid.*

38 I awoke one morning and found myself
famous.
*Entry in memoranda, on the success
of 'Childe Harold.'*

**BYRON, HENRY JAMES, English
dramatist, Jan. 1834–11 April, 1884**

39 Life's too short for chess. *Our Boys, 1.*

**CAESAR, GAIUS JULIUS, Roman
statesman, 12 July 102 B.C.–15
March, 44 B.C.**

40 Gallia est omnis divisa in partes tres. –
All Gaul is divided into three parts.
De Bello Gallico – On the Gallic War, I. i.

41 Iacta alea est. – The die is cast.
On crossing the Rubicon, 49 B.C.

42 Veni, vidi, vici. – I came, I saw, I
conquered.
*Letter after victory at Zela in Asia Minor,
47 B.C.*

43 Et tu, Brute? – You too, Brutus?
As he was being assassinated.

**CAINE, SIR THOMAS HENRY
HALL, English novelist, 14 May,
1853–31 Aug. 1931**

44 I reject the monstrous theory that while
a man may redeem the past a woman
never can. *The Eternal City, VI. xviii.*

**CALHOUN, JOHN CALDWELL,
US statesman, 18 March, 1782–31
March, 1850**

45 The very essence of a free government
consists in considering offices as public

trusts, bestowed for the good of the country, and not for the benefit of an individual or a party.
Speech, 13 Feb. 1835.

CALIGULA, GAIUS CAESAR, Roman Emperor, A.D. 12–41

1 Utinam populus Romanus unam cervicem haberet! – Would that the Roman people had but one neck!
Suetonius, Caligula, xxx.

CALLIMACHUS, Greek poet and librarian, 310?–240? B.C.

2 Μέγα βιβλίον, μέγα κακόν – Great book, great evil.
Atributed.

CALVERLEY (formerly BLAYDS), CHARLES STUART, English poet, 22 Dec. 1831–17 Feb, 1884

3 I love to gaze upon a child;
A young bud bursting into blossom;
Artless, as Eve yet unbeguiled,
And agile as a young opossum:
And such was he. A calm-brow'd lad,
Yet mad, at moments, as a hatter.
Gemini and Virgo.

4 Thou who, when fears attack,
Bidst them avaunt, and Black
Care, at the horseman's back
Perching, unseatest;
Sweet, when the morn is grey;
Sweet when they've cleared away
Lunch; and at close of day
Possibly sweetest.
Ode to Tobacco.

5 Grinder, who serenely grindest
At my door the Hundredth Psalm.
Lines on hearing the Organ.

6 The sports, to which with boyish glee
I sprang erewhile, attract no more;
Although I am but sixty-three
Or four.
Changed.

7 O my own, my beautiful, my blue-eyed!
To be young once more, and bite my thumb
At the world and all its cares with you, I'd
Give no inconsiderable sum.
First Love.

8 I deal in every ware in turn,
I've rings for buddin' Sally
That sparkle like those eyes of her'n;
I've liquor for the valet.
Wanderers.
(Parody of Tennyson's *The Brook*.)

9 The auld wife sat at her ivied door,
(Butter and eggs and a pound of cheese)
A thing she had frequently done before;
And her spectacles lay on her apron'd knees.
Ballad.

10 In moss-prankt dells which the sunbeams flatter.
Lovers, and a Reflection.

CAMBRONNE, PIERRE JACQUES ÉTIENNE, COMTE, French General, 26 Dec. 1770–8 Jan. 1842

11 La garde meurt, mais elle ne se rend pas. – The Guard dies, but does not surrender.
At Waterloo, 18 June, 1815.
(His real answer, according to French authorities, was 'shorter and not less forcible.')

CAMDEN, WILLIAM, English antiquary, 2 May, 1551–9 Nov. 1623

12 Betwixt the stirrup and the ground
Mercy I asked, mercy I found.
Epitaph for a Man killed by falling from his Horse.

CAMPBELL, IGNATIUS ROY DUNNACHIE, South African poet, 2 Oct. 1902–22 April, 1957

13 They use the snaffle and the curb all right,
But where's the bloody horse?
On some South African Novelists.

CAMPBELL, JANE MONTGOMERY, English translator, 1817–15 Nov. 1878

14 We plough the fields, and scatter
The good seed on the land,
But it is fed and watered
By God's almighty hand.
We plough the Fields.

15 He paints the wayside flower,
He lights the evening star.   *Ibid.*

**CAMPBELL, JOSEPH, Irish poet,
1879–13 July, 1944**

16 As a white candle
In a holy place,
So is the beauty
Of an aged face.   *The Old Woman.*

**CAMPBELL, THOMAS, Scottish
poet, 27 July, 1777–15 June, 1844**

17 'Tis distance lends enchantment to the
view.   *The Pleasures of Hope, I. 7.*

18 Hope, for a season, bade the world
farewell,
And Freedom shrieked – as Kosciusko
fell!   *Ibid, 381.*

19 What though my winged hours of bliss
have been,
Like angel-visits, few and far between.
        Ibid, II. 377.

20 Lochiel, Lochiel! beware of the day
When the Lowlands shall meet thee in
battle array!   *Lochiel's Warning, I.*

21 'Tis the sunset of life gives me mystical
lore,
And coming events cast their shadows
before.   *Ibid, 55*

22 A chieftain to the Highlands bound
Cries 'Boatman, do not tarry!
And I'll give thee a silver pound
To row us o'er the ferry.'
        Lord Ullin's Daughter.

23 Ye Mariners of England
That guard our native seas,
Whose flag has braved, a thousand
years,
The battle and the breeze –
Your glorious standard launch again
To match another foe!
And sweep through the deep,
While the stormy winds do blow –
While the battle rages loud and long,
And the stormy winds do blow.
        Ye Mariners of England.

24 Britannia needs no bulwarks,
No towers along the steep;
Her march is o'er the mountain waves,
Her home is on the deep.   *Ibid.*

25 The meteor flag of England
Shall yet terrific burn,
Till danger's troubled night depart
And the star of peace return.   *Ibid.*

26 There was silence deep as death,
And the boldest held his breath
For a time.   *Battle of the Baltic.*

27 On Linden, when the sun was low,
All bloodless lay the untrodden snow,
And dark as winter was the flow
Of Iser, rolling rapidly.   *Hohenlinden.*

28 Wave, Munich! all thy banners wave,
And charge with all thy chivalry!   *Ibid*

29 Our bugles sang truce – for the night-
cloud had lowered,
And the sentinel stars set their watch in
the sky;
And thousands had sunk on the ground
overpowered,
The weary to sleep, and the wounded to
die.   *The Soldier's Dream.*

30 There came to the beach a poor exile of
Erin.   *Exile of Erin.*

31 O leave this barren spot to me!
Spare, woodman, spare the beechen
tree.   *The Beech-Tree's Petition.*

32 To live in hearts we leave behind
Is not to die.   *Hallowed Ground, 35.*

33 Star that bringest home the bee,
And sett'st the weary labourer free!
        Song to the Evening Star.

**CAMPION, THOMAS, English
poet, 12 Feb. 1567–1 March, 1620**

34 Follow thy fair sun, unhappy shadow.
        Follow thy Fair Sun.

35 Follow your Saint, follow with accents
sweet;
Haste you, sad notes, fall at her flying
feet.   *Follow your Saint.*

1 Good thoughts his only friends;
   His wealth a well-spent age;
   The earth his sober inn,
   And quiet pilgrimage.
                    The man Upright of Life.

2 When thou must home to shades of
      under ground,
   And there arriv'd, a new admired guest,
   The beauteous spirits do ingirt thee
      round,
   White Iope, blithe Helen, and the rest.
                    When thou must Home.

3 Never love unless you can
   Bear with all the faults of man:
   Men will sometimes jealous be,
   Though but little cause they see;
   And hang the head, as discontent,
   And speak what straight they will
      repent.   *Never Love.*

4 There is a garden in her face
   Where roses and white lilies blow.
                    There is a Garden in her Face.

CANNING, GEORGE, English Prime Minister and wit, 11 April, 1770–8 Aug. 1827

5 Needy Knife-grinder! whither are you
      going?
   Rough is the road, your wheel is out of
      order –
   Bleak blows the blast; – your hat has got
      a hole in't.
   So have your breeches.
                    *The Friend of Humanity and the
                    Knife-Grinder.*

6 Story! God bless you! I have none to tell,
   Sir.   *Ibid.*

7 *I* give thee sixpence! I will see thee
   damned first.   *Ibid.*

8 And finds, with keen discriminating
      sight,
   Black's not so black; – nor white so *very*
   white.   *New Morality, 199.*

9 But of all plagues, good Heaven, thy
      wrath can send,
   Save, save, oh save me from the *candid
   friend*!   *Ibid, 210.*

10 Here's to the Pilot that weathered the
       storm (Pitt.)
    Song for the inauguration of the Pitt Club.

11 In matters of commerce the fault of the
       Dutch
    Is offering too little and asking too
       much.
    The French are with equal advantage
       content,
    So we.clap on Dutch bottoms just
       twenty per cent.
        *Despatch to British Ambassador at the
                        Hague, 31 Jan. 1826.*

12 A sudden thought strikes me, let us
    swear an eternal friendship.
                    The Rovers, I. i.

13 I called the New World into existence to
    redress the balance of the Old.
        The King's Message, 12 Dec. 1826.

CAREW, THOMAS, English poet, 1595?–1640

14 He that loves a rosy cheek,
    Or a coral lip admires;
    Or from star-like eyes doth seek
    Fuel to maintain his fires:
    As old Time makes these decay,
    So his flames must waste away.
                    Disdain returned.

15 Then fly betimes, for only they
    Conquer Love, that run away.
                    Conquest by Flight.

CAREY, HENRY, English poet, 1693?–4 Oct. 1743

16 Namby Pamby's little rhymes,
    (Ambrose Phillips.)
    Little jingles, little.chimes.
                    Namby Pamby.

17 Of all the girls that are so smart,
    There's none like pretty Sally;
    She is the.darling of my heart,
    And she lives in our alley.
                    Sally in our Alley.

18 Of all the days that's in the week
    I dearly love but one day –
    And that's the day that comes betwixt
    A Saturday and Monday.   *Ibid.*

19 Aldeborontiphoscophornio!
Where left you Chrononhotonthologos?
Chrononhotonthologos, I. i.

**CARLETON, WILL, US poet, 21
Oct. 1845–18 Dec. 1912**

20 Things at home are crossways, and
Betsey and I are out.
Betsey and I are out.

**CARLYLE, THOMAS, Scottish
author, 4 Dec. 1795–4 Feb. 1881**

21 How does the poet speak to men, with
power, but by being still more a man
than they? *Essays. Burns.*

22 It can be said of him (Scott), when he
departed, he took a Man's life along
with him. No sounder piece of British
manhood was put together in that
eighteenth century of Time.
Ibid, Sir Walter Scott.

23 He who first shortened the labour of
copyists by device of *Movable Types* was
disbanding hired armies, and cashiering
most Kings and Senates, and creating a
whole new democratic world: he had
invented the art of printing.
Sartor Resartus, I. v.

24 Man is a tool-using animal. *Ibid.*

25 Be not the slave of words: is not the
distant, the dead, while I love it, and
long for it, and mourn for it, here, in the
genuine sense, as truly as the floor I
stand on? *Ibid, viii.*

26 Do the duty which lies nearest thee,
which thou knowest to be a duty! Thy
second duty will already have become
clearer. *Ibid, II. ix.*

27 Produce! Were it but the pitifulest
infinitesimal fraction of a product,
produce it in God's name. *Ibid.*

28 'Speech is silvern, Silence is golden'; or,
as I might rather express it, Speech is of
Time, Silence is of Eternity.
Ibid, III. iii.

29 A whiff of grapeshot.
History of the French Revolution, I. v. iii.

30 The seagreen Incorruptible.
(Robespierre.) *Ibid, II. iv. iv.*

31 The history of the world is but the
biography of great men.
*Heroes and Hero-Worship, i.
The Hero as Divinity.*

32 The true university of these days is a
collection of books.
Ibid, V. The Hero as Man of Letters

33 The Dismal Science. (Political
Economy.) *Latter-Day Pamphlets, I.
The Present Time.*

34 A Parliament speaking through
reporters to Buncombe and the twenty-
seven millions, mostly fools.
Ibid, VI. Parliaments.

35 Work is the grand cure of all the
maladies and miseries that ever beset
mankind.
*Rectorial Address at Edinburgh, 2 April,
B1866.*

36 The Public is an old woman. Let her
maunder and mumble. *Journal, 1835.*

37 The unspeakable Turk.
Letter to G. Howard, 24 Nov. 1876.

38 So here hath been dawning
Another blue Day:
Think, wilt thou let it
Slip useless away? *To-day.*

39 What is Hope? A smiling rainbow
Children follow through the wet;
'Tis not here, still yonder, yonder:
Never urchin found it yet. *Cui Bono.*

40 What is Man? A foolish baby,
Vainly strives, and fights, and frets;
Demanding all, deserving nothing;
One small grave is what he gets. *Ibid.*

**CARNEY, JULIA A. FLETCHER,
US teacher, 1823–1908.**

41 Little drops of water, little grains of
sand,

Make the mighty ocean and the pleasant
land.
So the little minutes, humble though
they be,
Make the mighty ages of eternity.
Little Things.
(This has been wrongly attributed to E.
C. Brewer, D. C. Colesworkthy,
Charles Mackay, and Frances S.
Osgood.)

1 Little deeds of kindness, little words of
love,
Help to make earth happy, like the
heaven above.   *Ibid.*
(Later reading of 2nd line, 'Make this
earth an Eden.')

CARROLL, LEWIS (CHARLES LUTWIDGE DODGSON), English mathematician and author, 27 Jan. 1832–14 Jan. 1898.

2 She has the bear's ethereal grace,
The bland hyena's laugh,
The footstep of the elephant,
The neck of the giraffe;
I love her still, believe me,
Though my heart its passion hides;
'She's all my fancy painted her,'
But oh! *how much besides!*
College Rhymes. My Fancy.

3 'What is the use of a book,' thought
Alice, 'without pictures or
conversations?'
Alice's Adventures in Wonderland, i.

4 Curiouser and curiouser!   *Ibid, ii.*

5 'I'll be judge, I'll be jury,' said cunning
old Fury;
'I'll try the whole cause, and condemn
you to death.'   *Ibid, iii.*

6 'You are old, Father William,' the
young man said,
'And your hair has become very white;
And yet you incessantly stand on your
head –
Do you think, at your age, it is right?'
Ibid, v.

7 'In my youth,' Father William replied to
his son,

'I feared it might injure the brain;
But now that I'm perfectly sure I have
none,
Why, I do it again and again.'   *Ibid.*

8 He only does it to annoy,
Because he knows it teases.   *Ibid, vi.*

9 I speak severely to my boy,
I beat him when he sneezes;
For he can thoroughly enjoy
The pepper when he pleases!   *Ibid.*

10 Take care of the sense, and the sounds
will take care of themselves.   *Ibid, ix.*

11 "Reeling and Writhing, of course, to
begin with,' the Mock Turtle replied;
'and then the different branches of
Arithmetic – Ambition, Distraction,
Uglification, and Derision.'   *Ibid.*

12 When the sands are all dry, he is gay as a
lark,
And will talk in contemptuous tones of
the Shark:
But, when the tide rises and sharks are
around,
His voice has a timid and tremulous
sound.   *Ibid, x.*

13 Soup of the evening, beautiful soup!
Ibid.

14 They told me you had been to her,
And mentioned me to him:
She gave me a good character,
But said I could not swim.   *Ibid, xii.*

15 Stating that he would not stand it,
Stating in emphatic language
What he'd be before he'd stand it.
*Phantasmagoria. Hiawatha's
Photographing.*

16 Child of the pure unclouded brow
And dreaming eyes of wonder!
*Through the Looking-Glass and What
Alice found there, introduction.*

17 'Twas brillig, and the slithy toves
Did gyre and gimble in the wabe
All mimsy were the borogoves,
And the mome raths outgrabe.
Ibid, i. Jabberwocky.

18 He left it dead, and with its head
He went galumphing back. *Ibid.*

19 'And hast thou slain the Jabberwock?
Come to my arms, my beamish boy!
O frabjous day! Callooh! Callay!
He chortled in his joy. *Ibid.*

20 Curstey while you're thinking what to
say. It saves time. *Ibid, ii.*

21 'You may call it "nonsense" if you like,'
she (the Red Queen) said, 'but *I've* heard
nonsense, compared with which that
would be as sensible as a dictionary!'
Ibid.

22 'If seven maids with seven mops
Swept it for half a year,
Do you suppose,' the Walrus said,
'That they could get it clear?'
'I doubt it,' said the Carpenter,
And shed a bitter tear.
Ibid, iv. The Walrus and the Carpenter.

23 'The time has come,' the Walrus said,
'To talk of many things;
Of shoes – and ships – and sealing wax –
Of cabbages – and kings –
And why the sea is boiling hot –
And whether pigs have wings.' *Ibid.*

24 'A loaf of bread,' the Walrus said,
'Is what we chiefly need:
Pepper and vinegar besides
Are very good indeed.' *Ibid.*

25 The Carpenter said nothing but
'The butter's spread too thick!' *Ibid.*

26 'I weep for you,' the Walrus said:
'I deeply sympathise.' *Ibid.*

27 The rule is, jam to-morrow and jam
yesterday – but never jam to-day.
Ibid, v.

28 Consider what a great girl you are.
Consider what a long way you've
come to-day. Consider what o'clock it
is. Consider anything, only don't cry!
Ibid.

29 They gave it to me – for an un-birthday
present. *Ibid. vi.*

30 I said it very loud and clear;
I went and shouted in his ear. *Ibid.*

31 I must have two, you know – to come
and go. One to come, and one to go.
Ibid, vii.

32 You might as well try to stop a
Bandersnatch! *Ibid.*

33 It's as large as life, and twice as natural!
Ibid.

34 I'll tell thee everything I can:
There's little to relate.
I saw an aged, aged man,
A-sitting on a gate.
'Who are you, aged man?' I said,
'And how is it you live?'
And his answer trickled through my
head
Like water through a sieve. *Ibid. viii.*

35 But I was thinking of a plan
To dye one's whiskers green,
And always use so large a fan
That they could not be seen. *Ibid.*

36 He would answer to 'Hi!' or to any loud
cry,
Such as 'Fry me!' or 'Fritter my wig!'
To 'What-you-may-call-um!' or 'What-
was-his-name!'
But especially 'Thing-um-a-jig!'
The Hunting of the Snark, fit i.

37 His intimate friends called him 'Candle-
ends,'
And his enemies 'Toasted-cheese.'
Ibid.

38 Then the bowsprit got mixed with the
rudder sometimes. *Ibid, fit ii.*

39 Its habit of getting up late you'll agree
That it carries too far when I say
That it frequently breakfasts at five
o'clock tea,
And dines on the following day. *Ibid.*

40 I said it in Hebrew – I said it in Dutch –
I said it in German and Greek:
But I wholly forgot (and it vexes me
much)
That English is what you speak!
Ibid, fit iv.

1   They sought it with thimbles, they
     sought it with care;
    They pursued it with forks and hope;
    They threatened its life with a railway
     share;
    They charmed it with smiles and soap.
Ibid, fit v.

2   'Transportation for life' was the
    sentence it gave,
    'And *then* to be fined forty pound.'
Ibid, fit vi.

3   In the midst of the word he was trying
    to say,
    In the midst of his laughter and glee,
    He had softly and suddenly vanished
    away –
    For the Snark *was* a Boojum, you see.
Ibid, fit viii.

4   He thought he saw a Banker's Clerk
    Descending from a bus:
    He looked again, and found it was
    A Hippopotamus:
    'If this should stay to dine,' he said,
    'There won't be much for us!'
Sylvie and Bruno, vii.

CARRUTH, WILLIAM HERBERT, US poet, 5 April, 1859–15 Dec. 1924

5   Some call it Evolution,
    And others call it God.
Each in his own Tongue.

CARRYL, CHARLES EDWARD, US author, 30 Dec. 1841–3 July, 1920.

6   A capital ship for an ocean trip
    Was the 'Walloping Window-blind.'
    No gale that blew dismayed her crew
    Or troubled the Captain's mind.
Davy and the Goblin, a Nautical Ballad.

CARTER, HENRY, English author, died 30 July, 1806.

7   True patriots all; for be it understood
    We left our country for our country's
    good.
*Prologue on opening the Theatre
at Sydney, Botany Bay.*

CARY, PHOEBE, US poetess, 4 Sept. 1824–31 July, 1871

8   And though hard be the task,
    'Keep a stiff upper lip.'
Keep a Stiff Upper Lip.

CASWALL, EDWARD, English clergyman, 15 July, 1814–2 Jan. 1878

9   Days and moments quickly flying
    Blend the living with the dead;
    Soon shall you and I be lying
    Each within our narrow bed.   *Hymn.*

10 Jesus, the very thought of Thee
    With sweetness fills my breast.   *Hymn.*

CATO, MARCUS PORCIUS ('THE CENSOR'), Roman statesman, 234–149 B.C.

11 Delenda est Carthago. – Carthage must
    be destroyed.
*Words with which he ended every speech
in the Senate.*

CATULLUS, GAIUS VALERIUS, Roman poet, 84–54? B.C.

12 Lugete, O Veneres Cupidinesque,
    Et quantumst hominum venustiorum.
    Passer mortuus est meae puellae,
    Passer, deliciae meae puellae.
    – Mourn, O Loves and Cupids, and all
     loveliest of mortals,
    My girl's sparrow is dead, the sparrow,
     my girl's pet.   *Carmina – Songs, iii.*

13 Qui nunc it per iter tenebricosum
    Illuc, unde negant redire quemquam.
    – Which now goes along the dark path
    to that place whence they say none
    returns.   *Ibid.*

14 Vivamus, mea Lesbia, atque amemus,
    Rumoresque senum severiorum
    Omnes unius aestimemus assis.
    Soles occidere et redire possunt:
    Nobis cum semel occidit brevis lux
    Nox est perpetua una dormienda.
    – Let us live, my Lesbia, and love, and
    value the talk of over-serious old men
    at a single farthing. Suns can set and
    return; for us, when once our brief day

has gone, there is the sleep of one
unending night. *Ibid, v.*

15 Da mi basia mille, deinde centum,
Dein mille altera, dein secunda centum,
Deinde usque altera mille, deinde
centum.
– Give me a thousand kisses, then a
hundred, then another thousand, then
a second hundred, then yet another
thousand, then a hundred. *Ibid.*

16 Odi et amo. Quare id faciam, fortasse
requiris.
Nescio, sed fieri sentio et excrucior.
– I hate and love. Why I do it, perhaps
you ask. I know not, but I feel it and
am tortured. *Ibid, lxxxv.*

17 Multas per gentes et multa per aequora
vectus
Advenio has miseras, frater, ad infernas.
– Passing through many peoples and
over many seas I come brother, to
these sad obsequies. *Ibid, ci*

18 Atque in perpetuum, frater, ave atque
vale.
– And for ever, brother, hail and
farewell! *Ibid.*

**CAVELL, EDITH LOUISA,
English nurse, 4 Dec. 1865–12 Oct.
1915.**

19 Patriotism is not enough. I must have no
hatred or bitterness towards anyone.
Before her execution by the Germans.

**CELANO, THOMAS OF, Italian
mystic, died 1255?**

20 Dies irae, dies illa, solvet saeclum in
favilla.
– Day of wrath, that day, the world shall
dissolve in ashes. *Hymn.*

**CENTLIVRE, SUSANNAH,
English actress and dramatist,
1667?–1 Dec. 1723**

21 The real Simon Pure.
A Bold Stroke for a Wife, V. i.

**CERVANTES SAAVEDRA,
MIGUEL DE, Spanish novelist,
baptised 9 Oct. 1547, died 23 April,
1616.**

22 El Caballero de la Triste Figura. – The
Knight of the Rueful Countenance.
Don Quixote, I. xix.

23 Paciencia y barajar. – Patience, and
shuffle the cards. *Ibid, II. xxiii.*

24 Bien haya el que inventó el sueño, capa
que cubre todos los humanos
pensamientos. – Blessed be he who
invented sleep, a cloak that covers all a
man's thoughts. *Ibid, lxviii.*

**CHAMBERLAIN, JOSEPH,
English statesman, 8 July, 1836–2
July, 1914.**

25 Provided that the City of London
remains as it is at present, the clearing-
house of the world.
Speech, Guildhall, London, 19 Jan. 1904.

26 Learn to think Imperially. *Ibid.*

27 The day of small nations has long passed
away. The day of Empires has come.
Speech, Birmingham, 12 May, 1904.

**CHAMBERS, CHARLES
HADDON, English dramatist, 22
April, 1860–28 March, 1921**

28 The long arm of coincidence.
Captain Swift, II.

**CHANDLER, JOHN, English
clergyman, 16 June, 1806–1 July,
1876**

29 Conquering kings their titles take
From the foes they captive make:
Jesu, by a nobler deed,
From the thousands He hath freed.
Hymn from the Latin.

**CHAPMAN, ARTHUR, US author,
25 June, 1873–4 Dec. 1935**

30 Out where the handclasp's a little
stronger,

Out where the smile dwells a little
longer,
That's where the West begins.
Out where the West begins.

CHAPMAN, GEORGE, English dramatist, 1559?–12 May, 1634

1 Give me a spirit that on this life's rough
sea
Loves t'have his sails fill'd with a lusty
wind,
Even till his sail-yards tremble, his
masts crack,
And his rapt ship run on her side so low
That she drinks water, and her keel
ploughs air.
*The Conspiracy of Charles, Duke
of Byron, III. i.*

2 And let a scholar all Earth's volumes
carry,
He will be but a walking dictionary.
Tears of Peace, 265.

3 His (Homer's) naked Ulysses, clad in
eternal fiction.
The Odysseys of Homer, epistle dedicatory.

CHARLES I, English King, 19 Nov. 1600–30 Jan. 1649

4 Never make a defence or apology before
you be accused.
Letter to Lord Wentworth, 3 Sept. 1636.

CHARLES II, English King, 29 May, 1630–6 Feb. 1685

5 As good as a play!
*On the Lords debating Lord Ross's Divorce
Bill, 1670.*

6 I fear, gentlemen, I am an
unconscionable time a-dying.
On his death-bed.

7 Let not poor Nelly starve. (Of Nell
Gwynn.)   *Ibid.*

CHATHAM, WILLIAM PITT, 1ST EARL OF, English Prime Minister, 15 Nov. 1708–11 May, 1778

8 The atrocious crime of being a young
man . . . I shall neither attempt to
palliate nor deny.
Speech, House of Commons, 27 Jan. 1741.

9 Confidence is a plant of slow growth in
an aged bosom: youth is the season of
credulity.   *Ibid, 14 Jan. 1766.*

10 Where law ends, tyranny begins.
Speech, House of Lords, 9 Jan. 1770.

11 We have a Calvinistic creed, a Popish
liturgy, and an Arminian clergy.
Ibid, 19 May, 1772.

12 If I were an American, as I am an
Englishman, while a foreign troop was
landed in my country, I never would
lay down my arms, – never – never –
never!   *Ibid, 18 Nov. 1777.*

13 The poorest man may in his cottage bid
defiance to all the forces of the Crown.
It may be frail – its roof may shake –
the wind may blow through it – the
storm may enter – the rain may enter –
but the King of England cannot enter –
all his force dares not cross the
threshold of the ruined tenement!
Speech on the Excise Bill.

CHATTERTON, THOMAS, English poet, 20 Nov. 1752–24 Aug. 1770.

14 O sing unto my roundelay,
O drop the briny tear with me,
Dance no more at holy-day,
Like a running river be.
My love is dead,
Gone to his death-bed,
All under the willow-tree.
Minstrel's Song.

CHAUCER, GEOFFREY, English poet, 1340?–25 Oct. 1400.

15 The lyf so short, the craft so long to
lerne,
Th' assay so hard, so sharp the
conquering.
The Parlement of Foules, I.

16 Flee fro the prees, and dwelle with
sothfastnesse.   *Truth, I.*

17 O moral Gower, this booke I directe
To thee. *Troilus and Criseyde, V 1856.*

18 Of alle the floures in the mede,
Than love I most these floures white and
rede,
Swiche as men callen daysies in our
toun.
The Legend of Good Women, Prologue, 41.

19 Whan that Aprille with his shoures sote
The droghte of Marche hath perced to
the rote.
The Canterbury Tales. Prologue, I.

20 And smale fowles maken melodye
That slepen al the night with open yë.
Ibid, 9.

21 And of his port as meke as is a mayde.
Ibid, 69.

22 He was a verray parfit gentil knight.
Ibid, 72.

23 He was as fresh as is the month of May.
Ibid, 92.

24 Ful wel she song the service divyne,
Entuned in hir nose ful semely;
And Frensh she spak ful faire and fetisly,
After the scole of Stratford atte Bowe,
For Frensh of Paris was to hir unknowe.
Ibid, 122.

25 What sholde he studie, and make
himselven wood,
Upon a book in cloistre alwey to poure,
Or swinken with his handes, and
laboure,
As Austin bit? How shal the world be
served?
Lat Austin have his swink to him
reserved. *Ibid, 184.*

26 A Clerk ther was of Oxenford also,
That un-to logik hadde longe y-go.
Ibid, 285.

27 For him was lever have at his beddes
heed
Twenty bokes, clad in blak or reed,
Of Aristotle and his philosophye,
Than robes riche, or fithele, or gay
sautrye. *Ibid, 293.*

28 And gladly wold he lerne, and gladly
teche. *Ibid, 308.*

29 No-wher so bisy a man as he ther nas,
And yet he semed bisier than he was.
Ibid, 321.

30 It snewed in his hous of mete and
drinke. *Ibid, 345.*

31 With many a tempest hadde his berd
been shake. *Ibid, 406.*

32 His studie was but litel on the Bible.
Ibid, 438.

33 She was a worthy womman all hir lyve,
Housbondes at chirche-dore she hadde
fyve,
Withouten other companye in youthe.
Ibid, 459.

34 But Cristes lore, and his apostles twelve,
He taughte, and first he folwed it
himselve. *Ibid, 527.*

35 And whan that he wel dronken hadde
the wyn,
Than wolde he speke no word but
Latyn. *Ibid, 637.*

36 His walet lay biforn him in his lappe,
Bret-ful of pardoun come from Rome al
hoot. *Ibid, 686.*

37 The bisy larke, messager of day,
Saluëth in hir song the morwe gray;
And fyry Phebus ryseth up so brighte,
That al the orient laugheth of the lighte.
Ibid, The Knightes Tale, 633.

38 The smyler with the knyf under the
cloke. *Ibid, 1141.*

39 Up roose the sonne, and up roos
Emelye. *Ibid, 1415.*

40 What is this world? what asketh man to
have?
Now with his love, now in his colde
grave
Allone, with-outen any companye.
Ibid, 1919

1 Thou lokest as thou woldest finde an hare,
For ever up-on the ground I see thee stare. *Ibid, Sir Thopas. Prologue, 6.*

2 This may wel be rym dogerel.
Ibid, The Tale of Melibeus. Prologue 7.

CHEKHOV, ANTON PAVLOVITCH, Russian author, 17 Jan. 1860–2 July, 1904

3 Love, friendship, respect, do not unite people as much as a common hatred for something. *Note-books.*

CHERRY, ANDREW, Irish dramatist, 11 Jan. 1762–12 Feb. 1812

4 Till next day,
There she lay,
In the Bay of Biscay, O!
The Bay of Biscay.

CHESTERFIELD, PHILIP DORMER STANHOPE, 4TH EARL OF, English statesman, 22 Sept. 1694–24 March, 1773.

5 Be wiser than other people if you can, but do not tell them so.
Letters to his Son, 19 Nov. 1745.

6 An injury is much sooner forgotten than an insult. *Ibid, 9 Oct. 1746.*

7 Advice is seldom welcome; and those who want it the most always like it the least. *Ibid, 29 Jan. 1748.*

8 A man of sense only trifles with them (women), plays with them, humours and flatters them, as he does with a sprightly and forward child; but he neither consults them about, nor trusts them with, serious matters.
Ibid, 5 Sept. 1748.

9 Women are much more like each other than men: they have, in truth, but two passions, vanity and love.
Ibid, 19 Dec. 1749.

10 Tyrawley and I have been dead these two years; but we don't choose to have it known.
Boswell, Life of Johnson, an. 1773.

11 Give Dayrolles a chair. *Last Words.*

CHESTERTON, GILBERT KEITH, English author, 29 May, 1874–14 June. 1936

12 For the front of the cover shows somebody shot,
And the back of the cover will tell you the plot. *Commercial Candour.*

13 White founts falling in the courts of the sun,
And the Soldan of Byzantium is smiling as they run *Lepanto.*

14 Strong gongs groaning as the guns boom far,
Don John of Austria is going to the war. *Ibid.*

15 But the world is more full of glory Than you can understand.
The Mortal Answers.

16 Talk about the pews and steeples
And the Cash that goes therewith!
But the souls of Christian peoples . . .
Chuck it, Smith!
(F. E. Smith.)
Antichrist, or the Reunion of Christendom: An Ode.

17 And I dream of the days when work was scrappy,
And rare in our pockets the mark of the mint,
When we were angry and poor and happy,
And proud of seeing our names in print.
A Song of Defeat.

18 You never loved the sun in heaven as I have loved the rain. *The Last Hero.*

19 The strangest whim has seized me . . .
After all
I think I will not hang myself to-day.
A Ballade of Suicide.

20 And Noah he often said to his wife when he sat down to dine,

'I don't care where the water goes if it doesn't get into the wine.'
Wine and Water.

21 Before the Roman came to Rye or out to Severn strode,
The rolling English drunkard made the rolling English road.
The Rolling English Road.

22 For there is good news yet to hear and fine things to be seen,
Before we go to Paradise by way of Kensal Green.
Ibid.

23 Tea, although an Oriental,
Is a gentleman at least;
Cocoa is a cad and coward,
Cocoa is a vulgar beast.
The Song of Right and Wrong.

24 Before the gods that made the gods
Had seen their sunrise pass,
The White Horse of the White Horse Vale
Was cut out of the grass.
The Ballad of the White Horse, I. I.

25 The devil's walking parody
Of all four-footed things. *The Donkey.*

26 There is a great deal of difference between the eager man who wants to read a book, and the tired man who wants a book to read.
Charles Dickens, v.

27 A good joke is the one ultimate and sacred thing which cannot be criticised. Our relations with a good joke are direct and even divine relations.
Preface to Dicken's Pickwick Papers.

28 A man's good work is effected by doing what he does; a woman's by being what she is. *Robert Browning, ii.*

29 The two things that a healthy person hates most between heaven and hell are a woman who is not dignified and a man who is.
All Things considered. Cockneys and their Jokes.

30 If a thing is worth doing it is worth doing badly.
What's Wrong with the World.
Folly and Female Education.

31 Hardy became a sort of village atheist brooding and blaspheming over the village idiot.
The Victorian Age in Literature, ii.

CHEVALIER, ALBERT, English actor, 21 March, 1861–10 July, 1923

32 There ain't a lady in the land,
As I'd swop for my dear old Dutch.
My Old Dutch.

CHOATE, RUFUS, US statesman, 1 Oct. 1799–13 July, 1859

33 Its constitution the glittering and sounding generalities of natural right which make up the Declaration of Independence.
Letter to the Maine Whig Committee,
9 Aug. 1856.

CHORLEY, HENRY FOTHERGILL, English musical critic, 15 Dec. 1808–16 Feb. 1872.

34 God the All-terrible! King, Who ordainest
Great winds Thy clarions, the lightnings Thy sword. *God the All-Terrible.*

CHURCHILL, CHARLES, English clergyman and poet, Feb. 1731–4 Nov. 1764

35 He mouths a sentence as curs mouth a bone. *The Rosciad, 322.*

36 Be England what she will,
With all her faults, she is my country still. *The Farewell, 27.*

37 Apt alliteration's artful aid.
The Prophecy of Famine, 86.

38 He for subscribers baits his hook.
And takes your cash; but where's the book?
No matter where; wise fear, you know,
Forbids the robbing of a foe;

But what, to serve our private ends,
Forbids the cheating our friends?
(Of Dr. Johnson and his dictionary.)
The Ghost, III. 801.

CHURCHILL, SIR WINSTON LEONARD SPENCER, English Prime Minister, 30 Nov. 1874–24 Jan. 1965

1 It cannot in the opinion of His Majesty's Government be classified as slavery in the extreme acceptance of the word without some risk of terminological inexactitude.
Speech, House of Commons, 22 Feb. 1906.

2 I would say to the House, as I have said to those who have joined this Government : 'I have nothing to offer but blood, toil, tears and sweat.'
Ibid, 13 May, 1940.

3 We shall not flag or fail. We shall go on to the end, we shall fight in France, we shall fight on the seas and oceans, we shall fight with growing confidence and growing strength in the air, we shall defend our island, whatever the cost may be, we shall fight on the beaches, we shall fight on the landing grounds, we shall fight in the fields and in the streets, we shall fight in the hills; we shall never surrender.
Ibid, 4 June, 1940.

4 Let us therefore brace ourselves to our duties, and so bear ourselves that, if the British Empire and its Commonwealth last for a thousand years, men will still say, 'This was their finest hour.'
Ibid, 18 June, 1940.

5 The gratitude of every home in our island, in our Empire, and indeed throughout the world, except in the abodes of the guilty, goes out to the British airmen who, undaunted by odds, unwearied in their constant challenge and mortal danger, are turning the tide of the world war by their prowess and by their devotion. Never in the field of human conflict was so much owed by so many to so few.
Ibid, 20 Aug. 1940.

6 Undoubtedly this process means that these two great organisations of the English-speaking democracies, the British Empire and the United States, will have to be somewhat mixed up together in some of their affairs for mutual and general advantage. For my own part, looking out upon the future, I do not view the process with any misgivings. I could not stop it if I wished; no one can stop it. Like the Mississippi, it just keeps rolling along. Let it roll. Let it roll on full flood, inexorable, irresistible, benignant, to broader lands and better days.
Ibid.

7 Give us the tools, and we will finish the job.
Broadcast address, 9 Feb. 1941.

8 It becomes still more difficult to reconcile Japanese action with prudence or even with sanity. What kind of a people do they think we are?
Speech, US Congress, 26 Dec. 1941.

9 When I warned them (the French) that Britain would fight on alone whatever they did, their generals told their Prime Minister and his divided Cabinet, 'In three weeks England will have her neck wrung like a chicken.' Some chicken; some neck.
Speech, Canadian Senate and House of Commons, 30 Dec. 1941.

CIBBER, COLLEY, English Poet Laureate, 6 nov. 1671–12 Dec. 1757

10 Off with his head – so much for Buckingham!
Shakespeare's Richard III (altered), IV. iii.

11 Conscience avaunt, Richard's himself again.
Ibid, V. iii.

12 Perish the thought!
Ibid, V.

13 One had as good be out of the world as out of the fashion.
Love's Last Shift, II.

14 O say! What is that thing called Light, Which I can ne'er enjoy?
The Blind Boy.

CICERO, MARCUS TULLIUS, Roman Orator, 3 Jan. 106 B.C.–7 Dec. 43 B.C.

15 Silent enim leges inter arma. – For laws are dumb in the midst of arms.
Pro Milone – On Behalf of Milo, iv.

16 Salus populi suprema est lex. – The good of the people is the highest law.
De Legibus – On Laws, III. iii.

17 Quousque tandem abutere, Catilina, patientia nostra? – How long, pray, will you abuse our patience, Catiline?
In Catilinam – Against Catiline, I. i.

18 O tempora! O mores! – What times! What ways of life! *Ibid.*

19 Abiit, excessit, evasit, erupit. – He departed, he withdrew, he escaped, he broke forth. *Ibid, II. i.*

20 Spartam nactus es; hanc orna. – Sparta is yours; be an ornament to her.
Epistolae ad Atticum – Letters to Atticus, IV. vi.

21 Cedant arma togae, concedant laurea laudi.
– Let arms give place to the civic gown, and the laurel-wreath to praise.
De Officiis – On Duties, I. xxii.

22 O fortunatam natam me consule Romam!
– O lucky Roman State, born in my consulate! *Juvenal, Satires, x. 122.*

CLARE, JOHN, English poet, 13 July, 1793–20 May, 1864

23 Here sparrows build upon the trees,
And stockdove hides her nest;
The leaves are winnowed by the breeze
Into a calmer rest:
The blackcap's song was very sweet,
That used the rose to kiss;
It made the Paradise complete:
My early home was this.
My Early Home.

24 If life had a second edition, how I would correct the proofs. *Letter to a friend.*

CLARK, CHARLES HEBER, see ADELER, MAX

CLARKE, McDONALD (THE 'MAD POET'), US poet, 18 June, 1798–5 March, 1842

25 Whilst twilight's curtain spreading far,
Was pinned with a single star.
Death in Disguise, 227.

CLAY, HENRY, US statesman, 12 April, 1777–29 June, 1852

26 Sir, I would rather be right than be President. *Speech, 1850.*

CLEMENS, SAMUEL LANGHORNE, see TWAIN, MARK

CLEVELAND, STEPHEN GROVER, US President, 18 March, 1837–24 June, 1908

27 Your every voter, as surely as your chief magistrate, exercises a public trust.
Inaugural Address, 4 March, 1885.

28 However plenty silver dollars may become, they will not be distributed as gifts among the people.
First Annual Message, 8 Dec. 1885.

CLIVE OF PLASSEY, ROBERT CLIVE, BARON, English administrator, 29 Sept. 1725–22 Nov. 1774.

29 By God, Mr. Chairman, at this moment I stand astonished at my own moderation!
At Parliamentary inquiry into his conduct in India, 1773.

CLOUGH, ARTHUR HUGH, English poet, 1 Jan. 1819–13 Nov. 1861

30 Grace is given of God, but knowledge is bought in the market.
The Bothie of Tober-na-Vuolich, iv.

31 Where lies the land to which the ship would go ?

Far, far ahead, is all her seamen know.
Where lies the Land.

1 Say not the struggle naught availeth,
The labour and the wounds are vain,
The enemy faints not, nor faileth,
And as things have been they remain.
Say not the Struggle naught availeth.

2 For while the tired waves, vainly
breaking,
Seem here no painful inch to gain,
Far back, through creeks and inlets
making,
Comes silent, flooding in, the main.
Ibid.

3 And not by eastern windows only,
When daylight comes, comes in the
light;
In front, the sun climbs slow, how
slowly,
But westward, look, the land is bright.
Ibid.

4 Thou shalt have one God only; who
Would be at the expense of two?
The Latest Decalogue.

5 Thou shalt not kill; but need'st not strive
Officiously to keep alive. *Ibid.*

**COBBETT, WILLIAM, English
author, 9 March, 1762–18 June, 1835**

6 The great wen. (London.)
Rural Rides, 1821.

7 To be poor and independent is very
nearly an impossibility.
Advice to Young Men, ii.
To a Young Man.

**COBORN, CHARLES (COLIN
WHITTON McCALLUM),
English comedian, 4 Aug. 1852–23
Nov. 1945**

8 Two lovely black eyes,
Oh! what a surprise!
Only for telling a man he was wrong,
Two lovely black eyes!
Two Lovely Black Eyes.

**COCKBURN, ALICIA or ALISON
RUTHERFORD, Scottish poetess, 8
Oct. 1713–22 Nov. 1794.**

9 I've seen the smiling
Of Fortune beguiling;
I've felt all its favours, and found its
decay:
Sweet was its blessing,
Kind its caressing;
But now 'tis fled – fled far away.
The Flowers of the Forest.

**COKE, SIR EDWARD, English
Chief Justice, 1 Feb. 1552–3 Sept.
1634**

10 The gladsome light of jurisprudence.
Institutes: Commentary upon Littleton.
First Institute, epilogus.

11 They (corporations) cannot commit
treason, nor be outlawed, nor
excommunicate, for they have no souls.
Case of Sutton's Hospital, 10 Rep. 32.

12 Six hours in sleep, in law's grave study
six,
Four spend in prayer, the rest on Nature
fix. *Epigram.*

**COLBY, FRANK MOORE, US
author, 10 Feb. 1865–3 March, 1925**

13 I have found some of the best reasons I
ever had for remaining at the bottom
simply by looking at the men at the top.
Essays, II.

**COLERIDGE, HARTLEY, English
author, 19 Sept. 1796–6 Jan. 1849**

14 She is not fair to outward view
As many maidens be;
Her loveliness I never knew
Until she smiled on me.
O then I saw her eye was bright,
A well of love, a spring of light.
Song. She is not Fair.

15 Her very frowns are fairer far
Than smiles of other maidens are. *Ibid.*

COLERIDGE, MARY ELIZABETH, English authoress, 23 Sept. 1861–25 Aug. 1907

16 We were young, we were merry, we
    were very, very wise,
  And the door stood open at our feast,
  When there pass'd us a woman with the
    West in her eyes,
  And a man with his back to the East.
                                    Unwelcome.

COLERIDGE, SAMUEL TAYLOR, English poet, 21 Oct. 1772–25 July, 1834

17 It is an ancient Mariner,
  And he stoppeth one of three.
                The Ancient Mariner, part i.

18 He holds him with his glittering eye.
                                    Ibid.

19 The bride hath paced into the hall,
  Red as a rose is she.   *Ibid.*

20 The ice was here, the ice was there,
  The ice was all around:
  It cracked and growled and roared and
    howled,
  Like noises in a swound.   *Ibid.*

21 Nor dim nor red, like God's own head,
  The glorious sun uprist.   *Ibid, part ii.*

22 The fair breeze blew, the white foam
    flew,
  The furrow followed free;
  We were the first that ever burst
  Into that silent sea.   *Ibid.*

23 As idle as a painted ship
  Upon a painted ocean.   *Ibid.*

24 Water, water, everywhere.
  Nor any drop to drink.   *Ibid.*

25 The Night-mare Life-in-Death was she,
  Who thicks man's blood with cold.
                            Ibid, part iii.

26 'The game is done! I've won! I've won!'
  Quoth she, and whistles thrice.   *Ibid.*

27 The sun's rim dips; the stars rush out:
  At one stride comes the dark.   *Ibid.*

28 Till clomb above the eastern bar
  The hornèd moon, with one bright star
  Within the nether tip.   *Ibid.*

29 Alone, alone, all, all alone,
  Alone on a wide, wide sea!
                            Ibid, part iv.

30 The many men, so beautiful!
  And they all dead did lie;
  And a thousand thousand slimy things
  Lived on; and so did I.   *Ibid.*

31 The moving moon went up the sky,
  And nowhere did abide:
  Softly she was going up,
  And a star or two beside.   *Ibid.*

32 A spring of love gushed from my heart,
  And I blessed them unaware.   *Ibid.*

33 Oh sleep! it is a gentle thing,
  Beloved from pole to pole.   *Ibid, part v.*

34 A noise like of a hidden brook
  In the leafy month of June,
  That to the sleeping woods all night
  Singeth a quiet tune.   *Ibid.*

35 Quoth he, 'The man hath penance done,
  And penance more will do.'   *Ibid.*

36 Like one that on a lonesome road
  Doth walk in fear and dread,
  And having once turned round walks
    on,
  And turns no more his head;
  Because he knows a frightful fiend
  Doth close behind him tread.
                            Ibid, part vi.

37 Brown skeletons of leaves that lag
  My forest brook along.   *Ibid, part vii.*

38 O Wedding-Guest! this soul hath been
  Alone on a wide wide sea:
  Sol only 'twas, that God himself
  Scarce seemed there to be.   *Ibid.*

39 I pass like night from land to land;
  I have strange power of speech. *Ibid.*

1 He prayeth well, who loveth well
Both man and bird and beast.   *Ibid.*

2 He prayeth best who loveth best
All things both great and small.   *Ibid.*

3 A sadder and a wiser man,
He rose the morrow morn.   *Ibid.*

4 And the spring comes slowly up this
way.   *Christabel, part i.*

5 A sight to dream of, not to tell!   *Ibid.*

6 Alas! they had been friends in youth;
But whispering tongues can poison
truth;
And constancy lives in realms above;
And life is thorny, and youth is vain;
And to be wroth with one we love
Doth work like madness in the brain.
                              Ibid, part ii.

7 They stood aloof, the scars remaining,
Like cliffs which had been rent asunder;
A dreary sea now flows between.   *Ibid.*

8 In Xanadu did Kubla Khan
A stately pleasure-dome decree:
Where Alph, the sacred river, ran
Through caverns measureless to man
Down to a sunless sea.   *Kubla Khan.*

9 A savage place! as holy and enchanted
As e'er beneath a waning moon was
haunted
By woman wailing for her demon-
lover.   *Ibid.*

10 Five miles meandering with a mazy
motion.   *Ibid.*

11 Ancestral voices prophesying war.
                                       Ibid.

12 For he on honey-dew hath fed,
And drunk the milk of Paradise.   *Ibid.*

13 In the hexameter rises the fountain's
silvery column:
In the pentameter aye falling in melody
back.   *The Ovidian Elegiac Metre.*

14 From his brimstone bed at break of day
A-walking the Devil is gone,

To visit his snug little farm the earth,
And see how his stock goes on.
                          The Devil's Thoughts.

15 His jacket was red and his breeches were
blue,
And there was a hole where the tail came
through.   *Ibid.*

16 He saw a cottage with a double coach-
house,
A cottage of gentility:
And the devil did grin, for his darling
sin
Is pride that apes humility.   *Ibid.*

17 All thoughts, all passions, all delights,
Whatever stirs this mortal frame,
All are but ministers of Love,
And feed his sacred flame.   *Love.*

18 All this long eve, so balmy and serene,
Have I been gazing on the western sky,
And its peculiar tint of yellow green:
And still I gaze – and with how blank an
eye!
And those thin clouds above, in flakes
and bars,
That give away their motion to the stars;
Those stars, that glide behind them or
between,
Now sparkling, now bedimmed, but
always seen:
Yon crescent moon, as fixed as if it grew
In its own cloudless, starless lake of
blue;
I see them all so excellently fair,
I see, not feel, how beautiful they are!
                      Dejection: An Ode, 2.

19 Trochee trips from long to short:
From long to long in solemn sort
Slow Spondee stalks; strong foot! yet ill
able
Ever to come up with Dactyl trisyllable.
Iambics march from short to long;
With a leap and a bound the swift
Anapaests throng;
One syllable long, with one short at
each side,
Amphibrachys hastes with a stately
stride;
First and last being long, middle short,
Amphimacer
Strikes his thundering hoofs like a proud
high-bred racer.   *Metrical Feet.*

20 The Knight's bones are dust,
And his good sword rust; –
His soul is with the saints, I trust.
The Knight's Tomb.

21 Verse, a breeze mid blossoms straying,
Where Hope clung feeding, like a bee –
Both were mine! Life went a-maying
With Nature, Hope, and Poesy,
When I was young! *Youth and Age.*

22 I counted two and seventy stenches,
All well defined, and several stinks.
Cologne.

23 Stop, Christian passer-by! – Stop, child
of God,
And read with gentle breast. Beneath
this sod
A poet lies, or that which once seem'd
he.
O, lift one thought in prayer for S.T.C.
Epitaph.

24 Swans sing before they die – 'twere no
bad thing
Did certain persons die before they sing.
Epigram on a Volunteer Singer.

25 Clothing the palpable and familiar
With golden exhalations of the dawn.
The Death of Wallenstein, I. i.

26 A little child, dear brother Jem,
That lightly draws its breath,
And feels its life in every limb,
What should it know of death?
*Lines contributed to Wordsworth's
We are Seven.*

27 Not the poem which we have *read*, but
that to which we *return*, with the
greatest pleasure, possesses the genuine
power, and claims the name of *essential*
poetry. *Biographia Literaria, i.*

28 Our myriad-minded Shakespeare.
Ibid, xv.

29 I wish our clever young poets would
remember my homely definitions of
prose and poetry; that is, prose = words
in their best order; – poetry the *best*
words in the best order.
Table Talk, 12 July, 1827.

30 The man's desire is for the woman; but
the woman's desire is rarely other than
for the desire of the man.
Ibid, 23 July, 1827.

31 Summer has set in with its usual
severity.
*Quoted in Lamb's Letter to V. Novello,
9 May, 1826.*

**COLLINGS, JESSE, English
politician, 9 Jan. 1831–20 Nov. 1920**

32 Three acres and a cow.
Land reform slogan, 1885.

**COLLINS, WILLIAM, English
poet, 25 Dec. 1721–12 June, 1759.**

33 How sleep the brave, who sink to rest
By all their country's wishes blest!
Ode written in the Year 1746.

34 By fairy hands their knell is rung,
By forms unseen their dirge is sung;
There Honour comes, a pilgrim grey,
To bless the turf that wraps their clay,
And Freedom shall awhile repair
To dwell a weeping hermit there! *Ibid.*

35 If aught of oaten stop, or pastoral song
May hope, O pensive Eve, to soothe
thine ear. *Ode to Evening.*

36 Now air is hush'd, save where the weak-
ey'd bat,
With short shrill shriek flits by on
leathern wing,
Or where the beetle winds
His small but sullen horn. *Ibid.*

37 With eyes uprais'd, as one inspired.
Pale Melancholy sate retir'd.
The Passions, 57.

38 O Music, sphere-descended maid!
Ibid, 95.

39 To fair Fidele's grassy tomb
Soft maids and village hinds shall bring
Each op'ning sweet of earliest bloom,
And rifle all the breathing Spring.
Dirge in Cymbeline.

COLMAN, GEORGE (THE YOUNGER), English dramatist, 21 Oct. 1762–17 Oct. 1836.

1 When taken,
To be well shaken.
The Newcastle Apothecary.

2 Says he, 'I am a handsome man, but I'm a gay deceiver.'
Unfortunate Miss Bailey.

COLTON, CHARLES CALEB, English author, 1780?–28 April, 1832

3 Men will wrangle for religion; write for it; fight for it; die for it; anything but – live for it.
Lacon, I. No. 25

4 Imitation is the sincerest of flattery
Ibid, No 217

5 Examinations are formidable even to the best prepared, for the greatest fool may ask more than the wisest man can answer.
Ibid, No. 322.

COLUM, PADRAIC, Irish author, 8 Dec. 1881–11 Jan. 1972

6 Oh, to have a little house!
To own the hearth and stool and all!
An Old Woman of the Roads.

CONGREVE, WILLIAM, English dramatist, 10 Feb. 1670–19 Jan. 1729.

7 Thou liar of the first magnitude.
Love for Love, II. v.

8 Music hath charms to soothe a savage breast,
To soften rocks, or bend a knotted oak.
The Mourning Bride, I. i.

9 Heav'n has no rage like love to hatred turn'd,
Nor Hell a fury like a woman scorn'd.
Ibid, III. viii.

10 If there's delight in love, 'tis when I see
That heart, which others bleed for, bleed for me.
The Way of the World, III. xii.

11 Let us be very strange and well-bred: Let us be as strange as if we had been married a great while, and as well-bred as if we were not married at all.
Ibid, IV. v.

12 Defer not till to-morrow to be wise,
To-morrow's sun to thee may never rise.
Letter to Cobham.

CONNELL, JAMES, Irish author, 1852–8 Feb. 1929

13 Then raise the scarlet standard high!
Beneath its shade we'll live and die!
Though cowards flinch, and traitors jeer,
We'll keep the Red Flag flying here!
The Red Flag.

CONRAD, JOSEPH (TEODOR JOSEF KONRAD KORZENIOWSKI), Anglo-Polish novelist, 3 Dec. 1857–3 Aug. 1924

14 A work that aspires, however humbly, to the condition of art should carry its justification in every line.
The Nigger of the Narcissus, preface.

15 Women's rougher, simpler, more upright judgment embraces the whole truth, which their tact, their mistrust of masculine idealism, ever prevents them from speaking in its entirety.
Chance, I. v.

CONSTABLE, HENRY, English poet, 1562–9 Oct. 1613

16 Diaphenia, like the daffadowndilly,
White as the sun, fair as the lily,
Heigh-ho, how I do love thee!
Diaphenia.

CONSTANT DE REBECQUE, HENRI BENJAMIN, French politician, 25 Oct. 1767–8 Dec. 1830

17 Je ne suis pas la rose, mais j'ai vécu avec elle. – I am not the rose, but I have lived with her.
Attributed.

COOK, ELIZA, English poetess, 24 Dec. 1818–23 Sept. 1889

18 I love it, I love it; and who shall dare
To chide me from loving that old arm-
chair? *The Old Arm-Chair.*

COOLIDGE, CALVIN, US President, 4 July, 1872–5 Jan. 1933

19 There is no right to strike against the
public safety by anybody, anywhere,
any time.
Telegram to Samuel Gompers, 14 Sept. 1919.

20 They hired the money, didn't they?
Of the Allies' war debts to US.

COOPER, ANTHONY ASHLEY, see SHAFTESBURY

CORBET, RICHARD, Bishop successively of Oxford and of Norwich, 1582–28 July, 1635

21 Farewell, rewards and fairies,
Good housewives now may say,
For now foul sluts in dairies
Do fare as well as they.
And though they sweep their hearths no
less
Than maids were wont to do,
Yet who of late for cleanliness
Finds sixpence in her shoe?
Farewell, Rewards and Fairies.

CORNFORD, FRANCES CROFTS, English poetess, 30 March 1886–19 Aug. 1960.

22 O why do you walk through the fields
in gloves,
Missing so much and so much?
O fat white woman whom nobody
loves,
Why do you walk through the fields in
gloves? *To a Lady seen from the Train.*

CORNUEL, ANNE BIGOT DE, French wit, 1614–Feb. 1694

23 Il n'y a pas de héros pour un valet de
chambre. – No man is a hero to his
valet.
Letter of Mlle Aïssé, 13 Aug. 1728.

CORNWALL, BARRY, see PROCTER, BRYAN WALLER

CORY, WILLIAM JOHNSON, English poet, 9 Jan. 1823–11 June, 1892

24 All beauteous things for which we live
By laws of time and space decay.
But oh, the very reason why
I clasp them, is because they die.
Mimnermus in Church

25 Somewhere beneath the sun,
These quivering heart-strings prove it,
Somewhere there must be one
Made for this soul, to move it.
Amaturus

26 They told me, Heraclitus, they told me
you were dead;
They brought me bitter news to hear
and bitter tears to shed.
I wept as I remembered how often you
and I
Had tired the sun with talking and sent
him down the sky.
(Paraphrase from Callimachus).
Heraclitus.

27 Still are thy pleasant voices, thy
nightingales, awake;
For Death, he taketh all away, but them
he cannot take. *Ibid.*

COTTON, NATHANIEL, English poet and doctor, 1705–2 Aug. 1788

28 Thus hand in hand through life we'll go;
Its checker'd paths of joy and woe
With cautious steps we'll tread.
The Fireside, 13.

29 Yet still we hug the dear deceit.
Visions in Verse. Content.

COUÉ, ÉMILE, French doctor, 26 Feb. 1857–2 July, 1926

30 Tous les jours, à tous points de vue, je
vais de mieux en mieux. – Every day,
from every point of view, I am getting
better and better.
Formula for auto-suggestion.

COUSIN, VICTOR, French philosopher, 28 Nov. 1792–13 Jan. 1867

1 L'art pour l'art. – Art for art's sake.
Sorbonne lectures, xxii.

COWLEY, ABRAHAM, English author, 1618–28 July, 1667

2 His *faith,* perhaps, in some nice tenets might
Be wrong; his *life,* I'm sure, was in the right *On the Death of Crashaw.*

3 The thirsty earth soaks up the rain,
And drinks, and gapes for drink again;
The plants suck in the earth, and are
With constant drinking fresh and fair.
From Anacreon. Drinking.

4 Fill all the glasses there, for why
Should every creature drink but I?
Why, man of morals, tell me why?
Ibid.

5 Love in her sunny eyes doth basking play;
Love walks the pleasant mazes of her hair;
Love does on both her lips for ever stray,
And sows and reaps a thousand kisses there:
In all her outward parts Love's always seen;
But oh! he never went within.
The Change.

6 The monster London.
Essays in Verse and Prose, ii. Of Solitude, II.

COWLEY, HANNAH, English dramatist, 1743–11 March, 1809

7 But what is woman? – only one of Nature's agreeable blunders.
Who's the Dupe? II. ii.

8 Five minutes! Zounds! I have been five minutes too late all my lifetime!
The Belle's Stratagem, I. i.

COWPER, WILLIAM, English poet, 15 Nov. 1731–25 April, 1800

9 No dancing bear was so genteel,
Or half so *dégagé.* *On himself.*

10 There goes the parson, oh! illustrious spark,
And there, scarce less illustrious, goes the clerk!
On observing some Names of Little Note recorded in the Biographica Britannica.

11 Regions Caesar never knew
Thy posterity shall sway,
Where his eagles never flew,
None invincible as they.
Boadicea: an Ode.

12 Ages elaps'd ere Homer's lamp appear'd
And ages ere the Mantuan swan was heard:
To carry nature lengths unknown before,
To give a Milton birth, ask'd ages more.
Table Talk, 556.

13 How much a dunce that has been sent to roam
Excels a dunce that has been kept at home. *The Progress of Error, 415.*

14 'Tis hard if all is false that I advance –
A fool must now and then be right, by chance. *Conversation, 95.*

15 A moral, sensible, and well-bred man
Will not affront me, and no other can.
Ibid, 193.

16 Pernicious weed! whose scent the fair annoys,
Unfriendly to society's chief joys,
Thy worst effect is banishing for hours
The sex whose presence civilizes ours.
Ibid, 251.

17 I cannot talk with civet in the room,
A fine puss-gentleman that's all perfume. *Ibid, 283.*

18 Absence of occupation is not rest,
A mind quite vacant is a mind distress'd.
Retirement, 623.

19 I praise the Frenchman, his remark was
   shrewd   (La Bruyère.)
   How sweet, how passing sweet, is
   solitude!
   But grant me still a friend in my retreat,
   Whom I may whisper – solitude is
   sweet.   *Ibid, 739.*

20 I am monarch of all I survey,
   My right there is none to dispute.
                    *Verses supposed to be written by
                            Alexander Selkirk.*

21 O solitude! where are the charms
   That sages have seen in thy face?   *Ibid.*

22 The path of sorrow, and that path alone,
   Leads to the land where sorrow is
   unknown.
   An Epistle to a Protestant Lady in France.

23 With outstretch'd hoe I slew him at the
   door,
   And taught him NEVER TO COME
   THERE NO MORE.
   (Of a viper that attacked three kittens.)
                            The Colubriad.

24 Toll for the brave –
   The brave that are no more:
   All sunk beneath the wave,
   Fast by their native shore.
           On the Loss of the Royal George.

25 A land-breeze shook the shrouds,
   And she was overset;
   Down went the Royal George
   With all her crew complete.   *Ibid.*

26 John Gilpin was a citizen
   Of credit and renown.
   A train-band captain eke was he
   Of famous London town.   *John Gilpin.*

27 That, though on pleasure she was bent,
   She had a frugal mind.   *Ibid.*

28 So, fair and softly, John he cried,
   But John he cried in vain.   *Ibid.*

29 Away went Gilpin – who but he?
   His fame soon spread around –
   He carries weight! he rides a race!
   'Tis for a thousand pound!

30 My hat and wig will soon be here –
   They are upon the road.   *Ibid.*

31 Said John – It is my wedding-day,
   And all the world would stare,
   If wife should dine at Edmonton,
   And I should dine at Ware!   *Ibid.*

32 I sing the Sofa.
               The Task, I. The Sofa, I.

33 God made the country, and man made
   the town.   *Ibid, 749.*

34 Oh for a lodge in some vast wilderness,
   Some boundless contiguity of shade,
   Where rumour of oppression and deceit,
   Of unsuccessful or successful war,
   Might never reach me more.
               Ibid, II. The Timepiece, I.

35 Slaves cannot breathe in England; if
   their lungs
   Receive our air, that moment they are
   free;
   They touch our country, and their
   shackles fall.   *Ibid, 40.*

36 England, with all thy faults I love thee
   still,
   My country!   *Ibid, 206.*

37 There is a pleasure in poetic pains
   Which only poets know.   *Ibid, 285.*

38 Variety's the very spice of life,
   That gives it all its flavour.   *Ibid, 606.*

39 I was a stricken deer, that left the herd
   Long since.   *Ibid, III. The Garden, 108.*

40 Who loves a garden loves a greenhouse
   too.   *Ibid, 566.*

41 Now stir the fire, and close the shutters
   fast,
   Let fall the curtains, wheel the sofa
   round,
   And while the bubbling and loud-
   hissing urn
   Throws up a steamy column, and the
   cups,
   That cheer but not inebriate, wait on
   each,
   So let us welcome peaceful ev'ning in.
           Ibid, IV. The Winter Evening, 36.

1 O Winter, ruler of th' inverted year.
Ibid, 120.

2 With spots quadrangular of diamond form,
Ensanguin'd hearts, clubs typical of strife,
And spades, the emblem of untimely graves. *Ibid, 217.*

3 There is in souls a sympathy with sounds;
And, as the mind is pitch'd, the ear is pleas'd
With melting airs, or martial, brisk, or grave:
Some chord in unison with what we hear
Is touch'd within us, and the heart replies.
Ibid, VI. The Winter Walk at Noon, I.

4 Knowledge is proud that he has learn'd so much;
Wisdom is humble that he knows no more. *Ibid, 96.*

5 Books are not seldom talismans and spells. *Ibid, 98.*

6 I would not enter on my list of friends
(Tho' grac'd with polish'd manners and fine sense,
Yet wanting sensibility; the man
Who needlessly sets foot upon a worm.
Ibid, 560.

7 For public schools 'tis public folly feeds.
Tirocinium, 250.

8 An honest man, close-button'd to the chin,
Broadcloth without, and a warm heart within. *An Epistle to Joseph Hill, 62*

9 The poplars are fell'd, farewell to the shade
And the whispering sound of the cool colonnade. *The Poplar-Field.*

10 O that those lips had language! Life has pass'd
With me but roughly since I heard thee last.
On the Receipt of my Mother's Picture, I.

11 By disappointment every day beguil'd,
Dupe of *to-morrow* even from a child.
Ibid, 40.

12 For 'tis a truth well known to most,
That whatsoever thing is lost,
We seek it, ere it come to light,
In ev'ry cranny but the right.
The Retired Cat, 95.

13 Mary! I want a lyre with other strings.
Sonnet to Mrs. Unwin.

14 But misery still delights to trace
Its semblance in another's case.
The Castaway.

15 Oh! for a closer walk with God.
Olney Hymns, i.

16 What peaceful hours I once enjoy'd
How sweet their mem'ry still!
But they have left an aching void,
The world can never fill. *Ibid.*

17 There is a fountain fill'd with blood
Drawn from Emmanuel's veins;
And sinners, plung'd beneath that flood,
Lose all their guilty stains. *Ibid, xv.*

18 Can a woman's tender care
Cease, toward the child she bare?
Yes, she may forgetful be,
Yet will I remember thee. *Ibid, xviii.*

19 God moves in a mysterious way,
His wonders to perform;
He plants His footsteps in the sea,
And rides upon the storm. *Ibid, xxxv.*

20 Behind a frowning providence
He hides a smiling face. *Ibid.*

CRABBE, GEORGE, English poet and clergyman, 24 Dec. 1754–3 Feb. 1832

21 On Mincio's banks, in Caesar's bounteous reign,
If Tityrus found the Golden Age again,
Must sleepy bards the flattering dream prolong,
Mechanic echoes of the Mantuan song?
From Truth and Nature shall we widely stray,

Where Virgil, not where Fancy, leads
the way? *The Village, I. 15.*
(These lines were rewritten in this form
by Dr. Johnson.)

22 Yes, thus the muses sing of happy
swains,
Because the Muses never knew their
pains:
They boast their peasants' pipes; but
peasants now
Resign their pipes and plod behind the
plough. *Ibid, 21.*

23 By such examples taught, I paint the
Cot,
As Truth will paint it, and as Bards will
not. *Ibid, 53.*

24 Rank weeds, that every art and care
defy,
Reign o'er the land and rob the blighted
rye:
There thistles stretch their prickly arms
afar,
And to the ragged infant threaten war;
There poppies nodding, mock the hope
of toil,
There the blue bugloss paints the sterile
soil;
Hardy and high, above the slender
sheaf,
The slimy mallow waves her silky leaf;
O'er the young shoot the charlock
throws a shade,
And clasping tares cling round the sickly
blade. *Ibid, 67.*

25 Oh! rather give me commentators plain,
Who with no deep researches vex the
brain;
Who from the dark and doubtful love to
run,
And hold their glimmering tapers to the
sun.
The Parish Register, I. introduction, 89.

26 Books cannot always please, however
good;
Minds are not ever craving for their
food.
The Borough, letter xxiv. Schools, 402.

27 Grave Jonas Kindred, Sybil Kindred's
sire,

Was six feet high, and look'd six inches
higher.
Tales, vi. The Frank Courtship, I.

28 When the coarse cloth she saw, with
many a stain,
Soil'd by rude hinds who cut and came
again. *Ibid, vii. The Widow's Tale, 25.*

29 The ring so worn, as you behold,
So thin, so pale, is yet of gold:
The passion such it was to prove;
Worn with life's cares, love yet was
love. *His Mother's Wedding Ring.*

CRAIK, DINAH MARIA MULOCK, English authoress, 20 April, 1826–12 Oct. 1887

30 It's a bonnie bay at morning,
And bonnier at the noon,
But it's bonniest when the sun draps
And red comes up the moon;
When the mist creeps o'er the
Cumbraes,
And Arran peaks are grey,
And the great black hills, like sleepin'
kings,
Sit grand roun' Rothesay Bay.
Rothesay Bay.

31 Could ye come back to me, Douglas,
Douglas!
In the old likeness that I knew,
I would be so faithful, so loving,
Douglas,
Douglas, Douglas, tender and true.
Too Late.

CRASHAW, RICHARD, English poet, 1613?–21 Aug. 1649

32 Whoe'er she be
That not impossible she
That shall command my heart and me.
Wishes to his Supposed Mistress.

33 Where'er she lie
Locked up from mortal eye,
In shady leaves of destiny. *Ibid.*

34 Life that dares send
A challenge to his end,
And when it comes say 'Welcome,
Friend.' *Ibid.*

1 Two walking baths; two weeping
motions;
Portable and compendious oceans.
Saint Mary Magdalene, or
The Weeper, 19.

2 Nympha pudica Deum vidit, et erubuit.
– The conscious water saw its God, and
blushed. *Epigrammata Sacra.*
Aquae in Vinum Versae. – Sacred
Epigrams. The Water turned into Wine.
(Latin and translation both by
Crashaw.)

CRAWFORD, FRANCIS MARION,
US novelist, 2 Aug. 1854–9 April,
1909.

3 What is charm? It is what the violet has
and the camelia has not.
Children of the King, v.

CROCKETT, DAVID, US farmer,
17 Aug. 1786–6 March, 1836

4 Don't shoot, colonel. I'll come down: I
know I'm a gone coon.
Story of a treed raccoon.

CROMWELL, OLIVER, Lord
Protector, 25 April, 1599–3 Sept.
1658

5 I beseech you, in the bowels of Christ,
think it possible you may be mistaken.
Letter to the General Assembly of the
Church of Scotland, 3 Aug. 1650.

6 What shall we do with this bauble?
There, take it away. (Of the Mace.)
When dismissing Parliament,
20 April, 1653.

7 It is not my design to drink or to sleep,
but my design is to make what haste I
can to be gone. *Dying Words.*

CROSS, MRS., *see* **Eliot, George**

CROWNE, JOHN, English
dramatist, 1640?–1703?

8 There is no hiding love from lover's
eyes. *The Destruction of Jerusalem,*
part I. IV. i.

CUMBERLAND, RICHARD,
Bishop of Peterborough, 15 July,
1631–9 Oct. 1718

9 It is better to wear out than to rust out.
Bishop George Horne, A Duty of
Contending for the Faith.

CUNNINGHAM, ALLAN, Scottish
poet, 7 Dec. 1784–30 Oct. 1842

10 The sun rises bright in France,
And fair sets he;
But he has tint the blythe blink he had
In my ain countree.
The Sun rises bright in France.

11 A wet sheet and a flowing sea,
A wind that follows fast,
And fills the white and rustling sail,
And bends the gallant mast.
A wet Sheet and a flowing Sea.

12 While the hollow oak our palace is,
Our heritage the sea. *Ibid.*

13 Wha the deil hae we got for a king,
But a wee, wee German lairdie!
The Wee, Wee German Lairdie.

14 It's hame, and it's hame, hame fain wad
I be,
An' it's hame, hame, hame, to my ain
countree! *Hame, Hame, Hame.*
(This and the preceding quotation are
based on older poems.)

CURRAN, JOHN PHILPOT, Irish
judge, 24 July, 1650–14 Oct. 1817

15 The condition upon which God hath
given liberty to man is eternal vigilance.
Speech on the right of election of Lord Mayor
of Dublin, 10 July, 1790.

DANIEL, SAMUEL, English Poet
Laureate, 1562–14 Oct. 1619

16 Care-charmer Sleep, son of the sable
Night,
Brother to Death, in silent darkness
born. *Sonnets to Delia, liv.*

DANTE, ALIGHIERI, Italian poet, May, 1265–14 Sept. 1321

17 Lasciate ogni speranza, voi ch' entrate!
 – All hope abandon, ye who enter!
  *La Divina Commedia – The Divine
   Comedy. Inferno, iii. 9.*

18 Questi non hanno speranza di morte.
 – These have not hope of death.
  Ibid, 46.

19 Onorate l'altissimo poeta.
 – Honour the greatest poet.
  Ibid, iv. 80.

20 Nessun maggior dolore,
 Che ricordarsi del tempo felice
 Nella miseria.
 – No greater sorrow that to recall in our
 misery
 the time when we were happy.
  Ibid, v. 121.

21 E 'n la sua volontate è nostra pace.
 – And in His will is our peace.
  Paradiso, iii. 85.

22 L'amor che move il sole e l'altre stelle.
 – The love that moves the sun and the
 other stars. *Ibid, xxxiii. 145.*

DANTON, GEORGES JACQUES, French politician, 28 Dec. 1759–5 April, 1794.

23 De l'audace, encore de l'audace, et
 toujours de l'audace! – Boldness, again
 boldness, and always boldness!
 *Speech to Legislative Committee of General
 Defence, 2 Sept. 1792.*

DARWIN, CHARLES ROBERT, English naturalist, 12 Feb. 1809–19 April, 1882

24 I have called this principle, by which
 each slight variation, if useful, is
 preserved, by the term Natural
 Selection. *The Origin of Species, iii.*

25 The expression often used by Mr.
 Herbert Spencer, of the Survival of the
 Fittest, is more accurate, and is
 sometimes equally convenient. *Ibid.*

DARWIN, ERASMUS, English scientist, 12 Dec. 1731–18 April, 1802

26 Soon shall thy arm, unconquer'd steam!
 afar
 Drag the slow barge, or drive the rapid
 car;
 Or on wide-waving wings expanded
 bear
 The flying chariot through the field of
 air. *The Botanic Garden, I. i. 289.*

D'AVENANT SIR WILLIAM, English Poet Laureate, Feb. 1606–7 April, 1668

27 The lark now leaves his wat'ry nest
 And, climbing, shakes his dewy wings.
  Song.

DAVIES, SIR JOHN, English poet, baptised 16 April, 1659, died 7 Dec. 1626

28 Wedlock, indeed, hath oft compared
 been
 To public feasts, where meet a public
 rout,
 Where they that are without would fain
 go in,
 And they that are within would fain go
 out.
  *Contention betwixt a Wife, a Widow,
   and a Maid.*

DAVIES, WILLIAM HENRY, English poet, 3 July, 1871–26 Sept. 1940

29 What is this life if, full of care,
 We have no time to stand and stare.
  Leisure.

30 Sweet stay-at-Home, sweet Well-
 content. *Sweet Stay-at-Home.*

31 A rainbow and a cuckoo's song
 May never come together again;
 May never come
 This side the tomb. *A Great Time.*

DAVIS, THOMAS OSBORNE, Irish poet, 14 Oct. 1814–16 Sept. 1845

1 Come in the evening, or come in the morning,
Come when you're looked for, or come without warning. *The Welcome.*

DECATUR, STEPHEN, US naval commander, 5 Jan. 1779–22 March, 1820

2 Our country! In her intercourse with foreign nations may she always be in the right; but our country, right or wrong.
Toast given at Norfolk, Virginia, April, 1816.

DEFFAND, MARIE ANNE DE VICHY-CHAMROND, MARQUISE DU, French authoress, 25 Dec. 1697–23 Sept. 1780.

3 Il n'y a que le premier pas qui coûte. – It is only the first step which is troublesome.
Letter to d'Alembert, 7 July, 1763.

DEFOE, DANIEL, English author, 1660?–26 April, 1731

4 He bade me observe it, and I should always find, that the calamities of life were shared among the upper and lower part of mankind; but that the middle station had the fewest disasters.
Robinson Crusoe, part I.

5 Wherever God erects a house of prayer,
The Devil always builds a chapel there;
And 'twill be found upon examination,
The latter has the largest congregation.
The True-Born Englishman, I. I.

6 No danger can their daring spirit pall,
Always provided that their belly's full.
Ibid, II. 13.

7 No panegyric need their praise record;
An Englishman ne'er wants his own good word. *Ibid, 152*

DEKKER, THOMAS, English dramatist, 1570?–1641?

8 Art thou poor, yet hast thou golden slumbers?
O sweet content!
Art thou rich, yet is thy mind perplexed?
O punishment! *Patient Grissill, I.*

9 To add to golden numbers, golden numbers. *Ibid.*

10 Work apace, apace, apace, apace;
Honest labour bears a lovely face. *Ibid.*

11 Golden slumbers kiss your eyes,
Smiles awake you when you rise
Sleep, pretty wantons, do not cry,
And I will sing a lullaby. *Ibid, IV. ii.*

12 The best of men
That e'er wore earth about him was a sufferer;
A soft, meek, patient, humble, tranquil spirit,
The first true gentleman that ever breathed. *The Honest Whore, I. 1. ii.*

DE LA MARE, WALTER JOHN, English poet, 25 April, 1873–22 June, 1956

13 Slowly, silently, now the moon
Walks the night in her silver shoon.
Silver.

14 Softly along the road of evening,
In a twilight dim with rose,
Wrinkled with age, and drenched with dew,
Old Nod, the shepherd, goes. *Nod.*

15 Here lies a most beautiful Lady,
Light of step and heart was she;
I think she was the most beautiful lady
That ever was in the West Country.
Epitaph.

16 Look thy last on all things lovely
Every hour. *Farewell.*

17 Since that all things thou wouldst praise
Beauty took from those who loved them
In other days. *Ibid.*

18 Oh, no man knows
Through what wild centuries
Roves back the rose.   *All that's Past.*

19 Far are the shades of Arabia
Where the princes ride at noon.
                    Arabia.

20 'Is there anybody there?' said the
   Traveller,
Knocking on the moonlit door.
                    The Listeners.

DE MORGAN, AUGUSTUS, English mathematician, 1806–18 March, 1871.

21 Great fleas have little fleas upon their
   backs to bite 'em,
And little fleas have lesser fleas, and so *ad
infinitum.*
And the great fleas themselves, in turn,
   have greater fleas to go on;
While these again have greater still, and
   greater still, and so on.
            A Budget of Paradoxes, p. 377.

DENHAM, SIR JOHN, English poet, 1615–10 March, 1669

22 O, could I flow like thee, and make thy
   stream
My great example, as it is my theme!
Though deep, yet clear; though gentle,
   yet not dull;
Strong without rage; witout o'erflowing
full.
(Of the Thames.)   *Cooper's Hill, 189.*

DENMAN, THOMAS DENMAN, 1ST BARON, LORD CHIEF JUSTICE, 23 Feb. 1779–22 Sept. 1854

23 Trial by jury itself, instead of being a
security to persons who are accused,
will be a delusion, a mockery, and a
snare.
In O'Connell v. the Queen, 4 Sept. 1844.

DENNIS, JOHN, English critic, 1657–6 Jan. 1734

24 A man who could make so vile a pun
would not scruple to pick a pocket.
                    Attributed.

25 They will not let my play run, and yet
they steal my thunder!
*On hearing his own effects used in another
play.*

DE QUINCEY, THOMAS, English author, 15 Aug. 1785–8 Dec. 1859

26 If once a man indulge himself in murder,
very soon he comes to think little of
robbing; and from robbing he next
comes to drinking and Sabbath-
breaking, and from that to incivility and
procrastination.
Murder Considered as One of the Fine Arts.

27 It is notorious that the memory
strengthens as you lay burdens upon it,
and becomes trustworthy as you trust it.
*Confessions of an English Opium-Easter,
part I.*

DESCARTES, RENÉ, French philosopher, 31 March, 1596–11 Feb. 1650

28 Cogito, ergo sum. – I think, therefore I
am.
*Discours de la Méthode – Discourse of
Method.*

DIBDIN, CHARLES, English song writer, 4 March, 1745–25 July, 1814

29 There's a sweet little cherub that sits up
aloft,
To keep watch for the life of poor Jack.
                    Poor Jack.

30 And did you not hear of a jolly young
waterman,
Who at Blackfriar's Bridge used for to
ply?
He feather'd his oars with such skill and
dexterity,
Winning each heart, and delighting each
eye.   *The Jolly Young Waterman.*

31 Here, a sheer hulk, lies poor Tom
Bowling,
The darling of our crew;
No more he'll hear the tempest
howling,
For death has broach'd him to.
                    Tom Bowling.

1 Faithful below he did his duty,
But now he's gone aloft. *Ibid.*

2 Did you ever hear of Captain Wattle?
He was all for love, and a little for the
bottle. *Captain Wattle and Miss Roe.*

**DIBDIN, THOMAS, English
dramatist, 21 March, 1771–16 Sept.
1841**

3 O, it's a snug little island!
A right little, tight little island!
The Snug Little Island.

**DICKENS, CHARLES, English
novelist, 7 Feb. 1812–9 June, 1870**

4 He had used the word in its Pickwickian
sense. (Blotton.) *Pickwick Papers, i.*

5 Not presume to dictate, but broiled fowl
and mushrooms – capital thing! (Jingle.)
Ibid, ii.

6 Kent – apples, cherries, hops, and
women. (Jingle.) *Ibid.*

7 A rare old plant is the Ivy green.
Song, Ibid, vi.

8 'It wasn't the wine,' murmured Mr.
Snodgrass, in a broken voice. 'It was the
salmon.' *Ibid, viii.*

9 I wants to make your flesh creep. (Joe,
the fat boy.) *Ibid.*

10 Can I unmoved see thee dying
On a log,
Expiring frog! *Ode, Ibid, xv.*

11 Mr. Weller's knowledge of London was
extensive and peculiar. *Ibid, xx.*

12 The wictim o' connubiality, as Blue
Beard's domestic chaplain said, with a
tear of pity, ven he buried him. (Sam
Weller.) *Ibid.*

13 It's over, and can't be helped, and that's
one consolation, as they always say in
Turkey, ven they cuts the wrong man's
head off. (Sam Weller.) *Ibid, xxiii.*

14 Dumb as a drum vith a hole in it. (Sam
Weller.) *Ibid, xxv.*

15 Wen you're a married man, Samivel,
you'll understand a good many things as
you don't understand now; but vether
it's worth while goin' through so much
to learn so little, as the charity-boy said
ven he got to the end of the alphabet, is a
matter o' taste. (Old Weller.)
Ibid. xxvii.

16 A double glass o' the inwariable. (Old
Weller.) *Ibid, xxxiii.*

17 She's a-swellin' wisibly before my wery
eyes. (Old Weller.) *Ibid.*

18 'Little to do, and plenty to get, I
suppose?' said Sergeant Buzfuz with
jocularity.
'Oh, quite enough to get, sir, as the
soldier said ven they ordered him three
hundred and fifty lashes,' replied Sam.
'You must not tell us what the soldier,
or any other man, said, sir,' interposed
the judge; 'it's not evidence.'
Ibid, xxxiv.

19 'Yes, I have a pair of eyes,' replied Sam,
'and that's just it. If they wos a pair o'
patent double million magnifyin' gas
microscopes of hextra power, p'raps I
might be able to see through a flight o'
stairs and a deal door; but bein' only
eyes, you see, my wision's limited.'
Ibid.

20 Vy worn't there a alleybi! (Old Weller.)
Ibid.

21 If he damned hisself in confidence, o'
course that was another thing. (Old
Weller.) *Ibid, xliii.*

22 Anythin' for a quiet life, as the man said
wen he took the sitivation at the
lighthouse. (Sam Weller.) *Ibid.*

23 Which is your partickler wanity? (Sam
Weller.) *Ibid, xlv.*

24 Oliver Twist has asked for more!
(Bumble.) *Oliver Twist, ii.*

25 The Artful Dodger. *Ibid, viii.*

26 'If the law supposes that,' said Mr. Bumble . . . 'the law is a ass – a idiot.' *Ibid, li.*

27 Here's richness! (Squeers.) *Nicholas Nickleby, v.*

28 A demd, damp, moist, unpleasant body. (Mantalini.) *Ibid, xxxiv.*

29 She is come at last – at last – and all is gas and gaiters! (The old gentleman.) *Ibid, xlix.*

30 My life is one demd horrid grind. (Mantalini.) *Ibid, lxiv.*

31 He has gone to the demnition bow-wows. (Mantalini.) *Ibid.*

32 Is the old min agreeable (Dick Swiveller.) *The Old Curiosity Shop, ii.*

33 What is the odds so long as the fire of soul is kindled at the taper of conwiviality, and the wing of friendship never moults a feather! (Dick Swiveller.) *Ibid.*

34 Codlin's the friend, not Short. (Codlin.) *Ibid, xix.*

35 'There are strings,' said Mr. Tappertit, ' . . . in the human heart that had better not be wibrated.' *Barnaby Rudge, xxii.*

36 Any man may be in good spirits and good temper when he's well dressed. There ain't much credit in that. (Mark Tapley.) *Martin Chuzzlewit, v.*

37 Some credit in being jolly. (Mark Tapley.) *Ibid.*

38 With affection beaming in one eye, and calculation shining out of the other.' *Ibid, viii.*

39 Let us be moral. Let us contemplate existence. (Pecksniff.) *Ibid, ix.*

40 'Mrs. Harris,' I says, 'leave the bottle on the chimley-piece, and don't ask me to take none, but let me put my lips to it when I am so dispoged.' (Mrs. Gamp.) *Ibid, xix.*

41 He'd make a lovely corpse. (Mrs. Gamp.) *Ibid, xxv.*

42 Our backs is easy ris. We must be cracked-up, or they rises, and we snarls . . . You'd better crack us up, you had! (Chollop.) *Ibid, xxxiii.*

43 Oh Sairey, Sairey, little do we know wot lays afore us! (Mrs. Gamp.) *Ibid, xl.*

44 'Bother Mrs. Harris!' said Betsey Prig. . . . 'I don't believe there's no sich a person!' *Ibid, xlix.*

45 'But the words she spoke of Mrs. Harris, lambs could not forgive. No, Betsey!' said Mrs. Gamp, in a violent burst of feeling, 'nor worms forget!' *Ibid.*

46 In came Mrs. Fezziwig, one vast substantial smile. *A Christmas Carol, stave ii.*

47 'God bless us every one!' said Tiny Tim. *Ibid, iii.*

48 Oh, let us love our occupations, Bless the squire and his relations, Live upon our daily rations, And always know our proper stations. *The Chimes, 2nd quarter.*

49 He's tough, ma'am, tough, is J. B. Tough, and devilish sly! (Major Bagstock.) *Dombey and Son, vii.*

50 When found, make a note of. (Captain Cuttle.) *Ibid, xv.*

51 Train up a fig-tree in the way it should go, and when you are old sit under the shade of it. (Captain Cuttle.) *Ibid, xix.*

52 'I am a lone lorn creetur,' were Mrs. Gummidge's words, . . . 'and everything goes contrairy with me.' *David Copperfield, iii.*

1 She's been thinking of the old 'un! (Mr.
Peggotty.)   *Ibid.*

2 Barkis is willin'. (Barkis.)   *Ibid, v.*

3 'In case anything turned up,' which was
his (Micawber's) favourite expression.
                                            Ibid, xi.

4 I never will desert Mr. Micawber. (Mrs.
Micawber.)   *Ibid, xii.*

5 Annual income twenty pounds, annual ·
expenditure nineteen nineteen six, result
happiness. Annual income twenty
pounds, annual expenditure twenty
pounds ought and six, result misery.
(Micawber.)   *Ibid.*

6 'I'm a very umble person . . . . My
mother is likewise a very umble person.
We live in a numble abode, Master
Copperfield, but have much to be
thankful for.' (Uriah Heep.)   *Ibid, xvi.*

7 'I should be happy, myself, to propose
two months, . . . but I have a partner,
Mr. Jorkins. (Spenlow.)   *Ibid, xxiii.*

8 I'm Gormed – and I can't say no fairer
than that! (Mr. Peggotty.)   *Ibid, lxiii.*

9 A London particular. . . . A fog.
(Guppy.)   *Bleak House, iii.*

10 Educating the natives of Borrioboola-
Gha, on the left bank of the Niger.
(Mrs. Jellyby.)   *Ibid, iv.*

11 Not to put too fine a point upon it.
(Snagsby.)   *Ibid, xi.*

12 He wos wery good to me, he wos. (Jo.)
                                              Ibid.

13 'It is,' says Chadband, 'the ray of rays,
the sun of suns, the moon of moons, the
star of stars. It is the light of Terewth.'
                                            Ibid, xxv.

14 Far better hang wrong fler than no fler.
(The debilitated cousin of the
Dedlocks.)   *Ibid, liii.*

15 Facts alone are wanted in life.
(Gradgrind.)   *Hard Times, I. i.*

16 Whatever was required to be done, the
Circumlocution Office was beforehand
with all the public departments in the art
of perceiving – HOW NOT TO DO
IT.   *Little Dorrit, I. x.*

17 Papa, potatoes, poultry, prunes, and
prism, are all very good words for the
lips: especially prunes and prism. (Mrs.
General.)   *Ibid, II. v.*

18 It is a far, far better thing that I do, than I
have ever done; it is a far, far better rest
that I go to, than I have ever known.
(Sidney Carton.)
                    A Tale of Two Cities, II. xv.

19 Mr. Podsnap settled that whatever he
put behind him he put out of existence.
                        Our Mutual Friend, I. xi.

20 The question about everything (with
Podsnap) was, would it bring a blush to
the cheek of a young person?   *Ibid.*

21 Who comes here?
A Grenadier.
What does he want?
A pot of beer.   *Ibid, II. ii.*

**DICKINSON, EMILY
ELIZABETH, US poetess, 10 Dec.
1830–15 May, 1886**

22 I asked no other thing,
No other was denied.
I offered Being for it;
The mighty merchant smiled.

23 Brazil? He twirled a button,
Without a glance my way:
'But, madam, is there nothing else
That we can show to-day?'
                      Poems, part I. Life, xii.

24 How dreary to be somebody!
How public, like a frog
To tell your name the livelong day
To an admiring bog!   *Ibid, xxvii.*

25 I never saw a moor,
I never saw the sea;
Yet know I how the heath looks,
And what a wave must be.
            Ibid, part IV. Time and Eternity, xvii.

26 This quiet Dust was Gentlemen and
Ladies,
And Lads and Girls;
Was laughter and ability and sighing,
And frocks and curls.
Ibid, part V. The Single Hound, lxxiv.

**DIDEROT, DENIS, French scholar,
5 Oct. 1713–30 July, 1784**

27 L'esprit de l'escalier. – Staircase wit (i.e.
the retort which is thought of too late).
*Paradoxe sur le Comédien. – The Paradox
of the Comedian.*

**DILLON, WENTWORTH, see
Roscommon, Earl of.**

**DIONYSIUS OF
HALICARNASSUS, Greek
historian, 1st century B.C.**

28 'ιστορία φιλοσοφία
ε'στίν ε'κ ﻻαραδειγμάτων.
– History is philosophy derived from
examples.
Ars Rhetorica. – Art of Rhetoric, XI. ii.

**DISRAELI, BENJAMIN, 1ST
EARL OF BEACONSFIELD,
English Prime Minister, 21 Dec.
1804–19 April, 1881**

29 I will sit down now, but the time will
come when you will hear me.
*Maiden speech, House of Commons, 7 Dec.
1837.*

30 The noble Lord is the Prince Rupert of
Parliamentary discussion. (Lord
Stanley.)
*Speech, House of Commons, 24 April,
1844.*

31 The right honourable gentleman caught
the Whigs bathing, and walked away
with their clothes. (Sir Robert Peel.)
Ibid, 28 Feb. 1845.

32 The question is this: Is man an ape or an
angel? My lord, I am on the side of the
angels. *Ibid, Oxford, 25 Nov. 1864.*

33 I believe that without party
Parliamentary government is
impossible.
Ibid, Manchester, 3 April, 1872.

34 A university should be a place of light,
of liberty, and of learning.
Ibid, House of Commons, 11 March, 1873.

35 He is a great master of gibes and flouts
and jeers. (The Marquis of Salisbury.)
Ibid, 5 Aug. 1874.

36 Lord Salisbury and myself have brought
you back peace – but a peace I hope with
honour. *Ibid, 16 July, 1878.*

37 A sophistical rhetorician, inebriated
with the exuberance of his own
verbosity. (Gladstone.)
Ibid, Knightsbridge, 27 July, 1878.

38 Adventures are to the adventurous.
Ixion in Heaven, II. ii.

39 No Government can be long secure
without a formidable Opposition.
Coningsby, II. i.

40 Youth is a blunder; Manhood a struggle;
Old Age a regret. *Ibid, III. i.*

41 London is a modern Babylon.
Tancred, V. v.

42 The gondola of London. (A hansom.)
Lothair, xxvii.

43 I have always thought that every
woman should marry, and no man.
Ibid, XXX

**D'ISRAELI, ISAAC, English
antiquary, 11 May, 1766–19 Jan.
1848**

44 There is an art of reading, as well as an
art of thinking, and an art of writing.
Literary Character, xi.

**DOBELL, SYDNEY THOMPSON,
English poet, 5 April, 1824–22 Aug.
1874**

45 The murmur of the mourning ghost,
That keeps the shadowy kine,
'Oh, Keith of Ravelston,
The sorrows of thy line!'
A Nuptial Eve.

DOBSON, HENRY AUSTIN, English author, 18 Jan. 1840–2 Sept. 1921

1 Time goes, you say? Ah no!
Alas, Time stays, *we* go.
The Paradox of Time.

2 The ladies of St. James's!
They're painted to the eyes,
Their white it stays for ever,
Their red it never dies:
But Phyllida, my Phyllida!
Her colour comes and goes;
It trembles to a lily, –
It wavers to a rose.
The Ladies of St. James's.

3 I intended an Ode,
And it turn'd to a Sonnet.   *Urceus exit.*

DODDRIDGE, PHILIP, English clergyman, 26 June, 1702–26 Oct. 1751

4 Live while you live, the epicure would say,
And seize the pleasures of the present day;
Live while you live, the sacred preacher cries,
And give to God each moment as it flies.
Lord, in my views let both united be;
I live in pleasure when I live to thee.
Epigram on his Family Arms, 'Dum Vivimus Vivamus.'

5 O God of Jacob, by whose hand
Thy people still are fed.
Scripture Paraphases, ii.
(Later altered to 'O God of Bethel.')

DODGE, MARY ABIGAIL, see Hamilton, Gail

DODGSON, CHARLES LUTWIDGE, see Carroll, Lewis

DONATUS, AELIUS, Roman grammarian, 4th century A.D.

6 Pereant qui ante nos nostra dixerunt. –
Perish those who have said our remarks before us.
St. Jerome, Commentary on Ecclesiastes, i.

DONNE, JOHN, Dean of St. Paul's, 1571–31 March, 1631

7 Go and catch a falling star,
Get with child a mandrake root,
Tell me, where all past years are,
Or who cleft the Devil's foot.   *Song.*

8 For God's sake hold your tongue and let me love.   *The Canonization.*

9 And whilst our souls negotiate there,
We like sepulchral statues lay;
All day, the same our postures were,
And we said nothing, all the day.
The Ecstasy.

10 I long to talk with some old lover's ghost,
Who died before the god of love was born.   *Love's Deity.*

11 No spring nor summer beauty hath such grace
As I have seen in one autumnal face.
Elegies, ix. The Autumnal.

12   Her pure and eloquent blood
Spoke in her cheeks, and so distinctly wrought
That one might almost say her body thought.
Of the Progress of the Soul. The Second Anniversary, 244.

DONNELLY, IGNATIUS, US politician, 3 Nov. 1831–1 Jan. 1901.

13 The Democratic Party is like a mule – without pride of ancestry or hope of posterity.
Speech, Minnesota Legislature.

DOOLEY, MR. (FINLEY PETER DUNNE), US humorist, 10 July, 1867–30 June, 1919

14 Th' dead ar-re always pop'lar.
On Charity.

15 Life'd not be worth livin' if we didn't keep our inimies.
On New Year's Resolutions.

16 Vice . . . is a creature of such heejus
mien. . . . that the more ye see it th'
better ye like it.
The Crusade against Vice.

DOSTOIEVSKY, FEODOR
MIKHAILOVITCH, Russian
novelist, 11 Nov. 1821–9 Feb. 1881

17 Man is a pliable animal, a being who
gets accustomed to everything.
The House of the Dead, I. ii.

DOUDNEY, SARAH, English
authoress, 15 Jan. 1843–15 Dec. 1926

18 Listen to the water-mill;
Through the livelong day,
How the clicking of its wheel
Wears the hours away!
The Lesson of the Water-Mill.

19 And a proverb haunts my mind
As a spell is cast –
'The mill cannot grind
With the water that is past.' *Ibid.*

DOW, LORENZO, US preacher, 16
Oct. 1777–2 Feb. 1834

20 You can and you can't – You shall and
you shan't – You will and you won't –
You'll be damned if you do – And you'll
be damned if you don't. (Defining
Calvinism.)
Reflections on the Love of God.

DOWSON, ERNEST
CHRISTOPHER, English poet,
2 Aug. 1867–23 Feb. 1900

21 They are not long, the weeping and the
laughter,
Love and desire and hate:
I think they have no portion in us after
We pass the gate. *Vitae Summa Brevis.*

22 And I was desolate and sick of an old
passion. *Non sum qualis eram.*

23 I have been faithful to thee, Cynara! in
my fashion. *Ibid.*

DOYLE, SIR ARTHUR CONAN,
English author, 22 May, 1859–7
July, 1930

24 'Wonderful!' I ejaculated.
'Commonplace,' said Holmes.
A Study in Scarlet, iii.

25 An experience of women which extends
over many nations and three separate
continents. *The Sign of Four, ii.*

26 You know my methods. Apply them.
Ibid, vi.

27 You see, but you do not observe.
The Adventures of Sherlock Holmes. A
Scandal in Bohemia.

28 The case has, in some respects, been not
entirely devoid of interest.
Ibid, A Case of Identity.

29 Singularity is almost invariably a clue.
The more featureless and commonplace
a crime is, the more difficult it is to
bring it home.
Ibid, The Boscombe Valley Mystery.

30 A little monograph on the ashes of one
hundred and forty different varieties of
pipe, cigar, and cigarette tobacco. *Ibid.*

31 A man should keep his little brain attic
stocked with all the furniture that he is
likely to use, and the rest he can put
away in the lumber-room of his library,
where he can get it if he wants it.
Ibid, The Five Orange Pips.

32 It is my belief, Watson, founded upon
my experience, that the lowest and vilest
alleys of London do not present a more
dreadful record of sin than does the
smiling and beautiful countryside.
Ibid, The Copper Beeches.

33 A long shot, Watson; a very long shot!
The Memoirs of Sherlock Holmes. Silver
Blaze.

34 'The curious incident of the dog in the
night-time.'
'The dog did nothing in the night-time.'
'That was the curious incident,'
remarked Sherlock Holmes. *Ibid.*

1 'Excellent!' I cried. 'Elementary,' said
he.   *Ibid, The Crooked Man.*

2 He is the Napoleon of crime.
                Ibid, The Final Problem.

3 But here, unless I am mistaken, is our
client.   *His Last Bow. Wisteria Lodge.*

4 The natives were Cucama Indians, an
amiable but degraded race, with mental
powers hardly superior to the average
Londoner. (Professor Challenger.)
                        The Lost World, iv.

5 What of the bow?
The bow was made in England:
Of true wood, of yew wood,
The wood of English bows.
        *The White Company. The Song of the
                                    Bow.*

6 The Grenadiers of Austria are proper
men and tall.   *Cremona.*

**DOYLE, SIR FRANCIS
HASTINGS CHARLES, 2ND
BARONET, English poet, 21 Aug.
1810–8 June, 1888**

7 Last night, among his fellow roughs,
He jested, quaffed, and swore;
A drunken private of the Buffs,
Who never looked before.
To-day, beneath the foeman's frown,
He stands in Elgin's place,
Ambassador from Britain's crown,
And type of all her race.
                The Private of the Buffs.

8 Vain, mightiest fleets of iron framed;
Vain, those all-shattering guns;
Unless proud England keep, untamed,
The strong heart of her sons.   *Ibid.*

**DRAKE, SIR FRANCIS, English
Admiral, 1540?–28 Jan. 1596**

9 There's plenty of time to win this game,
and to thrash the Spaniards too.
        *When the Armada was sighted as he was at
                        bowls, 20 July, 1588.*

**DRAYTON, MICHAEL, English
poet, 1563–23 Dec. 1631**

10 Had in him those brave translunary
things,
That the first poets had.   (Marlowe.)
        *To Henry Reynolds, of Poets and Poesy,
                                    106.*

11 For that fine madness still he did retain
Which rightly should possess a poet's
brain.   *Ibid, 109.*

12 Fair stood the wind for France
When we our sails advance,
Nor now to prove our chance
Longer will tarry.
                The Ballad of Agincourt.

13 O, when shall Englishmen
With such acts fill a pen,
Or England breed again
Such a King Harry?   *Ibid.*

14 Since there's no help, come let us kiss
and part.   *Sonnets, lxi.*

15 Now at the last gasp of Love's latest
breath,
When, his pulse failing, Passion
speechless lies,
When Faith is kneeling by his bed of
death,
And Innocence is closing up his eyes,
Now if thou wouldst, when all have
given him over,
From death to life thou mightst him yet
recover.   *Ibid.*

**DRINKWATER, JOHN, English
author, 1 June, 1882–25 March, 1937**

16 I never went to Mamble
That lies above the Teme,
So I wonder who's in Mamble,
And whether people seem
Who breed and brew along there
As lazy as the name.   *Mamble.*

17 And not a girl goes walking
Along the Cotswold lanes
But knows men's eyes in April
Are quicker than their brains.
                    Cotswold Love.

DRUMMOND, THOMAS, English administrator, 10 Oct. 1797–15 April, 1840

18 Property has its duties as well as its rights.
Letter to the Earl of Donoughmore, 22 May, 1838.

DRUMMOND, WILLIAM (OF HAWTHORNDEN), Scottish poet, 13 Dec. 1585–4 Dec. 1649.

19 Phœbus, arise,
And paint the sable skies,
With azure, white, and red. *Song.*

20 Woods cut, again do grow,
Bud doth the rose, and daisy, winter done,
But we once dead no more do see the sun. *Song*

DRYDEN, JOHN, English Poet Laureate, 9 Aug. 1631–1 May, 1700.

21 An horrid stillness first invades the ear,
And in that silence we the tempest fear.
Astraea Redux, 7.

22 Whate'er he did was done with so much ease,
In him alone 'twas natural to please.
Absalom and Achitophel, I. 27.

23 Of these the false Achitophel was first,
A name to all succeeding ages curst.
Ibid, 150.

24 A daring pilot in extremity,
Pleased with the danger, when the waves went high
He sought the storms; but, for a calm unfit,
Would steer too nigh the sands to boast his wit. *Ibid, 159.*

25 Great wits are sure to madness near allied,
And thin partitions do their bounds divide. *Ibid, 163.*

26 Bankrupt of life, yet prodigal of ease.
Ibid, 168.

27 And all to leave what with his toil he won
To that unfeather'd two-legg'd thing, a son. *Ibid, 169.*

28 Resolv'd to ruin or to rule the state.
Ibid, 174.

29 But wild ambition loves to slide, not stand,
And fortune's ice prefers to virtue's land. *Ibid, 198.*

30 The wished occasion of the Plot he takes;
Some circumstances finds, but more he makes. *Ibid, 208.*

31 For politicians neither love nor hate.
Ibid, 223.

32 The people's prayer, the glad diviner's theme,
The young men's vision, and the old men's dream! *Ibid, 238.*

33 Than a successive title, long and dark,
Drawn from the mouldy rolls of Noah's ark. *Ibid, 301.*

34 A man so various that he seem'd to be
Not one, but all mankind's epitome:
Stiff in opinions, always in the wrong,
Was everything by starts and nothing long;
But in the course of one revolving moon,
Was chymist, fiddler, statesman, and buffoon. *Ibid, 545.*

35 So over-violent or over-civil
That every man with him was God or Devil. *Ibid, 557.*

36 In squandering wealth was his peculiar art;
Nothing went unrewarded but desert.
Beggared by fools whom still he found too late,
He had his jest, and they had his estate.
Ibid, 559.

37 Did wisely from expensive sins refrain
And never broke the Sabbath but for gain. *Ibid, 587.*

1 During his office treason was no crime,
The sons of Belial had a glorious time.
Ibid, 597.

2 His tribe were God Almighty's
gentlemen. *Ibid, 645.*

3 Beware the fury of a patient man.
Ibid, 1005.

4 Made still a blund'ring king of melody;
Spurr'd boldly on, and dash'd through
thick and thin,
Through sense and nonsense, never out
nor in. *Ibid, II. 413.*

5 All human things are subject to decay,
And, when fate summons, monarchs
must obey. *MacFlecknoe, I.*

6 The rest to some faint meaning make
pretence,
But Shadwell never deviates into sense.
Ibid, 19.

7 And torture one poor word ten
thousand ways. *Ibid, 208.*

8 She fear'd no danger, for she knew no
sin. *The Hind and the Panther, I. 4.*

9 For truth has such a face and such a
mien,
As to be lov'd needs only to be seen.
Ibid, 33.

10 By education most have been misled;
So they believe, because they so were
bred,
The priest continues what the nurse
began,
And thus the child imposes on the man.
Ibid, III. 389.

11 For Tom the Second reigns like Tom the
First. *Epistle to Mr. Congreve, 48.*

12 Be kind to my remains; and O defend,
Against your judgment, your departed
friend! *Ibid, 72.*

13 Better to hunt in fields, for health
unbought,
Than fee the doctor for a nauseous
draught.

The wise, for cure, on exercise depend;
God never made his work for man to
mend.
To John Driden of Chesterton, 92.

14 Wit will shine
Through the harsh cadence of a rugged
line.
To the Memory of Mr. Oldham, 15.

15 While yet a young probationer,
And candidate of heav'n.
To the Memory of Mrs. Killigrew, 15.

16 When rattling bones together fly
From the four corners of the sky.
Ibid, 184.

17 Here lies my wife: here let her lie!
Now she's at rest, and so am I.
Epitaph intended for Dryden's wife.

18 Three poets, in three distant ages born,
Greece, Italy, and England did adorn,
The first in loftiness of thought
surpass'd;
The next, in majesty; in both the last:
The force of Nature could no further go,
To make a third, she join'd the former
two.
Lines printed under a Portrait of Milton.

19 From harmony, from heavenly
harmony,
This universal frame began:
From harmony to harmony
Through all the compass of the notes it
ran,
The diapason closing full in Man.
A song for St. Cecilia's Day.

20 None but the brave deserves the fair.
Alexander's Feast, 15.

21 With ravish'd ears
The monarch hears;
Assumes the god,
Affects to nod,
And seems to shake the spheres.
Ibid, 37.

22 Bacchus' blessings are a treasure,
Drinking is the soldier's pleasure;
Rich the treasure,
Sweet the pleasure,
Sweet is pleasure after pain. *Ibid, 56.*

23 And thrice he routed all his foes, and
thrice he slew the slain. *Ibid, 68.*

24 Fallen, fallen, fallen, fallen,
Fallen from his high estate,
And weltering in his blood. *Ibid, 77.*

25 Sigh'd and look'd, and sigh'd again.
Ibid, 120.

26 And, like another Helen, fir'd another
Troy. *Ibid, 154.*

27 Oxford to him a dearer name shall be
Than his own Mother University.
Thebes did his green unknowing youth
engage,
He chooses Athens in his riper age.
Prologue to the University of Oxford.

28 For Art may err, but Nature cannot
miss.
Fables. The Cock and the Fox, 452.

29 He trudg'd along unknowing what he
sought,
And whistled as he went, for want of
thought.
Ibid, Cymon and Iphigenia, 84.

30 Of seeming arms to make a short essay,
Then hasten to be drunk, the business of
the day. *Ibid, 407.*

31 Happy who in his verse can gently steer
From grave to light, from pleasant to
severe. *The Art of Poetry, i. 75.*

32 Happy the man, and happy he alone,
He who can call to-day his own:
He who, secure within, can say,
To-morrow, do thy worst, for I have
liv'd to-day.
Imitation of Horace III. xxix. 65.

33 Not heav'n itself upon the past has
pow'r;
But what has been, has been, and I have
had my hour. *Ibid, 71.*

34 I can enjoy her while she's kind;
But when she dances in the wind,
And shakes the wings, and will not stay,
I puff the prostitute away. (Of Fortune.)
Ibid, 81.

35 Pains of love be sweeter far
Than all other pleasures are.
Tyrannic Love, IV. i.

36 But Shakespeare's magic could not
copied be;
Within that circle none durst walk but
he. *The Tempest, prologue.*

37 I am as free as Nature first made man,
Ere the base laws of servitude began,
When wild in woods the noble savage
ran.
The Conquest of Granada, part I. I. i.

38 Forgiveness to the injured does belong;
For they ne'er pardon who have done
the wrong. *Ibid, part II. i. ii.*

39 When I consider life, 'tis all a cheat;
Yet, fool'd with hope, men favour the
deceit;
Trust on, and think to-morrow will
repay:
To-morrow's falser than the former
day;
Lies worse, and, while it says, we shall
be blest
With some new joys, cuts off what we
possest.
Strange cozenage! None would live past
years again,
Yet all hope pleasure in what yet remain;
And from the dregs of life think to
receive
What the first sprightly running could
not give. *Aurengzebe, IV. i.*

40 Errors, like straws, upon the surface
flow;
He who would search for pearls must
dive below. *All for Love, prologue.*

41 Men are but children of a larger growth.
Ibid, IV. i.

42 There is a pleasure sure
In being mad, which none but madmen
know! *The Spanish Friar, II. i.*

43 He was the man who of all modern, and
perhaps ancient poets, had the largest
and most comprehensive
soul. (Shakespeare.)
Essay of Dramatic Poesy.

1 He was naturally learn'd; he needed not the spectacles of books to read Nature; he looked inwards, and found her there.
Ibid.

2 He is many times flat, insipid; his comic wit degenerating into clenches, his serious swelling into bombast. But he is always great when some occasion is presented to him.
Ibid.

3 Here is God's plenty. (Of Chaucer's 'Canterbury Tales.')
Fables, preface.

4 Cousin Swift, you will never be a poet.
Johnson's Life of Swift.

DUDLEY, SIR HENRY BATE, English clergyman and journalist, 25 Aug. 1745–1 Feb. 1824

5 Wonders will never cease.
Letter to Garrick, 13 Sept. 1776.

DUFFERIN, COUNTESS OF, see Sheridan, Helen Selina

DUFFIELD, GEORGE, US clergyman, 12 Sept. 1818–6 July, 1888

6 Stand up! stand up for Jesus!
Soldiers of the Cross.

DUMAS, ALEXANDRE (THE ELDER), French novelist, 24 July, 1802–5 Dec. 1870.

7 Cherchez la femme. – Look for the woman.
Les Mohicans de Paris. – The Mohicans of Paris, III. x.

DU MAURIER, GEORGE LOUIS PALMELLA BUSSON, English artist and novelist, 6 March, 1834–6 Oct. 1896

8 I have no talent for making new friends, but oh, such a genius for fidelity to old ones.
Peter Ibbetson.

9 I don't know much about his ability, but he's got a very good beside manner.
Punch, 15 March, 1884.

10 A little work, a little play
To keep us going – and so, good-day!
A little warmth, a little light,
Of love's bestowing – and so, good-night!
A little fun, to match the sorrow
Of each day's growing – and so, good-morrow!
A little trust that when we die
We reap our sowing! and so – good-bye!
Trilby, part VIII.

DUNBAR, WILLIAM, Scottish poet, 1465?–1530?

11 All love is lost but upon God alone.
The Merle and the Nightingale.

12 Our plesance here is all vain glory,
This fals world is but transitory,
The flesh is bruckle, the Feynd is slee:–
Timor Mortis conturbat me
Lament for the Makaris.

13 London, thou art the flower of cities all!
London.

DUNNE, FINLEY PETER, see Dooley, Mr.

DYER, SIR EDWARD, English courtier, 1540–1607

14 My mind to me a kingdom is;
Such present joys therein I find,
That it excels all other bliss
That earth affords or grows by kind:
Though much I want which most would have,
Yet still my mind forbids to crave.
My Mind to me a Kingdom is.

DYER, JOHN, Welsh poet, baptised 13 Aug. 1699, buried 15 Dec. 1757

15 Ever charming, ever new,
When will landscape tire the view?
Grongar Hill, 5.

16 A little rule, a little sway,
A sunbeam in a winter's day,
Is all the proud and mighty have
Between the cradle and the grave.
Ibid, 89.

EDISON, THOMAS ALVA, US scientist, 11 Feb. 1847–18 Oct. 1931

17 Genius is one per cent. inspiration and ninety-nine per cent. perspiration
Newspaper interview.

EDWARDS, OLIVER, English lawyer, 1711–1791

18 You are a philosopher, Dr. Johnson. I have tried too in my time to be a philosopher; but I don't know how, cheerfulness was always breaking in.
Boswell's Life of Johnson, an. 1778.

EDWARDS, RICHARD, English poet, 1523?–31 Oct. 1566

19 The falling out of faithful friends renewing is of love. *Amantium Irae.*

ELIOT, GEORGE (MARY ANN or MARIAN EVANS, MRS. CROSS), English novelist, 22 Nov. 1819–22 Dec. 1880.

20 Animals are such agreeable friends – they ask no questions, they pass no criticisms.
Scenes of Clerical Life. Mr. Gilfil's Love Story, vii.

21 It's but little good you'll do a-watering last year's crop. *Adam Bede, xviii.*

22 We hand folks over to God's mercy, and show none ourselves. *Ibid, xlii.*

23 The law's made to take care o' raskills.
The Mill on the Floss, III. iv.

24 The happiest women, like the happiest nations, have no history. *Ibid, VI. iii.*

25 Men's men: gentle or simple, they're much of a muchness.
Daniel Deronda, IV. xxxi.

26 O may I join the choir invisible
Of those immortal dead who live again
In minds made better by their presence.
The Choir Invisible.

ELIOT, THOMAS STEARNS, Anglo-American poet, 26 Sept. 1888–4 Jan. 1965

27 When the evening is spread out against the sky
Like a patient etherised upon a table.
The Love Song of J. Alfred Prufrock.

28 The yellow fog that rubs its back upon the window-panes. *Ibid.*

29 I am aware of the damp souls of housemaids
Sprouting despondently at area gates.
Morning at the Window.

30 Wearily, as one would turn to nod good-bye to Rochefoucauld,
If the street were time and he at the end of the street.
The Boston Evening Transcript.

31 O the moon shone bright on Mrs. Porter
And on her daughter
They wash their feet in soda water.
The Waste Land, III. The Fire Sermon.

32 When lovely woman stoops to folly and
Paces about her room again, alone,
She smoothes her hair with automatic hand,
And puts a record on the gramophone.
Ibid.

33 This is the way the world ends
Not with a bang but a whimper.
The Hollow Men.

34 And when you reach the scene of crime
– *Macavity's not there!*
Macavity: the Mystery Cat.

ELIZABETH I, English Queen. 7 Sept. 1533–24 March, 1603

35 I know I have the body of a weak and feeble woman, but I have the heart and stomach of a king, and of a king of England too.
Speech at Tilbury on the approach of the Spanish Armada, 1588.

1 All my possessions for a moment of
time. *Last words.*
(See also Ralegh, Sir Walter.)

**ELLERTON, JOHN, English
hymn-writer, 16 Dec. 1826–15 June,
1893**

2 Now the labourer's task is o'er;
Now the battle-day is past;
Now upon the farther shore
Lands the voyager at last.
Now the Labourer's Task.

**ELLIOT, JEAN or JANE, Scottish
poetess, 1727–29 March, 1805**

3 I've heard them lilting at our yowe-
milking –
Lasses a-lilting before dawn of day;
But now they are moaning on ilka green
loaning –
The Flowers of the Forest are a' wede
away. *The Flowers of the Forest.*

**ELLIOTT, CHARLOTTE, English
hymn-writer, 17 March, 1789–22
Sept. 1871**

4 Christian, seek not yet repose;
Hear they guardian angel say,
'Thou art in the midst of foes:
Watch and pray.'
Christian, seek not yet Repose.

**ELLIOTT, EBENEZER, English
poet, 17 March, 1781–1 Dec. 1849**

5 When wilt thou save the people?
Oh, God of mercy, when?
Not kings and lords, but nations!
Not thrones and crowns, but men!
The People's Anthem.

**ELLIS, GEORGE ('SIR GREGORY
GANDER'), English poet, 1753–10
April, 1815**

6 Snowy, Flowy, Blowy,
Showery, Flowery, Bowery,
Hoppy, Croppy, Droppy,
Breezy, Sneezy, Freezy.
The Twelve Months.

**ELLIS, HENRY HAVELOCK,
English psychologist, 2 Feb. 1859–8
July, 1939**

7 The tide turns at low water as well as at
high. *Impressions and Comments, I. 103.*

**EMERSON, RALPH WALDO, US
author, 25 May, 1803–27 April, 1882**

8 There is properly no history; only
biography. *Essays. History.*

9 A foolish consistency is the hobgoblin of
little minds. *Ibid. Self-Reliance.*

10 To be great is to be misunderstood.
Ibid.

11 All mankind love a lover. *Ibid, Love.*

12 The only reward of virtue is virtue; the
only way to have a friend is to be one.
Ibid, Friendship.

13 Beware when the great God lets loose a
thinker on this planet. *Ibid, Circles.*

14 Nothing great was ever achieved
without enthusiasm. *Ibid.*

15 Language is fossil poetry.
Ibid, The Poet.

16 Every hero becomes a bore at last.
Representative Men. Uses of Great Men.

17 Give me health and a day, and I will
make the pomp of emperors ridiculous.
Nature, iii.

18 Hitch your wagon to a star.
Society and Solitude. Civilisation.

19 Never read any book that is not a year
old. *Ibid, Books.*

20 If a man can write a better book, preach
a better sermon, or make a better
mouse-trap, than his neighbour, though
he build his house in the woods, the
world will make a beaten path to his
door. *Attributed.*

21 The hand that rounded Peter's dome,

And groined the aisles of Christian
Rome,
Wrought in a sad sincerity;
Himself from God he could not free;
He builded better than he knew;–
The conscious stone to beauty grew.
The Problem.

22 Earth proudly wears the Parthenon
As the best gem upon her zone.   *Ibid.*

23 The frolic architecture of the snow.
The Snowstorm.

24 Here once the embattled farmers stood,
And fired the shot heard round the
world.
*Hymn sung at the Completion of the
Concord Monument.*

25 So nigh is grandeur to our dust,
So near is God to man,'
When Duty whispers low, *Thou must,*
The youth replies, *I can.*
Voluntaries, iii.

26 If the red slayer thinks he slays,
Or if the slain thinks he is slain,
They know not well the subtle ways
I keep, and pass, and turn again.
Brahma.

27 I am the doubter and the doubt,
And I the hymn the Brahmin sings.
Ibid.

ENGLISH, THOMAS DUNN, US
author, 29 June, 1819–1 April, 1902

28 Don't you remember sweet Alice, Ben
Bolt,–
Sweet Alice whose hair was so brown,
Who wept with delight when you gave
her a smile,
And trembled with fear at your frown?
Ben Bolt.

ENNIUS, Roman poet, 239?–169? B.C.

29 Unus homo nobis cunctando restituit
rem.
– One man by delaying saved the State
for us.   *Annals, XII.*
(Of Quintus Fabius Maximus, Roman
general.)

ERSKINE, HENRY, Scottish
lawyer, 1 Nov. 1746–8 Oct. 1817

30 The rule of the road is a paradox quite,
Both in riding and driving along;
If you keep to the left, you are sure to be
right,
If you keep to the right you are wrong.
The Rule of the Road.

ESTIENNE, HENRI, French
scholar, 1528–March, 1598

31 Si jeunesse savait; si vieillesse pouvait. –
If youth knew; if age could.
Les Prémices, Épigramme cxci.

EUCLID, Greek mathematician,
about 300 B.C.

32 δὲ απεκρίνατο, μὴ ειναι βασιλικὴν
ατραπὸν επὶ γεωμετρίαν,
– But he answered that there was no
royal road to geometry. (When Ptolemy
asked if there was not a shorter method.)
*Proclus, Commentary on Euclid, prologue
G 20.*

EURIPIDES, Greek dramatist,
484?–406 B.C.

33 'Η γλῶσσ' ομώμοχ', η δὲ φρὴν
ανώμοτος.
– My tongue has sworn it, but my
mind's unsworn.   *Hippolytus, 612.*

34 'Ασφαλὴς γάρ εστ' αμείνων η θρασὺς
στρατηλάτης.
– A reliable general is better than a
dashing one.
Phœnissae. – The Phœnician Maidens, 599.

35 Θάλασσα κλύζει πάντα τανθρώπων
κακά.
– The sea washes all man's ills away.
*Iphignenia in Tauris – Iphigenia among the
Tauri, 1193.*

EUWER, ANTHONY
HENDERSON, US author, 11 Feb.
1877–

36 As a beauty I'm not a great star.
Others are handsomer far;
But my face – I don't mind it
Because I'm behind it;
It's the folks out in front that I jar.
Limerick.

EVANS, ABEL, English cleric, 1679–18 Oct. 1737

1 Under this stone, Reader, survey
Dead Sir John Vanbrugh's house of clay,
Lie heavy on him, Earth, for he
Laid many heavy loads on thee!
Epitaph on Vanbrugh, architect and dramatist.

EVANS, MARY ANN OR MARIAN, see Eliot, George

EVELYN, JOHN, English diarist, 31 Oct. 1620–27 Feb. 1706

2 A studious decliner of honours and titles. *Diary, introduction.*

3 I saw *Hamlet Prince of Denmark* played; but now the old plays begin to disgust this refined age. *Ibid, 26 Nov. 1661.*

EVERETT, DAVID, US author, 29 March, 1770–21 Dec. 1813

4 You'd scarce expect one of my age
To speak in public on the stage;
And if I chance to fall below
Demosthenes or Cicero,
Don't view me with a critic's eye,
But pass my imperfections by.
Large streams from little fountains flow,
Tall oaks from little acorns grow.
Lines written for a School Declamation.

FABER, FREDERICK WILLIAM, English cleric, 28 June, 1814–26 Sept. 1863

5 Angels of Jesus, angels of light,
Singing to welcome the pilgrims of the night! *Hark! hark, my soul!*

6 Small things are best;
Grief and unrest
To rank and wealth are given;
But little things
On little wings
Bear little souls to heaven
Written in a Little Lady's Little Album.

FARMER, EDWARD, English poet, 1809?–1876

7 I have no pain, dear mother, now; but, oh! I am so dry:

Just moisten poor Jim's lips once more;
and, mother, do not cry!
The Collier's Dying Child.

FARQUHAR, GEORGE, Irish dramatist, 1678–29 April, 1707

8 Lady Bountiful.
The Beaux' Stratagem, dramatis personæ.

9 I believe they talked of me, for they laughed consumedly. *Ibid, III. i.*

10 'Twas for the good of my country that I should be abroad. *Ibid, ii.*

11 Spare all I have, and take my life.
Ibid, V. ii.

FERRIAR, JOHN, Scottish doctor, 21 Nov. 1761–4 Feb. 1815

12 Now cheaply bought for thrice their weight in gold.
Illustrations of Sterne. Bibliomania, 65.

FEUERBACH, LUDWIG ANDREAS, German philosopher, 28 July, 1804–13 Sept. 1872

13 Der Mensch ist was er isst. – Man is what he eats.
Preface to Moleschott's Lehre der Nahrungsmittel für das Volk.

FIELD, EUGENE, US author, 2 or 3 Sept. 1850–4 Nov. 1895

14 A little peach in the orchard grew.
The Little Peach.

15 So shut your eyes while mother sings
Of wonderful sights that be,
And you shall see the beautiful things
As you rock on the misty sea
Where the old shoe rocked the
fishermen three,
Wynken,
Blynken,
And Nod. *Dutch Lullaby.*

16 The little toy dog is covered with dust,
But sturdy and staunch he stands;
And the little toy soldier is red with rust,
And his musket moulds in his hands;

Time was when the little toy dog was new,
And the soldier was passing fair;
And that was the time when our Little
Boy Blue
Kissed them and put them there.
Little Boy Blue.

17 Where the Dinkey-Bird is singing
In the Amfalula-Tree.
The Dinkey-Bird.

FIELDING, HENRY, English author, 22 April, 1707–8 Oct. 1754

18 Love and scandal are the best sweeteners of tea.
Love in Several Masques, IV. xi.

19 All Nature wears one universal grin.
Tom Thumb the Great, I. i.

20 To sun myself in Huncamunca's eyes.
Ibid, iii.

21 Lo, when two dogs are fighting in the streets,
With a third dog one of the two dogs meets;
With angry teeth he bites him to the bone,
And this dog smarts for what that dog has done. *Ibid, vi.*

22 Oh! the roast beef of England,
And old England's roast beef.
The Grub Street Opera, III. iii.

23 Never trust the man who hath reason to suspect that you know he hath injured you. *Jonathan Wild, III. iv.*

24 Thwackum was for doing justice, and leaving mercy to heaven.
Tom Jones, III. x.

25 An amiable weakness. *Ibid, X. viii.*

FISHER OF KILVERSTONE, JOHN ARBUTHNOT FISHER, 1ST BARON, English admiral, 25 Jan. 1841–10 July, 1920

26 Sack the lot!
Letter to the Times, 2 Sept. 1919.

FITZGERALD, EDWARD, English translator, 31 March, 1809–14 June, 1883

27 Awake! for Morning in the Bowl of Night
Has flung the Stone that puts the Stars to flight,
And Lo! the Hunter of the East has caught
The Sultán's Turret in a Noose of Light.
Rubáiyát of Omar Khayyám, ed. I. I.

28 Come, fill the Cup, and in the Fire of Spring
The Winter Garment of Repentance fling:
The Bird of Time has but a little way
To fly – and Lo! the Bird is on the Wing.
Ibid, 7.

29 Each Morn a thousand Roses brings, you say:
Yes, but where leaves the Rose of Yesterday? *Ibid, ed. IV. 9.*

30 Here with a Loaf of Bread beneath the Bough,
A Flask of Wine, a Book of Verse – and Thou
Beside me singing in the Wilderness –
And Wilderness is Paradise enow.
Ibid, ed. I. II.

31 A Book of Verses underneath the Bough,
A Jug of Wine, a Loaf of Bread – and Thou
Beside me singing in the Wilderness –
Oh, Wilderness were Paradise enow!
Ibid, ed. IV. 12.

32 Ah, take the Cash, and let the Credit go,
Nor heed the rumble of a distant Drum!
Ibid, 13.

33 The Worldly Hope men set their Hearts upon
Turns Ashes– or it prospers; and anon,
Like Snow upon the Desert's dusty Face
Lighting a little Hour or two – is gone.
Ibid, ed. I. 14.

34   This batter'd Caravanserai
Whose Doorways are alternate Night
and Day. *Ibid, 16.*

1 They say the Lion and the Lizard keep
The Courts where Jamshyd gloried and
drank deep;
And Bahrám, that great Hunter – the
Wild Ass
Stamps o'er his Head, and he lies fast
asleep. *Ibid, 17.*

2 I sometimes think that never blows so
red
The Rose as where some buried Caesar
bled;
That every Hyacinth the Garden wears
Dropt in its Lap from some once lovely
Head. *Ibid, 18.*

3 *To-morrow?* – Why, To-morrow I may
be
Myself with Yesterday's Sev'n
Thousand Years. *Ibid, 20.*

4 Oh, come with old Khayyám, and leave
the Wise
To talk; one thing is certain, that Life
flies;
One thing is certain, and the Rest is Lies;
The Flower that once has blown for ever
dies. *Ibid, 26.*

5 Myself when young did eagerly
frequent
Doctor and Saint, and heard great
Argument
About it and about: but evermore
Came out by the same Door as in I
went. *Ibid, 27.*

6 I came like Water, and like Wind I go.
Ibid, 28.

7 Into this Universe, and *why* not
knowing,
Nor *whence,* like Water willy-nilly
flowing:
And out of it, as Wind along the Waste,
I know not *whither,* willy-nilly blowing.
Ibid, 29.

8 There was a Door to which I found no
Key:
There was a Veil past which I could not
see. *Ibid, 32.*

9 One Moment in Annihilation's Waste,
One Moment, of the Well of Life to
taste–

The Stars are setting and the Caravan
Starts for the Dawn of Nothing – Oh,
make haste! *Ibid, 38.*

10 The Grape that can with Logic absolute
The Two-and-Seventy jarring Sects
confute. *Ibid, 43.*

11 'Tis all a Chequer-board of Nights and
Days
Where Destiny with Men for Pieces
plays:
Hither and thither moves, and mates,
and slays,
And one by one back in the Closet lays.
Ibid, 49.

12 The Ball no Question makes of Ayes or
Noes,
But Right or Left as strikes the Player
goes;
And He that toss'd Thee down into the
Field,
He knows about it all – HE knows – HE
knows! *Ibid, 50.*

13 The Moving Finger writes; and, having
writ,
Moves on: nor all thy Piety nor Wit
Shall lure it back to cancel half a Line,
Nor all thy Tears wash out a Word of it.
Ibid, 51.

14 And that inverted Bowl we call the Sky,
Whereunder crawling coop't we live and
die,
Lift not thy hands to *It* for help – for It
Rolls impotently on as Thou or I.
Ibid, 52.

15 Oh Thou, who didst with Pitfall and
with Gin
Beset the Road I was to wander in,
Thou wilt not with Predestination
round
Enmesh me, and impute my Fall to Sin?
Ibid, 57.

16 Oh, Thou, who Man of baser Earth
didst make,
And who with Eden didst devise the
Snake;
For all the Sin wherewith the Face of
Man
Is blacken'd, Man's Forgiveness give –
and take! *Ibid, 58.*

17 Said one – 'Folks of a surly Tapster tell,
And daub his Visage with the Smoke of
Hell;
They talk of some strict Testing of us –
Pish!
He's a Good Fellow, and 'twill all be
well.'   *Ibid, 64.*

18 I often wonder what the Vintners buy
One half so precious as the Goods they
sell.   *Ibid, 71.*

19 Alas, that Spring should vanish with the
Rose!
That Youth's sweet-scented Manuscript
should close!   *Ibid, 72.*

20 Ah Love! could thou and I with Fate
conspire
To grasp this sorry Scheme of Things
entire,
Would not we shatter it to bits – and
then
Re-mould it nearer to the Heart's
Desire!   *Bid, 73.*

21 And when Thyself with shining Foot
shall pass
Among the Guests Star-scatter'd on the
Grass,
And in thy joyous Errand reach the Spot
Where I made one – turn down an
empty Glass!   *Ibid, 75.*

22 And when like her, O Saki, you shall
pass.   *Ibid, ed. IV. 101.*

23 A Mr. Wilkinson, a clergyman.
                          Line parodying Wordsworth.

**FITZSIMMONS, ROBERT,
English pugilist, 4 June, 1862–22
Oct. 1917**

24 The bigger they come, the harder they
fall.
               *Before his fight with Jeffries in San
               Francisco, 25 July, 1902.*

**FLECKER, JAMES ELROY,
English poet, 5 Nov. 1884–3 Jan.
1915**

25 A ship, an isle, a sickle moon –
With few but with how splendid stars

The mirrors of the sea are strewn
Between their silver bars!
                    A Ship, an Isle, a Sickle Moon.

26 For pines are gossip pines the wide
world through.   *Brumana.*

27 With her fair and floral air and the love
that lingers there,
And the streets where the great men
go.   (Oxford.)   *The Dying Patriot.*

28 I have seen old ships sail like swans
asleep
Beyond the village which men still call
Tyre.   *The Old Ships.*

29 Sweet to ride forth at evening from the
wells,
When shadows pass gigantic on the
sand,
And softly through the silence beat the
bells
Along the Golden Road to Samarkand.
                                 Hassan, V. ii.

**FLEMING, MARGARET, English
infant prodigy, 15 Jan. 1803–19 Dec.
1811**

30 A direful death indeed they had
That would put any parent mad
But she was more than usual calm
She did not give a singel dam.
                                 Journal, 29.

31 I am now going to tell you the horrible
and wretched plaege that my
multiplication table gives me; the most
devilish thing is 8 time 8 and 7 time 7; it
is what nature itselfe cant endure.
                                    Ibid, 47.

**FLETCHER, ANDREW, Scottish
patriot, 1655–Sept. 1716**

32 If a man were permitted to make all the
ballads, he need not care who should
make the laws of a nation.
               *Letter to the Marquis of Montrose, and
                                        Others.*

FLETCHER, JOHN, English dramatist, born Dec. 1579, buried 29 Aug. 1625

1 Care-charming Sleep, thou easer of all
    woes,
Brother to Death, sweetly thyself
    dispose
On this afflicted prince; fall like a cloud
In gentle showers; give nothing that is
    loud
Or painful to his slumbers; – easy, light,
And as a purling stream, thou son of
    night,
Pass by his troubled senses; sing his pain
Like hollow murmuring wind or silver
    rain;
Into this prince gently, oh, gently slide,
And kiss him into slumbers like a bride!
                           Valentinian, V. ii.

2 God Lyaeus, ever young,
Ever honour'd, ever sung;
Stain'd with blood of lusty grapes,
In a thousand lusty shapes.   *Ibid, viii.*

3 Weep no more, nor sigh, nor groan;
Sorrow calls no time that's gone;
Violets plucked the sweetest rain
Makes not fresh nor grow again.
                     The Queen of Corinth, III. ii.

4 Hence, all you vain delights,
As short as are the nights
Wherein you spend your folly!
There's naught in this life sweet,
If man were wise to see't,
But only Melancholy,
O sweetest Melancholy!
                         The Nice Valour, III. iii.

5 Fountain heads and pathless groves,
Places which pale passion loves.   *Ibid.*

6 Man is his own star, and the soul that
    can
Render an honest and a perfect man
Commands all light, all influence, all
    fate.
Nothing to him falls early, or too late.
Our acts our angels are, or good or ill,
Our fatal shadows that walk by us still.
                         Upon an Honest Man's Fortune.

7 Primrose, first-born child of Ver,
Merry sprintime's harbinger,
With her bells dim.
                         The Two Noble Kinsmen, I. j.

FOCH, FERDINAND, Marshal of France, 2 Oct. 1851–20 March, 1929

8 Mon centre cède, ma droite recule,
situation excellente. J'attaque!—My
centre is yielding, my right is
withdrawing. Situation excellent. I
shall attack.
                    *Message to Joffre, First Battle of the
                         Marne, Sept. 1914*

FOOTE, SAMUEL, English dramatist, baptised 27 Jan. 1720, died 21 Oct. 1777

9 Born in a cellar . . . and living in a
garret.   *The Author, II.*

10 So she went into the garden to cut a
cabbage leaf to make an applie pie; and
at the same time a great she-bear,
coming up the street, pops its head into
the shop. 'What! no soap?' so he died,
and she very imprudently married the
barber; and there were present the
Picninnies, and the Joblillies, and the
Garyulies, and the Grand Panjandrum
himself, with the little round button at
top, and they all fell to playing the
game of catch as catch can, till the
gunpowder ran out at the heels of their
boots.
                    Nonsense written as a memory test.

FORD, JOHN, English dramatist, baptised 17 April, 1586, died 1639?

11 We can drink till all look blue.
                         The Lady's Trial, II. ii.

FORD, LENA GUILBERT, U.S. poetess, died 1918

12 Keep the home fires burning, while
    your hearts are yearning,
Though your lads are far away they
    dream of home;
There's a silver lining through the dark
    clouds shining,
Turn the dark cloud inside out, till the
    boys come home.
                    Keep the Home Fires Burning.

FORGY, HOWELL MAURICE, U.S. naval chaplain, 18 Jan. 1908–

13 Praise the Lord and pass the ammunition.
At Pearl Harbour, 7 Dec. 1941.

FOSS, SAM WALTER, U.S. librarian, 19 June, 1858–26 Feb. 1911

14 W'en you see a man in woe,
Walk right up and say, 'hullo.'
Say 'hullo' and 'how d'ye do.'
'How's the world a-usin' you?'   *Hullo.*

FOSTER, STEPHEN COLLINS, U.S. song-writer, 4 July, 1826–13 Jan. 1864

15 The day goes by like a shadow o'er the heart,
With sorrow where all was delight;
The time has come when the darkies have to part;
Then my old Kentucky home, good night!   *My Old Kentucky Home.*

16 'Way down upon de Swanee Ribber.
The Old Folks at Home.

17 All up and down de whole creation,
Sadly I roam,
Still longing for de old plantation,
And for de old folks at home.   *Ibid.*

18 Hard times, come again no more.
Song.

19 I'm coming, I'm coming,
For my head is bending low,
I hear the gentle voices calling
'Poor old Joe.'   *Poor old Joe.*

20 He had no wool on de top of his head,
In de place where de wool ought to grow.   *Uncle Ned.*

FOUCHÉ, JOSEPH, Duke of Otranto, French politician, 29 May, 1763–25 Dec. 1820

21 C'est plus qu'un crime; c'est une faute.—It is worse than a crime; it is a blunder.
Of the murder of the Duc d'Enghien by Napoleon in 1804.

FOX, CHARLES JAMES, English statesman, 24 Jan. 1740—13 Sept. 1806

22 How much the greatest event it is that ever happened in the world! and how much the best! [the fall of the Bastille.]
Letter to Fitzpatric, 30 July, 1789.

FRANCE, ANATOLE (Jacques Anatole Thibault), French author, 16 April, 1844—12 Oct. 1924

23 Le bon critique est celui qui raconte les adventures de son âme au milieu des chefs-d'œuvre.—The good critic is he who relates the adventures of his soul among masterpieces.
La Vie littéraire—The Literary Life, preface.

FRANCIS I, King of France, 12 Sept. 1494—31 March, 1547

24 Tout est perdu fors l'honneur,—All is lost except honour.
Traditional words after defeat and capture at Pavia, 1525.

FRANKLIN, BENJAMIN, U.S. statesman and philosopher, 17 Jan. 1706—17 April, 1790

25 Remember that time is money.
Advice to a Young Tradesman.

26 There never was a good war or a bad peace.
Letter to Josiah Quincy, II Sept. 1773.

27 Yes, we must, indeed, all hang together, or, most assuredly, we shall all hang separately.
At signing of the Declaration of Independence, 4 July, 1776.

28 He has paid dear, very dear, for his whistle.   *The Whistle.*

29 He (the sun) gives light as soon as he rises. (Advocating daylight saving.)
An Economical Project.

30 Here Skugg lies snug
As a bug in a rug.
Letter to Miss G. Shipley, 26 Sept. 1772.

FREDERICK II, THE GREAT, King of Prussia, 24 Jan. 1712—17 Aug. 1786

1 Hunde, wollt ihr ewig lebel?—Dogs, would you live for ever?
When the Guards hesitated, at Kolin, 18 June, 1757.

FREEMAN, JOHN, poet, 29 Jan. 1880—23 Sept. 1929

2 It was the lovely moon—she lifted
Slowly her white brow among
Bronze cloud-waves that ebbed and drifted
Faintly, faintlier afar.
It was the Lovely Moon.

FREEMAN, THOMAS, English epigrammatist, fl. 1614

3 I love thee, Cornwall, and will ever,
And hope to see thee once again!
For why?—thine equal knew I never
For honest minds and active men.
Encomion Cornubiae.

FRERE, JOHN HOOKHAM, 21 May, 1769–7 Jan. 1846

4 The feather'd race with pinions skim the air—
Not so the mackerel, and still less the bear!
Progress of Man, 34

FROHMAN, CHARLES, U.S. theatrical manager, 17 June, 1860–7 May, 1915

5 Why fear death? It is the most beautiful adventure in life.
Before going down in the Lusitania.

FROST, ROBERT LEE, U.S. poet, 26 March 1875–29 Jan. 1963

6 I'm going out to clean the pasture spring;
I'll only stop to rake the leaves away
(And wait to watch the water clear, I may):
I shan't be gone long.—You come too.
The Pasture.

7 Something there is that doesn't love a wall
Mending Wall.

8 My apple trees will never get across
And eat the cones under his pines, I tell him.
He only says, 'Good fences make good neighbours.'
Ibid.

9 I shall be telling this with a sigh
Somewhere ages and ages hence:
Two roads diverged in a wood, and I—
I took the one less travelled by,
And that has made all the difference.
The Road not taken.

FULLER, THOMAS, cleric, June, 1608–16 Aug. 1661

10 A little skill in antiquity inclines a man to Popery; but depth in that study brings him about again to our religion.
The Holy and Profane State.
The True Church Antiquary.

11 They that marry ancient people, merely in expectation to bury them, hang themselves in hope that one will come and cut the halter.
Ibid. Of marriage.

12 Light, God's eldest daughter, is a principal beauty in a building.
Ibid. Of Building.

13 A proverb is much matter decocted into few words.
The History of the Worthies of England, ii.

GAINSBOROUGH, THOMAS, English painter, baptised 14 May, 1727, died 2 Aug. 1788

14 We are all going to heaven, and Van Dyck is of the company.
Last words.

GALILEI, GALILEO, Italian scientist, 15 Feb. 1564–8 Jan. 1642

15 Eppur si muove.—Yet it does move.
Traditional words after being forced to recant his doctrine that the earth moves round the sun.

GANDER, SIR GREGORY, see Ellis, George

GARFIELD, JAMES ABRAM, U.S. President, 19 Nov. 1831–19 Sept. 1881

16 Fellow citizens! God reigns, and the Government at Washington still lives!
Speech on the assassination of Lincoln, 1865.

GARRICK, DAVID, English actor, 19 Feb. 1717–20 Jan. 1779

17 Heart of oak are our ships,
Heart of oak are our men:
We always are ready,
Steady, boys, steady!
We'll fight and we'll conquer again and again. *Heart of Oak.*

18 Here lies Nolly Godsmith, for shortness call'd Noll,
Who wrote like an angel, but talk'd like poor Poll.
Impromptu epitaph on Goldsmith.

19 A fellow-feeling makes one wondrous kind.
Prologue on quitting the Theatre, 1776.

GARRISON, WILLIAM LLOYD, U.S. reformer, 10 Dec. 1805–24 May, 1879

20 I am in earnest—I will not equivocate—I will not excuse—I will not retreat a single inch—and I will be heard.
The Liberator, 1 Jan. 1832.

GARTH, SIR SAMUEL, doctor, 1661–18 Jan. 1719

21 Hard was their lodging, homely was their food;
For all their luxury was doing good.
Claremont, 148.

GASKELL, ELIZABETH CLEGHORN, novelist, 29 Sept. 1810–12 Nov. 1865

22 A man is *so* in the way in the house.
Cranford, i.

23 Bombazine would have shown a deeper sense of her loss. *Ibid., vii.*

GAY, JOHN, poet, baptised 16 Sept. 1685, died 4 Dec. 1732

24 All in the Downs the fleet was moor'd.
Sweet William's Farewell to Black-eyed Susan, I.

25 Adieu!' she cries; and wav'd her lily hand. *Ibid., 48.*

26 Life is a jest; and all things show it.
I thought so once; but now I know it.
My own Epitaph.

27 Where yet was ever found a mother,
Who'd giver her booby for another?
Fables, I, iii. The Mother, the Nurse, and the Fairy, 33.

28 And when a lady's in the case,
You know, all other things give place.
Ibid., 1. The Hare and many Friends, 41.

29 O ruddier than the cherry!
O sweeter than the berry!
O nymph more bright
Than moonshine night,
Like kidlings blithe and merry!
Acis and Galatea, ii.

30 'Tis woman that seduces all mankind,
By her we first were taught the wheedling arts.
The Beggar's Opera, i. ii

31 By keeping men off, you keep them on.
Ibid., viii.

32 For on the rope that hangs my dear
Depends poor Polly's life. *Ibid., x.*

33 If the heart of a man is deprest with cares,
The mist is dispell'd when a woman appears. *Ibid., II. iii.*

34 The fly that sips treacle is lost in the sweets. *Ibid., viii.*

35 How happy could I be with either
Were t'other dear charmer away!
Ibid., xiii

1 One wife is too much for most husbands
to hear
But two at a time there's no mortal can
bear.   *Ibid., III. xi.*

2 The charge is prepar'd; the lawyers are
met;
The judges all rang'd (a terrible show!).
                                   Ibid., xiii.

GEORGE II, KING, 10 Nov. 1683–25 Oct. 1760

3 Oh! he is mad, is he? Then I wish he
would *bite* some other of my generals.
                                   Of General Wolfe.

4 Non, j'aurai des maitresses. – No, I shall
have mistresses.
*When the dying Queen urged him marry
again.*
(Her reply was 'Ah! mon Dieu! cela
n'empêche pas.' – 'Good Lord, that
doesn't prevent it.')

GEORGE V, English King, 3 June, 1865–20 Jan. 1936

5 How is the Empire?   *Last words.*

GEORGE, HENRY, US economist, 2 Sept. 1839–29 Oct. 1897

6 A crank is a little thing that makes
revolutions.   *Attributed.*

GIBBON, EDWARD, English historian, 27 April, 1737–16 Jan. 1794

7 History; which is, indeed, little more
than the register of the crimes, follies,
and misfortunes of mankind.
Decline and Fall of the Roman Empire, iii.

8 If a man were called to fix the period in
the history of the world during which
the condition of the human race was
most happy and prosperous, he would,
without hesitation, name that which
elapsed from the death of Domitian to
the accession of Commodus.   *Ibid.*

9 Corruption, the most infallible
symptom of constitutional liberty.
                                   Ibid, xxi.

10 In every deed of mischief he had a heart
to resolve, a head to contrive, and a
hand to execute. (Andronicus I.)
                                   Ibid, xlviii.

11 I sighed as a lover, I obeyed as a son.
                                   Autobiography.

GIBBONS, THOMAS, English dissenting minister, 31 May, 1720–22 Feb. 1785

12 That man may last, but never lives,
Who much receives, but nothing gives;
Whom none can love, whom none can
thank, –
Creation's blot, creation's blank.
                                   When Jesus dwelt.

GIFFORD, RICHARD, English cleric, 1725–1 March, 1807

13 Verse softens toil, however rude the
sound;
She feels no biting pang the while she
sings,
Nor, as she turns the giddy wheel
around,
Revolves the sad vicissitude of things
                                   Contemplation.

GIFFORD, WILLIAM, English editor of the 'Quarterly,' April, 1756–31 Dec. 1826

14 His namby-pamby madrigals of love.
                                   The Baviad, 176.

15 The ropy drivel of rheumatic brains.
                                   Ibid, 279.

GILBERT, SIR WILLIAM SCHWENCK, English dramatist, 18 Nov. 1836–29 May, 1911

16 There were captains by the hundred,
there were baronets by dozens.
                          Bab Ballads. Ferdinando and Elvira.

17 Then I waved the turtle soup
enthusiastically round me.   *Ibid.*

18 Oh, I am a cook and a captain bold,
And the mate of the *Nancy* brig,
And a bo'sun tight, and a midshipmite,

And the crew of the captain's gig.
Ibid, The Yarn of the 'Nancy Bell.'

19 Then they began to sing
That extremely lovely thing
'*Scherzando! ma non troppo, ppp.'*
Ibid, The Story of Prince Agib.

20 The padre said, 'Whatever have you
been and gone and done?'
Ibid, Gentle Alice Brown.

21 She may very well pass for forty-three
In the dusk, with a light behind her!
Trial by Jury.

22 And many a burglar I've restored
To his friends and his relations.   *Ibid.*

23 Time was when Love and I were well
acquainted.   *The Sorcerer, I.*

24 Fled gilded dukes and belted earls before
me –
Ah me, I was a pale young curate then!
Ibid.

25 Now to the banquet we press;
Now for the eggs and the ham;
Now for the mustard and cress,
Now for the strawberry jam!   *Ibid.*

26 'Though "Bother it," I may
Occasionally say,
I never use a big, big D.'
'What, never?'
'No, never!'
'What, *never?*'
'Hardly ever!'   *HMS Pinafore, I.*

27 And so do his sisters and his cousins and
his aunts!   *Ibid.*

28 When I was a lad I served a term
As office boy to an Attorney's firm.
I cleaned the windows and I swept the
floor,
And I polished up the handle of the big
front door.
I polished up that handle so carefullee
That now I am the ruler of the Queen's
Navee!   *Ibid.*

29 I always voted at my party's call,
And I never thought of thinking for
myself at all.   *Ibid.*

30 Things are seldom what they seem,
Skim milk masquerades as cream.
Ibid, II.

31 He is an Englishman!
For he himself has said it,
And it's greatly to his credit,
That he is an Englishman!   *Ibid.*

32 For he might have been a Roosian,
A French, or Turk, or Proosian,
Or perhaps Itali-an!   *Ibid.*

33 When constabulary duty's to be done,
A policeman's lot is not a happy one.
The Pirates of Penzance, II.

34 When the enterprising burglar's not a-
burgling.   *Ibid.*

35 If you're anxious for to shine in the high
aesthetic line as a man of culture rare.
Patience, I.

36 The meaning doesn't matter if it's only
idle chatter of a transcendental kind.
Ibid.

37 If this young man expresses himself in
terms too deep for *me*,
Why, what a very singularly deep
young man this deep young man must
be!   *Ibid.*

38 An attachment *à la* Plato for a bashful
young potato, or a not-too-French
French bean.   *Ibid.*

39 The consequence was he was lost
totally,
And married a girl in the *corps de bally*!
Ibid, II.

40 By no endeavour
Can magnet ever
Attract a Silver Churn!   *Ibid.*

41 A most intense young man,
A soulful-eyed young man,
An ultra-poetical, super-aesthetical,
Out-of-the-way young man!   *Ibid.*

42 Francesca di Rimini, miminy, piminy,
Je-ne-sais-quoi young man!   *Ibid.*

43 A greenery-yallery, Grosvenor Gallery
Foot-in-the-grave young man!   *Ibid.*

1 Bow, bow, ye lower middle classes!
Iolanthe, I.

2 A pleasant occupation for
A rather susceptible Chancellor! *Ibid.*

3 I often think it's comical
How nature always does contrive
That every boy and every gal
That's born into the world alive
Is either a little Liberal
Or else a little Conservative. *Ibid, II.*

4 The House of Peers, throughout the
war,
Did nothing in particular
And did it very well. *Ibid.*

5 Politics we bar,
They are not our bent;
On the whole we are
Not intelligent. *Princess Ida, I.*

6 We will hang you, never fear,
Most politely, most politely! *Ibid.*

7 Man's a ribald – Man's a rake,
Man is Nature's sole mistake! *Ibid, II.*

8 Oh, don't the days seem lank and long
When all goes right and nothing goes
wrong,
And isn't your life extremely flat
With nothing whatever to grumble at! *Ibid, III.*

9 Pooh-Bah (Lord High Everything Else).
The Mikado, Dramatis Personae.

10 I can trace my ancestry back to a
protoplasmal primordial atomic
globule. *Ibid, I.*

11 As some day it may happen that a victim
must be found,
I've got a little list – I've got a little list
Of society offenders who might well be
underground,
And who never would be missed – who
never would be missed! *Ibid.*

12 My object all sublime
I shall achieve in time –
To let the punishment fit the crime.
Ibid, II.

13 I drew my snickersnee! *Ibid.*

14 Something lingering, with boiling oil in
it, I fancy. *Ibid.*

15 Merely corroborative detail, intended to
give artistic verisimilitude to an
otherwise bald and unconvincing
narrative. *Ibid.*

16 The flowers that bloom in the spring,
Tra la,
Have nothing to do with the case. *Ibid.*

17 All baronets are bad. *Ruddigore, I.*

18 Cheerily carols the lark
Over the cot.
Merrily whistles the clerk
Scratching a blot. *Ibid.*

19 Some word that teems with hidden
meaning – like 'Basingstoke.' *Ibid, II.*

20 It's a song of a merryman, moping
mum,
Whose soul was sad, and whose glance
was glum,
Who sipped no sup, and who craved no
crumb,
As he sighed for the love of a ladye.
The Yeoman of the Guard, I.

21 He led his regiment from behind –
He found it less exciting.
The Gondoliers, I.

22 Of that there is no manner of doubt –
No probable, possible shadow of
doubt –
No possible doubt whatever. *Ibid.*

23 A taste for drink, combined with gout,
Had doubled him up for ever. *Ibid.*

24 Oh, 'tis a glorious thing, I ween,
To be a regular Royal Queen!
No half-and-half affair, I mean,
But a right-down regular Royal Queen!
Ibid.

25 Take a pair of sparkling eyes. *Ibid, II.*

26 When everyone is somebodee,
Then no one's anybody. *Ibid.*

27 There was an old man of St. Bees,
Who was stung in the arm by a wasp.
When asked, 'Does it hurt?'
He replied, 'No, it doesn't.
I'm so glad it wasn't a hornet.'
Limerick.

**GILLILAN, STRICKLAND, US
journalist, 1869–1954**

28 Bilin' down his repoort, wuz Finnigin!
An' he writed this here: 'Muster
Flannigan:
Off ag'in, on ag'in,
Gone ag'in. – Finnigin.'
Finnigin to Flannigan.

**GILMAN, CHARLOTTE
PERKINS STETSON, US author,
3 July, 1860–11 Aug. 1935**

29 Cried all, 'Before such things can come,
You idiotic child,
You must alter Human Nature!'
And they all sat back and smiled.
Similar Cases.

30 I do not want to be a fly;
I want to be a worm! *A Conservative.*

**GLADSTONE, WILLIAM
EWART, English Prime Minister,
29 Dec. 1809–19 May, 1898**

31 Decision by majorities is as much an
expedient as lighting by gas.
Speech, House of Commons, 21 Jan. 1858.

32 These gentlemen (the Irish Land League)
wish to march through rapine to the
disintegration and dismemberment of
the Empire.
Speech, Knowsley, 27 Oct. 1881.

33 An old parliamentary hand.
Speech, House of Commons, 21 Jan. 1886.

34 All the world over, I will back the
masses against the classes.
Speech, Liverpool, 28 June, 1886.

**GLOUCESTER, WILLIAM
HENRY, DUKE OF, 14 Nov.
1743–25 Aug. 1805**

35 Another damned, thick, square book!
Always scribble, scribble, scribble! Eh!
Mr. Gibbon? *Attributed.*

**GODLEY, ALFRED DENNIS,
English scholar, 22 Jan. 1856–27
June, 1925**

36 What is this that roareth thus?
Can it be a Motor Bus?
Yes, the smell and hideous hum
Indicat Motorem Bum. *Motor Bus.*

**GOETHE, JOHANN WOLFGANG
VON, German poet, 28 Aug.
1749–22 March, 1832**

37 Kennst du das Land, wo die Zitronen
blühn?
Im dunkeln Laub die Gold-Orangen
glühn,
Ein sanfter Wind vom blauen Himmel
weht,
Die Myrte still und hoch der Lorbeer
steht.
– Knowest thou the land where the
lemon-trees bloom? In the dark foliage
the golden oranges gleam, a soft wind
blows from the blue heavens, the
myrtle is still and the laurel stands
high. *Wilhelm Meister, III. i.*

38 Ohne Hast, aber ohn Rast. – Without
haste, but without rest. *Motto.*

39 Mehr Licht! – More light!
Attributed dying words.

**GOLDBERG, ISAAC, US critic, 1
Nov. 1887–14 July, 1938**

40 Diplomacy is to do and say
The nastiest thing in the nicest way.
The reflex.

**GOLDSMITH, OLIVER, Irish poet,
10 Nov. 1728–4 April, 1774**

41 The king himself has follow'd her, –
When she has walk'd before.
Elegy on Mrs. Mary Blaize.

42 The doctors found, when she was dead, –
Her last disorder mortal.

43 A night-cap deck'd his brows instead of
bay,
A cap by night – a stocking all the day!
Description of an Author's Bedchamber.

1 Remote, unfriended, melancholy, slow.
The Traveller, I.

2 Where'er I roam, whatever realms to
see,
My heart untravell'd fondly turns to
thee;
Still to my brother turns with ceaseless
pain,
And drags at each remove a lengthening
chain. *Ibid, 7.*

3 Such is the patriot's boast, where'er we
roam,
His first, best country ever is, at home.
Ibid, 73.

4 But winter ling'ring chills the lap of
May. *Ibid, 172.*

5 Laws grind the poor, and rich men rule
the law. *Ibid, 386.*

6 Taught by the Power that pities me,
I learn to pity them.
Edwin and Angelina, or The Hermit.

7 Man wants but little here below,
Nor wants that little long. *Ibid.*

8 The naked every day he clad,
When he put on his clothes.
Elegy on the Death of a Mad Dog.

9 The dog, to gain some private ends,
Went mad, and bit the man. *Ibid.*

10 The man recover'd of the bite,
The dog it was that died. *Ibid.*

11 When lovely woman stoops to folly,
And finds too late that men betray,
What charm can soothe her melancholy,
What art can wash her guilt away?
The only art her guilt to cover,
To hide her shame from every eye,
To give repentance to her lover,
And wring his bosom, is – to die.
Song. The Vicar of Wakefield, xxix.

12 Sweet Auburn! loveliest village of the
plain. *The Deserted Village, 1.*

13 The hawthorn bush, with seats beneath
the shade,
For talking age and whisp'ring lovers
made. *Ibid, 13.*

14 The bashful virgin's sidelong looks of
love,
The matron's glance that would those
looks reprove. *Ibid, 29.*

15 Ill fares the land, to hast'ning ills a prey,
Where wealth accumulates, and men
decay:
Princes and lords may flourish, or may
fade;
A breath can make them, as a breath has
made;
But a bold peasantry, their country's
pride,
When once destroy'd, can never be
supplied. *Ibid, 51.*

16 His best companions, innocence and
health;
And his best riches, ignorance of wealth.
Ibid, 61.

17 How happy he who crowns in shades
like these,
A youth of labour with an age of ease.
Ibid, 99.
(1st edition has 'How blest is he.')

18 The watchdog's voice that bay'd the
whisp'ring wind,
And the loud laugh that spoke the
vacant mind. *Ibid, 121.*

19 A man he was to all the country dear,
And passing rich with forty pounds a
year. *Ibid, 141.*

20 Wept o'er his wounds, or tales of
sorrow done,
Shoulder'd his crutch, and show'd how
fields were won. *Ibid, 157.*

21 Careless their merits, or their faults to
scan,
His pity gave ere charity began.
Thus to relieve the wretched was his
pride,
And e'en his failings lean'd to virtue's
side. *Ibid, 161.*

22 And, as a bird each fond endearment
tries

To tempt its new-fledg'd offspring to
the skies,
He tried each art, reprov'd each dull
delay,
Allur'd to brighter worlds, and led the
way. *Ibid, 167.*

23 Truth from his lips prevail'd with
double sway,
And fools, who came to scoff, remain'd
to pray. *Ibid, 179.*

24 Even children follow'd with endearing
wile,
And pluck'd his gown, to share the
good man's smile. *Ibid, 183.*

25 As some tall cliff, that lifts its awful
form,
Swells from the vale, and midway leaves
the storm,
Though round its breast the rolling
clouds are spread,
Eternal sunshine settles on its head.
Ibid, 189.

26 A man severe he was, and stern to view;
I knew him well, and every truant
knew;
Well had the boding tremblers learn'd to
trace
The day's disasters in his morning face;
Full well they laugh'd, with
counterfeited glee,
At all his jokes, for many a joke had he;
Full well the busy whisper, circling
round,
Convey'd the dismal tidings when he
frown'd;
Yet he was kind; or if severe in aught,
The love he bore to learning was in
fault. *Ibid, 197.*

27 In arguing too, the parson own'd his
skill,
For e'en though vanquish'd, he could
argue still;
While words of learned length and
thund'ring sound
Amazed the gazing rustics rang'd
around,
And still they gaz'd, and still the wonder
grew,
That one small head could carry all he
knew. *Ibid, 211.*

28 The white-wash'd wall, the nicely
sanded floor,
The varnish'd clock that click'd behind
the door;
The chest contriv'd a double debt to
pay,
A bed by night, a chest of drawers by
day. *Ibid, 227.*

29 The twelve good rules, the royal game
of goose. *Ibid, 232.*

30 Her modest looks the cottage might
adorn,
Sweet as the primrose peeps beneath the
thorn. *Ibid, 329.*

31 In all the silent manliness of grief.
Ibid, 384.

32 Thou source of all my bliss, and all my
woe.
That found'st me poor at first, and
keep'st me so. *Ibid, 413.*

33 Here lies our good Edmund, whose
genius was such,
We scarcely can praise it, or blame it too
much;
Who, born for the Universe, narrow'd
his mind,
And to party gave up what was meant
for mankind.
(Edmund Burke.) *Retaliation, 29.*

34 Though equal to all things, for all things
unfit,
Too nice for a statesman, too proud for
a wit:
For a patriot, too cool; for a drudge,
disobedient;
And too fond of the *right* to pursue the
expedient.
(Same.) *Ibid, 37.*

35 Here lies David Garrick, describe me,
who can,
An abridgment of all that was pleasant
in man. *Ibid, 93.*

36 On the stage he was natural, simple,
affecting;
'Twas only that when he was off he was
acting. (Same.) *Ibid, 101.*

1 He cast off his friends, as a huntsman his
pack,
For he knew when he pleas'd he could
whistle them back.
(Same.) *Ibid, 107.*

2 Here Reynolds is laid, and to tell you
my mind,
He has not left a better or wiser behind;
His pencil was striking, resistless, and
grand;
His manners were gentle, complying,
and bland. *Ibid, 137.*

3 When they talk'd of their Raphaels,
Correggios, and stuff,
He shifted his trumpet, and only took
snuff. (Same.) *Ibid, 145.*

4 Hope, like the gleaming taper's light,
Adorns and cheers our way;
And still, as darker grows the night,
Emits a brighter ray. *The Captivity, II.*

5 All our adventures were by the fire-side,
and all our migrations from the blue bed
to the brown. *The Vicar of Wakefield, i.*

6 They would talk of nothing but high
life, and high-lived company, with
other fashionable topics, such as
pictures, taste, Shakespeare, and the
musical glasses. *Ibid, ix.*

7 I love everything that's old; old friends,
old times, old manners, old books, old
wines. *She Stoops to Conquer, I.*

8 The very pink of perfection. *Ibid.*

9 In a concatenation accordingly. *Ibid.*

10 This is Liberty-hall, gentlemen.
Ibid, II.

11 There is no arguing with Johnson; for
when his pistol misses fire, he knocks
you down with the butt end of it.
Boswell's Life of Johnson, an. 1769.

12 If you were to make little fishes talk,
they would talk like whales.
(To Johnson.) *Ibid, an. 1773.*

**GOLDWYN, SAMUEL, US film
producer, 27 Aug. 1882–31 Jan. 1974**

13 Include me out. *Attributed.*

**GORDON, ADAM LINDSAY,
Australian poet, 19 Oct. 1833–24
June, 1870**

14 No game was ever worth a rap
For a rational man to play,
Into which no accident, no mishap,
Could possibly find its way.
Ye Wearie Wayfarer, fytte 4.

15 Life is mostly froth and bubble,
Two things stand like stone,
Kindness in another's trouble,
Courage in your own. *Ibid, fytte 8.*

16 I should live the same life over, if I had
to live again;
And the chances are I go where most
men go. *The Sick Stockrider.*

**GORE-BOOTH, EVA SELENA,
Irish poetess, 22 May, 1870–30 June,
1926**

17 But the little waves of Breffny have
drenched my heart in spray,
And the little waves of Breffny go
stumbling through my soul.
The Little Waves of Breffny.

**GOSCHEN, GEORGE JOACHIM
GOSCHEN, 1ST VISCOUNT,
English statesman, 10 Aug. 1831–7
Feb. 1907**

18 Our splendid isolation, as one of our
colonial friends was good enough to call
it. *Speech at Lewes, 26 Feb. 1896.*
(The phrase 'splendidly isolated' was
used by G. E. Foster and by Sir Wilfred
Laurier in the Canadian House of
Commons earlier that year.)

**GRAHAM, HARRY JOCELYN
CLIVE, English author, 23 Dec.
1874–30 Oct. 1936**

19 Father heard his children scream,
So he threw them in the stream,
Saying, as he drowned the third,

'Children should be seen, not heard!'
Ruthless Rhymes. The Stern Parent.

20 Billy, in one of his nice new sashes,
Fell in the fire and was burnt to ashes;
Now, although the room grows chilly,
I haven't the heart to poke poor Billy.
Ibid, Tender-Heartedness.

**GRAHAM, JAMES, see Montrose,
Marquis of**

**GRAHAM, ROBERT (later
CUNNINGHAME-GRAHAM),
Scottish poet, 1735?–1797?**

21 If doughty deeds my lady please,
Right soon I'll mount my steed.
If Doughty Deeds.

**GRAHAME, JAMES, Scottish poet,
22 April, 1765–14 Sept. 1811**

22 Hail, Sabbath! thee I hail, the poor
man's day. *The Sabbath, 29.*

**GRAHAME, KENNETH, English
author, 3 March, 1859–6 July, 1932**

23 The burglars vanished silently into the
laurels, with horrid implications!
The Golden Age. The Burglars.

24 Believe me, my young friend, there is
nothing – absolutely nothing – half so
much worth doing as simply messing
about in boats.
The Wind in the Willows, i.

**GRAINGER, JAMES, English
doctor, 1721?–16 Dec. 1766**

25 Now, Muse, let's sing of rats.
The Sugar Cane.

(Quoted by Boswell from the MS. Not in
the printed version.)

**GRANT, SIR ROBERT, Governor
of Bombay, 1779–9 July, 1838**

26 Our Shield and Defender, the Ancient of
Days,
Pavilioned in splendour, and girded
with praise. *O worship the King.*

**GRANT, ULYSSES SIMPSON, US
President, 27 April, 1822–23 July,
1885**

27 No terms except an unconditional and
immediate surrender can be accepted. I
propose to move immediately upon
your works.
*To General Buckner, Fort Donelson,
16 Feb. 1862.*

28 I propose to fight it out on this line, if it
takes all summer.
Despatch to Washington, 11 May, 1864.

**GRAVES, ALFRED PERCEVAL,
Irish author, 22 July, 1846–27 Dec.
1931**

29 Och! Father O'Flynn, you've the
wonderful way wid you.
Father O'Flynn.

30 Checkin' the crazy ones,
Coaxin' onaisy ones
Liftin' the lazy ones on wid the stick.
Ibid.

**GRAY, THOMAS, English poet, 26
Dec, 1716–30 July, 1771**

31 Ye distant spires, ye antique towers.
*Ode on a Distant Prospect of Eton
College, 1.*

32 They hear a voice in every wind,
And snatch a fearful joy. *Ibid, 39.*

33 Alas, regardless of their doom,
The little victims play!
No sense have they of ills to come,
Nor care beyond to-day. *Ibid, 51.*

34 To each his suff'rings: all are men,
Condemn'd alike to groan;
The tender for another's pain,
Th'unfeeling for his own.
Yet ah! why should they know their
fate?
Since sorrow never comes too late,
And happiness too swiftly flies.
Thought would destroy their paradise.
No more; where ignorance is bliss,
'Tis folly to be wise. *Ibid, 91.*

1 Daughter of Jove, relentless power,
Thou tamer of the human breast,
Whose iron scourge and torturing hour
The bad affright, afflict the best.
Hymn to Adversity.

2 What female heart can gold despise?
What cat's averse to fish?
Ode on the Death of a Favourite Cat.

3 A fav'rite has no friend. *Ibid.*

4 The curfew tolls the knell of parting
day,
The lowing herd winds slowly o'er the
lea,
The ploughman homeward plods his
weary way,
And leaves the world to darkness and to
me.
Elegy written in a Country Churchyard, 1.

5 Now fades the glimmering landscape on
the sight,
And all the air a solemn stillness holds,
Save where the beetle wheels his
droning flight,
And drowsy tinklings lull the distant
folds. *Ibid, 5.*

6 Each in his narrow cell for ever laid
The rude forefathers of the hamlet sleep.
Ibid, 15.

7 The breezy call of incense-breathing
morn. *Ibid, 17.*

8 Let not ambition mock their useful toil,
Their homely joys, and destiny obscure;
Nor grandeur hear with a disdainful
smile,
The short and simple annals of the poor.
Ibid, 29.

9 The boast of heraldry, the pomp of
pow'r,
And all that beauty, all that wealth e'er
gave,
Awaits alike th' inevitable hour,
The paths of glory lead but to the grave.
Ibid, 33.

10 Where through the long-drawn aisle and
fretted vault
The pealing anthem swells the note of
praise. *Ibid, 39.*

11 Can storied urn or animated bust
Back to its mansion call the fleeting
breath?
Can honour's voice provoke the silent
dust,
Or flatt'ry soothe the dull cold ear of
death? *Ibid, 41.*

12 Hands, that the rod of empire might
have sway'd,
Or wak'd to ecstasy the living lyre.
Ibid, 47.

13 Full many a gem of purest ray serene
The dark unfathom'd caves of ocean
bear:
Full many a flower is born to blush
unseen,
And waste its sweetness on the desert
air. *Ibid, 53.*

14 Some village Hampden, that with
dauntless breast
The little tyrant of his fields withstood;
Some mute inglorious Milton here may
rest,
Some Cromwell guiltless of his
country's blood. *Ibid, 57.*

15 Forbade to wade through slaughter to a
throne,
And shut the gates of mercy on
mankind. *Ibid. 67*

16 Far from the maddening crowd's
ignoble strife
Their sober wishes never learn'd to
stray;
Along the cool sequester'd vale of life
They kept the noiseless tenor of their
way *Ibid, 73*

17 For who to dumb forgetfulness a prey,
This pleasing anxious being e'er
resign'd,
Left the warm precincts of the cheerful⹁
day,
Nor cast one longing ling'ring look
behind? *Ibid, 85.*

18 Brushing with hasty steps the dews
away
To meet the sun upon the upland lawn.
Ibid, 99.

19 Here rests his head upon the lap of earth
A youth to fortune and to fame
unknown.
Fair Science frown'd not on his humble
birth,
And Melancholy mark'd him for her
own.   *Ibid, The Epitaph.*

20 Large was his bounty, and his soul
sincere,
Heav'n did a recompense as largely
send:
He gave to Mis'ry all he had, a tear,
He gain'd from Heav'n ('twas all he
wish'd) a friend.   *Ibid.*

21 No farther seek his merits to disclose,
Or draw his frailties from their dread
abode,
(There they alike in trembling hope
repose),
The bosom of his Father and his God.
Ibid.

22 Rich windows that exclude the light,
And passages that lead to nothing.
A Long Story, 7.

23 The meanest flowret of the vale,
The simplest note that swells the gale,
The common sun, the air, the skies,
To him are opening paradise.
*Ode on the Pleasures arising from
Vicissitude, 49.*

24 The bloom of young desire and purple
light of love.
The Progress of Poesy, 41.

25 Nor second he, that rode sublime
Upon the seraph-wings of ecstasy,
The secrets of th' abyss to spy.
He pass'd the flaming bounds of place
and time:
The living throne, the sapphire-blaze.
Where angels tremble while they gaze,
He saw; but blasted with excess of light,
Closed his eyes in endless night.
(Milton.)   *Ibid, 95.*

26 Two coursers of ethereal race,
With necks in thunder clothed, and
long-resounding pace.   *Ibid, 105.*

27 Bright-eyed Fancy, hovering o'er,
Scatters from her pictured urn
Thoughts that breathe and words that
burn.   *Ibid, 108.*

28 Ruin seize thee, ruthless King!
Confusion on thy banners wait.
The Bard, 1.

29 Weave the warp, and weave the woof,
The winding-sheet of Edward's race.
Ibid, 49.

30 Fair laughs the morn, and soft the
zephyr blows,
While proudly riding o'er the azure
realm
In gallant trim the gilded vessel goes,
Youth on the prow, and Pleasure at the
helm.   *Ibid, 71.*

31 Ye towers of Julius, London's lasting
shame,
With many a foul and midnight murther
fed.   *Ibid, 87.*

32 Iron-sleet of arrowy shower
Hurtles in the darkn'd air.
The Fatal Sisters.

33 Too poor for a bribe, and too proud to
importune;
He had not the method of making a
fortune.   *Sketch of his own Character.*

GREELEY, HORACE, US journalist, 3 Feb. 1811–29 Nov. 1872

34 Go West, young man, and grow up
with the country.   *Hints toward Reform.*

GREEN, MATTHEW, English poet, 1696–1737

35 To cure the mind's wrong bias, Spleen,
Some recommend the bowling-green;
Some, hilly walks; all, exercise;
Fling but a stone, the giant dies
Laugh and be well.   *The Spleen, 89.*

GREENE, ALBERT GORTON, US poet, 10 Feb. 1802–3 Jan. 1868

36 Old Grimes is dead; that good old man
We never shall see more:

He used to wear a long, black coat,
All button'd down before.   *Old Grimes.*

GREENE, ROBERT, English author, July, 1558–3 Sept. 1592

1 Weep not, my wanton, smile upon my
knee;
When thou art old their's grief enough
for thee.
Mother's wag, pretty boy,
Father's sorrow, father's joy.
                    Sephestia's Song.

GREGORY I., THE GREAT, Pope and Saint, 540?–10 March, 604

2 Non Angli, sed angeli. – Not Angles,
but angels.
*Traditional words on seeing English captives
                            at Rome.*

GRELLET, STEPHEN (ÉTIENNE DE GRELLET), Franco-American Quaker, 2 Nov. 1773–16 Nov. 1855

3 I expect to pass through this world but
once. Any good thing therefore that I
can do, or any kindness that I can show
to any fellow-creature, let me do it now;
let me not defer or neglect it, for I shall
not pass this way again.   *Attributed.*

(Authorship of this much disputed.)

GRENFELL, JULIAN HENRY FRANCIS, English soldier, 3 March, 1888–26 May, 1915

4 The fighting man shall from the sun
Take warmth, and life from the glowing
earth;
Speed with the light-foot winds to run,
And with the trees to newer birth.
                        Into Battle.

GREY OF FALLODON, EDWARD, 1ST VISCOUNT, English statesman, 25 April, 1862–7 Sept. 1933

5 The lamps are going out all over
Europe; we shall not see them lit again
in our lifetime.
        On the eve of war, 3 Aug. 1914.

GRIFFIN, GERALD, Irish author, 12 Dec. 1803–12 June, 1840

6 Dear were her charms to me,
Dearer her laughter free,
Dearest her constancy, –
Eileen Aroon!   *Eileen Aroon.*

GUEDALLA, PHILIP, English historian, 12 March, 1889–16 Dec. 1944

7 The work of Henry James has always
seemed divisible by a simple dynastic
arrangement into three reigns: James I,
James II, and the Old Pretender.
                Supers and Supermen.

8 The cheerful clatter of Sir James Barrie's
cans as he went round with the milk of
human kindness.   *Some Critics.*

GUITERMAN, ARTHUR, US author, 20 Nov., 1871–11 Jan. 1943

9 Bores of the dreariest hue,
Bringers of worry and care,
Watch us respond to our cue, –
'Exit, pursued by a bear.'
            The Shakespearean Bear.

GURNEY, DOROTHY FRANCES, English poetess, 1858–1932

10 The kiss of the sun for pardon,
The song of the birds for mirth,
One is nearer God's Heart in a garden
Than anywhere else on earth.
                        God's Garden

HABBERTON, JOHN, US author, 24 Feb. 1842–24 Feb. 1921

11 Want to shee the wheels go wound.
                    Helen's Babies, i.

HABINGTON, WILLIAM, 4 or 5 Nov. 1605–30 Nov. 1654

12 The starres, bright cent'nels of the skies.
*Castara, 1. A Dialogue between Night and
Araphil, 3.*

HAIG, DOUGLAS HAIG, EARL, 19 June, 1861–29 Jan. 1928

13 Every position must be held to the last man; there must be no retirement. With our backs to the wall, and believing in the justice of our cause, each one of us must fight to the end.
Order to the British troops, 12 April, 1918.

HALE, EDWARD EVERETT, US cleric, 3 April, 1822–10 June, 1909

14 To look up and not down,
To look forward and not back,
To look out and not in, and
To lend a hand. *Ten Times One is Ten.*

HALE, SARAH JOSEPH BUELL, US author, 24 Oct. 1788–30 April, 1879

15 Mary had a little lamb,
Its fleece was white as snow,
And everywhere that Mary went
The lamb was sure to go.
Mary's Lamb.

HALL, JOSEPH, Bishop of Norwich, 1 July, 1574–8 Sept. 1656

16 Moderation is the silken string running through the pearl chain of all virtues.
Christian Moderation, Introduction.

HALLECK, FITZ-GREENE, US poet, 8 July, 1790–19 Nov. 1867

17 Green be the turf above thee,
Friend of my better days!
None knew thee but to love thee,
Nor named thee but to praise.
On the Death of Joseph Rodman Drake.

HAMILTON, COUNT ANTHONY, English soldier and author, 1646 ?–21 April, 1720

18 Bélier, mon ami, lui dit le géant en l'interrompant, je ne comprends rien à tout cela. Si tu voulois bien commencer par le commencement, tu me ferois plaisir; car tous ces récits qui commencent par le milieu ne font que m'embrouiller l'imagination. – 'My dear Ram,' interrupted the giant, 'I have not the least notion what you are talking about. If you would have the kindness to begin at the beginning, I should be vastly obliged; all these stories that begin in the middle simply fog my wits.' *Le Bélier – The Ram.*

HAMILTON, GAIL (MARY ABIGAIL DODGE), US essayist, 31 March, 1833–17 Aug. 1896

19 The total depravity of inanimate things.
Epigram.

HAMILTON, WILLIAM, Scottish poet, 1704–25 March, 1754

20 Busk ye, busk ye, my bonny bonny bride,
Busk ye, busk ye, my winsome marrow. *The Braes of Yarrow.*

HAMILTON, WILLIAM GERARD, English politician, 28 Jan. 1729–16 July, 1796

21 Johnson is dead. – Let us go to the next best: – there is nobody; no man can be said to put you in mind of Johnson.
Boswell's Life of Johnson, an. 1784.

HANKEY, KATHERINE, English hymn-writer, 1834–1911

22 Tell me the old, old story.
The Old, Old Story.

HARDENBERG, FRIEDRICH LEOPOLD VON, see Novalis

HARDY, THOMAS, English author, 2 June, 1840–11 Jan. 1928

23 A nice unparticular man.
Far from the Madding Crowd, viii.

24 A lover without indiscretion is no lover at all. *The Hand of Ethelberta, xx.*

25 Dialect words – those terrible marks of the beast to the truly genteel.
The Mayor of Casterbridge, xx.

26 A little one-eyed blinking sort o'place.
Tess of the D'Urbervilles, i.

1 Always washing and never getting
finished. *Ibid, iv.*

2 'Justice' was done, and the President of
the Immortals (in Aeschylean phase) had
ended his sport with Tess. *Ibid, lix.*

3 Life's little ironies. *Title of Volume.*

4 Time and circumstance, which enlarge
the views of most men, narrow the
views of women almost invariably.
Jude the Obscure, vi.

5 When I came back from Lyonnesse
With magic in my eyes.
When I set out for Lyonesse.

6 What of the faith and fire within us
Men who march away?
Men who march away.

7 Only a man harrowing clods
In a slow silent walk
With an old horse that stumbles and
nods
Half asleep as they stalk.
In Time of 'The Breaking of Nations.'

8 Yet this will go onward the same
Though Dynasties pass. *Ibid.*

9 When the Present has latched its postern
behind my tremulous stay. *Afterwards.*

10 He was a man who used to notice such
things. *Ibid.*

11 This is the weather the cuckoos like,
And so do I. *Weathers.*

HARE, MAURICE E., 1889–1967

12 There was a young man who said,
'Damn!
At last I've found out what I am
A creature that moves
In determinate grooves,
In fact not a bus but a tram.' *Limerick.*

**HARINGTON, SIR JOHN, English
author, 1561–20 Nov. 1612**

13 Treason doth never prosper; what's the
reason?

For if it prosper, none dare call it
treason. *Epigrams, IV. 5.*

**HARRIS, CHARLES K., US
composer, 1 May, 1865–22 Dec. 1930**

14 Many a heart is aching, if you could read
them all.
Many the hopes that have vanished,
after the ball. *After the Ball.*

**HARRIS, JOEL CHANDLER, US
author, 8 Dec. 1848–3 July, 1908**

15 Tar-Baby ain't sayin' nuthin', en Brer
Fox, he lay low. *Uncle Remus, ii.*

16 Ez soshubble ez a baskit er kittens.
Ibid, iii.

17 Bred en bawn in a brier-patch, Brer
Fox. *Ibid, iv.*

18 Lounjun 'roun' en suffer'n. *Ibid, xii.*

19 I'm de'f in one year, en I can't hear out'n
de udder. *Ibid, xix.*

20 Oh, what shill we go w'en de great day
comes,
Wid de blowin' er de trumpits en de
bangin' er de drums?
How many po' sinners'll be kotched out
late
En find no latch ter de golden gate?
Uncle Remus. His Songs, i.

**HARTE, FRANCIS BRETT, US
author, 25 Aug. 1836–5 May, 1902**

21 Which I wish to remark,
And my language is plain,
That for ways that are dark
And for tricks that are vain,
The heathen Chinee is peculiar.
Plain Language from Truthful James.

22 With the smile that was childlike and
bland. *Ibid.*

23 Then Abner Dean of Angels raised a
point of order – when
A chunk of old red sandstone took him
in the abdomen,

And he smiled a kind of sickly smile and
curled up on the floor,
And the subsequent proceedings
interested him no more.
The Society upon the Stanislaus.

24 Do I sleep? Do I dream?
Do I wander and doubt?
Are things what they seem?
Or is visions about?
Further Language from Truthful James.

25 If of all words of tongue and pen,
The saddest are, 'It might have been,'
More sad are these we daily see:
'It is, but hadn't ought to be.'
Mrs. Judge Jenkins.

**HASKINS, MINNIE LOUISE,
English teacher and author, 12
May, 1875–3 Feb. 1957**

26 And I said to the man who stood at the
gate of the year:
'Give me a light that I may tread safely
into the unknown.'
And he replied:
'Go out into the darkness and put your
hand into the hand of God.
That shall be to you better than light and
safer than a known way.'
God knows.

**HAWES, STEPHEN, English poet,
died 1523?**

27 For though the day be never so longe,
At last the belles ringeth to evensonge.
Passetyme of Pleasure, xlii.

**HAWKER, ROBERT STEPHEN,
English cleric, 3 Dec. 1803–15 Aug.
1875**

28 And have they fixed the where and
when?
And shall Trelawny die?
Here's twenty thousand Cornish men
Will know the reason why!
Song of the Western Men.

**HAWKINS, SIR ANTHONY
HOPE, see Hope, Anthony**

**HAWTHORNE, NATHANIEL, US
author, 4 July, 1804–18 or 19 May,
1864**

29 Selfishness is one of the qualities apt to
inspire love. This might be thought out
at great length.
American Note-Books, 1840.

30 Life is made up of marble and mud.
The House of the Seven Gables, ii

**HAY, IAN (JOHN HAY BEITH),
English author, 17 April, 1876–22
Sept. 1952**

31 A good story is at present going the
round of the clubs, . . . anent a certain
well-known but absent-minded Peer of
the Realm.
The Right Stuff, iii.

32 Funny peculiar, or funny ha-ha?
Housemaster, III.

**HAY, JOHN, US author, 8 Oct.
1838–1 July, 1905**

33 A keerless man in his talk was Jim,
And an awkward hand in a row,
He never flunked, and he never lied, –
I reckon he never knowed how.
Jim Bludso.

**HAZLITT, WILLIAM, English
essayist, 10 April, 1778–18 Sept. 1830**

34 The art of pleasing consists in being
pleased. *The Round Table. On Manner.*

35 He (Coleridge) talked on for ever; and
you wished him to talk on for ever.
*Lectures on the English Poets. On the
Living Poets.*

36 It is better to be able neither to read nor
write than to be able to do nothing else.
*Table Talk. On the Ignorance of the
Learned.*

37 There is not a more mean, stupid,
dastardly, pitiful, selfish, spiteful,
envious, ungrateful animal than the
Public. It is the greatest of cowards, for
it is afraid of itself.
Ibid. On Living to Oneself.

1   His worst is better than any other
person's best.   (Scott.)
The Spirit of the Age. Sir Walter Scott.

2   When I take up a work that I have read
before (the oftener the better) I know
what I have to expect. The satisfaction is
not lessened by being anticipated.
The Plain Speaker. On reading Old Books.

3   No young man believes he shall ever
die.
On the Feeling of Immortality in Youth.

4   As we advance in life, we acquire a
keener sense of the value of time.
Nothing else, indeed, seems of any
consequence; and we become misers in
this respect.   *Ibid.*

**HEBER, REGINALD, Bishop of
Calcutta, 21 April, 1783–3 April,
1826**

5   Failed the bright promise of your early
day!   *Palestine.*

6   No hammers fell, no ponderous axes
rung;
Like some tall palm the mystic fabric
sprung.
Majestic silence!   *Ibid.*

7   Brightest and best of the sons of the
morning,
Dawn on our darkness, and lend us
thine aid.   *Epiphany.*

8   When spring unlocks the flowers to
paint the laughing soil.
Seventh Sunday after Trinity.

9   The Son of God goes forth to war,
A kingly crown to gain;
His blood-red banner streams afar:
Who follows in His train?
The Son of God goes forth to War.

10 From Greenland's icy mountains,
From India's coral strand,
Where Afric's sunny fountains
Roll down their golden sand.
Missionary Hymn.

11 Though every prospect pleases,
And only man is vile.   *Ibid.*

12 The heathen in his blindness
Bows down to wood and stone.   *Ibid.*

**HEMANS, FELICIA DORETHEA,
English poetess, 25 Sept. 1793–16
May, 1835**

13 The stately homes of England
How beautiful they stand!
Amidst their tall ancestral trees,
O'er all the pleasant land.
The Homes of England.

14 The boy stood on the burning deck,
Whence all but he had fled.   *Casabianca.*

15 There came a burst of thunder sound –
The boy – oh! where was he?   *Ibid.*

16 They grew in beauty, side by side,
They fill'd one home with glee; –
Their graves are sever'd, far and wide,
By mount, and stream, and sea.
The Graves of a Household.

17 Not there, not there, my child!
The Better Land.

18 Eye hath not seen it, my gentle boy!
Ibid.

**HENLEY, WILLIAM ERNEST,
English author, 23 Aug. 1849–11
July, 1903**

19 Far in the stillness a cat
Languishes loudly.
In Hospital, vii. Vigil.

20 Valiant in velvet, light in ragged luck,
Most vain, most generous, sternly
critical,
Buffoon and poet, lover and sensualist:
A deal of Ariel, just a streak of Puck,
Much Anthony, of Hamlet most of all,
And something of the Shorter-
Catechist. (R. L. Stevenson.)ˋ
Ibid, xxv., Apparition.

21 Out of the night that covers me,
Black as the Pit from pole to pole,
I thank whatever gods may be
For my unconquerable soul.
*Echoes, iv. In Memoriam R. T. Hamilton
Bruce, 1846–99.*

22 Under the bludgeonings of chance
My head is bloody, but unbowed.
Ibid.

23 I am the master of my fate:
I am the captain of my soul. *Ibid.*

24 A late lark twitters from the quiet skies.
*Ibid, xxxv. In Memoriam Margaritae
Sorori.*

25 Or ever the knightly years were gone
With the old world to the grave,
I was a King in Babylon
And you were a Christian Slave.
Ibid, xxxvii. To W. A.

26 What have I done for you,
England, my England?
What is there I would not do,
England, my own?
Rhymes and Rhythms, xxv.

**HENRI IV, King of France, 13 Dec.
1553–14 May, 1610**

27 Paris vaut bien une messe. – Paris is well
worth a mass. *Attributed.*

28 The wisest fool in Christendom. (Of
James I of England.) *Ibid.*

**HENRY, O. (WILLIAM SYDNEY
PORTER(, US author, 11 Sept.
1862–5 June, 1910**

29 If men knew how women pass the time
when they are alone, they'd never
marry. *Memoirs of a Yellow Dog.*

30 Turn up the lights; I don't want to go
home in the dark. *Last Words.*

**HENRY, PATRICK, US statesman,
29 May, 1736–6 June, 1799**

31 Tarquin and Caesar each had his Brutus,
Charles the First his Cromwell, and
George the Third ('Treason!' cried the
Speaker) – *may profit by their example.* If
this be treason, make the most of it.
*Speech in Virginia House of Burgesses,
29 May, 1765.*

32 I am not a Virginian, but an American.
*Speech in First Continental Congress,
14 Oct. 1774.*

33 Is life so dear, or peace so sweet, as to be
purchased at the price of chains and
slavery? Forbid it, Almighty God! I
know not what course others may
take, but as for me, give me liberty, or
give me death!
*Speech in Virginia Convention, 23 March,
1775.*

**HERBERT, SIR ALAN PATRICK,
English author and MP, 24 Sept.
1890–11 Nov. 1971**

34 Not huffy or stuffy, nor tiny or tall,
But fluffy, just fluffy, with no brains at
all. *I like them Fluffy.*

35 Holy deadlock. *Title of novel.*

36 I regard the pub as a valuable institution.
*Letter to the Electors of Oxford University,
1935.*

**HERBERT, GEORGE, English poet
and cleric, born 3 April, 1593,
buried 3 March, 1633**

37 Dare to be true: nothing can need a lie;
A fault which needs it most grows two
thereby. *The Church Porch, 77.*

38 Do all things like a man, not sneakingly:
Think the king sees thee still; for his
King does. *Ibid, 121.*

39 Pulpits and Sundays, sorrow dogging
sin,
Afflictions sorted, anguish of all sizes,
Fine nets and strategems to catch us in,
Bibles laid open, millions of surprises.
Sin.

40 O day most calm, most bright.
Sunday.

41 Sweet day, so cool, so calm, so bright,
The bridal of the earth and sky. *Virtue.*

42 Sweet spring, full of sweet days and
roses,
A box where sweets compacted lie.
Ibid.

1 Only a sweet and virtuous soul,
Like seasoned timber, never gives;
But though the whole world turn to
coal,
Then chiefly lives.   *Ibid.*

2 Love is swift of foot;
Love's a man of war,
And can shoot,
And can hit from far.   *Discipline.*

3 Do well, and right, and let the world
sink.
*A Priest to the Temple or the Country
Parson, xxix.*

**HERRICK, ROBERT, English poet
and cleric, baptised 24 Aug. 1591,
buried 15 Oct. 1674**

4 I sing of brooks, of blossoms, birds, and
bowers:
Of April, May, of June, and July
flowers.
I sing of maypoles, hock-carts, wassails,
wakes,
Of bridegrooms, brides, and of their
bridal cakes.
I write of youth, of love, and have access
By these, to sing of cleanly-
wantonness.
Hesperides. The Argument of his Book.

5 A sweet disorder in the dress
Kindles in clothes a wantonness.
Ibid, Delight in Disorder.

6 A winning wave (deserving note)
In the tempestuous petticoat:
A careless shoe-string, in whose tie
I see a wild civility:
Do more bewitch me, than when art
Is too precise in every part.   *Ibid.*

7 Gather ye rosebuds while ye may,
Old Time is till a-flying,
And this same flower that smiles to-day
To-morrow will be dying.
*Ibid. To the Virgins, to make much of
Time.*

8 Bid me to live, and I will live
Thy Protestant to be:
Or bid me love, and I will give
A loving heart to thee.
*Ibid, To Anthea, who may command him
any Thing.*

9 Fair daffodils, we weep to see
You haste away so soon:
As yet the early-rising sun
Has not attain'd his noon.
Ibid, To Daffodils.

10 Her pretty feet
Like snails did creep
A little out, and then,
s if they started at bo-peep,
Did soon draw in again.
Ibid, Upon her Feet.

11 Her eyes the glow-worm lend thee,
The shooting-stars attend thee
And the elves also,
Whose little eyes glow
Like the sparks of fire, befriend thee.
Ibid, The Night-piece, to Julia.

12 Whenas in silks my Julia goes,
Then, then, methinks, how sweetly
flows
That liquefaction of her clothes.
Ibid, Upon Julia's Clothes.

13 Attempt the end, and never stand to
doubt;
Nothing's so hard but search will find it
out.   *Ibid, Seek and find.*

14 Here a little child I stand,
Heaving up my either hand;
Cold as paddocks though they be,
Here I lift them up to thee,
For a benison to fall
On our meat and on us all. Amen.
*Noble Numbers. Another Grace for a
Child.*

**HESIOD, Greek poet, 8th century
B.C.**

15 Πλέον ημισυ παντός – The half is
more than the whole.
Works and Days, 40.

**HEYWOOD, JOHN, English
epigrammatist, 1497?–1580?**

16 Let the world slide, let the world go:
A fig for care, and a fig for woe!
If I can't pay, why I can owe,
And death makes equal the high and
low.   *Be Merry Friends.*

HEYWOOD, THOMAS, English dramatist, 1572?–Aug. 1641

17 Pack clouds away and welcome day,
With night we banish sorrow.
Pack Clouds Away.

HICKSON, WILLIAM EDWARD, English nonconformist preacher, 7 Jan. 1803–22 March, 1870

18 Nor on this land alone –
But be God's mercies known
From shore to shore.
Lord, make the nations see
That men should brothers be,
And form one family
The wide world o'er.
God bless our Native Land.
(Sometimes used as a stanza of 'God Save the King.')

19 If at first you don't succeed,
Try, try again.   *Try and try again.*

HILL, AARON, English poet, 10 Feb. 1685–8 Feb. 1750

20 First, then, a woman will, or won't,
depend on't;
If she will do't, she will; and there's an
end on't.
But if she won't, since safe and sound
your trust is,
Fear is affront, and jealousy injustice.
Epilogue to Zara.

21 Tender-handed stroke a nettle,
And it stings you for your pains;
Grasp it like a man of mettle,
And it soft as silk remains.

'Tis the same with common natures:
Use 'em kindly, they rebel;
But be rough as nutmeg-graters,
And the rogues obey you well.
Verses written on a window in Scotland.

HIPPOCLIDES, Greek notable, 6 century B.C.

22 Ου φροντὶς Ἱπποκλείδη – Hippoclides
does not care.   *Herodotus, VI. 129.*

HIPPOCRATES, Greek doctor, 460?–357? B.C.

23 Ὁ βίος βραχύς, η δὲ τέχνη μακρή
– Life is short and art is long.
Aphorisms, I. I.
(Commonly quoted in Latin, 'Ars longa, vita brevis.')

HOBBES, THOMAS, English philosopher, 5 April, 1588–4 Dec. 1679

24 For words are wise men's counters,
they do but reckon by them; but they
are the money of fools.
Leviathan, I. iv.

25 Sudden glory is the passion which
maketh those grimaces called laughter.
Ibid, vi.

26 No arts; no letters; no society; and
which is worst of all, continual fear and
danger of violent death; and the life of
man solitary, poor, nasty, brutish, and
short.   *Ibid, xiii.*

HOCH, EDWARD WALLIS, US politician, 17 March, 1849–2 June, 1925

27 There is so much good in the worst of
us,
And so much bad in the best of us,
That it hardly becomes any of us
To talk about the rest of us.
Good and Bad.

HODGSON, RALPH, English poet, 9 Sept. 1871–3 Nov. 1962

28 Time, you old gipsy man,
Will you not stay,
Put up your caravan
Just for one day?
Time, You Old Gipsy Man.

29 Wondering, listening,
Listening, wondering,
Eve with a berry
Halfway to her lips.   *Eve.*

HOFFMAN, AUGUST HEINRICH, VON FALLERSLEBEN, German poet and philologist, 2 April, 1798–19 Jan. 1874

1 Deutschland, Deutschland über alles. – Germany, Germany over all. *Song.*

HOGG, JAMES (THE ETTRICK SHEPHERD), Scottish poet, baptised 9 Dec. 1770, died 21 Nov. 1835

2 Bonny Kilmeny gaed up the glen.
Kilmeny, I.

3 Cam ye by Athol, lad wi' the philabeg?
Bonnie Prince Charlie.

4 Bird of the wilderness,
Blithesome and cumberless,
Sweet be thy matin o'er moorland and lea!
Emblem of happiness,
Blest is thy dwelling-place–
O to abide in the desert with thee!
The Skylark.

5 My love she's but a lassie yet. *Song.*

6 Where the pools are bright and deep,
Where the grey trout lies asleep,
Up the river and o'er the lea,
That's the way for Billy and me.
A Boy's Song.

HOLLAND, SIR RICHARD, Scottish poet, fl. 1450.

7 O Dowglas, O Dowglas, tendir and trewe! *Buke of the Howlat, 31.*

HOLMES, OLIVER WENDELL, US author, 29 Aug. 1809–7 Oct. 1894

8 Ay, tear her tattered ensign down!
Long has it waved on high,
And many an eye has danced to see
That banner in the sky. *Old Ironsides.*

9 Nail to the mast her holy flag,
Set every threadbare sail,
And give her to the god of storms,
The lightning and the gale. *Ibid.*

10 Their discords sting through Burns and Moore
Like hedgehogs dressed in lace.
The Music-Grinders.

11 And silence, like a poultice, comes
To heal the blows of sound. *Ibid.*

12 And, since, I never dare to write
As funny as I can. *The Height of the Ridiculous.*

13 When the last reader reads no more.
The Last Reader.

14 The freeman casting with unpurchased hand
The vote that shakes the turrets of the land. *Poetry, a Metrical Essay.*

15 Have you heard of the wonderful one-horse shay,
That was built in such a logical way
It ran a hundred years to a day?
The Deacon's Masterpiece.

16 A thought is often original, though you have uttered it a hundred times.
The Autocrat of the Breakfast Table, i.

17 The axis of the earth sticks out visibly through the centre of each and every town or city. *Ibid, vi.*

18 The world's great men have not commonly been scholars, nor its scholars great men. *Ibid.*

HOME, JOHN, Scottish poet, 21 Sept. 1722–5 Sept. 1808

19 My name is Norval; on the Grampian hills
My father feeds his flocks; a frugal swain,
Whose constant cares were to increase this store,
And keep his only son, myself, at home.
Douglas, II. i.

20 Like Douglas conquer, or like Douglas die. *Ibid, V. i.*

HOMER, Greek poet, about 900 B.C.

21 Μῆνιν αειδε, θεά, Πηληϊάδεω 'Αχιλῆος.
– Sing, goddess, the wrath of Achilles,
son of Peleus. *Iliad, i. I.*

22 Βῆ δ' ακέων παρὰ θῖνα
πολυφλοίσβοιο θαλάσσης.
– He went in silence along the shore of the
loud-sounding sea. *Ibid, 34.*

23 Τὸν δ' απαμειβόμενος προσέφη πόδας
ωκὺς 'Αχιλλεύς.
– And swift-footed Achilles answered
him and said. *Ibid, 84.*

24 Ἔπεα πτερόεντα.
– Winged words. *Ibid, 201.*

25 Ἐπὶ οινοπα πόντον.
– Over the wine-dark sea. *Ibid, 350.*

26 Ποῖόν σε επος φύγεν ερκος οδόντων;
– What a word has escaped the barrier of
thy teeth! *Ibid, iv. 350.*

27 Οιη περ φύλλων γενεή, τοίη δὲ καὶ
ανδρῶν.
– As the generation of leaves, so also is
that of men. *Ibid, vi. 146.*

28 Αιὲν αριστεύειν καὶ υπειροχον εμμεναι
αλλων.
– Always to excel, and be distinguished
above others. *Ibid, 208.*

29 'Αλλ' ητοι μὲν ταῦτα θεῶν εν γούνασι
κεῖται.
– But verily these things lie on the knees
of the gods. *Ibid, xvii. 514.*

30 Πολλῶν δ' ανθρώπων ιδεν αστεα καὶ
νόον εγνω.
– Many were the men whose cities he
saw and whose mind he learned. *Odyssey, i. 4.*

31 Ημος δ' ηριγένεια φάνη ροδοδάκτυλος
ηώς.
– But when rosy-fingered dawn, child
of the morning, appeared. *Ibid, ii. I.*

32 Ἑξῆς δ' εζόμενοι πολιὴν αλα τύπτον
ερετμοις.

– And sitting in order they smote the
hoary sea with their oars. *Ibid, ix. 104.*

33 Τέτλαθι δή, κραδίη καὶ κύντερον
αλλο ποτ' ετλης.
– Bear, O my heart; thou hast born yet a
harder thing. *Ibid, xx. 18.*

HOOD, THOMAS, English poet, 23 May, 1799–3 May, 1845

34 They went and told the sexton and
The sexton toll'd the bell.
Faithless Sally Brown.

35 Ben Battle was a soldier bold,
And used to war's alarms:
But a cannon-ball took off his legs,
So he laid down his arms!
Faithless Nelly Gray.

36 For here I leave my second leg
And the Forty-Second Foot! *Ibid.*

37 Spring it is cheery,
Winter is dreary,
Green leaves hang, but the brown must
fly;
When he's forsaken,
Wither'd and shaken,
What can an old man do but die? *Ballad.*

38 I remember, I remember,
The house where I was born,
The little window where the sun
Came peeping in at morn.
I remember, I remember.

39 I remember, I remember,
The fir trees dark and high;
I used to think their slender tops
Were close against the sky:
It was a childish ignorance,
But now 'tis little joy
To know I'm farther off from heav'n
Than when I was a boy. *Ibid.*

40 Two stern-faced men set out from Lynn
Through the cold and heavy mist,
And Eugene Aram walked between
With gyves upon his wrist.
The Dream of Eugene Aram.

41 Boughs are daily rifled
By the gusty thieves,

And the Book of Nature
Getteth short of leaves.   *The Seasons.*

1 Our very hopes belied our fears,
Our fears our hopes belied –
We thought her dying when she slept,
And sleeping when she died!
            The Death-Bed.

2 Seem'd washing his hands with invisible
soap,
In imperceptible water.
        Miss Kilmansegg. Her Christening.

3 With fingers weary and worn,
With eyelids heavy and red,
A woman sat, in unwomanly rags,
Plying her needle and thread –
Stitch! stitch! stitch!
In poverty, hunger, and dirt,
And still with a voice of dolorous pitch
She sang the 'Song of the Shirt'!
            The Song of the Shirt.

4 It is not linen you're wearing out
But human creatures' lives.   *Ibid.*

5 Oh! God! that bread should be so dear,
And flesh and blood so cheap.   *Ibid.*

6 My tears must stop, for every drop
Hinders needle and thread!   *Ibid.*

7 But evil is wrought by want of thought,
As well as want of heart.
            The Lady's Dream.

8 One more Unfortunate,
Weary of breath,
Rashly importunate,
Gone to her death!

Take her up tenderly,
Lift her with care;
Fashioned so slenderly,
Young, and so fair. *The Bridge of Sighs.*

9 Alas! for the rarity
Of Christian charity
Under the sun!   *Ibid.*

**HOOKER, RICHARD, English
theologian, 1554?–2 Nov. 1600**

10 To live by one man's will became the
cause of all men's misery.
            Ecclesiastical Polity, I.

**HOPE, ANTHONY (SIR
ANTHONY HOPE HAWKINS),
English novelist, 9 Feb. 1863–8 July,
1933**

11 'Bourgeois,' I observed, 'is an epithet
which the riff-raff apply to what is
respectable, and the aristocracy to what
is decent.'   *Dolly Dialogues, xvii.*

12 His foe was folly and his weapon wit.
        On memorial to W. S. Gilbert.

**HOPE, LAURENCE (ADELA
FLORENCE NICOLSON),
English poetess, 9 April, 1865–4
Oct. 1904**

13 Less than the dust beneath thy chariot
wheel.
    Indian Love Lyrics. Less than the Dust.

14 Pale hands I loved beside the Shalimar,
Where are you now? Who lies beneath·
your spell? *Ibid, Pale Hands I loved.*

**HOPKINS, GERARD MANLEY,
English poet and cleric, 28 July,
1844–8 June, 1889**

15 The world is charged with the grandeur
of God.   *God's Grandeur.*

16 Glory be to God for dappled things –
For skies of couple-colour as a brindled
cow;
For rose-moles all in stipple upon trout
that swim.   *Pied Beauty.*

17 Margaret, are you grieving
Over Goldengrove unleaving?
Leaves, like the things of man, you
With your fresh thoughts care for, can
you? *Spring and Fall: to a young child.*

18 What would the world be, once bereft
Of wet and of wildness? Let them be
left,
O let them be left, wildness and wet;
Long live the weeds and wilderness yet.
            Inversnaid.

**HOPKINSON, JOSEPH, US Judge,
12 Nov. 1770–15 Jan. 1842**

19 Hail, Columbia! happy land!
Hail, ye heroes! heaven-born band!

Who fought and bled in Freedom's
cause. *Hail, Columbia.*

HORACE (QUINTUS HORATIUS FLACCUS), Roman poet, 8 Dec. 65 B.C.–27 Nov. 8 B.C.

20   Mutato nomine de te
Fabula narratur.
– Change the name, and the story is told
about you. *Satires, I. i. 69.*

21 Hoc genus omne.
– All this sort. *Ibid, ii. 2.*

22 Faenum habet in cornu.
– He is dangerous (*lit.* He has hay on his
horn). *Ibid, iv. 34.*

23   Ad unguem
Factus homo.
– A highly accomplished person (*lit.*
made to the nail, from the testing of
marble work by drawing the nail over
it). *Ibid, v. 32.*

24 Sic me servavit Apollo.
– So Apollo preserved me. *Ibid, ix. 78.*

25 Carpe diem, quam minimum credula
postero.
– Seize the present day, trusting the
morrow as little as may be.
Odes, I. xi. 8.

26 Integer vitae scelerisque purus.
– The man of upright life and pure from
guilt. *Ibid, xxii. I.*

27   Neque semper arcum
Tendit Apollo
– Nor does Apollo always keep his bow
strung. *Ibid, II. x. 19.*

28 Eheu fugaces, Postume, Postume,
Labunter anni.
– Alas, Postumus, Postumus, the
fleeting years glide past. *Ibid, xiv. I.*

29 Odi profanum vulgus et arceo.
– I hate the vulgar throng and drive
them from me. *Ibid, III. i. 1.*

30 Dulce et decorum est pro patria mori.
– It is a sweet and glorious thing to die
for one's country. *Ibid, ii. 13.*

31 Si fractus illabatur orbis
Impavidum ferient ruinae.
– If the heavens were to break and fall,
the ruins would strike him
undismayed. *Ibid, iii. 7.*

32 Exegi monumentum aere perennius.
– I have completed a memorial more
lasting than brass. *Ibid, xxx. 1.*

33 Vixere fortes ante Agamemnona
Multi.
– Many brave men lived before
Agamemnon. *Ibid, IV. ix. 25.*

34   Rem facias, rem
Si possis, recte, si non, quocumque
modo rem.
– Make money, money, honestly if you
can; if not, by any means at all, make
money. *Epistles, I. i. 66.*

35 Quidquid delirant reges plectuntur
Achivi.
– Whatever madness the kings commit,
the Greeks suffer for it. *Ibid, ii. 14.*

36 Dimidium facti qui coepit habet.
– He who has begun has half done.
Ibid, 40.

37 Rusticus expectat dum defluat amnis.
– Like the yokel, waits for the river to
flow away. *Ibid, 42.*

38 Semper avarus eget.
– The miser is always in want. *Ibid, 56.*

39 Ira furor brevis est.
– Anger is a short madness. *Ibid, 62.*

40 Naturam expelles furca, tamen usque
recurret.
– Though you drive nature out with a
pitchfork, she will ever return.
Ibid, x. 24.

41 Caelum, non animum, mutant qui trans
mare currunt.
– They change their climate, not their
soul, who run beyond the sea.
Ibid, xi. 27.

42 Genus irritabile vatum.
– The touchy race of poets.
Ibid, II. ii. 102.

1   Brevis esse laboro,
Obscurus fio.
– I struggle to be brief, and become
obscure.   *Ars Poetica, 25.*

2 Parturiunt montes, nascetur ridiculus
   mus.
– The mountains are in labour; there will
be born a ridiculous mouse.   *Ibid, 139.*

3 Laudator temporis acti.
– Praiser of times past.   *Ibid, 173.*

4   Exemplaria Graeca
Nocturna versate manu, versate diurna.
– Con the pages of Greek models day
and night.   *Ibid, 268.*

5 Indignor, quandoque bonus dormitat
   Homerus.
– I think it shame when the worthy
Homer nods.   *Ibid. 359.*

**HOUGHTON, RICHARD
MONCKTON MILNES, 1ST
BARON, English poet and
politician, 19 June, 1809–11 Aug.
1885**

6 But on and up, where Nature's heart
Beats strong amid the hills.
     Tragedy of the Lac de Gaube, 2.

7 But the beating of my own heart
Was all the sound I heard.
           The Brookside.

8 A fair little girl sat under a tree,
Sewing as long as her eyes could see;
Then smoothed her work, and folded it
   right,
And said, 'Dear work, good-night,
   good-night.'
      Good-Night and Good-Morning.

**HOUSMAN, ALFRED EDWARD,
English scholar and poet, 26 March,
1859–30 April, 1936**

9 Loveliest of trees, the cherry now
Is hung with bloom along the bough.
        A Shropshire Lad, ii.

10 Clay lies still, but blood's a rover.
        Ibid, iv. Reveille.

11 When I was one-and-twenty
I heard a wise man say,
'Give crowns and pounds and guineas
But not your heart away.'   *Ibid, xiii.*

12 To-day, the road all runners come,
Shoulder-high we bring you home,
And set you at your threshold down,
Townsman of a stiller town.
   Ibid, xix. To an Athlete dying Young.

13 And silence sounds no worse than cheers
After death has stopped the ears. *Ibid.*

14 They carry back bright to the coiner the
   mintage of man,
The lads that will die in their glory and
   never be old.   *Ibid, xxiii.*

15 Dust's your wages, son of sorrow,
But men may come to worse than dust.
         Ibid, xliv.

16 By brooks too broad for leaping
The lightfoot boys are laid.   *Ibid, liv.*

17 And malt does more than Milton can
To justify God's ways to man.
Ale, man, ale's the stuff to drink
For fellows whom it hurts to think.
         Ibid, lxii.

18 Pass me the can, lad; there's an end of
   May.   *Last Poems, ix.*

19 May will be fine next year as like as not:
Oh ay, but then we shall be twenty-
four.   *Ibid.*

20 The fairies break their dances
And leave the printed lawn.   *Ibid, xxi.*

21 The pence are here and here's the fair,
But where's the lost young man?
         Ibid, xxxv.

22 These, in the day when heaven was
   falling,
The hour when earth's foundations fled,
Followed their mercenary calling
And took their wages and are dead.
   *Ibid, xxxviii. Epitaph on an Army of
         Mercenaries.*

23 Even when poetry has a meaning, as it
usually has, it may be inadvisable to

draw it out. . . . Perfect understanding will sometimes almost extinguish pleasure.
The Name and Nature of Poetry.

HOWARD, HENRY, see Surrey, Earl of

HOWARTH, ELLEN CLEMENTINE, US author, 20 May, 1827–1899

24 'Tis but a little faded flower. *Song.*

HOWE, JULIA WARD, US reformer, 27 May, 1819–17 Oct. 1910

25 Mine eyes have seen the glory of the coming of the Lord;
He is trampling out the vintage where the grapes of wrath sorted;
He hath loosed the fateful lightning of His terrible, swift sword;
His truth is marching on.
Battle Hymn of the Republic.

26 In the beauty of the lilies Christ was born across the sea. *Ibid.*

HOWELLS, WILLIAM DEAN, US author, 1 March, 1837–11 May, 1920

27 Tossing his mane of snows in wildest eddies and tangles,
Lion-like March cometh in, hoarse, with tempestuous breath.
Earliest Spring.

HOWITT, MARY, English author, 12 March, 1799–30 Jan. 1888

28 'Will you walk into my parlour?' said a spider to a fly:
' 'Tis the prettiest little parlour that ever you did spy;
The way into my parlour is up a winding stair,
And I have many curious things to show when you are there.'
The Spider and the Fly.

HOYLE, EDMOND, English writer on whist, 1672–29 Aug. 1769

29 When in doubt, win the trick.
Whist. Twenty-four Short Rules for Learners.

HUBBARD, ELBERT, US author, 19 June, 1856–7 May, 1915

30 Life is just one damned thing after another.
A Thousand and One Epigrams, 137.

HUGHES, THOMAS, English novelist, 20 Oct. 1822–22 March, 1896

31 Life isn't all beer and skittles; but beer and skittles, or something better of the same sort, must form a good part of every Englishman's education.
Tom Brown's Schooldays, I. ii.

HUME, DAVID, Scottish historian, 26 April, 1711–25 Aug. 1776

32 Avarice, the spur of industry.
Essays. Of Civil Liberty.

33 Custom, then, is the great guide of human life.
Inquiry concerning Human Understanding, V. i.

HUNT, GEORGE WILLIAM, English song-writer, 1829?–3 March, 1904

34 We don't want to fight, but by jingo if we do,
We've got the ships, we've got the men, we've got the money too. *Song.*

HUNT, JAMES HENRY LEIGH, English author, 19 Oct. 1784–28 Aug. 1859

35 Where the light woods go seaward from the town. *The Story of Rimini, i. 18.*

36 The two divinest things this world has got,
A lovely woman in a rural spot!
Ibid, iii. 257.

37 Abou Ben Adhem (may his tribe increase)
Awoke one night from a deep dream of peace. *Abou Ben Adhem.*

38 Write me as one who loves his fellow men. *Ibid.*

1 And lo! Ben Adhem's name led all the
rest.   *Ibid.*

2 Green little vaulter in the sunny grass.
To the Grasshopper and the Cricket.

3 Jenny kissed me when we met,
Jumping from the chair she sat in.
Rondeau.

4 This Adonis in loveliness was a
corpulent man of fifty. (The Prince
Regent.)
The Examiner, 22 March, 1812.

**HUTCHESON, FRANCIS, Scottish
philosopher, 8 Aug. 1694–1746**

5 That action is best, which procures the
greatest happiness for the greatest
numbers.
*Inquiry into the Original of our Ideas of
Beauty and Virtue, II. iii. 8.*

**HUXLEY, ALDOUS LEONARD,
English novelist, 26 July, 1894–22
Nov. 1963**

6 There are not enough *bon mots* in
existence to provide any industrious
conversationalist with a new stock for
every social occasion.
Point Counter Point, vii.

**HUXLEY, THOMAS HENRY,
English scientist, 4 May, 1825–29
June, 1895**

7 The great end of life is not knowledge
but action.   *Technical Education.*

8 It is the customary fate of new truths to
begin as heresies and to end as
superstitions.
*The Coming of Age of the Origin of
Species.*

**IBSEN, HENRIK JOHAN,
Norwegian dramatist, 20 March,
1828–28 May, 1906**

9 You should never put on your best
trousers when you go out to fight for
freedom and truth.
An Enemy of the People, V.

10 With vines leaves in his hair.
Hedda Gabler, II.

**INGE, CHARLES, English cleric, 2
May, 1868–13 April, 1957**

11 This very remarkable man
Commends a most practical plan:
You can do what you want
If you don't think you can't,
So don't think you can't think you can.
On Monsieur Coué.

**INGE, WILLIAM RALPH, Dean of
St. Paul's, 6 June, 1860–26 Feb. 1954**

12 Public opinion, a vulgar, impertinent,
anonymous tyrant who deliberately
makes life unpleasant for anyone who is
not content to be the average man.
*Outspoken Essays, 1st series. Our Present
Discontents.*

13 The modern town-dweller has no God
and no Devil; he lives without awe,
without admiration, without fear. *Ibid.*

14 A man may build himself a throne of
bayonets, but he cannot sit on it.
*Marchant, Wit and Wisdom of
Dean Inge, 108.*

15 The nations which have put mankind
and posterity most in their debt have
been small States – Israel, Athens,
Florence, Elizabethan England.
Ibid, 181.

**INGELOW, JEAN, English poetess,
17 March, 1820–20 July, 1897**

16 But two are walking apart for ever,
And wave their hands for a mute
farewell.   *Divided.*

17 Play uppe 'The Brides of Enderby.' *The
High Tide on the Coast of
Lincolnshire, 1571.*

**INGERSOLL, ROBERT GREEN,
US lawyer, 11 Aug. 1833–21 July,
1899**

18 An honest God is the noblest work of
man.   *Gods, I.*

INGRAM, JOHN KELLS, Irish economist, 7 July, 1823–1 May, 1907

19 Who fears to speak of Ninety-eight?
Who blushes at the name?
When cowards mock the patriot's fate,
Who hangs his head for shame?
The Memory of the Dead.

IRVING, WASHINGTON, US author, 3 April, 1783–28 Nov. 1859

20 The almighty dollar, that great object of
universal devotion throughout our land,
seems to have no genuine devotees in
these peculiar villages.
Wolfert's Roost. The Creole Village.

21 A sharp tongue is the only edged tool
that grows keener with constant use.
The Sketch-Book. Rip Van Winkle.

22 They who drink beer will think beer.
Ibid, Stratford.

JACKSON, HELEN HUNT, US author, 15 Oct. 1830–12 Aug. 1885

23 Oh, write of me, not 'Died in bitter
pains,'
But 'Emigrated to another star!'
Emigravit.

JAMES 1, English King, 19 June, 1566–27 March, 1625

24 A custom loathsome to the eye, hateful
to the nose, harmful to the brain,
dangerous to the lungs, and in the black,
stinking fume thereof nearest
resembling the horrible Stygian smoke
of the pit that is bottomless.
A Counterblast to Tobacco.

25 No bishop, no king. *Attributed.*

JAMES, HENRY, US author, 15 April, 1843–28 Feb. 1916

26 He was worse than provincial – he was
parochial. (Thoreau.)
Life of Nathaniel Hawthorne, iv.

27 The time-honoured bread-sauce of the
happy ending. *Theatricals, 2nd series.*

JEFFERSON, THOMAS, US President, 13 April, 1743–4 July, 1826

28 The God who gave us life gave us
liberty at the same time.
*Summary View of the Rights of British
America.*

29 We hold these truths to be self-evident,
– that all men are created equal; that
they are endowed by their Creator
with certain unalienable rights; that
among these are life, liberty, and the
pursuit of happiness.
Declaration of Independence.

30 Error of opinion may be tolerated when
reason is left free to combat it.
First Inaugural Address, 4 March, 1801.

31 Peace, commerce, and honest friendship
with all nations, – entangling alliances
with none. *Ibid.*

JEFFREY, FRANCIS, LORD, Scottish lawyer and critic, 23 Oct. 1773–26 Jan. 1850

32 Here lies the preacher, judge, and poet,
Peter,
Who broke the laws of God, and man,
and metre. *On Peter Robinson.*

33 This will never do. (On Wordsworth's
Excursion).
Edinburgh Review, Nov. 1814.

JEROME, JEROME KLAPKA, English author, 2 May, 1859–14 June, 1927

34 I like work; it fascinates me. I can sit and
look at it for hours. I love to keep it by
me: the idea of getting rid of it nearly
breaks my heart.
Three Men in a Boat, xv.

35 Love is like the measles; we all have to
go through it.
*Idle Thoughts of an Idle Fellow. On Being
in Love.*

JERROLD, DOUGLAS WILLIAM, English author, 3 Jan. 1803–8 June, 1857

1 Love's like the measles – all the worse when it comes late in life.
A Philanthropist.

2 Earth is here (in Australia) so kind, that just tickle her with a hoe and she laughs with a harvest. *A Land of Plenty.*

JOHNSON, LIONEL PIGOT, English poet, 15 March, 1867–4 Oct. 1902

3 The saddest of all kings
Crowned, and again discrowned.
By the Statue of King Charles at Charing Cross.

4 There Shelley dreamed his white Platonic dreams. *Oxford.*

JOHNSON, PHILANDER CHASE, US journalist, 6 Feb. 1866–18 May, 1939

5 Cheer up, the worst is yet to come.
Shooting Stars.

JOHNSON, ROSSITER, US author, 27 Jan. 1840–3 Oct. 1931

6 O for a lodge in a garden of cucumbers!
O for an iceberg or two at control!
O for a vale which at midday the dew cumbers!
O for a pleasure trip up to the Pole!
Ninety-nine in the Shade.

JOHNSON, SAMUEL, English lexicographer, 18 Sept. 1709–13 Dec. 1784

7 Here falling houses thunder on your head,
And here a female atheist talks you dead.
London, 17.

8 Of all the griefs that harass the distress'd,
Sure the most bitter is a scornful jest.
Ibid, 166.

9 This mournful truth is ev'rywhere confess'd,
Slow rises worth by poverty depress'd.
Ibid, 176.

10 Prepare for death if here at night you roam,
And sign your will before you sup from home. *Ibid, 224.*

11 Let observation with extensive view
Survey mankind from China to Peru.
The Vanity of Human Wishes, I.

12 There mark what ills the scholar's life assail,
Toil, envy, want, the patron, and the jail. *Ibid, 159.*

13 He left the name, at which the world grew pale,
To point a moral, or adorn a tale.
Ibid, 221.

14 In life's last scene what prodigies surprise,
Fears of the brave, and follies of the wise!
From Marlb'rough's eyes the streams of dotage flow,
And Swift expires a driv'ler and a show.
Ibid, 315.

15 Must helpless man, in ignorance sedate,
Roll darkling down the torrent of his fate? *Ibid, 345.*

16 When Learning's triumph o'er her barb'rous foes
First rear'd the Stage, immortal Shakespeare rose;
Each change of many-colour'd life he drew,
Exhausted worlds, and then imagin'd new:
Existence saw him spurn her bounded reign,
And panting Time toil'd after him in vain.
Prologue at the Opening of the Theatre in Drury Lane, I.

17 For we that live to please, must please to live. *Ibid, 54.*

18 I put my hat upon my head
And walk'd into the Strand,
And there I met another man
Whose hat was in his hand.
Parodies of the Hermit of Warkworth, ii.
(Another version is:–
As with my hat upon my head
I walk'd along the Strand,
I there did meet another man
With his hat in his hand.)

19 Phrase that time has flung away,
Uncouth words in disarray:
Trickt in antique ruff and bonnet,
Ode and elegy and sonnet.
*Lines written in Ridicule of Thomas
Warton's Poems.*

20 If the man who turnips cries,
Cry not when his father dies,
'Tis a proof that he had rather
Have a turnip than his father.
Burlesque of Lines by Lope de Vega.

21 How small, of all that human hearts
endure,
That part which laws or kings can cause
or cure,
Still to ourselves in every place
consign'd,
Our own felicity we make or find:
With secret course, which no loud
storms annoy,
Glides the smooth current of domestic
joy.
Added to Goldsmith's Traveller, 429.

22 That trade's proud empire hastes to
swift decay,
As ocean sweeps the laboured mole
away;
While self-dependent power can time
defy,
As rocks resist the billows and the sky.
*Added to Goldsmith's Deserted Village,
427.*

23 No place affords a more striking
conviction of the vanity of human
hopes, than a public library.
The Rambler, 23 March, 1751.

24 I am not yet so lost in lexicography, as
to forget that words are the daughters of

earth, and that things are the sons of
heaven.
*Dictionary of the English Language,
Preface.*

25 *Lexicographer* – A writer of dictionaries,
a harmless drudge. *Ibid, definitions.*

26 *Oats* – A grain, which in England is
generally given to horses, but in
Scotland supports the people. *Ibid.*

27 *Patron* – Commonly a wretch who
supports with insolence. and is paid
with flattery. *Ibid.*

28 *Pension* – An allowance made to anyone
without an equivalent. In England it is
generally understood to mean pay given
to a state hireling for treason to his
country. *Ibid.*

29 Ye who listen with credulity to the
whispers of fancy, and pursue with
eagerness the phantoms of hope; who
expect that age will perform the
promises of youth, and that the
deficiencies of the present day will be
supplied by the morrow; attend to the
history of Rasselas, Prince of Abyssinia.
Rasselas, i.

30 Marriage has many pains, but celibacy
has no pleasures. *Ibid, xxvi.*

31 The stream of time, which is continually
washing the dissoluble fabricks of other
poets, passes without injury by the
adamant of Shakespeare.
Edition of Shakespeare, preface.

32 That man is little to be envied whose
patriotism would not gain force upon
the plain of Marathon, or whose piety
would not grow warmer among the
ruins of Iona.
*Journey to the Western Islands. Inch
Kenneth.*

33 Whoever wishes to attain an English
style, familiar but not coarse, and
elegant but not ostentatious, must give
his days and nights to the volumes of
Addison.
Lives of the English Poets. Addison.

1 To be of no church is dangerous.
Religion, of which the rewards are
distant, and which is animated only by
Faith and Hope, will glide by degrees
out of the mind, unless it be invigorated
and reimpressed by external ordinances,
by stated calls to worship, and the
salutary influence of example.
Ibid. Milton.

2 That stroke of death, which has eclipsed
the gaiety of nations, and impoverished
the public stock of harmless pleasure.
(Garrick's death.)   *Ibid, Edmund Smith.*

3 Nullum quod tetigit non ornavit. – He
touched nothing that he did not adorn.
Epitaph on Goldsmith.

4 Sir, we are a nest of singing birds.
(Pembroke College, Oxford.)
Boswell's Life of Johnson, an. 1730.

5 Like the Monument. (When asked how
he felt on the ill success of his tragedy,
Irene.)   *Ibid, an. 1749.*

6 A man may write any time, if he will set
himself doggedly to it.   *Ibid, an. 1750.*

7 Wretched un-idea'd girls.
Ibid, an. 1753.

8 This man I thought had been a lord
among wits, but I find he is only a wit
among lords. (Lord Chesterfield.)
Ibid, an. 1754.

9 They teach the morals of a whore, and
the manners of a dancing master. (Lord
Chesterfield's *Letters*.)   *Ibid.*

10 Is not a Patron, my Lord, one who looks
with unconcern on a man struggling for
life in the water, and when he has
reached ground, encumbers him with
help? The notice which you have been
pleased to take of my labours, had it
been early, had been kind; but it has
been delayed till I am indifferent, and
cannot enjoy it; till I am solitary, and
cannot impart it; till I am known, and do
not want it.
Ibid, Letter to Lord Chesterfield, 1755.

11 Ignorance, Madam, pure ignorance.
(When asked why he defined *pastern* as
'the knee of a horse' in his dictionary.)
Ibid, an. 1755.

12 A man, Sir, should keep his friendship
in constant repair.   *Ibid.*

13 Being in a ship is being in jail, with the
chance of being drowned. . . . A man in
a jail has more room, better food, and
commonly better company.
Ibid, an. 1759.

14 That, Sir, I find, is what a very great
many of your countrymen cannot help.
(When Boswell said that he could not
help coming from Scotland.)
Ibid, an. 1763.

15 Another charge was, that he did not love
clean linen; and I have no passion for it.
(Of Kit Smart.)   *Ibid.*

16 You *may* abuse a tragedy, though you
cannot write one. You may scold a
carpenter who has made you a bad table,
though you cannot make a table. It is
not your trade to make tables.   *Ibid.*

17 Consider, Sir, how insignificant this
will appear a twelve-month hence.
Ibid.

18 The noblest prospect which a
Scotchman ever sees, is the high road
that leads him to England.   *Ibid.*

19 A man ought to read just as inclination
leads him; for what he reads as a task
will do him little good.   *Ibid.*

20 If he does really think that there is no
distinction between virtue and vice,
why, Sir, when he leaves our houses let
us count our spoons.   *Ibid.*

21 Sir, a woman's preaching is like a dog's
walking on his hinder legs. It is not done
well; but you are surprised to find it
done at all.   *Ibid.*

22 For my part I mind my belly very
studiously and very carefully; for I look

upon it, that he who does not mind his belly, will hardly mind anything else.
Ibid.

23 It was not for me to bandy civilities with my sovereign   *Ibid, an. 1767.*

24 Sir, we *know* our will is free, and *there's* an end on't.   *Ibid, an. 1769.*

25 It matters not how a man dies, but how he lives.   *Ibid.*

26 That fellow seems to me to possess but one idea, and that is a wrong one.
Ibid, an. 1770.

27 Why, Sir, if you were to read Richardson for the story, your impatience would be so much fretted that you would hang yourself.
Ibid, an. 1772.

28 Much may be made of a Scotchman, if he be *caught* young.   *Ibid.*

29 No, Sir, do *you* read books *through*? (When asked if he had read a new book through.)   *Ibid, an. 1773.*

30 My dear Sir, never accustom your mind to mingle virtue and vice. The woman's a whore, and there's an end on't.   *Ibid.*

31 There are few ways in which a man can be more innocently employed than in getting money.   *Ibid, an. 1775.*

32 A man will turn over half a library to make one book.   *Ibid.*

33 Patriotism is the last refuge of a scoundrel.   *Ibid.*

34 Knowledge is of two kinds. We know a subject ourselves, or we know where we can find information upon it.   *Ibid.*

35 In lapidary inscriptions a man is not upon oath.   *Ibid.*

36 There is nothing which has yet been contrived by man, by which so much happiness is produced as by a good tavern or inn.   *Ibid, an. 1776.*

37 No man but a blockhead ever wrote except for money.   *Ibid.*

38 Sir, you have but two topics, yourself and me, and I am sick of both.   *Ibid.*

39 Sir, it is not so much to be lamented that Old England is lost, as that the Scotch have found it.   *Ibid.*

40 If I had no duties, and no reference to futurity, I would spend my life in driving briskly in a postchaise with a pretty woman.   *Ibid, an. 1777.*

41 Depend upon it, Sir, when a man knows he is to be hanged in a fortnight, it concentrates his mind wonderfully.
Ibid.

42 No, Sir, when a man is tired of London he is tired of life; for there is in London all that life can afford.   *Ibid.*

43 All argument is against it; but all belief is for it. (Of the appearance of men's spirits after death.)   *Ibid, an. 1778.*

44 All censure of a man's self is oblique praise. It is in order to show how much he can spare.   *Ibid.*

45 Claret is the liquor for boys; port for men; but he who aspires to be a hero must drink brandy.   *Ibid, an. 1779.*

46 Worth seeing? yes; but not worth going to see. (Of the Giant's Causeway.)
Ibid.

47 Greek, Sir, is like lace; every man gets as much of it as he can.   *Ibid, an. 1780.*

48 Sir, I have two very cogent reasons for not printing any list of subscribers; – one, that I have lost all the names, – the other, that I have spent all the money. (Anecdote of 1763, referring to his edition of Shakespeare.)   *Ibid, an. 1781.*

49 My dear friend, clear your *mind* of cant. You may *talk* as other people do: you may say to a man, 'Sir I am your most humble servant.' You are *not* his most humble servant.   *Ibid, an. 1783.*

1 It might as well be 'Who drives fat oxen
should himself be fat.' (Parodying the
line from Brooke's *Earl of Essex* 'Who
rules o'er freemen should himself be
free.')   *Ibid, an. 1784.*

2 Sir, I have found you an argument; but I
am not obliged to find you an
understanding.   *Ibid.*

3 Preserve me from unseasonable and
immoderate sleep.
Prayers and Meditations.

4 Books that you may carry to the fire,
and hold readily in your hand, are the
most useful after all.
*Hawkins, Apophthegms, Sentiments,
Opinions.*

5 Dictionaries are like watches; the worst
is better than none, and the best cannot
be expected to go quite true.
Mrs. Piozzi, Anecdotes of Johnson.

6 Difficult do you call it, Sir? I wish it
were impossible. (Of the performance
of a celebrated violinist.)
W. Seward, Anecdotes.

**JONES, JOHN PAUL, Scottish
adventurer who became US naval
officer, 6 July, 1747–18 July, 1792**

7 I have not yet begun to fight.
*When summoned to surrender, as his ship
was sinking, 1779.*

**JONES, SIR WILLIAM, oriental
scholar, 28 Sept. 1746–27 April, 1794**

8 Seven hours to law, to soothing slumber
seven,
Ten to the world allot, and all to
Heaven.
In place of Sir E. Coke's lines, 68:12

**JONSON, BEN, English Poet
Laureate, 1572–6 Aug. 1637**

9 Underneath this stone doth lie
As much beauty as could die;
Which in life did harbour give
To more virtue than doth live.
Epitaph on Elizabeth, L. H.

10 Drink to me only with thine eyes,
And I will pledge with mine;
Or leave a kiss but in the cup,
And I'll not look for wine.   *To Celia.*

11 Have you seen but a bright lily grow,
Before rude hands have touch'd it?
Have you mark'd but the fall o' the
snow
Before the soil hath smutch'd it?

O so white! O so soft! O so sweet is she!
Celebration of Charis, iv. Her Triumph.

12 Soul of the age!
The applause! delight! the wonder of our
stage!
My Shakespeare, rise; I will not lodge
thee by
Chaucer, or Spenser, or bid Beaumont
lie
A little further, to make thee a room.
To the Memory of Shakespeare.

13 Or sporting Kyd, or Marlowe's mighty
line.   *Ibid.*

14 And though thou hadst small Latin, and
less Greek.   *Ibid.*

15 He was not of an age, but for all time.
Ibid.

16 Sweet Swan of Avon!   *Ibid.*

17 It is not growing like a tree
In bulk, doth make men better be.
*A Pindaric Ode on the Death of Sir H.
Morison.*

18 Queen and huntress, chaste and fair,
Now the sun is laid to sleep,
Seated in thy silver chair,
State in wonted manner keep:
Hesperus entreats thy light,
Goddess excellently bright.
Cynthia's Revels, V. iii.

19 Still to be neat, still to be drest,
As you were going to a feat.
Epicoene; or The Silent Woman, I. i.

20 I remember the players have often
mentioned it as an honour in
Shakespeare that in his writing

(whatsoever he penned) he never blotted out a line. My answer hath been 'Would he had blotted a thousand.'
Timber, or Discoveries made upon Men and Matters.

21 For I loved the man, and do honour his memory, on this side idolatry, as much as any.   *Ibid.*

JULIAN THE APOSTATE (FLAVIUS CLAUDIUS JULIANUS), Roman Emperor, 331–26 June, 363

22 Vicisti, Galilaee. – Thou has conquered, O Galilean.   *Attributed dying words.*

JUNIUS (pseudonym of writer never identified), fl, 1770.

23 The liberty of the press is the *Palladium* of all the civil, political, and religious rights of an Englishman.
Letters, dedication.

JUNOT, ANDOCHE, Marshal of France, 23 Oct. 1771–29 July, 1813

24 Moi je suis mon ancêtre. – I am my own ancestor.
When created Duke of Abrantes.

JUVENAL (DECIMUS JUNIUS JUVENALIS), Roman satirist, A.D. 60?–140?

25 Quidquid agunt homines, votum timor ira voluptas
Gaudia discursus, nostri farrago libelli est.
– Whatever men do, wishes, fears, anger, pleasures, joys, goings to and fro, is the medley of my book.
Satires, i. 85.

26 Nemo repente fuit turpissimus
– No one ever became thoroughly bad all at once.   *Ibid, ii. 83.*

27 Res angusta domi.
– Straitened means at home.
Ibid, iii. 165.

28 Rara avis in terris nigroque simillima cycno.

– A rare bird on the earth and very like a black swan.   *Ibid, vi. 165.*

29 Hoc volo, sic jubeo, sit pro ratione voluntas.
– This is my wish, thus I command. Let my will take the place of reason.
Ibid, 223.

30   Quis custodiet ipsos Custodes?
– Who is to guard the guards themselves?   *Ibid, 347.*

31 Scribendi cacoethes.
– The itch for writing   *Ibid, vii. 52.*

32 Crambe repetita.
– Cabbage served up again.   *Ibid, 154.*

33 Nobilitas sola est atque unica virtus.
– Virtue is the sole and only nobility.
Ibid, viii. 20.

34 Panem et circenses.
– Bread and games.   *Ibid, x. 81.*

35 Mens sana in corpore sano.
– A sound mind in a sound body.
Ibid, 356.

KANT, IMMANUEL, German philosopher, 22 April, 1724–12 Feb. 1804

36 Ich soll niemals anders verfahren, als so, dass ich auch wollen könne, meine Maxime solle ein allgemeines Gesetz werden. – I am never to act otherwise than so that I could also will that my maxim should become a universal law.
Grundlegung zur Metaphysik der Sitten. – Foundations of a Metaphysic of Morals, i.

KARR, JEAN BAPTISTE ALPHONSE, French novelist, 24 Nov. 1808–30 Sept. 1890

37 Plus ça change, plus c'est la même chose. – The more it changes the more it is the same thing.
Les Guêpes, Jan. 1849.

38 Si l'on veut abolir la peine de mort en ce cas, que MM. les assassins commencent.

– If it is intended to abolish the death penalty in this case, let the gentlemen who do the murders take the first step.
Ibid.

KEATS, JOHN, English poet, 29 or 31 Oct. 1795–23 Feb. 1821

1 Here are sweet peas, on tip-toe for a flight. *I stood tip-toe upon a Little Hill.*

2 To one who has been long in city pent,
'Tis very sweet to look into the fair
And open face of heaven.
To one who has been long.

3 Much have I travell'd in the realms of gold,
And many goodly states and kingdoms seen.
On first looking into Chapman's Homer.

4 Then felt I like some watcher of the skies
When a new planet swims into his ken;
Or like stout Cortez when with eagle eyes
He star'd at the Pacific – and all his men
Look'd at each other with a wild surmise –
Silent, upon a peak in Darien. *Ibid.*

5 They sway'd about upon a rocking-horse,
And thought it Pegasus.
Sleep and Poetry, 186.

6 A thing of beauty is a joy for ever:
Its loveliness increases; it will never
Pass into nothingness; but still will keep
A bower quiet for us, and a sleep
Full of sweet dreams, and health, and quiet breathing. *Endymion, I. I.*

7 Love in a hut, with water and a crust,
Is – Love, forgive us! – cinders, ashes, dust;
Love in a palace is perhaps at last
More grievous torment than a hermit's fast. *Lamia, ii. I.*

8 Philosophy will clip an angel's wings.
Ibid, 234.

9 So the two brothers and their murder'd man
Rode past fair Florence. *Isabella, 27.*

10 St. Agnes' Eve – Ah, bitter chill it was!
The owl, for all his feathers, was a-cold.
The Eve of St. Agnes, I.

11 The silver, snarling trumpets 'gan to chide. *Ibid, 4.*

12 As though a rose should shut, and be a bud again. *Ibid, 27.*

13 A heap
Of candied apple, quince, and plum, and gourd;
With jellies soother than the creamy curd,
And lucent syrops, tinct with connamon;
Manna and dates, in argosy transferr'd
From Fez; and spiced dainties, every one,
From silken Samarcand to cedar'd Lebanon. *Ibid, 30.*

14 My heart aches, and a drowsy numbness pains
My sense, as though of hemlock I had drunk. *Ode to a Nightingale, I.*

15 O for a beaker full of the warm South,
Full of the true, the blushful Hippocrene,
With beaded bubbles winking at the brim,
And purple-stainèd mouth;
That I might drink, and leave the world unseen,
And with thee fade away into the forest dim. *Ibid, 2.*

16 Where youth grows pale, and spectre-thin, and dies. *Ibid, 3.*

17 Away! away! for I will fly to thee,
Not charioted by Bacchus and his pards,
But on the viewless wings of Poesy,
Though the dull brain perplexes and retards. *Ibid, 4.*

18 I cannot see what flowers are at my feet,
Nor what soft incense hangs upon the boughs. *Ibid, 5.*

19 Darkling I listen; and for many a time
I have been half in love with easeful Death. *Ibid, 6.*

20 Thou wast not born for death, immortal
Bird!
No hungry generations tread thee
down;
The voice I hear this passing night was
heard
In ancient days by emperor and clown:
Perhaps the self-same song that found a
path
Through the sad heart of Ruth, when,
sick for home,
She stood in tears amid the alien corn;
The same that oft-times hath
Charm'd magic casements, opening on
the foam
Of perilous seas, in faery lands forlorn.
Ibid, 7.

21 Thou still unravish'd bride of quietness,
Thou foster-child of silence and slow
time.   *Ode on a Grecian Urn, I.*

22 Heard melodies are sweet but those
unheart
Are sweeter; therefore, ye soft pipes,
play on;
Not to the sensual ear, but, more
endear'd,
Pipe to the spirit ditties of no tone.
Ibid, 2.

23 For ever wilt thou love, and she be fair!
Ibid.

24 'Beauty is truth, truth beauty,' – that is
all
Ye know on earth, and all ye need to
know.   *Ibid, 5.*

25 And there shall be for thee all soft
delight
That shadowy thought can win,
A bright torch, and a casement ope at
night,
To let the warm Love in!
Ode to Psyche, 64.

26 Ever let the fancy roam,
Pleasure never is at home.   *Fancy, 1.*

27 Where's the eye, however blue,
Doth not weary? Where's the face
One would meet in every place?
Where's the voice, however soft,
One would hear so very oft?   *Ibid, 72.*

28 Bards of Passion and of Mirth,
Ye have left your souls on earth!
Have ye souls in heaven too,
Double lived in regions new?
*Ode (written in a volume of Beaumont and
Fletcher), 1.*

29 Souls of poets dead and gone,
What Elysium have ye known,
Happy field or mossy cavern
Choicer than the Mermaid Tavern?
Lines on the Mermaid Tavern, 1.

30 Season of mists and mellow fruitfulness,
Close bosom-friend of the maturing
sun.   *To Autumn, 1.*

31 Sometimes whoever seeks abroad may
find
Thee sitting careless on a granary floor,
Thy hair soft-lifted by the winnowing
wind.   *Ibid, 2.*

32 Deep in the shady sadness of a vale
Far sunken from the healthy breath of
morn,
Far from the fiery noon, and eve's one
star,
Sat grey-hair's Saturn, quiet as a stone,
Still as the silence round about his lair;
Forest on forest hung about his head
Like cloud on cloud.   *Hyperion, I, 1.*

33 As when, upon a tranced summer night,
Those green-rob'd senators of mighty
woods,
Tall oaks, branch-charmed by the
earnest stars,
Dream, and so dream all night without a
stir.   *Ibid, 72.*

34 When I have fears that I may cease to be
Before my pen has glean'd my teeming
brain.   *Sonnet. When I have Fears.*

35 In a drear-nighted December,
Too happy, happy tree,
Thy branches ne'er remember
Their green felicity.
Stanzas. In a Drear-nighted December.

36 O what can ail thee, knight-at-arms,
Alone and palely loitering?
The sedge has wither'd from the lake,
And no birds sing.
La Belle Dame sans Merci, 1.
(Another version of line 1 is:–
Ah, what can ail thee, wretched wight.)

1 Bright star, would I were steadfast as
thou art –
Not in lone splendour hung aloft the
night
And watching, with eternal lids apart,
Like nature's patient, sleepless Eremite,
The moving waters at their priestlike
task
Of pure ablution round earth's human
shores. *Sonnet. Bright Star.*

2 The imagination of a boy is healthy, and
the mature imagination of a man is
healthy; but there is a space of life
between in which the soul is in a
ferment, the character undecided, the
way of life uncertain, the ambition
thick-sighted: thence proceeds
mawkishness. *Endymion, preface.*

3 O for a life of sensations rather than of
thoughts!
Letter to Benjamin Bailey, 22 Nov. 1817.

4 Poetry should surprise by a fine excess,
and not by singularity; it should strike
the reader as a wording of his own
highest thoughts, and appear almost a
remembrance.
Letter to John Taylor, 27 Feb. 1818.

5 Here lies one whose name was writ in
water. *Epitaph for himself.*

**KEBLE, JOHN, English cleric and
professor of poetry, 25 April,
1792–29 March, 1866**

6 We need not bid, for cloister'd cell,
Our neighbour and our work farewell.
The Christian Year. Morning.

7 The trivial round, the common task,
Will furnish all we ought to ask. *Ibid.*

8 Abide with me from morn till eve,
For without Thee I cannot live;
Abide with me when night is nigh,
For without Thee I dare not die.
Ibid, Evening.

9 The voice that breathed o'er Eden,
That earliest wedding day.
Holy Matrimony.

**KEMBLE, JOHN PHILIP, English
actor, 1 Feb. 1757–26 Feb. 1823**

10 I give thee all – I can no more,
Tho' poor the offering be;
My heart and lute are all the store
That I can bring to thee.
Lodoiska, III. i.

11 Perhaps it was right to dissemble your
love,
But – Why did you kick me downstairs?
An Expostulation.

**KEMPIS, THOMAS À, Augustinian
monk, 1379?–1471?**

12 Sic transit gloria mundi. – So passes
away the glory of the world.
*De Imitatione Christi – On the Imitation of
Christ, iii. 6.*

**KEN or KENN, THOMAS, English
bishop, July, 1637–19 March, 1711**

13 Awake my soul, and with the sun
The daily stage of duty run.
Morning hymn.

14 Praise God, from whom all blessings
flow. *Morning and Evening Hymn.*

**KENNEDY, JOHN
FITZGERALD, US President, 29
May 1917–22 Nov. 1963**

15 Let us never negotiate out of fear. But
let us never fear to negotiate.
Inaugural Address, 20 Jan. 1961.

**KERR, ORPHEUS C., see Newell,
Robert Henry**

**KETHE, WILLIAM, Protestant
cleric, died 1608?**

16 All people that on earth do dwell,
Sing to the Lord with cheerful voice.
Psalm 100.

**KEY, FRANCIS SCOTT, US
lawyer, 1 Aug. 1779–11 Jan. 1843**

17 Oh, say, can you see, by the dawn's
early light,

What so proudly we hailed at the
twilight's last gleaming?
Whose broad stripes and bright stars,
through the perilous fight,
O'er the ramparts we watched, were so
gallantly streaming;
And the rocket's red glare, the bombs
bursting in air,
Gave proof through the night that our
flag was still there;
Oh, say, does that star-spangled banner
yet wave
O'er the land of the free and the home of
the brave? *The Star-Spangled Banner.*

**KILMER, JOYCE, US poet, 6 Dec.
1886–30 July, 1918**

18 I think that I shall never see
A poem lovely as a tree. *Trees.*

19 Poems are made by fools like me,
But only God can make a tree. *Ibid.*

**KING, BENJAMIN FRANKLIN,
US humorist, 1857–1894**

20 Nothing to do but work,
Nothing to eat but food,
Nothing to wear but clothes
To keep one from going nude.
The Pessimist.

**KING, STODDARD, US author, 19
Aug. 1889–13 June, 1933**

21 There's a long, long trail a-winding
Into the land of my dreams.
The Long Long Trail.

**KINGSLEY, CHARLES, English
cleric and author, 12 June, 1819–23
Jan. 1875**

22 O Mary, go and call the cattle home
Across the sands of Dee.
The Sands of Dee.

23 Three fishers went sailing away to the
west. *The Three Fishers.*

24 For men must work, and women must
weep,
And the sooner it's over, the sooner to
sleep. *Ibid.*

25 Airly Beacon, Airly Beacon;
Oh the pleasant sight to see
Shires and towns from Airly Beacon,
While my love climbed up to me!
Airly Beacon.

26 Be good, sweet maid, and let who will
be clever;
Do noble things, not dream them, all
day long:
And so make life, death, and that vast
for-ever
One grand, sweet song. *A Farewell.*
(Another version is:–
Be good, sweet maid, and let who can
be clever;
Do lovely things, not dream them, all
day long.)

27 Oh! that we two were maying.
The Saint's Tragedy, II. ix.

28 Young blood must have its course, lad,
And every dog his day.
The Water Babies. Young and Old.

29 God grant you find one face there,
You loved when all was young. *Ibid.*

30 I once had a sweet little doll, dears,
The prettiest doll in the world;
Her cheeks were so red and so white,
dears,
And her hair was so charmingly curled.
Ibid, My Little Doll.

31 Yet for old sakes' sake she is still, dears,
The prettiest doll in the world. *Ibid.*

32 Do the work that's nearest,
Though it's dull at whiles,
Helping, when you meet them,
Lame dogs over stiles. *The Invitation.*

**KIPLING, RUDYARD, English
author, 30 Dec. 1865–18 Jan. 1936**

33 Don't dance or ride with General Bangs
– a most immoral man.
A Code of Morals.

34 For sixty takes to seventeen,
Nineteen to forty-nine. *My rival.*

35 And a woman is only a woman, but a
good Cigar is a Smoke. *The Betrothed.*

1 Something lost behind the Ranges. Lost and waiting for you. Go! *The Explorer.*

2 Who hath desired the Sea? – the sight of salt water unbounded –
The heave and the halt and the hurl and the crash of the comber wind-hounded? *The Sea and the Hills.*

3 So and no otherwise – so and no otherwise – hillmen desire their Hills. *Ibid.*

4 There's never a law of God or man runs north of Fifty-Three. *The Rhyme of the Three Sealers.*

5 Predestination in the stride o' yon connectin'-rod. *McAndrew's Hymn.*

6 For you muddled with books and pictures, an' china an' etchin's an' fans,
And your rooms at college was beastly – more like a whore's than a man's. *The 'Mary Gloster.'*

7 Stiff-necked Glasgow beggar! I've heard he's prayed for my soul,
But he couldn't lie if you paid him, and he'd starve before he stole. *Ibid.*

8 The Liner she's a lady, an' she never looks nor 'eeds –
The Man-o'-War's 'er 'usband, an' 'e gives 'er all she needs. *The Liner she's a Lady.*

9 You have heard the beat of the off-shore wind,
And the thresh of the deep-sea rain;
You have heard the song – how long? how long?
Pull out on the trail again! *The Long Trail.*

10 Pull out, pull out, on the Long Trail – the trail that is always new! *Ibid.*

11 Fair is our lot – O goodly is our heritage! *A Song of the English.*

12 We have fed our sea for a thousand years
And she calls us, still unfed,
Though there's never a wave of all her waves
But marks our English dead. *The Song of the Dead, ii.*

13 If blood be the price of admiralty,
Lord God, we ha' paid in full! *Ibid.*

14 Daughter am I in my mother's house,
But mistress in my own. *Our Lady of the Snows.*

15 Winds of the World, give answer! They are whimpering to and fro –
And what should they know of England who only England know? *The English Flag.*

16 Never was isle so little, never was sea so lone,
But over the scud and the palm-trees an English flag has flown. *Ibid.*

17 And those that were good shall be happy: they shall sit in a golden chair;
They shall splash at a ten-league canvas with brushes of comet's hair. *When Earth's Last Picture is painted.*

18 And each, in his separate star,
Shall draw the Thing as he sees It for the God of Things as
They are! *Ibid.*

19 Oh, East is East, and West is West, and never the twain shall meet,
Till Earth and Sky stand presently at God's great Judgment Seat. *The Ballad of East and West.*

20 He trod the ling like a buck in spring, and he looked like a lance in rest. *Ibid.*

21 Then ye returned to your trinkets; then ye contented your souls
With the flannelled fools at the wicket or the muddied oafs at the goals. *The Islanders.*

22 Take up the White Man's Burden. *The White Man's Burden.*

23 Your new-caught, sullen peoples,
Half devil and half child. *Ibid.*

24 God of our fathers, known of old,
Lord of our far-flung battle-line. *Recessional.*

25 The tumult and the shouting dies;
The Captains and the Kings depart;

Still stands Thine ancient sacrifice,
An humble and a contrite heart.
Lord God of Hosts, be with us yet,
Lest we forget – lest we forget! *Ibid.*

26 Such boastings as the Gentiles use
Or lesser breeds without the Law. *Ibid.*

27 In a ram-you-damn-you liner with a
brace of bucking screws.
The Three-Decker.

28 Till the Devil whispered behind the
leaves, 'It's pretty but is it art?'
The Conundrum of the Workshops.

29 There are nine and sixty ways of
constructing tribal lays,
And every single one of them is right.
In the Neolithic Age.

30 When 'Omer smote 'is bloomin' lyre,
He'd 'eard men sing by land an' sea;
An' what he thought 'e might require,
'E went an' took – the same as me!
When 'Omer smote 'is Bloomin' Lyre.

31 For the sin ye do by two and two ye
must pay for one by one. *Tomlinson.*

32 The female of the species is more deadly
than the male.
The Female of the Species.

33   And all unseen
Romance brought up the nine-fifteen.
The King.

34 They have cast their burden upon the
Lord, and – the Lord
He lays it on Martha's Sons!
The Sons of Martha.

35 Then it's Tommy this, an' Tommy that,
an' 'Tommy, 'ow's yer soul?'
But it's 'Thin red line of 'eroes' when
the drums begin to roll. *Tommy.*

36 We aren't no thin red 'eroes, nor we
aren't no blackguards too,
But single men in barricks, most
remarkable like you. *Ibid.*

37 So 'ere's *to* you, Fuzzy-Wuzzy, at your
'ome in the Soudan;

You're a pore benighted 'eathen but a
first-class fightin' man.
Fuzzy-Wuzzy.

38 'E's all 'ot sand an' ginger when alive,
An' 'e's generally shammin' when 'e's
dead. *Ibid.*

39 The uniform 'e wore
Was nothin' much before,
An' rather less than 'arf o' that be'ind.
Gunga Din.

40 Though I've belted you and flayed you,
By the livin' Gawd that made you,
You're a better man than I am, Gunga
Din. *Ibid.*

41 When you're wounded and left on
Afghanistan's plains,
And the women come out to cut up
what remains,
Jest roll to your rifle and blow out your
brains
An' go to your Gawd like a soldier.
The Young British Soldier.

42 On the road to Mandalay,
Where the flyin'-fishes play,
An' the dawn comes up like thunder
outer China 'crost the Bay! *Mandalay.*

43 But that's all shove be'hind me – long
ago an' fur away,
An' there ain't no buses runnin' from the
Bank to Mandalay. *Ibid.*

44 Ship me somewheres east of Suez,
where the best is like the worst,
Where there aren't no Ten
Commandments an' a man can raise a
thirst. *Ibid.*

45 Back to the Army again, sergeant,
Back to the Army again.
Back to the Army again.

46 But to stand an' be still to the *Birkenhead*
drill is a damn' tough bullet to chew,
An' they done it, the Jollies – 'Er
Majesty's Jollies – soldier an' sailor too!
Soldier an' Sailor too.

47 An' I learned about women from 'er!
The Ladies.

1 When you get to a man in the case,
They're like as a row of pins –
For the Colonel's Lady an' Judy
O'Grady
Are sisters under their skins.   *Ibid.*

2 For to admire an' for to see,
For to be'old this world so wide –
It never done no good to me,
But I can't drop it if I tried!
                              For to admire.

3 Duke's son – cook's son – son of a
hundred kings –
(Fifty thousand horse and foot going to
Table Bay!)
Each of 'em doing his country's work
(and who's to look after their things?)
Pass the hat for your credit's sake,
and pay – pay – pay!
                    The Absent-Minded Beggar.

4 Boots – boots – boots – boots – movin'
up and down again!   *Boots.*

5 The bachelor may risk 'is 'ide
To 'elp you when you're downed;
But the married man will wait beside
Till the ambulance comes round.
                         The Married Man.

6 Of all the trees that grow so fair,
Old England to adorn,
Greater are none beneath the Sun
Than Oak, and Ash, and Thorn.
                            A Tree Song.

7 My new-cut ashlar takes the light
Where crimson-blank the windows
flare.   *My New-cut Ashlar.*

8 Mithras, God of the Morning, our
trumpets waken the Wall!
                         A Song to Mithras.

9 Nine hundred and ninety-nine can't bide
The shame or mocking or laughter,
But the Thousandth Man will stand by
your side
To the gallows-foot – and after!
                         The Thousandth Man.

10 Down to Gehenna or up to the Throne
He travels the fastest who travels alone.
                              The Winners.

11 In telegraphic sentences, half nodded to
their friends,
They hint a matter's inwardness – and
there the matter ends.
And while the Celt is talking from
Valencia to Kirkwall,
The English – ah, the English! – don't
say anything at all.   *The Puzzler.*

12 And the end of the fight is a tombstone
white with the name of the late
deceased,
And the epitaph drear: 'A fool lies here
who tried to hustle the East.'
              Chapter Headings. The Naulahka.

13 If you can keep your head when all
about you
Are losing theirs and blaming it on you.
                                   If —.

14 If you can meet with Triumph and
Disaster
And treat those two impostors just the
same.   *Ibid.*

15 If you can talk with crowds and keep
your virtue,
Or walk with Kings – nor lose the
common touch.   *Ibid.*

16 If you can fill the unforgiving minute
With sixty seconds' worth of distance
run,
Yours is the Earth and everything that's
in it,
And – which is more – you'll be a Man,
my son!   *Ibid.*

17 Brother and Sisters, I bid you beware
Of giving your heart to a dog to tear.
                         The Power of the Dog.

18 We get the hump –
Cameelious hump –
The hump that is black and blue!
              *Just So Verses. How the Camel
                              got his Hump.*

19 The cure for this ill is not to sit still,
Or frowst with a book by the fire;
But to take a large hoe and a shovel also,
And dig till you gently perspire.   *Ibid.*

20 And I'd like to roll to Rio
Some day before I'm old.
          Ibid. The Beginning of the Armadilloes.

21 We must go back with Policeman Day –
Back from the City of Sleep.
The City of Sleep.

22 But you the unhoodwinked wave shall
test – the immediate gulf condemn –
Except ye owe the Fates a jest, be slow
to jest with them. *Poseidon's Law.*

23 Splendaciously mendacious rolled the
Brass-bound Man ashore. *Ibid.*

24 Watch the wall, my darling, while the
Gentlemen go by! *A Smuggler's Song.*

25 And when your back stops aching and
your hands begin to harden,
You will find yourself a partner in the
Glory of the Garden.
The Glory of the Garden.

26 Take my word for it, the silliest woman
can manage a clever man; but it needs a
very clever woman to manage a fool.
*Plain Tales from the Hills. Three and – an
Extra.*

27 But that is another story. *Ibid.*

28 Never praise a sister to a sister, in the
hope of your compliments reaching the
proper ears. *Ibid. False Dawn.*

29 Nice but nubbly.
*Just-So Stories. How the Whale got his
Throat.*

30 A man of infinite-resource-and-
sagacity. *Ibid.*

31 An Elephant's Child – who was full of
'satiable curtiosity.
Ibid, The Elephant's Child.

32 This is too butch for be. *Ibid.*

33 'Tisn't beauty, so to speak, nor good
talk necessarily. It's just IT.
Traffics and Discoveries. Mrs. Bathurst.

**KNOX, JOHN, Scottish reformer,
1505–24 Nov. 1572**

34 The First Blast of the Trumpet Against
the Monstrous Regiment of Women.
Title of pamphlet, 1558.

**KNOX, RONALD ARBUTHNOT,
English cleric, 17 Feb. 1888–24 Aug.
1957**

35 There once was a man who said, 'God
Must think it exceedingly odd
If he finds that this tree
Continues to be
When there's no one about in the Quad.'
Limerick.
(The following reply was written by an
unknown author:–
Dear Sir,
Your astonishment's odd:
I am always about in the Quad.
And that's why the tree
Will continue to be,
Since observed by
Yours faithfully,
God.)

**KNOX, WILLIAM, Scottish poet,
17 Aug. 1789–12 Nov. 1825**

36 Oh why should the spirit of mortal be
proud! *Mortality, I.*

**LA COSTE, MARIE RAVENEL
DE, US poetess, 1849–1936**

37 Tenderly bury the fair young dead,
Pausing to drop on his grave a tear;
Carve on the wooden slab at his head,
'Somebody's darling slumbers here.'
Somebody's Darling.

**LAMB, CHARLES, English
essayist, 10 Feb. 1775–27 Dec. 1834**

38 The human species, according to the
best theory I can form of it, is composed
of two distinct races, *the men who borrow,*
and *the men who lend.*
Essays of Elia. The Two Races of Men.

39 A clear fire, a clean hearth, and the
rigour of the game.
Ibid, Mrs. Battle's Opinions on Whist.

40 Coleridge holds that man cannot have a
pure mind who refuses apple-
dumplings. I am not certain but he is
right. *Ibid, Grace before Meat.*

41 'Presents,' I often say, 'endear Absents.'
Ibid, A Dissertation upon Roast Pig.

1 I can read anything which I call a *book.*
There are things in that shape which I
cannot allow for such. In this catalogue
of *books which are no books – biblia a-biblia*
– I reckon Court Calendars,
Directories, Pocket Books, Draught
Boards bound and lettered at the back,
Scientific Treatises, Almanacks; Statues
at Large; the works of Hume, Gibbon,
Robertson, Beattie, Soame Jenyns, and
generally, all those volumes which 'no
gentleman's library should be without':
the Histories of Flavius Josephus (that
learned Jew), and Paley's Moral
Philosophy.
*Last Essays of Elia. Detached Thoughts on
Books and Reading.*

2 Things in books' clothing. *Ibid.*

3 It (a pun) is a pistol let off at the ear; not
a feather to tickle the intellect. *Ibid,*
Popular Fallacies. That the Worst
Puns are the Best.

4 An Oxford scholar, meeting a porter
who was carrying a hare through the
streets, accosts him with this
extraordinary question, 'Prithee,
friend, is that thy own hare, or a wig?'
Ibid.

5 An archangel a little damaged.
(Coleridge.) *Letter to Wordsworth, 26*
April, 1816.

6 The greatest pleasure I know, is to do a
good action by stealth and to have it
found out by accident.
Table Talk by the late Elia.
The Athenaeum, 4 Jan. 1834.

7 I have had playmates, I have had
companions,
In my days of childhood, in my joyful
schooldays
All, all are gone, the old familiar faces.
The Old Familiar Faces.

8 Who first invented work, and bound the
free
And holyday-rejoicing spirit down
To the ever-haunting importunity
Of business in the green fields, and the
town–

To plough, loom, anvil, spade – and oh!
most sad,
To that dry drudgery at the desk's dead
wood? *Work.*

9 Thou straggler into loving arms,
Young-climber up of knees,
When I forget thy thousand ways,
Then life and all shall cease.
Parental Recollections.

**LAMB, WILLIAM, see
MELBOURNE, VISCOUNT**

**LAMPTON, WILLIAM JAMES,
English journalist, 1859–30 May,
1917**

10 Same old slippers,
Same old rice,
Same old glimpse of
Paradise. *June Weddings.*

**LANDON, LETITIA ELIZABETH
(MRS. MACLEAN), English
poetess, 14 Aug. 1802–15 Oct. 1838**

11 As beautiful as woman's blush, –
As evanescent too. *Apple Blossoms.*

**LANDOR, WALTER SAVAGE,
English author, 30 Jan. 1775–17
Sept. 1864**

12 Ah, what avails the sceptred race!
Ah, what the form divine. *Rose Aylmer.*

13 Rose Aylmer, whom these wakeful eyes
May weep, but never see,
A night of memories and of sighs
I consecrate to thee. *Ibid.*

14 Browning! Since Chaucer was alive and
hale,
No man hath walk'd along our roads
with step
So active, so inquiring eye, or tongue
So varied in discourse.
To Robert Browning.

15 I strove with one, for none was worth
my strife;
Nature I loved; and next to Nature, Art;

I warm'd both hands before the fire of
life;
It sinks, and I am ready to depart.
I strove with None.

16 Stand close around, ye Stygian set,
With Dirce in one boat convey'd!
Or Charon, seeing, may forget
That he is old, and she a shade. *Dirce.*

17 Proud word you never spoke, but you
will speak
Four not exempt from pride some future
day.
Resting on one white hand a warm wet
cheek
Over my open volume you will say,
'This man loved *me*!' then rise and trip
away. *Proud Word you never spoke.*

18 George the First was always reckoned
Vile, but viler George the Second;
And what mortal ever heard
Any good of George the Third?
When from earth the Fourth descended
God be praised, the Georges ended!
Epigram.

19 I shall dine late; but the dining-room
will be well lighted, the guests few and
select.
*Imaginary Conversations. Archdeacon Hare
and Walter Landor.*

**LANE, GOERGE MARTIN, US
professor of Latin, 24 Dec. 1823–30
June, 1897**

20 The waiter roars it through the hall:
'We don't give bread with one fish-ball!'
One Fish-ball.

**LANG, ANDREW, Scottish author,
31 March 1844–20 July, 1912**

21 St. Andrews by the Northern Sea,
A haunted town it is to me.
Almae Matres.

22 There's a joy without canker or cark,
There's a pleasure eternally new,
'Tis to gloat on the glaze and the mark
Of china that's ancient and blue.
Ballade of Blue China.

23 The surge and thunder of the Odyssey.
The Odyssey.

24 *I* am the batsman and the bat,
I am the bowler and the ball,
The umpire, the pavilion cat,
The roller, pitch, and stumps, and all.
Brahma.
(Parody of Emerson, *95:27*)

**LANGHORNE, JOHN, English
cleric and poet, March, 1735–1
April, 1779**

25 Cold on Canadian hills or Minden's
plain,
Perhaps that parent mourn'd her soldier
slain;
Bent o'er her babe, her eye dissolv'd in
dew,
The big drops mingling with the milk
he drew,
Gave the sad presage of his future years,
The child of misery, baptis'd in tears.
The Country Justice, I. 161.

**LANGLAND, WILLIAM, English
priest and poet, 1332?–1400?**

26 In a somer seson whan soft was the
sonne. *The Vision of William concerning
Piers the Plowman, B Text, prologue, I.*

**LANIER, SIDNEY, US poet, 3 Feb.
1842–7 Sept. 1881**

27 Into the woods my Master went,
Clean forspent, forspent.
Into the woods my Master came,
Forspent with love and shame.
But the olives they were not blind to
Him;
The little grey leaves were kind to Him;
The thorn-tree had a mind to Him
When into the woods He came.
A Ballad of Trees and the Master.

**LANIGAN, GEORGE THOMAS,
US journalist, 10 Dec. 1845–5 Feb.
1886**

28 For the Ahkoond I mourn,
Who wouldn't?

He strove to disregard the message stern,
But he Ahkoodn't.
Threnody for the Ahkoond of Swat.

LA ROCHEFOUCAULD-LIANCOURT, FRANÇOIS ALEXANDRE FRÉDÉRIC, DUC DE, 11 Jan. 1747–24 March, 1827

1 Non, Sire, c'est une révolution. – No, Sire, it is a revolution.
When Louis XVI asked 'Is it a revolt?' on getting news of the fall of the Bastille, 1789.

LATIMER, HUGH, Bishop of Worcester, 1485?–16 Oct. 1555

2 Be of good comfort, Master Ridley, and play the man; we shall this day light such a candle by God's grace in England, as I trust shall never be put out.
As he and Ridley were being burned at Oxford for heresy.

LAUDER, SIR HARRY, Scottish comedian, 4 Aug. 1870–26 Feb. 1950

3 I love a lassie.　　　　　*Song.*

4 Roamin' in the gloamin'.　　*Song.*

5 If you can say'It's a braw bricht moonlicht nicht'
Y're a' richt, ye ken.
Just a Wee Deoch-an-doris.

LAWRENCE, DAVID HERBERT, English author, 11 Sept. 1885–2 March, 1930

6 I never saw a wild thing
Sorry for itself.　　　　*Self-Pity.*

LAWRENCE, THOMAS EDWARD (LAWRENCE OF ARABIA), English soldier, 15 Aug. 1888–19 May, 1935

7 I loved you, so I drew these tides of men into my hands and wrote my will across the sky in stars.
The Seven Pillars of Wisdom, dedication.

LAZARUS, EMMA, US poetess, 22 July, 1849–19 Nov. 1887

8 Give me your tired, your poor,
Your huddled masses yearning to breathe free,
The wretched refuse of your teeming shore,
Send these, the homeless, tempest-tossed, to me:
I lift my lamp beside the golden door.
The New Colossus.
(Lines inscribed on the Statue of Liberty.)

LEACOCK, STEPHEN BUTLER, Anglo-Canadian economist and humorist, 30 Dec. 1869–28 March, 1944

9 Lord Ronald said nothing; he flung himself from the room, flung himself upon his horse, and rode madly off in all directions.
Nonsense Novels. Gertrude the Governess.

10 Then he too Ajax on the one hand leaped (or possibly jumped) into the fight wearing on the other hand yes certainly a steel corslet (or possibly a bronze under-tunic) and on his head of course yes without doubt he had a helmet with a tossing plume taken from the mane (or perhaps extracted from the tail) of some horse which once fed along the banks of the Scamander (and it sees the herd and raises its head and paws the ground).
Behind and Beyond. Homer and Humbug.
(Parody of Homer.)

11 The up-to-date clean-shaven snoopopathic man. . . . How one would enjoy seeing a man – a real one with Nevada whiskers and long boots – land him one solid kick from behind.
Further Foolishness. The Snoopopaths.

12 The salesman should select from his wardrobe (or from his straw valise) a suit of plain, severe design, attractive and yet simple, good and yet bad, long and at the same time short, in other words, something that is expensive but cheap.
The Garden of Folly. The Perfect Salesman.

LEAR, EDWARD, English author and artist, 12 May, 1812–29 Jan. 1888

13 'How pleasant to know Mr. Lear!'
Who has written such volumes of stuff!
Some think him ill-tempered and queer,
But a few think him pleasant enough.
Nonsense Songs, preface.

14 There was an old man with a beard,
Who said, 'It is just as I feared!
Two Owls and a Hen
Four Larks and a Wren
Have all built their nests in my beard.'
Book of Nonsense.

15 The Owl and the Pussy-Cat went to sea
In a beautiful pea-green boat,
They took some honey, and plenty of money,
Wrapped up in a five-pound note.
The Owl and the Pussy-Cat.

16 Far and few, far and few,
Are the lands where the Jumblies live;
Their heads are green, and their hands are blue,
And they went to sea in a sieve.
The Jumblies.
(Also occurs in *The Dong with a Luminous Nose*.)

17 Ploffskin, Pluffskin, Pelican jee,
We think no Birds so happy as we!
Plumpskin, Ploshkin, Pelican jill,
We think so then, and we thought so still. *The Pelican Chorus.*

18 On the Coast of Coromandel
Where the early pumpkins blow,
In the middle of the woods,
Lived the Yonghy-Bonghy-Bò.
Two old chairs and half a candle, –
One old jug without a handle, –
These were all his worldly goods.
The Courtship of the Yonghy-Bonghy-Bò.

19 He has gone to fish, for his Aunt Jobiska's
Runcible cat with crimson whiskers.
The Pobble who has no Toes.

20 And she said, – 'It's a fact the whole world knows.

That Pobbles are happier without their toes.' *Ibid.*

21 Who, or why, or which, or *what*, is the Akond of SWAT? *The Akond of Swat.*

LEASE, MARY ELIZABETH, US lecturer, 11 Sept. 1853–29 Oct. 1933

22 Kansas had better stop raising corn and begin raising hell. *Attributed.*

LEE, HENRY, US soldier, 29 Jan. 1756–25 March, 1818

23 First in war, first in peace, and first in the hearts of his countrymen.
Resolution on Washington, House of Representatives, Dec. 1799.

LEE, NATHANIEL, English dramatist, born 1653?–buried 6 May, 1692

24 Then he will talk – good gods, how he will talk!
The Rival Queens or the Death of Alexander the Great, I. iii.

25 When Greeks joined Greeks, then was the tug of war! *Ibid, IV. ii.*

LE GALLIENNE, RICHARD, English poet, 20 Jan. 1866–14 Sept. 1947

26 She's somewhere in the sunlight strong,
Her tears are in the falling rain,
She calls me in the wind's soft song,
And with the flowers she comes again.
Song.

27 What of the darkness? Is it very fair?
What of the Darkness.

LEIGH, HENRY SAMBROOKE, English author, 29 March, 1837–16 June, 1883

28 In form and feature, face and limb,
I grew so like my brother
That folks got taking me for him,
And each for one another. *The Twins.*

29 And when I died – the neighbours came
And buried brother John! *Ibid.*

1 I know where little girls are sent
For telling taradiddles.   *Only Seven.*

LELAND, CHARLES GODFREY, US author, 15 Aug. 1824–20 March, 1903

2 Hans Breitmann gife a barty –
Where ish dat barty now?
Hans Breitmann's Party.

3 All goned afay mit de Lager Beer –
Afay in de Ewigkeit!   *Ibid.*

LENIN (VLADIMIR ILITCH ULIANOV), Russian statesman, 22 April, 1870–21 Jan. 1924

4 It is true that liberty is precious – so precious that it must be rationed.
Attributed.

L'ESTRANGE, SIR ROGER, English pamphleteer, 17 Dec. 1616–11 Dec. 1704

5 Though this may be play to you, 'tis death to us.
Fables from Several Authors, 398.

LEWIS, DAVID, Welsh poet, born 1683?–buried 8 April, 1760

6 And when with envy Time transported
Shall think to rob us of our joys,
You'll in your girls again be courted,
And I'll go wooing in my boys.
Song to Winfreda.
(Authorship uncertain. Wrongly attributed to J. G. Cooper.)

LINCOLN, ABRAHAM, US President, 12 Feb, 1809–15 April, 1865

7 In giving freedom to the slave we assure freedom to the free, – honourable alike in what we give and what we preserve.
Annual Message to Congress, 1 Dec. 1862.

8 That this nation, under God, shall have a new birth of freedom, and that government of the people, by the people, for the people, shall not perish from the earth.
Address, Gettysburg, 19 Nov. 1863.

9 I claim not to have controlled events, but confess plainly that events have controlled me.
Letter to A. G. Hodges, 4 Apr. 1864.

10 I have not permitted myself, gentlemen, to conclude that I am best man in the country; but I am reminded in this connection of a story of an old Dutch farmer, who remarked to a companion once that it was not best to swap horses when crossing a stream.
Reply to National Union League, 9 June, 1864.

11 With malice towards none; with charity for all; with firmness in the right, as God gives us to see the right, let us strive on to finish the work we are in; to bind up the nation's wounds; to care for him who shall have borne the battle, and for his widow and his orphan – to do all which may achieve and cherish a just and lasting peace among ourselves and with all nations.
Second Inaugural Address, 4 March, 1865.

12 The Lord prefers common-looking people. That is the reason He makes so many of them.
J. Morgan, Our Presidents, vi.

13 People who like this sort of thing will find this the sort of thing they like.
Criticism of an unreadably sentimental book.

LINDSAY, NICHOLAS VACHEL, US poet, 10 Nov. 1879–5 Dec. 1931

14 The banjos rattled, and the tambourines
Jing-jing-jingled in the hands of Queens!
General Booth enters Heaven.

15 Then I saw the Congo, creeping
through the black,
Cutting through the jungle with a
golden track.   *The Congo, I.*

LINLEY, GEORGE, English composer, 1798–10 Sept. 1865

16 Ever of theee I'm fondly dreaming.
Ever of Thee.

17 Tho' lost to sight, to mem'ry dear
Thou ever wilt remain.
(The first line is older and of unknown
origin.) *Song.*

LIVY (TITUS LIVIUS), Roman historian, 59 BC–AD 17

18 Vae victis. – Woe to the vanquished.
History of Rome, V. xlviii.

LLOYD GEORGE, DAVID LLOYD GEORGE, 1ST EARL, English Prime Minister, 17 Jan. 1863–26 March, 1945.

19 What is our task? To make Britain a fit
country for heroes to live in.
Speech, Wolverhampton, 24 Nov. 1918.

LOCKE, JOHN, English philosopher, 29 Aug. 1632–28 Oct. 1704

20 All men are liable to error; and most
men are, in many points, by passion or
interest, under temptation to it.
*Essay on the Human Understanding,
XX. 17.*

LOCKER-LAMPSON, FREDERICK, English poet, 29 May, 1821–30 May, 1895

21 And many are afraid of God –
And more of Mrs. Grundy.
The Jester's Plea.

LODGE, THOMAS, English author, 1558?–1625

22 Love in my bosom, like a bee,
Doth suck his sweet.
Love in my Bosom.

23 Heigh-ho, would she were mine!
Rosaline.

LONGFELLOW, HENRY WADSWORTH, US poet, 27 Feb. 1807–24 March, 1882

24 Tell me not, in mournful numbers,
Life is but an empty dream!
For the soul is dead that slumbers,
And things are not what they seem.

25 Life is real! Life is earnest!
And the grave is not its goal;
Dust thou art, to dust returnest,
Was not spoken of the soul.
A Psalm of Life.

26 Art is long, and Time is fleeting,
And our hearts, though stout and brave,
Still, like muffled drums, are beating
Funeral marches to the grave. *Ibid.*

27 Trust no future, howe'er pleasant!
Let the dead Past bury its dead!
Act, act in the living present!
Heart within, and God o'erhead! *Ibid.*

28 Lives of great men all remind us
We can make our lives sublime,
And, departing, leave behind us
Footprints on the sands of time. *Ibid.*

29 Let us, then, be up and doing,
With a heart for any fate;
Still achieving, still pursuing,
Learn to labour and to wait. *Ibid.*

30 There is a Reaper whose name is Death,
And, with his sickle keen,
He reaps the bearded grain at a breath,
And the flowers that grow between.
The Reaper and the Flowers.

31 It was the schooner Hesperus,
That sailed the wintry sea;
And the skipper had taken his little
daughter,
To bear him company.
The Wreck of the Hesperus.

32 Blue were her eyes as the fairy-flax.
Ibid.

33 Under a spreading chestnut tree
The village smithy stands;
The smith, a mighty man is he,
With large and sinewy hands;
And the muscles of his brawny arms
Are strong as iron bands.
The Village Blacksmith.

34 His brow is wet with honest sweat,
He earns whate'er he can,
And looks the whole world in the face,
For he owes not any man. *Ibid.*

1 Something attempted, something done,
Has earned a night's repose.   *Ibid.*

2 Standing with reluctant feet,
Where the brook and river meet,
Womanhood and childhood fleet!
                    Maidenhood.

3 The shades of night were falling fast,
As through an Alpine village passed
A youth, who bore, 'mid snow and
ice, A banner with the strange device,
Excelsior!   *Excelsior*

4 Beside the ungather'd rice he lay,
His sickle in his hand. *The Slave's Dream.*

5 Between the dark and the daylight,
When the night is beginning to lower,
Comes a pause in the day's occupations,
That is known as the Children's Hour.
                    The Children's Hour.

6 And the night shall be filled with music,
And the cares that infest the day
Shall fold their tents like the Arabs,
And as silently steal away.
                    The Day is Done.

7 I shot an arrow in the air,
It fell to earth, I knew not where.
                    The Arrow and the Song.

8 And the song, from beginning to end,
I found again in the heart of a friend.
                                    Ibid.

9 Though the mills of God grind slowly,
    yet they grind exceeding small;
Though with patience He stands
    waiting, with exactness grinds He all.
                    Retribution.

10 This is the forest primeval.
                    Evangeline, prelude.

11 Silently one by one, in the infinite
    meadows of heaven
Blossomed the lovely stars, the forget-
me-nots of the angels.   *Ibid., I. iii.*

12 Build me straight, O worthy Master!
Staunch and strong, a goodly vessel,
That shall laugh at all disaster,
And with wave and whirlwind wrestle!
                    The Building of the Ship.

13 Thou too, sail on, O ship of State
Sail on, O union, strong and great!
Humanity with all its fears,
With all its hopes of future years,
Is hanging breathless on thy fate!   *Ibid.*

14 'Wouldst thou' – so the helmsman
    answered, –
'Learn the secret of the sea?
'Only those who brave its dangers
Comprehend its mystery!'
                    The Secret of the Sea.

15 As unto the bow the cord is,
So unto the man is woman,
Though she bends him, she obeys him,
Though she draws him, yet she follows,
Useless each without the other!
                    The Song of Hiawatha, X.

16 Archly the maiden smiled, and with
eyes overrunning with laughter,
Said, in a tremulous voice, 'Why don't
you speak for yourself, John?'
                    The Courtship of Miles Standish, III.

17 The heights by great men reached and
    kept
Were not attained by sudden flight,
But they, while their companions slept,
Were toiling upward in the night.
                    The Ladder of Saint Augustine.

18 A boy's will is the wind's will,
And the thoughts of youth are long,
long thoughts.   *My Lost Youth.*

19 A Lady with a Lamp shall stand
In the great history of the land,
A noble type of good,
Heroic womanhood.   *Santa Filomena.*

20 Ships that pass in the night, and speak
    each other in passing,
Only a signal shown and a distant voice
    in the darkness;
So on the ocean of life we pass and speak
    one another,
Only a look and a voice; then darkness
    again and a silence.
                    *Tales of a Wayside Inn, III. The
                    Theologian's Tale. Elizabeth, iv.*

21 There was a little girl
Who had a little curl

Right in the middle of her forehead;
And when she was good
She was very, very good,
But when she was bad she was horrid.
There was a Little Girl.

LOOS, ANITA (MRS. JOHN EMERSON), US author, 26 April, 1893–

22 Kissing your hand may make you feel very good but a diamond bracelet lasts forever.
Gentlemen prefer Blondes, caption to frontispiece.
(The passage, in chapter iv, has 'very very good' and 'a diamond and safire bracelet.')

LOUIS XIV, King of France, 16 Sept., 1638–1 Sept. 1715

23 L'État, c'est moi. – I am the State.
Attributed.

LOVELACE, RICHARD, 1618–1658

24 I could not love thee, Dear, so much
Loved I not honour more.
To Lucasta, on going to the Wars.

25 Stone walls do not a prison make,
Nor iron bars a cage;
Minds innocent and quiet take
That for an hermitage:
If I have freedom in my love
And in my soul am free,
Angels alone, that soar above,
Enjoy such liberty.
To Althea from Prison.

LOVELL, MARIA ANNE, English dramatist, 16 July, 1803–2 April, 1877

26 Two souls with but a single thought,
Two hearts that beat as one.
Ingomar the Barbarian, II.
(Translated from the German of Von Münch Bellinghausen.)

LOVEMAN, ROBERT, US author, 11 April, 1864–10 July, 1923

27 It is not raining rain to me,
It's raining violets.
April Rain.

LOVER, SAMUEL, Irish author, 24 Feb. 1797–6 July, 1868

28 Reproof on her lip, but a smile in her eye.
Rory O'More, I.

29 When once the itch of literature comes over a man, nothing can cure it but the scratching of a pen.
Handy Andy, xxxvi.

LOWELL, JAMES RUSSELL, US author, 22 Feb. 1819–12 Aug, 1891

30 Once to every man and nation comes the moment to decide,
In the strife of Truth with Falsehood, for the good or evil side.
The Present Crisis.

31 And what is so rare as a day in June?
Then, if ever, come perfect days;
Then Heaven tries the earth if it be in tune,
And over it softly her warm ear lays.
The Vision of Sir Launfal, I. prelude.

32 An' you've gut to git up airly
Ef you want to take in God.
The Biglow Papers, 1st series, i.

33 He's been true to *one* party, – an' thet is himself.
Ibid., iii. What Mr. Robinson Thinks.

34 I *don't* believe in princerple,
But oh I *du* in interest.
Ibid., vi. The Pious Editor's Creed.

35 I scent which pays the best, an' then
Go into it baldheaded.
Ibid.

36 God makes sech nights, all white and still,
Fur'z you can look or listen.
Ibid., 2nd series, The Courtin'.

37 All kin' o' smily round the lips
An' teary round the lashes.
Ibid.

38 There is no good in arguing with the inevitable. The only argument available with an east wind is to put on your overcoat.
Democracy and Addresses.

LOWRY, ROBERT, US minister, 12 March, 1826–25 Nov. 1899

1 Yes, we'll gather at the river,
The beautiful, the beautiful river,
Gather with the saints at the river
That flows from the throne of God.
Shall we gather at the River?

LUCAN (MARCUS ANNAEUS LUCANUS), Roman poet, AD 39–65

2 Victrix causa deis placuit, sed victa
Catoni.
– The victorious cause was pleasing to
the Gods, but the vanquished to Cato.
Pharsalia, 128.

3 Magni nominis umbra.
– The shadow of a mighty name.
Ibid., 135

LUCRETIUS (TITUS LUCRETIUS CARUS), Roman poet, 99?–55? BC

4 Suave, mari magno turbantibus aequora
ventis,
E terra magnum alterius spectare
laborem.
– It is pleasant, when the sea is high and
the winds are dashing the waves about,
to watch from the land the struggles of
another.
*De Rerum Natura – On the Nature of
Things, 11. 1.*

LUTHER, MARTIN, German reformer, 10 Nov. 1483–18 Feb. 1546

5 Wenn ich gewisst hätte, dass so viel
Teufel auf mich gezielet hätten, als
Ziegel auf den Dächern waren zu
Worms, wäre ich dennoch eingeritten. –
If I had known that as many devils
would set on me as there are tiles on the
roofs in Worms, still I would have gone
there.
On approaching Worms, April, 1521.

6 Hier stehe ich! Ich kann nicht anders,
Gotte helfe mir! Amen. – Here I stand. I
can do no otherwise, God help me!
Amen.
Speech at Diet of Worms, 18 April, 1521.

7 Esto peccator et pecca fortiter, sed
fortius fide et gaude in Christo. – Be a
sinner and sin stoutly, but more stoutly
trust and rejoice in Christ.
Letter to Melanchthon.

LYDGATE, JOHN, English poet, 1370?–1451?

8 Sithe off oure language he was the
lodesterre. (Chaucer.)
The Fall of Princes, prologue, 252

LYLY, JOHN, English author, born 1554?–buried 30 Nov. 1606

9 Cupid and my Campaspe play'd
At cards for kisses: Cupid paid.
Campaspe, III. v.

10 None but the lark so shrill and clear!
Now at heaven's gates she claps her
wings,
The morn not waking till she sings.
Ibid., V. i.

LYTE, HENRY FRANCIS, English hymn-writer, 1 June, 1793–20 Nov. 1847

11 Abide with me; fast falls the eventide;
The darkness deepens; Lord, with me
abide:
When other helpers fail, and comforts
flee,
Help of the helpless, O abide with me.

12 Swift to its close ebbs out life's little day;
Earth's joys grow dim, its glories pass
away;
Change and decay in all around I see:
O Thou Who changest not, abide with
me.
Abide with me.

LYTTELTON, GEORGE LYTTELTON, 1ST BARON, English politician, 17 Jan. 1709–22 Aug. 1773

13 Where none admire, 'tis useless to excel;
Where none are beaux, 'tis vain to be a
belle.
Soliloquy of a Beauty in the Country.

LYTTON, EDWARD GEORGE EARLE LYTTON BULWER-LYTTON, 1ST BARON, English author, 25 May, 1803–18 Jan. 1873

14 Beneath the rule of men entirely great,
The pen is mightier than the sword.
Richelieu, 11. ii.

15 In the lexicon of youth, which fate reserves
For a bright manhood, there is no such word
As – *fail*. *Ibid.*

16 The brilliant chief, irregularly great,
Frank, haughty, rash, – the Rupert of debate. *The New Timon, 1. 6.*

17 Revolutions are not made with rose-water. *The Parisians, V. vii.*

LYTTON, EDWARD ROBERT BULWER-LYTTON, 1ST EARL OF (OWEN MEREDITH), 8 Nov. 1831–24 Nov. 1891

18 Genius does what it must, and Talent does what it can.
Last Words of a Sensitive Second-Rate Poet.

MACAULAY, THOMAS BABINGTON MACAULAY, BARON, English author, 25 Oct. 1800–28 Dec. 1859

19 The dust and silence of the upper shelf.
Essays. Milton.

20 Out of his surname they have coined an epithet for a knave. And out of his Christian name a synonym for the Devil. *Ibid. Machiavelli.*

21 The gallery in which the reporters sit has become a fourth estate of the realm.
Ibid. Hallam's Constitutional History.

22 We take this to be, on the whole, the worst similitude in the world. In the first place, no stream meanders, or can possibly meander, level with its fount. In the next place, if streams did meander level with their founts, no two motions can be less like each other than that of

meandering level and that of mounting upwards. (Referring to *177:18 infra*.)
Ibid. Mr. Robert Montgomery's Poems.

23 We know of no spectacle so ridiculous as the British public in one of its periodical fits of morality.
Ibid. Moore's Life of Lord Byron.

24 With the dead there is no rivalry. In the dead there is no change. Plato is never sullen. Cervantes is never petulant. Demosthenes never comes unseasonably. Dante never stays too long. No difference of political opinion can alienate Cicero. No heresy can excite the horror of Bossuet.
Ibid. Lord Bacon.

25 Every schoolboy knows who imprisoned Montezuma, and who strangled Atahualpa. *Ibid. Lord Clive.*

26 She (the Roman Catholic Church) may still exist in undiminished vigour when some traveller from New Zealand shall, in the midst of a vast solitude, take his stand on a broken arch of London Bridge to sketch the ruins of St. Paul's.
Ibid. Ranke's History of the Popes.

27 The Chief Justice was rich, quiet, and infamous. *Ibid. Warren Hastings.*

28 The great Proconsul. *Ibid.*

29 In order that he might rob a neighbour whom he had promised to defend, black men fought on the coast of Coromandel, and red men scalped each other by the Great Lakes of North America. *Ibid. Frederic the Great.*

30 He was a rake among scholars, and a scholar among rakes. (Richard Steele.)
Ibid. Aikin's Life of Addison.

31 The Puritan hated bear-baiting, not because it gave pain to the bear, but because it gave pleasure to the spectators. *History of England, I. ii.*

32 There were gentlemen and there were seamen in the navy of Charles the Second. But the seamen were not

gentlemen; and the gentlemen were not seamen. *Ibid., iii.*

1 Lars Porsena of Clusium
By the Nine Gods he swore
That the great house of Tarquin
Should suffer wrong no more.
Lays of Ancient Rome. Horatius, 1.

2 Then out spake brave Horatius,
The Captain of the Gate:
'To every man upon this earth
Death cometh soon or late.
And how can a man die better
Than facing fearful odds,
For the ashes of his fathers,
And the temples of his gods?' *Ib., 27.*

3 Then none was for a party;
Then all were for the State;
Then the great man helped the poor,
And the poor man loved the great:
Then lands were fairly portioned;
Then spoils were fairly sold;
The Romans were like brothers
In the brave days of old. *Ib., 32.*

4 Was none who would be foremost
To lead such dire attack:
For those behind cried 'Forward!'
And those before cried 'Back!' *Ibid., 50.*

5 O Tiber! father Tiber!
To whom the Romans pray,
A Roman's life, a Roman's arms,
Take thou in charge this day! *Ibid., 58.*

6 And even the ranks of Tuscany
Could scarce forbear to cheer. *Ibid., 60.*

7 How well Horatius kept the bridge
In the brave days of old. *Ibid., 70.*

8 In lordly Lacedaemon,
The city of two kings.
Ibid. The Battle of Lake Regillus, 2.

9 These be the great Twin Brethren
To whom the Dorians pray. *Ibid., 40.*

10 Press where ye see my white plume
shine, amidst the ranks of war,
And be your oriflamme to-day the
helmet of Navarre. *Ivry.*

11 Night sank upon the dusky beach, and
on the purple sea,
Such night in England ne'er had been,
nor e'er again shall be. *The Armada.*

MCCRAE, JOHN, Canadian doctor and poet, 30 Nov. 1872–28 Jan. 1918

12 In Flanders fields the poppies blow
Between the crosses, row on row.
In Flanders Fields.

MCCREERY, JOHN LUCKEY, US journalist, 21 or 31 Dec. 1835–6 Sept. 1906

13 There is no death! The stars go down
To rise upon some other shore,
And bright in heaven's jewelled crown
They shine for evermore.
There is no Death.

MACDONALD, GEORGE, Scottish author, 10 Dec. 1824–18 Sept. 1905

14 Where did you come from, baby dear?
Out of the everywhere into here. *Baby.*

15 Where did you get your eyes so blue?
Out of the sky as I came through. *Ibid*

MACKAY, CHARLES, Scottish journalist and song-writer, 27 March, 1814–24 Dec. 1889

16 The coin is spurious, nail it down.
John Littlejohn.

17 Old Tubal Cain was a man of might,
In the days when the earth was young.
Tubal Cain.

18 There's a good time coming, boys.
The Good Time Coming.

19 Cheer, boys! cheer! *Song.*

MACKINTOSH, SIR JAMES, Scottish philosopher, 24 Oct. 1765–30 May, 1832

20 The Commons, faithful to their system,
remained in a wise and masterly
inactivity. *Vindiciae Gallicae.*

21 The frivolous work of polished idleness.
Dissertation on Ethical Philosophy.
Remarks on Thomas Brown.

MACKLIN, CHARLES, Irish actor and dramatist, 1697?–11 July, 1797

22 The law is a sort of hocus-pocus science, that smiles in yer face while it picks yer pocket; and the glorious uncertainty of it is of mair use to the professors than the justice of it.   *Love à la Mode, II. i.*

MACLEAN, Mrs., see Landon, Letitia Elizabeth

MCLENNAN, MURDOCH, Scottish minister, 1701–1783

23 There's some say that we wan, some say that they wan,
Some say that nane wan at a', man;
But one thing I'm sure, that at Sheriffmuir
A battle there was which I saw, man:
And we ran, and they ran, and they ran, and we ran,
And we ran; and they ran awa', man.
                                  Sheriffmuir.

MACLEOD, NORMAN, Scottish minister, 3 June, 1812–16 June, 1872

24 Courage, brother! do not stumble,
Though thy path be dark as night;
There's a star to guide the humble:
'Trust in God, and do the right.'
                                  Trust in God.

MACMAHON, MARIE EDMÉ PATRICE MAURICE DE, Duke of Magenta, Marshal of France, 13 July, 1808–17 Oct. 1893

25 J'y suis, j'y reste. – Here I am, here I stay.
At the siege of Sevastopol, Sept. 1855.

MACNALLY, LEONARD, Irish dramatist, 1752–13 Feb. 1820

26 On Richmond Hill there lives a lass,
More sweet than May day morn,
Whose charms all other maids surpass,
A rose without a thorn.

This lass so neat, with smiles so sweet,
Has won my right good will,
I'd crowns resign to call thee mine,
Sweet lass of Richmond Hill.
                  The Lass of Richmond Hill.

MADDEN, SAMUEL, Irish author, 23 Dec. 1686–31 Dec. 1765

27 Words are men's daughters, but God's sons are things.
                  Boulter's Monument, 377.
(Said to have been insterted by Dr. Johnson.)

MAETERLINCK, MAURICE, COUNT, Belgian author, 29 Aug. 1862–1949

28 Il n'y a pas de morts. – There are no dead.
L'Oiseau Bleu. – The Blue Bird, IV. ii.

MAHONY, FRANCIS SYLVESTER, see Prout, Father

MAISTRE, JOSEPH MARIE, COMTE DE, French author, 1 April, 1754–26 Feb. 1821

29 Toute nation a le gouvernement qu'elle mérite. – Every nation has the government it deserves.
Letter from St. Petersburg, 27 Aug. 1811.

MALORY, SIR THOMAS, English author, fl. 1470

30 Thou wert never matched of earthly knight's hand; and thou wert the courteoust knight that ever bare shield; and thou wert the truest friend to thy lover that ever bestrad horse; and thou wert the truest lover of a sinful man that ever loved woman; and thou wert the kindest man that ever struck with sword; and thou wert the goodliest person that ever came among press of knights; and thou wert the meekest man and the gentlest that ever ate in hall among ladies; and thou wert the sternest knight to thy mortal foe that ever put spear in the rest. (Lancelot.)
                  Morte D'Arthur, XXI. xiii.

MANGAN, JAMES CLARENCE, Irish poet, 1 May, 1803–20 June, 1849

1 My dark Rosaleen!   *Dark Rosaleen.*

2 The fair hills of Éire, O.   *Title of Poem.*

MANN, HORACE, US educationist, 4 May, 1796–2 Aug. 1859

3 Lost, yesterday, somewhere between sunrise and sunset, two golden hours, each set with sixty diamond minutes. No reward is offered, for they are gone for ever.   *Lost, Two Golden Hours.*

4 Be ashamed to die until you have won some victory for humanity.
Commencement Address, Antioch College, 1859.

MANNERS, JOHN, see Rutland, Duke of

MANNYNG, ROBERT (ROBERT OF BRUNNE), English poet, 1264?–1340?

5 A gode womman is mannys blys.
Handlyng Synne.

MARCY, WILLIAM LEARNED, US Secretary for War, 12 Dec. 1786–4 July, 1857

6 They see nothing wrong in the rule that to the victors belong the spoils of the enemy.   *Speech, US Senate, Jan. 1832.*

MARKHAM, EDWIN, US poet, 23 April, 1852–7 March, 1940

7 Bowed by the weight of centuries he leans
Upon his hoe and gazes on the ground,
The emptiness of ages in his face,
And on his back the burden of the world.   *The Man with the Hoe.*

8 He drew a circle that shut me out –
Heretic, rebel, a thing to flout.

But Love and I had the wit to win:
We drew a circle that took him in.
Outwitted.

MARLOWE, CHRISTOPHER, English dramatist, 1564–1 June, 1593

9 From jigging veins of rhyming mother wits,
And such conceits as clownage keeps in pay,
We'll lead you to the stately tent of war,
Where you shall hear the Scuthian Tamburlaine
Threatening the world with high astounding terms,
And scourging kingdoms with his conquering sword.
Tamburlaine, part I. Prologue.

10 Our swords shall play the orator for us.
Ibid, I. ii.

11 "And ride in triumph through Persepolis!"
Is it not brave to be a king, Techelles?
Usumcasane and Theridamas,
Is it not passing brave to be a king,
"And ride in triumph through Persepolis"?   *Ibid, II. v.*

12 If all the pens that ever poets held
Had fed the feeling of their masters' thoughts,
And every sweetness that inspired their hearts,
Their minds, and muses on admirèd themes;
If all the heavenly quintessence they still
From their immortal flowers of poesy,
Wherein, as in a mirror, we perceive
The highest reaches of a human wit;
If these had made one poem's period,
And all combined in beauty's worthiness,
Yet should there hover in their restless heads
One thought, one grace one wonder, at the least,
Which into words no virtue no digest.
Ibid, V. i.

13 Now walk the angels on the walls of Heaven,

As sentinels to warn th' immortal souls
To entertain divine Zenocrate.
Ibid, part II. II. iv.

14 Holla, ye pampered jades of Asia!
What! can ye draw but twenty miles a
day! *Ibid, IV. iv.*

15 Was this the face that launched a
thousand ships
And burnt the topless towers of Ilium?
Sweet Helen, make me immortal with a
kiss.
Her lips suck forth my soul; see where it
flies! –
Come, Helen, come, give me my soul
again.
Here will I dwell, for Heaven is in these
lips,
And all is dross that is not Helena.
Doctor Faustus, xiv.

16 Oh, thou art fairer than the evening air
Clad in the beauty of a thousand stars.
Ibid.

17 Now hast thou but one bare hour to
live,
And then thou must be damned
perpetually!
Stand still, you ever-moving spheres of
Heaven
That time may cease, and midnight
never come. *Ibid, xvi.*

18 *O lente, lente currite noctis equi!*
The stars move still, time runs, the clock
will strike,
The Devil will come, and Faustus must
be damned.
O, I'll leap up to my God! Who pulls me
down?
See, see where Christ's blood streams in
the firmament! *Ibid.*

19 Ugly hell, gape not! come not, Lucifer!
I'll burn my books! Ah Mephistophilis!
Ibid.

20 Cut is the branch that might have grown
full straight,
And burnèd is Apollo's laurel bough,
That sometime grew within this learnèd
man. *Ibid.*

21 Infinite riches in a little room.
The Jew of Malta, I. i.

22 My men, like satyrs grazing on the
lawns,
Shall with their goat-feet dance the antic
hay. *Edward II, I. i.*

23 It lies not in our power to love or hate,
For will in us is over-ruled by fate.
When two are stripped, long ere the
course begin,
We wish that one should lose, the other
win;
And one especially do we affect
Of two gold ingots, like in each respect:
The reason no man knows; let it suffice,
What we behold is censured by our eyes.
Where both deliberate, the love is slight:
Who ever loved, that loved not at first
sight? *Hero and Leander, I. 167.*

24 Come live with me and be my love,
And we will all the pleasures prove
That hills and valleys, dales and fields,
Woods, or steepy mountain yields.
The Passionate Shepherd to his Love.

25 By shallow rivers, to whose falls
Melodious birds sing madrigals.
Ibid.

**MARMION, SHACKERLEY,
English dramatist, Jan. 1603–Jan.
1639**

26 What find you better or more
honourable than age? Take the
preheminence of it in everything: in an
old friend, in old wine, in an öld
pedigree. *The Antiquary, II. i.*

**MARQUIS, DONALD ROBERT
PERRY, US poet, 29 July, 1878–29
Dec. 1937**

27 A little while with grief and laughter,
And then the day will close;
The shadows gather . . . what comes
after
No man knows. *A Little While.*

28 it s cheerio
my deario

that pulls a
lady through
   archy and mehitable cheerio my deario
(Archy, a cockroach, cannot do
punctuation or capitals.)

1 To stroke a platitude until it purrs like
    an epigram.   *The Sun Dial.*

MARRIOTT, JOHN, English poet and clergyman, 1780–31 March, 1825

2 In a Devonshire lane as I trotted along
    T'other day, much in want of a subject
      for song;
    Thinks I to myself, I have hit on a
      strain –
    Sure marriage is much like a Devonshire
    lane.   *The Devonshire Lane.*

MARRYAT, FREDERICK, English captain in the Navy and novelist, 10 July, 1792–9 Aug. 1848

3 If you please, ma'am, it was a very little
    one. (Excusing her illegitimate baby.)
          Midshipman Easy, iii.

4 All zeal, Mrs. Easy.   *Ibid, ix.*

MARTIAL (MARCUS VALERIUS MARTIALIS), Roman poet, 40?–104?

5 Non amo te, Sabidi, nec possum dicere
    quare:
    Hoc tantum possum dicere, non amo te.
    – I do not love you, Sabidius, and I
    cannot say why:
    this only I can say, I do not love you.
          Epigrams, I xxxii.

6   Bonosque
    Soles effugere atque abire sentit,
    Qui nobis pereunt et imputantur.
    – And he feels that the good days are
    flying and passing away,
    those days that perish and are put down
    to our account.   *Ibid, V. xx.*

MARVELL, ANDREW, English poet and MP, 31 March, 1621–18 Aug. 1678

7 Where the remote Bermudas ride,
    In the ocean's bosom unespied. *Bermudas.*

8   The orange bright,
    Like golden lamps in a green night.
                  Ibid.

9 And all the way, to guide their chime,
    With falling oars they kept the time.
                  Ibid.

10 Had we but world enough, and time,
    This coyness, Lady, were no crime.
          To his Coy Mistress.

11 But at my back I always hear
    Time's winged chariot hurrying near;
    And yonder all before us lie
    Deserts of vast eternity.   *Ibid.*

12 The grave's a fine and private place,
    But none, I think, do there embrace.
                  Ibid.

13 Stumbling on melons, as I pass,
    Ensnared with flowers, I fall on grass.
        Thoughts in a Garden.

14 Annihilating all that's made
    To a green thought in a green shade.
                  Ibid.

15 Casting the body's vest aside,
    My soul into the boughs does glide.
                  Ibid.

16 The inglorious arts of peace.
    A Horatian Ode upon Cromwell's Return
                  from Ireland.

17 He nothing common did, or mean,
    Upon that memorable scene,
    But with his keener eye
    The axe's edge did try.   *Ibid.*

MARX, HEINRICH KARL, German socialist, 5 May, 1818–14 March, 1883

18 Die Religion . . . ist das Opium des

Volkes. – Religion . . . is the opium of the people.
Kritik der Hegelschen Rechtsphilosophie – Critique of the Hegelian Philosophy of Right, introduction.

MARY I, QUEEN, 18 Feb. 1516–17 Nov. 1558

19 When I am dead and opened, you shall find "Calais" lying in my heart.
Holinshed's Chronicles, III. 1160.

MASEFIELD, JOHN, English Poet Laureate, 1 June, 1878–12 May, 1967

20 Theirs be the music, the colour, the glory, the gold;
Mine be a handful of ashes, a mouthful of mould.
Of the maimed, of the halt and the blind in the rain and the cold –
Of these shall my songs be fashioned, my tales be told.   *A Consecration.*

21 I must go down to the seas again, to the lonely sea and the sky,
And all I ask is a tall ship and a star to steer her by.   *Sea-Fever.*

22 And all I ask is a merry yarn from a laughing fellow-rover,
And quiet sleep and a sweet dream when the long trick's over.   *Ibid.*

23 Dirty British coaster with a salt-caked smoke stack
Butting through the Channel in the mad March days,
With a cargo of Tyne coal,
Road-rail, pig-lead,
Firewood, iron-ware, and cheap tin trays.   *Cargoes.*

24 But I'm for toleration and for drinking at an inn,
Says the old bold mate of Henry Morgan.   *Captain Stratton's Fancy.*

25 I have seen dawn and sunset on moors and windy hills
Coming in solemn beauty like slow old tunes of Spain.   *Beauty.*

26 But the loveliest things of beauty God ever has showed to me,
Are her voice, and her hair, and eyes, and the dear red curve of her lips.   *Ibid.*

27 Laugh and be merry, remember, better the world with a song,
Better the world with a blow in the teeth of a wrong.
Laugh, for the time is brief, a thread the length of a span.
Laugh and be proud to belong to the old proud pageant of man.
Laugh and be Merry.

28 And he who gives a child a treat
Makes joy-bells ring in Heaven's street,
And he who gives a child a home
Builds palaces in Kingdom come.
The Everlasting Mercy.

MASON, WILLIAM, English poet, 12 Feb. 1724–7 April, 1797

29 The fattest hog of Epicurus' sty.
An Heroic Epistle, 24.

MASSINGER, PHILIP, English dramatist, 1583–March 1640

30 Her goodness does disdain comparison,
And, but herself, admits no parallel.
The Duke of Milan, IV. iii.

31 He that would govern others, first should be
The master of himself.
The Bondman, I. iii.

32 The devil turned precisian!
A New Way to pay Old Debts, I. i.

33 Some undone widow sits upon mine arm,
And takes away the use of 't; and my sword,
Glued to my scabbard with wronged orphans' tears,
Will not be drawn.   *Ibid, V. i.*

34 Death hath a thousand doors to let out life.
I shall find one.   *A Very Woman, V. iv.*

MAULE, SIR WILLIAM HENRY, English judge, 25 April, 1788–16 Jan. 1858

1 My lords, we are vertebrate animals, we are mammalia! My learned friend's manner would be intolerable in Almighty God to a black beetle.
In law court, opposing counsel being Sir Cresswell Cresswell.

MAXWELL, JAMES CLERK, English scientist, 13 June, 1831–5 Nov. 1879

2 Gin a body meet a body
Flyin' through the air,
Gin a body hit a body,
Will it fly? and where?
Ilka impact has its measure,
Ne'er a ane hae I,
Yet a' the lads they measure me,
Or, at least they try. *Rigid Body Sings.*

MEE, WILLIAM, English poet, 1788–29 May, 1862

3 She's all my fancy painted her;
She's lovely, she's divine. *Alice Gray.*

MELBOURNE, WILLIAM LAMB, 2ND VISCOUNT, English Prime Minister, 15 March, 1779–24 Nov. 1848

4 I wish I was as cocksure of anything as Tom Macaulay is of everything.
Attributed.

5 Things have come to a pretty pass when religion is allowed to invade the sphere of private life. *Ibid.*

MENANDER, Greek dramatist, 342?–291? B.C.

6 Φθείρουσιν ἤθη χρήσθ' ὁμιλίαι κακαί.
– Evil communications corrupt good manners. *Thais.*

MENCKEN, HENRY LOUIS, US critic, 12 Sept. 1880–29 Jan. 1956

7 The great artists of the world are never Puritans, and seldom even ordinarily respectable. *Prejudices, I. xvi.*

8 To be in love is merely to be in a state of perpetual anaesthesis – to mistake an ordinary young man for a Greek god or an ordinary young woman for a goddess. *Ibid.*

MEREDITH, GEORGE, English author, 12 Feb. 1828–18 May, 1909

9 I've studied men from my topsy-turvy
Close, and, I reckon, rather true.
Some are fine fellows: some, right scurvy:
Most, a dash between the two.
Juggling Jerry.

10 She is steadfast as a star,
And yet the maddest maiden:
She can wage a gallant war,
And give the peace of Eden. *Marian.*

11 And if I drink oblivion of a day,
So shorten I the stature of my soul.
Modern Love, xii.

12 Ah, what a dusty answer gets the soul
When hot for certainties in this our life!
Ibid, I.

13 Into the breast that gives the rose,
Shall I with shuddering fall?
Ode to the Spirit of Earth in Autumn.

14 Sweet as Eden is the air,
And Eden-sweet the ray.
Woodland Peace.

15 Under yonder beech-tree single on the green-sward,
Couched with her arms behind her golden head,
Knees and tresses folded to slip and ripple idly,
Lies my young love sleeping in the shade. *Love in the Valley.*

16 She whom I love is hard to catch and conquer,
Hard, but O the glory of the winning were she won! *Ibid.*

17 When her mother tends her before the laughing mirror,
Tying up her laces, looping up her hair.
Ibid.

18 Like the swinging May-cloud that pelts
   the flowers with hailstones
   Off a sunny border, she was made to
   bruise and bless.   *Ibid.*

19 Lovely are the curves of the white owl
   sweeping
   Wavy in the dusk lit by one large star.
   Lone on the fir-branch, his rattle-note
   unvaried,
   Brooding o'er the gloom, spins the
   brown eve-jar.   *Ibid.*

20 Brave in her shape, and sweeter
   unpossessed.   *Ibid.*

21 Pure from the night, and splendid for
   the day.   *Ibid.*

22 The song seraphically free
   Of taint of personality.
                          The Lark Ascending.

23 Enter those enchanted woods,
   You who dare.
                       The Woods of Westermain.

24 Around the ancient track marched, rank
   on rank,
   The army of unalterable law.
                          Lucifer in Starlight.

25 Thence had he the laugh
   . . . broad as ten thousand beeves
   At pasture!   *The Spirit of Shakespeare.*

26 I expect that Woman will be the last
   thing civilised by Man.
               The Ordeal of Richard Feveral, i.

27 He has a leg.   *The Egoist, ii.*

28 A dainty rogue in porcelain,   *Ibid, V*

29 Cynicism is intellectual dandyism.
                                 Ibid, vii.

30 A Phoebus Apollo turned fasting friar.
                                  Ibid, x.

31 Men may have rounded Seraglio Point:
   they have not yet doubled Cape Turk.
               Diana of the Crossways, i.

32 'Tis Ireland gives England her soldiers,
   her generals too.   *Ibid, ii.*

33 Ah could eat hog a solid hower!
   (Andrew Hedger.)   *Ibid, viii.*

34 "But how divine is utterance!" she said.
   "As we to the brutes, poets are to us."
                                Ibid, xvi.

35 None of your dam punctilio.
                   One of our Conquerors, i.

**MEREDITH, OWEN, see Lytton,
Earl of**

**MERRITT, DIXON LANIER, US
journalist, 9 July, 1879–1954**

36 A rare old bird is the pelican,
   His beak holds more than his belican.
   He can take in his beak
   Enough food for a week.
   I'm darned if I know how the helican!
                                  Limerick.

**MEYNELL, ALICE CHRISTIANA
GERTRUDE, English authoress, 22
Sept. 1847–27 Nov. 1922**

37 Thou art like silence unperplexed,
   A secret and a mystery
   Between one football and the next.
                           To the Beloved.

38 I must not think of thee; and, tired yet
   strong,
   I shun the thought that lurks in all
   delight –
   The thought of thee – and in the blue
   Heaven's height,
   And in the sweetest passage of a song.
                            Renouncement.

39 She walks – the lady of my delight –
   A shepherdess of sheep.
   Her flocks are thoughts. She keeps them
   white;
   She guards them from the steep.
                            The Shepherdess.

40 Flocks of the memories of the day draw
   near
   The dovecot doors of sleep.   *At Night.*

MICKLE, WILLIAM JULIUS, Scottish poet, 28 Sept. 1735–28 Oct. 1788

1 The dews of summer night did fall,
The moon, sweet regent of the sky,
Silver'd the walls of Cumnor Hall,
And many an oak that grew thereby.
Cumnor Hall.

MIDDLETON, RICHARD BARHAM, English author, 28 Oct. 1882–1 Dec. 1911

2 Why are her eyes so bright, so bright,
Why do her lips control
The kisses of a summer night
When I would love her soul?
Any Lover, Any Lass.

MIDDLETON, THOMAS, English dramatist, 18 April, 1580–4 July, 1627

3 Black spirits and white, red spirits and grey,
Mingle, mingle, mingle, you that mingle may! *The Witch, IV. iii.*

4 By many a happy accident.
No Wit, No Help, like a Woman's, IV. i.

MIDLANE, ALBERT, English hymn-writer, 23 Jan. 1825–27 Feb. 1909

5 There's a Friend for little children
Above the bright blue sky,
A Friend who never changes,
Whose love can never die. *Hymn.*

MILL, JOHN STUART, English philosopher, 20 May, 1806–8 May, 1873

6 When the object is to raise the permanent condition of a people, small means do not merely produce small effects; they produce no effect at all.
The Principles of Political Economy, II. xiii. 4.

7 The liberty of the individual must be thus far limited; he must not make himself a nuisance to other people.
Liberty, iii.

8 Unearned increment.
Dissertations and Discussions, IV. 299.

MILLAY, EDNA ST. VINCENT (MRS. EUGEN JAN BOISSEVAIN), US poetess, 22 Feb. 1892–19 Oct. 1950

9 My candle burns at both ends;
It will not last the night;
But, ah, my foes, and oh, my friends –
It gives a lovely light.
Figs from Thistles. First Fig.

10 Safe upon the solid rock the ugly houses stand:
Come and see my shining palace built upon the sand! *Ibid, Second Fig.*

11 I will be the gladdest thing under the sun!
I will touch a hundred flowers and not pick one. *Afternoon on a Hill.*

12 And if I loved you Wednesday,
Well, what is that to you?
I do not love you Thursday –
So much is true. *Thursday.*

13 And, "One thing there's no getting by –
I've been a wicked girl," said I;
"But if I can't be sorry, why,
I might as well be glad!" *The Penitent.*

MILLER, WILLIAM, Scottish poet, August, 1810–20 August, 1872

14 Wee Willie Winkie rins through the town,
Upstairs and downstairs in his nicht-gown,
Tirling at the window, crying at the lock,
"Are the weans in their bed, for it's now ten o'clock?" *Wee Willie Winkie.*

MILLS, JOHN, English banker, 16 Dec. 1821–26 Sept. 1896

15 Life's race well run,
Life's work well done,
Life's victory won,
Now cometh rest. *Epitaph.*
(There are various alternative versions, and authorship has been claimed for E. H. Parker, a US doctor who used the lines in his funeral ode on President Garfield.)

MILMAN, HENRY HART, Dean of St. Paul's and historian, 10 Feb. 1791–24 Sept. 1868

16 And the cold marble leapt to life a god.
The Belvidere Apollo.

MILNE, ALAN ALEXANDER, English author, 18 Jan. 1882–31 Jan. 1956

17 I do like a little bit of butter to my bread.
When we were very Young. The King's Breakfast.

18 James James
Morrison Morrison
Weatherby George Dupree
Took great
Care of his Mother
Though he was only three.
Ibid. Disobedience.

MILNES, RICHARD MONCKTON, see Houghton, Baron

MILTON, JOHN, English poet, 9 Dec. 1608–8 Nov. 1674

19 Let us with a gladsome mind
Praise the Lord, for he is kind,
For his mercies ay endure,
Ever faithful, ever sure. *Psalm 136*

20 It was the winter wild,
While the Heav'n-born child
All meanly wrapt in the rude manger lies.
On the Morning of Christ's Nativity, 29.

21 No war, or battle's sound
Was heard the world around. *Ibid, 53.*

22 While birds of calm sit brooding on the charmèd wave. *Ibid, 68.*

23 Time will run back, and fetch the age of gold. *Ibid, 135.*

24 The oracles are dumb. *Ibid, 173.*

25 No nightly trance, or breathed spell,
Inspires the pale-eyed priest from the prophetic cell. *Ibid, 179.*

26 So when the sun in bed,
Curtain'd with cloudy red,
Pillows his chin upon an orient wave.
Ibid, 229.

27 Blest pair of Sirens, pledges of Heav'n's joy,
Sphere-born harmonious sisters, Voice and Verse. *At a Solemn Music, 1.*

28 What needs my Shakespeare for his honour'd bones,
The labour of an age in piled stones,
Or that his hallow'd relics should be hid
Under a star-y-pointing pyramid?
Dear son of memory, great heir of fame,
What need'st thou such weak witness of thy name? *On Shakespeare.*

29 O nightingale, that on yon bloomy spray
Warbl'st at eve, when all the woods are still. *Sonnet. To the Nightingale.*

30 How soon hath Time, the subtle thief of youth,
Stoln on his wing my three and twentieth year!
Sonnet. On his being arrived to the Age of twenty-three.

31 All is, if I have grace to use it so,
As ever in my great Taskmaster's eye.
Ibid.

32 Hence, loathed Melancholy.
L'Allegro, 1.

33 Haste thee, nymph, and bring with thee
Jest, and youthful jollity,
Quips, and cranks, and wanton wiles,
Nods, and becks, and wreathed smiles.
Ibid, 25.

34 Sport that wrinkled Care derides,
And Laughter holding both his sides.
Come, and trip it as you go,
On the light fantastic toe. *Ibid, 31.*

35 The mountain nymph, sweet Liberty.
Ibid, 36.

36 To hear the lark begin his flight,
And singing startle the dull night,
From his watch-tower in the skies,
Till the dappled dawn doth rise.
Ibid, 41.

1 While the cock with lively din
Scatters the rear of darkness thin,
And to the stack, or the barn-door,
Stoutly struts his dames before.
Ibid, 49

2 Right against the eastern gate
Where the great sun begins his state.
Ibid, 59

3 Meadows trim with daisies pied,
Shallow brooks, and rivers wide;
Towers and battlements it sees
Bosom'd high in tufted trees,
Where perhaps some beauty lies,
The cynosure of neighbouring eyes.
Ibid, 75

4 Of herbs, and other country messes,
Which the neat-handed Phyllis dresses.
Ibid, 85.

5 Then to the spicy nut-brown ale.
Ibid, 100.

6 Tower'd cities please us then,
And the busy hum of men. *Ibid, 117.*

7 With store of ladies, whose bright eyes
Rain influence, and judge the prize
Or wit or arms. *Ibid, 121*

8 Such sights as youthful poets dream
On summer eves by haunted stream;
Then to the well-trod stage anon,
If Jonson's learned sock be on,
Or sweetest Shakespeare, Fancy's child,
Warble his native wood-notes wild.
Ibid, 129.

9 And ever, against eating cares,
Lap me in soft Lydian airs,
Married to immortal verse
Such as the meeting soul may pierce
In notes, with many a winding bout
Of linked sweetness long drawn out.
Ibid, 135

10 The melting voice through mazes
running,
Untwisting all the chains that tie
The hidden soul of harmony. *Ibid 142*

11 Hence, vain deluding joys,
The brood of Folly without father bred.
Il Penseroso, 1

12 The gay motes that people the
sunbeams. *Ibid, 8.*

13 Sober, steadfast, and demure. *Ibid, 32.*

14 And looks commercing with the skies,
Thy rapt soul sitting in thine eyes.
Ibid, 39.

15 And add to these retired Leisure,
That in trim gardens takes his pleasure.
Ibid, 49.

16 Sweet bird, that shunn'st the noise of
folly,
Most musical, most melancholy.
Ibid, 61.

17 To behold the wand'ring moon,
Riding near her highest noon,
Like one that had been led astray
Through the heaven's wide pathless
way;
And oft, as if her head she bow'd,
Stooping through a fleecy cloud.
Ibid, 67.

18 Oft, on a plat of rising ground,
I hear the far-off curfew sound,
Over some wide-water'd shore,
Swinging slow with sullen roar.
Ibid, 73.

19 Where glowing embers through the
room
Teach light to counterfeit a gloom,
Far from all resort of mirth,
Save the cricket on the hearth. *Ibid, 79.*

20 Sometime let gorgeous Tragedy
In sceptred pall come sweeping by,
Presenting Thebes, or Pelops' line,
Or the tale of Troy divine. *Ibid, 97*

21 Or bid the soul of Orpheus sing
Such notes as, warbled to the string,
Drew iron tears down Pluto's cheek.
Ibid, 105.

22 Or call up him that left half told
The story of Cambuscan bold.
Ibid, 109.

23 Where more is meant than meets the ear.
Ibid, 120.

24 Ending on the rustling leaves
With minute drops from the eaves.
Ibid, 129.

25 But let my due feet never fail
To walk the studious cloister's pale,
And love the high embowed roof,
With antique pillars massy proof,
And storied windows richly dight,
Casting a dim religious light.
There let the pealing organ blow
To the full-voiced quire below.
Ibid, 155.

26 Under the shady roof
Of branching elm star-proof.
Arcades, 88.

27 Above the smoke and stir of this dim
spot,
Which men call Earth.
Comus, 5.

28 An old and haughty nation proud in
arms.
Ibid, 33.

29 These my sky robes spun out of Iris'
woof.
Ibid, 83.

30 The star that bids the shepherd fold.
Ibid, 93.

31 Midnight shout and revelry,
Tipsy dance and jollity
Ibid, 103.

32 And, on the tawny sands and shelves,
Trip the pert fairies and the dapper
elves.
Ibid, 117.

33 Ere the blabbing eastern scout,
The nice Morn on the Indian steep
From her cabin'd loop-hole peep.
Ibid, 138.

34   When the grey-hooded Even
Like a sad votarist in palmer's weed,
Rose from the hindmost wheels of
Phoebus' wain.
Ibid, 188.

35 O welcome, pure-eyed Faith, white-
handed Hope,
Thou hovering angel girt with golden
wings.
Ibid, 213.

36 I took it for a faery vision
Of some gay creatures of the element,

That in the colours of the rainbow live,
And play i' the plighted clouds.
Ibid, 298.

37 I know each lane, and every alley green,
Dingle, or bushy dell, of this wild
wood,
And every bosky bourn from side to
side,
My daily walks and ancient
neighbourhood.
Ibid, 311.

38 With thy long levell'd rule of streaming
light.
Ibid, 340.

39 Virtue could see to do what virtue
would
By her own radiant light, though sun
and moon
Were in the flat sea sunk.
Ibid, 373.

40 He that has light within his own clear
breast
May sit i' th' centre and enjoy bright
day,
But he that hides a dark soul and foul
thoughts
Benighted walks under the midday sun;
Himself is his own dungeon.
Ibid, 381.

41 'Tis chastity, my brother, chastity:
She that has that is clad in complete
steel.
Ibid, 420.

42 Some say no evil thing that walks by
night
In fog, or fire, by lake, or moorish fen,
Blue meagre hag, or stubborn unlaid
ghost,
That breaks his magic chains at curfew
time,
No goblin, or swart faery of the mine,
Hath hurtful power o'er true virginity.
Ibid, 432.

43 How charming is divine philosophy!
Not harsh, and crabbed as dull fools
suppose,
But musical as is Apollo's lute,
And a perpetual feast of nectar'd sweets,
Where no crude surfeit reigns.
Ibid, 476.

44 And fill'd the air with barbarous
dissonance.
Ibid, 550.

1   I was all ear,
And took in strains that might create a
   soul
Under the ribs of death.   *Ibid, 560.*

2   If this fail,
The pillar'd firmament is rottenness,
And earth's base built on stubble.
               Ibid, 597.

3   The dull swain
Treads on it daily with his clouted
   shoon.   *Ibid, 634.*

4 Those budge doctors of the Stoic fur.
               Ibid, 707.

5 It is for homely features to keep home,
They had their name thence; coarse
   complexions
And cheeks of sorry grain will serve to
   ply
The sampler, and to tease the huswife's
   wool.
What need a vermeil-tinctured lip for
   that,
Love-darting eyes, or tresses like the
   morn?   *Ibid, 748.*

6 Sabrina fair,
Listen where thou art sitting
Under the glassy, cool, translucent
   wave,
In twisted braids of lilies knitting
The loose train of thy amber-dropping
   hair.   *Ibid, 859.*

7 Mortals that would follow me,
Love virtue, she alone is free,
She can teach ye how to climb
Higher than the sphery chime;
Or, if virtue feeble were,
Heaven itself would stoop to her.
              Ibid, 1018.

8 Yet once more, O ye laurels, and once
   more
Ye myrtles brown, with ivy never sere,
I come to pluck your berries harsh and
   crude,
And with forc'd fingers rude,
Shatter your leaves before the
   mellowing year.   *Lycidas, 1*

9   He knew
Himself to sing, and build the lofty
   rhyme.   *Ibid, 10.*

10 Without the meed of some melodius
   tear.   *Ibid, 14.*

11 Under the opening eyelids of the morn.
               Ibid, 26.

12 But, O the heavy change, now thou art
   gone,
Now thou art gone, and never must
   return!   *Ibid, 37.*

13 The gadding vine.   *Ibid, 40.*

14 And strictly meditate the thankless
   Muse.   *Ibid, 66.*

15 To sport with Amaryllis in the shade,
Or with the tangles of Neaera's hair.
               Ibid, 69.

16 Fame is the spur that the clear spirit doth
   raise
(That last infirmity of noble mind)
To scorn delights, and live laborious
   days;
But the fair guerdon when we hope to
   find,
And think to burst out into sudden
   blaze,
Comes the blind Fury with th' abhorred
   shears
And slits the thin-spun life.   *Ibid, 70.*

17 Fame is no plant that grows on mortal
   soil.   *Ibid, 78.*

18 Last came, and last did go
The Pilot of the Galilean lake,
Two massy keys he bore of metals twain
(The golden opes, the iron shuts amain).
              Ibid, 108.

19 Blind mouths! that scarce themselves
   know how to hold
A sheep-hook.   *Ibid, 119.*

20 And, then they list, their lean and flashy
   songs
Grate on their scrannel pipes of
   wretched straw;
The hungry sheep look up, and are not
   fed,

But, swoln with wind and the rank mist
    they draw,
Rot inwardly, and foul contagion
    spread.   *Ibid, 123.*

21 But that two-handed engine at the door
Stands ready to smite once, and smite no
    more.   *Ibid, 130.*

22 Throw hither all your quaint enamell'd
    eyes,
That on the green turf suck the honied
    showers
And purple all the ground with vernal
    flowers.
Bring the rathe primrose that forsaken
    dies,
The tufted crow-toe, and pale
    jessamine,
The white pink, and the pansy freak'd
    with jet,
The glowing violet,
The musk-rose, and the well-attir'd
    woodbine,
With cowslips wan that hang the
    pensive head,
And every flower that sad embroidery
    wears:
Bid amaranthus all his beauty shed,
And daffadillies fill their cups with tears,
To strew the laureate hearse where
    Lycid lies.   *Ibid, 139*

23 So sinks the day-star in the ocean bed,
And yet anon repairs his drooping head,
And tricks his beams, and with new-
    spangled ore
Flames in the forehead of the morning
    sky.   *Ibid, 168.*

24 At last he rose, and twitch'd his mantle
    blue:
To-morrow to fresh woods, and
    pastures new.   *Ibid, 192*

25 Captain or Colonel, or Knight in arms.
    *Sonnet. When the Assault was intended to
                                the City.*

26 The great Emathian conqueror bid spare
The house of Pindarus, when temple
    and tower
Went to the ground.   *Ibid.*

27 Killed with report that old man
    eloquent.
    Sonnet. To the Lady Margaret Ley.

28 That would have made Quintilian stare
    and gasp.
    *Sonnet. On the Detraction which followed
        upon my writing certain Treatises.*

29 License they mean when they cry
    liberty.   *Sonnet. On the same.*

30 Avenge, O Lord, thy slaughter'd saints,
    whose bones
Lie scatter'd on the Alpine mountains
    cold.
    Sonnet. On the late Massacre in Piedmont.

31 When I consider how my light is spent,
Ere half my days, in this dark world and
    wide,
And that one talent which is death to
    hide
Lodg'd with me useless, though my soul
    more bent
To serve therewith my Maker, and
    present
My true account, lest He returning
    chide,
Doth God exact day-labour, light
    denied,
I fondly ask: but Patience, to prevent
That murmur, soon replies, God doth
    not need
Either man's work or His own gifts;
    who best
Bear His mild yoke, they serve Him
    best: His state
Is kingly. Thousands at His bidding
    speed
And post o'er land and ocean without
    rest:
They also serve who only stand and
    wait.   *Sonnet. On his Blindness.*

32 Methought I saw my late espousèd
    Saint.   *Sonnet. On his Deceased Wife.*

33 New Presbyter is but old Priest writ
    large.
    *Sonnet. On the New Forcers of Conscience
                under the Long Parliament.*

34   Peace hath her victories
No less renowned than war.
    *Sonnet. To the Lord General Cromwell,
                        May, 1652.*

1 Of Man's first disobedience, and the
    fruit
 Of that forbidden tree, whose mortal
    taste
 Brought death into the world, and all
    our woe,
 With loss of Eden, till one greater Man
 Restore us, and regain the blissful seat,
 Sing, heav'nly Muse.
                                                            Paradise Lost, 1. 1.

2 Things unattempted yet in prose or
    rhyme.   *Ibid, 16.*

3   What in me is dark
 Illumine, what is low raise and support;
 That to the highth of this great
    argument
 I may assert eternal Providence,
 And justify the ways of God to men.
                                                            Ibid, 22.

4 As far as angels' ken.   *Ibid, 59.*

5   Yet from those flames
 No light, but rather darkness visible
 Serv'd only to discover sights of woe,
 Regions of sorrow, doleful shades,
    where peace
 And rest can never dwell, hope never
    comes
 That comes to all.   *Ibid, 62.*

6   What though the field be lost?
 All is not lost; th' unconquerable will,
 And study of revenge, immortal hate,
 And courage never to submit or yield:
 And what is else not to be overcome?
                                                            Ibid, 105.

7   To be weak is miserable
 Doing or suffering.   *Ibid, 157.*

8 And out of good still to find means of
    evil.   *Ibid, 165.*

9   Farewell happy fields
 Where joy for ever dwells: Hail horrors,
    hail.   *Ibid, 249.*

10 The mind is its own place, and in itself
 Can make a heav'n of hell, a hell of
    heav'n.   *Ibid, 254.*

11 Better to reign in hell, than serve in
    heav'n.   *Ibid, 263.*

12 His spear, to equal which the tallest pine
 Hewn on Norwegian hills, to be the
    mast
 Of some great ammiral, were but a
    wand,
 He walk'd with to support uneasy steps
 Over the burning marl.   *Ibid, 292.*

13 Thick as autumnal leaves that strow the
    brooks
 In Vallombrosa, where th' Etrurian
    shades
 High overarch'd imbower.   *Ibid, 302.*

14 Busiris and his Memphian chivalry.
                                                            Ibid, 307.

15 Awake, arise, or be for ever fall'n!
                                                            Ibid, 330.

16   And when night
 Darkens the streets, then wander forth
    the sons
 Of Belial, flown with insolence and
    wine.   *Ibid, 500.*

17 Th' imperial ensign, which, full high
    advanc'd,
 Shone like a meteor, streaming to the
    wind.   *Ibid, 536.*

18 Sonorous metal blowing martial sounds:
 At which the universal host up sent
 A shout that tore hell's concave, and
    beyond
 Frighted the reign of Chaos and old
    Night.   *Ibid, 540.*

19   Anon they move
 In perfect phalanx to the Dorian mood
 Of flutes and soft recorders.   *Ibid, 549.*

20   What resounds
 In fable or romance of Uther's son
 Begirt with British and Armoric
    knights;
 And all who since, baptis'd or infidel,
 Jousted in Aspramont or Montalban,
 Damasco, or Marocco, or Trebisond,
 Or whom Biserta sent from Afric shore
 When Charlemain with all his peerage
    fell
 In Fontarabbia.   *Ibid, 579.*

21   His form had yet not lost
 All her original brightness, nor appear'd

Less than archangel ruined, and th'
    excess
Of glory obscur'd.   *Ibid, 591.*

22   The sun . . .
In dim eclipse disastrous twilight sheds
On half the nations, and with fear of
    change
Perplexes monarchs.   *Ibid, 594.*

23 Thrice he assay'd, and thrice in spite of
    scorn,
Tears, such as angels weep, burst forth.
                       Ibid, 619.

24   Who overcomes
By force, hath overcome but half his
    foe.   *Ibid, 648.*

25   Let none admire
That riches grow in hell; that soil may
    best
Deserve the previous bane.   *Ibid, 690.*

26   How he fell
From heav'n, they fabl'd, thrown by
    angry Jove
Sheer o'er the crystal battlements: from
    morn
To **noon he** fell, from noon to dewy
    eve,
A summer's day; and with the setting
    sun
Dropt from the zenith like a falling star,
On Lemnos th' Aegean isle. *Ibid, 740.*

27   Faery elves,
Whose midnight revels, by a forest side
Or fountain some belated peasant sees,
Or dreams he sees, while overhead the
    moon
Sits arbitress.   *Ibid, 781.*

28 High on a throne of royal state, which
    far
Outshone the wealth of Ormus and of
    Ind,
Or where the gorgeous East with richest
    hand
Showers on her kings barbaric pearl and
    gold,
Satan exalted sat, by merit rais'd
To that bad eminence.   *Ibid, 11. 1.*

29 My sentence is for open war: of wiles
More unexpert, I boast not. *Ibid, 51.*

30   When the scourge
Inexorably, and the torturing hour
Calls us to penance.   *Ibid, 90.*

31 Which if not victory is yet revenge.
                       Ibid, 105.

32 Belial, in act more graceful and humane;
A fairer person lost not heav'n; he
    seemed
For dignity compos'd and high exploit:
But all was false and hollow; though his
    tongue
Dropt manna, and could make the
    worse appear
The better reason, to perplex and dash
Maturest counsels.   *Ibid, 109.*

33   For who would lose,
Though full of pain, this intellectual
    being,
Those thoughts that wander through
    eternity,
To perish rather, swallowed up and lost
In the wide womb of uncreated night,
Devoid of sense and motion? *Ibid, 146.*

34 His red right hand.   *Ibid, 174.*

35 Unrespited, unpitied, unreprived,
Ages of hopeless end.   *Ibid, 185.*

36   The never-ending flight
Of future days.   *Ibid, 221.*

37   With grave
Aspect he rose, and in his rising seem'd
A pillar of state; deep on his front
    engraven
Deliberation sat and public care;
And princely counsel in his face yet
    shone
Majestic though in ruin.   *Ibid, 300.*

38 And through the palpable obscure find
    out
His uncouth way.   *Ibid, 406.*

39   Long is the way
And hard, that out of hell leads up to
    light.   *Ibid, 432.*

40 Others apart sat on a hill retir'd
In thoughts more elevate, and reason'd
    high

Of providence, foreknowledge, will,
and fate,
Fix'd fate, free will, foreknowledge
absolute,
And found no end, in wand'ring mazes
lost.   *Ibid, 557.*

1 Vain wisdom all, and false philosophy.
                                   Ibid, 565.

2 A gulf profound as that Serbonian bog,
Betwixt Damiata and Mount Casius
old,
Where armies whole have sunk: the
parching air
Burns frore, and cold performs th' effect
of fire.   *Ibid, 592.*

3 O'er many a frozen, many a fiery Alp,
Rocks, caves, lakes, fens, bogs, dens,
and shades of death.   *Ibid, 620.*

4 Gorgons and Hydras, and Chimaeras
dire.   *Ibid, 628.*

5   The other shape,
If shape it might be call'd that shape had
none
Distinguishable in member, joint, or
limb,
Or substance might be call'd that
shadow seem'd,
For each seem'd either; black it stood as
night,
Fierce as ten furies, terrible as hell,
And shook a dreadful dart; what seem'd
his head
The likeness of a kingly crown had on.
                                   Ibid, 666.

6 Whence and what art thou, execrable
shape?   *Ibid, 681.*

7 Incens'd with indignation Satan stood
Unterrifi'd, and like a comet burn'd,
That fires the length of Ophiuchus huge
In th' arctic sky, and from his horrid hair
Shakes pestilence and war.   *Ibid, 707.*

8   Their fatal hands
No second stroke intend.   *Ibid, 712.*

9 So frown'd the mighty combatants, that
hell
Grew darker at their frown.   *Ibid, 719.*

10   On a sudden open fly
With impetuous recoil and jarring sound
Th' infernal doors, and on their hinges
grate
Harsh thunder.   *Ibid, 879.*

11 For hot, cold, moist, and dry, four
champions fierce,
Strive here for mastery.   *Ibid, 898.*

12   So eagerly the fiend
O'er bog or steep, through strait,
rough, dense, or rare,
With head, hands, wings, or feet
pursues his way,
And swims or sinks, or wades, or
creeps, or flies.   *Ibid, 947.*

13 With ruin upon ruin, rout on rout,
Confusion worse confounded.
                                   Ibid, 995.

14 So he with difficulty and labour hard
Mov'd on, with difficulty and labour he.
                                   Ibid, 1021.

15 Hail, holy light, offspring of heav'n
first-born.   *Ibid, 111. 1.*

16 Those other two equall'd with me in
fate,
So were I equall'd with them in renown,
Blind Thamyris and blind Maeonides,
And Tiresias and Phineus, prophets old.
                                   Ibid, 33.

17   Thus with the year
Seasons return, but not to me returns
Day, or the sweet approach of ev'n or
morn,
Or sight of vernal bloom, or summer's
rose,
Or flocks, or herds, or human face
divine;
But cloud instead, and ever-during dark
Surrounds me, from the cheerful ways
of men
Cut off, and for the book of knowledge
fair
Presented with a universal blank
Of nature's works to me expung'd and
ras'd,
And wisdom at one entrance quite shut
out.   *Ibid, 40.*

18 Dark with excessive bright.   *Ibid, 380.*

19   Eremites and friars,
White, black and grey, with all their
trumpery.   *Ibid, 474.*

20 Into a Limbo large and broad, since
called
The Paradise of Fools, to few unknown.
                                Ibid, 495.

21   At whose sight all the stars
Hide their diminished heads.
                             Ibid, IV. 34.

22 Me miserable! which way shall I fly
Infinite wrath, and infinite despair?
Which way I fly is hell; myself am hell;
And in the lowest deep a lower deep
Still threat'ning to devour me opens
wide,
To which the hell I suffer seems a
heav'n.   *Ibid, 73.*

23 So farewell hope, and with hope
farewell fear,
Farewell remorse: all good to me is lost;
Evil, be thou my good.   *Ibid, 108.*

24 Sabean odours from the spicy shore
Of Araby the blest.   *Ibid, 162.*

25 Thence up he flew, and on the Tree of
Life,
The middle tree and highest there that
grew,
Sat like a cormorant.   *Ibid, 194.*

26 A heaven on earth.   *Ibid, 208.*

27 Flowers of all hue, and without thorn
the rose.   *Ibid, 256.*

28 For contemplation he and valour
form'd,
For softness she and sweet attractive
grace,
He for God only, she for God in him:
His fair large front and eye sublime
declar'd
Absolute rule.   *Ibid, 297.*

29   Implied
Subjection, but requir'd with gentle
sway,

And by her yielded, by him best
receiv'd,
Yielded with coy submission, modest
pride,
And sweet reluctant amorous delay.
                                Ibid, 307.

30 Adam the goodliest man of men since
born
His sons, the fairest of her daughters
Eve.   *Ibid, 323.*

31 Imparadis'd in one another's arms.
                                Ibid, 506.

32 Now came still evening on, and twilight
grey
Had in her sober livery all things clad;
Silence accompanied, for beast and bird,
They to their grassy couch, these to
their nests
Were slunk, all but the wakeful
nightingale;
She all night slong her amorous descant
sung;
Silence was pleas'd: now glow'd the
firmament
With living sapphires: Hesperus, that led
The starry host, rode brightest, till the
moon
Rising in clouded majesty, at length
Apparent queen unveil'd her peerless
light,
And o'er the dark her silver mantle
threw.   *Ibid, 598.*

33 With thee conversing I forget all time,
All seasons and their change, all please,
alike.
Sweet is the breath of morn, her rising
sweet,
With charm of earliest birds; pleasant the
sun
When first on this delightful land he
spreads
His orient beams, on herb, tree, fruit,
and flower,
Glist'ring with dew; fragrant the fertile
earth
After soft showers; and sweet the
coming on
Of grateful evening mild, then silent
night
With this her solemn bird and this fair
moon,

And these the gems of heav'n, her starry train. *Ibid, 639.*

1   Eas'd the putting off
These troublesome disguises which we wear. *Ibid, 739.*

2 Hail wedded love, mysterious law, true source
Of human offspring, sole propriety
In Paradise of all things common else. *Ibid, 750.*

3 His thus intent Ithuriel with his spear
Touch'd lightly; for no falsehood can endure
Touch of celestial temper. *Ibid, 810.*

4 Not to know me argues yourselves unknown. *Ibid, 830.*

5   Abash'd the devil stood
And felt how awful goodness is, and saw
Virtue in her shape how lovely. *Ibid, 846.*

6 But wherefore thou alone? Wherefore with thee
Came not all hell broke loose? *Ibid, 917.*

7 Like Teneriff or Atlas unremov'd. *Ibid, 987.*

8 Now morn her rosy steps in th' eastern clime
Advancing, sow'd the earth with orient pearl,
When Adam wak'd, so custom'd, for his sleep
Was aery light, from pure digestion bred. *Ibid, V. 1.*

9 My fairest, my espous'd, my latest found,
Heav'n's last best gift, my ever new delight. *Ibid, 18.*

10 Best image of myself and dearer half. *Ibid, 95.*

11 These are thy glorious words, Parent of Good! *Ibid, 153.*

12 Him first, him last, him midst, and without end. *Ibid, 165.*

13 A wilderness of sweets. *Ibid, 294.*

14 So saying, with dispatchful looks in haste
She turns, on hospitable thoughts intent. *Ibid, 331.*

15 No fear lest dinner cool. *Ibid, 396.*

16 Thrones, dominations, princedoms, virtues, powers. *Ibid, 601.*

17 So spake the seraph Abdiel, faithful found
Among the faithless, faithful only he. *Ibid, 893.*

18 All night the dreadless angel unpursu'd
Through heav'n's wide champain held his way, till morn,
Wak'd by the circling hours, with rosy hand
Unbarr'd the gates of light. *Ibid, VI. 1.*

19 Arms on armour clashing bray'd
Horrible discord, and the madding wheels
Of brazen chariots rag'd; dire was the noise
Of conflict. *Ibid, 209.*

20 He onward came; far off his coming shone. *Ibid, 768.*

21 More safe I sing with mortal voice, unchang'd
To hoarse or mute, though fall'n on evil days,
On evil days though fall'n, and evil tongues. *Ibid, VII. 24.*

22   Still govern thou my song,
Urania, and fit audience find, though few. *Ibid, 30.*

23 The angel ended, and in Adam's ear
So charming left his voice, that he awhile
Thought him still speaking, still stood fix'd to hear. *Ibid, VIII. 1.*

24 Liquid lapse of murmuring streams. *Ibid, 263.*

25 And feel that I am happier than I know. *Ibid, 282.*

26 Grace was in all her steps, heav'n in her
    eye,
  In every gesture dignity and love.
                      Ibid, 488.

27 Her virtue and the conscience of her
    worth,
  That would be woo'd, and not unsought
    be won.   *Ibid, 502.*

28   The amorous bird of night
  Sung spousal, and bid haste the evening
    star
  On his hill top, to light the bridal lamp.
                      Ibid, 518.

29   So absolute she seems
  And in herself complete, so well to
    know
  Her own, that what she wills to do or
    say,
  Seems wisest, virtuousest, discreetest,
    best.   *Ibid, 547.*

30 Accuse not Nature, she hath done her
    part;
  Do thou but thine.   *Ibid, 561.*

31 To whom the angel with a smile that
    glow'd
  Celestial rosy red, love's
    proper hue.   *Ibid, 618.*

32 Since first this subject for heroic song
  Pleas'd me long choosing, and
    beginning late.   *Ibid, IX. 25.*

33 The serpent subtlest beast of all the field.
                      Ibid, 86.

34 For solitude sometimes is best society,
  And short retirement urges sweet
    return.   *Ibid, 249.*

35 As one who long in populous city pent,
  Where houses thick and sewers annoy
    the air.   *Ibid, 445.*

36   Hope elevates, and joy
  Brightens his crest.   *Ibid, 633.*

37 God so commanded, and left that
    command
  Sole daughter of his voice. *Ibid, 652.*

38 Earth felt the wound, and Nature from
    her seat

Sighing through all her works gave
    signs of woe,
  That all was lost.   *Ibid, 782.*

39 O fairest of creation, last and best
  Of all God's works, creature in whom
    excell'd
  Whatever can to sight or thought be
    form'd
  Holy, divine, good, amiable, or sweet!
  How art thou lost, how on a sudden
    lost,
  Defac'd, deflower'd, and now to death
    devote?   *Ibid, 896.*

40   A pillar'd shade
  High overarch'd, and echoing walks
    between.   *Ibid, 1106.*

41   Yet shall I temper so
  Justice with mercy, as may illustrate
    most
  Them fully satisfied, and thee appease.
                    Ibid, x. 77.

42 Demoniac frenzy, moping melancholy,
  And moon-struck madness.
                  Ibid, XI. 485.

43 And over them triumphant Death his
    dart
  Shook, but delay'd to strike, though oft
    invok'd
  With vows, as their chief good, and final
    hope.   *Ibid, 491.*

44 So may'st thou live, till like ripe fruit
    thou drop
  Into thy mother's lap.   *Ibid, 535.*

45 Nor love thy life, nor hate; but what
    thou liv'st
  Live well, how long or short permit to
    heav'n.   *Ibid, 553.*

46 A bevy of fair women.   *Ibid, 582.*

47 The brazen throat of war had ceased to
    roar,
  All now was turn'd to jollity and game,
  To luxury and riot, feast and dance.
                  Ibid, 713.

48 Some natural tears they dropp'd, but
    wip'd them soon;

The world was all before them, where
to choose
Their place of rest, and Providence their
guide:
They hand in hand with wand'ring steps
and slow,
Through Eden took their solitary way.
Ibid, XII. 645.

1   Satan, bowing low
His grey dissimulation, disappear'd.
Paradise Regained, I. 497.

2   Beauty stands
In the admiration only of weak minds
Led captive.   *Ibid, II. 220.*

3 Of fairy damsels met in forest wide
By knights of Logres, or of Lyones,
Lancelot or Pelleas, or Pellenore.
Ibid, 359.

4 Of whom to be disprais'd were no small
praise.   *Ibid, III. 56.*

5 Syene, and where the shadow both way
falls,
Meroe, Nilotic isle.   *Ibid, IV. 70.*

6   The childhood shows the man,
As morning shows the day.   *Ibid, 220.*

7 Athens, the eye of Greece, mother of
arts
And eloquence.   *Ibid, 240.*

8 See there the olive grove of Academe,
Plato's retirement, where the Attic bird
Trills her thick-warbl'd notes the
summer long.   *Ibid, 244.*

9 Thence to the famous orators repair,
Those ancient, whose resistless
eloquence
Wielded at will that fierce democratie,
Shook the arsenal and fulmin'd over
Greece,
To Macedon, and Artaxerxes' throne.
Ibid, 267.

10 Deep vers'd in books and shallow in
himself.   *Ibid, 327.*

11   Till morning fair
Came forth with pilgrim steps in amice
grey.   *Ibid, 426.*

12   He unobserv'd
Home to his mother's house private
return'd.   *Ibid, 638.*

13 A little onward lend thy guiding hand
To these dark steps, a little further on.
Samson Agonistes, I.

14 Eyeless in Gaza at the mill with slaves.
Ibid, 41.

15 O dark, dark, dark, amid the blaze of
noon,
Irrecoverably dark, total eclipse
Without all hope of day.   *Ibid, 80.*

16 Just are the ways of God,
And justifiable to men;
Unless there be who think not God at
all.   *Ibid, 293.*

17 What boots it at one gate to make
defence
And at another to let in the foe?
Ibid, 560.

18 But who is this, what thing of sea or
land?
Female of sex it seems,
That so bedeck'd, ornate, and gay,
Comes this way sailing
Like a stately ship
Of Tarsus, bound for th' isles
Of Javan or Gadier,
With all her bravery on, and tackle trim,
Sails fill'd, and streamers waving,
Courted by all the winds that hold them
play,
An amber scent of odorous perfume
Her harbinger.   *Ibid, 710.*

19 He's gone, and who knows how he may
report
Thy words by adding fuel to the flame?
Ibid, 1350.

20 For evil news rides post, while good
news baits.   *Ibid, 1538.*

21 Nothing is here for tears, nothing to
wail
Or knock the breast, no weakness, no
contempt,
Dispraise, or blame, nothing but well
and fair,

And what may quiet us in a death so
noble. *Ibid, 1721.*

22 Calm of mind, all passion spent.
Ibid, 1758.

23 A poet soaring in the high region of his
fancies with his garland and singing
robes about him.
*The Reason of Church Government, II.
Introduction.*

24 By labour and intent study (which I take
to be my portion in this life) joined
with the strong propensity of nature, I
might perhaps leave something so
written to after times, as they should
not willingly let it die. *Ibid.*

25 He who would not be frustrate of his
hope to write well hereafter in laudable
things ought himself to be a true poem.
Apology for Smectymnuus.

26 Truth is as impossible to be soiled by
any outward touch as the sunbeam.
The Doctrine and Discipline of Divorce.

27 To which (rhetoric) poetry would be
made subsequent, or indeed rather
precedent, as being less subtle and fine,
but more simple, sensuous and
passionate. *Tractate of Education.*

28 As good almost kill a man as kill a good
book; who kills a man kills a
reasonable creature, God's image; but
he who destroys a good book kills
reason itself, kills the image of God, as
it were in the eye. *Areopagitica.*

29 A good book is the precious life-blood
of a master spirit, embalmed and
treasured up on purpose to a life
beyond life. *Ibid.*

30 I cannot praise a fugitive and cloistered
virtue, unexercised and unbreathed,
that never sallies out and sees her
adversary, but slinks out of the race,
where that immortal garland is to be
run for, not without dust and heat.
Ibid.

31 Our sage and serious poet Spenser. *Ibid.*

32 Lords and Commons of England,
consider what nation it is whereof ye
are and whereof ye are the governors: a
nation not slow and dull, but of a
quick, ingenious, and piercing spirit,
acute to invent, subtle and sinewy to
discourse, not beneath the reach of any
point the highest that human capacity
can soar to. *Ibid.*

33 Now once again, by all concurrence of
signs and by the general instinct of
holy and devout men, as they daily and
solemnly express their thoughts, God
is decreeing to begin some new and
great period in his Church, even to the
reforming of Reformation itself. What
does He then but reveal himself to his
servants, and as his manner is, first to
his Englishmen? *Ibid.*

34 Methinks I see in my mind a noble and
puissant nation rousing herself like a
strong man after sleep, and shaking her
invincible locks. Methinks I see her as
an eagle mewing her mighty youth,
and kindling her undazzled eyes at the
full midday beam. *Ibid.*

35 Let her and Falsehood grapple; who ever
knew Truth put to the worse in a free
and open encounter? *Ibid.*

36 Rhyme being no necessary adjunct or
true ornament of poem or good verse,
in longer works especially, but the
invention of a barbarous age, to set off
wretched matter and lame metre.
The Verse. Preface to Paradise Lost, 1668.

**MOLIÈRE (JEAN BAPTISTE
POQUELIN), French dramatist,
15 Jan. 1622–17 Feb. 1673.**

37 Nous avons changé tout cela. – We have
changed all that.
*Le Médecin malgré lui – The Doctor in spite
of himself, II. vi.*

38 Il y a plus de quarante ans que je dis de la
prose sans que j'en susse rien. – For
more than forty years I have been
talking prose without knowing it.
*Le Bourgeois Gentilhomme – The Citizen
turned Gentleman, II. iv.*

1 Que diable allait-il faire dans cette
galère? – What the devil should he be
doing in that galley? *Les Fourberies de
Scapin – The Knavery of
Scapin, II. vii.*

MONKHOUSE, WILLIAM
COSMO, English art critic and
poet, 18 March, 1840–2 July, 1901

2 There was an old party of Lyme,
Who married three wives at one time.
When asked, "Why the third?"
He replied, "One's absurd,
And bigamy, sir, is a crime!" *Limerick.*

MONRO, HAROLD EDWARD,
English poet, 14 March, 1879–16
March, 1932

3 Silence is scattered like a broken glass,
The minutes prick their ears and run
about,
Then one by one subside again and pass
Sedately in, monotonously out.
Solitude.

4 She nestles over the shining rim,
Buries her chin in the creamy sea;
Her tail hangs loose; each drowsy paw
Is doubled under each bending knee.
Milk for the Cat.

MONSELL, JOHN SAMUEL
BEWLEY, Irish priest, 2 March,
1811–9 April, 1875

5 Fight the good fight
With all thy might;
Christ is thy strength, and Christ thy
right. *Fight of Faith.*

MONTAGU, LADY MARY
WORTLEY, English authoress,
baptised 26 May, 1689, died 21 Aug.
1762

6 Let this great maxim be my virtue's
guide, –
In part she is to blame that has been
tried:
He comes too near that comes to be
denied.
(Last line from Overbury, 186:4)
The Lady's Resolve.

7 And we meet, with champagne and a
chicken, at last. *The Lover.*

8 Be plain in dress, and sober in your diet;
In short, my deary! kiss me, and be
quiet.
A Summary of Lord Lyttelton's Advice.

9 Satire should, like a polished razor keen,
Wound with a touch that's scarcely felt
or seen.
*To the Imitator of the First Satire of Horace,
Book II.*

10 This world consists of men, women,
and Herveys. *Letters, I. 67.*

MONTAIGNE, MICHAEL
EYQUEM DE, French essayist, 28
Feb. 1533–13 Sept. 1592

11 Quand je me jouë à ma chatte, qui scait,
si elle passe son temps de moy plus que
je ne fay d'elle? – When I play with my
cat, who knows whether I do not make
her more sport than she makes me?
Essais, II. xii.

12 Peu d'hommes ont esté admiréz par
leurs domestiques. – Few men have been
admired by their servants. *Ibid, III. ii.*

13 Miserable à mon gré, qui n'a chez soy,
où estre à soy: où se faire
particulierement la cour: où se cacher. –
Miserable, to my thinking, is he who in
his home has no place where he can be
his sole company; where he can invite
his mind; where he can lurk secure.
Ibid, iii.

14 Il en advient ce qui se voit aux cages, les
oyseaux qui en sont dehors, desperent
d'y entrer; et d'un pareil soing en sortir,
ceux qui sont au dedans. – It happens as
with cages: the birds outside despair to
get in, and those inside despair of
getting out. (Of marriage.) *Ibid, V.*

15 Tout le monde me recognoist en mon
livre, et mon livre en moy. – All the
world knows me in my book, and my
book in me. *Ibid.*

MONTGOMERY, JAMES, English poet, 4 Nov. 1771–30 April, 1854

16 Here in the body pent,
Absent from Him I roam,
Yet nightly pitch my moving tent
A day's march nearer home.
At Home in Heaven.

MONTGOMERY, ROBERT, English clergyman and poet, 1807– 3 Dec. 1855

17 The solitary monk who shook the world.
Luther. Man's Need and God's Supply, 68.

18 The soul aspiring pants its source to mount
As streams meander level with their fount.
The Omnipresence of the Deity, I. 339.

MONTROSE, JAMES GRAHAM, 1ST MARQUIS OF, Scottish soldier, 1612–21 May, 1650

19 He either fears his fate too much,
Or his deserts are small,
That dares not put it to the touch,
To gain or lose it all.
My Dear and Only Love.
(An alternative version is:–
That puts it not unto the touch
To win or lose it all.)

20 I'll make thee glorious by my pen,
And famous by my sword. *Ibid.*

MOORE, EDWARD, English dramatist, 22 March, 1712–1 March, 1757

21 I am rich beyond the dreams of avarice.
The Gamester, II. ii.

MOORE, GEORGE, Irish author, 24 Feb. 1852–21 Jan. 1933

22 Acting is therefore the lowest of the arts, if it is an art at all. *Mummer-Worship.*

23 All reformers are bachelors.
The Bending of the Bough, I.

MOORE, JULIA A., US poetess, 1847–1920

24 'Lord Byron' was an Englishman
A poet I believe,
His first works in old England
Was poorly received.
Perhaps it was 'Lord Byron's' fault
And perhaps it was not.
His life was full of misfortunes,
Ah, strange was his lot.
Sketch of Lord Byron's Life.

MOORE, THOMAS, Irish poet, 28 May, 1779–25 Feb. 1852

25 How shall we rank thee upon glory's page?
Thou more than soldier and just less than sage. *To Thomas Hume.*

26 Row, brothers, row, the stream runs fast,
The Rapids are near and the daylight's past. *A Canadian Boat Song.*

27 A Persian's Heav'n is easily made,
'Tis but black eyes and lemonade.
Intercepted Letters, vi.

28 Go where glory waits thee,
But, while fame elates thee,
Oh! still remember me.
Irish Melodies. Go where Glory waits thee.

29 When he, who adores thee, has left but the name
Of his faults and his sorrows behind.
Ibid. When he who adores thee.

30 The harp that once through Tara's halls
The soul of music shed,
Now hangs as mute on Tara's walls,
As if that soul were fled.
Ibid, The Harp that once through Tara's Halls.

31 Rich and rare were the gems she wore,
And a bright gold ring on her wand she bore.
Ibid, Rich and Rare were the Gems she wore.

32 There is not in the wide world a valley so sweet

As that vale in whose bosom the bright
waters meet.
Ibid, The Meeting of the Waters.

1 Believe me, if all those endearing young
charms,
Which I gaze on so fondly to-day.
*Ibid, Believe me, if all those endearing
Young Charms.*

2 No, the heart that has truly lov'd never
forgets,
But as truly loves on to the close,
As the sun-flower turns on her god,
when he sets,
The same look which she turn'd when
he rose. *Ibid.*

3 And to know, when far from the lips we
love,
We've but to make love to the lips we
are near. *Ibid, 'Tis Sweet to think.*

4 But there's nothing half so sweet in life
As love's young dream.
Ibid, Love's Young Dream.

5 Lesbia hath a beaming eye,
But no one knows for whom it
beameth.
Ibid, Lesbia hath a Beaming Eye.

6 Eyes of most unholy blue!
Ibid, By that Lake whose Gloomy Shore.

7 She is far from the land where her young
hero-sleeps,
And lovers are round her, sighing:
But coldly she turns from their gaze,
and weeps,
For her heart in his grave is lying.
Ibid, She is far from the Land.

8 'Tis the last rose of summer
Left blooming alone;
All her lovely companions
Are faded and gone.
Ibid, The Last Rose of Summer.

9 Then awake! – the heavens look bright,
my dear,
'Tis never too late for delight, my dear,
And the best of all ways
To lengthen our days,
Is to steal a few hours from the night,
my dear! *Ibid, The Young May Moon.*

10 The Minstrel Boy to the war is gone,
In the ranks of death you'll find him;
His father's sword he has girded on,
And his wild harp slung behind him.
Ibid, The Minstrel Boy.

11 You may break, you may shatter the
vase, if you will,
But the scent of the roses will hang
round it still.
*Ibid, Farewell! – But whenever you
welcome the Hour.*

12 The time I've lost in wooing,
In watching and pursuing
The light, that lies
In woman's eyes.
Had been my heart's undoing.
Ibid. The Time I've lost in wooing.

13 My only books
Were woman's looks,
And folly's all they've taught me. *Ibid.*

14 Oft, in the stilly night,
Ere Slumber's chain has bound me,
Fond Memory brings the light
Of other days around me;
The smiles, the tears,
Of boyhood's years,
The words of love then spoken;
The eyes that shone,
Now dimm'd and gone,
The cheerful hearts now broken!
National Airs. Oft in the Stilly Night.

15 I feel like one
Who treads alone
Some banquet-hall deserted,
Whose lights are fled,
Whose garlands dead,
And all but he departed! *Ibid.*

16 Oh! ever thus, from childhood's hour,
I've seen my fondest hopes decay;
I never lov'd a tree or flow'r,
But 'twas the first to fade away.
I never nurs'd a dear gazelle,
To glad me with its soft black eye,
But when it came to know me well,
And love me, it was sure to die!
Lalla Rookh. The Fire-Worshippers, 1.
279.

17 "Come, come," said Tom's father, 'at your time of life,
There's no longer excuse for thus playing the rake –
It is time you should think, boy, of taking a wife' –
"Why, so it is, father – whose wife shall I take?"   *A Joke Versified.*

18 The minds of some of our own statesmen, like the pupil of the human eye, contract themselves the more, the stronger light there is shed upon them.
Corruption and Intolerance, preface.

MORDAUNT, THOMAS OSBERT, 1730–1809

19 Sound, sound the clarion, fill the fife,
Throughout the sensual world proclaim,
One crowded hour of glorious life
Is worth an age without a name.
Verses written during the War, 1756–1763.
(Quoted as anonymous by Scott in *Old Mortality*, xxxiii. 'To all' being put for 'Throughout.')

MORE, HANNAH, English authoress, 2 Feb. 1745–7 Sept., 1833

20 He liked those literary cooks
Who skim the cream of others' books;
And ruin half an author's graces
By plucking *bon-mots* from their places
Florio, 123.

MORE, SIR THOMAS, English lord Chancellor and Saint, 7 Feb., 1478–6 July, 1535

21 For men use, if they have an evil tourne, to write it in marble: and whoso doth us a good tourne we write it in dust.
Richard III.

22 Is not this house (the Tower of London) as nigh heaven as mine own?
Roper, Life of Sir Thomas More, 83.

23 I pray you, Master Lieutenant, see me safe up, and for my coming down let me shift for myself.
Words on mounting the scaffold.

MOREHEAD, JOHN MORLEY, US statesman, 4 July, 1796–27 Aug. 1866

24 It's a long time between drinks.
Remark to the Governor of South Carolina when Morehead was Governor of North Carolina.

MORELL, THOMAS, English author, 18 March, 1703–19 Feb. 1784

25 See, the conquering hero comes!
Sound the trumpets, beat the drums
Joshua, part iii.
(Lines wrongly ascribed to Nathaniel Lee.)

MORLEY, CHRISTOPHER DARLINGTON, US author, 5 May, 1890–28 March, 1957

26 There is no prince or prelate
I envy – no, not one.
No evil can befall me –
By God, I have a son!   *Secret Laughter.*

MORLEY, JOHN VISCOUNT, 24 Dec. 1838–23 Sept. 1932

27 Literature, the most seductive, the most deceiving, the most dangerous of professions.   *Burke, i.*

28 Every man of us has all the centuries in him, though their operations be latent, dim, and very various.
Life of Gladstone, 11. vi.

29 The great business of life is, to be, to do, to do without, and to depart.
Address on aphorisms, Edinburgh, Nov. 1887.

MORRIS, CHARLES, English song-writer, 1745–11 July, 1838

30 Solid men of Boston, make no long orations;
Solid men of Boston, banish strong potations.   *Billy Pit and the Farmer.*

31 If one must have a villa in summer to dwell,
Oh, give me the sweet shady side of Pall Mall!   *The Contrast.*

MORRIS, GEORGE POPE, US journalist and poet, 10 Oct. 1802–6 July, 1864

1 Woodman, spare that tree!
Touch not a single bough!
In youth it sheltered me,
And I'll protect it now.
Woodman, spare that Tree.

2 A song for our banner! The watchword recall
Which gave the Republic her station:
'United we stand, divided we fall!'
It made and preserves us a nation!
The union of lakes, the union of lands,
The union of States non can sever,
The union of hearts, the union of hands,
And the flag of our Union for ever!
The Flag of our Union.

MORRIS, WILLIAM, English artist and poet, 24 March, 1834–3 Oct. 1896

3 Pray but one prayer for me 'twixt thy closed lips,
Think but one thought of me up in the stars. *Summer Dawn.*

4 And ever she sung from noon to noon,
Two red roses across the moon.
Two Red Roses across the Moon.

5 My lady seems of ivory
Forehead, straight nose, and cheeks that be
Hollow'd a little mournfully.
Beata mea Domina! Praise of my Lady.

6 I know a little garden close
Set thick with lily and red rose,
Where I would wander if I might
From dewy dawn to dewy night,
And have one with me wandering.
The Life and Death of Jason, IV. 577.

7 The idle singer of an empty day.
The Earthly Paradise. An Apology.

8 Dreamer of dreams, born out of my due time,
Why should I strive to set the crooked straight? *Ibid.*

9 Love is enough: though the world be a-waning,
And the woods have no voice but the voice of complaining,
Though the sky be too dark for dim eyes to discover
The gold-cups and daisies fair blooming thereunder. *Love is enough, i.*

10 Wilt thou do the deed and repent it?
thou hadst better never been born:
Wilt thou do the deed and exalt it? then
thy fame shall be outworn:
Thou shalt do the deed and abide it, and
sit on thy throne on high,
And look on to-day and to-morrow as
those that never die.
Sigurd the Volsung, ii. 10.

MORTON, THOMAS, English dramatist, 1764?–28 March, 1838

11 Push on – keep moving.
A Cure for the Heartache, 11. i.

12 Approbation from-Sir Hubert Stanley is praise indeed. *Ibid, V. ii.*

13 Always ding, dinging Dame Grundy
into my ears – what will Mrs. Grundy
say? What will Mrs. Grundy think?
Speed the Plough, I. i.

MOSS, THOMAS, English poet and clergyman, 1740?–6 Dec. 1808

14 A pamper'd menial forc'd me from the door. *The Beggar, 15*

MOTHERWELL, WILLIAM, Scottish poet, 13 Oct. 1797–1 Nov. 1835

15 I've wandered east, I've wandered west,
Through mony a weary way;
But never, never can forget
The love o'life's young day.
Jeanie Morrison.

MOTLEY, JOHN LOTHROP, US historian, 15 April, 1814–29 May, 1877

16 Give us the luxuries of life, and we will dispense with its necessities.
O. W. Holmes's Autocrat of the Breakfast Table, vi.

MULOCK, DINAH MARIA, see Craik

MUNRO, HECTOR HUGH, see Saki

MUNRO, NEIL, Scottish author, 3 June, 1864–22 Dec. 1930

17 It was chust sublime.
The Vital Spark, Wee Teeny.

MUNSTER, ERNST FRIEDRICH HERBERT, COUNT VON, Hanovarian politician, 1766–1839

18 Absolutism tempered by assassination. (Description of the Russian Constitution.) *Letter.*

MURPHY, ARTHUR, Irish dramatist, 27 Dec. 1727–18 June, 1805

19 Above the vulgar flight of common souls. *Zenobia, V. i.*

MYERS, FREDERIC WILLIAM HENRY, English author, 6 Feb. 1843–17 Jan. 1901

20 Christ, I am Christ's, and let the name suffice you;
Aye, for me, too, it greatly hath sufficed.
Lo, with no winning words would I entice you,
Paul hath no honour and no friend but Christ. *Saint Paul.*

NAIRNE, CAROLINA OLIPHANT, BARONESS, Scottish poetess, 16 Aug. 1766–26 Oct. 1845

21 I'm wearin' awa' John,
Like snaw-wreaths in thaw, John;
I'm wearin' awa'
To the land o' the leal.
There's nae sorrow there, John;
There's neither cauld nor care, John;
The day's aye fair
In the land o' the leal.
The Land o' the Leal.

22 The Laird o' Cockpen he's proud and he's great,

His mind is ta'en up with the things o' the State. *The Laird o' Cockpen.*

23 Favour wi' wooin' was fashous to seek. *Ibid.*

24 A penniless lass wi' a lang pedigree. *Ibid.*

25 Oh Charlie is my darling, my darling, my darling,
Oh, Charlie is my darling, the young Chevalier. *Charlie is my Darling.*

26 Wi' a hundred pipers an' a', an' a'. *The Hundred Pipers.*

27 Better lo'ed ye canna be,
Will ye no come back again?
Will ye no come back again?

NAPIER, SIR CHARLES JAMES, English soldier and administrator, 10 Aug. 1782–29 Aug. 1853

28 Peccavi. (I have sinned = I have Sind.)
Punning dispatch after victory of Hyderabad in Sind, 1843.

NAPOLEON BONAPARTE, Emperor of France, 15 Aug. 1769–5 May, 1821

29 Soldats, songez que, du haut de ces pyramides, quarante siècles vous contemplent. – Soldiers, consider that, from the summit of these pyramids, forty centuries look down upon you.
Speech before the Battle of the Pyramids, 21 July, 1798.

30 Du sublime au ridicule il n'y a qu'un pas. – From the sublime to the ridiculous there is only one step.
After the retreat from Moscow, 1812.

31 La carrière ouverte aux talents. – The career open to talents.
On St. Helena, 1817.

32 L'Angleterre est une nation de boutiquiers. – England is a nation of shopkeepers. *Attributed.*

33 Tout soldat français porte dans sa giberne le bâton de maréchal de France.

– Every French soldier carries in his cartridge-pouch the baton of a marshal of France. *Ibid.*

NASH, OGDEN, US poet, 19 Aug. 1902 – 19 May, 1971

1 I think that I shall never see
A billboard lovely as a tree.
Song of the Open Road.

2 A girl who is bespectacled,
She may not get her nectacled.
Lines written to console those Ladies distressed by the Lines 'Men seldom make Passes, etc.'

3 I sit in an office at 244 Madison Avenue,
And say to myself You have a responsible job, havenue?
Spring comes to Murray Hill.

4 But the old men know when an old man dies. *Old Men.*

NASH or NASHE, THOMAS, English author, November, 1567–1601

5 Spring, the sweet spring, is the year's pleasant king;
Then blooms each thing, then maids dance in a ring,
Cold doth not sting, the pretty birds do sing:
Cuckoo, jug-jug, pu-we, to-witta-woo!
Spring.

6 Brightness falls from the air;
Queens have died young and fair;
Dust hath closed Helen's eye.
A Lament in Time of Plague.

NEALE, JOHN MASON, English clergyman and author, 24 Jan. 1818–6 Aug. 1866

7 Jerusalem the golden,
With milk and honey blest,
Beneath thy contemplation
Sink heart and voice oppressed.
Hymn from the Latin of Bernard of Morlaix.

8 Brief life is here our portion.
Hymn from same.

9 Art thou weary, art thou languid,
Art thou sore distressed.
Hymn from the Greek.

10 Christian, dost thou see them
On the holy ground,
How the troops of Midian
Prowl and prowl around.
Hymn from same.

11 Good King Wenceslas looked out
On the Feast of Stephen;
When the snow lay round about,
Deep and crisp and even.
Good King Wenceslas.

12 Bring me flesh and bring me wine,
Bring me pine-logs hither. *Ibid.*

NELSON, HORATIO NELSON, VISCOUNT, English admiral, 29 Sept. 1758–21 Oct. 1805

13 Westminster Abbey or victory!
At Battle of Cape St. Vincent, 14 Feb. 1797.

14 It is warm work; and this day may be the last to any of us at a moment. But mark you! I would not be elsewhere for thousands.
At Battle of Copenhagen, 2 April, 1801

15 I really do not see the signal! *Ibid.*
(putting the telescope to his blind eye).

16 England expects that every man will do his duty.
Signal from flagship at Trafalgar, 21 Oct. 1805.

17 Thank God, I have done my duty.
Dying words.

NERO (NERO CLAUDIUS CAESAR), Roman Emperor, 15 Dec. 37–9 June, 68

18 Qualis artifex pereo! – What an artist perishes in me! *Dying words.*

NESBIT EDITH (MRS HUBERT BLAND), English authoress, 19 Aug. 1858–4 May, 1924

19 The chestnut's proud, and the lilac's pretty,

The poplar's gentle and tall,
But the plane tree's kind to the poor dull
city –
I love him best of all.
Child's Song in Spring.

NEWBOLT, SIR HENRY JOHN, English poet, 6 June, 1862–19 April, 1938

20 Take my drum to England, hang et by
the shore,
Strike et when your powder's runnin'
low;
If the Dons sight Devon, I'll quit the
port o'Heaven,
An' drum them up the Channel as we
drummed them long ago.
Drake's Drum

21 All night long in a dream untroubled of
hope
He brooded, clasping his knees.
He fell among Thieves.

22 To set the cause above renown,
To love the game beyond the prize,
To honour, while you strike him down,
The foe that comes with fearless eyes.
Clifton Chapel.

23 'Qui procul hinc,' the legend's writ, –
The frontier-grave is far away –
'Qui ante diem periit:
Sed miles, sed pro patria. *Ibid.*
(Who died far from here, before his
time, but as a soldier, for his country.)

24 A bumping pitch and a blinding light,
An hour to play and the last man in.
Vitaï Lampada.

25 The sand of the desert is sodden red, –
Red with the wreck of a square that
broke;–
The Gatling's jammed and the Colonel
dead,
And the regiment blind with dust and
smoke.
The river of death has brimmed his
banks,
And England's far, and Honour a name,
But the voice of a schoolboy rallies the
ranks:
'Play up! play up and play the game!'
Ibid.

NEWELL, ROBERT HENRY ('ORPHEUS C. KERR'), US author, 13 Dec. 1836–July, 1901

26 Dog Hollow, in the Green Mount State,
Was his first stopping-place;
And then Skunk's Misery displayed
Its sweetness and its grace.
The American Traveller.

NEWLAND, ABRAHAM, English banker, 23 April, 1730–21 Nov. 1807

27 Beneath this stone old Abraham lies;
Nobody laughs and nobody cries
Where he is gone and how he fares,
Nobody knows, and nobody cares.
His own epitaph.

NEWMAN, JOHN HENRY, English Cardinal, 21 Feb. 1801–11 Aug. 1890

28 Lead, kindly Light, amid the encircling
gloom,
Lead Thou me on;
The night is dark, and I am far from
home;
Lead Thou me on.
Keep Thou my feet; I do not ask to see
The distant scene, – one step enough for
me. *Lead Kindly Light.*

29 And with the morn those angel faces
smile
While I have loved long since, and lost
awhile. *Ibid.*

NEWTON, SIR ISAAC, English scientist, 25 Dec. 1642–20 March, 1727

30 I do not know what I may appear to the
world, but to myself I seem to have been
only like a boy playing on the sea-shore,
and diverting myself in now and then
finding a smoother pebble or a prettier
shell than ordinary, whilst the great
ocean of truth lay all undiscovered
before me.
Brewster's Memoirs of Newton, II. xxvii.

31 O Diamond! Diamond! thou little
knowest the mischief done!
*To a dog that destroyed papers representing
years of work.*

NEWTON, JOHN, English clergyman, 24 July, 1725–21 Dec. 1807

1 Glorious things of thee are spoken,
Zion, city of our God. *Hymn.*

NICOLSON, ADELA FLORENCE, see Hope, Laurence

NOBLES, MILTON, US actor and dramatist, 28 Sept. 1847–14 June, 1924

2 The villain still pursued her.
The Phœnix, I. iii.

NOEL, THOMAS, English poet, 11 May, 1799–16 May, 1861

3 Rattle his bones over the stones;
He's only a pauper, whom nobody
owns! *The Pauper's Drive.*

NORRIS, JOHN, English clergyman, 1657–1711

4 How fading are the joys we dote upon, –
Like apparitions seen and gone:
But those which soonest take their
flight,
Are the most exquisite and strong,
Like angels' visits, short and bright;
Mortality's too weak to bear them long.
The Parting, 19.

NORTON, CAROLINE ELIZABETH SARAH, English poetess, 1808–15 June, 1877

5 My beautiful, my beautiful! that
standest meekly by,
With thy proudly-arched and glossy
neck, and dark and fiery eye!
Fret not to roam the desert now, with all
thy winged speed:
I may not mount on thee again! – thou'rt
sold, my Arab steed! *The Arab's
Farewell to his Steed.*

NOVALIS (FRIEDRICH LEOPOLD VON HARDENBERG), German author, 2 May, 1772–25 March, 1801

6 Gott-trunkener Mensch. – A God-
intoxicated man. *Said of Spinoza.*

NOYES, ALFRED, English author, 16 Sept. 1880–28 June, 1958

7 Apes and ivory, skulls and roses, in
junks of old Hong-Kong,
Gliding over a sea of dreams to a
haunted shore of song.
Apes and Ivory.

8 Calling as he used to call, faint and far
away,
In Sherwood, in Sherwood, about the
break of day. *Sherwood.*

9 There's a barrel-organ carolling across a
golden street
In the City as the sun sinks low.
The Barrel-Organ.

10 Come down to Kew in Lilac-time, in
lilac-time, in lilac-time;
Come down to Kew in lilac-time (it isn't
far from London!)
And you shall wander hand in hand with
love in summer's wonderland;
Come down to Kew in lilac-time (it isn't
far from London!) *Ibid.*

11 The wind was a torrent of darkness
among the gusty trees.
The moon was a ghostly galleon tossed
upon cloudy seas,
The road was a ribbon of moonlight
over the purple moor,
And the highwayman came riding –
Riding – riding –
The highwayman came riding, up to the
old inn-door. *The Highwayman, i.*

12 Down to the valley she came, for far and
far below in the dreaming meadows
Pleaded ever the Voice of voices, calling
his love by her golden name;
So she arose from her home in the hills,
and down through the blossoms that
danced with their shadows,
Out of the blue of the dreaming
distance, down to the heart of her lover
she came. *Orpheus and Eurydice, i.*

13 God, how the dead men
Grin by the wall,
Watching the fun
Of the Victory Ball. *A Victory Dance.*

OAKELEY, FREDERICK, English priest, 5 Sept. 1802–29 Jan. 1880

14 O come, all ye faithful,
Joyful and triumphant,
O come ye, O come ye to Bethlehem.
Hymn from Latin Adeste Fideles.

O'CASEY, SEAN, Irish dramatist, 30 March 1880–18 Sept. 1964

15 The whole world is in a state of chassis.
Juno and the Paycock, I. i.

OGILVY, JAMES, 1ST EARL OF SEAFIELD, Lord Chancellor of Scotland, 1664–15 Aug. 1730

16 Now there's ane end of ane old sang.
At the Act of Union of the Parliaments.

O'KEEFFE, JOHN, Irish dramatist, 24 June, 1747–4 Feb. 1833

17 Amo, amas, I love a lass,
As cedar tall and slender;
Sweet cowslip's grace
Is her nominative case,
And she's of the feminine gender.
Agreeable Surprise, II. ii.

O'KELLY, DENNIS, English racehorse owner, 1720?–28 Dec. 1787

18 It will be Eclipse first, the rest nowhere.
At Epsom, 3 May, 1769.

OLDHAM, JOHN, English poet, 9 Aug. 1653–9 Dec. 1683

19 Racks, gibbets, halters, were their arguments.
Satires upon the Jesuits, I. Garnet's Ghost, 176.

OLDYS, WILLIAM, English antiquary, 14 July, 1696–15 April, 1761

20 Busy, curious, thirsty fly,
Drink with me, and drink as I.
Busy, Curious, Thirsty Fly

OMAR KHAYYAM, see Fitzgerald, Edward

O'NEILL, MOIRA (MRS, N. H. SKRINE), Irish authoress, 1864–22 Jan. 1955

21 Over here in England I'm helpin' wi' the hay,
An' I wisht I was in Ireland the livelong day;
Weary on the English hay, an' sorra take the wheat.
Och! Corrymeela an' the blue sky over it.
Corrymeela.

OPIE, JOHN, English painter, May, 1761–9 April, 1807

22 I mix them with my brains, sir.
When asked with what he mixed his colours.

ORCZY, EMMUSKA or EMMA MAGDALENA ROSALIA MARIE JOSEPHA BARBARA, BARONESS (MRS. MONTAGU BARSTOW), Anglo-Hungarian novelist, 23 Sept. 1865–12 Nov. 1947

23 We seek him here, we seek him there,
Those Frenchies seek him everywhere.
Is he in heaven? – Is he in hell?
That demmed, elusive Pimpernel?
The Scarlet Pimpernel, xii.

O'REILLY, JOHN BOYLE, Irish author, 28 June, 1844–10 Aug. 1890

24 You may grind their souls in the self-same mill,
You may bind them, heart and brow;
But the poet will follow the rainbow still,
And his brother will follow the plough.
The Rainbow's Treasure.

25 The organised charity, scrimped and iced,
In the name of a cautious, statistical Christ.
In Bohemia.

O'SHAUGHNESSY, ARTHUR WILLIAM EDGAR, English poet, 14 March, 1844–30 Jan. 1881

26 We are the music-makers,
And we are the dreamers of dreams,
Wandering by lone sea-breakers,

And sitting by desolate streams;
World-losers and world-forsakers,
On whom the pale moon gleams:
Yet we are the movers and shakers
Of the world for ever, it seems.   *Ode.*

1 One man with a dream, at pleasure,
Shall go forth and conquer a crown:
And three with a new song's measure
Can trample an empire down.   *Ibid.*

**OTWAY, THOMAS, English
dramatist, 3 March, 1652–14 April,
1685**

2 O woman! lovely woman! Nature made
thee
To temper man: we had been brutes
without you;
Angels are painted fair, to look like you;
There's in you all that we believe of
heaven, –
Amazing brightness, purity, and truth,
Eternal joy, and everlasting love.
      Venice Preserved, I. i.

3 What mighty ills have not been done by
woman!
Who was't betrayed the Capitol? A
woman!
Who lost Mark Antony the world? A
woman!
Who was the cause of a long ten years'
war,
And laid at last old Troy in ashes?
Woman!
Destructive, damnable, deceitful
woman!   *The Orphan, III. i.*

**OVERBURY, SIR THOMAS,
English poet, 1581–15 Sept. 1613**

4   In part to blame is she
Which hath without consent been only
tried;
He comes too near that comes to be
denied.   *A Wife, 26.*

**OVID (PUBLIUS OVIDIUS
NASO), Roman poet, 20 March, 43
B.C.–17 A.D.**

5 Forsitan et nostrum nomen miscebitur
istis.
– Perhaps our name too will be mingled
with these.   *Ars Amatoria, iii. 339.*

6 Medio tutissimus ibis.
– You will go most safely in the middle.
      Metamorphoses, ii. 137.

7   Video meliora, proboque;
Deteriora sequor.
– I see better things and approve them; I
follow the worse.   *Ibid, vii. 20.*

8 Tempus edax rerum.
– Time, the devourer of things.
      Ibid, xv. 234.

**OWEN, JOHN, Welsh
epigrammatist, 1560?–1622**

9 God and the doctor we alike adore
But only when in danger, not before;
The danger o'er, both are alike requited,
God is forgotten, and the doctor
slighted.   *Epigrams.*

**OWEN, ROBERT, English social
reformer, 14 May, 1771–17 Nov.
1858**

10 All the world is queer save thee and me,
and even thou art a little queer.
      *On separating from his business partner,
      William Allen, 1828.*

**OXENSTIERNA, AXEL
GUSTAFSSON, COUNT,
Swedish Chancellor, 16 June,
1583–28 Aug. 1654.**

11 Behold, my son, with how little
wisdom the world is governed.
      Letter to his son, 1648.

**OXFORD, EDWARD DE VERE,
17TH EARL OF, English poet, 2
April, 1550–24 June, 1604.**

12 If women could be fair and yet not fond.
      Women's Changeableness.

**OXFORD AND ASQUITH, EARL
OF, see Asquith**

**PAINE, THOMAS, English
political pamphleteer, 29 Jan.
1737–8 June, 1809**

13 These are the times that try men's souls.
      The American Crisis, No. 1.

14 The final event to himself (Mr. Burke) has been that, as he rose like a rocket, he fell like the stick.
Letter to the Addressers on the Late Proclamation, 1792.

15 The sublime and the ridiculous are often so nearly related, that it is difficult to class them separately. One step above the sublime makes the ridiculous; and one step above the ridiculous makes the sublime again.
The Age of Reason, II. 20.

PALAFOX Y MELZI, JOSÉ DE, DUKE OF SARAGOSSA, Spanish soldier, 1780–15 Feb. 1847

16 Guerra al cuchillo. – War to the knife.
Reply when summoned to surrender Saragossa, 1808.

PALEY, WILLIAM, ARCHDEACON OF CARLISLE, July, 1743–25 May, 1805

17 Who can refute a sneer?
Moral Philosophy, V ix.

PARKER, DOROTHY (MRS. ALAN CAMPBELL), US authoress, 22 Aug. 1893–7 June, 1967

18 Where's the man could ease a heart Like a satin gown? *The Satin Dress.*

19 Four be the things I'd been better without:
Love, curiosity, freckles, and doubt.
Inventory.

20 Guns aren't lawful;
Nooses give;
Gas smells awful;
You might as well live. *Résumé.*

21 Down from Caesar past Joyson-Hicks
Echoes the warning, ever new;
Though they're trained to amusing tricks,
Gentler, they, than the pigeon's coo,
Careful, son, of the cursed two –
Either one is a dangerous pet;
Natural history proves it true –
Women and elephants never forget.
Ballade of Unfortunate Mammals.

22 Excuse my dust. *Her own epitaph.*

PARKER, MARTIN, English ballad-monger, died 1656?

23 Ye gentlemen of England
That live at home at ease,
Ah! little do you think upon
The dangers of the seas.
Ye Gentlemen of England.

PARNELL, THOMAS, English poet, 1679–Oct. 1718

24 Still an angel appear to each lover beside,
But still be a woman to you.
When thy Beauty appears.

25 Remote from man, with God he passed the days,
Prayer all his business, all his pleasure praise. *The Hermit, 5.*

26 We call it only pretty Fanny's way.
An Elegy to an Old Beauty, 34.

PARR, SAMUEL, English schoolmaster, 26 Jan. 1747–6 March, 1825

27 Ay, now that the old lion is dead, every ass thinks he may kick at him.
Boswell's Life of Johnson, an. 1784.

PASCAL, BLAISE, French author, 19 June, 1623–19 Aug. 1662

28 Le nez de Cléopâtre: s'il eût été plus court, toute la face de la terre aurait changé. – If Cleopatra's nose had been shorter, the whole face of the world would have been changed.
Pensées, sect. ii. 162.

29 Le cœur a ses raisons que la raison ne connaît point. – The heart has its reasons of which reason knows nothing.
Ibid, sect. iv. 277.

PATER, WALTER HORATIO, English author, 4 Aug. 1839–30 July, 1894

30 She is older than the rocks among which she sits; like the vampire, she has been

dead many times, and learned the secrets of the grave; and has been a diver in deep seas, and keeps their fallen day about her; and trafficked for strange webs with Eastern merchants: and, as Leda, was the mother of Helen of Troy, and, as Saint Anne, the mother of Mary; and all this has been to her but as the sound of lyres and flutes, and lives only in the delicacy with which it has moulded the changing lineaments, and tinged the eyelids and the hands. (Mona Lisa).
The Renaissance. Leonardo da Vinci.

1 All art constantly aspires towards the condition of music.   *Ibid, Giorgione.*

2 To burn always with this hard, gemlike flame, to maintain this ecstasy, is success in life.   *Ibid, Conclusion.*

3 In truth all art does but consist in the removal of surplusage, from the last finish of the gem-engraver blowing away the last particles of invisible dust, back to the earliest divination of the finished work to be, lying somewhere, according to Michelangelo's fancy, in the rough-hewn block of stone.
Appreciations. Style.

PATMORE, COVENTRY KERSEY DIGHTON, English poet, 23 July, 1823–26 Nov. 1896

4 Ah, wasteful woman, she who may
On her sweet self set her own price,
Knowing man cannot choose but pay,
How has she cheapened paradise;
How given for nought her priceless gift,
How spoil'd the bread and spill'd the wine,
Which, sent with due, respective thrift,
Had made brutes men, and men divine.
The Angel in the House, I. iii. prelude 3, Unthrift.

5 'I saw you take his kiss!' 'Tis true.'
'O, modesty!' 'Twas strictly kept:
He thought me asleep; at least, I knew
He thought I thought he thought I slept.'   *Ibid, viii. prelude 3, The Kiss.*

6 Why, having won her, do I woo?
Because her spirit's vestal grace

Provokes me always to pursue,
But, spirit-like, eludes embrace.
Ibid, xii. prelude 1, The Married Lover.

7 My little Son, who look'd from thoughtful eyes
And moved and spoke in quiet grown-up wise.
The Unknown Eros, I. x. The Toys.

8 If I were dead, you'd sometimes say, 'Poor Child!'
Ibid, xiv. If I were Dead.

9 This is to say, my dear Augusta,
We've had another awful buster:
Ten thousand Frenchmen sent below!
Thank God from whom all blessings flow.
Epigram on message sent by King William of Prussia to his Queen, Aug. 1870.

PAYNE, JOHN HOWARD, US actor and dramatist, 9 June, 1791–9 April, 1852

10 Mid pleasures and palaces though we may roam,
Be it ever so humble, there's no place like home.
Clari, the Maid of Milan. Home, Sweet Home.

PEACOCK, THOMAS LOVE, English author, 18 Oct. 1785–23 Jan. 1866

11 Seamen three! what men be ye?
Gotham's three Wise Men we be.
Whither in your bowl so free?
To rake the moon from out the sea.
The bowl goes trim. The moon doth shine,
And our ballast is old wine.
Nightmare Abbey, xi. The Men of Gotham.

12 The mountain sheep are sweeter,
But the vallley sheep are fatter;
We therefore deemed it meeter
To carry off the latter.
The Misfortunes of Elphin, xi. The War Song of Dinas Vawr.

PEEL, SIR ROBERT, 2ND BARONET, English Prime Minister, 5 Feb. 1788–2 July, 1850

13 It takes three generations to make a gentleman.   *Attributed.*

PEELE, GEORGE, English dramatist, 1558?–1597?

14 Fair and fair, and twice so fair,
As fair as any may be;
The fairest shepherd on our green,
A love for any lady.
                        The Arraignment of Paris, I. ii.

15 My merry, merry, merry roundelay
Concludes with Cupid's curse, –
They that do change old love for new,
Pray gods they change for worse!   *Ibid.*

16 His golden locks time hath to silver turn'd;
O time too swift, O swiftness never ceasing!
His youth 'gainst time and age hath ever spurn'd,
But spurn'd in vain; youth waneth by increasing.   *Polyhymnia. Sonnet.*

17 His helmet now shall make a hive for bees,
And, lovers' sonnets turn'd to holy psalms,
A man-at-arms must now serve on his knees,
And feed on prayers, which are age's alms.   *Ibid.*

PEMBROKE, HENRY HERBERT, 10TH EARL OF, 3 July, 1734–26 Jan. 1794

18 Dr. Johnson's sayings would not appear so extraordinary, were it not for his *bow-wow way.*
Boswell's Life of Johnson, an. 1775, note.

PENN, WILLIAM, Founder of Pennsylvania, 14 Oct. 1644–30 July, 1718

19 No pain, no palm; no thorns, no throne; no gall, no glory; no cross, no crown.
                        No Cross, No Crown.

PEPYS, SAMUEL, English diarist, 23 Feb. 1633–26 May, 1703

20 And so to bed.
                        Diary, 6 May, 1660, et passim.

21 This morning came home my fine camlet cloak, with gold buttons, and a silk suit, which cost me much money, and I pray God to make me able to pay for it.   *Ibid, 1 July, 1660.*

22 My wife, who, poor wretch, is troubled with her lonely life.   *Ibid, 19 Dec. 1662.*

23 Went to hear Mrs. Turner's daughter play on the harpsichon; but, Lord! it was enough to make any man sick to hear her; yet was I forced to commend her highly.   *Ibid, 1 May, 1663.*

24 Saw a wedding in the church . . . and strange to see what delight we married people have to see these poor fools decoyed into our condition.
                        Ibid, 25 Dec. 1665.

25 Home, and, being washing-day, dined upon cold meat.   *Ibid, 4 April, 1666.*

26 To church; and with my mourning, very handsome, and new periwig, make a great show.   *Ibid, 31 March, 1667.*

PERICLES, Greek statesman, 493?–429 B.C.

27 Φιλοκαλοῦμεν τε γὰρ μετ' ευτελείας καὶ φιλοσοφοῦμεν ανευ μαλακίας.
– For we are lovers of the beautiful without extravagance, and cultivate our minds without effeminacy.
                        Thucydides, II. xl.

28 'Ανδρῶν γὰρ επιφανῶν πᾶσα γῆ τάφος. –
For to famous men the whole earth is a sepulchre.   *Ibid, xliii.*
(Both quotations from his Funeral Oration over the Athenian dead in the first year of the Peloponnesian War, 431 B.C.)

PERRONET, EDWARD, English Methodist preacher, 1726–2 Jan. 1792

1 All hail, the power of Jesus' name!
Let angels prostrate fall;
Bring forth the royal diadem,
To crown Him Lord of All.
Hymn on the Resurrection.

PERSIUS (AULUS PERSIUS FLACCUS), Roman poet, 4 Dec. A.D. 34 –24 Nov. 62

2 Virtutem videant, intabescantque
relicta.
– Let them look on Virtue, and pine
away because they have abandoned
her.   *Satires, iii. 38.*

3 Venienti occurrite morbo.
– Meet the disease as it approaches.
Ibid, 64.

PÉTAIN, HENRI PHILIPPE, Marshal of France, 24 April, 1856–23 July, 1951

4 Ils ne passseront pas. – They shall not
pass.   *At the defence of Verdun, 1916.*

PETRONIUS ARBITER, Roman satirist, died A.D. 65

5 Horatii curiosa felicitas. – The studied
felicity of Horace.   *Satyricon, cxviii.*

PHELPS, EDWARD JOHN, US lawyer and diplomat, 11 July, 1822–9 March, 1900

6 The man who makes no mistakes does
not usually make anything
*Speech at Mansion House, London,
24 Jan. 1899.*

PHILIPS, AMBROSE, English poet and MP, 1675?–18 June, 1749

7 The flowers, anew, returning seasons
bring!
But beauty faded has no second spring.
The First Pastoral, 55.

PHILIPS, JOHN, English poet, 30 Dec. 1676–15 Feb. 1709

8 Happy the man who, void of cares and
strife,
In silken or in leathern purse retains
A Splendid Shilling.
The Splendid Shilling, I.

PHILLIPS, STEPHEN, English poet, 28 July, 1864–9 Dec. 1915

9 A man not old, but mellow, like good
wine.   *Ulysses, III. ii.*

PHILLIPS, WENDELL, US reformer, 29 Nov. 1811–2 Feb. 1884

10 One on God's side is a majority.
Speech at Brooklyn, 1 Nov. 1859.

PHILLPOTTS, EDEN, English author, 4 Nov. 1862–29 Dec. 1960

11 Then old man's talk o' the days behind
'e,
Your darter's youngest darter to mind
'e;
A li'l dreamin', a li'l dyin':
A li'l lew corner o' airth to lie in.
Man's Days.

12 He never went out of bounds at all,
from fear and also from goodness, but
cheefly from fear.
The Human Boy Again. The Qwarry.

PINDAR, Greek poet, 522?–422? B.C.

13 Αριστον μὲν υδωρ.
– Water is best.   *Olympian Odes, i.*

14 Αι τε λιπαραὶ καὶ ιοστέφανοὶ καὶ
αοίδιμοι, 'Ελλάδος ερεισμα, κλειναὶ'
Αθᾶναι, δαιμονιον πτολίεθρον.
– Shining and violet-crowned and
celebrated in song, bulwark of Greece,
famous Athens, divine city. *Fragment.*

PINDAR, PETER, see Wolcot, John

PINERO, SIR ARTHUR WING, English dramatist, 24 May, 1855–23 Nov. 1934

15 From forty to fifty a man is at heart
either a stoic or a satyr.
The Second Mrs. Tanqueray, 1.

PITT, WILLIAM, English Prime Minister, 28 May, 1759–23 Jan. 1806

16 Necessity is the plea for every
infringement of human freedom. It is
the argument of tyrants; it is the creed of
slaves.
Speech, House of Commons, 18 Nov. 1783.

17 England has saved herself by her
exertions; and will, as I trust, save
Europe by her example.
*Speech, Lord Mayor's Banquet,
9 Nov. 1805.*

18 Roll up that map (of Europe); it will not
be wanted these ten years.
On hearing of the battle of Austerlitz.

19 O my country! how I leave my country!
(*Or* how I love my country!)
Last words, by common account.

20 I think I could eat one of Bellamy's veal
pies.
Last words, according to an old waiter.

PITT, WILLIAM, see Chatham, Earl of

PITT, WILLIAM, English dockyard official, 1790?–1840

21 One night came on a hurricane,
The sea was mountains rolling
When Barney Buntline turned his quid,
And said to Billy Bowling:
'A strong nor'-wester's blowing, Bill;
Hark! don't ye hear it roar now!
Lord help 'em, how I pities them
Unhappy folks on shore now!'
The Sailor's Consolation.

POE, EDGAR ALLAN, US author, 19 Jan. 1809–7 Oct. 1849

22 All that we see or seem
Is but a dream within a dream.
A Dream Within a Dream.

23 I was a child and she was a child,
In this kingdom by the sea,
But we loved with a love that was more
than love –
I and my Annabel Lee –
With a love that the winged seraphs of
heaven
Coveted her and me. *Annabel Lee.*

24 Once upon a midnight dreary, while I
pondered, weak and weary,
Over many a quaint and curious volume
of forgotten lore,
While I nodded, nearly napping,
suddenly there came a tapping,
As of someone gently rapping.
The Raven.

25 Deep into the darkness peering, long I
stood there, wondering, fearing,
Doubting, dreaming dreams no mortal
ever dared to dream before. *Ibid.*

26 Take thy beak from out my heart, and
take thy form from off my door!
Quoth the Raven, "Nevermore." *Ibid.*

27 Helen, thy beauty is to me
Like those Nicaean barks of yore,
That gently, o'er a perfumed sea,
The weary, wayworn wanderer bore
To his own native shore.

28 On desperate seas long wont to roam,
Thy hyacinth hair, thy classic face,
Thy Naiad airs, have brought me home
To the glory that was Greece
And the grandeur that was Rome.
To Helen.

POMPADOUR, JEANNE ANTOINETTE POISSON LE NORMANT D'ÉTIOLES, MARQUISE DE, Mistress of Louis XV, 29 Dec. 1721–15 April, 1764

29 Après nous le déluge. – After us the
deluge.
After the battle of Rossbach, 5 Nov. 1757.

POOLE, JOHN, English dramatist, born 1786?, buried 10 Feb. 1872

30 I hope I don't intrude. *Paul Pry, I. ii.*

POPE, ALEXANDER, English poet, 21 May, 1688–30 May, 1744

1 Happy the man, whose wish and care
  A few paternal acres bound,
  Content to breathe his native air
  In his own ground.   *Ode on Solitude*

2 Thus let me live, unseen, unknown,
  Thus unlamented let me die,
  Steal from the world, and not a stone
  Tell where I lie.   *Ibid.*

3 Where'er you walk, cool gales shall fan
    the glade,
  Trees, where you sit, shall crowd into a
    shade:
  Where'er you tread, the blushing
    flowers shall rise
  And all things flourish where you turn
    your eyes.   *Pastorals. Summer, 73.*

4 'Tis with our judgments as our watches,
    none
  Go just alike, yet each believes his own.
      Essay on Criticism, 9.

5 Pride, the never-failing vice of fools.
      Ibid, 204.

6 A little learning is a dangerous thing;
  Drink deep, or taste not the Pierian
    spring:
  There shallow draughts intoxicate the
    brain,
  And drinking largely sobers us again.
      Ibid, 215.

7 Hills peep o'er hills, and Alps on Alps
    arise!   *Ibid, 232.*

8 Whoever thinks a faultless piece to see,
  Thinks what ne'er was, nor is, nor e'er
    shall be.   *Ibid, 253.*

9 True wit is nature to advantage dress'd,
  What oft was thought, but ne'er so well
    express'd.   *Ibid, 297.*

10 Words are like leaves; and where they
    most abound,
  Much fruit of sense beneath is rarely
    found.   *Ibid, 309.*

11 Such labour'd nothings, in so strange a
    style,

Amaze th' unlearn'd, and make the
    learned smile.   *Ibid, 326.*

12 Be not the first by whom the new are
    tried,
  Nor yet the last to lay the old aside.
      Ibid, 335.

13   Some to church repair
  Not for the doctrine, but the music
    there.   *Ibid, 342.*

14 These equal syllables alone require,
  Though oft the ear the open vowels tire;
  While expletives their feeble aid do join;
  And ten low words oft creep in one dull
    line.   *Ibid, 344.*

15 Where'er you find 'the cooling western
    breeze,'
  In the next line, it 'whispers through the
    trees';
  If crystal streams 'with pleasing
    murmurs creep,'
  The reader's threaten'd (not in vain)
    with] p':
  Then, at the last and only couplet
    fraught
  With some unmeaning thing they call a
    thought,
  A needless Alexandrine ends the song,
  That, like a wounded snake, drags its
    slow length along.   *Ibid, 350.*

16 True ease in writing comes from art, not
    chance,
  As those move easiest who have learn'd
    to dance.
  'Tis not enough no harshness gives
    offence,
  The sound must seem an echo to the
    sense:
  Soft is the strain when zephyr gently
    blows,
  And the smooth stream in smoother
    numbers flows;
  But when loud surges lash the sounding
    shore,
  The hoarse, rough verse should like a
    torrent roar.
  When Ajax strives some rock's vast
    weight to throw,
  The line too labours, and the words
    move slow:

Not so when swift Camilla scours the
plain,
Flies o'er the' unbending corn, and
skims along the main.   *Ibid, 362.*

17 For fools admire, but men of sense
approve.   *Ibid, 391.*

18 But let a lord once own the happy lines,
How the wit brightens! how the style
refines!   *Ibid, 420.*

19 To err is human, to forgive, divine. *Ibid,*
525.

20 The bookful blockhead, ignorantly
read,
With loads of learned lumber in his
head.   *Ibid, 612.*

21 For fools rush in where angels fear to
tread.   *Ibid, 625.*

22 What dire offence from amorous causes
springs,
What mighty contests rise from trivial
things,
I sing.   *The Rape of the Lock, i. I.*

23 And all Arabia breathes from yonder
box.

24 On her white breast a sparkling cross
she wore,
Which Jews might kiss, and infidels
adore.   *Ibid, ii. 7.*

25 If to her share some female errors fall,
Look at her face, and you'll forget them
all.   *Ibid, 17.*

26 Fair tresses man's imperial race insnare,
And beauty draws us with a single hair.
Ibid, 27.

27 Here thou, great Anna! whom three
realms obey,
Dost sometimes counsel take – and
sometimes tea.   *Ibid, iii. 7.*

28 At every word a reputation dies.
Ibid, 16.

29 The hungry judges soon the sentence
sign,

And wretches hang that jurymen may
dine.   *Ibid, 21.*

30 'Let spades be trumps!' she said, and
trumps they were.   *Ibid, 46.*

31 Coffee, which makes the politician wise,
And see through all things with his half-
shut eyes.   *Ibid, 117.*

32 The meeting points the sacred hair
dissever
From the fair head, for ever, and for
ever!   *Ibid, 153.*

33 Not louder shrieks to pitying heaven are
cast,
When husbands or when lap-dogs
breathe their last.   *Ibid, 157.*

34 Sir Plume, of amber snuff-box justly
vain,
And the nice conduct of a clouded cane.
Ibid, iv. 123.

35 Charms strike the sight, but merit wins
the soul.   *Ibid, v. 34.*

36 A brave man struggling in the storms of
fate,
And greatly falling with a falling State.
Prologue to Addison's Cato, 21.

37 Proud Nimrod first the bloody chase
began,
A mighty hunter, and his prey was man.
Windsor Forest, 61.

38 Nor fame I slight, nor for her favours
call;
She comes unlook'd for, if she comes at
all.   *The Temple of Fame, 513.*

39 Achilles' wrath, to Greece the direful
spring
Of woes unnumber'd, heavenly
goddess, sing!   *Homer's Iliad, i. 1.*

40 She moves a goddess, and she looks a
queen.   *Ibid, iii. 1.*

41 True friendship's laws are by this rule
exprest,
Welcoming the coming, speed the
parting guest.
Homer's Odyssey, xv. 83.

1 What beckoning ghost along the
moonlight shade
Invites my steps, and points to yonder
glade?
Elegy to the Memory of an Unfortunate
Lady, 1.

2 Ambition first sprung from your blest
abodes,
The glorious fault of angels and of gods.
Ibid, 13.

3 By foreign hands thy dying eyes were
closed,
By foreign hands thy decent limbs
composed,
By foreign hands thy humble grave
adorn'd,
By strangers honour'd, and by strangers
mourn'd. *Ibid, 51.*

4 So peaceful rests, without a stone, a
name,
What once had beauty, titles, wealth,
and fame.
How loved, how honour'd once, avails
thee not,
To whom related, or by whom begot;
A heap of dust alone remains of thee,
'Tis all thou art, and all the proud shall
be! *Ibid, 69.*

5 Speed the soft intercourse from soul to
soul,
And waft a sigh from Indus to the Pole.
Eloisa to Abelard, 57.

6 Love, free as air, at sight of human ties,
Spreads his light wings, and in a
moment flies. *Ibid, 75.*

7 And love th' offender, yet detest th'
offence. *Ibid, 192.*

8 How happy is the blameless vestal's lot!
The world forgetting, by the world
forgot. *Ibid, 207*

9 One thought of thee puts all the pomp
to flight,
Priests, tapers, temples, swim before
my sight. *Ibid, 273.*

10 He best can paint them who shall feel
them most. *Ibid, 366.*

11 Such were the notes thy once-loved poet
sung,
Till death untimely stopp'd his tuneful
tongue.
Epistle to Robert Earl of Oxford, 1.

12 Poetic justice, with her lifted scale,
Where, in nice balance, truth with gold
she weighs,
And solid pudding against empty praise.
The Dunciad, i. 52.

13 Now night descending, the proud scene
was o'er,
But lived, in Settle's numbers, one day
more. *Ibid, 89.*

14 While pensive poets painful vigils keep,
Sleepless themselves to give their
readers sleep. *Ibid, 93.*

15 Next, o'er his books his eyes began to
roll,
In pleasing memory of all he stole.
Ibid, 127.

16 And gentle Dulness ever loves a joke.
Ibid, ii. 34.

17 Lo! where Maeotis sleeps, and hardly
flows
The freezing Tanais through a waste of
snows. *Ibid, iii. 87.*

18 All crowd, who foremost shall be
damned to fame. *Ibid, 158.*

19 Silence, ye wolves! while Ralph to
Cynthia howls,
And makes night hideous – Answer
him, ye owls! *Ibid, 165.*

20 A wit with dunces, and a dunce with
wits. *Ibid, iv. 90.*

21 The right divine of kings to govern
wrong. *Ibid, 188.*

22 Stretch'd on the rack to a too easy chair.
Ibid, 342.

23 Even Palinurus nodded at the helm.
Ibid, 614,

24 Religion blushing veils her sacred fires,
And unawares morality expires.

Nor public flame, nor private, dares to
shine,
Nor human spark is left, nor glimpse
divine!
Lo! thy dread empire, Chaos! is restor'd;
Light dies before thy uncreating word;
Thy hand, great Anarch! lets the curtain
fall,
And universal darkness buries all.
Ibid, 649.

25 Awake, my St. John! leave all meaner
things
To low ambition and the pride of kings.
Let us (since life can little more supply
Than just to look about us, and to die)
Expatiate free o'er all this scene of man;
A mighty maze! but not without a plan.
Essay on Man. Epistle i. 1.

26 Eye Nature's walks, shoot folly as it
flies,
And catch the manners living as they
rise:
Laugh where we must, be candid where
we can;
But vindicate the ways of God to man.
Ibid, 13.

27 Heaven from all creatures hides the
book of Fate. *Ibid, 77.*

28 Who sees with equal eye, as God of all,
A hero perish, or a sparrow fall,
Atoms or systems into ruin hurl'd,
And now a bubble burst, and now a
world. *Ibid, 87.*

29 Hope springs eternal in the human
breast:
Man never is, but always to be blest.
Ibid, 95.

30 Lo, the poor Indian! whose untutor'd
mind
Sees God in clouds, or hears Him in the
wind;
His soul proud science never taught to
stray
Far as the solar walk or milky way.
Ibid, 99.

31 But thinks, admitted to that equal sky,
His faithful dog shall bear him
company. *Ibid, 111.*

32 Why has not man a microscopic eye?
For this plain reason, man is not a fly.
Ibid, 193.

33 Die of a rose in aromatic pain.
Ibid, 200.

34 The spider's touch, how exquisitely
fine!
Feels at each thread, and lives along the
line. *Ibid, 217.*

35 All are but parts of one stupendous
whole,
Whose body Nature is, and God the
soul. *Ibid, 267.*

36 Warms in the sun, refreshes in the
breeze,
Glows in the stars, and blossoms in the
trees. *Ibid, 271.*

37 All nature is but art, unknown to thee;
All chance, direction which thou canst
not see;
All discord, harmony not understood;
All partial evil, universal good:
And, spite of pride, in erring reason's
spite,
One truth is clear, Whatever is, is right.
Ibid, 289.

38 Know then thyself, presume not God to
scan,
The proper study of mankind is man.
Ibid, Epistle ii. 1.

39 Chaos of thought and passion, all
confused;
Still by himself abused or disabused;
Created half to rise, and half to fall;
Great lord of all things, yet a prey to all;
Sole judge of truth, in endless error
hurl'd:
The glory, jest, and riddle of the world!
Ibid, 13.

40 Vice is a monster of so frightful mien,
As, to be hated, needs but to be seen;
Yet seen too oft, familiar with her face,
We first endure, then pity, then
embrace. *Ibid, 217.*

41 Behold the child, by nature's kindly
law,

Pleased with a rattle, tickled with a
straw:
Some livelier plaything gives his youth
delight,
A little louder, but as empty quite:
Scarfs, garters, gold, amuse his riper
stage,
And beads and prayer-books are the
toys of age:
Pleased with this bauble still, as that
before;
Till tired he sleeps, and life's poor play is
o'er. *Ibid, 275.*

1 For forms of government let fools
contest;
What'er is best administer'd is best:
For modes of faith let graceless zealots
fight;
He can't be wrong whose life is in the
right:
In faith and hope the world will
disagree,
But all mankind's concern is charity.
Ibid, Epistle iii. 303.

2 O happiness! our being's end and aim!
Good, pleasure, ease, content! whate'er
thy name:
That something still which prompts th'
eternal sigh,
For which we bear to live, or dare to die.
Ibid, Epistle iv. 1.

3 Order is heaven's first law. *Ibid, 49.*

4 Worth makes the man, and want of it
the fellow:
The rest is all but leather or prunella.
Ibid, 203.

5 What can ennoble sots, or slaves, or
cowards?
Alas! not all the blood of all the
Howards. *Ibid, 215.*

6 An honest man's the noblest work of
God. *Ibid, 248.*

7 And more true joy Marcellus exiled
feels,
Than Caesar with a senate at his heels.
Ibid, 257.

8 If parts allure thee, think how Bacon
shined,

The wisest, brightest, meanest of
mankind:
Or, ravish'd with the whistling of a
name,
See Cromwell, damn'd to everlasting
fame! *Ibid, 281.*

9 Slave to no sect, who takes no private
road,
But looks through nature up to nature's
God. *Ibid, 331.*

10 Form'd by thy converse happily to steer
From grave to gay, from lively to
severe. *Ibid, 379.*

11 Thou wert my guide, philosopher, and
friend. *Ibid, 390.*

12 To observations which ourselves we
make,
We grow more partial for the observer's
sake. *Moral Essays. Epistle, i. 11.*

13 Like following life through creatures
you dissect,
You lose it in the moment you detect.
Ibid, 29.

14 'Tis from high life high characters are
drawn,
A saint in crape is twice a saint in lawn.
Ibid, 135.

15 'Tis education forms the common mind,
Just as the twig is bent, the tree's
inclined. *Ibid, 149.*

16 'Odious! in woollen! 'twould a saint
provoke!'
(Were the last words that poor Narcissa
spoke). *Ibid, 246.*

17 'One would not, sure, be frightful when
one's dead –
And – Betty – give this cheek a little
red.' *Ibid, 250.*

18 And you, brave Cobham, to the latest
breath,
Shall feel your ruling passion strong in
death. *Ibid, 262.*

19 Whether the charmer sinner it, or saint
it,
If folly grow romantic, I must paint it.
Ibid, Epistle ii. 15.

20 Choose a firm cloud before it fall, and in
it
Catch, ere she change, the Cynthia of
this minute. *Ibid, 19.*

21 Fine by defect, and delicately weak.
Ibid, 43.

22 With too much quickness ever to be
taught:
With too much thinking to have
common thought. *Ibid, 97.*

23 Virtue she finds too painful to
endeavour,
Content to dwell in decencies for ever.
Ibid, 163.

24 Men, some to business, some to
pleasure take;
But every woman is at heart a rake.
Ibid, 215.

25 See how the world its veterans rewards!
A youth of frolics, an old age of cards.
Ibid, 243.

26 She who ne'er answers till a husband
cools,
Or, if she rules him, never shows she
rules;
Charms by accepting, by submitting
sways,
Yet has her humour most when she
obeys. *Ibid, 261.*

27 And mistress of herself, though China
fall. *Ibid, 268.*

28 Woman's at best a contradiction still.
Ibid, 270.

29 Who shall decide when doctors
disagree? *Ibid, Epistle iii. 1.*

30 But thousands die, without or this or
that,
Die, and endow a college or a cat.
Ibid, 95.

31 The ruling passion, be it what it will,
The ruling passion conquers reason still.
Ibid, 153.

32 Rise, honest muse! and sing the Man of
Ross. *Ibid, 250.*

33 Where London's column, pointing at
the skies
Like a tall bully, lifts the head and lies.
Ibid, 339.

34 To rest, the cushion and soft dean invite,
Who never mentions hell to ears polite.
Ibid, Epistle iv. 149.

35 Statesman, yet friend to truth! of soul
sincere,
In action faithful, and in honour clear;
Who broke no promise, served no
private end,
Who gained no title, and who lost no
friend.
Ibid, Epistle v. To Mr. Addison, 67

36 Shut, shut the door, good John!
fatigued, I said;
Tie up the knocker, say I'm sick, I'm
dead.
*Epistle to Dr. Arbuthnot or Prologue to the
Satires, 1.*

37 Fire in each eye, and papers in each
hand,
They rave, recite, and madden round
the land. *Ibid, 5.*

38 Is there a parson, much bemused in
beer,
A maudlin poetess, a whyming peer,
A clerk, foredoom'd his father's soul to
cross,
Who pens a stanza, when he should
engross? *Ibid, 15.*

39 Fired that the house reject him, "Sdeath!
I'll print it.
And shame the fools. *Ibid, 61.*

40 No creature smarts so little as a fool.
Ibid, 84.

41 Destroy his fib or sophistry – in vain!
The creature's at his dirty work again.
Ibid, 91.

42 As yet a child, nor yet a fool to fame,
A lisp'd in numbers, for the numbers
came. *Ibid, 127.*

43 This long disease, my life. *Ibid, 132.*

1 And he, whose fustian's so sublimely
  bad
  It is not poetry, but prose run mad.
                                    Ibid, 187.

2   Were there one whose fires
  True genius kindles, and fair fame
  inspires;
  Blest with each talent, and each art to
  please,
  And born to write, converse, and live
  with ease;
  Should such a man, too fond to rule
  alone,
  Bear, like the Turk, no brother near the
  throne,
  View him with scornful, yet with
  jealous eyes,
  And hate for arts that caused himself to
  rise;
  Damn with faint praise, assent with civil
  leer,
  And, without sneering, teach the rest to
  sneer;
  Willing to wound, and yet afraid to
  strike,
  Just hint a fault, and hesitate dislike;
  Alike reserved to blame, or to
  commend,
  A timorous foe, and a suspicious friend;
  Dreading e'en fools, by flatterers
  besieged,
  And so obliging, that he ne'er obliged;
  Like Cato, give his little senate laws,
  And sit attentive to his own applause;
  While wits and Templars every sentence
  raise,
  And wonder with a foolish face of
  praise –
  Who but must laugh, if such a man there
  be?
  Who would not weep, if Atticus were
  he?   *Ibid, 193.*

3 Cursed be the verse, how well soe'er it
  flow,
  That tends to make one worthy man my
  foe.   *Ibid, 283.*

4 Satire or sense, alas! can Sporus feel,
  Who breaks a butterfly upon a wheel?
                                    Ibid, 307.

5 This painted child of dirt, that stinks and
  stings.   *Ibid, 310.*

6 Eternal smiles his emptiness betray,
  As shallow streams run dimpling all the
  way.   *Ibid, 315.*

7 Wit that can creep, and pride that licks
  the dust.   *Ibid, 333.*

8 The lines are weak, another's pleased to
  say,
  Lord Fanny spins a thousand such a day.
            *Satires and Epistles of Horace Imitated,
                              Bk. II. Satire i. 6.*

9 The feast of reason and the flow of soul.
                                    Ibid, 128.

10 One simile, that solitary shines
   In a dry desert of a thousand lines.
                  Ibid, Bk. II. Epistle i. III.

11 Waller was smooth; but Dryden taught
   to join
   The varying verse, the full-resounding
   line,
   The long majestic march and energy
   divine.   *Ibid, 267.*

12 Even copious Dryden wanted, or
   forgot,
   The last and greatest art, the art to blot.
                                    Ibid, 280.

13 The many-headed monster of the pit.
                                    Ibid, 305.

14 The vulgar boil, the learned roast an
   egg.   *Ibid, Epistle ii. 85.*

15 Do good by stealth, and blush to find it
   fame.   *Epilogue to the Satires,
                              dialogue i. 136.*

16 Vain was the chief's, the sage's pride!
   They had no poet, and they died.
            Imitations of Horace, Odes, IV. ix.

17 Teach me to feel another's woe,
   To hide the fault I see;
   That mercy I to others show
   That mercy show to me.   *The Universal
                                       Prayer.*

18 Heaven, as its purest gold, by tortures
   tried!
   The saint sustain'd it, but the woman
   died.   *Epitaph on Mrs. Corbet.*

19 Of manners gentle, of affections mild;
In wit, a man; simplicity, a child:
With native humour tempering virtuous
  rage,
Form'd to delight at once and lash the
  age.   *Epitaph on Mr. Gay.*

20 Nature and Nature's laws lay hid in
  night:
God said, 'Let Newton be!' and all was
  light.
     Epitaph intended for Sir Isaac Newton.

21 'Has she no faults, then (Envy says),
  sir?'
Yes, she has one, I must aver:
When all the world conspires to praise
  her,
The woman's deaf, and does not hear.
          On a Certain Lady at Court.

22 Dear, damn'd, distracting town,
  farewell!   *A Farewell to London, 1.*

23 You beat your pate and fancy wit will
  come:
Knock as you please, there's nobody at
  home.   *Epigram.*

24 I am his Highness' dog at Kew;
Pray tell me, sir, whose dog are you?
     *On the Collar of a Dog which I gave to his
               Royal Highness.*

25 I never knew any man in my life who
could not bear another's misfortunes
perfectly like a Christian.
          Thoughts on Various Subjects.

26 When men grow virtuous in their old
age, they only make a sacrifice to God of
the devil's leavings.   *Ibid.*

27 'Blessed is the man who expects
nothing, for he shall never be
disappointed' was the ninth beatitude
which a man of wit . . . added to the
eighth.
     Letter to Wm. Fortescue, 23 Sept. 1725.

**POPE, WALTER, English
astronomer, 1630?–25 June, 1714**

28 If I live to be old, for I find I go down,
Let this be my fate: in a country town

May I have a warm house with a stone at
  the gate,
And a cleanly young girl to rub my bald
  pate.
May I govern my passion with an
  absolute sway,
And grow wiser and better as my
  strength wears away,
Without gout or stone, by a gentle
  decay.   *The Old Man's Wish.*

**PORSON, RICHARD, Professor of
Greek, 25 Dec. 1759–25 Sept. 1808**

29 When Dido found Aeneas would not
  come,
She mourned in silence, and was Di-do-
  dum.   *Epigram on Latin gerunds.*

30 I went to Strasburg, where I got drunk
With that most learn'd professor,
  Brunck.
I went to Wortz, where I got more
  drunken
With that more learn'd professor,
  Ruhnken.
     Richard Porson, by M. L. Clarke, p. 16.

31 The Germans in Greek
Are sadly to seek;
Not five in five score,
But ninety-five more;
All; save only Hermann,
And Hermann's a German.   *Ibid, p. 69.*

**PORTER, WILLIAM SYDNEY, see
HENRY, O.**

**PRAED, WINTHROP
MACKWORTH, English poet, 26
July, 1802–15 July, 1839**

32 Some lie beneath the churchyard stone,
And some before the Speaker.
          Schools and Schoolfellows.

33 Tom Mill was used to blacken eyes
Without the fear of sessions;
Charles Medlar loathed false quantities
As much as false professions;
Now Mill keeps order in the land,
A magistrate pedantic;
And Medlar's feet repose unscanned
Beneath the wide Atlantic.   *Ibid.*

1   He must walk – like a god of old story
Come down from the home of his rest;
He must smile – like the sun in his glory
On the buds he loves ever the best;
And oh! from its ivory portal
Like music his soft speech must flow! –
If he speak, smile, or walk like a mortal,
My own Araminta, say "No!"
A Letter of Advice.

2   His talk was like a stream, which runs
With rapid change from rocks to roses:
It slipped from politics to puns,
It passed from Mahomet to Moses;
Beginning with the laws which keep
The planets in their radiant courses,
And ending with some precept deep
For dressing eels, or shoeing horses.
The Vicar.

3   The ice of her Ladyship's manners,
The ice of his Lordship's champagne.
Good-night to the Season.

PRIMROSE, ARCHIBALD PHILIP, see Rosebery, Earl of

PRIOR, MATTHEW, English poet and diplomatist, 21 July, 1664–18 Sept. 1721

4   The merchant, to secure his treasure,
Conveys it in a borrow'd name:
Euphelia serves to grace my measure;
But Chloe is my real flame.   *An Ode.*

5   Be to her virtues very kind;
Be to her faults a little blind;
Let all her ways be unconfin'd;
And clap your padlock – on her mind.
An English Padlock, 78.

6   The end must justify the means.
Hans Carvel, 67.

7   To John I ow'd great obligation;
But John unhappily thought fit
To publish it to all the nation:
Sure John and I are more than quit.
Epigram.

8   No longer shall the bodice, aptly lac'd
From thy full bosom to thy slender
waist,

That air and harmony of shape express,
Fine by degrees, and beautifully less.
Henry and Emma, 427.

9   Abra was ready ere I call'd her name;
And, though I call'd another, Abra
came.
Solomon on the Vanity of the World, ii.
362.

10 For hope is but the dream of those that
wake.   *Ibid, iii. 102.*

11 Cur'd yesterday of my disease,
I died last night of my physician.
The Remedy Worse than the Disease.

12 For, as our different ages move,
'Tis so ordain'd (would Fate but mend
it!),
That I shall be past making love
When she begins to comprehend it.
To a Child of Quality, Five Years Old.
The Author then Forty.

13 Nobles and heralds, by your leave,
Here lies what once was Matthew Prior;
The son of Adam and of Eve:
Can Bourbon or Nassau claim higher?
Epitaph.

PROCTER, ADELAIDE ANN, English poetess, 30 Oct. 1825–2 Feb. 1864

14 Seated one day at the organ,
I was weary and ill at ease.
A Lost Chord.

15 But I struck one chord of music,
Like the sound of a great Amen.   *Ibid.*

PROCTER, BRYAN WALLER ('BARRY CORNWALL'), English poet, 21 Nov. 1787–5 Oct. 1874

16 The sea! the sea! the open sea!
The blue, the fresh, the ever free!
The Sea.

17 I'm on the sea! I'm on the sea!
I am where I would ever be,
With the blue above and the blue below,
And silence whereso'er I go.   *Ibid.*

18 I never was on the dull, tame shore
But I loved the great sea more and more.
Ibid.

PROUT, FATHER (FRANCIS SYLVESTER MAHONY), Irish author, 1804–18 May, 1866

19 'Tis the bells of Shandon,
That sound so grand on
The pleasant waters
Of the River Lee. *The Bells of Shandon.*

PROWSE, WILLIAM JEFFREY, English poet, 6 May, 1836–17 April, 1870

20 Though the latitude's rather uncertain,
And the longitude also is vague,
The persons I pity who know not the city,
The beautiful city of Prague.
The City of Prague.

PUTNAM, ISRAEL, US General, 7 Jan. 1718–29 May, 1790

21 Don't one of you fire until you see the white of their eyes.
At Bunker Hill, 17 June, 1775.

QUARLES, FRANCIS, English poet, baptised 8 May, 1592, died 8 Sept. 1644

22 Sweet Phosphor, bring the day;
Light will repay
The wrongs of night;
Sweet Phosphor, bring the day!
Emblems, I. xiv.

23 Be wisely worldly, be not worldly wise.
Ibid, II. ii.

24 My soul, sit thou a patient looker-on;
Judge not the play before the play is done:
Her plot hath many changes; every day
Speaks a new scene; the last act crowns the play. *Epigram. Respice Finem.*

25 We'll cry both arts and learning down,
And hey! then up go we!
The Shepherd's Oracles. Song of Anarchus.

QUILLER-COUCH, SIR ARTHUR THOMAS, Professor of English, 21 Nov. 1863–12 May, 1944

26 Know you her secret none can utter?
– Hers of the Book, the tripled Crown?
Still on the spire the pigeons flutter;
Still by the gateway haunts the gown;
Still on the street from corbel and gutter,
Faces of stone look down. *Alma Mater.*

27 It was bellows to mend with Roberts –
starred three for a penalty kick:
But he chalked his cue and gave 'em the butt, and Oom Paul marked the trick –
'Offside – No Ball – and at fourteen all!
Mark Cock! and two for his nob!'
When W. G. ran clean through his lee
and beat him twice with a lob.
The Famous Ballad of the Jubilee Cup.

28 The lion is the beast to fight,
He leaps along the plain,
And if you run with all your might
He runs with all his mane.
Sage Counsel.

29 To be, or the contrary? Whether the former or the latter be preferable would seem to admit of some difference of opinion; the answer in the present case being of an affirmative or of a negative character according as to whether one elects on the one hand to mentally suffer the disfavour of fortune, albeit in an extreme degree, or on the other to boldly envisage adverse conditions in the prospect of eventually bringing them to a conclusion. (Hamlet's soliloquy jargonised.)
The Art of Writing, lecture v.

QUINCY, JOSIAH, US politician, 4 Feb. 1772–1 July, 1864

30 If this Bill (for the admission of Orleans Territory as a State) passes, it is my deliberate opinion that it is virtually a dissolution of the Union; that it will free the States from their moral obligation; and, as it will be the right of all, so it will be the duty of some, definitely to prepare for a separation, – amicably if they can, violently if they must.
Abridged Congressional Debates,
14 Jan. 1811.

RABELAIS, FRANÇOIS, French author, 1494?–9 April, 1553?

1 L'appétit vient en mangeant. – Appetite comes with eating. *Works, I. v.*

2 Je m'en vais chercher un grand peut-être. – I go in quest of a great Perhaps.
Traditional deathbed saying.

3 Tirez le rideau, la farce est jouée. – Ring down the curtain, the farce is played.
Ibid.

RACINE, JEAN, French dramatist, Dec. 1639–21 April, 1699

4 Ce n'est plus une ardeur dans mes veines cachée;
C'est Vénus toute entière à sa proie attachée.
– It is no long a passion hidden in my veins; it is Venus's very self fastened on her prey. *Phèdre, I. iii.*

RALEGH *or* RALEIGH, SIR WALTER, English soldier and author, 1552?–29 Oct. 1618

5 If all the world and love were young,
And truth in every shepherd's tongue,
These pretty pleasures might me move
To live with thee, and by thy love.
The Nymph's reply to the Passionate Shepherd.

6 Silence in love bewrays more woe
Than words, though ne'er so witty;
A beggar that is dumb, you know,
May challenge double pity.
The Silent Lover.

7 As you came from the holy land
Of Walsinghame,
Met you not with my true love
By the way as you came?
Walsinghame.

8 How shall I know your true love,
That have met many a one
As I went to the holy land,
That have come, that have gone. *Ibid.*

9 Give me my scallop-shell of quiet,
My staff of faith to walk upon,

My scrip of joy, immortal diet,
My bottle of salvation,
My gown of glory, hope's true gage,
And thus I'll take my pilgrimage.
The Pilgrimage.

10 Methought I saw the grave where Laura lay. *Verses to Edmund Spenser.*

11 Go, Soul, the body's guest,
Upon a thankless arrant;
Fear not to touch the best,
The truth shall be thy warrant:
Go, since I needs must die,
And give the world the lie. *The Lie.*

12 Fain would I climb, yet fear I to fall.
Said to have been written on a window-pane in the presence of Queen Elizabeth, who wrote underneath:–
If thy heart fails thee, climb not at all.

13 Even such is Time, that takes in trust
Our youth, our joys, our all we have,
And pays us but with earth and dust;
Who in the dark and silent grave,
When we have wander'd all our ways,
Shuts up the story of our days;
But from this earth, this grave, this dust,
My God shall raise me up, I trust.
Written the night before his death.

14 O eloquent, just, and mightie Death! whom none could advise, thou hast perswaded; what none hath dared, thou hast done; and whom all the world hath flattered, thou only hast cast out of the world and despised: thou hast drawne together all the farre stretched greatnesse, all the pride, crueltie, and ambition of men, and covered it all over with these two narrow words. *Hic jacet!*
Historie of the World, Bk. v. part i. ad fin.

15 So the heart be right, it is no matter which way the head lieth.
When laying his head on the block.

RALEIGH, SIR WALTER ALEXANDER, Professor of English, 6 Sept. 1861–13 May, 1922

16 I wish I loved the Human Race;
I wish I loved its silly face;

I wish I liked the way it walks;
I wish I liked the way it talks;
And when I'm introduced to one
I wish I thought *What Jolly Fun!*
Laughter from a Cloud. Wishes of an
Elderly Man.

17 In an examination those who do not
wish to know ask questions of those
who cannot tell.
Ibid, Some Thoughts on Examinations.

RAMSAY, ALLAN, Scottish poet,
15 Oct. 1686–7 Jan. 1758

18 Farewell to Lochaber, and farewell my
Jean,
Where heartsome with thee I hae mony
day been;
For Lochaber no more, Lochaber no
more,
We'll maybe return to Lochaber no
more. *Lochaber No More.*

RANDALL, JAMES RYDER, US
poet, 1 Jan. 1839–14 Jan. 1908

19 The despot's heel is on thy shore,
Maryland!
His torch is at thy temple door,
Maryland!
Avenge the patriotic gore
That fleck'd the streets of Baltimore,
And be the battle queen of yore,
Maryland, my Maryland!
Maryland, My Maryland.

RANKIN, JEREMIAH EAMES, US
Minister, 2 Jan. 1828–28 Nov. 1904

20 God be with you till we meet again.
Hymn.

READE, CHARLES, English
novelist, 8 June, 1814–11 April, 1884

21 Courage, camarade! Le diable est mort.
– Courage, comrade! The devil is dead.
The Cloister and the Hearth, xxiv.

REMARQUE, ERICH MARIA
(ERICH PAUL REMARK),
German author, 22 June, 1898–25
Sept. 1970

22 Im Westen nichts Neues. – All quiet on

the Western front (*lit.* No news in the
West). *Title of novel.*

REYNOLDS, FREDERIC, English
dramatist, 1 Nov. 1764–16 April,
1841

23 How goes the enemy? (Said by Mr.
Ennui, 'the time-killer.')
The Dramatist, 1.

REYNOLDS, SIR JOSHUA,
English portrait-painter, 16 July,
1723–23 Feb. 1792

24 If you have great talents, industry will
improve them: if you have but moderate
abilities, industry will supply their
deficiency. *Discourses, ii.*

25 A mere copier of nature can never
produce anything great. *Ibid, iii.*

RHOADES, JAMES, English
author, 9 April, 1841–16 March,
1923

26 Is he gone to a land of no laughter,
The man who made mirth for us all?
On the Death of Artemus Ward.

RHODES, CECIL JOHN, South
African statesman, 5 July, 1853–
26 March, 1902

27 The unctuous recititude of my
countrymen.
Speech at Port Elizabeth, 24 Dec. 1896.

28 Educational relations make the strongest
tie.
Will, establishing the Rhodes Scholarships.

29 So little done, so much to do.
Last words.

RHODES, WILLIAM BARNES,
English banker and dramatist,
25 Dec. 1772–1 Nov. 1826

30 'Who dares this pair of boots displace,
Must meet Bombastes face to face.'
Thus do I challenge all the human race.
Bombastes Furioso, iv.

RHYS, ERNEST PERCIVAL,
Welsh author, 17 July, 1859–25 May, 1946

1 Wales England wed; so I was bred.
'Twas merry London gave me breath.
I dreamt of love, and fame: I strove. But
Ireland taught me love was best:
And Irish eyes and London cries, and
streams of Wales may tell the rest.
What more than these I ask'd of Life I
am content to have from Death.
An Autobiography.

RICE, GRANTLAND, US author,
1 Nov. 1880–1954

2 For when the One Great Scorer comes
to write against your name,
He marks – not that you won or lost –
but how you played the game.
Alumnus Football.

RICE, SIR STEPHEN, Irish judge,
1637–16 Feb. 1715

3 I will drive a coach and six through the
Act of Settlement.
Macaulay's History of England, xii.

RICHARDSON, ROBERT,
Australian poet, 7 Jan. 1850–4 Oct. 1901

4 Warm summer sun, shine friendly here;
Warm western wind, blow kindly here;
Green sod above, rest light, rest light –
Good-night, Annette! Sweetheart,
good-night! *Annette.*

RILEY, JAMES WHITCOMB, US
poet, 7 Oct. 1849–22 July, 1916

5 Onc't there was a little boy wouldn't say
his pray'rs –
An' when he went to bed at night, away
up stairs,
His mammy heerd him holler, an' his
daddy heerd him bawl,
An' when they turn't the kivvers down,
he wasn't there at all!
An' they seeked him in the rafter-room,
an' cubby-hole, an' press,
An' seeked him up the chimbly-flue, an'
aver'wheres, I guess;

But all they ever found was thist his
pants an' roundabout!
An' the Gobble-uns'll git you
Ef you
Don't
Watch
Out! *Little Orphant Annie.*

ROCHE, SIR BOYLE, Irish
politician, 1743–5 June, 1807

6 What has posterity done for us?
Speech in Irish Parliament, 1780.

7 Mr. Speaker, I smell a rat; I see him
forming in the air and darkening the
sky; but I'll nip him in the bud.
Attributed.

ROCHESTER, JOHN WILMOT,
2ND EARL OF, English poet, 10 April, 1647–26 July, 1680

8 Here lies a great and mighty king,
Whose promise none relies on;
He never said a foolish thing,
Nor ever did a wise one.
Written on Charles II's bedchamber door.
(There are various versions, the first two
lines being commonly given as:–
Here lies our sovereign lord the king,
Whose word no man relies on.)

9 For pointed satire I would Buckhurst
choose,
The best good man with the worst-
natured muse.
An Allusion to Horace, Satire x. Bk. I.

10 A merry monarch, scandalous and poor.
On the King.

11 For all men would be cowards if they
durst. *A Satire Against Mankind.*

12 I cannot change, as others do,
Though you unjustly scorn,
Since that poor swain that sighs for you,
For you alone was born;
No, Phillis, no, your heart to move
A surer way I'll try, –
And to revenge my slighted love
Will still love on, and die. *Constancy.*

RODGER, ALEXANDER, Scottish poet, 16 July, 1784–26 Sept. 1846

13 My mither men't my auld breeks,
And wow, but they were duddy!
And sent me to get Mally shod
At Tobin Tamson's smiddy.
Robin Tamson's Smiddy.

ROGERS, SAMUEL, English poet, 30 July, 1763–18 Dec. 1855

14 Oh! she was good as she was fair.
None – none on earth above her!
As pure in thought as angels are,
To know her was to love her.
Jacqueline, i. 68.

15 But there are moments which he calls his own.
Then, never less alone than when alone,
Those that he loved so long and sees no more,
Loved and still loves – not dead – but gone before,
He gathers round him.
Human Life, 755.

16 Mine be a cot beside the hill;
A beehive's hum shall soothe my ear;
A willowy brook, that turns a mill,
With many a fall shall linger near.
A Wish.

17 That very law which moulds a tear
And bids it trickle from its source,
That law preserves the earth a sphere
And guides the planets in their course.
On a Tear.

18 Ward has no heart, they say, but I deny it:
He has a heart, and gets his speeches by it. *Epigram upon Lord Dudley.*

ROLAND DE LA PLATIÈRE, MARIE JEANNE PHLIPON, MADAME, French revolutionary, 18 March, 1754–8 Nov. 1793

19 O Liberté! comme on t'a jouée! – O Liberty! how thou hast been played with! (*Or* O Liberté! que de crimes on commet en ton nom! – O Liberty! what crimes are committed in thy name!)
At execution, viewing the statue of Liberty from the scaffold.

ROOSEVELT, FRANKLIN DELANO, US President, 30 Jan. 1882–12 April, 1945

20 The forgotten man at the bottom of the economic pyramid.
Broadcast address, 7 April, 1932.

21 I pledge you – I pledge myself – to a new deal for the American people.
Speech at Convention, Chicago, 2 July, 1932.

22 In the field of world policy I would dedicate this nation to the policy of the good neighbour.
First Inaugural Address, 4 March, 1933.

ROOSEVELT, THEODORE, US President, 27 Oct. 1858–6 Jan. 1919

23 I wish to preach, not the doctrine of ignoble ease, but the doctrine of the strenuous life.
Speech, Hamilton Club, Chicago, 10 April, 1899.

24 There is a homely adage which runs, 'Speak softly and carry a big stick; you will go far.' If the American nation will speak softly and yet build and keep at a pitch of the highest training a thoroughly efficient navy, the Monroe Doctrine will go far.
Speech, Minnesota State Fair, 2 Sept. 1901

25 A man who is good enough to shed his blood for his country is good enough to be given a square deal afterward. More than that no man is entitled to, and less than that no man shall have.
Speech, Springfield, Illinois, 4 July, 1903.

26 No man is justified in doing evil on the ground of expediency.
The Strenuous Life. Latitude and Longitude Among Reformers.

ROSCOMMON, WENTWORTH DILLON, 4TH EARL OF, Irish author, 1633?–Jan. 1685

27 And choose an author as you choose a friend. *Essay on Translated Verse, 96.*

1 Immodest words admit of no defence,
For want of decency is want of sense.
Ibid, 113.

ROSEBERY, ARCHIBALD PHILIP PRIMROSE, 5TH EARL OF, English Prime Minister, 7 May, 1847–21 May, 1929

2 There is no need for any nation, however great, leaving the Empire, because the Empire is a Commonwealth of Nations.
Speech at Adelaide, 18 Jan. 1884.

3 It is beginning to be hinted that we are a nation of amateurs.
Rectorial Address, Glasgow, 16 Nov. 1900.

4 I must plough my furrow alone.
*Speech, City of London Liberal Club,
19 July, 1901.*

ROSS, ALEXANDER, Scottish poet, 13 April, 1699–20 May, 1784

5 Woo'd, and married, and a',
Married, and woo'd, and a'!
And was she nae very weel aff,
That was woo'd, and married, and a'?
Woo'd, and Married, and A'.

ROSSETTI, CHRISTINA GEORGINA, English poetess, 5 Dec. 1830–29 Dec. 1894

6 Rest, rest, for evermore
Upon a mossy shore;
Rest, rest at the heart's core
Till time shall cease:
Sleep that no pain shall wake,
Night that no morn shall break
Till joy shall overtake
Her perfect peace.
Dream Land.

7 My heart is like a singing bird
Whose nest is in a watered shoot;
My heart is like an apple-tree
Whose boughs are bent with thick-set fruit;
My heart is like a rainbow shell
That paddles in a halcyon sea;
My heart is gladder than all these
Because my love is come to me.
A Birthday.

8 Remember me when I am gone away,
Gone far away into the silent land.
Remember.

9 Better by far that you should forget and smile
Than that you should remember and be sad.
Ibid.

10 When I am dead, my dearest,
Sing no sad songs for me;
Plant thou no roses at my head,
Nor shady cypress tree:
Be the green grass above me
With showers and dewdrops wet;
And if thou wilt, remember,
And if thou wilt, forget.
Song.

11 Does the road wind up-hill all the way?
Yes, to the very end.
Up-Hill.

ROSSETTI, DANTE GABRIEL, English poet, 12 May, 1828–9 April, 1882

12 The blessed damozel leaned out
From the gold bar of Heaven;
Her eyes were deeper than the depth
Of waters stilled at even;
She had three lilies in her hand,
And the stars in her hair were seven.
The Blessed Damozel.

13 Her hair that lay along her back
Was yellow like ripe corn.
Ibid.

14 As low as where this earth
Spins like a fretful midge.
Ibid.

15 And the souls mounting up to God
Went by her like thin flames.
Ibid.

16 'We two,' she said, 'will seek the groves
Where the lady Mary is,
With her five handmaidens, whose names
Are five sweet symphonies,
Cecily, Gertrude, Magdalen,
Margaret and Rosalys.'
Ibid.

17 Look in my face: my name is Might-have-been;
I am also called No-more, Too-late, Farewell.
The House of Life. A Superscription.

18 Was it a friend or foe that spread these
lies?
Nay, who but infants question in such
wise?
'Twas one of my most intimate
enemies.   *Fragment.*

**ROUGET DE LISLE, CLAUDE
JOSEPH, French author, 10 May,
1760–26 June, 1836**

19 Allons, enfants de la patrie,
Le jour de gloire est arrivé.
– Come, children of our country, the
day of glory has arrived.
                                    The Marseillaise.

**ROUSSEAU, JEAN JACQUES,
French author, 28 June, 1712–2 July,
1778**

20 L'homme est né libre, et partout il est
dans les fers. – Man is born free, and
everywhere he is in fetters.
                                    Du contrat social, i.

**ROUTH, MARTIN JOSEPH,
President of Magdalen College,
Oxford, 18 Sept. 1755–22 Dec. 1854**

21 Always verify your references.
                                    Attributed.

**ROWE, NICHOLAS, English Poet
Laureate, baptised 30 June, 1674,
died 6 Dec. 1718**

22 At length the morn and cold indifference
came.   *The Fair Penitent, I. i.*

23 Is this that haughty, gallant, gay
Lothario?   *Ibid, V. i.*

**RUSKIN, JOHN, English art critic
and author, 8 Feb. 1819–20 Jan. 1900**

24 It is far more difficult to be simple than
to be complicated, far more difficult to
sacrifice skill and cease exertion in the
proper place, than to expend both
indiscriminately.
              Modern Painters, I. 1. iii. 5.

25 To see clearly is poetry, prophecy, and
religion, all in one.
                        Ibid, III. IV. xvi. 28.

26 All travelling becomes dull in exact
proportion to its rapidity.
                            Ibid, xvii. 24.

27 Mountains are the beginning and the
end of all natural scenery.
                            Ibid, IV. V. xx. 1.

28 The purest and most thoughtful minds
are those which love colour the most.
              The Stones of Venice, II. v. 30.

29 There is no wealth but life.
                            Unto this Last, 77.

30 Life being very short, and the quiet
hours of it few, we ought to waste
none of them in reading valueless
books.   *Sesame and Lilies, preface.*

31 Engraving, then, is, in brief terms, the
Art of Scratch.
                    Ariadne Florentina, lecture i.

32 I have seen, and heard, much of
Cockney impudence before now; but
never expected to hear a coxcomb ask
two hundred guineas for flinging a pot
of paint in the public's face. (On
Whistler's 'Nocturne in Black and
Gold.')   *Fors Clavigera, letter lxxix.*

33 Trust thou thy Love: if she be proud, is
she not sweet?
Trust thou thy Love: if she be mute, is
she not pure?
Lay thou thy soul full in her hands, low
at her feet;
Fail, Sun and Breath! – yet, for thy
peace, she shall endure.
                            Trust Thou Thy Love.

**RUSSELL, GEORGE WILLIAM,
see Æ**

**RUSSELL, JOHN RUSSELL, 1ST
EARL, English Prime Minister, 18
Aug. 1792–28 May, 1878**

34 Among the defects of the Bill, which
were numerous, one provision was
conspicuous by its presence and another
by its absence.
Address to his constituents, 7 April, 1859.

1 One man's wit, and all men's wisdom.
Definition of a proverb.
(Sometimes quoted as 'The wisdom of
many and the wit of one.')

RUTILIUS NAMATIANUS, CLAUDIUS, Roman poet, 5th century A.D.

2 Urbem fecisti quod prius orbis erat.
– Thou has made a city what was a
world before. (Of Rome.)
De Reditu Suo – On his Return, i. 66.

RUTLAND, JOHN JAMES ROBERT MANNERS, 7TH DUKE OF, English politician, 13 Dec. 1818–4 Aug. 1906

3 Let wealth and commerce, laws and
learning die,
But leave us still our old nobility.
England's Trust, iii. 227.

SAKI (HECTOR HUGH MUNRO), English author, 18 Dec. 1870– 14 Nov. 1916

4 The cook was a good cook, as cooks go;
and as cooks go she went.
Reginald. Reginald on Besetting Sins.

5 Waldo is one of those people who would
be enormously improved by death.
*Beasts and Super-Beasts. The Feast of
Nemesis.*

SALLUST (GAIUS SALLUSTIUS CRISPUS), Roman historian, 86–35 B.C.

6 Alieni appentens, sui profusus.
– Coveting other men's wealth lavish of
his own.
Bellum Catilinae – The War of Catiline, v.

7 Idem velle atque idem nolle, ea demum
firma amicitia est.
– To desire the same and to reject the
same, that indeed is true friendship.
Ibid, xx.

SALVANDY, NARCISSE ACHILLE, COMTE DE, French statesman, 11 June, 1795–15 Dec. 1856

8 Nous dansons sur un volcan.
– We are dancing on a volcano.
*At a fete given by the Duke of Orleans to the
King of Naples before the revolution in
1830.*

SANDBURG, CARL, US poet, 6 Jan. 1878–22 July, 1967

9 The fog comes
on little cat feet. *Fog.*

SARGENT, EPES, US author, 27 Sept. 1813–30 Dec. 1880

10 A life on the ocean wave,
A home on the rolling deep. *Song.*

SASSOON, SIEGFRIED LORRAINE, English author, 8 Sept. 1886–1 Sept. 1967

11 Everyone suddenly burst out singing.
Everyone Sang.

SAVAGE, RICHARD, English poet, 1697?–1 Aug. 1743

12 He lives to build, not boast, a generous
race:
No tenth transmitter of a foolish face.
The Bastard, 7.

SCHILLER, JOHANN CHRISTOPH FRIEDRICH VON, German author, 10 Nov. 1759– 9 May, 1805

13 Mit der Dummheit kämpfen Götter
selbst vergebens.
– With stupidity the gods themselves
struggle in vain.
*Die Jungfrau von Orleans – The Maid of
Orleans, III. vi.*

SCHNECKENBURGER, MAX, German song-writer, 17 Feb. 1819–3 May, 1849

14 Lieb' Vaterland, magst ruhig sein,

Fest steht und treu die Wacht am Rhein!
– Dear Fatherland, you may be secure;
firm and true stands the watch on the
Rhine!

Die Wacht am Rhein – The Watch on the
Rhine.

SCOTT, ALEXANDER, Scottish poet, 1525?–1584?

15 They would have all men bound and thrall
To them, and they for to be free.

Of Womankind, 49.

SCOTT, ROBERT FALCON, English Antarctic explorer, 6 June, 1868–March, 1912

16 We are in a desperate state, feet frozen,
etc. No fuel and a long way from food,
but it would do your heart good to be in
our tent, to hear our songs and the
cheery conversation.

Farewell letter to Sir J. M. Barrie.

SCOTT, SIR WALTER, BARONET, Scottish author, 15 Aug. 1771–21 Sept. 1832

17 The way was long, the wind was cold,
The Minstrel was infirm and old;
His wither'd cheek, and tresses grey,
Seem'd to have known a better day.

The Lay of the Last Minstrel,
introduction, 1.

18 If thou would'st view fair Melrose
aright,
Go visit it by the pale moonlight.

Ibid, ii. 1.

19 In peace, Love tunes the shepherd's reed;
In war, he mounts the warrior's steed;
In halls, in gay attire is seen;
In hamlets, dances on the green.
Love rules the court, the camp, the
grove,
And men below, and saints above;
For love is heaven, and heaven is love.

Ibid, 10.

20 The meeting of these champions proud
Seem'd like the bursting thundercloud.

Ibid, iii. 5.

21 Her blue eyes sought the west afar,
For lovers love the western star.

Ibid, 24.

22 Call it not vain; they do not err,
Who say, that when the Poet dies,
Mute Nature mourns her worshipper,
And celebrates his obsequies.

Ibid, V. 1.

23 True love's the gift which God has given
To man alone beneath the heaven:
It is not fantasy's hot fire,
Whose wishes, soon as granted, fly;
It liveth not in fierce desire,
With dead desire it doth not die;
It is the secret sympathy,
The silver link, the silken tie,
Which heart to heart, and mind to mind,
In body and in soul can bind.   *Ibid, 13.*

24 Breathes there the man, with soul so
dead,
Who never to himself hath said,
This is my own, my native land!
Whose heart hath ne'er within him
burn'd,
As home his footsteps he hath turn'd,
From wandering on a foreign strand!
If such there breathe, go, mark him
well;
For him no Minstrel raptures swell;
High though his titles, proud his name,
Boundless his wealth as wish can claim;
Despite those titles, power, and pelf,
The wretch, concentrated all in self,
Living, shall forfeit fair renown,
And, doubly dying, shall go down
To the vile dust, from whence he
sprung,
Unwept, unhonour'd, and unsung.

Ibid, vi. 1.

25 O Caledonia! stern and wild,
Meet nurse for a poetic child!
Land of brown heath and shaggy wood,
Land of the mountain and the flood,
Land of my sires!   *Ibid, 2.*

26 That day of wrath, that dreadful day,
When heaven and earth shall pass away.

Ibid, 31. Hymn for the Dead.

27 His square-turn'd joints, and strength of
limb,

Show'd him no carpet knight so trim,
But in close fight a champion grim,
In camps a leader sage.   *Marmion, i. 5.*

1 Just at the age 'twixt boy and youth,
When thought is speech, and speech is
truth.   *Ibid, ii. introduction.*

2 In the lost battle,
Borne down by the flying,
Where mingles war's rattle
With groans of the dying.   *Ibid, iii. 11.*

3 Such dusky grandeur cloth'd the height,
Where the huge Castle holds its state,
And all the steep slope down,
Whose ridgy back heaves to the sky,
Pil'd deep and massy, close and high,
Mine own romantic town. (Edinburgh.)
               Ibid, iv. 30.

4 The gallant Frith the eye might note,
Whose islands on its bosom float,
Like emeralds chas'd in gold.   *Ibid.*

5 Cried 'Where's the coward that would
not dare
To fight for such a land!'   *Ibid.*

6 O, young Lochinvar is come out of the
west,
Through all the wide Border his steed
was the best.   *Ibid, v. 12. Lochinvar.*

7 So faithful in love, and so dauntless in
war,
There never was knight like the young
Lochinvar.   *Ibid.*

8 He staid not for brake, and he stopp'd
not for stone,
He swam the Eske river where ford
there was none.   *Ibid.*

9 For a laggard in love, and a dastard in
war,
Was to wed the fair Ellen of brave
Lochinvar.   *Ibid.*

10 With a smile on her lips, and a tear in her
eye.   *Ibid.*

11 Fierce he broke forth. 'And dar'st thou
then
To beard the lion in his den,
The Douglas in his hall?'   *Ibid, vi. 14.*

12 O what a tangled web we weave,
When first we practise to deceive.
               Ibid, 17.

13 O Woman! in our hours of ease,
Uncertain, coy, and hard to please,
And variable as the shade
By the light quivering aspen made;
When pain and anguish wring the brow
A ministering angel thou!   *Ibid, 30.*

14 Charge, Chester, charge! On, Stanley,
on!'
Were the last words of Marmion.
               Ibid, 32.

15 O, for a blast of that dread horn,
On Fontarabian echoes borne.
               Ibid, 33.
(*Rob Roy*, ii, has 'O for the voice of that
wild horn.')

16 The stubborn spear-men still made good
Their dark impenetrable wood,
Each stepping where his comrade stood,
The instant that he fell.   *Ibid, 34.*

17 The stag at eve had drunk his fill,
Where danced the moon on Monan's
rill.   *The Lady of the Lake, i. 1.*

18 Woe worth the chase, woe worth the
day,
That costs thy life, my gallant grey!
               Ibid, 9.

19 In listening mood, she seem'd to stand,
The guardian Naiad of the strand.
               Ibid, 17.

20 And ne'er did Grecian chisel trace
A Nymph, a Naiad, or a Grace
Of finer form, or lovelier face!   *Ibid, 18.*

21 A foot more light, a step more true,
Ne'er from the heath-flower dash'd the
dew;
E'en the slight harebell raised its head,
Elastic from her airy tread.   *Ibid.*

22 On his bold visage middle age
Had slightly press'd its signet sage,
Yet had not quench'd the open truth
And fiery vehemence of youth;
Forward and frolic glee was there,
The will to do, the soul to dare.
               Ibid, 21.

23 Soldier, rest! thy warfare o'er,
Dream of fighting fields no more:
Sleep the sleep that knows not breaking,
Morn of toil, nor night of waking.
Ibid, 31.

24 Hail to the Chief who in triumph
advances! *Ibid, ii. 19, Boat Song.*

25 Speed, Malise, speed! the dun deer's
hide
On fleeter foot was never tied.
Ibid, iii, 13.

26 Like the dew on the mountain,
Like the foam on the river,
Like the bubble on the fountain
Thou art gone, and for ever!
Ibid, 16. Coronach.

27 These are Clan-Alpine's warriors true;
And, Saxon, – I am Roderick Dhu!
Ibid, v. 9.

28 Come one, come all! this rock shall fly
From its firm base as soon as I.
Ibid, 10.

29 And the stern joy which warriors feel
In foemen worthy of their steel. *Ibid.*

30 O, Brignal banks are wild and fair,
And Greta woods are green,
And you may gather garlands there
Would grace a summer queen.
Rokeby, iii, 16.

31 A weary lot is thine, fair maid. *Ibid, 28.*

32 O! many a shaft, at random sent,
Finds mark the archer little meant!
And many a word, at random spoken,
May soothe or wound a heart that's
broken! *The Lord of the Isles, v. 18.*

33 But answer came there none.
The Bridal of Triermain, iii, 10.

34 O hush thee, my babie, thy sire was a
knight,
Thy mother a lady, both lovely and
bright. *Lullaby of an Infant Chief.*

35 Come as the winds come, when
Forests are rended,

Come as the waves come, when
Navies are stranded.
Pibroch of Donuil Dhu.

36 Twist ye, twine ye! even so
Mingle human bliss and woe.
Guy Mannering, iii, The Spindle Song.

37 Come fill up my cup, come fill up my
can,
Come saddle my horses, and call up my
man;
Come open your gates, and let me gae
free,
I daurna stay langer in bonny Dundee.
Rob Roy, xxiii.
(Slightly different version in *The Doom of
Devorgoil*, II. i.)

38 Proud Maisie is in the wood,
Walking so early;
Sweet Robin sits on the bush,
Singing so rarely.
The Heart of Midlothian, xl.

39 Look not thou on beauty's charming,
Sit thou still when kings are arming,
Taste not when the wine-cup glistens,
Speak not when the people listens,
Stop thine ear against the singer,
From the red gold keep thy finger;
Vacant heart and hand and eye,
Easy live and quiet die.
The Bride of Lammermoor, ii.

40 When Israel, of the Lord beloved,
Out of the land of bondage came,
Her fathers' God before her moved,
An awful guide in smoke and flame.
Ivanhoe, xxxix. Rebecca's Hymn.

41 March, march, Ettrick and Teviotdale,
Why the deil dinna ye march forward in
order?
March, march, Eskdale and Liddesdale,
All the Blue Bonnets are bound for the
Border.
The Monastery, xxv. Border March.

42 The lark, his lay who thrill'd all day,
Sits hush'd his partner nigh;
Breeze, bird, and flower confess the
hour,
But where is County Guy?
Quentin Durward, iv.

1 Come weal, come woe, we'll gather and
go,
And live or die with Charlie.
Redgauntlet, xi.

2 'Pro-di-gi-ous!' exclaimed Dominie
Samson. *Guy Mannering, xiv.*

3 Among the sea of upturned faces.
Rob Roy, xx.

4 My foot is on my native heath, and my
name is MacGregor! *Ibid, xxxiv.*

5 Jock, when ye hae naething else to do,
ye may be aye sticking in a tree; it will
be growing, Jock, when ye're sleeping.
The Heart of Midlothian, viii.

6 It's ill speaking between a fou man and a
fasting.
*Redgauntlet letter xi. Wandering Willie's
Tale.*

7 (Miss Austen) had a talent for describing
the involvements and feelings and
characters of ordinary life which is to me
the most wonderful I ever met with.
The Big Bow-Wow strain I can do
myself like any now going; but the
exquisite touch which renders ordinary
commonplace things and characters
interesting, from the truth of the
description and the sentiment, is denied
to me. *Journal, 14 March, 1826.*

**SCOTT, WILLIAM, BARON
STOWELL, English lawyer,
17 Oct. 1745–28 Jan. 1836**

8 A dinner lubricates business.
*Boswell's Life of Johnson (1835 edition),
an. 1781.*

9 The elegant simplicity of the three per
cents.
*Campbell's Lives of the Lord Chancellors,
X. ccxii.*

SEAFIELD, EARL OF, see Ogilvy

**SEARS, EDMUND HAMILTON,
US clergyman, 6 April, 1810–16 Jan.
1876**

10 It came upon the midnight clear,
That glorious song of old.
The Angels' Song.

**SEDLEY, SIR CHARLES, English
dramatist, 1639?–20 Aug. 1701**

11 When change itself can give no more,
'Tis easy to be true.
Reasons for Constancy.

12 Love still has something of the sea
From whence his mother rose.
Love still has something of the Sea.

13 Phyllis is my only joy,
Faithless as the winds or seas,
Sometimes cunning, sometimes coy,
Yet she never fails to please. *Phyllis.*

**SEEGER, ALAN, English soldier
and poet, 22 June, 1888–4 July, 1916**

14 I have a rendezvous with Death
At some disputed barricade.
I have a Rendezvous with Death.

**SELDEN, JOHN, English jurist,
16 Dec. 1584–30 Nov. 1654**

15 Old friends are best. King James used to
call for his old shoes; they were easiest
for his feet. *Table Talk. Friends.*

16 Commonly we say a judgment falls
upon a man for something in him we
cannot abide. *Ibid, Judgments.*

17 Ignorance of the law excuses no man;
not that all men know the law, but
because 'tis an excuse every man will
plead, and no man can tell how to
refute him. *Ibid, Law.*

18 Pleasures are all alike, simply considered
in themselves. He that takes pleasure to
hear sermons enjoys himself as much
as he that hears plays. *Ibid, Pleasure.*

19 A King is a thing men have made for
their own sakes, for quietness' sake.
Just as in a family one man is appointed
to buy the meat. *Ibid, Of a King.*

**SEWARD, THOMAS, English
clergyman, 1708–4 March, 1790**

20 Seven wealthy towns contend for
Homer dead,

Through which the living Homer
begg'd his bread.   *Attributed.*

SEWARD, WILLIAM HENRY, US statesman, 16 May, 1801–10 Oct. 1872

21 There is a higher law than the
Constitution.
Speech in US Senate, 11 March, 1850.

SHADWELL, THOMAS, English Poet Laureate, 1642?–19 Nov. 1692

22 I'll do't instantly, in the twinkling of a
bed-staff.   *The Virtuoso, I. i.*

SHAFTESBURY, ANTHONY ASHLEY COOPER, 3RD EARL OF, English philosopher, 26 Feb. 1671–4 Feb. 1713

23 'Twas the saying of an ancient sage, that
humour was the only test of gravity; and
gravity, of humour. For a subject which
would not bear raillery was suspicious;
and a jest which would not bear a
serious examination was certainly false
wit.
*Characteristicks. Essay on the Freedom of
Wit and Humour, 5.*
(The sage was Gorgias, in Aristotle,
Rhetoric, III. xviii.)

SHAKESPEARE, WILLIAM, English dramatist, baptised 26 April, 1564, died 23 April, 1616

The text used in the following
quotations is that of Clark and Wright's
Cambridge Shakespeare as reproduced in
the Globe Edition of 1911.

ALL'S WELL THAT ENDS WELL

24   Love all, trust a few,
Do wrong to none: be able for thine
enemy
Rather in power than use, and keep thy
friend
Under thy own life's key: be check'd for
silence,
But never tax'd for speech.
All's Well that Ends Well, I. i. 73.

25   'Twere all one
That I should love a bright particular
star
And think to wed it, he is so above me.
Ibid, 96.

26 The hind that would be mated by the
lion
Must die for love.   *Ibid, 102.*

27 Our remedies oft in ourselves do lie,
Which we ascribe to heaven: the fated
sky
Gives us free scope, only doth backward
pull
Our slow designs when we ourselves are
dull.   *Ibid, 231.*

28 Oft expectation fails and most oft there
Where most it promises, and oft it hits
Where hope is coldest and despair most
fits.   *Ibid, II. i. 145.*

29 From lowest place when virtuous things
proceed,
The place is dignified by the doer's deed.
Ibid, iii. 132.

30 A young man married is a man that's
marr'd.   *Ibid, 315.*

31 The web of our life is of a mingled yarn,
good and ill together.   *Ibid, IV. iii. 83.*

32 There's place and means for every man
alive.   *Ibid, 375.*

33 Praising what is lost
Makes the remembrance dear.
Ibid, V. iii. 19.

ANTONY AND CLEOPATRA

34 There's beggary in the love that can be
reckon'd.
Antony and Cleopatra, I. i. 15.

35 In nature's infinite book of secrecy
A little can I read.   *Ibid, ii. 9.*

36 The nature of bad news infects the teller.
Ibid, 99.

37 Where's my serpent of old Nile?
Ibid, v. 25.

1
                My salad days,
When I was green in judgment.
                        Ibid, 73.

2 The barge she sat in, like a burnish'd
   throne,
   Burn'd on the water: the poop was
   beaten gold;
   Purple the sails, and so perfumed that
   The winds were love-sick with them;
   the oars were silver,
   Which to the tune of flutes kept stroke,
   and made
   The water which they beat to follow
   faster,
   As amorous of their strokes. For her
   own person,
   It beggar'd all description. *Ibid, ii. 196.*

3   I saw her once
   Hop forty paces through the public
   street;
   And having lost her breath, she spoke,
   and panted,
   That she did make defect perfection,
   And, breathless, power breathe forth.
                        Ibid, 233.

4 Age cannot wither her, nor custom stale
   Her infinite variety.   *Ibid, 240.*

5 Though it be honest, it is never good
   To bring bad news.   *Ibid, v. 85.*

6 Come, thou monarch of the vine
   Plumpy Bacchus with pink eyne!
                        Ibid, vii. 120.

7 Who does i' the wars more than his
   captain can,
   Becomes his captain's captain: and
   ambition,
   The soldier's virtue, rather makes choice
   of loss,
   Than gain which darkens him.
                        Ibid, III. i. 21.

8 Celerity is never more admired
   Than by the negligent.   *Ibid, vii. 25.*

9   He wears the rose
   Of youth upon him.   *Ibid, xiii. 20.*

10 I found you as a morsel cold upon
    Dead Caesar's trencher   *Ibid, 116.*

11 Let's have one other gaudy night.
                        Ibid, 183.

12 To business that we love we rise betime,
    And go to't with delight.
                        Ibid, IV. iv. 20.

13   I have yet
    Room for six scotches more.
                        Ibid, vii. 9.

14 Sometime we see a cloud that's
    dragonish
    A vapour sometime like a bear or lion,
    A tower'd citadel, a pendent rock,
    A forked mountain, or blue promontory
    With trees upon't.   *Ibid, xiv. 2.*

15 Unarm, Eros; the long day's task is
    done,
    And we must sleep.   *Ibid, 35.*

16 I am dying, Egypt, dying; only
    I here importune death awhile, until
    Of many thousand kisses the poor last
    I lay upon thy lips.   *Ibid, xv. 18.*

17 O, wither'd is the garland of the war,
    The soldier's pole is fall'n: young boys
    and girls
    Are level now with men; the odds is
    gone,
    And there is nothing left remarkable
    Beneath the visiting moon.   *Ibid, 64.*

18   What's brave, what's noble,
    Let's do it after the high Roman fashion,
    And make death proud to take us.
                        Ibid, 86.

19 His legs bestrid the ocean: his rear'd arm
    Crested the world: his voice was
    propertied
    As all the tuned spheres, and that to
    friends;
    But when he meant to quail and shake
    the orb,
    He was as rattling thunder. For his
    bounty,
    There was no winter in't; an autumn
    'twas
    That grew the more by reaping: his
    delights
    Were dolphin-like; they show'd his back
    above

The elements they lived in: in his livery
Walk'd crowns and crownets; realms and islands were
As plates dropp'd from his pocket.
Ibid, V. ii. 82.

20 Finish, good lady; the bright day is done,
And we are for the dark. *Ibid, 193.*

21   I shall see
Some squeaking Cleopatra boy my greatnèss. *Ibid, 219.*

22 His biting is immortal; those that do die
of it seldom or never recover. *Ibid, 247.*

23 I wish you joy o' the worm. *Ibid, 281.*

24 Give me my robe, put on my crown; I have
Immortal longings in me. *Ibid, 283.*

25 If thou and nature can so gently part,
The stroke of death is as a lover's pinch
Which hurts, and is desired. *Ibid, 297.*

26 Dost thou not see my baby at my breast,
That sucks the nurse asleep? *Ibid, 312.*

27 Now boast thee, death, in thy possession lies
A lass unparallel'd. Downy windows, close;
And golden Phœbus never be beheld
Of eyes again so royal! *Ibid, 318.*

28 It is well done, and fitting for a princess
Descended of so many royal kings.
Ibid, 329.

AS YOU LIKE IT

29 Fleet the time carelessly, as they did in
the golden world.
As You Like It, I. i. 124.

30 How now, wit! whither wander you?
Ibid, ii. 60.

31 Well said: that was laid on with a trowel.
Ibid, 112.

32 My pride fell with my fortunes.
Ibid, 264.

33 *Celia.* Not a word?
Rosalind. Not one to throw at a dog.
Ibid, iii. 2.

34 O, how full of briers is this working-day world! *Ibid, 12.*

35 Beauty provoketh thieves sooner than gold. *Ibid, 112.*

36 We'll have swashing and a martial outside,
As many other mannish cowards have
That do outface it with their semblances. *Ibid, 122.*

37 Sweet are the uses of adversity,
Which, like the toad, ugly and venomous,
Wears yet a precious jewel in its head:
And this our life exempt from public haunt
Finds tongues in trees, books in the running brooks,
Sermons in stones and good in everything. *Ibid, II. i. 1.*

38   The big round tears
Coursed one another down his innocent nose
In piteous chase. *Ibid, 38.*

39   Thou makest a testament
As worldlings do, giving thy sum of more
To that which had too much. *Ibid, 47.*

40 Sweep on, you fat and greasy citizens.
Ibid, 55.

41 For in my youth I never did apply
Hot and rebellious liquors to my blood.
Ibid, iii. 48.

42 Therefore my age is as a lusty winter,
Frosty, but kindly. *Ibid, 52.*

43 O good old man, how well in thee appears
The constant service of the antique world,
When service sweat for duty, not for meed!
Thou art not for the fashion of these times,

When none will sweat but for
promotion. *Ibid, 56.*

1 Ay, now am I in Arden; the more fool I;
when I was at home, I was in a better
place: but travellers must be content.
Ibid, iv. 16.

2 If thou remember'st not the slightest
folly
That ever love did make thee run into,
Thou hast not loved. *Ibid, 34.*

3 We that are true lovers run into strange
capers. *Ibid, 54.*

4 Under the greenwood tree
Who loves to lie with me,
And turn his merry note
Unto the sweet bird's throat,
Come hither, come hither, come hither:
Here shall he see
No enemy
But winter and rough weather.
Ibid, v. 1.

5 I can suck melancholy out of a song, as a
weasel sucks eggs. *Ibid, 12.*

6 Who doth ambition shun
And loves to live i' the sun,
Seeking the food he eats,
And pleased with what he gets.
Ibid, 40.

7 And rail'd on Lady Fortune in good
terms,
In good set terms. *Ibid, vii. 16.*

8 Call me not fool till heaven hath sent me
fortune. *Ibid, 19.*

9 And then he drew a dial from his poke,
And, looking on it with lack-lustre eye,
Says very wisely, 'It is ten o'clock:
Thus we may see,' quoth he, 'how the
world wags.' *Ibid, 20.*

10 And so, from hour to hour, we ripe and
ripe,
And then, from hour to hour, we rot
and rot;
And thereby hangs a tale. *Ibid, 26.*

11 My lungs began to crow like
chanticleer,

That fools should be so deep-
contemplative,
And I did laugh sans intermission
An hour by his dial. *Ibid, 30.*

12 Motley's the only wear. *Ibid, 34.*

13 And says, if ladies be but young and fair,
They have the gift to know it: and in his
brain,
Which is as dry as the remainder biscuit
After a voyage, he doth strange places
cramm'd
With observation, the which he vents
In mangled forms. *Ibid, 37.*

14 I must have liberty
Withal, as large a charter as the wind,
To blow on whom I please. *Ibid, 47.*

15 The 'why' is plain as way to parish
church. *Ibid 52.*

16 Whate'er you are
That in this desert inaccessible,
Under the shade of melancholy boughs,
Lose and neglect the creeping hours of
time. *Ibid, 109.*

17 All the world's a stage,
And all the men and women merely
players:
They have their exits and their
entrances;
And one man in his time plays many
parts,
His acts being seven ages. At first the
infant,
Mewling and puking in the nurses'
arms.
And then the whining school-boy, with
his satchel
And shining morning face, creeping like
snail
Unwillingly to school. And then the
lover,
Sighing like furnace, with a woeful
ballad
Made to his mistress' eyebrow. Then a
soldier,
Full of strange oaths and bearded like the
pard,
Jealous in honour, sudden and quick in
quarrel,
Seeking the bubble reputation

Even in the cannon's mouth. And then the justice,
In fair round belly with good capon lined,
With eyes severe and beard of formal cut,
Full of wise saws and modern instances;
And so he plays his part. The sixth stage shifts
Into the lean and slipper'd pantaloon,
With spectacles on nose and pouch on side,
His youthful hose, well saved, a world too wide
For his shrunk shank; and his big manly voice
Turning again towards childish treble, pipes
And whistles in his sound. Last scene of all,
That ends this strange eventful history,
Is second childishness and mere oblivion,
Sans teeth, sans eyes, sans taste, sans everything.   *Ibid, 139.*

18 Blow, blow, thou winter wind,
Thou art not so unkind
As man's ingratitude;
Thy tooth is not so keen,
Because thou art not seen,
Although thy breath be rude. *Ibid, 174.*

19 Most friendship is feigning, most loving
mere folly.   *Ibid, 181.*

20 The fair, the chaste and unexpressive
she.   *Ibid, III. ii. 10.*

21 Hast any philosophy in thee, shepherd?
   Ibid, 22.

22 He that wants money, means and
content is without three good friends.
   Ibid, 25.

23 Truly thou art damned, like an ill-
roasted egg all on one side. *Ibid, 38.*

24 This is the very false gallop of the
verses.   *Ibid, 119.*

25 O wonderful, wonderful, and most
wonderful! and yet again wonderful,
and after that, out of all hooping!
   Ibid, 201.

26 Speak, sad brow and true maid.
   Ibid, 227.

27 Do you not know I am a woman? when
I think, I must speak.   *Ibid, 263.*

28 I do desire we may be better strangers.
   Ibid, 275.

29 *Jacques.* What stature is she of?
Orlando. Just as high as my heart.
   Ibid, 285.

30 Time travels in divers paces with divers
persons. I'll tell you who Time ambles
withal, who Time trots withal, who
Time gallops withal and who he stands
still withal.   *Ibid, 325.*

31 Every one fault seeming monstrous till
his fellow-fault came to match it.
   Ibid, 372.

32 Truly, I would the gods had made thee
poetical.   *Ibid, iii. 16.*

33 I am not a slut, though I thank the gods I
am foul.   *Ibid, 38.*

34 If ever, – as that ever may be near, –
You meet in some fresh cheek the power
of fancy,
Then shall you know the wounds
invisible
That love's keen arrows make.
   Ibid, iv. 28.

35   Down on your knees,
And thank heaven, fasting, for a good
man's love.   *Ibid, 57.*

36 Dead shepherd, now I find thy saw of
might,
'Who ever loved that loved not at first
sight?'
(Quoting Marlowe's 'Hero and
Leander.' See 157:23.)

37 It is a melancholy of mine own,
compounded of many simples,
extracted from many objects, and
indeed the sundry contemplation of my
travels, in which my often rumination
wraps me in a most humorous sadness.
   Ibid, IV. i. 16.

1 I had rather have a fool to make me
merry than experience to make me sad.
Ibid, 28.

2 Very good orators, when they are out,
they will spit. *Ibid, 75*

3 Men have died from time to time and
worms have eaten them, but not for
love. *Ibid, 106.*

4 Men are April when they woo,
December when they wed: maids are
May when they are maids, but the sky
changes when they are wives.
Ibid, 147.

5 The horn, the horn, the lusty horn
Is not a thing to laugh to scorn.
Ibid, ii. 18.

6 Chewing the food of sweet and bitter
fancy. *Ibid, iii. 102.*

7 It is meat and drink to me to see a
clown. *Ibid, V. i. 11.*

8 No sooner met but they looked, no
sooner looked but they loved, so sooner
loved but they sighed, no sooner sighed
but they asked one another the reason,
no sooner knew the reason but they
sought the remedy. *Ibid, ii. 36.*

9 O, how bitter a thing it is to look into
happiness through another man's eyes!
Ibid, 47.

10 It is to be all made of sighs and tears.

It is to be all made of faith and service.

It is to be all made of fantasy,
All made of passion and all made of
wishes,
All adoration, duty, and observance,
All humbleness, all patience and
impatience,
All purity, all trial, all observance. (Of
love.) *Ibid, 90.*

11 It was a lover and his lass,
With a hey, and a ho, and a hey nonino,
That o'er the green corn-field did pass

In the spring time, the only pretty ring
time,
When birds do sing, hey ding a ding,
ding:
Sweet lovers love the spring.
Ibid, iii. 17.

12 An ill-favoured thing, sir, but mine
own. *Ibid, iv. 60.*

13 O Sir, we quarrel in print, by the book;
as you have books for good manners: I
will name you the degrees. The first, the
Retort Courteous; the second, the Quip
Modest; the third, the Reply Churlish;
the fourth, the Reproof Valiant; the
fifth, the Countercheck Quarrelsome;
the sixth, the Lie with Circumstance; the
seventh, the Lie Direct. *Ibid, 94.*

14 Your If is the only peace-maker; much
virtue in If. *Ibid, 107.*

15 He uses his folly like a stalking-horse
and under the presentation of that he
shoots his wit. *Ibid, III.*

16 If it be true that good wine needs no
bush, 'tis true that a good play needs
no epilogue. *Ibid, epilogue, 3.*

THE COMEDY OF ERRORS

17 The pleasing punishment that women
bear.
The Comedy of Errors, I. i. 47.

18 A wretched soul, bruised with
adversity. *Ibid, II. i. 34.*

19 They brought one Pinch, a hungry lean-
faced villain,
A mere anatomy, a mountebank,
A threadbare juggler and a fortune-
teller,
A needy, hollow-eyed, sharp-looking
wretch,
A living dead man. *Ibid, V. i. 237.*

CORIOLANUS

20 My gracious silence, hail!
Coriolanus, II. i. 192.

21   Look, sir, my wounds!
I got them in my country's service,
    when
Some certain of your brethren roar's and
    ran
From the noise of our own drums.
                        Ibid, iii. 57.

22   Bid them wash their faces
And keep their teeth clean.   *Ibid, 66.*

23 I thank you for your voices: thank you:
Your most sweet voices.   *Ibid, 179.*

24 Hear you this Triton of the minnows?
    mark you
His absolute 'shall'?   *Ibid, III. i. 89.*

25 His nature is too noble for the world:
He would not flatter Neptune for his
    trident,
Or Jove for's power to thunder.
                        Ibid, 255.

26 You common cry of curs! whose breath
    I hate
As reek o' the rotten fens, whose loves I
    prize
As the dead carcasses of unburied men
That do corrupt my air, I banish you!
                        Ibid, iii. 120.

27   O, a kiss
Long as my exile, sweet as my revenge!
                        Ibid, V. iii. 44.

28   Chaste as the icicle
That's curdied by the frost from purest
    snow
And hangs on Diana's temple. *Ibid, 65.*

29 If you have writ your annals true, 'tis
    there,
That, like an eagle in a dovecot, I
Flutter'd your Volscians in Corioli:
Alone I did it.   *Ibid, vi. 114.*

CYMBELINE

30 Hark, hark! the lark at heaven's gate
    sings,
And Phœbus 'gins arise,
His steeds to water at those springs
On chaliced flowers that lies;

And winking Mary-buds begin
To ope their golden eyes:
With every thing that pretty is,
My lady sweet, arise.
                Cymbeline, II. iii. 21.

31   There be many Caesars,
Ere such another Julius. Britain is
A world by itself; and we will nothing
    pay
For wearing our own noses.
                        Ibid, III. i. 11.

32 The natural bravery of your isle, which
    stands
As Neptune's park, ribbed and paled in
With rocks unscaleable and roaring
    waters.   *Ibid, 18.*

33 Prouder than rustling in unpaid-for silk.
                        Ibid, iii. 24.

34   Slander,
Whose edge is sharper than the sword,
    whose tongue
Outvenoms all the worms of Nile,
    whose breath
Rides on the posting winds and doth
    belie
All corners of the world.   *Ibid, iv. 35.*

35 I have not slept one wink.   *Ibid, 103.*

36   Weariness
Can snore upon the flint, when resty
    sloth
Finds the down pillow hard.
                        Ibid, vi. 33.

37   With fairest flowers
Whilst summer lasts and I live here,
    Fidele,
I'll sweeten thy sad grave: thou shalt not
    lack
The flower that Æ like thy face, pale
    primrose, nor
The azured harebell, like thy veins, no,
    nor
The leaf of eglantine, whom not to
    slander,
Out-sweeten'd not thy breath.
                        Ibid, IV. ii. 220.

38 Thersites' body is as good as Ajax',
When neither are alive.   *Ibid, 252.*

219

1 Fear no more the heat o' the sun,
Nor the furious winter's rages;
Thou thy worldly task hast done,
Home art gone, and ta'en thy wages:
Golden lads and girls all must,
As chimney-sweepers, come to dust.
Ibid, 258.

2 The sceptre, learning, physic, must
All follow this, and come to dust.
Ibid, 268.

3 Fear no more the lightning-flash,
Nor the all-dreaded thunder-stone;
Fear not slander, censure rash;
Thou hast finish'd joy and moan:
All lovers young, all lovers must
Consign to thee, and come to dust.
Ibid, 270.

HAMLET

4 For this relief much thanks.
Hamlet, I. i. 8.

5 But in the gross and scope of my
opinion,
This bodes some strange eruption to our
state.   *Ibid, 67.*

6   Whose sore task
Does not divide the Sunday from the
week.   *Ibid, 75.*

7   This sweaty haste
Doth make the night joint-labourer with
the day.   *Ibid, 78.*

8 In the most high and palmy state of
Rome,
A little ere the mightiest Julius fell,
The graves stood tenantless and the
sheeted dead
Did squeak and gibber in the Roman
street.   *Ibid, 113.*

9 We do it wrong, being so majestical,
To offer it the show of violence.
Ibid, 143.

10 And then it started like a guilty thing
Upon a fearful summons.   *Ibid, 148.*

11 Whether in sea or fire, in earth or air,
The extravagant and erring spirit hies
To his confine.   *Ibid, 153*

12 Some say that ever 'gainst that season
comes
Wherein our Saviour's birth is
celebrated,
The bird of dawning singeth all night
long:
The nights are wholesome; then no
planets strike,
No fairy takes, nor witch hath power to
charm,
So hallow'd and so gracious is the time.
Ibid, 158.

13 But, look, the morn, in russet mantle
clad,
Walks o'er the lew of yon high eastward
hill.   *Ibid, 166.*

14 With an auspicious and a dropping eye,
With mirth in funeral and with dirge in
marriage,
In equal scale weighing delight and dole.
Ibid, ii. 11.

15 A little more than kin, and less than
kind.   *Ibid, 65.*

16 Thou know'st 'tis common; all that lives
must die,
Passing through nature to eternity.
Ibid, 72.

17 Seems, madam! nay, it is; I know not
'seems.'
'Tis not alone my inky cloak, good
mother,
Nor customary suits of solemn black.
Ibid, 76.

18 But I have that within which passeth
show;
These but the trappings and the suits of
woe.   *Ibid, 85.*

19 O, that this too too solid flesh would
melt,
Thaw and resolve itself into a dew!
Or that the Everlasting had not fix'd
His canon 'gainst self-slaughter! O God!
God!
How weary, stale, flat and unprofitable,
Seem to me all the uses of this world!
Ibid, 129.

20 So excellent a king; that was, to this,

Hyperion to a satyr; so loving to my
mother
That he might not beteem the winds of
heaven
Visit her face too roughly. *Ibid, 139.*

21   Why, she would hang on him,
As if increase of appetite had grown
By what it fed on. *Ibid, 143.*

22 Frailty, thy name is woman!
Ibid, 146.

23 A beast, that wants discourse of reason.
Ibid, 150.

24 It is not nor it cannot come to good.
Ibid, 158.

25 Thrift, thrift, Horatio! the funeral baked
meats
Did coldly furnish forth the marriage
tables. *Ibid, 180.*

26 In my mind's eye, Horatio. *Ibid, 185.*

27 He was a man, take him for all in all,
I shall not look upon his like again.
Ibid, 187.

28 In the dead vast and middle of the night.
Ibid, 198.

29 A countenance more in sorrow than in
anger. *Ibid, 232.*

30 While one with moderate haste might
tell a hundred. *Ibid, 238.*

31 A sable silver'd. *Ibid, 242.*

32 Give it an understanding, but no
tongue. *Ibid, 249.*

33 Foul play. *Ibid, 256.*

34 His greatness weigh'd, his will is not his
own;
For he himself is subject to his birth:
He may not, as unvalued persons do,
Carve for himself; for on his choice
depends
The safety and the health of this whole
state. *Ibid, iii. 17.*

35 The chariest maid is prodigal enough,
If she unmask her beauty to the moon:
Virtue itself 'scrapes not calumnious
strokes:
The canker galls the infants of the
spring,
Too oft before their buttons be
disclosed,
And in the morn and liquid dew of
youth
Contagious blastments are most
imminent. *Ibid, 36.*

36 Do not, as some ungracious pastors do,
Show me the steep and thorny way to
heaven;
Whiles, like a puff'd and reckless
libertine,
Himself the primrose path of dalliance
treads,
And recks not his own rede. *Ibid, 47.*

37 And these few precepts in thy memory
See thou character. Give thy thoughts
no tongue,
Nor any unproportion'd thought his
act.
Be thou familiar, but by no means
vulgar.
Those friends thou hast, and their
adoption tried,
Grapple them to thy soul with hoops of
steel. *Ibid, 58.*

38   Beware
Of entrance to a quarrel, but being in,
Bear't that the opposed may beware of
thee.
Give every man thy ear, but few thy
voice;
Take each man's censure, but reserve
thy judgment.
Costly thy habit as thy purse can buy,
But not express'd in fancy; rich, not
gaudy;
For the apparel oft proclaims the man.
Ibid 65.

39 Neither a borrower nor a lender be;
For loan oft loses both itself and friend,
And borrowing dulls the edge of
husbandry.
This above all: to thine own self be true,
And it must follow as the night the day,
Thou canst not then be false to any man.
Ibid, 75.

1 Ay, springes to catch woodcocks.
Ibid, 115.

2 Be somewhat scanter of your maiden
presence.   *Ibid, 121.*

3 *Hamlet.* The air bites shrewly; it is very
cold.
Horatio. It is a nipping and an eager air.
Ibid, iv. 1.

4 But to my mind, though I am native
here
And to the manner born, it is a custom
More honour'd in the breach than the
observance.   *Ibid, 14.*

5 Angels and ministers of grace defend us!
Be thou a spirit of health or goblin
damn'd,
Bring with thee airs from heaven or
blasts from hell,
Be thy intents wicked or charitable,
Thou comest in such a questionable
shape
That I will speak to thee.   *Ibid, 39.*

6 Hath oped his ponderous and marble
jaws.   *Ibid, 50.*

7   What may this mean,
That thou, dead corse, again in complete
steel
Revisit'st thus the glimpses of the
moon,
Making night hideous?   *Ibid, 51.*

8   Look, with what courteous action
It waves you to a more removed
ground.   *Ibid, 60.*

9 I do not set my life at a pin's fee;
And for my soul, what can it do to that,
Being a thing immortal as itself?
Ibid, 65.

10   Unhand me, gentlemen;
By heaven, I'll make a ghost of him that
lets me!   *Ibid, 84.*

11 Something is rotten in the state of
Denmark.   *Ibid, 90.*

12   But that I am forbid
To tell the secrets of my prison-house,

I could a tale unfold whose lightest word
Would harrow up thy soul, freeze thy
young blood,
Make thy two eyes, like stars, start from
their spheres,
Thy knotted and combined locks to
part,
And each particular hair to stand an end,
Like quills upon the fretful porpentine:
But this eternal blazon must not be
To ears of flesh and blood. List, list O
list!   *Ibid, v. 13.*

13 Murder most foul, as in the best it is;
But this most foul, strange and
unnatural.   *Ibid, 27.*

14   O my prophetic soul!
My uncle!   *Ibid, 40.*

15 O Hamlet, what a falling-off was there!
Ibid, 47.

16 But soft! methinks I scent the morning
air.   *Ibid, 58.*

17 Cut off even in the blossoms of my sin,
Unhousel'd, disappointed, unaneled,
No reckoning made, but sent to my
account
With all my imperfections on my head.
Ibid, 76.

18   Leave her to heaven
And to those thorns that in her bosom
lodge,
To prick and sting her.   *Ibid, 86.*

19 The glow-worm shows the matin to be
near,
And 'gins to pale his uneffectual fire.
Ibid, 89.

20   While memory holds a seat
In this distracted globe. Remember thee!
Yea, from the table of my memory
I'll wipe away all trivial fond records,
All saws of books, all forms, all
pressures past,
That youth and observation copied
there.   *Ibid, 97.*

21 O villain, villain, smiling, damned
villain!
My tables, – meet it is I set it down,

That one may smile, and smile, and be a villain;
At least I'm sure it may be so in
Denmark.   *Ibid, 106.*

22 There needs no ghost, my lord, come
from the grave
To tell us this.   *Ibid, 125.*

23 Wild and whirling words.   *Ibid, 133.*

24 There are more things in heaven and
earth, Horatio,
Than are dreamt of in your philosophy.
                                  Ibid, 166.

25 Rest, rest, perturbed spirit!   *Ibid, 182.*

26 The time is out of joint: O cursed spite,
That ever I was born to set it right.
                                  Ibid, 189.

27 Brevity is the soul of wit.
                                  Ibid, II. ii. 90.

28 More matter, with less art.   *Ibid, 95.*

29 That he is mad, 'tis true: 'tis true 'tis
pity;
And pity 'tis 'tis true.   *Ibid, 97.*

30 Doubt thou the stars are fire;
Doubt that the sun doth move;
Doubt truth to be a liar;
But never doubt I love.   *Ibid, 116.*

31 Still harping on my daughter.   *Ibid, 188.*

32 *Polonius.* What do you read, my lord?
Hamlet. Words, words, words.
                                  Ibid, 193.

33 Though this be madness, yet there is
method in't.   *Ibid, 207.*

34 On fortune's cap we are not the very
button.   *Ibid, 233.*

35 There is nothing either good or bad, but
thinking makes it so.   *Ibid, 255.*

36 Beggar that I am, I am even poor in
thanks.   *Ibid, 271.*

37 It goes so heavily with my disposition

that this goodly frame, the earth,
seems to me a sterile promontory, this
most excellent canopy, the air, look
you, this brave o'erhanging
firmament, this majestical roof fretted
with golden fire, why, it appears no
other thing to me than a foul and
pestilent congregation of vapours.
What a piece of work is a man! how
noble in reason! how infinite in faculty!
in form and moving how express and
admirable! in action how like an angel!
in apprehension how like a God! the
beauty of the world! the paragon of
animals! And yet, to me, what is this
quintessence of dust? man delights not
me: no, nor woman neither.   *Ibid, 304.*

38 I am but mad north-north-west: when
the wind is southerly I know a hawk
from a handsaw.   *Ibid, 397.*

39 The best actors in the world, either for
tragedy, comedy, history, pastoral,
pastoral-comical, historical-pastoral,
tragical-historical, tragical-comical-
historical-pastoral, scene individable,
or poem unlimited: Seneca cannot be
too heavy, nor Plautus too light.
                                  Ibid, 415.

40 Come, give us a taste of your quality.
                                  Ibid, 451.

41 The play, I remember, pleased not the
million; 'twas caviare to the general.
                                  Ibid, 456.

42 The mobled queen.   *Ibid, 525.*

43 They are the abstract and brief
chronicles of the time. (The players.)
                                  Ibid, 548.

44 Use every man after his desert, and who
should 'scape whipping?   *Ibid, 555.*

45 O, what a rogue and peasant slave am I!
                                  Ibid, 576.

46 What's Hecuba to him or he to Hecuba,
That he should weep for her?   *Ibid, 585.*

47 But I am pigeon-liver'd and lack gall
To make oppression bitter.   *Ibid, 605.*

1 Must, like a whore, unpack my heart
with words,
And fall a-cursing, like a very drab,
A scullion!   *Ibid, 614.*

2   The play's the thing
Wherein I'll catch the conscience of the
king.   *Ibid, 633.*

3   With devotion's visage
And pious action we do sugar o'er
The devil himself.   *Ibid, III. i. 47.*

4 To be or not to be: that is the question:
Whether 'tis nobler in the mind to suffer
The slings and arrows of outrageous
fortune,
Or to take arms against a sea of troubles,
And by opposing end them? To die: to
sleep;
No more; and by a sleep to say we end `
The heart-ache and the thousand natural
shocks
That flesh is heir to, 'tis a consummation
Devoutly to be wished. To die, to sleep:
To sleep: perchance to dream: ay, there's
the rub;
For in that sleep of death what dreams
may come
When we have shuffled off this mortal
coil,
Must gives us pause; there's the respect
That makes calamity of so long life;
For who would bear the whips and
scorns of time,
The oppressor's wrong, the proud
man's contumely,
The pangs of despised love, the law's
delay,
The insolence of office and the spurns
That patient merit of the unworthy
takes,
When he himself might his quietus make
With a bare bodkin? who would fardels
bear,
To grunt and sweat under a weary life,
But that the dread of something after
death,
The undiscover'd country from whose
bourn
No traveller returns, puzzles the will
And makes us rather bear those ills we
have
Than fly to others that we know not of?

Thus conscience does make cowards of
us all;
And thus the native hue of resolution
Is sicklied o'er with the pale cast of
thought,
And enterprises of great pitch and
moment
With this regard their currents turn
awry,
And lose the name of action.   *Ibid, 56.*

5   Nymph, in thy orisons
Be all my sins remember'd.   *Ibid, 89.*

6 Take these again; for to the noble mind
Rich gifts wax poor when givers prove
unkind.   *Ibid, 100.*

7 Get thee to a nunnery.   *Ibid, 122.*

8 What should such fellows as I do
crawling between earth and heaven?
                          Ibid, 130.

9 Be thou as chaste as ice, as pure as snow,
thou shalt not escape calumny.
                          Ibid, 140.

10 I have heard of your paintings too, well
enough; God has given you one face,
and you make yourselves another.
                          Ibid, 148.

11 O, what a noble mind is here
o'erthrown!
The courtier's, soldier's, scholar's, eye,
tongue, sword;
The expectancy and rose of the fair state,
The glass of fashion and the mould of
form,
The observed of all observers, quite,
quite down!   *Ibid, 158.*

12 Now see that noble and most sovereign
reason,
Like sweet bells jangled, out of tune and
harsh.   *Ibid, 165.*

13 Speak the speech, I pray you, as I
pronounced it to you, trippingly on the
tongue: but if you mouth it, as many of
your players do, I had as lief the town-
crier spoke my lines. Nor do not saw the
air too much with your hand, thus, but
use all gently.   *Ibid, ii. 1.*

14 Tear a passion to tatters, to very rags, to split the ears of the groundlings.
Ibid, 11.

15 It out-herods Herod. *Ibid, 16.*

16 Suit the action to the word, the word to the action; with this special observance, that you o'erstep not the modesty of nature. *Ibid, 20.*

17 The purpose of playing, whose end, both at the first and now, was and is, to hold, as 'twere, the mirror up to nature. *Ibid, 24.*

18 I have thought some of nature's journeymen had made men and not made them well, they imitated humanity so abominably. *Ibid, 38.*

19 A man that fortune's buffets and rewards
Hast ta'en with equal thanks. *Ibid, 72.*

20　　　　　　Give me that man
That is not passion's slave, and I will wear him
In my heart's core, ay, in my heart of heart,
As I do thee. *Ibid, 72.*

21 And my imaginations are as foul
As Vulcan's stithy. *Ibid, 88.*

22 Here's metal more attractive.
Ibid, 116.

23 This is miching mallecho; it means mischief. *Ibid, 147.*

24 *Ophelia.* 'Tis brief, my lord.
Hamlet. As woman's love. *Ibid, 164.*

25 The lady doth protest too much, methinks. *Ibid, 240.*

26 Let the galled jade wince, our withers are unwrung. *Ibid, 253.*

27 What, frighted with false fire!
Ibid, 277.

28 Why, let the stricken deer go weep,
The hart ungalled play;

For some must watch, while some must sleep:
So runs the world away. *Ibid, 282.*

29 The proverb is something musty.
Ibid, 359.

30 It will discourse most eloquent music.
Ibid, 374.

31 You would pluck out the heart of my mystery. *Ibid, 381.*

32 Very like a whale. *Ibid, 399.*

33 They fool me to the top of my bent.
Ibid, 401.

34 'Tis now the very witching time of night,
When churchyards yawn and hell itself breathes out
Contagion to this world. *Ibid, 406.*

35 I will speak daggers to her, but use none. *Ibid, 414.*

36 O, my offence is rank, it smells to heaven;
It hath the primal eldest curse upon't,
A brother's murder. *Ibid, iii. 36.*

37 May one be pardon'd and retain the offence? *Ibid, 56.*

38　　　　　　'Tis not so above;
There is no shuffling, there the action lies
In his true nature; and we ourselves compell'd,
Even to the teeth and forehead of our faults,
To give in evidence. *Ibid, 60.*

39　　　　　　About some act
That has no relish of salvation in't.
Ibid, 91.

40 My words fly up, my thoughts remain below:
Words without thoughts never to heaven go. *Ibid, 97.*

41 How now! a rat? Dead, for a ducat, dead! *Ibid, iv. 23.*

1 As false as dicers' oaths. *Ibid, 45.*

2 Look here, upon this picture, and on
this,
The counterfeit presentment of two
brothers.
See, what a grace was seated on this
brow;
Hyperion's curls; the front of Jove
himself;
An eye like Mars, to threaten and
command;
A station like the herald Mercury
New-lighted on a heaven-kissing hill;
A combination and a form indeed,
Where every go did seem to set his seal,
To give the world assurance of a man.
Ibid, 53.

3 You cannot call it love; for at your age
The hey-day in the blood is tame, it's
humble
And waits upon the judgment.
Ibid, 68.

4 A cutpurse of the empire and the rule,
That from a shelf the precious diadem
stole,
And put it in his pocket! *Ibid, 99.*

5 A king of shreds and patches. *Ibid, 102.*

6 This is the very coinage of your brain.
Ibid, 137.

7 My pulse, as yours, doth temperately
keep time,
And makes as healthful music: it is not
madness
That I have utter'd: bring me to the test.
Ibid, 140.

8 Lay not the flattering unction to your
soul. *Ibid, 145.*

9 Assume a virtue, if you have it not.
Ibid, 160.

10 I must be cruel, only to be kind.
Ibid, 178.

11 For 'tis the sport to have the enginer
Hoist with his own petar. *Ibid, 206.*

12   Diseases desperate grown
By desperate appliance are relieved,
Or not at all. *Ibid, IV. iii. 9.*

13 A certain convocation of politic worms
are e'en at him. *Ibid, 21.*

14 A man may fish with the worm that
hath eat of a king, and eat of the fish that
hath fed of that worm. *Ibid, 28.*

15 How all occasions do inform against
me,
And spur my dull revenge! What is a
man,
If his chief good and market of his time
Be but to sleep and feed? a beast, no
more.
Sure, he that made us with such large
discourse,
Looking before and after, gave us not
That capability and god-like reason
To fust in us unused. *Ibid, iv. 32.*

16   Some craven scruple
Of thinking too precisely on the event.
Ibid, 40.

17   Rightly to be great
Is not to stir without great argument,
But greatly to find quarrel in a straw
When honour's at the stake. *Ibid, 53.*

18 So full of artless jealousy is guilt,
It spills itself in fearing to be spilt.
Ibid, v. 19.

19 How should I your true love know
From another one?
By his cockle hat and staff,
And his sandal shoon. *Ibid, 23.*

20 We know what we are, but know not
what we may be. *Ibid, 42.*

21 When sorrows come, they come not
single spies,
But in battalions. *Ibid, 78.*

22 There's such divinity doth hedge a king,
That treason can but peep to what it
would. *Ibid, 123.*

23 To hell, allegiance! vows, to the blackest
devil!
Conscience and grace, to the
profoundest pit!
I dare damnation. *Ibid, 131.*

24 There's rosemary, that's for
remembrance; pray, love, remember:
and there is pansies, that's for thoughts.
Ibid, 175.

25 You must wear your rue with a
difference. *Ibid, 183.*

26 A very riband in the cap of youth.
Ibid, vii. 78.

27 One woe doth tread upon another's
heel,
So fast they follow. *Ibid, 164.*

28 Cudgel thy brains no more about it.
Ibid, V. i. 63.

29 Has this fellow no feeling of his
business? *Ibid, 73.*

30 The hand of little employment hath the
daintier sense. *Ibid, 77.*

31 How absolute the knave is! we must
speak by the card, or equivocation will
undo us. *Ibid, 148.*

32 The age is grown so picked that the toe
of the peasant comes so near the heel of
the courtier, he galls his kibe.
Ibid, 151.

33 Alas, poor Yorick! I knew him, Horatio:
a fellow of infinite jest, of most
excellent fancy. *Ibid, 202.*

34 Where be your gibes now? your
gambols? your songs? your flashes of
merriment, that were wont to set the
table in a roar. *Ibid, 208.*

35 To what base uses we may return,
Horatio! Why may not imagination
trace the noble dust of Alexander, till
he find it stopping a bung-hole?
Ibid, 223.

36 Imperious Caesar, dead and turn'd to
clay,
Might stop a hole to keep the wind
away. *Ibid, 236.*

37   Lay her i' the earth:
And from her fair and unpolluted flesh
May violets spring. *Ibid, 261.*

38 A ministering angel shall my sister be.
Ibid, 264.

39 Sweets to the sweet: farewell. *Ibid, 266.*

40 I thought thy bride-bed to have deck'd,
sweet maid,
And not have strew'd thy grave.
Ibid, 268.

41 For, though I am not splenetive and
rash,
Yet have I in me something dangerous.
Ibid, 284.

42   Nay, an thou'lt mouth,
I'll rant as well as thou. *Ibid, 306.*

43 Let Hercules himself do what he may,
The cat will mew and dog will have his
day. *Ibid, 314,*

44 There's a divinity that shapes our ends,
Rough-hew them how we will.
Ibid, ii. 10.

45 It did me yeoman's service. *Ibid, 36.*

46 Into a towering passion. *Ibid, 80.*

47 What imports the nomination of this
gentleman? *Ibid, 133.*

48 His purse is empty already; all's golden
words are spent. *Ibid, 136.*

49 The phrase would be more german to
the matter. *Ibid, 165.*

50 Not a whit, we defy augry; there's a
special providence in the fall of a
sparrow. *Ibid, 230.*

51 A hit, a very palpable hit. *Ibid, 292.*

52   This fell sergeant, death,
Is strict in his arrest. *Ibid, 347.*

53 Report me and my cause aright.
Ibid 350.

54 If thou didst ever hold me in thy heart,
Absent thee from felicity awhile,
And in this harsh world draw thy breath
in pain,
To tell my story. *Ibid, 357.*

1 The rest is silence.   *Ibid, 369.*

2 Now cracks a noble heart. Good-night,
sweet prince:
And flights of angels sing thee to thy
rest!   *Ibid, 370.*

JULIUS CAESAR

3 As proper men as ever trod upon's neat's
leather.   *Julius Caesar, I. i. 28.*

4 You blocks, you stones, you worse than
senseless things!   *Ibid, 40.*

5 Beware the ides of March.   *Ibid, ii. 19.*

6 I am not gamesome: I do lack some part
Of that quick spirit that is in Antony.
           Ibid, 28.

7 Set honour in one eye and death i' the
other,
And I will look on both indifferently.
           Ibid, 86.

8 Well, honour is the subject of my story.
I cannot tell what you and other men
Think of this life; but, for my single self,
I had as lief not be as live to be
In awe of such a thing as I myself.
           Ibid, 92.

9 Caesar said to me 'Darest thou, Cassius,
now
Leap in with me into this angry flood,
And swim to yonder point?' Upon the
word,
Accoutred as I was, I plunged in
And bade him follow.   *Ibid, 102.*

10   Ye gods, it doth amaze me
A man of such a feeble temper should
So get the start of the majestic world
And bear the palm alone.   *Ibid, 128.*

11 Why, man, he doth bestride the narrow
world
Like a Colossus, and we petty men
Walk under his huge legs and peep about
To find ourselves dishonourable graves.
Men at some time are masters of their
fates:

The fault, dear Brutus, is not in our
stars,
But in ourselves, that we are underlings.
           Ibid, 135.

12   Conjure with 'em,
Brutus will start a spirit as soon as
Caesar.
Now in the name of all the gods at once,
Upon what meat doth this our Caesar
feed,
That he is grown so great? Age, thou art
shamed!
Rome, thou hast lost the breed of noble
bloods!   *Ibid, 146.*

13 There was a Brutus once that would
have brook'd
The eternal devil to keep his state in
Rome
As easily as a king.   *Ibid, 159.*

14 Let me have men about me that are fat;
Sleek-headed men and such as sleep o'
nights:
Yond Cassius has a lean and hungry
look;
He thinks too much: such men are
dangerous.   *Ibid, 192.*

15 He is a great observer and he looks
Quite through the deeds of men.
           Ibid, 202.

16 Seldom he smiles, and smiles in such a
sort
As if he mock'd himself and scorn'd his
spirit
That could be moved to smile at any
thing.   *Ibid, 205.*

17 Lowliness is young ambition's ladder,
Whereto the climber-upward turns his
face;
But when he once attains the upmost
round,
He then unto the ladder turns his back,
Looks in the clouds, scorning the base
degrees
By which he did ascend.   *Ibid, II. i. 21.*

18 Between the acting of a dreadful thing
And the first motion, all the interim is
Like a phantasma, or a hideous dream:
The Genius and the mortal instruments

Are then in council; and the state of
man,
Like to a little kingdom, suffers then
The nature of an insurrection.   *Ibid, 63.*

19 For he will never follow any thing
That other men begin.   *Ibid, 151.*

20 A dish fit for the gods.   *Ibid, 173.*

21 But when I tell him he hates flatterers,
He says he does, being then most
flattered.   *Ibid, 207.*

22 You are my true and honourable wife,
As dear to me as are the ruddy drops
That visit my sad heart.   *Ibid, 288.*

23 Fierce fiery warriors fought upon the
clouds,
In ranks and squadrons and right form
of war.   *Ibid, ii. 19.*

24 When beggars die, there are no comets
seen;
The heavens themselves blaze forth the
death of princes.   *Ibid, 30.*

25 Cowards die many times before their
deaths;
The valiant never taste of death but
once.   *Ibid, 32.*

26 How hard it is for women to keep
counsel.   *Ibid, iv. 9.*

27 But I am constant as the northern star,
Of whose true-fix'd and resting quality
There is no fellow in the firmament.
   Ibid, III. i. 60.

28 Why, he that cuts off twenty years of life
Cuts off so many years of fearing death.
   Ibid, 101.

29   How many ages hence
Shall this our lofty scene be acted over
In states unborn and accents yet
unknown!   *Ibid, 111.*

30 O mighty Caesar! dost thou lie so low?
Are all thy conquests, glories, triumphs,
spoils,
Shrunk to this little measure?   *Ibid, 148.*

31 The choice and master spirits of this age.
   Ibid, 163.

32 Though last, not least in love.
   Ibid, 189.

33 O, pardon me, thou bleeding piece of
earth,
That I am meek and gentle with these
butchers!
Thou art the ruin of the noblest man
That ever lived in the tide of times.
   Ibid, 254.

34 Cry 'Havoc,' and let slip the dogs of
war.   *Ibid, 273.*

35 As Caesar loved me, I weep for him; as
he was fortunate, I rejoice at it; as he was
valiant, I honour him; but as he was
ambitious, I slew him. There is tears for
his love; joy for his fortune; honour for
his valour; and death for his ambition.
   Ibid, ii. 27.

36 Friends, Romans, countrymen, lend me
your ears;
I come to bury Caesar, not to praise
him.
The evil that men do lives after them;
The good is oft interred with their
bones.   *Ibid, 78.*

37 For Brutus is an honourable man;
So are they all, all honourable men.
   Ibid, 87.

38 When that the poor have cried, Caesar
hath wept:
Ambition should be made of sterner
stuff.   *Ibid, 96.*

39 O judgment! thou art fled to brutish
beasts,
And men have lost their reason.
   Ibid, 109.

40 But yesterday the word of Caesar might
Have stood against the world; now lies
he there,
And none so poor to do him reverence.
   Ibid, 123.

41 If you have tears, prepare to shed them
now.   *Ibid, 173.*

1 See what a rent the envious Casca made.
Ibid, 179.

2 This was the most unkindest cut of all.
Ibid, 187.

3 Ingratitude, more strong than traitors'
arms,
Quite vanquish'd him: then burst his
mighty heart.   *Ibid 189.*

4 O, what a fall was there, my
countrymen!   *Ibid, 194.*

5 I am no orator, as Brutus is;
But, as you know me all, a plain blunt
man.   *Ibid, 221.*

6 For I have neither wit, nor words, nor
worth,
Action, not utterance, nor the power of
speech,
To stir men's blood: I only speak right
on.   *Ibid, 225.*

7   Put a tongue
In every wound of Caesar that should
move
The stones of Rome to rise and mutiny.
Ibid, 232.

8 Tear him for his bad verses, tear him for
his bad verses.   *Ibid iii. 34.*

9 This is a slight unmeritable man,
Meet to be sent on errands.
Ibid, IV. i. 12.

10 When love begins to sicken and decay,
It useth an enforced ceremony.
There are no tricks in plain and simple
faith.   *Ibid, ii. 20.*

11   You yourself
Are much condemn'd to have an itching
palm.   *Ibid, iii. 9.*

12 I had rather be a dog, and bay the moon,
Than such a Roman.   *Ibid, 27.*

13 Away, slight man!   *Ibid, 37.*

14 There is no terror, Cassius in your
threats,
For I am arm'd so strong in honesty

That they pass by me as the idle wind,
Which I respect not.   *Ibid, 66.*

15 A friend should bear his friend's
infirmities,
But Brutus makes mine greater than
they are.   *Ibid, 86.*

16 Check'd like a bondman; all his faults
observed,
Set in a note-book, learn'd, and conn'd
by rote,
To cast into my teeth.   *Ibid, 97.*

17 There is a tide in the affairs of men,
Which, taken at the flood, leads on to
fortune;
Omitted, all the voyage of their life
Is bound in shallows and in miseries.
On such a full sea are we now afloat;
And we must take the current when it
serves,
Or lose our ventures.   *Ibid, 218.*

18 But for your words, they rob the Hybla
bees,
And leave them honeyless.
Ibid, V. i. 34.

19 For ever, and for ever, farewell, Cassius!
If we do meet again, why, we shall
smile;
If not, why then, this parting was well
made.   *Ibid, 117.*

20   O, that a man might know
The end of this day's business ere it
come!   *Ibid, 123.*

21 The last of all the Romans, fare thee
well!   *Ibid, iii. 99.*

22 This was the noblest Roman of them all.
Ibid, v. 68.

23 His life was gentle, and the elements
So mix'd in him that Nature might
stand up,
And say to all the world 'This was a
man!'   *Ibid, 73.*

KING HENRY IV, PART I

24 So shaken as we are, so wan with care.
King Henry IV. part I. 1. i. I.

25   In those holy fields
Over whose acres walk'd those blessed
  feet
Which fourteen hundred years ago were
  nail'd
For our advantage on the bitter cross.
Ibid, 24.

26 Let us be Diana's foresters, gentlemen of
the shade, minions of the moon.
Ibid, ii. 28.

27 What, in thy quips and thy quiddities?
Ibid, 50.

28 Old father antic the law.   *Ibid, 69.*

29 Thou hast damnable iteration, and art
indeed able to corrupt a saint. *Ibid, 101.*

30 'Tis my vocation, Hal; 'tis no sin for a
man to labour in his vocation.
Ibid, 117.

31 There's neither honesty, manhood, nor
good fellowship in thee. *Ibid, 155.*

32 Farewell, thou latter spring! farewell,
All-hallown summer! *Ibid, 177.*

33 If all the year were playing holidays,
To sport would be as tedious as to
  work.   *Ibid, 227.*

34 A certain lord, neat and trimly dress'd,
Fresh as a bridegroom; and his chin new
  reap'd
Show'd like a stubble-land at harvest-
  home;
He was perfumed like a milliner;
And 'twixt his finger and his thumb he
  held
A pouncet-box, which never and anon
He gave his nose and took't away again.
Ibid, iii. 33.

35 And as the soldiers bore dead bodies by,
He call'd them untaught knaves,
  unmannerly,
To bring a slovenly unhandsome corse
Betwixt the wind and his nobility.
Ibid, 42.

36   He made me mad
To see him shine so brisk and smell so
  sweet

And talk so like a waiting-gentlewoman
Of guns and drums and wounds, – God
  save the mark! –
And telling me the sovereign'st thing on
  earth
Was parmaceti for an inward bruise;
And that it was great pity, so it was,
This villainous salt-petre should be
  digg'd
Out of the bowels of the harmless earth,
Which many a good tall fellow had
  destroy'd
So cowardly; and but for these vile
  guns,
He would himself have been a soldier.
Ibid, 53.

37   The blood more stirs
To rouse a lion than to start a hare!
Ibid, 197.

38 By heaven, methinks it were an easy
  leap,
To pluck bright honour from the pale-
  faced moon,
Or dive into the bottom of the deep,
Where fathom-line could never touch
  the ground,
And pluck up drowned honour by the
  locks.   *Ibid, 201.*

39 Why, what a candy deal of courtesy
This fawning greyhound then did
  proffer me!   *Ibid, 251.*

40 I know a trick worth two of that.
Ibid, II. i. 40.

41 I am bewitched with the rogue's
company. If the rascal have not given
me medicines to make me love him, I'll
be hanged.   *Ibid, ii. 18.*

42 It would be argument for a week,
laughter for a month and a good jest
for ever.   *Ibid, 100.*

43   Falstaff sweats to death,
And lards the lean earth as he walks
  along.   *Ibid, 117.*

44 Out of this nettle, danger, we pluck this
flower, safety. *Ibid, iii. 10.*

1 Our plot is as good a plot as ever was laid; our friends true and constant; a good plot, good friends, and full of expectation; an excellent plot, very good friends. *Ibid, 18.*

2 I could brain him with his lady's fan. *Ibid, 25.*

3 A Corinthian, a lad of mettle, a good boy. *Ibid, iv. 13.*

4 I am not yet of Percy's mind, the Hotspur of the north; he that kills me some six or seven dozen of Scots at a breakfast, washes his hands, and says to his wife, 'Fie upon this quiet life! I want work.' *Ibid, 114.*

5 A plague of all cowards, I say. *Ibid, 128.*

6 There live not three good men unhanged in England; and one of them is fat and grows old. *Ibid, 142.*

7 Call you that backing of your friends? A plague upon such backing! *Ibid, 165.*

8 I am a Jew else, an Ebrew Jew. *Ibid, 198.*

9 I have peppered two of them; two I am sure I have paid, two rogues in buckram suits. I tell thee what, Hal, if I tell thee a lie, spit in my face, call me horse. Thou knowest my old ward; here I lay, and thus I bore my point. Four rogues in buckram let drive at me—. *Ibid, 211.*

10 O monstrous! eleven buckram men grown out of two! *Ibid, 243.*

11 Three misbegotten knaves in Kendal green. *Ibid, 245.*

12 Give you a reason on compulsion! if reasons were as plentiful as blackberries, I would give no man a reason upon compulsion, I. *Ibid, 263.*

13 Mark now, how a plain tale shall put you down. *Ibid, 281.*

14 No more of that, Hal, an thou lovest me! *Ibid, 312.*

15 A plague of sighing and grief! it blows a man up like a bladder. *Ibid, 365.*

16 I will do it in King Cambyses' vein. *Ibid, 426.*

17 That reverend vice, that grey iniquity, that father ruffian, that vanity in years. *Ibid, 499.*

18 Banish plump Jack, and banish all the world. *Ibid, 527.*

19 O monstrous! but one half-penny worth of bread to this intolerable deal of sack! *Ibid, 591.*

20 I am not in the roll of common men. *Ibid, III. i. 43.*

21 *Glendower.* I can call spirits from the vasty deep.
Hotspur. Why, so can I, and so can any man;
But will they come when you do call for them? *Ibid, 53.*

22 O, while you live, tell truth and shame the devil! *Ibid, 62.*

23 I had rather be a kitten and cry mew Than one of these same metre ballad-mongers. *Ibid, 130.*

24 Mincing poetry:
'Tis like the forced gait of a shuffling nag. *Ibid, 134.*

25 But in the way of bargain, mark ye me, I'll cavil on the ninth part of a hair. *Ibid, 139.*

26 And such a deal of skimble-skamble stuff. *Ibid, 154.*

27 I understand thy kisses and thou mine, And that's a feeling disputation. *Ibid, 205.*

28 And those musicians that shall play to you
Hang in the air a thousand leagues from hence. *Ibid, 226.*

29 Swear me, Kate, like a lady as thou art,
A good mouth-filling oath. *Ibid, 258.*

30 A fellow of no mark nor likelihood.
Ibid, ii. 45.

31 The skipping king, he ambled up and
down
With shallows jesters and rash bavin
wits. *Ibid, 60.*

32 He was but as the cuckoo is in June,
Heard, not regarded. *Ibid, 75.*

33 Company, villainous company, hath
been the spoil of me. *Ibid, iii. 10.*

34 Shall I not take mine ease at mine inn?
Ibid, 92.

35 That daff'd the world aside,
And bid it pass. *Ibid, IV. i. 96.*

36 I saw young Harry, with his beaver on,
His cuisses on his thighs, gallantly
arm'd,
Rise from the ground like feather'd
Mercury,
And vaulted with such ease into his seat,
As if an angel dropp'd down from the
clouds,
To turn and wind a fiery Pegasus
And witch the world with noble
horsemanship. *Ibid, 104.*

37 Doomsday is near; die all, die merrily.
Ibid, 134.

38 The cankers of a calm world and a long
peace. *Ibid, ii. 32.*

39 There's but a shirt and a half in all my
company; and the half shirt is two
napkins tacked together and thrown
over the shoulders like a herald's coat
without sleeves. *Ibid, 46.*

40 Food for powder, food for powder;
they'll fill a pit as well as better.
Ibid, 71.

41 I would 'twere bed-time, Hal, and all
well. *Ibid, V. i. 125.*

42 Honour pricks me on. Yea, but how if

honour prick me off when I come on?
how then? Can honour set a leg? no: or
an arm? no: or take away the grief of a
wound? no. Honour hath no skill in
surgery, then? no. What is honour? a
word. What is in that word honour?
what is that honour? air. A trim
reckoning! Who hath it? he that died o'
Wednesday. Doth he feel it? no. Doth he
hear it? no. 'Tis insensible, then? Yea, to
the dead. But will it not live with the
living? no. Why? detraction will not
suffer it. Therefore I'll none of it.
Honour is a mere scutcheon: and so ends
my catechism. *Ibid, 131.*

43 The time of life is short!
To spend that shortness basely were too
long. *Ibid, ii. 82.*

44 Two stars keep not their motion in one
sphere. *Ibid, 65.*

45 What, old acquaintance! could not all
this flesh
Keep in a little life? Poor Jack, farewell!
I could have better spared a better man.
Ibid, iv. 102.

46 Full bravely hast thou flesh'd
Thy maiden sword. *Ibid, 133.*

47 Lord, Lord, how this world is given to
lying! *Ibid, 150.*

48 I'll purge, and leave sack, and live
cleanly as a nobleman should do.
Ibid, 168.

KING HENRY IV, PART II

49 Even such a man, so faint, so spiritless,
So dull, so dead in look, so woe-begone,
Drew Priam's curtain in the dead of
night,
And would have told him half his Troy
was burnt.
King Henry IV, part II. 1. i. 70.

50 Yet the first bringer of unwelcome news
Hath but a losing office, and his tongue
Sounds ever after as a sullen bell,
Remember'd tolling a departed friend.
Ibid, 100.

1 I am not only witty in myself, but the cause that wit is in other men.
Ibid, ii. 11.

2 A rascally yea-forsooth knave. *Ibid, 42.*

3 We that are in the vaward of our youth.
Ibid, 198.

4 For my voice, I have lost it with halloing and singing of anthems. *Ibid, 212.*

5 It was alway yet the trick of our English nation, if they have a good thing, to make it too common. *Ibid, 241.*

6 If I do, fillip me with a three-man beetle.
Ibid, 255.

7 I can get no remedy against this consumption of the purse: borrowing only lingers and lingers it out, but the disease is incurable. *Ibid, 264.*

8 An habitation giddy and unsure Hath he that buildeth on the vulgar heart. *Ibid, iii. 89.*

9 Past and to come seem best; things present worst. *Ibid, 108.*

10 Away, you scullion! you rampallian! you fustilarian! I'll tickle your catastrophe. *Ibid, II. i. 65.*

11 He hath eaten me out of house and home. *Ibid, 80.*

12 Thou didst swear to me upon a parcel-gilt goblet, sitting in my Dolphin-chamber, at the round table, by a sea-coal fire, upon Wednesday in Wheeson week. *Ibid, 93.*

13 Let the end try the man. *Ibid, ii. 50.*

14   He was indeed the glass Wherein the noble youth did dress themselves. *Ibid, iii. 21.*

15 I beseek you now, aggravate your choler. *Ibid, iv. 175.*

16 By my troth, captain, these are very bitter words. *Ibid, 184.*

17 Is it not strange that desire should so many years outlive performance.
Ibid, 286.

18   O sleep, O gentle sleep, Nature's soft nurse, how have I frighted thee, That thou no more wilt weigh my eyelids down And steep my senses in forgetfulness?
Ibid, III. i. 5.

19 Wilt thou upon the high and giddy mast Seal up the ship-boy's eyes, and rock his brains In cradle of the rude imperious surge And in the visitation of the winds, Who take the ruffian billows by the top, Curling their monstrous heads and hanging them With deafening clamour in the slippery clouds, That, with the hurly, death itself awakes? *Ibid, 18.*

20 With all appliances and means to boot.
Ibid, 29.

21 Uneasy lies the head that wears a crown.
Ibid, 31.

22 Death, as the Psalmist saith, is certain to all; all shall die. How a good yoke of bullocks at Stamford fair? *Ibid, ii. 41.*

23 Accommodated; that is, when a man is, as they say, accommodated; or when a man is, being, whereby a' may be thought to be accommodated; which is an excellent thing. *Ibid, 85.*

24 We have heard the chimes at midnight.
Ibid, 228.

25 A man can die but once. *Ibid, 250.*

26 Lord, Lord, how subject we old men are to this vice of lying! *Ibid, 125.*

27 Against ill chances men are ever merry; But heaviness foreruns the good event.
Ibid, IV. ii. 81.

28 A peace is of the nature of a conquest; For then both parties nobly are subdued, And neither party loser. *Ibid, 89.*

29 He hath a tear for pity and a hand
Open as day for melting charity.
Ibid, iv. 31.

30 O polish'd perturbation! golden care!
That keep'st the ports of slumber open
wide
To many a watchful night! *Ibid, v. 23.*

31 Thy wish was father, Harry, to that
thought. *Ibid, 93.*

32   Commit
The oldest sins the newest kind of ways.
Ibid, 126.

33 A joint of mutton, and any pretty little
tiny kickshaws. *Ibid, V. i. 28.*

34 Not Amurath an Amurath succeeds,
But Harry Harry. *Ibid, ii. 48.*

35 A foutre for the world and worldlings
base!
I speak of Africa and golden joys. *Ibid,
iii. 103.*

36 Under which king, Besonian? speak, or
die. *Ibid, 119.*

37 I know thee not, old man: fall to thy
prayers;
How ill white hairs become a fool and
jester! *Ibid, v. 51.*

KING HENRY V

38 O for a Muse of fire, that would ascend
The brightest heaven of invention.
King Henry V., prologue, I.

39   Can this cockpit hold
The vasty fields of France? or may we
cram
Within this wooden O the very casques
That did affright the air at Agincourt?
Ibid, II.

40 Consideration, like an angel, came,
And whipp'd the offending Adam out of
him. *Ibid, I. i. 28.*

41 Turn him to any cause of policy,
The Gordian knot of it he will unloose,

Familiar as his garter: that, when he
speaks,
The air, a charter'd libertine, is still.
Ibid, 45.

42 And make her chronicle as rich with
praise
As is the ooze and bottom of the sea
With sunken wreck and sunless
treasuries. *Ibid, ii. 163.*

43   For so work the honey-bees,
Creatures that by a rule in nature teach
The act of order to a peopled kingdom.
They have a king and officers of sorts;
Where some, like magistrates, correct at
home,
Others, like merchants, venture trade
abroad,
Others, like soldiers, armed in their
stings,
Make boot upon the summer's velvet
buds,
Which pillage they with merry march
bring home
To the tent-royal of their emperor;
Who, busied in his majesty, surveys
The singing masons building roofs of
gold,
The civil citizens kneading up the
honey,
The poor mechanic porters crowding in
Their heavy burdens at the narrow gate,
The sad-eyed justice, with his surly
hum,
Delivering o'er to executors pale
The lazy yawning drone. *Ibid, 187.*

44   As 'tis ever common
That men are merriest when they are
from home. *Ibid, 271.*

45 Now all the youth of England are on
fire,
And silken dalliance in the wardrobe
lies. *Ibid, II. prologue, 1.*

46 I dare not fight; but I will wink and hold
out mine iron. *Ibid, i. 7.*

47 Though patience be a tired mare, yet she
will plod. *Ibid, 26.*

48 Base is the slave that pays. *Ibid, 100.*

1 He's in Arthur's bosom, if ever man
went to Arthur's bosom. A' made a
finer end and went away an it had been
any christom child; a' parted even just
between twelve and one, even at the
turning o' the tide; for after I saw him
fumble with the sheets and play with
flowers and smile upon his fingers' ends,
I knew there was but one way; for his
nose was as sharp as a pen, and a'
babbled of green fields.   *Ibid, iii. 9.*

2 Now I, to comfort him, bid him a'
should not think of God; I hoped there
was no need to trouble himself with
any such thoughts yet.   *Ibid, 21.*

3 Trust none.
For oaths are straws, men's faiths are
wafer-cakes,
And hold-fast is the only dog, my duck.
Ibid, 52.

4 Self-love, my liege, is not so vile a sin
As self-neglecting.   *Ibid, iv. 74.*

5 Once more unto the breach, dear
friends, once more;
Or close the wall up with our English
dead.
In peace there's nothing so becomes a
man
As modest stillness and humility:
But when the blast of war blows in our
ears,
Then imitate the action of the tiger;
Stiffen the sinews, summon up the
blood,
Disguise fair nature with hard-favour'd
rage.   *Ibid, III. i. 1.*

6   On, on, you noblest English,
Whose blood is fet from fathers of war-
proof!
Fathers that, like so many Alexanders,
Have in these parts from morn till even
fought
And sheathed their swords for lack of
argument.   *Ibid, 17.*

7 I see you stand like greyhounds in the
slips,
Straining upon the start.   *Ibid, 31.*

8 Men of few words are the best men.
Ibid, ii. 38.

9 I thought upon one pair of English legs
Did march three Frenchmen.
Ibid, vi. 158.

10 From camp to camp through the foul
womb of night
The hum of either army stilly sounds,
That the fix'd sentinels almost receive
The secret whispers of each other's
watch:
Fire answers fire, and through their paly
flames
Each battle sees the other's umber'd
face;
Steed threatens steed, in high and
boastful neighs
Piercing the night's dull ear; and from
the tents
The armourers, accomplishing the
knights,
With busy hammers closing rivets up,
Give dreadful note of preparation.
Ibid, IV. prologue, 1.

11 There is some soul of goodness in things
evil,
Would men observingly distil it out.
Ibid, i. 4.

12 Every subject's duty is the king's; but
every subject's soul is his own.
Ibid, 185.

13 Who with a body fill'd and vacant mind,
Gets him to rest, cramm'd with
distressful bread.   *Ibid, 286.*

14   O that we now had here
But one ten thousand of those men in
England
That do no work to-day!   *Ibid, iii. 16.*

15 If we are mark'd to die, we are enow
To do our country loss; and if to live,
The fewer men, the greater share of
honour.   *Ibid, 20.*

16 But if it be a sin to covet honour,
I am the most offending soul alive.
Ibid, 28.

17 This day is call'd the feast of Crispian.
He that outlives this day, and comes safe
home,

Will stand a tip-toe when this day is
named,
And rouse him at the name of Crispian.
Ibid, 40.

18   Then shall our names,
Familiar in his mouth as household
words,
Harry the king, Bedford and Exeter,
Warwick and Talbot, Salisbury and
Gloucester,
Be in their flowing cups freshly
remember'd.   *Ibid, 51.*

19 We few, we happy few, we band of
brothers.   *Ibid, 60.*

20 And gentlemen in England now a-bed
Shall think themselves accursed they
were not here,
And hold their manhoods cheap whiles
any speaks
That fought with us upon Saint
Crispin's day.   *Ibid, 64.*

21 There is occasions and causes why and
wherefore in all things.
     Ibid, V. i. 3.

22 All hell shall stir for this.   *Ibid, 72.*

23 For these fellows of infinite tongue, that
can rhyme themselves into ladies'
favours, they do always reason
themselves out again.   *Ibid, ii. 162.*

24 If he be not fellow with the best king,
thou shalt find the best king of good
fellows.   *Ibid, 260.*

KING HENRY VI, PART I

25 Hung be the heavens with black, yield
day to night!
     King Henry VI, part I, 1. i. 1.

26   Unbidden guests
Are often welcomest when they are
gone.   *Ibid, II. ii. 55.*

27 Between two hawks, which flies the
higher pitch;
Between two dogs, which hath the
deeper mouth;

Between two blades, which bears the
better temper;
Between two horses, which doth bear
him best;
Between two girls, which hath the
merriest eye;
I have perhaps some shallow spirit of
judgment;
But in these nice sharp quillets of the
law,
Good faith, I am no wiser than a daw.
     Ibid, iv. II.

28 She's beautiful and therefore to be
woo'd;
She is a woman, therefore to be won.
     Ibid, v. iii. 78.

KING HENRY VI, PART II

29 Could I come near your beauty with my
nails,
I'd set my ten commandments in your
face.
     King Henry VI, part II. 1. iii. 144.

30 Smooth runs the water where the brook
is deep.   *Ibid, III. i. 53.*

31 What stronger breastplate than a heart
untainted?
Thrice is he arm'd that hath his quarrel
just,
And he but naked, though lock'd up in
steel,
Whose conscience with injustice is
corrupted.   *Ibid, ii. 232.*

32 The gaudy, blabbing and remorseful
day
Is crept into the bosom of the sea.
     Ibid, IV. i. 1.

33 There shall be in England seven
halfpenny loaves sold for a penny: the
three-hooped pot shall have ten hoops;
and I will make it a felony to drink small
beer.   *Ibid, ii. 71.*

34 Is not this a lamentable thing, that the
skin of an innocent lamb should be
made parchment? that parchment,
being scribbled o'er, should undo a
man?   *Ibid, 84.*

1 Sir, he made a chimney in my father's house, and the bricks are alive at this day to testify it. *Ibid, 156.*

2 Thou hast most traitorously corrupted the youth of the realm in erecting a grammar school; and whereas, before, our forefathers had no other books but the score and tally, thou hast caused printing to be used, and, contrary to the king, his crown and dignity, thou hast built a paper-mill. *Ibid, vii. 35.*

3 Away with him, away with him! he speaks Latin. *Ibid, 62.*

KING HENRY VI, PART III

4 O tiger's heart wrapt in a woman's hide! *King Henry VI, part III. 1. iv. 137.*

5   Didst thou never hear That things ill got had ever bad success? And happy always was it for that son Whose father for his hoarding went to hell? *Ibid, II. ii. 45.*

6 O God! methinks it were a happy life, To be no better than a homely swain; To sit upon a hill, as I do now, To carve out dials quaintly, point by point, Thereby to see the minutes how they run, How many make the hour full complete; How many hours bring about the day; How many days will finish up the year; How many years a mortal man may live. *Ibid, v. 21.*

7 Gives not the hawthorn-bush a sweeter shade To shepherds looking on their silly sheep, Than doth a rich embroider'd canopy To kings that fear their subjects' treachery? *Ibid, 42.*

8 My crown is in my heart, not on my head; Not deck'd with diamonds and Indian stones, Nor to be seen: my crown is called content. *Ibid, III. i. 62.*

9 A little fire is quickly trodden out; Which, being suffer'd, rivers cannot quench. *Ibid, IV. viii. 7.*

10 Suspicion always haunts the guilty mind; The thief doth fear each bush an officer. *Ibid, V. vi. 11.*

11 Down, down to hell; and say I sent thee thither. *Ibid, 67.*

KING HENRY VIII

12   'Tis better to be lowly born, And range with humble livers in content, Than to be perk'd up in a glistering grief, And wear a golden sorrow. *King Henry VIII. II. iii. 19.* (A commonly accepted theory of the play's authorship gives this passage to Shakespeare and all those below to Fletcher.)

13 Orpheus with his lute made trees, And the mountain tops that freeze, Bow themselves when he did sing. *Ibid, III. i. 3.*

14 Heaven is above all yet; there sits a judge That no king can corrupt. *Ibid, 100.*

15 Farewell! a long farewell to all my greatness! This is the state of man: to-day he puts forth The tender leaves of hopes; to-morrow blossoms, And bears his blushing honours thick upon him; The third day comes a frost, a killing frost, And, when he thinks, good easy man, full surely His greatness is a-ripening, nips his root, And then he falls, as I do. *Ibid, ii. 351.*

16 Vain pomp and glory of this world, I hate ye: I fell my heart new open'd. O, how wretched

Is that poor man that hangs on princes'
favours!
There is, betwixt that smile we would
aspire to,
That sweet aspect of princes, and their
ruin,
More pangs and fears than wars of
women have:
And when he falls, he falls like Lucifer,
Never to hope again.   *Ibid, 365.*

17 A peace above all earthly dignities,
A still and quite conscience.   *Ibid, 379.*

18 Cromwell, I charge thee, fling away
ambition:
By that sin fell the angels.   *Ibid, 440.*

19 Love thyself last: cherish those hearts
that hate thee;
Corruption wins not more than
honesty.
Still in thy right hand carry gentle peace,
To silence envious tongues. Be just, and
fear not:
Let all the ends thou aim'st at be thy
country's,
Thy God's, and truth's.   *Ibid, 443.*

20 Had I but served my God with half the
zeal
I served my king, he would not in mine
age
Have left me naked to mine enemies.
                                Ibid, 455.

21 He gave his honours to the world again,
His blessed part to heaven, and slept in
peace.   *Ibid, IV. ii. 29.*

22 So may he rest; his faults lie gently on
him.   *Ibid, 31.*

23   He was a man
Of an unbounded stomach.   *Ibid, 33.*

24 Men's evil manners live in brass; their
virtues
We write in water.   *Ibid, 45.*

25 He was a scholar, and a ripe and good
one;
Exceeding wise, fair-spoken, and
persuading:
Lofty and sour to them that loved him
not;

But to those men that sought him sweet
as summer.   *Ibid, 51.*

26 Those twins of learning that he raised in
you,
Ipswich and Oxford.   *Ibid, 58.*

KING JOHN

27 Lord of thy presence and no land beside.
                        King John, I. i. 137.

28 For new-made honour doth forget
men's names.   *Ibid, 187.*

29 For courage mounteth with occasion.
                             Ibid, II. i. 82.

30 Saint George, that swinged the dragon,
and e'er since
Sits on his horse back at mine hostess'
door.   *Ibid, 288.*

31 Zounds! I was never so bethumped with
words
Since first I call'd my brother's father
dad.   *Ibid, 466.*

32   Here I and sorrows sit;
Here is my throne, bid kings come bow
to it.   *Ibid, III. i. 73.*

33 Thou wear a lion's hide! doff it for
shame,
And hang a calf's-skin on those recreant
limbs.   *Ibid, 128.*

34 Grief fills the room up of my absent
child,
Lies in his bed, walks up and down with
me,
Puts on his pretty looks, repeats his
words,
Remembers me of all his gracious parts,
Stuffs out his vacant garments with his
form.   *Ibid, iv. 93.*

35 Life is as tedious as a twice-told tale,
Vexing the dull ear of a drowsy man.
                              Ibid, 108.

36   When Fortune means to men most
good,
She looks upon them with a threatening
eye.   *Ibid, 119.*

1 Heat me these irons hot.   *Ibid, IV. i. 1.*

2 To gild refined gold, to paint the lily,
To throw a perfume on the violet,
To smooth the ice, or add another hue
Unto the rainbow, or with taper-light
To seek the beauteous eye of heaven to
garnish,
Is wasteful and ridculous excess.
Ibid, ii. 11.

3 And oftentimes excusing of a fault
Doth make the fault the worse by the
excuse.   *Ibid, 30.*

4 Another lean unwashed artificer.
Ibid, 201.

5 How oft the sight of means to do ill
deeds
Makes deeds ill done!   *Ibid, 219.*

6 This England never did, nor never shall,
Lie at the proud foot of a conqueror,
But when it first did help to wound
itself.   *Ibid, V. vii. 112.*

7 Come the three corners of the world in
arms,
And we shall shock them. Nought shall
make us rue,
If England to itself do rest but true.
Ibid, 116.

KING LEAR

8 *Lear.* So young, and so untender?
Cordelia. So young, my lord, and true.
King Lear, I. i. 108.

9 A still-soliciting eye.   *Ibid, 234.*

10 These late eclipses in the sun and moon
portend no good to us.   *Ibid, ii. 112.*

11 This is the excellent foppery of the
world, that, when we are sick in
fortune, – often the surfeit of our own
behaviour, – we make guilty of our
disasters the sun, the moon, and the
stars: as if we were villains by
necessity; fools by heavenly
compulsion; knaves, thieves, and
treachers, by spherical predominance;

drunkards, liars, and adulterers, by an
enforced obedience of planetary
influence; and all that we are evil in, by
a divine thrusting on.   *Ibid, 129.*

12 My cue is villainous melancholy, with a
sigh like Tom o' Bedlam.   *Ibid, 147.*

13 Ingratitude, thou marble-hearted fiend,
More hideous when thou show'st thee
in a child
Than the sea-monster!   *Ibid, iv. 281.*

14 How sharper than a serpent's tooth it is
To have a thankless child.   *Ibid, 310.*

15 Striving to better, oft we mar what's
well.   *Ibid, 369.*

16 Thou whoreson zed! thou unnecessary
letter!   *Ibid, II. ii. 69.*

17 I have seen better faces in my time
Than stands on any shoulder that I see
Before me at this instant.   *Ibid, 99.*

18 Fortune, good night: smile once more;
turn thy wheel!   *Ibid, 180.*

19 Hysterica passio, down, thou climbing
sorrow,
Thy element's below.   *Ibid, iv. 57.*

20 That sir which serves and seeks for gain,
And follows but for form,
Will pack when it begins to rain,
And leave thee in the storm.
Ibid, 79.

21   You are old;
Nature in you stands on the very verge
Of her confine.   *Ibid, 148.*

22 And let not women's weapons, water-
drops,
Stain my man's cheeks!   *Ibid, 280.*

23 Blow, winds, and crack your cheeks!
rage! blow!
You cataracts and hurricanoes, spout
Till you have drench'd our steeples,
drown'd the cocks!
You sulphurous and thought-executing
fires,
Vaunt-couriers to oak-cleaving
thunderbolts,

Singe my white head! And thou, all-
shaking thunder,
Smite flat the thick rotundity o' the
world!
Crack nature's moulds, all germens spill
at once,
That make ungrateful man!
Ibid, III. ii. 1.

24 I tax you not, you elements, with
unkindness. *Ibid, 16.*

25 A poor, infirm, weak, and despised old
man. *Ibid, 20.*

26 There was never yet fair woman but she
made mouths in a glass. *Ibid, 35.*

27 Things that love night
Love not such nights as these; the
wrathful skies
Gallow the very wanderers of the dark.
Ibid, 42.

28 I am a man
More sinn'd against than sinning.
Ibid, 59.

29 O, that way madness lies; let me shun
that. *Ibid, iv. 21.*

30 Poor naked wretches, whersoe'er you
are,
That bide the pelting of this pitiless
storm,
How shall your houseless heads and
unfed sides,
Your loop'd and window'd raggedness,
defend you
From seasons such as these? *Ibid, 28.*

31 Take physic, pomp;
Expose thyself to feel what wretches
feel. *Ibid, 33.*

32 Out-paramoured the Turk. *Ibid, 94.*

33 'Tis a naughty night to swim in.
Ibid, 115.

34 The green mantle of the standing pool.
Ibid, 139.

35 But mice and rats and such small deer,
Have been Tom's food for seven long
year. *Ibid, 144.*

36 The prince of darkness is a gentleman.
Ibid, 148.

37 Poor Tom's a-cold. *Ibid, 152.*

38 I'll talk a word with this same learned
Theban. *Ibid, 162.*

39 Child Rowland to the dark tower came,
His word was still, – Fie, foh, and fum.
I smell the blood of a British man.
Ibid, 187.

40 The little dogs and all,
Tray, Blanch, and Seeet-heart, see, they
bark at me. *Ibid, vi. 65.*

41 Mastiff, greyhound, mongrel grim,
Hound or spaniel, brach or lym,
Or bobtail tike or trundle-tail. *Ibid, 71.*

42 The worst is not
So long as we can say 'This is the worst.'
Ibid, IV. i. 29.

43 As flies to wanton boys, are we to gods,
They kill us for their sport. *Ibid, 38.*

44 You are not worth the dust which the
rude wind
Blows in your face. *Ibid, ii. 30.*

45 Wisdom and goodness to the vile seem
vile:
Filths savour but themselves. *Ibid, 38*

46 Patience and sorrow strove
Who should express her goodliest.
Ibid, iii. 18.

47 It is the stars,
The stars above us, govern our
conditions. *Ibid, 34.*

48 How fearful
And dizzy 'tis to cast one's eyes so low!
The crows and choughs that wing the
midway air
Show scarce so gross as beetles: half way
down
Hangs one that gathers samphire,
dreadful trade!
The fishermen, that walk upon the
beach,
Appear like mice; and yond tall
anchoring bark,

Diminish'd to her cock; her cock, a
buoy
Almost too small for sight: the
murmuring surge
That on the unnumber'd idle pebbles
chafes,
Cannot be heard so high.   *Ibid, vi. 11.*

1 Ay, every inch a king.   *Ibid, 109.*

2 The wren goes to 't, and the small gilded
fly
Does lecher in my sight.   *Ibid, 114.*

3 Give me an ounce of civet, good
apothecary, to sweeten my imagination.
  Ibid, 132.

4 See how yond justice rails upon yond
simple thief. Hark, in thine ear: change
places; and handy-dandy, which is the
justice, which is the thief?
  Ibid, 155.

5 Through tatter'd clothes small vices do
appear;
Robes and furr'd gowns hide all.
  Ibid, 168.

6   Mine enemy's dog,
Though he had bit me, should have
stood that night
Against my fire.   *Ibid, vii. 36.*

7 I am a very foolish fond old man,
Fourscore and upward, not an hour
more or less;
And, to deal plainly,
I fear I am not in my perfect mind.
  Ibid, 60.

8   Men must endure
Their going hence, even as their coming
hither:
Ripeness is all.   *Ibid, V. ii. 9.*

9   Come, let's away to prison:
We two alone will sing like birds i' the
cage:
When thou dost ask me blessing, I'll
kneel down,
And ask of thee forgiveness: so we'll
live,
And pray, and sing, and tell old tales,
and laugh

At gilded butterflies, and hear poor
rogues
Talk of court news; and we'll talk with
them too,
Who loses and who wins; who's in,
who's out;
And take upon's the mystery of things,
As if we were God's spies.
  Ibid, iii. 8.

10 Upon such sacrifices, my Cordelia,
The gods themselves throw incense.
  Ibid, 20.

11 The gods are just, and of our pleasant
vices
Make instruments to plague us.
  Ibid, 170.

12 The wheel is come full circle.   *Ibid, 174.*

13   Her voice was ever soft,
Gentle and low, an excellent thing in
woman.   *Ibid, 272.*

14 I have seen the day, with my good
biting falchion
I would have made them skip.
  Ibid, 276.

15 And my poor fool is hang'd! No, no, no
life!
Why should a dog, a horse, a rat, have
life,
And thou no breath at all? Thou'lt come
no more.
Never, never, never, never, never!
  Ibid, 305.

16 Vex not his ghost: O, let him pass! he
hates him much
That would upon the rack of this tough
world
Stretch him out longer.   *Ibid, 313.*

KING RICHARD II

17 Old John of Gaunt, time-honour'd
Lancaster.   *King Richard II, I. i. 1.*

18 A jewel in a ten-times-barr'd-up chest
Is a bold spirit in a loyal breast.
Mine honour is my life; both grow in
one;

Take honour from me, and my life is
done. *Ibid, 180.*

19 We were not born to sue, but to
command. *Ibid, 196.*

20 That which in mean men we intitle
patience
Is pale cold cowardice in noble breasts.
Ibid, ii. 33.

21 The daintiest last, to make the end most
sweet. *Ibid, iii. 68.*

22 Truth hath a quiet breast. *Ibid, 96.*

23   This must my comfort be,
The sun that warms you here shall shine
on me. *Ibid, 144.*

24 How long a time lies in one little word!
Ibid, 213.

25 Things sweet to taste prove in digestion
sour. *Ibid, 236.*

26 All places that the eye of heaven visits
Are to the wise man ports and happy
havens. *Ibid, 275.*

27 O, who can hold a fire in his hand
By thinking on the frosty Caucasus?
Or cloy the hungry edge of appetite
By bare imagination of a feast?
Or wallow naked in December snow
By thinking on fantastic summer's heat?
O, no! the apprehension of the good
Gives but a greater feeling to the worse.
Ibid, 294.

28 Methinks I am a prophet new inspired
And thus expiring do foretell of him:
His rash fierce blaze of riot cannot last,
For violent fires soon burn out
themselves;
Small showers last long, but sudden
storms are short;
He tires betimes that spurs too fast
betimes. *Ibid, II. i. 31.*

29 This royal throne of kings, this scepter'd
isle,
This earth of majesty, this seat of Mars,
This other Eden, demi-paradise,
This fortress built by Nature for herself

Against infection and the hand of war,
This happy breed of men, this little
world,
This precious stone set in the silver sea,
Which serves it in the office of a wall
Or as a moat defensive to a house,
Against the envy of less happier lands,
This blessed plot, this earth, this realm,
this England. *Ibid, 40.*

30 England, bound in with the triumphant
sea,
Whose rocky shore beats back the
envious siege
Of watery Neptune, is now bound in
with shame,
With inky blots and rotten parchment
bonds:
That England, that was wont to conquer
others,
Hath made a shameful conquest of itself.
Ibid, 61.

31 Can sick men play so nicely with their
names? *Ibid, 84.*

32 I am a stranger here in Gloucestershire:
These high wild hills and rough uneven
ways
Draws out our miles and makes them
wearisome. *Ibid, iii. 3.*

33 I count myself in nothing else so happy
As in a soul remembering my good
friends. *Ibid, 46.*

34 Evermore thanks, the exchequer of the
poor. *Ibid, 65.*

35 Things past redress are now with me
past care. *Ibid, 171.*

36 Eating the bitter bread of banishment.
Ibid, III. i. 21.

37 Not all the water in the rude rough sea
Can wash the balm from an anointed
king. *Ibid, ii. 54.*

38 O, call back yesterday, bid time return.
Ibid, 69.

39   Of comfort no man speak:
Let's talk of graves, of worms and
epitaphs;

243

Make dust our paper and with rainy eyes
Write sorrow on the bosom of the earth,
Let's choose executors and talk of wills.
Ibid, 144.

1 For God's sake let us sit upon the
ground
And tell sad stories of the death of kings:
How some have been deposed; some
slain in war;
Some haunted by the ghosts they have
deposed;
Some poison'd by their wives; some
sleeping kill'd;
All murder'd: for within the hollow
crown
That rounds the mortal temples of a
king
Keeps Death his court and there the
antic sits,
Scoffing his state and grinning at his
pomp,
Allowing him a breath, a little scene,
To monarchize, be fear'd and kill with
looks,
Infusing him with self and vain conceit,
As if this flesh which walls about our life
Were brass impregnable, and humour'd
thus
Comes at the last and with a little pin
Bores through his castle wall, and
farewell king! *Ibid, 155.*

2 What must the king do now? must he
submit?
The king shall do it: must he be
deposed?
The king shall be contented: must he
lose
The name of king? o' God's name, let it
go:
I'll give my jewels for a set of beads,
My gorgeous palace for a hermitage,
My gay apparel for an almsman's gown,
My figured goblets for a dish of wood,
My sceptre for a palmer's walking-staff,
My subjects for a pair of carved saints
And my large kingdom for a little grave,
A little little grave, an obscure grave.
Ibid, iii. 143.

3 If I dare eat, or drink, or breathe, or live,
I dare meet Surrey in a wilderness,
And spit upon him, whilst I say he lies,
And lies, and lies. *Ibid, IV. i. 73.*

4 And there at Venice gave
His body to that pleasant country's earth
And his pure soul unto his captain
Christ,
Under whose colours he had fought so
long. *Ibid, 97.*

5 Peace shall go sleep with Turks and
infidels. *Ibid, 139.*

6 You may my glories and my state
depose,
But not my griefs; still am I king of
those. *Ibid, 192.*

7 I am sworn brother, sweet,
To grim Necessity, and he and I
Will keep a league till death. *Ibid, Vi. i.*
20.

8 As in a theatre the eyes of men,
After a well-graced actor leaves the
stage,
Are idly bent on him that enters next,
Thinking his prattle to be tedious. *Ibid,*
ii. 23.

9 How sour sweet music is,
When time is broke and no proportion
kept!
So is it with the music of men's lives.
Ibid, V. 42.

KING RICHARD III.

10 Now is the winter of our discontent
Made glorious summer by the sun of
York. *King Richard III, I. i. 1.*

11 Our stern alarums changed to merry
meetings,
Our dreadful marches to delightful
measures.
Grim-visaged war hath smooth'd his
wrinkled front. *Ibid, 7.*

12 I, that am curtail'd of this fair
proportion,
Cheated of feature by dissembling
nature,
Deform'd, unfinish'd, sent before my
time
Into this breathing world, scarce half
made up,

And that so lamely and unfashionable
That dogs bark at me as I halt by them.
Ibid, 18.

13 In this weak piping time of peace.
Ibid, 24

14 I am determined to prove a villain.
Ibid, 30.

15 Was ever woman in this humour woo'd?
Was ever woman in this humour won?
Ibid, ii. 228.

16 And thus I clothe my naked villainy
With old odd ends stolen out of holy
writ;
And seem a saint, when most I play the
devil. *Ibid, iii. 336.*

17 O, I have pass'd a miserable night,
So full of ugly sights, of ghastly dreams,
That, as I am a Christian faithful man,
I would not spend another such a night,
Though 'twere to buy a world of happy
days,
So full of dismal terror was the time!
Ibid, iv. 2.

18 Lord, Lord! methought, what pain it
was to drown!
What dreadful noise of waters in mine
ears!
What ugly sights of death within mine
eyes!
Methought I saw a thousand fearful
wrecks;
Ten thousand men that fishes gnaw'd
upon;
Wedges of gold, great anchors, heaps of
pearl,
Inestimable stones, unvalued jewels,
All scatter'd in the bottom of the sea:
Some lay in dead men's skulls; and, in
those holes
Where eyes did once inhabit, there were
crept,
As 'twere in scorn of eyes, reflecting
gems,
Which woo'd the slimy bottom of the
deep,
And mock'd the dead bones that lay
scatter'd by. *Ibid, 21.*

19 So wise so young, they say, do never
live long. *Ibid, III. i. 79.*

20 High-reaching Buckingham grows
circumspect. *Ibid, IV. ii. 31.*

21 Their lips were four red roses on a stalk,
Which in their summer beauty kiss'd
each other. *Ibid, iii. 12.*

22 The sons of Edward sleep in Abraham's
bosom. *Ibid, 38.*

23 An honest tale speeds best being plainly
told. *Ibid, iv. 358.*

24 Harp not on that string. *Ibid, 364.*

25 True hope is swift, and flies with
swallow's wings;
Kings it makes gods, and meaner
creatures kings. *Ibid, V. ii. 23.*

26 The king's name is a tower of strength.
Ibid, iii. 12.

27 O coward conscience, how dost thou
afflict me! *Ibid, 179.*

28 My conscience hath a thousand several
tongues,
And every tongue brings in a several
tale,
And every tale condemns me for a
villain. *Ibid, 193.*

29 A horse! a horse! my kingdom for a
horse! *Ibid, iv. 7 and 13.*

30 Slave, I have set my life upon a cast,
And I will stand the hazard of the die:
I think there be six Richmonds in the
field. *Ibid, 9.*

LOVE'S LABOUR'S LOST

31 Spite of cormorant devouring Time.
Love's Labour's Lost, I. i. 4.

32 Why, all delights are vain; but that most
vain,
Which with pain purchased doth inherit
pain. *Ibid, 72.*

33 Light seeking light doth light of light
beguile. *Ibid, 77.*

1   Study is like the heaven's glorious sun
    That will not be deep-search'd with
    saucy looks:
    Small have continual plodders ever won
    Save base authority from others' books.
    Ibid, 84.

2   At Christmas I no more desire a rose
    Than wish a snow in May's new-fangled
    mirth.   *Ibid, 105.*

3   Devise, wit; write, pen; for I am for
    whole volumes in folio.   *Ibid, ii. 192.*

4   Remuneration! O, that's the Latin word
    for three farthings.   *Ibid, III. i. 140.*

5   A very beadle to a humorous sigh.
    Ibid, 177.

6   This wimpled, whining, purblind,
    wayward boy;
    This senior-junior, giant-dwarf, Dan
    Cupid;
    Regent of love-rhymes, lord of folded
    arms,
    The anointed sovereign of sighs and
    groans
    Liege of all loiterers and malcontents.
    Ibid, 181.

7   He hath never fed of the dainties that are
    bred in a book; he hath not eat paper, as
    it were; he hath not drunk ink.
    Ibid, IV ii. 25.

8   A lover's eyes will gaze an eagle blind;
    A lover's ear will hear the lowest sound,
    When the suspicious head of theft is
    stopp'd:
    Love's feeling is more soft and sensible
    Than are the tender horns of cockled
    snails;
    Love's tongue proves dainty Bacchus
    gross in taste:
    For valour, is not Love a Hercules,
    Still climbing trees in the Hesperides?
    Subtle as Sphinx; as sweet and musical
    As bright Apollo's lute, strung with his
    hair;
    And when Love speaks, the voice of all
    the gods
    Make heaven drowsy with the
    harmony.   *Ibid, iii. 334.*

9   From women's eyes this doctrine I
    derive:
    They sparkle still the right Promethean
    fire;
    They are the books, the arts, the
    academes,
    That show, contain, and nourish all the
    world.   *Ibid, 350.*

10 He draweth out the thread of his
    verbosity finer than the staple of his
    argument.   *Ibid, V. i. 18.*

11 Priscian a little scratched, 'twill serve.
    Ibid, 31.

12 They have been at a great feast of
    languages, and stolen the scraps.
    Ibid, 39.

13 In the posteriors of this day, which the
    rude multitude call the afternoon.
    Ibid, 94.

14 In russet yeas and honest kersey noes.
    Ibid, ii. 413.

15 A jest's prosperity lies in the ear
    Of him that hears it, never in the tongue
    Of him that makes it.   *Ibid, 871.*

16 When daisies pied and violets blue
    And lady-smocks all silver-white
    And cuckoo-buds of yellow hue
    Do paint the meadows with delight,
    The cuckoo then, on every tree,
    Mocks married men; for thus sings he,
    Cuckoo;
    Cuckoo, cuckoo: O word of fear,
    Unpleasing to a married ear. *Ibid, 904.*

17 The words of Mercury are harsh after
    the songs of Apollo.   *Ibid, 940.*

MACBETH

18 *First Witch.* When shall we three meet
    again
    In thunder, lightning, or in rain?
    Second Witch. When the hurly-burly's
    done,
    When the battle's lost and won.
    Macbeth, I. i. 1

19 Fair is foul, and foul is fair.   *Ibid, 11.*

20 What bloody man is that?   *Ibid, ii. 1.*

21 Sleep shall neither night nor day
Hang upon his pent-house lid;
He shall live a man forbid:
Weary se'nnights nine times nine
Shall he dwindle, peak and pine.
                        Ibid, iii. 19.

22 The weird sisters.   *Ibid, 32.*

23   What are these
So wither'd and so wild in their attire,
That look not like the inhabitants o' the
earth,
And yet are on't?   *Ibid, 39.*

24 If you can look into the seeds of time,
And say which grain will grow and
which will not.   *Ibid, 58.*

25 Stands not within the prospect of belief.
                        Ibid, 7.

26 The earth hath bubbles, as the water has,
And these are of them.   *Ibid, 79.*

27   The insane root
That takes the reason prisoner.   *Ibid, 84.*

28 And oftentimes, to win us to our harm,
The instruments of darkness tell us
truths,
Win us with honest trifles, to betray's
In deepest consequence.   *Ibid, 123.*

29   Why do I yield to that suggestion
Whose horrid image doth unfix my hair
And makes my seated heart knock at my
ribs
Against the use of nature? Present fears
Are less than horrible imaginings.
                        Ibid, 134.

30   Come what come may,
Time and the hour runs through the
roughest day.   *Ibid, 146.*

31   Nothing in his life
Became him like the leaving it; he died
As one that had been studied in his death
To throw away the dearest thing he
owed,
As 'twere a careless trifle.   *Ibid, iv. 7.*

32   There's no art
To find the mind's construction in the
face;
He was a gentleman on whom I built
An absolute trust.   *Ibid, 11.*

33   Yet I do fear thy nature;
It is too full o' the milk of human
kindness.   *Ibid, v. 17.*

34   What thou wouldst highly,
That wouldst thou holily; wouldst not
play false,
And yet wouldst wrongly win.
                        Ibid, 21.

35 That no compunctions visitings of
nature
Shake my fell purpose.   *Ibid, 46.*

36 Your face, my thane, is as a book where
men
May read strange matters.   *Ibid, 63.*

37   Look like the innocent flower,
But be the serpent under't.   *Ibid, 66.*

38 This castle hath a pleasant seat; the air
Nimbly and sweetly recommends itself
Unto our gentle senses.   *Ibid, vi. 1.*

39 Coign of vantage.   *Ibid, 7.*

40 If it were done when 'tis done, then
'twere well
It were done quickly: if the assassination
Could trammel up the consequence, and
catch
With his surcease success; that but this
blow
Might be the be-all and the end-all here,
But here, upon this bank and shoal of
time,
We'ld jump the life to come.
                        Ibid, vii. 1.

41   We but teach
Bloody instructions, which, being
taught, return
To plague the inventor: this even-
handed justice
Commends the ingredients of our
poison'd chalice
To our own lips.   *Ibid, 8.*

1   Besides, this Duncan
Hath borne his faculties so meek, hath
   been
So dear in his great office, that his
   virtues
Will pleade like angels, trumpet-
   tongued, against
The deep damnation of his taking-off;
And pity, like a naked new-born babe,
Striding the blast, or heaven's cherubim,
   horsed
Upon the sighless couriers of the air,
Shall blow the horrid deed in every eye.
                  Ibid, 16.

2   I have no spur
To prick the sides of my intent, but only
Vaulting ambition, which o'erleaps
   itself
And falls on the other.   *Ibid, 25.*

3   I have bought
Golden opinions from all sorts of
   people.   *Ibid, 32.*

4 Letting I 'dare not' wait upon 'I would,'
Like the poor cat i' the adage.   *Ibid, 44.*

5 I dare do all that may become a man;
Who dares do more is none.   *Ibid, 46.*

6   I have given suck, and know
How tender 'tis to love the babe that
   milks me:
I would, while it was smiling in my
   face,
Have pluck'd my nipple from his
   boneless gums,
And dash'd the brains out, had I so
   sworn as you
Have done to this.   *Ibid, 54.*

7 *Macbeth.*   If we should fail?
Lady Macbeth.   We fail!
But screw your courage to the sticking-
   place,
And we'll not fail.   *Ibid, 59.*

8 Memory, the warder of the brain.
                   Ibid, 65.

9 Away, and mock the time with fairest
   show:
False face must hide what the false heart
   doth know.   *Ibid, 81.*

10   There's husbandry in heaven;
Their candles are all out.   *Ibid, II. i. 4.*

11   Merciful powers,
Restrain in me the cursed thoughts that
   nature
Gives way to in repose.   *Ibid, 7.*

12   Shut up
In measureless content.   *Ibid, 15.*

13 Is this a dagger which I see before me,
The handle toward my hand? Come, let
   me clutch thee.
I have thee not, and yet I see thee still.
Art thou not, fatal vision, sensible
To feeling as to sight? or art thou but
A dagger of the mind, a false creation,
Proceeding from the heat-oppressed
   brain?   *Ibid, 33.*

14   Thou sure and firm-set earth,
Hear not my steps, which way they
   walk, for fear
The very stones prate of my
   whereabout.   *Ibid, 56.*

15 Hear it not, Duncan; for it is a knell
That summons thee to heaven or to hell.
                 Ibid, 63.

16 It was the owl that shriek'd, the fatal
   bellman
Which gave the stern'st good-night.
               Ibid, ii. 3.

17   The attempt and not the deed
Confounds us.   *Ibid, 11.*

18 Consider it not so deeply.   *Ibid, 30.*

19 I had most need of blessing, and 'Amen'
Stuck in my throat.   *Ibid, 32.*

20   These deeds must not be thought
After these ways; so, it will make us
   mad.   *Ibid, 33.*

21 Methought I heard a voice cry 'Sleep no
   more!
Macbeth does murder sleep', the
   innocent sleep,
Sleep that knits up the ravell'd sleave of
   care,
The death of each day's life, sore
   labour's bath,

Balm of hurt minds, great nature's
second course,
Chief nourisher in life's feast   *Ibid, 35.*

22   Infirm of purpose!
Give me the daggers.   *Ibid, 52.*

23 Will all great Neptune's ocean wash this
blood
Clean from my hand? No, this my hand
will rather
The multitudinous seas incarnadine,
Making the green one red.   *Ibid, 60.*

24 Go the primrose way to the everlasting
bonfire.   *Ibid, iii. 23.*

25 The labour we delight in physics pain.
                              Ibid, 54.

26 Confusion now hath made his
masterpiece!
Most sacrilegious murder hath broke
ope
The Lord's anointed temple, and stole
thence
The life o' the building.   *Ibid, 71.*

27 Shake off this downy sleep, death's
counterfeit,
And look on death itself!   *Ibid, 81.*

28 The wine of life is drawn, and the mere
lees
Is left this vault to brag of.   *Ibid, 100.*

29 Who can be wise, amazed, temperate
and furious,
Loyal and neutral, in a moment?
                              Ibid, 113.

30 A falcon, towering in her pride of place,
Was by a mousing owl hawk'd at and
kill'd.   *Ibid, iv. 12.*

31 I must become a borrower of the night
For a dark hour or twain.
                          Ibid, III. i. 26.

32 *First Murderer.* We are men, my liege.
Macbeth. Ay, in the catalogue ye go for
men;
As hounds and greyhounds, mongrels,
spaniels, curs,

Shoughs, water-rugs and demiwolves
are clept
All by the name of dogs.   *Ibid, 91.*

33   I am one, my liege,
Whom the vile blows and buffets of the
world
Have so incensed that I am reckless what
I do to spite the world.   *Ibid, 108.*

34   Things without all remedy
Should be without regard: what's done
is done.   *Ibid, ii. 11.*

35 We have scotch'd the snake, not kill'd it.
                              Ibid, 13.

36   Duncan is in his grave;
After life's fitful fever he sleeps well
Treason has done his worst: nor steel,
nor poison,
Malice domestic, foreign levy, nothing,
Can touch him further.   *Ibid, 22.*

37 But in them nature's copy's not eterne.
                              Ibid, 38.

38 The shard-borne beetle with his drowsy
hums
Hath rung night's yawning peal.
                              Ibid, 42.

39 A deed of dreadful note.   *Ibid, 44.*

40 Be innocent of the knowledge, dearest
chuck,
Till thou applaud the deed.   *Ibid, 45.*

41   Light thickens; and the crow
Makes wing to the rooky wood:
Good things of day begin to droop and
drowse;
Whiles night's black agents to their
preys do rouse.   *Ibid, 50.*

42 Things bad begun make strong
themselves by ill.   *Ibid, 55.*

43 Now spurs the lated traveller apace
To gain the timely inn.   *Ibid, iii. 6.*

44 But now I am cabin'd, cribb'd,
confined, bound in
To saucy doubts and fears.   *Ibid, iv. 24.*

1 Now, good digestion wait on appetite,
And health on both!   *Ibid, 38.*

2 Thou canst not say I did it: never shake
Thy gory locks at me.   *Ibid, 50.*

3 The air-drawn dagger.   *Ibid, 62.*

4   The time has been,
That, when the brains were out, the
        man would die,
And there an end; but now they rise
        again;
With twenty mortal murders on their
        crowns,
And push us from our stools.   *Ibid, 78.*

5 What man dare, I dare:
Approach thou like the rugged Russian
        bear,
The arm'd rhinocerus, or the Hyrcan
        tiger;
Take any shape but that, and my firm
        nerves
Shall never tremble.   *Ibid, 99.*

6   Hence, horrible shadow!
Unreal mockery, hence!   *Ibid, 106.*

7 You have displaced the mirth, broke the
        good meeting,
With most admired disorder
                        Ibid, 109.

8 Stand not upon the order of your going,
But go at once.   *Ibid, 119.*

9 *Macbeth.*   What is the night?
Lady Macbeth. Almost at odds with
        morning, which is which.   *Ibid, 126.*

10   I am in blood
Stepp'd in so far that, should I wade no
        more,
Returning were as tedious as go o'er.
                        Ibid, 136.

11 Double, double, toil and trouble;
Fire burn and cauldron bubble.
                        Ibid, IV. i. 10.

12 By the pricking of my thumbs,
Something wicked this way comes.
Open, locks,
Whoever knocks!   *Ibid, 44.*

13 How now, you secret, black, and
        midnight hags!   *Ibid, 48.*

14 A deed without a name.   *Ibid, 49.*

15 But yet I'll make assurance double sure,
And take a bond of fate.   *Ibid, 83.*

16 Macbeth shall never vanquished be until
Great Birnam wood to high Dunsinane
        hill
Shall come against him.   *Ibid, 92.*

17 What, will the line stretch out to the
        crack of doom?   *Ibid, 117.*

18   When our actions do not,
Our fears do make us traitors.
                        Ibid, ii. 3.

19 Angels are bright still, though the
        brightest fell.   *Ibid, iii. 22.*

20 Pour the sweet milk of concord into
        hell,
Uproar the universal peace, confound
All unity on earth.   *Ibid, 98.*

21 Stands Scotland where it did?
                        Ibid, 164.

22 Give sorrow words: the grief that does
        not speak
Whispers the o'erfrought heart and bids
        it break.   *Ibid, 209.*

23 What, all my pretty chickens and their
        dam
At one fell swoop?   *Ibid, 218.*

24 *Malcolm.* Dispute it like a man.
        Macduff. I shall do so;
But I must also feel it as a man:
I cannot but remember such things
        were,
That were most precious to me.
                        Ibid, 220.

25 O, I could play the woman with mine
        eyes
And braggart with my tongue!
                        Ibid, 230.

26 Out, damned spot! out, I say!
                        Ibid, V. i. 39.

27 Fie, my lord, fie! a soldier, and afeard?
Ibid, 41.

28 Yet who would have thought the old
man to have had so much blood in him.
Ibid, 44.

29 All the perfumes of Arabia will not
sweeten this little hand.   *Ibid, 57.*

30 The devil damn thee black, thou cream-
faced loon!
Where got'st thou that goose look?
Ibid, iii. 11.

31 I have lived long enough: my way of life
Is fall'n into the sear, the yellow leaf:
And that which should accompany old
age,
As honour, love, obedience, troops of
friends,
I must not look to have; but, in their
stead,
Curses, not loud but deep, mouth-
honour, breath,
Which the poor heart would fain deny,
and dare not.   *Ibid, 22.*

32 Canst thou not minister to a mind
diseased,
Pluck from the memory a rooted
sorrow,
Raze out the written troubles of the
brain
And with some sweet oblivious antidote
Cleanse the stuff'd bosom of that
perilous stuff
Which weighs upon the heart? *Ibid, 40.*

33 Throw physic to the dogs; I'll none of it.
Ibid, 47.

34 I would applaud thee to the very echo,
That should applaud again.   *Ibid, 53.*

35 Hang out our banners on the outward
walls:
The cry is still 'They come.'
Ibid, V. 1.

36 The time has been, my senses would
have cool'd
To hear a night-shriek; and my fell of
hair
Would at a dismal treatise rouse and stir

As life were in't: I have supp'd full with
horrors;
Direness, familiar to my slaughterous
thoughts,
Cannot once start me.   *Ibid, 10.*

37 To-morrow, and to-morrow, and to-
morrow,
Creeps in this petty pace from day to
day
To the last syllable of recorded time,
And all our yesterdays have lighted fools
The way to dusty death. Out, out, brief
candle!
Life's but a walking shadow, a poor
player
That struts and frets his hour upon the
stage
And then is heard no more: it is a tale
Told by an idiot, full of sound and fury,
Signifying nothing.   *Ibid, 19.*

38 I 'gin to be aweary of the sun. *Ibid, 49.*

39   Blow wind! come, wrack!
At least we'll die with harness on our
back.   *Ibid, 51.*

40 They have tied me to a stake; I cannot
fly,
But, bear-like, I must fight the course.
Ibid, vii. 1.

41 I bear a charmed life.   *Ibid, viii. 12.*

42 And be these juggling fiends no more
believed,
That palter with us in a double sense;
That keep the word of promise to our
ear,
And break it to our hope.   *Ibid, 19.*

43 Live to be the show and gaze o' the time.
Ibid, 24.

44   Lay on, Macduff,
And damn'd be him that first cries 'Hold,
enough!'   *Ibid, 33.*

MEASURE FOR MEASURE

45 Heaven doth with us as we with torches
do,
Not light them for themselves; for if our
virtues

Did not go forth of us, 'twere all alike
As if we had them not. Spirits are not
finely touch'd
But to fine issues.
Measure for Measure, I. i. 33.

1 I hold you as a thing ensky'd and
sainted. *Ibid, iv. 34.*

2   A man whose blood
Is very snow-broth; one who never feels
The wanton stings and motions of the
sense. *Ibid, 57.*

3   Our doubts are traitors
And make us lose the good we oft might
win
By fearing to attempt. *Ibid, 77.*

4 The jury, passing on the prisoner's life,
May in the sworn twelve have a thief or
two
Guiltier than him they try.
Ibid, II. i. 19.

5 Some rise by sin, and some by virtue
fall. *Ibid, 38.*

6 This will last out a night in Russia
When nights are longest there.
Ibid, 139.

7 Condemn the fault, and not the actor of
it? *Ibid, ii. 37.*

8 No ceremony that to great ones 'longs,
Not the king's crown, nor the deputed
sword,
The marshal's truncheon, nor the
judge's robe,
Become them with so half as good a
grace
As mercy does. *Ibid, 59.*

9 Why, all the souls that were were forfeit
once;
And He that might the vantage best
have took
Found out the remedy. How would you
be,
If He, which is the top of judgment,
should
But judge you as you are? *Ibid, 73.*

10   O, it is excellent
To have a giant's strength; but it is
tyrannous
To use it like a giant. *Ibid, 107.*

11   But man, proud man,
Drest in a little brief authority,
Most ignorant of what he's most
assured,
His glassy essence, like an angry ape,
Play such fantastic tricks before high
heaven
As make the angels weep. *Ibid, 117.*

12 That in the captain's but a choleric
word,
Which in the soldier is flat blasphemy.
Ibid, 130.

13 The miserable have no other medicine
But only hope. *Ibid, III. i. 2.*

14 Be absolute for death; either death or life
Shall thereby be the sweeter. Reason
thus with life:
If I do lose thee, I do lose a thing
That none but fools would keep: a
breath thou art,
Servile to all the skyey influences.
Ibid, 5.

15 Palsied eld. *Ibid, 36.*

16 The sense of death is most in
apprehension;
And the poor beetle, that we tread upon,
In corporal sufferance finds a pang as
great
As when a giant dies. *Ibid, 78.*

17   If I must die,
I will encounter darkness as a bride,
And hug it in mine arms. *Ibid, 83.*

18 Ay, but to die, and go we know not
where;
To lie in cold obstruction and to rot;
This sensible warm motion to become
A kneaded clod; and the delighted spirit
To bathe in fiery floods, or to reside
In thrilling region of thick-ribbed ice;
To be imprison'd in the viewless winds,
And blown with restless violence round
about
The pendent world! *Ibid, 118.*

19 The weariest and most loathed worldly
life
That age, ache, penury and
imprisonment
Can lay on nature is a paradise
To what we fear of death.   *Ibid, 129.*

20 Virtue is bold, and goodness never
fearful.   *Ibid, 215.*

21 There, at the moated grange, resides this
dejected Mariana.   *Ibid, 277.*

22 Take, O, take those lips away
That so sweetly were forsworn;
And those eyes, the break of day,
Lights that do mislead the morn:
But my kisses bring again, bring again;
Seals of love, but seal'd in vain, seal'd in
vain.   *Ibid, IV. i. 1.*

23 Every true man's apparel fits your thief.
                                     Ibid, ii. 46.

24 A forted residence 'gainst the tooth of
time
And razure of oblivion.   *Ibid, V. i. 12.*

25 They say, best men are moulded out of
faults;
And, for the most, become much more
the better
For being a little bad.   *Ibid, 444.*

THE MERCHANT OF VENICE

26 Nature hath framed strange fellows in
her time:
Some that will evermore peep through
their eyes
And laugh like parrots at a bag-piper,
And other of such vinegar aspect
That they'll not show their teeth in way
of smile,
Though Nestor swear the jest be
laughable.
       The Merchant of Venice, I. i. 51.

27 I hold the world but as the world,
Gratiano;
A stage where every man must play a
part,
And mine a sad one.   *Ibid, 77.*

28 Why should a man, whose blood is
warm within,
Sit like his grandsire cut in alabaster?
                                     Ibid, 83.

29 There are a sort of men whose visages
Do cream and mantle like a standing
pond.   *Ibid, 88.*

30 As who should say 'I am Sir Oracle,
And when I ope my lips let no dog
bark!'   *Ibid, 93.*

31 Gratiano speaks an infinite deal of
nothing, more than any man in all
Venice. His reasons are as two grains of
wheat hid in two bushels of chaff: you
shall seek all day ere you find them, and
when you have them, they are not
worth the search.   *Ibid, 114.*

32 In my school-days, when I had lost one
shaft,
I shot his fellow of the self-same flight
The self-same way with more advised
watch,
To find the other forth, and by
adventuring both
I oft found both.   *Ibid, 140.*

33 They are as sick that surfeit with too
much as they that starve with nothing.
                                     Ibid, ii. 5.

34 If to do were as easy as to know what
were good to do, chapels had been
churches and poor men's cottages
princes' palaces.   *Ibid, 13.*

35 God made him, and therefore let him
pass for a man.   *Ibid, 60.*

36 I dote on his very absence.   *Ibid, 119.*

37 Ships are but boards, sailors but men:
there be land-rats and water-rats,
water-thieves and land-thieves.
                                     Ibid, iii. 22.

38 How like a fawning publican he looks!
I hate him for he is a Christian,
But more for that in low simplicity
He lends out money gratis and brings
down
The rate of usance here with us in
Venice.

If I can catch him once upon the hip,
I will feed fat the ancient grudge I bear
him.   *Ibid, 42.*

1 Even there where merchants most do
congregate.   *Ibid, 50.*

2 The devil can cite Scripture for his
purpose.   *Ibid, 99.*

3 A goodly apple rotten at the heart:
O, what a goodly outside falsehood
hath!   *Ibid, 102.*

4 Still have I borne it with a patient shrug,
For sufferance is the badge of all our
tribe.   *Ibid, 110.*

5 You call me misbeliever, cut-throat
dog,
And spit upon my Jewish gaberdine.
                                       Ibid, 112.

6 Shall I bend low and in a bondman's
key,
With bated breath and whispering
humbleness.   *Ibid, 124.*

7 O father Abram, what these Christians
are,
Whose own hard dealings teaches them
suspect
The thoughts of others!   *Ibid, 161.*

8 I like not fair terms and a villain's mind.
                                       Ibid, 181.

9 Mislike me not for my complexion,
The shadow'd livery of the burnish'd
sun.   *Ibid, II. i. 1.*

10 O heavens, this is my true-begotten
father!   *Ibid, ii. 37.*

11 It is a wise father that knows his own
child.   *Ibid, 80.*

12 There is some ill a-brewing towards my
rest,
For I did dream of money-bags to-
night.   *Ibid, v. 17.*

13 And the vile squealing of the wry-
neck'd fife.   *Ibid, 30.*

14   All things that are,
Are with more spirit chased than
enjoy'd.   *Ibid, vi. 12.*

15 But love is blind and lovers cannot see
The pretty follies that themselves
commit.   *Ibid, 36.*

16 What, must I hold a candle to my
shames?   *Ibid, 41.*

17 My daughter! O my ducats! O my
daughter!
Fled with a Christian! O my Christian
ducats!   *Ibid, viii. 15.*

18 Let him look to his bond.
                          Ibid, III. i. 49, 50 and 52.

19 I am a Jew. Hath not a Jew eyes? hath
not a Jew hands, organs, dimensions,
senses, affections, passions?   *Ibid, 62.*

20 The villainy you teach me, I will
execute, and it shall go hard but I will
better the instruction.   *Ibid, 76.*

21 I would not have given it for a
wilderness of monkeys.   *Ibid, 127.*

22   He makes a swan-like end,
Fading in music.   *Ibid, ii. 44.*

23 Tell me where is fancy bred,
Or in the heart or in the head?
How begot, how nourished?   *Ibid, 63.*

24 In law, what plea so tainted and corrupt
But, being season'd with a gracious
voice,
Obscures the show of evil? In religion,
What damned error, but some sober
brow
Will bless it and approve it with a text?
                                       Ibid, 75.

25 There is no vice so simple but assumès
Some mark of virtue on his outward
parts.   *Ibid, 81.*

26 Thus ornament is but the guilded shore
To a most dangerous sea; the beauteous
scarf
Veiling an Indian beauty; in a word,

The seeming truth which cunning times put on
To entrap the wisest. *Ibid, 97.*

27 An unlesson'd girl, unschool'd, unpractised;
Happy in this, she is not yet so old
But she may learn. *Ibid, 161.*

28 Here are a few of the unpleasant'st words
That ever blotted paper. *Ibid, 254.*

29 I never did repent for doing good,
Nor shall not now. *Ibid, iv. 10.*

30 I'll not answer that:
But, say, it is my humour.
Ibid, IV. i. 42.

31 A harmless necessary cat. *Ibid, 55.*

32 What, wouldst thou have a serpent sting thee twice? *Ibid, 69.*

33 The quality of mercy is not strain'd,
It droppeth as the gentle rain from heaven
Upon the place beneath: it is twice blest;
It blesseth him that gives and him that takes:
'Tis mightiest in the mightiest: it becomes
The throned monarch better than his crown;
His sceptre shows the force of temporal power,
The attribute to awe and majesty,
Wherein doth sit the dread and fear of kings;
But mercy is above this sceptred sway;
It is enthroned in the hearts of kings,
It is an attribute to God himself;
And earthly power doth then show likest God's
When mercy seasons justice. Therefore, Jew,
Though justice be thy plea, consider this,
That, in the course of justice, none of us
Should see salvation: we do pray for mercy;
And that same prayer doth teach us all to render
The deeds of mercy. *Ibid, 184.*

34 Wrest once the law to your authority:
To do a great right, do a little wrong.
Ibid, 215.

35 A Daniel come to judgment! yea, a Daniel! *Ibid, 223.*

36 'Tis not in the bond. *Ibid, 262.*

37 For, as thou urgest justice, be assured
Thou shalt have justice, more than thou desirest. *Ibid, 315.*

38 A second Daniel, a Daniel, Jew!
Now, infidel, I have thee on the hip.
Ibid, 333.

39 I thank thee, Jew, for teaching me that word. *Ibid, 341.*

40 You take my house when you do take the prop
That doth sustain my house; you take my life
When you do take the means whereby I live. *Ibid, 375.*

41 He is well paid that is well satisfied.
Ibid, 415.

42 You taught me first to beg; and now methinks
You teach me how a beggar should be answer'd. *Ibid, 439.*

43 How sweet the moonlight sleeps upon this bank!
Here will we sit and let the sounds of music
Creep in our ears: soft stillness and the night
Become the touches of sweet harmony.
Sit, Jessica. Look how the floor of heaven
Is thick inlaid with patines of bright gold:
There's not the smallest orb which thou behold'st
But in his motion like an angel sings,
Still quiring to the young-eyed cherubins;
Such harmony is in immortal souls;
But whilst this muddy vesture of decay
Doth grossly close us in, we cannot hear it. *Ibid, V. i. 54.*

1 I am never merry when I hear sweet
   music.   *Ibid, 69.*

2 The man that hath no music in himself,
   Nor is not moved with concord of sweet
   sounds,
   Is fit for treasons, stratagems, and spoils;
   The motions of his spirit are dull as
   night
   And his affections dark as Erebus:
   Let no such man be trusted.   *Ibid, 83.*

3 How far that little candle throws his
   beams!
   So shines a good deed in a naughty
   world.   *Ibid, 90.*

4 How many things by season season'd
   are
   To their right praise and true perfection!
                                  Ibid, 107.

THE MERRY WIVES OF WINDSOR

5 I will make a Star-chamber matter of it.
        The Merry Wives of Windsor, I. i. 1.

6 I had rather than forty shillings I had my
   Book of Songs and Sonnets here.
                                  Ibid, 205.

7 'Convey' the wise it call. 'Steal!' foh! a
   fico for the phrase!   *Ibid, iii. 32.*

8 Here will be an old abusing of God's
   patience and the king's English.
                                  Ibid, iv. 5.

9 We burn daylight.   *Ibid, II. i. 54.*

10 Faith, thou hast some crotchets in thy
   head.   *Ibid, 159.*

11 Why, then the world's mine oyster,
   Which I with sword will open.
                                  Ibid, ii. 2.

12 I cannot tell what the dickens his name
   is.   *Ibid, III. ii. 19.*

13 O, what a world of vile ill-favour'd
   faults
   Look handsome in three hundred
   pounds a-year!   *Ibid, iv. 32.*

14 I have a kind of alacrity in sinking.
                                  Ibid, v. 13.

15 As good luck would have it.   *Ibid, 84.*

16 The rankest compound of villainous
   smell that ever offended nostril.
                                  Ibid, 93.

17 A man of my kidney.   *Ibid, 117.*

18 Vengeance of Jenny's case!
                                  Ibid, IV. i. 64.

19 They say there is divinity in odd
   numbers, either in nativity, chance or
   death.   *Ibid, V. i. 3.*

A MIDSUMMER NIGHT'S DREAM

20 But earthlier happy is the rose distill'd,
   Than that which withering on the virgin
   thorn
   Grows, lives and dies in single
   blessedness.
        A Midsummer Night's Dream, I. i. 76.

21   For aught that I could ever read,
   Could ever hear by tale or history,
   The course of true love never did run
   smooth.   *Ibid, 132.*

22 O hell! to choose love by another's eyes.
                                  Ibid, 140.

23 Swift as a shadow, short as any dream;
   Brief as the lightning in the collied
   night,
   That, in a spleen, unfolds both heaven
   and earth,
   And ere a man hath power to say
   'Behold!'
   The jaws of darkness do devour it up:
   So quick bright things come to
   confusion.   *Ibid, 144.*

24 Love looks not with the eyes, but with
   the mind;
   And therefore is wing'd Cupid painted
   blind.   *Ibid, 234.*

25 Masters, spread yourselves.   *Ibid, ii. 16.*

26 A part to tear a cat in.   *Ibid, 31.*

27 This is Ercles' vein. *Ibid, 42.*

28 I am slow of study. *Ibid, 69.*

29 I will roar you as gently as any sucking
dove; I will roar you as 'twere any
nightingale. *Ibid, 84.*

30 A proper man, as one shall see in a
summer's day. *Ibid, 88.*

31 Since once I sat upon a promontory,
And heard a mermaid on a dolphin's
back
Uttering such dulcet and harmonious
breath
That the rude sea grew civil at her song
And certain stars shot madly from their
spheres,
To hear the sea-maid's music.
Ibid, II. i. 149.

32 And the imperial votaress passed on,
In maiden meditation, fancy-free.
Yet mark's I where the bolt of Cupid
fell:
It fell upon a little western flower,
Before milk-white, now purple with
love's wound,
And maidens call it love-in-idleness.
Ibid, 163.

33 I'll put a girdle round about the earth
In forty minutes. *Ibid, 175.*

34 I know a bank where the wild thyme
blows,
Where oxlips and the nodding violet
grows,
Quite over-canopied and luscious
woodbine,
With sweet musk-roses and with
eglantine. *Ibid, 249.*

35 A lion among ladies, is a most dreadful
thing; for there is not a more fearful
wild-fowl than your lion living.
Ibid, III. i. 31.

36 A calendar, a calendar! look in the
almanac; find out moonshine, find out
moonshine. *Ibid, 54.*

37 What hempen homespuns have we
swaggering here? *Ibid, 79.*

38 Bless thee, Bottom! bless thee! thou are
translated. *Ibid, 121.*

39 Lord, what fools these mortals be!
Ibid, ii. 115.

40 So we grew together,
Like to a double cherry, seeming parted,
But yet an union in partition;
Two lovely berries moulded on one
stem. *Ibid, 208.*

41 She was a vixen when she went to
school;
And though she be but little, she is
fierce. *Ibid, 324.*

42 I have a reasonable good ear in music.
Let's have the tongs and the bones.
Ibid, IV. i. 30.

43 I have an exposition of sleep come upon
me. *Ibid, 41.*

44 My hounds are bred out of the Spartan
kind,
So flew'd, so sanded, and their heads are
hung
With ears that sweep away the morning
dew;
Crook-knee'd, and dew-lapp'd like
Thessalian bulls;
Slow in pursuit, but match's in mouth
like bells. *Ibid, 123.*

45 The lunatic, the lover and the poet
Are of imagination all compact.
Ibid, V. i. 7.

46 The lover, all as frantic,
Sees Helen's beauty in a brow of Egypt:
The poet's eye, in a fine frenzy rolling,
Doth glance from heaven to earth, from
earth to heaven;
And as imagination bodies forth
The forms of things unknown, the
poet's pen
Turns them to shapes and gives to airy
nothing
A local habitation and a name.
Ibid, 10.

47 Or in the night, imagining some fear,
How easy is a bush supposed a bear!
Ibid, 21.

1 Very tragical mirth.   *Ibid, 57.*

2 That is the true beginning of our end.
   Ibid, 111.

3 Whereat, with blade, with bloody
   blameful blade,
   He bravely broach'd his boiling bloody
   breast.   *Ibid, 147.*

4 The best in this kind are but shadows;
   and the worst are no worse, if
   imagination amend them.   *Ibid, 214.*

5 The iron tongue of midnight hath told
   twelve.   *Ibid, 370.*

MUCH ADO ABOUT NOTHING

6 He hath indeed better bettered
   expectation.
   Much Ado about Nothing, I. i. 15.

7 He is a very valiant trencher-man.
   Ibid, 51.

8 There's a skirmish of wit between them.
   Ibid, 63.

9 He wears his faith but as the fashion of
   his hat.   *Ibid, 75.*

10 My dear Lady Disdain.   *Ibid, 119.*

11 Benedick the married man.   *Ibid, 270.*

12 I have a good eye, uncle; I can see a
   church by daylight.   *Ibid, II. i. 86.*

13 Speak low, if you speak love.   *Ibid, 103.*

14 Friendship is constant in all other things
   Save in the office and affairs of love:
   Therefore all hearts in love use their
      own tongues;
   Let every eye negotiate for itself
   And trust no agent.   *Ibid, 182.*

15 Silence is the perfectest herald of joy: I
   were but little happy, if I could say how
   much.   *Ibid, 316.*

16 There was a star danced, and under that
   was I born.   *Ibid, 349.*

17 Is it not strange that sheeps' guts should
   hale souls out of men's bodies?
   Ibid, iii. 61.

18 Sigh no more, ladies, sigh no more,
   Men were deceivers ever,
   One foot on sea and one on shore,
   To one thing constant never.   *Ibid, 64.*

19 Sits the wind in that corner?   *Ibid, 102.*

20 Shall quips and sentences and these
   paper bullets of the brain awe a man
   from the career of his humour? No, the
   world must be peopled. When I said I
   would die a bachelor, I did not think I
   should live till I were married.
   Ibid, 248.

21 Disdain and scorn ride sparkling in her
   eyes.   *Ibid, III. i. 51.*

22 Taming my wild heart to thy loving
   hand.   *Ibid, 112.*

23 Everyone can master a grief but he that
   has it.   *Ibid, ii. 28.*

24 Are you good men and true?   *Ibid, iii. 1.*

25 To be a well-favoured man is the gift of
   fortune; but to write and read comes by
   nature.   *Ibid, 14.*

26 *Second Watch.* How if a' will not stand?
   Dogberry. Why, then, take no note of
   him, but let him go; and presently call
   the rest of the watch together and
   thank God you are rid of a knave.
   Ibid, 27.

27 For the watch to babble and talk is most
   tolerable and not to be endured.
   Ibid, 36.

28 The most peaceable way for you, if you
   do take a thief, is to let him show
   himself what he is and steal out of your
   company.   *Ibid, 61.*

29 I thank God I am as honest as any man
   living that is an old man and no
   honester than I.   *Ibid, v. 15.*

30 Comparisons are odorous.   *Ibid, 18.*

31 If I were as tedious as a king, I could find it in my heart to bestow it all of your worship. *Ibid, 23.*

32 A good old man, sir; he will be talking: as they say, When the age is in, the wit is out. *Ibid, 37.*

33 O, what men dare do! what men may do! what men daily do, not knowing what they do! *Ibid, IV. i. 19.*

34   I have mark's
A thousand blushing apparitions
To start into her face, a thousand innocent shames
In angel whiteness beat away those blushes. *Ibid, 160.*

35   For it so falls out
That what we have we prize not to the worth
Whiles we enjoy it, but being lack'd and lost,
Why, then we rack the value, then we find
The virtue that possession would not show us
While it was ours. *Ibid, 219.*

36 The idea of her life shall sweetly creep Into his study of imagination,
And every lovely organ of her life
Shall come apparell'd in more precious habit,
More moving-delicate and full of life,
Into the eye and prospect of his soul,
Than when she lived indeed. *Ibid, 226.*

37 Masters, it is proved already that you are little better than false knaves; and it will go near to be thought so shortly. *Ibid, ii. 22.*

38 Flat burglary as ever was committed. *Ibid, 52.*

39 O villain! thou wilt be condemned into everlasting redemption for this. *Ibid, 58.*

40 O that he were here to write me down an ass! *Ibid, 77.*

41 A fellow that hath had losses, and one

that hath two gowns and everything handsome about him. *Ibid, 87.*

42 Patch grief with proverbs. *Ibid, V. i. 17.*

43 For there was never yet philosopher That could endure the toothache patiently. *Ibid, 35.*

44 I was not born under a rhyming planet. *Ibid, ii. 40.*

45 Done to death by slanderous tongues. *Ibid, iii. 3.*

OTHELLO

46 A fellow almost damn'd in a fair wife; That never set a squadron in the field, Nor the divisions of a battle knows More than a spinster. *Othello, I. i. 21.*

47 The bookish theoric. *Ibid, 24.*

48 But I will wear my heart upon my sleeve For daws to peck at. *Ibid, 64.*

49 You are one of those that will not serve God, if the devil bid you. *Ibid, 107.*

50 Your daughter and the Moor are now making the beast with two backs. *Ibid, 117.*

51 The wealthy curled darlings of our nation. *Ibid, ii. 68.*

52 Most potent, grave, and reverend signiors,
My very noble and approved good masters. *Ibid, iii. 76.*

53 The very head and front of my offending Hath this extent, no more. *Ibid, 80.*

54   Rude am I in my speech,
And little bless'd with the soft phrase of peace;
For since these arms of mine had seven years' pith,

Till now some nine moons wasted, they
have used
Their dearest action in the tented field.
Ibid, 81.

1   I will a round unvarnish'd tale deliver
Of my whole course of love.   *Ibid, 90.*

2   A maiden never bold;
Of spirit so still and quiet, that her
motion
Blush'd at herself.   *Ibid, 94.*

3   Wherein I spake of most diastrous
chances,
Of moving accidents by flood and field,
Of hairbreadth 'scapes i' th' imminent
deadly breach.   *Ibid, 134.*

4   Antres vast and deserts idle,
Rough quarries, rocks and hills whose
heads touch heaven.   *Ibid, 140.*

5   And of the Cannibals that each other eat,
The Anthropophagi and men whose
heads
Do grow beneath their shoulders.
Ibid, 143.

6   My story being done,
She gave me for my pains a world of
sighs:
She swore, in faith, 'twas strange, 'twas
passing strange,
'Twas pitiful, 'twas wondrous pitiful:
She wish'd she had not heard it, yet she
wish'd
That heaven had made her such a man:
she thank'd me,
And bade me, if I had a friend that loved
her,
I should but teach him how to tell my
story,
And that would woo her. Upon this
hint I spake:
She loved me for the dangers I had
pass'd,
And I loved her that she did pity them.
This only is the witchcraft I have used.
Ibid, 158.

7   I do perceive here a divided duty.
Ibid, 181.

8   To mourn a mischief that is past and
gone

Is the next way to draw new mischief
on.   *Ibid, 204.*

9   The robb'd that smiles steals something
from the thief.   *Ibid, 208.*

10 The tyrant custom, most grave senators,
Hath made the flinty and steel couch of
war
My thrice-driven bed of down.
Ibid, 230.

11 Put money in thy purse.   *Ibid, 345.*

12 The food that to him now is as luscious
as locusts, shall be to him shortly as
bitter as coloquintida.   *Ibid, 354.*

13 Framed to make women false.
Ibid, 404.

14 I am not merry; but I do beguile,
The thing I am, by seeming otherwise.
Ibid, II. i. 122.

15 To suckle fools and chronicle small beer.
Ibid, 161.

16 O most lame and impotent conclusion!
Ibid, 162.

17 I have very poor and unhappy brains for
drinking: I could wish courtesy would
invent some other custom of
entertainment.   *Ibid, iii. 34.*

18 Potations pottle-deep.   *Ibid, 57.*

19 And let me the canakin clink;
A soldier's a man;
A life's but a span;
Why, then, let a soldier drink.   *Ibid, 72.*

20 Silence that dreadful bell: it frights the
isle
From her propriety.   *Ibid, 175.*

21 But men are men; the best sometimes
forget.   *Ibid, 241.*

22   Cassio, I love thee;
But never more be officer of mine.
Ibid, 248.

23 Reputation, reputation, reputation! O, I

have lost my reputation! I have lost the immortal part of myself, and what remains is bestial. *Ibid, 262.*

24 O God, that men should put an enemy in their mouths to steal away their brains! *Ibid, 292.*

25 Come, come, good wine is a good familiar creature, if it be well used. *Ibid, 313.*

26 How poor are they that have not patience! What wound did ever heal but by degrees? *Ibid, 376.*

27 Excellent wretch! Perdition catch my soul, But I do love thee! and when I love thee not, Chaos is come again. *Ibid, III. iii. 90.*

28 Good name in man and woman, dear my lord, Is the immediate jewel of their souls: Who steals my purse steals trash; 'tis something, nothing; 'Twas mine, 'tis his, and has been slave to thousands; But he that filches from me my good name Robs me of that which not enriches him And makes me poor indeed. *Ibid, 155.*

29 O, beware, my lord, of jealousy; It is the green-eyed monster which doth mock The meat it feeds on. *Ibid, 164.*

30 I am declined Into the vale of years. *Ibid, 265.*

31 O curse of marriage, That we can call these delicate creatures ours, And not their appetites! I had rather be a toad, And live upon the vapour of a dungeon, Than keep a corner in the thing I love For others' uses. *Ibid, 268.*

32 Trifles light as air

Are to the jealous confirmations strong As proofs of holy writ. *Ibid, 322.*

33 Not poppy, nor mandragora, Nor all the drowsy syrups of the world, Shall ever medicine thee to that sweet sleep Which thou owedst yesterday. *Ibid, 330.*

34 He that is robb'd, not wanting what is stol'n, Let him not know't, and he's not robb'd at all. *Ibid, 342.*

35 O, now for ever Farewell the tranquil mind! farewell content! Farewell the plumed troop, and the big wars That make ambition virtue! O, farewell! Farewell the neighing steed, and the shrill trump, The spirit-stirring drum, the ear-piercing fife, The royal banner, and all quality, Pride, pomp and circumstance of glorious war! And, O you mortal engines, whose rude throats The immortal Jove's dread clamours counterfeit, Farewell! Othello's occupation's gone! *Ibid, 347.*

36 Be sure of it; give me the ocular proof. *Ibid, 360.*

37 No hinge nor loop To hang a doubt on. *Ibid, 365.*

38 On horror's head horrors accumulate. *Ibid, 370.*

39 Take note, take note, O world, To be direct and honest is not safe. *Ibid, 377.*

40 But this denoted a foregone conclusion. *Ibid, 428.*

41 Like to the Pontic sea, Whose icy current and compulsive course Ne'er feels retiring ebb, but keeps due on

To the Propontic and the Hellespont,
Even so my bloody thoughts, with
violent pace,
Shall ne'er look back, ne'er ebb to
humble love,
Till that a capable and wide revenge
Swallow them up.   *Ibid, 453.*

1 I would have him nine years a-killing.
                         Ibid, IV. i. 188.

2 But yet the pity of it, Iago! O Iago, the
pity of-it, Iago!   *Ibid, 206.*

3 But, alas, to make me
A fixed figure for the time of scorn
To point his slow unmoving finger at.
                              Ibid, ii. 53.

4   O thou weed,
Who art so lovely fair and smell'st so
sweet
That the sense aches at thee, would thou
hadst ne'er been born!   *Ibid, 67.*

5 O heaven, that such companions
thou'ldst unfold,
And put in every honest hand a whip
To lash the rascals naked through the
world.   *Ibid, 141.*

6 'Tis neither here not there. *Ibid, iii. 59.*

7 He hath a daily beauty in his life
That makes me ugly.   *Ibid, V. i. 19.*

8   This is the night
That either makes me or fordoes me
quite.   *Ibid, 128.*

9 It is the cause, it is the cause, my soul, –
Let me not name it to you, you chaste
stars! –
It is the cause.   *Ibid, ii. 1.*

10 Put out the light, and then put out the
light;
If I quench thee, thou flaming minister,
I can again thy former light restore,
Should I repent me; but once put out thy
light,
Thou cunning pattern of excelling
nature,
I know not where is that Promethean
heat
That can thy light relume.   *Ibid, 7.*

11 Had all his hairs been lives, my great
revenge
Had stomach for them all.   *Ibid, 74.*

12 She was too fond of her most filthy
bargain.   *Ibid, 157.*

13   Curse his better angel from his side
And fall to reprobation.   *Ibid, 208.*

14 Every puny whisper gets my sword.
                              Ibid, 244.

15 Here is my journey's end, here is my
butt,
And very sea-mark of my utmost sail.
                              Ibid, 267.

16 Soft you; a word or two before you go.
I have done the state some service, and
they know't.
No more of that. I pray you, in your
letters,
Speak of me as I am; nothing extenuate,
Nor set down aught in malice: then
must you tell
Of one that loved not wisely but too
well;
Of one not easily jealous, but being
wrought
Perplex'd in the extreme; of one whose
hand,
Like the base Indian, threw a pearl away
Richer than all his tribe; of one whose
subdued eyes,
Albeit unused to the melting mood,
Drop tears as fast as the Arabian trees
Their medicinal gum. Set you down
this;
And say besides, that in Aleppo once,
Where a malignant and a turban'd Turk
Beat a Venetian and traduced the state,
I took by the throat the circumcised
dog,
And smote him, thus.   *Ibid, 338.*

PERICLES

17 See where she comes, apparell'd like the
spring!   *Pericles, I. i. 12.*

18 'Tis time to fear when tyrants seem to
kiss.   *Ibid, ii. 79.*

19 *Third Fisherman.* Master, I marvel how
the fishes live in the sea.
First Fisherman. Why, as men do a-land;
the great ones eat up the little ones.
Ibid, II. i. 29.

20　No, I will rob Tellus of her weed,
To strew thy green with flowers: the
yellows, blues,
The purple violets, and marigolds,
Shall as a carpet hang upon thy grave,
While summer days do last. Ay me!
poor maid,
Born in a tempest, when my mother
died,
This world to me is like a lasting storm,
Whirring me from my friends.
Ibid, IV. i. 14.

POEMS

21 Hunting he loved, but love he laugh'd to
scorn.　　　*Venus and Adonis, 4.*

22 Bid me discourse, I will enchant thine
ear,
Or, like a fairy, trip upon the green,
Or, like a nymph, with long dishevell'd
hair,
Dance on the sands, and yet no footing
seen:
Love is a spirit all compact of fire,
Not gross to sink, but light, and will
aspire.　　　*Ibid, 145.*

23 Round-hoof'd, short-joined, fetlocks
shag and long,
Broad breast, full eye, small head and
nostril wide,
High crest, short ears, straight legs and
passing strong,
Thin mane, thick tail, broad buttock,
tender hide:
Look, what a horse should have he did
not lack,
Save a proud rider on so proud a back.
Ibid, 295.

24 Love comforteth like sunshine after rain,
But Lust's effect is tempest after sun;
Love's gentle spring doth always fresh
remain,
Lust's winter comes ere summer half be
done:

Love surfeits not, Lust like a glutton
dies;
Love is all truth, Lust full of forged lies.
Ibid, 799.

25 Lo, here the gentle lark, weary of rest,
From his moist cabinet mounts up on
high,
And wakes the morning.　　*Ibid, 853.*

26 Beauty itself doth of itself persuade
The eyes of men without an orator.
The Rape of Lucrece, 29.

27 For greatest scandal waits on greatest
state.　　　　　　　*Ibid, 1006.*

28 To the onlie begetter of these insuing
sonnets.　　*Sonnets, dedication.*

29 From fairest creatures we desire
increase,
That thereby beauty's rose might never
die.　　　　　　　　*Ibid, i.*

30 Thou art thy mother's glass, and she in
thee
Calls back the lovely April of her prime.
Ibid, iii.

31 And stretched metre of an antique song.
Ibid, xvii.

32 Shall I compare thee to a summer's day?
Thou art more lovely and more
temperate:
Rough winds do shake the darling buds
of May,
And summer's lease hath all too short a
date.　　　　　　　*Ibid, xviii.*

33 But thy eternal summer shall not fade.
Ibid.

34 The painful warrior famoused for fight,
After a thousand victories once foil'd,
Is from the book of honour razed quite,
And all the rest forgot for which he
toil'd.　　　　　　　*Ibid, xxv.*

35 When in disgrace with fortune and
men's eyes
I all alone beweep my outcast state.
Ibid, xxix.

263

1 Wishing me like to one more rich in
  hope,
Featur'd like him, like him with friends
  possess'd,
Desiring this man's art and that man's
  scope,
With what I most enjoy contented least.
                                    Ibid.

2 When to the sessions of sweet silent
  thought,
I summon up remembrance of things
  past,
I sigh the lack of many a thing I sought,
And with old woes new wail my dear
  time's waste:
Then can I drown an eye, unused to
  flow,
For precious friends hid in death's
  dateless night,
And weep afresh love's long since
  cancell'd woe,
And moan the expense of many
  avanish'd sight.   *Ibid, xxx.*

3 But if the while I think on thee, dear
  friend,
All losses are restored and sorrows end.
                                    Ibid.

4 Full many a glorious morning have I
  seen
Flatter the mountain-tops with
  sovereign eye,
Kissing with golden face the meadows
  green,
Gilding pale streams with heavenly
  alchemy.   *Ibid, xxxiii.*

5 Why didst thou promise such a
  beauteous day
And make me travel forth without my
  cloak?   *Ibid, xxxiv.*

6 Not marble, nor the gilded monuments
Of princes, shall outlive this powerful
  rhyme.   *Ibid, lv.*

7 Being your slave, what should I do but
  tend
Upon the hours and times of your
  desire?
I have no precious time at all to spend,
Nor services to do, till you require.

Nor dare I chide the world-without-end
  hour
Whilst I, my sovereign, watch the clock
  for you,
Nor think the bitterness of absence sour
When you have bid your servant once
  adieu.   *Ibid, lvii.*

8 So true a fool is love that in your will,
Though you do any thing, he thinks no
  ill.   *Ibid.*

9 Like as the waves make towards the
  pebbled shore,
So do our minutes hasten to their end.
                            Ibid, lx.

10 When I have seen the hungry ocean gain
Advantage on the kingdom of the shore.
                           Ibid, lxiv.

11 Tired with all these, for restful death I
  cry.   *Ibid, lxvi.*

12 And art made tongue-tied by authority,
And folly doctor-like controlling skill,
And simple truth miscall'd simplicity,
And captive good attending captain ill.
                                    Ibid.

13 That time of year thou mayst in me
  behold
When yellow leaves, or none, or few, do
  hang
Upon those boughs which shake against
  the cold,
Bare ruin'd choirs, where late the sweet
  birds sang.
In me thou see'st the twilight of such
  day
As after sunset fadeth in the west,
Which by and by black night doth take
  away,
Death's second self, that seals up all in
  rest.   *Ibid, lxxiii.*

14 Was it the proud full sail of his great
  verse,
Bound for the prize of all too precious
  you.   *Ibid, lxxxvi.*

15 Farewell! thou art too dear for my
  possessing,
And like enough thou know'st thy
  estimate.   *Ibid, lxxxvii.*

16 Thus have I had thee, as a dream doth
flatter,
In sleep a king, but waking no such
matter.   *Ibid.*

17 Ah, do not, when my heart hath 'scaped
this sorrow,
Come in the rearward of a conquer'd
woe;
Give not a windy night a rainy morrow,
To linger out a purposed overthrow.
                                Ibid, xc.

18 They that have power to hurt and will
do none,
That do not do the thing they most do
show,
Who, moving others, are themselves as
stone.
Unmoved, cold, and to temptation
slow,
They rightly do inherit heaven's graces
And husband nature's riches from
expense;
They are the lords and owners of their
faces,
Others, but stewards of their excellence.
                                Ibid, xciv.

19 For sweetest things turn sourest by their
deeds;
Lilies that fester smell far worse than
weeds.   *Ibid.*

20 From you have I been absent in the
spring,
When proud-pied April dress'd in all his
trim
Hath put a spirit of youth in every thing.
                                Ibid, xcviii.

21 To me, fair friend, you never can be old,
For as you were when first your eye I
eyed,
Such seems your beauty still. Three
winters cold
Have from the forests shook three
summers' pride,
Three beauteous springs to yellow
autumn turn'd.   *Ibid, civ.*

22 Ah! yet doth beauty, like a dial-hand,
Steal from his figure and no pace
perceived.   *Ibid.*

23 When in the chronicle of wasted time
I see descriptions of the fairest wights,
And beauty making beautiful old rhyme
In praise of ladies dead and lovely
knights.   *Ibid, cvi.*

24 O, never say that I was false of heart,
Though absence seem'd my flame to
qualify.   *Ibid, cix.*

25 Alas, 'tis true I have gone here and there
And made myself a motley to the view.
                                Ibid, cx.

26   My nature is subdued
To what it works in, like the dyer's
hand.   *Ibid, cxi.*

27 Let me not to the marriage of true minds
Admit impediments. Love is not love
Which alters when it alteration finds.
                                Ibid, cxvi.

28 Love's not Time's fool, though rosy lips
and cheeks
Within his bending sickle's compass
come.   *Ibid.*

29 The expense of spirit in a waste of shame
Is lust in action; and till action, lust
Is perjured, murderous, bloody, full of
blame,
Savage, extreme, rude, cruel, not to
trust.   *Ibid, cxxix.*

30 Mad, in pursuit and in possession so;
Had, having, and in quest to have,
extreme;
A bliss in proof, and proved, a very
woe;
Before, a joy proposed; behind, a
dream.
All this the world well knows; yet none
knows well
To shun the heaven that leads men to
this hell.   *Ibid.*

31 That full star that ushers in the even.
                                Ibid, cxxxii.

32 Two loves I have of comfort and
despair,
Which like two spirits do suggest me
still:

The better angel is a man right fair,
The worser spirit a woman colour'd ill.
Ibid, cxliv.

1 Crabbed age and youth cannot live
together:
Youth is full of pleasance, age is full of
care;
Youth like summer morn, age like
winter weather;
Youth like summer brave, age like
winter bare.
The Passionate Pilgrim, xii.

2 Good friend, for Jesu's sake forbear
To dig the dust enclosed here.
Blest be the man that spares these
stones,
And curst be he that moves my bones.
His own epitaph.

ROMEO AND JULIET

3 A pair of star-cross'd lovers.
Romeo and Juliet, prologue, 6.

4 I do not bite my thumb at you, sir, but I
bite my thumb, sir.   *Ibid, I. i. 57.*

5 Gregory, remember thy swashing blow.
Ibid, 69.
11

6 An hour before the worshipp'd sun
Peer'd forth the golden window of the
east.   *Ibid, 125.*

7 Saint-seducing gold.   *Ibid, 220.*

8 When well apparell'd April on the heel
Of limping winter treads.
Ibid, ii. 27.

9 One fire burns out another's burning,
One pain is lessen'd by another's
anguish.   *Ibid, 46.*

10 Thou wilt fall backward when thou
comest to age.   *Ibid, iii. 56.*

11 That book in many's eyes doth share the
glory,
That in gold clasps locks in the golden
story.   *Ibid, 91.*

12 For I am proverb'd with a grandsire
phrase.   *Ibid, iv. 37.*

13 O, then, I see Queen Mab hath been
with you.
She is the fairies' midwife, and she
comes
In shape no bigger than an agate-stone
On the fore-finger of an alderman,
Drawn with a team of little atomies
Athwart men's noses as they lie asleep;
Her waggon-spokes made of long
spinners' legs,
The cover of the wings of grasshoppers,
The traces of the smallest spider's web,
The collars of the moonshine's watery
beams,
Her whip of cricket's bone, the lash of
film,
Her waggoner a small grey-coated gnat,
Not half so big as a round little worm
Prick'd from the lazy finger of a maid;
Her chariot is an empty hazel-nut
Made by the joiner squirrel or old grub,
Time out o' mind the fairies'
coachmakers.
And in this state she gallops night by
night
Through lovers' brains, and then they
dream of love;
O'er courtiers' knees, that dream of
court'sies straight,
O'er lawyers' fingers, who straight
dream on fees,
O'er ladies' lips, who straight on kisses
dream.   *Ibid, 53.*

14   True, I talk of dreams,
Which are but children of an idle brain,
Begot of nothing but vain fantasy.
Ibid, 96.

15 For you and I are past our dancing days.
Ibid, v. 33.

16 O, she doth teach the torches to burn
bright!
It seems she hangs upon the cheek of
night
Like a rich jewel in an Ethiope's ear;
Beauty too rich for use, for earth too
dear!   *Ibid, 46.*

17 We have a trifling foolish banquet
towards.   *Ibid, 124.*

18 Young Adam Cupid, he that shot so
trim,
When King Cophetua loved the beggar-
maid. *Ibid, II. i. 13.*

19 He jests at scars that never felt a wound.
Ibid, ii. 1.

20 See, how she leans her cheek upon her
hand!
O, that I were a glove upon that hand,
That I might touch that cheek! *Ibid, 23.*

21 O Romeo, Romeo! wherefore art thou
Romeo? *Ibid, 33.*

22 What's in a name? that which we call a
rose
By any other name would smell as
sweet. *Ibid, 43.*

23   At lovers' perjuries,
They say, Jove laughs. *Ibid, 92.*

24 But trust me, gentlemen, I'll prove
more true
Than those that have more cunning to
be strange. *Ibid, 100.*

25 *Romeo.* Lady, by yonder blessed moon I
swear
That tips with silver all these fruit-tree
tops –
Juliet. O, swear not by the moon, the
inconstant moon,
That monthly changes in her circled
orb,
Lest that thy love prove likewise
variable. *Ibid, 107.*

26 The God of my idolatry. *Ibid, 114.*

27 It is too rash, too unadvised, too sudden;
Too like the lightning, which doth cease
to be
Ere one can say 'It lightens.' *Ibid, 118.*

28 Love goes toward love, as schoolboys
from their books,
But love from love, toward school with
heavy looks. *Ibid, 156.*

29 How silver-sweet sound lovers' tongues
by night,
Like softest music to attending ears!
Ibid, 166.

30 Good night, good night! parting is such
sweet sorrow,
That I shall say good night till it be
morrow. *Ibid, 185.*

31 For nought so vile that on the earth doth
live
But to the earth some special good doth
give,
Nor aught so good but strain'd from
that fair use
Revolts from true birth, stumbling on
abuse:
Virtue itself turns vice, being
misapplied;
And vice sometimes by action dignified.
Ibid, iii. 17.

32 Care keeps his watch in every old man's
eye,
And where care lodges, sleep will never
lie. *Ibid, 35.*

33 O flesh, flesh, how art thou fishified!
Ibid, iv. 39.

34 I am the very pink of courtesy. *Ibid, 61.*

35 These violent delights have violent ends.
Ibid, vi. 9.

36 Too swift arrives as tardy as too slow.
Ibid, 15.

37 Here comes the lady: O, so light a foot
Will ne'er wear out the everlasting flint.
Ibid, 16.

38 A word and a blow. *Ibid, III. i. 43.*

39 A plague o' both your houses.
Ibid, 94 and 103.

40 No, 'tis not so deep as a well, nor so
wide as a church-door; but 'tis enough,
'twill serve. *Ibid, 99.*

41 Gallop apace, you fiery-footed steeds,
Towards Phoebus' lodging: such a
waggoner
As Phaethon would whip you to the
west,
And bring in cloudy night immediately,
Spread thy close curtain, love-
performing night,

That runaways' eyes may wink, and
Romeo
Leap to these arms, untalk'd of and
unseen.   *Ibid, ii. 1.*

1 Give me my Romeo; and, when he shall
die,
Take him and cut him out in little stars,
And he will make the face of heaven so
fine
That all the world will be in love with
night
And pay no worship to the garish sun.
Ibid, 21.

2 Adversity's sweet milk, philosophy.
Ibid, iii. 55.

3 Night's candles are burnt out, and
jocund day
Stands tiptoe on the misty mountain
tops.   *Ibid, v. 9.*

4 Villain and he be many miles asunder.
Ibid, 82.

5 A beggarly account of empty boxes.
Ibid, V. i. 45.

6 My poverty, but not my will, consents.
Ibid, 75.

7   Beauty's ensign yet
Is crimson in thy lips and in thy cheeks,
And death's pale flag is not advanced
there.   *Ibid, iii. 94.*

8   Eyes, look your last!
Arms, take your last embrace!
Ibid, 112.

THE TAMING OF THE SHREW

9 As Stephen Sly and old John Naps of
Greece
And Peter Turph and Henry Pimpernell
And twenty more such names and men
as these
Which never were nor no man ever saw.
The Taming of the Shrew, induction, ii. 95.

10 No profit grows where is no pleasure
ta'en:
In brief, sir, study what you most affect.
Ibid, I. i. 39.

11 'Tis a very excellent piece of work,
madam lady: would 'twere done!   *Ibid, 258.*

12 I must dance bare-foot on her wedding
day
And for your love to her lead apes in
hell.   *Ibid, ii. 33.*

13 This is the way to kill a wife with
kindness.   *Ibid, IV. i. 211.*

14 And as the sun breaks through the
darkest clouds,
So honour peereth in the meanest habit.
Ibid, iii. 175.

15 A woman moved is like a fountain
troubled,
Muddy, ill-seeming, thick, bereft of
beauty.   *Ibid, V. ii. 142.*

16 Such duty as the subject owes the prince
Even such a woman oweth to her
husband.   *Ibid, 155.*

THE TEMPEST

17 He hath no drowning mark upon him;
his complexion is perfect gallows.
The Tempest I. i. 32.

18 In the dark backward and abysm of
time.   *Ibid, ii. 50.*

19   Like one,
Who having into truth, by telling of it,
Made such a sinner of his memory,
To credit his own lie.   *Ibid, 99.*

20   My library
Was dukedom large enough.   *Ibid, 109.*

21 Knowing I loved my books, he
furnish'd me
From mine own library with volumes
that
I prize above my dukedom.   *Ibid, 166.*

22 From the still-vex'd Bermoothes.
Ibid, 229.

23 I will be correspondent to command
And do my spiriting gently.   *Ibid, 297.*

24 You taught me language; and my profit
   on't
   Is, I know how to curse. The red plague
   rid you
   For learning me your language!
   Ibid, 363.

25 Come unto these yellow sands,
   And then take hands:
   Courtsied when you have and kiss'd
   The wild waves whist.   *Ibid, 376.*

26 Full fathom five thy father lies;
   Of his bones are coral made;
   Those are pearls that were his eyes:
   Nothing of him that doth fade
   But doth suffer a sea-change
   Into something rich and strange.
   Ibid, 396.

27 The fringed curtains of thine eye
   advance
   And say what thou seest yond.
   Ibid, 408.

28   At the first sight
   They have changed eyes.   *Ibid, 440.*

29 Fie, what a spendthrift is he of his
   tongue!   *Ibid, II. i. 24.*

30 They'll take suggestion as a cat laps
   milk.   *Ibid, 288.*

31 A very ancient and fish-like smell.
   Ibid, ii. 27.

32 Misery acquaints a man with strange
   bedfellows.   *Ibid, 41.*

33 Well, here's my comfort. (*Drinks.*)
   Ibid, 47.

34 No more dams I'll make for fish;
   Nor fetch in firing
   At requiring:
   Nor scrape trencher, nor wash dish:
   'Ban, 'Ban, Cacaliban
   Has a new master: get a new man.
   Ibid, 184.

35   For several virtues
   Have I liked several women; never any
   With so full soul, but some defect in her

Did quarrel with the noblest grace she
   owed
   And put it to the foil.   *Ibid, III. i.. 42.*

36 *Ferdinand.* Here's my hand.
   Miranda. And mine, with my heart in't.
   Ibid, 89.

37 I am in case to justle a constable.
   Ibid, ii. 30.

38 He that dies pays all debts.   *Ibid, 140.*

39 Be not afeard; the isle is full of noises,
   Sounds and sweet airs, that give delight
   and hurt not.   *Ibid, 144.*

40 Our revels now are ended. These our
   actors,
   As I foretold you, were all spirits and
   Are melted into air, into thin air:
   And, like the baeless fabric of this
   vision,
   The cloud-capp'd towers, the gorgeous
   palaces,
   The solemn temples, the great globe
   itself,
   Yea, all which it inherit, shall dissolve
   And, like this insubstantial pageant
   faded,
   Leave not a rack behind. We are such
   stuff
   As dreams are made on, and our little
   life
   Is rounded with a sleep.
   Ibid, IV. i. 148.

41 I do begin to have bloody thoughts.
   Ibid, 220.

42 With foreheads villainous low.
   Ibid, 250.

43 Ye elves of hills, brooks, standing lakes
   and groves,
   And ye that on the sands with printless
   foot
   Do chase the ebbing Neptune and do fly
   him
   When he comes back.   *Ibid, V. i. 33.*

44 And deeper than did ever plummet
   sound
   I'll drown my book.   *Ibid, 56.*

1 Where the bee sucks, there suck I:
In a cowslip's bell I lie;
There I couch when owls do cry.
On the bat's back I do fly
After summer merrily.
Merrily, merrily shall I live now
Under the blossom that hangs on the
obough. *Ibid, 88.*

2 How beauteous mankind is! O brave
new world,
That has such people in't! *Ibid, 183.*

TIMON OF ATHENS

3 But flies an eagle flight, bold and forth
on,
Leaving no tract behind.
Timon of Athens, I. i. 49.

4 'Tis not enough to help the feeble up,
But to support him after. *Ibid, 107.*

5 I wonder men dare trust themselves
with men. *Ibid, ii. 44.*

6 Here's that which is too weak to be a
sinner, honest water, which ne'er left
man i' the mire. *Ibid, 59.*

7 I'll example you with thievery:
The sun's a thief, and with his great
attraction
Robs the vast sea: the moon's an arrant
thief,
And her pale fire she snatches from the
sun:
The sea's a thief, whose liquid surge
resolves
The moon into salt tears: the earth's a
thief,
That feeds and breeds by a composture
stolen
From general excrement: each thing's a
thief. *Ibid, IV. iii. 438.*

TITUS ANDRONICUS

8 Sweet mercy is nobility's true badge.
Titus Andronicus, I. i. 119.

9 She is a woman, therefore may be
woo'd;

She is a woman, therefore may be won;
She is Lavinia, therefore must be loved.
What, man! more water glideth by the
mill
Than wots the miller of; and easy it is
Of a cut loaf to steal a shive, we know.
Ibid, II. i. 82.

10 Come, and take choice of all my library,
And so beguile thy sorrow.
Ibid, IV. i. 34.

11 The eagle suffers little birds to sing,
And is not careful what they mean
thereby. *Ibid, iv. 83*

12 If one good deed in all my life I did,
I do repent it from my very soul.
Ibid, v. iii. 189.

TROILUS AND CRESSIDA

13 I have had my labour for my travail.
Troilus and Cressida, I. i. 71.

14 Women are angels, wooing:
Things won are done; joy's soul lies in
the doing.
That she beloved knows nought that
knows not this:
Men prize the thing ungain'd more than
it is. *Ibid, ii. 312.*

15 The baby figure of the giant mass
Of things to come at large.
Ibid, iii. 345.

16 I am giddy; expectation whirls me
round.
The imaginary relish is so sweet
That it enchants my sense.
Ibid, III. ii. 19.

17 To be wise and love
Exceeds man's might. *Ibid, 163.*

18 Welcome ever smiles,
And farewell goes out sighing.
Ibid, iii. 168.

19 One touch of nature makes the whole
world kin. *Ibid, 175.*

20 And give to dust that is a little gilt
More laud than gilt o'erdusted.
Ibid, 178.

21 And, like a dew-drop from the lion's
mane,
Be shook to air. *Ibid, 224.*

22 There's language in her eye, her cheek,
her lip,
Nay, her foot speaks; her wanton spirits
look out
At every joint and motive of her body.
Ibid, IV. v. 55.

23 Now they are clapper-clawing one
another. *Ibid, V. iv. 1.*

TWELFTH NIGHT

24 If music be the food of love, play on;
Give me excess of it, that, surfeiting,
The appetite may sicken, and so die.
That strain again! it had a dying fall:
O, it came o'er my ear like the sweet
sound,
That breathes upon a bank of violets,
Stealing and giving odour!
Twelfth Night, I. i. 1.

25 I am sure care's an enemy to life.
Ibid, iii. 2.

26 Speaks three or four languages word for
word without book. *Ibid, 27.*

27 I am a great eater of beef and I believe
that does harm to my wit. *Ibid, 89.*

28 Wherefore are these things hid?
Ibid, 133.

29 Is it a world to hide virtues in?
Ibid, 140.

30 Many a good hanging prevents a bad
marriage. *Ibid, v. 20.*

31 Good my mouse of virtue, answer me.
Ibid, 69.

32 'Tis beauty truly blent, whose red and
white
Nature's own sweet and cunning hand
laid on. *Ibid, 257.*

33 Make me a willow cabin at your gate,
And call upon my soul within the house;
Write loyal cantons of contemned love
And sing them loud even in the dead of
night;
Halloo your name to the reverberate
hills
And make the babbling gossip of the air
Cry out 'Olivia!' *Ibid, 287.*

34 Farewell, fair cruelty. *Ibid, 307.*

35 Not to be a-bed after midnight is to be
up betimes. *Ibid, II. iii. 1.*

36 O, mistress mine, where are you
roaming?
O, stay and hear; your true love's
coming,
That can sing both high and low:
Trip no further, pretty sweeting;
Journeys end in lovers meeting,
Every wise man's son doth know.
Ibid, 40.

37 In delay there lies no plenty;
Then come kiss me, sweet and twenty,
Youth's a stuff will not endure. *Ibid, 51.*

38 He does it with a better grace, but I do it
more natural. *Ibid, 88.*

39 *Sir Toby.* Dost thou think, because thou
art virtuous, there shall be no more
cakes and ale?
Clown. Yes, by Saint Anne, and ginger
shall be hot i' the mouth too. *Ibid, 123.*

40 My purpose is, indeed, a horse of that
colour. *Ibid, 181.*

41 It gives a very echo to the seat
Where Love is throned. *Ibid iv. 21.*

42 Let still the woman take
An elder than herself; so wears she to
him,
So sways she level in her husband's
heart:
For, boy, however we do praise
ourselves,
Our fancies are more giddy and unfirm,
More longing, wavering, sooner lost
and worn,
Than women's are. *Ibid, 30.*

1 Then let thy love be younger than
 thyself,
 Or thy affection cannot hold the bent.
 Ibid, 37.

2 The spinsters and the knitters in the sun
 And the free maids that weave their
 thread with bones
 Do use to chant it: it is silly sooth,
 And dallies with the innocence of love,
 Like the old age. *Ibid, 45.*

3 Come away, come away, death,
 And in sad cypress let me be laid;
 Fly away, fly away, breath;
 I am slain by a fair cruel maid.
 My shroud of white, stuck all with yew,
 O, prepare it!
 My part of death, no one so true
 Did share it. *Ibid, 52.*

4 *Duke.* And what's her history?
 Viola. A blank, my lord. She never told
 her love,
 But let concealment, like a worm i' the
 bud,
 Feed on her damask cheek: she pined in
 thought,
 And with a green and yellow
 melancholy
 She sat like patience on a monument,
 Smiling at grief. *Ibid, 112.*

5 I am all the daughters of my father's
 house,
 And all the brothers too. *Ibid, 123.*

6 Be not afraid of greatness: some are born
 great, some achieve greatness and some
 have greatness thrust upon 'em.
 Ibid, v. 156.

7 O world, how apt the poor are to be
 proud. *Ibid, III. i. 138.*

8 O, what a deal of scorn looks beautiful
 In the contempt and anger of his lip!
 Ibid, 157.

9 Love sought is good, but given
 unsought is better. *Ibid, 168.*

10 Let there be gall enough in thy ink,
 though thou write with a goose-pen, no
 matter. *Ibid, ii. 51.*

11 I think we do know the sweet Roman
 hand. *Ibid, iv. 30.*

12 Why, this is very midsummer madness.
 Ibid, 61.

13 If this were played upon a stage now, I
 could condemn it as an improbable
 fiction. *Ibid, 140.*

14 Still you keep o' the windy side of the
 law. *Ibid, 181.*

15 Fare thee well; and God have mercy
 upon one of our souls. He may have
 mercy upon mine; but my hope is
 better, and so look to thyself.
 Ibid, 183.

16 An I thought he had been valiant and so
 cunning in fence, I'ld have seen him
 damned ere I'ld have challenged him.
 Ibid, 311.

17 Out of my lean and low ability
 I'll lend you something. *Ibid, 378.*

18 I hate ingratitude more in a man
 Than lying, vainness, babbling,
 drunkenness,
 Or any taint of vice whose strong
 corruption
 Inhabits our frail blood. *Ibid, 388.*

19 *Clown.* What is the opinion of
 Pythagoras concerning wild fowl?
 Malvolio. That the soul of our grandam
 might haply inhabit a bird.
 Ibid, IV. ii. 54.

20 Thus the whirligig of time brings in his
 revenges. *Ibid, V. i. 384.*

21 When that I was and a little tiny boy,
 With hey, ho, the wind and the rain,
 A foolish thing was but a toy,
 For the rain it raineth every day.
 Ibid, 398.

**THE TWO GENTLEMEN OF
 VERONA**

22 Home-keeping youth have ever homely
 wits.
 The Two Gentlemen of Verona, I. i. 2.

23 I have no other but a woman's reason;
   I think him so because I think him so.
                        Ibid, ii. 23.

24 Put forth their sons to seek preferment
   out:
   Some to the wars, to try their fortune
   there;
   Some to discover islands far away;
   Some to the studious universities.
                        Ibid, iii. 6.

25 O, how this spring of love resembleth
   The uncertain glory of an April day!
                        Ibid, 84.

26 He makes sweet music with the
   enamell'd stones,
   Giving a gentle kiss to every sedge
   He overtaketh in his pilgrimage.
                        Ibid, II. vii. 28.

27 Except I be by Sylvia in the night,
   There is no music in the nightingale.
                        Ibid III. i. 178.

28 A man I am cross'd with adversity.
                        Ibid, IV. i. 12.

29 Who is Sylvia? what is she,
   That all our swains commend her?
                        Ibid, ii. 39.

30 Is she kind as she is fair?
   For beauty lives with kindness. *Ibid, 44.*

31 How use doth breed a habit in a man.
                        Ibid, V. iv. 1.

32   O heaven! were man
   But constant, he were perfect.
                        Ibid, 110.

THE WINTER'S TALE

33 Two lads that thought there was no
   more behind
   But such a day to-morrow as to-day,
   And to be boy eternal.
                The Winter's Tale, I. ii. 63.

34 We were as twinn'd lambs that did frisk
   i' the sun,
   And bleat the one at the other: what we
   changed

Was innocence for innocence: we knew
   not
   The doctrine of ill-doing, nor dream'd
   That any did.   *Ibid, 67.*

35 A sad tale's best for winter.
                        Ibid, II. i. 25.

36 The silence often of pure innocence
   Persuades when speaking fails.
                        Ibid, ii. 41.

37   What's gone and what's past help
   Should be past grief.
                        Ibid, III. ii. 223.

38 Exit, pursued by a bear.
                Ibid, iii. 58, stage direction.

39 I would there were no age between
   sixteen and three-and-twenty, or that
   youth would sleep out the rest; for there
   is nothing in the between but getting
   wenches with child, wronging the
   ancientry, stealing, fighting. *Ibid, 59.*

40 When daffodils begin to peer,
   With heigh! the doxy over the dale,
   Why, then comes in the sweet o' the
   year;
   For the red blood reigns in the winter's
   pale.   *Ibid, IV. iii. 1.*

41 A snapper-up of unconsidered trifles.
                        Ibid, 26.

42 Jog on, jog on, the foot-path way,
   And merrily hent the stile-a:
   A merry heart goes all the day,
   Your sad tires in a mile-a.   *Ibid, 132.*

43 For you there's rosemary and rue; these
   keep
   Seeming and savour all the winter long.
                        Ibid, iv. 74.

44   Here's flowers for you;
   Hot lavender, mints, savory, marjoram;
   The marigold, that goes to bed wi' the
   sun
   And with him rises weeping: these are
   flowers
   Of middle summer, and I think they are
   given
   To men of middle age.   *Ibid, 103.*

1
　　　　　　　　O Proserpina,
For the flowers now, that frighted thou
　　let'st fall
From Dis's waggon! daffodils
That come before the swallow dares,
　　and take
The winds of March with beauty;
　　violets dim,
But sweeter than the lids of Juno's eyes
Or cytherea's breath; pale primroses,
That die unmarried, ere they can behold
Bright Phœbus in his strength – a
　　malady
Most incident to maids; bold oxlips and
The crown imperial; lilies of all kinds,
The flower-de-luce being one!
　　　　　　　　　　　　Ibid, 116.

2
　　　　　　　　What you do
Still betters what is done. When you
　　speak, sweet,
I'ld have you do it ever: when you sing,
I'ld have you buy and sell so, so give
　　alms,
Pray so; and, for the ordering your
　　affairs,
To sing them too: when you do dance, I
　　wish you
A wave o' the sea, that you might ever
　　do
Nothing but that; move still, still so,
And own no other function.　*Ibid, 135.*

3
　　　　　　Good sooth, she is
The queen of curds and cream.
　　　　　　　　　　　　Ibid, 160.

4 I think there is not half a kiss to choose
Who loves another best.　　*Ibid, 175.*

5 Lawn as white as driven snow. *Ibid, 220.*

6 Will you buy any tape,
Or lace for your cape,
My dainty duck, my dear-a?
Any silk, any thread,
Any toys for your head,
Of the new'st and finest, finest wear-a?
　　　　　　　　　　　　Ibid, 322.

7 The selfsame sun that shines upon his
　　court
Hides not his visage from our cottage
　　but
Looks on alike.　　　　　*Ibid, 454.*

8 Let me have no lying: it becomes none
but tradesmen.　　　　　*Ibid, 743.*

SHAW, GEORGE BERNARD,
Irish dramatist, 26 July, 1856–
2 Nov. 1950

9 We have no more right to consume
happiness without producing it than to
consume wealth without producing it.
　　　　　　　　　　　　Candida, 1.

10 I'm only a beer teetotaller, not a
champagne teetotaller.　　*Ibid, III.*

11 We don't bother much about dress and
manners in England, because as a
nation we don't dress well and we've
no manners.　　*You never can tell, I.*

12 When we want to read of the deeds that
are done for love, whither do we turn?
To the murder column.
　　　Three Plays for Puritans, preface.

13 When a stupid man is doing something
he is ashamed of, he always declares
that it is his duty.　*Caesar and Cleopatra,*
　　　　　　　　　　　　　　　　III.

14 A lifetime of happiness! No man alive
could bear it; it would be hell on earth.
　　　　　　　　Man and Superman, I.

15 You think that you are Ann's suitor; that
you are the pursuer and she the
pursued; that it is your part to woo, to
persuade, to prevail, to overcome.
Fool: it is you who are the pursued, the
marked-down quarry, the destined
prey.　　　　　　　　　*Ibid, II.*

16 There are two tragedies in life. One is
not to get your heart's desire. The
other is to get it.　　　　*Ibid, IV.*

17 Do not do unto others as you would
they should do unto you. Their tastes
may not be the same.
　　　Ibid, Maxims for Revolutionists, 227.

18 Marriage is popular because it combines
the maximum of temptation with the
maximum of opportunity.　*Ibid, 231.*

19 The reasonable man adapts himself to
the world: the unreasonable one
persists in trying to adapt the world to
himself. Therefore all progress
depends on the unreasonable man.
Ibid, 238.

20 Home is the girl's prison and the
woman's workhouse. *Ibid, 240.*

21 Every man over forty is a scoundrel.
Ibid, 242.

22 A man is like a phonograph with half a
dozen records. You soon get tired of
them all; and yet you have to sit at table
whilst he reels them off to every new
visitor. *Getting Married.*

23 Not bloody likely. *Pygmalion, II.*

24 With the single of exception of Homer,
there is no eminent writer, not even Sir
Walter Scott, whom I can despise so
entirely as I despise Shakespeare when I
measure my mind against his.
Dramatic Opinions and Essays, II. 52.

**SHEALE, RICHARD, English
ballad-writer, 16th century**

25 For when his legs were smitten off,
He fought upon his stumps.
Ballad of Chevy Chase, II. x.

**SHEFFIELD, JOHN, see
Buckingham and Normanby, 1st
Duke of**

**SHELLEY, PERCY BYSSHE,
English poet, 4 Aug. 1792–8 July,
1822**

26 How wonderful is Death,
Death and his brother Sleep.
Queen Mab, I.

27 With hue like that when some greater
painter dips
His pencil in the gloom of earthquake
and eclipse. *The Revolt of Islam, v. 23.*

28 My name is Ozymandias, king of kings:
Look on my works, ye Mighty, and
despair! *Ozymandias.*

29 Most wretched men
Are cradled into poetry by wrong,
They learn in suffering what they teach
in song. *Julian and Maddalo, 543.*

30 I could lie down like a tired child
And weep away the life of care
Which I have borne and yet must bear
Till death like sleep might steal on me.
Stanzas written in Dejection, near Naples.

31 Men of England, wherefore plough
For the lords who lay ye low?
Wherefore weave with toil and care
The rich robes your tyrants wear?
Song to the Men of England.

32 O wild West Wind, thou breath of
Autumn's being,
Thou, from whose unseen presence the
leaves dead
Are driven, like ghosts from an
enchanter fleeing.
Ode to the West Wind, 1.

33 Thou who didst waken from his
summer dreams
The blue Mediterranean, where he lay,
Lulled by the coil of his crystalline
streams. *Ibid, 3.*

34 O, wind,
If Winter comes, can Spring be far
behind? *Ibid, 5.*

35 I arise from dreams of thee
In the first sweet sleep of night,
When the winds are breathing low,
And the stars are shining bright.
The Indian Serenade.

36 Nothing in the world is single;
All things by a law divine
In one spirit meet and mingle.
Why not I with thine?
Love's Philosophy.

37 Hell is a city much like London –
A populous and a smoky city.
Peter Bell the Third, III. Hell, 1.

38 When a man marries, dies, or turns
Hindoo,
His best friends hear no more of him.
Letter to Maria Gisborne, 235.

1 A Sensitive Plant in a garden grew,
And the young winds fed it with silver
dew.   *The Sensitive Plant, I. 1.*

2 That orbed maiden with white fire
laden,
Whom mortals call the moon,
Glides glimmering o'er my fleece-like
floor,
By the midnight breezes strewn.
The Cloud.

3 I am the daughter of earth and water,
And the nursling of the sky;
I pass through the pores of the ocean and
shores;
I change, but I cannot die.   *Ibid.*

4 Hail to thee, blithe spirit!
Bird thou never wert.   *To a Skylark.*

5 And singing still dost soar, and soaring
ever singest.   *Ibid.*

6 Like an unbodied joy whose race is just
begun.   *Ibid.*

7 We look before and after
And pine for what is not:
Our sincerest laughter
With some pain is fraught;
Our sweetest songs are those that tell of
saddest thought.   *Ibid.*

8 I fear thy kisses, gentle maiden,
Thou needest not fear mine;
My spirit is too deeply laden
Ever to burden thine.
To —. I fear thy Kisses.

9 I dreamed that, as I wandered by the
way,
Bare winter suddenly was changed the
spring,
And gentle odours led my steps astray,
Mixed with a sound of waters
murmuring.   *The Question.*

10 There grew pied wind-flowers and
violets,
Daisies, those pearled Arcturi of the
earth,
The constellated flower that never sets.
Ibid.

11 Art thou pale for weariness
Of climbing heaven and gazing on the
earth,
Wandering companionless
Among the stars that have a different
birth, –
And ever changing, like a joyless eye
That finds no object worth its
constancy?   *To the Moon.*

12 As long as skies are blue, and fields are
green,
Evening must usher night, night urge
the morrow,
Month follow month with woe, and
year wake year to sorrow.
Adonais, 21.

13 A pardlike spirit beautiful and swift.
Ibid, 32.

14 He has outsoared the shadow of our
night;
Envy and calumny and hate and pain,
And that unrest which men miscall
delight,
Can touch him not and torture not
again;
From the contagion of the world's slow
stain
He is secure, and now can never mourn
A heart grown cold, a head grown grey
in vain.   *Ibid, 40.*

15 He is a portion of the loveliness
Which once he made more lovely.
Ibid, 43.

16 The One remains, the many change and
pass;
Heaven's light forever shines, Earth's
shadows fly;
Life, like a dome of many-coloured
glass,
Stains the white radiance of eternity.
Ibid, 52.

17 The soul of Adonais, like a star,
Beacons from the abode where the
Eternal are.   *Ibid, 55.*

18 Swiftly walk over the western wave,
Spirit of Night!   *To Night.*

19 Music, when soft voices die,

Vibrates in the memory –
Odours, when sweet violets sicken,
Live within the sense they quicken.
           To —. Music, when Soft voices die.

20 Rarely, rarely, comest thou,
   Spirit of Delight!   *Song.*

21 The desire of the moth for the star,
   Of the night for the morrow,
   The devotion to something afar
   From the sphere of our sorrow.
       To —. One Word is too often profaned.

22 When the lamp is shattered
   The light in the dust lies dead –
   When the cloud is scattered
   The rainbow's glory is shed.
   When the lute is broken,
   Sweet tones are remembered not;
   When the lips have spoken,
   Loved accents are soon forgot.
           Lines: When the Lamp is shattered.

23 Forms more real than living man,
   Nurslings of immortality!
           Prometheus Unbound, I. 737.

24   All love is sweet,
   Given or returned. Common as light is
      love,
   And its familiar voice wearies not ever.

   They who inspire it are most fortunate,
   As I am now; but those who feel it most
   Are happier still.   *Ibid, II. v. 40.*

25 The world's great age begins anew,
   The golden years return,
   The earth doth like a snake renew
   Her winter weeds outworn:
   Heaven smiles, and faiths and empires
      gleam,
   Like wrecks of a dissolving dream.
                      Hellas, 1060

26 Oh, cease! must hate and death return?
   Cease! must men kill and die?
   Cease! drain not to its dregs the urn
   Of bitter prophecy.
   The world is weary of the past,
   Oh, might it die or rest at last!
                      Ibid, 1096.

27 Poetry is the record of the best and

happiest moments of the happiest and
best minds.   *A Defence of Poetry.*

28 Poets are the unacknowledged
   legislators of the world.   *Ibid.*

29 It might make one in love with death, to
   think that one should be buried in so
   sweet a place.   *Adonais, preface.*

SHERIDAN, HELEN SELINA, Countess of Dufferin, 1807–13 June, 1867

30 I'm sitting on the stile, Mary,
   Where we sat, side by side.
           The Lament of the Irish Emigrant.

31 They say there's bread and work for all,
   And the sun shines always there –
   But I'll not forget old Ireland,
   Were it fifty times as fair!   *Ibid.*

SHERIDAN, PHILIP HENRY, US General, 6 March, 1831–5 Aug. 1888

32 If I owned Texas and Hell, I would rent
   out Texas and live in Hell.
           At officers' mess, Fort Clark,
                      Texas, 1855.

SHERIDAN, RICHARD BRINSLEY, English dramatist and politician, 30 Oct. 1751–7 July, 1816

33 Illiterate him, I say, quite from your
   memory. (Mrs. Malaprop.)
                      The Rivals, I. ii.

34 'Tis safest in matrimony to begin with a
   little aversion. (Same.)   *Ibid.*

35 A progeny of learning. (Same.)   *Ibid.*

36 If I reprehend anything in this world, it
   is the use of my oracular tongue, and a
   nice derangement of epitaphs. (Same.)
                      Ibid, III. iii.

37 As headstrong as an allegory on the
   banks of the Nile. (Same.)

38 No caparisons, miss, if you please.
   Caparisons don't become a young
   woman. (Same.)   *Ibid, IV. ii.*

1 You are not like Cerberus, three gentlemen at once, are you? (Same.)
Ibid.

2 My valour is certainly going! – it is sneaking off! – I feel it oozing out as it were at the palms of my hands!
Ibid, V. iii.

3 I own the soft impeachment. (Mrs. Malaprop.)
Ibid.

4 Had I a heart for falsehood framed, I ne'er could injure you.
The Duenna, I. v.

5 You shall see them on a beautiful quarto page, where a neat rivulet of text shall meander through a meadow of margin.
The School for Scandal, I. i.

6 Here's to the maiden of bashful fifteen;
Here's to the widow of fifty;
Here's to the flaunting extravagant quean,
And here's to the housewife that's thrifty.
Let the toast pass, –
Drink to the lass.
I'll warrant she'll prove an excuse for the glass.
Ibid, III. iii.

7 An unforgiving eye, and a damned disinheriting countenance! *Ibid, IV. i.*

8 No scandal about Queen Elizabeth, I hope? *The Critic, II. i.*

9 The Spanish fleet thou canst not see – because
– It is not yet in sight! *Ibid, ii.*

10 All that can be said is, that two people happened to hit on the same thought – and Shakespeare made use of it first, that's all. *Ibid, III. i.*

11 An oyster may be crossed in love! *Ibid.*

12 You write with ease, to show your breeding,
But easy writing's curst hard reading.
Clio's Protest.

13 The Right Honourable gentleman is indebted to his memory for his jests, and to his imagination for his facts.
Replying to Mr. Dundas, in the House of Commons.

SHIRLEY, JAMES, English dramatist, born 18 Sept. 1596, buried 29 Oct. 1666

14 The glories of our blood and state
Are shadows, not substantial things;
There is no armour against fate;
Death lays his icy hand on kings:
Sceptre and crown
Must tumble down,
And in the dust be equal made
With the poor crooked scythe and spade.
The Contention of Ajax and Ulysses, iii.

15 Only the actions of the just
Smell sweet, and blossom in their dust.
Ibid.

SIDNEY, SIR PHILIP, English soldier, statesman, and poet, 30 Nov. 1554–17 Oct. 1586

16 My true love hath my heart and I have his,
By just exchange one for the other given. *Arcadia, III.*

17 Have I caught my heav'nly jewel.
Astrophel and Stella, song ii.

18 'Fool!' said my Muse to me, 'look in thy heart, and write.' *Ibid, sonnet i.*

19 With how sad steps, O Moon, thou climb'st the skies!
How silently, and with how wan a face!
Ibid, sonnet xxxi.

20 Come Sleep! O Sleep, the certain knot of peace,
The baiting-place of wit, the balm of woe,
The poor man's wealth, the prisoner's release,
Th' indifferent judge between the high and low. *Ibid, sonnet xxxix.*

21 With a tale forsooth he cometh unto you, with a tale which holdeth children

from play, and old men from the
chimney corner.   *The Defence of Poesy.*

22 Thy necessity is yet greater than mine.
*On giving his water-bottle to a wounded
soldier, when he himself had received his
death wound at the battle of Zutphen,
22 Sept. 1586.*

**SIMONIDES OF CEOS, Greek
poet, 556?–468? B.C.**

23 ω ξεῖν', αγγειλον Λακεδαιμονίοις οτι
τῇδε κείμεθα, τοῖς κείνων ρήμασι
πειθόμενοι.
– Stranger, tell the Lacedaemonians that
we lie here obedient to their orders.
*Epitaph on the Spartan dead at
Thermopylae.*

**SKELTON, JOHN, English poet,
1460?–21 June, 1529**

24 With solace and gladness,
Much mirth and no madness
All good and no badness;
So joyously,
So maidenly,
So womanly
Her demeaning.
To Mistress Margaret Hussey.

25 Steadfast of thought,
Well made, well wrought,
Fare may be sought,
Ere that y can find
So courteous, so kind,
As merry Margaret,
This midsummer flower,
Gentle as falcon,
Or hawk of the tower.   *Ibid.*

**SMART, CHRISTOPHER, English
poet, 11 April, 1722–21 May, 1771**

26 Strong is the lion – like a coal
His eyeball – like a bastion's mole
His chest against his foes.
Song to David, 76.

27 And now the matchless deed's achiev'd,
Determined, dared, and done.   *Ibid, 84.*

**SMILES, SAMUEL, English social
reformer, 23 Dec. 1812–16 April,
1904**

28 We often discover what *will* do, by
finding out what will not do; and
probably he who never made a mistake
never made a discovery.   *Self-Help, xi.*

29 A place for everything, and everything
in its place.   *Thrift, v.*

**SMITH, ADAM, Scottish political
economist, 5 June, 1723–17 July,
1790**

30 To found a great empire for the sole
purpose of raising up a people of
customers may at first sight appear a
project fit only for a nation of
shopkeepers. It is, however, a project
altogether unfit for a nation of
shopkeepers; but extremely fit for a
nation whose Government is influenced
by shopkeepers.
Wealth of Nations, II. IV. vii. 3.

**SMITH, ALEXANDER, Scottish
poet, 31 Dec. 1830–5 Jan. 1867**

31 Like a pale martyr in his shirt of fire.
A Life Drama, ii.

32 In winter, when the dismal rain
Came down in slanting lines,
And Wind, that grand old harper, smote
His thunder-harp of pines.   *Ibid.*

**SMITH, ARABELLA EUGENIA,
US teacher, 1844–24 July, 1916**

33 If I should die to-night,
My friends would look upon my quiet
face,
Before they laid it in its resting-place,
And deem that death had left it almost
fair.   *If I should die to-night.*

**SMITH, F. E., see Birkenhead, 1st
Earl of**

**SMITH, GOLDWIN, English
historian, 13 Aug. 1823–7 June, 1910**

34 King Nebuchadnezzar was turned out to
grass

With oxen, horses and the savage ass.
The King surveyed the unaccustomed
 fare
With an inquiring but disdainful air
And murmured as he cropped the
 unwonted food,
'It may be wholesome but it is not
 good.'
 Lines parodying Newdigate Prize poems.

SMITH, HORACE, English parodist, 31 Dec. 1779–12 July, 1849

1 Who makes the quartern loaf and
 Luddites rise?
 Who fills the butchers' shops with large
 blue flies?
 (Parody of W. T. Fitzgerald.)
  Rejected Addresses, i. Loyal Effusion.

2 'What are they fear'd on? fool! 'od rot
 'em!'
 Were the last words of Higginbottom.
 (Parody of Scott.)
  Ibid, ix. A Tale of Drury Lane.

3 In the name of the Prophet – figs!
  Ibid, x. Johnson's Ghost.

SMITH, JAMES, English parodist, 10 Feb. 1775–24 Dec. 1839

4 I saw them go: one horse was blind,
 The tails of both hung down behind,
 Their shoes were on their feet.
 (Parody of Wordsworth.)
  Rejected Addresses, ii. The Baby's Début.

5 John Richard William Alexander Dwyer
 Was footman to Justinian Stubbs,
 Esquire.
 (Parody of Crabbe.)
  Ibid, xvii. The Theatre.

SMITH, JOHN, GOVERNOR OF VIRGINIA, baptised 9 Jan. 1580, died 21 June, 1631

6 Why should the brave Spanish soldier
 brag, The sun never sets in the Spanish
 dominions, but ever shineth on one part
 or other we have conquered for our
 king?
  Advertisements for the Unexperienced
    Planters, xv.

SMITH, LANGDON, US journalist, 4 Jan. 1858–1908

7 When you were a tadpole and I was a
 fish,
 In the Palaeozoic time. *Evolution.*

SMITH, LOGAN PEARSALL, Anglo-American author, 18 Oct. 1865–2 March, 1946

8 There are two things to aim at in life:
 first, to get what you want; and after
 that, to enjoy it. Only the wisest of
 mankind achieve the second.
  Afterthoughts, i. Life and Human Nature.

9 A best-seller is the gilded tomb of a
 mediocre talent.
  Ibid, v. Art and Letters.

10 People say that life is the thing, but I
 prefer reading. *Ibid, vi. Myself.*

SMITH, SAMUEL FRANCIS, US clergyman, 21 Oct. 1808–16 Nov. 1895

11 My country, 'tis of thee,
 Sweet land of liberty,
 Of thee I sing:
 Land where my fathers died,
 Land of the pilgrims' pride,
 From every mountain-side
 Let freedom ring. *America.*

SMITH, SYDNEY, English clergyman, 3 June, 1771–22 Feb. 1845

12 We shall generally find that the
 triangular person has got into the square
 hole, the oblong into the triangular, and
 a square person has squeezed himself
 into the round hole.
  Sketches of Moral Philosophy, ix.

13 The motto I proposed for the
 (*Edinburgh*) *Review* was: *Tenui musam
 meditamur avena* – 'We cultivate
 literature upon a little oatmeal.'
  Works, I. preface.

14 The attempt of the Lords to stop the progress of reform reminds me very forcibly of the great storm of Sidmouth, and of the conduct of the excellent Mrs. Partington on that occasion.
Speech, Taunton, 11 Oct. 1831.

15 I have no relish for the country; it is a kind of healthy grave.
Letter to Miss G. Harcourt, 1838.

16 Poverty is no disgrace to a man, but it is confoundedly inconvenient.
Wit and Wisdom of Rev. Sydney Smith, 89.

17 It requires a surgical operation to get a joke well into a Scotch understanding.
Lady Holland's A Memoir of the Rev. Sydney Smith, I. ii.

18 I heard him speak disrespectfully of the Equator.
Ibid.

19 That garret of the earth – that knuckle-end of England – that land of Calvin, oatcakes, and sulphur. (Scotland.) *Ibid.*

20 As the French say, there are three Sexes, – men, women, and clergymen.
Ibid, ix.

21 Heat, ma'am! It was so dreadful here, that I found there was nothing left for it but to take off my flesh and sit in my bones. *Ibid.*

22 Live always in the best company when you read. *Ibid, x.*

23 He (Macaulay) has occasional flashes of silence, that make his conversation perfectly delightful. *Ibid.*

24 I never read a book before reviewing it; it prejudices a man so.
H. Pearson, The Smith of Smiths, iii.

25 Serenely full, the epicure would say, Fate cannot harm me, – I have dined to-day. *Recipe for Salad.*

SMOLLETT, TOBIAS GEORGE, Scottish novelist, baptised 19 March, 1721, died 17 Sept. 1771

26 He was formed for the ruin of our sex.
Roderick Random, xxii.

27 Hark ye, Clinker, you are a most notorious offender. You stand convicted of sickness, hunger, wretchedness, and want.
Humphrey Clinker, letter to Sir Watkin Phillips, 24 May.

28 The Great Cham of literature, Samuel Johnson.
Letter to John Wilkes, 16 March, 1759.

SOLON, Greek lawgiver, 640?–558? B.C.

29 Γηράσκω δ' αιεὶ πολλὰ διδασκόμενος.
– But I grow old always learning many things. *Plutarch, Solon, xxxi.*

SOMERVILLE, WILLIAM, English poet, 2 Sept. 1675–17 July, 1742

30 The chase, the sport of kings; Image of war, without its guilt.
The Chase, i. 13.

SOPHOCLES, Greek dramatist, 495?–406 B.C.

31 Πολλὰ τὰ δεινὰ κουδὲν ανθ ρῶπου δεινότερον πέλει.
– Wonders are many, and nothing is more wonderful than man.
Antigone, 332.

32 'Ἔρως ανίκατε μάχαν.
– Love, unconquered in battle.
Ibid, 781.

33 'Ἔφη αυτὸς μὲν οιους δεῖ ποιεῖν, Ευριπίδην δὲ οιοι εισίν.
– I portray men as they ought to be portrayed, but Euripides portrays them as they are.
Aristotle, Poetics, xxv.

SOUTHERNE, THOMAS, English dramatist, 1660–22 May, 1746

34 Pity's akin to love. *Oroonoko, II. ii.*

SOUTHEY, ROBERT, English Poet Laureate, 12 Aug. 1774– 21 March, 1843

35 How beautiful is night!

A dewy freshness fills the silent air;
No mist obscures, nor cloud, nor speck, nor stain,
Breaks the serene of heaven.
Thalaba the Destroyer, I. I.

1 And Sleep shall obey me,
And visit thee never,
And the Curse shall be on thee
For ever and ever.
The Curse of Kehama, II. 14.

2 My days among the Dead are past;
Around me I behold,
Where'er these casual eyes are cast,
The mighty minds of old;
My never-failing friends are they,
With whom I converse day by day.
(Written in his library.)
My Days among the Dead are Past.

3 How does the water
Come down at Lodore?
The Cataract of Lodore.

4 It was a summer evening,
Old Kaspar's work was done,
And he before his cottage door
Was sitting in the sun,
And by him sported on the green
His little grandchild Wilhelmine.
The Battle of Blenheim.

5 'But what good came of it at last?'
Quoth little Peterkin.
'Why, that I cannot tell,' said he,
'But 'twas a famous victory.' *Ibid.*

6 Till the vessel strikes with a shivering shock, –
'Oh Christ! it is the Inchcape Rock!'
The Inchcape Rock.

7 Sir Ralph the Rover tore his hair;
He curst himself in his despair. *Ibid.*

8 You are old, Father William, the young man cried,
The few locks which are left you are grey;
You are hale, Father William, a hearty old man,
Now tell me the reason, I pray.
The Old Man's Comforts.

9 From his brimstone bed at break of day
A walking the Devil is gone,
To look at his little snug farm of the World,
And see how his stock went on.
The Devil's Walk, 1.

10 His coat was red and his breeches were blue,
And there was a hole where his tail came through. *Ibid, 3.*

11 He pass'd a cottage with a double coach-house,
A cottage of gentility!
And he own'd with a grin
That his favourite sin
Is pride that apes humility. *Ibid, 8.*

12 Blue, darkly deeply beautifully blue,
In all its rich variety of shades.
Madoc in Wales, v. Lincoya, 102.

13 The Satanic School.
The Vision of Judgment, preface.

14 The march of intellect.
Colloquies on the Progress and Prospects of Society, xiv.

SOUTHWELL, ROBERT, English Jesuit and poet, 1561?–21 Feb. 1595

15 As I in hoary winter's night stood shivering in the snow,
Surprised I was with sudden heat which made my heart to glow;
And lifting up a fearful eye to view what fire was near,
A pretty Babe all burning bright did in the air appear. *The Burning Babe.*

SPENCER, HERBERT, English philosopher, 27 April, 1820–8 Dec. 1903

16 Education has for its object the formation of character.
Social Statics, II. xvii. 4.

17 No one can be perfectly free till all are free; no one can be perfectly moral till all are moral; no one can be perfectly happy till all are happy. *Ibid, IV. xxx. 16.*

18 Science is organised knowledge.
Education, ii.

19 Survival of the fittest.
Principles of Biology, III. xii. Indirect Equilibration, 165, et passim.

20 The Republican form of government is the highest form of government; but because of this it requires the highest type of human nature – a type nowhere at present existing.
Essays. The Americans.

SPENCER, WILLIAM ROBERT, English poet, 1769–24 Oct. 1834

21 Too late I stayed – forgive the crime;
Unheeded flew the hours;
How noiseless falls the foot of Time
That only treads on flowers!
Lines to Lady Anne Hamilton.

SPENSER, EDMUND, English Poet Laureate, 1552?–16 Jan. 1599

22 To Kerke the narre, from God more farre,
Has bene an old-sayd sawe,
And he, that strives to touch a starre,
Oft stombles at a strawe.
The Shepheard's Calender, Julye, 97.

23 A gentle Knight was pricking on the plaine.   *The Faerie Queene, I. i. I.*

24 And on his breast a bloodie Crosse he bore,
The deare remembrance of his dying Lord.   *Ibid, 2.*

25 The noblest mind the best contentment has.   *Ibid, 35.*

26 A bold bad man.   *Ibid, 37.*

27 Her angels face
As the great eye of heaven, shyned bright,
And made a sunshine in the shady place.
Ibid, iii. 4.

28 Sleepe after toyle, port after stormie seas,
Ease after warre, death after life,
does greatly please.   *Ibid, ix. 40.*

29 How over that same dore was likewise writ,
Be bolde, be bolde, and every where *Be bold.*

Another yron dore, on which was writ,
Be not too bold.   *Ibid, xi. 54.*

30 Dan Chaucer, well of English undefyled,
On Fames eternall beadroll worthie to be fyled.   *Ibid, IV. ii. 32.*

31 Full little knowest thou, that hast not tride,
What hell it is in suing long to bide:
To loose good dayes, that might be better spent;
To wast long nights in pensive discontent;
To speed to day, to be put back to morrow;
To feed on hope, to pine with feare and sorrow;
To have thy Princes grace, yet want her Peeres;
To have thy asking, yet waite manie yeares;
To fret thy soule with crosses and with cares;
To easte thy heart though comfortlesse dispaires;
To fawne, to crowche, to waite, to ride, to ronne,
To spend, to give, to want, to be undonne.
Unhappie wight, borne to disastrous end,
That doth his life in son long tendance spend!   *Mother Hubbards Tale, 895.*

32 What more felicitie can fall to creature
Then to enjoy delight with libertie.
Muiopotmos, 209.

33 For of the soule the bodie forme doth take;
The soule is forme, and doth the bodie make.
An Hymn in Honour of Beautie, 132.

34 The woods shall to me answer, and my Eccho ring.   *Epithalamion, 18.*

1 Sweet Themmes! runne softly, till I end
   my Song. *Prothalamion, 18.*

2 At length they all to mery London
   came,
   To mery London, my most kyndly
   Nurse. *Ibid, 127.*

3 I was promis'd on a time,
   To have reason for my rhyme;
   From that time unto this season,
   I received nor rhyme nor reason.
   Lines on his promised pension.

**SPOONER, WILLIAM
ARCHIBALD, Warden of New
College, Oxford, 22 July, 1844–
29 Aug. 1930**

4 Kinquering Congs their titles take.
   *Announcing hymn in New College chapel,
   1879.*

5 Let us drink to the queer old Dean.
   Attributed.

6 Sir, you have tasted two whole worms;
   you have hissed all my mystery lectures
   and been caught fighting a liar in the
   quad; you will leave by the next town
   drain. *Ibid.*
   (The first of the above is said to be the
   only genuine 'spoonerism', all others
   being invented.)

**SPRING-RICE, SIR CECIL
ARTHUR, English diplomatist,
27 Feb. 1859–14 Feb. 1918**

7 I vow to thee, my country – all earthly
   things above –
   Entire and whole and perfect the service
   of my love. *I vow to thee, my Country.*

8 And her ways are ways of gentleness,
   and all her paths are peace. *Ibid.*

**SQUIRE, SIR JOHN COLLINGS,
English author, 2 April, 1884–
20 Dec. 1958**

9 It did not last: the Devil howling *Ho,
   Let Einstein be,* restored the status quo.
   *Answer to Pope's couplet on Newton,
   199:20.*

10 But I'm not so think as you drunk I am.
   Ballade of Soporific Absorption.

**STANLEY, SIR HENRY
MORTON, English explorer,
29 June, 1841–10 May, 1904**

11 Dr. Livingstone, I presume?
   *On meeting him at Ujiji, Central Africa,
   10 Nov. 1871.*

**STANTON, CHARLES E., US
soldier, 1859–1933**

12 Lafayette, we are here.
   *Address on behalf of the American
   Expeditionary Force, at the tomb of
   Lafayette, 4 July, 1917.*
   (Often wrongly attributed to General
   Pershing.)

**STANTON, EDWIN
McMASTERS, US statesman,
19 Dec. 1814–24 Dec. 1869**

13 Now he belongs to the ages.
   At the deathbed of President Lincoln.

**STANTON, FRANK LEBBY, US
author, 22 Feb. 1857–7 Jan. 1927**

14 Sweetes' li'l' feller –
   Everybody knows;
   Dunno what ter call 'im,
   But he mighty lak' a rose!
   Sweetes' Li'l' Feller.

**STEELE, SIR RICHARD, Irish
author, baptised 12 March, 1672,
died 1 Sept. 1729.**

15 Though her mien carries much more
   invitation than command, to behold her
   is an immediate check to loose
   behaviour; to love her is a liberal
   education. *The Tatler, 49.*

16 The insupportable labour of doing
   nothing. *Ibid, 54.*

17 Reading is to the mind what exercise is
   to the body. *Ibid, 147.*

18 Will Honeycomb calls these over-
   offended ladies the outrageously
   virtuous. *The Spectator, 266.*

STEPHEN, JAMES KENNETH, English parodist, 25 Feb. 1859–3 Feb. 1892

19 Two voices are there: one is of the deep;
It learns the storm-cloud's thunderous melody,
Now roars, now murmurs with the changing sea,
Now bird-like pipes, now closes soft in sleep;
And one is of an old half-witted sheep
Which bleats articulate monotony,
And indicates that two and one are three,
That grass is green, lakes damp, and mountains steep:
And, Wordsworth, both are thine.
Lapsus Calami. A Sonnet.

20 When the Rudyards cease from Kipling
And the Haggards Ride no more.
Ibid, To R. K.

21 Ah! Matt.; old age has brought to me
Thy wisdom, less thy certainty;
The world's a jest, a joy's a trinket:
I knew that once: but now – I think it.
Ibid, Senex to Matt. Prior.

STERNE, LAURENCE, English clergyman and author, 24 Nov. 1713–18 March, 1768

22 Go, poor devil, get thee gone; why should I hurt thee? This world surely is wide enough to hold both thee and me. (Uncle Toby to the fly.)
Tristram Shandy, II. xii.

23 'Our armies swore terribly in Flanders,' cried my Uncle Toby, 'but nothing to this.'
Ibid, III. xi.

24 Of all the cants which are canted in this canting world, though the cant of hypocrites may be the worst, the cant of criticism is the most tormenting!
Ibid, xii.

25 'He shall not die, by G —,' cried my uncle Toby. – The Accusing Spirit, which flew up to heaven's chancery with the oath, blushed as he gave it in; and the Recording Angel, as he wrote it down, dropped a tear upon the word, and blotted it out for ever.
Ibid, VI. viii.

26 'They order,' said I, 'this matter better in France.'
A Sentimental Journey, I.

27 'God tempers the wind,' said Maria, 'to the shorn lamb.'
Ibid, Maria.

STEVENS, GEORGE ALEXANDER, English author, 1710–6 Sept. 1784

28 Cease, rude Boreas, blustering railer!
List, ye landsmen, all to me;
Messmates, hear a brother sailor
Sing the dangers of the sea.
The Storm.

STEVENSON, ROBERT LOUIS, Scottish author, 13 Nov. 1850–3 Dec. 1894

29 In marriage, a man becomes slack and selfish, and undergoes a fatty degeneration of his moral being.
Virginibus Puerisque, i.

30 Times are changed with him who marries; there are no more by-path meadows, where you may innocently linger, but the road lies long and straight and dusty to the grave.
Ibid, ii.

31 To marry is to domesticate the Recording Angel. Once you are married, there is nothing left for you, not even suicide, but to be good.
Ibid.

32 The cruellest lies are often told in silence.
Ibid, iv.

33 Old and young, we are all on our last cruise.
Ibid, Crabbed Age and Youth.

34 For God's sake give me the young man who has brains enough to make a fool of himself!
Ibid.

35 Books are good enough in their own way, but they are a mighty bloodless substitute for life.
Ibid, An Apology for Idlers.

1 Extreme *busyness*, whether at school or college, kirk or market, is a symptom of deficient vitality.   *Ibid.*

2 There is no duty we so much underrate as the duty of being happy.   *Ibid.*

3 Even if the doctor does not give you a year, even if he hesitates about a month, make one brave push and see what can be accomplished in a week.
                    Ibid, Aes Triplex.

4 To travel hopefully is a better thing than to arrive, and the true success is to labour.   *Ibid, El Dorado.*

5 I have thus played the sedulous ape to Hazlitt, to Lamb, to Wordsworth, to Sir Thomas Browne, to Defoe, to Hawthorne, to Montaigne, to Baudelaire and to Obermann.
                    Memories and Portraits, iv.

6 A Penny Plain and Twopence Coloured.
                    Ibid.

7 Here lies one who meant well, tried a little, failed much:– surely that may be his epitaph, of which he need not be ashamed.
                    Across the Plains. A Christmas Sermon.

8 Give us grace and strength to forbear and to persevere. Give us courage and gaiety and the quiet mind, spare us to our friends, soften to us our enemies.
                    Prayer.

9 Fifteen men on the Dead Man's Chest–
   Yo-ho-ho, and a bottle of rum!
   Drink and the devil had done for the rest –
   Yo-ho-ho, and a bottle of rum!
                    Treasure Island, i.

10 Tip me the black spot.   *Ibid, iii.*

11 Am I no a bonny fighter? (Alan Breck.)
                    Kidnapped, x.

12 Nothing like a little judicious levity. (Michael Finsbury.)
                    The Wrong Box, vii.
   (Written by Stevenson and his stepson Lloyd Osborne.)

13 In winter I get up at night
   And dress by yellow candle-light.
   In summer, quite the other way,
   I have to go to bed by day.
                    A Child's Garden of Verses: Bed in Summer.

14 A child should always say what's true,
   And speak when he is spoken to,
   And behave mannerly at table:
   At least as far as he is able.
                    Ibid, Whole Duty of Children.

15 When I am grown to man's estate
   I shall be very proud and great,
   And tell the other girls and boys
   Not to meddle with my toys.
                    Ibid, Looking Forward.

16 The pleasant land of counterpane.
                    The Land of Counterpane.

17 The friendly cow, all red and white,
   I love with all my heart:
   She gives me cream with all her might
   To eat with apple-tart.   *Ibid, The Cow.*

18 The world is so full of a number of things,
   I'm sure we should all be as happy as kings.   *Ibid, Happy Thought.*

19 And ever again, in the wink of an eye,
   Painted stations whistle by.
                    Ibid, From a Railway Carriage.

20 Go, little book, and wish to all,
   Flowers in the garden, meat in the hall,
   A bin of wine, a spice of wit,
   A house with lawns enclosing it,
   A living river by the door,
   A nightingale in the sycamore!
                    Underwoods, I. Envoy.

21 Under the wide and starry sky,
   Dig the grave and let me lie.
   Glad did I live and gladly die,
   And I laid me down with a will.

22 This be the verse you grave for me:
Here he lies where he longed to be;
Home is the sailor, home from sea,
And the hunter home from the hill.
Ibid, Requiem.

23 If I have faltered more or less
In my great task of happiness.
Ibid, The Celestial Surgeon.

24 Lord, thy most pointed pleasure take
And stab my spirit broad awake;
Or, Lord, if too obdurate I,
Choose thou, before that spirit die,
A piercing pain, a killing sin,
And to my dead heart run them in! *Ibid.*

25 The untented Kosmos my abode,
I pass, a wilful stranger:
My mistress still the open road
And the bright eyes of danger.
Ibid, Youth and Love.

26 I will make you brooches and toys for
your delight
Of bird-song at morning and star-shine
at night. *Ibid, xi.*

27 In the highlands, in the country places,
Where the old plain men have rosy
faces,
And the young fair maidens
Quiet eyes. *Ibid, xvi.*

28 Trusty, dusky, vivid, true,
With eyes of gold and bramble-dew,
Steel-true and blade-straight,
The great artificer
Made my mate. *Ibid. My Wife.*

29 Blows the wind to-day, and the sun and
the rain are flying,
Blows the wind on the moors to-day
and now,
Where about the graves of the martyrs
the whaups are crying,
My heart remembers how!
Ibid, To S. R. Crockett.

**STEVENSON, WILLIAM, Fellow
of Christ's College, Cambridge,
1530?–1575**

30 I cannot eat but little meat,
My stomach is not good;

But sure I think that I can drink
With him that wears a hood.
Though I go bare, take ye no care,
I am nothing a-cold:
I stuff my skin so full within
Of jolly good ale and old.
Back and side go bare, go bare,
Both foot and hand go cold;
But belly, God send thee good ale
enough,
Whether it be new or old.
Gammer Gurton's Needle, II. song.
(The authorship of this is disputed.)

**STIRLING, EARL OF, see
Alexander, Sir William**

**STONE, SAMUEL JOHN, English
clergyman, 25 April, 1839–19 Nov.
1900**

31 The Church's one foundation
Is Jesus Christ her Lord.

**STOWE, HARRIET ELIZABETH
BEECHER, U.S. authoress, 14 June
1811–1 July, 1896**

32 'Never was born!' persisted Topsy;
'never had no father, nor mother, nor
nothin'. I was raised by a speculator.'
Uncle Tom's Cabin, xx.

33 'Do you know who made you?'
'Nobody, as I knows on,' said the child,
with a short laugh . . . . 'I 'spect I
grow'd. Don't think nobody never
made me. *Ibid.*

34 I's wicked – I is. I's mighty wicked,
anyhow. I can't help it. *Ibid.*

**STOWELL, BARON, see Scott,
William**

**SUCKLING, SIR JOHN, English
poet, baptised 10 Feb. 1609, died
1642**

35 Her feet beneath her petticoat
Like little mice, stole in and out,
As if they fear'd the light.
Ballad upon a Wedding.

36 Her lips were red, and one was thin,

Compar'd to that was next her chin
(Some bee had stung it newly).   *Ibid*

1 Why so pale and wan, fond lover?
 Prithee, why so pale?
 Will, when looking well can't move her,
 Looking ill prevail?
                          Aglaura, iv. i. song.

2 Quit, quit, for shame, this will not
 move,
 This cannot take her;
 If of herself she will not love,
 Nothing can make her:
 The Devil take her!   *Ibid.*

3 Out upon it, I have loved
 Three whole days together
 And am like to love three more,
 If it prove fair weather.
                          A Poem with the Answer.

**SURREY, HENRY HOWARD, Earl
of, 1517?–21 Jan. 1547**

4 The soote season, that bud and bloom
 forth brings,
 With green hath clad the hill, and eke the
 vale.   *Description of Spring.*

5 But oft the words come forth awry of
 him that loveth well.
 *Description of the Fickle Affections, Pangs,
 and Slights of Love*

**SURTEES, ROBERT SMITH,
English sporting novelist, 1803–
16 March, 1864**

6 Full o' beans and benevolence!
                          Handley Cross, xxvii

7 Hellish dark, and smells of cheese!
                          Ibid, 1.

8 There is no secret so close as that
 between a rider and his horse.
                          Mr. Sponge's Sporting Tour, xxxi.

9 The only infallible rule we know is, that
 the man who is always talking about
 being a gentleman never is one.
                          Ask Mamma, i.

**SWIFT, JONATHAN, Dean of St.
Patrick's, Irish satirist, 30 Nov.
1667–19 Oct. 1745**

10 Read all the prefaces of Dryden,
 For them our critics much confide in,
 (Tho' merely writ at first for filling
 To raise the volume's price, a shilling).
                          On Poetry, 251.

11 Hobbes clearly proves that every
 creature
 Lives in a state of war by nature.
                          Ibid, 319

12 So, naturalists observe, a flea
 Hath smaller fleas that on him prey;
 And these have smaller fleas to bite 'em,
 And so proceed *ad infinitum*.
                          Ibid, 337.

13 Yet malice never was his aim;
 He lash'd the vice, but spared the name;
 No individual could resent,
 Where thousands equally were meant.
                          On the Death of Dr. Swift, 512.

14 The two noblest of things, which are
 sweetness and light.
                          The Battle of the Books, preface.

15 He (the Emperor) is taller by almost the
 breadth of my nail than any of his court,
 which alone is enough to strike an awe
 into the beholders.
                          Gulliver's Travels. Voyage to Lilliput, ii.

16 And he gave it for his opinion, that
 whoever could make two ears of corn or
 two blades of grass to grow upon a spot
 of ground where only one grew before,
 would deserve better of mankind, and
 do more essential service to his country,
 than the whole race of politicians put
 together.
                          Ibid, Voyage to Brobdingnag, vii.

17 He had been eight years upon a project
 for extracting sunbeams out of
 cucumbers, which were to be put into
 vials hermetically sealed, and let out to
 warm the air in raw inclement summers.
                          Ibid, Voyage to Laputa, v.

18 I said the thing which was not.
                          Ibid, Voyage to the Houyhnhms, iii.

19 I have been assured by a very knowing American of my acquaintance in London, that a young healthy child well nursed is at a year old a most delicious, nourishing, and wholesome food, whether stewed, roasted, baked, or boiled, and I make no doubt that it will equally serve in a fricassee, or a ragout.
A Modest Proposal for preventing the Children of Ireland from being a Burden to their Parents or Country.

20 The reason why so few marriages are happy, is, because young ladies spend their time in making nets, not in making cages. *Thoughts on Various Subjects.*

21 A nice man is a man of nasty ideas. *Ibid.*

22 Proper words in proper places, make the true definition of a style.
Letter to a young clergyman, 9 Jan. 1720.

23 Not die here in a rage, like a poisoned rat in a hole.
Letter to Bolingbroke, 21 March, 1729.

24 Good God! what a genius I had when I wrote that book. (Of 'The Tale of a Tub.')
Walter Scott, Memoirs of Jonathan Swift, ii.

25 I shall be like that tree, I shall die at the top. *Ibid., vii.*

26 Ubi saeva indignatio ulterius cor lacerare nequit. – Where fierce indignation can no more tear his heart.
Inscription on Swift's grave.

SWINBURNE, ALGERNON CHARLES, English poet, 5 April, 1837–10 April, 1909

27 I have put my days and dreams out of mind,
Days that are over, dreams that are done. *The Triumph of Time.*

28 The strong sea-daisies feast on the sun. *Ibid.*

29 I will go back to the great sweet mother, Mother and lover of men, the sea.

I will go down to her, I and no other, Close with her, kiss her and mix her with me. *Ibid.*

30 I shall never be friends again with roses. *Ibid.*

31 Let us go hence, my songs; she will not hear. *A Leave-taking.*

32 I have lived long enough, having seen one thing, that love hath an end;
Goddess and maiden and queen, be near me now and befriend.
Hymn to Proserpine.

33 Yea, is not even Apollo, with hair and harpstring of gold,
A bitter God to follow, a beautiful God to behold? *Ibid.*

34 Thou hast conquered, O pale Galilean; the world has grown grey from Thy breath. *Ibid.*

35 Kissing her hair I sat against her feet. *Rondel.*

36   Change in a trice
The lilies and languors of virtue
For the raptures and roses of vice.
Dolores.

37 O splendid and sterile Dolores, Our Lady of Pain. *Ibid.*

38 From too much love of living,
From hope and fear set free,
We thank with brief thanksgiving
Whatever gods may be
That no life lives for ever;
That dead men rise up never;
That even the weariest river
Winds somewhere safe to sea.
The Garden of Proserpine.

39 Shall I strew on thee rose or rue or laurel?
Ave atque vale. In memory of Charles Baudelaire.

40 Glory to Man in the Highest! for Man is the master of things. *Hymn of Man.*

41 Maiden, and mistress of the months and stars

Now folded in the flowerless fields of
heaven. *Atalanta in Calydon.*

1 When the hounds of spring are on
winter's traces,
The mother of months in meadow or
plain
Fills the shadows and windy places
With lisp of leaves and ripple of rain.
Ibid, Chorus.

2 And in green underwood and cover
Blossom by blossom the spring begins.
Ibid.

3 He weaves, and is clothed with derision;
derision;
Sows, and he shall not reap;
His life is a watch or a vision
Between a sleep and a sleep. *Ibid.*

4 Hope thou not much, and fear thou not
at all. *Hope and Fear.*

**SYMONDS, JOHN
ADDINGTON, English critic,
5 Oct. 1840–19 April, 1893**

5 These things shall be! A loftier race
Than e'er the world hath known, shall
rise,
With flame of freedom in their souls
And light of knowledge in their eyes.
New and Old. A Vista.

**SYMONS, ARTHUR, English poet
and critic, 28 Feb. 1865–22 Jan. 1945**

6 I have ever held that the rod with which
popular fancy invests criticism is
properly the rod of divination: a hazel-
switch for the discovery of buried
treasure, not a birch-twig for the
castigation of offenders.
*An Introduction to the Study of Browning,
preface.*

**TACITUS, CORNELIUS, Roman
historian, 55?–117?**

7 Omne ignotum pro magnifico est. –
Everything unknown is taken as
marvellous. *Agricola, xxx.*

8 Ubi solitudinem faciunt, pacem

appellant. – Where they make a desert,
they call it peace. *Ibid.*

9 Felix . . . opportunitate mortis. –
Fortunate in the occasion of his death
Ibid, xlv.

10 Omnium consensu capax imperit
imperasset. – Would by all have been
reckoned competent to rule, had he not
been emperor.
(Of Galba.) *Histories, I. xlix*

11 Sine ira et studio. – without rancour or
partiality. *Annals, I. i*

**TALFOURD, SIR THOMAS
NOON, English judge and author,
26 May, 1795–13 March, 1854**

12 'Tis a little thing
To give a cup of water; yet its draught
Of cool refreshment, drain'd by fever'd
lips,
May give a shock of pleasure to the
frame
More exquisite than when nectarean
juice
Renews the life of joy in happiest hours.
Ion, I. ii.

**TALLEYRAND–PÉRIGORD,
CHARLES MAURICE DE, French
statesman, 13 Feb. 1754–17 May,
1838**

13 C'est le commencement de la fin. – It is
the beginning of the end.
*Remark to Napoleon after battle of Leipzig,
18 Oct. 1813.*

14 Vous ne jouez donc pas le whist,
monsieur? Hélas! quelle triste vieillesse
vous vous preparez! – You do not then
play whist, sir? Alas, what a sad old age
you are preparing for yourself!
When reproached for his addiction to cards.

15 Ils n'ont rien appris, ni rien oublié. –
They have learned nothing and
forgotten nothing. *Attributed.*

16 Pas trop de zèle. – Not too much zeal.
Ibid.

17 Noir comme le diable,
Chaud comme l'enfer,
Pur comme un ange,
Doux comme l'amour.
– Black as the devil,
Hot as hell,
Pure as an angel,
Sweet as love. *Recipe for coffee.*

TANNAHILL, ROBERT, Scottish poet, 3 June, 1774–17 May, 1810

18 She's modest as ony, and blithe as she's
bonny;
For guileless simplicity marks her its ain:
And far be the villain, divested of
feeling,
Wha'd blight in its bloom the sweet
flower o' Dumblane.
The Flower o' Dumblane.

19 When gloamin treads the heels o' day,
And birds sit courin on the spray,
Alang the flow'ry hedge I stray,
To meet mine ain dear somebody.
Mine ain Dear Somebody.

TATE, NAHUM, Irish author, Poet Laureate, 1652–12 Aug. 1715

20 Permit the transports of a British Muse,
And pardon raptures that yourselves
infuse.
As Poet Laureate to the Parliament, 1701.

TAYLOR, ANNE (MRS. GILBERT), English poetess, 30 Jan. 1782–20 Dec. 1866

21 Who ran to help me when I fell,
And would some pretty story tell,
Or kiss the place to make it well?
My Mother.
Original Poems. My Mother.

22 Meddlesome Matty. *Ibid, Title.*

23 I thank the goodness and the grace
Which on my birth have smiled,
And made me, in these Christian days,
A happy English child.
Hymns for Infant Minds. A Child's Hymn
of Praise.

TAYLOR, BAYARD, US author, 11 Jan. 1825–19 Dec. 1878

24 Till the sun grows cold,
And the stars are old,
And the leaves of the Judgment Book
unfold. *Bedouin Song.*

TAYLOR, SIR HENRY, English author, 18 Oct. 1800–27 March, 1886

25 The world knows nothing of its greatest
men. *Philip Van Artefelde, part I. I. v.*

26 He that lacks time to mourn, lacks time
to mend. *Ibid.*

27 Such souls,
Whose sunken visitations daze the
world,
Vanish like lightning, but they leave
behind
A voice that in the distance far away
Wakens the slumbering ages. *Ibid, vii.*

TAYLOR, JANE, English poetess, 23 Sept. 1783–13 April, 1824

28 Twinkle, twinkle, little star,
How I wonder what you are!
Up above the world so high,
Like a diamond in the sky!
Rhymes for the Nursery. The Star.

TAYLOR, JEREMY, Bishop of Down and Connor, baptised 15 Aug. 1613, died 13 Aug. 1667

29 The sun reflecting upon the mud of
strands and shores is unpolluted in his
beam. *Holy Living, i. 3.*

30 Desperate by too quick a sense of
constant infelicity. *Holy Dying, i. 5.*

31 He that loves not his wife and children,
feeds a lioness at home and broods a
nest of sorrows.
Sermons. Married Love.

TEASDALE, SARA (MRS. ERNST B. FILSINGER), US poetess, 8 Aug. 1884–29 Jan. 1933

32 When I am dead and over me bright
April
Shakes out her rain-drenched hair.
I shall not care.

1 Redbud, buckberry,
  Wild plum-tree
  And proud river sweeping
  Southward to the sea.   *Redbirds.*

2 Strephon's kiss was lost in jest,
  Robin's lost in play,
  But the kiss in Colin's eyes
  Haunts me night and day.   *The Look.*

TEMPLE, SIR WILLIAM, English statesman and author, 1628–27 Jan. 1699

3 When all is done, human life is, at the
  greatest and the best, but like a froward
  child, that must be played with and
  humoured a little to keep it quiet till it
  falls asleep, and then the care is over.
                                  Essay on Poetry.

TENNYSON, ALFRED TENNYSON, 1ST BARON, English Poet Laureate, 6 Aug. 1809–6 Oct. 1892

4 Her court was pure; her life serene;
  God gave her peace; her land reposed;
  A thousand claims to reverence closed
  In her as Mother, Wife, and Queen.
                                  To the Queen.

5 Airy, fairy Lilian.   *Lilian.*

6 She only said, 'My life is dreary,
  He cometh not,' she said;
  She said, 'I am aweary, aweary,
  I would that I were dead!'   *Mariana.*

7 Dower'd with the hate of hate, the scorn
  of scorn,
  The love of love.   *The Poet.*

8 He thought to quell the stubborn hearts
  of oak,
  Madman!   *Buonaparte.*

9 A happy bridesmaid makes a happy
  bride.   *The Bridesmaid.*

10 To many-tower'd Camelot.
                          The Lady of Shalott, i.

11 'The curse is come upon me,' cried
   The Lady of Shalott.   *Ibid, iii.*

12 Across the walnuts and the wine.
                          The Miller's Daughter.

13 O mother Ida, many-fountained Ida,
   Dear mother Ida, hearken ere I die.
                                Oenone, 22.

14 Self-reverence, self-knowledge, self-
   control.
   These three alone lead life to sovereign
   power.   *Ibid, 142.*

15 Her manners had not that repose
   Which stamps the caste of Vere de Vere.
                      Lady Clara Vere de Vere.

16 Kind hearts are more than coronets,
   And simple faith than Norman blood.
                                    Ibid.

17 You must wake and call me early, call
   me early, mother dear;
   To-morrow 'ill be the happiest time of
   all the glad New Year;
   Of all the glad New Year, mother, the
   maddest merriest day;
   For I'm to be Queen o' the May,
   mother, I'm to be Queen o' the May.
                                The May Queen.

18   A land
   In which it seemed always afternoon.
                              The Lotos-Eaters.

19 Music that gentlier on the spirit lies,
   Than tir'd eyelids upon tir'd eyes.
                          Ibid, Choric Song, i.

20 The spacious times of great Elizabeth.
                      A Dream of Fair Women, 7.

21 A daughter of the gods, divinely tall,
   And most divinely fair.   *Ibid, 87.*

22 A land of settled government,
   A land of just and old renown,
   Where freedom slowly broadens down
   From precedent to precedent.
                              You ask me why.

23 She stood, a sight to make an old man
   young.   *The Gardener's Daughter, 140.*

24 In teacup-times of hood and hoop,
   Or while the patch was worn.
                          The Talking Oak, 16.

25 And drunk delight of battle with my
 peers,
 Far on the ringing plains of windy Troy.
 Ulysses, 16.

26 I am a part of all that I have met.
 Ibid, 18.

27 To follow knowledge like a sinking star,
 Beyond the utmost bound of human
 thought. *Ibid, 31.*

28 To strive, to seek, to find, and not to
 yield. *Ibid, 70.*

29 The woods decay, the woods decay and
 fall,
 The vapours weep their burthen to the
 ground,
 Man comes and tills the field and lies
 beneath,
 And after many a summer dies the
 swan. *Tithonus, I.*

30 The Gods themselves cannot recall their
 gifts. *Ibid, 49.*

31 In the Spring a livelier iris changes on
 the burnish'd dove;
 In the Spring a young man's fancy
 lightly turns to thoughts of love.
 Locksley Hall, 19.

32 He will hold thee, when his passion shall
 have spent its novel force,
 Something better than his dog, a little
 dearer than his horse. *Ibid, 49.*

33 This is truth the poet sings,
 That a sorrow's crown of sorrow is
 remembering happier things.
 Ibid, 75.

34 Heard the heavens fill with shouting,
 and there rain'd a ghastly dew
 From the nations' airy navies grappling
 in the central blue. *Ibid, 123.*

35 Till the war-drum throbb'd no longer,
 and the battle-flags were furl'd,
 In the Parliament of man, the Federation
 of the world. *Ibid, 127.*

36 Knowledge comes, but wisdom lingers.
 Ibid, 141.

37 Woman is the lesser man, and all thy
 passions, match'd with mine,
 Are as moonlight unto sunlight, and as
 water unto wine. *Ibid, 151.*

38 Let the great world spin for ever down
 the ringing grooves of change. *Ibid, 182.*

39 Better fifty years of Europe than a cycle
 of Cathay. *Ibid, 184.*

40 And o'er the hills, and far away,
 Beyond their utmost purple rim,
 Beyond the night, across the day,
 Thro' all the world she follow'd him.
 The Departure.

41 Make Thou my spirit pure and clear
 As are the frosty skies,
 Or this first snowdrop of the year
 That in my bosom lies. *St. Agnes' Eve.*

42 My strength is as the strength of ten,
 Because my heart is pure. *Sir Galahad.*

43 O plump head-waiter at The Cock
 To which I most resort,
 How goes the time? 'Tis five o'clock.
 Go fetch a pint of port.
 Will Waterproof's Lyrical Monologue, 1.

44 Cophetua sware a royal oath:
 'This beggar maid shall be my queen!'
 The Beggar Maid.

45 He clasps the crag with crooked hands.
 The Eagle.

46 The wrinkled sea beneath him crawls.
 Ibid.

47 God made Himself an awful rose of
 dawn. *The Vision of Sin, iii. and v.*

48 Break, break, break,
 On thy cold grey stones, O Sea!
 And I would that my tongue could utter
 The thoughts that arise in me.
 Break, break, break.

49 And the stately ships go on
 To their haven under the hill;
 But O for the touch of a vanish'd hand,
 And the sound of a voice that is still!
 Ibid.

1 But the tender grace of a day that is dead
Will never come back to me. *Ibid.*

2 The myriad shriek of wheeling ocean-
fowl,
The league-long roller thundering on
the reef. *Enoch Arden, 579.*

3 And when they buried him the little port
Had seldom seen a costlier funeral.
Ibid, 910.

4 I chatter, chatter, as I flow
To join the brimming river,
For men may come and men may go,
But I go on for ever. *The Brook.*

5 What does little birdie say
In her nest at peep of day?
Sea Dreams, 281.

6 With prudes for proctors, dowagers for
deans,
And sweet girl-graduates in their golden
hair. *The Princess, prologue, 141.*

7 A rosebud set with little wilful thorns,
And sweet as English air could make
her, she. *Ibid, 153.*

8 And blessings on the falling out
That all the more endears,
When we fall out with those we love
And kiss again with tears!
Ibid, ii. song.

9 Jewels five words long
That on the stretch'd forefinger of all
Time
Sparkle for ever. *Ibid, 355.*

10 Sweet and low, sweet and low,
Wind of the western sea. *Ibid, iii. song.*

11 The splendour falls on castle walls
And snowy summits old in story:
The long light shakes across the lakes,
And the wild cataract leaps in glory.
Blow, bugle, blow, set the wild echoes
flying,
Blow, bugle; answer, echoes, dying,
dying, dying. *Ibid, iv. song.*

12 The horns of Elfland faintly blowing.
Ibid.

13 Tears, idle tears, I know not what they
mean,
Tears from the depth of some divine
despair
Rise in the heart, and gather to the eyes,
In looking on the happy Autumn fields,
And thinking of the days that are no
more. *Ibid, song.*

14 Dear as remember'd kisses after death,
And sweet as those by hopeless fancy
feign'd
On lips that are for others; deep as love,
Deep as first love, and wild with all
regret;
O Death in Life, the days that are no
more. *Ibid.*

15 O Swallow, Swallow, flying, flying
South. *Ibid, song.*

16 O tell her, Swallow, thou that knowest
each,
That bright and fierce and fickle is the
South,
And dark and true and tender is the
North. *Ibid.*

17 Thy voice is heard thro' rolling drums,
That beat to battle where he stands.
Ibid, song.

18 Man is the hunter; woman is his game.
Ibid, v. 147.

19 Home they brought her warrior dead:
She nor swoon'd, nor utter'd cry:
All her maidens, watching, said,
'She must weep or she will die.'
Ibid, vi. song.

20 Rose a nurse of ninety years,
Set his child upon her knee –
Like summer tempest came her tears –
'Sweet my child, I live for thee.'
Ibid.

21 Ask me no more: the moon may draw
the sea. *Ibid, vii. song.*

22 Come down, O maid, from yonder
mountain height. *Ibid, 177.*

23 Myriads of rivulets hurrying thro' the
lawn,

The moan of doves in immemorial elms,
And murmuring of innumerable bees.
Ibid, 205.

24 Not once or twice in our rough island-story,
The path of duty was the way to glory:
He that walks it, only thirsting
For the right, and learns to deaden
Love of self, before his journey closes,
He shall find the stubborn thistle bursting
Into glossy purples, which outredden
All voluptuous garden-roses.
Ode on the Death of the Duke of Wellington, vii.

25 Half a league, half a league,
Half a league onward,
All in the valley of Death
Rode the six hundred.
The Charge of the Light Brigade.

26 Some one had blunder'd. *Ibid.*

27 Theirs not to make reply,
Theirs not to reason why,
Theirs but to do and die. *Ibid.*

28 Cannon to right of them,
Cannon to left of them,
Cannon in front of them
Volley'd and thunder'd. *Ibid.*

29 Sea-king's daughter from over the sea,
Alexandra! *A Welcome to Alexandra.*

30 And the parson made it his text that week, and he said likewise,
That a lie which is half a truth is ever the blackest of lies,
That a lie which is all a lie may be met and fought with outright,
But a lie which is part a truth is a harder matter to fight. *The Grandmother, 8.*

31 Bessy Marris's barne! tha knaws she laäid it to meä.
Mowt a beän, mayhap, for she wur a bad un, sheä.
Northern Farmer. Old Style.

32 Doänt thou marry for munny, but goä wheer munny is!
Northern Farmer. New Style.

33 All along the valley, stream that flashes white. *In the Valley of Cauteretz.*

34 Speak to Him thou for He hears, and Spirit with Spirit can meet –
Closer is He than breathing, and nearer than hands and feet.
The Higher Pantheism.

35 Flower in the crannied wall,
I pluck you out of the crannies,
I hold you here, root and all, in my hand,
Little flower – but *if* I could understand
What you are, root and all, and all in all,
I should know what God and man is.
Flower in the Crannied Wall.

36 O mighty-mouth'd inventor of harmonies,
O skill'd to sing of Time or Eternity,
God-gifted organ-voice of England,
Milton, a name to resound for ages.
Milton. Alcaics.

37 O you chorus of indolent reviewers.
Hendecasyllabics.

38 I hold it truth, with him who sings
To one clear harp in divers tones,
That men may rise on stepping-stones
Of their dead selves to higher things.
In Memoriam, i.

39 I do but sing because I must,
And pipe but as the linnets sing.
Ibid, xxi.

40 The Shadow cloak'd from head to foot,
Who keeps the keys of all the creeds.
Ibid, xxiii.

41 'Tis better to have loved and lost
Than never to have loved at all.
Ibid, xxvii.

42 O yet we trust that somehow good
Will be the final goal of ill. *Ibid, liv.*

43 But what am I?
An infant crying in the night:
An infant crying for the light:
And with nò language but a cry. *Ibid.*

44 Nature, red in tooth and claw. *Ibid, lvi.*

1 So many worlds, so much to do,
So little done, such things to be.
Ibid, lxxiii.

2 When rosy plumelets tuft the larch,
And rarely pipes the mounted thrush;
Or underneath the barren bush
Flits by the sea-blue bird of March.
Ibid, xci.

3 There lives more faith in honest doubt,
Believe me, than in half the creeds.
Ibid, xcvi.

4 Ring out the old, ring in the new,
Ring, happy bells, across the snow:
The year is going, let him go;
Ring out the false, ring in the true.
Ibid, cvi.

5 Ring out old shapes of foul disease;
Ring out the narrowing lust of gold;
Ring out the thousand wars of old,
Ring in the thousand years of peace.
Ibid.

6 And thus he bore without abuse
The grand old name of gentleman.
Ibid, cxi.

7 Move upward, working out the beast,
And let the ape and tiger die.
Ibid, cxviii.

8 One God, one law, one element,
And one far-off divine event,
To which the whole creation moves.
Ibid, conclusion.

9 Faultily faultless, icily regular, spendidly
null. *Maud, I. ii.*

10 That oil'd and curl'd Assyrian bull.
Ibid, vi. 6.

11 O let the solid ground
Not fail beneath my feet
Before my life has found
What some have found so sweet.
Ibid, xi. I.

12 Birds in the high Hall-garden
When twilight was falling,
Maud, Maud, Maud, Maud,
They were crying and calling.
Ibid, xii. I.

13 I know the way she went
Home with her maiden posy.
For her feet have touch'd the meadows
And left the daisies rosy. *Ibid, 6.*

14 Gorgonised me from head to foot
With a stony British stare. *Ibid, xiii. 2.*

15 Rosy is the West,
Rosy is the South,
Roses are her cheeks,
And a rose her mouth. *Ibid, xvii.*

16 There is none like her, none.
Ibid, xviiil. I.

17 Come into the garden, Maud,
For the black bat, night, has flown,
Come into the garden, Maud,
I am here at the gate alone. *Ibid, xxii. I.*

18 Queen rose of the rosebud garden of
girls. *Ibid, 9.*

19 She is coming, my own, my sweet;
Were it ever so airy a tread,
My heart would hear her and beat,
Were it earth in an earthy bed;
My dust would hear her and beat,
Had I lain for a century dead;
Would start and tremble under her feet,
And blossom in purple and red.
Ibid, 11.

20 O that 'twere possible
After long grief and pain
To find the arms of my true love
Round me once again! *Ibid, II. iv. 1.*

21 Wearing the white flower of a blameless
life,
Before a thousand peering littlenesses,
In that fierce light that beats upon a
throne. *Idylls of the King, dedication.*

22 Clothed in white samite, mystic,
wonderful.
Ibid, The Coming of Arthur, 284.
(Also *The Passing of Arthur*, 199)

23 From the great deep the great deep he
goes. *Ibid, 410.*

24   Lightly was her slender nose
Tip-tilted like the petal of a flower.
Ibid, Gareth and Lynette, 576.

25 It is the little rift within the lute,
That by and by will make the music
mute,
And ever widening slowly silence all.
Ibid, Merlin and Vivien, 388.

26 Dafaming and defacing, till she left
Not even Lancelot brave, nor Galahad
clean. *Ibid, 802.*

27 For men at most differ as Heaven and
earth,
But women, worst and best, as Heaven
and Hell. *Ibid, 812.*

28 Elaine the fair, Elaine the lovable,
Elaine, the lily maid of Astolat.
Ibid, Lancelot and Elaine, 1.

29   To me
He is all fault who hath no fault at all:
For who loves me must have a touch of
earth. *Ibid, 131.*

30   In me there dwells
No greatness, save it be some far-off
touch
Of greatness to know well I am not
great. *Ibid, 447.*

31 His honour rooted in dishonour stood,
And faith unfaithful kept him falsely
true. *Ibid, 871.*

32 He makes no friend who never made a
foe. *Ibid, 1082.*

33 Too late, too late! ye cannot enter now.
Ibid, Guinevere, 168.

34 To reverence the King, as if he were
Their conscience, and their conscience as
their King,
To break the heathen and uphold the
Christ,
To ride abroad redressing human
wrongs,
To speak no slander, no, nor listen to it.
Ibid, 465.

35 To love one maiden only, cleave to her,
And worship her by years of noble
deeds,
Until they won her. *Ibid, 472.*

36 We needs must love the highest when
we see it. *Ibid, 655.*

37 I found Him in the shining of the stars,
I mark'd Him in the flowering of His
fields,
But in His ways with men I find Him
not. *Ibid, The Passing of Arthur, 9.*

38 So all day long the noise of battle roll'd
Among the mountains by the winter
sea. *Ibid, 170.*

39 Authority forgets a dying king.
Ibid, 289.

40 When every morning brought a noble
chance,
And every chance brought out a noble
knight. *Ibid, 398.*

41 The old order changeth, yielding place
to new,
And God fulfils himself in many ways,
Lest one good custom should corrupt
the world. *Ibid, 408.*

42 If thou shouldst never see my face again,
Pray for my soul. More things are
wrought by prayer
Than this world dreams of. Wherefore,
let thy voice
Rise like a fountain for me night and
day. *Ibid, 414*

43 For so the whole round earth is every
way
Bound by gold chains about the feet of
God. *Ibid, 422.*

44 To the island-valley of Avilion;
Where falls not hail, or rain, or any
snow,
Nor ever wind blows loudly; but it lies
Deep-meadow'd, happy, fair with
orchard lawns,
And bowery hollows crown'd with
summer sea. *Ibid, 427.*

45 And the sun went down, and the stars
came out far over the summer sea.
The Revenge, ix.

46 God of battles, was ever a battle like this
in the world before? *Ibid.*

47 Sink me the ship, Master Gunner – sink
her, split her in twain!

Fall into the hands of God, not into the hands of Spain! *Ibid, xi.*

1 All the charm of all the Muses often flowering in a lonely word. *To Virgil.*

2 I salute thee, Mantovano, I that loved thee since my day began, Wielder of the stateliest measure ever moulded by the lips of man. *Ibid.*

3 Row us out from Desenzano, to your Sirmione row! So they row'd, and there we landed – 'O venusta Sirmio!' *'Frater ave atque vale.'*

4 Follow the Gleam. *Merlin and the Gleam.*

5 Sunset and evening star, And one clear call for me! And may there be no moaning of the bar, When I put out to sea. *Crossing the Bar.*

6 Twilight and evening bell, And after that the dark! And may there be no sadness of farewell When I embark. *Ibid.*

7 I hope to see my Pilot face to face When I have crost the bar. *Ibid.*

TERENCE (PUBLIUS TERENTIUS AFER), Roman dramatist, 195?–159 B.C.

8 Hinc illae lacrimae. – Hence these tears. *Andria – The Maid of Andros, 126.*

9 Davus sum, non Oedipus. – I'm Davus, not Oedipus. (i.e. I can't solve riddles.) *Ibid, 194.*

10 Amantium irae amoris integratio est. – The quarrels of lovers are the renewal of love. *Heauton Timoroumenos – The Self-Tormentor, 77.*

11 Quot homines, tot sententiae. – So many men, so many opinions. *Phormio, 454.*

TERTULLIAN (QUINTUS SEPTIMIUS FLORENS TERTULLIANUS), Roman theologian, A.D. 150?–220?

12 Certum est quia impossibile est. – It is certain because it is impossible. *De Carne Christi – Concerning the Flesh of Christ, II. v.* (Commonly misquoted 'Credo quia impossibile' – 'I believe because it is impossible.')

THACKERAY, WILLIAM MAKEPEACE, English novelist, 18 July, 1811–24 Dec. 1863

13 Fashnable fax and polite annygoats. *The Yellowplush Papers, part 1. title.*

14 There are some meannesses which are too mean even for man – woman, lovely woman alone, can venture to commit them. *A Shabby-Genteel Story, iii.*

15 This I set down as a positive truth. A woman with fair opportunities and without an absolute hump, may marry whom she likes. *Vanity Fair, iv.*

16 Them's my sentiments. *Ibid, xxi.*

17 Darkness came down on the field and city: and Amelia was praying for George who was lying on his face, dead, with a bullet through his heart. *Ibid, xxxii.*

18 I think I could be a good woman if I had five thousand a year. *Ibid, xxxvi.*

19 Ah! Vanitas Vanitatum! Which of us is happy in this world? Which of us has his desire? or, having it, is satisfied? – Come, children, let us shut up the box and the puppets, for our play is played out. *Ibid, last words.*

20 Remember, it's as easy to marry a rich woman as a poor woman. *Pendennis, xxviii.*

21 'Tis strange what a man may do, and a woman yet think him an angel. *Henry Esmond, vii.*

22 The true pleasure of life is to live with
your inferiors.   *The Newcomes, ix.*

23 What money is better bestowed than
that of a schoolboy's tip?   *Ibid, xvi.*

24 As the last bell struck, a peculiar sweet
smile shone over his face, and he lifted
up his head a little, and quickly said,
'Adsum!' and fell back. It was the word
we used at school, when names were
called; and lo, he, whose heart was as
that of a little child, had answered to
his name, and stood in the presence of
The Master.   *Ibid, lxxx.*

25 Dick (Idle) only began by playing pitch-
and-toss on a tomb-stone. . . . From
pitch-and-toss he proceeded to
manslaughter, if necessary: to highway
robbery; to Tyburn and the rope there.
       Roundabout Papers. Turnbridge Toys.

26 Little we fear
Weather without,
Sheltered about
The Mahogany Tree.
       The Mahogany Tree.

27 Charlotte, having seen his body
Borne before her on a shutter,
Like a well-conducted person,
Went on cutting bread-and-butter.
       The Sorrows of Werther.

28 Ho, pretty page, with the dimpled chin,
That never has known the barber's
   shear,
All your wish is woman to win,
This is the way that boys begin, –
Wait till you come to Forty Year.
       The Age of Wisdom.

29 There were three sailors of Bristol City
Who took a boat and went to sea.
       Little Billee.

30 There was gorging Jack and guzzling
   Jimmy,
And the youngest he was little Billee.
       Ibid.

**THAYER, ERNEST LAWRENCE,
US. Poet, 14 Aug. 1863–21 Aug.
1940**

31 Oh, somewhere in this favoured land
the sun is shining bright;
The band is playing somewhere, and
somewhere hearts are light,
And somewhere men are laughing, and
little children shout,
But there is no joy in Mudville – great
Casey has struck out.   *Casey at the Bat.*

**THEOCRITUS, Greek poet, 3rd
century B.C.**

32 ῎Εαρ θ' ορόωσα Νύχεια.
– And Nycheia with Spring in her eyes.
       Idylls, xiii. 45.

**THIBAULT, JACQUES
ANATOLE, see France, Anatole**

**THOMAS, PHILIP EDWARD,
English poet, 3 March, 1878–
9 April, 1917**

33 If I should ever by chance grow rich
I'll buy Codham, Cockridden, and
   Childerditch,
Roses, Pyrgo, and Lapwater,
And let them all to my elder daughter.
       If I should ever by Chance.

**THOMPSON, FRANCIS, English
poet, 18 Dec. 1859–13 Nov. 1907**

34 The hills look over on the South,
And southward dreams the sea;
And with the sea-breeze hand in hand
Came innocence and she.   *Daisy.*

35 Summer set lip to earth's bosom bare,
And left the flushed print in a poppy
there.   *The Poppy.*

36 Look for me in the nurseries of Heaven.
       To my Godchild.

37 I fled Him, down the nights and down
the days;
I fled Him, down the arches of the years;
I fled Him, down the labyrinthine ways
Of my own mind, and in the mist of
tears

I hid from Him, and under running
laughter. *The Hound of Heaven.*

1 Virtue may unlock hell, or even
A sin turn in the wards of Heaven
(As ethics of the text-book go),
So little men their own deeds know.
Epilogue to 'A Judgment in Heaven.'

2   Thou canst not stir a flower
Without troubling of a star.
The Mistress of Vision.

3 O world invisible, we view thee,
O world intangible, we touch thee,
O world unknowable, we know thee.
The Kingdom of God.

4   Upon thy so sore loss
Shall shine the traffic of Jacob's ladder
Pitched betwixt Heaven and Charing
Cross. *Ibid.*

5 Know you what it is to be a child? . . . It
is to believe in love, to believe in
loveliness, to believe in belief; it is to be
so little that the elves can reach to
whisper in your ear; it is to turn
pumpkins into coaches, and mice into
horses, lowness into loftiness, and
nothing into everything, for each child
has its fairy godmother in its own soul.
Shelley.

6 The universe is his box of toys. He
dabbles his fingers in the day-fall. He is
gold-dusty with tumbling amidst the
stars. He makes bright mischief with the
moon. (Of Shelley.) *Ibid.*

**THOMPSON, WILLIAM
HEPWORTH, Master of Trinity
College, Cambridge, 27 March,
1810–1 Oct. 1886**

7 We're none of us infallible – not even the
youngest among us.
Remark to a Junior Fellow.

**THOMSON, JAMES, Scottish poet,
11 Sept. 1700–27 Aug. 1748**

8 Come, gentle Spring, ethereal mildness,
come. *The Seasons. Spring, 1.*

9 Delightful task! to rear the tender
thought,
To teach the young idea how to shoot.
Ibid, 1152.

10 An elegant sufficiency, content
Retirement, rural quiet, friendship,
books,
Ease and alternate labour, useful life,
Progressive virtue, and approving
Heaven! *Ibid, 1161..*

11 Or sighed and looked unutterable
things. *Ibid, Summer, 1188.*

12 While Autumn nodding o'er the yellow
plain
Comes jovial on. *Ibid, Autumn, 2.*

13   Loveliness
Needs not the foreign aid of ornament,
But is when unadorned adorned the
most. *Ibid, 204.*

14   There studious let me sit,
And hold high converse with the
mighty dead –
Sages of ancient time, as gods revered.
Ibid, Winter, 431.

15 The kiss, snatched hasty from the
sidelong maid. *Ibid, 625.*

16 A pleasing land of drowsyhed it was:
Of dreams that wave before the half-
shut eye;
And of gay castles in the clouds that
pass,
For ever flushing round a summer sky.
The Castle of Indolence, i. 6.

17 A little, round, fat, oily man of God.
Ibid, 69.

18 Oh! Sophonisba, Sophonisba, Oh!
Sophonisba, III. ii.
(Altered after the second edition to
O Sophonisba! I am wholly thine.)

19 When Britain first, at Heaven's
command,
Arose from out the azure main,
This was the charter of the land,
And guardian angels sung this strain –
'Rule, Britannia, rule the waves;

Britons never will be slaves.'
Alfred: a Masque, II. v.
(Authorship also claimed for David
Mallet, who collaborated with Thomson
in the masque.)

THOMSON, JAMES, Scottish poet, 23 Nov. 1834–3 June, 1882

20 As we rush, as we rush in the train,
The trees and the houses go wheeling
back,
But the starry heavens above that plain
Come flying on our track.
Sunday at Hampstead, x.

21 Give a man a pipe he can smoke,
Give a man a book he can read:
And his home is bright with a calm
delight,
Though the room be poor indeed.
Gifts.

22 The City is of Night; perchance of
Death,
But certainly of Night.
The City of Dreadful Night.

THOREAU, HENRY DAVID, US essayist, 12 July, 1817–6 May, 1862

23 The mass of men lead lives of quiet
desperation. *Walden. Economy.*

24 I have lived some thirty years on this
planet, and I have yet to hear the first
syllable of valuable or even earnest
advice from my seniors. *Ibid.*

25 Beware of all enterprises that require
new clothes. *Ibid.*

26 Simplify, simplify.
Ibid, Where I lived and what I lived for.

27 I never found the companion that was so
companionable as solitude.
Ibid, Solitude.

28 Love your life, poor as it is. You may
perhaps have some pleasant, thrilling,
glorious hours, even in a poorhouse.
Ibid, Conclusion.

29 Some circumstantial evidence is very

strong, as when you find a trout in the
milk. *Journal, 11 Nov. 1854.*

30 That man is the richest whose pleasures
are the cheapest. *Ibid, 11 March, 1856.*

THORPE, ROSE HARTWICK, US authoress, 18 July, 1850–19 July, 1939

31 As she climbed the dusty ladder on
which fell no ray of light, – Up and up,
her white lips saying, Curfew shall not
ring to-night.'
Curfew must not ring to-night.

THRING, GODFREY, English clergyman, 25 March, 1823–13 Sept. 1903

32 Fierce raged the tempest o'er the deep.
Hymn.

THUCYDIDES, Greek historian, 460?–400? B.C.

33 Κτῆμα ες αεί
– A possession for ever.
History, I. xxii.

THURLOW, EDWARD THURLOW, 2ND BARON, English poet, 10 June, 1781–4 June, 1829

34 Did you ever expect a corporation to
have a conscience, when it has no soul to
be damned, and no body to be kicked?
Attributed.

TICKELL, THOMAS, English poet, 1686–23 April, 1740

35 There taught us how to live; and (oh!
too high
The price for knowledge) taught us how
to die.
On the Death of Mr. Addison, 81.

36 I hear a voice you cannot hear,
Which says I must not stay;
I see a hand you cannot see,
Which beckons me away.
Colin and Lucy.

TILLOTSON, JOHN ROBERT, Archbishop of Canterbury, baptised 10 Oct. 1630, died 22 Nov. 1694

1 If God were not a necessary Being of himself, He might almost seem to be made for the use and benefit of men.
Sermon 93.

TOBIN, JOHN, English dramatist, 28 Jan. 1770–8 Dec. 1804

2 The man who lays his hand upon a woman,
Save in the way of kindness, is a wretch
Whom 'twere gross flattery to name a coward. *The Honeymoon, II. i.*

TOLSTOY, COUNT LEO NIKOLAIEVICH, Russian author, 9 Sept. 1828–21Nov. 1910

3 Pure and complete sorrow is as impossible as pure and complete joy.
War and Peace, XV i

4 All happy families resemble one another; every unhappy family is unhappy in its own way.
Anna Karenina, I. i.

TOPLADY, AUGUSTUS MONTAGUE, English clergyman, 4 Nov. 1740–14 Aug. 1778

5 Rock of Ages, cleft for me,
Let me hide myself in Thee.
Rock of Ages.

TRAHERNE, THOMAS, English poet, 1637?–27 Sept. 1674

6 You never enjoy the world aright, till the sea itself floweth in your veins, till you are clothed with the heavens, and crowned with the stars.
Centuries of Meditation, i. 29.

7 The Men! O what venerable and reverend creatures did the aged seem! Immortal Cherubims! And the young men glittering and sparkling Angels, and maids strange seraphic pieces of life and beauty! Boys and girls tumbling in the street, and playing, were moving jewels. *Ibid, iii. 3.*

TRAILL, HENRY DUFF, English author, 14 Aug. 1842–21 Feb. 1900

8 Look in my face. My name is Used-to-was;
I am also called Played-out and Done-to-death,
And It-will-wash-no-more.
After Dilettante Concetti, viii.
(Parody of D.G. Rossetti, 206:17.)

TRAPP, JOSEPH, Professor of Poetry at Oxford, Nov. 1679–22 Nov. 1747

9 The King, observing with judicious eyes,
The state of both his universities,
To Oxford sent a troop of horse, and why?
That learned body wanted loyalty;
To Cambridge books, as very well discerning
How much that loyal body wanted learning.
Epigram on George I's donation of a library to Cambridge.
(Sir William Browne's answer is 35:29 *supra*.)

TRENCH, FREDERIC HERBERT, Irish poet, 26 Nov. 1865–11 June, 1923

10 Come let us make love deathless, thou and I. *To Ardilia, vi.*

11 But when Night is on the hills, and the great Voices
Roll in from sea,
By starlight and by candlelight and dreamlight
She comes to me.
Ibid, ix. She comes not when Noon is on the Roses.

12 O dreamy, gloomy, friendly Trees.
Poem.

TRENCH, RICHARD CHENEVIX, Archbishop of Dublin, 5 Sept. 1807–28 March, 1886

13 England, we love thee better than we know. *Gibraltar.*

TROLLOPE, ANTHONY, English novelist, 24 April, 1815–6 Dec. 1882

14 Not only humble but umble, which I look upon to be the comparative, or, indeed, superlative degree.
Doctor Thorne, iv.

15 A Man who desires to soften another man's heart, should always abuse himself. In softening a woman's heart, he should abuse her.
Last Chronicle of Barset, xliv.

16 It's dogged as does it. *Ibid, lxi.*

TRUMBULL, JOHN, US poet, 13 April, 1750–11 May, 1831

17 For any man with half an eye
What stands before him may espy;
But optics sharp it needs, I ween,
To see what is not to be seen.
McFingal, i. 65.

18 What has posterity done for us,
That we, lest they their rights should lose,
Should trust our necks to gripe of noose? *Ibid, ii. 124.*

TUER, ANDREW WHITE, English publisher, 24 Dec. 1838–24 Feb. 1900

19 English as she is spoke.
Title of reprint of Portuguese-English conversation guide.

TUPPER, MARTIN FARQUHAR, English author, 17 July, 1810– 29 Nov. 1889

20 Well-timed silence hath more eloquence than speech.
Proverbial Philosophy, 1st series. Of Discretion.

21 A good book is the best of friends, the same to-day and for ever.
Ibid, Of Reading

22 A babe in a house is a well-spring of pleasure. *Ibid, Of Education.*

TURGENEV, IVAN SERGEIEVITCH, Russian novelist, 9 Nov. 1818–3 Sept. 1883

23 I agree with no man's opinions. I have some of my own.
Fathers and Sons, xiii.

24 Go and try to disprove death. Death will disprove you, and that's all!
Ibid, xxvii.

25 Whatever a man prays for, he prays for a miracle. Every prayer reduces itself to this: 'Great God, grant that twice two be not four.' *Prayer.*

TURNER, WILLIAM JAMES REDFERN, English poet, 13 Oct. 1889–18 Nov. 1946

26 When I was but thirteen or so
I went into a golden land,
Chimborazo, Cotopaxi
Took me by the hand. *Romance.*

TWAIN, MARK (SAMUEL LANGHORNE CLEMENS), US author, 30 Nov. 1835–21 April, 1910

27 They spell it Vinci and pronounce it Vinchy; foreigners always spell better than they pronounce.
The Innocents Abroad, xix.

28 This poor little one-horse town.
Sketches. The Undertaker's Chat.

29 The statements was interesting, but tough.
The Adventures of Huckleberry Finn, xvii.

30 Cauliflower is nothing but cabbage with a college education.
Pudd'nhead Wilson's Calendar.

31 In Boston they ask, How much does he know? In New York, How much is he worth? In Philadelphia, Who were his parents?
What Paul Bourget thinks of us.

32 There ain't a-going to *be* no core.
Tom Sawyer Abroad, i.

1 A classic is something that everybody
wants to have read and nobody wants
to read.
Speeches. The Disappearance of Literature.

2 The reports of my death are greatly
exaggerated.
Cable from Europe to the Associated Press.

UDALL, NICHOLAS, English schoolmaster, born 1505, buried 23 Dec. 1556

3 As long liveth the merry man (they say)
As doth the sorry man, and longer by a
day. *Ralph Roister Doister, 1. i.*

UMBERTO I, King of Italy, 14 March, 1844–29 July, 1900

4 È un incidente del mestiere. – It is one of
the incidents of the profession.
After escaping assassination.

UNTERMEYER, LOUIS, US author, 1 Oct. 1885–21 Dec. 1977

5 God, though this life is but a wraith,
Although we know not what we use,
Although we grope with little faith,
Give me the heart to fight – and lose.
Prayer.

VANBRUGH or VANBURGH, SIR JOHN, English dramatist and architect, baptised 24 Jan. 1664, died 26 March, 1726

6 Much of a Muchness.
The Provoked Husband, 1. i.

VANDIVER, WILLARD DUNCAN, US Congressman, 30 March, 1854–30 May, 1932

7 I come from a state that raises corn and
cotton and cockleburs and Democrats,
and frothy eloquence neither convinces
nor satisfies me. I am from Missouri.
You have got to show me.
*Speech at a naval banquet in Philadelphia,
1899.*

VAUGHAN, HENRY, Welsh poet, 17 April, 1622–23 April, 1695

8 'Tis now clear day: I see a rose
Bud in the bright east, and disclose
The pilgrim sun. *The Search.*

9 Happy those early days! when I
Shin'd in my angel-infancy.
Before I understood this place
Appointed for my second race,
Or taught my soul to fancy aught
But a white celestial thought.
The Retreat.

10 And in those weaker glories spy
Some shadows of eternity. *Ibid.*

11 But felt through all this fleshy dress
Bright shoots of everlastingness. *Ibid.*

12 My soul, there is a country
Far beyond the stars. *Peace.*

13 I saw Eternity the other night,
Like a great ring of pure and endless
light,
All calm, as it was bright;
And round beneath it, Time in hours,
days, years,
Driv'n by the spheres
Like a vast shadow mov'd; in which the
world
And all her train were hurl'd.
The World.

14 They are all gone into the world of light,
And I alone sit lingering here.
They are all gone.

15 I see them walking in an air of glory,
Whose light doth trample on my days;
My days, which are at best but dull and
hoary,
Mere glimmering and decays. *Ibid.*

16 I cannot reach it; and my striving eye
Dazzles at it, as at eternity. *Childhood.*

VAUX OF HARROWDEN, THOMAS VAUX, 2nd Baron, 1510–Oct. 1556

17 For Age with stealing steps,
Hath clawed me with his clutch.
The Aged Lover renounceth Love.

VERE, EDWARD DE, see Oxford

**VICTORIA, QUEEN OF
ENGLAND, 24 May, 1819–22 Jan.
1901**

18 We are not amused.
When an equerry told a questionable story at Windsor.

**VILLIERS, GEORGE, see
Buckingham, 2nd Duke of**

**VILLON, FRANÇOIS, French poet,
1431–1485?**

19 Mais où sont les neiges d'antan?
– But where are the snows of yester-year?
*Ballade des dames du temps jadis –
Ballade of Old-time Ladies.*

**VINCENT OF LERINS, Saint, died
A.D. 450?**

20 Quod semper, quod ubique, quod ab omnibus creditum est.
– What always, what everywhere, what by everyone has been believed.
(Definition of catholicity.)
Commonitorium, ii.

**VIRGIL or VERGIL (PUBLIUS
VERGILIUS MARO), Roman poet,
15 Oct. 70–21 Sept. 19 B.C.**

21 Tityre, tu patulae recubans sub tegmine fagi
Silvestrem tenui musam meditaris avena.
– You, Tityrus, reclining under cover of a spreading beech tree, practise the woodland muse on a slender reed.
Eclogues (Bucolics), i. 1.

22 Et penitus toto divisos orbe Britannos.
– And the Britons wholly sundered from all the world. *Ibid, 66.*

23 Arcades ambo.
– Arcadians both. *Ibid, vii. 4.*

24 Non omnia possumus omnes.
–We cannot all do all things. *Ibid, viii. 63.*

25 Ultima Thule.
– Farthest Thule. *Georgics, I. 30.*

26 Felix, qui potuit rerum cognoscere causas.
– Happy he who has been able to learn the causes of things. *Ibid, II. 490.*

27 Sed fugit interea, fugit irreparabile tempus.
– But meanwhile it is flying, time is flying that cannot be recalled. *Ibid, III. 284.*

28 Arma virumque cano.
– Arms and the man I sing. *Aeneid, I. i.*

29 Forsan et haec olim meminisse juvabit.
– Perhaps even these things it will some day give pleasure to recall. *Ibid, 203.*

30 Mens sibi conscia recti.
– A mind conscious of its rectitude. *Ibid, 604.*

31 Non ignara mali miseris succurrere disco.
– Not ignorant of ill do I learn to aid the wretched. *Ibid, 630.*

32 Timeo Danaos et dona ferentes.
– I fear the Greeks even when they bring gifts. *Ibid, II. 49.*

33 In utrumque paratus.
– Prepared for either event. *Ibid, 61.*

34 Crimine ab uno
Disce omnes.
– From one piece of villainy judge them all. *Ibid, 65.*

35 Horresco referens.
– I shudder to recall it. *Ibid, 204.*

36 Tacitae per amica silentia lunae.
– Amid the friendly silence of the still moon. *Ibid, 255.*

37 Quantum mutatus ab illo.
– How changed from him whom we knew. *Ibid, 274.*

1 Dis aliter visum.
– The will of the gods was otherwise.
Ibid, 428.

2 Auri sacra fames.
– Accursed hunger for gold.
Ibid, III. 57.

3 Monstrum horrendum, informe,
ingens, cui lumen ademptum.
– A monster frightful, shapeless, huge,
bereft of sight. *Ibid., 658.*

4   Varium et mutabile semper
Femina.
– A fickle and changeable thing is
woman ever. *Ibid., IV. 569.*

5 Possunt, quia posse videntur.
– They are able because they seem to be
able. *Ibid., V. 231.*

6   Facilis descensus Averno:
Noctes atque dies patet atri janua Ditis;
Sed revocare gradum, superasque
evadere ad auras,
Hoc opus, hic labor est.
– Easy is the descent to Avernus; night
and day stands open the gate of gloomy
Pluto; but to recall the step, and pass out
to the upper air – this is the toil, this the
labour. *Ibid., VI. 126.*

7 Parcere subjectis et debellare superbos.
– To spare the humbled and subdue the
proud. *Ibid., 853.*

8 O mihi praeteritos referat si Juppiter
annos.
– O, if Jupiter would restore to me the
years that are past! *Ibid., VIII. 560.*

9 Macte nova virtute, puer, sic itur ad
astra.
– Good luck to your youthful valour,
boy. Such is the way to the stars.
Ibid., IX. 641.

10 Sic vos non vobis mellificatis apes.
– So do you bees make honey, not for
yourselves. *Attributed.*

11 Mantua me genuit, Calabri rapuere,
tenet nunc
Parthenope. Cecini pascua, rura, duces.

– Mantua bore me, the Calabrians
carried me off,
Naples holds me now. I sang of
pastures, farms, leaders.
His own epitaph.

**VOLTAIRE, FRANÇOIS MARIE
AROUET DE, French author and
philosopher, 21 Nov. 1694–30 May,
1778**

12 Si Dieu n'existait pas, il faudrait
l'inventer.
– If God did not exist, it would be
necessary to invent Him.
*Épîtres, xcvi. A l'auteur du livre des trois
imposteurs. – Letters, xcvi. To the Author
of the Book of the Three Impostors.*

13 Tout est pour le mieux dans le meilleur
des mondes possibles.
– All is for the best in the best of possible
worlds. (Dr. Pangloss.) *Candide, i.*

14 Dans ce pays-ci, il est bon de tuer de
temps en temps un amiral pour
encourager les autres.
– In this country (England) it is good to
kill an admiral from time to time, to
encourage the others. (In allusion to the
shooting of Admiral Byng.)
Ibid., xxiii.

15 Cela est bien dit, répondit Candide,
mais il faut cultiver notre jardin.
– 'That is well said,' replied Candide,
'but we must cultivate our garden.' (i.e.
we must attend to our own affairs.)
Ibid, xxx.

16 Ils ne se servent de la pensée que pour
autoriser leurs injustices, et n'emploient
les paroles que pour déguiser leurs
pensées.
– They use thought only to warrant
their injustice, and employ words only
to conceal their thoughts.
*Dialogue xiv. Le Chapon et la poularde. –
The Capon and the Pullet.*

**WADE, JOSEPH AUGUSTINE,
Irish composer, 1796?–15 July, 1845**

17 Meet me by moonlight alone.
Meet me by Moonlight.

WALLACE, WILLIAM ROSS, US poet, 1819–5 May, 1881

18 But a mightier power and stronger
Man from his throne has hurled,
And the hand that rocks the cradle
Is the hand that rules the world.
The Hand that rules the World.

WALLAS, GRAHAM, sociologist, 31 May, 1858–10 Aug. 1932

19 Just as it is impossible to sing, or to
speak a foreign language, well, with
one's mouth and throat in a
'gentlemanly' position, so it may prove
to be the case that one cannot think
effectively if one's main purpose in life is
to be a gentleman.
The Great Society, x.

WALLER, EDMUND, English poet, 3 March, 1606–21 Oct. 1687

20 The yielding marble of her snowy
breast.
On a Lady passing through a Crowd of People.

21 So was the huntsman by the bear
oppress'd
Whose hide he sold—before he caught
the beast!
Battle of the Summer Islands, ii. 38.

22 That which her slender waist confin'd
Shall now my joyful temples bind;
No monarch but would give his crown
His arms might do what this has done.
On a Girdle.

23 A narrow compass! and yet there
Dwelt all that's good, and all that's fair:
Give me but what this riband bound,
Take all the rest the sun goes round.
Ibid.

24 Others may use the ocean as their road,
Only the English make it their abode.
Of a War with Spain, 25.

25 For all we know
Of what the blessed do above
Is, that they sing, and that they love.
While I listen to thy Voice.

26 Go, lovely rose!
Tell her, that wastes her time and me,
That now she knows,
When I resemble her to thee,
How sweet and fair she seems to be.
Go, Lovely Rose.

27 The soul's dark cottage, batter'd and
decay'd,
Lets in new light through chinks that
time has made;
Stronger by weakness, wiser men
become,
As they draw near to their eternal home.
Leaving the old, both worlds at once
they view
That stand upon the threshold of the
new. *On the foregoing Divine Poems.*

WALPOLE, HORACE or HORATIO, 4th EARL OF ORFORD, author, 24 Sept. 1717– 2 March, 1797

28 It is charming to totter into vogue.
Letters. To George Augustus Selwyn, 2 Dec. 1765.

29 This world is a comedy to those that
think, a tragedy to those that feel.
Ibid, To Sir Horace Mann, 31 Dec. 1769.

WALPOLE, SIR ROBERT, 1st EARL OF ORFORD, English Prime Minister, 26 Aug. 1676– 18 March, 1745

30 All those men have their price.
(Referring to 'pretended patriots.'
Usually misquoted as 'All men have
their price.')
W. Coxe, Memoirs Of Walpole, IV. 369.

31 They now ring the bells, but they will
soon wring their hands.
On the declaration of war with Spain, 1739.

32 The balance of power.
Speech in House of Commons, 13 Feb. 1741.

WALSH, WILLIAM, English poet, 1663–18 March, 1708

33 And sadly reflecting
That a lover forsaken

A new love may get,
But a neck when once broken
Can never be set.
The Despairing Lover, 17.

1 I can endure my own despair,
But not another's hope.
Of all the Torments.

WALTON, IZAAK, English writer on angling, 9 Aug. 1593–15 Dec. 1683

2 Some innocent, harmless mirth, of which, if thou be a severe, sour-complexioned man, then I here disallow thee to be a competent judge.
The Compleat Angler. Epistle to the Reader.

3 I am, Sir, a Brother of the Angle.
Ibid, viii.

4 Thus use your frog . . . . Put your hook, I mean the armingwire, through his mouth, and out at his gills; and then with a fine needle and silk sew the upper part of his leg, with only one stitch, to the arming-wire of your hook; or tie the frog's leg, above the upper joint, to the armed-wire; and, in so doing, use him as though you loved him, that is, harm him as little as you may possibly, that he may live the longer. *Ibid, viii.*

5 This dish of meat is too good for any but anglers, or very honest men. *Ibid.*

6 And (blessing) upon all that are lovers of virtue; and dare trust in His providence; and be quiet; and go a-Angling.
Ibid, xxi.

WARBURTON, WILLIAM, Bishop of Gloucester, 24 Dec. 1698–7 June, 1779

7 Orthodoxy is my doxy; heterodoxy is another man's doxy.
Remark to Lord Sandwich. Priestly, Memoirs, I. 372.

WARD, ARTEMUS (CHARLES FARRAR BROWNE), US humorist, 26 April, 1834–6 March, 1867

8 I now bid you a welcome adoo.
Artemus Ward his Book. The Shakers.

9 My pollertics, like my religion, bein of a exceedin accommodatin character.
Ibid, The Crisis.

10 N.B. – This is rote Sarcasticul.
Ibid, A Visit to Brigham Young.

11 I girdid up my Lions and fled the Seen.
Ibid.

12 Did you ever hav the measels, and if so *how many?* *Ibid, The Census.*

13 Do me eyes deceive me earsight? Is it some dreams? *Ibid, Moses the Sassy.*

14 I'm not a politician and my other habits air good. *Ibid, Fourth of July Oration.*

15 Why is this thus? What is the reason of this thusness? *Artemus Ward's Lecture.*

WARE, EUGENE FITCH, US lawyer, 29 May, 1841–1911

16 Oh, dewy was the morning, upon the first of May,
And Dewey was the admiral, down in Manila Bay;
And dewy were the Regent's eyes, them royal orbs of blue,
And do we feel discouraged? We do not think we do! *Manila.*

WARMAN, CY, US journalist, 22 June, 1855–7 April, 1914

17 Every daisy in the dell knows my secret, knows it well,
But yet I dare not tell, sweet Marie.
Sweet Marie.

WARREN, SAMUEL, English lawyer and novelist, 23 May, 1807–29 July, 1877

18 There is probably no man living, though ever so great a fool, that cannot do *something* or other well.
Ten Thousand a Year, xxviii.

WASHBURN, HENRY STEVENSON, US author, 10 June, 1813–1903

19 We shall meet, but we shall miss him,
There will be one vacant chair.
The Vacant Chair.

WASHINGTON, GEORGE, US President, 22 Feb. 1732–14 Dec. 1799

20 Father, I cannot tell a lie, I did it with
my little hatchet. *Attributed.*

21 We must consult Brother Jonathan
(Jonathan Trumbull, Governor of
Connecticut).
*Frequent remark during War of
Independence.*
(Hence the use of 'Brother Jonathan' for
typical American.)

22 It is our true policy to steer clear of
permanent alliances with any portion of
the foreign world.
Farewell Address, 17 Sept. 1796.

WATKYNS, ROWLAND, English author, fl. 1662

23 I love him not; but shew no reason can
Wherefore, but this, *I do not love the man.*
*Flamma sine Fumo: or Poems without
Fictions. Antipathy.*

WATSON, SIR WILLIAM, English poet, 2 Aug. 1858–11 Aug. 1935

24 Man looks at his own bliss, considers it,
Weighs it with curious fingers; and 'tis
gone. *The Fatal Scrutiny.*

25 Too avid of earth's bliss, he was of those
Whom Delight flies because they give
her chase. *Byron the Voluptuary.*

26 O be less beautiful, or be less brief.
Autumn.

27 The staid, conservative
Came-over-with-the-Conqueror type
of mind. *A Study in Contrasts, i. 42.*

28 April, April,
Laugh thy girlish laughter;

Then, the moment after,
Weep thy girlish tears! *April.*

WATTS, ISAAC, English hymn-writer, 17 July, 1674–25 Nov. 1748

29 Let dogs delight to bark and bite.
*Divine Songs for Children, xvi. Against
Quarrelling.*

30 But, children, you should never let
Such angry passions rise;
Your little hands were never made
To tear each other's eyes. *Ibid.*

31 Birds in their little nests agree.
*Ibid, xvii. Love between Brothers and
Sisters.*

32 How doth the little busy bee
Improve each shining hour,
And gather honey all the day
From every opening flower.
Ibid, xx. Against Idleness and Mischief.

33 For Satan finds some mischief still
For idle hands to do. *Ibid.*

34 'Tis the voice of the sluggard; I hear him
complain,
'You have wak'd me too soon, I must
slumber again.'
As the door on its hinges, so he on his
bed,
Turns his sides and his shoulders and his
heavy head.
Moral Songs, i. The Sluggard.

35 Our God, our help in ages past,
Our hope for years to come,
Our shelter from the stormy blast,
And our eternal home. *Psalm, xc.*
(The substitution of 'O' for 'Our' was
made by John Wesley.)

36 A thousand ages in thy sight
Are like an evening gone,
Short as the watch that ends the night
Before the rising sun. *Ibid.*

37 Time, like an ever-rolling stream,
Bears all its sons away. *Ibid.*

38 Hark! from the tombs a doleful sound.
A Funeral Thought.

WEATHERLY, FREDERIC EDWARD, English song writer, 4 Oct. 1848–7 Sept. 1929

1 Where are the boys of the old Brigade?
The Old Brigade.

2 Then steadily, shoulder to shoulder,
Steadily, blade by blade!
Ready and strong, marching along,
Like the boys of the old Brigade.
Ibid.

3 Roses are flow'ring in Picardy,
But there's never a rose like you!
Roses of Picardy.

WEAVER, see Wever

WEBBER, BYRON, English author, 1838–1913

4 Hands across the sea!
Feet on British ground!
The old blood is bold blood, the wide
world round.   *Hands across the Sea.*

WEBSTER, DANIEL, US statesman, 18 Jan. 1782–24 Oct. 1852

5 Liberty and Union, now and for ever,
one and inseparable.
Speech in Senate, 26 Jan. 1830.

6 He touched the dead corpse of public
credit, and it sprang upon its feet.
Eulogy on Alexander Hamilton,
10 March, 1831

7 On this question of principle, while
actual suffering was yet afar off, they
(the Colonies) raised their flag against a
power to which, for purposes of
foreign conquest and subjugation,
Rome in the neight of her glory is not
to be compared, – a power which has
dotted over the surface of the whole
globe with her possessions and military
posts, whose morning drum-beat,
following the sun, and keeping
company with the hours, circles the
earth with one continuous and
unbroken strain of the martial airs of
England.
Speech in Senate, 7 May, 1834.

8 I was born an American; I will live an
American; I shall die an American.
Ibid, 17 July, 1850.

WEBSTER, JOHN, English dramatist, 1580?–1625?

9 Is not old wine wholesomest, old
pippins toothsomest, old wood burn
brightest, old linen wash whitest? Old
soldiers, sweetheart, are surest, and old
lovers are soundest.
Westward Hoe, II. ii.

10 Call for the robin redbreast and the
wren,
Since o'er shady groves they hover,
And with leaves and flowers do cover
The friendless bodies of unburied men.
The White Devil, V. iv.

11 Cover her face; mine eyes dazzle: she
died young.
The Duchess of Malfi, IV. ii.

WELLINGTON, ARTHUR WELLESLEY, 1ST DUKE OF, English Field Marshal and Prime Minister, 29 April or 1 May, 1769–14 Sept. 1852

12 Nothing except a battle lost can be half
so melancholy as a battle won.
Despatch, 1815.

13 There is no mistake; there has been no
mistake; and there shall be no mistake.
Letter to Mr. Huskisson.

14 Up, Guards, and at them!
Attributed order
at Waterloo, 18 June, 1815.
(His own account was that he said 'Stand
up, Guards!' and then gave the order to
attack.)

15 I never saw so many shocking bad hats
in my life.
On seeing the first Reformed Parliament.

16 The whole art of war consists in getting
at what is on the other side of the hill.
Attributed.

17 I care not one twopenny damn what
becomes of the ashes of Napoleon
Buonaparte.   *Ibid.*

18 The battle of Waterloo was won on the
playing fields of Eton.   *Ibid.*

WELLS, HERBERT GEORGE,
English author, 21 Sept. 1866–
13 Aug. 1946

19 I was thinking jest what a Rum Go
everything is.   *Kipps, III. iii. 8.*

20 Sesquippledan verboojuice.
                          Mr. Polly, i. 5.

21 The world may discover that all its
common interests are being managed
by one concern, while it still fails to
realise that a world government exists.
          A Short History of the World, lix.

22 The shape of things to come.
                          Title of book.

WESLEY, CHARLES, English
Methodist preacher, 18 Dec. 1707–
29 March, 1788

23 Jesus, lover of my soul,
Let me to Thy bosom fly,
While the nearer waters roll,
While the tempest still is high.
          Jesus, Lover of my Soul.

24 Cover my defenceless head
With the shadow of Thy wing.   *Ibid.*

25 Gentle Jesus, meek and mild,
Look upon a little child,
Pity my simplicity,
Suffer me to come to Thee.
          Gentle Jesus, Meek and Mild.

WESLEY, JOHN, English founder
of Methodism, 17 June, 1703–
2 March, 1791

26 Certainly this (neatness of apparel) is a
duty, not a sin. 'Cleanliness is, indeed,
next to godliness.
          Sermons, xciii. On Dress.

27 I look upon all the world as my parish.
          Journal, 11 June, 1739.

28 Do all the good you can,
By all the means you can,

In all the ways you can,
In all the places you can,
At all the times you can,
To all the people you can,
As long as ever you can.
                          Rule of Conduct.

WESSEL, HORST, Nazi storm
trooper, 9 Oct. 1907–23 Feb. 1930

29 Die Fahnen hoch! – die Reihen dicht
geschlossen!
– Up with the Colours! – Close fast the
ranks!   *Horst Wessel Song.*

WESTBURY, RICHARD
BETHELL, 1ST BARON, Lord
Chancellor, 30 June, 1800–20 July,
1873

30 Then, sir, you will turn it over once
more in what you are pleased to call
your mind. (Retort to a solicitor.)
          T. A. Nash, Life of Lord Westbury, II.
                          292.

31 A silly old man who does not
understand even his silly old trade. (Of
a witness from the Herald's College.)
                          Attributed.

WESTCOTT, EDWARD NOYES,
US author, 27 Sept. 1846–31 March,
1898

32 Do unto the other feller the way he'd
like to do unto you an' do it fust.
                          David Harum, xx.

WEVER or WEAVER, RICHARD,
English dramatist, fl.1565?

33 In a herber green, asleep where as I lay,
The birds sang sweet in the middes of
the day;
I dreamed fast of mirth and play;
In youth is pleasure, in youth is
pleasure.   *Lusty Juventus.*

WHATELY, RICHARD,
Archbishop of Dublin, 1 Feb.
1787–1 Oct. 1863

34 Happiness is no laughing matter.
                Apophthegms, page 218.

WHEWELL, WILLIAM, Master of Trinity College, Cambridge, 24 May, 1794–6 March, 1866

1 Hence no force however great can stretch a cord however fine, into an horizontal line which is accurately straight.
Elementary Treatise on Mechanics, 1st edition, page 44.
(Instance of unconscious versification.)

WHISTLER, JAMES ABBOTT McNEILL, US painter, 10 July, 1834–17 July, 1903

2 No, I ask it for the knowledge of a lifetime. (When asked in a legal action, 'For two days' labour, you ask two hundred guineas?')
The Gentle Art of making Enemies, 5.

3 I am not arguing with you – I am telling you.
Ibid, 51.

4 Why drag in Velasquez? (To an enthusiast who said she knew of only two painters in the world, himself and Velasquez.)
D. C. Seitz, Whistler Stories, 27.

5 I'm lonesome. They are all dying. I have hardly a warm personal enemy left.
Ibid, 47.

WHITE, JOSEPH BLANCO, Irish author, 11 July, 1775–20 May, 1841

6 Mysterious Night! when our first parent knew
Thee from report divine, and heard thy name,
Did he not tremble for this lovely frame,
This glorious canopy of light and blue?
To Night.

7 If Light can thus deceive, wherefore not Life?
Ibid.

WHITEFIELD, GEORGE, English Methodist preacher, 16 Dec. 1714–30 Sept. 1770

8 Hark! the herald-angels sing
Glory to the new-born King.
Altered opening lines of Charles Wesley's Christmas Hymn.

WHITEHEAD, WILLIAM, English Poet Laureate, baptised 12 Feb. 1715, died 14 April, 1785

9 Yes, I'm in love, I feel it now,
And Celia has undone me!
And yet I'll swear I can't tell how
The pleasing plague stole on me.
The Je ne sais quoi.

10 Her voice, her touch, might give th' alarm –
'Twas both, perhaps, or neither!
In short, 'twas that provoking charm
Of Celia all together.
Ibid.

11 Say, can you listen to the artless woes
Of an old tale, which every schoolboy knows?
The Roman Father, prologue, 9.

WHITING, WILLIAM, English hymn-writer, 1 Nov. 1825–1878

12 O hear us when we cry to Thee
For those in peril on the sea.
Eternal Father Strong to save.

WHITMAN, WALT (WALTER), US poet, 31 May, 1819–26 March, 1892

13 I loafe and invite my soul.
Song of Myself, i.

14 I think I could turn and live with animals, they are so placid and self-contain'd;
I stand and look at them long and long.
They do not sweat and whine about their condition;
They do not lie awake in the dark and weep for their sins;
They do not make me sick discussing their duty to God;
Not one is dissatisfied – not one is demented with the mania of owning things;
Not one kneels to another, nor to his kind that lived thousands of years ago;
Not one is respectable or industrious over the whole earth.
Ibid, xxxii.

15 I sound my barbaric yawp over the roofs of the world.
Ibid, lii.

16 Out of the cradle endlessly rocking,
Out of the mocking-bird's throat, the
musical shuttle.
Out of the Cradle endlessly rocking.

17 O Captain! my Captain! our fearful trip
is done,
The ship has weather'd every rack, the
prize we sought is won,
The port is near, the bells I hear, the
people all exulting,
While follow eyes the steady keel, the
vessel grim and daring;
But O heart! heart! heart!
O the bleeding drops of red,
Where on the deck my Captain lies,
Fallen cold and dead.
O Captain! My Captain!

**WHITTIER, JOHN GREENLEAF,
US poet, 17 Dec. 1807–7 Sept. 1892**

18 For of all sad words of tongue or pen,
The saddest are these: 'It might have
been!' *Maud Muller.*

19 Blessings on thee, little man,
Barefoot boy, with cheek of tan!
The Barefoot Boy.

20 Old Floyd Ireson, for his hard heart,
Tarred and feathered and carried in a
cart
By the women of Marblehead.
Skipper Ireson's Ride.

21 Dinna ye hear it? – dinna ye hear it?
The pipes o' Havelock sound!
The Pipes at Lucknow.

22 'Shoot, if you must, this old grey head,
But spare your country's flag,' she said.
Barbara Frietchie.

23 'Who touches a hair of yon grey head
Dies like a dog! March on!' he said.
Ibid.

**WHUR, CORNELIUS, English
Methodist minister, 1782–
12 March, 1853**

24 Will not a beauteous landscape bright –
Or music's soothing sound,
Console the heart – afford delight,
And throw sweet peace around?

They may, but never comfort lend
Like an accomplished female friend!
Village Musings. The Female Friend.

**WHYTE-MELVILLE, GEORGE
JOHN, Scottish author, 19 June,
1821–5 Dec. 1878**

25 We always believe our first love is our
last, and our last love our first.
Katerfelto, xiv.

26 The swallows are making them ready to
fly,
Wheeling out on a windy sky:
Good-bye, Summer, good-bye, good-
bye. *Good-bye, Summer.*

27 Wrap me up in my tarpaulin jacket,
And say a poor buffer lies low.
The Tarpaulin Jacket.

**WILBERFORCE, SAMUEL,
Bishop of Winchester, 7 Sept.
1805–19 July, 1873**

28 If I were a cassowary
On the plains of Timbuctoo,
I would eat a missionary,
Coat and bands and hymn-book too.
Attributed.

**WILCOX, ELLA WHEELER, US
poetess, 5 Nov. 1850–30 Oct. 1919**

29 Laugh, and the world laughs with you;
Weep, and you weep alone;
For the sad old earth must borrow its
mirth,
But has trouble enough of its own.
Solitude.

30 So many gods, so many creeds,
So many paths that wind and wind,
When just the art of being kind
Is all the sad world needs.
The World's Need.

31 No question is ever settled
Until it is settled right.
Settle the Question Right.

WILDE, OSCAR FINGAL O'FLAHERTIE WILLS, Irish author, 16 Oct. 1854–30 Nov. 1900

1 There is no such thing as a moral or an immoral book. Books are well written, or badly written. That is all.
The Picture of Dorian Gray, preface.

2 All art is quite useless. *Ibid.*

3 The only way to get rid of a temptation is to yield to it. *Ibid, ii.*

4 He knew the precise psychological moment when to say nothing. *Ibid.*

5 Meredith is a prose Browning, and so is Browning. *The Critic as Artist, I.*

6 As long as war is regarded as wicked, it will always have its fascination. When it is looked upon as vulgar, it will cease to be popular. *Ibid, II.*

7 There is no sin except stupidity. *Ibid.*

8 I can resist everything except temptation. *Lady Windermere's Fan, I.*

9 A man who knows the price of everything, and the value of nothing. (Definition of a cynic.) *Ibid, III.*

10 Experience is the name everyone gives to his mistakes. *Ibid.*

11 One should never trust a woman who tells one her real age. A woman who would tell one that, would tell one anything.
A Woman of No Importance, I.

12 I have nothing to declare except my genius. *At New York Custom House.*

13 I suppose that I shall have to die beyond my means.
When confronted with a large fee for an operation.

14 Tread lightly, she is near
Under the snow,
Speak gently, she can hear
The daisies grow. *Requiescat.*

15 Yet each man kills the thing he loves,
By each let this be heard,
Some do it with a bitter look,
Some with a flattering word.
The coward does it with a kiss,
The brave man with a sword.
The Ballad of Reading Gaol, i. 7.

16 The vilest deeds like poison-weeds
Bloom well in prison-air:
It is only what is good in Man
That wastes and withers there:
Pale Anguish keeps the heavy gate
And the Warder is Despair. *Ibid, v. 5.*

17 Down the long and silent street,
The dawn, with silver-sandaled feet,
Crept like a frightened girl.
The Harlot's House.

WILLARD, EMMA HART, US educationist, 23 Feb. 1787–15 April, 1870

18 Calm and peaceful shall we sleep,
Rocked in the cradle of the deep.
The Cradle of the Deep.

WILLIAM III (of Orange), King, 4 Nov. 1650–8 March, 1702

19 There is one certain means by which I can be sure never to see my country's ruin: I will die in the last ditch.
D. Hume, History of England, lxv.

20 Every bullet has its billet.
John Wesley's Journal, 6 June, 1765.

WILLS, WILLIAM GORMAN, Irish dramatist, 28 Jan. 1828–13 Dec. 1891

21 I'll sing thee songs of Araby,
And tales of fair Cashmere,
Wild tales to cheat thee of a sigh,
Or charm thee to a tear.
I'll sing thee Songs of Araby.

WILSON, JOHN, English bookseller, died 1889 ·

22 O for a Booke and a shadie nooke,
Eyther in-a-doore or out;
With the grene leaves whisp'ring overhede,

Or the Streete cryes all about.
Where I maie Reade all at my ease,
Both of the Newe and Olde;
For a jollie goode Booke whereon to
looke
Is better to me than Golde.
For a catalogue of second-hand books.

**WILSON, THOMAS, Bishop of
Sodor and Man, 20 Dec. 1663–
7 March, 1755**

23 It costs more to revenge (injuries) than
to bear them.
Maxims of Piety and Morality, 303.

**WILSON, THOMAS WOODROW,
US President, 28 Dec. 1856–3 Feb.
1924**

24 There is such a thing as a man being too
proud to fight.
*Address to foreign-born citizens,
10 May, 1915.*

25 The world must be made safe for
democracy. *Address to Congress asking
for declaration of war, 2 April, 1917.*

**WIMPERIS, ARTHUR HAROLD,
English dramatist, 3 Dec. 1874–
14 Oct. 1953**

26 I've gotter motter –
Always merry and bright!
Look around and you will find
Every cloud is silver-lined;
The sun will shine
Although the sky's a grey one.
I've often said to meself, I've said,
'Cheer up, cully, you'll soon be dead!
A short life and a gay one!'
The Arcadians, III. My Motter.

**WITHER, GEORGE, English poet,
11 June, 1588–2 May, 1667**

27 Shall I, wasting in despair,
Die, because a woman's fair?
Or make pale my cheeks with care
'Cause another's rosy are?
Be she fairer than the day
Or the flowery meads in May,
If she think not well of me,
What care I how fair she be?
The Author's Resolution in a Sonnet.

28 If she slight me when I woo,
I can scorn and let her go. *Ibid.*

**WOLCOT, JOHN ('PETER
PINDAR'), English poet, baptised
9 May, 1738, died 14 Jan. 1819**

29 What rage for fame attends both great
and small!
Better be d—d than mentioned not at all!
*More Lyric Odes to the Royal
Academicians, viii.*

30 Care to our coffin adds a nail, no doubt;
And ev'ry grin so merry, draws one out.
Expostulatory Odes, xv.

**WOLFE, CHARLES, Irish poet,
14 Dec. 1791–21 Feb. 1823**

31 Not a drum was heard, not a funeral
note,
As his corse to the rampart we hurried.
The Burial of Sir John Moore.

32 But he lay like a warrior taking his rest
With his martial cloak around him.
Ibid.

33 We carved not a line, and we raised not a
stone,
But we left him alone with his glory.
Ibid.

**WOLFE, JAMES, English General,
2 Jan. 1727–13 Sept. 1759**

34 I would rather have written those lines
(Gray's *Elegy*) than take Quebec.
*The night before he was killed on the Plains
of Abraham.*

**WOLSEY, THOMAS, English
Cardinal and Lord Chancellor,
1475?– 29 Nov. 1530**

35 Had I served my God as diligently as I
have served the king, He would not
have given me over in my grey hairs.
*To Sir William Kingston, on the day of his
death.*

**WOODWORTH, SAMUEL, US
poet, 13 Jan. 1784–9 Dec. 1842**

36 The old oaken bucket, the iron-bound
bucket,

The moss-covered bucket, which hung
in the well.   *The Old Oaken Bucket.*

WOOLF, ADELINE VIRGINIA, English authoress, 25 Jan. 1882– 28 March, 1941

1 Those comfortably padded lunatic
asylums which are known,
euphemistically, as the stately homes of
England.
      The Common Reader. Lady Dorothy
      Nevill.

2 A room of one's own.   *Title of book.*

WORDSWORTH, DAME ELIZABETH, Principal of Lady Margaret Hall, Oxford, 22 June, 1840–30 Nov. 1932

3 If all the good people were clever,
And all clever people were good,
The world would be nicer than ever
We thought that it possibly could.
      Good and Clever.

4 But somehow, 'tis seldom or never
The two hit it off as they should,
The good are so harsh to the clever,
The clever, so rude to the good!   *Ibid.*

WORDSWORTH, WILLIAM, English Poet Laureate, 7 April, 1770–23 April, 1850

5 In that sweet mood when pleasant
thoughts
Bring sad thoughts to the mind.
      Lines Written in Early Spring.

6 And 'tis my faith that every flower
Enjoys the air it breathes.   *Ibid.*

7 Nor less I deem that there are Powers
Which of themselves our minds impress;
That we can feed this mind of ours
In a wise passiveness.
      Expostulation and Reply.

8 Up! up! my friend, and quit your books;
Or surely you'll grow double.
      The Tables Turned.

9 Come forth into the light of things,
Let Nature be your teacher.   *Ibid.*

10 One impulse from a vernal wood
May teach you more of man,
Of Moral evil and of good,
Than all the sages can.   *Ibid.*

11   Sensations sweet
Felt in the blood, and felt along the
heart.
      Lines Composed a Few Miles above Tintern
      Abbey, 27.

12 That best portion of a good man's life,
His little, nameless, unremembered acts,
Of kindness and of love.   *Ibid, 33.*

13   The sounding cataract
Haunted me like a passion.   *Ibid, 76.*

14   I have learned
To look on nature, not as in the hour
Of thoughtless youth; but hearing
oftentimes
The still, sad music of humanity,
Nor harsh nor grating, though of ample
power
To chasten and subdue. And I have felt
A presence that disturbs me with the joy
Of elevated thoughts: a sense sublime
Of something far more deeply
interfused,
Whose dwelling is the light of setting
suns,
And the round ocean and the living air,
And the blue sky, and in the mind of
man.   *Ibid, 88.*

15 Knowing that Nature never did betray
The heart that loved her.   *Ibid, 122.*

16 A primrose by a river's brim
A yellow primrose was to him,
And it was nothing more.
      Peter Bell, I. 249.

17 All silent and all damned!   *Ibid, II. 516.*

18 What fond and wayward thoughts will
slide
Into a lover's head! –
'O mercy!' to myself I cried,
'If Lucy should be dead!'
      Strange Fits of Passion have I known.

19 She dwelt among the untrodden ways
Beside the springs of Dove,

A maid whom there were none to
praise:
And very few to love:

20 A violet by a mossy stone
Half hidden from the eye!
Fair as a star, when only one
Is shining in the sky.
She dwelt among the Untrodden Ways.

21 But she is in her grave, and, oh,
The difference to me!   *Ibid.*

22 No motion has she now, no force;
She neither hears nor sees,
Rolled round in earth's diurnal course,
With rocks, and stones, and trees.
A Slumber did my Spirit seal.

23 The stars of midnight shall be dear
To her; and she shall lean her ear
In many a secret place
Where rivulets dance their wayward
round,
And beauty born of murmuring sound
Shall pass into her face.
Three Years she grew.

24 One that would peep and botanize
Upon his mother's grave.
A Poet's Epitaph.

25 And you must love him, ere to you
He will seem worthy of your love.
Ibid.

26 The sweetest thing that ever grew
Beside a human door.   *Lucy Gray.*

27 Drink, pretty creature, drink!
The Pet Lamb.

28 She gave me eyes, she gave me ears;
And humble cares, and delicate fears;
A heart, the fountain of sweet tears;
And love, and thought, and joy.
The Sparrow's Nest.

29 My heart leaps up when I behold
A rainbow in the sky
My Heart leaps up.

30 The child is father of the man.   *Ibid.*

31 The cattle are grazing,

Their heads never raising;
There are forty feeding like one.
Written in March.

32 Sweet childish days, that were as long
As twenty days are now. *To a Butterfly.*

33 As high as we have mounted in delight
In our dejection do we sink as low.
*The Leech-Gatherer; or, Resolution and
Independence, 4.*

34 I thought of Chatterton, the marvellous
boy,
The sleepless soul that perished in his
pride;
Of him who walked in glory and in joy
Followed his plough, along the
mountain-side:
By our own spirits are we deified;
We poets in our youth begin in gladness;
But thereof comes in the end
despondency and madness.   *Ibid, 7.*

35 Earth has not anything to show more
fair.
Sonnet, composed upon Westminster Bridge.

36 This City now doth like a garment wear
The beauty of the morning.   *Ibid.*

37 Dear God! the very houses seem asleep;
And all that mighty heart is lying still!
Ibid.

38 Once did she hold the gorgeous East in
fee.
*Sonnet, on the Extinction of the Venetian
Republic.*

39 Men are we, and must grieve when even
the shade
Of that which once was great, is passed
away.   *Ibid.*

40 Plain living and high thinking are no
more:
The homely beauty of the good old
cause
Is gone; our peace, our fearful
innocence,
And pure religion breathing household
laws.
*Sonnet. O Friend! I know not which Way I
must look.*

317

1 Milton! thou should'st be living at this
   hour:
   England hath need of thee: she is a fen
   Of stagnant waters.
   Sonnet. London, 1802.

2 Thy soul was like a star, and dwelt
   apart:
   Thou hadst a voice whose sound was
   like the sea:
   Pure as the naked heavens, majestic,
   free,
   So didst thou travel on life's common
   way,
   In cheeful godliness; and yet thy heart
   The lowliest duties on herself did lay.
   Ibid.

3 We must be free or die, who speak the
   tongue
   That Shakespeare spake; the faith and
   morals hold
   Which Milton held.
   Sonnet. It is not to be thought of.

4 And stepping westward seemed to be
   A kind of heavenly destiny.
   Stepping Westward.

5 A voice so thrilling ne'er was heard
   In springtime from the cuckoo-bird,
   Breaking the silence of the seas
   Among the farthest Hebrides.
   The Solitary Reaper.

6 For old, unhappy, far-off things,
   And battles long ago.   *Ibid.*

7 The music in my heart I bore,
   Long after it was heard no more.   *Ibid.*

8   The good old rule
   Sufficeth them, the simple plan,
   That they should take, who have the
   power,
   And they should keep who can.
   Rob Roy's Grave.

9 The swan on still St. Mary's Lake
   Float double, swan and shadow.
   Yarrow Unvisited.

10 O Cuckoo! shall I call thee bird,
   Or but a wandering voice?
   To the Cuckoo.

11 She was a phantom of delight
   When first she gleamed upon my sight.
   She was a Phantom of Delight.

12 A dancing shape, an image gay,
   To haunt, to startle, and waylay.   *Ibid.*

13 A creature not too bright or good
   For human nature's daily food;
   For transient sorrows, simple wiles,
   Praise, blame, love, kisses, tears, and
   smiles.   *Ibid.*

14 A perfect woman, nobly planned,
   To warn, to comfort, and command.
   Ibid.

15 I wandered lonely as a cloud
   That floats on high o'er vales and hills,
   When all at once I saw a crowd,
   A host of golden daffodils;
   Beside the lake, beneath the trees.
   Fluttering and dancing in the breeze.
   I wandered Lonely as a Cloud.

16 For oft, when on my couch I lie
   In vacant or in pensive mood,
   They flash upon that inward eye
   Which is the bless of solitude;
   And then my heart with pleasure fills,
   And dances with the daffodils.   *Ibid.*

17 Spade! with which Wilkinson hath tilled
   his lands.   *To the Spade of a Friend.*

18 Stern daughter of the voice of God!
   Ode to Duty.

19 Thou dost preserve the stars from
   wrong;
   And the most ancient heavens, through
   Thee, are fresh and strong.   *Ibid.*

20 The light that never was, on sea or land;
   The consecration, and the poet's dream.
   *Elegiac Stanzas suggested by a Picture of
   Peele Castle in a Storm.*

21 But an old age serene and bright,
   And lovely as a Lapland night,
   Shall lead thee to thy grave.
   To a Young Lady.

22   Where the statue stood

Of Newton, with his prism and silent face,
The marble index of a mind forever
Voyaging through strange seas of thought alone. *The Prelude, III. 61.*

23 Bliss was it in that dawn to be alive,
But to be young was very heaven!
Ibid, XI. 108.

24 Who is the happy Warrior? Who is he
That every man in arms should wish to be? *Character of the Happy Warrior.*

25 Who, doomed to go in company with Pain,
And Fear, and Bloodshed, miserable train!
Turns his necessity to glorious gain.
Ibid.

26 But who, if he be called upon to face
Some awful moment to which Heaven has joined
Great issues, good or bad for human kind,
Is happy as a lover. *Ibid.*

27 Nuns fret not at their convent's narrow room,
And hermits are contented with their cells. *Sonnet. Nuns fret not.*

28 The world is too much with us; late and soon,
Getting and spending, we lay waste our powers:
Little we see in Nature that is ours.
Sonnet. The World is too much with us.

29   Great God! I'd rather be
A Pagan suckled in a creed outworn;
So might I, standing on this pleasant lea,
Have glimpses that would make me less forlorn;
Have sight of Proteus rising from the sea;
Or hear old Triton blow his wreathèd horn. *Ibid.*

30 The rainbow comes and goes,
And lovely is the rose.
Ode on Intimations of Immortality.

31 The sunshine is a glorious birth;

But yet I know, where'er I go,
That there hath passed away a glory
from the earth. *Ibid.*

32 The cataracts blow their trumpets from the steep. *Ibid.*

33 The winds come to me from the fields of sleep. *Ibid.*

34 Whither is fled the visionary gleam?
Where is it now, the glory and the dream? *Ibid.*

35 Our birth is but a sleep and a forgetting:
The soul that rises with us, our life's star,
Hath had elsewhere its setting,
And cometh from afar:
Not in entire forgetfulness,
And not in utter nakedness,
But trailing clouds of glory do we come
From God, who is our home:
Heaven lies about us in our infancy!
Shades of the prison-house begin to close
Upon the growing boy,
But he beholds the light, and whence it flows
He sees it in his joy;
The youth, who daily farther from the east
Must travel, still is Nature's priest,
And by the vision splendid
Is on his way attended;
At length the man perceives it die away,
And fade into the light of common day.
Ibid.

36 As if his whole vocation
Were endless imitation. *Ibid.*

37 And custom lie upon thee with a weight,
Heavy as frost, and deep almost as life!
Ibid.

38 Those obstinate questionings
Of sense and outward things,
Fallings from us, vanishings;
Blank misgivings of a creature
Moving about in worlds not realised,
High instincts before which our mortal nature
Did tremble like a guilty thing surprised. *Ibid.*

1   Truths that wake
To perish never.   *Ibid.*

2 Hence, in a season of calm weather,
Though inland far we be,
Our souls have sight of that immortal
sea
Which brought us hither.   *Ibid.*

3 In years that bring the philosophic
mind.   *Ibid.*

4 To me the meanest flower that blows
can give
Thoughts that do often lie too deep for
tears.   *Ibid.*

5 Two voices are there; one is of the sea,
One of the mountains; each a mighty
voice:
In both from age to age thou didst
rejoice,
They were thy chosen music, Liberty!
*Sonnet. Thought of a Briton on the
Subjugation of Switzerland.*

6   The good die first,
And they whose hearts are dry as
summer dust
Burn to the socket.
The Excursion, I. 500.

7 A man he seems of cheerful yesterdays
And confident to-morrows.
Ibid, VII. 557.

8   The Gods approve
The depth, and not the tumult, of the
soul.   *Laodamia, 74.*

9 An ampler ether, a diviner air.
Ibid, 105.

10 Ethereal minstrel! Pilgrim of the sky!
To a Skylark.

11 Type of the wise who soar, but never
roam,
True to the kindred points of heaven and
home.   *Ibid.*

12 Scorn not the Sonnet. Critic, you have
frowned,
Mindless of its just honours; with this
key

Shakespeare unlocked his heart.
Sonnet. Scorn not the Sonnet.

13 Nature's old felicities.   *The Trossachs.*

14 And Lamb, the frolic and the gentle,
Has vanished from his lonely hearth.
*Extempore Effusion upon the Death of
James Hogg.*

15 How fast has brother followed brother,
From sunshine to the sunless land!   *Ibid.*

16 And thou art long, and lank, and
brown,
As is the ribbed sea sand.
Lines added to Coleridge's Ancient Mariner.

17 And listens like a three years' child.
Ibid.

18 Poetry is the spontaneous overflow of
powerful feelings: it takes its origin
from emotion recollected in tranquillity.
Lyrical Ballads, preface.

WORK, HENRY CLAY, US songwriter, 1 Oct. 1832–8 June, 1884

19 Bring the good old bugle, boys, we'll
sing another song;
Sing it with a spirit that will start the
world along,
Sing it as we used to sing it – fifty
thousand strong,
As we were marching through Georgia.
Marching through Georgia.

20 Father, dear father, come home with me
now,
The clock in the steeple strikes one.
Come Home, Father.

WOTTON, SIR HENRY, English diplomat and poet, 1568–Dec. 1639

21 How happy is he born and taught
That serveth not another's will;
Whose armour is his honest thought,
And simple truth his utmost skill.
The Character of a Happy Life.

22 And entertains the harmless day
With a religious book, or friend.   *Ibid.*

23 Lord of himself, though not of lands,
And, having nothing, yet hath all. *Ibid.*

24 You meaner beauties of the night,
That poorly satisfy our eyes
More by your number than your light
You common people of the skies;
What are you, when the moon shall rise?
On his Mistress, the Queen of Bohemia.

25 He first deceased; she for a little tried
To live without him, liked it not, and
died.
*Upon the Death of Sir Albertus Morton's
Wife.*

26 An ambassador is an honest man sent to
lie abroad for the good of his country.
Written in a friend's album.

**WYATT, SIR THOMAS, English
poet, born 1503? buried 11 Oct. 1542**

27 And wilt thou leave me thus?
Say nay, say nay, for shame!
Poems from the Devonshire MS. part I. xii.

28 Forget not yet the tried intent
Of such a truth as I have meant;
My great travail so gladly spent
Forget not yet! *Ibid, xxvii.*

**XENOPHON, Greek historian,
430?–355? B.C.**

29 θάλαττα θάλαττα. – The sea! the sea!
Anabasis, IV. vii.
(Transliterated Thalatta, thalatta. Shout
of Greek soldiers when they sighted
the Euxine on their homeward march.)

**XERXES, King of Persia, 519?–465
B.C.**

30 My men have become women, and my
women men.
*When Queen Artemisia's ship sank another
at Salamis, 480 B.C.*

**YEATS, WILLIAM BUTLER, Irish
poet, 13 June, 1865–28 Jan. 1939**

31   The land of faery,
Where nobody gets old and godly and
grave,

Where nobody gets old and crafty and
wise,
Where nobody gets old and bitter of
tongue.
The Land of Heart's Desire.

32 Had I the heavens' embroidered cloths,
Enwrought with golden and silver light.
He wishes for the Cloths of Heaven.

33 I have spread my dreams under your
feet;
Tread softly, because you tread on my
dreams. *Ibid.*

34 When you are old and grey and full of
sleep,
And nodding by the fire, take down this
book. *When you are Old.*

35 She bid me take life easy, as the grass
grows on the weirs;
But I was young and foolish, and now
am full of tears.
Down by the Salley Gardens.

36 I will arise and go now, and go to
Innisfree,
And a small cabin build there, of clay
and wattles made;
Nine bean-rows will I have there, a hive
for the honey-bee,
And live alone in the bee-loud glade.
The Lake Isle of Innisfree.

37 When I play on my fiddle in Dooney,
Folk dance like a wave of the sea.
The Fiddler of Dooney.

**YOUNG, ANDREW, Scottish
schoolmaster, 23 April, 1807–
30 Nov. 1889**

38 There is a happy land,
Far, far away,
Where saints in glory stand,
Bright, bright as day.
There is a Happy Land.

**YOUNG, EDWARD, English poet,
baptised 3 July, 1683, died 5 April,
1765**

39 Tired Nature's sweet restorer, balmy
sleep!

He, like the world, his ready visit pays
Where fortune smiles; the wretched he
forsakes.   *Night Thoughts, Night i. I.*

1 Night, sable goddess! from her ebon
throne
In rayless majesty, now stretches forth
Her leaden sceptre o'er a slumb'ring
world.   *Ibid, 18.*

2 Procrastination is the thief of time.
Ibid, 393.

3 At thirty, man suspects himself a fool;
Knows it at forty, and reforms his plan:
At fifty chides his infamous delay,
Pushes his prudent purpose to resolve;
In all the magnanimity of thought
Resolves; and re-resolves; then, dies the
same.   *Ibid, 417.*

4 All men think all men mortal but
themselves.   *Ibid, 424.*

5 Who does the best his circumstance
allows,
Does well, acts nobly; angels could no
more.   *Ibid, Night ii. 90.*

6 Some for renown, on scraps of learning
dote,
And think they grow immortal as they
quote.
Love of Fame, Satire i. 89.

7   Be wise with speed;
A fool at forty is a fool indeed.
Ibid, Satire ii. 282.

8 For her own breakfast she'll project a
scheme,

Nor take her tea without a stratagem.
Ibid, Satire vi. 187.

9 How commentators each dark passage
shun,
And hold their farthing candle to the
sun.   *Ibid, Satire vii. 97.*

10 Their feet through faithless leather met
the dirt,
And oftener chang'd their principles
than shirt.
To Mr. Pope, Epistle i. 277.

11 Accept a miracle instead of wit, –
See two dull lines with Stanhope's pencil
writ.
*Lines written with Lord Chesterfield's
diamond pencil.*

**ZAMOYSKI, JAN, Chancellor of
Poland, 1541–3 June, 1605**

12 The king reigns, but does not govern.
Speech in Polish Parliament, 1605.

**ZANGWILL, ISRAEL, Jewish
novelist, 14 Feb. 1864–1 Aug. 1926**

13 Scratch the Christian and you find the
pagan – spoiled.
The Children of the Ghetto, II. vi.

**ZOLA, ÉMILE ÉDOUARD
CHARLES ANTOINE, French
novelist, 2 April, 1840–29 Sept. 1902**

14 J'accuse. – I accuse.
*Title of open letter to President of France in
connection with the Dreyfus case, 13 Jan.
1898.*

THE BIBLE

The text used in the following quotations is that of the Authorised Version, except in a few instances which are indicated by notes.

THE OLD TESTAMENT

15 And God said, Let there be light: and there was light.   *Genesis, i. 3.*

16 It is not good that the man should be alone.   *Ibid, ii. 18.*

17 Bone of my bones, and flesh of my flesh.   *Ibid, 23.*

18 Ye shall be as gods, knowing good and evil.   *Ibid, iii. 5.*

19 In the sweat of thy face shalt thou eat bread.   *Ibid, 19.*

20 For dust thou art, and unto dust shalt thou return.   *Ibid.*

21 The mother of all living.   *Ibid, 20.*

22 Am I my brother's keeper?   *Ibid, iv. 9.*

23 My punishment is greater than I can bear.   *Ibid, 13.*

24 There were giants in the earth in those days.   *Ibid, vi. 4.*

25 But the dove found no rest for the sole of her foot.   *Ibid, viii. 9.*

26 Whoso sheddeth man's blood, by man shall his blood be shed.   *Ibid, ix. 6.*

27 Even as Nimrod the mighty hunter before the Lord.   *Ibid, x. 9.*

28 In a good old age.   *Ibid, xv. 15.*

29 His hand will be against every man, and every man's hand against him.   *Ibid, xvi. 12.*

30 Shall not the Judge of all the earth do right?   *Ibid, xviii. 25.*

31 Esau selleth his birthright for a mess of pottage.
(In the Genevan Bible.)   *Ibid, xxv. chapter heading.*

32 The voice of Jacob's voice, but the hands are the hands of Esau.   *Ibid, xxvii. 22.*

33 This is none other but the house of God, and this is the gate of heaven.   *Ibid, xxviii. 17.*

34 I will not let thee go, except thou bless me.   *Ibid, xxxii. 26.*

35 Behold, this dreamer cometh.   *Ibid, xxxvii. 19.*

36 Jacob saw that there was corn in Egypt.   *Ibid, xlii. 1.*

37 Bring down my grey hairs with sorrow to the grave.   *Ibid, 38.*

38 Ye shall eat of the fat of the land.   *Ibid, xlv. 18.*

39 Few and evil have the days of the years of my life been.   *Ibid, xlvii. 9.*

40 Unstable as water, thou shalt not excel.   *Ibid, xlix. 4.*

41 Now there arose up a new king over Egypt, which knew not Joseph.   *Exodus, i. 8.*

42 Who made thee a prince and a judge over us?   *Ibid, ii. 14.*

1 I have been a stranger in a strange land.
Ibid, 22.

2 A land flowing with milk and honey.
Ibid, iii. 8.

3 Darkness which may be felt. *Ibid, x. 21.*

4 And they spoiled the Egyptians.
Ibid, xii. 36.

5 Thou shalt give life for life, eye for eye, tooth for tooth, hand for hand, foot for foot. *Ibid, xxi. 23.*

6 Thou shalt not seethe a kid in his mother's milk. *Ibid, xxiii. 19.*

7 Thou shalt love thy neighbour as thyself. *Leviticus, xix. 18.*

8 The Lord bless thee, and keep thee: The Lord make his face shine upon thee, and be gracious unto thee: The Lord lift up his countenance upon thee, and give thee peace. *Numbers, vi. 24.*

9 Let me die the death of the righteous, and let my last end be like his! *Ibid, 10.*

10 Be sure your sin will find you out.
Ibid, xxxii. 23.

11 Thou shalt love the Lord thy God with all thine heart, and with all thy soul, and with all thy might.
Deuteronomy, vi. 5.

12 Thou shalt not muzzle the ox when he treadeth out the corn. *Ibid, xxv. 4.*

13 In the morning thou shalt say, Would God it were even! and at even thou shalt say, Would God it were morning!
Ibid, xxviii. 67.

14 Jeshurun waxed fat, and kicked.
Ibid, xxxii. 15.

15 As thy days, so shall thy strength be.
Ibid, xxxiii. 25.

16 The eternal God is my refuge, and underneath are the everlasting arms.
Ibid, 27

17 Hewers of wood and drawers of water.
Joshua, ix. 21.

18 I am going the way of all the earth.
Ibid, xxiii. 14.

19 I arose a mother in Israel. *Judges, v, 7.*

20 The stars in their courses fought against Sisera. *Ibid, 20.*

21 She brought forth butter in a lordly dish. *Ibid, 25.*

22 Why tarry the wheels of his chariots?
Ibid, 28.

23 Have they not divided the prey; to every man a damsel or two? *Ibid, 30.*

24 Faint, yet pursuing them. *Ibid, viii. 4.*

25 He smote them hip and thigh.
Ibid, xv. 8.

26 The Philistines be upon thee, Samson.
Ibid, xvi. 9.

27 Whither thou goest, I will go; and where thou lodgest, I will lodge: thy people shall be my people, and thy God my God: Where thou diest, will I die, and there will I be buried: the Lord do so to me, and more also, if ought but death part thee and me. *Ruth, i. 16.*

28 Speak, Lord; for thy servant heareth.
1 Samuel, iii. 9.

29 Quit yourselves like men. *Ibid, iv. 9.*

30 Is Saul also among the prophets?
Ibid, x. 11.

31 A man after his own heart.
Ibid, xiii. 14.

32 Agag came unto him delicately. And Agag said, Surely the bitterness of death is past. *Ibid, xv. 32.*

33 Saul hath slain his thousands, and David his ten thousands. *Ibid, xviii. 7.*

34 Tell it not in Gath, publish it not in the streets of Askelon. *2 Samuel, i. 20.*

35 Saul and Jonathan were lovely and pleasant in their lives, and in their death they were not divided. *Ibid, 23.*

36 How are the mighty fallen in the midst of the battle! *Ibid, 25.*

37 Thy love to me was wonderful, passing the love of women. *Ibid, 26.*

38 Smote him under the fifth rib. *Ibid, ii. 23.*

39 Tarry at Jericho until your beards be grown. *Ibid, x. 5.*

40 The poor man had nothing, save one little ewe lamb. *Ibid, xii. 3.*

41 Thou art the man. *Ibid, 7.*

42 Would God I had died for thee, O Absalom, my son, my son! *Ibid, xviii, 33.*

43 A proverb and a byword among all people. *1 Kings, ix. 7.*

44 Behold, the half was not told me. *Ibid, x. 7.*

45 My father hath chastised you with whips, but I will chastise you with scorpions. *Ibid, xii. 11.*

46 He slept with his fathers. *Ibid, xiv. 20.*

47 How long halt ye between two opinions? *Ibid, xviii. 21.*

48 He is talking, or he is pursuing, or he is in a journey, or peradventure he sleepeth, and must be awaked. *Ibid, 27.*

49 There ariseth a little cloud out of the sea, like a man's hand. *Ibid, 44.*

50 A still small voice. *Ibid, xix. 12.*

51 Hast thou found me, O mine enemy? *Ibid, xxi. 20.*

52 And a certain man drew a bow at a venture, and smote the king of Israel between the joints of his harness. *Ibid, xxii. 34.*

53 Is it well with the child? And she answered, It is well. *2 Kings. iv. 26.*

54 There is death in the pot. *Ibid, 40.*

55 Are not Abana and Pharpar, rivers of Damascus, better than all the waters of Israel? *Ibid, v. 12.*

56 Is thy servant a dog, that he should do this great thing? *Ibid, viii. 13.*

57 The driving is like the driving of Jehu, the son of Nimshi; for he driveth furiously. *Ibid, ix. 20.*

58 The man whom the king delighteth to honour. *Esther, vi. 9.*

59 From going to and fro in the earth, and from walking up and down in it. *Job, i. 7.*

60 Naked came I out of my mother's womb, and naked shall I return thither: the Lord gave, and the Lord hath taken away; blessed be the name of the Lord. *Ibid, 21.*

61 Skin for skin, yea, all that a man hath, will he give for his life. *Ibid, ii. 4.*

62 There the wicked cease from troubling, and there the weary be at rest. *Ibid, iii. 17.*

63 Man is born unto trouble, as the sparks fly upward. *Ibid, v. 7.*

64 My days are swifter than a weaver's shuttle, and are spent without hope. *Ibid, vii. 6.*

65 No doubt but ye are the people, and wisdom shall die with you. *Ibid, xii. 2.*

66 Man that is born of a woman is of few days, and full of trouble. *Ibid, xiv. 1.*

67 Miserable comforters are ye all. *Ibid, xvi. 2.*

1 The king of terrors. *Ibid, xviii. 14.*

2 I am escaped with the skin of my teeth.
Ibid, xix. 20.

3 I know that my redeemer liveth.
Ibid, 25.

4 Seeing the root of the matter is found in
me. *Ibid, 28.*

5 My desire is . . . that mine adversary
had written a book. *Ibid, xxxi. 35.*

6 Who is this that darkeneth counsel by
words without knowledge?
Ibid, xxxviii. 2.

7 When the morning stars sang together,
and all the sons of God shouted for joy.
Ibid, 7.

8 Canst thou bind the sweet influences of
Pleiades, or loose the bands of Orion?
Ibid, 31.

9 He saith among the trumpets, Ha, ha;
and he smelleth the battle afar off, the
thunder of the captains, and the
shouting. *Ibid, xxxix. 25.*

10 Canst thou draw out leviathan with an
hook? *Ibid, xli. 1.*

11 As hard as a piece of the nether
millstone. *Ibid, 24.*

12 He maketh the deep to boil like a pot.
Ibid, 31

13 Why do the heathen rage, and the people
imagine a vain thing? ***Psalms,** ii. 1*

14 Out of the mouth of babes and
sucklings. *Ibid, viii. 2.*

15 Thou hast made him a little lower than
the angels. *Ibid, 5.*

16 The fool hath said in his heart, There is
no God. *Ibid, xiv. 1. and liii. 1.*

17 He that sweareth to his own hurt, and
changeth not. *Ibid, xv. 4.*

18 The lines are fallen unto me in pleasant
places; yea, I have a goodly heritage.
Ibid, xvi, 6.

19 Keep me as the apple of the eye, hide me
under the shadow of thy wings.
Ibid, xvii. 8.

20 Yea, he did fly upon the wings of the
wind. *Ibid, xviii. 10.*

21 The heavens declare the glory of God;
and the firmament showeth his
handiwork. *Ibid, xix. 1.*

22 Day unto day uttereth speech, and night
unto night showeth knowledge.
Ibid, 2.

23 More to be desired are they than gold,
yea, than much fine gold: sweeter also
than honey and the honeycomb.
Ibid, 10.

24 He maketh me to lie down in green
pastures: he leadeth me beside the still
waters. *Ibid, xxiii. 2.*

25 Though I walk through the valley of the
shadow of death. *Ibid, 4.*

26 Thy rod and thy staff they comfort me.
Ibid.

27 Weeping may endure for a night, but
joy cometh in the morning.
Ibid, xxx. 5.

28 My times are in thy hand.
Ibid, xxxi. 15.

29 Eschew evil, and do good: seek peace,
and ensue it.
(Book of Common Prayer rendering.)
Ibid, xxxiv. 14.

30 I have been young, and now am old; yet
have I not seen the righteous forsaken,
nor his seed begging bread.
Ibid, xxxvii. 25.

31 Flourishing like a green bay tree.
(Book of Common Prayer rendering.)
Ibid, 36.

32 He heapeth up riches, and knoweth not who shall gather them. *Ibid, xxxix. 6.*

33 Blessed is he that considereth the poor.
Ibid, xli. 1.

34 As the hart panteth after the water brooks. *Ibid, xlii. 1.*

35 Deep calleth unto deep. *Ibid, 7.*

36 My tongue is the pen of a ready writer.
Ibid, xlv. 1.

37 God is our refuge and strength, a very present help in trouble. *Ibid, xlvi. 1.*

38 Man being in honour abideth not: he is like the beasts that perish.
Ibid, xlix. 12.

39 The cattle upon a thousand hills.
Ibid, l. 10.

40 A broken and a contrite heart, O God, thou wilt not despise. *Ibid, li. 17.*

41 Oh that I had wings like a dove!
Ibid, lv. 6.

42 But it was even thou, my companion, my guide, and mine own familiar friend. (Book of Common Prayer rendering.) *Ibid, 14.*

43 We took sweet counsel together.
Ibid, 14.

44 Vain is the help of man.
Ibid, lx. 11 and cviii. 12.

45 His enemies shall lick the dust.
Ibid, lxii. 9.

46 He putteth down one, and setteth up another. *Ibid, lxxv. 7.*

47 They go from strength to strength.
Ibid, lxxxiv. 7.

48 For a day in thy courts is better than a thousand. I had rather be a doorkeeper in the house of God, than to dwell in the tents of wickedness. *Ibid, 10.*

49 Mercy and truth are met together; righteousness and peace have kissed each other. *Ibid, lxxxv. 10.*

50 For a thousand years in thy sight are but as yesterday when it is past, and as a watch in the night. *Ibid, xc. 4.*

51 We spend our years as a tale that is told.
Ibid, 9.

52 The days of our years are threescore years and ten; and if by reason of strength they be fourscore years, yet is their strength labour and sorrow; for it is soon cut off, and we fly away.
Ibid, 10.

53 So teach us to number our days, that we may apply our hearts unto wisdom.
Ibid, 12.

54 I will say of the Lord, He is my refuge and my fortress: my God; in him will I trust. *Ibid, xci. 2.*

55 Nor for the pestilence that walketh in darkness; nor for the destruction that wasteth at noonday. *Ibid, 6.*

56 As for man, his days are as grass: as a flower of the field, so he flourisheth.
Ibid, ciii. 15.

57 For the wind passeth over it, and it is gone; and the place thereof shall know it no more. *Ibid, 16.*

58 Wine that maketh glad the heart of man.
Ibid, civ. 15.

59 They that go down to the sea in ships, that do business in great waters.
Ibid, cvii. 23.

60 They reel to and fro, and stagger like a drunken man, and are at their wit's end.
Ibid, 27.

61 I said in my haste, All men are liars.
Ibid, cxvi. 11.

62 Precious in the sight of the Lord is the death of his saints. *Ibid, 15.*

1 This is the day which the Lord hath made; we will rejoice and be glad in it. *Ibid, cxviii. 24.*

2 Thy word is a lamp unto my feet, and a light unto my path. *Ibid, cxix. 105.*

3 The sun shall not smite thee by day, nor the moon by night. *Ibid, cxxi. 6.*

4 Except the Lord build the house, they labour in vain that build it. *Ibid, cxxvii. 1.*

5 He giveth his beloved sleep. *Ibid, 2.*

6 Happy is the man that hath his quiver full of them. *Ibid, 5.*

7 Thy children like the olive branches round about thy table. (Book of Common Prayer rendering.) *Ibid, cxxviii. 3.*

8 Behold, how good and how pleasant it is for brethren to dwell together in unity! *Ibid, cxxxiii. 1.*

9 We hanged our harps upon the willows. *Ibid, cxxxvii. 2.*

10 How shall we sing the Lord's song in a strange land? *Ibid, 4.*

11 If I forget thee, O Jerusalem, let my right hand forget her cunning. *Ibid, 5.*

12 If I take the wings of the morning, and dwell in the uttermost parts of the sea. *Ibid, cxxxix. 9.*

13 I am fearfully and wonderfully made. *Ibid, 14.*

14 Put not your trust in princes. *Ibid, cxlvi. 3.*

15 Surely in vain the net is spread in the sight of any bird. **Proverbs,** *i. 17.*

16 Wisdom crieth without; she uttereth her voice in the streets. *Ibid, 20.*

17 Her ways are ways of pleasantness, and all her paths are peace. *Ibid, iii. 17.*

18 The path of the just is as the shining light, that shineth more and more unto the perfect day. *Ibid, iv. 18.*

19 Go to the ant, thou sluggard; consider her ways, and be wise. *Ibid, vi. 6.*

20 Yet a little sleep, a little slumber, a little folding of the hands to sleep. *Ibid, 10.*

21 As an ox goeth to the slaughter. *Ibid, vii. 22.*

22 Wisdom is better than rubies. *Ibid, viii. 11.*

23 Stolen waters are sweet, and bread eaten in secret is pleasant. *Ibid, ix. 17.*

24 A wise son maketh a glad father: but a foolish son is the heaviness of his mother. *Ibid, x. 1.*

25 In the multitude of counsellors there is safety. *Ibid, xi. 14 and xxiv. 6.*

26 As a jewel of gold in a swine's snout, so is a fair woman which is without discretion. *Ibid, 22.*

27 A righteous man regardeth the life of his beast; but the tender mercies of the wicked are cruel. *Ibid, xii. 10.*

28 Hope deferred maketh the heart sick. *Ibid, xiii. 12.*

29 The way of transgressors is hard. *Ibid, 15.*

30 He that spareth the rod hateth his son. *Ibid, 24.*

31 The heart knoweth his own bitterness; and a stranger doth not intermeddle with his joy. *Ibid, xiv. 10.*

32 A soft answer turneth away wrath. *Ibid, xv. 1.*

33 A merry heart maketh a cheerful countenance. *Ibid, 13.*

34 Better is a dinner of herbs where love is, than a stalled ox and hatred therewith. *Ibid, 17.*

35 A word spoken in due season, how
good it is! *Ibid, 23.*

36 Pride goeth before destruction, and an
haughty spirit before a fall.
Ibid, xvi. 18.

37 The hoary head is a crown of glory, if it
be found in the way of righteousness.
Ibid, 31.

38 He that repeateth a matter separateth
very friends. *Ibid, xvii. 9.*

39 A merry heart doeth good like a
medicine. *Ibid, 22.*

40 He that hath knowledge spareth his
words. *Ibid, 27.*

41 Even a fool, when he holdeth his peace,
is counted wise. *Ibid, 28.*

42 Whoso findeth a wife findeth a good
thing. *Ibid, xviii. 22.*

43 There is a friend that sticketh closer than
a brother. *Ibid, 24.*

44 He that hath pity upon the poor lendeth
unto the Lord. *Ibid, xix. 17.*

45 Wine is a mocker, strong drink is
raging. *Ibid, xx. 1.*

46 Every fool will be meddling. *Ibid, 3.*

47 It is naught, it is naught, saith the buyer:
but when he is gone his way, then he
boasteth. *Ibid, 14.*

48 It is better to dwell in a corner of the
housetop, than with a brawling woman
in a wide house. *Ibid, xxi. 9.*

49 A good name is rather to be chosen than
great riches. *Ibid, xxii. 1.*

50 Train up a child in the way he should go:
and when he is old, he will not depart
from it. *Ibid, 6.*

51 Riches certainly make themselves
wings. *Ibid, xxiii. 5.*

52 Look not thou upon the wine when it is
red. *Ibid, 31.*

53 At the last it biteth like a serpent, and
stingeth like an adder. *Ibid, 32.*

54 As cold waters to a thirsty soul, so is
good news from a far country.
Ibid, xxv. 25.

55 Answer not a fool according to his folly,
lest thou also be like unto him.
Ibid, xxvi. 4.

56 Answer a fool according to his folly, lest
he be wise in his own conceit. *Ibid, 5.*

57 The sluggard is wiser in his own conceit
than seven men that can render a reason.
Ibid, 16.

58 Whoso diggeth a pit shall fall therein.
Ibid, 27.

59 Boast not thyself of to-morrow; for
thou knowest not what a day may bring
forth. *Ibid, xxvii. 1.*

60 Faithful are the wounds of a friend.
Ibid, 6.

61 A continual dropping in a very rainy day
and a contentious woman are alike.
Ibid, 15.

62 Iron sharpeneth iron; so a man
sharpeneth the countenance of his
friend. *Ibid, 17.*

63 Though thou shouldest bray a fool in a
mortar among wheat with a pestle, yet
will not his foolishness depart from him.
Ibid, 22.

64 The wicked flee when no man pursueth:
but the righteous are bold as a lion.
Ibid, xxviii.1.

65 He that maketh haste to be rich shall not
be innocent. *Ibid, 20.*

66 Where there is no vision, the people
perish. *Ibid, xxix. 18.*

67 The horseleach hath two daughters,
crying, Give, give. *Ibid, xxx. 15.*

1 The way of an eagle in the air; the way of a serpent upon a rock; the way of a ship in the midst of the sea; and the way of a man with a maid. *Ibid, 19.*

2 The spider taketh hold with her hands, and is in king's palaces. *Ibid, 28.*

3 Who can find a virtuous woman? for her price is far above rubies. *Ibid, xxxi. 10.*

4 Her children arise up, and call her blessed. *Ibid, 28.*

5 Vanity of vanities; all is vanity.
Ecclesiastes, i. 2.

6 What profit hath a man of all his labour which he taketh under the sun? *Ibid, 3.*

7 One generation passeth away, and another generation cometh: but the earth abideth for ever. *Ibid, 4.*

8 All the rivers run into the sea; yet the sea is not full. *Ibid, 7.*

9 There is no new thing under the sun.
Ibid, 9.

10 All is vanity and vexation of spirit.
Ibid, 14.

11 He that increaseth knowledge increaseth sorrow. *Ibid, 18.*

12 One event happeneth to them all.
Ibid, ii. 14.

13 To everthing there is a season, and a time to every purpose under the heaven.
Ibid, iii. 1.

14 A threefold cord is not quickly broken.
Ibid, iv. 12.

15 God is in heaven, and thou upon earth: therefore let thy words be few.
Ibid, v. 2.

16 Better is it that thou shouldest not vow, than that thou shouldest vow and not pay. *Ibid, 5.*

17 A good name is better than precious ointment; and the day of death than the day of one's birth. *Ibid, vii. 1.*

18 It is better to go to the house of mourning than to go to the house of feasting. *Ibid, 2.*

19 As the crackling of thorns under a pot, so is the laughter of the fool. *Ibid, 6.*

20 Say not thou, What is the cause that the former days were better than these? for thou dost not enquire wisely concerning this. *Ibid, 10.*

21 Be not righteous overmuch. *Ibid, 16.*

22 God hath made man upright; but they have sought out many inventions.
Ibid, 29.

23 A living dog is better than a dead lion.
Ibid, ix. 4.

24 Whatsoever thy hand findeth to do, do it with thy might. *Ibid, 10.*

25 The race is not to the swift, nor the battle to the strong, neither yet bread to the wise, nor yet riches to men of understanding, nor yet favour to men of skill; but time and chance happeneth to them all. *Ibid, 11.*

26 Dead flies cause the ointment of the apothecary to send forth a stinking savour. *Ibid, x. 1.*

27 For a bird of the air shall carry the voice, and that which hath wings shall tell the matter. *Ibid, 20.*

28 Cast thy bread upon the waters: for thou shalt find it after many days.
Ibid, xi. 1.

29 In the place where the tree falleth, there it shall be. *Ibid, 3.*

30 Truly the light is sweet, and a pleasant thing it is for the eyes to behold the sun.
Ibid, 7.

31 Rejoice, O young man, in thy youth.
Ibid, 9.

32 Remember now thy Creator in the days of thy youth, while the evil days come not, nor the years draw nigh, when thou shalt say, I have no pleasure in them.
Ibid, xii. 1.

33 And the grasshopper shall be a burden, and desire shall fail: because man goeth to his long home, and the mourners go about the streets. *Ibid, 5.*

34 Or ever the silver cord be loosed, or the golden bowl be broken, or the pitcher be broken at the fountain, or the wheel broken at the cistern. *Ibid, 6.*

35 Then shall the dust return to the earth as it was: and the spirit shall return unto God who gave it. *Ibid, 7.*

36 Of making many books there is no end; and much study is weariness of the flesh.
Ibid, 12.

37 Let us hear the conclusion of the whole matter: Fear God, and keep his commandments: for this is the whole duty of man. *Ibid, 13.*

38 Let him kiss me with the kisses of his mouth: for thy love is better than wine.
The Song of Solomon, i. 2.

39 Stay me with flagons, comfort me with apples: for I am sick of love. *Ibid, ii. 5.*

40 For, lo, the winter is past, the rain is over and gone; The flowers appear on the earth; the time of the singing of birds is come, and the voice of the turtle is heard in our land. *Ibid, 11.*

41 Take us the foxes, the little foxes, that spoil the vines. *Ibid, 15.*

42 Until the day break, and the shadows flee away. *Ibid, 17.*

43 Who is she that looketh forth as the morning, fair as the moon, clear as the sun, and terrible as an army with banners? *Ibid, vi. 10.*

44 Set me as a seal upon thine heart, as a seal upon thine arm: for love is strong as

death; jealousy is cruel as the grave.
Ibid, viii. 6.

45 Many waters cannot quench love.
Ibid, 7.

46 The ox knoweth his owner, and the ass his master's crib. **Isaiah, i. 3.**

47 Though your sins be as scarlet, they shall be as white as snow. *Ibid, 18.*

48 They shall beat their swords into plowshares, and their spears into pruninghooks; nation shall not lift up sword against nation, neither shall they learn war any more.
*Ibid, ii. 4 and **Micah, iv. 3.***

49 Grind the faces of the poor.
Ibid, iii. 15.

50 Woe unto them that call evil good, and good evil. *Ibid, v. 20.*

51 Wizards that peep, and that mutter.
Ibid, viii. 19.

52 The wolf also shall dwell with the lamb, and the leopard shall lie down with the kid. *Ibid, xi. 6.*

53 How art thou fallen from heaven, O Lucifer, son of the morning!
Ibid, xiv. 12.

54 Watchman, what of the night?
Ibid, xxi. 11.

55 Let us eat and drink; for to-morrow we shall die. *Ibid, xxii. 13.*

56 Whose merchants are princes.
Ibid, xxiii. 8.

57 For precept must be upon precept, precept upon precept; line upon line, line upon line; here a little, and there a little. *Ibid, xxviii. 10.*

58 The desert shall rejoice, and blossom as the rose. *Ibid, xxxv. 1.*

59 Set thine house in order.
Ibid, xxxviii. 1.

1 All flesh is grass.   *Ibid, xl. 6.*

2 A bruised reed shall he not break, and the smoking flax shall he not quench.
    Ibid, xlii. 3.

3 There is no peace, saith the Lord, unto the wicked.   *Ibid, xlviii.* 22.

4 How beautiful upon the mountains are the feet of him that bringeth good tidings, that publisheth peace.
    Ibid, lii. 7.

5 A man of sorrows, and acquainted with grief.   *Ibid, liii. 3.*

6 All we like sheep have gone astray.
    Ibid, 6.

7 He is brought as a lamb to the slaughter.
    Ibid, 7.

8 Seek ye the Lord while he may be found, call ye upon him while he is near.
    Ibid, lv. 6.

9 For my thoughts are not your thoughts, neither are your ways my ways, saith the Lord.   *Ibid, 8.*

10 All our righteousnesses are as filthy rags; and we all do fade as a leaf.
    Ibid, lxiv. 6.

11 Saying, Peace, peace; when there is no peace.   **Jeremiah,** *v. 14 and viii. 11.*

12 Is there no balm in Gilead?
    Ibid, viii. 22.

13 Can the Ethiopian change his skin, or the leopard his spots?   *Ibid, xiii. 23.*

14 Is it nothing to you, all ye that pass by? behold, and see if there be any sorrow like unto my sorrow.
    Lamentations, *i. 12.*

15 As if a wheel had been in the midst of a wheel.   **Ezekiel,** *x. 10.*

16 The fathers have eaten sour grapes, and the children's teeth are set on edge.
    Ibid, xviii. 2.

17 Can these bones live?   *Ibid, xxxvii. 3.*

18 Cast into the midst of a burning fiery furnace.   **Daniel,** *iii. 6.*

19 Thou art weighed in the balances, and art found wanting.   *Ibid, v. 27.*

20 According to the law of the Medes and Persians, which altereth not.
    Ibid, vi. 12.

21 The Ancient of days.   *Ibid, vii. 13.*

22 Many shall run to and fro, and knowledge shall be increased.
    Ibid, xii. 4.

23 They have sown the wind, and they shall reap the whirlwind.
    Hosea, *viii. 7.*

24 I have multiplied visions, and used similitudes.   *Ibid, xii. 10.*

25 Your old men shall dream dreams, your young men shall see visions.
    Joel, *ii. 28.*

26 They shall sit every man under his vine and under his fig tree.   **Micah,** *iv. 4.*

27 Write the vision, and make it plain upon tables, that he may run that readeth it.
    Habakkuk, *ii. 2.*

28 Who hath despised the day of small things?   **Zechariah,** *iv. 10.*

29 I was wounded in the house of my friends.   *Ibid, xiii. 6.*

30 But unto you that fear my name shall the Sun of righteousness arise with healing in his wings.   **Malachi,** *iv. 2.*

THE NEW TESTAMENT

31 The voice of one crying in the wilderness, Prepare ye the way of the Lord, make his paths straight.
    Matthew, *iii. 3.*

32 O generation of vipers, who hath

warned you to flee from the wrath to come? *Ibid, 7.*

33 And now also the axe is laid unto the root of the trees.
*Ibid, 10 and **Luke**, iii. 9.*

34 Man shall not live by bread alone, but by every word that proceedeth out of the mouth of God. *Ibid, iv. 4.*

35 Blessed are the meek: for they shall inherit the earth. *Ibid, v. 5.*

36 Blessed are the pure in heart: for they shall see God. *Ibid, 8.*

37 Blessed are the peacemakers: for they shall be called the children of God.
Ibid, 9.

38 Ye are the salt of the earth: but if the salt have lost his savour, wherewith shall it be salted? *Ibid, 13.*

39 Ye are the light of the world. A city that is set on an hill cannot be hid. *Ibid, 14.*

40 Let your light so shine before men, that they may see your good works, and glorify your Father which is in heaven.
Ibid, 16.

41 Whosoever shall say, Thou fool, shall be in danger of hell fire. *Ibid, 22.*

42 Till thou hast paid the uttermost farthing. *Ibid, 26.*

43 An eye for an eye, and a tooth for a tooth. *Ibid, 38.*

44 Whosoever shall smite thee on thy right cheek, turn to him the other also.
Ibid, 39.

45 Love your enemies. *Ibid, 44.*

46 He maketh his sun to rise on the evil and on the good, and sendeth rain on the just and on the unjust. *Ibid, 45.*

47 When thou doest alms, let not thy left hand know what thy right hand doeth.
Ibid, vi. 3.

48 Our Father which art in heaven, Hallowed be thy name. Thy kingdom come. Thy will be done in earth, as it is in heaven. Give us this day our daily bread. And forgive us our debts, as we forgive our debtors. And lead us not into temptation, but deliver us from evil: For thine is the kingdom, and the power, and the glory, for ever. Amen.
Ibid, 9.

49 Where moth and rust doth corrupt, and where thieves break through and steal.
Ibid, 19.

50 Where your treasure is, there will your heart be also. *Ibid, 21.*

51 No man can serve two masters.
Ibid, 24.

52 Ye cannot serve God and mammon.
Ibid.

53 Which of you by taking thought can add one cubit unto his stature? *Ibid, 27.*

54 Consider the lilies of the field, how they grow; they toil not, neither do they spin. *Ibid, 28.*

55 Seek ye first the kingdom of God, and his righteousness; and all these things shall be added unto you. *Ibid, 33.*

56 Take therefore no thought for the morrow; for the morrow shall take thought for the things of itself. Sufficient unto the day is the evil thereof. *Ibid, 34.*

57 Judge not, that ye be not judged.
Ibid, vii. 1.

58 Why beholdest thou the mote that is in thy brother's eye, but considerest not the beam that is in thine own eye?
Ibid, 3.

59 Neither cast ye your pearls before swine. *Ibid, 6.*

60 Ask, and it shall be given you; seek, and ye shall find; knock, and it shall be opened unto you. *Ibid, 7.*

1 What man is there of you, whom if his son ask bread, will he give him a stone? *Ibid, 9.*

2 Therefore all things whatsoever ye would that men should do to you, do ye even so to them: for this is the law and the prophets. *Ibid, 12.*

3 Wide is the gate, and broad is the way, that leadeth to destruction, and many there be which go in thereat. *Ibid, 13.*

4 Strait is the gate, and narrow is the way, which leadeth unto life, and few there be that find it. *Ibid, 14.*

5 Beware of false prophets, which come to you in sheep's clothing, but inwardly they are ravening wolves. *Ibid, 15.*

6 By their fruits ye shall know them. *Ibid, 20.*

7 For he taught them as one having authority, and not as the scribes. *Ibid, 29.*

8 There shall be weeping and gnashing of teeth. *Ibid, viii. 12.*

9 The foxes have holes, and the birds of the air have nests; but the Son of man hath not where to lay his head. *Ibid, 20.*

10 Let the dead bury their dead. *Ibid, 22.*

11 The harvest truly is plenteous, but the labourers are few. *Ibid, ix. 37.*

12 Freely ye have received, freely give. *Ibid, x. 8.*

13 Be ye therefore wise as serpents, and harmless as doves. *Ibid, 16.*

14 The very hairs of your head are all numbered. *Ibid, 30.*

15 He that findeth his life shall lose it: and he that loseth his life for my sake shall find it. *Ibid, 39.*

16 What went ye out into the wilderness to see? A reed shaken with the wind? *Ibid, xi. 7.*

17 Wisdom is justified of her children. *Ibid, 19.*

18 Come unto me, all ye that labour and are heavy laden, and I will give you rest. *Ibid, 28.*

19 He that is not with me is against me. *Ibid, xii. 30 and **Luke**, xi. 23.*

20 Empty, swept, and garnished. *Ibid, 44.*

21 The last state of that man is worse than the first. *Ibid, 45.*

22 Some seeds fell by the way side. *Ibid, xiii. 4.*

23 An enemy hath done this. *Ibid, 28.*

24 When he had found one pearl of great price. *Ibid, 46.*

25 A prophet is not without honour, save in his own country, and in his own house. *Ibid, 57.*

26 Be of good cheer; it is I; be not afraid. *Ibid, xiv. 27.*

27 If the blind lead the blind, both shall fall into the ditch. *Ibid, xv. 14.*

28 The dogs eat of the crumbs which fall from their masters' table. *Ibid, 27.*

29 Thou art Peter, and upon this rock I will build my church; and the gates of hell shall not prevail against it. *Ibid, xvi. 18.*

30 Get thee behind me, Satan. *Ibid, 23.*

31 It is good for us to be here. *Ibid, xvii. 4.*

32 Except ye be converted, and become as little children, ye shall not enter into the kingdom of heaven. *Ibid, xviii. 3.*

33 But whoso shall offend one of these little ones which believe in me, it were better for him that a millstone were hanged about his neck and that he were drowned in the depth of the sea. *Ibid, 6.*

34 If thine eye offend thee, pluck it out, and cast it from thee: it is better for thee to enter into life with one eye, rather than having two eyes to be cast into hell fire.
Ibid, 9.

35 Where two or three are gathered together in my name, there am I in the midst of them. *Ibid, 20.*

36 Until seventy times seven. *Ibid, 22.*

37 What therefore God hath joined together, let not man put asunder.
Ibid, xix. 6.

38 Thou shalt love thy neighbour as thyself. *Ibid, 19.*

39 It is easier for a camel to go through the eye of a needle, than for a rich man to enter into the kingdom of God.
Ibid, 24.

40 With men this is impossible; but with God all things are possible. *Ibid, 26.*

41 But many that are first shall be last; and the last shall be first. *Ibid, 30.*

42 Borne the burden and heat of the day.
Ibid, xx. 12.

43 The stone which the builders rejected, the same is become the head of the corner. *Ibid, xxi. 42.*

44 For many are called, but few are chosen.
Ibid, xxii. 14.

45 Render therefore unto Caesar the things which are Caesar's; and unto God the things that are God's. *Ibid, 21.*

46 Ye pay tithe of mint and anise and cummin. *Ibid, xxiii. 23.*

47 Blind guides, which strain at a gnat, and swallow a camel. *Ibid, 24.*

48 Whited sepulchres, which indeed appear beautiful outward, but are within full of dead men's bones. *Ibid, 27.*

49 Wars and rumour of wars. *Ibid, xxiv. 6.*

50 For nation shall rise against nation, and kingdom against kingdom. *Ibid, 7.*

51 The abomination of desolation.
Ibid, 15.

52 Wheresoever the carcase is, there will the eagles be gathered together.
Ibid, 28.

53 Eating and drinking, marrying and giving in marriage. *Ibid, 38.*

54 Well done, thou good and faithful servant. *Ibid, xxv. 21.*

55 Unto every one that hath shall be given, and he shall have abundance: but from him that hath not shall be taken away even that which he hath. *Ibid, 29.*

56 I was a stranger, and ye took me in.
Ibid, 35.

57 Thirty pieces of silver. *Ibid, xxvi. 15.*

58 Watch and pray, that ye enter not into temptation: the spirit indeed is willing, but the flesh is weak. *Ibid, 41.*

59 All they that take the sword shall perish with the sword. *Ibid, 52.*

60 Thy speech bewrayeth thee. *Ibid, 73.*

61 He saved others; himself he cannot save.
Ibid, xxvii. 42.

62 Eli, Eli, lama sabachthani? that is to say, My God, my God, why hast thou forsaken me? *Ibid, 46.*

63 The sabbath was made for man, and not man for the sabbath. ***Mark****, ii. 27.*

64 If a house be divided against itself, that house cannot stand. *Ibid, iii. 25.*

65 He that hath ears to hear, let him hear.
Ibid, iv. 9.

66 My name is Legion. *Ibid, v. 9.*

67 Clothed, and in his right mind.
Ibid, 15.

1 I see men as trees, walking.
Ibid, viii. 24.

2 What shall it profit a man, if he shall gain the whole world, and lose his own soul? *Ibid, 36.*

3 Where their worm dieth not, and the fire is not quenched. *Ibid, ix. 44.*

4 Suffer the little children to come unto me, and forbid them not: for of such is the kingdom of God. *Ibid, x. 14.*

5 Which devour widows' houses, and for a pretence make long prayers.
Ibid, xii. 40.

6 Go ye into all the world, and preach the gospel to every creature. *Ibid, xvi. 15.*

7 Glory to God in the highest, and on earth peace, good will toward men.
Luke, ii. 14.

8 Physician, heal thyself. *Ibid, iv. 23.*

9 The only son of his mother, and she was a widow. *Ibid, vii. 12.*

10 No man, having put his hand to the plough and looking back, is fit for the kingdom of God. *Ibid, ix. 62.*

11 The labourer is worthy of his hire.
Ibid, x. 7.

12 He passed by on the other side.
Ibid, 31.

13 Go, and do thou likewise. *Ibid, 37.*

14 But one thing is needful: and Mary hath chosen that good part, which shall not be taken away from her. *Ibid, 42.*

15 Thou fool, this night thy soul shall be required of thee. *Ibid, xii. 20.*

16 Let your loins be girded about, and your lights burning. *Ibid, 35.*

17 Friend, go up higher. *Ibid, xiv. 10.*

18 For whosoever exalteth himself shall be abased; and he that humbleth himself shall be exalted. *Ibid, 11.*

19 I have married a wife, and therefore I cannot come. *Ibid, 20.*

20 The poor, and the maimed, and the halt, and the blind. *Ibid, 21.*

21 Go out into the highways and hedges, and compel them to come in. *Ibid, 23.*

22 Rejoice with me; for I have found my sheep which was lost. *Ibid, xv. 6.*

23 Joy shall be in heaven over one sinner that repenteth, more than over ninety and nine just persons, which need no repentance. *Ibid, 7.*

24 Wasted his substance with riotous living. *Ibid, 13.*

25 And he would fain have filled his belly with the husks that the swine did eat.
Ibid, 16.

26 I cannot dig; to beg I am ashamed.
Ibid, xvi. 3.

27 The children of this world are in their generation wiser than the children of light. *Ibid, 8.*

28 Make to yourselves friends of the mammon of unrighteousness. *Ibid, 9.*

29 There was a certain rich man, which was clothed in purple and fine linen, and fared sumptuously every day. *Ibid, 19.*

30 Between us and you there is a great gulf fixed. *Ibid, 26.*

31 We are unprofitable servants: we have done that which was our duty to do.
Ibid, xvii. 10.

32 The kingdom of God is within you.
Ibid, 21.

33 Remember Lot's wife. *Ibid, 32.*

34 God, I thank thee, that I am not as other men are, extortioners, unjust, adulterers, or even as this publican.
Ibid, xviii. 11.

35 God be merciful to me a sinner.
Ibid, 13.

36 Out of thine own mouth will I judge
thee. *Ibid, xix. 22.*

37 For if they do these things in a green
tree, what shall be done in the dry?
Ibid, xxiii. 31.

38 Father, forgive them; for they know not
what they do. *Ibid, 34.*

39 Whose shoe's latchet I am not worthy to
unloose. *John, i. 27.*

40 Can there any good thing come out of
Nazareth? *Ibid, 46.*

41 The wind bloweth where it listeth, and
thou hearest the sound thereof, but canst
not tell whence it cometh, and whither it
goeth. *Ibid, iii. 8.*

42 God so loved the world, that he gave his
only begotten Son, that whosoever
believeth in him should not perish, but
have everlasting life. *Ibid, 16.*

43 Men loved darkness rather than light,
because their deeds were evil. *Ibid, 19.*

44 He was a burning and a shining light.
Ibid, v. 35.

45 Judge not according to the appearance.
Ibid, vii. 24.

46 He that is without sin among you, let
him first cast a stone at her. *Ibid, viii. 7.*

47 The truth shall make you free. *Ibid, 32.*

48 The night cometh, when no man can
work. *Ibid, ix. 4.*

49 The hireling fleeth, because he is an
hireling, and careth not for the sheep.
Ibid, x. 13.

50 I am the resurrection, and the life.
Ibid, xi. 25.

51 For the poor always ye have with you.
Ibid, xii. 8.

52 A new commandment I give unto you,
That ye love one another. *Ibid, xiii. 34.*

53 Let not your heart be troubled: ye
believe in God, believe also in me.
Ibid, xiv. 1.

54 In my Father's house are many
mansions. *Ibid, 2.*

55 Greater love hath no man than this, that
a man lay down his life for his friends.
Ibid, xv. 13.

56 What I have written I have written.
Ibid, xix. 22.

57 Silver and gold have I none; but such as I
have give I thee. *Acts, iii. 6.*

58 Thy money perish with thee.
Ibid, viii. 20.

59 Breathing out threatenings and
slaughter. *Ibid, ix. 1.*

60 It is hard for thee to kick against the
pricks. *Ibid, 5.*

61 God is no respecter of persons.
Ibid, x. 34.

62 Come over into Macedonia, and help
us. *Ibid, xvi. 9.*

63 Certain lewd fellows of the baser sort.
Ibid, xvii. 5.

64 For in him we live, and move, and have
our being. *Ibid, 28.*

65 Gallio cared for none of those things.
Ibid, xviii. 17.

66 Great is Diana of the Ephesians.
Ibid, xix. 34.

67 It is more blessed to give than to receive.
Ibid, xx. 35.

68 A citizen of no mean city.
Ibid, xxi. 39.

69 Brought up in this city at the feet of
Gamaliel. *Ibid, xxii. 3.*

1 With a great sum obtained I this freedom. *Ibid, 28.*

2 Hast thou appealed unto Caesar? Unto Casesar shalt thou go. *Ibid, xxv. 12*

3 Paul, thou art beside thyself; much learning doth make thee mad. *Ibid, xxvi. 24*

4 Words of truth and soberness. *Ibid, 25*

5 For this thing was not done in a corner. *Ibid, 26.*

6 Almost thou persuadest me to be a Christian. *Ibid, 28.*

7 They cast four anchors out of the stern, and wished for the day. *Ibid, xxvii. 29.*

8 A law unto themselves. **Romans,** *ii. 14.*

9 (As some affirm that we say) Let us do evil, that good may come. *Ibid, iii. 8.*

10 The wages of sin is death. *Ibid, vi. 23.*

11 And we know that all things work together for good to them that love God. *Ibid, viii. 28.*

12 If God be for us, who can be against us? *Ibid, 31.*

13 For I am persuaded that neither death, nor life, nor angels, nor principalities, nor powers, nor things present, nor things to come, Nor height, nor depth, nor any other creature, shall be able to separate us from the love of God, which is in Christ Jesus our Lord. *Ibid, 38.*

14 Be not wise in your own conceits. *Ibid, xii. 16.*

15 Vengeance is mine; I will repay, saith the Lord. *Ibid, 19.*

16 Therefore if thine enemy hunger, feed him; if he thirst, give him drink: for in so doing thou shalt heap coals of fire on his head. *Ibid, 20.*

17 Be not overcome of evil, but overcome evil with good. *Ibid, 21.*

18 The powers that be are ordained of God. *Ibid, xiii. 1*

19 The night is far spent, the day is at hand. *Ibid, 12*

20 None of us liveth to himself. *Ibid, xiv 7*

21 Absent in body, but present in spirit. **1 Corinthians,** *v 3*

22 Know ye not that a little leaven leaveneth the whole lump? *Ibid, 6*

23 It is better to marry than to burn. *Ibid, vii. 9*

24 I am made all things to all men. *Ibid, ix. 22*

25 But I keep under my body, and bring it into subjection. *Ibid, 27*

26 All things are lawful for me, but all things are not expedient. *Ibid, x. 23*

27 For the earth is the Lord's, and the fulness thereof. *Ibid, 26.*

28 If a woman have long hair, it is a glory to her. *Ibid, xi. 15.*

29 Though I speak with the tongues of men and of angels, and have not charity, I am become as sounding brass, or a tinkling cymbal. *Ibid, xiii. 1.*

30 When I was a child, I spake as a child, I understood as a child, I thought as a child. but when I became a man, I put away childish things. *Ibid, 11*

31 For now we see through a glass, darkly; but then face to face. *Ibid, 12*

32 And now abideth faith, hope, charity, these three; but the greatest of these is charity. *Ibid, 13.*

33 Let all things be done decently and in order. *Ibid, xiv. 40.*

34 Let us eat and drink; for to-morrow we die. *Ibid, xv. 32.*

35 Behold, I show you a mystery; We shall not all sleep, but we shall all be changed, In a moment, in the twinkling of an eye, at the last trump. *Ibid, 51*

36 O death, where is thy sting? O grave, where is thy victory? *Ibid, 55*

37 Quit you like men, be strong. *Ibid, xvi. 13*

38 Not of the letter, but of the spirit. *2 Corinthians, iii. 6*

39 For we walk by faith, not by sight. *Ibid, v. 7*

40 God loveth a cheerful giver. *Ibid, ix. 7.*

41 For ye suffer fools gladly, seeing ye yourselves are wise. *Ibid, xi. 19.*

42 A thorn in the flesh. *Ibid, xii. 7*

43 And he said unto me, My grace is sufficient for thee: for my strength is made perfect in weakness. *Ibid, 9*

44 The right hands of fellowship. *Galatians, ii. 9.*

45 God is not mocked: for whatsoever a man soweth, that shall he also reap. *Ibid, vi. 7*

46 Let us not be weary in well-doing. *Ibid, 9.*

47 Be ye angry, and sin not: let not the sun go down upon your wrath. *Ephesians, iv. 26.*

48 Put on the whole armour of God. *Ibid, vi. 11.*

49 For me to live is Christ, and to die is gain. *Philippians, i. 21.*

50 Work out your own salvation with fear and trembling. *Ibid, ii. 12.*

51 Whose God is their belly, and whose glory is in their shame. *Ibid, iii. 19.*

52 The peace of God, which passeth all understanding. *Ibid, iv 7*

53 Whatsoever things are true, whatsoever things are honest, whatsoever things are just, whatsoever things are pure, whatsoever things are lovely, whatsoever things are of good report; if there be any virtue, and if there be any praise, think on these things. *Ibid, 8*

54 Touch not, taste not, handle not. *Colossians, ii. 21*

55 Labour of love. *1 Thessalonians, i. 3*

56 Study to be quiet. *Ibid, iv. 11*

57 Pray without ceasing. *Ibid, v. 17*

58 Prove all things; hold fast that which is good. *Ibid, 21.*

59 Not greedy of filthy lucre. *1 Timothy, iii. 3.*

60 Drink no longer water, but use a little wine for thy stomach's sake and thine often infirmities. *Ibid, v. 23.*

61 The love of money is the root of all evil. *Ibid, vi. 10.*

62 Fight the good fight. *Ibid, 12.*

63 Science falsely so called. *Ibid, 20.*

64 I have fought a good fight, I have finished my course, I have kept the faith. *2 Timothy, iv. 7*

65 Unto the pure all things are pure. *Titus, i. 15.*

66 Faith is the substance of things hoped for, the evidence of things not seen. *Hebrews, xi. 1.*

67 Whom the Lord loveth he chasteneth. *Ibid, xii. 6.*

68 Let brotherly love continue. *Ibid, xiii. 1.*

69 Be not forgetful to entertain strangers: for thereby some have entertained angels unawares *Ibid, 2.*

1 Jesus Christ the same yesterday, and to-
day, and for ever.   *Ibid, 8.*

2 The tongue can no man tame; it is an
unruly evil.   *James, iii. 8.*
(Commonly misquoted, 'The tongue is
an unruly member.')

3 Resist the devil, and he will flee from
you.   *Ibid, iv. 7.*

4 Honour all men. Love the brotherhood.
Fear God. Honour the king.
        1 Peter, ii. 17.

5 Giving honour unto the wife, as unto
the weaker vessel.   *Ibid, iii. 7*

6 Charity shall cover the multitude of
sins.   *Ibid, iv. 8.*

7 Be sober, be vigilant; because your
adversary the devil, as a roaring lion,
walketh about, seeking whom he may
devour.   *Ibid, v. 8.*

8 The dog is turned to his own vomit
again; and the sow that was washed to
her wallowing in the mire.
        2 Peter, ii. 22.

9 Bowels of compassion.   *1 John, iii. 17.*

10 God is love.   *Ibid, iv. 8.*

11 There is no fear in love; but perfect love
casteth out fear.   *Ibid, 18.*

12 Be thou faithful unto death, and I will
give thee a crown of life.
        Revelation, ii. 10.

13 He shall rule them with a rod of iron.
        Ibid, 27.

14 I know thy works, that thou art neither
cold nor hot: I would thou wert cold or
hot.   *Ibid, iii. 15.*

15 He went forth conquering, and to
conquer.   *Ibid, vi. 2*

16 And I looked, and behold a pale horse:
and his name that sat on him was Death.
        Ibid, 8.

17 And I saw a new heaven and a new
earth: for the first heaven and the first
earth were passed away; and there was
no more sea.   *Ibid, xxi. 1*

18 And God shall wipe away all tears from
their eyes; and there shall be no more
death, neither sorrow, nor crying,
neither shall there be any more pain: for
the former things are passed away. And
he that sat upon the throne said, Behold,
I make all things new.   *Ibid, xxi. 4.*

19 I am Alpha and Omega, the beginning
and the end, the first and the last.
        Ibid, xxii. 13.

THE APOCRYPHA

20 Great is truth, and mighty above all
things.   *1 Esdras, iv. 41.*

21 Miss not the discourse of the elders.
        Ecclesiasticus, viii. 9.

22 He that toucheth pitch shall be defiled
therewith.   *Ibid, xiii. 1.*

23 As the clear light is upon the holy
candlestick, so is the beauty of the face
in ripe age.   *Ibid, xxvi. 17*

24 Whose talk is of bullocks.
        Ibid, xxxviii. 25.

25 Let us now praise famous men, and our
fathers that begat us.   *Ibid, xliv. 1*

26 It was an holy and good thought.
        2 Maccabees, xii. 45

27 And Nicanor lay dead in his harness.
        Ibid, xv. 28.

THE BOOK OF COMMON PRAYER

28 We have left undone those things which
we ought to have done; And we have
done those things which we ought not
to have done.
        Morning Prayer. General Confession.

29 The noble army of Martyrs.
        Ibid, Te Deum.

30 O all ye Works of the Lord, bless ye the lord: praise him, and magnify him for ever *Ibid, Benedicite*

31 Give peace in our time, O Lord. *Ibid, Versicles.*

32 Whose service is perfect freedom. *Ibid, Second Collect, for Peace.*

33 Have mercy upon us miserable sinners. *Litany.*

34 From envy, hatred, and malice, and all uncharitableness. *Ibid.*

35 The world, the flesh, and the devil. *Ibid.*

36 From battle and murder, and from sudden death. *Ibid.*

37 All sorts and conditions of men. *Prayer for All Conditions of Men.*

38 Read, mark, learn, and inwardly digest. *Collect for the Second Sunday in Advent.*

39 Jews, Turks, Infidels, and Heretics. *Third Collect for Good Friday.*

40 Renounce the devil and all his works. *Baptism of Infants.*

41 The pomps and vanity of this wicked world. *Catechism.*

42 To keep my hands from picking and stealing. *Ibid.*

43 To do my duty in that state of life, unto which it shall please God to call me. *Ibid.*

44 An outward and visible sign of an inward and spiritual grace. *Ibid.*

45 If any of you know cause or just impediment. *Solemnisation of Matrimony.*

46 Brute beasts that have no understanding. *Ibid*

47 Let him now speak, or else hereafter for ever hold his peace. *Ibid.*

48 To have and to hold from this day forward, for better for worse, for richer for poorer, in sickness and in health, to love and to cherish, till death us do part. *Ibid.*

49 To love, cherish, and obey. *Ibid.*

50 With this ring I thee wed, with my body I thee worship, and with all my worldly goods I thee endow. *Ibid.*

51 Those whom God hath joined together let no man put asunder. *Ibid.*

52 Laid violent hands upon themselves. *Burial of the Dead.*

53 Man that is born of a woman hath but a short time to live, and is full of misery. *Ibid.*

54 In the midst of life we are in death. *Ibid.*

55 We therefore commit his body to the ground; earth to earth, ashes to ashes, dust to dust; in sure and certain hope of the Resurrection to eternal life. *Ibid.*

56 We therefore commit his body to the deep, to be turned into corruption, looking for the resurrection of the body (when the Sea shall give up her dead). *Form of Prayer to be used at the Burial of the Dead at Sea.*

57 Of Works of Supererogation. *Articles of Religion. Title of Article xiv.*

58 A fond thing vainly invented. *Ibid, xxii. Of Purgatory.*

59 A man may not marry his Grandmother. *Table of Kindred and Affinity.*

341

AUTHORSHIP
UNKNOWN

EARLY ENGLISH

1 Þæs oferoede, þisses swa mæg!
– That was got over, so may this be!
Deor's Lament

2 Hige sceal þe heardra, heorte þe cenre,
Mod sceal þe mare, þe ure mægen lytlað
– Spirit shall be the stouter, heart the
bolder, courage shall be the greater, as
our might lessens.
The Battle of Maldon, 312.

3 Sumer is icumen in,
Lhude sing cuccu! *Cuckoo Song.*

4 Everyman, I will go with thee, and be
thy guide,
In thy most need to go by thy side.
(Knowledge.) *Everyman, 522.*

BALLADS

5 I saw the new moon late yestreen
Wi' the auld moon in her arm.
Sir Patrick Spens

6 Yestreen the Queen had four Maries,
The night she'll hae but three;
There was Marie Seaton, and Marie
Beaton,
And Marie Carmichael, and me.
The Queen's Maries.

7 As I was walking all alane
I heard twa corbies making a mane.
The tane unto the tither did say,
'Whar sall we gang and dine the day?'
The Twa Corbies.

8 This ae nighte, this ae nighte,
Every nighte and alle,
Fire and fleet, and candle-lighte,
And Christe receive thy saule.
A Lyke-Wake Dirge

9 I wish I were where Helen lies,
Night and day on me she cries;
O that I were where Helen lies,
On fair Kirkconnell lea!
Helen of Kirkconnell.

10 I lighted down my sword to draw,
I hackèd him in pieces sma',
I hackèd him in pieces sma',
For her sake that died for me. *Ibid.*

11 Fight on, my men, Sir Andrew says,
A little I'm hurt, but yet not slain;
I'll but lie down and bleed awhile,
And then I'll rise and fight again.
Ballad of Sir Andrew Barton.

SONGS AND CAROLS

12 God rest you merry, gentlemen,
Let nothing you dismay.
God rest you Merry.

13 Please her the best you may,
She looks another way.
Alas and well-a-day!
Phillida flouts me.
The Disdainful Shepherdess.

14 There is a lady sweet and kind,
Was never face so pleased my mind;
I did but see her passing by,
And yet I love her till I die.
There is a Lady Sweet and Kind.

15 My love in her attire doth show her wit,
It doth so well become her;
For every season she hath dressings fit,
For Winter, Spring, and Summer.
No beauty she doth miss
When all her robes are on:
But Beauty's self she is
When all her robes are gone. *Madrigal.*

16 I saw my Lady weep,
And Sorrow proud to be advancèd so
In those fair eyes where all perfections
keep.
*John Dowland's Third Book of Songs or
Airs, iii.*

17 Weep you no more, sad fountains;
What need you flow so fast?
Look how the snowy mountains
Heaven's sun doth gently waste!
Ibid, viii

18 Love not me for comely grace,
For my pleasing eye or face,
Nor for any outward part,
No, nor for a constant heart.
Love not me for Comely Grace.

19 Over the mountains
And over the waves,
Under the fountains
And under the graves;
Under floods that are deepest,
Which Neptune obey,
Over rocks that are steepest,
Love will find out the way.
Love will find out the Way.

20 Begone, dull Care! I prithee begone
from me!
Begone, dull Care! thou and I shall
never agree. *Begone Dull Care.*

21 Though little, I'll work as hard as a
Turk,
If you'll give me employ,
To plough and sow, and reap and mow,
And be a farmer's boy.
The Farmer's Boy.

22 And this is law, I will maintain,
Unto my dying day, Sir,
That whatsoever king shall reign,
I will be the Vicar of Bray, Sir.
The Vicar of Bray.

23 God save our gracious king,
Long live our noble king,
God save the king!
Send him victorious,
Happy and glorious,
Long to reign over us,
God save the king!
God save the Kiing.
(Authorship claimed for Henry Carey and
for James Oswald.)

24 'Where are you going, my pretty maid?'
'I am going a-milking, sir,' she said.
Where are you going, my Pretty Maid?

25 'What is your fortune, my pretty maid?'
'My face is my fortune, sir,' she said.
'Then I won't marry you, my pretty
maid.'
'Nobody asked you, sir,' she said.
Ibid.

26 The noble Duke of York,
He had ten thousand men,
He marched them up to the top of the
hill,
And he marched them down again.
When they were up, they were up,
And when they were down, they were
down,
And when they were only half-way up,
They were neither up nor down.
The Noble Duke of York.

27 It is good to be merry and wise,
It is good to be honest and true,
It is best to be off with the old love,
Before you are on with the new.
Songs of England and Scotland, II. 73.

28 From the lone sheiling of the misty
island
Mountains divide us, and the waste of
seas –
Yet still the blood is strong, the heart is
Highland,
And we in dreams behold the Hebrides.
Canadian Boat Song.

29 Oh, ye'll tak' the high road, and I'll tak'
the low road,
And I'll be in Scotland afore ye,
But me and my true love will never
meet again,
On the bonny, bonny banks o' Loch
Lomond.
The Bonny Banks o' Loch Lomond.

30 Farewell and adieu to you, fair Spanish
Ladies,
Farewell and adieu to you, Ladies of
Spain,
For we've received orders to sail for old
England,

But we hope in a short time to see you again.
We'll rant and we'll roar, all o'er the
  wild ocean,
We'll rant and we'll roar, all o'er the
  wild seas,
Until we strike soundings in the
  Channel of Old England,
From Ushant to Scilly is thirty-five
  leagues.   *Spanish Ladies.*

1 Casey Jones, he mounted to the cabin,
Casey Jones, with his orders in his hand!
Casey Jones, he mounted to the cabin,
Took his farewell trip into the promised
  land.   *Casey Jones.*

2 Frankie and Johnny were lovers, O
  Lordy, how they could love.
Swore to be true to each other, true as
  the stars above;
He was her man, and he done her
  wrong.   *Frankie and Johnny*

EPIGRAMS

3 Had you seen these roads before they
  were made,
You would lift up your hands and bless
  General Wade.
              *On roads made in the
              Scottish highlands, 1726–1729.*

4 Great Chatham, with his sabre drawn,
Stood waiting for Sir Richard Strachan;
Sir Richard, longing to be at 'em,
Stood waiting for the Earl of Chatham.
        On the Walcheren Expedition, 1809.

5 On Waterloo's ensanguined plain,
Full many a gallant man was slain,
But none, by bullet or by shot,
Fell half so flat as Walter Scott.
        On Walter Scott's 'Field of Waterloo.'

6 I come first. My name is Jowett.
I am the Master of the College.
Everything that is, I know it.
If I don't, it isn't knowledge.
                   The Balliol Masque.

7 My name is George Nathaniel Curzon.
I am a most superior person.   *Ibid.*

LIMERICKS

8 There was a young lady of Riga,
Who went for ride on a tiger;
They returned from the ride
With the lady inside,
And a smile on the face of the tiger.

9 There was a young man of Devizes,
Whose ears were of different sizes;
The one that was small
Was no use at all;
The other won hundreds of prizes.

10 There was an old man of Khartoum,
Who kept two black sheep in his room.
'They remind me,' he said,
'Of two friends who are dead.'
But he never would tell us of whom.

11 There was a young man of Boulogne,
Who sang a most topical song.
It wasn't the words
That frightened the birds,
But the horrible *double entendre*.

12 There was a young curate of Salisbury,
Whose manners were quite halisbury-
  scalisbury;
He ran about Hampshire
Without any pampshire,
Till the vicar compelled him to
  walisbury.
(Salisbury=Sarum,
  Hampshire=Hants.)

13 There was an old man of Nantucket
Who kept all his cash in a bucket,
But his daughter, named Nan,
Ran away with a man,
And as for the bucket, Nantucket.

14 There was a young lady named Bright,
Who could travel much faster than light.
She started one day
In the relative way,
And came back on the previous night.

15 There's a wonderful family called Stein,
There's Gert and there's Epp and there's
  Ein;
Gert's poems are bunk,
Epp's statues are junk,
And no one can understand Ein.
(Gertrude Stein, Jacob Epstein, Albert
  Einstein.)

EPITAPHS AND INSCRIPTIONS

16 What we gave, we have;
What we spent, we had;
What we left, we lost.
Epitaph on the Earl of Devon, 1419

17 Here sleeps in peace a Hampshire
grenadier,
Who caught his death by drinking cold
small beer;
Soldiers, take heed from his untimely
fall,
And when you're hot, drink strong, or
not at all.
From a Winchester churchyard

18 Here lie I, Martin Elginbrodde;
Hae mercy o' my soul, Lord God;
As I wad do, were I Lord God,
And ye were Martin Elginbrodde.
*Quoted by George MacDonald in 'David
Elginbrod.'*

19 Here lies a poor woman who always
was tired,
She lived in a house where help wasn't
hired.
The last words she said were: 'Dear
friends, I am going
Where washing ain't wanted, nor
sweeping, nor sewing;
And everything there is exact to my
wishes,
For where folk don't eat there's no
washing of dishes.
In heaven loud anthems for ever are
ringing,
But having no voice I'll keep clear of the
singing.
Don't mourn for me now, don't mourn
for me never;
I'm going to do nothing for ever and
ever.'
The Tired Woman's Epitaph

20 This is the grave of Mike O'Day
Who died maintaining his right of way.
His right was clear, his will was strong,
But he's just as dead as if he'd been
wrong. *Modern*

21 Give me a good digestion, Lord,
And also something to digest;
Give me a healthy body, Lord,
With sense to keep it at its best;
Give me a healthy mind, good Lord,
To keep the good and pure in sight,
Which seeing sin is not appalled
But finds a way to set it right;
Give me a mind that is not bored,
That does not whimper, whine, or sigh;
Don't let me worry overmuch
About the fussy thing called I.
Give me a sense of humour, Lord,
Give me the grace to see a joke,
To get some happiness from life
And pass it on to other folk.
Prayer found in Chester Cathedral.

PARODIES

22 Ye gods! annihilate but space and time
And make two lovers happy.
*Martinus Scriblerus on the Art of Sinking
in Poetry, xi.*

23 And thou Dalhousie, the great God of
War,
Lieutenant-Colonel to the Earl of Mar.
(Both of these are often ascribed to
Pope.) *Ibid.*

24 He killed the noble Mudjokivis.
Of the skin he made him mittens,
Made them with the fur side inside
Made them with the skin side outside.
He, to get the warm side inside,
Put the inside skin side outside.
He, to get the cold side outside,
Put the warm side fur side inside.
That's why he put the fur side inside,
Why he put the skin side outside,
Why he turned them inside outside.
The Modern Hiawatha

WEATHER AND CALENDAR RHYMES

25 First it rained, and then it snew,
Then it friz, and then it thew
And then it friz again.

26 Please to remember
The fifth of November,
Gunpowder treason and plot;
I see no reason
Why gunpowder treason
Should ever be forgot.
On Guy Fawkes Day.

345

1 Christmas is coming, the geese are
   getting fat,
   Please put a penny in an old man's hat.
   If you haven't got a penny, a ha'penny
   will do,
   If you haven't got a ha'penny, God bless
   you.   *Beggar's rhyme.*

2 Thirty days hath September,
   April, June, and November;
   All the rest have thirty-one,
   Excepting February alone,

Which has but twenty-eight days clear,
And twenty-nine at each leap year.
(Many different versions.)   *Old rhyme.*

3 The Ram, the Bull, the Heavenly
   Twins,
   And next the Crab, the Lion shines,
   The Virgin, and the Scales,
   The Scorpion, Archer, and He-Goat,
   The Man that bears the Watering-Pot,
   And Fish with glittering tails.
                    Signs of the Zodiac

PROVERBS

COLLECTIONS OF PROVERBS
REFERRED TO

Opposite each proverb is indicated either the earliest of the standard collections in which it appears, or the century of its earliest-noted appearance in literature. References in brackets are to older forms of what is in essentials the same proverb. In many cases, of course, the proverb is older than any reference given.

A. H.	A. Henderson, *Scottish Proverbs, 1832.*
B.	H. G. Bohn, *A Handbook of Proverbs,* 1855.
C.	J. Clarke, *Paroemiologia Anglo-Latina,* 1639.
C. R.	W. Camden, *Remaines Concerning Britaine,* 1614.
D.	M. A. Denham, *A Collection of Proverbs and Popular Sayings relating to the Seasons, the Weather, and Agricultural Pursuits,* 1846.
D. F.	D. Fergusson, *Scottish Proverbs,* 1641.
F.	T. Fuller, *Gnomologia: Adagies and Proverbs.* 1732.
G. H.	G. Herbert, *Outlandish Proverbs,* 1640; 2nd edition entitled *Jacula Prudentum,* 1651.
H.	J. Heywood, *A Dialogue containing the number in effect of all the Proverbs in the English Tongue,* 1546.
I.	R. Inwards, *Weather Lore: A Collection of Proverbs, Sayings and Rules concerning the Weather,* 1869.
J. H.	J. Howell, *Proverbs,* 1659.
K.	J. Kelly, *Complete Collection of Scottish Proverbs,* 1721.
L.	V. S. Lean, *Collectanea,* 1902–4.
P. R. A.	B. Franklin, *Poor Richard's Almanack,* 1758.
R.	J. Ray, *English Proverbs,* 1670 and later editions.
T. D.	T. Draxe, *Bibliotheca Scholastica Instructissima, or A Treasury of Ancient Adagies and Sententious Proverbs,* 1616.
W. H.	W. C. Hazlitt, *English Proverbs and Proverbial Phrases,* 1869.

PROVERBS

1 A bad bush is better than the open field.
R.

2 A bad excuse is better than none.
16th cent.

3 A bad penny always comes back.
19th cent.

4 A bad workman quarrels with his tools.
G. H.

5 A baker's wife may bite of a bun,
A brewer's wife may drink of a tun,
A fishmonger's wife may feed of a
conger,
But a servingman's wife may starve for
hunger. *16th cent.*

6 A bald head is soon shaven. *R.*

7 A barber learns to shave by shaving
fools. *R.*

8 A bargain is a bargain. *16th cent.*

9 A barley-corn is better than a diamond
to a cock. *16th cent.*

10 A beggar can never be bankrupt. *C.*

11 A beggar's purse is bottomless. *16th cent.*

12 A belly full of gluttony will never study
willingly. *R.*

13 A bird in the hand is worth two in the
bush. *Latin*

14 A bit in the morning is better than
nothing all day. *R*

15 A black hen lays a white egg. *French*

16 A black (=dark) man is a jewel (*or* pearl)
in a fair woman's eye. *R. (16th cent.)*

17 A black plum is as sweet as a white.
T.D.

18 A blate (=shy) cat makes a proud
mouse. *D. F.*

19 A blind man cannot judge colours.
Latin

20 A blind man will not thank you for a
looking-glass. *F.*

21 A blustering night, a fair day. *G. H.*

22 A boaster and a liar are all one. *14th cent*

23 A bonny bride is soon buskit
(=dressed). *D. F.*

24 A book that is shut is but a block. *F.*

25 A borrowed loan should come laughing
home. *F.*

26 A bow long bent grows weak. *H.*

27 A bribe will enter without knocking.
T. D.

28 A broken friendship may be soldered,
but will never be sound. *F.*

29 A broken sleeve holdeth the arm back.
15th cent.

30 A bully is always a coward. *19th cent.*

31 A bushel of March dust is worth a king's
ransom. *16th cent.*

32 A buxom widow must be either
married, buried, or shut up in a convent.
Spanish

33 A carrion kite will never be a good
hawk. *16th cent.*

1 A cat has nine lives. *H.*

2 A cat in gloves catches no mice.
16th cent.

3 A cat may look at a king. *H.*

4 A cat's walk: a little way and back.
W. H.

5 A child may have too much of his
mother's blessing. *C.*

6 A chip of the old block. *17th cent.*

7 A city that parleys is half gotten. *G. H.*

8 A civil denial is better than a rude grant.
F.

9 A close mouth catches no flies. *Italian*

10 A cock is crouse on his ain midden (*or*
bold on his own dunghill) *Latin*

11 A cold hand and a warm heart. *L.*

12 A cold May and a windy
Makes a full barn and a findy (=solid).
R.

13 A collier's cow and an alewife's sow are
always well fed. *R.*

14 A covetous man is good to none, but
worst to himself. *Latin*

15 A crab of the wood is sauce very good
For a crab of the sea.
The wood of a crab is good for a drab
That will not her husband obey. *J. H.*

16 A cracked bell can never sound well.
F.

17 A crafty knave needs no broker. *H.*

18 A creaking gate (*or* door) hangs long.
(Used figuratively of long-lived
invalids.) *18th cent.*

19 A cup in the pate is a mile in the gate
(=way). *17th cent.*

20 A curst cow has short horns. *Latin*

21 A danger foreseen is half avoided. *F.*

22 A dear ship stands long in the haven.
D. F.

23 A diligent scholar, and the master's
paid. *G. H.*

24 A dog will not howl if you beat him
with a bone. *K. (J. H.)*

25 A dog's nose and a maid's knees are
always cold. *R. (J. H.)*

26 A drowning man will catch at a straw.
17th cent.

27 A dry May and a dripping June
Bring all things into tune. *I.*

28 A dwarf on a giant's shoulder sees
further of the two. *Latin*

A fair bride is soon busked, *see* A bonny
bride, etc.

29 A fair day in winter is the mother of a
storm. *G. H.*

30 A fair exchange is no robbery.
17th cent. (H.)

31 A famine in England begins at the horse-
manger. (=When oats are dear.)
R. (C. R.)

32 A fat housekeeper makes lean executors.
G. H.

33 A fault confessed is half redressed.
16th cent.

34 A fool and his money are soon parted.
16th cent.

35 A fool knows more in his own house
than a wise man in another's. *G. H.*

36 A fool may ask more questions in an
hour than wise man can answer in seven
years. *R.*

37 A fool may give a wise man counsel.
K. (14th cent.)

38 A fool will not give his bauble for the Tower of London. *16th cent.*

39 A fool's bolt is soon shot. *13th cent.*

40 A forced kindness deserves no thanks. *F.*

41 A foul morn may turn to a fair day. *F.*

42 A fox is not taken twice in the same snare. *Greek*

43 A friend in court is better than a penny in purse. *15th cent.*

44 A friend in need is a friend indeed. *Latin*

45 A friend is never known till needed. *14th cent.*

46 A friend to all is a friend to none. *Greek*

47 A friend's frown is better than a fool's smile. *J. H.*

48 A full belly neither fights nor flies well. *G. H.*

49 A ganging fit is aye getting. (= A going foot is always getting.) *K.*

50 A gift long waited for is sold, not given. *F.*

51 A good beginning makes a good ending. *14th cent.*

52 A good conscience is a continual feast. *T. D.*

53 A good deed is never lost. *T. D.*

54 A good example is the best sermon. *F.*

55 A good face is a letter of recommendation. *17th cent.*

56 A good face needs no band, and a pretty wench no land. *R.*

57 A good horse cannot be of a bad colour. *17th cent.*

58 A good Jack makes a good Jill. *C. R.*

59 A good lather is half the shave. *F.*

60 A good man can no more harm than a sheep. *C.R.*

61 A good name keeps its lustre in the dark. *R.*

62 A good neighbour, a good morrow. *15th cent.*

63 A good paymaster never wants workmen. *F.*

64 A good shift may serve long, but it will not serve ever. *R.*

65 A good surgeon must have an eagle's eye, a lion's heart, and a lady's hand. *R.*

66 A good tale ill told is marred in the telling. *Latin*

67 A good tale is none the worse for being twice told. *K.*

68 A good thing is soon snatched up. *R.*

69 A good wife and health is a man's best wealth. *F.*

70 A good wife makes a good husband. *H.*

71 A great city, a great solitude. *Greek*

72 A great dowry is a bed full of brambles. *G. H.*

73 A great fortune is a great slavery. *Latin*

74 A great ship asks deep waters. *G. H.*

75 A green winter (*or* Christmas) makes a fat churchyard. *R.*

76 A green wound is soon healed. *R.*

77 A growing youth has a wolf in his belly. *17th cent.*

78 A grunting horse and a groaning wife seldom fail their master. *H.*

79 A guilty conscience needs no accuser. *18th cent. (16th cent.)*

1 A hair of the dog that bit you. (=A drink to cure the effect of a previous debauch.) *H.*

2 A handful of good life is better than a bushel of learning. *G. H.*

3 A head like a snake,
A neck like a drake,
A back like a beam,
A belly like a bream,
A foot like a cat.
A tail like a rat. (Points of a good greyhound.) *R.*

4 A heavy purse makes a light heart. *16th cent.*

5 A hedge between keeps friendship green. *18th cent.*

6 A high building, a low foundation. *C. R.*

7 A honey tongue, a heart of gall. *16th cent.*

8 A hook's well lost to catch a salmon. *J. D.*

9 A horse stumbles that has four legs. *G. H.*

10 A hungry man is an angry man. *J. H.*

11 A king without learning is but a crowned ass. *16th cent.*

12 A lame traveller should get out betimes. *F.*

13 A lawyer never goes to law himself. *Italian*

14 A lazy sheep thinks its wool heavy. *F.*

15 A lazy youth, a lousy age. *18th cent.*

16 A leg of a lark is better than the body of a kite. *H.*

17 A liar is not believed when he speaks the truth. *Latin*

18 A lie begets a lie. *F.*

19 A light purse makes a heavy heart. *16th cent.*

20 A light-heeled mother makes a heavy-heeled daughter. *R.*

21 A lion may be beholden to a mouse. *17th cent.*

22 A lion's skin is never cheap. *17th cent.*

23 A lisping lass is good to kiss. *R.*

24 A little body doth often harbour a great soul. *R.*

25 A little good is soon spent. *C. R.*

26 A little house well filled.
A little land well tilled,
And a little wife well willed. *R.*

27 A little of everything is nothing in the main. *F.*

28 A little pot is soon hot. *H.*

29 A long tongue is a sign of a short hand. (=Lavish promise is followed by poor performance.) *G. H.*

30 A low hedge is easily leaped over. *C. R.*

31 A mackerel sky and mares' tails
Make lofty ships carry low sails. *I.*

32 A mackerel sky is never long dry. *I.*

33 A maid oft seen, and a gown oft worn,
Are disesteemed and held in scorn. *R.*

34 A maid that laughs is half taken. *R.*

35 A maiden with many wooers often chooses the worst. *K.*

36 A man, a horse, and a dog are never weary of each other's company. *18th cent.*

37 A man among children will be long a child, a child among men will be soon a man. *F.*

38 A man at sixteen will prove a child at sixty. *F.*

39 A man can do no more than he can. *R.*

40 A man cannot whistle and drink at the same time. *16th cent.*

41 A man is as old as he feels, and a woman as old as she looks. *19th cent.*

42 A man is known by the company he keeps. *17th cent.*

43 A man is weal or woe as he thinks himself so. *K.*

44 A man knows his companion in a long journey and a little inn. *F.*

45 A man may bear till his back break. *C.*

46 A man may love his house well, though he ride not on the ridge. (=Does not proclaim it from the house-top.) *H.*

47 A man may woo where he will, but he will wed where his hap is. *D. F.*

48 A man of many trades begs his bread on Sundays. *F.*

49 A man of straw is worth a woman of gold. *16th cent.*

50 A man of words and not of deeds is like a garden full of weeds. *J. H.*

51 A man surprised is half beaten. *F.*

52 A man without a smiling face must not open a shop. *Chinese*

53 A man's best fortune, or his worst, is a wife. *J. H.*

A man's house is his castle, *see* An Englishman's house, etc.

54 A May flood never did good. *C.*

55 A miss is as good as a mile. *19th cent.*

56 A moneyless man goes fast through the market. *F.*

57 A mouse in time may bite in two a cable. *H.*

58 A new broom sweeps clean. *H.*

59 A nice wife and a back door
Do often make a rich man poor.
(The wife spends and the servants steal.) *15th cent.*

60 A nod from a lord is a breakfast for a fool. *F.*

61 A nod is as good as a wink to a blind horse. *19th cent.*

A peck of March dust is worth a king's ransom, *see* A bushel, etc.

62 A penny for your thoughts. *H.*

63 A penny saved is a penny gained (*or* got). *17th cent.*

64 A pennyweight of love is worth a pound of law. *K.*

65 A pitiful look asks enough. *G. H.*

66 A poor man's table is soon spread. *T. D.*

67 A pound of care will not pay an ounce of debt. *16th cent.*

68 A pretty kettle of fish (=a muddle). *18th cent.*

69 A proud man hath many crosses. *F.*

70 A quiet conscience sleeps in thunder. *F.*

71 A ragged colt may make a good horse. *H.*

72 A rainbow in the morning is the shepherd's warning;
A rainbow at night is the shepherd's delight. *I.*

73 A right Englishman knows not when a thing is well. *R.*

74 A rolling eye, a roving heart. *17th cent.*

1 A rolling stone gathers no moss. *H.*

2 A runaway monk never praises his convent. *Italian*

3 A saint abroad and a devil at home. *17th cent.*

4 A scald (=scabby) head is soon broken. *15th cent.*

5 A Scot, a rat, and a Newcastle grindstone travel all the world over. *17th cent.*

6 A Scottish man is wise behind the hand. (=Afterwards.) *D. F.*

7 A Scottish mist will wet an Englishman to the skin. *C.*

8 A ship and a woman are ever repairing. *G. H.*

9 A short horse is soon curried. *14th cent.*

10 A short life and a merry one. *17th cent.*

11 A small leak will sink a great ship. *F.*

12 A small pack becomes a small pedlar. *French*

13 A smiling boy seldom proves a good servant. *R.*

14 A snow year, a rich year. *G. H.*

15 A solitary man is either a brute or an angel./or either a God or a beast.) *F.*

16 A stern chase is a long chase *19th cent.*

17 A stick is quickly found to beat a dog with. *16th cent.*

18 A stitch in time saves nine. *F.*

19 A storm in a teacup. *19th cent.*

20 A straight stick is crooked in the water. *17th cent.*

21 A swarm of bees in May is worth a load of hay,
But a swarm in July is not worth a fly. *R.*

22 A tale never loses in the telling. *K. (T. D.)*

23 A tale twice told is cabbage twice sold. *F.*

24 A thief knows a thief as a wolf knows a wolf. *T. D.*

25 A tocherless (=dowerless) dame sits long at hame. *K.*

26 A toom (=empty) purse makes a blate (=shy) merchant. *R.*

27 A traveller may lie by authority. *14th cent.*

28 A true jest is no jest. *14th cent.*

29 A watched pot never boils. *19th cent.*

30 A whistling woman and a crowing hen Are neither fit for God nor men. *K.*

31 A white wall is a fool's paper. *16th cent.*

32 A wife brings but two good days, her wedding day and death day. *Greek*

33 A wight =strong) man never wanted a weapon. *D. F.*

34 A wild goose never laid a tame egg. *B.*

35 A wilful man will have his way. *19th cent.*

36 A wise man changes his mind, a fool never will. *17th cent.*

37 A woman, a dog (*or ass*), and a walnut tree,
The more you beat them, the better they'll be.
(Several versions with 'spaniel' for 'dog.') *R. (16th cent.)*

38 A woman conceals what she knows not. *G. H.*

39 A woman is an angel at ten, a saint at fifteen, a devil at forty, and a witch at fourscore. *17th cent.*

40 A woman is to be from her house three times: when she is christened, married, and buried. *G.*

41 A woman's advice is a poor thing, but he is a fool who does not take it. *Spanish*

42 A woman's mind and winter wind change oft. *C.*

43 A woman's strength is in her tongue. *J. H.*

44 A woman's tongue is the last thing about her that dies. *17th cent.*

45 A woman's work is never done. *R.*

46 A wonder lasts but nine days. *H. (14th cent.)*

47 A word spoken is past recalling. *16th cent.*

48 A work ill done must be done twice. *J. H.*

49 A young courtier, an old beggar. *16th cent.*

50 A young man should not marry yet, an old man not at all. *Greek*

51 Accidents will happen in the best-regulated families. *19th cent.*

52 Actions speak louder than words. *20th cent.*

53 Adversity makes a man wise, not rich. *R.*

54 Afraid of his own shadow. *16th cent.*

55 After a storm comes a calm. *16th cent.*

56 After death, the doctor. (Too late.) *16th cent.*

57 After dinner sit awhile; after supper walk a mile. *16th cent.*

58 After meat, mustard. (When it is of no use.) *16th cent.*

59 Age and wedlock tames man and beast. *C. R.*

60 Agree, for the law is costly. *C. R.*

61 Agues come on horseback, but go away on foot *17th cent.*

62 Alike every day makes a clout (=rag) on Sunday. (=If you always wear your best clothes they will soon wear out.) *K.*

63 All are good lasses, but whence come the bad wives? *K.*

64 All are not friends that speak us fair. *C.*

65 All are not merry that dance lightly. *15th cent.*

66 All cats are grey in the dark. *H.*

67 All covet, all lose. *13th cent.*

68 All doors open to courtesy. *F.*

69 All fellows at football. (=On the playing-field, all are on equality.) *16th cent.*

70 All fish are not caught with flies. *16th cent.*

71 All flesh is not venison. *G. H.*

72 All his geese are swans. *16th cent.*

73 All is fair in love and war. *17th cent.*

74 All is fish that comes to net. *16th cent.*

75 All is lost that is put in a riven dish. *C.*

76 All is not gold that glitters. *Latin*

77 All is not lost that is in danger. *R.*

78 All is over but the shouting. *19th cent.*

79 All is well that ends well. *15th cent.*

80 All is well with him who is beloved of his neighbours. *G. H.*

81 All lay load on the willing horse. *R. (H.)*

355

1 All Lombard Street to a China orange. (Lombard Street is a banking centre.)
19th cent. (18th cent.)

2 All men can't be first. *F.*

3 All men can't be masters. *H.*

4 All my eye and Betty Martin. (=All humbug.) *18th cent.*

5 All promises are either broken or kept. *16th cent.*

6 All roads lead to Rome. *14th cent.*

7 All Stuarts are not sib (=related) to the king. *K.*

8 All tarred with the same brush. *19th cent.*

9 All the keys hang not at one man's girdle. *H.*

10 All the months in the year curse a fair Februeer. *R.*

11 All the world and his wife. *18th cent.*

12 All things are difficult before they are easy. *F.*

13 All things come to those who wait. *French*

14 All truths are not to be told. *14th cent.*

15 All weapons of war cannot arm fear. *16th cent.*

16 All work and no play makes Jack a dull boy. *J. H.*

17 Almost and Very (*or* Well) nigh saves many a lie. *C.*

18 Almost was never hanged. *C.*

19 Alms never make poor. *G. H.*

20 Always in the saddle, never on his way. (Of equestrian statues.) *16th cent.*

21 Always taking out of the meal-tub, and never putting in, soon comes to the bottom. *18th cent.*

22 An ague in the spring is physic for a king. *J. H.*

23 An ape's an ape, a varlet's a varlet. Though they be clad in silk or scarlet. *F. (16th cent.)*

24 An apple a day keeps the doctor away. *20th cent.*

25 An apple, an egg, and a nut, you may eat after a slut. *R.*

26 An artist lives everywhere. *16th cent.*

27 An ass is but an ass, though laden with gold. *17th cent.*

28 An ass loaded with gold climbs to the top of the castle. *F.*

29 An atheist is one point beyond the devil. *F.*

30 An egg will be in three bellies in twenty-four hours. *R.*

31 An empty sack cannot stand upright. *17th cent.*

32 An English summer, three hot days and a thunderstorm. *19th cent.*

33 An Englishman is never happy but when he is miserable, a Scotchman never at home but when he is abroad, and an Irishman never at peace but when he is fighting. *19th cent.*

34 An Englishman's house is his castle. *R.*

35 An honest man's word is as good as his bond. *R.*

36 An hour in the morning is worth two in the evening. *B.*

37 An idle youth, a needy age. *G. H.*

38 An ill stake standeth longest. *J. H.*

39 An ill wound is cured, not an ill name. *G. H.*

40 An inch in a miss is as good as an ell. *C. R.*

41 An iron hand in a velvet glove. *French*

42 An oak is not felled at one stroke. *15th cent.*

43 An old cat laps as much as a young kitten. *C. R.*

44 An old cat sports not with her prey. *G. H.*

45 An old dog bites sore. *H.*

46 An old fox needs no craft. *C.*

47 An old head on young shoulders. *C.*

48 An old knave is no babe. *H.*

49 An old man is a bed full of bones. *R.*

50 An old man never wants a tale to tell. *F.*

51 An old physician and a young lawyer. (Are best.) *G. H.*

52 An old poacher makes the best keeper. *19th cent. (14th cent.)*

53 An old soldier, an old fool. *French*

54 An open door may tempt a saint. *J. H.*

55 An ounce of discretion is worth a pound of learning. *R.*

56 An ounce of fortune is worth a pound of forecast. *17th cent.*

57 An ounce of mother-wit is worth a pound of clergy (=learning). *17th cent.*

58 An ounce of wit that's bought is worth a pound that's taught. *F.*

59 An ox is taken by the horns, and a man by the tongue. *G. H.*

60 An unbidden guest knows not where to sit. *14th cent.*

61 Anger and haste hinder good counsel. *B.*

62 Another's bread costs dear. *G. H.*

63 Any port in a storm. *18th cent.*

64 Anything for a quiet life. *R.*

65 Ars est celare artem. – Art lies in concealing art. *Latin*

66 As a man is friended, so the law is ended. *16th cent.*

67 As bald as a coot. *15th cent.*

68 As calm as a clock. *19th cent.*

69 As clean as a whistle. *19th cent.*

70 As close as wax. *18th cent.*

71 As cold as charity. *17th cent.*

72 As cross as a bear with a sore head. *19th cent.*

73 As cross as nine highways. *B.*

74 As cross as two sticks. *19th cent.*

75 As dead as a door-nail. *14th cent.*

76 As dead as mutton. *18th cent.*

77 As drunk as a lord. *17th cent.*

78 As drunk as a mouse. *14th cent.*

79 As drunk as a wheelbarrow. *R.*

80 As dry as a bone. *16th cent.*

81 As dull (*or* dead) as ditchwater. *18th cent.*

82 As fine as fivepence. *16th cent.*

83 As fit as a fiddle. *R.*

84 As flat as a pancake. *18th cent. (16th cent.)*

85 As full as an egg is of meat. *16th cent.*

As good be hanged for a sheep as a lamb, *see* As well be hanged, etc.

1 As good be out of the world as out of the fashion. **C.**

2 As good lost as found. **H.**

3 As good play for nought as work for nought. **H.**

4 As jolly as a sandboy. *19th cent.*

5 As large as life. *18th cent.*

6 As lazy as Ludlam's dog, that leaned his head against a wall to bark. **R.**

7 As lean as a rake. *14th cent.*

8 As like as two peas. *16th cent.*

9 As mad as a hatter. *19th cent.*

10 As mad as a March hare. *14th cent.*

11 As melancholy as a cat. *16th cent.*

12 As melancholy as a sick monkey. *19th cent.*

13 As merry as a cricket. **H.**

14 As merry as a grig. *18th cent.*

15 As merry as mice in malt. **C.**

16 As mild as a lamb. *16th cent.*

17 As neat as a new pin. *18th cent.*

18 As nimble as a cow in a cage. **H.**

19 As nimble as an eel in a sandbag. **F.**

20 As old as Paul's (*or* Paul's steeple). *17th cent.*

21 As old as the hills. *19th cent.*

22 As plain as a pikestaff. (Originally 'packstaff,' with which the pedlar carried his pack over his shoulder.) *16th cent.*

23 As plain as the nose on a man's face. **C.**

24 As poor as a church mouse. **J. H.**

25 As poor as Job. *14th cent.*

26 As proud as a peacock. *13th cent.*

27 As proud as Lucifer. *14th cent.*

28 As quick as thought. *13th cent.*

29 As quiet as a mouse. *17th cent.*

30 As red as a turkey-cock. *17th cent.*

31 As right as a trivet. *19th cent.*

32 As right as ninepence. *19th cent.*

33 As right as rain. *19th cent.*

34 As seasonable as snow in summer (*or* harvest). *16th cent.*

35 As sick as a dog. *16th cent.*

36 As slender in the middle as a cow in the waist. **R.**

37 As slippery as an eel. *15th cent.*

38 As soft as butter. *16th cent.*

39 As soft as silk. *14th cent.*

40 As soon as man is born he begins to die. *German*

41 As soon goes the young sheep as the old to market (*or* pot). *16th cent.*

42 As sore fight wrens as cranes. **D. F.**

43 As sound as a bell. *16th cent.*

44 As sound as a trout (*or* roach). *13th cent.*

45 As sure as a gun. *17th cent.*

46 As sure as death. *16th cent.*

47 As sure as eggs is eggs. *17th cent.*

48 As sure as God made little apples. *19th cent.*

49 As sure as God's in Gloucestershire. *17th cent.*

50 As sweet as a nut. *16th cent.*

51 As the day lengthens the cold strengthens. *R.*

52 As the fool thinks, so the bell clinks. *17th cent.*

53 As the goodman saith, so say we, But as the goodwife saith, so must it be. *R.*

54 As the old cock crows, the young one learns. *14th cent.*

55 As the touchstone trieth gold, so gold trieth men. *F. (16th cent.)*

56 As they brew, so let them drink (*or* bake). *16th cent. (13th cent.)*

57 As true as a turtle to her mate. *15th cent.*

58 As true as God's in heaven. *R.*

59 As true as Gospel. *16th cent.*

60 As true as steel. *14th cent.*

61 As true as the dial to the sun. *17th cent.*

62 As ugly as sin. *19th cent.*

63 As warm (*or* hot) as toast. *15th cent.*

64 As weak as water. *14th cent.*

65 As welcome as flowers in May. *17th cent.*

66 As welcome as water in one's shoes. *J. H.*

67 As well as the beggar knows his dish (*or* bag). *H.*

68 As well be hanged for a sheep as a lamb. *R.*

69 As wise as a man of Gotham. (Gotham was proverbial for folly.) *J. H.*

70 As you make your bed, so you must lie on it. *16th cent.*

71 As your wedding-ring wears, your cares will wear away. *R.*

72 Ask a kite for a feather, and she'll say, she has but just enough to fly with. *F.*

73 Ask much to have a little. *G. H.*

74 Ask my fellow if I be a thief. *H.*

75 Ask no questions and you will be told no lies. *18th cent.*

76 Ask the mother if the child be like his father. *F.*

77 At a great bargain, pause. *G. H.*

78 At a round table there's no dispute of place. *R.*

79 At court, everyone for himself. *14th cent.*

80 At Easter let your clothes be new, Or else be sure you will it rue. *L.*

81 At every dog's bark seem not to awake. (=Do not fuss about trifles.) *H.*

82 At latter Lammas. (=Never.) *16th cent.*

83 At length the fox is brought to the furrier. *G. H.*

84 At open doors dogs come in. *D. F.*

85 At the end of the game you'll see who's the winner. *F. (G. H.)*

86 Athanasius contra mundum. – Athanasius against the world. *Latin*

87 Audi alteram partem. – Hear the other side. *Latin*

88 Autre temps, autre mœurs. – Other times, other manners. *French*

89 Away goes the devil when he finds the door shut against him. *Italian*

90 Bacchus hath drowned more men than Neptune. *F.*

1 Bachelor's fare: bread and cheese and kisses. *18th cent.*

2 Bachelors' wives and maids' children are always well taught. *H.*

3 Back may trust but belly won't. (=You can wait for clothes, but not for food.) *19th cent.*

4 Bad is the best. *16th cent.*

5 Bare as the birch at Yule even. *19th cent.*

6 Bare walls make giddy housewives. *C. R.*

7 Bare words make no bargain. *C.*

8 Barking dogs seldom bite. *16th cent.*

9 Barnaby bright, Barnaby bright: The longest day and the shortest night. (St. Barnabas' day, 11 June, *J. H.* in Old Style reckoned longest.)

10 Bashfulness is an enemy to poverty. *Latin*

11 Be a friend to thyself, and others will befriend thee. *K.*

12 Be as you would seem to be. *G. H.*

13 Be it better, be it worse, Be ruled by him that bears the purse. *14th cent.*

14 Be just before you are generous. *18th cent.*

15 Be long sick, that you may be soon hale. *K.*

16 Be not too bold with your betters. *J. H.*

17 Be not too hasty to outbid another. *R.*

18 Be still, and have thy will. *16th cent. (15th cent.)*

19 Be sure before you marry of a house wherein to tarry. *Italian*

20 Bear and forbear. *16th cent.*

21 Bear wealth, poverty will bear itself. *D. F.*

22 Bear with evil, and expect good. *G. H.*

23 Beauty draws more than oxen. *G. H.*

24 Beauty is but a blossom. *T. D.*

25 Beauty is but skin-deep. *17th cent.*

26 Beauty is potent, but money is omnipotent. *R.*

27 Beauty will buy no beef. *F.*

28 Beauty without bounty avails nought. *16th cent.*

29 Bees that have honey in their mouths have stings in their tails. *15th cent.*

30 Before one can say Jack Robinson. *18th cent.*

31 Before you make a friend eat a bushel of salt with him. *Latin*

32 Beggars cannot be choosers. *H.*

33 Being on sea, sail; being on land, settle. *G. H.*

34 Believe well and have well. *H.*

35 Bells call others to church, but go not themselves. *G. H. (16th cent.)*

36 Benefits please, like flowers, while they are fresh. *G. H.*

37 Best is best cheap. (=The best bargain.) *H.*

38 Best to bend while 'tis a twig. *16th cent.*

39 Better a clout (=patch) than a hole out. *C. R.*

40 Better a finger off than always aching. *13th cent.*

41 Better a fortune in a wife than with a wife. *K.*

42 Better a lean peace than a fat victory.
17th cent.

43 Better a little fire to warm us, than a great one to burn us. *16th cent.*

44 Better a mischief than an inconvenience. *C.*

45 Better a mouse in the pot than no flesh at all. *C. R.*

Better a wee bush than nae bield (=no shelter), *see* A bad bush, etc.

46 Better an egg to-day than a hen to-morrow. *Italian*

47 Better an empty house than an ill tenant. *F.*

48 Better an open enemy than a false friend. *17th cent.*

49 Better bairns greet (=children weep) than bearded men. *D. F.*

50 Better be a fool than a knave. *G. H.*

51 Better be alone than in bad company. *C. (15th cent.)*

52 Better be an old man's darling than a young man's warling (=object of contempt). *H.*

53 Better be born lucky than rich. *C.*

54 Better be envied than pitied. *Greek*

55 Better be happy than wise. *H.*

56 Better be stung by a nettle than pricked by a rose. (=Better be wronged by an enemy than by a friend.) *J. H.*

57 Better be sure than sorry. *19th cent.*

58 Better be ill spoken of by one before all than by all before one. *J. H.*

59 Better be poor than wicked. *B.*

60 Better be the head of a dog than the tail of a lion. *R.*

61 Better be the head of the yeomanry than the tail of the gentry. *C.*

62 Better be unmannerly than troublesome. *J. H.*

63 Better bow than break.
15th cent. (14th cent.)

64 Better buy than borrow. *D. F.*

65 Better come at the latter end of a feast than the beginning of a fray. *H.*

66 Better cut the shoe than pinch the foot. *F.*

67 Better die a beggar than live a beggar. *R.*

68 Better early than late. *13th cent.*

69 Better give a shilling than lend a half a crown. *J. H.*

70 Better go about than fall into a ditch. *J. H.*

71 Better go away longing than loathing. *F.*

72 Better go to bed supperless than rise in debt. *R.*

73 Better go to heaven in rags than to hell in embroidery. *F.*

74 Better good afar off than evil at hand. *G. H.*

75 Better have an old man to humour than a young rake to break your heart. *W. H.*

76 Better have one plough going than two cradles. *16th cent.*

77 Better hazard once than be always in fear. *F.*

78 Better keep now than seek anon. *J. H.*

79 Better kiss a knave than be troubled with him. *C. R.*

1 Better late than never.   *Greek.*

2 Better leave than lack.   *H.*

3 Better lose a jest than a friend.
    16th cent.

4 Better luck next time.   *19th cent.*

5 Better my hog dirty home than no hog at all.   *R.*

6 Better one house filled than two spilled (=spoiled). (Said when two unpleasant people marry.)   *R.*

7 Better one's house too little one day than too big all the year after.   *R.*

8 Better pay the butcher than the doctor.
    19th cent.

9 Better ride on an ass that carries me than a horse that throws me.   *G. H.*

10 Better say Here it is than Here it was.
    D. F.

11 Better sell than live poorly.   *F.*

12 Better sit idle than work for nothing.
    17th cent.

13 Better sit still than rise up and fall.
    15th cent.

14 Better small fish than an empty dish. *R.*

15 Better some of a pudding than none of a pie.   *R.*

16 Better spare at brim than at bottom. (=Save early and avoid being in want later.)   *H.*

17 Better spare to have of thine own than ask of other men.   *G. H.*

18 Better speak to the master than the man.
    17th cent.

19 Better suffer ill than do ill.   *C.*

20 Better the devil you know than the devil you don't know.   *19th cent.*

21 Better the foot slip than the tongue.
    16th cent.

22 Better the last smile than the first laughter.   *H.*

23 Better unborn than untaught.
    H. (13th cent.)

24 Better untaught than ill taught.   *R.*

25 Better wear out shoes than sheets. (Sound men wear out shoes, sick men sheets.)   *K.*

26 Better wed over the mixen (=dung-heap) than over the the moor. (=Choose a partner from near at home.)   *D. F.*

27 Between Scylla and Charybdis.   *Greek*

28 Between the beetle (=mallet) and the block.   *16th cent.*

29 Between the devil and the deep sea.
    17th cent.

30 Between the hammer and the anvil.
    Latin

31 Between two stools one falls to the ground.   *Latin*

32 Between you and me and the post (*or* bedpost). (=In confidence.)   *19th cent.*

33 Beware beginnings.   *C.*

34 Beware of a silent dog and still water.
    Latin

35 Beware of after-claps.   *16th cent.*

36 Beware of breed. (=Ill breed.)   *R.*

37 Beware of Had I wist.   *14th cent.*

38 Beware of the forepart of a woman, the hind part of a mule, and all sides of a priest.   *16th cent.*

39 Beware of the man of one book.   *Latin*

40 Birchen twigs break no ribs.   *C.*

41 Birds of a feather flock together.
16th cent.

42 Birth is much, but breeding is more. *C.*

43 Bis dat qui cito dat.
– He gives twice who gives quickly.
Latin.

44 Biting and scratching is Scots folk's
wooing. *D. F.*

45 Bitter pills may have wholesome effects.
F.

46 Black will take no other hue. *H.*

47 Blessings are not valued till they are
gone. *F.*

48 Blind man's holdiay. (=Twilight.)
16th cent.

49 Blood is thicker than water.
(=Relationship is a strong bond.)
19th cent.

50 Blood will have blood. *16th cent.*

51 Blow first and sip afterwards. *R.*

52 Blow the wind never so fast,
It will lower at the last. *F.*

53 Blushing is virtue's colour. *17th cent.*

54 Born on Monday, fair in the face;
Born on Tuesday, full of God's grace;
Born on Wednesday, sour and sad;
Born on Thursday, merry and glad;
Born on Friday, worthily given;
Born on Saturday, work hard for your
living;
Born on Sunday, you will never know
want.
(*See* Monday's child, etc.) *19th cent.*

55 Born on the wrong side of the blanket.
(=Illegitimate.) *18th cent.*

56 Borrowed garments never sit well. *F.*

57 Both together do best of all. *C.*

58 Bought wit is best, but may cost too
much. *R.*

59 Boys will be boys. *17th cent.*

60 Boys will be men. *D. F.*

61 Brag is a good dog, but Holdfast is a
better. *R.*

62 Bread is the staff of life. *17th cent.*

63 Bridges were made for wise men to
walk over and fools to ride over. *R.*

64 Bring a cow to the hall and she'll run to
the byre. *D. F.*

65 Building and marrying of children are
great wasters. *G. H.*

66 Building is a sweet impoverishing.
G. H.

67 Business is business. *18th cent.*

68 Butter is gold in the morning, silver at
noon, and lead at night. *16th cent.*

69 Butter is mad twice a year. (When very
hard or very soft.) *17th cent.*

70 Buy at a fair but sell at home. *T. D.*

71 By hook or by crook (=By fair means
or foul.) *H. (14th cent.)*

72 By the street of By and by one arrives at
the house of Never. *Spanish*

73 By Tre, Pol, and Pen,
You shall know the Cornish men.
(Cornish prefixes.) *R.*

74 Cadgers are aye cracking of
crooksaddles. (=Carriers are always
talking of pack-saddles. – People tend to
talk 'shop.') *D. F.*

75 Caesar's wife must be above suspicion.
Latin

76 Calf love, half love; old love, cold love.
19th cent.

77 Call me cousin, but cozen me not. *R.*

78 Call no man happy till he dies. *17th cent.*

1 Calm weather in June sets corn in tune.
16th cent.

2 Cards are the devil's books. *17th cent.*

3 Care is no cure. *16th cent.*

4 Care killed a cat. *16th cent.*

5 Cast ne'er a clout till May be out. *F.*

6 Cast not out the foul water till you bring in the clean. *D. F.*

7 Cat will after kind. *H. (13th cent.)*

8 Cats eat what hussies (=housewives) spare. (=What is niggardly saved is often squandered.) *16th cent.*

9 Cauld kail het again. (=Cold cabbage warmed up.) *Latin*

10 Caveat emptor. – Let the buyer beware. (=The quality of the article is his concern.) *Latin*

11 Change of weather is the discourse of fools. *J. H.*

12 Charity begins at home. *14th cent.*

13 Che sarà, sarà.
– What will be, will be. *Italian*

14 Cheat me in the price but not in the goods. *F.*

15 Cheese it is a peevish elf,
It digests all things but itself. *Latin*

16 Children and chicken must be always picking. *16th cent.*

17 Children and fools have merry lives. *C.*

18 Children and fools speak the truth. *H.*

19 Children are certain cares, but uncertain comforts. *C.*

20 Children are poor men's riches. *R.*

21 Children pick up words as pigeons pease,

And utter them again as God shall please. *R.*

22 Children should be seen and not heard. *19th cent.*

23 Children suck the mother when they are young, and the father when they are old. *R.*

24 Children, when little, make parents fools; when great, mad. *G. H.*

25 Choose a horse made, and a wife to make. *G. H.*

26 Choose a wife rather by your ear than your eye. *F.*

27 Choose for yourself and use for yourself. *C.*

28 Choose neither woman nor linen by candle-light. *16th cent.*

29 Choose none for thy servant who have served thy betters. *G. H.*

30 Christmas comes but once a year.
But when it comes it brings good cheer. *16th cent.*

31 Church work goes on slowly. *17th cent.*

32 Cider is treacherous because it smiles in the face and then cuts the throat. *17th cent.*

33 Circumstances alter cases. *19th cent.*

34 Civility costs nothing. *19th cent.*

35 Claw me, and I'll claw thee. (Of mutual flattery.) *16th cent.*

36 Clergymen's sons always turn out badly. *19th cent.*

37 Cloudy mornings turn to clear evenings. *H.*

38 Cold broth hot again, that loved I never;
Old love renewed again, that loved I ever. *F.*

39 Cold of complexion, good of condition.
R.

40 Cold pudding settles love. *17th cent.*

41 Cold weather and crafty knaves come out of the north. *J. H.*

42 Come day, go day, God send Sunday. (The sluggard's wish.) *K.*

43 Come not to counsel uncalled. *16th cent.*

44 Command your man and do it yourself. *R.*

45 Common fame is a common liar. *17th cent.*

46 Common fame is seldom to blame. *R.*

47 Comparisons are odious. *15th cent.*

48 Conceited (=ingenious) goods are quickly spent. *R.*

49 Confess and be hanged. *16th cent.*

50 Confession is good for the soul. *K.*

51 Constant dropping wears away the stone. *Greek*

52 Content is the philosopher's stone, that turns all it touches into gold. *F.*

53 Content lodges oftener in cottages than palaces. *F.*

54 Cool words scald not the tongue. *F.*

55 Corruptio optimi pessima.
– Corruption of best is worst. *Latin*

56 Counsel breaks not the head. *G. H.*

57 Counsel is no command. *F.*

58 Courtesy on one side only lasts not long. *G. H.*

59 Courting and wooing bring dallying and doing. *C. R.*

60 Covetousness brings nothing home. *C.*

61 Covetousness bursts the sack.
19th cent. (16th cent.)

62 Craft against craft makes no living.
G. H.

63 Craft must have clothes, but truth loves to go naked. *F.*

64 Credit keeps the crown of the causeway. (=Is not ashamed to show itself.) *K.*

65 Creditors have better memories than debtors. *J. H.*

66 Critics are like brushers of noblemen's clothes. *G. H.*

67 Crooked logs make straight fires.
17th cent.

68 Cross the stream where it is ebbest (=shallowest). *17th cent.*

69 Crosses are ladders to heaven. *T. D.*

70 Crows are never the whiter for washing themselves. *K.*

71 Cucullus non facit monachum.
– The cowl does not make the monk.
Latin.

72 Cunning (=skill) is no burden.
16th cent.

73 Curiosity is ill manners in another's house. *F.*

74 Curses, like chickens, come home to roost. *14th cent.*

75 Custom is second nature. *14th cent.*

76 Custom is the plague of wise men and the idol of fools. *B.*

77 Custom makes all things easy.
16th cent.

78 Custom without reason is but ancient error. *17th cent.*

79 Dally not with money or women.
G. H.

1 Danger and delight grow on one stock.
16th cent.

2 Dangers are overcome by dangers.
G. H.

3 Daughters and dead fish are no keeping wares. *F.*

4 Dawted (=petted) daughters make daidling (=silly) wives. *19th cent.*

5 De gustibus non est disputandum. – There is no disputing about tastes.
Latin

6 De minimis non curat lex. – The law does not concern itself about trifles.
Latin

7 De mortuis nil nisi bonum. – Concerning the dead (speak) nothing but good. *Latin*

8 Dead men don't bite. *Latin*

9 Dead men tell no tales. *17th cent.*

10 Dead mice feel no cold. *R.*

11 Death and marriage make term day.
D. F.

12 Death defies the doctor. *K.*

13 Death is the grand leveller. *F.*

14 Death keeps no calendar. *G. H.*

15 Death pays all debts. *16th cent.*

16 Death's day is doom's day. *16th cent.*

17 Deaths foreseen come not. *G. H.*

18 Debt is better than death. *J. H.*

19 Debt is the worst poverty. *F.*

20 Debtors are liars. *G. H.*

21 Deeds are fruits, words are but leaves.
T. D.

22 Deeds are males and words are females.
16th cent.

23 Deem the best till the truth be tried out.
15th cent.

24 Delays are dangerous. *14th cent.*

25 Deliberating is not delaying. *F.*

26 Denying a fault doubles it. *17th cent.*

27 Dependence is a poor trade. *F.*

28 Desert and reward seldom keep company. *17th cent.*

29 Desires are nourished by delays. *T. D.*

30 Despair gives courage to a coward. *F.*

31 Desperate diseases must have desperate remedies (*or* cures). *Latin*

32 Diamond cut diamond. (Of people matched in cunning.) *17th cent.*

33 Diet cures more than doctors. *19th cent.*

34 Diffidence is the right eye of prudence.
F.

35 Diligence is the mother of good luck.
17th cent.

36 Dinners cannot be long where dainties want. *H.*

37 Discreet women have neither eyes nor ears. *G. H.*

38 Discretion is the better part of valour.
16th cent.

39 Diseases are the interests of pleasures. *R.*

40 Disgraces are like cherries, one draws another. *G. H.*

41 Dissembled sin is double wickedness.
T. D.

42 Divide et impera.
– Divide and rule. *Latin*

43 Do and undo, the day is long enough.
C.

44 Do as I say, not as I do. *H.*

45 Do as most men do, and men will speak well of you. *H.*

46 Do as you would be done by. *16th cent.*

47 Do as you're bidden and you'll never bear blame. *R.*

48 Do evil and look for the like. *16th cent.*

49 Do it well that thou mayest not do it twice. *F.*

50 Do not all you can; spend not all you have; believe not all you hear; and tell not all you know. *B.*

51 Do not halloo till you are out of the wood. *19th cent.*

52 Do not keep a dog and bark yourself. *16th cent.*

53 Do not meet troubles half-way. *16th cent.*

54 Do not put all your eggs in one basket. *18th cent.*

55 Do not spur a free horse. *Latin.*

56 Do on the hill as you would do in the hall. *D. F.*

57 Do the likeliest and hope the best. *D. F.*

58 Do well and have well. *14th cent.*

59 Do what thou oughtest and come what can come. *J. H.*

60 Do wrong once and you'll never hear the end of it. *17th cent.*

61 Dog does not eat dog. *18th cent.*

62 Dogs bark as they are bred. *K.*

63 Dogs bark before they bite. *H.*

64 Dogs that bark at a distance never bite. *C. R.*

65 Dogs wag their tails not so much in love to you as to your bread. *17th cent.*

66 Draff is good enough for swine. *16th cent.*

67 Drawn wells are seldom dry. (=Things are improved by use.) *C.*

68 Drawn wells have sweetest water. *C.*

69 Dreams go by contraries. *15th cent.*

70 Dree out (=endure)the inch as you have done the span. *K.*

71 Drift is as bad as unthrift. *J. H.*

72 Drink only with the duck. (=Water only..) *14th cent.*

73 Drink wine, and have the gout; drink none, and have the gout. *16th cent.*

74 Drive the nail that will go. *17th cent.*

75 Drunken folks seldom take harm. *18th cent.*

76 Dry bread at home is better than roast meat abroad. *G. H.*

77 Dulce bellum inexpertis. – War is pleasant to those who have not tried it. *Latin*

78 Dumb folks get no lands. *14th cent.*

79 Dummy (=a dumb man) cannot lie. *D. F.*

80 Each bird loves to hear himself sing. *H.*

81 Each cross hath its inscription. *C.*

82 Early master, soon knave (=servant). (Early independence causes extravagance, making employment necessary.) *14th cent.*

83 Early to bed and early to rise Makes a man healthy, wealthy, and wise. *C. (16th cent.)*

84 Ease and success are fellows. *14th cent.*

85 East, west, home's best. *B.*

1 Easy come, easy go. (Of quickly acquired fortunes.) *19th cent.*

2 Eat at pleasure, drink by measure. *French*

3 Eat to live, but do not live to eat. *Latin*

4 Eaten bread is forgotten. *C. R.*

5 Eating and scratching wants but a beginning. (Said to people who have a poor appetite.) *K.*

6 Education begins a gentleman, conversation completes him. *F.*

7 Ἐγγύη πάρα δ'ἄτη – (Act as) surety; ruin is at hand. *Greek*

8 Either a feast or a fast. *F.*

9 Empty vessels make the most sound (*or* noise.) *16th cent.*

10 England is the paradise of women, the hell of horses, and the purgatory of servants. *D. F. (16th cent.)*

11 Enough is as good as a feast. *15th cent.*

12 Envy never enriched any man. *R. (T. D.)*

13 Envy shoots at others and wounds herself. *16th cent.*

14 Even a fly hath its spleen. *Latin.*

15 Even a worm will turn. *H.*

16 Even reckoning makes long friends. *H.*

17 Evening red and morning grey
Help the traveller on his way;
Evening grey and morning red
Bring down rain upon his head. *D.*

18 Ever drunk, ever dry. *16th cent.*

19 Ever sick of the slothful guise,
Loth to bed and loth to rise. *C.*

20 Every ass loves to hear himself bray. *F.*

21 Every bean hath its black. *C.*

22 Every bird likes its own nest best. *French*

23 Every cloud has a silver lining. *19th cent.*

24 Every dog has his day. *H.*

25 Every dog is a lion at home. *Italian*

26 Every door may be shut but death's door. *Italian*

27 Every herring must hang by its own gill. *C.*

28 Every honest miller has a golden thumb. *R. (16th cent.)*

29 Every horse thinks his own pack heaviest. *F.*

30 Every Jack has his Jill. *R.*

31 Every little helps. *18th cent.*

32 Every man at forty is a fool or a physician. *R.*

33 Every man can rule (*or* tame) a shrew but he who has her. *H.*

34 Every man for himself, and God for us all. *H.*

35 Every man has his faults. *C.*

36 Every man is a fool sometimes, and none at all times. *K.*

37 Every man is best known to himself. *T. D.*

38 Every man is the architect of his own fortune. *Latin*

39 Every man must eat a peck of dirt before he dies. *C.*

40 Every man to his trade. *Greek*

41 Every miller draws water to his own mill. *R. (16th cent.)*

42 Every one can keep house better than her mother till she trieth. *F.*

43 Every one is kin to the rich man. *Italian*

44 Every one to his taste, as the old woman said when she kissed her cow. *H.*

45 Every one's faults are not written in their foreheads. *R.*

46 Every path hath a puddle. *G. H.*

47 Every shoe fits not every foot. *17th cent.*

48 Every sin brings its punishment with it. *G. H.*

49 Every tub must stand on its own bottom. *16th cent.*

50 Every white hath its black, and every sweet its sour. *18th cent.*

51 Everybody's business is nobody's business. *17th cent.*

52 Everything hath an end, and a pudding hath two. *16th cent.*

53 Everything is the worse for wearing. *C.*

54 Everything must have a beginning. *16th cent.*

55 Evil to him that evil thinks. *16th cent.*

56 Ex Africa semper aliquid novi. – Out of Africa always something new. *Latin*

57 Ex nihilo nihil fit. – Nothing comes of nothing. *Latin*

58 Ex pede Herculem. – From his foot (you may know) Hercules. (=A small piece shows the quality fo the whole.) *Latin*

59 Ex ungue leonem. – By his claw (you may know) the lion. *Latin*

60 Example is better than precept. *Latin*

Exchange is no robbery, *see* A fair exchange, etc.

61 Experience is the mistress of fools. *16th cent.*

62 Extreme right is extreme wrong. *Latin*

63 Extremes meet. *18th cent.*

64 Face to face the truth comes out. *F.*

65 Facts are stubborn things. *18th cent.*

66 Faint heart never won fair lady. *16th cent.*

67 Fair and foolish, little and loud, Long and lazy, black and proud; Fat and merry, lean and sad, Pale and peevish, red and bad. (Of women's colours.) *16th cent.*

68 Fair and softly goes far. *14th cent.*

69 Fair folk are aye fushionless (=pithless]. *K.*

70 Fair in the cradle and foul in the saddle. *C.*

71 Fair maidens wear no purses. (=A girl is not expected ot pay her shot.) *K.*

72 Fair play's a jewel. *19th cent.*

73 Fair words break no bones. *15th cent.*

74 Fair words butter no parsnips. *C.*

75 Fair words make fools fain (=pleased). *(H. 13th cent.)*

76 Fall not out with a friend for a trifle. *C.*

77 Fame is but the breath of the people. *F.*

78 Familiarity breeds contempt. *Latin*

79 Far-fetched and dear bought is good for ladies. *H.*

80 Far fowls have fair feathers. *K.*

81 Far from eye, far from heart. *13th cent.*

1 Fast bind, fast find.   *H.*

2 Fat paunches make lean pates.   *Greek*

3 Fat sorrow is better than lean sorrow.
(=Better be rich and miserable than
poor and miserable.)   *R.*

4 Fate leads the willing but drives the
stubborn.   *Latin*

5 Faults are thick where love is thin.   *J. H.*

6 Feather by feather the goose is plucked.
    Italian

7 February fill dyke.   *16th cent.*

8 February makes a bridge, and March
breaks it.   *G. H.*

9 Feed a cold and starve a fever.   *19th cent.*

10 Feed by measure and defy the physician.
    H.

11 Festina lente.
– Hasten slowly.   *Latin*

12 Few words are best.   *16th cent.*

13 Few words to the wise suffice.   *H.*

14 Fiat experimentum in corpore vili.
– Let the experiment be made on a
worthless body.   *Latin*

15 Fiat justitia, ruat coelum.
– Let justice be done, though heaven
fall.   *Latin*

16 Fields have eyes, and woods have ears.
    13th cent.

17 Finding's keeping.   *19th cent.*

18 Fine feathers make fine birds.
Fine words butter no parsnips, *see* Fair
words, etc.   *R.*

19 Finis coronat opus.
– The end crowns the work.   *Latin*

20 Fire is a good servant but a bad master.
    17th cent.

21 Fire that is closest kept burns most of all.
    Latin

22 First catch your hare. (Misquotation
from a cookery-book.)   *18th cent.*

23 First come, first served.   *16th cent.*

24 First creep and then go (=walk).
    15th cent.

25 First deserve and then desire.   *C. R.*

26 First think and then speak.   *C.*

27 First thrive and then wive.   *C.*

28 Fish and company stink in three days.
    16th cent.

29 Fish is cast away that is cast in dry pools.
    H.

30 Fish must swim thrice – once in the
water, a second time in the sauce, and a
third time in wine in the stomach.   *French*

31 Five hours sleepeth a traveller, seven a
scholar, eight a merchant, and eleven
every knave.   *17th cent.*

32 Fling dirt enough, and some will stick.
    Latin

33 Follow love and it will flee,
Flee love and it will follow thee.
    R. (16th cent.)

34 Follow not truth too near the heels, lest
it dash out thy teeth.   *G. H.*

35 Follow the river and you'll get to the
sea.   *F.*

36 Fools and bairns should not see half-
done work.   *K.*

37 Fools and madmen speak the truth.
    17th cent.

38 Fools are fain of flittin. (=Fond of
moving.)   *D. F.*

39 Fools build houses, and wise men buy
them.   *R.*

40 Fools cut their fingers, but wise men cut their thumbs. (=The folly of wise men is greater.) *18th cent.*

41 Fools make feasts and wise men eat them. *C. (16th cent.)*

42 Fools tie knots and wise men loose them. *C.*

43 For a flying enemy make a golden (*or* silver) bridge. *French*

44 For a morning rain leave not your journey. *16th cent.*

45 For age and want, save while you may! No morning sun lasts a whole day. *P. R. A.*

46 For every evil under the sun There is a remedy or there is none: If there be one, try and find it; If there be none, never mind it. *W. H.*

47 For want of a nail the shoe is lost; for want of a shoe the horse is lost; for want of a horse the rider is lost. *G. H.*

48 For want of company, welcome trumpery. *R.*

49 Forbearance is no acquittance. *H.*

50 Forbid a thing, and that we will do. *14th cent.*

51 Forewarned, forearmed. *Latin*

52 Forgive and forget. *H.*

53 Forgive any sooner than thyself. *Spanish*

54 Fortiter in re, suaviter in modo. – Strong in action, gentle in method. *Latin*

55 Fortune can take from us nothing but what she gave us. *Latin*

56 Fortune favours fools. *Latin*

57 Fortune favours the brave. *Latin*

58 Fortune knocks once at least at every man's gate. *W. H.*

59 Foul in the cradle and fair in the saddle. *C. R.*

60 Four eyes see more than two. *Latin*

61 Friends are like fiddle-strings, they must not be screwed too tight. *B.*

62 Friends are thieves of time. *17th cent.*

63 Friends may meet, but mountains never greet. *R. (16th cent.)*

64 Friends tie their purses with a cobweb thread. *B.*

65 Friendships multiply joys and divide griefs. *B.*

66 From a choleric man withdraw a little; from him that says nothing, for ever. *G. H.*

67 From hell, Hull and Halifax, good Lord deliver us. (Beggars' saying, Hull and Halifax being of old very strict in enforcing the law against them.) *16th cent.*

68 From pillar to post (*or* post to pillar). (=From whipping-post to pillory.) *15th cent.*

69 Frost and fraud both end in foul. *C. R.*

70 Full of courtesy, full of craft. *C. (16th cent.)*

71 Gadding gossips shall dine on the pot-lid. *F.*

72 Game is cheaper in the market than in the fields and woods. *F.*

73 Gaming, women, and wine, while they laugh, they make men pine. *G. H.*

74 Gear (=property) is easier gained than guided. *R.*

75 Gentility is but ancient riches. *G. H.*

1 Gentility without ability is worse than plain beggary. *R.*

2 Gentry sent to market will not buy one bushel of corn. *16th cent.*

3 Get a name to rise early, and you may lie all day. *K.*

4 Giff gaff (=one gift for another) makes good friends. *R.*

5 Give a bairn his will, and a whelp his fill, and none of these two will thrive. *K.*

6 Give a dog a bad name and hang him. *K.*

7 Give a lie twenty-four hours' start, and you can never overtake it. *L.*

8 Give a loaf, and beg a shive (=slice). *R.*

9 Give a man luck, and throw him into the sea. *C.*

10 Give a thief rope enough, and he'll hang himself. *R.*

11 Give a thing and take again
And you shall ride in hell's wain. *R.*

12 Give and spend, and God will send. *B.*

13 Give him an inch, and he'll take an ell.
17th cent. (H.)

Give him rope enough and he'll hang himself, *see* Give a thief rope, etc.

14 Give losers leave to speak (*or* talk). *H.*

15 Give me a child for the first seven years, and you may do what you like with him afterwards. (A Jesuit saying.) *L.*

16 Give never the wolf the wether to keep.
D. F.

17 Give the devil his due. *16th cent.*

18 Giving much to the poor doth increase a man's store. *G. H.*

19 Glasses and lasses are brittle ware. *K.*

20 Gluttony kills more than the sword.
16th cent.

21 Γνῶθι σεαυτόν
– Know thyself. *Greek*

22 Go down the ladder when thou marriest a wife; go up when thou choosest a friend. *R.*

23 Go farther and fare worse. *H.*

24 Go not for every grief to the physician, for every quarrel to the lawyer, nor for every thirst to the pot. *G. H.*

25 Go to bed with the lamb, and rise with the lark. *16th cent.*

26 God comes to see us without a bell.
Spanish

27 God comes with leaden feet, but strikes with iron hands. *16th cent.*

28 God defend me from my friends; from my enemies I can defend myself.
17th cent. (15th cent.)

29 God heals and the doctor takes the fee.
G. H.

30 God help the poor, for the rich can help themselves. *K.*

31 God help the rich, the poor can beg.
J. H.

32 God helps them that help themselves.
G. H. (16th cent.)

33 God is better pleased with adverbs than with nouns. (=With what is done well and lawfully.) *16th cent.*

34 God makes and apparel shapes, but it is money that finishes the man. *R.*

35 God never sends mouths but he sends meat. *H.*

36 God send you joy, for sorrow will come fast enough. *T. D.*

37 God send me a friend that may tell me of my faults; if not, an enemy, and he will. *R.*

38 God sends cold after clothse. (=He supplies men according to their needs.) *H.*

39 God sends fortune to fools. *H.*

40 God sends meat and the devil sends cooks. *16th cent.*

41 God tempers the wind to the shorn lamb. *French*

42 God's mill grinds slow but sure. *Greek*

43 Gold goes in at any gate except heaven's. *R.*

44 Good advice is beyond price. *Latin*

45 Good ale is meat, drink and cloth. *17th cent.*

46 Good ale will make a cat speak. *R.*

47 Good and quickly seldom meet. *G. H.*

48 Good clothes open all doors. *F.*

49 Good company on the road is the shortest cut. *Italian*

50 Good harvests make men prodigal, bad ones provident. *R*

51 Good in the mouth and bad in the maw. *17th cent.*

52 Good is good, but better carries it. *G. H.*

53 Good masters make good servants. *19th cent.*

54 Good men (*or* people) are scarce. *17th cent.*

55 Good riding at two anchors, men have told,
For if one break the other may hold. *Greek*

56 Good swimmers at length are drowned. *G. H.*

57 Good take-heed doth surely speed. *C.*

58 Good to fetch a sick man sorrow and a dead man woe. (Said to those who loiter on errands.) *R.*

59 Good ware makes quick markets. *Latin*

60 Good weight and measure is heaven's treasure. *F.*

61 Good will should be taken for part payment. *D. F.*

62 Good wine needs no bush. (The old sign of a tavern was a bunch of ivy.) *16th cent.*

63 Good words cost nought. *16th cent.*

64 Good words without deeds
Are rushes and reeds. *J. H.*

65 Good workmen are seldom rich. *G. H.*

66 Goods are theirs who enjoy them. *16th cent.*

67 Gossiping and lying go together. *F.*

68 Grasp all, lose all. *18th cent.*

69 Great barkers are no biters. *C. R.*

70 Great boast, small roast. *H.*

71 Great bodies move slowly. *K.*

Great cry and little wool, *see* Much cry, etc.

72 Great men's sons seldom do well. *Latin*

73 Great minds think alike. *20th cent. (17th cent.)*

74 Great spenders are bad lenders. *C.*

75 Great strokes make not sweet music. *G. H.*

76 Great talkers are great liars. *18th cent.*

1 Great trees are good for nothing but shade.   *G. H.*

2 Great trees keep down little ones.   *F.*

3 Great winds blow upon high hills.
                    16th cent.

4 Greedy folk have long arms.   *K.*

5 Grey hairs are death's blossoms.   *R.*

6 Gutta cavat lapidem non vi sed saepe cadendo.
– The drop hollows the stone not by force but by often falling.   *Latin*

7 Had I fish, is good without mustard. (A retort to those who talk of what they would do if they had so-and-so.) *C. R.*

8 Hae ye gear, hae ye nane,
Tine heart and a's gane.
(=Have you goods, have you none, lose heart and all's gone.)   *B.*

9 Hail brings frost in the tail.   *C.*

10 Hair and hair makes the carle's
(=fellow's) head bare.
(=A large store may be brought to nothing by taking away a little at a time.)   *C.*

11 Half a loaf is better than no bread.   *H.*

Half the world knows not how the other half lives, *see* One half of the world, etc.

12 Hall binks are sliddery. (=Hall benches are slippery. The favour of the great is uncertain.)   *D. F.*

13 Handsome is that handsome does.
                R. (16th cent.)

14 Hang him that hath no shift and him that hath one too many.   *K.*

15 Hanging and wiving go by destiny.   *H.*

16 Hap (=good luck) and a halfpenny are world's gear (=goods) enough.   *C.*

17 Happy is he that is happy in his children.
                F.

18 Happy is he whose friends were born before him. (=He who has a position ready-made.)   *R.*

19 Happy is the bride the sun shines on, and the corpse the rain rains on.
                17th cent.

20 Happy is the child whose father goes to the devil. (And leaves a great estate got by extortion.)   *16th cent.*

21 Happy is the country which has no history.   *19th cent.*

22 Happy is the wooing that is not long a-doing.   *16th cent.*

23 Happy man be his dole. (=May happiness be his lot.)   *H.*

24 Hard fare makes hungry bellies.   *C.*

25 Hard with hard never made good wall. (=Mortar is needed. Refractory spirits will not agree.) *Latin*

26 Hard words break no bones.   *16th cent.*

27 Hares may pull dead lions by the beard.
                Latin

28 Harm watch, harm catch.   *15th cent.*

29 Harvest comes not every day, though it come every year.   *F.*

30 Haste and wisdom are things far odd.
                H.

31 Haste comes not alone. (There is always some trouble with it.)   *G. H.*

32 Haste is from hell (*or* the devil.)*17th cent.*

33 Haste makes waste.   *H.*

34 Haste trips up its own heels.   *F.*

35 Hasty climbers have sudden falls.
             R. (16th cent.)

36 Hasty gamesters oversee themselves. *R.*

37 Hate not at the first harm.   *C.*

38 Hatred is blind, as well as love. *F.*

39 Have a horse of thine own and thou mayest borrow another. *J. H.*

40 Have an eye to the main chance. *16th cent.*

41 Have but few friends, though many acquaintances. *J. H.*

42 Have God and have all. *D. F.*

43 Have not thy cloak to make when it begins to rain. *F. (C)*

44 Hawks will not pick hawks' eyes out. *16th cent.*

45 He begins to die that quits his desires. *G. H.*

46 He brings a staff to break his own head. *16th cent.*

47 He can give little to his servant who licks his own trencher. *G. H.*

48 He can ill be master that never was scholar. *C.*

49 He cannot say Bo to a goose. *16th cent.*

50 He cannot speak well that cannot hold his tongue. *F. (17th cent.)*

51 He carries fire in one hand and water in the other. *15th cent.*

52 He carries well to whom it weighs not. *G. H.*

53 He commands enough that obeys a wise man. *G. H.*

54 He complains wrongfully on the sea that twice suffers shipwreck. *G. H.*

55 He could eat me without salt. (=He hates me bitterly.) *K.*

56 He dances well to whom fortune pipes. *16th cent*

57 He deserves not the sweet that will not taste the sour. *Latin*

He dwells far from neighbours that is fain to praise himself, *see* He hath ill neighbours, etc.

58 He giveth twice that gives in a trice. *Latin*

59 He goes a great voyage that goes to the bottom of the sea. *F.*

60 He goes far that never turns. *H.*

61 He goes long barefoot that waits for dead men's shoes. *H.*

62 He goes not out of his way that goes to a good inn. *G. H.*

63 He has a good estate, but that the right owner keeps it from him. *R.*

64 He has a great fancy to marriage that goes to the devil for a wife. *F.*

65 He has brought his pigs to a fine market. *J. H. (16th cent.)*

66 He has but a short Lent that must pay money at Easter. *F. (J. H.)*

67 He has a fault of a wife that marries mam's pet. *K.*

68 He has much prayer but little devotion. *H.*

69 He has not a penny to bless himself with. *H.*

70 He has not lost all who has one cast left. *F.*

71 He has wit at will that with an angry heart can hold him still *D. F.*

72 He hath ill neighbours that is fain to praise himself. *16th cent.*

73 He has great need of a fool that plays the fool himself. *G. H.*

74 He hath no leisure who useth it not. *G. H.*

1 He hath not lived that lives not after
death.   *G. H.*

2 He hath slept well that remembers not
he hath slept ill.   *F.*

3 He is a fool that forgets himself.
    14th cent.

4 He is a fool that is not melancholy once a
day.   *R.*

5 He is a fool that marries at Yule,
For when the corn's to shear the bairn's
   to bear.   *K.*

6 He is a fool who makes his doctor his
heir.   *Latin*

7 He is a good friend that speaks well of us
behind our backs.   *R.*

8 He is a good man whom fortune makes
better.   *F.*

9 He is a good physician who cures
himself.   *15th cent.*

10 He is a great necromancer, for he asks
counsel of the dead. (=Of books.)
    G. H.

11 He is an ill cook that cannot lick his own
fingers.   *H.*

12 He is an ill guest that never drinks to his
host.   *R.*

13 He is blind enough who sees not
through the holes of a sieve.   *R.*

14 He is born in a good hour who gets a
good name.   *15th cent.*

15 He is either dead or teaching school.
    Greek

16 He is happy that thinks himself so. *Latin*

17 He is idle that might be better
employed.   *F.*

18 He is lifeless that is faultless.   *H.*

19 He is no man's enemy but his own.   *C.*

20 He is not a wise man who cannot play
the fool on occasion.   *F. (16th cent.)*

21 He is not laughed at that laughs at
himself first.   *F.*

22 He is not poor that hath little, but he
that desireth much.   *G. H.*

23 He is not wise that is not wise for
himself.   *Latin*

24 He is only bright that shines by himself.
    G. H.

25 He is poor indeed that can promise
nothing.   *R. (C)*

26 He is rich enough that wants nothing.
    Latin

27 He is unworthy to live who lives only
for himself.   *F.*

28 He is wise enough that can keep himself
warm.   *H.*

29 He is wise that is ware in time. *14th cent.*

30 He is wise that knows when he is well
enough.   *H.*

31 He knows enough that can live and hold
his peace.   *16th cent.*

32 He laughs best that laughs last. *18th cent.*

33 He laughs ill that laughs himself to
death.   *C.*

34 He lives long that lives well.   *16th cent.*

35 He lives unsafely that looks too near on
things.   *G. H.*

36 He loses his thanks who promises and
delays.   *T. D.*

37 He loseth indeed that loseth at last.   *F.*

38 He loseth nothing that loseth not God.
    G. H.

39 He loves me for little that hates me for
naught.   *D. F.*

40 He makes a rod for his own back.
H. (14th cent.)

41 He may freely receive courtesies that knows how to requite them.   *R.*

42 He may ill run that cannot go (=walk.)   *H.*

43 He may well be contented who needs neither borrow nor flatter. *R. (15th cent.)*

44 He must have iron nails that scratches a bear.   *R.*

45 He must have leave to speak who cannot hold his tongue.   *D. F.*

46 He must needs swim that is held up by the chin.   *H.*

47 He must rise betimes that will cozen with the devil.   *J. H.*

48 He must rise early that would please everybody.   *R.*

49 He must stoop that hath a low door.   *R.*

50 He never broke his hour that kept his day.   *R.*

51 He never lies but when the holly is green. (=He lies always.)   *D. F.*

52 He never tint (=lost) a cow that grat (=wept) for a needle.   *D. F.*

53 He preaches well that lives well.
17th cent.

54 He preacheth patience that never knew pain.   *B.*

55 He quits his place well that leaves his friend there.   *G. H.*

56 He rides sure that never fell.   *15th cent.*

57 He rises over early that is hanged ere noon.   *D. F.*

58 He should have a long spoon that sups with the devil.   *14th cent.*

59 He sits full still that has riven breeks (=trousers).   *D. F.*

60 He sits not sure that sits too high.
17th cent.

61 He smells best that smells of nothing.
Latin

62 He stands not surely that never slips.
G. H.

63 He sups ill who eats up all at dinner.
French

64 He teacheth ill who teacheth all.   *J. H.*

65 He that asketh faintly beggeth a denial.
Latin

66 He that believes all, misseth; he that believes nothing, hits not.   *G. H.*

67 He that bewails himself hath the cure in his hands.   *G. H.*

68 He that bites on every weed must needs light on poison.   *C.*

69 He that blames would buy.   *G. H.*

70 He that blows in the dust fills his eyes with it.   *G. H.*

71 He that borrows must pay again with sham or loss.   *R.*

72 He that brings up his son to nothing, breeds a thief.   *F.*

73 He that burns his house warms himself for once.   *G. H.*

74 He that burns most shines most.
G. H.

75 He that buys a house ready wrought hath many a pin and nail for nought.
C. R.

76 He that buys land buys many stones;
He that buys flesh buys many bones;
He that buys eggs buys many shells;
He that buys good ale buys nothing else.
R.

1 He that by the plough would thrive
Himself must either hold or drive. _R._

2 He that can make a fire well can end a
quarrel. _G. H._

3 He that can stay obtains. _French_

4 He that cannot abide a bad market
deserves not a good one. _R._

5 He that cannot make sport should mar
none. _K._

6 He that cannot pay, let him pray. _R._

7 He that chastiseth one amendeth many.
_T. D._

8 He that comes first to the hill may sit
where he will. _D. F._

9 He that cometh last to the pot is the
soonest wroth. _H._

10 He that commits a fault thinks everyone
speaks of it. _G. H._

11 He that could know what would be dear
Need be a merchant but one year. _H._

12 He that counts all costs will ne'er put
plough in the earth. _D. F._

13 He that desires honour is not worthy of
honour. _17th cent._

14 He that does bidding deserves no
dinging (=beating). _D. F._

15 He that does not love a woman sucked a
sow. _F._

16 He that does you an ill turn will never
forgive you. _K._

17 He that doth lend doth lose his friend.
W. H. (17th cent.)

18 He that doth nothing doth ever amiss.
17th cent.

19 He that doth what he should not shall
feel what he would not.
G. H. (16th cent.)

20 He that doth what he will doth not what
he ought. _G. H._

21 He that eats till he is sick must fast till he
is well. _F._

22 He that falls to-day may rise to-
morrow. _17th cent._

23 He that feareth every bush must never
go a-birding. _16th cent._

24 He that fears death lives not. _G. H._

25 He that fears you present will hate you
absent. _F._

26 He that fights and runs away may live to
fight another day. _Greek_

27 He that gains well and spends well needs
no account book. _G. H._

28 He that gapeth till he be fed,
Well may he gape until he be dead. _H._

29 He that gives me small gifts would have
me live. _French_

30 He that goes barefoot must not plant
thorns. _G. H._

31 He that goes to bed thirsty riseth
healthy. _G. H._

32 He that goeth far hath many encounters.
_G. H._

33 He that goeth out with often loss
At last comes home by weeping cross.
_R._

34 He that gropes in the dark finds that he
would not. _J. H._

35 He that handles thorns shall prick his
fingers. _R._

36 He that has a wife has a master. _K._

37 He that has no children knows not what
is love. _17th cent._

38 He that has no gear to tine (=goods to
lose) has shins to pine (=to suffer pain).

(=Corporal punishment may be used when the offender cannot pay a fine.) *D. F.*

39 He that has two hoards will get a third. *D. F.*

40 He that hath a good harvest may be content with some thistles. *C.*

41 He that hath a head of wax must not walk in the sun. *G. H.*

42 He that hath an ill name is half hanged. *H.*

43 He that hath but one eye must be afraid to lose it. *G. H.*

44 He that hath it and will not keep it,
He that wants it and will not seek it,
He that drinks and is not dry,
Shall want money as well as I. *J. H.*

45 He that hath lost his credit is dead to the world. *G. H.*

46 He that hath no head needs no hat. *R.*

47 He that hath no ill fortune is troubled with good. *G. H.*

48 He that hath no money needeth no purse. *T. D.*

49 He that hath nothing is not contented. *R.*

50 He that hath one hog makes him fat; and he that hath one son makes him a fool. *G. H.*

51 He that hath plenty of goods shall have more. *H.*

52 He that hath right, fears; he that hath wrong, hopes. *G. H.*

53 He that hath shipped the devil must make the best of him. *R.*

54 He that hath some land must have some labour. *C.*

55 He that hath time, and looks for time, loseth time. *C. R. (16th cent.)*

56 He that hears much and speaks not at all, shall be welcome both in bower and hall. *R.*

57 He that hides can find. *15th cent.*

58 He that hopes not for good fears not evil. *G. H.*

59 He that is a master must serve. *G. H.*

60 He that is angry at a feast is rude. *G. H.*

61 He that is angry without a cause, must be pleased without amends. *H.*

62 He that is born to be hanged shall never be drowned. *G. R.*

63 He that is busy is tempted by but one devil; he that is idle, by a legion. *F.*

64 He that is down, down with him. *C.*

65 He that is fallen cannot help him that is down. *G. H.*

66 He that is fed at another's hand may stay long ere he be full. *G. H.*

67 He that is foolish in the fault, let him be wise in the punishment. *G. H.*

68 He that hath done ill once will do it again. *B.*

69 He that is ill to himself will be good to nobody. *K.*

70 He that is in a town in May loseth his spring. *G. H.*

71 He that is master of himself will soon be master of others. *B.*

72 He that is not handsome at twenty, nor strong at thirty, nor rich at forty, nor wise at fifty, will never be handsome, strong, rich, or wise. *G. H.*

73 He that is once born, once must die. *G. H.*

74 He that is too secure (=over-confident) is not safe. *F.*

1 He that kisseth his wife in the market-place shall have many teachers. *C. R.*

2 He that knows little soon repeats it. *R.*

3 He that knows nothing doubts nothing. *G. H.*

4 He that labours and thrives spins gold. *G. H.*

5 He that lends gives. *G. H.*

6 He that lies on the ground can fall no lower. *Latin*

7 He that lives ill, fear follows him. *G. H.*

8 He that lives in hope danceth without music. *G. H.*

9 He that lives most dies most. *G. H.*

10 He that lives not well one year sorrows seven after. *G. H.*

11 He that lives well is learned enough. *G. H.*

12 He that loseth his due gets not thanks. *G. D.*

13 He that loseth his wife and sixpence hath lost a tester (=sixpenny piece). *R.*

14 He that loves glass without G, Take away L and that is he. *R.*

15 He that loves the tree loves the branch. *G. H.*

16 He that makes a good war makes a good peace. *G. H.*

17 He that makes a thing too fine breaks it. *G. H.*

18 He that makes himself a sheep shall be eaten by the wolf. *G. H. (16th cent.)*

19 He that marries a widow and three children marries four thieves. *R.*

20 He that marries a widow will often have a dead man's head thrown in his dish. *H.*

21 He that marries ere he be wise will die ere he thrive. *H.*

22 He that marries for wealth sells his liberty. *G. H.*

23 He that marries late marries ill. *G. H. (16th cent.)*

24 He that may not do as he would must do as he may. *Latin*

25 He that mischief hatcheth mischief catcheth. *C. R.*

26 He that mocks a cripple ought to be whole. *16th cent.*

27 He that never climbed never fell. *H.*

28 He that once deceives is ever suspected. *G. H.*

29 He that once hits will ever be shooting. *G. H.*

30 He that passeth a winter's day escapes an enemy. *French*

31 He that pays last never pays twice. *R.*

32 He that pities another remembers himself. *G. H.*

33 He that praiseth himself spattereth himself. *G. H.*

34 He that preacheth giveth alms. *G. H.*

35 He that promises too much means nothing. *F.*

36 He that pryeth into every cloud may be stricken with a thunderbolt. *R.*

37 He that puts on a public gown must put off a private person. *F.*

He that reckons without his host must reckon twice, *see* To reckon without one's host.

38 He that respects not is not respected.
G. H.

39 He that riseth first is first dressed.
G. H.

40 He that runs fast will not run long. B.

41 He that runs in the dark may well
stumble. R.

42 He that saveth his dinner will have the
more for his supper.
(=The man who saves when young will
have more to spend when he is old.)
French

43 He that seeks trouble never misses.
G. H.

44 He that sends a fool means to follow
him. G. H.

45 He that serves everybody is paid by
nobody. 17th cent.

46 He that serves well need not be afraid to
ask his wages. G. H.

47 He that shames shall be shent
(=disgraced). D. F.

48 He that shoots oft shall at last hit the
mark. Latin

49 He that shows his purse longs to be rid
of it. C.

50 He that sings on Friday will weep on
Sunday. G. H.

51 He that spares the bad injures the good.
Latin

52 He that speaks me fair and loves me not,
I'll speak him fair and trust him not.
T. D.

53 He that speaks sows, and he that holds
his peace gathers. G. H.

54 He that stays in the valley shall never get
over the hill. R.

55 He that strikes with his tongue must
ward with his head. G. H.

56 He that studies his content wants it.
G. H.

57 He that stumbles and falls not mends his
pace. G. H.

58 He that takes not up a pin slights his
wife. G. H.

59 He that talks much of his happiness
summons grief. G. H.

60 He that talks to himself speaks to a fool.
K.

61 He that teaches himself has a fool for his
master. 17th cent.

62 He that tells a secret is another's servant.
G. H.

63 He that tells his wife news is but newly
married. G. H.

64 He that thinks too much of his virtues
bids others think of his vices. W. H.

65 He that travels far knows much. R.

66 He that was born under a three-
halfpenny (or threepenny) planet shall
never be worth two pence (or a groat).
R.

67 He that will eat the kernel must crack
the nut. Latin

68 He that will France (or England) win
must with Scotland first begin.
16th cent.

69 He that will enter into Paradise must
have a good key. G. H.

70 He that will not be counselled cannot be
helped. C.

71 He that will not be ruled by his own
dame shall be ruled by his stepdame.
(=Those who cannot be prevailed upon
by gentle means must have harsher
treatment.) H.

72 He that will not be saved needs no
preacher. R.

381

1 He that will not have peace, God gives him war.   *G. H.*

2 He that will not stoop for a pin shall never be worth a pound.   *R.*

3 He that will not when he may, when he will he shall have nay.   *H. (10th cent.)*

4 He that will thrive must ask leave of his wife.   *H. (15th cent.)*

5 He that will thrive must rise at five, He that hath thriven may lie till seven.   *16th cent.*

6 He that will to Cupar maun (=must) to Cupar. (=Wilful people must have their way. The Fife courts of Justice were formerly at Cupar.)   *K.*

7 He that winketh with the one eye and looketh with the other, I will not trust him though he were my brother.   *H.*

8 He that wipes the child's nose kisseth the mother's cheek.   *G. H.*

9 He that woos a maid must come seldom in her sight, But he that woos a widow must woo her day and night.   *C.*

10 He that would be old long must be old betimes.   *17th cent. (16th cent.)*

11 He that would be well needs not go from his own house.   *G. H.*

12 He that would hang his dog gives out first that he is mad.   *R. (16th cent.)*

13 He that would have good luck in horses must kiss the parson's wife.   *R.*

14 He that would have what he hath not should do what he doth not.   *H.*

15 He that would know what shall be must consider what hath been.   *F.*

16 He that would learn to pray, let him go to sea.   *R.*

17 He that would live for aye must eat sage in May.   *R.*

18 He that would live in peace and rest Must hear and see and say the best.   *R.*

19 He that would no evils do must shun all things that long (=belong) thereto.   *C.*

20 He that would the daughter win Must with the mother first begin.   *R.*

21 He thinks not well that thinks not again.   *G. H.*

22 He to whom God gave no sons the devil gives nephews.   *B.*

23 He warms too near that burns.   *G. H.*

24 He was a bold man that first ate an oyster.   *17th cent.*

25 He was hanged that left his drink behind him. (Only a man running for his life would do so.)   *R.*

26 He was scant (=short) of news that told his father was hanged.   *K.*

27 He who commences many things finishes but few.   *Italian*

28 He who does not rise early never does a good day's work.   *T. D.*

29 He who lies down with dogs will rise with fleas.   *Latin*

30 He who never was sick dies the first fit.   *F.*

31 He who pays the piper may call the tune.   *17th cent.*

32 He who rides on a tiger can never dismount.   *Chinese*

33 He who says what he likes shall hear what he does not like.   *Latin*

34 He who swells in prosperity will shrink in adversity.   *B.*

35 He wrongs not an old man that steals his supper from him.   *G. H.*

36 Heads I win, tails you lose.   *17th cent.*

37 Health and money go far. *G. H.*

38 Health and wealth create beauty. *B.*

39 Health and sickness surely are men's double enemies. *G. H.*

40 Health is better than wealth. *16th cent.*

41 Health is not valued till sickness comes. *F.*

42 Hear all parties. *H.*

43 Hear and see and be still. *15th cent.*

44 Hear twice before you speak once. *B.*

45 Hearken to reason, or she will be heard. *G. H.*

46 Hearts may agree though heads differ. *F.*

Heaven helps those that help themselves, *see* God helps them, etc.

47 Hell and Chancery are always open. *F.*

48 Hell is full of good meanings and wishes. *G. H.*

Hell is paved with good intentions, *see* The road to hell, etc.

49 Hell is wherever heaven is not. *17th cent.*

50 Help, hands! for I have no lands. *16th cent.*

51 Help me to salt, help me to sorrow. *19th cent.*

52 Here to-day and gone to-morrow. *P. R. A.*

53 Hereafter comes not yet. *H.*

54 Heresy may be easier kept out than shook off. *G. H.*

55 Hew not too high lest the chips fall in thine eye. *14th cent.*

56 Hide nothing from thy minister, physician, and lawyer. *G. H. (16th cent.)*

57 High places have their precipices.

High words break no bones, *see* Hard words, etc. *F.*

58 His bark is worse than his bite. *Latin*

59 His bashful mind hinders his good intent. *R.*

60 His bread is buttered on both sides. (=He is well-to-do.) *R.*

61 His hair grows through his hood. (=He is in want.) *15th cent.*

62 His heart is in his boots (*formerly* hose). *15th cent.*

63 His heart is in his mouth. *16th cent.*

64 His money burns a hole in his pocket. (=He feels a strong desire to spend it.) *16th cent.*

65 His wits are wool-gathering. (=He is absent-minded.) *16th cent.*

66 History repeats itself. *19th cent.*

67 Hold fast when you have it. *H.*

68 Hold your hands off other folks' bairns, till you get some of your own. *B.*

69 Home is home, be it never so homely. *H.*

70 Homer sometimes nods. *Latin*

71 Honest men marry soon, wise men not at all. *R.*

72 Honesty is the best policy. *16th cent.*

73 Honesty may be dear bought, but can never be an ill pennyworth. *K.*

74 Honey in the mouth saves the purse. *Italian*

75 Honey is dear bought if licked off thorns. *12th cent.*

76 Honey is sweet, but the bee stings. *G. H.*

1 Honi soit qui mal y pense.
 – Shame take him that shame thinketh.
French

2 Honour and ease are seldom bedfellows.
C.

3 Honour and profit lie not in one sack.
G. H.

4 Honour will buy no beef. *17th cent.*

5 Honour without profit is a ring on the
finger. *Spanish*

6 Honours change manners. *Latin*

7 Hope for the best and prepare for the
worst. *16th cent.*

8 Hope is a good breakfast but a bad
supper. *17th cent.*

9 Hope is a lover's staff. *B.*

10 Hope is as cheap as despair. *F.*

11 Hope is the poor man's bread. *Italian*

12 Hope well and have well. *16th cent.*

13 Hot love is soon cold. *H.*

14 Humanum est errare.
 – To err is human. *Latin*

15 Humble hearts have humble desires.
G. H.

16 Hunger breaks through stone walls. *H.*

17 Hunger finds no fault with the cookery.
F.

18 Hunger is the best sauce. *Latin*

19 Hunger makes dinners, pastime
suppers. *G. H.*

20 Hungry bellies have no ears. *Latin*

21 Hungry dogs will eat dirty puddings.
H.

22 Hungry flies bite sore. *H.*

23 Husbands are in heaven whose wives
scold not. *H.*

24 Hypocrisy is a homage that vice pays to
virtue. *French*

25 I am very wheamow (=nimble) said the
old woman, when she stepped into the
milk-bowl. *R.*

26 I can see as far into a millstone as
another. *H.*

27 I cannot be your friend and your flatterer
too. *17th cent.*

28 I gave the mouse a hole, and she is
become my heir. *G. H.*

29 I had rather have your room than your
company. *16th cent.*

30 I have other fish to fry. (=Other
business to attend to.) *17th cent.*

31 I know him not though I should meet
him in my dish. *17th cent.*

32 I know no more than the man in the
moon about it. *19th cent.*

33 I know no more than the Pope of Rome
about it. *R.*

34 I live, and lords do no more. *16th cent.*

35 I love my friends well, but myself
better. *French.*

36 I love thee like pudding, if thou wert pie
I'd eat thee. *R.*

37 I may see him need, but I'll not see him
bleed. *C.*

38 I pensieri stretti ed il viso sciolto.
 – The thoughts close and the
countenance open. *Italian*

39 I say little (*or* nothing) but I think the
more. *H. (15th cent.)*

40 I stout (=proud) and thou stout, who
shall bear the ashes out? *H.*

41 I taught you to swim, and now you'd drown me. *F.*

42 I was not born yesterday. *19th cent.*

43 I wept when I was born, and every day shows why. *G. H.*

44 I will either grind or find. *R.*

45 I will keep no more cats than will catch mice. *R.*

46 I will neither meddle nor make. *16th cent.*

47 I will not change a cottage in possession for a kingdom in reversion. *R.*

48 I will not keep a dog and bark myself. *16th cent.*

49 I will not make a toil of a pleasure. *17th cent.*

50 I will not make my dish-clout my table-cloth. *R.*

51 I will not pull the thorn out of your foot and put it into my own. *R.*

52 I will trust him no further than I can fling him. *R.*

53 I wot well how the world wags, he is most loved that hath most bags. *R.*

54 I would not call the king my cousin. (=I would be so happy.) *K.*

55 I would not touch him with a pair of tongs. *R.*

56 Idle brains are the devil's workshop. *R.*

57 Idle folks have the least leisure. *19th cent.*

58 Idle men are dead all their life long. *F.*

59 Idle people take the most pains. *R.*

60 Idleness is the key of beggary. *R.*

61 Idleness is the parent of all vice (*or* the root of all evil). *15th cent.*

62 Idleness makes the wit rust. *F.*

63 Idleness must thank itself if it go barefoot. *R.*

64 If a good man thrive, all thrive with him. *G. H.*

65 If a man deceive me once, shame on him; if he deceive me twice, shame on me. *K.*

66 If a woman were little as she is good A peascod would make her a gown and a hood. *Italian*

67 If all fools wore white caps we should seem a flock of geese. *G. H.*

68 If all men say that thou art an ass, then bray. *T. D.*

69 If an ass goes a-travelling, he'll not come home a horse. *F.*

70 If anything stay, let work stay. *R.*

71 If Candlemas day be fair and bright, (2 Feb.) Winter will have another flight; If on Candlemas day it be shower and rain, Winter is gone and will come not again. *R.*

72 If every man mend one, all shall be amended. *H.*

73 If folly were grief, every house would weep. *G. H.*

74 If fools went not to market, bad wares would not be sold. *Spanish*

75 If great men would have care of little ones, both would last long. *G. H.*

76 If hope were not, heart would break. *13th cent.*

77 If I had not lifted up the stone, you had not found the jewel. *R.*

78 If Ifs and Ans were pots and pans There'd be no trade for tinkers. *19th cent.*

1 If it were not for the belly the back
might wear gold.   *F.*

2 If Jack's in love, he's no judge of Jill's
beauty.   *F.*

3 If Janiveer's calends be summerly gay,
'Twill be winterly weather till the
calends of May.   *F.*

4 If money be not thy servant, it will be
thy master.   *17th cent.*

5 If my shirt knew my design, I'd burn it.
F (17th cent.)

6 If on the eighth of June it rain,
It foretells a wet harvest, men sain.   *F.*

7 If one sheep leap o'er the dyke (=ditch),
all the rest will follow.   *K.*

8 If one will not another will; so are all
maidens married.   *H.*

9 If physic do not work, prepare for the
kirk.   *R.*

10 If St. Paul's be fine and clear (25 Jan.)
It doth betide a happy year.
16th cent. (14th cent.)

11 If St. Vitus's day be rainy weather
(15 June)
It will rain for thirty days together.   *D.*

12 If the adder could hear and the
blindworm could see,
Neither man nor beast would ever go
free.   *19th cent.*

13 If the beard were all, the goat might
preach.   *17th cent.*

14 If the bed could tell all it knows, it
would put many to the blush.   *J. H.*

15 If the brain sows not corn, it plants
thistles.   *G. H.*

16 If the cap fits, wear it.   *18th cent.*

17 If the cock goes crowing to bea.
He's sure to rise with a watery head.
(=It will rain.)   *D.*

18 If the counsel be good, no matter who
gave it.   *F.*

19 If the devil find a man idle, he'll set him
to work.   *K.*

20 If the doctor cures, the sun sees it; but if
he kills, the earth hides it.   *K.*

21 If the dog bark, go in; if the bitch bark,
go out.   *R.*

22 If the first of July it be rainy weather,
'Twill rain, more or less, for four weeks
together.   *F.*

23 If the grass grow in Janiveer,
It grows the worse for't all the year.   *R.*

24 If the ice will bear a maman before
Christmas, it will not bear a goose
after.   *I.*

25 If the laird slight the lady, so will all the
kitchen boys.   *K.*

26 If the lion's skin cannot, the fox's shall.
(=If force will not answer, craft
will.)   *French*

27 If the mountain will not come to
Mahomet, Mahomet must go to the
mountain.   *R.*

28 If the oak's before the ash,
Then you'll only get a splash;
If the ash precedes the oak,
Then you may expect a soak.   *W. H.*

29 If the old dog barks, he gives counsel.
G. H.

30 If the pills were pleasant, they would not
want gilding.   *F. (T. D.)*

31 If the sky falls we shall catch (*or* have)
larks.   *H.*

32 If the staff be crooked, the shadow
cannot be straight.   *G. H.*

33 If the sun in red should set.
The next day surely will be wet;
If the sun should set in grey,
The next will be a rainy day.   *I.*

34 If the twenty-fourth of August be fair
and clear,
Then hope for a prosperous autumn that
year. *F.*

35 If the wise erred not, it would go hard
with fools. *G. H.*

36 If there be a rainbow in the eve,
It will rain and leave;
But if there be a rainbow in the morrow,
It will neither lend nor borrow. *R.*

37 If there were no knaves and fools, all the
world would be alike. *F.*

38 If things were to be done twice, all
would be wise. *G. H.*

39 If thou dealest with a fox, think of his
tricks. *F.*

40 If thou hast not a capon, feed on an
onion. *R.*

41 If we are bound to forgive an enemy, we
are not bound to trust him. *F.*

42 If wind blows on you through a hole,
Make your will and take care of your
soul. *P. R. A.*

43 If wise men play the fool, they do it with
a vengeance. *B.*

44 If wishes were horses, beggars would
ride. *K.*

45 If ye would know a knave, give him a
staff. *G. H.*

46 If you always say No, you'll never be
married. *K.*

47 If you are too fortunate, you will not
know yourself; if you are too
unfortunate, nobody will know you. *F.*

48 If you beat spice it will smell the
sweeter. *F.*

49 If you can kiss the mistress, never kiss
the maid. *R.*

50 If you cannot bite, never show your
teeth. *R.*

51 If you don't like it, you may lump (=put
up with) it. *19th cent.*

52 If you drink in your pottage, you'll
cough in your grave. *R.*

53 If you make a jest, you must take a jest.
18th cent.

54 If you have done no ill the six days, you
may play the seventh. *F.*

55 If you have no enemies, it is a sign
fortune has forgot you. *F.*

56 If you kill one flea in March you kill a
hundred. *L.*

57 If you leap into a well, Providence is not
bound to fetch you out. *F.*

58 If you lie upon roses when young, you'll
lie upon thorns when old. *F.*

59 If you pay not a servant his wages, he
will pay himself. *F.*

60 If you put nothing into your purse, you
can take nothing out. *F.*

61 If you run after two hares, you will
catch neither. *Latin*

62 If you sing before breakfast, you'll cry
before night. *16th cent.*

63 If you squeeze a cork, you will get but
little juice. *F.*

64 If you swear, you'll catch no fish.
17th cent.

If you touch pot you must touch penny,
see Touch pot, etc.

65 If you trust before you try,
You may repent before you die.
R. (16th cent.)

66 If you want a thing well done, do it
yourself. *L.*

67 If you want a thing done, go; if not,
send. *P. R. A.*

68 If you wish good advice, consult an old
man. *Portuguese*

1 If you wish to live and thrive,
Let the spider run alive. *19th cent.*

2 If you would fruit have,
You must bring the leaf to the grave.
(=Transplant in autumn.) *R.*

3 If you would know secrets, look for
them in grief or pleasure. *G. H.*

4 If you would know the value of money,
try to borrow some. *G. H.*

5 If you would live well for a week, kill a
hog; if you would live well for a month,
marry; if you would live well all your
life, turn priest. *19th cent.*

6 If you would make an enemy, lend a
man money, and ask it of him again.
Portuguese

7 If you would wish the dog to follow
you, feed him. *B.*

8 If your ear burns, someone is talking
about you. *H.*

9 If your hand be bad, mend it with good
play. (At cards.) *F.*

10 If youth knew what age would crave, it
would both get and save. *R.*

11 Ignorance is the mother of devotion.
16th cent.

12 Ignorance is the mother of impudence.
B.

13 Ignotum per ignotius. – (Explaining)
what is unknown by what is still more
unknown. *Latin*

14 Il faut reculer pour mieux sauter.
– One must draw back in order to leap
better. *French*

15 Ill beef ne'er made good broo (=broth).
K.

16 Ill comes in ells and goes out by inches.
G.H.

17 Ill comes upon waur's [=worse's] back.
K.

18 Ill doers are ill deemers. *K.*

19 Ill-gotten gains [or goods] seldom
prosper. *16th cent.*

20 Ill-gotten goods thrive not to the third
heir. *Latin*

21 Ill gotten, ill spent. *Latin*

22 Ill luck is good for something. *C. R.*

23 Ill natures never want a tutor. *F.*

24 Ill news travels fast [or comes apace].
16th cent.

25 Ill ware is never cheap. *G. H.*

26 Ill weeds grow apace. *French*

27 Ill will never said well. *15th cent.*

28 In a calm sea every man is a pilot. *R.*

29 In a good house all is quickly ready.
G. H.

30 In a retreat the lame are foremost.
G. H.

31 In a thousand pounds of law there is not
an ounce of love. *R.*

32 In all games it is good to leave off a
winner. *F.*

33 In an ermine spots are soon discovered.
F.

34 In April, come he will; (The cuckoo.)
In May, he sings all day;
In June he alters his tune;
In July he prepares to fly;
In August, go he must;
If he stay till September,
'Tis as much as the oldest man can ever
remember. *I.*

35 In at one ear and out at the other.
14th cent.

36 In choosing a wife and buying a sword
we ought not to trust another. *G. H.*

37 In dock, out nettle. (Signifying inconstancy.) *14th cent.*

38 In doing we learn. *G. H.*

39 In every art it is good to have a master. *G. H.*

40 In every country the sun rises in the morning. *G. H.*

41 In fair weather prepare for foul. *F.*

42 In for a penny, in for a pound. *17th cent.*

43 In giving and taking it is easy mistaking. *B.*

44 In love is no lack. *15th cent.*

45 In love's wars, he who flieth is conqueror. *F.*

46 In March, the birds begin to search; In April, the corn begins to fill; In May, the birds begin to lay. *W. H.*

47 In my own city my name, in a strange city my clothes procure me respect. *R.*

48 In settling an island, the first building erected by a Spaniard will be a church; by a Frenchman, a fort; by a Dutchman, a warehouse; and by an Englishman, an alehouse. *18th cent.*

49 In space comes grace. *H.*

50 In sports and journeys men are known. *G. H.*

51 In the coldest flint there is hot fire. *16th cent.*

52 In the country of the blind the one-eyed man is king. *16th cent.*

53 In the deepest water is the best fishing. *R.*

54 In the end things will mend. *J. H.*

55 In the grave, dust and bones jostle not for the wall. *F.*

56 In the house of the fiddler all fiddle. *G. H.*

57 In the husband wisdom, in the wife gentleness. *G. H.*

58 In the old of the moon, a cloudy morning bodes a fair afternoon. *R.*

59 In the world, who knows not to swim goes to the bottom. *G. H.*

60 In time of prosperity friends will be plenty; In time of adversity not one among twenty. *J. H.*

61 In trust is treason. *15th cent.*

62 In vain he craves advice that will not follow it. *R.*

63 In vino veritas. – In wine there is truth. *Latin.*

64 Industry is fortune's right hand, and frugality her left. *R.*

65 Inglese italianato è un diavolo incarnato. – An Englishman Italianate is a devil incarnate. *Italian*

66 Injuries don't use to be written on ice. *F.*

67 Innocence itself sometimes hath need of a mask. *F.*

68 Innocent actions carry their warrant with them. *F.*

69 Interest will not lie. *17th cent.*

70 Into the mouth of a bad dog often falls a good bone. *C.*

71 It chances in an hour, that happens not in seven years. *16th cent.*

72 It cost more to do ill than to do well. *G. H.*

73 It early pricks that will be a thorn. *14th cent.*

1 It is a bad cause that none dare speak in.
　　　　　　　　　　　　　　　　C.

2 It is a bad cloth that will take no colour.
　　　　　　　　　　　　　　　　H.

3 It is a bad sack that will abide no
clouting.　　　　　　　　　　　H.

4 It is a bold (or wily) mouse that breeds
(or nestles) in the cat's ear.　15th cent.

5 It is a dear collop that is cut out of thine
own flesh.　　　　　　　　　　H.

6 It is a foolish sheep that makes the wolf
his confessor.　　　　　　　　　R.

7 It is a good horse that never stumbles,
And a good wife that never grumbles.
　　　　　　　　　　　　　　　　R.

8 It is a good tongue that says no ill, and a
better heart that thinks none.　K.

9 It is a hard-fought field where none
escapes.　　　　　　　　　　　H.

10 It is a hard winter when one wolf eats
another.　　　　　　　　　16th cent.

11 It is a long lane that has no turning.　R.

12 It is a pain both to pay and pray.　D. F.

13 It is a poor dog that is not worth the
whistling.　　　　　　　　　　H.

14 It is a poor heart that never rejoices.
　　　　　　　　　　　　19th cent.

15 It is a poor stake that cannot stand one
year in the ground.　　　　　　H.

16 It is a proud horse that will not bear his
own provender.　　　　　　　　H.

17 It is a rank courtesy when a man is
forced to give thanks for his own.　R.

18 It is a sad burden to carry a dead man's
child.　　　　　　　　　　17th cent.

19 It is a sad house where the hen crows
louder than the cock.　　　16th cent.

20 It is a sair dung (=sore beaten) bairn that
dare not greet (=weep).

21 It is a silly bargain where nobody gets.
　　　　　　　　　　　F. (16th cent.)

22 It is a silly fish that is caught twice with
the same bait.　　　　　　　　F.

23 It is a silly goose that comes to the fox's
sermon.　　　　　　　　　16th cent.

24 It is a sin to belie the devil.　16th cent.

25 It is a sin to steal a pin.　　19th cent.

26 It is a wise child that knows its own
father.　　　18th cent. (16th cent.)

27 It is always term time in the court of
conscience.　　　　　　　　　F.

28 It is an ill battle (or army) where the
devil carries the colours.　R. (C.)

29 It is an ill bird that fouls its own nest.
　　　　　　　　　　　　13th cent.

30 It is an ill counsel that hath no escape.
　　　　　　　　　　　　　G. H.

31 It is an ill procession where the devil
bears the cross (or holds the candle).
　　　　　　　　　　　　　T. D.

32 It is an ill wind that blows nobody good.
　　　　　　　　　　　　　　　H.

33 It is as hard to please a knave as a knight.
　　　　　　　　　　　　　　　R.

34 It is better to marry a shrew than a
sheep.　　　　　　　　　16th cent.

35 It is better to hear the lark sing than the
mouse squeak (or cheep).　　B.

36 It is comparison that makes men
miserable.　　　　　　　　　　F.

37 It is day still while the sun shines.　R.

38 It is easier to build two chimneys than to
maintain one.　　　　　　　G. H.

39 It is easier to fall than rise.   *C. R.*

40 It is easier to pull down than to build up.
    16th cent.

41 It is easier to raise the devil than to lay
him.   *18th cent.*

42 It is easy to be wise after the event.
    17th cent.

43 It is easy to bowl down hill.   *C.*

44 It is easy to rob an orchard when none
keeps it.   *C.*

45 It is good beating proud folks, for they
will not complain.   *C.*

46 It is good fishing in troubled waters.
    16th cent.

47 It is good sheltering under an old hedge.
    R.

48 It is good sleeping in a whole skin.   *H.*

49 It is good to be merry and wise. (Said
when merriment becomes foolish.)   *H.*

50 It is good to be near of kin to an estate.
    R.

51 It is good to beware by other men's
harms.   *Latin*

52 It is good to fear the worst, the best will
be the welcomer (*or* save itself).   *T. D.*

53 It is good to have a hatch before the
door. (=To keep silence.)   *H.*

54 It is good to have some friends both in
heaven and in hell.   *G. H.*

55 It is Greek to me. (=Unintelligible.)
    16th cent.

56 It is hard to halt before a cripple. (He
will soon see if you are shamming.)
    14th cent.

57 It is hard to be wretched, but worse to
be known so.   *G. H.*

58 It is hard to laugh and cry both with a
breath.   *C.*

59 It is hard to please all.   *15th cent.*

60 It is hard to sit in Rome and strive
against the Pope.   *D. F.*

61 It is hard to wive and thrive both in a
year.   *15th cent.*

62 It is ill fishing before the net.
(=Anticipating gains.)   *H.*

63 It is ill healing of an old sore.   *H.*

64 It is ill jesting with edged tools.
    16th cent.

65 It is ill putting a naked sword in a
madman's hand.   *H.*

66 It is ill speaking between a full man and a
fasting.   *D. F.*

67 It is ill striving against the stream.
    13th cent.

68 It is ill taking the breeks off a
Hielandman.   *19th cent.*

69 It is ill to drive black hogs in the dark.
    R.

70 It is ill waiting for dead men's shoes.
    16th cent.

71 It is lawful to learn even from an enemy.
    Latin

72 It is love that makes the world go round.
    French

73 It is merry in hall when beards wag all.
    14th cent.

74 It is merry when gossips meet.   *C.*

75 It is merry when knaves meet.   *H.*

76 It is more easy to praise poverty than to
bear it.   *H.*

77 It is more pain to do nothing than
something.   *G. H.*

1 It is never too late to mend. *17th cent.*

2 It is no more pity to see a woman weep than to see a goose go barefoot. *16th cent.*

3 It is no play where one greets (=weeps) and another laughs. *D. F.*

4 It is no sin to sell dear, but a sin to give ill measure. *K.*

5 It is no time to stoop when the head is off. *D. F.*

6 It is no use crying over spilt milk. *J. H.*

7 It is not all butter that the cow yields. *H.*

8 It is not as thy mother says, but as thy neighbours say. *F.*

9 It is not good to want and to have. *D. F.*

10 It is not how long, but how well we live. *R.*

11 It is not lost that a friend gets. *D. F.*

12 It is not lost that comes at last. *17th cent.*

13 It is not the suffering, but the cause, that makes a martyr. *17th cent.*

14 It is not What is she, but What has she. *17th cent.*

15 It is safe taking a shive (=slice) of a cut loaf. *R. (16th cent.)*

16 It is the men who make a city. *Greek*

17 It is the nature of the beast. *R.*

18 It is the pace that kills. *19th cent.*

19 It is the unforeseen (*or* unexpected) that always happens. *19th cent.*

20 It is too late to grieve when the chance is past. *C. R.*

21 It is too late to spare when the bottom is bare (*or* when all is spent). *Latin*

22 It is very hard to shave an egg. *C.*

23 It is wit to pick a lock and steal a horse, but wisdom to let them alone. *J. H.*

24 It matters not what religion an ill man is of. *F.*

25 It must be true that all men say. *H.*

26 It never rains but it pours. *19th cent. (18th cent.)*

27 It never troubles a wolf how many the sheep be. *17th cent.*

28 It signifies nothing to play well if you lose. *F.*

29 It takes all sorts to make a world. *17th cent.*

30 It takes two to make a quarrel. *19th cent.*

31 It will be all the same a hundred years hence. *B.*

32 Jack is as good as his master. *19th cent.*

33 Jack of all trades and master of none. *18th cent.*

34 Jack Sprat could eat no fat,
His wife could eat no lean;
And so, betwixt them both, you see,
They licked the platter clean. *C.*

35 Jack would be a gentleman if he could speak French. *H.*

36 Janiveer (=January) freeze the pot by the fire. *R.*

37 Joan is as good as my lady in the dark. *17th cent.*

38 Jouk and let the jaw gae by. (=Dodge and let the splash go past.) *K.*

39 Jove laughs at lovers' perjuries. *Latin*

40 Judex damnatur ubi nocens absolvitur.
– The judge is condemned when the
guilty is acquitted.   *Latin*

41 Justice pleaseth few in their own house.
                                        G. H.

42 Kame sindle, kame sair. (=Comb
seldom, comb sore.)   *D. F.*

43 Keek in my kail pot, glower in my
ambry. (=Peer in my cabbage pot, stare
in my cupboard. Said to those who pry
officiously.)   *K.*

44 Keep a calm sough. (=Keep a quiet
tongue.)   *19th cent.*

45 Keep a thing seven years and you will
find a use for it.   *17th cent.*

46 Keep counsel thyself first.   *C.*

47 Keep good men company and you shall
be of the number.   *G. H.*

48 Keep some till more come.   *R.*

49 Keep something for a sore foot. (=Save
for age or distress.)   *K.*

50 Keep the common road, and thou'rt
safe.   *F.*

51 Keep your ain fish-guts for your ain sea-
maws (=gulls). (=Keep your leavings
for your own friends.)   *K.*
Keep your breath to cool your porridge,
see Save your breath, etc.

52 Keep your eyes wide open before
marriage and half shut afterwards.
                                  P. R. A.

53 Keep your mouth shut and your eyes
open.   *18th cent.*

54 Keep your shop and your shop will keep
you.   *17th cent.*

55 Kick an attorney downstairs and he'll
stick to you for life.   *L.*

56 Kindle not a fire that you cannot
extinguish.   *B. (16th cent.)*

57 Kindness cannot be bought for gear
(=goods).   *D. F.*

58 Kindness is lost that is bestowed on
children and old folks.   *C.*

59 Kindnesses, like grain, increase by
sowing.   *B.*

60 Kings and bears oft worry their keepers.
                                   D. F.

61 King's chaff is worth other men's corn.
                                   D. F.

62 Kings have long arms.   *Greek*

63 Kings have many ears and many eyes.
                                    Greek

64 Kiss and be friends.   *14th cent.*

65 Kissing goes by favour.   *C. R.*

66 Kitchen physic is the best physic.
                                 16th cent.

67 Kitty Swerrock where she sat,
Come reach me this, come reach me
   that.
(Said to lazy girls who ask for things to
be reached to them.)   *K.*

68 Knavery may serve a turn, but honesty
never fails.   *R.*

69 Knaves and fools divide the world.   *R.*

70 Knaves imagine nothing can be done
without knavery.   *F.*

71 Knowledge is folly, except grace guide
it.   *G. H.*

72 Knowledge is no burden.   *G. H.*

73 Knowledge is power.
                     19th cent. (17th cent.)

74 Knowledge makes one laugh, but
wealth makes one dance.   *G. H.*

75 Knowledge without practice makes but
half an artist.   *F.*

1 Κόινὰ τά τῶν φίλων.
– The things of friends are in common.
Greek

2 Laborare est orare.
– To work is to pray. *Latin*

3 Labour as long-lived, pray as ever dying. *G. H.*

4 Lad's love (=southernwood) is lassies' delight, and if lads won't love, lassies will flite (=scold). *19th cent.*

5 Lad's love's a busk of broom, hot awhile and soon done. *R.*

6 Land was never lost for want of an heir. *R.*

7 Lasses are lads' leavings. *R.*

8 Last but not least. *16th cent.*

9 Last make fast. (When going through a gate.) *J. H.*

10 Late repentance is seldom true. *Latin*

11 Laugh and grow fat. *16th cent.*

12 Law, logic, and Switzers may be hired to fight for anybody. *16th cent.*

13 Law makers should not be law breakers. *17th cent. (14th cent.)*

14 Law catches flies, but lets hornets go free. *15th cent.*

15 Lawsuits consume time, and money, and rest, and friends. *G. H.*

16 Lawyers' houses are built on the heads of fools. *G. H.*

17 Lazy folk take the most pains. *18th cent.*

18 Leal heart lied never. *18th cent.*

19 Lean liberty is better than fat slavery. *F.*

20 Learn weeping and thou shalt gain laughing. *G. H.*

21 Learn wisdom by the follies of others. *B.*

22 Learning makes a good man better and an ill man worse. *F.*

23 Least said soonest mended. *15th cent.*

24 Least talk most work. *17th cent.*

25 Leave a jest when it pleases you best. *G. H.*

26 Leave is light. (=It is an easy matter to ask leave.) *H.*

27 Leave off while the play is good. *14th cent.*

28 Leave off with an appetite. *16th cent.*

29 Lend and lose; so play fools. *R.*

30 Lend not horse, nor wife, nor sword. *16th cent.*

31 Lend your money and lose your friend. *R.*

32 Less of your courtesy and more of your purse. *C.*

33 Let all live as they would die. *G. H.*

34 Let alone makes many a loon. (=Neglect makes many a rascal.) *D F.*

35 Let another's shipwreck be your sea-mark. *17th cent.*

36 Let bygones be bygones. *17th cent. (H.)*
Let every herring hang by its own tail, *see* Every herring, etc.

37 Let every pedlar carry his own pack (*or* burden). *J. H.*

38 Let him that is cold blow at the coal. *H.*

39 Let him that would be happy for a day, go to the barber; for a week, marry a wife; for a month, buy him a new horse; for a year, build him a new house; for all his lifetime, be an honest man. *Italian*

40 Let his own wand ding (=rod beat)him.
(=Let him bear the results of his own
folly.) *K.*

41 Let not a child sleep upon bones. (=On
the nurse's lap.) *R.*

42 Let not your tongue cut your throat. *B.*

43 Let patience (=a kind of dock) grow in
your garden alway. *H.*

44 Let sleeping dogs lie. *14th cent.*

45 Let that flee (=fly) stick to the wall.
18th cent.

46 Let that which is lost be for God.
Spanish

47 Let the cobbler stick to his last. *Latin*

48 Let the world slide (*or* wag) . *16th cent.*

49 Let them laugh that win. *H.*

50 Let well alone. *14th cent.*

51 Let your letter stay for the post, not the
post for the letter. *R.*

52 Let your purse be your master. *C.*

53 Liars begin by imposing upon others,
but end by deceiving themselves. *B.*

54 Liars should have good memories.
Latin

55 Life is half spent before we know what it
is. *G. H.*

56 Life is made up of little things. *L.*

57 Life is sweet. *14th cent.*

58 Life lies not in living but in liking. *R.*

59 Life without a friend is death without a
witness. *G. H.*

60 Life would be too smooth if it had no
rubs in it. *F.*

61 Light burdens, long borne, grow heavy.
H.

62 Light cares speak, great ones are dumb.
Latin

63 Light gains make heavy purse. (Because
light gains come often, great only
occasionally.) *H.*

64 Lightly come, lightly go. *15th cent.*

65 Like a bull in a china shop. *19th cent.*

66 Like a dying duck in a thunderstorm.
18th cent.

67 Like a house on fire. (=Rapidly.)
19th cent.

68 Like a fish out of water. *Latin*

69 Like a hen on a hot griddle. (=Fidgety.)
19th cent.

70 Like a red rag to a bull. *16th cent.*

71 Like a toad under a harrow.
19th cent. (13th cent.)

72 Like author, like book. *R.*

73 Like blood, like good, and like age,
make the happiest marriage. *C.*

74 Like cures like. *Latin*

75 Like father, like son. *14th cent.*

76 Like herrings in a barrel. (=Packed
close.) *19th cent.*

77 Like lips, like lettuce. (Of an ass eating
thistles.) *Latin*

78 Like master, like man. *Latin*

79 Like mother, like daughter. *16th cent.*

80 Like punishment and equal pain both
key and keyhole do sustain. *C.*

81 Like the curate's egg, good in parts.
19th cent.

82 Like water off a duck's back. *19th cent.*

83 Like will to like. *Latin*

395

1 Likely lies in the mire when Unlikely gets over. *D. F.*

2 Likeness causeth liking. *C.*

3 Lilies are whitest in a blackamoor's hand. *F.*

4 Listeners hear no good of themselves. *R.*

5 Littera scripta manet. – The written letter remains. *Latin*

6 Little and often fills the purse. *17th cent.*

7 Little birds that can sing and won't sing must be made to sing. *R.*

8 Little by little as the cat ate the flickle [=flitch]. *H.*

9 Little goods, little care. *T. D.*

10 Little intermeddling makes good friends. *D. F.*

11 Little journeys and good cost bring safe home. *G. H.*

12 Little kens the wife that sits by the fire How the wind blows cold in Hurle-burle-swyre. (=Those in shelter know little of others' troubles. Hurle-burle-swyre is a Scottish mountain pass.) *D. F.*

13 Little knoweth the fat sow what the lean doth mean. *H.*

14 Little pitchers have long (*or* wide) ears. *G. H. (H.)*

15 Little sticks kindle the fire, great ones put it out. *G. H.*

16 Little strokes fell great oaks. *16th cent.*

17 Little thieves are hanged, but great ones escape. *C.*

18 Little things are pretty. *R.*

19 Little things please little minds. *Latin*

20 Live and learn. *C.*

21 Live and let live. *Dutch*

22 Living well is the best revenge. *G. H.*

23 London Bridge was made for wise men to go over and fools to go under. (The old bridge was dangerous for light wherries to shoot.) *C.*

24 Long a widow weds with shame. *J. H.*

25 Long absent, soon forgotten. *T. D.*

26 Long beards heartless, Painted hoods witless, Gay coats graceless Makes England Thriftless. (A taunting rhyme made up by the Scots.) *16th cent.*

27 Long foretold, long last; Short notice, soon past. (Of the barometer.) *19th cent.*

28 Long looked for comes at last. *15th cent.*

29 Long-tongued wives go long with bairn. (=They tell everyone as soon as it is in prospect.) *R.*

30 Look at your corn in May, And you'll come weeping away; Look at the same in June, And you'll come home in another tune. *C.*

31 Look before you leap. *14th cent.*

32 Look high and fall low. *R.* Look not a gift horse in the mouth, *see* Never look, etc.

33 Look on the bright side. *19th cent.* Look to the main chance, *see* Have an eye, etc.

34 Lookers-on see most of the game. *16th cent.*

35 Lose an hour in the morning and you'll be all day hunting for it. *19th cent.*

36 Lose nothing for want of asking. *16th cent.*

37 Losers are always in the wrong.   B.

38 Loth to bed and loth out of it.   D. F.

39 Loth to drink and loth to leave it off.
                                          D. F.

40 Love and a cough cannot be hid.   Latin

41 Love and business teach eloquence.
                                          G. H.

42 Love and lordship like no fellowship.
                                          Latin

43 Love and pride stock Bedlam.   F.

44 Love asks faith, and faith asks firmness.
                                          G. H.

45 Love begets love.   Latin

46 Love comes in at the window and goes
   out at the door.   C. R.

47 Love does much but money does all.
                                          French

48 Love is blind.   14th cent.

49 Love is full of trouble (or fear).
                       16th cent. (14th cent.)

50 Love is lawless.   Latin

51 Love is never without jealousy.
                               17th cent.

52 Love is not found in the market.   G. H.

53 Love is sweet in the beginning but sour
   in the ending.   T. D.

54 Love is the loadstone of love.   F.

55 Love is the true price of love.   G. H.

56 Love laughs at locksmiths.   19th cent.

57 Love lives in cottages as well as in
   courts.   R. (16th cent.)

58 Love locks no cupboards.   C.

59 Love makes all hearts gentle.   G. H.

60 Love makes one fit for any work. G. H.

61 Love me little, love me long.   H.

62 Love me, love my dog.   Latin

63 Love of lads and fire of chats (=chips) is
   soon in and soon out.   15th cent.

64 Love rules his kingdom without a
   sword.   G. H.

65 Love will creep where it cannot go
   (=walk). (Originally 'Kind (=Nature)
   will creep,' kind being later mistaken for
   kindness or love.)   17th cent.

66 Love will find a way.   16th cent.

67 Love your neighbour, yet pull not down
   your hedge.   G. H.

68 Lovers live by love as larks live by leeks.
                                          H.

69 Loving comes by looking.   C.

70 Lucky men need no counsel.   B.

71 Lucy light, Lucy light,
   The shortest day and the longest night.
   (St. Lucy's Day, 21 Dec. in Old Style,
   was reckoned shortest.)   R.

72 Maidens must be mild and meek, swift
   to hear and slow to speak.   K.

73 Maidens should be mim till they're
   married, and then they may burn kirks.
                                          K.

74 Maids say nay and take.   R. (16th cent.)

75 Maids want nothing but husbands, and
   when they have them they want
   everything.   R.

76 Make a virtue of necessity.   Latin

77 Make hay while the sun shines.   H.

78 Make not balks of good ground. (Do
   not waste opportunities.)   C. R.

79 Make not mickle (=much) of little.
                                          D. F.

1 Make not thy tail broader than thy wings. (=Do not have too many attendants.) *J. H.*

2 Make not two sorrows of one. *H.*

3 Make the best of a bad bargain. *R.*

4 Make yourself all honey and the flies will devour you. *Italian*

5 Malice is mindful. *C.*

6 Malt is above meal (*or* wheat) with him. (=He is drunk.) *H.*

7 Man doth what he can, and God what He will. *T. D.*

8 Man is a bubble. *Greek*

9 Man is the measure of all things. *Greek*

10 Man proposes, God disposes. *Latin*

11 Man, woman, and devil, are the three degrees of comparison. *F.*

12 Manchester bred: long in the arms, and short in the head. *W. H.*

13 Manners maketh man (*or* Manners make the man). *14th cent.*

14 Man's extremity is God's opportunity. *17th cent.*

15 Many a good cow hath a bad calf. *H.*

16 Many a little makes a mickle (=great). *Greek*

17 Many a man speirs the gate (=asks the way] he knows full well. *D. F.*

18 Many a one for land takes a fool by the hand. (=Marries her or him.) *R. (C.)*

19 Many a true word is spoken in jest. *14th cent.*

20 Many blame the wife for their own thriftless life. *B.*

21 Many estates are spent in the getting,

Since women, for tea, forsook spinning and knitting,
And men, for punch, forsook hewing and splitting. *P. R. A.*

22 Many go out for wool and come home shorn. *Spanish*

23 Many hands make light work. *Latin*

24 Many have been ruined by buying good pennyworths. *F.*

25 Many hips and haws, many frosts and snaws. *D.*

26 Many kinsfolk and few friends. *H.*

27 Many kiss the child for the nurse's sake. *H. (13th cent.)*

28 Many kiss the hand they wish cut off. *G. H.*

29 Many sands will sink a ship. *C.*
Many strokes fell great oaks, *see* Little strokes, etc.

30 Many talk of Robin Hood that never shot in his bow,
And many talk of Little John that never did him know. *R.*

31 Many things grow in the garden that were never sown there. *Spanish*

32 Many would be cowards if they had courage enough. *F.*

33 March borrows of April
Three days, and they be ill. *F.*

34 March comes in like a lion and goes out like a lamb. *R.*

35 March in Janiveer, Janiveer in March I fear. *R.*

36 March many weathers. *R.*

37 March wind and May sun
Makes clothes white and maids dun. *R.*

38 March winds and April showers
Bring forth May flowers. *D.*

39 Marriage is a lottery. *17th cent.*

40 Marriage is honourable, but housekeeping is a shrew. *R.*

41 Marriages are made in heaven. *16th cent.*

42 Marriage, with peace, is this world's paradise; with strife, this life's purgatory. *17th cent.*

43 Marry first and love will follow. *17th cent.*

44 Marry in haste, and repent at leisure. *16th cent.*

45 Marry in Lent, live to repent. *19th cent.*

46 Marry in May, you'll rue it for aye. *Latin*

47 Marry with your match. *Latin*

48 Marry your son when you will, your daughter when you can. *G. H.*

49 May bees don't fly this month. (A retort to people who say 'Maybe.') *K.*

50 Measure is a merry mean. *14th cent.*

51 Measure thrice before you cut once. *Italian*

52 Meat and matins (*or* mass) hinder no man's journey. *C.*

53 Meat is much, but manners is more. *C.*

54 Μηδὲν αγαν.
   – Nothing too much. *Greek*

55 Men are blind in their own cause. *D. F.*

56 Men are not to be measured by inches. *F.*

57 Men cut large thongs of other men's leather. *Latin*

58 Men have faults, women only two: There's nothing good they say, and nothing good they do. *17th cent.*

59 Men leap over where the hedge is lowest. *H.*

60 Men may meet, but mountains never. *16th cent.*

61 Men muse as they use. *R.*

62 Mend your clothes and you may hold out this year. *G. H.*

63 Merry is the feast-making till we come to the reckoning. *R.*

64 Merry meet, merry part. *R.*

65 Mettle is dangerous in a blind horse. *R.*

66 Mickle (=big) head, little wit. *D. F.*

67 Might is right. *14th cent.*

68 Milk says to wine, Welcome friend. *G. H.*

69 Mills and wives are ever wanting. *Italian*

70 Mint (=give warning) ere you strike. *D. F.*

71 Mischief comes by the pound and goes away by the ounce. *F. (16th cent.)*

72 Misfortunes come on wings and depart on foot. *B.*

73 Misfortunes never come singly. *14th cent.*

74 Misreckoning is no payment. *H.*

75 Mocking is catching. *R.*

76 Monday for wealth,
   Tuesday for health,
   Wednesday the best day of all:
   Thursday for crosses,
   Friday for losses,
   Saturday no luck at all. (Days for marrying.) *19th cent.*

77 Monday's child is fair of face,
   Tuesday's child is full of grace,
   Wednesday's child is full of woe,

Thursday's child has far to go,
Friday's child is loving and giving,
Saturday's child works hard for its
living;
But the child who is born on the
Sabbath day
Is lucky and happy and good and gay.
19th cent.

1 Money begets money. *Italian*

2 Money is often lost for want of money.
T. D.

3 Money is round and rolls away. *Italian*

4 Money is the sinews of war. *Latin*

5 Money makes the man. *Greek*

6 Money makes the mare to go. *16th cent.*

7 Money talks. *17th cent.*

8 More belongs to marriage than four bare
legs in a bed. *H.*

9 More hair than wit. (Long hair was
supposed to denote lack of brains.)
16th cent.

10 More haste less speed. *H.*

11 More have repented speech than silence.
G. H.

12 More know Tom Fool than Tom Fool
knows. *18th cent.*

13 More than enough is too much.
17th cent.

14 More than we use is more than we want.
F.

15 Morning dreams are true. *Latin*

16 Much bruit, little fruit. *French.*

17 Much coin, much care. *Latin*

18 Much cry and little wool. *15th cent.*

19 Much water goes by the mill the miller
knows not of. *H.*

20 Much would have more. *14th cent.*

21 Muck and money go together. *R.*

22 Murder will out. *14th cent. (13th cent.)*

23 Music helps not the toothache. *G. H.*

24 Must is a king's word. *17th cent.*

25 My belly thinks my throat cut. (=I am
hungry.) *16th cent.*

26 My son's my son till he gets him a wife,
My daughter's my daughter all her life.
R.

27 Name not a rope in his house that
hanged himself. *G. H.*

28 Names and natures do often agree. *C.*

29 Nature abhors a vacuum. *17th cent.*

30 Nature does nothing in vain. *17th cent.*

31 Nature draws more than ten oxen. *R.*

32 Nature has given us two ears, two eyes,
and but one tongue; to the end we
should hear and see more than we speak.
Greek

33 Nature passes nurture. *16th cent.*

34 Nature requires five,
Custom taketh seven,
Idleness takes nine,
And Wickedness eleven. (Hours of
sleep.) *D.*

35 Naughty boys sometimes make good
men. *17th cent.*

36 Ne sutor ultra crepidam.
– Let not the cobbler go beyond his last.
Latin

37 Near is my coat, but nearer is my shirt
(*or* Near is my kirtle (*or* petticoat) but
nearer is my smock.) *Latin*

38 Near is my shirt, but nearer is my skin.
16th cent.

39 Nearest the heart, nearest the mouth.
(When one person is named instead of
another by mistake.) *D. F.*

40 Nearest the King, nearest the widdie
(=gallows). *D. F.*

41 Necessity is the mother of invention.
16th cent.

42 Necessity knows no law. *Latin*

43 Neck or nothing. *R.*

44 Need makes the old wife trot. *15th cent.*

45 Needles and pins, needles and pins,
When a man's married his trouble
begins. *19th cent.*

46 Needs must when the devil drives.
15th cent.

47 Neither fish nor flesh nor good red
herring. *H.*

48 Neither great poverty not great riches
will hear reason. *B.*

49 Neither praise nor dispraise thyself; thy
actions serve the turn. *G. H.*

50 Never a barrel the better herring.
(=Nothing to choose between them.)
H.

51 Never ask pardon before you are
accused. *B.*

52 Never be ashamed to eat your meat.
Latin

53 Never cast dirt into that fountain of
which thou hast sometime drunk. *R.*

54 Never catch at a falling knife or a falling
friend. *19th cent.*

55 Never cross a bridge till you come to it.
19th cent.

56 Never draw your dirk when a dunt
(=blow) will do. *A. H.*

57 Never is a long day. *14th cent.*

58 Never judge from appearances.
16th cent.

59 Never look a gift horse in the mouth.
Latin

60 Never put off till to-morrow what may
be done to-day. *14th cent.*

61 Never refuse a good offer. *R.*

62 Never say die. *19th cent.*

63 Never sigh, but send. *R.*

64 Never too old (*or* late) to learn. *R.*

65 Never trouble trouble till trouble
troubles you. *19th cent.*

66 Never venture out of your depth till you
can swim. *B.*

67 Never was cat or dog drowned, that
could but see the shore. *Italian*

New brooms sweep clean, *see* A new
broom, etc.

68 New lords, new laws. *16th cent.*

69 Night is the mother of counsel. *Greek*

70 Nine tailors make a man. *17th cent.*

71 No better than she should be.
(=Immoral.) *17th cent.*

72 No butter will stick to his bread.
(=Everything goes wrong with him.)
H.

73 No case: abuse the plaintiff's attorney.
17th cent.

74 No churchyard is so handsome that a
man would desire straight to be buried
there. *G. H.*

75 No day passeth without some grief. *R.*

76 No fence against a flail. *R.*

77 No folly to being in love. *R.*

401

1 No fool like an old fool. *H.*

2 No friend like the penny. *Spanish*

3 No gains without pains. *16th cent.*

4 No garden without its weeds. *F.*

5 No joy without annoy (*or* alloy). *C.*

6 No living man all things can. *Latin*

7 No lock will hold against the power of gold. *G. H.*

8 No longer pipe, no longer dance. (Of people who are kind only while getting benefits.) *C. R.*

9 No man can both sup and blow at once. *D. F.*

10 No man can play the fool so well as the wise man. *D. F.*

11 No man cries stinking fish. *F.*

12 No man hath a worse friend than he brings from home. *R.*

13 No man is a match for a woman till he is married. *19th cent.*

14 No man is born wise. *17th cent.*

15 No man is his craft's master the first day. *C.*

16 No man is wise at all times. *Latin*

17 No man loveth his fetters, be they made of gold. *H.*

18 No man will another in the oven seek, except that himself have been there before. (Often said of mother and daughter.) *H.*

19 No mill, no meal. *Greek*

20 No mischief but a woman or a priest is at the bottom of it. *Latin*

21 No money, no Swiss. (Swiss mercenaries will not fight unless they are paid.) *French*

22 No names, no pack drill. *20th cent.*

23 No news is good news. *Italian*

No pains, no gains, *see* No gains without pains.

24 No penny, no paternoster. (=Priests will not serve without payment.) *16th cent.*

25 No profit to honour, no honour to religion. *G. H.*

26 No receiver, no thief. *H.*

27 No remedy but patience. *T. D.*

28 No rose without a thorn. *15th cent.*

29 No safe wading in an unknown waster. *C.*

30 No sunshine but hath some shadow. *R.*

31 No sweet without sweat. *C.*

32 No taxation without representation. *18th cent.*

33 No time like the present. *17th cent.*

34 No weather is ill if the wind be still. *C.*

35 No wisdom like silence. *Greek*

36 Nodum in scirpo quaerere. – To seek for a knot in a bulrush. (=To find difficulties where there are none.) *Latin*

37 None is offended but by himself. *Latin*

38 None knows the weight of another's burden. *G. H.*

39 None so blind as those who won't see. *16th cent.*

40 None so deaf as those who won't hear. *16th cent.*

41 None so old that he hopes not for a year of life. *Latin*

42 Northampton stands on other men's

legs. (Because it is the centre of the boot trade.) *17th cent.*

43 Not God above gets all men's love.
Greek

44 Not to advance is to go back. *Latin*

45 Not to be fit to hold a candle to him. (=Not to be compared with him. From the custom of holding candles before shrines.) *18th cent.*

46 Not to be sneezed at. (=Not to be despised.) *19th cent.*

47 Nothing dries sooner than a tear. *Latin*

48 Nothing for nothing. *18th cent.*

49 Nothing hath no savour. *H.*

50 Nothing have, nothing crave. *J. H.*

51 Nothing is certain but death and the taxes. *L.*

52 Nothing is certain but uncertainty.
Latin

53 Nothing is impossible to a willing heart.
H.

54 Nothing like leather. (In the cobbler's opinion. = Each believes in his own trade.) *17th cent.*

55 Nothing must be done hastily but killing of fleas. *R.*

56 Nothing so bad but it might have been worse. *19th cent.*

57 Nothing so crouse (=pert) as a new washen louse. (Of ragged people who get new clothes.) *D. F.*

58 Nothing succeeds like success.
19th cent.

59 Nothing venture, nothing have (*or* win).
17th cent. (14th cent.)

60 Nothing worse than a familiar enemy. (=One belonging to one's household.)
14th cent.

61 Nulla dies sine linea.
– No day without a line. (From a tradition regarding the industry of the painter Apelles.) *Latin*

62 Nurture is above nature. *French*

63 Oaks may fall when reeds stand the storm. *F.*

64 Obedience is much more seen in little things than in great. *F.*

65 Obscurum per obscurius.
– The obscure (explained) by the more obscure. *Latin*

66 Of a pig's tail you can never make a good shaft. *G. H.*

67 Of all tame beasts I hate sluts. *R.*

68 Of enough men leave. (=If there are no leavings, there can hardly have been enough.) *D. F.*

69 Of evil grain no good seed can come.
R. (T. D.)

70 Of him that speaks ill, consider the life more than the word. *G. H.*

71 Of idleness comes no goodness. *R.*

72 Of little meddling cometh great rest (*or* ease.) *H. (14th cent.)*

73 Of saving cometh having. *T. D.*

74 Of soup and love, the first is the best.
F.

75 Of sufferance cometh ease (*or* rest).
14th cent.

76 Of thy sorrow be not too sad, of thy joy be not too glad. *15th cent.*

77 Of two evils choose the least. *14th cent.*

78 Of wine the middle, of oil the top, of honey the bottom, is the best. *Latin*

79 Often and little eating makes a man fat.
R.

1 Often to the water, often to the tatter. (Of linen.) *R.*

2 Old age is honourable. *B.*

3 Old age, though despised, is coveted by all. *B.*

4 Old and tough, young and tender. *R.*

5 Old-bees yield no honey. *R.*

6 Old friends and old wine are best. *T. D.*

7 Old maids lead apes in hell. *16th cent.*

8 Old men and travellers may lie by authority. *C. R.*

9 Old men are twice children. *Greek*

10 Old men go to death; death comes to young men. *G. H.*

11 Old men, when they scorn young, make much of death. *G. H.*

12 Old men will die and children soon forget. *16th cent.*

13 Old muck-hills will bloom. *R.*

14 Old porridge is sooner heated than new made. (= Old lovers are sooner reconciled than new loves begun.) *R.*

15 Old praise dies unless you feed it. *G. H.*

16 Old sin makes new shame. *14th cent.*

Omelets are not made without breaking of eggs, *see* You cannot make an omelet, etc.

17 On Candlemas Day throw candle and candlestick away. *R.*

18 On painting and fighting look aloof. (One is dangerous, the other loses effect close at hand.) *G. H.*

19 On St. Valentine all the birds of the air in couples do join. (St. Valentine's Day, 14 Feb.) *14th cent.*

20 On the first of April
Hunt the gowk another mile.
(Gowk=cuckoo, here=April fool.) *D.*

21 On Valentine's day will a good goose lay. (14 Feb.) *R.*

22 Once a knave and ever a knave. *J. H.*

23 Once a parson, always a parson. *19th cent.*

24 Once bitten, twice shy. *19th cent.*

25 Once in ten years one man hath need of another. *16th cent.*

26 Once wood and aye the waur. (= Once mad and always the worse. Recovery from madness is seldom complete.) *D. F.*

27 One and none is all one. (= One is negligible.) *Spanish*

28 One beats the bush, and another catches the birds. *14th cent.*

29 One beggar is enough at a door. *C.*

30 One beggar is woe that another by the door should go. *14th cent.*

31 One, but that one a lion. *Greek*

32 One cannot be in two places at once. *17th cent.*

33 One day of pleasure is worth two of sorrow. *F.*

34 One enemy is too many, and a hundred friends too few. *German*

35 One eye of the master sees more than ten of the servants'. *G. H.*

36 One eye-witness is better than ten ear-witnesses. *Latin*

37 One father is more than a hundred schoolmasters. *G. H.*

38 One flower makes no garland. *G. H.*

39 One fool makes many.   *G. H.*

40 One foot is better than two crutches. *G. H.*

41 One for sorrow,
Two for mirth,
Three for a wedding,
Four for a birth. (Omens from
magpies.)   *D.*

42 One God, no more, but friends good
store.   *C.*

43 One good turn deserves (*or* asks *or*
requires) another.   *15th cent.*

44 One hair of a woman draws more than a
team of oxen.   *16th cent.*

45 One half of the world does not know
how the other half lives.   *G. H.*

46 One hand washeth the other, and both
the face.   *Latin*

47 One hour to-day is worth two
to-morrow.   *F.*

48 One hour's sleep before midnight is
worth two after.   *G. H.*

49 One ill weed mars a whole pot of
pottage.   *H.*

50 One ill word asketh another.   *H.*

51 One law for the rich and another for the
poor.   *19th cent.*

52 One lie makes many.   *Latin.*

53 One mad action is not enough to prove a
man mad.   *F.*

54 One man may steal a horse while
another may not look over a hedge.
19th cent. (H.)

55 One man's meat is another man's
poison.   *Latin*

56 One may know by your nose what
pottage you love. (=Strong drink.)
16th cent.

57 One may see day at a little hole.   *H.*

58 One mule scrubs another.   *Latin*

59 One must draw the line somewhere.
19th cent.

60 One nail drives out another.   *13th cent.*

61 One of these days is none of these days.
B.

62 One pair of legs is worth two pairs of
hands.   *16th cent.*

63 One scabbed sheep infects a whole flock.
Latin

64 One slumber invites another.   *G. H.*

65 One swallow does not make a summer.
Greek

66 One sword keeps another in the sheath.
G. H.

67 One tale is good till another is told.
F. (16th cent.)

68 One to-day is worth two to-morrows.
17th cent.

69 One tongue is enough for a woman.   *R.*

70 One volunteer is worth two pressed
men.   *18th cent.*

71 One year a nurse, and seven years the
worse.   *R.*

72 One year of joy, another of comfort,
and all the rest of content. (A marriage
wish.)   *R.*

73 Opinion rules the world.   *17th cent.*

74 Opportunity makes the thief.
13th cent.

75 Οὐδὲ Ἡρακλῆς πρὸς δύο.
– Not even Hercules could contend
against two.   *Greek*

76 Our last garment is made without
pockets.   *Italian*

1 Our sins and our debts are often more than we think. *J. H.*

2 Out of debt, out of danger. *C.*

3 Out of sight, out of mind. *13th cent.*

4 Out of the frying-pan into the fire. *H.*

5 Oxford for learning, London for wit, Hull for women, and York for a tit (=horse). *W. H.*

6 Pain past is pleasure. *16th cent.*

7 Painted pictures are dead speakers. *R.*

8 Painters and poets have leave to lie. *16th cent.*

9 Pale moon doth rain, red moon doth blow,
White moon doth neither rain nor snow. *C.*

10 Pardon all but thyself. *G. H.*

11 Past cure, past cure. *16th cent.*

12 Paternoster built churches, and Our Father pulls them down. *17th cent.*

13 Patience is a flower that grows not in every garden. *H.*

14 Patience is a plaster for all sores. *C. (14th cent.)*

15 Patience, money, and time bring all things to pass. *G. H.*

16 Pay beforehand was never well served. *16th cent.*

17 Pay what you owe, and what you're worth you'll know. *F.*

18 Peace makes plenty. *15th cent.*

19 Peebles for pleasure. *19th cent.*

20 Penny and penny laid up will be many. *C.*

21 Penny wise, pound foolish. *C. R.*

22 Pens may blot, but they cannot blush. *16th cent.*

23 Pension never enriched a young man. *G. H.*

24 People who live in glass houses should never throw stones. *G. H.*

25 Pigs love that lie together. *R.*

26 Pigs might fly, but they are very unlikely birds. *19th cent.*

27 Plain dealing is a jewel, though they that use it commonly die beggars. *16th cent.*

28 Plain dealing is praised more than practised. *C.*

29 Play with your peers. (Said to young folk who are cheeky to their elders.) *D. F.*

30 Play, women and wine undo men laughing. *J. H.*

31 Pleasant hours fly fast. *F.*

32 Please the eye and plague the heart. *17th cent.*

33 Pleasing ware is half sold. *G. H.*

34 Pleasure has a sting in its tail. *17th cent.*

35 Plenty makes dainty. *R.*

36 Plough deep while others sleep
And you shall have corn to sell and to keep. *D. (J. H.)*

37 Poeta nascitur, non fit.
– A poet is born, not made. *Latin*

38 Poets are born, but orators are made. *Latin*

39 Poor and liberal, rich and covetous. *G. H.*

40 Poor folk are fain (=glad) of little. *D. F.*

41 Poor folks' friends soon misken (=fail to know them). *K.*

406

42 Poor men seek meat for their stomach; rich men stomach for their meat.
16th cent.

43 Poor men's tables are soon spread.　　R.

44 Possession is nine (*or* eleven) points of the law.　　*17th cent.*

45 Post hoc; ergo propter hoc.
– After this; therefore on account of this.
Latin

46 Pour not water on a drowned mouse.
　　C.

47 Poverty breeds strife.　　R.

48 Poverty is in want of much, avarice of everything.　　*Latin*

49 Poverty is no sin.　　G. H.

50 Poverty is no vice but an inconvenience.
16th cent.

51 Poverty is not a shame, but the being ashamed of it is.　　F.

52 Poverty is the mother of all arts and trades.　　*17th cent.*

53 Poverty is the mother of health.
14th cent.

54 Poverty parteth fellowship (*or* friends).
14th cent.

55 Practice makes perfect.　　*Latin*

56 Practise what you preach.　　*17th cent.*

57 Praise day at night, and life at the end.
　　G. H.

58 Praise makes good men better and bad men worse.　　F. (*17th cent.*)

59 Praise to the face is open disgrace.　　L.

60 Prayers and provender hinder no man's journey.　　G. H.

61 Prettiness makes no pottage.　　R.

62 Prevention is better than cure.　　*Latin*

63 Pride and grace dwell never in one place.
　　F.

64 Pride breakfasted with Plenty, dined with Poverty, and supped with Infamy.
P. R. A.

65 Pride feels no cold.　　R.

66 Pride goes before, and shame follows after.　　*14th cent.*

67 Pride is as loud a beggar as want, and a great deal more saucy.　　F.

68 Pride will have a fall.　　*16th cent.*

69 Proffered service stinks.　　*Latin*

70 Promise is debt.　　*14th cent.*

71 Promises and pie-crusts are made to be broken.　　*18th cent.*

72 Prospect is often better than possession.
　　F.

73 Prove thy friend ere thou have need.
15th cent.

74 Proverbs are the daughters of daily experience.　　*Dutch*

75 Provide for the worst, the best will save itself.　　H.

76 Providence is better than rent.　　G. H.

77 Public money is like holy water, everyone helps himself to it.　　*Italian*

78 Public reproof hardens shame.　　F.

79 Puff not against the wind.　　C. R.

80 Punctuality is the politeness of princes.
French

81 Punctuality is the soul of business.　　B.

82 Put a coward to his mettle, and he'll fight the devil.　　K.

83 Put not thy hand between the bark and the tree. (=Do not meddle in family matters.)　　H.

1 Put that in your pipe and smoke it.
(=Put up with it.) *19th cent.*

2 Put your shoulder to the wheel.
17th cent.

3 Quality without quantity is little
thought of. *K.*

4 Quarrelling dogs come halting home.
K.

5 Quartan agues kill old men and cure
young. *Italian*

6 Queen Anne is dead. (=The news is
stale.) *18th cent.*

7 Qui facit per alium facit per se.
– He who does a thing through another
does it himself. *Latin*

8 Quick at meat, quick at work. *C.*

9 Quickly come, quickly go. *17th cent.*

10 Quietness is best. *A. H.*

11 Quos Deus vult perdere, prius
dementat.
– Whom God wishes to destroy He first
makes mad. *Latin*

12 Quot homines, tot sententiae.
– So many men, so many opinions.
Latin

13 Rain before seven: fine before eleven.
19th cent.

14 Rain, rain, go to Spain,
Fair weather come again. *J. H.*

15 Raise no more spirits than you can
conjure down. *C.*

16 Rather sell than be poor. *R.*

17 Rats desert a sinking ship (*or* a falling
house). *17th cent.*

18 Raw dads (=chunks) make fat lads. *K.*

19 Ready money is a ready medicine.
16th cent.

20 Ready money will away. *R.*

21 Reason lies between the spur and the
bridle. *G. H.*

22 Reason rules all things. *T. D.*

23 Reckless youth makes rueful age.
16th cent.

24 Red sky at night, shepherd's delight:
Red sky in the morning, shepherd's
warning. *16th cent.*

25 Religion is the best armour, but the
worst cloak. *F.*

26 Remove an old tree and it will die.
16th cent.

27 Repentance comes too late. *15th cent.*

28 Reserve the master-blow. (=Do not
teach all your skill, lest your pupil
overreach you.) *J. H.*

29 Respect a man, he will do the more.
J. H.

30 Respice finem. – Look to the end.
Latin

31 Revenge is sweet. *16th cent.*

32 Rice for good luck, and bauchles (=old
shoes) for bonny bairns.
(Referring to the wedding custom.)
19th cent.

33 Rich folk have many friends. *K.*

34 Rich men have no faults. *F.*

35 Riches are but the baggage of fortune.
J. H.

36 Riches are gotten with pain, kept with
care, and lost with grief. *16th cent.*

37 Riches are like muck, which stink in a
heap, but spread abroad make the earth
fruitful. *16th cent.*

38 Riches bring oft harm, and ever fear.
H.

39 Riches serve a wise man but command a fool. *French*

40 Ride softly that you may get home the sooner. *R.*

41 Right wrongs no man. *A. H.*

42 Rome was not built in a day. *Latin*

43 Rue and thyme grow both in one garden. *K.*

44 Rule youth well, for age will rule itself. *D. F.*

45 Sadness and gladness succeed each other. *C.*

Safe bind, safe find, *see* Fast bind, etc.

46 St. Bartholomew brings the cold dew. (24 Aug.)

47 St. Benedick, sow thy pease, or keep them in thy rick. (21 March.) *R.*

48 St. Matthie sends sap into the tree. (St. Matthias's day=24 Feb.) *R.*

49 St. Swithin's day, if thou dost rain, (15 July.)
For forty days it will remain;
St. Swithin's day, if thou be fair,
For forty days 'twill rain na mair. *16th cent.*

50 St. Thomas grey, St. Thomas grey, (21 Dec.)
The longest night and the shortest day. *19th cent.*

51 Salmon and sermon have their season in Lent. *J. H.*

52 Salt seasons all things. *J. H.*

53 Salus populi suprema est lex.
– The safety of the people is the highest law. *Latin*

54 Samson was a strong man, but he could not pay money before he had it. *J. H.*

55 Satan reproves (*or* rebukes) sin. *17th cent.*

56 Save a thief from the gallows and he will cut your throat. *C. R.*

57 Save something for the man that rides on the white horse. (=For white-haired old age.) *C.*

58 Save your breath to cool your porridge. *16th cent.*

59 Say as men say, but think to yourself. *C.*

60 Say no ill of the year till it be past. *G. H.*

61 Say to pleasure, Gentle Eve, I will none of your apple. *G. H.*

62 Say well is good but Do well is better. *C.*

63 Say well or be still. *15th cent.*

64 Saying is one thing and doing another. *H.*

65 Scald not your lips in another man's pottage. *R. (16th cent.)*

66 Scatter with one hand, gather with two. *J. H.*

67 Schoolboys are the reasonablest people in the world; they care not how little they have for their money. *R.*

68 Score twice before you cut once. (=Plan carefully before taking an irrevocable step.) *17th cent.*

69 Scorn at first makes after-love the more. *B.*

70 Scorning is catching. *R.*

11 Scotsmen aye reckon frae an ill hour. *K.*

72 Scratch a Russian and you'll find a Tartar. *19th cent.*

Scratch me and I'll scratch you, *see* You scratch my back, etc.

73 Se non è vero, è molto ben trovato.
– If it is not true, it is very well invented. *Italian*

1 Search not too curiously lest you find trouble. *J. H.*

2 Second thoughts are best. *Latin*

3 See a pin and let it lie,
You'll want a pin before you die.
See a pin and pick it up,
All the day you'll have good luck.
19th cent.

4 See Naples and then die. *Italian*

5 Seeing is believing. *C.*

6 Seek till you find, and you'll not lose your labour. *R.*

7 Seek your salve where you get your sore. *D. F.*

8 Seldom comes a better. (When a bad one goes.) *13th cent.*

9 Seldom seen, soon forgotten. *14th cent.*

10 Self do, self have. *H.*

11 Self-love is a mote in every man's eye. *R.*

12 Self-praise is no recommendation. *17th cent.*

13 Self-preservation is the first law of nature. *17th cent.*

14 Send a fool to the market, and a fool he'll return. *16th cent.*

15 Send a wise man on an'errand, and say nothing to him. *14th cent.*

16 Servants should put on patience when they put on a livery. *F.*

17 Servants should see all and say nothing. *18th cent.*

18 Service is no inheritance. *15th cent.*

19 Service without reward is punishment. *G. H.*

20 Set a beggar on horseback and he'll ride to the devil (*or* to the gallows *or* ride a gallop.) *16th cent.*

21 Set a stout heart to a stey brae (=steep hill). *K.*

22 Set a thief to catch a thief. *R.*

23 Set good against evil. *G. H.*

24 Set the saddle on the right horse. *T. D.*

25 Set trees poor and they will grow rich, set them rich and they will grow poor. *R.*

26 Seven hours' sleep will make a clown forget his design. *F.*

27 Seven may be company but nine are confusion. *F. (17th cent.)*

28 Shame in a kindred cannot be avoided. *C. R.*

29 Shameless (*or* shameful) craving must have shameful nay. *H.*

30 Share and share alike. *17th cent.*

31 She that is born a beauty is half married. *F.*

32 Shear your sheep in May and shear them all away. *R.*

33 Ships fear fire more than water. *G. H.*

34 Short acquaintance brings repentance. *R.*

35 Short and sweet. *16th cent.*

36 Short pleasure, long lament. *15th cent.*

37 Short reckonings are soon cleared. *F.*

38 Short reckonings make long friends. *16th cent.*

39 Short rede (=counsel), good rede. *13th cent.*

40 Short shooting loseth the game. *H.*

41 Show me a liar and I will show you a thief.   *17th cent.*

42 Show me not the meat, but show me the man.   *C.*

43 Show me the man, and I'll show you the law.   *D. F.*

44 Si vis pacem, para bellum.
– If you want peace, prepare for war.   *Latin*

45 Sickness is felt, but health not at all.   *F.*

46 Sickness tells us what we are.   *F.*

47 Silence gives consent.   *14th cent.*

48 Silence is golden.   *19th cent. (G. H.)*

49 Silence is the best ornament of a woman.   *R. (16th cent.)*

50 Silence was never written down.   *Italian*

51 Silence seldom doth harm.   *R.*

52 Silks and satins put out the kitchen fire.   *G. H.*

53 Sins are not known till they be acted.   *G. H.*

54 Sit in your place, and none can make you rise.   *G. H.*

55 Six hours for a man, seven for a woman, and eight for a fool. (Of sleep.)   *18th cent.*

56 Six of one and half a dozen of the other.   *19th cent.*

57 Slander leaves a scar behind it.   *T. D.*

58 Sleep without supping and wake without owing.   *G. H.*

59 Sloth is the key to poverty.   *17th cent.*

60 Slow and (*or* but) sure.   *C. (T. D.)*

61 Slow at meat, slow at work.   *K.*

62 Sluts are good enough to make slovens' pottage.   *C.*

63 Small birds must have meat. (=Children must be fed.)   *C.*

64 Small invitation will serve a beggar.   *B.*

Small pitchers have wide ears, *see* Little pitchers, etc.

65 Small profits and quick returns. *19th cent.*

66 Small rain lays great dust.   *R.*

67 Small sorrows speak; great ones are silent.   *Latin*

68 Smoke follows the fairest.   *Greek*

69 Sneeze on a Monday, you sneeze for danger;
Sneeze on a Tuesday, you kiss a stranger;
Sneeze on a Wednesday, you sneeze for a letter;
Sneeze on a Thursday, for something better;
Sneeze on a Friday, you sneeze for sorrow;
Sneeze on a Saturday, see your sweetheart to-morrow;
Sneeze on a Sunday, your safety seek,
The Devil will have you the whole of the week.   *W. H.*

70 So got, so gone.   *R.*

71 So many countries, so many customs.   *R. (11th cent.)*

72 So many servants, so many enemies.   *Latin*

73 So we have the chink, we will bear with the stink.   *Latin*

74 Soft fire makes sweet malt.   *16th cent.*

75 Soft words and hard arguments.   *R.*

76 Some are wise and some are otherwise.   *J. H.*

77 Some evils are cured by contempt.   *G. H.*

1 Some have hap (=luck), some stick in the gap.   *C.*

2 Sometimes the best gain is to lose.   *G. H.*

3 Somewhat is better than nothing.   *H.*

4 Soon crooketh the tree that good gambrel would be. (Gambrel=butcher's bent hanger for carcases.)   *15th cent.*

5 Soon enough if well enough.   *Latin*

6 Soon got, soon spent.   *H.*

7 Soon hot, soon cold.   *15th cent.*

8 Soon learnt, soon forgotten.   *14th cent.*

9 Soon ripe, soon rotten.   *Latin*

10 Sorrow and an evil life maketh soon an old wife.   *C.*

11 Sorrow comes unsent for.   *Latin*

12 Sorrow is dry.   *French*

13 Sorrow is good for nothing but sin.   *J. H.*

14 Sorrow will pay no debt.   *R.*

15 Sow with the hand, and not with the whole sack.   *Greek*

16 Spare the rod and spoil the child.   *C. (Bible.)*

17 Spare to speak and spare to speed.   *14th cent.*

18 Spare well and spend well.   *16th cent.*

19 Spare when you're young, and spend when you're old.   *R.*

20 Sparing is the first gaining.   *16th cent.*

21 Speak fair and think what you will   *C. R.*

22 Speak fitly or be silent wisely.   *G. H. (C.)*

23 Speak not of my debts unless you mean to pay them.   *G. H.*

24 Speak well of the dead.   *Latin*

25 Speak well of your friend, of your enemy say nothing.   *B.*

26 Speak when you're spoken to; come when you're called.   *R.*

27 Spectacles are death's arquebuse.   *G. H.*

28 Speech is the picture of the mind.   *R.*

29 Speed the plough!   *17th cent. (15th cent.)*

30 Spend and be free, but make no waste.   *C.*

31 Spend and God will send.   *14th cent.*

32 Spend not where you may save; spare not where you must spend.   *R.*

33 Spies are the ears and eyes of princes.   *G. H.*

34 Spit in your hands and take better hold.   *H.*

35 Sport is sweetest when there be no spectators.   *C.*

36 Spread the table, and contention will cease.   *R.*

37 Standing pools gather filth.   *C.*

38 Stay a little, and news will find you.   *G. H.*

39 Stay a while, that we may end the sooner.   *G. H.*

40 Step after step the ladder is ascended.   *G. H.*

41 Sticks and stones may break my bones, but words will never hurt me.   *19th cent.*

42 Still waters run deep.   *19th cent. (14th cent.)*

43 Stolen pleasures are sweetest. *17th cent.*

44 Stone-dead hath no fellow. *17th cent.*

45 Straws show which way the wind blows. *17th cent.*

46 Stretch your arm no further than your sleeve will reach. *16th cent.*

47 Stretch your legs according to your coverlet. *G. H. (13th cent.)*

48 Strike while the iron is hot. *14th cent.*

49 Success is never blamed. *F.*

50 Such beginning, such end. *H.*

51 Such welcome, such farewell. *H.*

52 Sue a beggar and get a louse. *C.*

53 Suffer and expect. *G. H.*

54 Sunday's child is full of grace,
Monday's child is full in the face,
Tuesday's child is solemn and sad,
Wednesday's child is merry and glad,
Thursday's child is inclined to thieving,
Friday's child is free in giving,
Saturday's child works hard for its living.
(Days of birth. *See* Monday's child, etc.) *19th cent.*

55 Sus Minervam.
– A pig (teaching) Minerva. (=Teach your grandmother.) *Latin*

56 Sweep before your own door. *17th cent.*

57 Sweet discourse makes short days and nights. *R.*

58 Sweet meat will have sour sauce. *H. (15th cent.)*

59 Sweetest wine makes sharpest vinegar. *16th cent.*

60 Sweetheart and Honeybird keeps no house. *R.*

61 Swine, women and bees cannot be turned. *R.*

62 Tailors and writers must mind the fashion. *F.*

63 Tak awa' Aberdeen and twal' mile round aboot, an' far (=where) are ye? (On Aberdeen's importance.) *19th cent.*

64 Tak your ain will, an' then ye'll no die o' the pet (=ill humour). *K.*

65 Take a farthing from a thousand pounds, it will be a thousand pounds no longer. *18th cent.*

66 Take away fuel, take away flame. *C.*

67 Take away my good name and take away my life. *R.*

68 Take care of the pence and the pounds will take care of themselves. *18th cent.*

69 Take heed is a good rede (= counsel). *16th cent.*

70 Take heed of a person marked, and a widow thrice married. (Marked=with some natural defect.) *G. H.*

71 Take heed of a stepmother: the very name of her sufficeth. *G. H.*

72 Take heed of an ox before, an ass behind, and a monk on all sides. *Spanish*

73 Take heed of enemies reconciled and of meat twice boiled. *R.*

74 Take heed of the vinegar of sweet wine. *G. H.*

75 Take heed you find not that you do not seek. *R.*

76 Take not a musket to kill a butterfly. *W. H.*

77 Take the bit and the buffet with it. (=Put up with some ill usage where you get advantage.) *K.*

78 Take things as they come. *17th cent.*

79 Take things as you find them. *L.*

1 Take time by the forelock. *16th cent.*

2 Take time while time is, for the time will away. *R. (16th cent.)*

3 Take your wife's first advice and not her second. *17th cent.*

4 Take your will of it, as the cat did of the haggis. *K.*

5 Talk is but talk; but 'tis money buys lands. *R.*

6 Talk of an angel and you'll hear his wings. *L.*

7 Talk of the devil, and he'll appear. *17th cent.*

8 Talking pays no toll. *G. H.*

9 Tarry-long brings little home. *F.*

10 Teach your grandmother to suck eggs. *18th cent. (16th cent.)*

11 Teaching others teacheth yourself. *F.*

12 Tell a lie and find the truth. *Spanish*

13 Tell me with whom thou goest and I'll tell thee what thou doest. *16th cent.*

14 Tell (=count) money after your own father. *C. (T. D.)*

15 Tell not all you know, nor do all you can. *Italian*

16 Tell that to the Marines. (Expressing incredulity.) *19th cent.*

17 Tell the truth and shame the devil. *16th cent.*

18 Tempora mutantur, nos et mutamur in illis.
– Times change and we change with them. *Latin*

19 Tempus fugit.
– Time flies. *Latin*

20 Thank you for nothing. *16th cent.*

21 That cock won't fight. (=That story won't be accepted.) *19th cent.*

22 That fish will soon be caught that nibbles at every bait. *F.*

23 That is a game that two can play at. *19th cent.*

24 That is but an empty purse that is full of other men's money. *R.*

25 That is well spoken that is well taken. *16th cent.*

26 That suit is best that best suits me. *C.*

27 That which doth blossom in the spring will bring forth fruit in the autumn. *T. D.*

28 That which is easily done is soon believed. *R.*

29 That which is evil is soon learned. *C.*

30 That which proves too much proves nothing. *F.*

31 That which two will takes effect. *Latin*

32 That which was bitter to endure may be sweet to remember. *F.*

33 The absent are always in the wrong. *G. H.*

34 The ass that brays most eats least. *R.*

35 The axe goes to the wood where it borrowed its helve. *F.*

36 The bait hides the hook. *F.*

37 The beggar may sing before the thief. *Latin*

38 The belly hates a long sermon. *F.*

39 The belly is not filled with fair words. *C.*

40 The belly teaches all arts. *Latin*

41 The best bred have the best portion. *G. H.*

42 The best fish swim near the bottom.   C.

43 The best horse needs breaking, and the aptest child needs teaching.   C.

44 The best is behind.   *16th cent.*

45 The best mirror is an old friend.   R.

46 The best of friends must part.   *17th cent.*

47 The best of the sport is to do the deed and say nothing.   G. H.

48 The best patch is off the same cloth.   F.

49 The best physicians are Dr. Diet, Dr. Quiet, and Dr. Merryman.   *Latin*

50 The best remedy against an ill man is much ground between.   G. H.

51 The best smell is bread, the best savour salt, the best love that of children.   G. H.

52 The best thing for the inside of a man is the outside of a horse. (=Riding exercise.)   *19th cent.*

53 The best things are worst to come by.   C.

54 The best throw of the dice is to throw them away.   *16th cent.*

55 The better the day the better the deed.   *17th cent.*

56 The better workman, the worse husband.   T. D.

57 The black ox has trod on his foot. (=Care has come on him.)   H.

58 The blind eat many a fly.   *15th cent.*

59 The body is sooner dressed than the soul.   G. H.

60 The boot is on the other leg. (=Things are the other way about.)   *19th cent.*

61 The boughs that bear most hang lowest.   *17th cent.*

62 The brother had rather see the sister rich than make her so.   R.

63 The burnt child dreads the fire.   *14th cent.*

64 The busiest men have the most leisure.   *19th cent*

65 The buyer needs a hundred eyes, the seller not one.   *Italian*

66 The calf, the goose, the bee: The world is ruled by these three. (=Parchment, pen, and wax.)   *17th cent.*

67 The calmest husbands make the stormiest wives.   *17th cent.*

68 The camel going to seek horns lost his ears.   *Latin*

69 The cat and dog may kiss, yet are none the better friends.   *13th cent.*

70 The cat is hungry when a crust contents her.   R.

71 The cat knows whose lips she licks.   *Latin*

72 The cat would eat fish but would not wet her feet.   *13th cent.*

73 The chamber of sickness is the chapel of devotion.   T. D.

74 The charitable gives out at the door and God puts in at the window.   R.

75 The chickens are the country's, but the city eats them.   G. H.

76 The child says nothing but what it heard by the fire.   G. H.

77 The children in Holland take pleasure in making
What the children in England take pleasure in breaking.   *19th cent.*

78 The clartier (=dirtier) the cosier.   *19th cent.*

79 The coaches won't run over him. (=He is in jail.)   R.

1 The comforter's head never aches.
G. H.

2 The common horse is worst shod. *H.*

3 The company makes the feast.
17th cent.

4 The covetous spends more than the
liberal. *G. H.*

5 The cow knows not what her tail is
worth till she hath lost it. *G. H.*

6 The crow thinks her own bird fairest.
16th cent.

7 The cuckold is the last that knows of it.
C. R.

8 The cuckoo comes in April,
Sings a song in May;
Then in June another tune,
And then she flies away. *W. H.*

9 The cunning wife makes her husband
her apron. *R.*

The cure is worse than the disease, *see*
The remedy, etc.

10 The danger past and God forgotten.
G. H.

11 The darkest hour is before the dawn.
17th cent.

12 The day has eyes and the night has ears.
D. F.

13 The day is short and the work is long.
15th cent.

14 The dead have few friends. *14th cent.*

15 The death of wolves is the safety of the
sheep. *16th cent.*

16 The devil always leaves a stink behind
him. *16th cent.*

17 The devil dances in an empty pocket.
15th cent.

18 The devil divides the world between
atheism and superstition. *G. H.*

19 The devil gets up to the belfry by the
vicar's skirts. *J. H.*

20 The devil is a busy bishop in his own
diocese. *16th cent.*

21 The devil is kind to his own. *17th cent.*

22 The devil is good when he is pleased.
C. (16th cent.)

23 The devil is in the dice. *R.*

24 The devil is not so black as he is painted.
16th cent.

25 The devil lies brooding in the miser's
chest. *F.*

26 The devil lurks behind the cross. *Spanish*

27 The devil take the hindmost. *17th cent.*

28 The devil tempts all, but the idle man
tempts the devil. *Turkish*

29 The devil was sick, the devil a monk
would be;
The devil was well, the devil a monk
was he. *Latin*

30 The devil wipes his tail with the poor
man's pride. *J. H.*

31 The devil's children have the devil's
luck. *R.*

32 The devil's meal is all bran. (=Ill-gotten
gains are disappointing.) *Italian*

33 The diligent spinner has a large shift.
(=Industry gives comfort.) *Spanish*

34 The dog that licks ashes trust not with
meal. *G. H.*

35 The eagle does not catch flies. *Latin*

36 The early bird catches the worm. *C. R.*

37 The earthen pot must keep clear of the
brass vessel. *F.*

38 The ebb will fetch off what the tide
brings in. *R.*

39 The effect speaks, the tongue needs not.
G. H.

40 The end crowns all. *Latin*

41 The end justifies the means. *17th cent.*

42 The end of fishing is not angling but catching. *F.*

43 The English never know when they are beaten. *19th cent.*

44 The Englishman weeps, the Irishman sleeps, but the Scotchman gangs while (=goes till) he gets it. *K.*

45 The envious man shall never want woe.
C. R.

46 The escaped mouse ever feels the taste of the bait. *G. H.*

47 The evening crowns the day.
17th cent.

48 The evils we bring on ourselves are the hardest to bear. *L.*

49 The exception proves (=tests) the rule.
17th cent.

50 The eye is bigger than the belly.
16th cent.

51 The eye is the pearl of the face.
16th cent.

52 The eye of the master will do more work than both his hands. *P. R. A.*

53 The eye that sees all things else sees not itself. *16th cent.*

54 The eyes have one language everywhere. *G. H.*

55 The face is the index of the heart (*or* mind). *Latin*

56 The fairer the hostess the fouler the reckoning. *J. H.*

57 The fairer the paper the fouler the blot.
F.

58 The fairest rose at last is withered.
16th cent.

59 The fairest silk is soonest stained.
16th cent.

The farthest way about is the nearest way home, *see* The longest way round, etc.

60 The fat is in the fire. *16th cent.*

61 The father to the bough, the son to the plough. (=If the father is hanged, the son inherits the land.) *16th cent.*

62 The feet of the deities are shod with wool. (As they bring judgment.) *Latin*

63 The fewer his years, the fewer his tears.
F.

64 The fire which lights us at a distance will burn us when near. *B.*

65 The first and last frosts are the worst.
G. H.

66 The first blow is half the battle.
18th cent.

67 The first blow makes the wrong, but the second makes the fray. *17th cent.*

68 The first breath is the beginning of death. *F.*

69 The first dish pleaseth all. *G. H.*

70 The first faults are theirs that commit them, the second theirs that permit them. *F.*

71 The first glass for thirst, the second for nourishment, the third for pleasure, and the fourth for madness. *16th cent.*

72 The first service a child doth his father is to make him foolish. *G. H.*

73 The first wife is matrimony, the second company, the third heresy. *Italian*

74 The first year let your house to your enemy; the second to your friend; the third, live in it yourself. *W. H.*

1 The fly sat upon the axletree of the chariot-wheel and said What a dust do I raise! *Greek*

2 The folly of one man is the fortune of another. *17th cent.*

3 The fool asks much, but he is more fool that grants it. *T. D.*

4 The fool is busy in everyone's business but his own. *F.*

5 The fool saith, Who would have thought it? *T. D.*

6 The fool wanders, the wise man travels. *F.*

7 The foot on the cradle and hand on the distaff is the sign of a good housewife. *Spanish*

8 The fox fares best when he is cursed. *17th cent.*

9 The fox knows much, but more he that catcheth him. *G. H.*

10 The fox may grow grey, but never good. *17th cent.*

11 The fox preys farthest from his hole. *J. H.*

12 The fox's wiles will never enter the lion's head. *16th cent.*

13 The friar preached against stealing, and had a goose (*or* pudding) up his sleeve. *G. H.*

14 The frog cannot out of her bog. *R.*

15 The frog said to the harrow, Cursed be so many lords. *13th cent.*

16 The full moon brings fair weather. *B.*

17 The further you go, the further behind. *15th cent.*

18 The gallows will have its own at last. *B.*

19 The game is not worth the candle. *G. H.*

20 The German's wit is in his fingers. *G. H.*

21 The goat must browse where she is tied. *G. H.*

22 The golden age never was the present age. *F.*

23 The good mother says not, Will you? but gives. *G. H.*

24 The good or ill hap of a good or ill life Is the good or ill choice of a good or ill wife. *F.*

25 The goodman is the last who knows what's amiss at home. *R.*

26 The gown is his that wears it, and the world his that enjoys it. *G. H.*

27 The grace of God is gear (=goods) enough. *D. F.*

28 The grapes are sour. *Greek.*

29 The great and the little have need of one another. *F.*

30 The great would have none great, and the little all little. *G. H.*

31 The greater the truth, the greater the libel. *18th cent.*

32 The greatest burdens are not the gainfullest. *R.*

33 The greatest clerks (=scholars) are not the wisest men. *Latin*

34 The greatest respect is due to children. *Latin*

35 The greatest step is that out of doors. *G. H.*

36 The greatest talkers are always the least doers. *C. R. (16th cent.)*

37 The greatest wealth is contentment with a little. *J. H.*

38 The groat is ill saved that shames the master. *C. R.*

39 The groundsel (=door sill) speaks not,
save what it heard of the hinges.   *G. H.*

40 The gull comes against the rain.
R. (T. D.)

41 The hand that gives gathers.   *J. H.*

42 The handsomest flower is not the
sweetest.   *B.*

43 The hare starts when a man least expects
it.   *14th cent.*

44 The hasty man never wants woe.
14th cent.

45 The head and feet keep warm,
The rest will take no harm.   *French*

46 The healthful man can give counsel to
the sick.   *G. H.*

47 The heart's letter is read in the eyes.
G. H.

48 The higher the ape goes, the more he
shows his tail.   *G. H. (16th cent.)*

49 The higher the plum tree, the riper the
plum;
The richer the cobbler, the blacker his
thumb.   *R.*

50 The higher up, the greater fall.
16th cent.

51 The highest branch is not the safest
roost.   *B.*

52 The highest flood has the lowest ebb.
16th cent.

53 The highway is never about.   *C.*

54 The hindmost dog may catch the hare.
16th cent.

55 The hog never looks up to him that
threshes down the acorns.   *F.*

56 The hole calls the thief.   *G. H.*

57 The horse that draws his halter is not
quite escaped.   *C.*

58 The horse thinks one thing, and he that
saddles him another.   *17th cent.*

59 The house goes mad when women gad.
19th cent.

60 The house is a fine house when good
folks are within.   *G. H.*

61 The house shows the owner.   *G. H.*

62 The ignorant hath an eagle's wings and
an owl's eyes.   *G. H.*

63 The iron entered into his soul. (From a
mistranslation in the Vulgate of Psalm
cv. 18, 'He was laid in iron.')   *Latin*

64 The Italians are wise before the deed, the
Germans in the deed, the French after
the deed.   *G. H.*

65 The Jews spend at Easter, the Moors at
marriages, the Christians in suits.
G. H.

66 The king can do no wrong.   *17th cent.*

67 The king can make a knight, but not a
gentleman.   *17th cent.*

68 The king never dies. (Legal **maxim.**)
Latin

69 The king's cheese goes half away in
parings. (Among his attendants.)   *J. H.*

70 The king's word is more than another
man's oath.   *16th cent.*

71 The lame goes as far as the staggerer.
G. H.

72 The lame post brings the truest news.
F.

73 The lame tongue gets nothing.   *C. R.*

74 The lapwing cries farthest from her nest.
16th cent.

75 The larks fall there ready roasted. [A
sluggard's dream.)   *French*

76 The last drop makes the cup run over.
17th cent.

1 The last straw breaks the camel's back.
                19th cent. (17th cent.)

2 The last suitor wins the maid.   *R.*

3 The least foolish is wise.   *G. H.*

4 The less wit a man has, the less he
knows that he wants it.   *F.*

5 The life of man is a winter's day and a
winter's way.   *R.*

6 The lion is not so fierce as he is painted.
                G. H. (T. D.)

7 The little cannot be great unless he
devour many.   *G. H.*

8 The lone sheep is in danger of the wolf.
                C.

9 The longest day must have an end.
                17th cent.

10 The longest way round is the nearest
way home.   *17th cent.*

11 The love of money and the love of
learning rarely meet.   *G. H.*

12 The love of the wicked is more
dangerous than their hatred.   *F.*

13 The lower millstone grinds as well as the
upper.   *R.*

14 The mad dog bites his master.   *F.*

15 The magician mutters, and knows not
what he mutters.   *R.*

16 The man shall have his mare again.
                16th cent.

17 The market is the best garden.   *G. H.*

18 The master absent and the house dead.
                G. H.

19 The master's eye makes the horse fat.
                Greek

20 The master's footsteps fatten the soil.
                J. H. (16th cent.)

21 The mill cannot grind with the water
that is past.   *G. H.*

22 The mind is the man.   *Latin*

23 The miserable man maketh a penny of a
farthing, and the liberal of a farthing
sixpence.   *G. H.*

24 The mob has many heads, but no brains.
                F.

25 The money you refuse will never do you
good.   *B.*

26 The moon does not heed the barking of
dogs.   *Latin*

27 The moon is a moon still, whether it
shine or not.   *F.*

28 The more cost the more honour.
                D. F. (16th cent.)

29 The more danger, the more honour.
                R. (16th cent.)

30 The more knave, the better luck.
                16th cent.

31 The more laws, the more offenders.
                Latin

32 The more light a torch gives, the shorter
it lasts.   *F.*

33 The more mischief the better sport.   *K.*

34 The more noble the more humble.
                T. D.

35 The more the merrier; the fewer the
better cheer (*or* fare).   *H.*

36 The more thy years, the nearer thy
grave.   *C. R.*

37 The more wit the less courage.   *F.*

38 The more women look in their glass, the
less they look to their house.   *G. H.*

39 The more you stir, the worse it will
stink.   *H.*

40 The morning hour has gold in its mouth. *German*

41 The mother of mischief is no bigger than a midge's wing. *D. F.·*

42 The mother-in-law remembers not that she was a daughter-in-law. *J. H.*

43 The mouse that has but one hole is quickly taken. *14th cent.*

44 The nearer the bone, the sweeter the flesh. *16th cent.*

45 The nearer the church, the farther from God. *14th cent.*

46 The nightingale and cuckoo sing both in one month. *C.*

47 The noblest vengeance is to forgive. *16th cent.*

48 The nurse is valued till the child has done sucking. *F.*

49 The nurse's tongue is privileged to talk. *R.*

50 The offender never pardons. *G. H.*

51 The offspring of those that are very young or very old lasts not. *G. H.*

52 The parings of a pippin are better than the whole crab. *F.*

53 The parson always christens his own child first. *R.*

54 The peacock hath fair feathers but foul feet. *T. D.*

55 The penny is well spent that saves a groat. *C. R.*

56 The persuasion of the fortunate sways the doubtful. *G. H.*

57 The pine wishes herself a shrub when the axe is at her root. *F.*

58 The pitcher goes so often to the well that it is broken at last. *14th cent.*

59 The plough goes not well if the ploughman hold it not. *G.*

60 The poor man pays for all. *C.*

61 The poor man's shilling is but a penny. (Because he buys at the dearest rate.) *K.*

62 The postern door makes thief and whore. *C. R.*

63 The pot calls the kettle black. *17th cent.*

64 The pride of the rich makes the labours of the poor. *C.*

65 The priest forgets that he was clerk. *16th cent.*

66 The prodigal robs his heir, the miser himself. *F.*

67 The proof of the pudding is in the eating. *C. R.*

68 The properer man, the worse luck. *R.*

69 The reasons of the poor weigh not. *G. H. (T. D.)*

70 The receiver is as bad as the thief. *17th cent.*

71 The remedy for injuries is not to remember them. *Italian*

72 The remedy for love is – land between. *Spanish*

73 The remedy is worse than the disease. *17th cent.*

74 The resolved mind hath no cares. *G. H.*

75 The rich knows not who is his friend. *G. H.*

76 The rich never want for kindred. *B.*

The river past and God forgotten, *see* The danger past, etc.

77 The road to hell is paved with good intentions. *19th cent. (16th cent.)*

1 The robin and the wren are God's cock and hen,
The martin and the swallow are God's bow and arrow. *19th cent.* ·

2 The rotten apple injures its neighbours. *Latin*

3 The rough net is not the best catcher of birds. *H.*

4 The same heat that melts the wax will harden the clay. *16th cent.*

5 The same knife cuts bread and fingers. *T. D.*

6 The sandal tree perfumes the axe that fells it. *Indian*

7 The scholar may waur (=worst) the master. *K.*

8 The Scot will not fight till he sees his own blood. *19th cent.*

9 The sea and the gallows refuse none. *18th cent.*

10 The sea complains it wants water. *C.*

11 The sea hath fish for every man. *16th cent.*

12 The sea refuses no river. *F.*

13 The shoe will hold with the sole. *H.*

14 The shortest answer is doing. *G. H.*

15 The sickness of the body may prove the health of the soul. *B.*

16 The sight of you is good for sore eyes. *18th cent.*

17 The sign invites you in, but your money must get you out. *F.*

18 The singing man keeps his shop in his throat. *G. H.*

19 The slothful man is the beggar's brother. *K.*

20 The sluggard makes his night till noon. *F.*

21 The sluggard's convenient season never comes. *F.*

22 The smith and his penny are both black. *G. H.*

23 The smith hath always a spark in his throat. (=Is always thirsty.) *R.*

24 The smoke of a man's own house is better than the fire of another. *Latin*

25 The snail slides up the tower at last, though the swallow mounteth it not. *F.*

26 The soul is not where it lives, but where it loves. *16th cent.*

27 The soul needs few things, the body many. *G. H.*

28 The still sow eats up all the draff. *15th cent.*

29 The sting is in the tail. *17th cent.*

30 The sting of a reproach is the truth of it. *F.*

31 The stone that lieth not in your way need not offend you. *F.*

32 The stream cannot rise above its source. *F.*

33 The subject's love is the king's life-guard. *Latin*

34 The submitting to one wrong brings on another. *Latin*

35 The sun can be seen by nothing but its own light. *F.*

36 The sun is never the worse for shining on a dunghill. *14th cent.*

37 The sun shines upon all alike. *16th cent.*

38 The swan sings before death. *Latin*

39 The table robs more than the thief.
         G. H.

40 The tailor makes the man. *17th cent.*

41 The tale runs as it pleases the teller. *F.*

42 The taste of the kitchen is better than the smell. *W. H.*

43 The thief is sorry he is to be hanged, but not that he is a thief. *F.*

44 The thin end of the wedge is to be feared. *19th cent.*

45 The third time pays for all. *16th cent.*

46 The thread breaks where it is weakest.
         G. H.

47 The thunderbolt hath but his clap.
         T. D.

48 The tide never goes out so far but it always comes in again. *19th cent.*

49 The tired ox treads surest. *Latin*

50 The tongue breaks bone, though itself has none. *13th cent.*

51 The tongue is ever turning to the aching tooth. *Italian*

52 The tongue is not steel yet it cuts. *H.*

53 The tongue of idle persons is never idle.
         F.

54 The tongue talks at the head's cost.
         G. H.

55 The treason is loved but the traitor is hated. *17th cent.*

56 The tree falls not at the first stroke.
         16th cent.

57 The truest jests sound worst in guilty ears. *R.*

58 The unexpected always happens. *Latin*

59 The vale discovereth the hill. *16th cent.*

60 The virtue of a coward is suspicion.
         G. H.

61 The war is not done so long as my enemy lives. *G. H.*

62 The way to an Englishman's heart is through his stomach. *19th cent.*

63 The way to be safe is never to feel secure. *F.*

64 The way to bliss lies not on beds of down. *C.*

65 The weakest goes to the wall. *15th cent.*

66 The Welshman keeps nothing till he has lost it. *17th cent.*

67 The wholesomest meat is at another man's cost. *J. H.*

68 The wife is the key of the house. *T. D.*

69 The wind keeps not always in one quarter. *C.*

70 The wine in the bottle does not quench thirst. *G. H.*

71 The wine will taste of the cask. *16th cent.*

72 The wise hand doth not all that the foolish mouth speaks. *G. H.*

73 The wish is father to the thought. *Latin*

74 The wolf eats oft of the sheep that have been warned. *G. H.*

75 The world is a ladder for some to go up and some down. *J. H.*

76 The world is his who enjoys it. *18th cent.*

77 The worse for the rider, the better for the bider. (=Where roads are muddy, the soil is good.) *C.*

78 The worse luck now, the better another time. *K.*

1 The worse the passage, the more welcome the port. *F.*

2 The worst of law is that one suit breeds twenty. *G. H.·*

3 The worst wheel of a cart creaks most. *15th cent.*

4 The worth of a thing is best known by the want of it. *R.*

5 The worth of a thing is what it will bring. *17th cent.*

6 The young pig grunts like the old sow. *R.*

7 There are as good fish in the sea as ever came out of it. *19th cent.*

8 There are black sheep in every flock (*or* fold). *19th cent.*

9 There are many ways to fame. *G. H.*

10 There are more maids than Malkin, and more men than Michael. *R.*

11 There are more men threatened than struck. *G. H.*

12 There are more ways to kill a dog than hanging. *R.*

13 There are more ways to the wood than one. *H.*

14 There are no birds in last year's nest. *Spanish*

15 There are no fans in hell. *Arabic.*

16 There are spots even on the sun. *19th cent.*

17 There are two sides to every question. *19th cent.*

18 There are wheels within wheels. (=Complex influences are at work.) *17th cent.*

19 There came nothing out of the sack but what was in it. *G. H.*

20 There is a devil in every berry of the grape. *17th cent.*

21 There is a good time coming. *19th cent.*

22 There is a measure in all things. *14th cent.*

23 There is a remedy for everything but death. *16th cent.*

24 There is a salve for every sore. *16th cent.*

25 There is a time for all things. *14th cent.*

26 There is a witness everywhere. *F.*

27 There is always a something. *19th cent.*

28 There is but an hour in a day between a good housewife and a bad. *R.*

29 There is but one good wife in the world, and every man thinks he has her. *17th cent.*

30 There is a difference between staring and stark blind (*or* mad). *H.*

31 There is falsehood in fellowship. *H.*

32 There is great force hidden in a sweet command. *G. H.*

33 There is honour among thieves. *18th cent.*

34 There is little for the rake after the besom (=broom). *D. F.*

35 There is luck in odd numbers. *16th cent.*

36 There is many a fair thing found false. *D. F.*

37 There is no fire without some smoke. *H.*

38 There is no general rule without some exception. *17th cent.*

39 There is no going to heaven in a sedan. *F.*

40 There is no jollity but hath a smack of folly in it. *G. H.*

41 There is no love lost between them. (=They hate each other, *but formerly* =They love mutually.) *17th cent.*

42 There is no medicine against death. *Latin*

43 There is no medicine for fear.

44 There is no pack of cards without a knave. *16th cent.*

45 There is no redemption from hell. *14th cent.*

46 There is no such flatterer as a man's self. *F.*

47 There is no tree but bears some fruit. *C.*

48 There is no venom to that of the tongue. *J. H.*

49 There is no wool so white but a dyer can make it black. *16th cent.*

50 There is nobody will go to hell for company. *G. H.*

51 There is reason in roasting of eggs. *J. H.*

52 There is who despises pride with a greater pride. *Greek*

53 There may be blue and better blue. *K.*

54 There needs a long time to know the world's pulse. *G. H.*

55 There was never a slut but had a slit, there was never a daw (=drab) but had twa. (Said to girls whose clothes have tears in them.) *K.*

56 There were no ill language if it were not ill taken. *G. H.*

57 There will be sleeping enough in the grave. *P. R. A.*

58 There would be no great ones if there were no little ones *G. H.*

59 There's many a slip 'twixt the cup and the lip. *Greek*

60 There's no mischief in the world done, But a woman is always one. (=A woman is at the bottom of it.) *R.*

61 They agree like bells; they want nothing but hanging. *R.*

62 They are far behind that may not follow. (Said to encourage those who are outstripped.) *K.*

63 They buy good cheap (=a bargain) that bring nothing home. *D. F.*

64 They cleave (*or* hang *or* hold) together like burrs. *H.*

65 They die well that live well. *C.*

They laugh best that laugh last, *see* He laughs best, etc.

66 They love dancing well that dance among thorns. *C. R.*

67 They love me for little that hate me for naught. *R.*

68 They love too much that die for love. *R.*

69 They must hunger in frost that will not work in heat. *H.*

70 They need much whom nothing will content. *C.*

71 They say so, is half a lie. *Italian*

72 They take a long day that never pay. *R.*

73 They talk of Christmas so long that it comes. *G. H.*

74 They that are bound must obey. *13th cent.*

75 They that be in hell ween there is none other heaven. *H.*

76 They that bourd wi' cats maun counts on scarts. (=They that jest with cats must count on scratches.) *A. H.*

1 They that have got good store of butter may lay it thick on their bread. *C.*

2 They that have no other meat Bread and butter are glad to eat. *C.*

3 They that live longest must die at last. *R.*

4 They that think none ill are soonest beguiled. *H.*

5 They that walk much in the sun will be tanned at last. *R. (16th cent.)*

6 They think a calf a muckle (=large) beast that never saw a cow. *A. H.*

7 They who live longest will see most. *Spanish*

8 They who love most are least set by. *J. H.*

9 They who would be young when they are old must be old when they are young. *R.*

10 Things are as they be taken. *C.*

11 Things at the worst will mend. *17th cent.*

12 Things done cannot be undone. *H.*

13 Things hardly attained are longer retained. *C.*

14 Things past cannot be recalled. *H.*

15 Things present are judged by things past. *16th cent.*

16 Things well fitted abide. *G. H.*

17 Think much, speak little, and write less. *Italian*

18 Think of ease, but work on. *G. H.*

19 Think to-day and speak to-morrow. *B.*

20 Think well of all men. *J. H.*

21 Think with the wise, but talk with the vulgar(=ordinary people). *Greek*

22 Thinking is very far from knowing. *B.*

23 This rule in gardening never forget, To sow dry and to set wet. *R.*

24 This world is nothing except it tend to another. *G. H.*

25 Though a lie be well dressed it is ever overcome. *G. H.*

26 Though I say it that should not. *16th cent.*

27 Though love is blind, yet 'tis not for want of eyes. *F.*

28 Though modesty be a virtue, yet bashfulness is a vice. *F.*

29 Though old and wise, yet still advise (=take counsel). *G. H.*

30 Though the sore be healed, yet a scar may remain. *F.*

31 Though the sun shines, leave not your cloak at home. *Spanish*

32 Thought is free. *14th cent.*

33 Threatened men (*or* folks) live long. *16th cent.*

34 Threats without power are like powder without ball. *18th cent.*

35 Three are too many to keep a secret, and too few to be merry. *F.*

36 Three failures and a fire make a Scotsman's fortune. *19th cent.*

37 Three great evils come out of the North, a cold wind, a cunning knave, and a shrinking cloth. *17th cent.*

38 Three helping one another bear the burden of six. *G. H.*

39 Three may keep counsel if two be away. *H.*

40 Three removes are as bad as a fire. *P. R. A.*

41 Three things drive a man out of his house – smoke, rain, and a scolding wife. *Bible*

42 Three women and a goose make a market. *Italian*

43 Thrift is good revenue. *Latin*

44 Thrift is the philosopher's stone. *F.*

45 Thursday come, and the week is gone. *G. H.*

46 Time and chance reveal all secrets. *18th cent.*

47 Time and thinking tame the strongest grief. *K.*

48 Time and tide wait for no man. *16th cent.*

49 Time fleeth away without delay. *C.*

50 Time is a file that wears and makes no noise. *Italian*

51 Time is money. *18th cent.*

52 Time is the rider that breaks youth. *G. H.*

53 Time lost cannot be won again (*or* Time past cannot be recalled). *14th cent.*

54 Time tries all things. *16th cent.*

55 Time trieth truth. *H.*

56 To a child all weather is cold. *G. H.*

57 To a crazy ship all winds are contrary. *G. H.*

58 To be a good spender God is the treasurer. *G. H.*

59 To a red man read thy rede, (=Give your counsel.)
With a brown man break thy bread,
At a pale man draw thy knife,
From a black man keep thy wife.
The red is wise, the brown trusty,
The pale envious, and the black lusty. (Refers to the different complexions.) *D. F.*

60 To add insult to injury. *Latin*

61 To be beloved is above all bargains. *G. H.*

62 To be born with a silver spoon in one's mouth. *C.*

63 To be in a person's bad (*or* good) books. (=In (*or* out of) favour.) *19th cent.*

64 To be in the wrong box. (=In an awkward position.) *16th cent.*

65 To be on one's last legs. (=Near death.) *16th cent.*

66 To be too busy gets contempt. *G. H.*

67 To be under a cloud. (=In disgrace.) *17th cent.*

68 To bear away the bell. (=To be first.) *14th cent.*

69 To bear two faces in one hood. (=To be double-faced.) *15th cent.*

70 To beat about the bush. (=To approach a subject indirectly.) *16th cent.*

71 To bend the bow of Ulysses. (=To emulate a great man's achievements.) *Greek*

72 To blow one's own trumpet. (=To praise onesel.) *16th cent.*

73 To break my head and then give me a plaster. *15th cent.*

74 To break Priscian's head. (=To be guilty of bad grammar. Priscian was a Latin grammarian.) *16th cent.*

75 To bring a noble to ninepence. (=To waste money. The noble was worth a third of £1.) *H.*

76 To bring haddock to paddock. (=To lose everything.) *H.*

427

1 To build castles in Spain.
(=Daydreams.) *15th cent.*

2 To build castles in the air.
(=Daydreams.) *16th cent.*

3 To burn one's boats. (=To commit
oneself irrevocably.) *19th cent.*

4 To burn the candle at both ends. *R.*

5 To bury the hatchet. (=To make peace.)
18th cent.

6 To buy a pig in a poke. *H.*

7 To buy and sell and live by the loss.
T. D.

8 To call a spade a spade. (=To speak
plainly.) *Latin*

9 To carry coals to Newcastle. (Newcastle
being a main source of coal.) *16th cent.*

10 To carry (*or* draw) water in a sieve.
Latin

11 To cast water into the sea (*or* Thames).
14th cent.

12 To catch a Tartar. (=To make a capture
that is beyond control.) *17th cent.*

13 To catch a weasel asleep. *19th cent.*

14 To comb one's head with a stool. (=To
thrash him.) *16th cent.*

15 To come from little good to stark
nought. *R.*

16 To come up to the scratch. (=To come
forward for an encounter.) *19th cent.*

17 To count one's chickens before they are
hatched. *16th cent.*

18 To cry out before one is hurt. *16th cent.*

19 To cry with one eye and laugh with the
other. *14th cent.*

20 To cut off one's nose to spite one's face.
French

21 To cut the coat according to the cloth.
(=To keep within one's means.) *H.*

22 To cut the grass (*or* ground) from under
a person's feet. (=To thwart him.)
16th cent.

23 To deceive oneself is very easy. *G. H.*

24 To deserve (*or* lie for) the whetstone.
(=To be a great liar, a whetstone round
the neck being the former penalty for
this.) *15th cent.*

25 To dig one's grave with one's teeth. (By
overeating.) *French*

26 To draw the long bow. (=To
exaggerate.) *R.*

27 To fiddle while Rome is burning. (=To
trifle during a crisis.) *17th cent.*

28 To find a mare's nest. (=A discovery
that amounts to nothing.) *16th cent.*

29 To fish for a herring and catch a sprat.
C.

30 To flog a dead horse. (=To argue on an
outworn theme.) *19th cent.*

31 To fry in one's own grease. *14th cent.*

32 To gain teacheth how to spend. *G. H.*

33 To give a thing and take a thing
Is to wear the devil's gold ring.
17th cent.

34 To haul over the coals. (=To call to
account.) *16th cent.*

35 To have a bee in one's bonnet. (=To be
crazy on some one point.) *17th cent.*

36 To have a bone in one's leg. (A joking
excuse.) *R.*

37 To have a crow to pluck (*or* pull) with
one. (=To have a complaint to make.)
15th cent.

38 To have a finger in the pie (=To be
concerned in the affair.) *16th cent.*

39 To have a rod in pickle for someone. [=To have punishment in store for him.) *16th cent.*

40 To have (*or* hold) a wolf by the ears. (So that you can neither hold nor let go.) *Greek*

41 To have bats in the belfry. (=To be crazy.) *20th cent.*

42 To have many (*or* other) irons in the fire. *16th cent.*

43 To have one's labour for one's pains. *16th cent.*

44 To have one foot in the grave. *16th. cent.*

45 To have the wrong sow by the ear. *H.*

46 To have two strings to one's bow. *15th cent.*

47 To heap Ossa upon Pelion. (Alluding to the attempt of the Giants to scale heaven.) *Greek*

48 To help a lame dog over a stile. *H.*

49 To hit the nail on the head. (=To speak to the point.) *16th cent.*

50 To hold a candle to the devil. (=To assist in evil.) *15th cent.*

51 To keep (*or* hold) one's nose to the grindstone. (=To work without stopping.) *H.*

52 To keep one's tongue between one's teeth. *17th cent.*

53 To keep the wolf from the door. (=To avert want.) *H.*

11 To kill the goose that lays the golden eggs. *Greek*

55 To kill two birds with one stone. *17th cent.*

56 To kiss the rod. (To submit meekly to correction.) *16th cent.*

57 To know how many beans make five. *18th cent.*

58 To know on which side one's bread is buttered. *H.*

59 To know where the shoe pinches. *14th cent.*

60 To know which way the wind blows. *H.*

61 To laugh on the wrong side of one's mouth (*or* face). *17th cent.*

62 To lay it on with a trowel. (=To flatter grossly.) *16th cent.*

63 To lay up for a rainy day. (=To provide for a time of want.) *16th cent.*

64 To lead one by the nose. (=To dominate him.) *Latin*

65 To leave no stone unturned. (=To try all methods.) *Greek*

66 To let the cat out of the bag. (=To disclose a secret.) *18th cent.*

67 To lick into shape. (=To train or mould.) *17th cent.*

68 To look as if butter would not melt in one's mouth. (=To look very innocent.) *16th cent.*

69 To look at both sides of a penny. (=To be very saving.) *19th cent.*

70 To look for a needle in a haystack. *Latin*

To lose the ship for a halfpennyworth of tar, *see* To spoil the ship, etc.

71 To make a mountain out of a molehill. *16th cent.*

72 To make a person turn in his grave. *19th cent.*

73 To make bricks without straw. *.Bible*

74 To make ducks and drakes of. (=To squander.) *16th cent.*

1 To make ends meet. (=To live within one's means.) *C.*

2 To make fish of one and flesh (*or* fowl) of another. (=To discriminate unfairly.) *C.*

3 To make two bites of a cherry. (=To do a small task in two stages.) *French*

4 To pay a person in his own coin. (=To retaliate in the same way as he has injured you.) *16th cent.*
To pile Ossa upon Pelion, *see* To heap Ossa, etc.

5 To play first (*or* second) fiddle. (=To take the leading (*or* subordinate) part.) *19th cent.*

6 To pour oil upon the waters. (=To compose a quarrel.) *19th cent.*

7 To promise and give nothing is comfort to a fool. *T. D.*

8 To put a spoke in one's wheel. (=To put an obstacle in the way. Reference is to the pin used to lock wheels.) *17th cent. (16th cent.)*

9 To put one's best foot foremost. (= To make a strong effort.) *17th cent.*

10 To put one's nose out of joint. (=To supplant him.) *16th cent.*

11 To put salt on a bird's tail. (Jokingly said to be a way of catching it.) *16th cent.*

12 To put the cart before the horse. *Latin*

13 To reckon without one's host. *16th cent. (15th cent.)*

14 To rob Peter to pay Paul. *14th cent.*

15 To run with the hare and hunt with the hounds. *19th cent. (15th cent.)*

16 To scare a bird is not the way to catch it. *C.*

17 To see which way the cat jumps. (=How events will turn out.) *19th cent.*

18 To send away with a flea in his ear. (=Peremptorily.) *H.*

19 To set the Thames on fire. (=To create a sensation.) *18th cent.*

20 To shut the stable door when the steed is stolen. *French*

21 To smell of the lamp. (=To show studied effort.) *Greek*

22 To sow one's wild oats. (=To indulge in youthful excesses.) *16th cent.*

23 To split hairs. (=To make fine distinctions.) *R.*

24 To spoil the ship (*originally* sheep) for a halfpennyworth of tar. *C. R.*

25 To stand in one's own light. (=To spoil one's own chances.) *H.*
To stew in one's own juice, *see* To fry in one's own grease.

26 To take a leaf out of one's book. (=To follow his example.) *19th cent.*

27 To take counsel of one's pillow. (=To allow a night's interval before making a decision.) *16th cent.*

28 To take one down a peg or two. (=To humble his pride.) *16th cent.*

29 To take one up before he is down. *16th cent.*

30 To take the bull by the horns. (=To face a difficulty.) *19th cent.*

31 To take the chestnuts out of the fire with the cat's paw. *16th cent.*

32 To take the gilt off the gingerbread. (=To make a thing less attractive.) *19th cent.*

33 To take the law into one's own hands. (=To act without authority.) *17th cent.*

34 To take the rough with the smooth. *15th cent.*

35 To take the will for the deed. *15th cent.*

36 To take the wind out of one's sails. (=To put him at a disadvantage.) *19th cent.*

37 To tell tales out of school. *H.*

38 To throw a sprat to catch a whale. (=To do a small favour in the hope of a great return.) *19th cent.*

39 To throw dust in one's eyes. (To mislead.) *T. D.*

40 To throw good money after bad. *19th cent.*

41 To throw the helve after the hatchet. (=To throw away what remains, because your losses have been so great.) *H.*

42 To turn an honest penny. (=To make money.) *H.*

43 To turn cat in pan. (=To change sides.) *17th cent.*

44 To turn over a new leaf. (=To amend one's ways.) *H.*

45 To wash a blackamoor white. (=To waste effort.) *Greek*

46 To wash dirty linen in public. (=To publish family scandals.) *19th cent.*

47 To wear one's heart upon one's sleeve. (=To make one's feelings apparent to everyone.) *17th cent.*

48 To wear the breeches. (Of a wife who dominates her husband.) *16th cent. (15th cent.)*

49 To wear the willow. (=To mourn the loss of a sweetheart.) *16th cent.*

50 To wet one's whistle. (=To have a drink.) *14th cent.*

51 Toasted cheese hath no master. *R.*

52 To-day a man, to-morrow a mouse. *R.*

53 To-day is Yesterday's pupil. *Latin*

54 To-day me, to-morrow thee. *13th cent.*

55 To-morrow come never. *R.*

56 To-morrow is a new day. *16th cent.*

57 Too many cooks spoil the broth. *16th cent.*

58 Too much breaks the bag. *Spanish*

59 Too much consulting confounds. *F.*

60 Too much of one thing is good for nothing. *14th cent.*

61 Too much praise is a burden. *17th cent.*

62 Too much taking heed is loss. *G. H.*

63 Too too will in two. (Friends that are too intimate will quarrel.) *R.*

64 Touch a galled horse, and he'll wince (or kick). *18th cent. (14th cent.)*

65 Touch pot, touch penny. (=No credit given.) *17th cent.*

66 Touch wood, it's sure to come good. (Touching wood is a charm to avert ill-luck after boasting.) *20th cent.*

67 Tout passe, tout casse, tout lasse. – All passes, all breaks, all wearies. *French*

68 Translators, traitors. *Italian*

69 Trash and trumpery is the highway to beggary. *R.*

70 Travel makes a wise man better, but a fool worse. *F.*

Tread on a worm and it will turn, *see* Even a worm, etc.

71 True blue will never stain. *J. H.*

72 True lovers are shy when people are by. *18th cent.*

73 Trust me, but look to thyself. *F.*

1 Trust not a horse's heel, nor a dog's tooth. *R.*

2 Trust not a new friend nor an old enemy. *K.*

3 Truth and oil are ever above. *G. H.*

4 Truth fears no colours. *R.*

5 Truth finds foes where it makes none. *R.*

6 Truth hath a good face, but bad clothes. *J. H.*

7 Truth is God's daughter. *F.*

8 Truth is stranger than fiction. *19th cent.*

9 Truth is truth to the end of the reckoning. *16th cent.*

10 Truth lies at the bottom of a well. *Greek*

11 Truth may be blamed but cannot be shamed. *16th cent.*

12 Truth needs not many words. *16th cent.*

13 Truth never grows old. *F.*

14 Truth and roses have thorns about them. *B.*

15 Truth seeks no corners. *16th cent.*

16 Try before you trust. *15th cent.*

17 Try your friend before you have need of him. *15th cent.*

18 Try your skill in gilt first, and then in gold. *C.*

19 Turkey, carps, hops, pickerel, and beer Came into England all in one year. (Pickerel=young pike. The year is supposed to be 1520.) *17th cent.*

20 Turn your money when you hear the cuckoo, and you'll never be without it during the year. *W. H.*

21 Two anons and a by and by is an hour and a half. *C. R.*

22 Two attorneys can live in a town when one cannot. *L.*

23 Two blacks do not make a white. (=Another's fault does not excuse your own.) *K.*

Two can play at that game, *see* That is a game, etc.

24 Two cats and a mouse,
Two wives in one house,
Two dogs and a bone,
Never agree in one. *R.*

25 Two daughters and a back door are three arrant thieves. (The daughters spend, and the servants filch.) *D. F.*

26 Two dogs fight for a bone, and a third runs away with it. *16th cent.*

27 Two dry sticks will kindle a green one. *R.*

28 Two ears to one tongue, therefore hear twice as much as you speak. *Greek*

29 Two eyes can see more than one. *C. R. (16th cent.)*

30 Two fools in one house (*or* bed) are too many. *16th cent.*

31 Two heads are better than one. *H.*

32 Two hungry meals make the third a glutton. *H.*

33 Two in distress make trouble less. *B.*

34 Two is company, three is none. *19th cent.*

Two may keep counsel if one be away, *see* Three may keep, etc.

35 Two negatives make an affirmative. *16th cent.*

36 Two of a trade can never agree. *R.*

37 Two Sir Positives can scarce meet without a skirmish. *F.*

38 Two sparrows on one ear of corn make an ill agreement. *G. H.*

39 Two things a man should never be angry at; what he can help, and what he cannot help. *K.*

40 Two things doth prolong thy life: A quiet heart and a loving wife. *17th cent.*

41 Two to one in all things against the angry man. *F.*

42 Two wrongs don't make a right. *19th cent.*

43 Under the blanket the black one is as good as the white. *F.*

44 Under the furze is hunger and cold, Under the broom is silver and gold. *R.*

45 Under water, famine; under snow, bread. *G. H.*

46 Unkissed, unkind. *16th cent.*

47 Unknown (*or* uncouth], unkissed. *14th cent.*

48. Unlucky in love, lucky at play. *18th cent.*

49 Unminded, unmoaned. *H.*

50 Unsound minds, like unsound bodies, if you feed, you poison. *G. H.*

51 Up hill spare me;
Down hill forbear me;
Plain way, spare me not,
Let me not drink when I am hot. (How to use a horse.) *F.*

52 Use legs and have legs. *R.*

Use makes perfectness, *see* Practice makes perfect.

53 Use the means, and God will give the blessing. *T. D.*

54 Vainglory blossoms but never bears. *F.*

55 Valour that parleys is near yielding. *G. H.*

56 Valour would fight, but discretion would run away. *R.*

57 Vanity is the sixth sense. *19th cent.*

58 Variety is pleasing. *Greek*

59 Varnishing hides a crack. *F.*

60 Venture not all in one bottom. *Latin*

61 Verbum sat sapienti.
− A word is enough to the wise. *Latin*

62 Vice makes virtue shine. *F.*

63 Vice ruleth where gold reigneth. *17th cent.*

64 Virtue and a trade are the best portion for children. *G. H.*

65 Virtue and happiness are mother and daughter. *B.*

66 Virtue is its own reward. *Latin*

67 Virtue never grows old. *G. H.*

68 Virtue which parleys is near a surrender. *18th cent.*

69 Virtues all agree, but vices fight one another. *F.*

70 Vows made in storms are forgotten in calms. *F.*

71 Vox et praeterea nihil.
− A voice and nothing besides. *Latin*

72 Vox populi vox Dei.
− The voice of the people is the voice of God. *Latin*

73 Wage will get a page. (=You will get servants if you have the money to hire them.) *K.*

74 Wake not a sleeping lion. *16th cent.*

75 Walls have ears. *17th cent.*

76 Want is the mother of industry. *B.*

77 Want makes strife 'twixt man and wife. *B.*

1 Want of wit is worse than want of wealth. *K.*

2 Want will be your master. *18th cent.*

3 Wanton kittens may make sober cats. *F.*

4 War, hunting, and law (*or* love) are as full of trouble as pleasure. *G. H.*

5 War is death's feast. *G. H.*

6 War makes thieves, and peace hangs them. *G. H.*

7 Wars bring scars. *R.*

8 Wash your hands often, your feet seldom, and your head never. *R.*

Waste makes want, *see* Wilful waste, etc.

9 Waste not, want not. *18th cent.*

10 Water, fire, and soldiers quickly make room. *G. H.*

11 We are born crying, live complaining, and die disappointed. *F.*

12 We are bound to be honest, but not to be rich. *W. H.*

13 We bachelors grin, but you married men laugh till your hearts ache. *R.*

14 We can drink of the burn when we cannot bite of the brae (=hill). (=People who lack bread can always get water.) *D. F.*

15 We can live without our friends, but not without our neighbours. *K.*

16 We can shape coat and sark (=shirt) for them, but we cannot shape their weird (=fate). *K.*

17 We cannot come to honour under coverlet. *G. H.*

18 We leave more to do when we die, than we have done. *G. H.*

19 We may give advice, but we cannot give conduct. *P. R. A.*

20 We must live by the quick, not by the dead. *16th cent.*

21 We must not lie down and cry, God help us. *17th cent.*

22 We never find that a fox dies in the dirt of his own ditch. (=Men are rarely hurt by the things they are accustomed to.) *R.*

23 We never miss the water till the well runs dry. *K.*

24 We see not what sits on our shoulder. *C.*

25 We shall lie all alike in our graves. *C.*

26 We shall see what we shall see. *19th cent.*

27 We soon believe what we desire. *Latin*

28 Weak food best fits weak stomachs. *15th cent.*

29 Weak men had need be witty. *C.*

30 Weal and woman never pan (=close together). *19th cent. (C.)*

31 Wealth is best known by want. *F.*

32 Wealth is like rheum, it falls on the weakest parts. *G. H.*

33 Wealth makes wit waver. *D. F.*

34 Wealth makes worship. *C.*

35 Wedlock is a padlock. *R.*

36 Weeds want no sowing. *F.*

37 Weening is not measure. *G. H.*

38 Weigh right, and sell dear. *16th cent.*

39 Weight and measure take away strife. *G. H.*

40 Welcome death, quoth the rat, when the trap fell. *J. H.*

41 Welcome evil, if thou comest alone. *G. H.*

42 Welcome is the best cheer. (=In hospitality the spirit is the thing.) *Greek*

43 Well begun is half done. *Latin*

44 Well may he smell fire whose gown burns. *G. H.*

45 Well to work and make a fire, It doth care and skill require. *R.*

46 Were there no hearers, there would be no backbiters. *G. H.*

47 What can you expect from a hog but a grunt. *Γ. R. A. (R).*

48 What can't be cured must be endured. *14th cent.*

49 What costs little is little esteemed. *17th cent.*

50 What God will no frost can kill. *R.*

51 What greater crime than loss of time? *F.*

52 What is bolder than a miller's neckcloth, which takes a thief by the throat every morning? *German*

53 What is bought is cheaper than a gift. *R.*

54 What is bred in the bone will not out of the flesh. *H. (13th cent.)*

55 What is done by night appears by day. *14th cent.*

56 What is got over the devil's back is spent under his belly. (=What is got by oppression is spent in luxury.) *17th cent.*

57 What is lost in the hundred (=district) will be found in the shire. *17th cent. (H.)*

58 What is new is not true, what is true is not new. *19th cent.*

59 What is sauce for the goose is sauce for the gander. *R.*

60 What is the good of a sun-dial in the shade? *F.*

61 What is worth doing is worth doing well. *19th cent.*

62 What man has done, man can do. *19th cent.*

63 What may be done at any time will be done at no time. *K.*

64 What one day gives another takes away from us. *G. H.*

65 What one knows, it is sometimes useful to forget. *Latin*

66 What soberness conceals, drunkenness reveals. *Latin*

67 What the eye doesn't see the heart doesn't grieve over. *19th cent. (H.)*

68 What the fool does in the end, the wise man does at the beginning. *19th cent.*

69 What the heart thinks the tongue speaks. *15th cent.*

70 What's yours is mine, and what's mine's my own. *18th cent.*

71 When a couple are newly married, the first month is honeymoon, or smick smack: the second is, hither and thither: the third is thwick thwack: the fourth, the devil take them that brought thee and I together. *R.*

72 When a dog is drowning, everyone offers him drink. *G. H.*

73 When a friend asks, there is no to-morrow. *G. H.*

74 When age is jocund, it makes sport for death. *G. H.*

1 When ale (*or* drink *or* wine) is in, wit is
out.   *H. (14th cent.)*

2 When all men have what belongs to
them it cannot be much.   *G. H.*

3 When all men speak, no man hears.   *K.*

4 When all sins grow old, covetousness is
young.   *G. H. (16th cent.)*

5 When April blows his horn, (=When it
thunders.)
It's good both for hay and corn.   *R.*

6 When at Rome do as the Romans do.
                                    Latin

7 When Candlemas day is come and gone,
(2 Feb.)
The snow lies on a hot stone.   *R.*

8 When caught by the tempest, whatever
it be,
If it lightens and thunders beware of a
tree.   *D.*

9 When children stand quiet they have
done some ill.   *G. H.*

When drink is in, wit is out, *see* When
ale is in, etc.

10 When Fortune knocks, open the door
                                    17th cent.

11 When Greek meets Greek, then comes
the tug of war. (Common misquotation
of 147:25 *supra*.)   *17th cent.*

12 When house and land are gone and
spent,
Then learning is most excellent.
                                    18th cent.

13 When I did well, I heard it never;
When I did ill, I heard it ever.   *K.*

14 When I lent I was a friend,
When I asked I was unkind.   *16th cent.*

15 When in doubt, leave out. (A newspaper
maxim.)   *20th cent.*

16 When it rains and the sun shines at the
same time, the devil is beating his wife.
                                    French

17 When it thunders the thief becomes
honest.   *Italian*

18 When love puts in, friendship is gone.
                                    17th cent.

19 When many strike on an anvil, they
must strike by measure.   *R.*

20 When need is highest, help is nighest.
                                    13th cent.

21 When one door shuts another opens.
                                    Spanish

22 When Oxford draws knife. England's
soon at strife.   *17th cent.*

23 When poverty comes in at the door,
love flies out at the window.   *17th cent.*

24 When round the moon there is a brugh,
(=halo.)
The weather will be cold and rough. *D.*

25 When sorrow is asleep wake it not.
                                    J. H.

26 When the belly is full, the bones would
be at rest.   *H.*

27 When the cat is away the mice will play.
                                    16th cent.

28 When the cat winketh, little wots the
mouse what the cat thinketh.   *R.*

29 When the clouds are upon the hills,
They'll come down by the mills.   *R.*

30 When the corn is in the shock,
The fish are on the rock.   *W. H.*

31 When the cuckoo comes she eats up all
the dirt. (=The mire dries up.)
                                    17th cent.

32 When the cuckoo comes to the bare
thorn,
Sell your cow and buy your corn:
But when she comes to the full bit,
Sell your corn and buy your sheep.   *R.*

33 When the cup is full, carry it even.
                                    14th cent.

34 When the devil is blind. (=Never.)
J. H.

35 When the fern is as high as a ladle,
You may sleep as long as you are able.
R.

36 When the fox preaches, beware the
geese. *H.*

37 When the goodman is from home, the
goodwife's table is soon spread. *R.*

38 When the gorse (*or* furze) is out of
bloom, kissing is out of fashion.
(Gorse is always in bloom.) *P. R. A.*

39 When the head aches, all the body is the
worse. *Latin*

40 When the husband drinks to the wife, all
would be well; when the wife drinks to
the husband, all is well. *R.*

41 When the mist comes from the hill,
Then good weather it doth spill;
When the mist comes from the sea,
Then good weather it will be. *D.*

42 When the moon's in the full, then wit's
in the wane. *D.*

43 When the sand doth feed the clay. (In a
wet summer.)
England woe and welladay!
When the clay doth feed the sand, (In a
dry summer.)
Then it is well with England. *R.*

44 When the sun is highest he casts the least
shadow. *F.*

45 When the sun sets bright and clear,
An easterly wind you need not fear. *D.*

46 When the sun sets in a bank,
A westerly wind we shall not want. *D.*

47 When the tree is fallen, all go with their
hatchet. *Greek*

48 When the wind is in the east
It's good for neither man nor beast.
J. H.

49 When the wind is in the north
The skilful fisher goes not forth. *D.*

50 When the wind is in the south
It blows the bait in the fish's mouth.
17th cent.

51 When the wind is in the west
The weather is at the best. *17th cent.*

52 When thieves fall out, honest men come
by their own. *H.*

53 When things are at the worst they will
mend. *16th cent.*

54 When thou dost hear a toll or knell.
Then think upon thy passing bell.
J. H.

55 When thy neighbour's house doth burn,
then look to your own. *Latin*

56 When war begins hell opens. *G. H.*

57 When we have gold we are in fear, when
we have none we are in danger. *R.*
When wine is in, wit is out, *see* When ale
is in, etc.

58 When wine sinks, words swim. *K.*

59 When you are an anvil, hold you still;
When you are a hammer, strike your
fill. *16th cent.*

When you are at Rome, do as Rome
does, *see* When in Rome, etc.

60 When you are well hold youself so. *K.*

61 When you bow, bow low. *Chinese*

62 When you can tread on nine daisies at
once, spring has come. *19th cent.*

63 When you christen the bairn, you
should know what to call it. *K.*

64 When you go to dance, take heed whom
you take by the hand. *C.*

65 When you have told (=counted) your
cards, you'll find you have gained but
little. *H.*

1 Where bees are, there is honey. *R.*

2 Where coin is not common, common (=provisions) must be scant. *H.*

11 Where God hath his church, the devil will have his chapel. *R. (16th cent.)*

4 Where God helps, nought harms. *14th cent.*

5 Where honour ceases, knowledge decreases. *C.*

6 Where it is well with me, there is my country. *Latin*

7 Where no fault is, there needs no pardon. *C.*

8 Where nothing is, a little doth ease. *H.*

9 Where nothing is, the king must lose his right. *H.*

10 Where shall the ox go but he must labour? *G. H.*

11 Where the bee sucks, honey, the spider sucks poison. *16th cent.*

12 Where the dam leaps over, the kid follows. *F.*

13 Where the devil cannot come, he will send. *German*

14 Where the heart is past hope, the face is past shame. *16th cent.*

15 Where the horse lies down, there some hairs will be found. *16th cent.*

16 Where the water is shallow no vessel will ride. *C.*

17 Where there are three physicians, there are two atheists. *Latin*

18 Where there is peace, God is. *G. H.*

19 Where there is whispering, there is lying. *R.*

20 Where there's a will there's a way. *G. H.*

21 Where vice is, vengeance follows. *C.*

22 Where your will is ready, your feet are light. *G. H.*

23 Whether the pitcher strikes the stone, or the stone the pitcher, it is bad for the pitcher. *17th cent.*

24 While the discreet advise, the fool doth his business. *G. H.*

25 While the dog (*or* hound) gnaws the bone, companions would he none. *Latin*

26 While the dust is on your feet, sell what you have bought. *R.*

27 While grass grows the horse starves. *Latin*

28 While the leg warmeth the boot harmeth. *H.*

29 While the tall maid is stooping, the little one hath swept the house. *Italian*

30 While there is life there is hope. *Latin*

31 White hands cannot hurt. *Spanish*

32 White silver draws black lines. *16th cent.*

33 Who can sing so merry a note As he that cannot change a groat? *H.*

34 Who chatters to you will chatter of you. *19th cent.*

35 Who draweth his sword against his prince must throw away the scabbard. *J. H.*

36 Who gives away his goods before he is dead, Take a beetle and knock him on the head. *R.*

37 Who gives to all, denies all. *G. H.*

38 Who goes a-borrowing goes a-sorrowing. *16th cent.*

39 Who goes a-mothering finds violets in the lane. (Parents visited on Mothering Sunday, Mid-Lent.) *20th cent.*

40 Who goes to bed supperless, all night tumbles and tosses. *Italian*

41 Who goes to Westminster for a wife, to Paul's for a man, and to Smithfield for a horse, may meet with a whore, a knave, and a jade. *J. H.*

42 Who hastens a glutton, chokes him. *G. H.*

43 Who hath none to still him, may weep out his eyes. *G. H.*

44 Who is worse shod than the shoemaker's wife? *H.*

45 Who keeps company with the wolf will learn to howl. *16th cent.*

46 Who knows most says least. *Italian*

47 Who lives by hope will die by hunger. *Italian*

48 Who marries does well, who marries not does better. *17th cent.*

49 Who marrieth for love without money, hath merry nights and sorry days. *R.*

50 Who may hold that will away? *H.*

51 Who meddleth in all things may shoe· the gosling. (=May waste his time.) *H.*

52 Who more busy than he that hath least to do? *T. D.*

53 Who more ready to call her neighbour scold, than the arrantest scold in the parish? *C.*

54 Who more than he is worth doth spend, He makes a rope his life to end. *R.*

55 Who preacheth war is the devil's chaplain. *R.*

56 Who spends more than he should, shall not have to spend when he would. *R.*

57 Who spits against heaven, it falls in his face. *G. H.*

58 Who swims in sin shall sink in sorrow. *16th cent.*

59 Who will not be ruled by the rudder must be ruled by the rock. *Italian*

60 Who will not keep a penny never shall have many. *C.*

61 Whom we love best, to them we can say least. *R.*

62 Whoredom and grace dwelt ne'er in one place. *K.*

63 Whoso hath but a mouth shall ne'er in England suffer drouth. (The rain will fill it.) *R.*

64 Wide will wear but tight will tear. *R.*

65 Widows are always rich. *R.*

66 Widows' children turn out well. *19th cent.*

67 Wife and children are bills of charges. *J. H.*

68 Wiles help weak folk. *D. F.*

69 Wilful waste makes woeful want. *K.*

70 Will is the cause of woe. *C.*

71 Will will have will, though will woe win. *H.*

72 Willows are weak, yet they bind other wood. *G. H.*

73 Win at first and lose at last. *R.*

74 Win gold and wear gold. *16th cent.*

75 Wine and wenches empty men's purses. *16th cent.*

76 Wine is a turncoat, first a friend, then an enemy. *G. H.*

77 Wine is old men's milk. *16th cent.*

1 Wine makes all sorts of creatures at table. *G. H.*

2 Wink and choose. *C.*

3 Wink at small faults. *C.*

Winter and wedlock tames man and beast, *see* Age and wedlock, etc.

4 Winter eateth what summer getteth. *15th cent.*

5 Winter finds out what summer lays up. *R.*

6 Winter never rots in the sky. *17th cent.*

7 Winter's thunder and summer's flood Never boded Englishman good. *R.*

8 Winter's thunder makes summer's wonder. *C. R.*

9 Winter weather and women's thoughts change oft. *15th cent.*

10 Wisdom sometimes walks in clouted shoes. *F.*

11 Wise men are caught with wiles. *C.*

12 Wise men care not for what they cannot have. *R.*

13 Wise men have their mouths in their hearts, fools their hearts in their mouths. *15th cent.*

14 Wise men learn by other men's mistakes; fools, by their own. *Latin*

15 Wise men make proverbs and fools repeat them. *18th cent.*

16 Wise men propose, and fools determine. *17th cent.*

17 Wishers and wolders (=woulders) be small householders. *16th cent.*

18 Wishes can never fill a sack. *Italian*

19 Wit once bought is worth twice taught. *R.*

20 With empty hands men may no hawks allure. *14th cent.*

21 With Latin, a horse, and money, thou wilt pass through the world. *Italian*

22 Without business, debauchery. *G. H.*

23 Without danger we cannot get beyond danger. *G. H.*

24 Wives must be had, be they good or bad. *C.*

25 Woe to the house where there is no chiding. *G. H.*

26 Woman is the woe of man. *Latin*

27 Women and dogs set men together by the ears. *16th cent.*

28 Women and hens by too much gadding are lost. *17th cent.*

29 Women and music should never be dated. *18th cent.*

30 Women and their wills are dangerous ills. *17th cent.*

31 Women and wine, game and deceit, Make the wealth small and the wants great. *K.*

32 Women are always in extremes. *C.*

33 Women are born in Wiltshire, brought up in Cumberland, lead their lives in Bedfordshire, bring their husbands to Buckingham, and die in Shrewsbury. *17th cent.*

34 Women are necessary evils. *16th cent.*

35 Women are saints in church, angels in the street, devils in the kitchen, and apes in bed. *16th cent.*

36 Women in state affairs are like monkeys in glass-shops. *J. H.*

37 Women laugh when they can and weep when they will. *G. H.*

38 Women must have the last word.
16th cent.

39 Women must have their wills when they live, because they make none when they die. *R.*

40 Women, priests, and poultry never have enough. *J. H.*

41 Women's jars breed men's wars.
17th cent.

42 Wonder is the daughter of ignorance.
17th cent. (16th cent.)

43 Wood half-burnt is easily kindled.
G. H.

44 Wood in a wilderness, moss in a mountain, and wit in a poor man's breast, are little thought of. *D. F.*

45 Words are but sands, it's money buys lands. *J. H.*

46 Words are but wind, but blows unkind.
J. H.

47 Words are wind. *13th cent.*

48 Words cut more than swords. *13th cent.*

49 Worse things happen at sea. *19th cent.*

50 Wranglers never want words. *R.*

51 Write down the advice of him who loves you, though you like it not at present.
17th cent.

52 Wrong never comes right. *19th cent.*

53 Years know more than books. *G. H.*

54 Yelping curs will raise mastiffs. *K.*

55 Yesterday will not be called again.
16th cent.

56 You are a fool to steal if you can't conceal. *B.*

57 You are a man among the geese when the gander is away. *R.*

58 You are come of a blood and so is a pudding. *D. F.*

59 You are good to fetch the devil a priest. (Said to those who loiter.) *K.*

60 You are of so many minds, you'll never be married. *K.*

61 You cackle often, but never lay an egg.
F.

62 You can call a man no worse than unthankful. *C.*

63 You can have no more of a cat than the skin. *16th cent.*

64 You cannot catch old birds with chaff.
R. (15th cent.)

65 You cannot drive a windmill with a pair of bellows. *G. H.*

66 You cannot eat your cake and have it.
H.

67 You cannot get blood (*or* water) out of a stone. *Latin*

68 You cannot know wine by the barrel.
G. H.

69 You cannot lose what you never had.
17th cent.

70 You cannot make a silk purse out of a sow's ear. *J. H.*

71 You cannot make an omelet without breaking eggs. *French*

72 You cannot make people honest (*or* sober) by Act of Parliament. *20th cent.*

73 You cannot see the city for the houses.
16th cent.

74 You cannot see the wood for the trees.
H.

75 You cannot teach an old dog new tricks.
C. R.

1 You have a head and so has a pin.
18th cent.

2 You know good manners, but you use but few. *R.*

3 You may be a wise man though you can't make a watch. *R.*

4 You may ding the deil (=beat the devil) into a wife, but you'll never ding him out of her. *K.*

5 You may go and shake your ears. (Expressing contempt.) *16th cent.*

6 You may know by a handful the whole sack. *F.*

7 You may know by a penny how a shilling spends. *R.*

8 You may poke a man's fire after you have known him seven years, but not before. *L.*

9 You may take a horse to the water, but you can't make him drink. *H.*

10 You may trust him with untold gold. *C.*

11 You might have knocked me down with a feather. (=I was greatly surprised.) *19th cent.*

12 You must ask your neighbour if you shall live in peace. *C.*

13 You must go into the country to hear what news at London. *R.*

14 You must look where it is not, as well as where it is. *F.*

15 You must lose a fly to catch a trout. *G. H.*

16 You must not let your mouse-trap smell of blood. *F.*

17 You must not pledge your own health. *R.*

18 You must take the fat with the lean. *R.*

19 You never know what you can do till you try. *19th cent.*

20 You never speak but your mouth opens. *R.*

21 You pay more for your schooling than your learning is worth. *C.*

22 You pays your money and you takes your choice. *L.*

23 You scratch my back and I'll scratch yours. *17th cent.*

24 You see what we must all come to, if we live. *R.*

25 You should never rub your eyes but with your elbow. (=Not at all.)

26 You think all is lost that goes beside your own mouth. *17th cent.*

27 You were born when wit was scant. *R.*

28 You were bred in Brazen-Nose College. (=You have plenty of assurance.) *F.*

29 You will never be mad, you are of so many minds. *R.*

30 You will scratch a beggar one day before you die. (=You will be a beggar.) *C.*

31 You would be over the stile ere you come at it. *H.*

32 You would do little for God if the devil were dead. *D. F.*

33 You would spy faults if your eyes were out. *R.*

34 Young cocks love no coops. *C. R.*

35 Young men may die, old men must. *16th cent.*

36 Young men think old men fools, and old men know young men to be so. *16th cent.*

37 Young men's knocks old men feel. (=We pay in age for what happened in youth.) *R.*

38 Young prodigal in a coach will be old
beggar barefoot.   F.

39 Young saint, old devil.   *15th cent.*

40 Your lips hang in your light. (=You talk
foolishly.)   H.

41 Your mind is chasing mice. (=Wool-
gathering.)   K.

42 Your trumpeter is dead. (Reproaching a
braggart.)   K.

43 Youth and age will never agree.   *D. F.*

44 Youth and white paper take any
impression.   R.

45 Youth will be served.   *19th cent.*

46 Youth will have its course (*or* swing).
16th cent.

47 Yule is come, and Yule is gone,
And we have feasted well;
So Jack must to his flail again,
And Jenny to her wheel.   D.

48 Zeal without knowledge is fire without
light.   F.

49 Zeal without prudence is frenzy.   F.

INDEX

A

A' that and a' that, for, 47:33
A-Angling, be quiet and go, 308:6
Abana and Pharpar, 325:55
Abased, shall be, 336:18
Abdiel, spake the seraph, 172:17
Abdomen, took him in the, 116:23
A-bed after midnight, 271:35
  gentlemen in England now, 237:20
Aberdeen, tak awa', 413:63
Abhorrence, my heart's, 37:30
Abide, nowhere did, 69:31
  our question, others, 19:15
  something in him we cannot, 212:16
  things well fitted, 426:16
  with me, 138:8, 152:11
Abiit, excessit, evasit, erupit, 67:19
Abilities, but moderate, 203:24
Ability, intellectual, 20:11
  out of my lean and low, 272:17
  Scotsman of your, 25:31
  [studies serve] for, 22:15
A-birding, must never go, 378:23
Able, as far as he is, 286:14
  because they seem to be, 306:5
Ablution, of pure, 138:1
Abode, English make [ocean], 307:24
  live in a numble, 84:6
Abodes, from your blest, 94:2
Abomination of desolation, 325:51
A-borrowing, who goes, 438:38
Abou Ben Adhem awoke, 126:37
Abound, where they most, 192:10
About it and about, 98:5
Above me, he is so, 213:25
  'tis not so, 225:38
  truth and oil are, 432:3
Abra was ready, 200:9
Abraham lies, old, 183:27
Abraham's bosom, sleep in, 245:22
Abram, O father, 254:7
Abroad, that I should be, 96:10

Absalom, my son, my son, 325:42
Absence, conspicuous by, 207:34
  dote on his very, 253:36
  makes the heart grow fonder, 26:12
  seem'd my flame to qualify, 265:24
  sour, bitterness of, 264:7
Absent are always in the wrong, 414:33
  in body, 338:21
  will hate you, 378: 25
Absents, presents endear, 143:41
Absolute for death, be, 252:14
  power corrupts, 15:2
  she seems, so, 172:29
  the knave is, how, 227:31
Absolutism tempered by assassination,
  181:18
Absurd man is the one, 26:1
Absurde, l'homme, 26:1
Abundance, he shall have, 325:55
A-burgling, burglar's not, 105:34
Abuse himself, should, 303:15
  stumbling on, 267:31
  the plaintiff's attorney, 401:73
Abused by most men, commonly, 47:42
  or disabused, by himself, 195:39
Abusing of God's patience, 256:8
Abyss, secrets of th', 113:25
Academe, olive grove of, 174:8
Accents are soon forgot, loved, 277:22
Accident, by many a happy, 162:4
  into which no, 110:14
Accidents by flood and field, moving,
  260:3
  will happen, 355:51
Accommodated, as they say, 234:23
Accommodatin character, 308:9
Account, a beggarly, 268:5
  book, needs no, 378:27
  present my true, 167:31
  put down to our, 158:6
  sent to my, 222:17

Accoutred as I was, 228:9
Accursed, think themselves, 237:20
Accuse, j', 322:14
Accused, before you are, 401:51
  before you be, 62:4
Accuser, needs no, 351:79
Accustomed to everything, 87:17
Achilles assumed, what name, 35:24
  swift-footed, 123:23
  the wrath of, 123:21
Achilles' wrath, 193:39
'Αχιλλεύς, πόδας ὠκύς, 123:23
Aching, better a finger off than always,
  360:40
Achitophel was first, false, 89:23
A-cold, I am nothing, 287:30
  poor Tom's, 241:37
Acorns, threshes down, 419:55
Acquaintance be forgot, auld, 45:77
  short, 410:34
  what, old, 233:45
Acquaintances, [have] many, 375:41
Acquent, when we were first, 45:42
Acquittance, forbearance is no, 371:50
Acres, a few paternal, 192:1
  and a cow, three, 71:32
Act crowns the play, last, 201:24
  in the living present, 149:27
  of Parliament, make people honest by,
    441:72
  of Settlement, through, 204:3
  otherwise, never to, 135:36
  that has no relish of salvation, 225:39
Acting and the first motion, between,
    228:18
  lowest of the arts, 179:22
  when he was off he was, 109:36
Action, do no sinful, 17:19
  done, no noble, 31:21
  how like an angel, in, 223:37
  lies in his true nature, 225:38
  lose the name of, 224:4
  nor utterance, 230:6
  not knowledge but, 128:7
  strong in, 371:54
  to the word, suit, 225:16
  used their dearest, 259:54
Actions are what they are, 47:43
  innocent, 389:68
  serve the turn, 401:49
  speak louder, 355:52
Active men, honest minds and, 102:3

Actor leaves, well-graced, 244:8
Actors in the world, best, 223:39
  were all spirits, 269:40
Acts, little, nameless, 316:12
  our angels are, our, 100:6
  the best, 23:24
  the four first, 28:13
A-cursing, like a very drab, 224:1
Adam and Eve were dispossessed, 32:4
  and of Eve, son of, 200:13
  dolve and Eve span, 23:30
  the goodliest man, 171:30
  whipp'd the offending, 235:40
Added unto you, all these things shall be,
    333:55
Adder could hear, if, 386:12
  stingeth like, 329:53
Adding one to one, goes on, 39:29
Addison, to the volumes of, 131:33
Adieu, bid your servant, 264:7
  for evermore, 47:27
  my native shore, 50:7
  she cries, 103:25
Administered is best, whate'er is best, 196:1
Admirable, how express and, 223:37
Admiral, good to kill an, 306:14
Admiralty, blood be the price of, 140:13
Admire an' for to see, for to, 142:2
  fools, 193:17
  where none, 152:13
Ado there was, much, 33:13
A-doing, not long, 374:22
Adonais, the soul of, 276:17
Adonis in loveliness, 128:4
Adoo, bid you a welcome, 308:8
Adoration, duty, and observance, all,
    218:10
Adores thee, he who, 177:29
Adorn, that he did not, 132:3
Adsum, and fell back, said, 299:24
Adullam, political Cave of, 33:26
'Αδύνατα εἰκότα, πρσαιρεῖσθαι, 18:9
Advance, not to, 403:44
Advantage, mutual and general, 66:6
Adventure, awfully big, 25:29
  meet the great, 24:12
  most beautiful, 102:5
Adventures are to the adventurous, 85:38
Adventuring both, by, 253:32
Adverbs, God is better pleased with, 372:33
Adversary had written a book, that mine,
    326:5

wealth a well-spent, 56:1
what a sad old, 290:14
when thou comest to, 266:10
will perform, expect, 131:29
will rule itself, 409:44
with stealing steps, 304:17
would crave, knew what, 388:10
would there were no, 273:39
Aged, aged man, I saw an, 59:34
    seem, reverend creatures, 302:7
Ages and ages hence, 102:9
Ages elapsed ere Homer's, 74:12
    his acts being seven, 216:17
    in thy sight, thousand, 309:36
    move, our different, 200:12
    now he belongs to, 284:13
    of hopeless end, 169:35
    passed away, forms of, 27:24
    the emptiness of, 156:7
    wakens the slumbering, 291:27
Agent, trust no, 258:14
Aggravate your choler, 234:15
Agincourt, at, 235:39
A-gley, gang aft, 44:12
Agony, swimmer in his, 52:18
Agree in one, never, 432:24
Agreeable, is the old min, 83:32
    not want people to be very, 21:31
Ague in the spring, 356:22
Agues come on horseback, 355:61
    cure young, 408:05
    go away on foot, 355:61
    kill old men, 408:5
Ahead, far far, 67:31
Ahkoond I mourn, for the, 145:28
A-hunting, we daren't go, 18:1
Aid, alliteration's artful, 65:37
    lend us thine, 118:7
Ail thee, what can, 137:36
Aim at, two things to, 280:8
Air, a charter'd libertine, 235:41
    a diviner, 320:9
    appear, did in the, 282:15
    are melted into, 269:40
    babbling gossip of, 271:33
    bites shrewdly, 222:3
    broke into a mist, 38:18
    burns frore, parching, 170:2
    did affright the, 335:39
    do not saw the, 224:13
    excellent canopy, the, 223:37
    fills the silent, 281:35

flyin' through the, 160:2
hang in the, 232:28
her fair and floral, 99:27
hurtles in the darken'd, 113:32
inquiring but disdainful, 279:34
is hush'd, 71:36
let out to warm the, 288:17
nimbly and sweetly recommends itself,
    247:38
nipping and an eager, 222:3
sightless couriers of, 248:1
sweet as Eden is the, 160:14
that do corrupt my, 219:26
wing the midway, 241:48
Airly Beacon, Airly Beacon, 139:25
Airly, gut to git up, 151:32
Airs, lap me in soft Lydian, 164:9
    melting, or martial, 76:3
Airth, li'l lew corner o', 190:11
Airts the wind can blaw, 45:35
Airy, fairy Lilian, 292:5
Aisle, the long-drawn, 112:10
Aisles of Christian Rome, 94:21
Ajax on the one hand leaped, 146:10
    strives, when, 192:16
Ajax', as good as, 219:38
A-killing, nine years, 262:1
Akond of Swat, the, 147:21
"Αλα τύπτον ἐρετμοῖς, 132:32
Alabaster, cut in, 253:28
Alacrity in sinking, 256:14
Alarm, might give the, 312:10
Alarums changed to merry meetings,
    244:11
Alas and well-a-day, 342:13
Alchemy, with heavenly, 264:4
Aldeborontiphoscophornio, 57:19
Alderman, fore-finger of, 266:13
Ale and old, jolly good, 287:30
    God send thee good, 287:30
    he that buys good, 377:76
    is in, when, 436:1
    is meat, drink, and cloth, 373:45
    man, ale's the stuff, 126:17
    spicy nut-brown, 164:5
    take it as tinkers do, 47:42
    take the size of pots, 48:6
    will make a cat speak, 373:46
Alea est jacta, 53:41
Aleppo once, in, 262:16
Alexander, noble dust of, 227:35
    she's gane, like, 46:19

Alexanders, like so many, 236:6
Alexandrine ends the song, 192:15
Algebra, hour o' th' day by, 48:7
Alice, remember sweet, 95:28
Alieni appetens, 208:6
Alike every day, 355:16
  in our graves, all, 434:25
  none go just, 192:4
  there should be none, 35:23
Alium, qui facit per, 408:7
Alive, in that dawn to be, 319:23
  looking as if she were, 38:19
  officiously to keep, 68:5
  'ot sand and ginger when, 141:38
  that he's no longer, 28:8
  when neither are, 219:38
All alike, sun shines upon, 422:37
  before one, by, 361:58
  have God and have, 375:42
  in all, take him for, 221:27
  men say, must be true, 392:25
  men speak, when, 436:3
  the proud shall be, 194:4
  things can, no living man, 402:6
  things, cannot all do, 305:24
  things to all men, 338:24
  things to pass, bring, 406:15
Allegiance, to hell, 226:23
Allegory, headstrong as, 277:37
Alley green, every, 165:37
  she lives in our, 56:17
Alleybi, vy worn't there a, 82:20
Alleys, lowest and vilest, 87:32
Alliances, steer clear of permanent, 309:22
  with none, entangling, 129:31
Alliteration's artful aid, 65:37
Allone, withouten any companye, 63:40
Alloy, no joy without, 402:5
All-terrible, God the, 65:34
Almanac, look in the, 257:36
Almighty's orders to perform, 15:7
Almost and Very nigh, 356:17
  was never hanged, 356:18
Alms, giveth, 380:34
  never make poor, 356:19
  when thou doest, 333:47
Almsman's gown, gay apparel for, 244:2
Aloft, now he's gone, 82:1
Alone, all, all alone, 69:29
  and palely loitering, 137:36
  better be, 36:51
  how women pass the time when they

are, 119:29
I did it, 219:29
if thou comest, 435:41
left blooming, 178:8
let well, 395:30
never less alone than when, 205:15
not good that the man should be, 323:16
on a wide wide sea, 69:29, 69:38
one who treads, 178:15
sit lingering, I, 304:14
who travels, 142:10
Aloof, they stood, 70:7
Alp, o'er many a frozen, 170:3
Alph, the sacred river, 70:8
Alpha and Omega, I am, 340:19
Alpine mountains cold, on, 167:30
  village, through an, 150:3
Alps on Alps arise, 192:7
Altereth not, law which, 332:20
Alters when it alteration finds, 265:27
Altitudo, to an O, 35:20
Always, what everywhere, what, 305:20
Amantium irae, 298:10
Amaranthus all his beauty shed, bid, 167:22
Amaryllis, to sport with, 166:15
Amateurs, nation of, 206:3
Amaze me, ye gods, it doth, 228:10
Ambassador from Britain's crown, 88:7
  is an honest man, 321:26
Ambition, distraction, 58:11
  first sprung, 94:2
  fling away, 239:18
  leave to low, 195:25
  loves to slide, 89:29
  mock, let not, 112:8
  should be made of sterner stuff, 229:38
  shun, who doth, 216:6
  the soldier's virtue, 214:7
  thick-sighted, the, 138:2
  vaulting, 248:2
  which o'erleaps itself, 248:2
Ambition's ladder, young, 228:17
Ambitions dwindle, swollen, 37:33
Ambitious, I slew him, 228:17
Ambled up and down, 233:31
Ambulance comes round, till, 142:5
Âme, aventures de son, 101:23
Amelia was praying for George, 298:17
Amemus, vivamus . . . atque, 60:14
Amen, sound of a great, 200:15
  stuck in my throat, 248:19
Amended, all shall be, 385:72

Angle, Brother of the, 308:3
Anglers, too good for any but, 308:5
Angles, but angels, not,114:2
Angli, sed angeli, non, 114:2
Angling but catching, not, 417:42
Angry, and sin not, be ye, 339:47
  at a feast, 379:60
  at, two things a man should never be,
    433:39
  man, against, 433:41
  man, hungry man is, 352:10
  without a cause, 379:61
  word, speak no, 17:19
Anguish keeps the heavy gate, 314:16
  lessen'd by another's, 266:9
  of all sizes, 119:39
Angusta domi, res, 135:27
Animal, man is a noble, 35:26
  man is a tool-using, 57:24
Animals are such agreeable friends, 93:20
  paragon of, 223:37
  turn and live with, 312:14
  we are vertebrate, 160:1
Anna, here thou, great, 193:27
Annabel Lee, I and my, 191:23
Annals, short and simple, 112:8
  true, writ your, 219:29
Anni labuntur, fugaces, 24:11, 125:28
Annihilating all that's made, 158:14
Annihilation's Waste, Moment in, 98:4
Annos, praeteritos referat si Juppiter, 306
Annoy, no joy without, 402:5
  only does it to, 58:8
Anons and a by and by, two, 432:21
Another, does a thing through, 408:7
  one good turn deserves, 405:43
Answer came there none, 211:33
  gets the soul dusty, 160:12
  is doing, shortest, 422:14
  rang, the silver, 36:8
  soft, 328:32
  to Hi, he would, 59:26
  trickled through my head, 59:34
  would not stay for, 22:7
Answered him and said, 123:23
Answers, she who ne'er, 197:26
Ant, go to the, 328:19
Ante nos nostra dixerunt, 86:6
Anthem, the pealing, 112:10
Anthems for ever are ringing, 345:19
  hallowing and singing of, 234:4
Anthropophagi, the, 460:5

"Ανθρωπος φύσει πολιτικὸν ξῶσν, 18:9
'Ανθρώπου δεινότερον, σύδέν, 281:31
Antic sits, there the, 244:1
Antidote, sweet oblivious, 251:32
Antiquity, little skill in, 102:10
Anvil, hammer and, 362:30
  when many strike on, 436:19
  when you are, 437:59
Any thing, though you do, 264:8
Anybody, anywhere, any time, 73:19
  no one's, 106:26
  there, is there, 81:20
'Απαμειβόμενος, τὸν δ', 123:23
Apart for ever, walking, 128:16
Ape and tiger die, let the, 296:7
  goes, the higher the, 419:48
  like an angry, 252:11
  or an angel, is man, 85:32
  played the sedulous, 286:5
Ape's an ape, 356:23
Apennine, wind-grieved, 38:2
Apes and ivory, 184:7
  in bed, 440:35
  in hell, lead, 268:12
  in hell, old maids lead, 404:7
  leave Now for dogs and, 39:28
Apes [bees], mellificatis, 306:10
Apollo, after the songs of, 246:17
  always keep his bow strung, nor does,
    125:27
  arcum tendit, 125:27
  comes leading, 19:19
  preserved me, so, 125:24
  sic me servavit, 125:24
  turned fasting friar, 161:30
  yea, is not even, 104:2
Apollo's laurel bough, 157:20
  lute, musical as, 246:8
Apollyon straddled, 42:9
Apology, never make, 62:4
Apostles shrank, while, 25:22
Apostolic blows and knocks, 48:13
Appalling to think of, 25:31
Apparel oft proclaims the man, 221:38
  shapes, 372:34
Apparition, was an, 20:13
Apparitions, a thousand blushing, 259:34
  seen and gone, 184:4
Appealed unto Caesar, 338:2
Appearance, according to, 337:45
Appearances, judge from, 401:58
Appetit vient en mangeant, 202:1

crested the world, 214:19
no further, stretch, 412:46
of coincidence, the long, 61:28
undone widow sits upon, 159:33
Arma, silent leges inter, 67:15
togae, cedant, 67:21
virumque cano, 305:28
Arm-chair, loving that old, 73:18
Armed, thrice is he, 237:31
with his primer, 34:12
Armies, disbanding hired, 57:23
of the ransomed saints, 17:24
swore terribly, our, 285:23
whole have sunk, where, 170:2
Arminian clergy, an 62:11
Armour, best, 408:25
of God, put on, 339:48
Armourers, accomplishing the knights,
236:10
Arms [*limbs*], greedy folk have long, 374:4
hug it in mine, 252:72
if one could fall into, 29:17
imparadis'd in one anothers', 171:31
kings have long, 393:62
leap to these, 267:41
long in, 398:12
lord of folded, 246:6
might do what this has done, his, 307:22
muscles of his brawny, 149:33
straggler into loving, 149:9
the everlasting, 324:16
Arms [*weapons*], against a sea, take, 224:4
and the man I sing, 305:28
every man in, 319:24
give place to the civic gown, let, 67:21
he laid down his, 123:35
nation proud in, 165:28
on armour clashing, 172:19
never would lay down, 62:12
Army again, back to the, 141:45
hum of either, 236:10
it is an ill, 390:28
of unalterable law, 161:24
with banners, terrible as, 331:43
A-roving, we'll go no more, 52:8
Arran peaks are grey, 77:30
Arrant, upon a thankless, 202:11
Array, lo! in bright, 27:24
meet thee in battle, 55:20
Arrears, pay glad life's, 40:6
Arrest, strict in his, 227:52
Arrive, better thing than, 286:4

Arrow into the air, shot, 150:7
Ars est celare artem, 357:65
longa, vita brevis, 121:23
Arsenal, shook the, 174:9
Art, a score of years to, 39:25
constantly aspires, 188:1
desiring this man's, 264:1
does but consist in the removal of
surplusage, 188:3
for art's sake, 74:1
her guilt to cover, 108:11
in every, 389:39
is long, 121:23, 149:26
is quite useless, all, 314:2
is too precise, 120:6
it's pretty but is it, 141:28
last and greatest, 198:12
lies in concealing art, 357:65
made tongue-tied by authority, 264:12
may err, 91:28
more matter with less, 223:28
next to Nature, 114:15
not chance, comes from, 192:16
of God, nature is the, 35:22
of reading, 85:44
pour l'art, 74:1
to find the mind's construction, 247:32
to please, each, 198:2
work that aspires to, 72:14
Artaxerxes' throne, 174:9
Artful Dodger, the, 83:25
Arthur's bosom, he's in, 236:6
Article, snuff'd out by an, 53:30
Artifex pereo, qualis, 182:18
Artificer, lean unwashed, 240:4
the great, 287:28
Artificial, all things are, 35:22
Artist lives everywhere, 356:26
makes but half, 393:75
perishes in me, what an, 182:18
Artists are never Puritans, great, 160:7
Arts, acting lowest of, 177:22
and eloquence, mother of, 174:7
and learning down, cry, 201:25
belly teaches all, 414:40
mother of all, 407:52
no; no letters, 121:26
of peace, inglorious, 158:16
that caused himself to rise, 198:2
Ascend, by which he did, 228:17
Ash precedes the oak, if, 386:28
Ashamed of, doing something he is, 274:13

to eat, never be, 401:52
Ashes, handful of, 159:20
Hope . . . turns, 97:33
monograph on, 87:30
of Napoleon, 310:17
out, who shall bear, 384:40
splendid in, 35:26
to ashes, 341:55
was burnt to, 111:20
Ashlar, my new-cut, 142:7
Asia, pampered jades of, 157:4
A-sorrowing, goes, 438:38
Aspect he rose, with grave, 169:37
Aspen, light quivering, 210:13
'Ασφαλὴς ἄρ ἐστ' ἀμείνων, 95:34
Ask and ask, we, 19:15
and it shall be given, 333:60
furnish all we ought to, 138:7
it of him again, 388:6
me no more, 294:21
me to take none, don't, 83:40
much to have a little, 359:73
of other men, 362:17
Asked no other thing, I, 84:22
Askelon, in the streets of, 324:34
Asketh faintly, he that, 377:65
Asking, for want of, 396:36
to have thy, 283:31
too much, 56:11
Asleep, and he lies fast, 98:1
as they stalk, half, 116:7
catch a weasel, 428:13
he thought me, 188:5
sucks the nurse, 215:26
till it falls, 292:3
very houses seem, 317:37
where as I lay, 311:33
Aspire, the rest bade, 37:26
Aspramont or Montalban, jousted in,
168:20
Ass behind [take heed of], 412:72
but a crowned, 352:11
goes a-travelling, if, 385:69
if all men say that thou art, 385:68
is but an ass, 356:27
[knoweth] his master's crib, 331:46
loaded with gold, 356:28
loves to hear himself, 368:20
stamps o'er his Head, 98:1
that brays most, 414:34
that carries me, 362:9
thinks he may kick at him 187.27

to write me down an, 259:40
Assassination could trammel up the
consequence, 247:40
tempered by, 181:18
Assassins commencement, que MM. les,
135:38
Asses who pull, mankind are, 53:33
Assis, unius aestimemus, 60:14
Assistance, cause that lacks, 23:33
Assurance double sure, make, 250:15
Assyrian bull, curl'd, 296:10
came down, 51:38
"Αστεα καὶ νόσν εγνω, ιδεν, 123:30
Astolat, lily maid of, 297:28
Astonished at my own moderation, 67:29
Astra, sic itur ad, 306:9
Astray, like sheep have gone, 332:6
that had been led, 164:17
Asunder, let no man put, 341:51
let not man put, 325:37
A-swellin' wisibly, 82:17
Asylums, padded lunatic, 316:1
Atahualpa, who strangled, 153:25
'Αθᾶναι, κλειναί, 190:14
Athanasius contra mundum, 359:86
Atheism and superstition, 416:18
inclineth to, 22:13
Atheist, a female, 130:7
is one point beyond the devil, 356:29
sort of village, 65:31
Atheists, there are two, 438:17
Athens, divine city, 190:14
he chooses, 91:27
maid of, 50:5
the eye of Greece, 174:7
Athol, cam ye by, 122:3
Atlantic, beneath the wide, 199:33
Atlas, like Teneriff or, 172:7
Atomies, team of little, 266:13
'Ατραπόν, μὴ ειναι βασιλικήν, 95:32
Attachment à la Plato, 105:38
Attack, I shall, 100:8
lead such dire, 154:4
Attained, things hardly, 426:13
Attempt and not the deed confounds us,
248:17
fearing to, 252:3
the end, 120:13
Attended, is on his way, 319:35
Attentions, these pleasing, 21:25
Attic, beauty crieth in an, 49:31
Attic bird trills, the, 174:8

stage, glory of, 18:14
Atticus were he, if, 198:2
Attire doth show her wit, in, 342:15
   walk in silk, 30:15
   wild in their, 247:23
Attorney, abuse, 401:73
   downstairs, kick, 393:55
Attorneys, can live, two, 432:22
Attractive and yet simple, 146:12
   metal more, 225:22
Attribute of a Scotsman, 25:32
Auburn, sweet, 108:12
Audace, toujours de l', 79:23
Audi alteram partem, 359:87
Augury, we defy, 227:50
August be fair, if the twenty-fourth of, 387:34
   go he must, in, 388:34
   to recommence in, 53:31
Augusta, my dear, 188:9
Auld acquaintance be forgot, 45:37
   lang syne, 45:37, 38, 39, 40
   man, lassie do wi' an, 46:13
Aunts, his cousins and his, 105:27
Auras, superasque evadere ad, 306:6
Auri sacra fames, 306:2
[Austen, Miss], had a talent, 212:7
Austin have his swink, lat, 63:25
Austria, Grenadiers of, 88:6
Author, choose an, 205:27
   like book, like, 395:72
Author's graces, ruin half, 179:20
Authority, as one having, 324:7
   drest in a little brief, 252:11
   forgets a dying king, 297:39
Autre temps, autre mœurs, 359:88
Autumn comes jovial on, 300:12
   fields, happy, 294:13
   hope for a prosperous, 387:34
   that grew the more by reaping, 214:19
Autumn's being, breath of, 275:32

Autumnal face, seen in one, 86:11
Avarice, beyond the dreams of, 177:21
   [in want] of everything, 407:48
   spur of industry, 127:32
Avarus eget, semper, 125:38
Ave atque vale, 61:18
Avena, musam meditamur, 280:13
   tenui meditaris, 305:21
Avenge, O Lord, thy slaughter'd saints, 167:30
Avenue, at 244 Madison, 182:3
Average man, content to be, 128:12
Averno, facilis descensus, 306:6
Avernus, descent to, 306:6
Aversion, begin with a little, 277:34
Avilion, island-valley of, 297:44
Avis in terris, rara, 135:28
Avoided, half, 350:21
Avon, sweet Swan of, 134:16
Awake my soul, 138:13
   seem not to, 359:81
Awaked, must be, 325:48
Away, away! for I will fly, 136:17
   with him, 238:3
Awe, enough to strike, 288:15
   lives without, 128:13
   of such a thing as I myself, in, 228:8
Aweary, aweary, I am, 292:6
   of the sun, to be, 251:38
Awoke one morning, I, 53:38
Axe goes to the wood, 414:35
   is at her root, 421:57
   is laid unto the root, 333:33
   that fells it, perfumes, 422:6
Axe's edge did try, 158:17
Axes rung, no ponderous, 118:6
Axis of the earth sticks out, 122:17
Axletree, fly sat upon, 418:1
Ayes or Noes, Question makes of, 98:12
Ayr, auld, 46:6

B

Babble and talk, to, 258:27
Babbled of green fields, 236:1

Babe all burning bright, 28:15
   bent o'er her, 145:25

Bandersnatch, try to stop a, 59:32
Bandits, those cut-throat, 46:14
Bands, strong as iron, 149:33
Bandy civilities, to, 133:23
Bane, that soil may best deserve the
   precious, 169:25
Banes, Willie Michie's, 45:31
Bang, many a, 48:17
Bangs, ride with General, 139:33
Banish all the world, 232:18
   plump Jack, 232:18
Banishing, worst effect is, 74:16
Banishment, bitter bread of, 243:36
Banjos rattled, the, 148:14
Bank, I know a, 257:34
Bank to Mandalay, from the, 141:43
Banker's Clerk, saw a, 60:4
Bankrupt, beggar can never be, 349:10
   of life, 89:26
Banks and braes o' bonnie Doon, 46:12
   are wild and fair, 211:30
   on the bonny, bonny, 343:29
Banner, a song for our, 180:2
   his blood-red, 118:9
   in the sky, that, 122:8
   royal, 261:35
   that star-spangled, 138:17
   torn but flying, 51:24
   with the strange device, 150:3
Banners, hang out our, 251:35
   wait, confusion on thy, 113:28
   wave, all thy, 55:28
Banquet, trifling foolish, 266:17
   we press, to the, 105:25
Banquet-hall deserted, 178:15
Bar, clomb above the eastern, 69:28
   no moaning of the, 298:5
   when I have crost the, 298:7
Barajar, paciencia y, 61:23
Barbarians all at play, young, 51:25
Barbarous age, invention of a, 175:36
Barber, go to, 394:39
   learns to shave, 349:7
   she very imprudently married the, 100:10
Barber's shear, known the, 299:28
Bards of old enjoyed, 30:1
   of Passion and of Mirth, 137:28
   will not, as, 77:23
Bare as the birch, 360:5
   though I go, 287:30
Barefoot, goes long, 375:61
   he that goes, 378:30

I must dance, 268:12
   if it go, 385:63
Bargain, bare words make no, 360:7
   her most filthy, 262:12
   in the way of, 232:25
   is a bargain, a, 349:8
   it is a silly, 390:21
   make the best of a bad, 398:3
   pause, at a great, 359:77
Bargains, above all, 427:61
Barge, drag the slow, 79:26
   she sat in, 214:2
Bark [of dog] as they are bred, dogs, 367:62
   at a distance, 367:64
   at every dog's, 359:81
   at me, see, they, 241:40
   before they bite, 367:63
   is worse than his bite, 383:58
   leaned his head against a wall to, 358:6
   myself, keep a dog and, 385:48
   watch-dog's honest, 52:15
   yourself, keep a dog and, 367:52
Bark [ship] is on the sea, my, 52:9
   tall anchoring, 241:48
Bark [of tree] and the tree, between, 407:83
Barkers are no biters, 373:69
Barking dogs seldom bite, 360:8
Barks of yore, Nicaean, 191:27
Barkis is willin', 84:2
Barley-corn is better, a, 349:9
Barn, full, and findy, 350:12
Barnaby bright, 360:9
Barn-door, stack, or the, 164:1
Barne, Bessy Marris's, 295:31
Baronets are bad, all, 106:17
   by dozens, 104:16
Barrel, know wine by, 441:68
   the better, never, 401:50
Barrel-organ carolling, 184:9
Barricade, at some disputed, 212:14
Barricks, single men in, 141:36
Barrie's cans, clatter of, 114:8
Bars, between their silver, 99:25
Barty, Breitmann gife a, 148:2
   now, where ish dat, 148:2
Base, from its firm, 211:28
Baser sort, lewd fellows of, 337:63
Bashfulness is a vice, 426:28
   is an enemy, 360:10
Basia mille, da mi, 61:15
Basin of nice smooth gruel, 21:28
Basingstoke, word . . . like, 106:19

Basket, all your eggs in one, 367:54
Bat, weak-ey'd, 71:36
Bathing, caught the Whigs, 85:31
Baths, two walking, 78:1
Baton of a marshal of France, 181:33
Bâton de maréchal de France, 181:33
Bats in the belfry, have, 429:41
Bastman and the bat, *I* am, 145:24
Battalions, but in, 226:21
Battered and decay'd, 307:27
Battle and murder, from, 341:36
   and the breeze, 55:23
   beat to, 294:17
   drunk delight of, 293:25
   half, 417:66
   he smelleth the, 326:9
   in the lost, 210:2
   in the midst of, 325:36
   it is an ill, 390:28
   knows, divisions of, 259:46
   like this, was ever a, 297:46
   lost, nothing except, 310:12
   lour, front o', 47:23
   news of, 22:1
   queen of yore, be, 203:19
   rages loud and long, 55:23
   roll'd, noise of, 297:38
   there was which I saw, 155:23
   won, melancholy as, 310:12
Battle's lost and won, when, 246:18
Battle-flags were furl'd, 293:35
Battle-day is past, 94:2
Battle-line, our far-flung, 140:24
Battlements, sheer o'er the crystal, 169:26
Battles, god of, 297:46
   long ago, 318:6
Bauble, do with this, 78:6
   pleased with this, 195:41
   will not give his, 351:38
Bauchles for bonny bairns, 408:32
Bay [*inlet*] at morning, bonnie, 77:30
   of Biscay, O, in the, 64:4
Bay, [*laurel*] instead of, 107:43
Bayonets, throne of, 128:14
Be as you would seem to be, 360:12
   I had as lief not, 228:8
   not afraid of greatness, 272:6
   or not to be, to, 224:4
   or the contrary, to, 201:29
   to do, to do without, and to depart, to,
     179:29
   what they will be, 47:43

Βη̄ δ' δκε῎ων παρὰ θι῀να, 123:22
Beach, there came to the, 55:30
   upon the dusky, 154:11
Beaches, we shall fight on, 66:3
Beacon, towns from Airly, 139:25
Beacons from the abode, 276:17
Beads and prayer-books, 195:41
Beak, can take in his, 161:36
   from out my heart, take thy, 191:26
   holds more than his belican, 161:36
Beaker full, O for a, 136:15
Be-all and the end-all, 247:40
Beam that is in thine own eye, 333:58
   the full midday, 175:34
Beameth, no one knows for whom it, 178:5
Beamish boy, my, 59:19
Beams, spreads his orient, 171:33
   tricks his, 167:23
Bean hath its black, 368:21
   not-too-French French, 105:38
Bean-rows will I have, nine, 321:36
Beans and benevolence, full o', 288:6
   make five, how many, 429:57
Bear [*animal*], dancing, 74:9
   exit, pursued by a, 114:99, 273:38
   oppress'd, huntsman by, 307:21
   rugged Russian, 250:5
   still less the, 102:4
   that scratches, 377:44
   with a sore head, 357:72
Bear [*endure*] and forbear, 360:20
   greater than I can, 323:23
Bear it, no man alive could, 247:14
   no mortal can, 104:1
   till his back break, 353:45
Bear's ethereal grace, 58:2
Bear-baiting, Puritan hated, 153:31
Beard of formal cut, 216:17
   Old Man with a, 147:14
   were all, if, 386:13
Bearded like the pard, 216:17
Beards be grown, until your, 325:39
   heartless, long, 396:26
   wag all, when, 391:73
Beast, before he caught, 307:21
   cocoa is a vulgar, 65:23
   it is the nature of, 392:17
   life of his, 328:27
   man and bird and, 70:1
   marks of the, 115:25
   that wants discourse of reason, 221:23
   with two backs, 259:50

supperless, goes to, 439:40
to the brown, blue, 110:5
two fools in one, 432:30
welcome to your gory, 46:22
with the lamb, go to, 372:25
Beddes heed, at his, 63:27
Bedfellows, seldom, 384:2
  with strange, 269:32
Bedfordshire, lead their lives in, 440:33
Bedimmed, now sparkling, now, 70:18
Bedlam, love and pride stock, 397:43
Beds of down, lies not on, 423:64
Bed-staff, in the twinkling of, 213:22
Bed-time, would 'twere, 233:41
Bee, bringest home the, 55:33
  calf, the goose, and, 415:66
  had stung it newly, 287:36
  how doth the little, 309:32
  in my bosom, like a, 149:22
  in one's bonnet, have, 428:35
  stings, honey is sweet but, 383:76
  sucks honey, where, 438:11
  sucks, where the, 270:1
Beech tree, under cover of, 305:21
  under yonder, 160:15
Beef, beauty will buy no, 360:27
  great eater of, 271:27
  ne'er made good broo, ill, 388:15
  of England, roast, 97:22
Beehive's hum, 205:16
Beer, a pot of, 84:21
  afay mit de Lager, 148:3
  and skittles, 127:31
  chronicle small, 260:15
  drinking cold small, 385:17
  felony to drink small, 237:33
  hops, pickerel, and, 432:19
  teetotaller, only a, 274:10
  they who drink, 129:22
  will think, 129:22
Bees are, where, 438:1
  in May, swarm of, 354:21
  make a hive for, 189:97
  make honey, so do, 306:10
  murmuring of innumerable, 294:23
  rob the Hybla, 230:18
  that have honey, 360:29
  yield no honey, old, 404:5
Beetle [insect], God to a black, 160:1
  shard-borne, 249:38
  thupon, 252:16
  wheels his droning flight, 112:5

winds his . . . horn, 71:36
Beetle [mallet] and the block, between,
  362:28
  with a three-man, 234:6
Beetles, scarce so gross as, 241:48
Beeves at pasture, ten thousand, 161:25
Befriend, be near me now and, 289:32
  thee, elves, 120:11
  thee, others will, 360:11
Beg I am ashamed, to, 336:26
  taught me first to, 255:42
Begetter, onlie, 263:28
Beggar barefoot, old, 443:38
  better die, 364:10
  can never be bankrupt, 349:10
  is enough, one, 404:29
  is woe, one, 404:30
  knows his dish, 359:67
  live a, 361:67
  may sing, 414:37
  old, 355:49
  on horseback, set, 410:20
  one day, scratch, 442:30
  pride is as loud, 407:67
  should be answer'd, how a, 255:42
  small invitation will serve, 411:64
  sue, 412:52
  that I am, 223:36
Beggar's brother, 422:19
  purse, a, 449:11
Beggared by fools, 89:36
Beggar-maid, loved the, 267:18
  shall be my queen, 293:44
Beggars cannot be choosers, 360:32
  commonly die, 406:27
  die, when, 229:24
  would ride, 387:44
Beggary, highway to, 431:69
  in the love, 213:34
  key of, 385:60
  worse than plain, 372:1
Begging bread, his seed, 326:30
Begin again, get up and, 38:12
  at the beginning, 115:18
  that other men, 229:19
Beginning and the end, 314:19
  everything must have, 369:54
  good, 351:51
  of the end, 290:3
  such end, such, 412:50
  wants but, 368:5
Beginnings, beware, 362:33

Begone, dull Care, 343:20
Begot, how nourished, how, 254:23
Begs his bread on Sundays, 353:48
Beguile the thing I am, 260:14
Beguiled, every day, 76:11
    soonest, 426:4
Begun has half done, who has, 125:36
    is half done, well, 435:43
    to fight, not yet, 134:7
Behave mannerly at table, 286:14
Behaviour, check to loose, 84:15
    surfeit of our own, 240:11
Behind him, whatever he put, 84:19
    it, because I'm, 95:36
    led his regiment from, 106:21
    less than 'arf o' that, 141:39
    me, Satan, get thee, 324:30
    they are far, 425:62
Behoving and unbehoving, 36:7
Being, a necessary, 302:1
    for it, I offered, 84:22
    lose this intellectual, 169:33
    move and have our, 337:64
    pleasing anxious, 112:17
    what she is, by, 65:28
Belfry, have bats in, 429:41
Belgium's capital, 50:11
Belial, in act more graceful, 169:32
    sons of, 90:1, 168:16
Belief is for it, all, 133:43
    within the prospect of, 247:25
Beliefs, forsaken, 20:3
Believe in belief, to, 300:5
    not all you hear, 367:50
    well and have well, 360:34
    what we desire, 434:27
Believed, by everyone, 305:20
    soon, 414:28
Believes all, he that, 377:66
    nothing, he that, 377:66
Believeth in him, whosoever, 337:42
Believing, seeing is, 410:5
Bell, as a sullen, 233:50
    clinks, so, 359:52
    cracked, 350:16
    merry as a marriage, 50:11
    silence that dreadful, 260:20
    sound as, 358:43
    struck, as the last, 299:24
    think upon thy passing, 437:54
    to bear away, 427:68
    twilight and evening, 298:6

    without, 372:26
Belle, 'tis vain to be a, 152:13
Bellies, egg will be in three, 356:30
    have no ears, hungry, 384:20
    hungry, 374:24
Bellman, fatal, 248:16
Bellows to mend, 201:27
    with a pair of, 441:65
Bellum inexpertis, dulce, 367:77
    para, 411:44
Bells call others to church, 360:35
    dim, with her, 100:7
    I hear, the, 313:17
    into a mist with, 38:18
    jangled, like sweet, 224:12
    of s:19
    ring, happy, 296:4
    ringeth to evensonge, 117:27
    they agree like, 425:61
    they now ring, 307:31
    through the silence beat, 99:29
Belly, eye is bigger than, 417:50
    fain have filled, 336:25
    full of gluttony, 349:12
    God send thee good ale, 287:30
    has a wolf in his, 351:77
    hates a long sermon, 414:38
    I mind my, 132:22
    if it were not for, 386:1
    in fair round, 216:17
    is full, when, 346:26
    is not filled, 414:39
    like a bream, 352:3
    neither fights nor flies well, full, 351:48
    spent under his, 435:56
    teaches all arts, 414:40
    thinks my throat cut, 400:25
    whose God is their, 339:51
    won't [trust], 360:3
Belly's full, provided that, 80:6
Belongs to them, when all men have what,
    436:2
Beloved from pole to pole, 69:33
    of his neighbours, 355:80
    sleep, giveth his, 328:5
    to be, 427:61
Below, Frenchmen sent, 188:9
Belted you, though I've, 141:40
Ben Battle was a soldier, 123:35
Ben Bolt, sweet Alice, 95:28
Bend while 'tis a twig, 360:38
Benedick the married man, 258:11

Benefits please while they are fresh, 360:36
Benison to fall, for a, 120:14
Bent, they are not our, 106:5
  to the top of my, 225:33
Berd been shake, hadde his, 63:31
Berkeley, Bishop, 53:28
  coxcombs vanquish, 34:15
Bermoothes, still-vex'd, 268:22
Bermudas ride, the remote, 158:7
Berries harsh and crude, 166:7
  moulded on one stem, two, 257:40
Berry halfway to her lips, 121:29
  made a better, 49:32
  sweeter than the, 103:29
Beseems him half so well, none, 22:3
Beside thyself, thou art, 338:3
Besides, how much, 58:2
Besom, after, 424:34
Bespectacled, girl who is, 182:2
Best, all is for the, 306:13
  and the last, 40:5
  better than any other person's, 118:1
  deem, 386:23
  fear not to touch, 202:11
  go to the next, 115:21
  hear and see and say, 382:18
  hope for, 384:7
  hope the, 367:57
  is behind, 415:44
  is best cheap, 360:37
  is like the worst, the, 141:44
  is worst, corruption of, 365:55
  is yet to be, 39:42
  learn and propagate, 20:4
  man in the country, 148:10
  men of few words are, 236:8
  not to seem, but to be, 16:11
  of, make, 398:3
  of us, bad in the, 121:27
  that action is, 128:5
  that has been known and said, 20:9
  that is known and thought, 20:4
  things are worst to come by, 415:53
  who does the, 322:5
  will be the welcomer, 391:52
  will save itself, 407:75
Bestial, what remains is, 260:23
Bestow it all of your worship, 259:31
Best-seller is the gilded tomb, 280:9
Bethel, O God of, 86:5
Bethlehem, little town of, 34:10
  O come ye to, 185:14

Betime, to business that we love we rise, 214:12
Betimes, he must rise, 377:47
  should get out, 352:12
  to be up, 271:35
Betray us in deepest consequence, 247:28
Betsey and I are out, 57:20
Better and better, getting, 73:30
  be, doth make men, 134:17
  be it, 360:13
  bettered expectation, 258:6
  book, can write a, 94:20
  carries it, 373:52
  for being a little bad, 253:25
  for worse, for, 341:48
  man than I am, 141:40
  or wiser behind, not left a, 110:2
  seldom comes, 410:8
  spared a better man, 233:45
  striving to, 240:15
  than she should be, no, 401:71
  than he knew, builded, 94:21
  the world with ablow, 159:27
  thing, far, far, 84:18
  things and approve them, I see, 186:7
  without, I'd been, 187:19
Betters, hold with your, 360:16
  who have served, 364:29
Betty Martin, my eye and, 356:4
Bewails himself, he that, 377:67
Beware by other men's harms, 391:51
  I bid you, 142:17
  when the great God lets loose a thinker, 94:13
Bewitch me, do more, 120:6
Bewitched with the rogue's company, 231:41
Bewrayeth thee, speech, 325:60
Bible, but litel on the, 63:32
Bibles laid open, 119:39
Biblia a-biblia, 144:1
Βιβλι´ον, υε´γα κακο´ν, 54:2
Bidden, do as you're, 367:47
Bidding, he that does, 378:14
Bider, better for, 423:77
Bier ye cannot fashion, better, 22:3
Bigamy, sir, is a crime, 176:2
Bigger they come, 99:24
Bilin' down his repoort, 107:28
Billboard lovely as a tree, 182:1
Billee, youngest he was little, 299:30
Billows, takes the ruffian, 234:19

Bills of charges, children are, 439:67
Billy and me, way for, 122:6
  heart to poke poor, 111:20
Bind, fast find, fast, 370:1
  them, heart and brow, 185:24
Biography is about chaps, 28:7
  no history, only, 94:8
βι΄ος βραχυ΄ς, δ, 121:23
Birch at Yule even, bare as,360:5
Birchen twigs break no ribs, 362:40
Bird, a rare, 135:28
  clung to, spray the, 38:10
  each fond endearment tries, 108:22
  early, 416:36
  immortal, 137:20
  un hand, a, 349:13
  in the sight of any, 328:15
  is on the Wing, 97:28
  it is an ill, 390:29
  like a singing, 206:7
  likes its own nest, 368:22
  loves to hear himself, 367:80
  might haply inhabit, 272:19
  of dawning, 220:12
  of March, sea-blue, 296:2
  of night, amorous, 173:28
  of the air, 330:27
  of the winderness, 122:4
  of Time has but a little way to fly, 97:28
  on the wing, like a, 32:3
  that shunn'st the noise of folly, 164:16
  thou never wert, 276:4
  to scare, 430:16
  trills, the Attic, 174:8
Bird's throat, the sweet, 216:4
Birdie say, does little, 294:5
Birds, another catches, 404:28
  begin to lay, 389:46
  begin to search, 389:46
  charm of earliest, 171:33
  choirs of singing, 42:17
  do sing, pretty, 182:5
  do sing, when, 218:11
  fine feathers make fine, 370:18
  frightened the, 344:11
  how can ye chant, 46:12
  i' the cage, like, 242:9
  in last year's nest, 424:14
  in the high Hall-garden, 296:12
  in their little nests agree, 309:31
  kill two, 429:55
  nest of singing, 132:4

  of feath, 361
  of cam sit roou, 163:22
  of th air, all, 404:19
  outside despair to get in, 176:14
  sang, late the sweet, 264:13
  sang sweet, 311:33
  sing, and no, 137:36
  sing madrigals, 157:25
  sit courin, 291:19
  so happy as we, no, 147:17
  that sing and won't sing, 396:7
  time of the singing of, 331:40
  to sing, suffers little, 270:11
  very unlikely, 406:26
  with chaff, catch old, 441:64
Bird-song at morning, 287:26
Birkenhead drill, to the, 141:46
Birnam wood to high Dunsinane hill,
    250:16
Birth, day of one's, 330:17
  have smiled, on my, 291:23
  he himself is subject to his, 221:34
  is but a sleep, our, 319:35
  is much, 363:42
  on his humble, 113:19
  repeats the story of her, 15:9
  revolts from true, 267:31
Birthright, selleth his, 323:31
Biscuit, as the remainder, 216:13
Bishop, and abbot, and prior, 24:4
  devil is a busy, 416:20
  no king, no, 129:25
Bisier than he was, he semed, 63:29
Bisy a man as he, no-wher so, 63:29
Bit [*piece*] and the buffet, take, 412:77
  in the morning, a, 349:14
Bit [*bite*] me, though he had, 242:6
  the man, went mad and, 108:9
Bitch bark, go out, if, 386:21
Bite, bark is worse than, 283:58
  dead men don't, 366:8
  delight to bark and, 309:29
  dogs bark before, 367:63
  'em, smaller fleas to, 288:12
  if you cannot, 387:50
  man recover'd of the, 108:10
  my thumb at you, 266:4
  never, 367:64
  of the brae, cannot, 434:14
  some other of my generals, 104:3
  upon their backs to, 81:21
Biters, barkers are no, 373:69

Bites him to the bone, 97:21
  of a cherry, two, 430:3
Biteth like a serpent, 329:53
Biting and scratching, 363:44
  is immortal, his, 215:22
Bitten, twice shy, once, 404:24
Bitter a thing uus, how, 17;9
  as coloquintida, 260:12
  to endure, 414:36
Bitterness, knoweth his own, 328:31
Black and proud, 369:67
  as he is painted, not so, 416:24
  as the devil, 291:17
  as the Pit, 118:21
  bean hath its, 368:21
  black's not so, 56:8
  creeping through the, 148:15
  dyer can make it, 425:49
  I am, 30:3
  [is] lusty, 427:59
  man is a jewel, 349:16
  man keep thy wife, from, 427:59
  men fought, 153:29
  one is as good as the white, 433:43
  smith and his penny, 422:22
  suits of solemn, 220:17
  to red began to turn, 49:23
  will take no other hue, 363:46
Blackamoor white, wash, 431:45
Blackamoor's hand, in, 396:3
Blackberries, plentiful as, 232:12
Blackbird 'tis to whistle, to a, 48:3
  what a boy you are, 35:17
Blackcap's song was very sweet, 67:23
Blackfriar's Bridge, at, 81:30
Blackguards, we aren't no, 141:36
Blacks do not make a white, two, 432:23
Bladder, like a, 232:15
Blade, bloody blameful, 258:3
  round the sickly, 77:24
  trenchant, 48:15
Blades, between two, 237:27
Blame, alike reserved to, 198:2
  fame is seldom to, 365:46
  in part she is to, 176:6
  is she, in part to, 186:4
  you'll never bear, 367:47
Blames would buy, he that, 377:69
Bland, childlike and, 116:22
  gentle, complying and, 110:2
Blank, creation's, 104:12
  my lord, a, 272:4

presented with a universal, 170:17
Blanket, under, 433:43
  wrong side of, 363:55
Blasphemy, in the solder is flat, 252:12
Blast, bleak blows the, 56:5
  in the cauld, 47:34
  striding the, 248:1
Blastments, contagious, 221:35
Blate cat, 349:18
Blaze think to burst out into sudden, 166:16
Blazon, this eternal, 222:12
Bleat the one at the other, 273:34
  bleats articulate monotony, 285:19
Bleed awhile, lie down and, 342:11
  for me, heart, 72:10
  I'll not see him, 384:37
Blent in one red burial, 50:16
Bless himself with, penny to, 375:69
  it and approve it, 254:24
  me, except thou, 323:34
  relaxes, 30:14
  thee and keep thee, 324:8
Blessed are the meek, 33:35
  are the peacemakers, 33:37
  are the ure in heart, 33:36
  [children call her], 330:4
  do above, what, 307:25
  is the man, 199:27
  them unaware, I, 69:32
  to give, more, 337:67
Blessedness, in single, 256:20
Blesseth him that gives, 255:33
Blessing, God will give, 433:53
  had most need of, 248:19
  sweet was its, 68:9
  thou dost ask me, 242:9
Blessings are not valued, 363:47
  flow from whom, 138:14, 188:9
  On the falling out, 294:8
  on your frosty pow, 45:42
Blest, always to be, 195:29
  it is twice, 255:33
Blind eat many a fly, 415:58
  enough, he is, 376:13
  in the country of, 389:52
  in their own cause, 399:55
  lead the blind, 324:27
  man cannot judge colours, 349:19
  man will not thank you, 349:20
  man's holiday, 363:48
  none so, 402:39
  old man of Scio's rocky isle, 51:33

staring and stark, 424:30
the halt and the, 159:20, 336:20
to Him, olives they were not, 145:27
with dust and smoke, 183:25
Blindly, never lov'd sae, 46:17
Blindworm could see, [if], 386:12
Blink, tint the blythe, 78:10
Bliss and woe, mingle human, 211:36
it excels all other, 92:14
looks at his own, 309:24
source of all my, 109:32
too avid of earth's, 309:25
was it, 319:23
way to, 423:64
where ignorance is, 111:34
winged hours of, 55:19
Blithesome and cumberless, 122:4
Block, beetle and, 362:28
book that is shut is, 349:24
chip of the old, 350:6
in the rough-hewn, 188:3
itself, the old, 43:35
you insensible, 24:2
Blockhead, bookful, 193:20
no man but a, 133:37
Blocks, you stones, you, 228:4
Blood and iron, 29:23
be shed, by man shall his, 323:26
be the price of admiralty, 140:13
clean from my hand, wash, 249:23
felt in the, 316:11
for his country, good enough to shed,
205:25
fountain fill'd with, 76:17
freeze thy young, 222:12
hey-day in the, 226:3
I smell the, 241:39
in him, so much, 251:28
inhabits our frail, 272:18
is bold blood, old, 310:4
is fet from fathers of warproof, 236:6
is strong, still the, 343:28
is tame, it's humble, 226:3
is thicker than water, 363:49
is very snow-broth, 252:2
is warm within, whose, 253:28
more stirs, 231:37
must have its course, young, 139:28
out of a stone, get, 441:67
pure and eloquent, 86:12
reigns, red, 273:40
simple faith than Norman, 292:16

smell of, 442:16
stepp'd in so far, in, 250:10
streams in the firmament, 157:18
summon up the, 236:5
till he sees his own, 422:8
to stir men's, 230:6
toil, tears, and sweat, 66:2
weltering in his, 91:24
whoso sheddeth man's, 323:26
will have blood, 363:60
with cold, thicks man's, 69:25
you are come of a, 441:58
Blood's a rover, 126:10
Bloody but unbowed, head, 119:22
likely, not, 275:23
man is that, what, 247:20
Bloom, blight in its, 291:18
is shed, its, 46:10
old muck-hills will, 404:13
on a woman, sort of, 25:30
sae fresh and fair, 46:12
sight of vernal, 170:17
sweet of earliest, 71:39
Blooms each thing, 182:5
Blossom, beauty is but, 360:24
bud bursting into, 54:3
by blossom, 290:2
in purple and red, 296:19
in the spring, 414:27
under the, 270:1
with pleasure, 38:10
Blossoms, birds, and bowers, 120:4
but never bears, 433:54
down through the, 184:12
straying, mid, 71:21
Blot, art to, 198:12
creation's, 104:12
scratching a, 106:18
the fouler the, 417:57
Blotted a thousand, would he had, 134:20
it out for ever, 285:25
out a line, never, 134:20
Blow [*puff*] at once, sup, and, 402:9
first, 363:51
kindly here, 204:4
on whom I please, to, 216:14
wind! come, wrack! 251:39
Blow [*knock*], but a word and a, 42:11
first, 417:66, 417:67
liberty's in every, 47:24
might be the be-all, 247:40
remember thy swashing, 266:5

Blowing, nor'-wester's, 191:21
Blown with reckless violence, 252:18
Blows [*puffs*] a man up, it, 232:15
nobody good, 390:32
the wind to-day, 287:29
Blows [*knocks*] [are] unkind, 441:46
Blue above and the blue below, 200:17
and better blue, 425:53
Beard's domestic chaplain, 82:12
darkly deeply beautifully, 282:12
grappling in the central, 293:34
Hobbs hints, 38:15
Presbyterian true, 48:11
ran the flash across, 40:16
till all look, 100:11
were her eyes, 149:32
will never stain, true, 431:71
Blue-eyed, beautiful, my, 54:7
Blunder free us, frae mony a, 45:23
it is a, 101:21
Blundered, some one had, 295:26
Blunders, one of Nature's, 74:7
Blush, beautiful as woman's, 144:11
put many to, 386:14
to find it fame, 198:15
unseen, born to, 112:13
would it bring a, 84:20
Blushed, saw its God, and, 78:2
Blushes, beat away those, 259:34
Blushing is virtue's colour, 363:53
Blut und Eisen, 29:23
Bo to a goose, say, 375:49
Boast, small roast, great, 373:70
Boaster and a liar, 349:22
Boasteth, when he is gone, 329:47
Boastings as the Gentiles use, 141:26
Boat and went to sea, took, 299:29
beautiful pea-green, 147:15
is on the shore, my, 52:9
speed, bonny, 32:3
Boatman, do not tarry, 55:22
Boats, messing about in, 111:24
to burn one's, 428:3
Bodice, aptly lac'd, 200:8
Bodie forme doth take, 283:33
Bodies by, bore dead, 231:35
hale souls out of, 258:17
move slowly, great, 373:71
of unburied men, 310:10
unsound, 433:50
Bodkin, with a bare, 224:4
Body and in soul, in, 209:23

and soul, overthrow of, 47:42
Charlotte, having seen his, 299:27
demd, damp, moist, 83:28
fill'd and vacant mind, 236:13
give me a healthy, 345:21
he is through your, 31:33
hit a body, gin a, 160:2
I keep under my, 338:25
I thee worship, with my, 341:50
is sooner dressed, 415:59
is the worse, all, 437:39
joint and motive of her, 271:22
little, 352:24
meet a body, gin a, 43:35, 160:2
[needs] many [things], 422:77
on a worthless, 370:14
pent, here in the, 177:16
perfect little, 33:18
sound mind in a sound, 135:35
Thersites', 219:38
thought, her, 86:12
to be kicked, no, 301:34
to that pleasant country's earth, gave his,
244:4
to the deep, commit, 341:56
to the ground, commit, 341:55
Body's vest aside, casting, 158:15
Bog, cannot out of her, 418:14
or steep, o'er, 170:12
profound as that Serbonian, 170:2
to an admiring, 84:24
Boil [an egg], the vulgar, 198:14
like a pot, maketh the deep to, 326:12
Boils, watched pot never, 354:29
Bois, n'irons plus aux, 23:34
Bokes, clad in blak or reed, 63:27
Bold and forth on, 270:3
bad man, a, 283:26
be not too, 283:20, 360:16
every where Be, 283:20
man, he was, 382:24
Boldest held his breath, 55:26
Boldness, again boldness, 79:23
Bolt is soon shot, fool's, 351:39
Bombast, serious swelling into, 92:2
Bombastes, must meet, 203:30
Bombazine would have shown, 103:23
Bombs bursting in air, 138:17
Bond, let him look to his, 254:18
'tis not in the, 255:36
word is as good as, 356:35
Bondman, check'd like a, 230:16

Bondman's key, in a, 254:6
Bone, as curs mouth, a, 65:35
  beat him with, 350:24
  dry as, 357:80
  in one's leg, have, 428:36
  of my bones, 323:17
  often falls a good, 389:70
  the nearer, 421:44
  tongue breaks, 423:50
Bone, what is bred in, 435:54
Bones are coral made, 269:26
  bed full of, 357:49
  buys many, 377:76
  curst be he that moves my, 266:2
  fair words break no, 369:73
  for his honour'd, 163:28
  full of dead men's, 325:48
  interred with their, 229:36
  live, can these, 332:17
  mock'd the dead, 245:18
  over the stones, rattle his, 184:3
  sit in my, 281:21
  sleep upon, 395:41
  stones may break, 412:41
  that lay scatter'd by, 245:18
  together fly, rattling, 90:16
  tongs and the, 257:42
  words break no, 374:26
  would be at rest, 436:26
Bonfire, everlasting, 249:24
Bon-mots from their places, plucking,
    179:20
  not enough, 128:6
Bonnet, bee in one's, 428:35
  in antique ruff and, 131:19
Bonnets, all the Blue, 211:41
Bonnie bay at morning, 77:30
  blithe as she's, 291:18
Bononcini, compar'd to, 49:34
Bonum, nil nisi, 366:7
Booby for another, give her, 103:27
Boojum, the Snark was a, 60:3
Book, a book's a, 49:39
  about, not throw this, 27:26
  all the world knows me in my, 176:15
  another damned, thick, square, 107:35
  as good almost kill a man as kill a good,
    175:28
  beware of the man of one, 362:39
  can write a better, 94:20
  dainties that are bred in, 246:7
  doth share the glory, 266:11

frowst with a, 142:19
genius I had when I wrote, 289:24
go, little, 286:20
great, great evil, 54:2
he can read, give a man, 301:21
he who destroys a good, 175:28
I can read anything which I call, 144:1
I directe to thee, 63:17
I never read a, 281:24
I'll drown my, 269:44
in cloistre, upon a, 63:25
is the best of friends, good, 303:21
is the precious life-blood, good, 175:29
like author, like, 395:72
medley of my, 135:25
moral or an immoral, 314:1
Nature was his, 30:18
no such thing as a moral, 314:1
of knowledge fair, 170:17
of Nature, the, 123:41
of secrecy, nature's, 213:35
of songs and sonnets, 256:6
of Verse, 97:30
of Verses, 97:31
quarrel by the, 218:13
take a leaf out of one's, 430:26
take down this, 321:34
that is not a year old, never read any,
    94:19
that is shut, 349:24
that mine adversary had written, 326:5
to make one, 133:32
to read, wants a, 65:26
wants to read a, 65:26
what is the use of, 58:3
where men may read strange matters,
    247:36
where's the, 65:38
with a religious, 320:22
word for word without, 271:26
Booke, a jollie goode, 314:22
  and a shadie nooke, 314:22
  go, little, 15:4
Bookful blockhead, 193:20
Books, all saws of, 222:20
  and pictures, muddled with, 140:6
  are good enough, 28:35
  are not seldom talismans and spells, 76:5
  are to be tasted, some, 22:16
  are well written, 314:1
  at the British Museum, 49:30
  authority from others', 246:1

cannot always please, 77:26
deep vers'd in, 174:10
devil's, 364:2
else appear so mean, all, 41:32
for good manners, 218:13
[I love] old, 110:7
I'll burn my, 157:19
in a person's bad, 427:63
in the running brooks, 215:37
knowing I loved, 268:21
lard their lean, 47:38
my only, 178:13
next o'er his, 194:15
of making many, 331:36
quit your, 316:8
reading valueless, 207:30
skim the cream of others', 179:20
spectacles of, 92:1
that you may carry to the fire, 134:4
[that you may] hold readily in your hand,
   134:4
the arts, the academes, 246:9
through, do you read, 133:29
were read, his, 27:33
which are no books, 144:1
years know more than, 441:53
you need, all the, 41:32
Books' clothing, things in, 144:2
Boot harmeth, 438:28
is on the other leg, 415:60
saddle, to horse, 37:24
Boots—boots—boots—boots, 142:4
displace pair of, 203:30
heart is in his, 383:62
ran out at the heels of, 100:10
Bo-peep, as if they started at, 120:10
Border, bound for the, 211:41
off a sunny, 161:18
she gaed o'er the, 46:19
through all the wide, 210:6
Bore, every hero becomes a, 94:16
Borealis race, like the, 46:10
Boreas, cease, rude, 285:28
Bores and *Bored*, two mighty tribes, 53:32
of the dreariest hue, 114:9
Born, as soon as a man is, 538:40
better never been, 180:10
better to be lowly, 238:12
crying, we are, 434:11
for you alone was, 204:12
he that is once, 379:73
I wept when I was, 385:43

in a cellar, 100:9
in a good hour, 376:14
natural to die as to be, 22:9
never was, 287:32
on the wrong side, 363:55
out of my due time, 180:8
under that I was, 258:16
when wit was scant, 442:27
with a silver spoon, 427:62
would thou hadst ne'er been, 262:4
yesterday, not, 385:42
Borogoves, mimsy were the, 58:17
Borrioboola-Gha, natives of, 84:10
Borrow another, thou mayest, 375:39
better buy than, 361:64
men who, 143:38
nor flatter, neither, 377:43
some [money] try to, 388:4
Borrowed garments, 363:56
Borrower nor a lender be, neither, 221:39
Borrowing dulls the edge of husbandry,
   221:39
only lingers it, 234:7
Borrows must pay, he that, 377:71
Bosom bare, to earth's, 299:35
cleanse the stuff'd, 251:32
fly, let me to Thy, 311:23
he's in Arthur's, 236:1
leaning across the, 33:17
lies, that in my, 293:41
of his Father, the, 113:21
wring his, 108:11
Bosoms, men's business and, 22:6
Bossuet, no heresy can excite the horror of,
   153:24
Boston, solid men of, 179:30
they ask, in, 303:31
this is good old, 31:31
Bo'sum tight, and a, 104:18
Botanize, peep and, 317:24
Both perhaps, or neither, 312:10
together do best, 363:57
Bother it, I may occasionally say, 105:26
Bottle, a little for the, 82:2
of salvation, 202:19
on the chimney-piece, 83:40
Bottom, better spare at brim than at, 362:16
bless thee! 257:38
goes to, 389:59
is bare, when, 392:21
not all in one, 433:60
remaining at the, 68:13

naughty, 400:35
of the old Brigade, 310:1, 310:2
tell the other, 286:15
the liquor for, 133:45
will be boys, 363:59
will be men, 363:60
Bracelet lasts forever, diamond, 151:22
Braces, damn, 30:14
Bracken, lift him from, 22:3
Bradford, there goes John, 32:8
Brae, cannot bite of, 434:14
  stey, 410:21
Braes, run about the, 45:29
Brag is a good dog, 363:61
Brain attic, his little, 87:31
  children of an idle, 266:14
  coinage of your, 226:6
  feared it might injure, 58:7
  glean'd my teeming, 137:34
  harmful to the, 129:24
  heat-oppressed, 248:13
  him with his lady's fan, 232:2
  madness in the, 70:6
  perplexes, dull, 136:17
  possess a poet's, 88:11
  sows not corn, if, 386:15
  warder of the, 248:8
  which is as dry, 216:13
  written troubles of, 251:32
Brains at all, with no, 119:34
  blow out your, 141:41
  cudgel thy, 227:28
  enough to make a fool of himself, 285:34
  mix them with my, 185:22
  out, dash'd the, 248:6
  quicker than their, 88:17
  rheumatic, 104:15
  rock his, 234:19
  steal away their, 261:24
  were out, when the, 250:4
Brake, he staid not for, 210:8
Branch, cut is the, 157:20
  highest, 419:51
  loves, 380:15
Branches, like the olive, 328:7
  ne'er remember, 137:35
Brandy, hero must drink, 133:45
  some are fou o', 44:10
Brass, become as sounding, 338:29
  impregnable, were, 244:1
  more lasting than, 125:32
  vessel, clear of, 416:37

where he carried his, 28:3
Brass-bound Man, rolled, 143:23
Bravado, met the sun's, 26:2
Brave and strong, we will be, 24:12
  fears of the, 130:14
  fortune favours, 371:57
  home of the, 138:17
  how sleep the, 71:33
  in her shape, 161:20
  man struggling, a, 193:36
  men, fair women and, 50:11
  none but the, 90:20
  toll for the, 75:24
  translunary things, 88:10
  what's noble, what's, 214:18
Bravery on, with all her, 174:18
Braw, that was, 42:2
Bray if all men say that thou art an ass,
    385:68
  loves to hear himself, 368:20
Brazen-Nose College, in, 442:28
Brazil, he twirled a button, 84:23
Breach, imminent deadly, 260:3
  once more unto, 236:5
  than the observance, more honour'd in
    the, 222:4
Bread, a Loaf of, 97:30, 97:31
  alone, not live by, 333:34
  and butter are glad to eat, 426:2
  and butter, cutting, 299:27
  and butter, smell of, 52:11
  and cheese and kisses, 360:1
  and fingers, cuts, 422:5
  and games, 135:34
  and work for all, 277:31
  at home, dry, 367:76
  better than no, 374:11
  bit of butter to, 163:17
  break thy, 427:59
  costs dear, another's, 357:62
  cramm'd with distressful, 236:13
  eaten in secret, 328:23
  give us this day our daily, 333:48
  half-pennyworth of, 232:19
  if his son ask, 324:1
  is buttered on both sides, 383:60
  is buttered, on which side, 429:58
  is the staff of life, 363:62
  lay it thick on, 426:1
  looked to government for, 43:34
  no butter will stick to, 401:72

Bridesmaid, happy, 292:9
Bridge, make a golden, 371:43
  never cross, 401:55
Bridges were made for wise men to walk
  over, 363:63
Bridle-reins a shake, gae, 47:25
Brief, I struggle to be, 126:1
  or be less, 309:26
Brier-patch, bred en bawn in, 116:17
Briers, how full of, 215:34
Brig, mate of the *Nancy*, 104:18
Brigade, boys of the old, 310:1, 310:2
Bright and beautiful, things, 17:18
  and fierce and fickle, 294:16
  both lovely and, 211:34
  bright as day, 321:38
  he is only, 376:24
  things come to confusion, 256:23
  young lady named, 344:14
Brightest and best, 118:7
Brightness, all her original, 168:21
  falls from the air, 182:6
Brignal banks are wild, 211:30
Brillig, 'twas, 58:17
Brim, better spare at, 362:16
  bubbles winking at, 136:15
Brimming, and bright, and large, 19:23
Brimstone bed, from his, 70:14, 282:9
Bring, what it will, 424:5
Bristol City, sailors of, 299:29
Britain a fit country, make, 149:19
  first, at Heaven's command, 300:19
  is a world by itself, 219:31
  is going to make war, 28:14
Britain's crown, from, 88:7
Britannia needs no bulwarks, 55:24
  rule the waves, 300:19
Britannos, divisos orbe, 305:22
Brither, lo'ed him like a, 46:8
British and Armoric knights, 168:20
  ground, feet on, 310:4
  man, blood of a, 241:39
  manhood, piece of, 57:22
Britons never will be slaves, 300:19
  wholly sundered from all the world,
  305:22
Broached, be bravely, 258:3
Broadcloth without, 76:8
Broken and a contrite heart, 327:40
  at last, [pitcher] is, 421:58
  made to be, 407:71
Broken-hearted, half, 49:36

ne'er been, 46:17
Broker, needs no, 350:17
Broo, ne'er made good, 388:15
Brooches, I will make you, 287:26
Brook along, my forest, 69:37
  and river meet, where, 150:2
  fast by a, 26:16
  is deep, where the, 237:30
  like of a hidden, 69:34
  that turns a mill, 205:16
Brooks, after the water, 327:34
  I sing of, 120:4
  too broad for leaping, 126:16
Broom, busk of, 394:5
  is silver and gold, under, 433:44
  sweeps clean, new, 353:58
Broth hot again, cold, 364:38
  too many cooks spoil, 431:57
Brother, closer than, 329:43
  followed brother, 320:15
  hail and farewell, 61:18
  I grew so like my, 147:28
  man, gently scan, 44:21
  near the throne, no, 198:2
  though he were my, 382:7
  turns, still to my, 108:2
Brother's keeper, am I my, 323:22
Brotherhood, crown thy good with, 26:4
  love the, 340:4
Brotherly love continue, 339:68
Brothers and their murder'd man, two,
  136:9
  be for a' that, 47:33
  too, all the, 272:5
  we band of, 237:19
Brow, grace was seated on this, 226:2
  in that victorious, 19:16
  is beld, now your, 45:42
  is wet, his, 149:34
  lifted slowly her white, 102:2
  on thine azure, 51:30
  pure unclouded, 58:16
  was brent, bonnie, 45:42
Brown [is] trusty, 427:59
  man break thy bread, with, 427:59
Browning, a prose, 314:5
  Since Chaucer was alive, 144:14
  some "Pomegranate," from, 35:30
Brows, gathering her, 46:5
Bruce has aften led, 46:22
Brugh, round the moon, 436:24
Bruise and bless, made to, 161:18

for an inward, 231:36
Bruit, little fruit, much, 400:16
Brunck, learn'd professor, 199:30
Brush, tarred with the same, 356:8
  work with so fine, 21:32
Brushers of noblemen's clothes, 365:66
Brushes of comet's hair, 140:17
Brute or an angel, 354:15
Brute, et tu, 53:43
Brutes men, had made, 188:4
  without you, we had been, 186:2
Brutus is an honourable man, 229:37
  once, there was a, 228:13
  Tarquin and Caesar each had his, 119:31
  the fault, dear, 228:11
  you too, 53:43
Bubble, man is, 398:8
  mostly froth and, 110:15
Bubbles, earth has, 247:26
  winking, beaded, 136:15
Buck in spring, like a, 140:20
Bucket, as for the, 344:13
  old oaken, 315:36
  which hung in the well, 315:36
Buckhurst choose, I would, 204:9
Buckingham, bring their husbands to,
    440:33
  high-reaching, 245:20
  so much for, 66:10
Buckram men grown out of two, eleven,
    232:10
  suits, rogues in, 232:9
Bud again, be a, 136:12
  and bloom forth brings, 288:4
  bursting, young, 54:3
  nip him in the, 204:7
Buds of May, darling, 263:32
  summer's velvet, 235:43
Buffer lies low, poor, 313:27
Buffet, take the bit and, 412:77
Buffoon, statesman and, 89:34
Buffs, private of the, 88:7
Bug in a rug, snug as, 101:30
Bugle, blow, 294:11
  bring the good old, 320:19
Bugles, blow out, you, 34:7
  sang truce, our, 55:29
Bugloss, the blue, 77:24
Build me straight, 150:12
  not boast, lives to, 208:12
  the house, except the Lord, 328:4
  up, easier to pull down than, 391:40

Builded better than he knew, 94:21
Building and marrying, 363:65
  erected, first, 389:48
  high, 352:6
  is a sweet impoverishing, 363:66
  principal beauty in, 102:12
Built in such a logical way, 122:15
Bull by the horns, take, 430:30
  curl'd Assyrian, 296:10
  in a china shop, 395:65
  like a red rag to, 395:70
Bullet, damn' tough, 141:46
  has its billet, 314:20
  or by shot, by, 344:5
  through his heart, 298:17
Bullets of the brain, paper, 258:20
Bullocks, how a good yoke of, 234:22
  whose talk is of, 340:24
Bully is always a coward, 349:30
  like a tall, 197:33
Bulrush, knot in, 402:36
Bulwark, the floating, 29:24
Bulwarks, Britannia needs no, 55:24
Bun, bite of a, 349:5
Bung-hole, stopping a, 227:35
Buoy, her cock a, 241:48
Burden and heat of the day, 325:42
  carry his own, 394:37
  cunning is no, 365:72
  it is a sad, 390:18
  the White Man's, 140:22
  thine, ever to, 276:8
  too much praise is, 431:61
  upon the Lord, cast, 141:34
  weight of another's, 402:38
Burdens, greatest, 418:32
  grow heavy, light, 395:61
  long borne, 395:61
Burglar, enterprising, 105:34
  I've restored, many a, 105:22
Burglars vanished silently, 111:23
Burglary, flat, 259:38
Burial blent, in one red, 50:16
Buried brother John, 147:29
  desire straight to be, 401:74
  him, when they, 294:3
  in so sweet a place, 277:29
  there will I be, 324:27
Burn [*fire*], better to marry than, 338:23
  shall yet terrific, 55:25
  us when near, will, 417:64
Burn [*stream*], girl that fords, 39:25

Burned on the water, 214:2
Burning bright, tiger, 30:5
Burns and Moore, through, 122:10
Burns most, fire that is closest kept, 370:21
  most shines most, he that, 377:74
  warms too near that, 382:23
Burnt child dreads the fire, 415:63
Burrs, hang together like, 425:64
Burthen of his song, this, 29:15
Bury Caesar, not to praise, 229:36
  them, in expectation to, 102:11
  this man there, 39:31
Bus but a tram, not a, 116:12
  can it be a Motor, 107:36
  descending from a, 60:4
Buses runnin', ain't no, 141:43
Bush, a bad, 349:1
  an officer, fear each, 238:10
  feareth every, 378:23
  good wine needs no, 373:62
  one beats, 404:28
  supposed a bear, how easy is a, 257:47
  to beat about, 427:70
  underneath the barren, 296:2
  worth two in the, 349:13
Busiest men have the most leisure, 415:64
Business but his own, everyone's, 418:4
  could not make dull, 18:14
  dinner lubricates, 212:8
  everybody's, 369:51
  home to men's, 22:6
  importunity of, 144:8
  in great waters, do, 327:59
  is business, 363:67
  no feeling of his, 227:29
  of the day, 91:30
  soul of, 407:81
  [take], some to, 197:24
  that we love, to, 214:12
  without, 440:22
Busiris and his Memphian chivalry, 168:14
Busk ye, busk ye, 115:20
Bust, animated, 112:11
Buster, had another awful, 188:9
Bustle, at noonday in the, 41:21
Busy, curious, thirsty fly, 185:20
  he that is, 379:63
  to be too, 427:66
  who more, 439:52
Busyness, extreme, 286:1

Butch for be, this is too, 143:32
Butcher, better pay, 362:8
  paints, want to know, 40:14
Butchers, gentle with these, 229:33
Butt end, knocks you down with, 110:11
  here is my, 262:15
Butter and eggs, 54:9
  got good store of, 426:1
  is gold in the morning, 363:68
  is mad twice a year, 363:69
  little bit of, 163:17
  she brought forth, 324:21
  soft as, 358:38
  that the cow yields, not all, 392:7
  will stick, no, 401:72
  would not melt in one's mouth, as if, 429:68
Butter's spread too thick, 59:25
Buttered on both sides, 383:60
Butterflies, laugh at gilded, 242:9
Butterfly, breaks a, 198:4
  I'd be a, 26:6
  musket to kill, 412:76
Button, he twirled a, 84:23
  with the little, 100:10
Button'd down before, all, 113:36
Buttons be disclosed, before, 221:35
Buy and sell so, have you, 274:2
  and sell, to, 428:7
  at a fair, 363:70
  Codham, I'll, 299:33
  good cheap, they, 425:63
  he that blames would, 377:69
  than borrow, better, 361:64
  what the Vintners, 99:18
  what would you, 27:22
Buyer beware, let, 364:10
  it is naught, saith, 329:47
  needs a hundred eyes, 415:65
Buys good ale, he that, 377:76
  nothing else, 377:76
Buzzing in my ears, is he, 40:2
By and by, street of, 363:72
  and by, two anons and, 432:12
Bygones be bygones, let, 394:36
By-path meadows, no more, 285:30
Byre, she'll run to, 363:64
Byron was an Englishman, 177:24
Byron's fault, perhaps it was, 177:24
Byword among all people, 325:43

C

books, [sent] to, 302:9
Cambuscan bold, story of, 164:22
Cambyses' vein, in King, 232:16
Came, I saw, I conquered, I, 53:42
Camel, easier for a, 325:39
  going to seek horns, 415:68
  swallow a, 325:47
Camel's back, breaks, 420:1
Camelot, many-tower'd, 292:10
Came-over-with-the-Conqueror type of
    mind, 309:27
Cameron, come hither, Evan, 22:2
Camilla scours the plain, 192:16
Camp to camp, from, 236:10
Campaspe play'd, Cupid and, 152:9
Can [be able] and you can't, you, 87:20
  no more, I, 138:10
  youth replies, I, 95:25
Can [vessel], come fill up my, 211:37
  pass me the, 126:18
Canadian hills, cold on, 145:25
Canakin clink, let me, 260:19
Candid where we can, be, 195:26
Candle and candlestick away, throw,
    404:17
  as a white, 55:16
  at both ends, burn, 428:4
  burns at both ends, 162:9
  devil holds, 390:31
  fit to hold, 49:34, 403:45
  game is not worth, 418:19
  hold their farthing, 322:9
  light such a, 146:2
  out, out brief, 251:37
  throws his beams, how far, 256:3
  to my shames, hold, 254:16
  to the devil, hold, 429:50
  two old chairs and half a, 147:18
Candle-ends, called him, 59:37
Candle-light, by yellow, 286:13
  choose neither a woman nor linen by,
    364:28
  colours seen by, 36:6
  fleet and, 342:8
Candlemas day be fair, if, 385:71
  day is come, when, 436:7
  day it be shower, if on, 385:71
  Day, on, 404:17
Candles are all out, their, 248:10
Candlestick, upon the holy, 340:23
Candlestick-maker much acquaints, 40:14
Cane, conduct of a clouded, 193:34

Canker galls the infants, 221:35
Cankers of a calm world, 233:38
Cannibals that each other eat, 260:5
Cannon in front of them, 295:28
  to right of them, 295:28
Cannon's mouth, even in, 216:17
  opening roar, 50:13
Canopy of light and blue, 312:6
  rich embroider'd, 238:7
Cant, clear your mind of, 133:49
Cantie wi' mair, 47:28
Cantons, write loyal, 271:33
Cants which are canted, 285:24
Canvas, splash at a ten-league, 140:17
Cap by night, a, 107:43
  fits, wear it, if, 386:16
Capa que cubre todos, 61:24
Capacity can soar to, highest that human,
    175:32
Caparisons don't become a young woman,
    277:38
  no, 277:38
Capax imperii nisi imperasset, 290:10
Cape, round the, 37:34
  St. Vincent to the North-west, 38:6
  Turk, not yet doubled, 161:31
Capers, lovers run into strange, 216:3
Capitol betrayed the, 186:3
Capon, if thou hast not, 387:40
  lined, with good, 216:17
Captain, becomes his captain's, 214:7
  bold, cook and a, 104:18
  can, more than his, 214:17
  lies, on the deck, 313:17
  my Captain, O, 313:17
  of the Gate, 154:2
  or Colonel, 167:25
Captains and the Kings depart, 140:25
  by the hundred, 104:16
  thunder of the, 326:9
Car, drive the rapid, 79:26
Caravan, put up your, 121:28
  starts for the Dawn of Nothing, 98:9
  the innumerable, 41:26
Caravanserai, batter'd, 97:34
Carcase is, wheresoever, 325:52
Carcasses of unburied men, 219:26
Card, speak by the, 227:31
Cardinal's chair, sat on, 24:4
Cards are the devil's books, 364:2
  shuffle the, 61:23
  when you have told, 437:65

without a knave, no, 425:44
Care, a fig for, 120:16
　and skill require, 435:45
　at the horseman's back, 54:4
　begone, dull, 343:20
　beyond to-day, no, 111:33
　bringers of worry and, 111:33
　for nobody, I, 29:15
　golden, 235:30
　Hippoclides does not, 121:22
　is no cure, 364:3
　is over, then the, 292:3
　keeps his watch, 267:32
　killed a cat, 364:4
　little goods, little, 396:9
　much coin, much, 400:17
　neither cauld nor, 181:21
　not for what they cannot have, 440:12
　now with me past, 243:35
　past cure, past, 406:11
　pound of, 353:67
　punch with, 34:9
　ravell'd sleeve of, 248:21
　so wan with, 230:24
　to our coffin adds a nail, 315:30
　weary fu' o', 46:12
　with judicious, 44:15
　woman's tender, 76:18
Care's an enemy to life, 271:25
Cared for none of those things, 337:65
Career, awe a man from the, 258:20
　open to talents, 181:31
　which might damage, 25:32
Cares, against eating, 164:9
　and strife, void of, 190:8
　are dumb, great, 395:62
　deprest with, 103:33
　humble, 317:28
　resolved mind hath no, 421:74
　speak, light, 395:62
　that infest the day, 150:6
　will wear away, 359:71
　with crosses and with, 283:31
　worn with life's, 77:29
Caressing, kind its, 68:9
Carpe diem, 125:25
Carpenter, I doubt it, said, 59:22
　you may scold, 132:16
Carriére ouverte aux talents, 181:31
Carries well, he, 375:52
Carry [the cup] even, 436:33
Cart before the horse, put, 430:12

carried in a, 312:20
Carthage must be destroyed, 60:11
Carve for himself, 220:34
Casbeen, across, 28:4
Case, no, 401:73
　semblance in another's, 76:14
　vengeance of Jenny's, 256:18
Casement ope at night, 137:25
Casements, charm'd magic, 137:20
Cases, circumstances alter, 364:33
Casey has struck out, 298:31
Casey Jones, he mounted to the cabin,
　　344:1
Cash in a bucket, kept, 344:13
　take the, 97:32
　takes your, 65:38
　that goes therewith, 64:16
Cashmere, tales of fair, 314:21
Cask, taste of, 423:73
Casques, cram the very, 235:39
Cassowary, if I were a, 313:28
Cast into the midst, 332:1
　left, has one, 375:70
Caste of Vere da Vere, 292:15
Castigation, birch-twig for, 290:6
Castitatem, de mihi, 20:17
Castle, called Doubting, 42:12
　climbs to the top of, 356:28
　hath a pleasant seat, 247:38
　holds its state, 210:3
　house is his, 356:34
　precipice-encurled, 38:2
Castles in Spain, build, 428:1
　in the air, build, 428:2
　in the clouds, gay, 300:16
Cat and dog may kiss, 415:69
　ate the flickle, 396:1
　blate, 349:18
　care killed, 364:4
　did of the haggis, as, 414:4
　feet, on little, 208:9
　hanging of his, 32:11
　harmless necessary, 255:31
　has nine lives, 350:1
　have no more of, 440:63
　i' the adage, like, 248:4
　in gloves, 350:2
　in pan, turn, 431:43
　in, part to tear a, 256:26
　is away, when, 436:27
　is hungry, 415:70
　it might have been, 24:8

jumps, see which way, 430:17
knows whose lips she licks, 415:71
languishes loudly, 118:19
laps as much, an old, 356:43
laps milk, as a, 269:30
may look at a king, 350:3
melancholy as, 358:11
or dog drowned, never, 401:67
out of the bag, let, 429:66
runcible, 147:19
speak, ale will make, 373:46
sports not, old, 356:44
when I play with my, 176:11
will after kind, 364:7
will mew, 227:43
winketh, when, 436:28
would eat fish, 415:72
Cat's averse to fish, what, 112:2
ear, breeds in, 390:4
paw, with, 430:31
walk, 350:4
Cataract, sounding, 316:13
Cataracts and hurricanoes, 240:23
blow their trumpets, 319:32
Catastrophe, tickle your, 234:10
Catch and conquer, hard to, 160:16
ere she change, 197:20
it, not the way to, 430:16
neither, you will, 387:61
Catcher, not the best, 422:3
Catcheth him, [knows] more, 418:9
Catechism, so ends my, 233:42
Cathay, cycle of, 293:39
Cato, like, 198:2
vanquished [cause pleasing] to, 152:2
Catoni, victa [placuit], 152:2
Cats are grey, all, 355:66
eat what hussies spare, 364:8
keep no more, 385:45
make sober, 434:3
they that bourd wi', 425:76
Cattle are grazing, 317:31
home, call the, 139:22
upon a thousand hills, 327:39
Caucasus, thinking on the frosty, 243:27
Cauldron bubble, 250:11
Cauliflower is nothing but, 303:30
Causas, rerum cognoscere, 305:26
Cause above renown, set the, 183:22
aright, report my, 227:53
beauty of the good old, 317:40
blind in their own, 399:55

I'll try the whole, 58:5
it is a bad, 390:1
my soul, it is the, 262:9
or just impediment, 341:45
that lacks assistance, 23:33
that makes the martyr, 392:13
they see, but little, 56:3
Causes, home of lost, 20:3
of things, learn, 305:26
springs, from amorous, 193:22
Causeway, keeps the crown of, 365:64
Cave of Adullam, political, 33:26
Caveat emptor, 364:10
Cavern, field or mossy, 137:29
Caverns measureless to man, 70:8
Caviare to the general, 223:41
Cavil on the ninth part, 232:25
Cease to be, that I may, 137:34
Cecily, Gertrude, Magdalen, 206:16
Cecrops, dear city of, 21:21
Celerity is never more admired, 214:8
Celia all together, of, 312:10
has undone me, 312:9
Celibacy has no pleasures, 131:30
Cell, each in his narrow, 112:6
for cloister'd, 138:6
from the prophetic, 163:25
Cellar, born in a, 100:9
Cells, contented with, 319:27
Celt is talking, while the, 142:11
Censure of a man's self, 133:44
take each man's, 221:38
Centre, cède, mon, 100:8
is yielding, my, 100:8
Logan is the Head, 33:27
may sit i' th', 165:40
Centum, dein secunda, 60:15
Centuries, bowed by the weight of, 156:7
in him, every man of us has all the,
125:21
look down upon you, forty, 181:29
through what wild, 81:18
Cerberus, you are not like, 278:1
Ceremony that to great ones 'longs, 252:8
useth an enforced, 230:10
Certain, it is, 298:12
nothing is, 403:51, 403:52
one thing is, 98:4
Certainties, begin with, 22:19
hot for, 160:12
Certum est, 298:12
Cervantes is never petulant, 153:24

Cervicem haberet, unam, 54:1
Chaff, catch old birds with, 440:64
  corn in, 50:1
  in two bushels of, 253:31
Chain, drags a lengthening, 108:2
Chains and slavery, 47:23
  bound by gold, 297:43
  breaks his magic, 165:42
  untwisting all the, 164:10
Chair, give Dayrolles a, 64:11
  jumping from the, 128:3
  rack of a too easy, 194:22
  seated in thy silver, 134:18
  sit in a golden, 140:17
  will be one vacant, 309:18
Chalice, our poison'd, 247:41
Challenge, thus do I, 203:30
  to his end, 77:34
Challenged, ere I'ld have, 272:16
Cham of literature, Great, 281:28
Chamber, shall take his, 41:26
Champ and chafe and toss, 18:17
Champagne and a chicken, 176:7
Champion, in close fight, 209:27
Champions proud, meeting of, 208:20
Chance, be right by, 74:14
  bludgeonings of, 119:22
  direction which thou canst not see,
    195:37
  every morning brought a noble, 297:40
  eye to the main, 375:40
  happeneth to them all, 330:25
  is past, when, 392:20
  to prove our, 88:12
Chancellor, susceptible, 106:3
Chancery, hell and, 383:47
Chances, against ill, 234:27
  in an hour, it, 389:71
  most disastrous, 260:3
Change and decay in all around, 152:12
  as others do, I cannot, 204:12
  but I cannot die, 276:3
  came o'er the spirit, 52:7
  for worse, 189:15
  itself can give no more, 212:11
  jamais, qui ne, 26:1
  O the heavy, 166:12
  plus ça, 135:37
  ringing grooves of, 293:38
  their climate, not their soul, 125:41
  with fear of, 169:22
  with them, we, 414:18

Changé tout cela, nous avons, 174:37
Changed all that, we have, 174:37
  from him whom we knew, 305:37
  we shall all be, 339:35
Changes, the more it, 135:37
  who never, 26:1
Changest not, Thou who, 152:12
Changeth not, sweareth and, 326:17
Channel, butting through, 159:23
  drum them up the, 183:20
Chanticleer, crow like, 216:11
Chaos and old Night, frighted the reign of,
    168:18
  is come again, 261:27
  of thought and passion, 195:39
  thy dread empire, 194:24
Chapel, devil will have, 438:3
Chapels had been churches, 253:34
Chaps, biography is about, 28:7
Character, formation of, 282:16
  gave me a good, 58:14
  of a negative, 200:29
Characters are drawn, high, 196:14
  of ordinary life, 212:7
Charge, Chester, charge, 210:14
  is prepar'd, the, 104:2
Charing Cross, betwixt Heaven and, 300:4
Chariot, bear the flying, 79:26
  is an empty hazel-nut, 266:13
Chariot-wheel, axletree of, 418:1
Chariots, wheels of brazen, 172:19
Charitable gives out at the door, 415:74
Charity began, pity gave ere, 108:21
  begins at home, 364:12
  cold as, 356:71
  for all, with, 148:11
  for melting, 234:29
  greatest of these is, 338:32
  have not, 338:29
  mankind's concern, 196:1
  of Christian, 124:9
  organised, 185:25
  shall cover the multitude of sins, 340:6
  the living need, 18:13
Charity-boy said, as the, 82:15
Charlemain with all his peerage, 168:20
Charles the Second, navy of, 153:32
Charlie is my darling, 181:25
  live or die with, 212:1
Charlock throws a shade, 77:24
Charm of all the Muses, all, 298:1
  that provoking, 312:10

what is, 78:3
Charmer away, t'other dear, 103:35
Charming, ever new, ever, 92:15
Charms by accepting, 197:26
   endearing young, 178:1
   strike the sight, 193:35
Charon, seeing, may forget, 145:16
Charybdis, Scylla and, 362:27
Chase, because they give, 309:25
   began, the bloody, 193:37
   stern, 54:10
   the sport of kings, 281:30
   woe worth the, 210:18
Chased than enjoy'd, with more spirit, 254:14
Chassis, in a state of, 185:15
Chaste as ice, 224:9
   as the icicle, 218:28
Chasteneth, whom the Lord loveth he, 339:67
Chastise you, I will, 325:45
Chastiseth one, he that, 378:7
Chastity, give me, 20:17
   my brother, chastity, 165:41
   of honour, that, 43:29
Chatham, with his sabre drawn, 344:4
Chatte, quand je me jouë à, 176:11
Chatter, as I flow, I, 294:4
   it's only idle, 104:36
   of you, will, 438:34
Chatters to you, who, 438:34
Chatterton, I thought of, 317:34
Chaucer, Dan, 283:30
   lodge thee by, 134:12
   to learned, 26:3
   was alive, since, 144:14
Chaud comme l'enfer, 291:17
Che sarà, sarà, 364:13
Cheap, ill ware is never, 388:25
   they buy good, 425:63
Cheaply bought, now, 96:12
Cheat me in the price, 364:14
Cheek a little red, give, 196:17
   bring a blush to, 84:20
   feed on her damask, 272:4
   he that loves a rosy, 56:14
   his wither'd, 208:17
   kisseth the mother's, 382:8
   meet in some fresh, 217:34
   of tan, with, 312:19
   smite thee on, 333:44
   that I might touch, 267:20

Cheeks, blood spoke in, 86:12
   crack your, 240:23
   of sorry grain, 166:5
   roses are her, 296:15
   rosy lips and, 265:28
   stain my man's, 240:22
   that be hallow'd, 180:5
   were so red and so white, 139:30
   with care, make pale, 315:27
Cheer, be of good, 324:26
   boys! cheer! 154:19
   brings good, 364:30
   but not inebriate, 74:41
   greet the unseen with, 40:21
   scarce forbear to, 154:6
   up, cully, 315:26
   up, the worst is yet, 130:5
   welcome is the best, 435:42
Cheerfulness was always breaking in, 93:18
Cheerio my deario, 157:28
Cheers, sounds no worse than, 125:13
Cheese, eggs and a pound of, 54:9
   it is a peevish elf, 364:15
   king's, 419:69
   smells of, 288:7
   toasted, 431:51
Chefs-d'œuvre, au milieu des, 101:23
Chequer-board of Nights and Days, 98:11
Cherchez la femme, 92:7
Cherries, disgraces are like, 366:40
Cherry, like to a double, 257:40
   make two bites of, 430:3
   now is hung, 125:9
   ruddier than the, 103:29
Cherub that sits up aloft, 81:29
Cherubim, heaven's, 248:1
Cherubims, immortal, 302:7
Cherubins, young-eyed, 255:43
Chess, life's too short for, 53:39
Chest against his foes, 278:26
   contriv'd a double debt to pay, 109:28
   of drawers by day, 109:28
   ten-times-barr'd-up, 242:18
Chest, Dead Man's, 286:9
Chesterton, dared attack, 27:31
Chestnut tree, a spreading, 149:33
Chestnut's proud, the, 182:19
Chestnuts out of the fire, take, 430:31
Chevalier, the young, 181:25
Chewed and digested, to be, 22:16
Chicken, champagne and a, 176:7
   children and, 364:16

Christians are, what these, 254:7
  awake, 49:35
  [spend] in suits, 419:65
Christmas comes but once a year, 364:30
  green, 351:75
  I no more desire a rose, at, 246:2
  if the ice will bear a man before, 386:24
  is coming, 346:1
  in middle of winter, 16:3
  they talk of, 425:73
Christo, fide et gaude in, 152:7
Chronicle as rich with praise, 235:42
Chronicles, abstract and brief, 223:43
Chrononhotonthologos, 57:19
Chuck [*darling*], dearest, 249:40
Chuck [*stop*] it, Smith, 64:16
Church by daylight, can see, 258:12
  call others to, 360:35
  plain as way to, 216:15
  repair, some to, 192:13
  some new and great period in his, 174.33
  the nearer, 421:45
  to be of no, 132:1
  upon this rock I will build, 324:29
  where God hath, 438:3
  work goes on slowly, 364:31
Church's one foundation, 287:31
Church-door, wide as a, 267:40
Churches, Paternoster built, 406:12
Churchyard is so handsome, no, 401:74
  makes a fat, 351:75
Churchyards yawn, when, 225:34
Churn, attract a Silver, 104:40
Cicero, fall below Demosthenes or, 96:4
  no difference can alienate, 153:24
Cider is treacherous, 364:32
Cigar is a Smoke, good, 139:35
Cinnamon, tinct with, 136:13
Circenses, panem et, 135:34
Circle none durst walk, within that, 91:36
  that shut me out, 156:8
  that took him in, 156:8
  wheel is come full, 242:12
Circumcised dog, the, 262:16
Circumlocution Office, the, 84:16
Circumspect, Buckingham grows, 245:20
Circumspice, si monumentum, 24:3
Circumstance allows, best, 322:5
Circumstances alter cases, 364:33
  finds, some, 89:30
Citadel, tower'd, 214:14
Cities, all, flower of, 92:13

he saw, men whose, 123:30
  please us, tower'd, 164:6
Citizen, John Gilpin was, 75:26
  of no mean city, 337:68
  the humblest, 40:24
Citizens, fat and greasy, 215:40
City, a great solitude, great, 351:71
  a rose-red, 42:20
  brought up in this, 337:69
  eats [chickens], 415:75
  for the houses, cannot see, 440:73
  is of Night, the, 300:22
  it is the men who make, 392:16
  my name, in my own, 389:47
  now doth like a garment wear, 317:36
  of dreadful height, 31:27
  of God, dear, 21:21
  of no mean, 337:68
  of our God, Zion, 184:1
  of two kings, 154:8
  pent, in populous, 173:35
  pent, long in, 136:2
  populous and a smoky, 275:37
  that is set on an hill, 333:39
  that parleys, 350:7
  thou hast made a, 208:2
  to the poor dull, 182:19
  who know not the, 200:20
  with her dreaming spires, 19:28
Civet, give me an ounce of, 242:3
  in the room, with, 74:17
Civic animal, man is, 18:9
Civic denial, 350:8
Civilised by Man, last thing, 160:26
Civilities, to bandy, 133:23
Civility costs nothing, 364:34
  I see a wild, 120:6
  of my knee, 35:19
Clad in silk or scarlet, 356:23
Claes look, gars auld, 44:13
Clamour, with deafening, 234:19
Clamours counterfeit, dread, 261:35
Clap, thunderbolt hath but, 423:47
Clapper-clawing one another, 48:24, 271:23
Claret is the liquor for boys, 133:45
Clarion, sound, sound the, 179:19
Clartier the cosier, 415:78
Classes, back the masses against, 106:34
  ye lower middle, 106:1
Classic, everybody want to have read,
  304:1
  face, thy, 191:28

ground, to tread on, 15:10
Claw me, and I'll claw thee, 364:35
Clay and wattles made, of, 320:36
  doth feed the sand, 437:43
  lies still, 126:10
  turf that wraps, 71:34
  will harden, 422:4
Clean as a whistle, 356:69
  linen, did not love, 132:15
Cleanliness is next to godliness, 310:26
Cleanly-wantonness, sing of, 120:4
Clear, though deep, yet, 81:22
Clearing-house of the world, 61:25
Cleave to her and worship her, 297:35
  together like burrs, 425:64
Cleopatra, some squeaking, 215:21
Cleopatra's nose — 187:28
Cléopâtre, le nez de, 187:28
Clergy, an Arminian, 62:11
  worth a pound of, 356:57
Clergyman, Wilkinson, a, 99:23
Clergymen, men, women and, 281:20
Clergymen's sons, 364:36
Clerk, merrily whistles the, 106:18
  saw a Banker's, 60:4
  ther was of Oxenford, 63:26
  there goes the, 74:10
  who pens a stanza, 197:38
Clerks, greatest, 418:33
Clever deils he'll mak them, 45:31
  let who will be, 139:26, 15:4
  people were good, [if], 316:3
  so rude to the good, 316:4
Client, here . . . is our, 88:3
Cliff, as some tall, 109:25
Cliffs which had been rent, like, 70:7
Climate, heaven for, 25:24
Climb, fain would I, 202:12
  not at all, 202:12
  teach ye how to, 166:7
Climbed, he that never, 380:27
Climbers, hasty, 374:35
Clime, a happy fireside, 46:4
  in some brighter, 23:35
Clive, what I like about, 28:8
Cloak around him, martial, 315:32
  at home, leave not, 426:31
  my fine camlet, 189:21
  not alone my inky, 220:17
  that covers, sleep, a, 61:24
  to make, have not, 375:43
  without my, 264:5

worst, 408:22
Clock, calm as, 356:68
  does strike, 48:7
  for you, watch the, 264:7
  in the steeple strikes one, 320:20
  look at the, 24:2
  that click'd behind the door, 109:28
  will strike, the, 157:18
Clods, a man harrowing, 116:7
Cloister's pale, studious, 165:25
Cloke, knyf under the, 63:38
Close as wax, 356:70
  little garden, 180:6
Closer is He than breathing, 294:34
Closes, pleasant orchard, 36:4
Closet lays, back in the, 98:11
Cloth, according to, 428:21
  it is a bad, 390:2
  meat, drink, and, 373:45
  off the same, 415:48
  she saw, coarse, 77:28
  shrinking, 426:37
Clothed, and in his right mind, 325:67
Clothes a wantonness, in, 120:5
  be new, let your, 359:80
  brushers of noblemen's, 365:66
  cold after, 373:38
  enterprises that require new, 300:25
  good, 373:48
  good smell of old, 34:6
  liquefaction of, 120:12
  mend your, 399:62
  nothing to wear but, 139:20
  pockets in none, 28:3
  procure me respect, 389:47
  through tatter'd, 242:5
  truth hath bad, 432:6
  walked away with their, 85:31
  when he put on, 108:8
  white, makes, 398:37
Clothing the palpable, 71:25
  things in books', 144:2
Cloths, heavens' embroidered, 320:32
Cloud, choose a firm, 197:20
  has a silver lining, 368:23
  inside out, turn the dark, 100:12
  is scattered, when, 277:22
  is silver-lined, every, 315:26
  nor speck, not stain, 281:35
  on cloud, like, 137:32
  out of the sea, little, 325:49
  pryeth into every, 380:36

that floats on high, 318:15
that's dragonish, 214:14
through a fleecy, 164:17
to be under, 427:67
wandered lonely as, 318:15
what a scowl of, 40:17
Cloudcuckooborough, 18:8
Clouds, above, those thin, 70:18
are spread, rolling, 109:25
are upon the hills, 436:29
away, pack, 121:17
fought upon the, 229:23
in the slippery, 234:19
looks in the, 228:17
on the wing, white, 18:2
play i' the plighted, 165:36
shining, through the dark, 100:12
stray, the white, 33:19
through rolling, 50:4
through the darkest, 268:14
would break, doubted, 40:20
Cloud-waves that ebbed, 102:2
Clout, cast ne'er, 364:5
than a hole, better, 360:39
on Sunday, makes a, 355:62
Clouting, will abide no, 390:3
Clown forget his design, make, 410:26
to see a, 218:7
Clubs, going the round of, 116:31
typical of strife, 76:2
Clutch, clawed me with his, 304:17
Coach and six, drive a, 204:3
Coaches won't run over him, 415:79
Coach-house, with a double, 70:16, 282:11
Coal, blow at, 394:38
whole world turn to, 120:1
with a cargo of Tyne, 159:23
Coals of fire, heap, 338:16
to haul over, 428:34
to Newcastle, carry, 428:9
Coaster, dirty British, 159:23
Coat according to the cloth, cut, 428:21
and sark, shape, 434:16
near is my, 400:37
riband to stick in, 37:25
was red, his, 282:10
wear a long, black, 113:36
without sleeves, herald's, 233:39
Coats, a hole in a' your, 46:2
graceless, gay, 395:26
Coaxin' onaisy ones, 111:30
Cobbler go beyond his last, let not, 400:36

stick to his last, 395:47
the richer the, 419:49
Cobham, you, brave, 196:18
Cock and hen, God's, 422:1
crows, as the old, 359:54
diminished to her, 241:48
goes crowing to bed, if, 386:17
is bold, 350:10
is crouse, 350:10
learns, young, 359:54
mark, 200:27
with lively din, 164:1
won't fight, that, 414:21
Cock, head-waiter at The, 293:43
Cockle hat and staff, by, 226:19
Cockpen, Laird o', 181:22
Cockpit hold the vasty fields, can this, 235:39
Cocks, drown'd the, 240:23
love no coops, young, 442:34
Cocksure, wish I was as, 160:4
Cocoa is a cad and coward, 65:23
is a vulgar beast, 65:23
Cod, home of the bean and, 31:31
Codlin's the friend, 82:34
Coelum, ruat, 370:15
Coepit habet dimidium, qui, 125:36
Cœur a ses raisons, 187:29
Coffee, which makes the politician wise, 193:31
Cogito, ergo sum, 81:28
Cohorts were gleaming, 51:38
Coil, shuffled off this mortal, 224:4
Coin is not common, where, 438:2
is spurious, 154:16
much care, much, 400:17
pay a person in his own, 430:4
Coincidence, long arm of, 61:28
Coiner, carry back bright to, 126:14
Cold a cold, we called, 28:2
after clothes, God sends, 373:38
all weather is, 427:56
as charity, 356:71
dead mice feel no, 366:10
doth not sting, 182:5
feed, 370:9
foot and hand go, 287:30
hand and a warm heart, 350:11
in the rain and the, 159:20
let him that is, 394:38
maid's knees are, 350:25
meat, dined upon, 189:25

nor hot, neither, 340:14
shake against the, 264:13
strengthens, 359:51
Coliseum, while stands the, 51:26
Collar, braw brass, 44:19
College, in Brazen-Nose, 442:28
  or a cat, endow a, 197:30
Collop, it is a dear, 390:5
Colonel dead, the, 183:25
Colonel's Lady an' Judy O'Grady, 142:1
Colonnade, sound of the cool, 76:9
Colonus, singer of sweet, 18:14
Coloquintida, bitter as, 260:12
Colossus, like a, 228:11
Colour, of a bad, 351:57
  those which love, 207:28
  virtue's, 363:53
  will take no, 390:2
Colours, cannot judge, 349:19
  seen by candle-light, 36:6
  truth fears no, 432:4
  under whose, 244:4
  up with the, 310:29
Colt, ragged, 353:71
Columbia! happy land! hail, 124:19
Column, London's, 197:33
  throws up a steamy, 74:41
Comb one's head with a stool, 428:14
Conbatants, frown'd the mighty, 170:9
Comber wind-hounded, the, 140:2
Combination and a form, 226:2
Come as the winds come, 211:35
  at it, ere you, 442:31
  hither, come hither, 216:4
  hither, Evan Cameron, 22:2
  lightly, 395:64
  one, come all, 211:28
  one to, and one to go, 59:31
  over into Macedonia, 337:62
  shape of things to, 310:22
  take things as they, 412:78
  to it, till you, 401:55
  to, what we must all, 442:24
  too, you, 102:6
  unto me, 324:18
  up to the scratch, 428:16
  what can come, 367:59
  what come may, 247:30
  when you're called, 412:26
  when you're looked for, 80:1
  without warning, 80:1
Comedy to those that think, 307:29

Comes at last, long looked for, 395:28
  see where she, 262:17
  to me, she, 302:11
Comet burn'd like a, 170:7
Cometh not, he, 292:6
Comets seen, there are no, 229:24
Comfort and command, to, 318:14
  and despair, of, 265:32
  another [year] of, 404:72
  be, this must my, 243:23
  here's my, 269:33
  him, to, 236:2
  lend, never, 313:24
  me, rod and thy staff, 326:26
  no man speak, of, 243:39
Comfortable, baith grand and, 25:26
Comforter's head never aches, 416:1
Comforters, miserable, 325:67
Comical, I often think it's, 106:3
Coming, my own, she is, 296:19
  shone, far off his, 172:20
  yet for a' that, 47:33
Command, correspondent to, 268:23
  counsel is no, 365:57
  in a sweet, 424:32
  not born to sue, but, 243:19
  to threaten and, 226:2
  your man, 364:44
Commandment I give, a new, 337:52
Commandments, aren't no Ten, 141:44
  in your face, set my ten, 237:29
  keep his, 330:37
Commands enough, he, 375:53
Commencement de la fin, 290:13
Commencer par la commencement, 115:18
Commences many things, who, 382:27
Commend her, forced to, 189:23
Commentators each dark passage shun,
    322:9
  plain, give me, 77:25
Commerce, in matters of, 56:11
Commit them, theirs that, 417:70
Commodus, to the accession of, 104:8
Common did or mean, nothing, 158:17
  if they have a good thing, to make it too,
    234:5
  men, in the roll of, 232:20
  natures, same with, 121:21
  things of friends are in, 394:1
  thou know'st 'tis, 220:16
  touch, nor lose the, 142:15
Common-looking people, the Lord

Conquered, I came, I saw, I, 53:42
    O Galilean, hast, 135:22
    thou hast, 289:34
Conquering, he went forth, 340:15
    so sharp the, 62:15
Conqueror bid spare, Emathian, 167:26
    he who flieth is, 389:45
    proud foot of, 240:6
Conquest, for purposes of foreign, 310:7
    of itself, shameful, 243:30
    of the nature of, 234:28
Conquests farther, spread, 46:19
    glories, triumphs, spoils, 229:30
Conscia recti, mens, 305:30
Conscience and grace, to the profoundest
    pit, 226:23
    as if he were, 297:34
    as their King, 297:34
    avaunt, 66:11
    does make cowards, 224:4
    good, 351:52
    guilty, 351:79
    hath a thousand several tongues, 245:28
    in the court of, 390:27
    O coward, 245:27
    of her worth, 173:27
    of the king, catch, 224:2
    sleeps, quiet, 353:70
    still and quiet, 239:17
    with injustice is corrupted, 237:31
Consecrate to thee, I, 144:13
Consent, silence gives, 411:47
Consented, whispering 'I will ne'er
    consent,' 52:14
Consequence, trammel up, 247:40
Consequences of them will be, 47:43
Conservative, or else a little, 106:3
Consider it not so deeply, 248:18
    wihat hath been, 382:15
    what o'clock it is, 59:28
Consideration, like an angel, came, 235:40
Consistency, a foolish, 94:9
Consolation, that's one, 82:13
Conspicuous by its absence, 207:34
Consipre, with Fate, 99:20
Constable, justle a, 269:37
Constabulary duty's to be done, 104:33
Constancy, dearest her, 114:6
    no object worth, 276:11
Constant as the northern star, 229:27
    never, to one thing, 258:18
    were man but, 273:32

Constitution, higher law than, 213:21
Consulate, born in my, 66:22
Consulting, too much, 431:59
Consumedly, they laughed, 96:9
Consummation devoutly to be wished,
    224:4
Contagion spread, foul, 166:20
Contemplation, beneath thy, 182:7
    he and valour form'd, for, 170:28
Contempt and anger of his lip, 272:8
    cured by, 411:77
    familiarity breeds, 369:78
    too busy gets, 427:66
Content, all the rest of, 404:72
    crown is called, 238:8
    farewell, 261:35
    he that studies his, 381:56
    in measureless, 248:12
    is the philosopher's stone, 365:52
    lodges oftener in cottages, 365:53
    nothing will, 425:70
    O sweet, 80:8
    to breathe his native air, 192:1
    wants, 381:56
    with equal advantage, 56:11
Contented, he that hath nothing is not,
    379:49
    least, with what I most enjoy, 264:1
    may well be, 376:43
    wi' little, 47:28
Contention will cease, 412:36
Contentment has, best, 283:25
    with a little, 418:37
Contests, what mighty, 193:22
Continents, three separate, 87:25
Contortions of the Sybil, 43:36
Contract themselves the more, 179:18
Contradiction, at best a, 197:28
Contrairy, everythink goes, 82:52
Contraries, dreams go by, 367:69
Contrary, runneth not to the, 29:25
Contrive, a head to, 104:10
Contumely, proud man's, 224:4
Convent, it was a stately, 27:24
    never praises his, 354:2
Conversation completes [a gentleman],
    368:6
Conversationalist, industrious, 128:6
Conversations, without pictures or, 58:3
Converse, form'd by thy, 196:10
    hold high, 300:14
    with whom I,

very pink of, 267:34
Courtier, heel of the, 227:24
  young, 355:49
Courtier's, soldier's, scholar's, 224:11
Courtiers throng, a thousand, 27:25
Courtiers' knees, o'er, 366:13
Courting and wooing, 365:59
Courts, a day in thy, 327:48
  in cottages as well as, 397:57
  those stately, 17:23
  where Jamshyd gloried, 98:1
Courtsied when you have, 269:25
Cousin, call me, 363:77
  not call the king, 385:54
Cover shows, front of the, 64:12
  will tell, back of, 64:12
Coverlet, according to, 412:47
  to honour under, 431:17
Covet, all lose, all, 355:67
Coveting other men's wealth, 208:6
Covetous man is good to none, 350:14
  spends more, 416:4
Covetousness brings nothing home, 365:60
  bursts the sack, 365:61
  is young, 436:4
Cow, all red and white, 286:17
  collier's, 350:13
  curst, 350:22
  hath a bad calf, good, 398:15
  I never saw a Purple, 42:18
  I wrote the Purple, 42:19
  in a cage, nimble as, 358:18
  in the waist, slender as, 358:36
  knows not, 416:5
  never saw, 426:6
  never tint, 376:52
  sell your, 436:32
  to the hall, bring, 363:65
  when she kissed, 368:44
  yields, not all butter, 392:7
Coward, flattery to name a, 302:2
  gives courage to, 366:30
  that would not dare, 210:5
  to his mettle, put, 406:82
  virtue of, 423:60
Cowardice, pale cold, 243:20
Cowards, all men would be, 204:11
  die many times, 229:25
  flinch, though, 72:13
  if they durst, be, 204:11
  many other mannish, 215:36
  many would be, 398:32

plague of all, 232:5
sots or slaves or, 196:5
the greatest of, 116:37
Cowl does not make the monk, 365:71
Cowslip's bell I lie, in, 270:1
  grace, sweet, 185:17
Cowslips wan that hang the pensive head,
  167:22
Coxcombs vanquish Berkeley, 34:15
Coy, and hard to please, 210:13
Coyness were no crime, 158:10
Cozen me not, 363:77
Cozenage, strange, 91:39
Crab [wild apple], better than the whole,
  421:52
  of the wood, 350:15
Crab [shell-fish] of the sea, 350:15
Crack us up, you'd better, 82:42
  varnishing hides, 433:59
Crackling of thorns, 330:19
Cradle and the grave, between, 92:16
  endlessly rocking, 312:51
  fair in, 369:70
  foot on, 418:7
  foul in, 371:59
  hand that rocks, 307:18
  of the deep, rocked in, 314:18
Cradles, better have one plough going than
  two, 361:76
Craft against craft, 365:62
  full of, 371:70
  must have clothes, 365:63
  so long to lerne, 62:15
Crag, castled, 50:17
  he clasps the, 293:45
Crambe repetita, 135:32
Cranes, as sore fight wrens as, 358:42
Crank is a little thing, a, 104:6
Crannies, pluck you out of, 295:3
Cranny but the right, ev'ry, 76:12
Crave, nothing, 403:50
Craving, shameless, 410:29
Crazy ones, checkin' the, 111:30
Creaking gate hangs long, 350:18
Creaks most, worst wheel, 424:3
Cream, she gives me, 286:17
  skim milk masquerades as, 108:30
Creation moves, to which the whole, 296:8
  up and down the whole, 101:17
Creation's blot, 104:12
  'dawn beheld, 51:30
Creator, remember now thy, 330:32

Creature, drink, pretty, 316:27
  good familiar, 261:25
  gospel to every, 336:6
  nor any other, 338:13
Creatures, from fairest, 263:29
  great and small, 17:18
  meanest of his, 39:39
  ours, call these delicate, 261:31
  wine makes all sorts of, 440:1
Credit, corpse of public, 310:6
  go, let the, 97:32
  he that hath lost, 379:45
  in being jolly, 82:37
  in that, an't much, 82:36
  it's greatly to his, 104:31
  keeps the crown of the causeway, 365:64
Creditors have better memories, 365:65
Creditum est, ab omnibus, 305:20
Credula postero, quam minimum, 125:25
Credulity, season of, 62:9
  who listen with, 131:29
Creed, a Calvinistic, 62:11
  outworn, suckled in, 319:29
  sapping a solemn, 50:19
Creeds, keys of all, 295:40
  so many, 313:30
  than in half the, 296:3
Creeks and inlets, through, 68:2
Creep and then go, 370:24
  make your flesh, 82:9
  shall sweetly, 258:36
  where it cannot go, 397:65
Creetur, a lone lorn, 82:52
Crest, joy brightens his, 173:36
Crew complete, with all her, 75:25
  darling of our, 81:31
  no gale dismayed, 60:6
Crib, ass his master's, 331:46
Cricket, merry as, 358:13
  on the hearth, 164:19
Cried in vain, John he, 75:28
Cries, night and day on me she, 342:9
Crime, featureless and commonplace, 87:29
  madden to, 51:32
  Napoleon of, 88:2
  of being a young man, 62:8
  plus qu'un, 10:21
  punishment fit the, 106:12
  reach the scene of, 93:34
  this coyness were no, 158:10
  what greater, 435:51
  worse than a, 10:21

Crimes, follies, and misfortunes, register
  of, 104:7
Crimine ab uno disce omnes, 305:34
Cripple, halt before, 391:56
  he that mocks, 380:26
Crispian, feast of, 238:17
Critic, in logic a great, 48:4
  the good, 101:23
  you have frowned, 320:12
Critic's eye, view me with, 96:4
Critical, sternly, 118:20
Criticism, cant of, 285:24
  definition of, 20:4
Criticisms, they pass no, 93:20
Critics!—appall'd I venture, 46:14
  are like brushers, 365:66
  before you trust in, 50:1
  much confide in, 288:10
Critique, le bon, 101:23
Cromwell, Charles the First [had his],
  119:31
  damned, see, 196:8
  guitless, some, 112:14
Crony, trusty, drouthy, 46:8
Crooked in the water, 354:20
  if the staff be, 386:32
  straight, set the, 180:8
Crooksaddles, cracking of, 363:74
Crop, a-watering last year's, 93:21
Cross as a bear, 356:72
  as nine highways, 356:73
  as two sticks, 356:74
  devil bears, 390:31
  e'en though it be a, 15:6
  hath its inscription, 367:81
  last at His, 25:22
  lurks behind, 416:26
  no crown, no, 189:19
  of Jesus, with the, 24:13
  on the bitter, 231:25
  she wore, sparkling, 193:24
Crosse he bore, a bloodie, 283:24
Crosses are ladders, 365:69
  between the, 154:12
  proud man hath, 353:69
Crossways, things at home are, 57:20
Crotchets in thy head, 256:10
Crouch, still bidding, 37:26
Crouse, nothing so, 403:57
Crow makes wing to the rooky wood,
  249:41
  thinks her own bird fairest, 416:6

Cups, in their flowing, 237:18
　that cheer, 74:41
Curate, I was a pale young, 104:24
Curates, long dust, will come, 34:3
Curds and cream, queen of, 274:3
Cure, better than, 406:62
　care is no, 364:3
　for this ill, the, 142:19
　in his hands, hath, 376:67
　past care, past, 406:11
Cured, what can't be, 435:48
　yesterday of my disease, 200:11
Cures, desperate, 366:31
　himself, physician who, 376:9
Curfew, hear the far-off, 164:18
　shall not ring to-night, 301:31
　time, breaks his magic chains at, 165:42
　tolls the knell, 112:4
Curiosity is ill manners, 365:73
Curious things to show, 127:28
Curiouser and curiouser, 58:4
Curl, who had a little, 150:21
Current, glides the smooth, 131:21
　when it serves, take, 230:17
　whose icy, 261:41
Currents, split his, 18:23
　turn awry, their, 224:4
Curs, yelping, 440:54
　you common cry of, 218:26
Curse, I know how to, 269:24
　is come upon me, 292:11
　primal eldest, 225:36
　shall be on thee, 282:1
　such a terrible, 24:5
Curses come home to roost, 365:74
　not loud but deep, 251:31
Curst, to all succeeding ages, 89:23
Curtain fall, lets the, 194:24
　ring down the, 202:3
　spread thy close, 267:41

twilight's, 67:25
Curtain'd with cloudy red, 163:26
Curtains, let fall the, 74:41
Curtiosity, full of 'satiable, 143:31
Curtsey while you're thinking, 59:20
Curves, lovely are the, 160:19
Curzon, George Nathaniel, 344:7
Custodes, quis custodiet, 135:30
Custodiet ipsos custodes, quis, 135:30
Custom is second nature, 365:75
　is the great guide, 127:33
　is the plague of wise men, 365:76
　lie upon thee, 319:37
　loathsome to the eye, 129:24
　makes all things easy, 365:77
　more honour'd in the breach, 222:4
　should corrupt the world, lest one good,
　　297:41
　stale her infinite variety, 214:4
　taketh seven, 400:34
　the tyrant, 260:10
　without reason, 365:78
Customs, so many, 411:71
Cut and came again, 77:28
　of all, most unkindest, 230:2
　off, it soon, 326:52
　once, before you, 399:51, 408:68
　shortest, 373:49
　their fingers, fools, 371:40
Cutpurse of the empire, 226:4
Cuts, not steel yet it, 423:52
Cycno, nigroque simillima, 135:28
Cymbal, tinkling, 338:29
Cynara, faithful to thee, 87:23
Cynicism is intellectual dandyism, 160:29
Cynosure of neighbouring eyes, 164:3
Cynthia of this minute, 197:20
Cypress, in sad, 272:3
　tree, shady, 206:10
Cytherea's breath, 274:1

D

D, never use a big, big, 104:26
Dacian mother, their, 51:25

Dactyl trisyllable, 70:19
Dad, call'd my brother's father, 239:31

Daddy heerd him bawl, 204:5
Dads make fat lads, raw, 408:18
Daffadillies fill their cups with tears, 167:22
Daffadowndilly, like the, 72:16
Daffed the world aside, 233:35
Daffodils begin to peer, 273:40
  dances with the, 318:16
  host of golden, 318:15
  that come before the swallow dares,
    274:1
  we weep to see, 12:9
Dagger, air-drawn, 250:3
  is this a, 248:13
  of the mind, 248:13
  smiles at the drawn, 16:1
Daggers, give me the, 249:22
  I will speak, 225:35
Daggers-drawing, been at, 48:24
Dainties, spiced, 136:13
  want, where, 366:36
Daintiest last, the, 243:21
Dainty, plenty makes, 406:35
Dairies, foul sluts in, 72:21
Daisies fair blooming, 180:9
  grow, hear the, 314:14
  pied, 246:16
  rosy, left the, 296:13
  those pearled Arcturi, 276:10
  tread on nine, 437:62
Daisy in the dell, every, 308:17
  winter done, rose and, 89:20
Dalhousie, the great God of War, 345:23
Dalliance in the wardrobe lies, 235:45
  primrose path of, 220:36
Dallying and doing, 365:59
Dam [mother] leaps over, where, 438:12
Dam [damn], did not give a singel, 99:30
Damaged, archangel a little, 144:5
Damasco, or Marocco, or Trebisond,
  168:20
Dame, our sulky sullen, 46:5
  tocherless, 354:25
  will not be ruled by his own, 381:71
Damiata and Mount Casius old, betwixt,
  170:2
Damn braces, 30:14
  not one twopenny, 310:17
  with faint praise, 198:2
  young man who said, 116:12
Damnation, I dare, 226:23
  of his taking-off, 248:1
Damnations, twenty-nine distinct, 37:31

Damned, all silent and all, 316:17
  be him that first cries, 251:44
  better be, 315:29
  first, see thee, 56:7
  hisself in confidence, 82:21
  I'ld have seen him, 272:16
  if you don't, be, 87:20
  perpetually, must be, 157:17
  thing after another, one, 127:30
  to fame, shall be, 194:18
  truly thou art, 217:23
Damning those they have no mind to,
  48:14
Damozel, the blessed, 206:12
Dams I'll make, no more, 269:34
Damsel or two, to every man, 324:23
Damsels met in forest, fairy, 174:3
Dance among thorns, 425:66
  and jollity, tipsy, 165:31
  like a wave of the sea, 320:37
  lightly, that, 355:65
  no longer, 402:8
  no more at holy-day, 62:14
  on with the, 50:12
  or ride with General Bangs, don't, 139:33
  riot, feast and, 173:47
  when you do, 274:2
  when you go to, 437:64
  who have learn'd to, 192:16
Dances, fairies break their, 126:20
  in the wind, she, 91:34
  well to whom fortune pipes, 375:56
Danceth without music, 380:8
Dancing days, past our, 266:15
  well, they love, 425:66
Dancing-master, manners of, 132:9
Dandyism, intellectual, 160:29
Daniel, a second, 255:38
  come to judgment, 255:35
Danger and delight, 366:1
  bright eyes of, 287:25
  foreseen, 350:27
  get beyond, 440:23
  lost that is in, 355:77
  only when in, 186:9
  out of debt, out of, 406:2
  out of this nettle, 231:44
  past, 416:10
  pleased with the, 89:24
  she fear'd no, 90:8
  sneeze for, 411:69
  the more honour, more, 420:29

we are in, 437:57
without, 440:23
Danger's troubled night, 55:25
Dangerous, have in me something, 227:41
such men are, 228:14
thing, little learning is a, 192:6
Dangers are overcome by dangers, 366:2
who brave, its, 150:14
Dansons sur un volcan, 208:8
Dante never stays too long, 153:24
Danube, rude hut by, 51:25
Dappled things, glory be to God for,
124:16
Dare do all that may become a man, 248:5
do, what men, 258:33
never grudge the throe, 39:43
'not' wait upon 'I would,' 248:4
what man dare, I, 250:5
you who, 160:23
Darien, upon a peak in, 136:4
Daring spirit pall, no danger can, 80:6
Dares do more is none, who, 248:5
Darest thou then, 210:11
Dark, after that the, 298:1
all cats are grey in, 355:66
and bright, best of, 51:36
and doubtful, from the, 77:25
and the daylight, between, 150:5
and true and tender, 294:16
at one strike comes, 69:27
children fear to go in, 22:8
dark, dark, 174:15
drive black hogs in, 391:69
ever-during, 170:16
go home in the, 119:30
good as my lady in, 392:37
he that gropes in, 378:34
he that runs in, 381:41
hellish, 288:7
illumine, what in me is, 168:3
irrecoverably, 174:15
wanderers of the, 241:27
we are for the, 215:20
with excess of bright, 170:18
Darkies have to part, 101:15
Darkness again and a silence, 150:20
as a bride, encounter, 252:17
born, in silent, 78:16
buries all, universal, 194:24
came down on the field, 298:17
dawn on our, 118:7
deepens, the, 152:11

do devour it, jaws of, 256:23
go out into the, 116:26
instruments of, 247:28
leaves the world to, 112:4
peering, into that, 191:25
prince of, 241:36
rather than light, 337:43
scatters the rear of, 164:1
visible, 168:5
walketh in, 326:55
what of the, 147:27
which may be felt, 324:3
Darling, Charlie is my, 181:25
of my heart, 56:17
old man's, 361:52
somebody's, 143:37
Darlings, wealthy curled, 259:51
Dart, feather on the fatal, 50:4
shook a dreadful, 170:5
Time shall throw a, 35:28
Darter's youngest darter, 190:11
Dastard in war, 210:9
Dat, bis dat cito, 363:43
Date, all too short, 263:32
Dated, women and music should never be,
440:29
Daughter am I in my mother's house,
140:14
Duke-and-a-Duchess's, 24:7
harping on my, 223:31
heavy-heeled, 352:20
let them all to, 298:33
like mother, like, 395:79
my daughter's my, 400:26
O my ducats! 254:17
of the gods, 292:21
of the voice of God, 318:18
taken his little, 149:31
when you can, [marry], 399:48
win, he that would, 382:20
Daughter-in-law, that she was, 421:42
Daughters and a back door, two, 432:25
and dead fish, 366:3
dawted, 366:4
none of Beauty's, 52:1
of my father's house, I am all the, 272:5
Dauntless in war, so, 210:7
David his ten thousands, 324:33
Daw but had twa, never, 425:55
Dawn and sunset, seen, 149:25
before, 416:11
comes up like thunder, 141:42

Deceit, we hug the dear, 73:29
Deceive, first we practise to, 210:12
  me once, if a man, 385:65
  me twice, if he, 385:65
  oneself, to, 428:23
Deceived, desire to be, 47:43
Deceiver, I'm a gay, 72:2
Deceivers ever, men were, 258:18
Deccives, he that once, 380:28
December, drear-nighted, 137:35
  seek roses in, 50:1
Decencies, content to dwell in, 197:23
Decency, want of, 206:1
Decent, to what is, 124:11
Decently and in order, 338:33
  things be done, 338:33
Decide, the moment to,
  who shall, 197:29
Deck, stood on the burning, 118:14
Declare, nothing to, 314:12
Decliner of honours and titles, 96:2
Dedans, ceux qui sont au, 176:14
Dee, across the sands of, 139:22
  lived on the river, 29:15
Dee [die], I wad, 22:25
Deed and abide it, do the, 180:10
  and repent it, do the, 180:10
  by the doer's, 213:29
  in all my life, one good, 270:12
  in every eye, blow the horrid, 248:1
  is never lost, good, 351:53
  of dreadful note, 249:39
  so shines a good, 256:3
  take the will for, 431:35
  the better the, 415:55
  till thou applaud, 249:40
  wise before, 419:64
  without a name, 250:14
Deed's achieved, matchless, 278:27
Deeds are fruits, 366:21
  are males, 366:22
  emblems of, 51:32
  ill done, makes, 240:5
  know, so little men their own, 300:1
  like poison-weeds, 314:16
  must not be thought, 248:20
  my lady please, doughty, 111:21
  not years, live in, 22:24
  of men, looks quite through, 228:15
  relate, these unlucky, 262:16
  turn sourest by, 265:19
  were evil, because, 337:43

which make up life, 36:18
  years of noble, 297:35
Deep a lower deep, in the lowest, 170:22
  almost as life, 319:37
  and crisp and even, 182:11
  and massy, close and high, 210:3
  calleth unto deep, 326:35
  cradle of the, 314:18
  dive into the bottom of, 231:38
  for me, in terms too, 104:37
  from the great deep to the great deep,
    296:23
  from the vasty, 232:21
  her home is on the, 55:24
  home on the rolling, 208:10
  in the shady sadness, 137:32
  slimy bottom of the, 245:18
  still waters run, 412:42
  sweep through the, 55:23
  tempest o'er the, 301:32
  there's danger on the, 26:11
  to boil, he maketh, 326:12
  young man, singularly, 104:37
Deeper than did ever plummet sound,
    269:44
Deer, a-chasing the wild, 46:3
  go weep, stricken, 225:28
  I was a stricken, 74:39
  rats and such small, 241:35
Defac'd deflower'd, and now to death
  devote, 173:39
Defaming and defacing, 297:26
Défauts de leur qualités, 22:31
Defect in her, some, 269:35
  of Henry King, chief, 28:1
  perfection, make, 214:3
Defects of their qualities, 22:31
Defence and ornament, 29:24
  at one gate to make, 174:17
  or apology, make a, 62:4
Defend, he had promised to, 153:29
  me from my friends, 372:28
Defender, I mean the Faith's, 49:33
Defer or neglect it, not, 114:3
Deficiency, supply their, 203:24
Defiled, shall be, 340:22
Deform'd, unfinish'd, 244:12
Dégagé, half so, 74:9
Degeneration, fatty, 285:29
Degree, in an extreme, 200:29
  suits with our, 36:4
Degrees, name you the, 218:13

is in the dice, 416:23
is kind to his own, 416:21
is not so black, 416:24
lies brooding, 416:25
lurks behind the cross, 416:26
make the best of, 379:53
man, woman, and, 398:11
one point beyond, 356:29
renounce the, 341:40
resist the, 340:3
shame, 414:17
sin to belie, 390:24
stood, abash'd the, 172:5
sups with, 377:58
synonym for the, 153:20
take her, the, 288:2
take the hindmost, 416:27
talk of, 414:7
tell truth and shame, 23:22
tempted by but one, 379:63
tempts all, 416:28
turned precisian, 159:32
was sick, 416:29
was well, 416:29
were dead, if, 442:32
when most I play, 245:16
whispered, till the, 141:28
will come, the, 157:18
will cozen, 377:47
will have his chapel, 438:3
will have you, 411:69
will send, 438:13
wipes his tail, 416:30
world, the flesh and, 341:35
you don't know, 362:20
you know, better, 362:20
your adversary, 340:7
Devil's back, got over, 435:56
chaplain, 439:55
children, 416:31
foot, who cleft, 86:7
gold ring, wear, 428:33
leavings, 199:26
meal is all bran, 416:32
walking parody, 65:25
workshop, 385:56
Devilish thing is 8 times 8, 99:31
Devils in the kitchen, 440:35
would set on me, as many, 152:5
Devizes, young man of, 344:9
Devon, glorious Devon, 32:4
if the Dons sight, 183:20

Devonshire lane, in a, 158:2
Devotion, chapel of, 415:73
I love to use at, 359:19
mother of, 388:11
much prayer but little, 375:68
object of universal, 129:20
to something afar, 277:21
Devotion's visage, with, 224:3
Devour many, unless he, 420:7
me, threat'ning to, 171:22
seeking whom he may, 340:7
Dew, brings the cold, 409:46
cumbers, at midday the, 130:6
dissolve itself into, 220:19
drenched with, 80:14
fed it with silver, 276:1
from the heath-flower dash'd, 210:21
glist'ring with, 171:33
rain'd a ghastly, 293:34
soft falls the, 27:23
to meet the morning, 20:1
walks o'er the, 220:13
Dewdrop from the lion's mane, 271:21
woman like a, 38:16
Dewey was the admiral, 308:16
Dew-lapped like Thessalian bulls, 257:44
Dews away, brushing, 112:18
of summer night, 162:1
Dewy was the morning, 308:16
Dexterity, such skill and, 81:30
Diable est mort, 203:21
Diadem, bring forth the, 190:1
stole, from a shelf, 226:4
Dial, an hour by his, 216:11
from his poke, drew, 216:9
to the sun, true as, 359:61
Dialect words, 115:25
Dials quaintly, carve out, 238:6
Diamond, better than a, 349:9
cut diamond, 366:32
form, of, 76:2
in the sky, like, 291:28
Diamond! O Diamond! 183:31
Diamonds, not deck'd with, 238:8
Diana, great is, 337:66
of the Ephesians, 337:66
Diana's foresters, 231:26
Diapason closing full, 90:19
Diavolo incarnato, 389:65
Dice, best throw of, 415:54
devil is in, 416:23
Dicere, hoc tantum possum, 158:5

Dickens, what the, 256:12
Dictate, not presume to, 82:5
Dictionaries are like watches, 134:5
  writer of, 131:2
Dictionary, a walking, 62:2
  sensible as a, 59:21
Did it, canst not say I, 250:?
  well, when I, 436:3
Διδασκόμευσς, πολλά, 201:29
Dido found Aeneas would not come,
  199:29
Die [perish], a Christian can, 16:6
  a little trust that when we, 92:10
  all, die merrily, 233:37
  all that lives must, 220:16
  and endow a college, 197:30
  and go we know not where, 252:18
  and there an end, 250:4
  as natural to, 22:9
  as those that never, 180:10
  at last, must, 426:3
  at the top, I shall, 289:25
  be ashamed to, 156:4
  because a woman's fair, 315:27
  before they sing, 71:24
  believes he shall ever, 118:3
  better how can a man, 154:2
  beyond my means, 314:13
  but once, a man can, 234:25
  by G——, he shall not, 285:25
  clasp them because they, 73:24
  disappointed, 11
  ere he thrive, 380:21
  for love, 425:68
  he begins to, 358:40, 375:45
  he does not, 27:32
  hearken ere I, 292:13
  here in a rage, 289:23
  if I should, 34:8
  if we are mark'd to, 236:15
  is gain to, 339:49
  is not to, 55:32
  is —— to, 108:11
  it was sure to, 178:16
  let me sing and, 53:25
  like Douglas, 122:20
  live as they would, 394:33
  make none when they, 441:39
  more to do when we, 434:18
  never say, 401:62
  not willingly let it, 175:24
  now that I come to, 40:2

of a rose, 195:33
of it seldom recover, those that do,
  215:22
old men must, 442:35
once born, once must, 379:73
or rest at last, 277:26
since I needs must, 202:11
still love on, and, 204:12
taught us how to, 301:35
to: to sleep; no more, 224:4
to-morrow we, 338:34
to-morrow we shall, 331:55
to-night, if I should, 279:33
unlamented let me, 192:2
unless you can, 36:7
well that live well, 425:65
where thou diest, will I,
who would wish to, 31:29
will be an awfully big adventure, to,
  25:29
with harness on our back, 251:39
without Thee I dare not, 138:8
Die [dice] is cast, 53:41
Died for me, for her sake that, 342:10
  for thee, would God I had, 325:42
  from time to time, men have, 218:3
  in bitter pains, 129:23
  last night of my physician, 200:11
  liked it not, and, 321:25
  o' Wednesday, he that, 233:42
  since little Willie, 16:7
  sleeping when she, 124:1
  the neighbours came, when I, 147:29
  to save us all, 17:10
Dies ere he knows it, 39:29
  last thing about her that, 355:44
  like a dog, 313:23
  matters not how a man, 133:25
  most, he that lives most, 380:9
  pays all debts, he that, 269:38
  the first fit, 382:30
  the same, then, 322:3
  when an old man, 182:4
Dies irae, dies illa, 61:20
  sine linea, nulla, 403:61
Diet cures more, 366:33
  Dr. Quiet, Dr., 415:49
  sober in your, 176:8
Dieu n'existait pas, si, 306:12
Difference, made all the, 102:9
  to me, the, 317:21
  wear your rue with, 227:25

Difficult, all things are, 356:12
do you call it, 134:6
Difficulty and labour, with, 170:14
Diffidence is the right eye, 366:34
Dig, I cannot, 336:26
till you gently perspire, 142:19
Digest, inwardly, 341:38
something to, 345:21
Digestion bred, from pure, 172:8
give me a good, 345:21
sour, prove in, 243:25
wait on appetite, 250:1
Digests all things but itself, 364:15
Dignified, man who is, 60:29
Dignity compos'd, for, 169:32
of history, 31:24
Diligence is the mother of good luck,
366:35
Dimidium facti, 125:36
Dine at Ware, I should, 75:31
if this should stay to, 60:4
late, I shall, 145:19
on the pot-lid, 371:71
that jurymen may, 193:29
Dined to-day, I have, 281:25
Dines on the following day, 59:39
Ding, chiels that winna, 45:27
the deil into a wife, 442:4
Dinging, deserves no, 378:14
Dingle, or bushy dell, 165:27
Dining-room will be well lighted, 145:19
Dinkey-Bird is singing, 99:17
Dinner cool, no fear lest, 172:15
eats up all at, 377:63
he that saveth, 381:42
lubricates business, 212:8
sit awhile, after, 355:57
Dinner-bell, tocsin of the soul, 53:27
Dinners cannot be long, 366:36
hunger makes, 384:19
Diocese, in his own, 416:20
Diplomacy is to do and say, 107:40
Dirce in one boat, with, 145:16
Directions, rode madly off in all, 146:9
Directories, Pocket Books, 144:1
Dirge is sung, 71:34
Dirk, never draw your, 401:56
Dirt, eat a peck of, 368:39
enough, fling, 370:32
feet met, 322:10
never cast, 401:53
of his own ditch, dies in, 434:22

painted child of, 198:5
Dirty work again, at his, 197:41
Dis aliter visum, 306:1
Dis's waggon, from, 274:1
Disappointed, never be, 199:27
Disappointment every day, by, 76:11
Disaster, laugh at all, 150:12
meet with Triumph and, 142:14
Disasters, had the fewest, 80:4
trace the day's, 109:26
Disclosure, sky makes no, 38:13
Discobulus, standeth, the, 49:31
Discontent, hang the head as, 36:3
in pensive, 283:31
winter of our, 244:10
Discord, bray'd horrible, 172:19
harmony not understood, 195:37
Discords sting, their, 122:10
Discouraged, do we feel, 308:16
Discourse, bid me, 263:22
dialect and, 48:24
of the elders, 340:21
subtle and sinewy to, 175:32
sweet, 412:57
with such large, 226:15
Discovery, never made a, 279:28
Discreet advise, while, 438:24
Discretion is the better part, 366:38
ounce of, 357:55
woman without, 328:26
would run away, 433:56
Discrowned, crowned and again, 130:3
Disdain and scorn, 258:21
my Dear Lady, 258:10
Disease is incurable, 234:7
meet the, 190:3
my life, long, 197:43
shapes of foul, 296:5
worse than, 421:73
Diseases are the interests, 366:39
desperate, 366:31
desperate grown, 226:12
remedy to all, 47:41
Disgrace, open, 407:59
with fortune, in, 263:35
Disgraces are like cherries, 366:40
Disguises which we wear, 172:1
Dish, empty, 362:14
fit for the gods, 229:20
in a lordly, 324:21
meet him in my, 384:31
nor wash, 269:34

510

Doctrines plain, makes all, 49:25
Dodger, the Artful, 83:25
Doers are ill deemers, ill, 388:18
  least, 418:36
Does a thing through another, 408:7
  'tis not what man, 38:7
Doest, tell thee what thou, 414:13
Doff it for shame, 239:33
Dog a bad name, give, 372:6
  and bark myself, keep, 385:48
  and bark yourself, keep, 367:52
  are you, whose, 199:24
  bark, go in, if, 386:21
  barks, if the old, 386:29
  better be the head of, 361:60
  beware of a silent, 362:34
  bites his master, mad, 420:14
  bites sore, old, 357:45
  brag is a good, 363:61
  curious incident of, 87:34
  does not eat dog, 367:61
  gnaws bone, while, 438:25
  has done, what that, 97:21
  has his day, every, 368:24
  he that would hang, 382:12
  hindmost, 419:54
  his day, every, 139:28
  I am his Highness', 199:24
  I had rather be a, 230:12
  into the mouth of a bad, 389:70
  is a lion at home, 368:25
  is drowning, when, 435:72
  is thy servant a, 325:56
  is turned to his own vomit, 340:8
  it is a poor, 390:13
  it was that died, 108:10
  little toy, 96:16
  living, 330:23
  love me, love my, 397:62
  man, a horse, and a, 352:36
  mine enemy's, 242:6
  more ways to kill, 424:12
  new tricks, teach an old, 441:75
  one of the two dogs meets, with a third,
    97:21
  over a stile, help, 428:48
  shall bear him company, 195:31
  sick as, 358:35
  smarts, this, 97:21
  something better than, 293:32
  that bit you, hair of, 352:1
  that licks ashes, 416:34

  to beat, 354:7
  to follow you, wish, 388:7
  to tear, giving your heart to a, 142:17
  to throw at a, 215:33
  went mad, the, 108:9
  will have his day, 227:43
  will not howl, 350:24
Dog Hollow, 183:26
Dog's tooth, [trust not], 432:1
  walking on his hinder legs, 132:21
Dogerel, may wel be rym, 64:2
Dogged as does it, it's, 303:16
Dogs, all by the name of, 249:32
  and a bone, two, 432:24
  and all, little, 241:40
  are fighting, two, 97:21
  bark as they are bred, 367:62
  bark at me, 244:12
  bark before they bite, 367:63
  between two, 237:27
  come in, at open doors, 359:84
  delight to bark, let, 309:29
  eat of the crumbs, 324:28
  fight for a bone, two, 432:26
  heed the barking of, 420:26
  hungry, 384:21
  lie, let sleeping, 395:44
  of war, let slip, 229:34
  over stiles, lame, 139:32
  quarrelling, 408:4
  seldom bite, barking, 360:8
  that bark at a distance, 367:64
  throw physic to, 251:33
  wag their tails, 367:65
  who lies down with, 382:29
Doing [is] another [thing], 409:64
  joy's soul lies in, 270:14
  or suffering, 168:17
  shortest answer is, 422:14
  then be up and, 149:29
  well, worth, 435:61
  what he does, by, 65:28
Δοκεῖν ἀριστος, ἀλλ' εἶναι, σύ γάρ, 16:12
Dole, happy man be his, 374:23
Doll, had a sweet little, 139:30
  in the world, prettiest, 139:30, 139:31
Dollar, the almighty, 129:20
Dollars, however plenty, 67:28
Dolore, nessun maggior, 79:20
Dolores, splendid and sterile, 289:37
Dolphin's back, mermaid on, 257:31
Dolphin-chamber, in my, 234:12

Dome, that rounded Peter's, 94:21
Domestiques, admirez par leurs, 176:12
Domina, beata mea, 180:5
Domitian, from the death of, 104:8
Don John of Austria, 64:14
Don, remote and ineffectual, 27:31
Dona ferentes, et, 305:32
Done at all, surprised to find it, 132:21
  at any time, may be, 435:63
  been and gone and, 105:20
  betters what is, 274:2
  by, do as you would be, 367:46
  cannot be undone, 426:12
  determined, dared and, 279:27
  for you, what have I, 119:26
  if you want a thing, 387:67
  is done, what's, 249:34
  it is well, 215:28
  may compute what's, 144:22
  quickly, well it were, 247:40
  so little, 203:29, 296:1
  something, 150:1
  we ought not to have, 340:28
  well begun is half, 435:43
  when 'tis done, if it were, 247:40
  would 'twere, 268:11
Done-to-death, called, 302:8
Doom, regardless of their, 111:34
  to the crack of, 250:17
Doom's day, death's day is, 366:16
Doomsday is near, 233:37
Doon, banks and braes o', 46:12
Dooney, on my fiddle in, 321:37
Door, before his cottage, 282:4
  beside a human, 317:26
  beside the golden, 146:8
  came out by the same, 98:5
  creaking, 350:18
  daughters and a back, 432:25
  forc'd me from the, 180:14
  form from off my, 191:26
  good John, shut the, 197:36
  have a hatch before, 391:53
  keep the wolf from, 429:53
  knocking on the moonlit, 81:20
  [love] goes out at, 397:46
  may be shut, every, 368:26
  may tempt, open, 357:54
  nice wife and a back, 353:59
  on its hinges, as, 309:34
  open the, 436:10
  sat at her ivied, 54:9

should go, another by, 404:30
shut the stable, 430:20
shut, when he finds, 359:89
shuts, when one, 436:21
stood open at our feast, 69:16
sweep before your, 412:56
Door, that hath a low, 377:49
  to which I found no key, 98:8
  world will make a beaten path to his,
    94:20
Doorkeeper, had rather be, 327:48
Door-nail, dead as, 357:75
Doors, dogs come in, at open, 359:89
  good clothes open, 373:48
  open to courtesy, all, 355:68
  [step] out of, 418:35
  th' infernal, 170:10
Doorways are alternate Night and Day,
    79:34
Dorian mood of flutes, 168:19
Dorians pray, to whom, 154:9
Dormienda, nox est perpetua, 60:14
Dormitat Homerus, bonus, 165:5
Dotage flow, streams of, 130:14
Dote on his very absence, 253:36
Doth not what he ought, 378:20
  what he should not, he that, 378:19
  what he will, he that, 378:20
Double, double, toil and trouble, 250:11
  entendre, horrible, 344:11
  lived in regions new, 137:28
  surely you'll grow, 316:8
Doubled him up for ever, 106:23
Doubt, do I wander and, 117:24
  doubter and the, 95:27
  leave out, when in, 436:15
  never stand to, 120:13
  no possible, 106:22
  on, to hang a, 261:37
  that indicates a, 24:9
  truth to be a liar, 223:30
  when in, 126:29
Doubtful, sways, 421:56
Doubting Castle, 42:12
Doubts and fears, saucy, 249:44
  are traitors, our, 252:3
  he shall end in, 22:19
  nothing, 380:3
Douglas, come back to me, 77:31
  conquer, like, 122:20
  in his hall, 210:11
Doux comme l'amour, 291:17

Dove found no rest, the, 323:25
  gently as any sucking, 257:29
  on the burnish'd, 293:31
  that I had wings like, 327:41
Dove, beside the springs of, 316:19
Doves, harmless as, 324:13
  moan of, 294:23
Dowagers for deans, 294:6
Dowglas, tendir and trewe, 122:7
Down [on ground], he that is, 42:15, 379:64
  help him that is, 379:65
  hill, easy to bowl, 391:43
  let me shift for myself, for my coming,
    179:23
  tale shall put you, 232:13
  with him, he that is down, 379:64
Down [high land], hill that skirts, 26:16
Downs, all in the, 103:24
Downstairs, why did you kick me, 138:11
Dowry, great, 351:72
Doxy over the dale, 273:40
Drab, good for, 350:15
Drachenfels, crag of, 50:17
Draff, eats up all, 422:28
  is good enough, 367:66
Drag in Velasquez, why, 312:4
Dragon, swinged the, 239:30
Dragon-fly on the river, 36:11
Drain, leave by the next town, 284:6
Drama, fifth shall close, 28:13
Drank deep, glories and, 98:1
Draught [drink], for a nauseous, 90:13
  of cool refreshment, 290:12
Draught [game] boards bound and lettered,
  144:1
Draughts intoxicate, shallow, 192:6
Draw in again, did soon, 120:10
Drawers of water, 324:17
Dread, walk in fear and, 69:36
  whence this secret, 15:14
Dreadful thing, acting of, 228:18
Dream all night without a stir, 137:33
  behind, a, 265:30
  but an empty, 149:24
  do I, 117:24
  doth flatter, as a, 265:16
  I saw, as in a, 27:24
  is past, when the, 36:7
  love's young, 178:4
  o'er the spirit of my, 52:7
  of fighting fields, 211:23
  of love, then they, 266:13

of, not to tell, to, 70:5
of peace, from a deep, 126:37
of those that wake, 200:10
one man with a, 186:1
perchance to, 224:4
phantasma, or a hideous, 228:18
prolong, flattering, 76:21
short as any, 256:23
the poet's, 318:20
untroubled of hope, 183:21
within a dream, 191:22
wrecks of a dissolving, 277:25
Dream'd of the devil, 18:3
  that, as I wandered, 276:9
Dreamer cometh, this, 323:35
  of dreams, 180:8
Dreaming, of thee I'm fondly, 148:16
Dreams are made on, as, 269:40
  are true, morning, 400:15
  full of sweet, 136:6
  go by contraries, 367:69
  he sees, 169:27
  his white Platonic, 130:4
  I have spread my, 321:33
  I talk of, 266:14
  into the land of, 139:21
  is it some, 308:13
  lies down to pleasant, 41:26
  may come, what, 224:4
  no mortal ever dared to dream, 191:25
  of thee, I arise from, 275:35
  old men shall dream, 332:25
  out of mind, put my, 289:27
  that are done, 289:27
  that wave before the half-shut eye,
    300:16
  to sell, there were, 27:22
  waken from his summer, 275:33
  you tread on my, 321:33
Dreamt that I dwelt in marble halls, 42:3
Dree out the inch, 367:70
Dress and manners, 274:11
  be plain in, 176:8
  sweet disorder in, 120:5
  this fleshly, 304:11
  well, we don't, 274:11
Dressed, first, 381:39
  in all his trim, 265:20
  when he's well, 83:35
Dressings fit, for every season, 342:15
Drest, still to be, 134:19
Dries sooner, nothing, 403:37

E

that sweep away the morning dew, 257:44
to hear, he that hath, 325:65
to one tongue, two, 432:28
walls have, 433:75
were of different sizes, 344:9
with ravish'd, 90:21
woods have, 370:16
Earthly things above, all, 284:7
Earthquake and eclipse, 275:27
Earthquake's spoil is sepulchred below, 50:10
Ear-witnesses, better than ten, 404:36
Earth a sphere, preserves, 205:17
  abideth for ever, 330:7
  affords or grows, that, 92:14
  after soft showers, fragrant, 171:33
  an Eden, make this, 58:1
  and heaven, crawling between, 224:8
  and man were gone, 33:30
  and sky, bridal of, 119:41
  and Sky stand presently, till, 140:19
  and water, daughter of, 276:3
  bleeding piece of, 229:33
  bowels of the harmless, 231:36
  circles the, 310:7
  confound all unity on, 250:20
  do dwell, that on, 138:16
  doth like a snake renew, 277:25
  doth live, on the, 267:31
  felt the wound, 173:38
  fruitful, make, 408:37
  gazing on the, 276:11
  girdle round about, 257:33
  going to and fro in, 325:59
  happy, help to make, 58:1
  has bubbles, 247:26
  has not anything to show, 317:35
  here, there is our, 38:21
  hides it, 386:20
  I will move, 18:6
  in an earthy bed, were it, 296:19
  in a sepulchre, whole, 189:28
  is here so kind, 130:2
  is the Lord's, 138:27
  it fell to, 150:7
  lards the lean, 231:43
  lat her i' the, 227:37
  left your souls on, 137:28
  lie heavy on him, 96:1
  must have a touch of, 297:29

nightly to the listening, 15:9
not like the inhabitants o', 247:23
or air, in, 220:11
passed away a glory from, 319:31
proudly wears the Parthenon, 95:22
sad old, 313:29
snug little farm the, 70:14
soaks up the rain, 74:3
spins, low as where, 206:14
spot which men call, 165:27
sure and firm-set, 248:14
the broken arcs, on, 39:40
the brown old, 39:40
the whole round, 297:43
they shall inherit, 333:35
this goodly frame, 232:37
this grave, this dust, this, 202:13
tideless and inert, 23:28
to earth, 341:55
upon the lap of, 113:19
was young, when the, 154:17
way of all the, 324:18
with ruin, man marks, 51:28
yours is the, 142:16
Earth's base built on stubble, 166:2
  diurnal course, in, 317:22
  foundations fled, when, 126:22
  human shores, round, 138:1
  shadows fly, 276:16
  smoothness rough, turns, 39:43
Ease after warre, 283:28
  and alternate labour, 300:10
  and success are fellows, 367:84
  cometh great, 403:72
  doctrine of ignoble, 205:23
  done with so much, 89:22
  in our hours of, 210:13
  live at home at, 187:23
  of sufferance cometh, 403:75
  prodigal of, 89:26
  think of, 426:18
Easily done, that which is, 414:28
East, daily farther from, 319:35
  in fee, hold the gorgeous, 317:38
  is East and West is West, 140:19
  Side, West Side, 29:29
  tried to hustle the, 142:12
  west, home's best, 367:85
  with his back to, 69:16
  with richest hand, gorgeous, 169:28
Easter let your clothes be new, at, 359:80
  must pay money at, 375:66

Elders, discourse of, 340:21
Eldorado, land of, 26:2
Elegant but not ostentatious, 131:33
Element, gay creatures of, 165:36
Element's below, thy, 240:19
Elementary, said he, 88:1
Elements, amidst the war of, 16:1
    I tax you not, 241:24
    so mix'd in him, 230:23
Elephant, footstep of the, 58:2
Elephant's Child, an, 143:31
Eleven, fine before, 408:13
    wickedness [takes], 400:34
Elfland, horns of, 294:12
Elginbrodde, Martin, 245:18
Eli, lama sabachthani, 325:62
Elizabeth, times of great, 292:20
Ell, as good as an, 357:40
    he'll take, 372:13
'Ελλάδο, ερεισμα, 190:14
Elm star-proof, branching, 165:26
Elms, in immemorial, 294:23
Eloquence neither convinces nor satisfies
    me, 304:7
    resistless, 174:9
    teach, 397:41
    than speech, more, 303:20
Eloquent, that old man, 167:27
'Elp you when you're downed, 142:5
Elsewhere for thousands, I would not be,
    182:14
Elucescebat quoth our friend, 39:36
Elves also, the, 120:11
    can reach to whisper in your ear, 300:5
    faery, 169:27
    of hills, brooks, 269:43
    the dapper, 165:32
Elysium have ye known, what, 137:29
Emathian conqueror, great, 167:26
Embalmed and treasured up, 175:29
Embark, when I, 298:6
Embarras des richesses, 17:25
Embattled farmers stood, 95:24
Embers through the room, 164:19
Embrace, eludes, 188:6
    endure, then pity, then, 195:40
    none do there, 158:12
    take your last, 268:8
Emelye, up roos, 63:39
Emeralds chas'd in gold, 210:4
Emigrated to another star, 129:23
Eminence, rais'd to that bad, 169:28

Ημισυ παντός, πλέον, 120:15
Emmanuel's veins, drawn from, 76:17
Emotion new, bounding at, 20:1
    recollected in tranquillity, 320:18
Emperor and clown, heard by, 137:20
    had he not been, 290:10
    tent-royal of, 235:43
Emperors ridiculous, make the pomp of,
    94:17
Empire, dismemberment of, 107:32
    down, trample an, 186:1
    how is the, 104:5
    is a Commonwealth, 206:2
    survey our, 51:35
    westward the course of, 28:13
Empires has come, day of, 61:27
Employ, if you'll give me, 343:21
Employed, might be better, 376:17
    more innocently, 133:31
Emptiness betray, smiles, 198:6
Emptor, caveat, 364:10
Empty dish, 362:14
    louder, but as, 195:41
    sack cannot stand, 356:31
    swept and garnished, 324:20
    vessels, 368:9
Enchanted, as holy and, 70:9
Enchantment, distance lends, 55:17
Enchantments of the Middle Age, 20:3
Encounter, free and open, 175:35
Encounters, hath many, 378:32
Encourage the others, to, 306:14
Encourager les autres, pour, 306:14
End, a' made a finer, 236:1
    and aim, our being's, 196:2
    be like his, let my last, 324:9
    born to disastrous, 283:31
    crowns the work, 370:19
    crowns all, 417:40
    everything hath, 369:52
    here is my journey's, 262:15
    justifies the means, 417:41
    look to, 408:30
    makes a swan-like, 254:22
    midst and without, 172:12
    most sweet, to make, 243:21
    must justify the means, 200:6
    of ane old sang, ane, 185:16
    of it, never hear, 367:60
    of this day's business, 230:20
    on't, there's an, 133:24, 133:30
    served no private, 197:35

such beginning, such, 412:50
the sooner, we may, 412:39
them, by opposing, 224:4
things will mend, in, 389:54
true beginning of our, 258:2
try the man, let the, 234:13
we shall go on to the, 66:3
wish it all at an, 44:1
yes, to the very, 206:11
Endearment tries, fond, 108:22
Endears, all the more, 294:8
Endeavour, by no, 105:40
  to learn, disinterested, 20:4
  too painful an, 197:23
Ending, bread-sauce of the happy, 129:27
  makes a good, 351:51
Endow, I thee, 341:50
Ends, burn the candle at both, 428:4
  divinity that shapes, 227:44
  meet, make, 430:1
  thou aim'st at, all, 239:19
  to gain some private, 108:9
  to serve our private, 65:38
Endure, for thy peace, she shall 207:33
  we first, 195:40
Endured, must be, 435:48
Enemies I can defend myself, from, 372:28
  if you have no, 387:55
  love your, 333:45
  men's double, 383:39
  my most intimate, 207:18
  naked to mine, 239:20
  reconciled, 412:73
  shall lick the dust, 327:45
  so many, 411:72
  soften to us our, 286:8
Enemy, be able for thine, 213:24
  better an open, 361:48
  bound to forgive, 387:41
  but his own, no man's, 376:19
  escapes, 380:30
  faints not, 68:1
  familiar, 403:60
  first, a friend, then, 439:76
  for a flying, 371:43
  found me, O mine, 325:51
  [God send me], 373:37
  hath done this, an, 324:23
  here shall he see no, 216:4
  how goes the, 203:23
  hunger, if thine, 338:16
  if you would make, 388:6

is too many, one, 404:34
learn even from, 391:71
left, hardly a warm, 312:5
let your house to, 417:74
lives, so long as, 423:61
not bound to trust, 387:41
say nothing, of, 412:25
[trust not] an old, 432:2
Energy divine, march and, 198:11
Engine at the door, two handed, 167:21
Engines, mortal, 261:35
England all in one year, into, 432:19
  at her roots, poison, 32:1
  bound in with the triumphant sea, 243:30
  bow was made in, 88:5
  breed again, 88:13
  but one ten thousand of those men in,
    236:14
  Channel of Old, 343:30
  children in, 415:77
  did adorn, Italy and, 90:18
  dress and manners in, 274:11
  Elizabethan, 128:15
  expects that every man will do his duty,
    182:16
  famine in, 350:31
  given to horses in, 131:26
  has saved herself, 191:17
  hath need of thee, 318:1
  her soldiers, Ireland gives, 161:32
  home, and beauty, 20:10
  is a nation of shopkeepers, 181:32
  is lost, Old, 133:39
  is the mother, 33:25
  is the paradise of women, 368:10
  it is well with, 437:43
  keep, unless proud, 88:8
  know, who only, 140:15
  knuckle-end of, 281:19
  martial airs of, 310:7
  men of, 275:31
  meteor flag of, 55:25
  mourns for her dead, 29:18
  my England, 119:26
  my own, 119:26
  ne'er had been, such night in, 154:11
  never did, not never shall, 240:6
  of a king of, 93:35
  Oh, to be in, 38:4
  over here in, 185:21
  road that leads him to, 132:18
  roast beef of, 97:22

'Επιφανῶν πᾶσα γῆ τάφος, 189:28
Epitaph, believe a woman or, 50:1
  drear, the, 142:12
  that may be his, 286:7
Epitaphs, derangement of, 277:36
  talking of, 24:3
  worms and, 243:39
Epitome, all mankind's, 89:34
Ἔπος φύγεν, ποῖόν σε, 123:26
Epp's statues are junk, 344:15
Equal knew I never, thine, 102:3
  men are created, 129:29
  to all things, 109:34
Equalled with me in fate, 170:16
Equator, speak disrespectfully of, 281:18
Equivocate, I will not, 102:20
Equivocation will undo us, 227:31
Ηρακλῆς πρὸς δύο, οὐδέ, 405:75
Ercles' vein, this is, 257:27
Erebus, dark as, 256:2
Eremite, patient sleepless, 138:1
Eremites and friars, 171:19
'Ερετμοῖς, αλα τύπτον, 123:32
Erin, a poor exile of, 55:30
Ερκος ὀδόντων, 123:26
Ermine, in, 388:33
'Eroes, thin red line of, 141:35
  we aren't no thin red, 141:36
Ἔρως ἀνίκατε μάχγν, 2081:32
Err is human, to, 193:19, 384:14
  with Pope, better to, 50:2
Errands, meet.to be sent on, 230:9
Errare, humanum est, 384:14
Error, all men are liable to, 149:20
  ancient, 365:78
  he was guilty of no, 34:13
  hurl'd, in endless, 195:39
  of opinion may be tolerated, 129:30
  than all the hosts of, 41:24
  under temptation to, 149:20
  what damned, 254:24
Errors fall, some female, 193:25
  like straws, 91:40
Erubuit, Deum vidit, et, 78:2
Erupit, excessit, evasit, 67:19
Eruption, bodes some strange, 220:5
Esau, hands of, 323:32
  selleth his birthright, 323:31
Escalier, l'esprit de l', 85:27
Escape, counsel that hath no, 390:30
Escaped, he, he broke forth, 67:19
  not quite, 419:57

Escapes, field where none, 390:9
  hairbreadth, 260:3
Eskdale and Liddesdale, 211:41
Espoused, my fairest, my, 172:9
Esprit de l'escalier, 85:27
Espy, what stands before him, 303:17
Essay, to make a short, 91:30
Essence, his glassy, 252:11
Estate, fallen from his high, 91:24
  he has a good, 375:63
  near of kin to, 391:50
  of the realm, fourth, 153:21
  they had his, 89:36
Estates are spent in the getting, 398:21
Esteemed, little, 435:49
Estimate, thou know'st thy, 264:15
Estre à soy, où, 176:13
État, c'est moi, 151:23
Eternal are, where the, 276:17
Eternity, dazzles at it, as at, 304:16
  deserts of vast, 158:11
  I saw, 304:13
  in an hour, 30:8
  mighty ages of, 57:41
  radiance of, 276:16
  some shadows of, 304:10
  thou pleasing-dreadful thought, 15:14
  through nature to, 220:16
  to man, intimates, 15:14
Eternity's sunrise, lives in, 30:10
Ἤδη χρήσθ', φθείρουσιν, 106:6
Ether, an ampler, 320:9
Ethics of the text-book, 300:1
Ethiopian change his skin, 332:13
Eton, playing fields of, 311:18
Etrurian shades, 168:13
Ettrick and Teviotdale, 211:41
Εὖ νικάτω, τόδ', 16:15
Eugene Aram walked between, 123:40
Ευρηκα, 18:5
Ευριπίδην οιοι εἰσὶ [ποιειν], 381:33
Euripides chorus-ending from, 39:37
  the human, 36:5
Europe, better fifty years of, 293:39
  by her example, save, 191:17
  is extinguished, glory of, 43:28
Evanish all like vapours, 17:23
Eve [woman], artless as, 54:3
  fairest of her daughters, 171:30
  gentle, 409:61
  span, Adam dolve and, 23:30
  with a berry, 121:29

523

good, 351:54
influence of, 132:1
is better, 369:60
may profit by, 119:31
Examples, derived from, 85:78
taught, by such, 77:23
Excel, always to, 123:28
thou shalt not, 323:40
'tis useless to, 152:13
Excellence, stewards of their, 265:18
Excellent, I cried, 88:1
Excelsior, strange device, 150:3
Exception proves the rule, 417:49
without some, 424:38
Excess, ocean of, 52:2
of it, give me, 271:24
surprise by a fine, 138:4
wasteful and ridiculous, 240:2
Exchange, by just, 278:16
fair, 350:30
Exciseman, deil's awa wi', 46:18
Exciting, found it less, 106:21
Excrement, stolen from general, 270:7
Excrucior, fieri sentio et, 61:16
Excuse, a bad, 349:2
every man will plead, 212:17
I will not, 102:20
make the fault the worse by, 240:3
Execute, a hand to, 104:10
Executors, delivering o'er to, 235:43
lean, 350:32
let's choose, 243:39
Exercise depend, for cure, on, 90:13
is to the body, what, 284:17
Exertion in the proper place, cease, 207:24
Exhalations of the dawn, 71:25
Exile, long as my, 219:27
Existence, contemplate, 83:39
put out of, 84:19
saw him spurn, 130:16
would exist, every, 33:30
Exit, pursued by a bear, 114:9, 273:33
Exits and their entrances, 216:17
Expect, I know what I have to, 118:2
suffer and, 412:53
Expectation, bettered, 258:6
fails, oft, 213:28
full of, 232:1
whirls me round, 270:16
Expects it, man least, 419:43
Expediency, the ground of, 205:26
Expedient, all things are not, 338:26

to pursue the, 109:34
Expenditure nineteen nineteen six, 84:5
Expense of two, who would be at, 68:4
Expensive but cheap, 146:12
Experience, daughters of daily, 407:74
is the mistress of fools, 369:61
name everyone gives to his mistakes,
314:10
to make me sad, 218:1
Experiment be tried, let, 370:14
Experimentum, flat, 370:14
Expert is one who knows, 481:1
Explanations, I do loathe, 25:23
Expletives their feeble aid do join, 192:14
Express her goodliest, 241:46
what I can ne'er, 51:27
Expressed, ne'er so well, 192:9
Expression, his favourite, 84:3
Extensive and peculiar, 82:11
Extent, no more, hath this, 259:53
Extenuate, nothing, 262:16
Extinguish, fire that you cannot, 393:56
Extortioners, unjust, 336:34
Extreme right is extreme wrong, 369:62
Extremes meet, 369:63
women are always in, 440:32
Extremity, man's, 398:14
Exuberance of his own verbosity, 85:37
Eye, a microscopic, 195:32
affection beaming in, 83:38
all my, 356:4
an unforgiving, 278:7
apple of the, 326:19
auspicious and a dropping, 220:14
beam that is in, 333:58
before the half-shut, 300:16
broad breast, full, 263:23
changing, like a joyless, 276:11
dark and fiery, 194:5
dazzles, my striving, 304:16
dissolv'd in dew, her, 145:25
doesn't see, what, 435:67
dust hath closed Helen's, 182:6
enter into life with one, 325:34
far from, 369:81
flash upon that inward, 318:16
for an eye, 333:43
for eye, 324:5
fringed curtains of, 269:27
glad me with its soft black, 178:16
half hidden from the, 317:20
has danced, many an, 121:8

of men, persuade, 263:26
of most unholy blue, 278:6
of wonder, dreaming, 58:16
one whose subdued, 262:16
ope their golden, 219:30
open, [keep], 393:53
out, pick hawks', 375:44
owl's, 419:62
pair of sparkling, 106:25
pearls that were his, 269:26
play the woman with mine, 250:25
poorly satisfy our, 321:24
quaint enamell'd, 167:22
quiet, 287:27
rain influence, bright, 164:7
rapt soul sitting in, 164:14
read in, 419:47
ride sparkling in, 258:21
see more, four, 371:60
see with mortal, 18:12
severe, with, 216:17
she gave me, 317:28
slumbers kiss your, 80:11
so blue, where did you get, 154:15
so bright, why are her, 162:2
so low, cast one's, 241:48
so shut your, 96:15
sought the west afar, 208:21
sparkle like those, 54:8

that shone, the, 178:14
the break of day, 253:22
the glow-worm lend, 120:11
they have changed, 269:28
through another man's, 218:9
throw dust in, 431:39
tir'd eyelids upon tir'd, 292:19
to be cast into hell, having two, 325:34
to discover, for dim, 180:9
to tear each other's, 209:30
two lovely black, 68:8
until you see the white of, 201:21
uprais'd, with, 71:37
used to blacken, 199:33
voice and her hair and, 159:26
weep out his, 439:43
were closed, thy dying, 194:3
were deeper, her, 206:12
were out, if your, 442:3
where you turn your, 192:3
which spake again, 50:11
wide open, keep, 393:52
with [dust], fills, 377:70
with eagle, 136:4
with his half-shut, 193:31
with Spring in her, 299:32
Eye-witness is better, one, 404:36
Εζόμενοι, εξῆς, 123:32

F

Fable or romance, resounds in, 168:20
Fabric, like the baseless, 269:40
   sprung, the mystic, 118:6
Fabricks, the dissoluble, 131:31
Fabula narratur, de te, 125:20
Face, a garden in her, 56:4
   again, never see my, 297:42
   beauty of an aged, 55:6
   beauty of the, 340:25
   climber-upward turns, 228:17
   cover her, 310:11
   divine, human, 170:17
   eye is the pearl of, 417:51
   fair in the, 363:54
   familiar with her, 195:40
   finer form or lovelier, 210:20
   full in, 412:54
   God has given you one, 224:10

good, 351:55, 6
he hides a smiling, 76:20
her angels, 283:27
I don't mind it, my, 95:36
in one autumnal, 86:11
in the public's, 207:32
is as a book, your, 247:36
is my fortune, my, 343:25
is past shame, 438:14
is the index, 417:55
it falls in his, 439:57
kissing with golden, 264:4
look in my, 206:17, 302:18
look on her, 193:25
look upon my quiet, 279:33
loved its silly, 202:16
make yourselves another, 224:10
mind's construction in, 247:32

must hide, false, 248:9
needs no band, good, 351:56
of heaven so fine, make, 268:1
one would meet in every place, 137:27
pass into her, 317:23
sees the other's umber'd, 236:10
she looket in my, 25:17
shine upon thee, make his, 324:8
shining morning, 216:17
smile shone over his, 299:24
so pleased my mind, 342:14
that fixed you, absent, 36:7
that launched a thousand ships, 157:15
that mist in my, 40:4
there, you find one, 139:29
to face, 369:64
to face, but then, 338:31
to spite one's, 428:20
to start into her, 259:34
too roughly, visit her, 220:20
transmitter of a foolish, 208:12
with his prism and silent, 318:22
with how wan a, 278:19
without a smiling, 353:52
wonder with a foolish, 198:2
Faces, bid them wash their, 219:22
   I have seen better, 240:17
   lords and owners of, 265:18
   of stone look down, 201:26
   of the poor, grind, 331:49
   old familiar, 144:7
   sea of upturned, 212:3
   smile, those angel, 183:29
   so many millions of, 35:23
   to bear two, 427:69
Facit per alium, qui, 408:7
Facts alone are wanted, 84:15
   are chiels that winna ding, 45:27
   are stubborn things, 369:65
   to his imagination for, 278:13
Faculty, how infinite in, 223:37
Fade away, the first to, 178:16
   nothing of him that doth, 269:26
Faded and gone, are, 178:8
Fading away, things are, 26:6
Faenum habet in cornu, 125:22
Faery, land of, 321:31
   lands forlorn, in, 137:20
   of the mine, swart, 165:42
Fagi, sub tegmine, 305:21
Fahnen hoch, die, 311:29
Fail, if we should, 248:7

no such word as, 153:15
Failed much, 286:7
Failings lean'd to virtue's side, 108:21
Fails, one sure, if another, 37:31
Failures and a fire, three, 426:36
Faint and far away, 184:8
   yet pursuing them, 324:24
Faintly, faintlier afar, 102:2
Fair [beautiful], all so excellently, 70:18
   all that's, 307:23
   and foolish, 369:67
   and softly, 75:28, 369:68
   and twice so fair, 189:14
   and yet not fond, 186:12
   anything to show more, 317:35
   deserves the, 90:20
   folk are aye fushionless, 369:69
   [for ever] she be, 137:23
   if thou be, 406:49
   in love, all is, 355:73
   is foul, 247:19
   is it very, 147:27
   most divinely, 292:21
   of face, 399:77
   she be, what care I how, 315:27
   speak us, 355:64
   the chaste, the, 217:20
   thing found false, 424:36
   to outward view, not, 68:14
   were it fifty times as, 277:31
   woman's eye, in, 349:16
   women and brave men, 50:11
Fair [market], here's the, 126:21
Fairer than that, say no, 84:8
   than the day, 315:27
   than the evening air, 157:16
Fairest of creation, 173:39
   of her daughters, 171:30
   smoke follows, 411:68
   thinks her own bird, 416:6
Fairies, beginning of, 25:28
   break their dances, 126:20
   rewards and, 73:21
   trip the pert, 165:32
Fairies' coachmakers, 266:13
   midwife, 266:13
Fairin, thou'll get thy, 46:11
Fairy, believes it was, 20:13
   godmother, child has, 300:5
   takes, no, 220:12
Faith and fire within us, 116:6
   and green fields, 28:10

and Hope, only by, 132:1
and hope the world will disagree in, 196:1
and service, made of, 218:10
asks firmness, 397:44
evidence of things not seen, 339:66
for modes of, 196:1
grope with little, 304:5
he wears his, 258:9
hope, charity, 338:32
I have kept the, 339:64
in honest doubt, more, 296:3
is fast, that his, 36:7
is kneeling by his bed, 88:15
is the substance of things hoped for, 339:66
might be wrong, 74:2
not by sight, by, 339:39
plain and simple, 230:10
pure-eyed, 165:35
shines equal, 33:29
such as do build, 48:12
than Norman blood, simple, 292:16
'tis my, 316:6
unfaithful, 297:31
we walk by, 339:39
with my childhood's,
Faithful, come, all ye, 185:14
ever sure, ever, 163:19
in love, so, 210:7
only he, among the faithless, 172:17
to thee, Cynara, 87:23
unto death, be, 340:12
Faithless as the winds, 212:13
faithful found among, 172:17
Faiths and empires gleam, 277:25
are wafer-cakes, 236:3
Falchion, good biting, 242:14
Falcon, towering in her pride of place, 249:30
Fall, fear I to, 202:12
from his untimely, 345:17
greater, 419:50
half to rise and half to, 195:39
haughty spirit before, 329:36
into the ditch, both shall, 324:27
it had a dying, 271:24
laugh at a, 38:12
low, look high and, 396:32
needs fear no, 42:15
out with those we love, 294:8
than rise, easier to, 391:39

the harder they, 99:24
therein, shall, 329:58
to rise, held we, 40:20
was there, what a, 230:4
Fallen, fallen, fallen, 91:24
he that is, 379:65
how are the mighty, 325:36
how art thou, 331:53
or be for ever, 168:15
Falling in melody back, 70:13
with a falling State, 193:36
Falling-off was there, what a, 222:15
Fallings from us, vanishings, 319:38
Falls, as I do, then he, 238:15
between two stools, 362:31
like Lucifer, 238:16
stumbles and, 381:57
sudden, 374:35
to-day, he that, 378:22
False again, prove, 49:25
and hollow, all was, 169:32
as dicers' oaths, 226:1
fair thing found, 424:36
ring out, 296:4
that I advance, all, 74:14
to any man, canst not then be, 221:39
Falsehood can endure touch of celestial temper, no, 172:3
framed heart for, 278:4
grapple, let her and, 175:35
hath goodly outside, 254:3
in fellowship, 424:31
Falstaff sweats to death, 231:43
Faltered more or less, 287:23
Fame, bandits in the paths of, 46:14
common, 365:45, 365:46
damned to everlasting, 196:8
elates thee, while, 177:28
great heir of, 163:28
I slight, nor, 193:38
inspires, fair, 198:2
is but the breath, 369:77
is no plant that grows on mortal soil, 166:17
is the spur, 166:16
many ways to, 424:9
nor yet a fool to, 197:42
rage for, 315:29
shall be damned to, 194:18
shall be outworn, thy, 180:10
soon spread around, 75:29
that wit could ever win, 42:6

titles, wealth and, 194:4
unknown, to, 113:19
was but a dream, lust of, 33:28
Fames eternall beadroll, on, 283:30
Familiar, but by no means vulgar, 221:37
but not coarse, 131:33
in his mouth as household words, 237:18
palpable and, 71:25
Familiarity breeds contempt, 369:78
Families, best-regulated, 355:51
resemble one another, happy, 302:4
Family, every unhappy, 302:4
form one, 121:18
Famine in England, 350:31
under water, 433:45
Famous, found myself, 53:38
men, let us now praise, 340:25
Fan, brain him with his lady's, 232:2
use so large a, 59:35
Fancies are more giddy, our, 271:42
Fancy, a young man's, 293:31
bred, where is, 254:23
bright-eyed, 113:27
feign'd, by hopeless, 294:14
not express'd in, 221:38
of most excellent, 227:33
painted her, all my, 82:1, 160:3
power of, 217:34
roam, ever let the, 137:26
sweet and bitter, 218:6
whispers of, 131:29
Fanny's way, only pretty, 187:26
Fans in hell, no, 424:15
Fantastic toe, the light, 163:34
tripped the light, 29:29
Fantasy, all made of, 218:10
nothing but vain, 266:14
Fantasy's hot fire, not, 209:23
Far and few, far and few, 147:16
between, short and, 29:28
far, away, 321:38
from eye, far from heart, 369:81
he that goeth, 378:32
that never turns, goes, 375:60
to go, has, 399:77
Fare, hard, 374:24
surveyed the unaccustomed, 279:34
thee well, for ever, 52:5
worse, go farther and, 372:23
Fared sumptuously every day, 336:29
Fares, how he, 183:27
Farewell! a long farewell, 238:15

and adieu to you, 343:30
content, 261:35
for a mute, 128:16
for ever, 230:19
goes out sighing, 270:18
hail, and, 61:18
need not bid, 138:6
no sadness of, 298:6
remorse, 171:23
such welcome, such, 412:51
to Lochaber, 203:18
Farce est jouée, 202:3
is played, the, 202:3
Fardels bear, who would, 224:4
Far-fetched and dear bought, 369:79
Farm, his little snug, 282:9
his snug little, 70:14
Farmer stood, embattled, 95:24
Farrago libelli, nostri, 135:25
Farther and fare worse, go, 372:23
Farthing, at a single, 60:14
from a thousand pounds, 412:65
maketh a penny of, 420:23
[maketh] sixpence of, 420:23
uttermost, 333:42
Farthings, Latin word for three, 246:4
Fashion, after the high Roman, 214:18
faithful in my, 87:23
glass of, 224:11
must mind, 412:62
out of, 358:1
out of the, 66:13
Fashioned so slenderly, 124:8
Fashnable fax, 298:13
Fast [quick] they follow, so, 227:27
we live, too, 19:20
Fast [go hungry], feast or, 368:8
till he is well, must, 378:21
Fasting, between a fou man and a, 212:6
Fat and greasy citizens, 215:40
and grows old, one is, 232:6
and kicked, waxed, 324:14
and merry, 369:67
could eat no, 392:34
friend, who's your, 41:23
is in the fire, 417:60
let me have men about me that are,
228:14
laugh and grow, 394:11
makes a man, 403:79
of others' works, 47:38
of the land, eat of, 323:38

oxen, who drives, 134:1
she help'd him to, 24:8
should himself be, 134:1
sow, little knoweth, 395:13
with the lean, take, 442:18
Fate, all influence, all, 100:6
cannot touch me, 281:25
conspire, with, 99:20
drives the stubborn, 370:4
equall'd with me in, 170:16
foreknowledge, will and, 169:40
hanging breathless on, 150:13
heart for every, 51:10
hides the book of, 195:27
in the storms of, 193:36
leads the willing, 370:4
let this be my, 199:28
master of my, 119:23
no armour against, 278:15
summons, when, 90:5
take a bond of, 250:15
too much, fears his, 177:19
torrent of his, 130:15
why should they know their, 111:34
with a heart for any, 149:29
Fates a jest, owe the, 143:22
masters of their, 228:11
Father, after your own, 414:14
bred, without, 164:11
child that knows, 390:26
dear father, 320:20
dies, cry not when, 131:20
goes to the devil, 374:20
heard his children scream, 110:19
is more, one, 404:77
it is a wise, 254:11
like son, like, 395:75
maketh a glad, 328:24
my true-begotten, 254:10
urged me sair, my, 24:17
was hanged, told his, 382:26
when they are old, [suck], 364:23
which art in heaven, 333:48
which is in heaven, glorify, 332:40
Father William, you are hale, 282:8
you are old, 58:6, 282:8
Fatherland, dear, 208:14
Fathers, ashes of his, 154:2
God of our, 140:24
of war-proof, 236:6
slept with his, 325:46
that begat us, 340:25

Fathom five, full, 269:26
Fauld, sheep are in the, 24:16
Fault, all fault who hath no, 297:29
and his sorrows, his, 177:29
and not the actor, condemn, 252:7
confessed, 350:33
doubles it, denying, 366:26
excusing of a, 240:3
he that commits, 378:10
I see, hide the, 198:17
is, where no, 438:7
or stain, without 33:18
seeming monstrous, 217:31
the glorious, 194:2
the worse, make, 240:3
which needs it, 119:37
Faultless, faultily, 296:9
lifeless that is, 376:18
piece to see, 192:8
Faults a little blind, to, 200:5
are not written in their foreheads, 369:45
are thick, 370:5
best men are moulded out of, 253:25
every man has, 368:35
first, 417:70
has she no, 199:21
I love thee, with all, 74:36
lie gently on him, 239:22
men have, 399:58
not for thy, 50:23
observed, all his, 230:16
of man, bear with, 56:3
rich men have no, 408:34
teeth and forehead of, 225:38
tell of my, 373:37
to scan, their, 108:21
vile ill-favour'd, 256:13
wink at small, 440:3
with all her, 65:36
you would spy, 442:33
Faustus must be damned, 157:18
Faute, c'est une, 101:21
Favour, kissing goes by, 393:65
wi' wooin' was fashous, 181:23
Favourite has no friend, 112:3
Favours call, nor for her, 193:38
hangs on princes', 238:16
I've felt all its, 68:9
Fawne, to crowche, to, 283:31
Fear and Bloodshed, 319:25
and danger, continual, 121:26
and trembling, with, 339:50

with silver-sandaled, 314:17
would not wet, 415:72
Felice, ricordarsi del tempo, 79:20
Felicem fuisse, 31:22
Felicitas, curiosa, 190:5
Felicite, what more, 283:32
Felicities, Nature's old, 320:13
Felicity, absent thee from, 227:54
  studied, 190:5
  their green, 137:35
  we make, our own, 131:21
Felix opportunitate mortis, 290:9
  qui potuit, 305:26
Fell, from morn to noon he, 169:26
  half so flat, 344:5
  help me when I, 291:21
  like the stick, 187:14
  never climbed, never, 380:27
  rides sure that never, 376:56
  the instant that he, 210:16
Fella, also on the unjust, 32:6
Feller, sweetes' li'l', 284:14
Fellow, he's a Good, 99:17
  I shot his, 253:32
  if I be a thief, ask my, 359:74
  many a good tall, 231:36
  of no mark, 233:30
  want of it the, 196:4
  with the best king, 237:24
Fellow-feeling makes one, 103:19
Fellow-rover, a laughing, 159:22
Fellows as I do, what should such, 224:8
  at football, all, 355:69
  Nature hath framed strange, 253:26
Fellowship, falsehood in, 424:32
  like no, 397:42
  right hands of, 339:44
Felt as a man, 26:18
Female of sex it seems, 174:18
  of the species, 141:32
Femina, varium et mutabile, 306:4
Feminine gender, she's of, 185:17
Femme, cherchez la, 92:7
Fen of stagnant waters, 318:1
  wild-fire dances on, 22:26
Fence against a flail, no, 401:76
  cunning in, 272:18
Fences make good neighbours, good, 102:8
Fere, my trusty, 45:40
Fern is as high as a ladle, 437:35
Ferry, row us o'er the, 54:22
Fers, il est dans les, 207:20

Festina lente, 370:11
Fetch you out, bound to, 387:57
Fetlocks shag and long, 263:23
Fetters, he [man] is in, 207:20
  no man loveth, 402:17
Feud, Fhairshon swore a, 22:5
Fever, after life's fitful, 249:36
  starve, 370:9
Few and evil have the days, 323:39
  and far between, 55:19
  and select, guests, 145:19
  fit audience find, though, 172:22
  owed by so many to so, 66:5
  there be that find it, 324:4
  we happy few, we, 237:19
Fewer men, the greater share of honour, 236:15
  the better cheer, the, 420:35
Feynd, is slee, the, 92:12
Fez, transferr'd from, 136:13
Fhairshon swore a feud, 22:5
Fib or sophistry, destroy, 197:41
Fickle and changeable, 306:4
Fiction, clad in eternal, 62:3
  condemn it as an improbable, 272:13
  stranger than, 432:8
Fiddle, all, 389:56
  fit as, 356:83
  play first, 430:5
  play second, 430:5
  when I play on my, 320:37
  while Rome is burning, 428:27
Fiddler, in the house of, 389:56
Fiddle-strings, friends are like, 371:61
Fidele's grassy tomb, 71:39
Fidelity, genius for, 92:8
Fie, foh, and fum, 241:39
  my lord, fie, 251:27
Field, better than the open, 349:1
  comes and tills, 293:29
  corner of a foreign, 34:8
  flood and, 260:3
  from the wet, 19:29
  hard-fought, 390:9
  in the tented, 259:54
  rush'd into the, 50:14
  set a squadron in, 259:46
Fields, a' babbled of green, 236:1
  are green, [as long as], 76:12
  dream of fighting, 211:23
  flowering of His, 297:37
  his study, 30:18

Finis coronat opus, 370:19
Finish, good lady, 215:20
Finishes but few [things], 382:27
Finnigin, gone ag'in, 106:28
Fir-branch, lone on the, 160:19
Fire, a clear, 143:39
  and fleet and candle-light, 342:8
  answers fire, 236:10
  as bad as, 426:40
  burn and cauldron bubble, 250:11
  burns out another's burning, one, 266:9
  burnt child dreads, 415:63
  by a sea-coal, 234:12
  cold performs th' effect of, 170:2
  don't one of you, 200:21
  fell in the, 111:20
  fretted with golden, 223:37
  frightened with false, 225:27
  in each eye, 197:37
  in his hand, hold, 243:27
  in his shirt of, 279:31
  in one hand, 375:51
  into, 406:4
  irons in, 429:42
  is a good servant, 370:20
  is not quenched, 336:3
  is quickly trodden out, little, 238:9
  kindle not, 393:56
  laden, with white, 276:2
  like a house on, 395:67
  like the sparks of, 120:11
  makes sweet malt, soft, 411:74
  now stir the, 74:41
  of another, better than, 422:24
  of chats, 397:63
  pale his ineffectual, 222:19
  put out the kitchen, 411:52
  set the Thames on, 430:19
  she snatches from the sun, 270:7
  ships fear, 410:33
  should have stood that night against my, 242:6
  that in the heart resides, 18:21
  that is closest kept, 370:21
  the fat is in, 417:60
  the right Promethean, 246:9
  there is hot, 389:51
  three failures and, 426:36
  to burn us, great, 361:43
  to warm us, little, 361:43
  was near, to view what, 282:15
  well, he that can make, 378:2

well may be smell, 435:44
well to work and make, 435:45
which lights us, 417:64
wife that sits by, 395:12
without light, 443:48
without some smoke, no, 424:37
you may poke a man's, 442:8
Fire-flames noondays kindle, 37:33
Fires burning, keep the home, 100:12
  fuel to maintain his, 56:14
  soon burn out, violent, 243:28
  straight, 365:68
  sulphurous and thought-executing, 240:23
  veils her sacred, 194:24
Fire-side, adventures were by, 110:5
  clime, a happy, 46:4
Firing, fetch in, 269:34
Firmament, brave o'erhanging, 223:37
  is rottenness, pillar'd, 166:2
  no fellow in, 229:27
  showeth his handiwork, 326:21
  the spacious, 15:8
  with living sapphires, glow'd, 171:32
First, all men can't be, 356:3
  and the last, 340:19
  building erected, 389:48
  come, first served, 370:23
  glass for thirst, 417:71
  him last, him, 172:12
  in the hearts, 147:23
  in war, first in peace, 147:23
  is the best, 403:74
  month is honeymoon, 435:71
  shall be last, 324:41
  that ever burst, the, 69:22
  there is no last nor, 37:22
  to the hill, comes, 378:8
  wife is matrimony, 417:73
  worse than the, 324:21
Fish, all is, 355:74
  and company stink, 370:28
  are not caught, all, 355:70
  are on the rock, 436:30
  best, 415:42
  better small, 362:14
  cries stinking, 402:11
  daughters and dead, 366:3
  for every man, 422:11
  had I, 374:7
  he has gone to, 147:19
  I was a, 280:7

in the sea, as good, 424:7
is cast away, 370:29
it is a silly, 390:22
kettle of, 353:68
must swim thrice, 370:30
no more land, say, 34:5
nor flesh, neither, 401:47
of one, make, 430:2
out of water, like, 395:68
that hath fed of that worm, eat of, 226:14
to fry, I have other, 384:30
will soon be caught, 414:22
with glittering tails, 346:3
you'll catch no, 387:64
Fish-ball, bread with one, 145:20
Fisher goes not forth, 437:49
Fishermen three, rocked, 96:15
Fishers went sailing, three, 167:26
Fishes gnaw'd upon, men that, 245:18
live, I marvel how, 263:19
talk, if you were to make little, 110:12
Fish-guts, keep your ain. 393:51
Fishified, how art thou, 267:33
Fishing before the net, 391:62
best, 389:53
end of, 417:42
in troubled waters, 391:46
Fishmonger's wife, 349:5
Fist instead of a stick, 48:2
Fit [*well, suitable*] as a fiddle, 356:83
audience find, though few, 172:22
for God nor man, neither, 354:30
Fit [*foot*], ganging, 351:47
Fithele, or gay sautrye, 63:27
Fitted abide, things well, 46:16
Fittest, survival of the, 79:25, 283:19
Five, how many beans make, 429:57
in five score, not, 199:31
must rise at, 382:5
nature requires, 400:34
thousand a year, if I had, 298:18
Fivepence, fine as, 356:82
Flag [*standard*] flying, keep the Red, 72:13
has braved, whose, 54:23
has flown, English 140:16
her holy, 122:9
of England, meteor, 55:25
of our Union for ever, 180:2
spare your country's, 312:22
was still there, our, 138:17
Flag [*lose vigour*] or fail, we shall not, 66:3
Flagons, stay me with, 330:39

Flail, no fence against, 401:76
Flame, Chloe, is my real, 200:4
feed his sacred, 70:17
hard, gemlike, 188:2
nor private, dares to shine, nor public, 194:24
so full of subtile, 27:19
take away, 412:66
Flames, through their paly, 236:10
must waste away, his, 56:14
went by her like thin, 206:15
Flanders fields, in, 154:12
Flat as a pancake, 356:84
insipid, many times, 92:2
Flatter, neither borrow nor, 376:43
Flattered, being then most, 229:21
Flatterer as a man's self, no such, 425:46
friend and, 425:46
Flatterers besieged, by, 198:2
tell him he hates, 229:21
Flattering with delicacy, 21:25
Flattery, is paid with, 131:27
sincerest of, 72:4
Flavour, gives it all its, 74:38
Flax shall he not quench, 332:2
Flea has smaller fleas, 288:12
in his ear, with, 430:18
in March, kill one, 387:56
Fleas have little fleas, great, 81:21
killing of, 403:55
rise with, 382:29
to go on, greater, 81:21
Fled, all but he had, 118:14
far away, now 'tis, 68:9
Him, I, 298:37
Flee [*run away*] fro the prees, 62:16
from you, [devil] will, 340:3
Flee [*fly*] stick to the wall, let, 395:45
Fleece was white as snow, 115:15
Fleet thou canst not see, Spanish, 278:9
was moor'd, 103:24
Fleets of iron framed, 88:8
sweep over thee, ten thousand, 57:28
Flesh and blood so cheap, 124:5
at all, no, 361:45
bring me, 182:12
could not all this, 233:45
creep, make your, 82:9
cut out of thine own, 390:5
fair and unpolluted, 227:37
he that buys, 376:76
how art thou fishified, 267:33

for powder, 233:40
have been Tom's, 241:35
he eats, seeking the, 216:6
homely was their, 103:21
nothing to eat but, 139:20
nourishing and wholesome, 289:19
that is as luscious, 260:12
Fool and his money, 350:32
answer a, 329:56
answer not, 329:55
asks much, 418:3
at forty is a fool indeed, 322:7
better be, 361:50
breakfast for, 353:60
by the hand, takes, 398:18
call me not, 216:8
comfort to, 430:7
does in the end, 435:68
doth his business, 438:24
for his master, has, 381:61
hath great need of, 375:73
hath said in his heart, 326:16
he is, 376:3, 376:4, 376:5, 376:6
he that sends, 381:44
he'll return, 410:14
himself, plays, 375:73
ill white hairs become, 234:37
in a mortar, bray, 329:63
in Christendom, wisest, 119:28
is busy, 418:4
is counted wise, 329:41
is hang'd, my poor, 242:15
knows more in his own house, 350:33
laughter of, 330:19
lies here, a, 142:12
like an old fool, no, 402:1
make him, 379:50
makes many, one, 404:39
may ask, greatest, 72:5
may ask more questions, 350:34
may give a wise man counsel, 350:35
me to the top of my bent, 225:33
must now and then be right, 74:14
no man can play, 402:10
of himself, brains enough to make,
    285:34
on occasion, play, 376:20
or a physician, 368:32
resolved to live a, 27:19
sees not the same, 30:13
smarts so little as, 197:40
some of the people, 25:21

sometimes, every man is, 368:36
speaks to a, 381:60
suspects himself a, 322:3
thinks, as, 359:52
though ever so great, 308:18
to make me merry, 218:1
to steal, you are, 440:56
to the market, send, 410:14
wanders, 418:6
who does not take it, 355:41
whosoever shall say, Thou, 333:41
will be meddling, every, 329:46
will not give his bauble, 350:36
Fool's bolt is soon shot, 350:37
Foolish in the fault, 379:67
is wise, least, 420:3
thing, never said, 204:8
to make him, 417:72
Foolishness depart from him, will not,
    329:63
Fools and bairns, 370:36
and madmen, 370:37
are fain of flittin, 370:38
are my theme, 49:38
at the wicket, flannelled, 140:21
built on the heads of, 394:16
by shaving, 349:7
contest, let, 196:1
determine, 440:17
discourse of, 364:11
dreading e'en, 198:2
fain, fair words make, 369:75
fortune favours, 371:56
gladly, ye suffer, 339:41
[have] their hearts in their mouths,
    440:13
idol of, 365:76
in one house, two, 432:30
it would go hard with, 387:35
[learn] by their own [mistakes], 440:14
mistress of, 369:61
never-failing vice of, 192:5
'od rot 'em, 280:2
repeat [proverbs], 440:15
rush in, 193:21
see these poor, 189:24
shame the, 197:39
should be so deep-contemplative, 216:11
so play, 394:29
the money of, 121:24
the Paradise of, 170:20
these mortals be, what, 257:39

think old men, 442:36
to go under, for, 395:23
to suckle, 260:15
twenty-seven millions, mostly, 57:34
went not to market, if, 385:74
who came to scoff, 109:23
wore white caps if, 385:67
would keep, none but, 252:14
yesterdays have lighted, 251:37
Foot, and the Forty-Second, 123:36
depart on, 399:72
feeble of, 32:7
for foot, 324:5
for the sole of her, 323:25
foremost, put one's best, 430:9
in the grave, one, 429:44
is better, one, 405:40
keep something for a sore, 393:49
less prompt, 20:1
lie at the proud, 240:6
like a cat, 352:3
make crouch beneath, 40:11
more light, a, 210:21
ox has trod on, 415:57
pinch, 361:66
shall pass, with shining, 99:21
shoe fits not every, 369:47
slip, better, 362:21
so light a, 267:37
speaks, her, 271:22
was never tied, on fleeter, 211:25
Football, all fellows at, 355:69
Footfall and the next, between one, 160:37
Footing seen, no, 263:22
Foot-in-the-grave young man, 104:43
Footman, was, 280:5
Foot-path way, jog on, 273:42
poor, narrow, 45:29
Footprints on the sands of time, 149:28
Footstep falls, where soft, 27:24
Footsteps, master's, 420:20
Foppery of the world, excellent, 240:11
For ever, and for ever, 193:32
Forbear and to persevere, 286:8
bear and, 360:20
for Jesus' sake, 266:2
me, down hill, 433:51
Forbearance ceases to be a virtue, 42:23
is no acquittance, 371:49
Forbid a thing, 371:50
it, Almighty God, 119:33
live a man, 247:20

Force hidden, great, 424:32
however great, no, 312:1
no argument but, 35:29
who overcomes by, 169:24
Ford there was none, where, 210:8
Forearmed, forewarned, 371:51
Forecast, worth a pound of, 356:56
Forefathers, the rude, 112:6
think of your, 15:5
Forehead, middle of her, 150:21
of ivory, 180:5
Foreheads villainous low, 269:42
written in, 369:45
Foreign hands, by, 194:3
troop was landed, 62:12
world, with any portion of, 309:22
Foreigners always spell better, 303:27
Foremost fighting fell, 50:14
none who would be, 154:4
Forest dim, fade away into, 136:15
on forest hung about his head, 137:32
primeval, this is, 156:10
Forests are rended, when, 211:35
of the night, in, 30:5
shook, from the, 265:21
Foretell, expiring do, 243:28
Foretold, long, 395:27
Forever, man has, 39:28
Forewarned, forearmed, 371:51
Forget and smile, better, 206:9
best sometimes, 260:21
best to, 40:15
forgive and, 371:52
if thou wilt, 206:10
lest we, 140:25
not yet, 320:28
sometimes useful to, 435:65
thee, if I, 328:11
them all, you'll, 193:25
women and elephants never, 187:21
Forgetful be, she may, 76:18
Forgetfulness a prey, to dumb, 112:17
not in entire, 319:35
steep my senses in, 234:18
sweets of, 26:17
Forget-me-nots of the angels, 150:11
Forgets, heart that has truly lov'd never,
178:2
himself, he is a fool that, 376:3
Forgetting, the world, 194:8
Forgive and forget, 371:52
any sooner than thyself, 371:53

divine to, 193:19
good to, 40:15
them as a Christian, 21:27
them, Father, 336:38
us our debts, 333:48
vengeance is to, 421:47
you, will never, 378:16
Forgiveness, ask of thee, 242:9
give — and take, 98:16
to the injured, 91:38
Forgot, all the rest, 263:34
Forgotten man, the, 205:20
nothing, 290:15
seldom seen, soon, 410:9
soon, 395:25
soon learnt, soon, 412:8
Forks and hope, with, 60:1
Forlorn, make me less, 319:29
Form and feature, in, 147:28
and moving how express and admirable,
in, 223:37
divine, what [avails], 144:12
lifts its awful, 109:25
mould of, 224:11
Former days were better, 330:20
or the latter, 200:29
Forms unseen, by, 71:34
vents in mangled, 216:13
Forsaken me, why hast thou, 325:62
when he's, 123:37
Forspent, clean, 145:27
with love and shame, 145:27
Forsworn, so sweetly were, 253:22
Fort, hold the, 30:17
Fortes ante Agamemnona, vixere, 125:33
Fortiter in re, 371:54
pecca, 152:7
Fortress built by Nature, 243:29
Fortunatam natam me consule, 66:22
Fortunate, I rejoice at it, 229:35
if you are too, 387:47
Fortune, adversity of, 31:22
and men's eyes, 263:35
and to fame unknown, to, 113:19
architect of his own, 368:38
baggage of, 408:35
beguiling, of, 66:9
can take from us, 371:55
favours fools, 371:56
favours the brave, 371:57
grit of, 258:25
good night, 240:18

great, 351:73
has forgot you, 387:55
he that hath no ill, 379:47
in a wife, better a, 360:41
knocks once, 371:58
knocks, when, 436:10
leads on to, 230:17
make a Scotsman's, 426:36
makes better, 376:8
man's best, 353:53
means to men most good, when, 239:36
method of making, 113:33
of another, 418:2
of outrageous, 224:4
ounce of, 356:56
pipes to whom, 375:56
rail'd on Lady, 216:7
sick in, 240:11
smiles, where, 320:39
till heaven hath sent me, 216:8
to fools, God sends, 373:39
troubled with good, 379:47
what is your, 342:25
Fortune's buffets and rewards, 225:19
cap we are not the very button, on,
223:34
golden smile, 45:26
ice prefers, 89:29
right hand, 389:64
Fortune's, pride fell with, 215:32
Fortune-teller, juggler and, 218:19
Forty, a fool at, 322:7
days it will remain, 409:49
devil at, 354:39
every man at, 368:32
every man over, 274:21
feeding like one, 317:31
knows it at, 322:3
rich at, 379:72
to fifty, from, 191:15
Year, till you come to, 298:28
years on, 32:7
Forty-nine, nineteen [takes] to, 139:34
Forty-three, pass for, 104:21
Forward and not back, look, 115:14
those behind cried, 154:4
Fou for weeks thegither, 46:8
I was na, 44:8
o' love divine, 44:10
Fought, from morn till even, 236:6
so long, he had, 244:4
with us upon St. Crispin's day, 237:20

Foul, frost and fraud both end in, 371:69
  is fair, 246:18
  strange, and unnatural, 222:13
  thank the gods I am, 217:33
Found, all they ever, 204:5
  Him in the shining of the stars, 297:37
  it, I have, 18:5
  less often sought than, 53:37
  me, hast thou, 325:51
  out by accident, 144:6
  while he may be, 332:8
Foundation, low, 352:6
Foundations quiver, hell's, 24:14
Fount, meander level with, 177:18
Fountain, cast dirt into, 401:53
  fill'd with blood, 76:17
  heads, 100:5
  like the bubble on, 211:26·
  troubled, like a, 268:15
Fountain's murmuring wave, 26:16
  silvery column, 70:13
Fountains, Afric's sunny, 118:10
  sad, 342:17
  under the, 342:19
Founts falling, white, 64:13
  level with their, 153:22
Four eyes see more, 371:60
  for a birth, 404:41
  grant that twice two be not, 303:25
Four-footed things, of all, 65:25
Fourscore, witch at, 354:39
Fourth estate of the realm, 153:21
  [glass] for madness, 417:71
Fowl and mushrooms, 82:5
  concerning wild, 272:19
Fowles maken melodys, smale, 63:20
Fowls have fair feathers, far, 369:80
Fox fares best when he is cursed, 418:8
  if thou dealest with, 387:39
  is brought to the furrier, 359:83
  is not taken twice, 351:40
  knows much, 418:9
  may grow grey, 418:10
  needs no craft, old, 356:46
  preaches, when, 437:36
  preys farthest, 418:11
  than that of the, 30:20
Fox's sermon, comes to, 390:23
  [skin] shall, 386:26
  wiles, 418:12
Foxes have holes, 324:9
  take us the, 330:41

that spoil the vines, 330:41
Frailties, draw his, 113:21
Frailty, thy name is woman, 220:22
Frame began, universal, 90:19
  stirs this mortal, 70:17
  tremble for this lovely, 312:6
France, I saw the Queen of, 43:28
  order this matter better in, 285:26
  sun rises bright in, 78:10
  vasty fields of, 235:39
  win, he that will, 381:68
Francesca di Rimini, 104:42
Frank, haughty, rash, 153:16
Frankie and Johnny were lovers, 344:2
Frater, ave atque vale, 61:18
Fraud, frost and, 371:69
Fray, beginning of, 361:65
  second [blow] makes, 417:67
Fredome is a nobill thing, 23:36
Free as Nature first made man, 91:37
Free, from God he could not, 94:21
  in my soul am, 151:25
  know our will is, 133:24
  man is born, 207:20
  neither man or beast would ever go,
    386:12
  or die, we must be, 318:3
  should himself be, 134:1
  that moment they are, 74:35
  the fresh, the ever, 200:17
  they for to be, 208:15
  thou art, 18:15
  till all are free, no one can be perfectly,
    282:17
  truth shall make you, 337:47
  yearning to breathe, 146:8
Freed, thousands He hath, 61:29
Freedom and truth, fight for, 128:9
  and whiskey gang thegither, 44:20
  flame of, 290:5
  infringement of, 191:16
  new birth of, 148:8
  obtained I this, 338:1
  ring, let, 280:11
  service is perfect, 340:32
  shall awhile repair, 71:34
  shrieked—as Kosciusko fell, 55:18
  slowly broadens down, 292:22
  to the free, assure, 148:7
  to the slave, in giving, 148:7
  yet thy banner, 50:24
Freedom's cause, bled in, 124:19

Freely ye have received, 324:12
Freeman casting . . . vote, 122:14
Freemen, who rules o'er, 134:1
Freeze the pot, Janiveer, 392:36
French, if he could speak, 392:35
    or Turk, or Proosian, 104:32
    [wise] after the deed, 419:64
Frenchman, a fort, 389:48
    I praise the, 75:19
Frenchmen, did march three, 236:9
    sent below, ten thousand, 188:9
Frensh of Paris was to hir unknowe, 63:24
    she spak ful faire, 63:24
Frenzy, demoniac, 173:42
    rolling, in a fine, 257:46
    zeal without prudence is, 443:49
Fresh and strong, through Thee, 318:19
    benefits please while, 360:36
Freshness, dewy, 281:35
Fret, living, we, 40:15
Friar, Apollo turned fasting, 160:30
    many a, 24:4
Friars, white, black and grey, 170:19
Fricassee or a ragout, in, 289:19
Friday, born on, 363:54
    for losses, 399:76
    he that sings on, 381:50
    sneeze on, 411:69
Friday's child, 399:77
Friend, a fav'rite has no, 112:3
    a suspicious, 198:2
    accomplished female, 313:24
Friend and your flatterer, 384:27
    as you choose a, 205:27
    asks, when, 435:73
    before you make, 360:31
    better lose a jest than, 362:3
    [catch at] a falling, 401:54
    Codlin's the, 82:34
    countenance of, 329:62
    defend . . . your departed, 90:12
    doth lose his, 378:17
    faithful are the wounds of, 329:60
    fall not out with, 369:76
    false, 361:48
    for little children, 162:5
    gets, not lost that, 392:11
    go up higher, 336:17
    God send me, 373:37
    good, 266:2
    grant me still a, 75:19
    guide, philosopher and, 196:11

hath a worse, 402:12
he is a good, 376:7
he makes no, 297:32
in an old, 157:26
in court, 351:41
in need, 351:42
in the heart of, 150:8
is never known till needed, 351:43
knows not who is, 421:75
like the penny, no, 402:2
lose your, 394:31
mine own familiar, 327:42
mirror is an old, 415:45
of my better days, 115:17
only way to have a, 94:12
or foe, was it a, 207:18
prove, 406:73
religious book, or, 320:22
save me from the candid, 51:27
say welcome, 77:34
should bear his friend's infirmities,
    230:15
speak well of, 412:25
that sticketh closer, 329:43
then an enemy, 439:76
there, leaves his, 376:55
to all, 351:44
to none, 351:44
to thy lover, truest, 155:30
to thyself, be, 360:11
tolling a departed, 233:50
trust not a new, 432:2
try your, 432:17
when I lent I was, 436:14
when thou choosest, 372:22
who lost no, 197:35
who never changes, 162:5
who's your fat, 40:23
Friend's frown is better, 351:45
Friended, as a man is, 356:66
Friends, again, never be, 289:30
    all are not, 355:64
    and his relations, to his, 104:22
    are best, old, 212:15, 404:6
    are lapp'd in lead, 25:20
    are like fiddle-strings, 371:61
    are thieves of time, 371:62
    backing of your, 232:7
    both in heaven and in hell, 391:54
    called him candle-ends, 59:37
    cheating of our, 65:38
    dead have few, 416:14

Full as an egg is of meat, 356:85
  man and a fasting, between, 391:66
  stay long ere he be, 379:66
Fulness thereof, and the 338:27
Fume, black, stinking, 129:24
Fun, I thought What jolly, 202:16
  watching the, 184:13
Function, own no other, 274:2
Funeral baked meats, 220:25
  seen a costlier, 294:3
  with mirth in, 220:14
Funny as I can, as, 122:12
  ha-ha, 116:32
  peculiar, 116:32
Furies, fierce as ten, 170:5
Furnace, burning fiery, 332:18
Furnaces, worship is your, 32:2
Furniture, stocked with all, 87:31
  superfluously fair, 17:23

Furrier, fox is bought to, 359:83
Furrow alone, plough my, 206:4
  followed free, the, 69:22
Further you go, the, 418:17
Fury, beware the, 90:3
  comes the blind, 166:16
  like a woman scorn'd, 72:9
Fury, said cunning old, 58:5
Furze is hunger, under, 433:44
  is out of bloom, 437:38
Fussy thing called I, 345:21
Fust, do it, 310:32
Fustian's so sublimely bad, 198:1
Fustilarian, you, 234:10
Future in the distance, 23:33
  trust no, 149:27
Futurity, no reference to, 133:40
Fuzzy-Wuzzy, 'ere's *to* you, 141:37

G

Gaberdine, upon my Jewish, 254:5
Gadding are lost, by too much, 440:28
Gaiety of nations, eclipsed, 132:2
Gain is to lose, best, 412:2
  laughing, thou shalt, 394:20
  teacheth how to spend, to, 428:32
  which darkens him, 214:7
Gained than guided, easier, 371:74
Gainfullest, greatest burdens are not 418:32
Gaining, first, 412:20
Gains, God bless all our, 36:4
  ill-gotten, 388:19
  light, 395:63
  well and spends well, 378:27
  without pains, no, 402:3
Gait, like the forced, 232:24
Gaiters, all is gas and, 82:29
Galahad clean, nor, 297:26
Galatians, great text in, 37:31
Gale, lightning and the, 122:9
  that blew dismayed, no, 60:6
Galère, que diable allait-il faire dans cette,
  176:1
Gales shall fan the glade, 192:3
Galilean, thou hast conquered, 135:22,
  289:34
Galilee, on deep, 51:38
Gall, pigeon-liver'd and lack, 223:47

Gallant men, nation of, 43:28
Galled horse, touch, 431:64
Gallery, greenery-yallery, Grosvenor,
  104:43
Galley, doing in that, 176:1
Galleys went, over the sea, 36:13
Gallia est omnis divisa, 53:40
Gallio cared for none, 337:65
Gallop apace, 267:41
  of the verses, false, 217:24
Galloped all three, we, 37:28
Gallops, in this state she, 266:13
Gallows, complexion is perfect 268:17
  he'll ride to, 410:20
  sea and, 422:9
  will have its own, 418:18
Gallows-foot—and after, to, 142:9
Galumphing back, he went, 59:18
Gamaliel, at the feet of, 337:69
Gambrel would be, good, 412:4
Game and deceit, 440:31
  at the end of, 359:85
  beyond the prize, love, 183:22
  how you played the, 204:2
  is cheaper in the market, 371:12
  is done, the, 69:26
  is not worth the candle, 418:19
  rigour of the, 143:39

Giants in the earth, there were, 323:24
Gibes, great master of, 85:35
  now, where be your, 227:34
Giddy, I am, 270:16
Giff gaff makes good friends, 372:4
Gift, cheaper than, 435:53
  long waited for, 351:50
  which God has given, 209:23
Giftie gie us, wad some Power, 45:23
Gifts, gives me small, 378:29
Gods themselves cannot recall, 293:30
  when they bring, 305:32
  will not be distributed as, 67:28
Gig, crew of the captain's, 104:18
Gilding pale streams, 264:4
  would not want, 386:30
Gilead, balm in, 332:12
Gill, hang by its own, 368:27
Gilpin, away went, 75:29
  was a citizen, John, 75:26
Gilt first, try your skill in, 432:18
  off the gingerbread, take, 430:32
Ginger shall be hot i' the mouth, 271:39
Gingerbread, gilt off, 430:32
Giraffe, neck of the, 58:2
Girdle, at one man's, 356:9
Girl, an unlesson'd, 255:27
  cleanly young, 199:28
  goes walking, not a, 88:17
  in the *corps de bally*, 104:39
  in the kiss of one, 40:19
  like a frightened, 314:17
  sat under a tree, 126:8
  that fords the burn, 39:25
  there was a little, 150:21
  unschool'd, unpractised, 255:27
  who is bespectacled, 182:2
  you are, what a great, 59:28
Girl-graduates, sweet, 294:6
Girls again be courted, in your, 148:6
  are sent, where little, 148:1
  between two, 237:27
  rosebud garden of, 296:18
  swear to never kiss, 39:33
  that are so smart, 56:17
  wretched un-idea'd, 132:7
Give a shilling, better, 361:69
  thing and take a thing, to, 428:33
  a thing and take again, 372:11
  and spend, 372:12
  daughters, crying, 329:67
  him an inch, 372:13

I thee, such as I have, 337:57
  than to receive, most blessed to, 337:67
  thee all I, 138:10
Given him over, all have, 88:15
  me over, he would not have, 315:35
Giver, cheerful, 339:40
Givers prove unkind, when, 224:6
Gives, he that lends, 380:6
  says not, Will you? 418:23
  to all, who, 438:37
  twice, he, 363:43
Giveth twice that giveth in a trice, 375:58
Giving and taking, in, 389:43
  free in, 414:54
Glad and gay, we will be, 24:12
  be not too, 403:76
  I might as well be, 162:13
Gladdest thing, I will be, 162:11
Glade, in the bee-loud, 320:36
  points to yonder, 194:1
Gladly wold he lerne, 63:28
Gladness, sadness and, 409:45
  with solace and, 278:24
Glance from heaven to earth, 257:46
  my way, without a, 84:23
  was glum, whose, 106:20
Glare, ever caught by, 50:6
Glasgow beggar, stiff-necked, 140:7
Glass, darkly, through a, 338:31
  dome of many coloured, 276:16
  excuse for the, 278:6
  for thirst, first, 417:71
  he was indeed the, 234:14
  houses, who live in, 406:24
  like a broken, 176:3
  more women look in, 420:38
  o' the inwariable, 82:16
  thou art thy mother's, 263:30
  turn down an empty, 99:21
  without G, loves, 380:14
Glasses and lasses, 372:19
  fill all the, 74:4
  the musical, 110:6
Gleam, follow the, 298:4
  visionary, 319:34
Glee, forward and frolic, 210:22
  of his laughter and, 60:3
  songs of pleasant, 30:2
  to which with boyish, 54:6
  with counterfeited, 109:26
Glen, down the rushy, 18:1
  Kilmeny gaed up the, 122:2

bid him a' should not think of, 236:2
bless all our gains, 36:4
bless the King, 49:33
bless us all, 49:33
bless us every one, 82:47
but for the grace of, 32:8
by your faithfully, 143:35
Cabots talk only to, 31:31
called the children of, 332:37
closer walk with, 76:15
comes to see us, 372:26
comes with leaden feet, 372:27
conscious water saw, 78:2
could have made a better, 48:32
daughter of the voice of, 318:18
dear city of, 21:21
declare the glory of, 326:21
did not exist, if, 306:12
did seem to set his seal, every, 226:2
disposes, 398:10
[doth] what He will, 398:7
doorkeeper in the house of, 326:48
each moment, give to, 86:4
ef you waunt to take in, 151:32
erects a house, wherever, 80:5
ever has showed to me, 159:26
exact day-labour, doth, 167:31
fall into the hands of, 297:47
fear, 330:37, 340:4
flows from the throne of, 152:1
for a Greek, 160:8
forgotten, 416:10
for us all, 368:34
from the love of, 338:13
fulfils himself in many ways, 297:41
grace is given of, 67:30
had I served my, 315:35
hath joined, what, 324:37
he could not free, himself from, 94:21
he passed the days, with, 187:25
heals, 372:29
help us, cry, 434:21
helps, where, 438:5
himself scarce seemed there to be, 69:38
his Father and his, 113:21
house of, 323:33
I'll leap up to my, 157:18
in clouds, sees, 195:30
in him, she for, 170:28
in the highest, to, 336:7
is an attribute to, 255:33
is forgotten, 186:9

is in heaven, 330:15
is love, 340:10
is my refuge, eternal, 324:16
is no respecter of persons, 337:61
is not mocked, 339:45
is our refuge, 326:37
is the treasurer, 427:58
is, where there is peace, 438:18
just are the ways of, 174:16
kills the image of, 174:28
let us worship, 44:15
lost be for, 395:46
loveth a cheerful giver, 339:40
made him, 253:35
made Himself an awful rose, 293:47
made little apples, sure as, 358:48
ade the country, 74:33
made them all, 17:18
make a sacrifice to, 199:26
makes and apparel shapes, 372:34
many are afraid of, 149:21
marble leapt to life a, 163:16
more farre, from, 283:22
moves in a mysterious way, 76:19
never made his work, 90:13
no more, one, 404:42
noblest work of, 196:6, 44:16
observes, sure that, 38:13
of all, as, 195:28
of Bethel, O, 86:5
of Hosts, Lord, 140:25
of Jacob, O, 86:5
of love was born, 86:10
of mercy, 94:5
of my idolatry, 267:26
of old story, like a, 200:1
of our fathers, 140:24
of War, great, 345:23
once was a man who said, 143:35
one law, one element, one, 296:8
only, he for, 170:28
only, shalt have one, 68:4
or a beast, 354:15
or Devil, with him was, 89:35
ordained of, 338:18
others call it, 60:5
our help in ages past, 309:35
out of the mouth of, 332:34
praise, 138:14
put your hand into the hand of, 113:26
puts in at the window, 415:74
reigns, 103:16

rest you merry, 340:12
save the king, 340:23
shall raise me up, 202:13
shall wipe away all tears, 340:18
shed His grace on thee, 26:4
so loved the world, 336:42
stop, child of, 71:23
tempers the wind, 285:27
that loseth not, 376:38
the All-terrible, 65:34
the farther from, 421:45
the soul, 195:35
there is no, 326:16
they shall see, 332:36
thy God my, 324:27
to a black beetle, 160:1
to behold, beautiful, 289:33
to follow, bitter, 289:33
to man, so near is, 95:25
to man, vindicate the ways of, 195:26
to men, justify the ways of, 168:3
to scan, presume not, 195:38
to Thee, nearer, 15:6
to them that love, 338:11
up to nature's, 196:9
voice of, 433:72
were not a necessary Being, if, 302:1
what I call, 40:10
who gave it, unto, 330:35
who gave us life, 129:28
who is our home, from, 319:35
who made thee mighty, 28:5
will not serve, 259:49
will send, spend and, 372:12, 412:31
will, what, 435:50
with the grandeur of, 124:15
ye believe in, 337:53
you would do little for, 442:32
God's Almighty hand, by, 54:14
and truth's thy, 239:19
daughter, truth is, 432:7
image, reasonable creature, 174:28
in Gloucestershire, sure as, 358:49
in heaven, true as, 359:58
in his heaven, 37:19
mercies, known, be, 121:18
opportunity, 398:14
plenty, here is, 92:3
side, one on, 190:10
ways to man, justify, 126:17
works, best of all, 173:39
God-intoxicated man, 184:6

Goddess and maiden and queen, 289:32
excellently bright, 134:18
she moves a, 193:40
Godliness, in cheerful, 318:2
Gods are just, the, 242:11
as flies to wanton boys are we to, 241:43
dish fit for the, 229:20
he swore, by the Nine, 154:1
in the name of all, 228:12
may be, I thank whatever, 118:21
may be, whatever, 289:38
on the knees of, 123:29
revered, [sages] as, 300:14
so many, 313:30
struggle in vain, 208:13
temples of his, 154:2
that made the gods, 65:24
themselves cannot recall, 293:30
was otherwise, will of the, 306:1
ye shall be as, 323:18
Goest, tell me with whom thou, 414:13
Goethe's wide . . . view, 18:20
Going to and fro in the earth, 325:59
where are you, 342:24
Gold, accursed hunger for, 306:2
against the power of, 402:7
all is not, 355:76
as its purest, 198:18
ass loaded with, 356:28
barbaric pearl and, 169:28
be they made of, 402:17
can buy you entrance, no, 42:6
despise, heart can, 112:2
guilt first and then, 432:18
goes in at any gate, 373:43
hair and harpstring of, 289:33
in the morning, 363:68
in the realms of, 136:3
is she not pure, 37:35
narrowing lust of, 296:5
patines of bright, 255:43
pearl to, 26:2
reigneth, where, 433:63
saint-seducing, 266:7
spins, 380:4
standard, demand for, 41:25
than much fine, 326:23
though laden with, 356:27
thrice their weight in, 96:12
to gild refined, 240:2
touchstone trieth, 359:55
trieth men, so, 359:55

trust him with untold, 442:10
turns all it touches into, 365:52
upon a cross of, 41:25
when we have, 437:57
win gold and wear, 439:74
woman of, 354:11
Gold-cups and daisies, 180:9
Golde, better to me than, 314:22
Golden Age, found the, 76:21
 numbers, add to, 80:9
 opes, the iron shuts, 166:18
Gold-Orangen glühn, die, 107:37
Goldsmith, here lies Nolly, 103:18
Gondola of London, 85:42
Gone, all, all, are, 144:7
 and for ever, art, 211:26
 before, not dead—but, 205:15
 far away, 206:8
 here and there, I have, 265:25
 not valued till, 363:47
 now thou art, 166:12
 poor devil, get thee, 285:22
Gongs groaning, strong, 64:14
Good action by stealth, do, 144:6
 afar off, better, 361:74
 against evil, set, 410:23
 amiable, or sweet, 173:39
 and evil, knowing, 323:18
 and final hope, chief, 173:43
 and gay, 399:77
 and how pleasant, how, 328:8
 and ill together, 213:31
 and market, his chief, 226:15
 and no badness, all, 278:24
 and pure, in sight, keep, 345:21
 and quickly seldom meet, 373:47
 and yet bad, 146:12
 apprehension of the, 243:27
 are so harsh to the clever, 316:4
 as a play, as, 62:5
 as his master, as, 392:32
 as she was fair, 205:14
 attending captain ill, captive, 264:12
 but it is not, 279:34
 came of it at last, what, 282:5
 crown thy, 26:4
 deed in all my life, one, 270:12
 deed, so shines a, 256:3
 die first, 320:6
 doth give, special, 267:31
 dwelth all that's, 307:23
 eschew evil, and do, 326:29

event, heaviness foreruns, 234:27
evil, [call], 331:50
except, 360:22
fellowship in thee, 231:31
folks are within, 419:60
for neither man nor beast, 436:18
for nothing, 431:60
for our country's 60:7
for us to be here, 324:31
grey, but never, 418:10
hold fast that which is, 339:58
hopes not for, 379:58
in everything, 215:37
in Man, only what is, 314:16
in parts, 395:81
in the worst of us, 121:27
injuries, 381:69
is good, 373:52
is oft interred with their bones, 229:36
is soon spent, little, 352:25
it might do, 42:14
luxury was doing, 103:21
man better, makes, 394:22
man can no more harm, 351:60
man, he is, 376:8
man, the best, 204:9
man thrive, if, 385:64
may come, do evil that, 338:9
means to men most, 239:36
men and true, are you, 258:24
men are scarce, 373:54
men better, makes, 406:58
men company, keep, 393:47
men, sometimes make, 400:35
money after bad, throw, 431:40
morning, bid me, 23:35
must associate, 43:24
never do you, 420:25
news yet to hear, 65:22
night, I shall say, 267:30
night, say not, 23:35
night, stern'st, 248:16
night, sweetheart, 204:4
noble type of, 150:19
not too bright or, 318:13
nothing left but to be, 285:31
of moral evil and of, 316:10
of my country, for, 96:10
of themselves, hear no, 395:4
old man, sir, a, 258:32
or bad, be they, 440:24
or bad for human kind, 319:26

can be long secure, no, 85:39
essence of free, 53:45
exists, world, 310:21
for forms of, 196:1
highest form of, 283:20
is impossible, 84:33
it deserves, has, 155:29
land of settled, 292:22
of the people, 148:8
Gowans fine, pu'd the, 45:39
Gowd for a' that, man's the, 47:31
Gower, O moral, 63:17
Gowk another mile, hunt, 404:20
Gown and a hood, peascod would make, 385:66
  burns, whose, 435:44
  by the gateway haunts, 200:26
  is his that wears it, 418:26
  like a satin, 187:18
  of glory, 202:9
  oft worn, 352:33
  pluck'd his, 109:24
  puts on a public, 380:37
Gowns, one that hath two, 258:41
Gr-r-r—you swine, 37:32
Grace and strength, give us, 286:8
  bear's ethereal, 58:2
  does it with a better, 271:38
  for comely, 342:18
  for sweet attractive, 170:28
  full of, 399:77, 412:54
  full of God's 363:54
  guide it, except, 393:71
  in space comes, 389:49
  inward and spiritual, 341:44
  is given of God, 67:30
  is sufficient, my, 339:43
  of a day, tender, 294:1
  of God, but for, 32:8
  of God is gear enough, 418:27
  quarrel with the noblest, 269:35
  their God—His, 45:32
  to have thy Princes, 283:31
  to use it so, if I have, 163:31
  was in all her steps, 173:26
Graceful and humane, in act, 169:32
Graces, inherit heaven's, 265:18
Gracious unto thee, be, 324:8
Gradum, revocare, 306:6
Grain at a breath, reaps, 149:30
  of evil, 403:69
  will grow, say which, 247:23

Grammar, heedless of, 24:6
Gramophone, puts a record on, 93:32
Grampian hills, on the, 122:19
Granary floor, careless on, 137:31
Grand and comfortable, baith, 25:26
Grandchild, his little, 282:4
Grandmother, may not marry, 341:59
  teach your, 414:10
Grandsire, sit like his, 253:28
Grange, at the moated, 253:21
Grant, rude, 350:8
Grants it, more fool that, 418:3
Grape, devil in every berry of, 424:20
  that can . . . Sects confute, 98:10
Grapes are sour, 418:28
  blood of lusty, 100:2
  fathers have eaten sour, 332:16
  of wrath are stored, 127:25
Grapeshot, a whiff of, 57:29
Grapple them to thy soul, 221:37
Grasp all, lose all, 373:68
  it like a man, 121:21
  reach should exceed, 39:34
Grass above me, green, 206:10
  destroy a blade of, 32.1
  from under, cut, 428:22
  grow in Janiveer, if, 386:23
  grows on the weirs, as, 320:35
  grows, while, 438:27
  I fall on, 158:13
  in the sunny, 128:2
  is green, that, 285:19
  kissed the lovely, 34:1
  star-scatter'd on, 99:21
  to grow, two blades of, 288:16
  turned out to, 279:34
  was cut out of the, 65:24
Grasshopper shall be a burden, 330:33
Grasshoppers, wings of 266:13
Grave [tomb], a little little, 244:2
  a tear, drop on his, 143:37
  adora'd, thy humble, 194:3
  as a carpet hang upon, 263:20
  as now my bed, on my, 35:27
  between the cradle and the, 92:16
  but she is in her, 317:21
  dark and silent, 206:13
  dig the, 286:21
  Duncan is in his, 249:36
  earliest at His, 25:22
  funeral marches to, 149:26
  ghost come from, 222:22

night, lamps in a, 158:8
peculiar tint of yellow, 70:18
sported on the, 282:4
thought in a green shade, 158:14
tree, do these things in, 337:37
trip upon the, 263:22
winter, 351:75
Greenhouse too, loves a, 75:40
Greenland's icy mountains, 118:10
Green-sward, single on, 160:15
Greet [salute] thee, how should I, 49:37
Greet [weep], bairn that dare not, 390:20
better bairns, 361:49
it gars me, 46:7
Greets, no play where one, 392:3
Grenadier, Hampshire, 345:17
Who comes here? A, 84:21
Grenadiers of Austria, 88:6
Greta woods are green, 211:30
Grew, as fixed as if it, 70:18
together, so we, 257:40
Grey, but not with years, 52:4
my gallant, 210:18
Greyhound, this fawning, 231:39
Greyhounds in the slips, 236:7
Griddle, hen on a hot, 395:69
Grief, acquainted with, 332:5
and laughter little while with, 157:27
and pain, after long, 296:20
canker and the, 53:36
enough for thee, 114:1
every one can master a, 258:23
fills the room up, 239:34
is past, 41:28
or pleasure, look for them in, 388:3
perk'd up in a glistering, 238:12
plague of sighing and, 232:5
should be past, 273:37
silent manliness of, 109:31
smiling at, 272:4
summons, 381:59
tame the strongest, 427:47
that does not speak, 250:22
with proverbs, patch, 259:42
without some, 401:75
Griefs [friendship] divide, 371:65
still am I king of, 244:6
that bow, 19:16
that harass, all, 130:8
Grieve, it is too late to, 392:20
Grieving, Margaret are you, 124:17
Grig, merry as, 358:14

Grimes is dead, old, 113:36
Grin, he own'd with a, 282:11
so merry, every, 315:30
vanquish Berkeley by, 34:15
wears one universal, 97:19
Grind, one demd horrid, 83:30
or find, either, 385:44
slowly, mills of God, 150:9
Grinder, who serenely grindest, 54:5
Grinds He all, with exactness, 150:9
lower millstone, 420:13
Grindstone, keep one's nose to, 429:51
Newcastle, 354:4
Groan, condemn'd alike to, 111:34
with bubbling, 51:29
Groat, cannot change, 438:33
is ill saved, 418:38
saves, 421:55
shall never want, 381:66
Grooves, down the ringing, 293:38
in determinate, 116:12
Gropes in the dark, he that, 378:34
Gross to sink, not, 263:22
Grossness, losing all its, 43:30
Ground between, much, 415:50
choose thy, 53:37
fathom-line could never touch, 231:38
from under, cut, 428:22
he that lies on, 380:6
I see thee stare, up-on, 64:1
make not balks of good, 397:78
not fail, solid, 296:11
on the holy, 182:10
plat of rising, 164:18
purple all the, 167:22
rise from the, 233:36
to a more removed, 222:8
to shades of under, 56:2
Groundlings, split the ears of, 225:14
Groundsel speaks not, 419:39
Grove, nightingale's song in, 26:17
of Academe, olive, 174:18
Groves, pathless, 100:5
standing lakes and, 269:43
they hover, o'er, 310:10
we two will seek, 206:16
Grow old along with me, 39:42
up with the country, 113:34
where de wool ought to, 101:20
Grow'd, I 'spect I, 287:33
Growing when ye're sleeping, 212:5
Growled, cracked and, 69:20

Grown-up wise, in quiet, 188:7
Grows the worse for't, [grass], 386:23
Growth, of a larger, 91:41
Grudge, feel fat the ancient, 253:38
Gruel, basin of nice smooth, 21:28
Grumble at, nothing whatever to, 106:8
Grumbles, wife that never, 390:7
Grundy, more [afraid] of Mrs., 149:21
  say, what will Mrs., 180:13
Grunt, expect from a hog, 435:47
Guard, dies, the, 44:11
  the guards, who is to, 135:30
Guards, and at them, up, 310:14
  them from the steep, 161:39
Gude or ill, no for only, 44:7
Gudeman, Robin Gray was, 25:17
Gude-willie waught, right, 45:40
Guerdon when we hope to find, 166:16
Guerra al cuchillo, 187:16
Guerre, ce n'est pas la, 31:30
Guess now who holds thee, 36:8
Guest, a new admired, 56:2
  he is an ill, 376:12
  unbidden, 357:60
  welcome the coming, 193:41
Guests few and select, 145:19
  speed the parting, 193:41
  Star-scatter'd on the Grass, 99:21
  unbidden, 237:26
Guide, go with thee and be thy, 342:4
  in smoke and flame, awful, 211:40
  philosopher, and friend, 196:11
Guided, easier gained than, 371:74
Guides, blind, 325:47
Guilders, a thousand, 39:27

Guilt away, wash her, 108:11
  full of artless jealousy, 226:18
  o'er the shoals of, 52:2
  pure from, 125:26
Guiltier than him they try, 252:4
Guilty ears, sound worse in, 423:57
  is acquitted, 393:40
  thing, started like, 220:10
  thing surprised, like, 319:38
Guinea's stamp, rank is but, 47:31
Gulf condemn, immediate, 143:22
  fixed, a great, 336:30
  profound as that Serbonian bog, 170:2
Gull comes against the rain, 419:40
Gum, their medicinal, 262:16
Gums, from his boneless, 248:6
Gun is laid aside, 16:7
  sure as, 358:45
  text of pike and, 48:12
  with his little wooden, 16:7
Gunga Din, 141:40
Gunner, Master, 297:47
Gunpowder ran out at the heels, 100:10
  treason and plot, 345:26
Guns, all-shattering, 88:8
  and drums and wounds, 231:26
  aren't lawful, 187:20
  boom far, as the, 64:14
  but for these vile, 231:36
Gustibus, de, 366:5
Gutta cavat lapidem, 374:6
Gutter, from corbel and, 201:26
Gyre and gimble in the wabe, 58:17

H

Ha, ha, among the trumpets, 326:9
Ha'penny will do, 346:1
Habit, costly thy, 221:38
  in more precious, 259:36
  in the meanest, 268:14
Habitation and a name, local, 257:46
  giddy and unsure, 234:8

Habits air good, my other, 308:14
Hack, some body to hew and, 48:15
Hacked him in pieces sma', 342:10
Had, having, and in quest to have, 265:30
  thee, thus, have I, 265:16
Haddock to paddock, bring, 427:76
Hag, blue meagre, 165:42

Haggards Ride no more, 285:20
Haggis, as the cat did of, 414:4
Hags, black and midnight, 250:13
Hail [shower] brings frost, 374:9
　　or rain, falls not, 297:44
Hail [greeting] and farewell, 61:18
　　to thee, blithe spirit, 276:4
Hailstones, pelts the flowers with, 16:18
Hair and hair, 374:10
　　dissever, sacred, 193:32
　　divide a, 48:4
　　draws us with a single, 193:26
　　from his horrid, 170:7
　　grows through his hood, 383:61
　　has become very white, 58:6
　　if a woman have long, 338:28
　　image doth unfix my, 247:29
　　is grey, my, 52:4
　　kissing her, 289:35
　　looping up her, 160:17
　　ninth part of a, 232:25
　　of a woman draws, 405:44
　　of the dog, 352:1
　　pleasant mazes of her, 74:5
　　rain-drenched, 29:32
　　Ralph the Rover tore, 282:7
　　smooths her, 93:32
　　soft-lifted, thy, 137:31
　　tangles of Neaera's, 166:15
　　than wit, more, 400:9
　　that is shining and free, 34:6
Hair, that lay along her back, 206:13
　　thy amber-dropping, 166:6
　　thy hyacinth, 191:28
　　to stand on end, each, 222:12
　　was so brown, whose, 95:28
　　was so charmingly curled, 139:30
　　who touches a, 313:23
　　with long dishevell'd, 263:22
　　with vine leaves in, 128:10
　　would rouse and stir, 251:36
Hairs are death's blossoms, grey, 374:5
　　become a fool, ill white, 235:37
　　bring down my grey, 323:37
　　in my grey, 315:35
　　of your head are all numbered, 324:14
　　split, 430:23
　　will be found, there, 438:15
Hale, you may be soon, 360:15
Half a dozen of the other, 411:56
　　a loaf is better, 374:11
　　dearer, 172:10

his foe, overcome but, 169:24
is more than the whole, 120:15
of the world, one, 405:45
was not told me, the, 325:44
Halifax, hell, Hull and, 371:67
Halisbury-scalisbury, 344:12
Hall, as you would do in, 367:56
　　binks are sliddery, 374:12
　　bring a cow to, 363:64
　　hung in the castle, 26:15
Halloo, do not, 367:51
Halls, dwelt in marble, 42:3
　　in gay attire, in, 209:19
　　those gorgeous, 17:23
Halt before a cripple, 391:56
　　by them, as I, 244:12
　　ye, how long, 325:47
Halting home, come, 408:4
Hame, hame, hame, it's, 78:14
　　kye's a' at, 25:16
Hamlet, forefathers of the, 112:6
　　is still, when the, 26:17
Hamlet most of all, of, 118:20
　　Prince of Denmark, saw, 96:3
Hamlets, dances on the green, in, 209:17
Hammer and the anvil, between, 362:30
　　when you are, 437:59
Hammers closing rivets up, 236:10
　　fell, no, 118:6
Hampden, some village, 112:14
Hampshire, he ran about, 344:12
Hand against him, every man's, 323:29
　　be bad, if your, 388:9
　　between, put not thy, 407:83
　　by God's almighty, 54:14
　　cold, 350:11
　　Cotopaxi took me by the, 303:26
　　doeth, what thy right, 333:47
　　doth not all, wise, 423:72
　　findeth to do, whatsoever, 330:24
　　for hand, 324:5
　　forget her cunning, my, 328:11
　　[have] a lady's, 351:65
　　heaving up my either, 120:14
　　here's my, 269:36
　　his red right, 169:34
　　in hand through life, 73:28
　　in hand with wand'ring steps, 173:48
　　infinity in palm of, 30:8
　　into the hand of God, put your, 117:26
　　iron, 357:41
　　kissing your, 51:22

confess and be, 365:49
ere noon, that is, 377:57
half, 379:42
himself, in his house that, 400:27
knows he is to be, 133:41
sorry he is to be, 423:43
that left his drink, 382:25
told his father was, 382:26
Hanging and wiving, 374:15
of his cat, 32:11
prevents a bad marriage, good, 271:30
want nothing but, 425:61
Hangs my dear, rope that, 103:32
Hanner, lost our little, 16:8
Hap and a halfpenny, 374:16
good or ill, 418:24
some have, 412:1
Happens not in seven years, 389:71
Happier than I know, feel that I am, 172:25
things, remembering, 293:33
Happiest women have no history, 93:24
Happiness for the greatest numbers,
greatest, 128:5
emblem of, 122:4
from life, get some, 345:21
great task of, 287:23
is no laughing matter, 311:34
is produced, so much, 133:36
lifetime of, 274:17
our being's end, 196:2
pursuit of, 129:29
right to consume, 274:9
talks much of, 381:59
through another man's eyes, 218:9
too swiftly flies, 111:34
without producing it, consume, 274:9
wreck of, 52:2
Happy and glorious, 343:23
angry and poor and, 64:17
as a lover, 319:26
as kings, all be as, 286:18
but when he is miserable, never, 356:33
could I be with either, 103:35
duty of being, 286:2
fields, farewell, 168:9
for a day, would be, 394:39
for you, it is, 21:25
he who crowns, 108:17
human race was most, 104:8
I were but little, 258:15
in his children, 374:17
in nothing else so, 243:33

is he, 374:17, 374:18
is he born and taught, 320:21
man be his dole, 374:23
swains, Muses sing of, 72:22
than wise, better be, 361:55
that thinks himself so, 376:16
the man, 91:32, 190:8, 192:1
those that were good shall be, 140:17
till all are, 282:17
till he dies, call no man, 363:78
time when we were, 79:20
to have been, 31:22
which of us is, 298:19
who has once been, 31:19
Harass'd, to attain, too, 19:20
Harbinger, perfume her, 174:18
Hard as a piece of the nether millstone,
326:11
nothing's so, 120:13
times, come again, 101:18
with hard, 374:25
Hardens a' within, it, 45:25
Harder thing, hast borne, 123:33
Hardest to bear, 417:48
Hardy became a sort of village atheist,
65:31
Hare, as thou woldest finde, 64:1
first catch your, 370:22
I like the hunting of, 31:20
it look'd like, 24:8
mad as a March, 358:10
may catch, 419:54
or a wig, thy own, 144:4
porter who was carrying, 144:4
run with, 430:15
starts, 419:43
to start a, 231:37
Harebell, like thy veins, 219:37
raised its head, 210:21
Hares may pull dead lions, 374:27
run after two, 387:61
Hark, hark! the lark, 219:30
Harm, at the first, 374:87
drunken folks seldom take, 367:75
rest will take no, 419:45
than a sheep, no more, 351:60
to win us to our, 247:28
watch, harm catch, 374:28
Harmless as doves, 324:13
Harmonies, inventor of, 295:36
Harmony, from heavenly, 90:19
hidden soul of, 164:10

is in immortal souls, 255:43
touches of sweet, 255:43
Harms, beware by other men's, 391:51
Harness, between the joints of, 325:52
  dead in his, 340:27
  on our back, with, 251:39
Harp not on that string, 245:24
  slung behind him, wild, 178:10
  that once through Tara's halls, 177:30
Harping on my daughter, 223:31
Harps, we hanged our, 328:9
Harpsichon, play on the, 189:23
Harris, bother Mrs., 83:44
  words she spoke of Mrs., 83:45
Harrow, frog said to, 418:15
Harry, I saw young, 233:36
  [succeeds] Harry, 235:34
  such a King, 88:13
  the king, 237:18
Harsh and crabbed, not, 165:43
  nor grating, nor, 316:14
Harshness gives offence, no, 192:16
Hart panteth, as the, 327:34
  ungalled play, 225:28
Harvest comes not every day, 374:29
  foretells a wet, 386:6
  he that hath a good, 379:40
  she laughs with a, 130:2
  truly is plenteous, 324:11
Harvests, good, 373:50
Has been, what has been, 191:33
Hast, ohne, 107:38
Haste and wisdom, 374:30
  away so soon, you, 120:9
  comes not alone, 374:31
  I can to be gone, make what, 78:7
  I said in my, 327:61
  is from hell, 107:36
  less speed, more, 400:10
  makes waste, 107:37
  mounting in hot, 50:15
  sweaty, 220:7
  trips up, 107:38
  with moderate, 221:30
  without, 107:38
Hasten slowly, 370:11
Hastily, nothing must be done, 403:55
Hasty, be not too, 360:17
  man never wants woe, 419:44
Hat and wig will soon be here, 75:30
  as the fashion of, 258:9
  for your credit's sake, pass the, 142:3

has got a hole in't, 56:5
in an old man's, 346:1
needs no, 379:46
upon my head, I put, 131:18
was in his hand, whose, 131:18
Hatch before the door, have, 391:53
Hatched, before they are, 428:17
Hatchet, all go with, 437:47
  did it with my, 309:20
  throw the helve after, 431:41
  to bury, 428:5
Hate and death return, must, 277:26
  and love, I, 61:16
  as long as they fear, let them, 15:1
  is blind, 375:38
  me for naught, 425:67
  not at the first harm, 375:37
  of hate, dower'd with, 292:7
  smile to those who, 52:10
  you absent, will, 378:25
Hates me for naught, 376:39
  that a healthy person, 65:29
Hath, all that a man, 325:61
  it and will not keep it, 379:44
  not, from him that, 325:55
  unto every one that, 325:55
Hatred for something, common, 64:3
  more dangerous than, 420:12
  or bitterness, no, 61:19
  therewith, ox and, 328:34
Hats, so many shocking bad, 310:15
Hatter, mad as, 54:3, 358:9
Haughty spirit before a fall, 329:36
Haul over the coals, 428:34
Haunt, exempt from public, 215:37
  to startle, and waylay, to, 318:12
Haunted by woman wailing, 70:9
Have and hold, to, 341:48
  not good to want and, 392:9
  of thine own, spare to, 362:17
  thee not, and yet I see thee, 248:13
  we prize not, what we, 259:35
  well, do well and, 367:58
  what asketh man to, 63:40
  what he hath not, would, 382:14
  what they cannot, 440:12
Havelock sound, pipes o', 313:21
Haven, stands long in, 350:22
  under the hill, to, 293:49
Havoc, cry, 229:34
Hawk from a handsaw, know, 223:38
  never be a good, 349:33

of the tower, 278:25
Hawked at and killed, 248:30
Hawks allure, men may no, 440:20
  between two, 237:27
  will not pick hawks' eyes out, 375:44
Hawthorn bush, with seats, 108:13
Hay [*grass*] and corn, good for, 436:5
  I'm helpin' wi' the, 185:21
  make, 397:77
  on his horn, he has, 125:22
  weary on the English, 185:21
  world is a bundle of, 53:33
  worth a load of, 354:21
Hay [*dance*], dance the antic, 157:22
Haystack, needle in, 429:70
Hazard of the die, stand, 245.30
  once, better, 361:77
He knows about it all, 98:12
Head aches, when, 437:39
  and feet keep warm, 419:45
  and nostril wide, small, 263:23
  and turns no more his, 69:36
  arms behind her golden, 160:15
  as gently lay my, 35:27
  bare, makes the carle's, 374:10
  break his own, 375:46
  break Priscian's, 427:74
  coals of fire on his, 338:16
  comforter's, 416:1
  counsel breaks not, 365:56
  cover my defenceless, 311:24
  four angels round my, 16:9
  from some once lovely, 98:2
  from the fair, 193:32
  grown grey in vain, 276:14
  hands, wings, or feet, with, 170:12
  he that hath no, 279:46
  here rests his, 113:19
  his heavy, 309:34
  if you can keep your, 142:13
  incessantly stand on, 58:6
  is a crown, hoary, 329:37
  is bending low, my, 101:19
  is off, when, 392:5
  is soon broken, scald, 354:4
  is soon shaven, bald, 349:6
  knock him on, 438:36
  lieth, which was the, 202:15
  like a snake, 352:3
  like God's own, 69:21
  mickle, 399:66
  must ward with his, 381:55

of yon grey, 313:23
off, cuts the wrong man's, 82:13
off with his, 66:10
on de top of his, 101:20
on young shoulders, old, 357:47
one small, 109:27
repairs his drooping, 167:23
she bow'd, as if, 164:17
short in, 398:12
singe my white, 240:23
take lodgings in a, 48:10
this old grey, 313:22
thrown in his dish, dead man's, 380:20
thunder on your, 130:7
to break my, 427:73
toys for your, 274:6
trickled through my, 59:34
uneasy lies the, 234:21
what seem'd his, 170:5
where to lay his, 324:9
with a stool, comb, 428:14
with all my imperfections on my, 222:17
you have, 442:1
Head's cost, talks at, 423:54
Heads and unfed sides, houseless, 241:30
  are better, two, 432:31
  are green, their, 147:16
  but no brains, many, 420:24
  curling their monstrous, 234:19
  differ, though, 383:46
  do grow beneath their shoulders, 260:5
  hide their diminished, 171:21
  hover in their restless, 156:12
  I win, tails you lose, 382:36
  never raising, 317:31
Headstrong as an allegory, 277:37
Head-waiter, plump, 293:43
Heal thyself, physician, 336:8
Healing in his wings, with, 332:30
  of an old sore, 391:63
Health and a day, give me, 94:17
  and money go far, 383:37
  and sickness, 383:39
  and wealth, 383:38
  innocence and, 108:16
  is better than wealth, 383:40
  is not valued, 383:41
  mother of, 407:53
  not [felt] at all, 411:45
  not pledge your own, 442:17
  of the soul, prove, 422:15
  unbought, for, 90:13

leaps up, my, 317:29
less bounding, 20:1
licht, werena my, 23:25
makes a heavy, 352:19
makes a light, 352:4
man after his own, 324:31
man could ease a, 187:18
merry, 328:33
my true love hath my, 278:16
nearest, 401:39
never won, faint, 369:66
new open'd, feel my, 238:16
now cracks a noble, 228:2
of a friend, found in, 150:8
of a man is deprest, 103:33
of gall, 352:7
of heart, in my, 225:20
of her sons, strong, 88:8
of man, maketh glad, 227:58
of oak are our ships, 103:17
open my, and you will see, 38:3
or in the head, in, 254:23
plague, 406:32
quiet, 433:40
quiver'd in his, 50:4
rake to break your, 361:75
remembers how, my, 287:29
rise in the, 294:13
roving, 353:74
run them in, to my dead, 287:24
Shakespeare unlocked his, 40:13, 320:12
sick, maketh, 328:28
softening a woman's, 303:15
soothe or wound a, 211:32
spring of love gushed from, 69:32
strings in the human, 83:35
taming my wild, 258:22
that has truly lov'd, 178:2
that I was false of, 265:24
that loved her, betray, 316:15
that thinks none [ill], 390:8
that's broken, wound, 211:32
the bolder, 342:2
thinks, what, 435:69
to a dog to tear, giving, 142:17
to a stey brae, stout, 410:21
to a willing, 403:53
to eat thy, 283:31
to glow, made my, 282:15
to heart, and mind to mind, 209:23
to move, your, 204:12
to poke poor Billy, 111:20

to resolve, 104:10
to soften another man's, 303:15
untainted, 237:31
untravell'd fondly turns, 108:2
upon my sleeve, wear, 259:48
upon one's sleeve, 431:47
was as that of a little child, 299:24
was in the sea, my, 25:17
was like to break, my, 25:17
was to an Englishman's, 423:62
weighs upon the, 251:32
which others bleed for, 72:10
whispers the o'erfraught, 250:22
winning each, 81:30
with an angry, 375:71
with pleasure fills, 318:16
with words, unpack my, 224:1
within, a warm, 76:8
within, and God o'erhead, 149:27
within blood-tinctured, 35:30
would break, 385:76
would fain deny, 251:31
would hear her and beat, 269:19
Heart's core, rest at, 206:6
core, wear him in, 225:20
Desire, nearer to, 99:20
in the Highlands, 46:3
letter, 419:47
undoing, my, 178:12
Heart-ache, end the, 224:4
Hearth, a clean, 143:39
and stool and all, 72:6
from his lonely, 320:14
Hearths, sweep their, 73:21
Hearts are dry as summer dust, 320:6
are light, somewhere, 299:31
are more than coronets, kind, 292:16
are yearning, while, 100:12
beat happily, thousand, 50:11
endure, that human, 131:21
ensanguined, 76:2
gentle, makes all, 397:59
humble, 384:15
in love use their own tongues, 258:14
in their mouths, 440:13
may agree, 383:46
men with Splendid, 34:4
now broken, cheerful, 178:14
of his countrymen, first in, 147:23
other lips and other, 42:5
quell the stubborn, 292:8
sweetness that inspired, 156:12

Honourable man, Brutus is, 229:37
  men, so are they all, 229:37
Honours, bears his blushing, 238:15
  change manners, 384:6
  mindless of its just, 320:12
  perish, piled-up, 37:33
  thick upon him, 238:15
  to the world, gave his, 239:21
Hood, hair grows through, 383:61
  him that wears a, 287:30
Hoods witless, painted, 396:26
Hook, bait hides, 414:36
  draw out leviathan with, 326:10
  for subscribers baits, 65:38
  or by crook, by, 363:71
  through his mouth, put, 308:4
Hook's well lost, 352:8
Hoop, times of hood and, 292:24
Hooping, out of all, 217:25
Hoot, come from Rome al, 63:36
Hop forty paces, saw her, 214:3
Hope abandon, all, 79:17
  again, never to, 238:16
  and fear set free, from, 289:38
  and Glory, land of, 28:5
  bade the world farewell, 55:18
  break it to our, 251:42
  but not another's, 308:1
  clung feeding, 71:21
  [days] spent without, 325:64
  deferred, 328:28
  dream untroubled of, 183:21
  elevates his crest, 173:36
  fool'd with, 91:39
  for the best, 384:7
  for years to come, 309:35
  he that lives in, 380:8
  he who would not be frustrate of, 175:25
  in sure and certain, 341:55
  is a good breakfast, 384:8
  is a lover's staff, 384:9
  is as cheap as despair, 384:10
  is better, my, 272:15
  is but the dream, 200:10
  is coldest, hits where, 213:28
  is swift, true, 245:25
  is the poor man's bread, 384:11
  less quick to spring, 20:1
  like the gleaming taper's light, 110:4
  men set their hearts upon, 97:33
  more rich in, 264:1
  never comes that comes to all, 168:5

  no other medicine but, 252:13
  nursing unconquerable, 19:27
  phantoms of, 131:29
  pursued it with forks and, 60:1
  repose, in trembling, 113:21
  springs eternal, 195:29
  thou not much, 290:4
  to feed on, 283:31
  well and have well, 384:12
  were not, if, 385:76
  what is, 57:39
  whence this pleasing, 15:14
  while there is life there is, 438:30
  white-handed, 165:35
  who lives by, 439:47
Hope's true gage, 202:9
Hoped for, substance of things, 339:66
Hopes and fears, for fifty, 39:37
  belied out fears, 124:1
  decay, seen my fondest, 178:16
  not for good, 379:58
  of future years, all, 150:13
  tender leaves of, 238:15
  that have vanished, 116:14
  vanity of human, 131:23
  will cling, to weakest, 42:4
Hoppy, Croppy, Droppy, 94:6
Hops and women, 82:6
Horace, felicity of, 190:5
  says is, what, 24:11
  whom I hated so, 50:23
Horatii curiosa felicitas, 190:5
Horatius kept the bridge, 154:7
  out spake brave, 154:2
Horde, now one polish'd, 53:32
Horn, blast of that dread, 210:15
  blow his wreathèd, 319:29
  small but sullen, 71:36
  the lusty horn, 218:5
  voice of that wild, 210:15
Hornet, glad it wasn't a, 107:27
Hornets go free, lets, 394:14
Hornie, Satan, Nick, auld, 44:17
Horns, curst cow has short, 350:20
  of Elfland, 294:12
  take the bull by, 430:30
Horrendum, informe, ingens, 306:3
Horresco referens, 305:35
Horrid, are they all, 21:22
  when she was bad she was, 150:21
Horror of falling into naught, 15:14
Horrors accumulate, on horror's head,

to live, one bare, 157:17
to-day, one, 405:47
Hour's sleep before midnight, one, 405:48
Hours away, wears the, 87:18
  bring about the day, how many, 238:6
  chase the glowing, 50:12
  fly fast, pleasant, 406:31
  I once enjoy'd, 76:16
  lose and neglect, 216:16
  lost, two golden, 156:3
  of bliss, winged, 55:19
  sleepeth a traveller, five, 370:31
  slow ye move, ye heavy, 47:30
  thrilling, glorious, 301:28
  unheeded flew the, 283:21
  wak'd by the circling, 172:18
Housbondes at chirche-dore, 63:33
House and home, out of, 234:11
  and land are gone, when, 436:12
  be divided against itself, 325:64
  better an empty, 361:47
  buy him a new, 394:39
  cannot stand, that, 325:64
  dead, 420:18
  desert a falling, 408:17
  doth burn, neighbour's, 437:55
  drive a man out of, 427:41
  every one can keep, 369:42
  except the Lord build, 328:4
  filled, better one, 362:6
  goes mad, 419:59
  he that burns, 377:73
  Honeybird keeps no, 412:60
  I will hold my, 27:28
  in a good, 388:29
  in a wide, 329:48
  in his own, 324:25
  in my Father's, 337:54
  in order, set thine, 331:59
  in the woods, though he build his, 94:20
  is a fine house, 419:60
  is his castle, 356:34
  it is a sad, 390:19
  justice pleaseth few in their own, 393:41
  knows more in his own, 350:35
  less they look to, 420:38
  looks to your own, 437:55
  man may love his, 353:46
  may I have a warm, 199:28
  not go from his own, 382:11
  of God, none other but, 323:33
  on fire, like, 395:67

prop that doth sustain, 255:40
ready wrought, buys, 377:75
shows the owner, 419:61
smoke of a man's own, 422:24
to have a little, 72:6
to your enemy, let, 417:74
to your friend, let, 417:74
too big all the year, 362:7
too little one day, 362:7
well filled, little, 352:26
where I was born, 123:38
wherein to tarry, 360:19
wife is the key of, 423:68
with lawns enclosing it, 286:20
woman is to be from, 355:40
you take my, 255:40
yourself, live in, 417:74
Householders, small, 440:17
Housekeeper, fat, 350:32
Housekeeping is a shrew, 399:40
Housemaids, damp souls of, 93:29
Houses, cannot see the city for, 441:73
  devour widows', 336:5
  fools build, 370:39
  plague o' both, 367:39
  seem asleep, very, 317:37
  stand, the ugly, 162:10
  thick and sewers, 173:35
  thunder, falling, 130:7
  wise men buy, 370:39
Housetop, in a corner of, 329:48
Housewife and a bad, between a good,
  424:28
  sign of a good, 418:7
  that's thrifty, 278:6
Housewives, make giddy, 360:6
  now may say, 73:21
How d'ye do, hullo and, 101:14
  not to do it, 84:16
Howards, blood of all the, 196:5
Hower, eat hog a solid, 101:33
Howl, will learn to, 439:45
Howled, roared and, 69:20
Hue like that, with, 275:27
  take no other, 363:46
Huffy or stuffy, not, 119:34
Hug the dear deceit, 73:29
Hulk, here, a sheer, 81:31
Hull and Halifax, from, 371:67
  for women, 406:5
Hullo, walk right up and say, 101:14
Hum, justice with his surly, 235:43

I

I am the doubter and the doubt, 95:27
  fussy thing called, 345:21
Iambics march from short, 70:19
Ibis, medio tutissimus, 186:6
Ice in June, 50:1
  of her Ladyship's manners, 200:3
  of his Lordship's champagne, 200:3
  region of thick ribbed, 252:18
  to smooth the, 240:2
  was all around, 69:20
  was here, the ice was there, 69:20
  will bear a man, if, 386:24
  written on, 389:66
Iceberg or two at control, 130:6
Icicle that's curdied by the frost, 219:28
Ida, dear mother, 292:13
  many-fountained, 292:13
Idea, possess but one, 133:26
  teach the young, 300:9
Idealism, mistrust of masculine, 72:15
Ideas, man of nasty, 289:21
Idem velle atque idem nolle, 208:7
Ides of March, beware the, 228:5
Idiot, blaspheming over the village, 65:31
  tale told by an, 251:37
Idle as a painted ship, as, 69:23
  better sit, 362:12
  brains, 385:56
  folks, 385:57
  hands to do, for, 309:33
  he that is, 379:63
  if the devil find a man, 386:19
  man tempts the devil, 416:28
  men are dead, 385:58
  people take the most pains, 385:39
  persons, tongue of, 423:53
  that might be better employed, he is, 376:17
Idleness comes no goodness, of, 403:71
  is the key of beggary, 385:60
  is the parent of all vice, 385:61

is the root of all evil, 385:61
  makes the wit rust, 385:62
  must thank itself, 385:63
  takes nine, 400:34
  work of polished, 155:21
Idolatries, bow'd to its, 50:20
Idolatry, on this side, 135:21
Idols, like old, 32:2
If, much virtue in, 218:14
Ifs and Ans were pots and pans, if, 385:78
Ignara mali, non, 305:31
Ignorance, a childish, 123:39
  daughter of, 441:42
  is bliss, where, 111:34
  is the mother, 388:11/12
  Madam, pure, 132:11
  of the law, 212:17
  sedate, in, 130:15
Ignorant has an eagle's wings, 419:62
  of ill, not, 305:31
  of what he's most assured, 252:11
Ignotum per ignotius, 388:13
  pro magnifico est, 290:7
Ilium, topless towers of, 157:15
Ill a-brewing towards my rest, 254:12
  better suffer, 362:19
  comes in by ells, 388:16
  comes upon waur's back, 388:17
  cure for this, 142:19
  deeds, means to do, 240:5
  doers are ill deemers, 388:18
  final goal of, 295:42
  gotten, ill spent, 388:21
  he that hath done, 379:68
  he thinks no, 264:8
  if you have done no, 387:54
  it costs more to do, 388:22
  make strong themselves by, 249:42
  man is, what religion, 392:24
  man worse, [makes], 394:22
  spoken of, better be, 361:58

they have done some, 436:9
to himself, he that is, 379:69
will never said well, 388:27
Ill-doing, doctrine of, 273:34
Ill-favoured thing, but mine own, 218:12
Ill-gotten gains, 388:19
Illiterate him, I say, 277:33
Ills a prey, to hast'ning, 108:15
away, washes all man's, 95:35
dangerous, 440:30
to come, no sense of, 111:33
we have, bear those, 224:4
Image gay, 318:12
of myself, best, 172:10
Imaginary, all our wants are, 31:21
Imagination all compact of, 257:45
amend them, 258:4
bodies forth, 257:46
into his study of, 259:36
of a boy, 138:2
of a man, mature, 138:2
to sweeten my, 242:3
Imaginations are as foul, 225:21
Imaginings, horrible, 247:29
Imitation, endless, 319:36
is the sincerest, 72:4
Immodest words admit of no defence,
206:1
Immortal man, a most, 139:33
Immortal as itself, being, 222:9
part of myself, lost, 260:23
think they grow, 322:6
Immortality, longing after, 15:14
nurslings of, 277:23
Immortals, President of the, 116:1
Impact has its measure, 160:2
Imparadis'd in one another's arms, 171:31
Impatience would be so much fretted,
133:27
Impavidum ferient ruinae, 125:31
Impeachment, own the soft, 278:3
Impediment, cause or just, 341:45
Impediments, admit, 265:27
to great enterprises, 22:11
Impera, divide et, 366:42
Imperfections by, pass my, 96:4
Imperially, learn to think, 61:26
Imperii, capax, 290:10
Implications, with horrid, 111:23
Importunate, rashly, 124:8
Importunity, ever-haunting, 144:8
Impossibile est, quia, 298:12

Impossibilities, plausible, 18:10
Impossibility, nearly an, 68:7
Impossible, because it is, 298:12
I wish it were, 134:6
nothing is, 403:53
with men this is, 325:40
Imposters, treat those two, 142:14
Impoverishing, sweet, 363:66
Impression, take any, 443:44
Impudence, Cockney, 207:32
mother of, 388:12
Impulse from a vernal wood, 316:10
of the moment, 21:25
this or that poor, 37:83
In at one ear, 388:35
I went, out by the same Door as, 98:5
who's out, who's, 242:9
Inactivity, wise and masterly, 154:20
Inanimate things, depravity of, 115:19
Incense, gods themselves throw, 242:10
hangs, what soft, 136:18
Inch a king, every, 242:1
dree out, 367:70
give him, 372:13
to gain, no painful, 68:2
Inchcape Rock, it is the, 282:6
Inches, goes out by, 388:16
Incident of the dog, 87:34
Incidente, è un, 304:4
Incidents, one of the, 304:4
Incivility and procrastination, 81:26
Inclination leads, read just as, 132:19
inclined to, sins they are, 48:14
Include me out, 110:13
Income twenty pounds, 84:5
will supply, moderate, 31:25
Inconvenience, no vice but, 407:50
poverty is, 407:50
Inconvenient, confoundedly, 281:16
Incorruptible, the seagreen, 57:30
Increase, we desire, 263:29
Increment, unearned, 162:8
Ind, wealth of Ormus and of, 169:28
Indpendence, Declaration of, 65:33
Independent, of being, 45:26
to be poor and, 68:7
Index of the heart, 417:55
India's coral strand, 118:10
Indian, like the base, 262:16
lo, the poor, 195:30
steep, on the, 165:33
Indifference, morn and cold, 207:22

It, it's just, 143:33
Italians are wise before the deed, 419:64
Italy, graved inside of it, 38:3
Itch of literature, 151:29
Iter tenebricosum, it per, 60:13
Iteration, damnable, 231:29

Ithuriel with his spear touch'd, 172:3
It-will-wash-no-more, and, 302:8
Ivory, little bit of, 21:32
Ivy green, rare old plant, 82:7
  never sere, with, 166:8

J

J'y suis, j'y reste, 155:25
Jabberwock, hast thou slain, 59:19
Jack, for the life of poor, 81:29
  has his Jill, every, 368:30
  makes a good Jill, good, 351:58
  must to his flail, 443:47
  of all trades, 392:33
  Robinson, before one can say, 360:30
  Sprat could eat no fat, 392:34
  there was gorging, 299:30
Jackdaw sat on . . . chair, 24:4
Jacket, in my tarpaulin, 313:27
  was red, his, 70:15
Jacob's ladder, traffic of, 300:4
  voice, voice is, 323:32
Jacta alea est, 53:41
Jade, whore, a knave, and, 439:41
Jades of Asia, pampered, 157:14
Jafeth, of the gentilman, 25:18
Jai, being in a ship is being in a, 132:13
  more room in a, 132:13
  the patron and the, 130:12
Jam to-day, never, 59:27
James, work of Henry, 114:7
James I, James II, and the Old Pretender, 114:7
Janiveer freeze the pot, 392:36
  if the grass grow in, 386:23
  in March I fear, 398:35
Janiveer's calends be summerly gay, if, 386:3
Janua Ditis, patet atri, 306:6
Japanese action with prudence, reconcile, 66:8
Jardin, il faut cultiver, 306:15
Javan or Gadire, isles of, 174:18

Jaw gae by, let, 392:38
Jaws, ponderous and marble, 222:6
Jealous confirmations, to, 261:32
  eyes, scornful yet, 198:2
  one not easily, 262:16
Jealousy, beware, my lord, of, 261:29
  full of artless, 226:18
  injustice, 121:20
  is cruel as the grave, 331:44
  never without, 397:51
Jeers, gibes and flouts and, 85:35
Jehu, like the driving of, 325:57
Jellies soother than the creamy curd, 136:13
Jenny kissed me, 128:3
  to her wheel, 443:47
Jenny's case, vengeance of, 256:18
Jericho, tarry at, 325:39
Jerusalem, if I forget thee, 328:11
  the golden, 182:7
  till we have built, 30:12
Jessamine, pale, 167:22
Jest, a scornful, 130:8
  and youthful jollity, 163:33
  be laughable, swear, 253:26
  better lose, 362:3
  except ye owe the Fates, 143:22
  fellow of infinite, 227:33
  for ever, good, 231:42
  he had his, 89:36
  if you make, 387:53
  is not jest, true, 354:28
  leave, 394:25
  life is a, 103:26
  put his whole wit in, 27:19
  true word is spoken in, 398:19
  with them, be slow to, 143:22

you must take, 387:53
Jest's prosperity lies in the ear of him that
hears it, 246:15
Jested, quaffed and swore, 88:7
Jester, become a fool and, 234:37
Jesters, with shallow, 233:31
Jesting with edged tools, 391:64
Jests sound worst, truest, 423:57
to his memory for, 278:13
Jesu, by a nobler deed, 61:29
Jesus Christ her Lord, is, 287:31
Christ the same, 340:1
gentle, 311:25
lover of my soul, 311:23
stand up for, 92:6
the blood of, 29:16
the very thought of Thee, 60:10
with the Cross of, 24:13
ye belong to, 17:19
Jesus' name, power of, 190:1
Jeunesse savait, si, 95:31
Jew, an Ebrew, 232:8
else, I am a, 232:8
eyes, hath not a, 254:19
Jewel, black man is, 349:16
caught my heav'nly, 278:17
fair play's a, 369:72
in a ten-times-barr'd-up chest, 242:18
in an Ethiope's ear, 266:16
in its head, precious, 215:37
of gold in a swine's snout, 328:26
of their souls, immediate, 261:28
you had not found, 385:77
Jewels five words long, 294:9
for a set of beads, 244:2
moving, 302:7
Jews might kiss, 193:24
spend at Easter, 419:65
Turks, Infidels, 341:39
Jhesus, that gentleman, 25:18
Jigging veins of rhyming mother wits,
156:9
Jill, every Jack has, 368:30
Jingo if we do, by, 126:34
Job, poor as, 358:25
Job, we will finish the, 66:7
you have a responsible, 182:3
Jobiska's, for his Aunt, 147:19
Joe, poor old, 101:19
Jog on, the foot-path way, 273:42
John Anderson my jo, 45:42
John Bull, greatest of all, 53:33

John Naps of Greece, old, 268:9
John of Gaunt, old, 242:17
John Richard William Alexander Dwyer,
280:5
Johnny Groat's, Maidenkirk to, 46:2
Johnson, imitation of, 43:36
is dead, 115:21
no arguing with, 110:11
put you in mind of, 115:21
the Great Cham, 281:28
Johnson's sayings, 189:18
Joined, whom God hath, 341:51
Joint, nose out of, 430:10
Joints, his square-turn'd, 209:27
Joke, Dulness ever loves a, 194:16
grace to see a, 345:21
had he, for many a, 109:26
relations with a good, 65:27
Jollies, 'er Majesty's, 141:46
they done it, the, 141:46
Jollity and game, turn'd to, 173:47
but hath a smack of folly, no, 425:40
Jolly as a sandboy, 358:4
credit in being, 83:37
Jonathan, consult Brother, 309:21
Jonson's learned sock, 164:8
Jordan's wave, on this side, 17:21
Jorkins, I have a partner, 84:7
Joseph, knew not, 323:41
Josephus, Histories of, 144:1
Jostle not, dust and bones, 389:55
Jouk and let the jaw gae by, 392:38
Jour de gloire est arrivé, 207:19
Journey closes, before his, 294:24
he is in a, 325:48
hinder no man's, 399:52, 406:60
in a long, 353:44
leave not your, 371:44
Journeys end in lovers' meeting, 271:36
little, 395:11
Jours, tous les, 73:30
Jove, daughter of, 112:1
for's power to thunder, 218:25
himself, front of, 226:2
laughs at lovers' perjuries, 392:39
laughs, at lovers' perjuries, 271:23
thrown by angry, 169:26
Jove's dread clamours, 261:35
Jowett, my name is, 344:6
Joy and moan, finish'd, 230:3
as it flies, who kisses, 30:10
at his fortune, 229:35

be unconfined, 50:12
brightens his crest, 173:36
chortled in his, 59:19
cometh in the morning, 326:27
current of domestic, 131:21
father's sorrow, father's, 114:1
for ever, a, 125:41
for ever dwells, where, 168:9
God send you, 372:36
he sees it in his, 319:35
like an unbodied, 276:6
one year of, 405:72
perfectest herald of, 258:15
Phyllis is my only, 212:13
pledges of Heav'n's, 163:27
proposed, before, 265:30
pure and complete, 302:3
shall be in heaven, 336:23
shall overtake, till, 206:6
shouted for, 326:7
snatch a fearful, 111:32
which warriors feel, 211:29
who bends to himself a, 30:10
without annoy, no, 402:5
without canker or cark, 145:22
Joy's trinket, 285:21
Joy-bells ring, makes, 159:28
Joyful and triumphant, 185:14
Joynson-Hicks, past, 187:21
Joys, Africa and golden, 234:35
    and destiny obscure, homely, 112:8
    friendships multiply, 371:65
    grow dim, earth's, 159:12
    hence, vain deluding, 164:11
    therein I find, present, 92:14
    three-parts pain, 39:43
    to rob us of our, 148:6
    we dote upon, how fading are, 184:4
Judex damnatur, 393:40
Judge you as you are, but, 258:9
    disallow thee to be a competent, 308:2
    in heaven, no, 20:2
    indifferent, 278:20
    is condemned, 393:40
    not, 333:57
    not according to the appearance, 337:45
    obey, the inward, 20:2
    of all the earth, 323:30
    over us, who made thee, 323:42
    that no king can corrupt, 238:14
    thee, will I, 336:26
Judge's robe, 252:8

Judged, that ye be not, 333:57
Judges all rang'd, 104:2
    soon the sentence sign, hungry, 193:29
Judgment Book, leaves of, 291:24
    Daniel come to, 225:35
    falls upon a man, 212:16
    green in, 214:1
    He which is the top of, 252:9
    reserve thy, 221:38
    Seat, God's great, 140:19
    shallow spirit of, 237:27
    thou art fled, 229:39
    waits upon the, 226:3
    women's rougher, 72:15
Judgments as our watches, with, 192:4
Jug without a handle, old, 147:18
Juice, get but little, 387:63
    nectarean, 290:12
Julia goes, in silks my, 120:12
Julius, ere such another, 219:31
    fell, mightiest, 220:8
    ye towers of, 113:31
July he prepares to fly, in, 388:34
    it be rainy weather, if the first of, 386:22
    swarm [of bees] in, 354:21
Jumblies live, where the, 147:16
June another tune, in, 416:8
    calm weather in, 364:1
    dripping, 350:27
    he alters his tune, in, 388:34
    in the leafy month of, 69:33
    it rain, if on the eight of, 386:6
    look at [corn] in, 395:30
    newly sprung in, 47:25
    rare as a day in, 151:31
    reared that bunch, 37:21
June's twice June, 37:29
Jungle, cutting through, 148:15
Juno's eyes, lids of, 274:1
Jurisprudence, light of, 68:10
Jury, I'll be judge, I'll be, 58:5
    passing on the prisoner's life, 252:4
    trial by, 81:23
Just, actions of the, 278:15
    and fear not, be, 239:19
    and on the unjust, on, 333:46
    before you are generous, be, 360:14
    it raineth on the, 32:6
    path of the, 328:18
    persons, ninety and nine, 336:23
    whatsoever things are, 339:53
Justice, as thou urgest, 255:37

be done, let, 370:15
be thy plea, though, 255:33
even-handed, 247:41
in the course of, 255:33
kind of wild, 22:10
pleaseth few, 393:41
sad-eyed, 235:43
thou shalt have, 255:37

was done, 116:2
was for doing, 97:24
which is the, 242:4
with her lifted scale, 194:12
with mercy, temper, 173:41
Justinian Stubbs, Esquire, 280:5
Justitia, fiat, 370:15

K

Kail het again, cauld, 364:9
Κακά, πάνα τἀνθρώπων, 95:35
Kalendas Graecas, ad, 21:20
Kame sindle, kame sair, 393:42
Kann nicht anders, ich, 152:6
Kansas had better stop raising corn, 147:22
Kaspar's work was done, 282:4
Keats, what porridge had, 38:15
    who kill'd John, 53:34
Keek in my kail pot, 393:43
Keel, follow eyes the, 312:17
    ploughs air, her, 62:1
Keep a thing seven years, 393:45
    and pass, and turn, 95:26
    it by me, I love to, 129:34
    it, hath it and will not, 379:44
    now, better, 361:78
    some till more come, 393:48
    something for a sore foot, 393:49
    to the right, if you, 95:30
    who can, they should, 318:8
    you, shop will, 393:54
Keeper, am I my brother's, 323:22
    poacher makes the best, 356:52
Keepers, oft worry their, 393:60
Keeping, finding's, 370:17
    men off, by, 103:31
Keerless man in his talk, 116:33
Κείμεθα, τῆδε, 278:23
Keith of Ravelston, 85:45
Ken, as far as angels' 168:4
Kens the wife, little, 395:12
Kensal Green, by way of, 65:22
Kent, apples, cherries, 82:6

Kentucky home, my old, 101:15
Kerke the narre, to, 283:22
Kernel, he that will eat, 381:67
Kettle black, pot calls, 421:63
    of fish, 339:67
Kew, come down to, 184:10
    his Highness' dog at, 199:24
Key and keyhole do sustain, 395:80
    must have a good, 381:69
    to which I found no, 98:8
    under thy own life's, 213:24
    with this, 320:12
    with this same, 40:13
Keys hang not, all, 356:9
    he bore, two massy, 116:18
Khartoum, old man of, 344:10
Khayyám, come with old, 98:4
Kibe, galls his, 227:32
Kick, a penalty, 200:27
    against the pricks, 337:60
    an attorney downstairs, 393:55
    land him one solid, 146:11
    me downstairs, why, 138:11
Kicked until they can feel, 48:22
    waxed fat and, 324:14
Kirkshaws, little tiny, 234:33
Kid follows, 438:12
    lie down with, 331:52
    thou shalt not seethe, 324:6
Kidlings blithe, than, 103:29
Kidney, man of my, 256:17
Kill a wife with kindness, 268:13
    and die, must men, 277:26
    thou shalt not, 68:5

dear as remember'd, 294:14
dream, straight on, 266:13
give me a thousand, 60:15
I fear thy, 276:8
I understand thy, 232:27
of a summer night, 162:2
of his mouth, with, 330:38
of many thousand, 214:16
play'd at cards for, 152:9
sows and reaps, 74:5
tears and smiles, 318:13
Kissing goes by favour, 393:65
her hair, 289:35
is out of season, 437:38
your hand, 151:22
Kitchen boys, so will all, 386:25
physic is the best, 393:66
taste of, 423:42
Kite, body of, 352:16
carrion, 349:33
for a feather, ask a, 359:72
Kitten, I had rather be a, 232:23
laps as much as, 356:43
Kittens, soshubble ez a baskit er, 116:16
wanton, 434:3
Kitty Swerrock where she sat, 393:67
Knave and ever a knave, once, 404:22
as hard to please, 390:3
be troubled with, 361:79
better be a fool than, 361:50
better kiss, 361:79
crafty, 350:17
cunning, 426:37
early master, soon, 367:82
eleven [hours sleepeth], 370:31
if ye would know, 387:45
is no babe, old, 356:48
no pack of cards without, 425:44
petty sneaking, 30:11
rascally yea-forsooth, 234:2
thank God, you are rid of, 258:26
the better luck, more, 420:30
Knavery, done without, 393:70
may serve a turn, 393:68
Knaves and fools divide the world, 393:69
and fools, if there were no, 387:37
come out of the north, 364:41
imagine nothing can be done without
knavery, 393:70
little better than false, 258:37
meet, merry when, 391:75
thieves, and treachers, 240:11

three misbegotten, 232:11
unmannerly, untaught, 231:35
Knee, bow'd . . . patient, 50:20
civility of my, 34:19
gomes schust to mine, 15:3
stand beside my, 22:2
Kneels to another, not one, 312:14
Knees and tresses folded, 160:15
brooded, clasping, 183:21
down on your, 219:35
maid's, 350:25
of the gods, on the, 123:29
on her apron'd, 54:10
young climber up of, 144:9
Knell is rung, their, 71:34
strikes like a rising, 50:11
that summons thee, 248:15
Knew not Joseph, which, 323:41
small head could carry all he, 109:27
Knife, catch at a falling, 401:54
cuts, same, 422:5
draw thy, 427:59
Knife-grinder, needy, 56:5
Knight, as hard to please a knave as, 390:33
every chance brought a noble, 297:40
in arms, Colonel or, 167:25
king can mak, 47:32
king can make, 419:67
many a, and many a squire, 24:4
of the Rueful Countenance, 61:22
so trim, carpet, 209:27
that ever bare shield, courteous, 155:30
there never was, 210:7
thy sire was a, 211:34
verray parfit gentil, 63:22
was pricking, 283:23
Knight's bones are dust, 71:20
Knight-at-arms, ail thee, 137:36
Knights, came among press of, 155:30
ladies dead and lovely, 265:23
of Logres, or of Lyones, 174:3
Knitters in the sun, 272:2
Knitting, forsook spinning and, 398:21
Knock, and it shall be opened, 324:30
as you please, 199:23
Knocked me down with a feather, 442:11
Knocker, tie up the, 197:36
Knocks, apostolic blows and, 48:13
open, locks, whoever, 250:12
young men's, 442:37
Knot in a bulrush, seek, 402:36
Knots, fools tie, 371:42

L

L and that is he, take away, 380:14
Laborare est orare, 394:2
Laborem, alterius spectare, 152:4
Labour, all ye that, 324:18
  and sorrow, their strength, 327:52
  and the wounds are vain, 68:1
  as long-lived, 394:3
  bears a lovely face, 80:10
  but he must, 438:10
  for my travail, had my, 270:14
  for one's pains, have, 429:43
  in vain that build it, they, 328:4
  insupportable, 284:16
  must have some, 379:54
  of love, 339:55
  this is the toil, this the, 306:6
  true success is to, 286:4
  we delight in, 249:25
  which he taketh, 330:6
  with difficulty and, 170:14
  you'll not lose, 410:6
Labour's bath, sore, 248:21
Laboure, as Austin bit, 63:25
Labourer free, sett'st the, 55:33
  is worthy of his hire, 336:11
Labourers are few, 324:11
Labours and thrives, he that, 380:4
Labyrinthine buds the rose, 36:15
Lace for your cape, 274:6
  Greek is like, 133:47
Lacedaemon, in lordly, 154:8
Lacedaemonians, tell the, 278:23
Laces, tying up her, 160:17
Lack, eat into itself, for, 48:15
  of many a thing, sigh, 264:2
Lacrimae, hinc illae, 298:8
Lad that's born to be king, 32:3
  when I was a, 104:28
Lad's love's a busk of broom, 394:5
  love is lassies' delight, 394:4
Ladder, climbed the dusty, 301:31

  go down, 372:22
  is ascended, 412:40
  traffic of Jacob's, 300:4
  world is, 423:75
Laden, labour and are heavy, 324:18
Ladies, ate in hall among, 155:30
  be but young and fair, 216:13
  dead, in praise of, 265:23
  good for, 369:79
  intellectual, lords of, 51:13
  of St. James's, 86:2
  of Spain, 342:30
  over-offended, 284:18
  spend their time in making nets, 289:20
  with store of, 164:7
Ladies' favours, rhyme themselves into,
    237:23
  lips, o'er, 266:13
Lads and Girls, 85:26
  and girls, golden, 230:1
  are far away, though, 100:12
  love of, 397:63
  raw dads make fat, 408:18
  that thought there was no more behind,
    273:33
  that will die in their glory, 125:14
  won't love, if, 394:4
Lads' leavings, lasses are, 394:7
Lady, a love for any, 189:14
  a most beautiful, 80:15
  here comes the, 267:37
  in the land, ain't a, 65:32
  Joan is as good as my, 392:37
  never won fair, 369:66
  of my delight, the, 160:39
  of Shallott, 292:11
  seems of ivory, my, 180:5
  sweet and kind, 342:14
  sweet, arise, my, 219:30
  through, pulls a, 157:28
  thy mother a, 211:34

with a Lamp, 150:19
Lady's in the case, when a, 103:28
Lady-smocks all silver-white, 246:16
Lafayette, we are here, 284:12
Laggard in love, 210:9
Laid me down with a will, 286:21
Laird o' Cockpen, 181:21
  slight the lady, if, 386:25
Lairdie, wee, wee German, 78:13
Lake of blue, starless, 70:18
  or moorish fen, by, 165:42
  on still St. Mary's, 318:9
ακεδαιμονίοις, αγγειλον, 278:23
Lakes, light shakes across, 294:11
Lamb, dwell with, 331:52
  go to bed with, 372:25
  goes out like, 398:34
  Mary had a little, 115:15
  mild as, 358:16
  save one little ewe, 325:40
  shorn, 373:41
  skin of an innocent, 237:34
  to the shorn, 285:27
  to the slaughter, as, 332:7
  was sure to go, 115:15
Lamb, the frolic and the gentle, 320:14
Lambs could not forgive, 82:45
  we were as twinn'd, 273:34
Lame and impotent conclusion, 260:16
  are foremost, 388:30
  goes as far, 419:71
  post brings the truest news, 419:72
  tongue gets nothing, 419:73
Lamely and unfashionable, 244:12
Lament, long, 410:36
Lammas, at latter, 359:82
Lamp, I lift my, 146:8
  in the evening, light, 27:27
  is shattered, when, 277:22
  Lady with a, 150:19
  smell, of, 430:21
  unto my feet, 328:2
Lamps, a thousand silver, 27:25
  are going out all over Europe, 114:5
  like golden, 158:8
  shone, bright the, 50:11
Lancaster, time-honour'd, 242:17
Lance in rest, looked like, 140:20
Lancelot brave, not even, 297:26
  or Pelleas, or Pellenore, 174:3
Land alone, on this, 121:18
  being on, settle, 360:33

between, remedy for love is, 421:72
charter of the, 300:19
England's the one, 34:4
flowing with milk and honey, 324:2
from the holy, 202:7
green and pleasant, 30:12
he that buys, 376:76
he that hath some, 379:54
ill fares the, 108:15
in a strange, 328:10
in this favoured, 298:31
in which it seemed always afternoon,
  292:18
into a golden, 303:26
into the promised, 344:1
into the silent, 206:8
is bright, look, the, 68:3
kennst du das, 107:37
know ye the, 51:32
knowest thou the, 107:37
marched into their, 22:5
Land, my native – good night, 50:8
  my own, my native, 209:24
  o' the leal, to the, 181:21
  o'er all the pleasant, 118:13
  of bondage, from, 211:40
  of brown heath, 209:25
  of drowsyhed, pleasing, 300:16
  of Eldorado, 26:2
  of Hope and Glory, 28:5
  of my sires, 209:25
  of old, London like a, 26:2
  of settled government, 292:22
  of the free, 138:17
  of the mountain and the flood, 209:25
  of the pilgrims' pride, 280:11
  reposed, her, 292:4
  she is far from the, 178:7
  some influence to, 27:32
  stranger in a strange, 324:1
  takes a fool, for, 398:18
  there is a happy, 320:38
  there shall be no more, 34:5
  to fight for such a, 210:5
  to land, like night from, 69:38
  to watch from the, 152:4
  was never lost, 394:6
  well tilled, little, 352:26
  went to the holy, 202:8
  where lies the, 67:31
  where my fathers died, 280:11
Landed, row'd and there we, 298:3

Landing grounds, fight on the, 66:3
Land-rats and water-rats, 240:37
Lands between us lie, what, 47:29
  dumb folks get no, 367:78
  envy of less happier, 243:29
  forlorn, faery, 137:21
  I have no, 383:50
  were fairly portioned, 154:3
Landscape bright, beauteous, 313:24
  fades the glimmering, 112:5
  tire the view, 92:15
Lane, I know each, 165:37
  in a Devonshire, 158:2
  in an English, 38:1
  it is a long, 390:11
Language, eyes have one, 417:54
  he was the lodesterre, off oure, 152:8
  in emphatic, 58:15
  in her eye, 271:22
  in fossil poetry, 94:15
  is plain, my, 116:21
  learning me your, 269:24
  there were no, 425:56
  you taught me, 269:24
Languages, great feast of, 250:20
  speaks three or four, 271:26
Languid, art thou, 182:9
Lap of May, chills the, 108:4
Lap-dogs breathe their last, 193:33
Lapidem, gutta cavat, 374:6
Lapland night, lovely as, 318:21
Lappe, biforn him in his, 63:36
Lapwater, Roses, Pyrgo and, 298:33
Lapwing cries most, 419:74
Larch, rosy plumelets tuft, 296:2
Lards the lean earth, 231:43
Large as life, 358:5
Lark at heaven's gate sings, 219:30
  begin his fight, hear, 163:36
  cheerily carols the, 106:18
  he is gay as a, 58:12
  his lay who thrill'd, 211:42
  leg of, 352:16
  lo, here the gentle, 263:25
  more blithe, no, 29:15
  now leaves his wat'ry nest, 79:27
  rise with, 372:25
  sing, better to hear, 390:35
  so shrill and clear, 152:10
  twitters, a late, 119:24
  weary of rest, 263:25
Lark's on the wing, 37:19

Larke, the bisy, 63:37
Larks and a Wren, four, 147:14
  fall there ready roasted, 419:75
  live by leeks, 397:68
  we shall catch, 386:31
Lars Porsena of Clusium, 154:1
Lash the rascals naked, 262:5
Lashes, teary round the, 151:37
Lass, a penniless, 181:24
  amo, amas, I love a, 185:17
  asked by his, 28:3
  drink to the, 278:6
  lisping, 352:23
  of Richmond Hill, 155:26
  so neat, this, 155:26
  unparallel'd, 215:27
Lasse, tout casse, tout, 431:67
Lasses a-lilting, 94:3
  all are good, 355:63
  are lads' leavings, 394:7
  glasses and, 372:19
  honest men and bonnie, 46:6
  then she made the, 44:3
Lassie do wi' an auld man, 46:13
  I lo'e best, the, 45:35
  I love a, 146:3
  lives, the bonnie, 45:35
  my love she's but, 45:43, 122:5
  service to my bonnie, 45:41
Lassies will fite, 394:4
Lassies' delight, 394:4
Last [at the end] and best of all God's works,
  173:39
  but not least, 394:8
  came and last did go, 166:18
  is commonly best, 47:39
  make fast, 394:9
  man, held to the, 115:13
  man in, 183:24
  not least in love, 229:32
  of all the Romans, 230:21
  shall be first, 324:41
  state of that man, 324:21
  to the pot, cometh, 378:9
Last [go on], but never lives, may, 104:12
Last [go on] long, both would, 385:75
  long foretold, long, 395:27
Last [block] cobbler stick to, 395:47
Late all my lifetime, five minutes too, 74:8
  and soon, 319:28
  better early than, 361:68
  falls early or too, 100:6

habit of getting up, 59:39
I stayed, too, 283:21
long choosing, and beginning, 173:32
than never, better, 362:1
to mend, never too, 392:1
too late, too, 297:33
worse when it comes, 130:1
Latent, dim and very various, operations
be, 179:28
Lather, good, 351:59
Latin, a horse, and money, with, 440:21
and less Greek, small, 134:14
he speaks, 238:3
was no more difficile, 48:3
word for three farthings, 246:4
Latitude's rather uncertain, 200:20
Latyn, speke no word but, 63:35
Laud than gilt o'erdusted, more, 271:20
Laudator temporis acti, 126:3
Laudi, concedant laurea, 66:21
Laugh and be merry, 159:27
and be proud, 159:27
and be well, 113:35
and cry, hard to, 391:58
and grow fat, 394:11
and the world laughs, 313:29
at any mortal thing, if I, 52:26
bland hyena's, 58:2
broad as ten thousand beeves, 160:25
broke into pieces, 25:28
like parrots, 253:26
on the wrong side of one's mouth, 429:61
sans intermission, 216:11
shall win, exploded, 34:15
that win, let them, 395:49
the loud, 108:18
to scorn, thing to, 218:5
where we must, 195:26
who but must, 198:2
with the other [eye], 428:19
Laughed at, he is not, 376:21
consumedly, they, 96:9
full well they, 109:26
in the sun, 34:1
when the first baby, 25:28
Laughing is heard on the hill, 30:4
somewhere men are, 298:31
women and wine undo men, 406:30
Laughs at himself first, 376:21
best that laughs last, 376:33
himself to death, 376:33
ill, he, 376:33

last, that, 376:32
one greets and another, 392:3
with a harvest, 130:2
Laughter and ability and sighing, 85:26
Laughter, eyes overrunning with, 150:16
first, 362:22
for a month, 231:42
free, dearer her, 114:6
grimaces called, 121:25
holding both his sides, 163:34
in the midst of his, 60:3
laugh thy girlish, 309:28
our sincerest, 276:7
shame or mocking or, 142:9
to a land of no, 203:26
under running, 298:37
waves' unnumbered, 16:12
weeping and, 87:21
Laura lay, grave where, 202:10
Laurea laudi, concedant, 66:21
Laurel, rose or rue or, 289:39
stands high, the, 107:37
trees are cut, 23:34
Laurels, once more, O ye, 166:8
worth all your, 53:35
Laurel-wreath to praise, 66:21
Lauriers sont coupés, 23:34
Lave o't, whistle o'er the, 46:1
Lavender, mints, savory, 273:44
Lavish of his own, 208:6
Law and the prophets, 324:2
army of unalterable, 160:25
breakers, 394:13
breeds without the, 141:26
catches flies, 394:14
divine, by a, 275:36
does not concern itself, 366:6
eleven points of, 406:44
ends, where, 62:10
for the rich, one, 404:51
heaven's first, 196:3
highest, 409:53
I'll show you, 411:43
I will maintain, this is, 342:22
ignorance of the, 212:17
in a thousand pounds of, 388:31
into one's own hands, take, 430:33
is a ass, the, 82:26
is a sort of hocus-pocus science, 155:22
is costly, 355:60
is ended, so, 356:66
lawyer never goes to, 352:13

logic, and Switzers, 394:12
makers, 394:13
my maxim should become a universal,
135:36
necessity knows no, 401:42
nine points of, 406:44
of God or man, never a, 140:4
of nature, first, 410:13
of the Medes and the Persians, 332:20
old father antic the, 231:28
rich men rule the, 108:5
seven hours, to, 134:8
sharp quillets of, 213:27
the highest, 66:16
there is a higher, 213:21
unto themselves, 338:8
Law, what plea, in, 254:24
which moulds a tear, 199:20
windy side of the, 272:14
worst of, 424:2
worth a pound of, 353:64
wrest once the, 255:34
Law's delay, the, 224:4
grave study, six in, 68:12
made to take care o' raskills, 93:23
Lawful, all things are, 338:26
Lawn, hurrying thro' the, 294:23
leave the printed, 126:20
upon the upland, 112:18
Lawns, fair with orchard, 297:44
Laws and learning die, 208:3
are dumb in the midst of arms, 66:15
breathing household, 317:40
care who should make, 99:32
grind the poor, 108:5
new lords, new 401:68
of God, broke the, 129:32
or kings can cause, 131:21
the more, 420:31
Lawsuits consume time, 394:15
Lawyer, [go not] for every quarrel to,
372:24
minister, physician, and, 383:56
never goes to law, 352:13
young, 356:51
Lawyers are met, the, 104:2
Lawyers' fingers, o'er, 266:13
houses, 394:16
Lay low, Brer Fox, he, 116:15
on, Macduff, 251:44
there she, 64:4
up for a rainy day, 429:63

Lays, constructing tribal, 141:29
Lazy as Ludlam's dog, 358:6
as the name, as, 88:16
folk take the most pains, 394:17
ones on, liftin' the, 111:30
youth, a lousy age, 352:15
Lea, o'er moorland and, 122:4
on this pleasant, 319:29
winds slowly o'er, 112:4
Lead [metal] at night, 363:68
friends are lapp'd in, 25:20
Lead [conduct] one by the nose, 429:64
Thou me on, 183:28
Leader is fairest, 18:19
sage, in camps, 209:27
Leaf, in the yellow, 53:36
out of one's book, take, 430:26
the sear, the yellow, 251:31
to the grave, bring, 388:2
turn over a new, 431:44
we all do fade as, 332:10
League [distance], for many a, 18:23
onward, half a, 294:25
League [compact] till death, keep a, 244:7
Leagues from hence, a thousand, 232:28
thirty-five, 342:30
Leak, small, 354:11
Leal heart lied never, 394:18
Leal, land o' the, 181:21
Lean and sad, 369:67
as a rake, 358:7
she help'd him to, 24:8
[sow] doth mean, what, 395:13
take the fat with, 442:18
wife could eat no, 392:34
Leaned his head against a wall, 358:6
Leap better, in order to, 388:14
for mankind, one giant, 18:11
in, darest thou, 228:9
into a well, if you, 387:57
it were an easy, 231:38
look before you, 395:31
over, men, 399:59
Leaped (or possibly jumped), 146:10
over, easily, 352:30
Lear, pleasant to know Mr., 147:13
Learn, in doing we, 389:38
it is lawful to, 391:71
live and, 395:20
never too old to, 401:64
not yet so old but she may, 255:27
weeping, 394:20

Learned and conn'd by rote, 230:16
 enough, 380:11
 evil is soon, 414:29
 he was naturally, 92:1
 man grew within this, 157:20
 nothing, have, 290:15
 smile, make the, 192:11
Learning, a little, 192:6
 a progeny of, 277:35
 bushel of, 352:2
 dote, on scraps of, 322:6
 doth make thee mad, 338:3
 is most excellent, 436:12
 is worth, than, 442:21
 just enough of, 49:40
 love he bore to, 109:26
 love of, 420:11
 loyal body wanted, 302:9
 makes a good man better, 394:22
 many things, 281:29
 of liberty and of, 85:34
 twins of, 239:26
 will be cast into the mire, 43:32
 worth a pound of, 356:55
Learning's triumph o'er her barb'rous foes
 130:16
Learnt, soon, 412:8
Least, last but not, 394:8
 of two evils choose, 403:77
 to do, that hath, 439:52
Leather, nothing like, 403:54
 of other men's, 399:57
 or prunella, but, 196:4
 Spanish or neat's, 48:22
 through faithless, 322:10
 trod upon neat's, 228:3
Leave [depart from] it off, loth to, 397:39
 me thus, wilt thou, 320:27
 of enough men, 403:68
 off while the play is good, 394:27
 off with an appetite, 394:28
 out, when in doubt, 436:15
 than lack, better, 362:2
Leave [permission] is light, 394:26
Leaven laveneth the whole lump, a little,
 338:22
Leaves and flowers do cover, with, 310:10
 away, rake the, 102:6
 brown skeletons of, 69:37
 dead are driven, 275:32
 generation of, 123:27
 getteth short of, 123:41

hang, green, 123:37
like the things of man, 124:17
lisp of, 290:1
in the rustling, 165:24
or none, yellow, 264:13
shatter your, 166:8
thick as autumnal, 168:13
whisp'ring overhede, 314:22
Lebanon, to cedar'd, 136:13
Leben, wollt ihr ewig, 102:1
Lecher in my sight, does, 242:2
Lectures, hissed all my mystery, 284:6
Lee, ran clean through, 200:27
Lee, waters of the river, 200:19
Leer, assent with civil, 198:2
Lees is left this vault, 249:28
Left [bequeathed] we lost, what we, 345:16
Left [side], if you keep to, 95:30
Leg, bone in one's, 428:36
 boot is on the other, 415:60
 he has a, 160:27
 here I leave my second, 123:36
 warmeth, while, 438:28
Leges inter arma, silent, 66:15
Legion, my name is, 325:66
 [tempted] by, 379:63
Legiones redde, 20:19
Legions, give me back, 20:19
Legislators, unacknowledged, 277:28
Legs and have legs, use, 433:52
 and passing strong, straight, 263:23
 bestrid the ocean, his, 214:19
 cannon-ball took off, 123:35
 in a bed, four bare, 400:8
 on one's last, 427:65
 on other men's, 402:42
 one pair of, 404:62
 one pair of English, 236:9
 stretch, 412:47
 that has four, 352:9
 walk under his huge, 228:11
 walking on his hinder, 132:21
 were smitten off, 275:25
Leisure, have the most, 415:64
 he hath no, 375:74
 least, 385:57
 retired, 164:15
Lemnos th'Aegean isle, on, 169:26
Lemon-trees bloom, where, 107:37
Lemonade, black eyes and, 177:27
Lend a man money, 388:6
 and lose, 394:29

half a crown, 361:69
he that doth, 378:17
men who, 143:38
nor borrow, neither, 387:36
not horse, nor wife, 394:30
you something, I'll, 272:17
your money, 394:31
Lenders, bad, 373:74
Lendeth unto the Lord, 329:44
Lends gives, he that, 380:5
Length along, drags its slow, 192:15
Lent [season], has but a short, 375:66
  have their season in, 409:51
  marry in, 399:45
Lent [gave loan] I was a friend, when I,
  436:14
Lente currite noctis equi, 157:18
Leonem, ex ungue, 369:59
Leopard [change] his spots, 332:13
  shall lie down with the kid, 331:52
Lerne, craft so long to, 62:15
  gladly wold be, 63:28
Lesbia hath a beaming eye, 178:5
  vivamus, mea, 60:14
Lesely, saw ye bonnie, 46:19
Less, the little, 38:8
Let alone, 394:34
  thee go, I will not, 323:34
  unfurnished, to be, 48:10
Letter, not of the, 339:38
  of recommendation, 351:55
  remains, written, 395:5
  sneeze for, 411:69
  stay for the post, 395:51
  thou unnecessary, 240:16
Lettuce, like lips, like, 395:77
Leveller, death is, 366:13
Leviathan, draw out, 326:13
Levity, a little judicious, 286:12
Levys at ese that frely levys, 23:36
Lewd fellows of the baser sort, 337:63
Lex, de minimis non curat, 366:6
  suprema est, 66:16, 409:53
Lexicographer, a harmless drudge, 131:25
Lexicography, lost in, 131:24
Lexicon of youth, in the, 153:15
Liar, boaster and, 349:22
  caught fighting a, 284:6
  fame is a common, 364:45
  is not believed, 352:17
  of the first magnitude, 72:7
  show me, 411:41

Liars, all men are, 327:61
  begin by imposing upon others, 395:53
  debtors are, 366:20
  end by deceiving themselves, 395:53
  great talkers are, 373:76
  should have good memories, 395:54
Libel, the greater the, 418:31
Libelli, nostri farrago, 135:25
Liberal, either a little, 106:3
  spends more than, 416:4
Liberté ! comme on t'a jouée ! 205:19
  l'arbre de la, 24:1
  que de crimes on commet en ton nom !
    205:19
Libertine, charter'd, 235:41
  puff'd and reckless, 220:36
Liberty and the pursuit of happiness, 129:29
  and Union, 310:5
  condition upon which God hath given,
    78:15
  enjoy such, 151:25
  give me, 119:33
  God who gave us life gave, 129:28
  how thou hast been played with ! 205:19
  I must have, 216:14
  is precious, 148:4
  lean, 394:19
  license they mean when they cry, 167:29
  mountain nymph, sweet, 163:35
  of the individual, 162:7
  of the press, 135:23
  sells his, 380:22
  sweet land of, 280:11
  symptom of constitutional, 104:9
  thy chosen music, 320:5
  tree of, 24:1
  what crimes are committed in thy name!
    205:19
Liberty's in every blow, 47:24
Liberty-hall, this is, 110:10
Libraries are not made, 29:22
Library, from mine own, 268:21
  lumber-room of his, 87:31
  public, 131:23
  should be without, no gentleman's, 144:1
  take choice of, 270:10
  turn over half a, 133:32
  was dukedom, my, 268:20
Libre, l'homme est né, 207:20
License they mean when they cry liberty,
  167:29
Licht, mehr, 107:39

under a weary, 224:4
unfulfilled, each, 40:7
unpleasant, makes, 128:12
Life upon a cast, set my, 245:30
    useful, 300:10
    voyage of their, 230:17
    was full of misfortunes, 177:24
    was gentle, his, 230:23
    was in the right, 74:2
    we've been long together, 23:35
    web of our, 213:31
    went a-maying, 71:21
    were in't as, 251:36
    what is, 79:29
    what more I ask'd of, 204:1
    wherefore not, 312:7
    while there is, 439:66
    white flower of a blameless, 296:21
    why should a dog, a horse, a rat, have,
        242:15
    will he give for him, 325:61
    will try his nerves, 38:13
    without a friend, 395:59
    would be too smooth, 395:60
    you take my, 255:40
Life'd not be worth livin', 86:15
[Life's] a poor player, 251:37
    arrears, pay glad, 40:6
    but a span, 260:19
    but a walking shadow, 251:37
    common way, travel on, 318:2
    feast, chief nourisher in, 248:21
    last scene, in, 130:14
    little day, ebbs out, 152:12
    little ironies, 116:3
    poor play is o'er, 195:41
    race well run, 162:15
    rough sea, on this, 62:1
    too short for chess, 53:39
Life-in-Death, Night-mare, 69:25
Lifeless that is faultless, 376:18
Lifetime, knowledge of a, 312:2
    sole work of a, 37:33
Life her with care, 124:8
Light [brightness], a little warmth, a little,
        92:10
    a spring of, 68:14
    a torch gives, more, 420:32
    and leading, men of, 43:33
    and there was, 323:15
    as if they fear'd, 287:35
    as soon as he rises, gives, 101:29

as the shining, 328:18
behind her, with a, 104:21
better than, 117:26
blasted with excess of, 113:25
blinding, 183:24
burning and a shining, 337:44
by her own radiant, 165:39
can thus deceive, if, 312:7
children of, 336:27
comes in the, 68:3
dies before thy uncreating word, 194:24
dim religious, 165:25
fell no ray of, 301:31
from these flames no, 168:5
gives a lovely, 162:9
gladsome, 68:10
gleaming taper's, 110:4
God's eldest daughter, 102:12
golden and silver, 320:32
hail, holy, 170:15
he beholds, 319:35
in a Noose of, 97:27
in fleecy flocks of, 33:19
in that fierce, 296:21
in the dust lies dead, 277:22
is, as the clear, 340:23
is spent, how my, 167:31
is sweet, 330:30
lead, kindly, 183:28
let there be, 323:15
lets in new, 307:27
more, 107:39
more by your number than, 320:24
much faster than, 344:14
nothing but its own, 422:35
of common day, fade into, 319:35
of liberty, and of learning, place of, 85:34
of Terewth, 84:13
of the bright world, 32:5
of the world, ye are, 333:39
of things, come forth into, 316:9
pure and endless, 304:13
put out the, 262:10
relume, that can thy, 262:10
restore, thy former, 262:10
rule of streaming, 165:38
seeking light doth light of light beguile,
        245:33
shakes, long, 294:11
so shine, let your, 333:40
stand in one's own, 430:25
that lies in woman's eyes, 178:12

that never was, 318:20
that thing called, 66:14
them for themselves, not, 251:45
there is shed, stronger, 179:18
thickens, 249:41
to counterfeit a gloom, teach, 164:19
unbarr'd the gates of, 172:18
unto my path, 328:2
unveil'd her peerless, 171:32
up the steeps of, 17:24
will repay the wrongs, 200:22
windows that exclude, 113:22
within he that has, 165:40
your lips hang in, 443:40
Light [not heavy], and will aspire, 263:22
of step and heart, 80:15
Lighte, orient laugheth of, 63:37
Lightens, ere one can say It, 267:27
if it, 436:8
Light-heeled mother, 352:20
Lighthouse, sitivation at, 82:22
Lighting a little Hour or two, 97:33
by gas, as much expedient as, 107:31
Lightly come, lightly go, 106:31
Lightning, brief as the, 256:23
loosed the fateful, 127:25
too like the, 267:27
vanish like, 291:27
Lightning-flash, fear no more, 230:3
Lightnings Thy sword, 65:34
Lights are fled, whose, 178:15
burning, your, 336:16
turn up the, 119:30
Like again, look upon his, 220:27
as two peas, 353:8
blood, like good, and like age, 395:73
cures like, 395:74
it, if you don't, 387:51
it not at present, you, 440:51
it the least, always, 64:7
look for the, 367:48
sort of thing they, 148:13
will to like, 395:83
Likeliest, do the, 367:57
Likelihood, of no mark nor, 233:30
Likely lies in the mire, 396:1
not bloody, 275:23
Likeness causeth liking, 395:2
in the old, 77:31
Likewise, go and do thou, 336:13
Liking, likeness causeth, 396:2
not in living but, 395:58

them, trouble of, 21:31
Lilac's pretty, the, 182:19
Lilac-time, to Kew in, 184:10
Lilies and languors of virtue, 289:36
are whitest, 396:3
breaking the golden, 36:11
in her hand, three, 206:12
in the beauty of, 127:26
of all kinds, 274:1
of the field, 333:54
roses and white, 56:4
that fester, 265:19
twisted braids of, 166:6
Lilting, I've heard them, 94:3
Lily and red rose, with, 180:6
fair as the, 72:16
seen but a bright, 134:11
to paint the, 240:2
trembles to a, 86:2
Limb, life in every, 71:27
strength of, 209:27
Limbo large and broad, a, 170:20
Limbs composed, thy decent, 194:3
great smooth marbly, 39:35
on those recreant, 239:33
Linden, when the sun was low, on, 55:27
Line, cadence of a rugged, 90:14
fight it out on this, 111:28
in one dull, 192:14
into an horizontal, 312:1
justification in every, 72:14
lives along the, 195:34
never blotted out a, 134:20
no day without, 403:61
one must draw, 404:59
stretch out, will the, 250:17
the full-resounding, 198:11
to cancel half a, 98:13
too labours, 192:16
upon line, 331:57
we carved not a, 315:38
Linea, nulla dies sine, 403:61
Lineaments, moulded the changing, 187:30
Linen, clothed in purple and fine, 336:29
did not love clean, 132:15
in public, wash dirty, 433:63
wash whitest, old, 310:9
you're wearing out, not, 124:4
Liner, ram-you-damn-you, 141:27
she's a lady, 140:8
Lines are fallen unto me, 304:3
are weak, 198:8

as lief the town-crier spoke my, 224:13
desert of a thousand, 198:10
own the happy, 193:18
rather have written those, 315:34
see two dull, 322:11
silver draws black, 438:32
Lingering, something, 106:14
Lining, cloud has a silver, 368:23
there's a silver, 100:12
Linnet courting, I heard, 33:16
Linnets sing, pipe but as, 295:39
Lion among ladies, 257:35
and the Lizard keep, 98:1
as a roaring, 340:7
be mated by the, 213:26
better than a dead, 330:23
by his claw, 369:59
comes in like, 398:34
in his den, beard the, 210:11
is dead, the old, 187:27
is not so fierce, 420:6
is the beast to fight, 200:28
may be beholden to a mouse, 352:21
one, but that one a, 404:31
strong is the, 278:26
tail of, 361:60
to rouse a, 231:37
wake not a sleeping, 433:74
Lioness at home feeds, 291:31
Lion's head, never enter, 418:12
hide, thou wear a, 239:33
mane, dewdrop from, 271:21
skin cannot, if, 386:26
skin is never cheap, 352:22
Lions by the beard, pull dead, 374:27
Lions [=loins], I girdid up my, 308:11
Lip admires, a coral, 56:14
contempt and anger of, 272:8
keep a stiff upper, 60:8
'twixt the cup and, 425:59
vermeil-tinctured, 166:5
Λιπαραὶ καὶ ἰοστέφανοι, 190:14
Lips and other hearts, other, 42:5
are now forbid, my, 26:7
away, take those, 253:22
cannot fail of taking their plie, 42:21
control, why do her, 162:2
crimson in thy, 268:7
drain'd by fever'd, 290:12
for ever stray, on, 74:5
good words for, 84:17
had language, those, 76:10

hang in your light, 443:40
have spoken, when, 277:22
Heaven is in these, 157:15
last I lay upon thy, 214:16
like lettuce, like, 395:77
moisten poor Jim's, 96:7
of man, moulded by, 298:2
red curve of her, 159:26
saying, her white, 301:31
scald not your, 409:65
she licks, whose, 415:71
smily round the, 151:37
suck forth my soul, 157:15
that are for others, 294:14
to it, put my, 82:40
'twixt thy closed, 180:3
we love, far from, 178:3
were four red roses, 245:21
were red, and one was thin, 287:36
when I ope my, 253:30
Liquor for the valet, I've, 54:8
Liquors, hot and rebellious, 215:41
Lisp'd in numbers, I, 197:42
Lisping lass, 352:23
List [roll], I've got a little, 106:11
List [listen] list, O list! 222:13
Listen, darkling I, 136:19
fur'z you can look or, 151:36
where thou art sitting, 166:6
Listeners hear no good, 396:4
Lit again, not see them, 114:5
Literature, itch of, 151:29
of the day, 48:19
the most seductive of professions, 179:27
we cultivate, 280:13
Lith in their neck, 20:15
Littera scripta manet, 396:5
Little and loud, 369:67
and often, 396:6
as she is good, 385:66
ask much to have, 359:73
by little, 396:8
cannot be great, 420:7
contented wi', 46:28
done, so, 203:29
doth ease, 438:8
effect after much labour, 21:32
fain of, 406:40
gained but, 437:65
goin' through so much to learn so, 82:15
good is soon spent, 352:25
goods, little care, 395:9

lovely and pleasant in, 325:35
may last, but never, 104:12
most, he that, 380:9
most, who thinks most, 22:24
not, he that fears death, 378:24
not well, he that, 380:10
nowhere, one really, 44:1
of great men, 149:28
of quiet desperation, 300:23
only for himself, 376:27
sublime, make our, 149:28
then chiefly, 120:1
unsafely, he, 376:35
well, he that, 380:11
well, preaches well that, 376:53
Liveth the merry man, as long, 304:3
to himself, none, 338:20
Living, makes no, 365:62
mother of all, 323:21
need charity, 18:13
plain, 317:40
too much love of, 289:38
well is the best revenge, 395:22
with the dead, blend, 60:9
work hard for, 363:54
Living-dead man, a, 218:19
Livingstone, I presume, 284:11
Livre, tout le monde me recognoist en
mon, 176:15
Lo'ed ye canna be, better, 181:27
Load, all lay, 355:81
Loadstone of love, 397:54
Loaf [bread] and Luddites rise, 280:1
give, 372:8
half, 373:11
of bread, the Walrus said, 59:24
shive of a cut, 392:15
to steal, of a cut, 270:9
Loaf [loiter] and invite my soul, 312:13
Loan, borrowed, 349:25
oft loses both itself and friend, 221:39
Loaning, on ilka green, 94:3
Loathing, better go away longing than,
361:71
Loaves sold for a penny, seven halfpenny,
237:33
Lob, beat him twice with, 200:27
Lobster boiled, like a, 48:23
Loch Lomond, banks o', 342:29
Lochaber no more, 203:18
Lochiel! beware of the day, 54:20
Lochinvar is come out of the west, 210:6

like the young, 210:7
Lock, crying at the, 162:14
it is wit to pick, 392:23
will hold, no, 402:7
Locks [hairs] are like the snow, 45:42
at me, shake thy gory, 250:2
his golden, 189:16
shaking her invincible, 174:34
to part, combined, 222:12
were like the raven, 45:42
which are left you are grey, 282:8
Locks [of door], open, 250:12
Locksmiths, love laughs at, 397:56
Lodesterre, off our language, 152:8
Lodge in a garden, O for a, 130:6
in some vast wilderness, 74:34
where thou lodgest, I will, 324:27
Lodging, hard was their, 103:21
Lodgings in a head, take, 48:10
Lodore, water come down at, 282:3
Lofty and sour to them that loved him not,
238:25
Log, dying on a, 82:10
Logan is the Head Centre, 33:27
Logic a great critic, in, 48:4
absolute, with, 98:10
and rhetoric [make men] able to
contend, 22:18
Logik hadde longe y-go, un-to, 63:26
Logs, crooked, 365:67
Loin, unlit lamp and ungirt, 39:32
Loins be girded about, your, 336:16
Loiterers, liege of all, 246:6
Loitering, palely, 137:36
Lombard Street, all, 356:1
London Bridge is falling down, 29:29
Bridge, on a broken arch of, 153:26
Bridge was made for wise men to go
over, 395:23
came, all to mery, 284:2
city much like, 275:37
for wit, 406:5
gave me breath, 204:1
hear what news at, 442:13
is a modern Babylon, 85:41
it isn't far from, 184:10
like a land of old, 26:2
Mr. Weller's Knowledge of, 82:11
my most kyndly Nurse, 284:2
particular, a, 84:9
the City of, 61:25
the monster, 74:6

thou are the flower, 92:13
town, famous, 75:26
    vilest alleys of, 87:32
    when a man is tired of, 133:42
London's column, 197:33
    lasting shame, 113:31
Londoner, to the average, 88:4
Lonesome road, one that on, 69:36
Long and at the same time short, 146:12
    and lank and brown, 320:16
    and lazy, 369:67
    as ever you can, as, 310:28
    or short permit to heav'n, how, 173:45
Longer by a day, 304:3
Longest way round, 420:10
Longing, better go away, 361:71
    wavering, more, 271:42
Longings, I have immortal, 215:24
Longitude also is vague, 200:20
Look about us, just to, 195:25
    aloof, on painting, 404:18
    and a voice, only a, 150:20
    asks enough, pitiful, 353:65
    at it for hours, 129:34
    at them, I stand and, 312:14
    avenge even a, 43:28
    before and after, 276:7
    before you leap, 395:31
    blue, till all, 100:11
    do it with a bitter, 314:15
    for, what we must, 20:11
    high and fall low, 396:32
    in thy heart, and write, 278:18
    lean and hungry, 228:14
    on the bright side, 395:33
    one longing ling'ring, 112:17
    that goose, 251:30
    thy last on all, 80:16
    to thyself, 272:15, 431:73
    up and not down, 115:14
    where it is not, 442:14
    which she turn'd, same, 178:2
    wore a bashful, 30:18
Looked again, and found, 60:4
    for, long, 396:28
    no sooner met but, 218:8
    unutterable things, 300:11
Looker-on, a patient, 200:24
Lookers-on see most, 395:34
Looking before and after, 226:15
    ill prevail, 288:1
    loving comes by, 397:69

Looking-glass, thank you for, 349:20
Looks another way, she, 342:13
    books were woman's, 178:13
    commercing with the skies, 164:14
    deep-search'd with saucy, 246:1
    her modest, 109:30
    kill with, 244:1
    on alike, 274:7
    puts on his pretty, 239:34
    reprove, would those, 108:14
    too near on things, 376:35
    with dispatchful, 172:14
Loon, makes many, 394:34
    thou cream-faced, 251:30
Loop-hole, her cabin'd, 165:33
Loose upon the world, let, 25:31
Lorbeer steht, hoch der, 107:37
Lord among wits, a, 132:8
    be thankit, 47:36
    bless thee, and keep thee, 324:8
    bless ye the, 340:30
    blessed be the name of, 325:60
    children of the, 17:19
    do so to me, 324:27
    drunk as, 356:77
    gave, the, 325:60
    glory of the coming of, 127:27
    hath taken away, 325:60
    High Everything Else, 106:9
    hunter before the, 323:27
    I will say of the, 327:54
    loveth he chasteneth, whom, 339:67
    neat and trimly dress'd, 231:34
    nod from a, 353:60
    of all, crown Him, 190:1
    of all things, great, 195:39
    of himself, 320:23
    of thy presence, 239:27
    once own, let a, 193:18
    praise the, 101:13
    precious in the sight of, 327:62
    remembrance of his dying, 283:24
    seek ye the, 332:8
    their God,—His Grace, 45:32
Lord Fanny spins a thousand, 198:8
Lord Tomnoddy is thirty-four, 34:11
Lords and Commons of England, 174:32
    cursed be so many, 418:15
    do no more, 384:34
    new laws, new, 401:68
    who lay ye low, 275:31
Lore, gives me mystical, 55:21

volume of forgotten, 191:24
Lose, all covet, all, 355:67
  all, grasp all, 373:68
  at last, 439:73
  best gain is to, 412:2
  heart to fight—and, 304:5
  if you, 392:28
  it, afraid to, 379:43
  it all, to gain or, 177:19
  it in the moment you detect, 196:13
  nothing for want of asking, 396:36
  tails you, 382:36
  what you never had, cannot, 440:69
  who may, 38:11
  wish that one should, 157:23
Loser, neither party, 234:28
Losers are always in the wrong, 397:37
  leave, give, 372:14
Loses and who wins, who, 242:9
Loseth his life for my sake, 324:15
  indeed that loseth at last, 376:37
  not God, that, 376:38
  nothing, he, 376:38
Losing theirs and blaming it on you, 142:13
Loss, deeper sense of her, 103:23
  enow to do our country, 236:15
  goeth out with often, 378:33
  live by, 428:7
  makes choice of, 214:7
  pay again with, 376:71
  upon thy so sore, 300:4
Losses are restored, all, 264:3
  God bless all our, 36:4
  that hath had, 258:41
Lost all, he has not, 375:70
  all is not, 168:6
  and waiting for you, 140:1
  and worn, sooner, 271:42
  as found, as good, 358:2
  be for God, 395:46
  being lack'd and, 258:35
  except honour, all is, 101:24
  how art thou, 173:39
  it, till he has, 423:66
  it, till she hath, 416:5
  our little Hanner, 16:8
  praising what is, 213:33
  that a friend gets not, 392:11
  that all was, 173:38
  that comes at last, not, 392:12
  that is in danger, not, 355:77
  that is put in a riven dish, 355:75

to have loved and, 295:41
  totally, he was, 104:39
  two golden hours, 156:3
  whatsoever thing is, 76:12
  you think all is, 442:26
Lot, fair is our, 140:11
  is thine, a weary, 211:31
  strange was his, 177:24
Lot's wife, remember, 336:33
Loth out of [bed], 397:38
  to bed and loth to rise, 368:19
Lothario, gallant, gay, 207:23
Lottery, marriage is, 399:39
Loud and clear, said it very, 59:30
Lounjun 'roun' en suffer'n, 116:18
Louse, get, 412:52
  new washen, 403:57
Love a bright particular star, 213:25
  a Hercules, is not, 246:8
  a lassie, I, 146:3
  a well of, 68:14
  all is fair in, 355:73
  all she loves is, 52:21
  all, trust a few, 213:24
  and a cough cannot be hid, 397:40
  and business, 397:41
  and desire and hate, 87:21
  and fame, I dreamt of, 204:1
  and I had the wit, 156:8
  and I were well acquainted, 104:23
  and it will flee, follow, 370:33
  and it will follow, flee, 370:33
  and lordship, 397:42
  and pride stock, Bedlam, 397:43
  and scandal, 97.18
  and thought, and joy, 317:28
  and to cherish, to, 341:48
  apt to inspire, 117:29
  asks faith, 397:44
  by my, 157:24
  be sweeter, pains of, 91:35
  be younger than thyself, 271:37
  begets love, 397:45
  begins to sicken and decay, 230:10
  best, whom we, 439:61
  bid me, 120:8
  brief as woman's, 225:24
  but her, and love for ever, 46:16
  but her for ever, 46:19
  but ministers of, 70:17
  by another's eyes, to choose, 256:22
  calf love, half, 363:76

calling his, 184:12
can never die, whose, 162:5
cantons of contemned, 271:33
casteth out fear, 340:11
cherish, and obey, 341:49
climbed up to me, my, 139:25
cold pudding settles, 364:40
comes in at the window, 397:46
comforteth like sunshine, 263:24
common as light is, 277:24
continue, brotherly, 339:68
could never change, we thought, 33:20
course of true, 256:21
curiosity, freckles, and doubt, 187:19
dallies with the innocence of, 272:2
deathless, let us make, 302:10
deeds that are done for, 274:12
deep as first, 294:14
did make thee run into, 216:2
die for, 425:68
[died], but not for, 218:3
divine, fou o', 44:10
does much, 397:47
ebb to humble, 261:41
far from the lips we, 178:3
find the arms of my true, 296:20
flies out at the window, 436:23
flowers and fruits of, 53:36
for a good man's, 217:35
for ever wilt thou, 137:23
for new, change old, 189:15
fortunate who inspire, 277:24
free as air, 194:6
get all men's, 403:43
given unsought is better, 272:9
God is, 340:10
goes in with Folly's dress, 42:6
goes toward love, 267:28
gushed from my heart, 69:32
hail wedded, 160:29
happier who feel it most, 277:28
hath an end, 289:32
hath my heart, my true, 278:16
hath no man, greater, 337:55
he bore to learning, 109:26
he laughed to scorn, 263:21
he was all for, 82:2
he will seem worthy of, 317:25
he would, and she would not, 33:13
her is a liberal education, to, 284:15
her till I die, I, 342:14
her, to know her was to, 205:14

her, to see her is to, 46:19
her, to see her was to, 46:16
her, you, who do not, 37:35
him best of all, I, 182:19
him, medicines to make me, 231:41
him not, I, 309:23
him, you must, 317:25
hold your tongue and let me, 86:8
I am sick of, 330:39
I feel it now, I'm in, 312:9
I hate and, 60:16
I laugh to scorn, 33:28
I shall be past making, 200:12
if I have freedom in, 151:25
if Jack's in, 386:2
if there's delight in, 72:10
in a hut, 136:7
in a palace, 136:7
in every gesture, 173:26
in her attire, my, 342:15
in her sunny eyes, 74:5
in my bosom, 149:22
in, to let the warm, 137:25
is a spirit all compact of fire, 263:22
is all truth, 263:24
is better than wine, 330:38
is blind, 254:15, 397:48
is blind, though, 426:27
is come to me, my, 206:7
is dead, my, 62:14
is, dinner of herbs where, 328:34
is enough, 180:9
is full of fear, 397:49
is full of trouble, 397:49
is heaven, 208:19
is lawless, 397:50
is like the measles, 129:35
is lost, all, 92:11
is merely, to be in, 160:8
is never without jealousy, 397:51
is no lack, in, 389:44
is not found in the market, 397:52
is not love which alters, 265:27
is of man's life a thing apart, man's, 31:23
is our last, believe our first, 313:25
is slight, when both deliberate, 157:23
is soon cold, hot, 381:13
is strong as death, 330:44
is sweet, given or returned, 277:24
is sweet in the beginning, 397:53
is swift of foot, 120:2
is the loadstone of love, 397:54

is the true price of love, 397:55
is thin, 370:5
is throned, seat where, 271:41
it, and long for it, 57:25
it, I love it, I, 72:18
joy and everlasting, 186:2
keep a corner in the thing I, 261:31
know, how should I your true, 226:18.
know your true, 202:8
knows not what is, 378:37
laggard in, 210:9
last, not least in, 229:32
laughs at locksmiths, 397:56
left the ancient, 30:1
lies my young, 160:15
little words of, 58:1
live, my Lesbia, and, 60:14
live with thee, and be thy, 202:5
lives in cottages, 397:57
locks no cupboards, 397:58
looks not with the eyes, 256:24
lost between them, no, 425:41
Lordy, how they could, 344:2
makes all hearts gentle, 397:59
makes one fit, 397:60
many waters cannot quench, 330:45
may get, a new, 307:33
may go all bare, 42:6
may lead Love in, 42:6
me and my true, 342:29
me for little, 425:67
me little, 397:61
me long, 397:61
me, love my dog, 397:62
me, sigh to those who, 51:10
me yet, you'll, 37:21
met you not with my true, 202:7
most, they who, 426:8
music the food of, 271:24
must die for, 213:26
must kiss that mortal's eyes, 42:6
my friends well, I, 384:35
my whole course of, 260:1
myself better, 384:35
never doubt I, 223:30
never seek to tell, 30:6
no folly to being in, 401:77
not an ounce of, 388:31
not Death, but, 36:8
not me for comely grace, 342:18
now with his, 63:40
O lyric, 40:9

o' life's young day, 180:15
of a ladye, sighed for, 106:20
of friends, laughter and, 27:30
of herself she will not, 288:2
of lads, 397
of love, the, 292:
of soup and, 403:74
of women, alas ! the, 52:20
of women, passing the, 325:37
off with the old, 342:27
office and affairs of, 258:14
old love, cold, 363:76
one another, that ye, 337:52
one maiden only, 297:35
only they conquer, 56:15
or hate, not in our power to, 157:23
our first, last, 313:25
our occupations, let us, 82:48
oyster may be crossed in, 278:11
pangs of despised, 224:4
pennyweight of, 353:64
permanent, interwreath, 27:32
pity's akin to, 281:34
prove likewise variable, 267:25
purple light of, 113:24
puts in, when, 436:18
remedy for, 421:72
renewal of, 298:10
renewed again, old, 364:38
renewing is of, 93:19
resembleth, spring of, 272:25
revenge my slighted, 204:12
right to dissemble, 138:11
rules his kingdom, 397:64
rules the court, the camp, 208:19
seals of, 253:22
seemed, so sweet, 33:20
she never told her, 272:4
she's but a lassie, my, 45:43, 122:5
sidelong looks of, 108:14
silence in, 202:6
so true a fool is, 264:12
soft eyes look'd, 50:11
sought is good, 272:9
speak low if you speak, 258:13
speaks, when, 246:8
still has something of the sea, 212:12
surfeits not, 263:24
that can be reckon'd, 213:34
that lingers there, 99:27
that makes the world go round, 391:72

needs not the foreign aid of ornament, 300:13
portion of the, 276:15
to believe in, 300:5
Lovely and a fearful thing, 52:20
and more temperate, more, 263:32
and pleasant in their lives, 325:35
on all things, 80:16
once he made more, 276:15
things, not dream them, do, 139:26
Lover, all as frantic, 257:46
all mankind love a, 94:6
and his lass, it was, 218:11
and sensualist, 118:20
forsaken, 307:33
give repentance to, 108:11
I sighed as a, 104:11
of trees, you, 38:1
pale and wan, fond, 288:1
sighing like furnace, 216:17
to the heart of her, 184:12
without indiscretion, 115:24
woman loves her, 52:21
Lover's ear will hear the lowest sound, 246:8
eyes will gaze an eagle blind, 246:8
head, slide into a, 316:18
staff, hope is, 384:9
Love-rhymes, regent of, 246:6
Lovers are round her, sighing, 178:7
are shy, true, 431:72
are soundest, old, 310:9
happy, make two, 345:22
live by love, 397:68
love the spring, 218:11
love the western star, 208:21
meeting, journeys end in, 271:36
must consign to thee, 220:3
pair of star-cross'd, 266:3
quarrels of, 298:10
we that are true, 216:3
whisp'ring, 108:13
Lovers' brains, through, 266:13
eyes, hiding love from, 78:8
perjuries, at, 267:23; 392:39
tongues by night, 367:29
Loves a rosy cheek, he that, 56:14
another best, who, 274:4
his fellow men, who, 126:38
I have, two, 265:32
I prize as the dead carcasses, 219:26
is love, all she, 52:21

kills the thing he, 314:15
me for little, 376:39
no-one who . . . unhappy, 25:27
not where it lives but where it, 422:26
on to the close, truly, 178:2
remain, if our, 38:1
woman whom nobody, 73:22
Lovesome thing, a garden is, 35:18
Lovest me, an thou, 232:14
Loveth best all things, 70:2
well both man and bird, 70:1
well, of him that, 288:5
Loving and giving, 399:77
comes by looking, 397:69
longest . . . when hope is gone, 21:29
mere folly, most, 217:19
never call it, 36:7
so faithful, so, 77:31
Low, he that is, 42:15
man seeks a little thing, 39:29
raise and support, what is, 168:3
soft, gentle and, 242:13
water, tide turns at, 94:7
Lowells talk only to Cabots, 31:31
Lower at the last, it will, 363:52
can fall no, 380:6
than the angels, 326:15
Lowlands shall meet thee, 55:20
Lowliness is young ambition's ladder, 228:17
Loyal and neutral, 249:29
Loyalties, impossible, 20:3
Loyalty, learned body wanted, 302:9
Lucifer, come not, 157:9
falls like, 238:16
proud as, 358:27
son of the morning, 331:53
Luck, all the day you'll have good, 410:3
another time, better, 423:78
devil's, 416:31
give a man, 372:9
in horses, have good, 382:13
in odd numbers, 424:35
is good for something, ill, 388:22
light in ragged, 118:20
more knave, better, 420:30
mother of good, 366:35
next time, better, 362:4
now, worse, 423:78
the worse, 421:68
would have it, as good, 256:15
Lucky and happy, 399:77

at play, 433;48
buttef be born, 361:53
men need no counsel, 397:70
Lucre, filthy, 339:59
Lucy light, 397:71
  should be dead, if, 316:18
Ludlam's dog, lazy as, 358:6
Lullaby, I will sing a, 80:11
Lulled by the coil, 275:33
Lumber, loads of learned, 193:20
  room of his library, 87:31
  room, stowed away in, 49:31
Lumen ademptum, cui, 306:3
Lump [piece] leaventh the whole, 338:22
Lump [put up with] it, you may, 387:51
Lunae, per amica silentia, 305:36
Lunatic, the lover, and the poet,
Luncheon, supper, dinner, 39:26
Lungs began to crow, 216:11
  dangerous to the, 129:24
  receive our air, 75:35
Lurk secure, where he can, 176:13
Luscious as locusts, as, 260:12
Lust full of forged lies, 263:24
  in action, 265:29
  is perjured, murderous, 265:29
  like a glutton dies, 263:24
Lust's effect is tempest, 263:24
  winter comes, 263:24
Lustre in the dark, keeps, 351:61
Lute is broken, when, 277:22

little rift within, 297:25
strung with his hair, 246:8
Luve thee still, I will, 47:26
Luve's like a red, red rose, 47:25
  like the melody, 47:25
Lux, cum semel occidit, 60:14
Luxuries of life, give us, 180:16
Luxury and riot, to, 173:47
  thinks it, 15:12
Lyaeus, ever young, god, 100:2
Lydian airs, soft, 164:9
Lyf so short, the, 62:15
[Lying], [falsehood], becomes none but
  tradesmen, 274:8
  gossiping and, 373:67
  let me have no, 274:48
  there is, 438:19
  this vice of, 234:26
  vainness, babbling, drunkeness, 272:18
  world, is given to, 233:47
Lying [reclining], shall you and I be, 60:9
  where he fell, leave him, 22:3
Lyme, old party of, 176:2
Lynn, set out from, 123:40
Lyones, knights of, 174:3
Lyonesse, came back from, 116:5
Lyre, smote 'is bloomin', 141:30
  wak'd to ecstasy the living, 112:12
  with other strings, 76:13
Lyres and flutes, sound of, 187:30
Lyve, worthy womman al hir, 63:33

M

Mab hath been with you, Queen, 266:13
Macassar, 'incomparable oil,' 52:12
Macaulay, cocksure as Tom, 160:4
  has occasional flashes of silence, 281:23
Macavity's not there, 93:34
Macbeth shall never vanquished be, 250:16
Macduff, lay on, 251:44
Macedon and Artaxerxes' throne, 174:9
Macedonia, come over into, 337:62
Machine, beauty of a great, 34:6
Machines, for making more, 32:2

Mackerel, not so the, 102:4
  sky, 352:31, 352:32
McTavish, against the clan, 22:5
Mad action, one mad, 405:53
  as a hatter, 358:9
  as a March hare, 358:10
  dog bites his master, 420:14
  enough to prove a man, 405:53
  fitter being sane than, 40:8
  gives out first that he is, 382:12
  He first makes, 408:11

he made me, 231:36
in pursuit and in possession, 265:30
is he? 104:3
it will make us, 248:20
north-north-west, but, 223:38
pleasure sure in being, 91:42
staring and stark, 424:30
world, my masters, 33:15
you will never be, 442:29
Made, fearfully and wonderfully, 328:13
me, nobody never, 287:33
men and not made them well, 225:18
Madman, thought to quell, 292:8
Madman's hand, sword in, 391:65
Madmen know, none but, 91:42
Madness, despondency and, 317:34
doth work like, 70:6
lies, that way, 241:29
moonstruck, 173:42
near allied, to, 89:25
that fine, 88:11
that I have utter'd, not, 226:7
though this be, 223:33
very midsummer, 272:12
Madrigals, birds sing, 157:25
namby-pamby, 104:14
Maeonides, blind, 170:16
Maeotis sleeps, lo! where, 194:17
Magic casements, charm'd, 137:20
in my eyes, with, 116:5
like thee, with a, 52:1
Magician mutters, 420:15
Magistrate pedantic, a, 199:33
Magistrates, correct at home, like, 235:43
Magnet ever attract, can, 105:40
of their course, 52:2
Magni nominis umbra, 152:3
Magnificent, it is, 31:30
Magnifique, c'est, 31:30
Magnify him for ever, 341:30
Magnitude, liar of the first, 72:7
Mahomet must go to the mountain, 386:27
Maid, be good, sweet, 139:26
come down, O, 294:22
from the sidelong, 300:15
hath swept, little, 438:29
he that woos, 382:9
is prodigal, chariest, 221:35
is stooping, tall, 438:29
last suitor wins, 420:2
my pretty, 343:24, 343:25
never kiss, 387:49

of Astolat, lily, 297:28
of Athens, ere we part, 50:5
oft seen, 352:33
sad brow and true, 217:26
slain by a fair cruel, 272:3
sphere-descended, 71:38
that laughs, 352:34
Maiden, and mistress, 289:41
gentle, 276:8
meditation, fancy-free, 257:32
never bold, 260:2
of bashful fifteen, 278:6
smiled, archly the, 150:16
that orbed, 276:2
the maddest, 160:10
with many wooers, 352:35
Maidenkirk to Johnny Groat's, 46:2
Maidenly, so joyously, so, 279:24
Maidens be, as many, 68:14
like moths, 50:6
married, so are all, 386:8
must be mild and meek, 397:72
should be mim, 397:73
watching, all her, 294:19
wear no purses, 369:71
young fair, 287:27
Maids and village hinds, 71:39
dance in a ring, 182:5
dun, [makes], 398:37
lead apes, old, 404:7
May when they are, 218:4
say nay and take, 397:74
strange seraphic pieces, 302:7
surpass, all other, 155:26
than Malkin, more, 424:10
that weave their thread with bones, 272:2
want nothing but husbands, 397:75
with seven mops, seven, 59:22
Maimed and set at naught, 49:31
Main, from out the azure, 300:19
silent, flooding in, 68:2
skims along the, 192:16
Maisie is in the wood, 211:38
Maîtresses, j'aurai des, 104:4
Majestic though in ruin, 169:37
Majestical, being so, 220:9
Majesty, attribute to awe and, 255:33
busied in his, 235:43
in rayless, 322:1
this earth of, 243:29
Majorities, decision by, 107:31
Majority, one on God's side is, 190:10

Make anything, does not, 190:6
　neither meddle nor, 385:46
Maker, serve therewith my, 167:31
Makes me or fordoes me, 262:8
　so many, reason, He, 148:12
Making, take pleasure in, 415:77
Maladies and miseries, cure of, 57:35
Malady most incident to maids, 274:1
Malcontents, loiterers and, 246:6
Male, more deadly than, 141:32
Malice domestic, 249:36
　is mindful, 398:5
　never was his aim, 288:13
　set down aught in, 262:16
　towards none, with, 148:11
Malkin, more maids than, 424:10
Mallecho, miching, 225:23
Mallow waves her silky leaf, 77:24
Malt does more than Milton, 126:17
　is above meal, 398:6
　makes sweet, 411:74
Mam's pet, marries, 375:67
Mamble, I never went to, 88:16
Mammon of unrighteousness, 336:28
　serve God and, 333:52
Mammy heerd him holler, 204:5
Man, a horse, and a dog, 352:26
　after his own heart, 324:31
　alive, means for every, 213:32
　all that may become, 248:5
　all the faults of, 56:3
　all things can, no, 402:6
　all this scene of, 195:25
　among children, 352:37
　assurance of a, 226:2
　at sixteen, 353:38
　being in honour abideth not, 327:28
　by courtesy a, 21:33
　call up my, 211:37
　can do no more than he can, 353:39
　child is father of, 317:30
　closing full in, 90:19
　comes and tills the field, 293:29
　could ease a heart, where's the, 187:18
　delights not me, 223:37
　dispute it like a, 250:24
　do all things like a, 119:38
　doth what he can, 398:7
　even such a, 233:49
　for the sabbath, not, 325:63
　from his throne has hurled, 307:18
　get a new, 269:34

has done, what, 435:62
he was her, 344:2
heaven had made her such, 260:6
his prey was, 193:37
in the case, get to, 142:1
in the moon, no more than, 384:32
is a bubble, 398:8
is . . . a civic animal, 18:9
is a noble animal, 35:26
is a pliable animal, 87:17
is a tool-using animal, 57:24
is as old as he feels, 353:41
is born unto trouble, 325:63
is his own star, 100:6
is Nature's sole mistake, 106:7
is so in the way, 103:22
[is taken] by the tongue, 357:59
is the hunter, 294:18
is the master of things, 289:40
is the measure, 398:9
is vile, only, 118:11
is what he eats, 96:13
let him pass for a, 253:35
let the end try the, 234:13
looks at his own bliss, 309:24
may do, strange what a, 298:21
may redeem the past, 53:44
must also feel it as a, 250:24
must helpless, 130:15
my son, you'll be a, 142:16
noblest work of, 128:18
nothing is more wonderful than, 281:31
of baser Earth didst make, 98:16
of God, round, fat, oily, 300:17
old proud pageant of, 159:27
perceives it die away, 319:35
play the, 146:2
proposes, 398:10
proud man, 252:11
recover'd of the bite, 108:10
restore us, greater, 168:1
show me, 414:42, 414:43
so can any, 232:21
study of mankind is, 195:38
tailor makes, 423:40
teach you more of, 316:10
that good old, 113:36
that is born of a woman, 325:66, 341:53
that is not passion's slave, 225:20
the less, I love not, 51:27
there I met another, 131:18
this is the state of, 238:15

half, 410:31
man, Benedick the, 258:11
men, wen you're a, 82:15
man will wait beside, 142:5
men laugh, 434:13
men, mocks, 246:16
mim till they're, 397:73
once you are, 285:31
one was never, 47:40
people have, delight, 189:24
till he is, 402:13
when a man's, 401:45
you'll never be, 387:46, 441:60
Marries at Yule, 376:5
dies, or turns Hindoo, 275:38
does well, who, 439:48
ere he be wise, 380:21
for wealth, 380:22
late marries ill, he'that, 380:23
not does better, who, 439:48
times are changed with him who, 285:30
Marrieth for love, without money, 439:49
Marrow, my winsome, 115:20
Marry a rich woman, as easy, 298:20
a shrew than a sheep, better, 390:34
ancient people, that, 102:11
be sure before your, 360:19
every woman should, 85:43
first, 399:43
for munny, doänt, 295:32
his Grandmother, Man may not, 341:59
if you would live well for a month, 388:5
in haste, 399:44
in Lent, 399:45
in May, 399:46
is to domesticate the Recording Angel,
   to, 285:31
no man [should], 85:43
not at all, wise men, 383:71
soon, honest men, 383:71
than to burn, better to, 338:23
they's never, 119:29
whom she likes, may, 298:15
with your match, 399:47
you, then I won't, 343:25
young man should not, 355:50
Marrying and giving in marriage, 325:53
Mars, an eye like, 226:2
this seat of, 243:29
Marshal, baton of a, 181:33
Martha's sons, Lord He lays it on, 141:34
Martin and the swallow, 422:1

Martyr, cause, that makes, 392:13
like a pale, 279:31
Martyrs, noble army of, 340:29
Marvel, match me such, 43:20
Mary, Anne the mother of, 187:30
is, where the lady, 206:16
right lyne of, 25:18
Mary had a little lamb, 114:15
Mary hath chosen that good part, 336:14
Mary, I want a lyre, 76:13
Mary Morison, ye are na, 44:2
Mary-buds, winking, 219:30
Maryland, my Maryland, 203:19
Masculine idealism, mistrust of, 72:15
Mask, hath need of, 389:67
Masons, the singing, 235:43
Mass [lump], figure of the giant, 270:15
untwine me from the, 36:18
Mass [eucharist], meat and, 399:52
Paris is well worth, 119:27
Masses against the classes, back, 107:34
your huddled, 146:8
Mast, bends the gallant, 78:11
nail to the, 122:9
of some great ammiral, 168:12
upon the high and giddy, 234:19
Master absent, 420:18
and make crouch, 40:11
as good as his, 392:32
better speak to, 362:18
cheese hath no, 431:51
eye of, 417:52
[fire is] a bad, 370:20
good to have, 389:39
has a fool for his, 381:61
has a new, 269:34
he can ill be, 375:48
he that has a wife has, 378:36
his craft's, 402:15
like man, like, 395:78
must serve, he that is, 379:59
O worthy, 150:12
of himself, 379:71
of himself, should be, 159:31
of my fate, I am, 119:23
of none, 392:33
of others, 379:71
of the College, 344:6
one eye of, 404:35
scholar may waur, 422:7
seldom fail their, 351:78
shames the, 418:38

612

soon knave, early, 367:82
stood in the presence of, 299:24
went, into the woods my, 145:27
Master's eye, 420:19
    footsteps, 420:20
    paid, 350:23
Master-blow, reserve, 408:28
Masters, all men can't be, 356:3
    make good servants, good, 373:53
    no man can serve two, 333:51
    noble and approved, 259:52
Mastery, strive here for, 170:11
Mastiff, greyhound, mongrel, grim, 241:41
Mastiffs, curs will raise, 441:54
Match for a woman, no man, 402:13
    it, fellow-fault came to, 217:31
    me such marvel, 43:20
Matched in mouth like bells, 257:44
    of earthly knight's hand, never, 155:30
Mate, artificer made my, 287:28
    of the *Nancy* brig, 104:18
    says the old bold, 159:24
Mathematics [makes] subtile, 22:18
Matin, sweet be thy, 122:4
Matins, meat and, 399:52
Matron's glance, 108:14
Matter ends, there the, 142:11
    more german to the, 227:49
    root of the, 326:4
    set off wretched, 175:36
    tell the, 330:27
    there was no, 53:28
    what he said, no, 53:28
    with less art, more, 223:28
    wrecks of, 16:1
Matthew, Mark, Luke, and John, 16:9
Matrimony, first wife is, 417:73
    safest in, 277:34
Matty, meddlesome, 291:22
Maud, Maud, Maud, Maud, 196:12
Maurice died, since, 33:21
Maw, bad in, 373:51
Mawkishness, proceeds, 138:2
Maxim be my virtue's guide, 176:6
    should become a universal law, my,
        135:36
Maxime solle ein allgemeines Gesetz
        werden, 135:36
May be out, till, 364:5
    bees don't fly, 399:49
    chills the lap of, 108:4
    cold, and windy, 350:12

crowned with milk-white, 33:19
dry, 350:27
flood never did good, 353:54
flowers, bring forth, 398:38
he sings all day, in, 388:34
in a town in, 379:70
look at your corn in, 396:30
marry in, 62:6
merry month of, 25:19
shear your sheep in, 410:32
sings a song in, 416:8
sun, March wind and, 398:37
swarm of bees in, 354:21
the birds begin to lay, in, 389:46
there's an end of, 126:18
till the kalends of, 386:3
will be fine next year, 126:19
May's new-fangled mirth, 246:2
May-cloud, the swinging, 161:18
Mayde, make as is a, 63:21
Maying, that we two were, 139:27
May-morn, till that, 40:16
Maypoles, I sing of, 120:4
Maze, a mighty, 195:25
Mazes lost, in wand'ring, 169:40
Mægen lytað, þe ure, 342:2
Me for him, got taking, 147:28
Meadow or plain, in, 290:1
Meadows, feet have touch'd, 296:13
    green, kissing, 264:4
    in the dreaming, 184:12
    of heaven, infinite, 150:11
    paint the, 246:16
    trim with daisies pied, 164:3
Meads in May, flowery, 315:27
Meal is all bran, devil's, 416:32
    malt is above, 398:6
    no mill, no, 402:19
    trust not with, 416:34
Meal-tub, taking out of, 356:21
Meals, two hungry, 432:32
Mean [*base*] even for man, too, 298:14
    nothing common did, or, 158:17
    stupid, dastardly, 117:37
Mean [*signify*], I know not what they,
        294:13
    not careful what they, 270:11
Mean [*middle*] measure is a merry, 398:50
Meandering, five miles, 70:10
Meanest of mankind, 196:8
Meaning doesn't matter, 105:36
    teems with hidden, 106:19

to some faint, 90:6
Meannesses which are too mean, 298:14
Means [agency] at all, by any, 125:34
    die beyond my, 314:13
    end justifies, 417:41
    end must justify, 200:6
    produce no effect, small, 162:6
    straitened, 135:27
    to boot, appliances and, 234:20
    to do ill, sight of, 240:5
    use the, 433:53
    you can, by all the, 311:28
Means [signifies] nothing, 380:35
Meant than meets the ear, more is, 164:23
    well, lies one who, 286:7
Measels, did you ever hav, 308:12
Measles, love is like, 129:25
    love's like the, 130:1
Measure in all things, 424:22
    is a merry mean, 399:40
    me, lads they, 160:2
    must strike by, 436:19
    of all things, 398:9
    serves to grace, 200:4
    shrunk to this little, 229:30
    sin to give ill, 392:4
    thrice, 399:51
    weening is not, 434:37
    wielder of the stateliest, 298:2
Measured, men are not to be, 399:56
Measures, not men, but, 43:25
Meat, abroad, roast, 367:76
    and canna eat, some hae, 47:36
    and drink to me, it is, 218:7
    and matins, 399:55
    and on us all, on our, 120:14
    and we can eat, we hae, 47:36
    ashamed to eat, 401:52
    cannot eat but little, 287:30
    doth this out Caesar feed, upon what,
        228:12
    drink, and cloth, 373:45
    for their stomach, seek, 407:42
    God sends, 372:35, 373:40
    in the hall, 286:20
    is much, 399:53
    it feeds on, mock, 261:29
    one man is appointed to buy, 212:19
    one man's, 405:55
    show me not, 411:42
    small birds must have, 411:63
    sweet, 412:58

that have no other, 426:2
this dish of, 308:5
twice boiled, 412:73
wholesomest, 423:67
Meats, funeral baked, 221:25
Meddle not make, neither, 385:46
Meddlesome Matty, 219:22
Meddleth in all things, 439:51
Meddling, of little, 403:72
Μηδὲν ἄγαν, 399:54
Medes and the Persians, law of, 332:20
Medicine against death, no, 425:42
    for fear, no, 425:43
    merry heart like, 329:39
    ready, 408:19
Medicines to make me love, 231:41
Medio tutissimus ibis, 186:6
Meditation, in maiden, 257:32
Mediterranean, the blue, 275:33
Meek and mild, 311:25
    blessed are, 333:35
    borne his faculties so, 248:1
    than fierce, safer being, 40:8
Meekest man and the gentlest, 155:30
Meet a body, gin a body, 47:35
    again, if we do, 230:19
    again, shall we three, 246:18
    again, till we, 203:20
    again, will never, 343:29
    and mingle, all things, 275:36
    him in my dish, though I should, 384:31
    make ends, 430:1
    me by moonlight, 306:17
    men may, 399:60
    merry part, merry, 399:64
    never the twain shall, 140:19
    thee, if I should, 49:37
    wheel-barrows tremble when, 45:29
Meeter, deemed it, 188:12
Meeting, broke the good, 250:7
Meke as is a mayde, 63:21
Melancholy as a cat, 358:11
    as a sick monkey, 358:12
    green and yellow, 272:4
    hence, loathed, 163:32
    mark'd him for her own, 113:19
    moping, 173:42
    most musical, most, 164:16
    nought so sweet, 47:37
    O sweetest, 99:4
    of mine own, 217:37
    once a day, 376:4

out of a song, suck, 216:5
sate retir'd, 71:37
villainous, 240:12
what charm can soothe, 108:11
Meliora, proboque, video, 186:7
Melodies are sweet, heard, 137:22
Melody, blund'ring kind of, 90:4
  luve's like the, 47:25
Melodye, smale fowles ihaken, 63:20
Melons, stumbling on, 158:13
Melrose aright, view fair, 209:18
Member, joint, or limb, in, 170:5
  unruly, 340:2
Même chose, plust c'est la, 135:37
Meminisse juvabit, haec, 305:29
Memorial, completed a, 125:32
Memories, a night of, 144:13
  flocks of the, 161:40
  have good, 395:54
Memory brings the light, 178:14
  dear son of, 163:28
  dear, to, 149:17
  do honour his, 135:21
  from the table of, 222:20
  holds a seat, while, 222:20
  how sweet their, 76:16
  made such a sinner of, 268:19
  of all he stole, 194:15
  of man runneth not, 29:25
  pluck from the, 251:32
  strengthens as you lay burdens upon it,
    81:27
  the warder of the brain, 248:8
  vibrates in the, 276:19
Men and women merely players, 216:17
  are but children, 91:41
  are created equal, 129:29
  are men, but, 260:21
  are not to be measured, 398:56
  are we and must grieve, 317:39
  as he, can be such, 20:2
  as trees, walking, see, 336:1
  at most differ as Heaven and earth,
    297:27
  betray, finds too late that, 108:11
  biography of great, 57:31
  busy hum of, 164:6
  but measures, not, 43:25
  cheerful ways of, 170:17
  dare trust themselves with men, I
    wonder, 270:5
  decay, 108:15

divine, [had made], 188:4
do a-land, as, 263:19
do, whatever, 135:25
enlarge the views of, 116:4
for fear of little, 18:1
for Pieces, with, 98:11
have become women, my, 321:30
have faults, 399:58
he had ten thousand, 343:26
I've studied, 160:9
in His ways with, 297:37
in the catalogue ye go for, 249:32
loved darkness, 337:43
may come and men may go, 294:4
must work, 139:24
not thrones and crowns but, 94:5
off, by keeping, 103:31
quit you like, 339:37
quit yourselves like, 324:29
should brothers be, 121:18
so beautiful, the many, 69:30
sorts and conditions of, 341:37
that were boys when I was, 27:28
the best of, 80:12
think all men mortal, all, 322:4
we've got the, 126:34
who march away, 116:6
whose cities he saw, 123:30
will sometimes jealous be, 56:3
women and Herveys, 176:10
Men's men, 93:25
Mend, at the worst will, 426:11
  in the end things will, 389:54
  lacks time to, 291:26
  never too late to, 392:1
  one, if every man, 385:72
  [things] will, 437:53
  work for man to, 90:13
Mendacious, splendaciously, 143:23
Mended, least said soonest, 394:23
Menial, a pamper'd, 180:14
Μῆνιν αειδε, θεά, 123:21
Mens sana in corpore sano, 135:35
  sibi conscia recti, 305:30
Mensch ist was er isst, 96:13
Mental powers hardly superior, 88:4
Mention her, we never, 26:7
Mentioned not at all, 315:29
Mephistophilis, ah, 157:19
Mercenary calling, followed, 126:22
Merchant, blate, 354:26
  but one year, be, 378:11

615

eight [hours sleepeth], 370:31
smiled, mighty, 84:22
Merchants are princes, 331:56
most do congregate, where, 254:1
Mercies ay endure, his, 163:19
tender, 328:27
Merciful, God be, 337:35
Mercury are harsh, words of, 246:17
like feather'd, 233:36
like the herald, 226:2
Mercy and truth are met, 327:49
become them with one half so good a
grace as, 252:8
hand folks over to God's, 93:22
I asked, mercy I found, 54:12
I to others show, 198:17
is above this sceptered sway, 255:33
is nobility's true badge, 270:8
is not strain'd, quality of, 255:33
render the deeds of, 255:33
seasons justice, 255:33
show to me, that, 198:17
shut the gates of, 112:15
temper justice with, 173:41
to heaven, leaving, 97:24
upon mine, he may have, 272:15
upon one of our souls, God have, 272:15
upon us, have, 341:33
we do pray for, 255:33
Meredith is a prose Browning, 314:15
Merit rais'd to that bad eminence, by,
169:28
takes, spurns that, 224:4
wins the soul, 193:35
Merits or their faults to scan, 108:21
to disclose, seek, 113:21
Mermaid, heard a, 257:31
Mermaid, done at the, 27:19
Tavern, choicer than, 137:29
Meroe, Nilotic isle, 174:5
Merrier, the more the, 420:35
Merriest when they are from home, 235:44
Merrily shall I live now, 270:1
Merriment, flashes of, 227:34
Merry, against ill chances, 234:27
all are not, 355:65
and bright, always, 315:26
and glad, 412:54
and wise, good to be, 343:27, 391:49
as a cricket, 358:13
as a grig, 358:14
as a marriage bell, 50:11

as mice in malt, 358:15
God rest you, 342:12
I am not, 260:14
in hall, it is, 391:73
man, as long liveth, 304:3
meet, merry part, 399:64
men, uprouse ye, 23:26
month of May, 25:19
too few to be, 426:35
when gossips meet, 391:74
when I hear sweet music, never, 256:1
when knaves meet, 391:75
Merryman, song of a, 106:20
Merryman, Dr Quiet and Dr., 415:49
Message stern, disregard, 145:28
Messe, vaut bien une, 119:27
Messes, other country, 164:4
Messing about in boats, 111:24
Mestiere, incidente del, 304:4
Met, all that I have, 293:26
many a one, that have, 202:8
never—or never parted, 46:17
night that first we, 26:10
'twas in a crowd, 26:8
Metal more attractive, 225:22
Metaphor, betrayed into no, 34:13
Metaphysic wit can fly, 48:9
Metaphysics is the finding of bad reasons,
32:9
Mete and drink, it snewed, 63:30
Meteor, shone like a, 168:17
Method, gentle in, 371:54
in't, there is, 223:33
Methods, you know my, 87:26
Metre, laws of God, and man, and, 129:32
set off wretched matter and lame, 175:36
stretched, 263:31
Mettle is dangerous, 399:65
lad of, 232:3
Metuant, oderint dum, 14:1
Mew, be a kitten and cry, 232:23
Mewing and puking, 216:17
Micawber, never will desert, 84:4
Mice and men, schemes o', 44:12
and rats and such small deer, 241:35
catches no, 350:2
feel no cold, dead, 366:10
fishermen appear like, 241:48
in malt, merry as, 358:15
into horses, turn, 300:5
like little, 287:35
mind is chasing, 443:41

616

than will catch, 385:45
will play, 436:27
Michael, more men than, 424:10
Microscopes, magnifyin' gas, 82:19
Midden, on his ain, 350:10
Middle Age, enchantments of, 20:3
age, given to men of, 273;44
age had slightly press'd its signet, 210:22
go most safely in, 186:6
station had the fewest disasters, 80:4
stories that begin in the, 115:18
Midge, like a fretful, 206:14
Midge's wing, no bigger than, 421:41
Midian, how the troops of, 182:10
Midlands, living in the, 27:27
Midnight, chimes at, 234:24
clear, upon the, 212:10
dreary, upon a, 191:24
iron tongue of, 258:5
never come, 157:17
Midnights, flashes struck from, 37·33
Midshipmite, and a, 104:18
Midst of them, am I in, 325:35
Midwife, fairies', 216:13
Mien, of so frightful, 195:40
of such heejus, 87:16
such a face and such a, 90:9
Mieux en mieux, je vais de, 73:30
tout est pour le, 306:13
Might [*strength*], a man of, 154:17
do it with thy, 330:24
exceeds man's, 270:17
fight with all thy, 176:5
is right, 399:67
lessens, as our, 342:2
Might [*could*] have been, it, 117:25, 313:18
Mightiest in the mightiest, 255:33
Mighty above all things, 340:20
fallen, how are the, 325:36
God who made thee, 28:5
Mild and meek, 397:72
as a lamb, 358:16
Mildest manner'd man, 52:22
Mildness, ethereal, 300:8
Mile in the gate, 350:19
miss is as good as, 353:55
round aboot twal', 412:63
Miles a day, draw but twenty, 157:14
draws out our, 243:32
Milieu, commencent par le, 115:18
Milk and honey blest, with, 182:7
and honey, flowing with, 324:2

crying over spilt, 392:6
he drew, drops mingling with the, 145:24
in his mother's, 324:6
of human kindness, 114:8, 247:33
of Paradise, drunk the, 70:12
says to wine, 399:68
wine is old men's, 439:77
Milk-bowl, stepped into, 384:25
Milky way, solar walk or, 195:30
Mill cannot grind, 87:19, 420:21
grinds slow, God's, 373:42
in the self-same, 185:24
more water glideth by, 270:9
much water goes by, 400:19
no meal, no, 402:19
water to his own, 368:41
Mille altera, dein, 61:15
Miller draws water, 368:41
every honest, 368:28
knows not of, 400:19
of, than wots the, 270:9
there was a jolly, 29:15
Miller's neckcloth, what is bolder than, 435:52
Milliner, perfumed like a, 231:34
Million, aiming at a, 39:29
Mills and wives, 399:69
of God grind slowly, 150:9
they'll come down by, 436:29
Millstone grinds lower, 420:13
nether, 326:11
see as far into, 384:26
were hanged about his neck, 324:33
Milton, a name to resound, 295:36
birth, give a, 74:12
can, more than, 126:17
held, faith and morals, 318:3
mute inglorious, 112:14
thou should'st be living, 318:1
Miminy, piminy, 105:42
Mimsy were the borogoves, 58:17
Mincio's banks, on, 76:21
Mind, and never brought to, 45:37
anything else, hardly, 132:22
bashful, 383:59
body fill'd and vacant, 236:13
bring the philosophic, 320:3
cannot have a pure, 143:40
come back into my, 27:27
concentrates his, 133:41
conscious of its rectitude, 305:30

innocent, harmless, 308:4
man who made, 203:26
very tragical, 258:1
you have displaced, 250:7
Misbeliever, you call me, 254:5
Mischief comes by the pound, 399:71
done, thou little knowest, 183:31
hatcheth mischief catcheth, he that,
380:25
in every deed of, 104:10
in the world, no, 425:60
it means, 225:23
mother of, 421:41
no, 402:20
on, draw new, 260:8
than an inconvenience, better, 361:44
that is past, mourn, 260:8
the more, 420:33
Miser is always in want, 125:38
[robs] himself, 421:66
Miser's chest, in, 416:25
Miserable have no other medicine, 252:13
makes men, 390:36
Miseris sucurrere disco, 305:31
Misers, we become, 117:4
Misery acquaints a man, 269:32
all he had, gave to, 113:20
cause of all men's, 124:10
full of, 341:53
still delights, 76:14
to recall in our, 79:20
Misfortune, most unhappy kind, 31:22
Misfortunes, bear another's, 199:25
come on wings, 399:72
never come singly, 399:73
Misgivings, blank, 319:38
Mishap, no accident, no, 110:14
Misquote, enough of learning to, 49:40
Misreckoning is no payment, 399:74
Miss, an inch in, 357:40
is as good as a mile, 353:55
him, we shall, 309:19
Missed, who never would be, 106:11
Missing so much, 73:22
Missionary, I would eat, 313:28
Missouri, I am from, 304:7
Mist and hum, out of the, 19:23
comes from the hill, 437:41
comes from the sea, 437:41
in my face, 40:4
is dispell'd, 103:33
obscures, no, 281:35

they draw, rank, 166:20
through the cold and heavy, 123:40
will wet, Scottish, 354:7
Mistake, he who never made, 279:28
there shall be no, 310:13
Mistaken, think it possible you may be,
78:5
Mistakes, learn by other men's, 440:14
man who makes no, 190:6
name everyone gives to, 314:10
Mistaking, it is easy, 389:43
Mistletoe hung in the castle hall, 26:15
Mistress, if you can kiss, 387:49
in my own [house], 140:14
mine, O, 271:36
of herself, 197:27
Mistresses, I shall have, 104:4
with great smooth marbly limbs, 39:35
Mists, season of, 137:30
Mithras, God of the Morning, 142:8
Mittens, made him, 345:24
Mix them with my brains, 185:22
Mixen, wed over, 362:26
Moab in the land of, 17:21
Moan the expense, 264:2
Moaning, now they are, 94:3
Moat defensive to a house, 243:29
Mob has many heads, 420:24
Mock on, 'tis all in vain, 30:7
on, Voltaire, Rousseau, 30:7
Mocked himself, as if he, 228:16
Mockery, hence, unreal, 250:6
Mocking is catching, 399:75
Mocking-bird's throat, 313:16
Mod sceal þe mare, 342:2
Moderation, astonished at, 67:29
is the silken string, 114:16
Modest as ony, she's, 291:18
Modesty be a virtue, 426:28
wore enough for, 41:29
Mole, like a bastion's, 279:26
sweeps the laboured, 131:22
Molehill, mountain out of, 429:71
Moment, face some awful, 319:26
give to God each, 86:4
great pitch and, 224:4
in Annihilation's Waste, 98:9
precise psychological, 314:4
Moments, best and happiest, 277:27
Monachum, cucullus non facit, 365:71
Monarch, a merry, 204:10
becomes the throned, 255:33

and I could keep this up, 15:4
behold the wand'ring, 164:17
beneath a waning, 70:9
beneath the visiting, 214:17
brings fair weather, full, 418:16
does not heed, 420:26
dog, and bay the, 230:12
doth blow, red, 406:9
doth neither rain nor snow, white, 406:9
doth rain, pale, 406:9
fair as, 331:45
from out the sea, rake, 188:11
from the pale-faced, 231:38
gleams, the pale, 185:26
I saw the new, 342:5
I swear, by yonder, 267:25
i' the cold o' the, 40:1
in her arm, auld, 342:5
in the old of, 389:58
is a moon still, 420:27
it was the lovely, 102:2
makes bright mischief with, 300:6
may draw the sea, 294:21
minions of the, 231:26
of moons, star of stars, 84:13
of one revolving, 89:34
red comes up the, 77:30
revisit'st thus the glimpses of, 222:7
rising in clouded majesty, 191:32
shall rise, what are you when, 321:24
shone bright on Mrs. Porter, 93:31
silence of the still, 305:36
silver'd the walls, 162:1
sits arbitress, the, 169:27
[smite thee] by night, nor, 328:3
swear not by the, 267:25
takes up the wonderous tale, 15:9
the horned, 69:28
the inconstant, 267:25
there is a brugh, round, 436:24
two red roses across, 180:4
under the solitary, 19:23
walks the night, 80:13
was a ghostly galleon, 184:11
went up the sky, 69:31
where danced the, 210:17
whom mortals call, 276:2
with how sad steps, 278:19
Moon's an arrant thief, 270:7
in the full, when, 437:42
Moonlight, meet me by, 306:17
sleeps, how sweet, 255:43

unto sunlight, as, 293:37
visit it by the pale, 209:18
Moons wasted, some nine, 259:54
Moonshine, find out, 257:36
Moonshine's watery beams, 266:13
Moor, I never saw a, 84:25
over the purple, 184:11
Moore, through Burns and, 122:10
Moors [spend] at marriages, 419:65
Moral being, degeneration of, 285:29
let us be, 83:39
till all are, 282:17
to point a, 130:13
Morality expires, unawares, 194:24
fits of, 153:23
Morals, man of, tell me why, 74:4
of a whore, 132:9
Morbo, venienti occurrite, 190:3
More a man than they, 57:21
also, so to me and, 324.27
and more about less and less, 48:1
asked for, 82:24
come, keep some till, 393:48
he will do, 408:29
than enough, 400:13
than we think, often, 406:1
than we use, 400:14
the little, 38:8
the merrier, the, 420:35
we'll do, 15:11
ye see it th' better ye like it, 87:16
Mores, O tempora, O, 67:18
Morgan, mate of Henry, 159:24
Morn a thousand Roses brings, 97:29
and cold indifference came, 207:22
approach of ev'n or, 170:17
fair laughs the, 113:30
far sunken from the healthy breath of, 137:32
foul, 351:41
her rosy steps in th'eastern clime, 172:8
in russet mantle clad, 220:13
incense-breathing, 112:7
lights that do mislead, 253:22
like a lobster boiled, 49:23
not waking till she sings, 152:10
of toil, nor night of waking, 211:23
salute the happy, 49:35
sun came peeping in at, 123:38
sweet is the breath of, 171:33
that vanished with, 33:28
the nice, 165:33

till night, worked and sung from, 29:15
under the opening eyelids of, 166:11
wak'd by the circling hours, 172:18
Morning, a bit in the, 349:14
air, I scent the, 222:16
almost at odds with, 250:9
an hour inmthe, 356:36
beauty of the, 317:36
cloudy, 389:58
come in the, 80:1
dawn, child of the, 123:31
early, up in the, 45:34
fair came forth with pilgrim steps, 174:11
grey, 368:17
hour, 421:40
in the Bowl of Night, 97:27
looketh forth as, 331:43
Lucifer, son of, 331:53
many a glorious, 264:4
Mithras, God of, 142:8
never glad confident, 37:27
red, 368:17
shows the day, as, 174:6
sons of the, 118:7
take the wings of, 328:12
thou shalt say, in, 324:13
wakes the, 263:25
won't go home till, 41:33
would God it were, 324:13
Morning's at seven, 37:19
no for me, up in, 45:34
Mornings, cloudy, 364:37
Morrison Morrison, James, 163:18
Morrow as little, trusting, 125:25
morn, he rose the, 70:3
no thought for, 333:56
supplied by the, 131:29
Morsel cold, found you as, 214:10
Mort, abolir la peine de, 135:38
Mortal be proud, why should the spirit of, 143:36
but themselves, think all, 322:4
her last disorder, 107:42
speak, smile, or walk like a, 200:1
Mortality, behold and fear, 27:20
trust to frail, 22:23
Mortals be, what fools, 257:39
that would follow me, 166:7
Morte, speranza di, 79:18
Mortis, felix opportunitate, 290:9
Mortis, il n'y a pas de, 155:28
Mortuis nil nisi bonum, de, 366:7

Moses, from Mahomet to, 200:2
Moss, gathers no, 354:1
in a mountain, 441:44
starved bank of, 40:6
Mote that is in thy brother's eye, 333:58
Motes that people the sunbeams, gay, 164:12
Moth and rust doth corrupt, 333:43
for the star, desire of, 277:21
Mother and daughter, 433:65
bore me, my, 30:3
didna speak, my, 25:17
first begin, with, 382:20
for her children, 29:18
good, 418:23
heaviness of his, 328:24
if the child be like his father, ask, 359:76
in Israel, I arose, 324:19
keep house better than, 369:42
light-heeled, 352:20
like daughter, like, 395:79
no father, nor, 287:32
of all living, 323:21
of months, 290:1
of Parliaments, 33:25
of the Free, 28:5
says, not as thy, 392:8
sings, while, 96:15
so loving to my, 220:20
tends her, when her, 160:17
to the great sweet, 289:29
took great care of, 163:18
was ever found a, 103:27
when they are young, suck, 364:23
Mother's blessing, too much of, 350:5
cheek, kisseth, 382:8
lap, into thy, 173:44
Mother-in-law remembers not, 421:42
Mother-wit, ounce of, 357:57
Moths, maidens, like, 50:6
Motion blush'd at herself, 260:2
has she now, no, 317:22
sensible warm, 252:18
with a mazy, 70:10
Motions, two weeping, 78:1
Motley to the view, made myself, 265:25
Motley's the only wear, 216:12
Motor Bus, can it be a, 107:36
Motorem Bum, indicat, 107:36
Motter, I've gotter, 315:26
Mould [earth], mouthful of, 159:20
Mould [shape], broke the, 18:7

Mount, and stream, and sea, 118:16
  on thee, I may not, 184:5
Mountain and the flood, 209:25
  cradle, his high, 19:23
  forked, 211:11
  height, from yonder, 294:22
  like the dew on, 211:26
  Nebo's lonely, 17:21
  out of the molehill, 429:71
  sheep are sweeter, 188:12
  tops, flatter the, 264:4
  tops, misty, 268:3
  tops that freeze, 238:13
  up the airy, 18:1
  will not come to Mahomet, 386:27
Mountains are in labour, 126:2
  beautiful upon, 332:4
  beginning and end of all scenery, 207:27
  by the winter sea, 297:38
  divide us, 343:28
  Greenland's icy, 118:10
  look on Marathon, 52:24
  never greet, 371:63
  never [meet], 399:60
  one of the, 320:5
  over the, 343:19
  snowy, 343:17
Mountain-side, from every, 280:11
Mountebank, mere anatomy, a, 218:19
Mounting in hot haste, 50:15
Mourn, countless thousands, 44:5
  for me never, don't, 345:19
  for the Ahkoond I, 145:28
  lacks time to, 291:26
  man was made to, 44:4
Mourners go about the streets, 331:33
Mourning, to the house of, 330:18
  very handsome, 189:26
Mouse a hole, I gave, 384:28
  beholden to, 352:21
  drunk as, 357:78
  escaped, 417:46
  for killing of a, 32:11
  in the pot, 361:45
  in time may bite, 353:57
  it is a bold, 390:4
  it is a wily, 390:4
  of virtue, good my, 271:31
  poor as a church, 358:24
  proud, 349:18
  quiet as, 358:29
  ridiculous, 126:2

squeak, [hear], 390:35
  that has but one hole, 421:43
  to-morrow a, 431:52
  water on a drowned, 407:46
  what the cat thinketh, little wots, 436:28
Mouse-trap, make a better, 94:20
  smell of blood, let, 442:16
Mouth, a rose her, 296:15
  butter would not melt in, 429:68
  close, 350:9
  could not ope, 48:5
  goes beside your own, 442:26
  gold in its, 421:40
  good in, 373:51
  hath the deeper, 237:27
  heart is in his, 383:63
  honey in, 383:74
  I'll rant, an thou'lt, 227:42
  it, if you, 224:13
  look a gift horse in, 401:59
  nearest, 401:39
  of babes, out of, 326:14
  opens, but your, 442:20
  out of thine own, 337:36
  purple-stained, 136:15
  shut, keep, 393:53
  speaks, foolish, 423:72
  whoso hath but, 439:63
  wrong side of, 429:61
Mouth-honour, breath, 251:31
Mouths a sentence, 65:35
  blind, 166:19
  God never sends, 372:35
  in a glass, made, 241:26
  in their hearts, 440:13
  put an enemy in, 261:24
Moutons, revenons à nos, 30:16
Move immediately, I propose to, 111:27
  yet it does, 102:15
Moves and mates, and slays, 98:11
  in a mysterious way, 76:19
Movin' up and down again, 142:4
Moving, keep, 180:11
Much for us, there won't be, 60:4
  he that desireth, 376:22
  I want, though, 92:14
  if I could say how, 258:15
  it cannot be, 436:2
  might be said on both sides, 16:2
  of a muchness, they're, 93:25
  owed by so many, so, 66:5
  that which had too, 215:39

to do, so, 296:1
to have a little, ask, 359:73
would have more, 400:20
Muchness, much of a, 304:6
Muck and money go together, 400:21
riches are like, 408:37
Muck-hills will bloom, old, 404:13
Mud, marble and, 117:30
Muddy, ill-seeming, thick, 268:15
Mudie's, British Museum and, 49:30
Mudjokivis, killed the noble, 345:24
Mudville, no joy in, 299:31
Mugwump of the final plot, 33:27
Mule, hind part of, 362:38
Party is like a, 86:13
scrubs another, one, 405:58
Multiplication table gives me, plaege that
my, 99:31
Multitude below live, 39:31
swinish, 43:32
Mumble, let her maunder and, 57:36
Munch on, crunch on, 39:26
Mundum, Athanasius contra, 359:86
Munich! all thy banners wave, 55:28
Munny is, goä wheer, 295:32
Muove, eppur si, 102:15
Murder and to rafish, to, 22:5
brother's, 225:36
column, to the, 274:12
undulges himself in, 81:26
me, will you let them, 40:12
most foul, 22:13
most sacrilegious, 249:26
will out, 400:22
Murdered man, brothers and, 136:9
Murders, gentlemen who do, 135:38
twenty mortal, 250:4
Murex up, who fished the, 38:15
Murmurs creep, with pleasing, 192:15
hear our mutual, 53:25
Murther, foul and midnight, 113:31
Mus, nascetur ridiculus, 126:2
Musam meditamur avena, 280:13
silvestrem, 305:21
Muscles of his brawny arms, 149:33
Muse [goddess], let's sing of rats, 111:25
meditate the thankless, 166:14
of fire, O for a, 235:28
of the many-twinkling feet, 51:31
practise the woodland, 305:21
rise, honest, 197:32
transports of a British, 291:20

worst-natured, 204:9
Muse [ponder] as they use, men, 399:61
Muses, all the charm of, 298:1
sing of happy swains, 77:22
Museum, books at the British, 49:30
Mushrooms, broiled fowl and, 82:5
Music arose with its voluptuous swell,
50:11
be the food of love, 271:24
creep in our ears, 255:43
discourse most eloquent, 225:30
fading in, 254:22
hath charms, 72:8
hear the sea-maid's, 257:31
helps not, 400:23
in himself, man that hath no, 256:2
in its roar, 51:27
in my heart I bore, 318:7
is, how sour sweet, 244:9
make not sweet, 373:75
makes as healthful, 226:7
makes sweet, 273:26
mute, will make, 297:25
night shall be filled with, 150:6
of men's lives, with, 244:9
on the waters, like, 52:1
one chord of, 200:15
shed, soul of, 177:30
sphere-descended, 71:38
that gentlier on the spirit lies, 292:19
the colou , the, 159:20
the condition of, 188:1
there, [for] the, 192:13
they were thy chosen, 320:5
though I'm full of, 42:17
to attending ears, 367:29
when I hear sweet, 256:1
when soft voices die, 276:19
Music's soothing sound, 313:24
Musical as is Apollo's lute, 165:43
Musicians that shall play to you, 232:28
Music-makers, we are the, 185:26
Musing there an hour, 52:24
Musket moulds in his hands, 96:16
take not, 412:76
Musk-roses, with sweet, 257:34
Must, Duty whispers low, Thou, 95:25
is a king's word, 400:24
Mustard, after meat, 355:58
and cress, now for, 105:25
good without, 374:7
Mutamur in illis, 414:18

Mutant, caelum, non animum, 125:41
Mutato nomine, 125:28
Mutatus ab illo, quantum, 305:37
Mute, is she not pure, 207:33
Mutiny, to rise and, 230:7
Mutter, wizards that, 331:51
Mutters, knows not what he, 420:15
Mutton, dead as, 357:76
  joint of, 235:33
Muzzle the ox, thou shalt not, 324:12
Myriad-minded Shakespeare, 71:28

Mytre still, 107:37
Myrtle, cypress and, 51:32
  is still, the, 107:37
Myrtles brown, ye, 166:8
Mystery, comprehend its, 150:14
  I show.you a, 339:35
  lost myself in a, 35:20
  of things, take upon's, 242:9
  pluck out the heart of, 225:31
Mystic, wonderful, 296:22

N

Nactus es, Spartam, 67:20
Nag, gait of a shuffling, 232:24
Naiad airs, thy, 191:28
  the guardian, 210:19
Nail drives out another, 405:60
  for want of, 371:47
  it down, 154:16
  made to the, 125:23
  on the head, hit, 429:49
  that will go, drive, 367:74
  to our coffin adds a, 315:30
Nailed for our advantage, 231:25
Nails, he must have iron, 377:44
Naked came I out of my mother's womb,
    325:60
  every day he clad, 108:8
  though lock'd up in steel, 237:31
Nakedness, not in utter, 319:35
Namby-pamby madrigals, 104:14
Namby Pamby's little rhymes, 56:16
Name Achilles assumed, what, 35:24
  age without a, 179:19
  Amos Cottle, what a, 50:3
  answered to his, 299:24
  as lazy as the, 88:16
  at which the world grew pale, 130:13
  blushes at the, 129:19
  by any other, 267:22
  by her golden, 184:12
  change the, 125:20
  deed without a, 250:14

filches from me my good, 261:28
gathered together in my, 325:35
gets a good, 376:14
give a dog a bad, 372:6
halloo your, 271:33
hallowed be thy, 333:48
has left but the, 177:29
he that hath an ill, 379:42
in a borrow'd, 200:4
in man and woman, good, 261:28
and in my own city my, 389:47
in print, see one's, 49:39
is better, good, 330:17
is MacGregor, my, 212:4
is Might-have-been, my, 206:17
is never heard, her, 26:7
is Norval, my, 122:19
is rather to be chosen, good, 329:49
is Used-to-was, my, 302:8
it to you, let me not, 262:9
keeps its lustre, good, 351:61
led all the rest, 128:1
local habitation and, 257:46
not an ill, 356:39
of her sufficeth, 412:71
out of his Christian, 153:20
power of Jesus', 190:1
proud his, 209:24
rouse him at the, 236:17
set down my, 42:8
shadow of a mighty, 152:3

to the pole, true as, 31:28
through the eye of, 335:39
Needles and pins, 401:45
Needs must, 401:46
Negatives, two, 325:39
Neglect, wise and salutary, 43:26
Negligent, celerity is never more admired
  than by, 214:8
Negotiate, never fear to, 138:15
Neiges d'antan, où sont, 305:19
Neighbour and our work, our, 138:6
  as thyself, love, 324:7, 325:38
  good, 351:62
  love your, 397:67
  policy of the good, 205:22
  that he might rob, 153:29
  you must ask, 442:12
Neighbourhood, ancient, 165:37
Neighbours, beloved of his, 355:80
  good fences make good, 102:8
  he hath ill, 375:72
  injures its, 422:2
  not [live] without, 434:15
  say, as thy, 392:9
Neighs, high and boastful, 236:10
Nelly starve, let not poor, 62:7
Νεφελοκοκκυγία, 18:8
Nephews, devil gives, 382:22
Neptune, chase the ebbing, 629:43
  drowned more men than, 359:90
  siege of watery, 243:30
  would not flatter, 219:25
Neptune's park, stands as, 219:32
Nerves at a strain, to keep, 38:12
  feels for my poor, 21:26
  life will try his, 38:13
  shall never tremble, my firm, 250:5
Nescio, sed fieri sentio, 61:16
Nest at peep of day, in her, 294:5
  bird likes its own, 368:22
  birds in làst year's, 424:14
  farthest from her, 419:74
  fouls its own, 390:29
  leaves his wat'ry, 79:27
  mare's, 428:28
  of singing birds, 132:4
  stockdove hides her, 67:27
Nestles over the shining rim, 176:4
Nestor swear the jest be laughable, 253:26
Nests, birds of the air have, 324:9
  in my beard, built, 147:14
  were slunk, to their, 171:32

Net, fishing before, 391:62
  is spread, in vain, 328:15
  rough, 422:3
  that comes to, 355:74
Nets and stratagems, fine, 119:39
Nettle, better be stung by, 361:56
  in dock, out, 389:37
  stroke a, 121:21
Neues, im Westen nichts, 203:22
Never, better late than, 362:1
  house of, 363:72
  is a long day, 401:57
  never—never, 62:12
  never, never, never, never, 242:13
  to come there no more, 75:23
  were nor no man ever saw, 268:9
  what? Hardly ever! 105:26
Nevermore, quoth the raven, 191:26
New, always something, 369:56
  amaist as weel's the, 44:13
  are tried, first by whom, 192:12
  before you are on with, 343:27
  ever charming, ever, 92:15
  I make all things, 340:18
  is not true, what is, 435:58
  or old, whether it be, 287:30
  ring in the, 296:4
  thing, there is no, 330:9
  World into existence, called the, 56:13
  Year, of all the glad, 292:17
  yielding place to, 297:41
New York, sidewalks of, 29:29
  [they ask], in, 303:31
New Zealand, traveller from, 153:26
Newcastle, carry coals to, 428:9
  grindstone, 354:5
News at London, hear what, 442:13
  baits, good, 174:20
  bringer of unwelcome, 233:50
  brings the truest, 419:72
  comes apace, ill, 388:24
  from a far country, good, 329:54
  he was scant of, 382:26
  is good news, no, 402:23
  nature of bad, 213:36
  never good to bring bad, 214:5
  of battle, 22:1
  rides post, evil, 174:20
  talk of court, 242:9
  tells his wife, 381:63
  to hear, bitter, 73:26
  travels fast, ill, 388:24

O

P

wedlock is, 434:35
Padre said, Whatever have you been and
gone, 104:20
Pagan, I'd rather be a, 319:29
spoiled, you find, 322:13
Page [sheet], beautiful quarto, 278:5
upon glory's, 177:25
Page [servant], ho, pretty, 298:28
wage will get, 433:73
Pageant, insubstantial, 269:40
Paid by nobody, 381:45
in full, God, we ha', 140:13
that is well satisfied, well, 255:41
till thou hast, 333:42
two I am sure I have, 232:9
Pain and anguish wring the brow, 210:13
darkness, and cold, 40:6
dear mother, now, no, 96:7
equal, 395:80
in aromatic, 195:33
in company with, 319:25
is fraught, with some, 276:7
is lessen'd, one, 266:9
joys three-parts, 39:43
labour physics, 249:25
neither shall there be any more, 340:18
never, knew, 376:54
no palm, no, 189:19
of finite hearts, 38:9
Our Lady of, 289:37
past is pleasure, 406:6
piercing, 287:24
tender for another's, 111:34
turns with ceaseless, 108:2
with pain purchased doth inherit, 245:32
Pains, have one's labour for, 429:43
never knew their, 77:22
no gains without, 402:3
of love be sweeter, 91:35
take the most, 385:59, 394:17
the immortal spirit must endure, 18:16
Paint, flinging a pot of, 207:32
it, I must, 196:19
them, he best can, 194:10
Painted on the wall, Duchess, 38:19
to the eyes, 86:2
Painter dips his pencil, 275:27
Painters and poets have leave to lie, 406:8
Painting and fighting look aloof, on, 404:18
Paintings, heard of your, 224:10
Pair of sparkling eyes, 106:25
Palace and prison on each hand, 50:21

for a hermitage, 244:2
see my shining, 162:10
Palaces, gorgeous, 269:40
in kings' 330:2
oftener in cottages than, 365:53
those golden, 17:23
Palaeozoic time, in the, 280:7
Pale and peevish, 369:67
and wan, why so, 288:1
for weariness, 276:11
[is] envious, 427:59
man draw thy knife, at, 427:59
young curate, I was a, 104:24
Paley's Moral Philosophy, 144:1
Palinurus nodded at the helm, 194:23
Pall, in sceptred, 164:20
Pall Mall, shady side of, 179:31
Palladium of all the civil, political rights,
135:23
Palliate, attempt to, 62:8
Palm [tree] alone, bear the, 228:10
like some tall, 118:6
trees, over the scud and, 140:16
Palm [hand], to have an itching, 230:11
Palmer's walking-staff, 244:2
weed, votarist in, 165:34
Pamere, mountain cradle in, 18:23
Pan, the great god, 36:11
Panaceas, beyond all their, 47:41
Pancake, as flat as, 356:84
Pandion, King, he is dead, 25:20
Panem et circenses, 135:34
Pang as great, finds a, 252:16
feels no biting, 104:13
learn, nor account, 39:43
Pangs, keen were his, 50:4
Panic's in thy breastie, 44:11
Panjandrum, the Grand, 100:10
Pansies, that's for thoughts, 227:24
Pansy freak'd with jet, 167:22
Pantaloon, lean and slipper'd, 216:17
Panted, she spoke and, 214:3
Papa, potatoes, poultry, 84:17
Paper bullets of the brain, 258:20
fool's, 354:31
he hath not eat, 246:7
just for a scrap of, 28:14
that ever blotted, 255:28
the fairer the, 417:57
Paper-mill, hast built a, 238:2
Papers in each hand, 197:37
Parable, took up his, 324:8

Παραδειγμάτων, φιλοσοφία ἐκ, 84:28
Paradise, and walked in, 17:17
  before we go to, 65:22
  complete, made the, 66:23
  drunk the milk of, 70:12
  enow, Wilderness is, 97:30
  enow, Wilderness were, 97:13
  has she cheapened, 188:4
  he that will enter into, 381:69
  same old glimpse of, 144:10
  this world's, 399:42
  to him are opening, 113:23
  to what we fear of death, 253:19
Parallel, but herself, admits no, 159:30
Paratus, in utrumque, 305:33
Parcell'd Oxus, shorn and, 18:23
Parcere subjectis, 306:7
Parchment, being scribbled o'er, 237:34
  bonds, rotten, 243:30
Pardon all but thyself, 406:10
  kiss of the sun for, 114:10
  never ask, 401:51
  there needs no, 438:7
Pardoned and retain the offence, be, 225:37
Pardons, offender never, 421:50
Pardoun, bret-ful of, 63:36
Pards, Bacchus and his, 136:17
Parent knew, when our first, 312:6
  mad, put any, 99:30
Parents fools, make, 364:24
  mad, [children] make, 364:24
  who were his, 303:31
Parfit gentil knight, 63:22
Parings, half away in, 419:69
Paris, Americans . . . go to, 18:4
  is well worth a mass, 119:27
  vaut bien une messe, 119:27
Parish, all the world as my, 310:27
Parleys, city that, 350:7
Parliament of man, in, 293:35
  speaking through reporters, 57:34
Parliamentary discussion, Prince Rupert of,
    85:30
  hand, an old, 106:33
Parliaments, mother of, 33:25
Parlour, walk into my, 127:28
Parmaceti for an inward bruise, 231:36
Parochial, he was, 129:26
Parody, devil's walking, 65:25
Paroles, n'emploient les, 306:16
Parritch, the halesome, 44:14
Parrots, laugh like, 253:26

Parsnips, butter no, 369:74
Parson, always a parson, once, 404:23
  always christens his own child first,
    421:53
  made it his text, 294:30
  much bemused in beer, 197:38
  own'd his skill, 109:27
  there goes the, 74:10
Parson's wife, must kiss, 382:13
Part, chosen that good, 336:14
  darkies have to, 101:15
  every man must play, 253:27
  friends must, 415:46
  of all that I have met, 293:26
  she hath done her, 173:30
  thee and me, ought but death, 324:27
  'tis hard to, 23:35
  to tear a cat in, 256:26
Parted, never met—or never, 46:17
  soon, 350:32
  when we two, 49:36
Partem, audi alteram, 359:88
Partial, we grow more, 196:12
Particle, that very fiery, 52:30
Parting is such sweet sorrow, 267:30
  was well made, 230:19
Partington, conduct of Mrs., 281:14
Partitions do their bounds divide, thin,
    89:25
Parthenon, earth proudly wears, 95:22
Pathenope, tenet nunc, 306:11
Partiality, without rancour or, 290:11
Particular, a London, 84:9
Partner, but I have a, 84:7
  find yourself a, 143:25
  nigh, hush'd his, 211:42
Parts allure thee, if, 196:8
  in all his gracious, 239:34
  one man in his time plays many, 215:17
Party gave up, to, 109:33
  none were for a, 154:3
  true to one, 151:33
  without, Parliamentary government,
    85:33
Pascua, rura, duces, cecini, 306:11
Pass and speak one another, 150:20
  by, all ye that, 332:14
  for forty-three, 104:21
  in the night, ships that, 150:20
  it on to other folk, 345:21
  like night from land to land, 69:38
  they shall not, 190:4

things have come to a pretty, 160:5
this way again, not, 114:3
Passage shun, each dark, 322:9
the worse the, 424:1
Passages that lead to nothing, 113:22
Passe son temps de moy, elle, 176:11
tout casse, tout, 431:67
Passed away, former things are, 340:18
by on the other side, 336:12
over, so he, 42:13
Passenjare, punch in the presence of, 34:9
Passer, deliciae meae puellae, 60:12
mortuus est, 60:12
Passer-by, stop, Christian, 71:23
Passeront pas, ils ne, 190:4
Passes, all breaks, all, 431:67
Passing by, see her, 342:14
Passing-bell, some cost a, 27:22
Passion, all made of, 218:10
discern infinite, 38:9
feel your ruling, 196:18
for it, I have no, 132:15
haunted me like a, 316:13
hidden in my veins, 202:4
into a towering, 227:46
loves, which pale, 100:5
may I govern my, 199:28
shall have spent, when, 293:32
sick of an old, 87:22
speechless lies, 88:15
spent, all, 174:22
the ruling, 197:31
to tatters, tear a, 225:14
Passions, all thoughts, all, 70:17
match'd with mine, 293:37
rise, such angry, 309:30
[women] have but two, 64:9
Passiveness, in a wise, 316:7
Past and to come seem best, 234:9
bury its dead, let the dead, 149:27
cannot be recalled, 428:14
has pow'r, upon the, 90:13
judged by things, 426:15
remembrance of things, 264:2
short notice, soon, 395:27
till [the year] be, 409:60
Pastoral, pastoral-comical, 223:39
Pastors, some ungracious, 220:36
Pastures, farms, leaders, I sang of, 306:11
in green, 326:24
new, fresh woods and, 167:24
Patch, best, 415:48

was worn, while the, 292:24
Pate, you beat your, 199:23
Paternoster built churches, 406:12
no penny, no, 402:24
Pates, lean, 370:2
Path hath a puddle, 369:46
of gold for him, 37:34
of the just, 328:18
to his door, a beaten, 94:20
Pathos and sublime, true, 46:4
Paths are peace, all her, 284:8, 328:17
of joy and woe, 73:28
straight, make his, 332:31
that wind, so many, 313:30
Patience, abusing of God's, 256:8
and impatience, all, 218:10
and shuffle the cards, 61:23
and sorrow strove, 241:46
aptitude à la, 42:2
be a tired mare, 235:47
grow, let, 395:43
he preacheth, 376:54
He stands waiting, with, 150:9
in mean men we intitle, 243:20
is a flower, 406:13
is a plaster, 406:14
money, and time, 406:15
no remedy but, 402:27
on a monument, like, 272:4
poor are they that have not, 261:26
put on, 410:16
to prevent that murmur, 167:31
will you abuse, 66:17
Patient etherised, like a, 93:27
man, fury of a, 90:3
Patientia nostra, abutere, 66:17
Patria mori, pro, 125:30
sed pro, 183:23
Patrie, enfants de la, 207:19
Patriot, too cool, for a, 109:34
Patriot's boast, such is, 108:3
fate, cowards mock, 129:19
Patriotism is not enough, 61:19
is the last refuge, 133:33
would not gain force, 131:32
Patriots all, true, 60:7
Patron and the jail, the, 130:12
commonly a wretch, 131:27
my Lord, is not a, 132:10
Paul hath no honour and no friend but
Christ, 181:20
thou art beside thyself, 338:3

Paul's for a man, goes to, 439:41
Paunches, fat, 370:2
Pauper, he's only a, 184:3
Pause in the day's occupations, 150:5
  must give us, 224:4
Pavement, archways and the, 22:1
Pavilioned in splendour, 111:26
Paw is doubled, each drowsy, 176:4
  with the cat's, 430:31
Pay again with shame or loss, 376:71
  and pray, pain both to, 390:12
  beforehand, 406:16
  for it, pray God to make me able to,
    189:21
  for one by one, 141:31
  given to a state hireling, 131:28
  he that cannot, 378:6
  himself, he will, 387:59
  if I can't, 120:16
  in his own coin, 430:4
  man cannot choose but, 188:4
  pay—pay, 142:3
  that never, 425:72
  unless you mean to, 412:23
  we will nothing, 219:31
  what you owe, 406:17
Paymaster, good, 351:63
Payment, taken for part, 373:61
Pays, base is the slave that, 235:48
  for all, third time, 423:45
  for all, poor man, 421:60
  last, he that, 380:31
  the best, scent which, 151:35
  twice, never, 380:31
Peace above all earthly dignities, 239:17
  all her paths are, 284:8, 328:17
  and ensue it, seek, 326:29
  and rest can never dwell, where, 168:5
  around, throw sweet, 313:24
Peace, better a lean, 361:42
  but when he is fighting, never at, 356:33
  calm world and a long, 233:38
  certain knot of, 278:20
  commerce, and honest friendship, 129:31
  deep dream of, 127:37
  for ever hold his, 341:37
  gathers, he that holds his, 381:53
  God gave her, 292:4
  hangs [thieves], 434:6
  hath her victories, 167:34
  he that will not have, 382:1
  her perfect, 206:6

I hope with honour, 85:36
if you shall live in, 442:12
if you want, 411:44
in His will is our, 79:21
in our time, give, 340:31
in thy right hand carry, 239:19
inglorious arts of, 158:16
is of the nature of a conquest, 234:28
just and lasting, 148:11
live and hold his, 376:31
[Lord] give thee, 324:8
Love tunes, in, 208:19
makes a good, 380:16
makes plenty, 406:18
[never was] a bad, 101:26
of Eden, give the, 160:10
of God, 339:52
on earth, 336:7
peace, saying, 332:11
perfect peace, 29:16
piping time of, 245:13
publisheth, 332:4
retrenchment and reform, 33:24
return, star of, 55:25
shall go sleep, 244:5
soft phrase of, 259:54
they call it, 290:8
thousand years of, 296:5
unto the wicked, no, 332:3
uproar the universal, 250:20
when he holdeth, 329:41
when there is no, 332:11
where there is, 438:18
within, whispers, 29:10
Peaceable way, most, 258:28
Peacemaker, If is the only, 218:14
Peacemakers, blessed are, 333:37
Peach in the orchard grew, 96:14
Peacock hath fair feathers, 421:54
  proud as, 358:26
Peak, silent upon a, 136:4
Peal, rung night's yawning, 249:38
Pearl away, threw a, 262:16
  black man is, 349:16
  heaps of, 245:18
  of great price, one, 324:24
  showers on her kings barbaric, 169:28
  sow'd the earth with orient, 172:8
Pearls before swine, cast, 333:59
  would search for, 91:40
Peas, here are sweet, 136:1
  like as two, 358:8

with a grandsire, 266:12
would be more german, 227:49
Φρὴν ἀνώμοτος, 95:33
Φροντὶς Ἱπποκλείδμ, οξ, 121:22
Φύλλων γενεή, οιη περ, 123:27
Phyllida, my, 86:2
Phyllis is my only joy, 212:13
neat-handed, 164:4
Physic do not work, if, 386:9
for a king, 356:22
kitchen, 393:66
pomp, take, 241:31
to the dogs, throw, 251:33
Physician, defy, 370:10
fool or, 368:32
go not for every grief to, 372:24
he is a good, 376:9
heal thyself, 336:8
old, 356:51
Physicians, best, 415:49
Where there are three, 438:17
Picardy, roses in, 310:3
Picket's off duty forever, 27:23
Picking and stealing, from, 341:42
must be always, 364:16
Pickle, have a rod in, 429:39
Pickwickian sense, in its, 82:4
Picture, look here upon this, 226:2
plac'd the busts between, 32:12
Pictures are dead speakers, 406:7
or conversations, without, 58:3
out, cutting all, 27:26
painted, 406:7
Pie, have a finger in, 428:32
I'd eat thee, if thou wert, 384:36
none, of, 362:15
Pieces of silver, thirty, 325:57
sma', hacked him in, 342:10
Pie-crusts, promises and, 406:71
Pier, I walk'd upon the, 24:10
Pierian spring, 192:6
Pies, one of Bellamy's veal, 191:20
Piety more prone, to, 17:22
nor Wit, all thy, 98:13
would not grow warmer, 131:32
Pig grunts, young, 424:6
in a poke, to buy, 428:6
[teaching] Minerva, 412:55
Pigs have wings, whether, 59:23
love that lie together, 406:25
might fly, 406:26
squeak, as naturally as, 48:3

to a fine market, brought, 375:65
Pikestaff, plain as, 358:22
Pilate, jesting, 22:7
Pilgrim grey, 71:34
steps in amice grey, with, 174:11
Pilgrimage, quiet, 56:1
take my, 202:9
Pilgrims of the night, 96:5
track the Phoenix, 28:4
Pillar of state, seem'd a, 169:37
to post, from, 371:68
Pillars massy proof, with, 165:25
Pillow hard, finds the down, 219:36
take counsel of, 430:27
Pills, bitter, 363:45
were pleasant, if, 386:30
Pilot, every man is, 388:28
face to face, see my, 298:7
here's to the, 56:10
in extremity, daring, 89:24
of the Galilean lake, 166:18
'tis a fearful night, 26:11
Pimpernel, demmed, elusive, 185:23
Pin and let it lie, see, 410:3
and nail for nought, many a, 376:75
and pick it up, see, 410:3
before you die, want, 410:3
he that takes not up, 381:58
neat as a new, 358:17
sin to steal a, 390:25
so has a, 442:1
will not stoop for, 382:2
with a little, 244:1
Pinch, they brought one, 218:19
Pinches, where the shoe, 429:59
Pindarus, the house of, 167:26
Pine [languish], dwindle, peak and, 247:20
for what is not, 276:7
look on Virtue and, 190:2
make men, 371:73
Pine [tree] were but a wand, tallest, 168:12
wishes herself a shrub, 421:57
Pine-logs hither, bring me, 182:12
Pines are gossip pines, 99:26
eat the cones under, 102:8
thunder-harp of, 279:32
Pinion, he nursed the, 50:4
Pinions skin the air, with, 102:4
Pink of courtesy, 267:34
of perfection, very, 110:8
the white, 167:22
Pinned with a single star, 67:25

Pins, like as a row of, 142:1
Pipe he can smoke, 300:21
  no longer, 402:8
  put that in your, 408:1
Piper, he who pays, 382:31
Pipers, wi' a hundred, 181:26
Pipes and whistles, 215:17
  boast their peasants', 77:22
  grate on their scrannel, 166:20
  o' Havelock sound, 312:21
  play on, ye soft, 137:22
Piping down the valleys, 30:2
Pippin, parings of, 421:52
Pippins toothsomest, old, 310:9
Pistol let off at the ear, 144:3
  misses fire, when, 110:11
Pit as well as better, fill, 233:40
  monster of the, 198:13
  that is bottomless, 129:24
  whoso diggeth, 328:58
Pitch [*throw*], a bumping, 183:24
  flies the higher, 237:27
  this one high, 20:2
Pitch [*tar*], he that toucheth, 340:22
Pitch-and-toss, began by playing, 298:25
Pitcher be broken at the fountain, 330:74
  goes so often to the well, 421:58
  it is bad for, 438:23
  strikes the stone, 438:23
Pitchers, little, 395:14
Pitfall and with Gin, with, 98:15
Pith, seven years', 259:54
Pitied, better be envied than, 361:54
Pities another, he that, 380:32
  them, how I, 191:21
Pitiful look asks enough, 353:65
  'twas wondrous, 260:6
Pity, challenge double, 202:6
  gave ere charity began, 108:21
  he hath a tear for, 234:29
  like a naked new-born babe, 248:1
  much his case, I, 45:32
  of it, Iago, 262:2
  so it was, great, 231:36
  them, I learn to, 108:6
  'tis 'tis true, 222:29
Pity's akin to love, 281:34
Place and means for every man, 213:32
  at home I was in a better, 216:1
  before I understood this, 304:9
  buried in so sweet, 277:29
  dwelt ne'er in one, 439:62

ere you can point, 46:10
fine and private, 158:12
for everything, 279:29
in a holy, 55:16
in her pride of, 249:30
in many a secret, 317:23
in the shady, 280:14
is dignified, 213:29
little one-eyed blinking sort o', 115:26
never in one, 406:63
never the time and, 40:18
no dispute of, 359:78
other things give, 103:28
savage, 70:9
sit in your, 411:54
thereof shall know it no more, 327:57
well, quits his, 376:55
Places at once, in two, 404:32
  change; handy-dandy, 242:4
  crammed, strange, 216:13
  in pleasant, 326:18
  that the eye of heaven visits, all, 243:26
  you can, in all the, 310:28
Placid and self-contain'd, 312:14
Plague o' both your houses, 267:39
  rid you, the red, 269:24
  stole on me, pleasing, 312:9
  that's his, 47:40
  us, instruments to, 242:11
Plagues thy wrath can send, 56:9
Plain as a pikestaff, 358:22
  as way to parish church, 216:15
  as the nose, 358:23
  blunt man, a, 230:5
  Camilla scours the, 192:16
  dealing is a jewel, 406:28
  nodding o'er the yellow, 300:12
  stretch'd upon the, 50:4
  upon tables, make it, 332:27
Plainly told, speeds best, 245:23
Plains, on the ringing, 293:25
  with his darling, 27:32
Plan, I was thinking of a, 59:35
  most practical, 128:11
  not without a, 195:25
  reforms his, 322:3
  simple, 318:8
Plane tree's kind, the, 182:19
Planet, born under a rhyming, 258:44
  born under a three-halfpenny, 381:66
  swims into his ken, new, 136:4
Planets, guides the, 205:17

Pledge with mine, I will, 134:9
Pleiades, influences of, 326:8
Plenty, breakfasted with, 406:64
 but just had, 44:8
 he that hath, 379:51
 here is God's, 92:3
 makes dainty, 406:35
 peace makes, 406:18
 though never so, 53:35
Plesance here is all vain glory, 92:12
Pliable animal, man is a, 87:17
Plie, fail of taking, 42:21
Plod, yet she will, 235:47
Plodders ever won, small, 246:1
Ploffskin, Pluffskin, 147:17
Plot [scheme], gunpowder treason and,
 345:26
 hath many changes, 200:24
 is as good a plot as ever was laid, 232:1
 Mogul and Mugwump of, 33:27
 signify, does the, 41:31
 will tell you the, 64:12
 wished occasion of, 89:30
Plot [ground], this blessed, 243:29
Plough and sow, to, 342:21
 brother will follow, 185:24
 deep while others sleep, 406:36
 following his, 317:34
 goes not well, 421:59
 going, better have one, 361:76
 having put his hand to, 336:10
 in the earth, put, 378:12
 loom, anvil, spade, 144:8
 plod behind the, 74:22
 son to, 417:61
 speed, 412:29
 wherefore, 275:31
 would thrive, he that by, 378:1
Ploughman hold it not, 421:59
 homeward plods, 112:4
Pluck it out, 324:34
 with one, crow to, 428:37
Plum, black, 349:17
 the riper the, 419:49
 tree, wild, 292:1
Plume shine, where ye see my white,
 154:10
Plumes at random thrown, 28:4
Plummet sound, deeper than, 269:44
Pluto, gate of gloomy, 306:6
Pluto's cheek, down, 164:21
Poacher makes the best keeper, 356:52

Pobbles are happier, 147:20
Pocket, burns a hole in, 383:64
 in an empty, 416:17
 it picks yer, 155:22
 put it in his, 226:4
 scruple to pick a, 81:24
Pockets, made without, 404:76
 rare in our, 64:17
Poem lovely as a tree, 139:18
 no true ornament of, 174:36
 ought himself to be a true, 174:25
 to which we return, 71:27
 unlimited, 223:39
 very pretty, 28:12
 which we have read, 71:27
Poem's period, made one, 156:12
Poems are made by fools, 139:19
Poesy, immortal flowers of, 156:12
 viewless wings of, 136:17
Poet, buffoon and, 118:20
 dies, when the, 209:22
 for I am a, 38:20
 honour the greatest, 79:19
 is born, not made, 406:37
 lies, beneath this sod, 71:23
 lunatic, the lover and, 257:45
 our sage and serious, 174:31
 preacher, judge and, 129:32
 sings, truth the, 293:33
 soaring in the high region of his fancies,
  174:23
 speak to men, how does, 57:21
 sung, once-loved, 194:11
 they had no, 198:16
 will follow the rainbow, 185:24
 you will never be a, 92:4
Poet's brain, should possess, 88:11
 dream, the, 318:20
 eye, in a fine frenzy rolling, 257:46
 pen turns them to shapes, 257:46
Poeta nascitur, 406:37
 onorate l'altissimo, 79:19
Poetess, a maudlin, 197:38
Poetic fields encompass me, 15:10
 justice, 194:12
 pains, pleasure in, 74:37
Poetical, would the gods had made thee,
 217:32
Poetry, but prose run mad, not, 198:1
 by wrong, cradled into, 275:29
 Fleshly School of, 41:30
 has a meaning, when, 126:23

giving much to, 372:18
God help, 372:30
grind the faces of, 331:49
have cried, when that, 229:38
he that considereth, 327:33
indeed, he is, 376:25
indeed, makes me, 261:28
infirm, weak, 241:25
labours of, 421:64
laws grind the, 108:5
make a rich man, 353:59
man had nothing, 325:40
man loved the great, 154:3
man pays for all, 421:60
man's bread, hope is, 384:11
man's day, 111:22
man's shilling, 421:61
man's table, 353:66
men seek meat, 406:42
men's riches, 364:20
men's tables, 406:43
rather sell than be, 408:16
simple annals of, 112:8
than wicked, better be, 361:59
thanks, the exchequer of, 243:34
that hath little, not, 376:22
that hath pity upon, 329:44
weigh not, reasons, of, 421:69
Poorhouse, glorious hours even in, 300:28
Pope [bishop] of Rome, no more than,
    384:33
        strive against, 391:60
Pope [poet], better to err with, 50:2
    Mr., very pretty poem, 28:12
Popery, inclines a man to, 102:10
Popish liturgy, a, 62:11
Poplar's gentle and tall, 182:19
Poplars are fell'd, 76:9
Poppies, a-flutter with, 38:2
    blow, the, 154:12
    nodding, 77:24
    pleasures are like, 46:10
Poppy, blindly scattereth her, 35:25
    flushed print in a, 298:35
    nor mandragora, 261:33
Populi, salus, 66:19, 409:53
Populus Romanus, utinam, 54:1
Porcelain, dainty rogue in, 160:28
Pores, pass through the, 276:3
Porpentine, quills upon the fretful, 222:12
Porridge, cool your, 409:58
    had John Keats, what, 38:15

is sooner heated, old, 404:14
Port [harbour] after stormie seas, 283:28
    in a storm, any, 356:63
    is near, the, 312:17
    the more welcome, 424:1
Port [wine] for men, 133:45
    go fetch a pint of, 293:43
Port [mien] as meke, of his, 63:21
Portal, from its ivory, 200:1
Porters, poor mechanic, 235:43
Portion for children, best. 433:64
    have the best, 414:41
    he wales a, 44:15
    in us, have no, 87:21
Portray men as they ought to be portrayed,
    I, 281:33
Ports and happy havens, 243:26
Positives, two Sir, 432:37
Possession, better than, 406:72
    for ever, a, 301:33
    is nine points, 406:44
    lies, in thy, 215:27
    would not show, virtue, 258:35
Possessions, all my, 94:1
Possest, cuts off what we, 91:39
Possibilities, unconvincing, 18:10
Possible, O that 'twere, 296:20
    with God all things are, 324:40
Possunt, quia posse videntur, 306:5
Post [mail], lame, 419:72
    o'er land and ocean, 167:31
    [stay] for the letter, 395:51
Post between you and me and, 362:32
    from pillar to, 371:68
Post hoc; ergo propter, 406:45
Postchaise, driving briskly in, 133:40
Posteriors of this day, 246:13
Posterity done, what has, 204:6, 303:18
    hope of, 86:13
    mankind and, 128:15
    shall sway, thy, 74:11
    think of your, 15:5
Postern door makes thief, 421:62
    latched its, 116:9
Postume, anni labuntur, 24:11
Postumus, Postumus, alas, 125:28
Postures were, same our, 84:9
Posy, with her maiden, 296:13
Pot by the fire, freeze, 392:36
    calls the kettle black, 421:63
    cometh last to, 376:55
    death in the, 325:54

is soon hot, little, 352:28
must keep clear, earthen, 416:37
never boils, watched, 354:29
shall have ten hoops, 237:33
young sheep to, 358:41
Potations, banish strong, 179:30
Potato, bashful young, 104:38
Potomac, quiet along the, 27:23
Pottage, if you drink in, 387:52
in another's man's, 409:65
mess of, 323:31
prettiness makes no, 406:61
whole pot of, 404:49
you love, what, 404:56
Pouch on side, 216:17
Poultice, silence like a, 122:11
Pouncet-box, held a, 231:34
Pound, comes by, 399:71
foolish, penny wise, 406:75
give thee a silver, 54:22
in for, 389:42
shall never be worth, 382:2
'tis for a thousand, 75:29
to be fined forty, 60:2
Pounds a year, rich with forty, 108:19
a year, three hundred, 256:13
a year, two hundred, 48:25
draw for a thousand, 16:5
take a farthing from a thousand, 412:65
will take care of themselves, 412:68
Pours, never rains but it, 392:26
[Poverty], being ashamed of, 406:51
breeds strife, 406:47
but not my will, 268:6
comes in at the door, 436:23
debt is the worst, 366:19
depress'd, worth by, 130:9
dined with, 406:64
enemy to, 360:10
great, 401:48
is in want of much, 406:48
is no disgrace, 281:16
is no sin, 406:49
is no vice, 406:50
is not a shame, 406:51
is the mother of all arts, 406:52
is the mother of health, 406:53
key to, 411:59
more easy to praise, 391:76
parteth fellowship, 406:54
parteth friends, 406:54
will bear itself, 360:21

Pow, blessings on your frosty, 45:42
Powder without ball, 426:34
Powder's runnin' low, when, 183:20
Power and stronger, mightier, 307:18
and the glory, 333:48
balance of, 307:32
doth then show likest God's, earthly,
255:33
force of temporal, 255:33
knowledge is, 393:73
lead life to sovereign, 292:14
of speech, strange, 69:33
pomp of, 112:9
proud Edward's, 47:23
relentless, 112:1
self-dependent, 131:22
shall fall short in, 36:18
tends to corrupt, 15:2
than use, rather in, 213:24
that pities me, 108:6
to chasten, of ample, 316:14
to hurt, that have, 265:18
Powers, deem that there are, 316:7
princedoms, virtues, 172:16
that be, 338:18
we lay waste our, 319:28
Poy, I haf von funny leedle, 15:3
Practice makes perfect, 406:55
what you preach, 406:52
Prague, beautiful city of, 200:20
Praise, all his pleasure, 187:25
as they turn from, 36:9
at the shout of, 24:14
blame, love, 318:13
damn with faint, 198:2
dies, old, 404:15
foolish face of, 198:2
girded with, 111:26
him and magnify him, 340:30
himself, is fain to, 375:72
if there be any, 339:53
it, or blame it too much, scarcely can,
109:33
makes good men better, 406:58
named thee but to, 115:17
nor dispraise thyself, neither, 401:49
oblique, 133:44
of whom to be disprais'd were no small,
174:4
record, no panegyric need, 80:7
swells the note of, 112:10
there were none to, 316:19

things thou wouldst, 80:17
to the face, 406:59
to their right, 256:4
too much, 431:61
world conspires to, 198:21
Praised more than practised, 406:28
Praiser of times past, 126:3
Praiseth himself, he that, 380:33
Praising what is lost, 213:33
Prattle to be tedious, thinking his, 244:8
Praxed's ear to pray, Saint, 39:25
Pray as ever dying, 394:3
he that would learn to, 382:16
let him, 378:6
one to watch and one to, 16:9
pain both to pay and, 390:12
remain'd to, 109:23
Saint Praxed's ear to, 39:35
so, so give alms, 274:2
to whom the Romans, 154:5
to work is to, 394:2
without ceasing, 339:57
Prayer all his business, 187:25
but little devotion, much, 375:68
doth teach us all, 255:33
erects a house of, 80:5
four [hours] spend in, 68:12
lift one thought in, 71:23
more things are wrought by, 297:42
pray but one, 180:3
reduces itself to this, 303:25
Prayers and provender hinder no man's
journey, 406:60
fall to thy, 234:37
feed on, 189:17
for a pretence make long, 336:5
which are age his alms, 189:17
wouldn't say his, 204:5
Prayeth best who loveth best, 70:2
well, he, 70:1
Prays for, whatever a man, 303:25
Preach again, never sure to, 26:5
goat might, 386:13
practise what you, 406:56
Preached against stealing, 418:13
as never sure, 26:5
Preacher cries, sacred, 86:4
here lies the, 130:10
needs no, 381:72
Preaches well that lives well, 376:53
Preacheth, he that, 380:34
Preaching, a woman's, 132:21

Precedent to precedent, from, 292:22
Precept, better than, 369:60
ending with some, 200:2
upon precept, 331:57
Precepts in thy memory, 221:37
Precincts, left the warm, 112:17
Precious, one half so, 99:18
to me, were most, 250:24
Precipices, high places have, 383:57
Precise in every part, too, 120:6
Precisian, devil turned, 159:32
Predestination in the stride, 140:5
round enmesh me, with, 98:15
Predominance, by spherical, 240:11
Prefaces, read all the, 288:10
Preferment out, to seek, 272:24
Prejudices a man so, it, 281:24
Premier pas, il n'y a que le, 80:3
Prentice han' she tried on man, 44:3
Preparation, dreadful note of, 236:10
no formal, 31:33
Prepared for either event, 305:33
Presbyter is but old Priest, new, 167:33
Presbyterian true blue, 48:11
Presence, lord of thy, 239:37
made better by their, 93:26
scanter of your maiden, 222:2
that disturbs me, 316:14
Present [now], act in the living, 149:29
are judged, things, 426:15
day, deficiencies of, 131:29
day, pleasures of, 86:4
day, seize the, 125:25
has latched its postern, 116:9
in spirit, 338:21
no time like, 402:33
nor things to come, things, 338:13
[seem] worst, things, 234:9
Present [gift], for an un-birthday, 59:29
Presentment, counterfeit, 226:2
Presents endear Absents, 143:41
President, rather be right than be, 67:26
Press, liberty of the, 135:23
Pressed men, worth two, 404:70
Pretender, God bless, 49:33
Prettiness makes no pottage, 406:61
Pretty is, every thing that, 219:30
little things are, 395:18
Prevention is better than cure, 406:62
Previous study, result of, 21:25
Prey, destined, 274:15
fastened on her, 202:4

have they not divided, 324:23
sports not with, 356:44
Preys do rouse, to their, 249:41
Priam's curtain, drew, 233:49
Price, all those men have, 307:30
cheat me in, 364:14
of everything, knows, 314:9
of love, true, 397:55
pearl of great, 324:24
raise the volume's, 288:10
set her own, 188:4
Prick and sting her, to, 222:18
Pricking, knight was, 283:23
Pricks, kick against, 337:60
Pride and grace, 406:63
breakfasted with Plenty, 406:64
crueltie, and ambition, 202:14
dined with Poverty, 406:64
feels no cold, 406:65
fell with my fortunes, 215:32
goes before, 406:66
goeth before destruction, 329:36
is as loud a beggar, 406:67
naething here but Highland, 45:33
never-failing vice, 192:5
not exempt from, 145:17
perished in his, 317:34
pomp, and circumstance, 261:35
poor man's, 416:30
that apes humility, 70:16, 282:11
that licks the dust, 198:7
vain was the sage's, 198:16
will have a fall, 406:68
with a greater pride, despises, 425:52
Priest, all sides of, 362:38
continues what the nurse began, 90:10
fetch the devil a, 440:59
forgets that he was clerk, 421:65
pale-eyed, 163:25
still is Nature's, 319:35
turn, 388:5
woman or, 402:20
writ large, old, 167:33
Priests, tapers, temples, 194:9
Prime, lovely April of her, 263:30
Primrose by a river's brim, 316:16
first-born child of Ver, 100:7
pale, 219:37
path of dalliance, 220:36
sweet as the, 109:30
that forsaken dies, rathe, 167:22
was to him, a, 316:16

way, go the, 249:24
Primroses that die unmarried, 274:1
Prince, draweth his sword against, 438:35
on this afflicted, 100:1
who made thee a, 323:42
Princerple, I don't believe in, 151:34
Princes and lords may flourish, 108·15
ears and eyes of, 412:33
put not your trust in, 328:14
sweet aspect of, 238:16
Princess, fitting for a, 239:19
Principalities, nor powers, 338:13
Principle, necessary, and fundamental, 29:26
rebels from, 43:31
Principles, chang'd their, 322:10
religious and moral, 20:11
Print it, 'sdeath! I'll, 197:39
it, some said, 42:14
left the flushed, 298:35
see one's name in, 49:39
seeing our names in, 64:17
Printing, invented the art of, 57:23
to be used, caused, 238:2
Prior, what once was Matthew, 200:13
Priscian a little scratched, 246:11
Priscian's head, to break, 427:74
Prison, let's away to, 242:9
make, walls do not, 151:25
Prison-air, bloom well in, 314:16
Prisoner's life, passing on, 252:4
Prison-house, secrets of my, 222:12
Private, drunken, 88:7
person, put off, 380:37
Privilege, for the glorious, 45:26
Prize, bound for the, 264:14
we sought is won, 312:17
Prizes, to offer glittering, 29:20
won hundreds of, 344:9
Probationer, a young, 90:15
Proceedings, subsequent, 116:23
Procession, it is an ill, 390:31
Proconsul, the great, 153:28
Procrastination is the thief of time, 322:2
Procul hinc, qui, 183:23
Prodigal in a coach, young, 443:38
make men, 373:50
robs his heir, 421:66
Prodigies, Africa and her, 35:21
surprise, what, 130:14
Pro-di-gi-ous ! 212:2
Produce it in God's name, 57:27

Product, infinitesimal fraction of a, 57:27
Profession, incidents of, 304:4
Professions, most dangerous of, 179:27
Professors, mair use to, 155:22
Proffered service stinks, 406:69
Profit a man, what shall it, 336:2
  hath a man, what, 330;6
  honour and, 384:5
  honour without, 384:5
Profits, small, 411:65
Profusus, sui, 208:6
Progeny of learning, a, 277:35
Proie attachée, à sa, 202:4
Project for extracting sunbeams, 288:17
Promethean heat, that, 262:10
Promise and give nothing, 430:7
  failed and bright, 118:5
  is debt, 406:70
  keep the word of, 251:42
  nothing, that can, 376:25
  who broke no, 197:35
Promised on a time, I was, 284:3
Promises and delays, who, 376:36
  and pie-crusts, 406:71
  are either broken or kept, 356:5
  too much, he that, 380:35
Promontory, sat upon a, 257:31
  sterile, 223:37
  with trees upon't, 214:14
Promotion, none will sweat but for, 215:43
Pronounce, spell better than they, 303:27
Proof, give me the ocular, 261:36
  of the pudding, 421:67
  that he had rather, 131:20
Proofs, how I would correct, 66:24
Prop, when you do take, 255:40
Proper man, a, 257:30
  men and tall, 88:6
  men as ever trod, 228:3
Properer man, the, 421:68
Property has its duties, 89:18
Prophecy, urn of bitter, 277:26
Prophet, in the name of, 280:3
  is not without honour, 324:25
  new inspired, I am, 243:28
Prophets, beware of false, 324:25
  old, Tiresias and Phineus, 170:16
  Saul also among, 324:30
Propontic, on to the, 261:41
Proportion, curtailed of this fair, 244:12
Propose, wy don't the men, 26:9
Propriety in Paradise, sole, 172:2

Propter hoc, ergo, 406:45
Prose and poetry, definitions, 71:29
  je dis de la, 174:38
  or rhyme, unattempted yet in, 168:2
  run mad, 198:1
  verse will seem, 41:32
  without knowing it, talking, 174:38
Proserpina, O, 274:1
Prospect is often better than possession,
    406:72
  noblest, 132:18
Prospect pleases, every, 118:11
Prosper, ill-gotten gains seldom, 388:19
  treason doth never, 116:13
Prosperity, in time of, 389:60
  swells in, 382:34
Prostitute away, puff the, 91:34
Protest too much, doth, 225:25
Protestant to be, thy, 120:8
Proteus rising from the sea, 319:29
Proud and great, be very, 286:15
  and he's great, he's, 181:22
  and mighty have, all, 92:16
  as a peacock, 358:26
  as Lucifer, 358:27
  folks, good beating, 391:45
  is she not sweet, 207:33
  man hath many crosses, 353:69
  to fight, too, 315:24
  to importune, too, 113:33
  word you never spoke, 145:17
Prouder than rustling in unpaid-for silk,
    219:33
Prove all things, 339:58
  thy friend, 406:73
Provender, bear his own, 390:16
Proverb and a byword, 325:43
  haunts my mind, 87:19
  is much matter, a, 102:13
  is something musty, 225:29
Proverbed, I am, 243:29
Proverbs are the daughters, 406:74
  patch grief with, 258:42
  wise men make, 440:15
Proves too much, 414:30
Provide for the worst, 406:75
Providence, assert eternal, 168:3
  behind a frowning, 76:20
  has sent me, 45:33
  is better than rent, 406:76
  is not bound, 387:57
  reason'd high of, 169:40

special, 227:50
their guide, 173:48
trust in His, 308:6
Provident, [make men], 373:50
Province, all knowledge to be my, 22:20
Provincial, worse than, 129:26
Prowl and prowl around, 182:10
Prows, with cleaving, 36:13
Prudence, right eye of, 366:34
Prudes for proctors, 294:6
Prunella, but leather or, 196:4
Prunes and prism, 84:17
Prussic acid, she drank, 24:7
Pryeth into every cloud, 380:36
Psalm, the Hundreth, 54:5
Psalmist saith, as the, 234:22
Psalms, turn'd to holy, 189:17
Πτολίεθρον, δαιμόνιον, 190:14
Pub as a valuable institution, 119:36
Public gown, puts on, 380:37
  is an old woman, the, 57:36
  like a frog, how, 84:24
  opinion, 128:12
  ridiculous as the British, 153:23
  to speak in, 96:4
  ungrateful animal, 116:37
Publican, like a fawning, 253:38
  or even as this, 336:34
Publish it not in the streets, 324:34
  it to all the nation, 200:7
Puck, just a streak of, 118:20
Pudding against empty praise, 194:12
  better some of, 362:15
  hath two [ends], 369:52
  love thee like, 384:36
  proof of, 421:67
  settles love, cold, 364:40
  so is a, 440:58
Pudding-race, chieftain o', 45:30
Puddings, eat dirty, 384:71
Puddle, path hath, 369:46
Puff not against the wind, 406:79
Pull down, easier to, 391:40
Pulpit, drum ecclesiastic, 48:2
Pulpits and Sundays, 119:39
Pulse, as yours, doth temperately keep
    time, my, 226:7
  failing, his, 88:15
  to know the world's, 425:54
Pumpkins blow, the early, 147:18
  into coaches, turn, 300:5
Pun, make so vile a, 81:24

not a feather to tickle the intellect, 144:3
  pistol let off at the ear, 144:3
Punch [drink], forsook hewing, for, 398:2
Punch [stamp], with care, 34:9
Punctilio, none of your, 160:35
Punctuality is the politeness of princes,
    406:80
  is the soul of business, 406:81
Punishment fit the crime, 106:12
  in itself is evil, 28:6
  is greater, my, 323:23
  is mischief, 28:6
  like, 395:80
  pleasing, 218:17
  sin brings its, 369:48
  wise in, 379:67
Puns, from politics to, 200:2
Pupil of the human eye, like, 179:18
Puppets, best and worst, are we, 37:22
  shut up the box and, 282:19
Pur comme un ange, 291:17
Pure all things are pure, unto, 339:65
  as an angel, 291:17
  as snow, 224:9
  from the night, 160:21
  in heart, blessed are, 332:36
  in thought as angels, 205:14
  mind, man cannot have, 143:40
  the real Simon, 61:21
  whatsoever things are, 339:53
Purer than the purest, 38:16
Purgatory, this life's, 399:42
Purge, and leave sack, 233:48
Purger of goods, violent, 47:42
Puritan hated bear-baiting, 153:31
Puritans, great artists never, 160:7
Purity, all trial, all, 218:10
Purple and fine linen, 336:29
  Cow, I never saw a, 42:18
  Cow, I wrote the, 42:19
  with love's wound, 257:32
Purples, which outredden, 294:24
Purpose, infirm of, 249:22
  pushes his prudent, 322:3
  shake my fell, 247:35
Purse be your master, let, 395:52
  beggar's, 349:11
  but an empty, 414:24
  can buy, costly as, 221:38
  consumption of the, 234:7
  empty, 33:14
  he that shows, 381:49

Q

Queens have died young and fair, 182:6
  in the hands of, 148:14
Queer, all the world is, 186:10
  ill-tempered and, 147:13
  thou art a little, 186:10
Queerest schap, der, 15:3
Quest, what thy, 33:17
Question is ever settled, no, 313:31
  makes of Ayes or Noes, 98:12
  others abide our, 18:15
  that is the, 223:41
  two sides to, 424:17
Questionings, obstinate, 319:38
Questions, ask no, 359:75
  fool may ask more, 350:34
  they ask no, 93:20
Quick as thought, 358:28
  at meat, quick at work, 408:8
  we must live by the, 434:20
Quickly come, quickly go, 408:9
  good and, 373:47
  who gives, 363:43
Quickness, with too much, 197:22
Quid, Buntline turned his, 191:21
Quidquid agunt homines, 135:25
Quiescence, he boasts his, 37:26
Quiet along the Potomac, 27:23
  as a mouse, 358:29

as a stone, 137:32
hours of [life] few, 207:30
life, anything for, 356:64
on the Western front, 203:22
she reposes, in, 19:24
study to be, 339:56
when children stand, 436:9
Quietness, bride of, 137:21
  is best, 408:10
Quietus make, might his, 224:4
Quince and plum and gourd, 136:13
Quintessence they still, heavenly, 156:12
Quintilian stare and gasp, made, 167:28
Quip Modest, second, 218:13
Quips, and cranks, and wanton wiles,
    163:33
  and sentences, 258:20
  and thy quiddities, 231:27
Quire, to the full-voiced, 165:25
Quit, more than, 200:7
  quit, for shame, 288:2
  you like men, 339:37
  yourselves like men, 324:29
Quiver full of them, hath, 328:6
Quocumque modo, si non, 125:34
Quote, grow immortal as they, 322:6
  it, kill you if you, 42:19
Quousque tandem, 66:17

R

Race, amiable but degraded, 88:4
  appointed for my second, 304:9
  build a generous, 208:12
  he rides a, 75:29
  is just begun, whose, 276:6
  is not to the swift, 330:25
  shall rise, loftier, 290:5
  slinks out of the, 174:30
  the feather'd, 102:4
  type of all her, 88:7
  well run, life's, 162:15
  what avails the sceptred, 144:12
Racer, proud high-bred, 70:19
Rack behind, leave not, 269:40

stretch'd on the, 194:22
Racks, gibbets, halters, 185:19
Radiance, stains the white, 276:16
Rage, Heav'n has no, 72:9
  puts all Heaven in, 30:9
  tempering virtuous, 199:19
  with hard-favour'd, 236:5
Raggedness, loop'd and window'd, 241:30
Rags, as filthy, 332:10
Railed on Lady Fortune, 216:7
Railer, blustering, 285:28
Raillery, would not bear, 213:23
Railway share, with a, 60:1
Raiment, in sparkling, 17:24

Rain, a mist and a weeping, 154:14
and leave, it will, 387:36
as I have loved the, 64:18
before seven, 408:13
bring down, 368:17
came down in slanting lines, 279:32
droppeth as the gentle, 255:33
earth soaks up, 74:3
for morning, 371:44
for four weeks, 386:22
for thirty days, 386:11
go to Spain, 408:14
gull comes against, 419:40
if thou dost, 409:49
is over and gone, 331:40
it is not raining, 151:27
it raineth every day, 272:21
it raineth on the just, 32:6
lays great dust, small, 411:66
makes not fresh, 100:3
na mair, 'twill, 409:49
on the just, sendeth, 333:46
rains on, corpse, 374:19
right as, 358:33
ripple of, 290:1
silver, 100:1
tears are in the falling, 147:26
the volleying, 19:29
thresh of the deep-sea, 140:9
when it begins to, 375:43
Rainbow, a smiling, 57:39
add another hue unto, 240:2
and a cuckoo's song, 79:31
at night, 353:72
comes and goes, 319:30
in the eve, 387:36
in the morning, 353:72
in the morrow, 387:36
in the sky, 317:29
live, in the colours of, 165:36
love unreturned has, 25:27
when I behold, 317:29
Rainbow's glory is shed, 277:22
lovely form, like, 46:10
Rained, and then it snew, 345:25
Rains and the sun shines, 436:16
but it pours, it never, 392:26
Raise the devil, easier to, 391:41
Raison ne conait point, 187:29
Rake among scholars, a, 153:30
lean as, 358:7
little for, 424:34

man's a, 106:7
thus playing the, 179:17
to break your heart, 361:75
woman is at heart a, 197:24
Ralph the Rover-tore his hair, 282:7
Ralph to Cynthia howls, 194:19
Ram, the Bull, the Heavenly Twins, 346:3
Rampallian, you, 234:10
Ramparts we watched, o'er, 138:17
Ran, and they ran, we, 115:23
certain of your brethren, roar'd and,
219:21
Rang, crab-tree and old iron, 48:17
Ranges, something lost behind, 140:1
Rank is but the guinea's stamp, 47:31
on rank, marched, 161:24
thee, how shall we, 177:25
Ranks and squadrons, in, 229:23
close fast the, 311:29
of Tuscany, even the, 154:6
schoolboy rallies, 183:25
Ransom, worth a king's, 349:31
Rant and we'll roar, we'll, 343:40
as well as thou, I'll, 227:42
Rap, ever yet worth a, 110:14
Raphaels, talk'd of their, 110:3
Rapidity, in proportion to, 207:26
Rapids are near, the, 177:26
Rapine, to march through, 107:32
Rapping, someone gently, 191:24
Rapture, first fine careless, 38:5
on the lonely shore, 51:27
Raptures and roses of vice, 289:36
that yourselves infuse, 291:20
Rara avis in terris, 135:28
Rare bird on the earth, 135:28
Rarely, rarely, comest thou, 277:20
Rarity, alas for the, 124:9
Rascals naked, to lash the, 262:5
Rash, not splenetive and, 227:41
too unadvised, too sudden, too, 267:27
Raskills, to take care o', 93:23
Rasselas, history of, 131:29
Rast, ohne, 107:38
Rat, how now! a, 225:41
I smell a, 204:7
in a hole, poisoned, 289:23
Raths outgrabe, the mome, 58:17
Rationed, so precious that it must be, 148:4
Rations, upon our daily, 83:48
Rats desert, 408:17
Muse, let's sing of, 111:25

Rattle, mingles war's, 210:2
  pleased with a, 195:41
Rave, recite, and madden, 197:37
Raven, locks were like the, 45:42
  'Nevermore', quoth, 191:26
Ray, Eden-sweet the, 160:14
  emits a brighter, 110:4
  of rays, sun of suns, 84:13
  on ray split the shroud, 40:17
Razor, like a polished, 176:9
Reach it, I cannot, 304:16
  me more, never, 75:34
  should exceed his grasp, 39:34
  me this, come, 393:67
Read anything which I call a *book*, I can,
  144:1
  blockhead ignorantly, 193:20
  books through, do you, 133:29
  everybody wants to have, 304:1
  in the best company, 281:22
  just as inclination leads, 132:19
  mark, learn, 341:38
  nobody wants to, 304:1
  nor write, better to be able neither to,
  117:36
  with gentle breast, 71:23
Reade all at my ease, 314:22
Reader reads no more, last, 122:13
  should strike the, 138:4
  easy writing's curst hard, 278:12
Reader's threaten'd, the, 192:15
Readeth, he may run that, 332:27
Reading, art of, 354:4
  I prefer, 280:10
  is to the mind, 284:17
  maketh a full man, 22:17
Reads as a task, what he, 132:19
Ready and strong, 310:2
  all is quickly, 388:29
  ere I call'd her name, 200:9
Real than living man, forms more, 277:23
  Realm, o'er the azure, 113:30
  to that mysterious, 41:26
Realms and islands were as plates, 214:19
  obey, whom three, 193:27
Reap and mow, 343:21
  that shall he also, 399:45
Reaper whose name is Death, 149:30
Reason, asked one another, 218:8
  can, shew no, 309:23
  capability and god-like, 226:15
  feast of, 198:9

for my rhyme, to have, 284:3
for this plain, 195:32
hearken to, 383:45
how noble in, 223:37
in roasting of eggs, 425:51
is left free, 129:30
knows nothing, of which, 187:29
lies between, 408:21
men have lost, 229:39
men that can render, 329:57
no other but a woman's, 273:23
noble and most sovereign, 224:12
now tell me the, 282:8
on compulsion, give, 232:12
prisoner takes the, 247:27
pursue my, 35:20
rules all things, 408:22
ruling passion conquers, 197:31
themselves out, 237:23
wants discourse of, 221:23
why, any other, 17:16
why I cannot tell, 35:16
why I clasp them, 73:24
why, theirs not to, 295:27
why, will know the, 117:28
will be heard, 383:45
Reason's spite, in erring, 195:37
Reasonable man adapts himself, 275:19
Reasonableness, sweet, 20:8
Reasons, finding of bad, 32:9
  two very cogent, 133:48
  we should drink, 17:16
  were as plentiful, 232:12
Rebel, use 'em kindly, they, 121:21
Rebellion, Rum, Romanism and, 42:16
Rebels from principle, 43:31
Rebuff, welcome each, 39:43
Recall, give pleasure to, 305:29
Recalled, past cannot be, 426:14
Recapture, he never could, 38:5
Received, freely ye have, 324:12
Receiver is as bad, 421:70
Receives, but nothing gives, 104:12
Reckless, so incensed that I am, 249:53
Reckon frae an ill hour, 409:71
  without one's host, 430:13
Reckoning, a trim, 233:42
  even, 368:16
  the fouler, 417:56
  till we come to, 399:63
  to the end of, 432:9
Reckonings, short, 410:37, 410:38

Recommendation, letter of, 351:55
  self-praise is no, 410:12
Recompense send, Heav'n did, 113:20
Records, wipe away all trivial fond, 222:20
  with half a dozen, 275:22
Recover, mightst him yet, 88:15
Recte, si possis, 125:34
Rectitude, conscious of, 305:30
  unctuous, 203:27
Reculer, il faut, 388:14
Recurret, tamen usque, 125:40
Red and bad, 369:67
  and white, whose, 271:32
  as a rose is she, 69:19
  as a turkey-cock, 358:30
  azure, white and, 89:19
  celestial rosy, 173:31
  Flag flying, keep the, 72:13
  is wise, 427:59
  it never dies, 86:2
  line of 'eroes, thin, 141:35
  making the green one, 249:23
  man read thy rede, to, 427:59
  men scalped each other, 153:29
  never blows so, 98:2
  nor dim nor, 69:21
  rag to a bull, like, 395:70
  with the wreck of a square, 183:25
Redbud, buckerry, 292:1
Rede, read thy, 427:59
  recks not his own, 221:36
  short rede, good, 410:39
  take heed is a good, 412:69
Redeemer liveth, I know my, 326:3
Redemption, condemned into everlasting,
    259:39
  from hell, no, 425:45
Redire quemquam, unde negant, 60:13
Redress, things past, 243:35
Redressed, half, 350:33
Reed, on a slender, 305:21
  shaken with the wind, 324:16
  shall he not break, 332:2
Reeds by the river, in the, 36:11
  stand the storm, 403:63
Reef, thundering on the, 294:2
Reek o' the rotten fens, 219:26
Reel to and fro, they, 327:60
Reeling and writhing, 58:11
References, verify your, 207:21
Refined age, disgust this, 96:3
Reform peace, retrenchment and, 33:24

stop the progress of, 281:14
Reformation, reforming of, 175:33
Reformers are bachelors, 177:23
Refuge and my fortress, my, 327:54
  and strength, God is, 327:37
Refuse a good offer, never, 401:61
  money you, 420:25
  the wretched, 146:8
Regard, should be without, 249:34
Regent's eyes, dewy were, 308:16
Reges, quidquid delirant, 125:35
Regiment from behind, led, 106:21
  of Women, Monstrous, 143:34
Regions Caesar never knew, 74:11
Regret, wild with all, 294:14
Regular, icily, 296:9
Reign over us, long to, 343:23
  spurn her bounded, 130:16
Reigns, but does not govern, 322:12
  like Tom the First, 90:11
Reihen dicht geschlossen, 311:29
Reject him, fired that the house, 197:39
Rejoice and be glad in it, 328:1
  O young man, 330:31
  with me, 336:22
Rejoices, heart that never, 390:14
Relate, there's little to, 59:34
Relations, direct and even divine, 65:27
Relative way, in the, 344:14
Release, prisoner's, 278:20
Relics, his hallow'd, 163:28
Relief much thanks, for this, 220:4
Relies on, promise none, 204:8
Religion blushing veils, 194:24
  bringeth minds to, 22:13
  brings him about again to our, 102:10
  is allowed to invade, 160:5
  is the best armour, 408:25
  is the opium, 158:18
  ist das Opium, 158:18
  matters not what, 392:24
  no honour to, 402:25
  pure, 317:40
  what damned error, in, 254:24
  will glide out of the mind, 132:1
  wrangle for, 72:3
Relish is so sweet, imaginary, 270:16
Rem, cunctando restituit, 95:29
  facias, rem, 125:34
Remain, as things have been, 68:1
Remains, be kind to my, 190:12
Remark, which I wish to, 116:21

Remarkable man, this very, 128:11
nothing left, 214:17
Remarks before us, said our, 86:6
Ρήμασι πειθόμενοι, 279:23
Remedies, desperate, 366:31
oft in ourselves do lie, 213:27
Remedy against an ill man, 415:50
but patience, no, 402:27
for everything but death, 424:23
for injuries, 421:71
for love, 421:72
is worse, 421:73
sought the, 218:8
there is, 371:46
things without all, 249:34
to all diseases, 47:41
worse than disease, 22:12
Remember and be sad, 206:9
as much as the oldest man can, 388:34
for years, to, 18:2
I remember, I, 123:38, 123:39
if thou wilt, 206:10
me, Oh! still, 177:28
me when I am gone, 206:8
please to, 345:26
such things were, cannot but, 250:24
sweet to, 414:36
thee, yet will I, 76:18
them, we will, 29:19
with tears, to, 18:2
Remembered, in their flowing cups, 237:18
Remembering you, we will be brave, 24:12
Remembers himself, 380:32
Remembrance, appear almost, 138:4
dear, makes, 213:33
I summon up, 264:2
Remote from man, 187:25
unfriended, melancholy, slow, 108:1
Re-mould it nearer to the Heart's Desire, 99:20
Remove an old tree, 408:26
Removes, three, 426:40
Remuneration! Latin word, 246:4
Rend pas, elle ne se, 54:11
Render unto Caesar, 325:44
Renown, equall'd with them in, 170:16
just and old, 292:22
of credit and, 75:26
shall forfeit fair, 209:24
some for, 322:6
Rent [payment], better than, 407:76
Rent [tear] the envious Casca made, 230:1

Repairing, ship and a woman are ever, 354:8
Repay, I will, 338:15
Repeateth a matter, that, 329:38
Repeats it, he that knows little soon, 380:2
Repent at leisure, 399:44
before you die, 387:65
for doing good, never did, 255:29
it from my very soul, 270:12
straight they will, 56:3
live to, 399:45
Repentance comes too late, 408:27
Garment of, 97:28
is seldom true, late, 394:10
need no, 336:23
short acquaintance brings, 410:34
Reply Churlish, third, 218:13
theirs not to make, 295:27
Report divine, from, 312:6
me and my cause aright, 227:53
Reporters sit, gallery in which, 153:21
Reports of my death, 304:2
Repose, earned a night's, 150:1
gives way to in, 248:11
in statue-like, 17:17
manners had not, 292:15
seek not yet, 94:4
Reprehend anything, if I, 277:36
Representation, no taxation without, 402:32
Reproach, sting of, 422:30
Reprobation, fall to, 262:13
Reproof on her lip, 151:28
public, 407:78
Valiant, fourth, 218:13
Republic her station, gave, 180:2
Republican form of government, 283:20
Republicans, we are, 42:16
Reputation dies, at every word a, 193:28
I have lost my, 260:23
seeking the bubble, 216:17
written out of, 28:11
Requited, both are alike, 186:9
Res angusta domi, 135:27
Researches, with no deep, 77:25
Resemble her to thee, 307:26
Resent, no individual could, 288:13
Reside in thrilling region, 252:18
Residence, a forted, 253:24
Resistance, wrong that needs, 23:33
Resisted, know not what's, 44:22
Resolution, native hue of, 224:4

Resolve, a heart to, 104:10
Resolves; and re-resolves, 322:3
Respect a man, 408:29
  greatest, 418:34
Respectable, genius found, 36:10
  not one is, 312:14
  seldom even ordinarily, 160:7
  to what is, 124:11
Respected, is not, 381:38
Respecter of persons, no, 337:61
Respects not, he that, 381:38
Rest [repose], absence of occupation is not, 74:18
  angels sing thee to, 228:2
  brave who sink to, 71:33
  cometh great, 408:72
  dove found no, 323:25
  far, far better, 84:58
  gets him to, 236:13
  I will give you, 324:18
  now cometh, 162:15
  now she's at, and so am I, 90:17
  of sufferance cometh, 403:75
  perturbed spirit, 223:25
  rest, for evermore, 206:6
  seals up all in, 264:13
  so may he, 239:22
  without, 107:38
Rest [remainder], name led all the, 128:1
  nowhere, Eclipse first, 185:18
  the sun goes round, take all, 307:23
Reste, j'y suis, j'y, 155:25
Resting-place, laid it in, 279:33
Result happiness, 84:5
Resurrection, hope of the, 341:55
  I am the, 337:50
  looking for, 341:56
Retained, longer, 426:13
Retirement, must be no, 115:13
  rural quiet, 300:10
  urges sweet return, short, 173:34
Retort Courteous, first, 218:13
Retreat, a friend in my, 75:19
  I will not, 102:20
  in, 388:30
Return, never must, 166:12
Returning were as tedious as go o'er, 250:10
Returns, quick, 411:65
  whence they say none, 60:13
Reveal himself to his servants, 175:33
Revelry by night, sound of, 50:11

Revels by a forest side, midnight, 169:27
  now are ended, 269:40
Revenge, best, 396:22
  capable and wide, 261:41
  had stomach, my, 262:11
  if not victory is yet, 169:31
  is sweet, 408:31
  kind of wild justice, 22:10
  spur my dull, 226:15
  study of, 168:6
  sweet as my, 219:27
  sweet is, 52:16
Revenges, times brings in, 272:20
Revenons à nos moutons, 30:16
Revenue, thrift is good, 427:43
Reverence, claims to, 292:4
  none so poor to do him, 229:40
Reviewers, chorus of indolent, 295:37
Reviewing, read a book before, 281:24
Révolution, c'est une, 146:1
Revolutions are not made with rose-water, 153:17
  that makes, 104:6
Reward, desert and, 366:28
  service without, 410:19
  virtue is its own, 433:66
Rewards and fairies, 73:21
  are distant, 132:1
Reynolds is laid, here, 110:2
Rhein, die Wacht am, 208:14
Rhetoric, he could not one, for, 48:5
Rhetorician, sophistical, 85:37
Rheumatic of shoulder, 32:7
Rhine, watch on the, 208:14
  wide and winding, 50:17
Rhinoceros, the arm'd, 250:5
Rhone, rushing of the arrowy, 50:18
Rhyme being no necessary adjunct, 175:36
  build the lofty, 166:9
  making beautiful old, 265:23
  nor reason, received nor, 284:3
  outlive this powerful, 264:6
  the rudder is of verses, 48:16
  themselves into ladies' favours, 237:23
  those that write in, 48:20
Rhymes, Namby Pamby's little, 56:16
Rhyming mother wits, 156:9
  planet, born under, 259:44
Rib, under the fifth, 325:38
Riband bound, what this, 307:23
  in the cap of youth, 227:26
  just for a, 37:25

Judge of all the earth do, 323:30
little, tight little, 82:3
of way, died maintaining, 345:20
or wrang, makes us, 44:6
or wrong, our country, 80:2
than be President, rather be, 67:26
there is none to dispute, 75:20
thirsting for the, 295:24
too fond of the, 109:34
was clear, his, 345:20
were worsted, though, 40:20
Whatever is, is, 195:37
whose life is in the, 196:1
with firmness in, 148:11
wrong never comes, 441:52
wrongs no man, 409:41
Righteous are bold as a lion, 329:64
cause, armour of, 41:24
die the death of, 324:9
forsaken, not seen, 326:30
man regardeth the life of his beast, 328:27
overmuch, be not, 330:21
Righteousness and peace have kissed,
327:49
arise, Sun of, 332:30
in the way of, 329:37
Righteousnesses are as filthy rags, 332:10
Rights, certain unalienable, 129:29
duties as well as, 89:18
should lose, lest they, 303:18
of an Englishman, 135:23
Rim, over the mountain's, 37:34
utmost purple, 293:40
Ring I thee wed, with this, 341:50
like a great, 304:13
on her wand, gold, 177:31
on the finger, 384:5
out the old, 296:4
so worn, 77:29
the bells, they now, 307:31
time, only pretty, 218:11
wear the devil's gold, 28:33
Ring-a-rosie, tots sang, 29:29
Rings for buddin' Sally, 54:8
Rio, I'd like to roll to, 142:20
Riot, rash fierce blaze of, 243:28
Riotous living, with, 336:24
Ripe, from hour to hour we, 216:10
soon rotten, soon, 412:9
Ripeness is all, 242:8
Riper stage, amuse his, 195:41
Rise again, now they, 250:4

and fight again, I'll, 342:11
and trip away, then, 145:17
at five, must, 382:5
betimes, he must, 377:47
early, get a name to, 372:8
early, he must, 377:48
early, who does not, 382:28
easier to fall than, 391:39
loth to, 368:19
none can make you, 411:54
on stepping-stones, 295:38
sun to thee may never, 72:12
to-morrow, may, 378:22
up and fall, 362:13
Rises, gives light as soon as he, 101:29
over early, he, 377:57
Riseth first, he that, 381:39
River, Alph the sacred, 70:8
and o'er the lea, up, 122:6
by the door, living, 286:20
Dee, lived on the, 29:15
even the weariest, 289:38
floated on, majestic, 19:23
follow, 370:35
he swam the Eske, 210:8
in the reeds by, 36:11
join the brimming, 294:4
like the foam on, 211:26
save the rush of, 27:23
sea refuseth no, 422:12
snow falls in the, 46:10
sweeping, proud, 292:1
to flow away, waits for, 125:37
we'll gather at the, 152:1
Rivers, by shallow, 157:25
cannot quench, 238:9
of Damascus, 325:55
run into the sea, all, 330:8
wide, brooks and, 164:3
Rivulets dance their wayward round,
317:23
myriads of, 294:23
Roach, sound as, 358:44
Road all runners come, 126:12
beset the, 98:15
keep the common, 393:50
lies long and straight, 285:30
made the rolling English, 65:21
my mistress still the open, 287:25
no royal, 95:32
one that on a lonesome, 69:36
rule of the, 95:30

holiday, to make a, 51:25
State, lucky, 67:22
this was the noblest, 230:22
Roman's life, a, 154:5
Romance, brought up the nine-fifteen, 141:33
Romans do, do as, 436:6
last of all the, 230:21
were like brothers, 154:3
Rome, aisles of Christian, 94:21
all roads lead to, 356:6
falls, when, 51:26
grandeur that was, 191:28
hard to sit in, 391:60
in the height of her glory, 310:7
is burning, fiddle while, 428:27
keep his state in, 228:13
palmy state of, 220:8
pardoun come from, 63:36
shall stand, 51:26
thou hast lost the breed, 228:14
was not built in a day, 409:42
when at, 436:6
Romeo, wherefore art thou, 267:21
Roof, high embowed, 165:25
majestical, 223:37
under the shady, 165:26
Roofs of gold, building, 235:43
Room be poor indeed, though, 301:21
convent's narrow, 319:27
for Shakespeare, make, 26:3
from my lonely, 22:4
grows chilly, although, 111:20
in a Montreal lumber, 49:31
of one's own, a, 316:2
paces about her, 93:32
quickly make, 434:10
rather have your, 384:29
riches in a little, 157:21
Rooms at college, was beastly, 140:6
Roosian, might have been a, 105:32
Roost, curses come home to, 365:74
not the safest, 419:51
Root and all, and all in all, 295:35
nips his, 238:15
of the matter is found in me, 326:4
the insane, 247:27
Rope enough, give a thief, 372:10
his life to end, makes, 439:54
name not, 400:27
that hangs my dear, 103:32
Rorke, me and Mamie, 29:29

Rosaleen, my dark, 156:1
Rose [verb] like a rocket, 187:14
Rose [flower] at last is withered, 417:58
blossom as the, 331:58
blows so red the, 98:2
breast that gives the, 160:13
brings, a thousand, 97:29
bud doth the, 89:20
bud in the bright east, 304:8
die of a, 195:33
distill'd, happy is, 256:20
English unofficial, 34:2
go, lovely, 15:4, 307:26
I am not the, 72:17
is she, red as a, 69:19
je ne suis pas la, 72:17
labyrinthine buds the, 36:15
like a red, red, 47:25
like you, never a, 310:3
lovely is, 319:30
mighty lak' a, 284:14
of dawn, an awful, 293:47
of summer, last, 178:8
of the rosebud garden, queen, 296:18
of Yesterday, leaves, 97:29
of youth, wears, 214:9
pricked by, 361:56
ravage with impunity, 36:16
roves back, the, 81:18
should shut, as though, 136:12
Spring should vanish with, 99:19
that which we call, 267:22
thick with lily and, 180:6
wavers to a, 86:2
without a thorn, 155:26
without a thorn, no, 402:28
without thorn the, 171:27
Rose Aylmer, 144:13
Rosebud set with little wilful thorns, 294:7
Rosebuds, gather ye, 120:7
Rosemary and rue, for you, 273:43
that's for remembrance, 227:24
Rose-moles all in stipple, 124:16
Rose-red city, 43:20
Roses across the moon, two red, 180:4
and white lilies, 56:4
are flow'ring in Picardy, 310:3
at my head, plant thou no, 206:10
friends again with, 289:30
in December, seek, 50:1
on a stalk, four, 245:21
roses, all the way, 38:17

strew on her, 19:24
sweet days and, 119:42
when young, lie upon, 387:58
wore a wreath of, 26:10
Rose-water, revolutions are not made with, 153:17
Ross, sing the Man of, 197:32
Rosy are, 'cause another's, 315:27
is the West, 296:15
Rot, from hour to hour we, 216:10
lie in cold obstruction and, 252:18
Rote, perced to the, 63:19
Rothesay Bay, grand roun', 77:30
Rotten in the state of Denmark, something, 222:11
soon ripe, soon, 412:9
Rotundity, smite flat, 240:23
Rough as nutmeg-graters, 121:21
with the smooth, take, 430:34
Rough-hew them how we will, 227:41
Roughs, among his fellow, 88:7
Round, attains the upmost, 228:17
hole, square person has squeezed himself into, 280:12
in heaven a perfect, 39:41
me once again, 296:20
Round, the trivial, 138:7
Roundelay, merry, merry, 189:15
sing unto my, 62:14
Round, hoof'd, short-jointed, 263:23
Rousseau, mock on, 30:7
Rout, where meet a public, 79:28
Rover, living a, 26:6
whither away, fair, 33:17
Row [oar], brothers, row, 177:26
us out from Desenzano, 298:3
Row [brawl], awkward hand in a, 117:33
Royal George, down went, 75:25
Rub, there's the, 224:4
Rubies, better than, 328:22
price is far above, 330:3
Rubs in it, if it had no, 395:60
Rudder, bowsprit got mixed with, 59:38
ruled by, 439:59
Ruddier than the cherry, 103:29
Rude grant, better than, 350:8
he that is angry at a feast is, 379:60
Rue [regret], be sure you will it, 359:80
it for aye, you'll, 399:46
nought shall make us, 240:7
Rue [plant] and thyme grow both, 409:43
with a difference, wear your, 227:25

Ruffian, that father, 232:17
Ruhnken, learn'd professor, 199:30
Ruin hurl'd, systems into, 195:28
is at hand, 368:7
majestic though in, 169:37
seize thee, 113:28
upon ruin, rout on rout, 170:13
Ruined, many have been, 398:24
Rule, a little sway, a little, 92:16
alone, too fond to, 198:2
declar'd absolute, 171:28
exception proves, 417:49
exprest, by this, 193:41
good old, 318:8
long levell'd, 165:38
of men entirely great, beneath, 153:14
of the road, 95:30
only infallible, 288:9
reckoned competent to, 290:10
the state, ruin or to, 89:28
them with a rod of iron, 340:13
without some exception, no, 424:38
Ruled by him, be, 360:13
by his stepdame, 381:71
Ruler of the Queen's Navee, 105:28
Rules all things, reason, 408:22
never shows she, 197:26
twelve good, 109:29
Rum [liquor], bottle of, 286:9
Romanism and Rebellion, 42:16
Rum [queer] Go everything is, what, 311:19
Rumination, my often, 217:37
Rumour of oppression, 75:34
Rumours of wars, 325:49
Run away, they conquer Love that, 56:15
he may ill, 377:42
long, will not, 381:40
that readeth, he may, 332:27
to and fro, many shall, 332:22
with all your might, 201:28
Runcible cat, 147:19
Running, first sprightly, 91:39
Runs away, fights and, 378:26
fast, he that, 381:40
in the dark, he that, 381:41
with all his mane, 201:28
Rupert of debate, the, 153:16
of Parliamentary discussion, Prince, 85:30
Rural spot, woman in a, 126:36
Rushes and reeds, 373:64
Rushing of the arrowy Rhone, 50:18

Russia, night in, 252:6
Russian, scratch, 409:72
Rust, his good sword, 71:20
  out, than to, 78:9
Rustics, amazed the gazing, 109:27
Rusticus expectat, 125:37

Rusty, for want of fighting, 48:15
Ruth, the sad heart of, 137:20
Rye, coming through the, 47:35
  rob the blighted, 72:24
Rym dogerel, may wel be, 64:2

S

S.T.C., in prayer for, 71:23
Sabbath day, born on, 399:77
  hail, 111:22
  never broke the, 89:37
  was made for man, 325:63
Sabean odours, 171:24
Sable silver'd, 221:31
Sabrina fair, 166:6
Sack [bag], came nothing out of, 424:19
  cannot stand, empty, 356:31
  covetousness bursts, 365:61
  it is a bad, 399:3
  know by a handful the whole, 442:6
  lie not in one, 384:3
  [sow] not with the whole, 412:15
  the lot, 97:26
  wishes can never fill, 440:18
Sack [wine], intolerable deal of, 232:19
  purge, and leave, 233:48
Sacrifice, an unpitied, 43:24
  Thine ancient, 140:25
Sacrifices, upon such, 242:10
Sacristan, he says no word, 20:9
Sad and bad and mad, how, 40:3
  be not too, 403:76
  brow and true maid, 217:26
  tires in a mile-a, 273:42
Sadder and a wiser man, 70:3
Saddest are these, 313:18
  when I sing, I'm, 26:14
Saddle, always in the, 356:20
  fair in, 371:59
  foul, in, 369:70
  on the right horse, 410:24
Saddles him, he that, 419:58
Sadness and gladness, 409:45

most humorous, 217:37
Saeclum in favilla, solvet, 61:20
Safe home, bring, 396:11
  to be direct and honest is not, 261:39
  too secure is not, 379:74
  up, see me, 179:23
  way to be, 432:63
Safest, just when we are, 39:37
Safety, against the public, 73:19
  pluck this flower, 231:44
Sage in May, must eat, 382:17
  just less than, 177:25
  thought as a, 26:18
Sages can, than all the, 316:10
  have seen in thy face, 75:21
  of ancient time, 300:14
Said it, he himself has, 105:31
  it in Hebrew, I, 59:40
  it very loud and clear, 59:30
  soonest mended, least, 394:23
Sail, proud full, 264:14
  set every threadbare, 122:9
  shall never stretch, 52:2
  white and rustling, 78:11
Sailor, hear a brother, 285:28
Sailors of Bristol City, 299:29
Sails advance, we our, 88:12
  carry low, 352:31
  crowding, thy white, 33:17
  fill'd, and streamers waving, 174:18
  fill'd, t'have his, 62:1
  purple the, 214:2
  take the wind out of, 431:36
Saint, able to corrupt a, 231:29
  abroad, 354:3
  at fifteen, 354:39

follow your, 55:35
George, that swinged the dragon, 239:30
in carpe, 196:14
in lawn, twice a, 196:14
my late espousèd, 167:32
old devil, young, 443:39
Provoke, 'twould a, 196:16
seem a, 245:16
sustain'd it, 198:18
St. Agnes' Eve, 136:10
St. Andrews by the Northern Sea, 145:21
St. Bartholomew brings the cold dew,
   409:46
St. Bees, old man of, 107:27
St. Benedick, sow thy pease, 409:47
St. Crispin's day, upon, 237:20
St. James's, ladies of, 86:2
St. Matthie sends sap, 409:48
St. Paul's be fine, if, 386:10
St. Paul's, old as, 358:20
St. Paul's, sketch the ruins of, 153:26
St. Swithin's day, 409.49
St. Thomas grey, 409:50
St. Valentine, on, 404:19
St. Valentine's day, 404:21
St. Vitus's day be rainy weather if, 386:11
Sainted, ensky'd and, 252:1
Saints at the river, gather with, 152:1
   death of his, 327:62
   in glory stand, 321:38
   pair of carved, 244:2
   soul is with the, 71:20
   the ransomed, 17:24
   thy slaughter'd, 167:30
   with my lost, 36:9
Sair, kame sindle, kame, 393:42
Sairey, little do we know, 83:43
Sake, for old sake's, 139:31
Saki, you shall pass, 99:22
Salad days, my, 214:1
Salesman should select, 146:12
Salisbury, young curate of, 344:12
Sally, none like pretty, 56:17
Salmon and sermon, 409:51
   it was the, 82:8
   to catch a, 352:8
Salt, eat me without, 375:55
   have lost his savour, 333:38
   help me to, 383:51
   of the earth, ye are, 333:38
   on a bird's tail, 430:11
   seasons all things, 409:52

with him, eat a bushel of, 360:31
Salt-petre, villainous, 231:36
Salus populi, 67:16, 409:53
Salutary neglect, wise and, 43:26
Salute thee, Mantonvano, I, 298:2
Salvation, no relish of, 225:39
   none of us should see, 255:33
   work out your own, 339:50
Salve for every sore, 424:24
   seek your, 410:7
Samarcand, from silken, 136:13
Samarkand, Golden Road to, 99:27
Same, it will be all the, 392:31
   old slippers, 144:10
   thing, the more it is, 135:37
   to desire the, 208:7
   to-day and for ever, 303:21
   yesterday and to-day, 340:1
Samite, clothed in white, 296:22
Samphire, one that gathers, 241:48
Sampler, serve to ply the, 166:5
Samson, exclaimed Dominie, 212:2
Samson, Philistines be upon thee, 324:26
   was a strong man, 409:54
Sana in corpore sano, mens, 135:35
Sand against the wind, throw, 30:7
   as is the ribbed sea, 320:16
   doth feed the clay, 437:43
   little grains of, 57:41
   palace built upon, 162:10
   roll down their golden, 118:10
   shadows pass gigantic on, 99:29
   through beds of, 19:23
   world in a grain of, 30:8
Sandal tree perfumes, 422:6
Sandboy, jolly as, 358:4
Sands and shelves, tawny, 165:32
   are all dry, when the, 58:12
   begin to hem, 19:23
   dance on the, 263:22
   ignoble things, 27:21
   many, 398:29
   of Dee, across the, 139:22
   unto these yellow, 269:25
   with printless foot, on, 269:43
Sandstone, chunk of old red, 116:23
Sane than mad, fitter being, 40:8
Sang, ane end of ane old, 185:16
Sapienti, verbum sat, 433:61
Sappho loved and sung, 52:23
Sarcasticul, this is rote, 308:10
Sashes, one of his nice new, 111:20

Sat side by side, where we, 277:30
Satan, bowing low, 174:1
  exalted sat, 169:28
  finds some mischief still, 309:33
  Nick, or Clootie, 44:17
  reproves sin, 409:55
  stood unterrifi'd, 170:7
  when ye tak him, 45:31
Satanic School, the, 282:13
Satire be my song, let, 49:38
  for pointed, 204:9
  or sense, 198:4
  should wound with a touch that's
    scarcely felt, 176:9
Saturday, born on, 367:54
  no luck at all, 399:76
  sneeze on, 411:69
Saturday's child, 399:77
Saturn, sat grey-haired, 137:32
Satyr, Hyperion to a, 220:20
Satyrs grazing on the lawns, 157:22
Sauce for the goose, 435:59
  hunger is the best, 384:18
  second time in, 370:30
  sour, 412:58
Saucy, great deal more, 407:67
Saul and Jonathan, 325:35
  also among the prophets, 324:30
  hath slain his thousands, 324:33
Sauter, pour mieux, 435:46
Savage, extreme, rude, 265:29
  in woods the noble, 91:37
Save, both get and, 388:10
  Europe by her example, 191:17
  himself he cannot, 325:61
  on'e own, matter enough, 38:22
  something for the man, 409:57
  while you may, 371:45
Saved, groat is ill, 418:38
  he that will not be, 381:72
  others, he, 325:61
  penny, 353:63
Saving cometh having, of, 403:73
Saviour of the world, 49:35
  stung, with trait'rous kiss, 25:22
Saviour's birth is celebrated, 220:12
Savour, keep seeming and, 273:43
  nothing hath no, 403:49
  salt, best, 415:51
Saw of might, I find thy, 217:36
Sawe, bene an old-sayd, 283:22
Saws, full of wise, 216:17

Say as men say, 409:59
  do as I, 366:44
  it that should not, 426:26
  least, to them, we can, 439:61
  little but I think the more, 384:39
  nothing, do the deed and, 415:47
  nothing good they, 399:58
  nothing, see all and, 410:17
  so, they, 425:71
  this only I can, 158:5
  well is good, 409:62
  well or be still, 409:63
Saying is one thing, 409:64
  things, effective mode of, 20:5
Says least, who knows most, 439:46
  no ill, tongue that, 390:8
  nothing, from him that, 37:66
  what he likes, he who, 382:33
Scabbard, must throw away, 438:35
Scald not your lips, 409:65
Scale, be geometric, 48:6
  weighing, in equal, 220:14
Scallop-shell of quiet, 202:9
Scan your brother man, 44:21
Scandal about Queen Elizabeth, no, 278:8
  love and, 97:18
  waits on greatest state, greatest, 263:27
Scandalous and poor, 204:10
Scar may remain, 426:30
  slander leaves, 411:57
Scarf, beauteous, 254:26
Scarfs, garters, gold, 195:41
Scars, he jests at, 267:19
  remaining, the, 70:7
  wars bring, 434:7
Scarts, count on, 425:76
Scatter with one hand, 409:66
Scelerisque purus, 125:26
Scene be acted over, lofty, 229:29
  every day speaks a new, 201:24
  individable, 223:39
  of all, last, 216:17
  see the distant, 183:28
  upon that memorable, 158:17
  was changed, the, 27:25
  was o'er, proud, 194:13
Scenery, end of all, 207:27
Scenes like these, from, 44:16
Scent of the roses will hang round it, 178:11
  the fair annoys, 74:16
Sceptre and crown, 278:14
  for a palmer's walking-staff, 244:2

her leaden, 322:1
learning, physic, 220:2
shows the force, 255:32
Scheme of Things, sorry, 99:20
she'll project a, 322.0
Schemes o' mice and men, 44:12
Scherzando, ma non troppo, 105:19
Scholar among rakes, a, 153:30
and a ripe and good one, 239:25
diligent, 350:23
gentleman and, 44:19
may waur the master, 422:7
seven [hours sleepeth], 370:31
that never was, 375:48
Scholar's life assail, ills, 130:12
Scholars great men, not commonly, 122:18
School, dead or teaching, 376:15
erecting a grammar, 238:2
tell tales out of, 431:37
unwillingly to, 216:17
when she went to, 257:41
with heavy looks, toward, 267:28
Schoolboy knows, every, 153:25, 312:11
voice of a, 183:25
whining, 216:17
with his satchel, 29:27
Schoolboys are the reasonablest people,
409:67
from their books, 267:28
Schooldays, in my joyful, 144:7
Schooling, pay more for, 442:21
Schoolmaster is abroad, 34:12
Schoolmasters, more than a hundred,
404:37
Schools, public, 'tis public folly feeds, 76:7
Schooner Hesperus, it was, 149:31
Schulin o' your weans, 45:31
Science falsely so called, 339:63
frown'd not fair, 113:19
is organised knowledge, 283:18
never taught to stray, 195:30
sort of hocus-pocus, 155:22
the Dismal, 57:33
Scientia potestas est, 22:21
Scio's rocky isle, of, 51:33
Scirpo, nodum in, 402:36
Scoff, fools who came to, 109:23
Scoffing his state, 244:1
Scold, call her neighbour, 439:53
in the parish, arrantest, 439:53
Scole of Stratford atte Bowe, 63:24
Scope, gives us free, 213:27

that man's, 264:1
Score and tally, 238:2
twice, 409:68
Scorer, the One Great, 204:2
Scorn and let her go, 315:28
at first, 409:69
looks beautiful, 272:8
of scorn, 292:7
to point, time of, 262:3
you unjustly, 204:12
Scorning is catching, 409:70
Scorpion, Archer, and He-Goat, 346:3
Scorpions, chastise you with, 325:45
Scot, a rat, and a Newcastle grindstone,
354:5
will not fight, 422:8
Scotch have found it, the, 133:39
understanding, get a joke well into,
281:17
Scotched the snake, 249:35
Scotches, room for six, 214:13
Scotchman ever sees, noblest prospect,
132:18
gangs while he gets it, 417:44
much may be made of, 133:28
never at home, 356:33
Scotia's food, chief of, 44:14
grandeur springs, 44:16
Scotland afore ye, I'll be in, 343:29
first begin, with, 381:68
supports the people in, 131:26
where it did, stands, 250:21
Scots, brither, 46:2
folk's wooing, 363:44
kills me some six or seven dozen of,
232:4
wha hae, 46:12
Scotsman, moral attribute of, 25:32
of your ability, 25:31
Scotsman's fortune, make, 426:36
Scotsmen aye reckon frae an ill hour,
409:71
Scott, not even Sir Walter, 275:24
so flat as Walter, 344:5
Scottish man is wise, 354:6
mist will wet, 354:7
Scoundrel, last refuge of, 133:33
man over forty is, 275:21
Scourge inexorably calls, 169:30
whose iron, 112:1
Scout, blabbing eastern, 165:33
Scrap of paper, just for a, 28:14

Scrappy, patchy and, 40:7
Scraps, stolen the, 246:12
Scratch a beggar, you will, 442:30
　Art of, 207:31
　come up to, 428:16
　my back, you, 442:23
Scratched, Priscian a little, 246:11
Scratching of a pen, 151:29
　wants but a beginning, 368:5
Screws, brace of bucking, 141:27
Scribble, always scribble, 107:35
Scribendi cacoethes, 135:31
Scribes, not as the, 324:7
Scrimped and iced, 185:25
Scrip of joy, 202:9
Scripture, devil can cite, 254:2
Scruple, some craven, 226:16
Scullion, a very drab, a, 224:1
　away, you, 234:10
Sculptor, and you, great, 39:25
Scurvy, some [are] right, 160:9
Scylla and Charybdis, between, 362:27
Scythe and spade, crooked, 278:14
Sea, a flowing, 78:11
　and one on shore, one foot on, 258:18
　and the gallows refuse none, 422:9
　and the sky, lonely, 159:21
　are we now afloat, on such, 230:17
　as good fish in, 424:7
　being on, sail, 360:33
　beneath him crawls, wrinkled, 293:46
　break, break, break, 293:48
　by the winter, 297:38
　cast water into, 428:11
　complains it wants water, 422:10
　complains wrongfully on, 375:54
　crept into the bosom of, 237:32
　crowned with summer, 297:44
　devil and the deep, 362:29
　down to a sunless, 70:8
　far over the summer, 297:45
　from over the, 295:29
　goes to the bottom of, 375:59
　grew civil, rude, 257:31
　hands across the, 310:4
　hath fish for every man, 422:11
　I never saw the, 84:25
　I'm on the, 200:17
　in a calm, 388:28
　in ships, go down to, 327:59
　in the bottom of the, 245:18
　in the rude rough, 243:37

into that silent, 69:22
is boiling hot, why the, 59:23
is not full, yet, 330:8
kingdom by the, 191:23
learn the secret of, 150:14
let him go to, 382:16
love still has something of, 212:12
Marathon looks on the, 52:24
more, loved the great, 201:18
mother and lover of men, 289:29
murmurs with the changing, 285:19
my bark is on the, 52:9
now flows between, dreary, 70:7
o'er a perfumed, 191:27
of dreams, over a, 184:7
of the loud-sounding, 123:22
of upturned faces, 212:3
on the purple, 154:11
one is of the, 320:5
ooze and bottom of, 235:42
or fire, whether in, 220:11
or land, never was on, 318:20
or land, what thing of, 174:18
our heritage the, 78:12
over the wine-dark, 123:25
paddles in a halcyon, 206:7
plants his footsteps in, 76:19
refuseth no river, 422:12
rising, nor sky clouding, 33:17
robs the vast, 270:7
rock on the misty, 96:15
run beyond the, 125:41
sailed the wintry, 149:31
set in the silver, 243:29
shall give up her dead, 341:56
sight of that immortal, 320:2
sing the dangers of, 285:28
smote the hoary, 123:32
so lone, never was, 140:16
southward dreams the, 299:34
southward to the, 292:1
sunk, in the flat, 165:39
the blue, the fresh, 200:16
the mirrors of the, 99:25
the open sea! the, 200:16
the sea!, the, 321:29
there was no more, 340:17
those in peril on the, 312:12
throw him into, 372:9
Sea, to a most dangerous, 254:26
　to shining sea, from, 26:4
　to Skye, over the, 32:3

of April's sowing, 37:21
Seeing is believing, 410:5
  worth, 133:46
Seek all day, you shall, 253:31
  and ye shall find, 333:60
  anon, better keep now than, 361:78
  another in the oven, 402:18
  him here, we, 185:13
  him, those Frenchies, 185:13
  it, wants it and will not, 379:44
  that you do not, 412:75
  till you find, 410:6
  ye first the kingdom of God, 333:55
  ye the Lord, 332:8
Seem, are things what they, 117:24
  seldom what they, 105:30
  things are not what they, 149:24
  to be, be as you would, 360:12
Seems, it is; I know not, 220:17
Seen and not heard, 364:22
  because thou art not, 217:18
  evidence of things not, 339:66
  fled the, 308:11
  needs but to be, 195:40
  needs only to be, 90:9
  one thing, having, 289:32
  seldom, 410:9
Sees it and does it, 39:29
  not itself, eye, 417:53
Seest yond, say what thou, 269:27
Self, all censure of, 133:44
  concentred all in, 209:24
  deaden love of, 295:24
  do, self have, 410:10
Self-honoured, self-secure, 19:16
Selfishness apt to inspire love, 117:29
Self-love is mote, 410:11
  is not so vile, 236:4
Self-neglecting, not so vile a sin as, 236:4
Self-praise is no recommendation, 410:12
Self-preservation is the first law, 410:13
Self-reverence, self-knowledge, self-
  control, 292:14
Self-schooled, self-scanned, 19:16
Self-slaughter, canon 'gainst, 220:19
Sell at home, 363:70
  better, 362:11
  dear, 434:38
  dear, no sin to, 392:4
  precious as the Goods they, 99:18
  than be poor, rather, 408:16
  what you have bought, 438:26

Seller [needs] not one [eye], 415:65
Semblances, outface it with, 215:36
Selves, of their dead, 295:38
Semper, quod ubique, quod, 305:20
Sempronius, we'll do more, 14:11
Senate laws, give his little, 198:2
Senators, green-rob'd, 137:33
  most grave, 260:10
Send, if not, 387:67
  never sigh, but, 401:63
Seneca cannot be too heavy, 223:39
Seniors, advice from my, 301:24
Sensations, for a life of, 138:3
  sweet, 316:11
Sense aches at thee, 262:4
  and motion, devoid of, 169:33
  and outward things, 319:38
  echo to the, 192:16
  enchants my, 270:16
  hath the daintier, 227:30
  much fruit of, 192:10
  never deviate into, 90:6
  one for, and one for rhyme, 48:20
  palter in a double, 251:42
  stings and motions of, 252:2
  sublime, 316:14
  take care of the, 58:10
  they quicken, within, 276:19
  to keep it at its best, 345:21
  too quick a, 291:30
  vanity is the sixth, 433:57
  want of, 206:1
Senseless things, worse than, 228:4
Senses, affections, passions, 254:19
  in forgetfulness, steep, 234:18
  pass by his troubled, 100:1
  unto our gentle, 247:38
  would have cool'd, 251:36
Sensibility, wanting, 76:6
Sensible as a dictionary, 59:21
  more soft and, 246:8
Sensitive Plant in a garden, 276:1
Sentence, he mouths a, 65:35
  raise, every, 198:2
Sentences, in telegraphic, 142:11
Sententiae, tot, 298:11, 408:12
Sentiments, them's my, 298:16
Sentinels almost receive, 236:10
Senum severiorum, rumoresque, 60:14
Separate us, able to, 338:13
Separately, all hang, 101:27
Separateth very friends, 329:38

launched a thousand, 157:15
sail like swans, 99:28
that pass in the night, 150:20
we've got the, 126:34
Shipwreck be your sea-mark, let another's, 394:35
twice suffers, 375:54
Shire, will be found in, 435:59
Shirt and a half, but, 233:39
knew my design, if, 386:5
near is my, 400:38
nearer is my, 400:37
oftener chang'd their principles than, 322:10
song of the, 124:3
Shive, beg, 372:8
it is safe taking, 392:15
Shock them, we shall, 240:7
with a shivering, 282:6
Shocks, thousand natural, 224:4
Shod, common horse is worst, 416:2
who is worse, 439:44
Shoe, better cut, 361:66
finds sixpence in her, 73:21
fits not every foot, 369:47
for want of, 371:47
is lost, 371:47
pinches, know where, 429:59
rocked the fishermen, 96:15
waits for dead men's, 370:61
will hold with the sole, 422:13
Shoe's latchet, 337:39
Shoemaker's wife, worse shod than, 439:44
Shoes and ships and sealing-wax, 59:23
better wear out, 362:25
call for his old, 212:15
dead men's, 391:70
walks in clouted, 440:10
were on their feet, 280:4
Shoe-string, a careless, 120:6
Shook off, easier kept out than, 383:54
Shoon, his sandal, 226:19
in her silver, 80:13
with his clouted, 166:3
Shoot, don't, colonel, 78:4
his sister, no more he'll, 16:7
if you must, 313:22
teach the young idea how to, 300:9
Shooting, short, 410:40
will ever be, 380:29
Shooting-stars attend thee, 120:11
Shoots oft, he that, 381:48

Shop, bull in a china, 395:65
keep your, 393:54
must not open, 353:52
Shopkeepers, Government is influenced by, 279:30
nation of, 181:32, 279:30
Shops, fills the butchers', 280:1
Shore, adieu ! my native, 50:7
beats back,.rocky, 243:30
but the guiled, 254:26
control stops with, 51:28
could but see, 401:67
fast by their native, 75:24
my boot is on the, 52:9
of song, haunted, 184:7
on the kingdom of, 264:10
rapture on lonely, 51:27
rise upon some other, 154:13
some wide-water'd, 164:18
surges lash the, 192:16
the dull, tame, 201:18
to his own native, 191:27
towards the pebbled, 264:9
unhappy folks on, 191:21
upon a mossy, 206:6
upon the farther, 94:2
upon the Irish, 47:27
went in silence along, 123:22
Shores, of the ocean and, 276:3
Shoreward blow, great winds, 19:17
Shorn, come home, 398:22
Short and far between, 29:28
and sweet, 410:35
as the watch, 309:36
hour ayont the twal', 44:9
Shorter it lasts, 320:32
Shorter-Catechist, something of the, 118:20
Shortness basely, spend that, 233:43
Shot, a very long, 87:33
heard round the world, 95:24
shows somebody, 64:12
so trim, he that, 267:18
Shoughs, water-rugs, and demi-wolves, 249:32
Should not, I say it that, 426:26
Shoulder, on a giant's, 350:28
rheumatic of, 32:7
stands on any, 240:17
to shoulder, 310:2
to the wheel, put, 408:2
what sits on our, 434:24

Shoulders, on young, 357:47
Shoures sote, with his, 63:19
Shout and revelry, midnight, 165:31
   that tore hell's concave, 168:18
Shouted in his ear, went and, 59:30
Shouting, all is over but, 353:78
Shove be'ind me, that's all, 141:43
Show, a terrible, 104:2
   and gaze o' the time, 251:43
   do not do the thing they most do, 265:18
   himself what he is, 258:28
   make a great, 189:26
   me, you have got to, 304:7
   that within which passeth, 220:18
   to-day, that we can, 84:23
Shower, iron-sleet of arrowy, 113:32
Showers and dewdrops wet, with, 206:10
   last long, small, 243:28
   suck the honied, 167:22
Showery, Flowery, Bowery, 94:6
Shreds and patches, king of, 226:5
Shrew, better to marry, 390:34
   every man can rule, 368:33
Shrewd, remark was, 75:19
Shrewsbury, die in, 440:33
Shriek, myriad, 294:2
   solitary, 52:18
   with short, shrill, 71:36
Shrieks, not louder, 193:33
Shroud of white, my, 272:3
Shrouds, land-breeze shook, 75:25
Shrug, with a patient, 254:4
Shudder to recall it, I, 305:35
Shuddering fall, with, 160:13
Shuffling, there is no, 225:38
Shun all things that long thereto, 382:19
Shut afterwards, half, 393:52
Shutter, borne before her on, 229:27
Shutters fast, close the, 75:41
Shuttle, swifter than a weaver's, 325:64
   the musical, 313:16
Shy, once bitten, twice, 404:24
   when people are by, 431:72
Sick as a dog, 358:35
   be long, 360:15
   eats till he is, 378:21
   give counsel to, 419:46
   he who never was, 382:30
   I was desolate and, 87:22
   man sorrow, fetch, 373:58
   men play so nicely, 243:31
   of both, I am, 133:38

that surfeit, as, 253:33
they do not make me, 312:14
   to hear her, 189:23
Sickle in his hand, his, 150:4
   keen with his, 119:30
Sickle's compass, bending, 265:28
Sickness and in health, in, 341:48
   chamber of, 415:73
   comes, till, 383:41
   health and, 383:39
   is felt, 411:45
   of the body, 422:15
   tells us what we are, 411:46
Side, hear the other, 359:87
   in thy most need to go by thy, 342:4
   keep o' the windy, 272:14
   look on the bright, 396:33
   nobody is on my, 21:26
   of one's face, wrong, 429:61
   of the hill, what is on the other, 310:16
   south and south-west, 48:4
   will stand by your, 142:9
Sides and his shoulders, turns, 309:34
   be said on both, 16:2
   of a penny, look at both, 429:69
   to every question, two, 424:17
Sidewalks of New York, 29:29
Sidney's sister, 35:28
Siècles vous contemplent, quarante, 181:29
Sieve, carry water in, 428:10
   like water through, 59:34
   sees not through the holes of, 376:13
   went to sea in a, 147:16
Sigh, beadle to a humorous, 246:5
   but send, never, 401:63
   like Tom o' Bedlam, 240:12
   no more, ladies, 258:18
   prompts th' eternal, 196:2
   some a light, 27:22
   to cheat thee of a, 314:21
   to those who love me, 52:10
   'twill cost a, 23:35
   waft a, 194:5
Sighed and look'd, 91:25
   and said among them, 44:2
   as a lover, I, 104:11
   deep, we have not, 40:7
   no sooner loved but, 218:8
Sighs and groans, sovereign of, 246:6
   and tears, made of, 218:10
   for my pains a world of, 260:6
   for you, swain that, 204:12

of memories and of, 144:13
on the Bridge of, 50:21
Sight, admit them in your, 21:27
at the first, 268:28
bereft of, 306:3
come seldom in her, 382:9
from my aching, 22:4
gleamed upon my, 318:11
it is not yet in, 278:9
keen discriminating, 56:8
loved not at first, 157:23, 217:36
many a vanish'd, 264:2
of you is good, 422:16
or thought be form'd, can to, 173:39
out of mind, out of, 406:3
swim before my, 194:9
tho' lost to, 149:17
to dream of, 70:5
to see, pleasant, 139:25
Sights, so full of ugly, 245:17
that be, wonderful, 96:15
Sign invites you in, 422:17
outward and visible, 341:44
Signal, do not see the, 182:15
shown, only a, 150:20
Signiors, grave and reverend, 259:52
Silence all, ever widening, 297:25
amid the friendly, 305:36
and tears, with, 49:37
be check'd for, 213:24
deep as death, 55:26
flashes of, 281:23
foster-child of, 137:21
gives consent, 411:47
in love bewrays more woe, 202:6
in that, 89:21
is golden, 57:28, 411:48
is of Eternity, 57:28
is scattered, 176:3
is the best ornament of a woman, 411:49
is the perfectest herald of joy, 258:15
like a poultice, 122:11
majestic, 118:6
more have repented speech than, 400:11
my gracious, 218:20
no wisdom like, 402:35
of pure innocence, 273:36
often told in, 285:32
round about his lair, 137:32
seldom doth harm, 411:51
sounds no worse, 126:13
the rest is, 228:1

unperplexed, like, 161:37
was never written down, 411:50
was pleas'd, 171:32
well-timed, 303:20
wheresoe'er I go, 200:17
ye wolves, 194:19
Silent and all damned, all, 316:17
wisely, be, 412:22
Sile attire, walk in, 30:15
fairest, 417:59
in unpaid-for, 219:33
or scarlet, clad in, 356:23
soft as, 358:39
Silks and satins put out, 411:52
my Julia goes, in, 120:12
Siller hae to spare, 30:15
Silly old man, a, 311:31
Silver and gold, 433:44
and gold have I none, 337:57
at noon, 363:68
draws black, white, 438:32
for a handful of, 37:25
that tips with, 267:25
thirty pieces of, 325:57
turn'd, time hath to, 189:16
Simile that solitary shines, 198:10
Similitude in the world, worst, 153:22
Similitudes, used, 332:24
Simon Pure, the real, 61:21
Simple, difficult to be, 207:24
Simples, compounded of many, 217:37
Simplicity, a child, [in], 199:19
elegant, 212:9
guileless, 291:18
pity my, 311:25
Simplify, simplify, 301:26
Sin brings its punishment, 369:48
dissembled, 366:41
dreadful record of, 87:32
except stupidity, no, 314:7
fell the angels, by that, 239:18
for a man to labour in his vocation, no, 231:30
good for nothing but, 412:13
he that is without, 337:46
his darling, 70:16
his favourite, 282:11
I impute to each, 39:32
impute my Fall to, 98:15
in the blossom of my, 222:17
is not appalled, seeing, 345:21
it is, 390:24, 390:25

273:39
man at, 353:38
Sixty, prove a child at, 353:38
seconds' worth of distance, 142:16
takes to seventeen, 139:34
Sixty-three, I am but, 54:6
Sizes, anguish of all, 119:39
Skeletons of leaves, brown, 69:37
Skies are blue, as long as, 276:12
as are the frosty, 293:41
cent'nels of the, 114:12
cloudless climes and starry, 51:36
commercing with the, 164:14
common people of, 321:24
from the quiet, 119:24
illumed the eastern, 17:17
of couple-colour, 124:16
paint the sable, 89:19
some watcher of, 136:4
sun, the air, the, 113:23
thou climb'st the, 278:19
watch-tower in the, 163:36
wrathful, 241:27
Skill, favour to men of, 330:25
in gilt first, try, 432:18
sacrifice, 207:24
Skim milk masquerades as cream, 105:30
Skimble-skamble stuff, 232:26
Skin, Ethiopian change his, 332:13
for skin, 325:61
is never cheap, lion's, 352:22
nearer is my, 400:38
no more of a cat than, 441:63
of my teeth, escaped with, 326:2
sleeping in a whole, 391:48
so full, I stuff my, 287:30
Skin-deep, beauty is but, 360:25
Skins, sisters under their, 142:1
Skip, would have made them, 242:14
Skipper had taken his little daughter, 149:31
Skipping king, the, 233:31
Skirmish, meet without, 432:37
Skulls and roses, 184:7
lay in dead men's, 245:18
Skunk's Misery displayed, 182:26
Sky, above the bright blue, 162:5
admitted to that equal, 195:31
air and the blue, 316:14
as I came through, out of, 154:15
at night, red, 408:24
be too dark, though, 180:9
blue ethereal, 15:8

Bowl we call the, 98:14
close against the, 123:39
darkening the, 204:7
falls, if, 386:31
flames in the forehead of the morning,
167:23
flushing round a summer, 300:16
four corners of the, 90:16
gazing on the western, 70:18
gives us free scope, 213:27
in th' arctic, 170:7
in the morning, red, 408:24
is ever clear, thy, 41:22
is never long dry, 352:32
mackerel, 352:31, 352:32
moving moon went up, 69:31
nursling of the, 276:3
of spring, a blue, 18:2
only one is shining in, 317:20
out on a windy, 313:26
over it, the blue, 185:21
pilgrim of the, 320:10
resist the billows and, 131:22
sent him down the, 73:26
set their watch in, 55:29
steal across the, 24:15
sweet regent of the, 162:1
which noticed all, 38:13
wide and starry, 286:21
wrote my will across, 146:7
Sky's a grey one, although, 315:26
above me, whatever, 52:10
Skye, over the sea to, 32:3
Slack and selfish, becomes, 285:29
Slain, hurt but yet not, 342:11
that in the field is, 48:19
the Jabberwock, 59:19
thinks he is slain, 95:26
thrice he slew the, 91:23
Slander, censure rash, 220:3
leaves a scar, 411:57
to speak no, 297:34
whom not to, 219:37
whose breath rides on the posting winds,
219:34
whose edge is sharper than the sword,
219:34
whose tongue outvenoms, 219:34
Slaughter, as a lamb to, 332:7
to wade through, 112:15
Slave, being your, 264:7
giving freedom to, 148:7

rogue and peasant, 223:35
that is not passion's, 225:20
that pays, base is, 235:48
to thousands, has been, 261:28
you were a Christian, 119:25
Slavery, chains and, 47:23, 119:33
  classified as, 66:1
  fat, 394:19
  great, 351:73
Slaves, at the mill with, 174:14
  cannot breathe in England, 75:35
  creed of, 191:16
  never will be, 300:19
Slayer thinks he slays, 95:26
Slays, moves and mates and, 98:11
Sleep a king, in, 265:16
  after toyle, 283:28
  an exposition of, 257:43
  and a forgetting, 319:35
  and a sleep, between, 290:3
  and a sweet dream, 159:22
  and feed, but to, 226:15
  and we must, 214:15
  as long as you are able, 437:35
  back from the City of, 143:21
  balmy, 321:39
  before midnight, one hour's, 405:48
  calm and peaceful, 314:18
  care-charmer, 78:16
  care-charming, 100:1
  closes soft in, 289:19
  come Sleep! O, 278:20
  Death and his brother, 275:26
  deep and dreamless, 34:10
  dovecot doors of, 161:40
  from the fields of, 319:33
  full of sweet dreams, 136:6
  giveth his beloved, 328:5
  grey and full of, 321:34
  he who invented, 61:24
  I can get nane, 45:36
  is a death, 35:27
  it is a gentle thing, 69:33
  Macbeth does murder, 248:21
  medicine thee to that, 261:33
  Nature's soft nurse, 234:18
  no more, voice cry, 248:21
  O gentle sleep, 234:18
  o' nights, such as, 228:14
  of night, first sweet, 275:35
  of one unending night, 60:14
  preserve me from, 134:3

rounded with, 269:40
seven hours', 410:26
shake off this downy, 249:27
shall neither night nor day, 247:21
shall obey me, 282:1
six hours in, 68:12
some must watch, while some must,
  225:28
sooner it's over, the sooner to, 139:24
that knits up, 248:21
that knows not breaking, 211:23
that no pain shall wake, 206:6
the brave, how, 71:33
the innocent, 248:21
till morn, no, 50:12
to give their readers, 194:14
to say we end, by a, 224:4
to wake, 40:20
unseasonable and immoderate, 134:2
visit thee never, 282:1
was aery light, his, 172:8
we shall not all, 339:35
while others, 406:36
will never lie, where care lodges, 267:32
without supping, 411:58
yet a little, 328:20
Sleepeth a traveller, five hours, 370:31
  peradventure he, 325:48
Sleeping dogs lie, let, 395:44
  enough in the grave, 425:57
  in a whole skin, 391:48
Sleepless themselves to give their readers
  sleep, 194:14
Sleeps in peace, here, 345:17
  till tired he, 195:41
  well, he, 249:36
Sleeve, broken, 349:29
  goose in his, 418:13
  heart upon one's, 431:47
  my heart upon my, 259:48
  pudding in his, 418:13
  will reach, than, 412:46
Slender, as cedar tall and, 185:17
  in the middle, as, 358:36
Slepen al the night, that, 63:20
Slept, dying when she, 124:1
  ill, remembers not he hath, 376:2
  in peace, 239:21
  one wink, I have not, 219:35
  well, he hath, 376:2
  while their companions, 150:17
  with his fathers, he, 325:46

Slew him at the door, I, 75:23
Sliddery, hall blinks are, 374:12
Slide, gently, oh gently, 100:1
Slight man, away, 230:13
　unmeritable man, 230:9
Slimy things, thousand, 69:30
Slings and arrows, the, 224:4
Slip and ripple idly, 160:15
　there's many a, 425:59
　useless away, let it, 57:38
Slippers, same old, 144:10
Slippery as an eel, 358:37
Slips, that never, 377:62
Slit, never a slut but had, 425:55
Slope down, all the steep, 210:3
Sloth is the key to poverty, 411:59
　resty, 219:36
Slothful guise, sick of, 368:19
　man, 422:19
Slough was Despond, 42:7
Slovens' pottage, to make, 411:62
Slow and sure, 411:60
　as tardy as too, 367:36
　at meat, slow at work, 411:61
　but sure, mill grinds, 373:42
　of study, I am, 257:28
　unfriended, melancholy, 108:1
Sluggard, go to the ant, 328:19
　is wiser in his own conceit, 329:57
　makes his night till noon, 422:20
　voice of the, 309:34
Sluggard's convenient season, 422:21
Slumber, a little, 328:20
　again, I must, 309:34
　invites another, one, 405:64
　open wide, keep'st the ports of, 235:30
　to soothing, 134:8
Slumber's chain has bound me, are, 178:14
Slumbers, hast thou golden, 80:8
　kiss him into, 100:1
　kiss your eyes, 80:11
Slut but had a slit, never, 425:53
　I am not a, 217:33
　you may eat after, 356:25
Sluts are good enough, 411:62
　I hate, 403:67
　in dairies, foul, 73:21
Sly, Stephen, 268:9
Sly, tough and devilish, 83:49
Small birds must have meat, 411:63
　for sight, almost too, 241:58
　grind exceeding, 150:9

things are best, 96:6
things, day of, 332:28
Smart, the girls that are so, 56:17
Smarts so little, no creature, 197:40
Smell, ancient and fish-like, 269:31
　and hideous hum, 107:36
　as sweet, would, 267:22
　better than, 423:42
　is bread, best, 415:51
　of bread and butter, 52:11
　of old clothes, 34:6
　of the lamp, 430:21
　so sweet, [see him], 231:36
　the sweeter, it will, 387:48
　villainous, 256:16
Smellest so sweet, 262:4
Smells best that smells of nothing, 377:61
　to heaven, it, 225:36
Smick smack, honeymoon or, 435:71
Smiddy, Robin Tamson's, 205:13
Smile and be a villain, 222:21
　better the last, 362:22
　could be moved to, 228:16
　dwells a little longer, where, 61:30
　fool's, 351:47
　Fortune's golden, 45:26
　good gigantic, 39:40
　in her eye, a, 151:28
　in way of, 253:26
　kind of sickly, 116:23
　on her lips, with a, 210:10
　one vast substantial, 83:46
　peculiar sweet, 299:24
　share the good man's, 109:24
　that glow'd, with a, 173:31
　that was childlike, 116:22
　to those who hate, 52:10
　upon my knee, 114:1
　we would aspire to, 238:16
　why, we shall, 230:19
　with a disdainful, 112:8
Smiled, all sat back and, 107:29
　on me, until she, 68:14
Smiles and soap, charmed it with, 60:1
　awake you when you rise, 80:11
　becks and wreathed, 163:33
　eternal, 198:6
　in such a sort, 228:16
　in the face, [cider], 364:32
　in yer face, 155:22
　of other maidens, than, 68:15
　seldom he, 228:16

meek, patient, 80:12
Softly goes far, fair and, 369:68
  she was going up, 69:31
Softness she and sweet attractive grace,
  for, 171:28
Soil, fatten, 420:20
  hath smutch'd it, before, 134:11
  paints the sterile, 77:24
  that grows on mortal, 166:17
  to paint the laughing, 118:8
Sojourns here, whoe'er, 45:32
Solace to man giffis, 23:36
Sold, not given, 351:50
  pleasing ware is half, 406:33
Soldan of Byzantium, 64:13
Soldat français porte dans sa giberne, tout,
  181:33
Soldered, friendship may be, 349:28
Soldier, an old fool, old, 357:53
  an' sailor too, 141:46
  and afeard, a, 251:27
  bold, Ben Battle was, 123:35
  carries in his cartridge-pouch, every
    French, 181:33
  drink, let a, 260:19
  go to your Gawd, like, 141:41
  is flat blasphemy, in, 252:12
  little toy, 96:16
  rest! thy warfare o'er, 210:23
  said, you must not tell us what, 82:18
  slain, mourn'd her, 145:25
  thou more than, 177:25
  would himself have been, 231:36
Soldier's a man, 260:19
  pole is fall'n, 214:17
Soldiers are surest, old, 310:9
  onward Christian, 24:13
  take heed, 345:17
Sole, shoe will hold with, 422:13
Sole e l'altre stelle, 79:22
Solemn and sad, 412:54
Soles effugere atque abire sentit, 158:6
  occidere et redire possunt, 64:14
Solid men of Boston, 179:30
Solitary, and cannot impart it, 132:10
  man, 354:15
Solitude, bliss of, 318:16
  companionable as, 301:27
  great, 351:71
  how sweet is, 75:19
  midst of a vast, 153:26
  sometimes is best society 173:34

where are the charms, 75:21
Solitudinem faciunt, ubi, 290:8
Somebody, how dreary to be, 84:24
  mine ain dear, 291:19
Somebody's darling, 143:37
Somer seson, in a, 145:26
Something attempted, something done,
  150:1
  or other well, cannot do, 308:18
  there is always, 424:27
Somewhat is better than nothing, 412:3
Somewhere hearts are light, 299:31
  there must be one, 73:25
Son, Absalom, my, 325:42
  by God, I have a, 179:26
  foolish, 328:24
  Fitzdotterel's eldest, 34:11
  gave his only begotten, 337:42
  hateth his, 328:30
  he that hath one, 379:50
  I obeyed as a, 104:11
  keep his only, 122:19
  like father, like, 395:75
  maketh a glad father, wise, 328:24
  my little, 188:7
  my son's my, 400:26
  of a hundred kings, 142:3
  of his mother, only, 336:9
  of man, 324:9
  to nothing, brings up, 377:72
  two-legg'd thing, a, 89:27
  when you will, marry, 399:48
Song, better the world with, 159:27
  for our banner, a, 180:2
  from beginning to end, 150:8
  govern thou my, 172:22
  hast no sorrow in thy, 41:22
  in want of a subject for, 158:2
  may hope, pastoral, 71:35
  metre of an antique, 263:31
  of old, glorious, 212:10
  of the birds for mirth, 114:10
  one grand sweet, 139:26
  saluëth in hir, 63:77
  sang a most topical, 344:11
  seraphically free, 161:22
  sing the Lord's, 328:10
  subject for heroic, 173:32
  sweetest passage of, 161:38
  that found a path, 137:20
  the burthen of his, 29:15
  the Syrens sang, what, 35:24

till I end my, 284:1
twice over, sings each, 38:5
we'll sing another, 320:19
what they teach in, 275:29
Song's measure, with a new, 106.1
Songs and cheery conversation, 209:16
be fashioned, of these, 159:20
cannot sing the old, 42:17
lean and flashy, 166:20
let us go hence, my, 289:31
may inspirit us, 37:26
of Araby, sing thee, 314:21
of pleasant glee, 30:2
our sweetest, 276:7
sing no sad, 206:10
Sonne, up roos the, 63:39
whan soft was the, 145:26
Sonnet, it turn'd to a, 86:3
ode and elegy and, 131:19
scorn not the, 320:12
Sonnets, book of songs and, 256:6
these insuing, 263:28
turn'd to holy psalms, 189:17
Sonorous metal blowing, 168:18
Sons away, bears all its, 309:37
clergymen's, 364:36
God gave no, 382:22
great man's, 373:72
of God shouted, 326:7
Soon enough if well enough, 412:5
got, soon spent, 412:6
Sooth, it is silly, 272:2
Sophisters, economists, and calculators,
43:28
Sophonisba, Oh, 300:18
Sordello's story, may hear, 36:14
Sore be healed, though, 426:30
eyes, good for, 422:16
healing of an old, 391:63
salve for every, 424:24
where you get your, 410:7
who themselves are, 50:1
Sores, plaster for all, 406:14
Sorrow, a little fun to match, 92:10
and an evil life, 412:10
be not too sad, of, 403:76
calls no time that's gone, 100:3
comes unsent for, 412:11
comes with years, ere, 36:1
down, thou climbing, 240:19
fat, 370:3
from the sphere of, 277:21

heart hath 'scaped, 265:17
help me to, 383:51
in thy song, hast no, 41:22
increaseth, 330:11
Is asleep, when, 436:23
is dry, 412:12
is good for nothing, 412:13
is unknown, where, 75:22
lean, 370:3
like unto my, 332;14
melt into, 51:32
never comes too late, 111:34
no greater, 79:20
nor crying, neither, 340:18
pine with fear and, 283:31
proud to be advanced, 343:16
pure and complete, 302:3
regions of, 168:5
rooted, 251:32
see if there be any, 332:14
sink in, 439:58
sneeze for, 411:69
so beguile thy, 270:10
son of, 126:15
sorrow's crown of, 293:33
such sweet, 267:30
than in anger, more in, 221:29
the path of, 75:22
there, there's nae, 181:21
to the grave, with, 323:37
wear a golden, 238:12
where all was delight, 101:15
will come fast enough, 372:36
will pay no debt, 412:14
with night we banish, 121:17
with rainy eyes write, 243:39
words, give, 250:22
worth two [days] of, 404:33
Sorrows are silent, great, 411:67
broods a nest of, 291:31
come, when, 226:21
for transient, 318:13
man of, 332:5
of one, make not two, 398:2
of thy line, 85:45
seven [years] after, 380:10
sit, here I and, 239:32
speak, small, 411:67
Sorry, better be sure than, 361:57
for itself, wild thing, 146:6
if I can't be, 162:13
man, as doth [live], 304:3

Sort, all this, 125:21
  of things, people who like this, 148:13
Sortir, d'un pareil soing en, 176:14
Sorts and sonditions, all, 341:37
  it takes all, 392:29
Sothfastnesse, dwell with, 62:16
Sots, what can ennoble, 196:5
Soudan, your 'ome in the, 141:37
Sough, keep a calm, 393:44
Sought, far may be, 279:25
  it with thimbles, 60:1
  unknowing what he, 91:29
Soul abides, in mystery, 19:21
  adventures of his, 101:23
  again, give me my, 157:15
  alive, most offending, 236:16
  aspiring pants, the, 177:18
  awake my, 138:13
  away, two to bear my, 16:9
  bruised with adversity, 218:18
  call upon my, 271:33
  captain of my, 119:23
  depth and not the tumult of, 320:8
  dusty answer gets the, 160:12
  even-balanc'd, 18:14
  eye and prospect of, 259:36
  flow of, 198:9
  for my unconquerable, 118:21
  for they have no, 68:11
  good for, 365:50
  hae mercy o' my, 345:18
  harbour a great, 352:24
  harmony is in immortal, 255:43
  harrow up thy, 222:12
  hath been alone, this, 69:38
  he that hides a dark, 165:40
  he's prayed for my, 140:7
  invite my, 312:13
  into the boughs does glide, 158:15
  iron entered into, 419:63
  is dead that slumbers, 149:24
  is his own, subject's, 236:12
  is in a ferment, 138:2
  is kindled, fire of, 83:33
  is mine, no coward, 33:29
  is not where it lives, 422:26
  is white, my, 30:3
  is with the saints, 71:20
  lay thou thy, 207:33
  lose his own, 336:2
  lover of my, 311:23
  made for this, 73:25

may pierce, meeting, 164:9
more bent to serve, my, 167:31
most comprehensive, 91:43
needs few things, 422:27
O my prophetic, 222:14
of our grandam, 172:19
of the age, 134:12
pray for my, 297:42
secured in her existence, 16:1
shall be required of thee, 336:15
shorten I the stature of, 160:11
sincere, his, 113:20
sit thou, my, 201:24
sitting in thine eyes, 164:14
sleepless, 317:34
so dead, with, 209:24
sooner dressed than, 415:59
stumbling through my, 110:17
sweet and virtuous, 120:1
take care of your, 387:42
that might create a, 166:1
that rises with us, 319:35
the body's guest, 202:11
to be damned, no, 301:34
to cross, father's, 197:38
to fancy aught, taught my, 304:9
Tommy, 'ow's yer, 141:35
unction to your, 226:8
was like a star, thy, 318:2
was not spoken of, 149:25
was sad, whose, 106:20
waters to a thirsty, 329:54
were fled, as if that, 177:30
what can it do to, 222:9
when I would love her, 162:2
why shrinks the, 15:14
with song, acquaints, 40:14
Soul's dark cottage, 307:27
[Soule] doth the bodie make, 283:33
  is forme, 283:33
  with crosses, fret thy, 283:31
Souls a sympathy with sounds, in, 76:3
  as free, our, 51:35
  flight of common, 181:19
  freedom in their, 290:5
  mounting up to God, 206:15
  negotiate there, our, 86:9
  out of men's bodies, hale, 258:17
  times that try men's, 186:13
  to heaven, little, 96:6
  to play with, 38:22
  to warn th'immortal, 156:13

vanish like lightning, 291:27
were forfeit once, all, 252:9
with but a single thought, two, 151:26
ye contented your, 140:21
you may grind their, 185:24
Soul-slides, boasts two, 39:39
Sound [noise] and fury, full of, 251:37
  beauty born of, 317:23
  burst of thunder, 118:15
  doleful, 209:38
  however rude the, 104:13
  I heard, all the, 126:7
  is forc'd, 30:1
  length and thund'ring, 109:27
  like the sweet, 271:24
  make the most, 368:9
  must seem an echo, 192:16
  save the rush, no, 27:23
  the whispering, 76:9
  therof, thou hearest, 337:41
  timid and tremulous, 58:12
  to heal the blows of, 122:11
  well, can never, 350:16
  with impetuous recoil and jarring, 170:10
Sound [healthy] as a bell, 358:43
  as a roach, 358:44
  as a trout, 358:44
Soundings, until we strike, 343:30
Sounds and sweet airs, 269:39
  blowing martial, 168:18
  concord of sweet, 256:2
  will take care of themselves, 58:10
Soup and love, of, 403:74
  I waved the turtle, 104:17
  of the evening, 58:13
Sour and sad, 363:54
  in the ending, 397:53
  will not taste, 375:57
Source, rise above its, 422:32
  to mount, pants its, 177:18
South Country, hills of, 27:27
  fierce and fickle is, 294:16
  full of the warm, 136:15
  rosy is the, 296:15
Sovereign, civilities with, 133:23
Sovereignest thing on earth, 231:36
Sow [pig], alewife's, 350:13
  by the ear, wrong, 429:45
  eats up all, still, 422:28
  like the old, 424:6
  little knoweth the fat, 396:13
  sucked, 178:15

that was washed, 340:8
Sow [seed] dry and set wet, 426:23
  one's wild oats, 430:22
  with the hand, 412:15
Sow's ear, silk purse out of, 111:70
Soweth, whatsoever a man, 339:45
Sowing, increase by, 393:59
  weeds want no, 434:36
Sown there, were never, 398:31
Sows, and he shall not reap, 290:3
Space and time, annihilate, 345:22
Spade a spade, to call, 428:8
  with which Wilkinson, 318:17
Spades, the emblem of untimely graves, 76:2
Spain, castles in, 428:1
  into the hands of, 297:47
Span, inch as you have done, 367:70
  less than a, 22:22
  thread the length of, 159:27
Spangled heavens, 15:8
Spaniard will be a church, first building erected by, 389:48
Spaniards too, thrash the, 88:9
Spaniel, brach, or lym, 241:41
Spanish soldier brag, 280:6
  to tell her in, 37:29
Spare all I have, 96:11
  at brim, better, 362:16
  how much he can, 133:44
  it is too late to, 392:21
  me not, plain way, 433:51
  me, up hill, 433:51
  not where you must spend, 412:32
  the humbled, 306:7
  to have of thine own, 362:17
  well and spend well, 412:18
  when you're young, 412:19
Spares the bad, he that, 381:51
Sparing is the first gaining, 412:20
Spark, illustrious, 74:10
  in his throat, hath, 42:23
  is left, nor human, 194:24
Sparkle for ever, 294:9
Sparks fly, upward, as the, 325:63
Sparrow fall, hero perish or a, 195:28
  in the fall of a, 227:50
  is dead, my girl's, 60:12
  my girl's pet, 60:12
Sparrows build upon the trees, 67:23
  on one ear of corn, two, 432:28
Sparta is yours, 67:20

ill gotten, ill, 388:21
little good is soon, 352:25
soon got, soon, 412:6
we had, what we, 345:16
when all is, 392:21
Speranza, lasciate ogni, 79:17
  questi non hanno, 79:18
Sphere, motion in one, 233:44
Spheres, as all the tuned, 214:19
  driv'n by the, 304:13
  seems to shake, 90:21
Sphinx, subtle as, 246:8
Spice, if you beat, 387:48
  of life, the very, 75:38
Spider run alive, let, 388:1
  sucks poison, 438:11
  taketh hold with her hands, 330:2
  to a fly, said a, 127:28
Spider's touch, 195:34
  web, smallest, 266:13
Spies are the ears and eyes, 412:33
  as if we were God's, 242:9
  come not single, 226:21
Spilled, two [houses], 362:6
Spills itslef in fearing to be spilt, 226:18
Spin, neither do they, 333:54
Spinner, diligent, 416:33
Spinster, knows more than, 259:46
Spinsters and the knitters, 272:2
Spire the pigeons flutter, on the, 201:26
Spires, with her dreaming, 19:28
  ye distant, 111:31
Spirit a woman, worser, 265:32
  beautiful and swift, 276:13
  blithe, 276:4
  bloweth and is still, 19:21
  broad awake, stab my, 287:24
  Brutus will start, 228:12
  die, before that, 287:24
  doth raise, clear, 166:16
  expense of, 265:29
  extravagant and erring, 220:11
  give me a, 62:1
  history of the human, 20:9
  is too deeply laden, 276:8
  is willing, 325:58
  lack some part of that quick, 228:6
  lies, gentlier on, 292:19
  life-blood of a master, 175:29
  motions of his, 256:2
  of health, be thou, 222:5
  of mortal be proud, why should the,

143:36
  of the, 339:38
  of the chainless Mind, 52:3
  pardlike, 276:13
  pipe to the, 137:22
  pure, make Thou my, 293:41
  quick, ingenious, and piercing, 175:32
  rest, perturbed, 223:25
  scorned his, 228:16
  shall be the stouter, 342:2
  shall return unto God, 331:35
  sing it with a, 320:19
  so still and quiet, 260:2
  the Accusing, 285:25
  to bathe in fiery floods, 252:18
  vexation of, 330:10
  with Spirit can meet, 295:34
Spiriting gently, do my, 268:23
Spiritless, so faint, so, 233:49
Spirits and white, black, 162:3
  are not finely touch'd, 251:45
  are we deified, by our own, 317:34
  choice and master, 229:31
  do ingirt thee, 56:2
  do suggest me, like, 265:32
  float above, whose, 52:2
  I can call, 232:21
  look out, wanton, 271:22
  raise no more, 408:15
Spit in your hands, 412:34
  upon my Jewish gaberdine, 254:5
  when they are out, 218:2
Spite, O cursed, 223:26
Spits against heaven, who, 439:57
Splash, you'll only get, 386:28
Splashing and paddling, 36:11
Spleen, fly hath, 368:14
  mind's wrong bias, 113:35
Splendid for the day, 161:21
Splendour, not in lone, 138:1
Splenetive and rash, not, 227:41
Splitting, forsook hewing and, 398:21
Spoil of me, hath been the, 233:33
Spoiled the Egyptians, 324:4
Spoils of the enemy, to the victors belong,
  156:6
  were fairly sold, 154:3
Spoke [speak], moved and, 188:7
Spoke [bar] in one's wheel, put, 430:8
Spoken, that is well, 414:25
Spondee stalks, slow, 70:19
Spoon, have a long, 377:58

in one's mouth, silver, 427:62
Spoons, let us count our, 132:20
Sport, best of, 415:47
  had ended his, 116:2
  he that cannot make, 378:5
  is sweetest, 412:35
  kill us for their, 241:43
  of kings, 281:30
  that wrinkled Care derides, 163:34
  whether I do not make her more, 176:11
  with Amaryllis in the shade, 166:15
  would be as tedious, 231:33
Sports and journeys, in, 389:50
  attract no more, 54:6
Sporus feel, can, 198:4
Spot, out, damned, 250:26
  stir of this dim, 165:27
  tip me the black, 286:10
  to me, leave this, 55:31
Spots are soon discovered, 388:33
  even on the sun, 424:16
  quadrangular, with, 76:2
Spousal, bird of night sung, 173:28
Sprat, catch, 428:29
  to catch a whale, 431:38
Spray [branch], on yon bloomy, 163:29
  the Bird clung to, 38:10
Spray [liquid], chafe and toss in, 19:17
Spread, table is soon, 353:66
  yourselves, 256:25
Spring, absent in the, 265:20
  apparell'd like, 262:17
  be far behind, can, 275:34
  begins, blossom by blossom, 290:2
  blue sky of, 18:2
  clean the pasture, 102:6
  come, gentle, 300:8
  comes slowly, 70:4
  courting his lady, in, 33:16
  flowers that bloom in, 106:16
  full of sweet days, 119:42
  goeth all in white, 33:19
  has come, 437:62
  in her eyes, with, 299:32
  in the Fire of, 97:28
  infants of the, 220:35
  it is cheery, 123:37
  loseth his, 379:70
  no second, 190:7
  rifle all the breathing, 71:39
  should vanish with the Rose, 99:19
  the sweet spring, 182:5

thou latter, 231:32
time, in the, 218:11
unlocks the flowers, 118:8
year's at the, 37:19
young man's fancy, in, 293:31
Springes to catch woodcocks, 222:1
Springs of Dove, beside, 316:19
  to yellow autumn turn'd, 265:21
Springtime's harbinger, 100:7
Sprouting despondently, 93:29
Spur a free horse, do not, 367:51
  and the bridle, between, 408:21
  to prick the sides, 248:2
Spurred boldly on, 90:4
Square hole, into the, 280:12
Squealing, the vile, 254:13
Squire and his relations, 83:48
Squirrel, by the joiner, 266:13
Stable door, shut, 430:20
Staff be crooked, if, 386:32
  give him, 387:45
  of faith, 202:9
  of life, bread is, 363:62
  to break his own head, 375:46
Stag at eve had drunk his fill, 210:17
Stage, actor leaves the, 244:8
  all the world's a, 216:17
  first rear'd the, 130:16
  glory of the Attic, 18:14
  he was natural, on the, 109:36
  if this were played upon, 272:13
  in public on the, 96:4
  shifts, the sixth, 216:17
  to the well-trod, 164:8
  where every man must play a part,
    253:27
  wonder of our, 134:12
Stagger like a drunken man, 327:60
Staggerer, as far as, 419:71
Stain, like a wound, felt, 43:29
  true blue will never, 431:71
  world's slow, 276:14
Stained, soonest, 417:59
Stains, lose all their guilty, 76:17
Stair, up a winding, 127:28
Stake, it is a poor, 390:15
  standeth longest, ill, 356:38
  still hae a, 44:18
  tied me to a, 251:40
Stalking-horse, uses his folly like, 218:15
Stamford fair, bullocks at, 234:22
Stampa, ruppe la, 18:7

Stand a tip-toe, 236:17
  and stare, time to, 79:29
  and wait, who only, 161:31
  close around, 145:16
  give me somewhere to, 18:6
  here I, 152:6
  how if a' will not, 258:26
  in one's own light, 430:25
  it, that he would not, 58:15
  not upon the order of your going, 250:8
  one year in the ground, 390:15
  up for Jesus, 92:6
Standard launch, glorious, 55:23
  raise the scarlet, 72:13
Stands not surely, 377:62
Stanhope's pencil, with, 322:11
Stanley, approbation from Sir Hubert,
    180:12
Stanza, when he should engross, pens a,
    197:38
Star and garter, take away, 22:4
  bid haste the evening, 173:28
  bright particular, 213:25
  catch a falling, 86:7
  constant as the northern, 229:27
  danced, there was a, 258:16
  each in his separate, 140:18
  emigrated to another, 129:23
  eve's one, 137:32
  fair as a, 317:20
  glittering like the morning, 43:28
  hitch your wagon to, 94:18
  I'm not a great, 95:36
  lights the evening, 55:15
  like a falling, 169:26
  like a sinking, 293:27
  lit by one large, 161:19
  love the western, 209:21
  man is his own, 100:6
  or two beside, and a, 69:31
  our life's, 319:35
  pinned with a single, 67:25
  sheds its ray, red, 23:26
  soul of Adonais, like, 276:17
  splendid, a, 40:17
  sunset and evening, 298:5
  that bids the shepherd fold, 165:30
  that bringest home, 55:33
  that ushers in the even, 265:31
  to steer her by, a, 159:21
  twinkle, little, 291:28
  with one bright, 69:28

without troubling of, 300:2
  would I were steadfast, 138:1
Star-chamber matter, 256:5
Stare, all the world would, 75:31
  stony British, 290.14
  time to stand and, 79:29
Starlight and by candlelight and
    dreamlight, 302:11
  into the frosty, 19:23
Star-proof, branching elm, 165:26
Starre, strives to touch, 283:22
Stars above us govern our conditions,
    241:47
  and sunbeams know, didst, 19:16
  are fire, doubt thou, 223:30
  are old, [till], 291:24
  are setting, 98:9
  are shining bright, 275:35
  beauty of a thousand, 157:16
  blesses his, 15:12
  blossomed the lovely, 150:11
  branch-charmed by, 137:33
  bright cent'nels, 114:12
  crowned with the, 302:6
  cut him out in little, 268:1
  emerge, new-bath'd, 19:23
  far, beyond the, 304:12
  fault is not in our, 228:11
  from wrong, preserve, 318:19
  give away their motion to, 70:18
  go by, silent, 34:10
  go down, the, 154:13
  glows in the, 195:36
  gold-dusty with tumbling amidst, 300:6
  in her hair were seven, 206:12
  in the shining of, 297:37
  in their courses, 324:20
  keep not their motion in one sphere,
    two, 233:44
  move still, the, 157:18
  of midnight shall be dear, 317:23
  on the sea, like, 51:38
  rush out, 67:27
  sang together, morning, 326:7
  shall fade away, 16:1
  shot madly from their spheres, 257:31
  stripes and bright, 138:17
  such is the way to, 306:9
  that have a different birth, 276:11
  the sentinel, 55:29
  to flight, that puts, 97:27
  up in the, 180:3

with how splendid, 99:25
  you chaste, 262:9
Star-shine at night, 287:26
Start me, direness cannot, 251:36
  straining upon the, 236:7
Starve for hunger, may, 349:5
  let not poor Nelly, 62:7
  with nothing, that, 253:33
Starved, feasted, despaired, 40:7
State, all were for the, 154:3
  expectancy and rose of, 224:11
  glories of our, 278:14
  high and palmy, 220:8
  his mind is ta'en up with the things o'
    the, 181:22
  I am the, 151:23
  in wonted manner keep, 134:18
  is kingly, His, 167:31
  of life, in that, 341:43
  of man, like to a little kingdom, 228:18
  safety and the health of this whole,
    221:34
  some service, done the, 262:16
  something rotten in, 222:11
  strange eruption to, 220:5
  to ruin or to rule, 89:28
  traduced the, 262:16
  whole machinery of, 34:13
States and kingdoms seen, 136:3
  small—Israel, Athens, 128:15
  unborn and accents yet unknown, in,
    229:29
Statesman, chymist, fiddler, 89:34
  too nice for a, 109:34
  yet friend to truth, 197:35
Statesmen, minds of some, 179:18
Stations, know our proper, 83:48
  whistle by, 286:19
Statues, like sepulchral, 86:9
Stature, one cubit unto, 333:53
Status quo, restored the, 284:9
Statutes at Large, 141:1
Staunch and strong, 150:12
Stay a little, 412:38
  a while, 412:39
  behind my tremulous, 116:9
  he that can, 378:3
  here I am, here I, 155:25
  if anything, 385:70
  langer, I daurna, 211:37
  says I must not, 301:36
Stay-at-Home, sweet, 79:30

Steadfast as a star, 160:10
  as thou, would I were, 138:1
Steadily, blade by blade, 310:2
  saw life, 18:14
Steady, boys, steady, 103:17
Steal a horse, one man may, 405:54
  a shive, of a cut loaf, 270:9
  away, silently, 150:6
  fico for the phrase, 256:7
  out of your company, 258:28
  you are a fool to, 441:56
Stealing, fighting, 373:39
  from picking and, 341:42
  preached against, 418:13
Stealth, do a good action by, 144:6
  do good by, 198:15
Steam, unconquer'd, 79:26
Steed, farewell the neighing, 261:35
  is stolen, when, 430:20
  mounts the warrior's, 209:19
  my Arab, 184:5
  soon I'll mount my, 111:21
  that knows his rider, 50:9
  threatens steed, 236:10
  was the best, his, 210:6
Steeds to water, his, 219:30
  you fiery-footed, 267:41
Steel, clad in complete, 165:41
  in complete, 222:7
  true as, 359:60
  which impell'd the, 50:4
  with hoops of, 221:37
  worthy of their, 211:29
Steel-true and blade-straight, 287:28
Steep, on Sunium's marbled, 53:25
  on the Indian, 165:33
Steeple, old as Paul's, 358:20
Steeples, drench'd our, 240:23
  talk about the, 64:16
Steer too nigh, would, 89:24
Stehe ich, hier, 152:6
Stein, wonderful family called, 344:15
Stenches, two and seventy, 71:22
Step after step, 412:40
  enough for me, one, 183:28
  greatest, 418:35
  more true, a, 210:21
  one small, for a man, 18:11
  only the first, 80:3
  so active, 144:14
  to recall, 306:6
Stepdame, rule by his, 381:71

Stephen, on the Feast of, 182:11
Stepmother, take heed of, 412:71
Stepping westward, 318:4
Steps, age with stealing, 304:17
   and slow, wand'ring 173:48
   brushing with hasty, 112:18
   hear not my, 248:14
   invites my, 194:1
Steps, to support uneasy, 168:12
   to these dark, 174:13
   with how sad, 278:19
Stern [strict] to view, 109:26
Stern [ship] chase is a long chase, 354:16
Stern-faced men, two, 123:40
Stewed, roasted, baked, or boiled, 289:19
Stick [rod], carry a big, 205:24
   is quickly found, 354:17
   kindle a green, 432:27
   straight, 354:20
   with fist unstead of, 48:2
Stick [cling], some [dirt] will, 370:32
   to you, he'll, 393:55
Sticking-place, screw your courage, to 248:7
Sticks and stones may break my bones, 412:41
   cross as two, 356:74
   kindle, little, 395:15
   put it out, great, 395:15
   two dry, 432:27
Stiff upper lip, keep a, 60:8
Stile, help a lame dog over, 429:48
   sitting on the, 277:30
   you would be over, 442:31
Stile-a, merrily hent the, 273:42
Stiles, lame dogs over, 139:32
Still, all white and, 151:36
   and have thy will, be, 360:18
   as the silence, 137:32
   he sits full, 376:59
   hear and see and be, 383:43
   him, hath none to, 439:43
   hold him, 375:71
   hold you, 437:59
   say well or be, 409:63
   to stand an' be, 141:46
Stillness, an horrid, 89:21
   far in the, 118:19
   holds, a solemn, 112:5
Sting, death, where is thy, 339:36
   is in the tail, 422:29
   that bids nor sit, 39:43

thee twice, serpent, 255:32
Stingeth like an adder, 329:53
Stings, armed in their, 235:43
   in their tails, 360:29
   never feels the wanton, 252:2
   you for your pains, 121:21
Stink, devil always leaves, 416:16
   in a heap, 408:37
   the worse it will, 420:39
   we will bear with, 411:73
Stinking fish, cries, 402:11
   savour, send forth, 330:26
Stinks, and several, 71:22
   and stings, 198:5
Stir, the more you, 420:39
Stirrup and the ground, betwixt the, 54:12
   I sprang to the, 37:28
Stitch in times saves nine, 354:18
   stitch! stitch! 124:3
Stithy, foul as Vulcan's, 225:21
Στῶ, δός μοι ποῦ, 18:6
18:6
Stock goes on, see how his, 70:14
   went on, see how his, 282:9
Stocking all the day, a, 107:43
Stoic fur, doctors of the, 166:4
   or a satyr, either a, 191:15
Stole, he's starve before he, 140:7
   in and out, 287:35
   memory of all he, 194:15
Stolen, not wanting what is, 261:34
   waters are sweet, 328:23
Stolen on his wing, 163:30
Stomach for their meat, 406:42
   for them all, had, 262:11
   in wine in, 370:30
   is not good, my, 287:30
   of an unbounded, 239:23
   through his, 423:62
Stomach's sake, wine for, 339:60
Stomachs, best fits weak, 434:28
Stone, are themselves as, 265:18
   beneath this, 183:27
   bows down to wood and, 118:12
   doth lie, underneath, 134:9
   drop hollows, 374:6
   fling but a, 113:35
   get blood out of, 440:67
   he stopp'd not for, 210:8
   if I had not lifted, 385:77
   let him first cast, 337:46
   philosopher's, 365:52

pipes of wretched, 166:20
tickled with a, 195:41
Strawberry jam, now for, 104:25
Strawe, oft stombles at a, 283:22
Straws show which way the wind blows, 412:45
Stream, as a purling, 100:1
  by haunted, 164:8
  cannot rise above, 422:32
  cross, 365:68
  like an ever-rolling, 309:37
  runs fast, the, 177:26
  striving against, 391:67
  swap horses when crossing, 148:10
  that flashest white, 294:33
Streams, by desolate, 185:26
  dam his, 18:23
  from little fountains flow, large, 96:4
  his crystalline, 275:33
  lapse of murmuring, 172:24
  meander level, 153:22, 177:18
  run dimpling, 198:6
Street, across a golden, 184:9
  down the long, 314:17
  narrow foot-path of, 45:29
  o'er the stony, 50:12
  of By and by, 363:72
  ringing down the, 22:1
  through the public, 214:3
  were time, if the, 93:30
Streete cryes all about, 314:22
Streets, gibber in the Roman, 220:8
  where the great men go, 99:27
Strength, adds to the thought, 32:12
  ancient and natural, 29:24
  be, so shall thy, 324:15
  is as the strength of ten, 293:42
  is made perfect in weakness, 339:43
  to strength, from, 327:47
  tower of, 245:26
  wears away, as my, 199:28
  with promise of, 33:18
  woman's, 355:43
Stretch him out longer, 242:16
Strew on her roses, 19:24
  on thee rose, shall I, 289:39
Strife, none was worth my, 144:15
  poverty breeds, 406:47
  take away, 434:39
Strike, afraid to, 198:2
  but delay'd to, 173:43
  by measure, must, 436:19

mint ere you, 399:70
no right to, 72:19
  while the iron is hot, 412:48
  your fill, 437:59
String, chewing little bits of, 28:1
  warbled to the, 164:21
Strings do scarcely move, 30:1
Stripes and bright stars, 138:17
Stripling Thames, crossing, 19:26
Strive, need'st not, 68:5
  to seek, to find, 292:18
Stroke, at the first, 423:56
  intend, no second, 170:8
  not felled at one, 356:42
Strokes, amorous of their, 214:2
  fell great oaks, little, 395:16
  great, 373:75
Strong at thirty, 379:72
  battle to the, 330:25
  man after sleep, like a, 174:34
  without rage, 81:22
Stronger by weakness, 307:27
Strove, a little while she, 52:14
  with none, I, 144:15
Struck, more men threatened than, 424:11
Struggle, in a contemptible, 43:24
  naught availeth, 68:1
Struggles of another, watch, 152:4
Struts and frets his hour, 251:37
  his dames before, 164:1
Stuarts are not sib, all, 356:7
Stubble-land, show'd like, 231:34
Studie was but litel on the bible, 63:32
  what sholde he, 63:25
Studies serve for delight, 22:15
Studio, sine ira et, 290:11
Studious let me sit, 300:14
Study is a weariness, much, 330:36
  is like the heaven's glorious sun, 246:1
  labour and intent, 174:24
  of mankind is man, 195:35
  to be quiet, 339:56
  what you most affect, 268:10
  willingly, will never, 349:12
Stuff, made of sterner, 229:38
  perilous, 251:32
  we are such, 269:40
Stumble, may well, 381:41
Stumbles and falls, he that, 381:57
  horse that never, 390:7
Stumps, fought upon his, 275:25
Stupidity, no sin except, 314:7

and moon were in the flat sea sunk, 165:39
and the other stars, 79:22
and the rain are flying, 287:29
as the dial to, 31:28
at the going down of, 29:19
before the rising, 309:36
begins his state, 164:2
benighted walks under the midday, 165:40
bosom-friend of the maturing, 137:30
can be seen by nothing but its own light, 422:35
candle to the, 322:9
clear as, 330:43
climbs slow, in front, 68:3
dead no more do see, 89:20
disclose the pilgrim, 304:8
doth gently waste, 342:17
doth move, doubt that, 223:30
drum-beat, following the, 310:7
follow thy fair, 55:34
for the eyes to behold, 330:30
glimmering tapers to, 77:25
go down upon your wrath, 339:47
goes to bed wi' the, 273:44
grows cold, till the, 291:24
had long since in the lap, 48:23
heat o' the, 220:1
himself grow dim, 16:1
in all his state, 17:17
in bed, the, 163:26
in dim eclipse, 169:22
in his glory, smile like, 200:1
in red should set, if, 386:33
in the courts of the, 64:13
is highest, when, 437:44
is laid to sleep, 134:18
is never the worse, 422:36
lasts, no morning, 371:45
laughed in the, 34:1
looked over the mountain's rim, 37:34
loves to live i' the, 216:6
many an evening, 26:16
must not walk in, 379:41
myself in Huncamunca's eyes, 97:20
never sets in the Spanish dominions, 280:6
of righteousness, 332:30
of the burnish'd, 254:9
peer'd forth, worshipp'd, 266:6
reflecting upon the mud, 291:29

rises bright in France, 78:10
rises in the morning, 389:40
sees it, 386:20
sets bright and clear, 437:45
sets in a bank, 437:46
shall not smite thee by day, 328:3
shines always there, 277:31
shines, day still while, 390:37
shines, make hay while, 397:77
shines on, bride, 374:19
shines, though, 426:31
shines upon all, 422:57
should set in grey, 386:33
sinks low, as the, 184:9
sitting in the, 282:4
somewhere beneath the, 73:25
spots even on, 424:16
take warmth, from the 114:4
that warms you here shall shine on me, 243:23
the early-rising, 120:9
the selfsame, 274:7
to feel the, 36:3
to meet the, 112:18
to rise, maketh his, 333:46
to the garish, 268:1
under the, 330:6, 330:8
uprist, the glorious, 69:21
views, descending, 30:21
walk much in, 426:5
warm summer, 204:4
warms in the, 195:36
went down and the stars came out, 297:45
white as the, 72:16
will be dimmed, glory of, 22:28
will shine, the, 315:26
with the dying, 32:5
you never loved the, 64:18
Sun's a thief, 270:7
bravado, met the, 26:2
rim dips, 69:27
Sunbeam, impossible to be soiled as, 174:26
in a winter's day, 92:16
Sunbeams flatter, which the, 54:10
motes that people, 164:12
out of cucumbers, 288:17
Sunday, born on, 363:54
from the week, does not divide, 220:6
God send, 364:42
killing of a mouse on, 32:11
makes a clout on, 355:62

sneeze on, 411:69
will weep on, 381:50
Sunday's child, 412:54
Sundays, begs his bread on, 353:48
pulpits and, 119:39
Sun-dial in the shade, 435:60
what is the good of, 435:60
Sun-flower turns to her god, 178:2
Sung, ever honour'd, ever, 100:2
from noon to noon, 180:4
Sunium's marbled steep, 52:25
Sunless land, from sunshine to, 320:15
Sunlight, somewhere in the, 147:26
Sunrise, lives in Eternity's, 30:10
pass, seen their, 65:24
Suns and universes ceased, 33:30
can set and return, 60:14
light of setting, 316:14
Sunset and evening star, 298:5
fadeth, after, 264:13
ran . . . reeking, 38:6
Sunset-touch, there's a, 39:37
Sunshine after rain, like, 263:24
but hath some shadow, no, 402:30
is a glorious birth, 319:31
made a, 283:27
settles on its head, 109:25
Sun-treader, 36:12
Sup and blow at once, 402:9
from home, before you, 130:10
sipped no, 106:20
Supererogation, Works of, 341:57
Superlative degree, 303:14
Superstition, atheism and, 416:18
Superstitions, end as, 128:8
Supper from him, steals, 382:35
good breakfast but a bad, 384:8
if ever I ate a good, 18:3
walk a mile, after, 355:57
will have more for, 381:42
Supperless, go to bed, 361:72
goes to bed, 439:40
Suppers, pastime [makes], 384:19
Supping, sleep without, 411:58
Supplied, can never be, 108:15
Support him after, to, 270:4
Sups ill, he, 376:63
Sure as a gun, 358:45
as death, 358:46
as eggs is eggs, 358:47
as God made little apples, 358:48
as God's in Gloucestershire, 358:49

slow and, 411:60
than sorry, better be, 361:57
Surety, [act as], 368:7
Surface flow, upon the, 91:40
Surfeit reigns, no crude, 165:43
Surge and thunder of the Odyssey, 145:23
rude imperious, 234:19
the murmuring, 241:48
Surgeon, good, 351:65
Surmise, with a wild, 136:4
Surname, out of his, 153:20
Surpass, her, nothing earthly could, 52:12
Surplusage, removal of, 188:3
Surprise, to no little, 24:5
what a, 68:8
Surprised is half beaten, man, 353:51
Surprises, millions of, 119:39
Surrender, dies but does not, 54:11
unconditional and immediate, 111:27
virtue is near, 433:68
we shall never, 66:3
Surrey in a wilderness, meet, 244:3
Survival of the fittest, 79:25
Sus Minervan, 412:55
Susceptible Chancellor, 106:2
Suspect, hath reason to, 97:23
the thoughts of others,
Suspected, ever, 254:7
Suspicion always haunts the guilty mind,
238:10
must be above, 363:75
virtue of a coward is, 423:60
Sutor ultra crepidam, ne, 400:36
Swaggering here, have we, 257:37
Swain, a frugal, 122:19
no better than a homely, 238:6
Swains commended her, all, 273:29
Swallow dares, before the, 274:1
does not make a summer one, 404:64
flying south, 294:15
mounteth it not, 422:25
thou that knowest each, 294:16
Swallow's wings, flies with, 245:25
Swallows are making them ready to fly,
313:26
Swan and shadow, double, 318:9
dies the, 293:29
float double, 318:9
of Avon, sweet, 134:16
sings before death, 422:32
Swanee Ribber, upon de, 101:16
Swans, all his geese are, 355:72

698

asleep, sail like, 99:28
sing before they die, 71:24
Swap horses when crossing, 148:10
Swashing and a martial outside, 215:36
Swat, the Akond of, 117:21
Sway, above this sceptred, 255:33
　requir'd with gentle, 170:29
　with an absolute, 199:28
Sways, by submitting, 197:26
Swear, if you, 387:64
　me, Kate, like a lady, 233:29
　to me, thou didst, 234:12
Sweareth to his own hurt, 326:17
Sweat and whine, do not, 312:14
　no sweet without, 402:31
　of thy face, in the, 323:19
　to grunt and, 224:4
　toil, tears and, 66:2
　wet with honest, 149:34
Sweats to death, Falstaff, 231:43
Sweep before your own door, 412:56
Sweeping, nor sewing, nor, 345:19
Sweet and fair she seems, how, 307:26
　and glorious thing, 125:30
　and low, 294:10
　as a nut, 359:50
　as English air could make her, 294:7
　as love, 291:17
　as summer, 239:25
　deserves not, 375:57
　doth suck his, 149:22
　[hath its] sour, 369:50
　how it was, 40:3
　in the beginning, 397:53
　is revenge, 52:16
　is she, O so, 134:11
　my own, my, 296:19
　naught in this life, 100:4
　nothing half so, 178:4
　short and, 410:35
　so strangely, 33:20
　than May day morn, more, 155:26
　things, both, 31:29
　two-and-twenty, 53:35
　what some have found so, 296:11
　when the morn is grey, 54:4
　without sweat, no, 402:31
Sweeter also than honey, 326:23
Sweetest [flower], not, 419:42
　stolen pleasures are, 412:43
　thing that ever grew, 317:26
　things turn sourest, 265:19

Sweetheart and Honeybird, 412:60
　to-morrow, see, 411:69
Sweeting, pretty, 271:36
Sweetness and it sgrace, 183:26
　and light, 20.7, 288.14
　long drawn out, 164:9
　that inspired, 156:12
　waste its, 112:13
Sweets compacted lie, where, 119:42
　feast of nectar'd, 165:43
　lost in the, 103:34
　to the sweet, 227:39
　wilderness of, 172:13
Swell, with its voluptuous, 50:11
Swept and garnished, 324:20
　it for half a year, 59:22
Swift [fast] arrives as tardy, too, 267:36
　race is not to, 330:25
Swift [Dean] expires a driv'ler, 130:14
　you will never be a poet, 92:4
Swiftness never ceasing, 189:16
Swim, he must needs, 376:46
　I taught you to, 385:41
　said I could not, 58:14
　till you can, 401:66
　to yonder point, 228:9
　who knows not to, 389:59
Swimmer, cry of some strong, 52:18
Swimmers, good, 373:56
Swims or sinks, or wades, 170:12
Swine did eat, husks that, 336:25
　good enough for, 367:66
　pearls before, 333:59
　women and bees, 412:61
Swine's snout, jewel in, 328:26
Swinish multitude, 43:32
Swink, lat Austin have his, 63:25
Swinken with his handes, 63:25
Swiss, no money, no, 402:21
Switzers, law, logic, and, 394:12
Swooned, nor utter's cry, 294:19
Swoop, at one fell, 250:23
Swop for my dear old Dutch, 65:32
Sword against his prince, draweth, 438:35
　against nation, lift up, 331:48
　all they that take, 325:59
　brave man with a, 314:15
　edge is sharper than, 219:34
　flesh'd thy maiden, 233:46
　glued to my scabbard, 159:33
　he has girded on, father's, 178:10
　his terrible, swift, 127:25

in a madman's hand, 391:65
in buying, 388:36
keeps another in the sheath, one, 404:66
kills more than, 372:20
lightnings Thy, 65:34
[make thee] famous by, 177:20
no flourishing with, 31:33
rules without, 397:64
rust, his good, 71:20
·shall perish with, 325:59
sleep in my hand, 30:12
the deputed, 252:8
to draw, I lighted down, 342:10
whipster gets my, 262:14
will open, I with, 256:11
Swords into plowshares, beat, 331:48
must have leaped, 43:28
shall play the orator, 156:10
sheated their, 236:6
words cut more than, 440:48
Swore, quaffed and, 88:7

terribly, our armies, 285:23
Sworn as you, had I so, 248:6
it, my tongue had, 95:33
Swound, like noises in a, 69:20
Sybil, contortions of the, 43:36
Syene, and . . . Meroe, 174:5
Syllable, hear the first, 300:24
Syllables require, equal, 192:14
Sylvia, except I be by, 273:27
who is, 273:29
Symmetry, frame thy fearful, 30:5
Sympathise, I deeply, 59:26
Sympathy, it is the secret, 209:23
with sounds, 76:3
Symphonies, five sweet, 206:16
Syne, auld lang, 45:37, 45:38, 45:39, 45:40
Syrens sang, what song, 35:25
Syrops, lucent, 136:13
Syrups of the world, drowsy, 261:33
System will decay, energies of our, 22:28

T

Table, at a round, 359:78
from their masters', 324:28
in a roar, set the, 227:34
is soon spread, goodwife's, 437:37
made you a bad, 132:16
poor man's, 353:66
robs more, 423:39
round about thy, 328:7
spread, 412:36
Table Bay, going to, 142:3
Table-cloth, make my dish-clout, 385:50
Tables are soon spread, poor men's, 406:43
not your trade to make, 132:16
Tadpole, when you were a, 280:7
Tail broader, make not thy, 398:1
came through, where, 70:15, 282:10
extracted from the, 146:10
hangs loose, her, 176:4
is worth, what her, 416:5
like a rat, 352:3
of a pig's, 403:66

salt on a bird's, 430:11
sting in its, 406:34
sting is in, 422:29
the more he shows, 419:48
thin mane, thick, 263:23
Tailor makes the man, 423:40
Tailors and writers, 412:62
make a man, nine, 401:70
Tails, dogs wag, 367:65
of both hung down, 280:4
Take heed whom you take, 437:64
her, this cannot, 288:2
one down a peg, 430:28
one up before he is down, 430:29
things as they come, 412:78
things as you find them, 412:79
thou in charge, 154:5
who have the power, 318:8
Take-heed doth surely speed, 373:57
Taken, are as they be, 426:10
away even that which he hath, 325:55

half, 352:34
if it were not ill, 425:56
that is well, 414:25
Taking out, always, 356:21
Tale, adorn a, 130:13
condemns me, every, 245:28
ill told, good, 351:66
is good, one, 404:67
is none the worse, good, 351:67
never losses in the telling, 354:22
or history, hear by, 256:21
round unvarnish'd, 260:1
runs as it pleases, 423:41
speeds best, honest, 245:23
shall put you down, plain, 232:13
tedious as a twice-told, 239:35
that is told, as a, 326:51
thereby hangs a, 216:10
to tell, never wants, 356:50
told by an idiot, 251:37
twice told, 354:23
unfold, I could a, 222:12
which holdeth children, 278:21
woes of an old, 312:11
Tale's best for winter, sad, 273:35
Talent, blest with each, 198:2
does what it can, 153:18
tomb of a mediocre, 280:9
which is death to hide, 167:31
Talents, career open to, 181:31
if you have great, 203:24
ouverts aux, 181:31
Tales be told [of these] 159:20
dead men tell no, 366:9
of fair Cashmere, 314:21
of sorrow done, 108:20
out of school, tell, 431:37
tell old, 242:9
Talismans and spells, books are, 76:5
Talk as other people do, 133:49
gods, how he will, 147:24
I long to, 86:10
is but talk, 414:5
is of bullocks, whose, 340:24
most work, least, 394:24
of an angel, 414:6
of many things, to, 59:23
of the devil, 414:7
on, you wished him to, 116:35
privileged to, 421:49
was like a stream, 200:2
with the vulgar, 426:21

with them too, we'll, 242:9
Talked like poor Poll, 103:18
of me, they, 96:9
on for ever, he, 116:35
Talkers, great, 373:76
greatest, 418:36
Talking about you, someone, 388:8
he is, 325:48
he will be, 252:32
pays no toll, 414:8
tired the sun with, 73:26
Talks, liked the way it, 202:16
to himself, he that, 381:60
you dead, atheist, 130:7
Tall, divinely, 292:21
maid is stooping, while, 438:29
not tiny or, 119:34
proper men and, 88:6
Taller by almost the breadth of my nail,
288:15
Tam! thou'll get thy fairin, 46:11
was glorious, 46:9
Tambourines jing-jing-jingled, 148:14
Tamburlaine, the Scythian, 156:9
Tamer of the human breast, 112:1
Tames man and beast, wedlock, 355:59
Tanais, the freezing, 194:17
Tane unto the tither did say, 342:7
Tanned at last, will be, 426:5
Tape, will you buy any, 274:6
Tapers to the sun, hold, 77:25
Τάφος, πᾶσα γῆ, 189:28
Tapping, there came a, 191:24
Tapster tell, of a surly, 99:17
Tar, halfpennyworth of, 430:24
Tara's halls, harp that once through, 177:30
Taradiddles, for telling, 148:1
Tares cling round the sickly blade, 77:24
Tarquin, great house of, 154:1
Tarred and feathered, 312:20
with the same brush, 356:8
Tarry at Jericho, 325:39
longer will, 88:12
the wheels, why, 324:22
Tarry-long brings little home, 414:9
Tarsus, stately ship of, 174:18
Tartar, to catch, 428:12
you'll find, 409:72
Tartarly, so savage and, 53:34
Task, at their priestlike, 138:1
hast done, wordly, 230:1
is done, long day's, 214:15

is o'er, labourer's, 94:2
sore, 220:6
the common, 138:7
though hard be the, 60:8
what he reads as a, 132:19
Taskmaster's eye, in my great, 163:31
Tasks in hours of insight will'd, 18:21
Tassie, fill it in a silver, 45:41
Taste, every one to his, 369:44
   not, handle not, 339:54
   of the kitchen, 423:42
   the whole, let me, 40:6
   things sweet to, 243:25
Tasted, some books to be, 22:16
Tastes may not be the same, 274:17
   no disputing about, 366:5
   of men, so various are, 16:14
Tatter, often to, 404:1
Taught by the Power, 108:6
   maids' children are always well, 360:2
   worth a pound that's, 356:58
   worth twice, 440:19
Tavern or inn, a good, 133:36
Taxation without representation, no,
   402:32
Taxes, death and, 403:51
Tea, although an Oriental, 64:23
   and sometimes [take], 193:27
   best sweeteners of, 97:18
   breakfasts at five o'clock, 59:39
   forsook spinning for, 398:21
   nor take her, 322:8
Teach your grandmother, 414:10
Teachers, shall have many, 380:1
Teaches himself, he that, 381:61
Teacheth ill who teacheth all, 376:64
Teaching others teacheth yourself, 414:11
Teacup, storm in, 354:19
Teacup-times of hood and hoop, 292:24
Tear [weep], charm thee to a, 314:21
   dries sooner than, 403:47
   drop the briny, 62:14
   in her eye, 210:10
   law which moulds a, 205:17
   meed of some melodious, 166:10
   shed a bitter, 59:22
Tear [rend] him for his bad verses, 230:8
Tears as fast, drop, 262:16
   baptis'd in, 145:25
   coursed one another, 215:38
   drew iron, 164:21
   droppings of warm, 36:5

for his love, 229:35
fountain of sweet, 317:28
hence these, 298:8
if you have, 229:41
idle tears, 294:13
in silence and, 49:36
in the mist of, 298:37
like summer tempest came, 294:20
must stop, my, 124:6
nothing is here for, 174:21
now am full of, 320:35
she stood in, 137:20
such as angels weep, 169:23
the fewer his, 417:63
they dropp'd, some natural, 173:48
to shed, bitter, 73:26
too deep for, 320:4
wash out a Word, 98:13
weep thy girlish, 309:28
wipe away all, 340:18
world as a vale of, 40:2
Teases, because he knows it, 58:8
Teche, lerne, and gladly, 63:28
Τεχνη μακρή, ή, 121:23
Tedious as a king, if I were, 258:31
Teeth are set on edge, 332:16
   barrier of thy, 123:26
   clean, keep their, 218:22
   dig one's grave with, 428:25
   gnashing of, 324:8
   keep one's tongue between, 429:52
   lest it dash out, 370:34
   never show your, 389:50
   not show their, 253:26
   sans eyes, sans, 216:17
   to cast into my, 230:16
   with the skin of my, 326:2
Teetotaller, only a beer, 274:10
Tell it not in Gath, 324:34
   me not, 149:24
   not all you know, 367:50, 414:15
   one anything, would, 314:11
   Sir, I have none to, 56:6
   that to the Marines, 414:16
   them so, do not, 64:5
   those who cannot, 203:17
   why, that I cannot, 282:5
   yet I dare not, 308:17
   you, anyhow, I can, 42:18, 42:19
Teller, as it pleases, 423:41
   bad news infects, 213:36
Telling, marred in the, 351:66

Theatre the eyes, as in a, 244:8
Theban, this same learned, 241:38
Thebes did his green unknowing youth
engage, 90:27
presenting, 164:20
Theft, suspicious head of, 246:8
Theme, fools are my, 49:38
Themes, muses on admired, 156:12
Themmes ! run softly, sweet, 284:1
Θεῶν ἐν γούνασι κεῖται, 123:29
Theoric, bookish, 259:47
Theory, reject the monstrous, 53:44
There, my child, not, 118:17
Thersites' body is as good, 219:38
Thetis, in the lap of, 48:23
Thew, friz, and then it, 345:25
They say so, is half a lie, 425:71
Thick and thin, through, 90:4
Thief, apparel fits your, 253:23
as bad as, 421:70
ask my fellow if I be, 359:74
becomes honest, 436:17
breeds, 376:72
by the throat, takes, 435:52
doth fear each bush, 238:10
each thing's a, 270:7
from the gallows, save, 409:56
hole calls, 419:56
I will show you, 411:41
if you do take a, 258:28
in the sworn twelve, 252:4
is sorry he is to be hanged, 423:43
justice rails upon, 242:4
knows a thief, 354:24
no receiver, no, 402:26
opportunity makes, 404:74
robs more than, 423:39
rope enough, give, 372:10
sing before, 414:37
[sorry] that he is, 423:43
steals something from, 260:9
the sun's a, 270:7
to catch a theif, set, 410:22
Thievery, example you with, 270:7
Thieves are hanged, little, 395:17
beauty provoketh, 215:35
break through and steal, 333:49
by the gusty, 123:41
escape, great, 395:17
fall out, when, 437:52
honour among, 424:33
marries four, 380:19

three arrant, 432:25
Thieving, inclined to, 412:54
Thighs, his cuisses on his, 233:36
Thimbles, sought it with, 60:1
Thin, but not too thin, 21:28
end of the wedge, 423:44
Thine, why not I with, 275:36
Thing as he sees It, draw, 140:18
far, far better, 84:18
that's quite another, 49:33
what a little, 18:2
which was not, said, 288:18
Things are as they be taken, 426:10
are the sons of heaven, 131:24
as They are, God of, 140:18
bright and beautiful. 17:18
full of a number of, 286:18
God's sons are, 155:27
can come, before such, 106:29
to come, mass of, 270:15
we have done those, 340:28
which we ought to have done, 340:28
who's to look after their, 142:3
Thing-um-a-jig, especially, 59:36
Think alike, great minds, 373:73
and then speak, 370:26
beer, who drink beer, 129:22
effectively, cannot, 307:19
him so because I think him so, 273:23
I'm not so, 284:10
Imperially, learn to, 61:26
it, I knew that once: but now—I, 285:21
much, speak little, 426:17
none ill, they that, 426:4
not well of me, if she, 315:27
of thee, I must not, 160:38
on thee, if the while I, 264:3
on these things, 339:53
so then, we, 147:17
the more, I, 384:39
therefore I am, I, 81:28
to yourself, 409:59
to-day, 426:19
well of all men, 426:20
what you will, 412:21
when it hurts to, 126:17
with the wise, 426:21
you can't, don't, 128:11
Thinker, God lets loose a, 94:13
Thinking, art of, 85:44
high, 317:40
is very far from knowing, 426:22

change oft, women's, 440:9
close, 384:38
covers all a man's, 61:24
dark soul and foul, 165:40
feeling of their masters', 156:12
fond and wayward, 316:18
his only friends, good, 56:1
his own highest, 138:4
intent, on hospitable, 172:14
joy of elevated, 316:14
long, long, 150:18
more elevate, in, 169:40
my bloody, 261:41
my slaughterous, 251:36
no tongue, give, 221:37
not breaths, 22:24
penny for your, 353:62
pleasant thoughts bring sad, 316:5
remain below, 225:40
restrain in me the cursed, 248:11
sensations rather than, 138:3
that arise in me, 293:48
that breathe, 113:27
that do often lie too deep for tears, 320:4
that nature gives way to, 248:11
that wander through eternity, 169:33
to conceal their, 306:16
will perish, 22:28
with your fresh, 124:17
yet, with any such, 236:2
Thousand, better than a, 327:48
pounds, draw for a, 16:5
pounds no longer, 412:65
slimy things, 69:30
such a day, spins, 198:8
ten thousand times ten, 17:24
then another, 60:15
years in thy sight, 327:50
years, thrice a, 16:10
Thousands at His bidding speed, 167:31
equally were meant, 288:13
had sunk, 55:29
slain his, 324:33
Thousandth Man will stand by your side,
142:9
Thread, any silk, any, 274:6
breaks, 423:46
feels at each, 195:34
with a cobweb, 371:64
Threatened men live long, 426:33
more men, 424:11
Threatenings and slaughter, 325:45

Threats, no terror in your, 230:14
without power, 426:34
Three are too many, 426:35
for a wedding, 404:41
gentlemen at once, 278:1
he stoppeth one of, 69:17
helping one another, 426:38
may keep counsel, 426:39
per cents, 212:9
removes are as bad, 426:40
she'll hae but, 342:6
though he was only, 163:18
whole days together, 288:3
women and a goose, 427:42
Threescore years and ten, 327:52
Threshold, dares nor cross, 62:13
of the new, upon, 307:27
set you at your, 126:12
Thrice he assay'd, 169:23
Thrift is good revenue, 427:43
is the philosopher's stone, 427:44
thrift, Horatio, 220:25
Thrive and then wive, 370:27
he that will, 382:4, 382:5
none of these two will, 372:5
with him, all, 385:64
Thriven, he that hath, 382:5
Throat, [cider] cuts, 364:32
cut a, 52:23
cut, belly thinks, 400:25
cut your, 409:56
shop in his, 422:18
to feel the fog in, 40:4
tongue cut your, 395:42
took by the, 262:16
Throe, dare, never grudge, 39:43
Throne, from her ebon, 322:1
he that sat upon, 340:18
here is my, 239:32
light that beats upon, 296:21
like a burnish'd, 214:2
of bayonets, 128:14
of royal state, on a, 169:28
on high, sit on, 180:10
through slaughter to, 112:15
up to the, 142:10
Thrones, dominations, princedoms,
virtues, powers, 172:16
Throw of the dice, best, 415:54
Thrush, pipes the mounted, 296:2
that's the wise, 38:5
Thule, farthest, 305:25

Thumb at the world, bite my, 54:7
 at you, bite my, 266:4
 golden, 368:28
 the blacker his, 419:49
 unto his nose, puts, 24:9
Thumbs, pricking of my, 250:12
 wise men cut their, 371:40
Thunder, all-shaking, 240:23
 clothed, necks in, 113:26
 grate harsh, 170:10
 he was as rattling, 214:19
 lightning, or in rain in, 242:17
 sleeps in, 353:70
 they steal my, 81:25
 winter's, 440:7, 440:8
Thunderbolt, hath but his clap, 423:47
 stricken with, 380:36
Thunderbolts, oak-cleaving, 240:23
Thundercloud, like the bursting, 208:20
Thunders, when it, 436:17
Thunder-stone, all-dreaded, 230:3
Thunderstorm, dying duck in, 395:66
 streams like, 50:24
 three hot days and, 356:32
Thursday, born on, 363:54
 come, 427:45
 for crosses, 399:76
 sneeze on, 411:69
Thursday's child, 399:77
Thus, why is this, 308:15
Thusness, reason of this, 308:15
Thwack, many a stiff, 48:17
Thwackum was for doing justice, 97:24
Thwick thwack, third [month] is, 435:71
Thyme blows, wild, 257:34
Tiber, father Tiber! 154:5
Tickle her with a hoe, 130:2
Tide always comes in again, 423:48
 at the turning o', 236:1
 brings in what, 416:38
 in the affairs of men, 230:17
 never goes out so far, 423:48
 rises, when the, 58:12
 turns at low water, 94:7
Tides of men, I drew these, 146:7
 seward flow, 18:17
Tidings, bringeth good, 332:4
 convey'd the dismal, 109:26
Tied, browse where she is, 418:21
Ties, at sight of human, 194:6
Tiger! burning bright, 30:5
 he who rides on, 382:32

Hycan, 250:5
 imitate the action of, 236:5
 smile on the face of, 344:8
 went for a ride on, 344:8
Tiger's heart wrapt in a woman's hide,
 238:4
Tight, must not be screwed too, 371:61
 will tear, 439:64
Tike or trundle-tail, 241:41
Tiles on the roofs, as there are, 152:5
Timber, like seasoned, 120:1
Timbuctoo, plains of, 313:28
Time a-dying, unconscionable, 62:6
 ambles withal, who, 217:30
 and age, 'gainst, 189:16
 and chance, happeneth, 330:25
 and chance reveal all, 427:46
 and circumstance, 116:4
 and me, wastes her, 307:26
 and nonsense scorning, 41:33
 and the hour, 247:30
 and the place, never, 40:18
 and thinking, 427:47
 and tide, 427:48
 backward and abysm of, 268:18
 bank and shoal of, 247:40
 bounds of place and, 113:25
 but for all, 134:15
 by heart-throbs, count, 22:24
 by the forelock, take, 414:1
 carelessly, fleet the, 215:29
 choose thine own, 23:35
 chronicle of wasted, 265:23
 chronicles of the, 223:43
 coming, a good, 154:18, 424:21
 cormorant devouring, 245:31
 creeping hours of, 216:16
 defy, power can, 131:22
 doth temperately keep, 226:7
 fleeth away, 427:49
 flies, 414:19
 footprints on the sands of, 149:28
 for a moment of, 94:1
 for all things, 424:25
 forefinger of all, 294:9
 'gainst the tooth of, 253:24
 gallops withal, who, 217:30
 give peace in our, 340:31
 goes, you say, 86:1
 had a glorious, 90:1
 half as old as, 42:20
 has made, chinks that, 307:27

Tiresias and Phineus, 170:16
Tithe of mint, ye pay, 325:46
Title, gained no, 197:35
  long and dark, successive, 89:33
  suit three, whatever, 44:17
Titles, decliner of honours and, 96:2
  high though his, 209:24
  take, kings their, 61:29
Tityre, tu, 305:21
Tityrus found the Golden Age, 76:21
Toad, I had rather be, 261:31
  ugly and venomous, 215:37
  under a harrow, like, 395:71
Toast of a' the town, yon, 44:2
  pass, let the, 278:6
  warm as, 359:63
Toasted-cheese, enemies, 59:37
Tobacco, devilish and damned, 47:42
  divine, rare, 47:41
  varieties of, 87:30
Tocherless dame, 354:25
Tocsin of the soul, 52:27
To-day a man, 431:52
  and gone to-morrow, here, 383:52
  and to-morrow, look on, 180:10
  better an egg, 361:46
  for I have liv'd, 90:32
  his own, can call, 90:32
  is worth, one, 404:68
  is Yesterday's pupil, 431:53
  me, to-morrow thee, 431:54
  one hour, 404:47
  was past and dead, 16:10
  what may be done, 401:60
Toe, light fantastic, 163:34
  lissom, clerical, 34:3
Toes, happier without, 147:20
Togae, cedant arma, 66:21
Together do best, both, 363:57
  must all hang, 101:27
Toil, envy, want, 130:12
  he won, what with, 89:27
  mock the hope of, 77:24
  mock their useful, 112:8
  not, neither do they spin, 333:54
  of a pleasure, make, 385:49
  verse softens, 104:13
Told, for being twice, 357:67
  me you had been to her, 58:14
  that left half, 164:22
  the sexton, went and, 123:34
  till another [tale] is, 404:67

Toledo trusty, 48:15
Tolerable and not to be endured, most,
    258:27
Toleration, I'm for, 159:24
Toll [of bell] for the brave, 75:24
  or knell, hear, 437:54
Toll [tax], talking pays no, 414:8
Toll'd the bell, sexton, 123:34
Tom Fool knows, than, 400:12
  more know, 400:12
Tom o' Bedlam, sigh like, 240:12
Tom, so no more of, 52:29
Tom the Second reigns, 90:11
Tomb, asleep within the, 31:26
  come this side the, 79:31
  Fidele's grassy, 71:39
  threefold, fourfold, 26:3
Tombs, hark! from the, 309:38
Tombstone white, a, 142:12
Tommy this, an' Tommy that, 141:35
Tomnoddy, My Lord, 34:11
To-morrow, and to-morrow, 251:37
  boast not thyself of, 329:59
  come never, 431:55
  defer not till, 72:12
  do thy worst, 90:32
  dupe of, 76:11
  I may be myself with Yesterday's, 98:3
  is a new day, 431:56
  put off till, 401:60
  there is no, 435:73
  to fresh woods, 167:24
  will repay, think, 91:39
  worth two, 404:47
To-morrow's falser than the former day,
    91:39
  sun to thee, 72:12
To-morrows, confident, 320:7
  worth two, 404:68
Tones are remembered not, sweet, 277:22
Tongs, not touch him with a pair of, 385:55
Tongue, better the foot slip than, 362:21
  between one's teeth, keep, 429:52
  breaks bone, 423:50
  brings in a several tale, every, 245:28
  but one, 400:32
  can no man tame, 340:2
  cannot hold his, 376:45
  cool words scald not, 365:54
  could utter, would that, 292:48
  cut your throat, let not, 395:42
  dropt manna, his, 169:32

709

it is, a haunted, 145:21
little one-horse, 303:28
man made the, 74:33
mine own romantic, 210:3
of Bethlehem, little, 34:10
or city, centre of each, 122:17
seaward from the, 127:35
surpasses, ne'er a, 46:6
townsman of a stiller, 126:12
Town-dweller, modern, 128:13
Towns contend, seven, 212:20
Toy dog is covered with dust, 96:16
foolish thing was but, 272:21
Toys for your delight, 287:26
not to meddle with, 286:15
Track, around the ancient, 160:24
come flying on our, 300:20
with a golden, 148:15
Tract behind, leaving no, 270:3
Trace abroad, venture, 235:43
every man to his, 368:40
gathers samphire, dreadful, 241:48
his silly old, 310:31
poor, 366:27
two of a, 432:36
Trade's proud empire, 131:22
Trades, jack of all, 392:33
man of many, 353:48
mother of all, 406:52
Tradesmen, becomes none but, 274:8
Trafficked for strange webs, 187:30
Tragedy, comedy, history, 223:38
gorgeous, 164:20
to those that feel, 307:29
you *may* abuse a, 132:16
Tragical-comical-historical-pastoral,
223:39
Trail again, pull out on, 140:9
a-winding, long, long, 139:21
pull out on the Long, 140:10
that is always new, 140:10
Train, as we rush in the, 300:20
attendant, for a, 45:26
her starry, 171:33
up a child, 329:50
who follows in His, 118:9
Train-band captain eke, 75:26
Traitor is hated, 423:55
Traitors, fears do make us, 250:18
jeer, 72:13
Traitors' arms, more strong than, 230:3
Tram, not a bus but a, 116:12

Trance, no nightly, 163:25
Tranquillity, recollected in, 320:18
Transcendental kind, of a, 104:36
Transgressors, way of, 328:29
Transit gloria mundi, sic, 138:12
Translated, thou art, 257:38
Translators, traitors, 431:68
Translunary things, brave, 88:10
Transmitter, no tenth, 208:12
Transportation for life, 60:2
Transports, permit the, 291:20
Trap fell, when, 435:40
Trash and trumpery, 431:69
Travail, my labour for my, 270:14
so gladly spent, 320:28
Travel all the world over, 354:5
forth, make me, 264:5
hopefully, to, 286:4
[makes] a fool worse, 431:70
makes a wise man better, 431:70
Travell'd, much have I, 136:3
Traveller, five hours sleepeth, 370:31
lame, 352:12
may lie, 354:27
on his way, help, 368:17
returns, no, 224:4
said the, 81:20
spurs the lated, 249:43
Travellers may lie, 404:8
must be content, 216:1
Travelling becomes dull, 207:26
Travels, contemplation of, 217:37
far, he that, 381:65
the fastest, he, 142:10
Tray, Blanch, and Sweet-heart, 241:40
Trays, iron-ware and cheap tin, 159:23
Tre, Pol, and Pen, 363:73
Treacle, fly that sips, 103:34
Tread, doth close behind him, 69:36
elastic from her airy, 210:21
every so airy a, 296:19
is on an Empire's dust, 50:10
lightly, she is near, 314:14
softly, 320:33
with cautious steps, 73:28
Treads on it daily, swain, 166:3
Treason can but peep, 226:22
doth never prosper, 116:13ˉ
gunpowder, 345:26
has done his worst, 249:36
if *this*, be, 119:31
is loved, 423:55

him no further, 385:2
him not, speak him fair and, 381:52
him with untold gold, 442:10
in him will I, 327:54
in princes, put not, 328:14
is treason, in, 389:61
it, trustworthy as you, 81:27
me, 431:73
me, gentleman, 267:24
none, 236:3
that's purer than pearl, 40:19
the man, never, 97:23
themselves with men, I wonder men
  dare, 270:5
try before you, 432:16
Trusted, let no such man be, 256:2
Trusts, offices as public, 53:45
Trusty, dusky, vivid, true, 287:28
Truth and Nature, from, 76:21
  and oil are ever above, 432:3
  and roses have thorns, 432:14
  and shame the devil, tell, 232:22
  and soberness, 338:4
  as I have meant, such, 320:28
  be tried out, till, 366:23
  brightness, purity and, 186:2
  cannot be shamed, 432:11
  children and fools speak, 364:18
  comes out, 369:64
  fears no colours, 432:4
  find, 414:12
  finds foes, 432:5
  fools and madmen speak, 370:37
  friend to, 197:35
  from his lips prevail'd, 109:23
  great is, 340:20
  has such a face, 90:9
  hath a good face, 432:6
  hath a quiet breast, 243:22
  [hath] bad clothes, 432:6
  his utmost skill, 320:21
  I hold it, 295:38
  in every shepherd's tongue, 202:5
  in wine there is, 389:63
  is as impossible to be soiled, 174:26
  [is] beauty, 137:24
  is clear, one, 195:37
  is God's daughter, 432:7
  is marching on, His, 127:25
  is stranger than fiction, 432:8
  is truth to the end, 432:9
  lay all undiscovered, 183:30

lie which is half a, 294:30
lies at the bottom of a well, 432:10
loves to go naked, 365:63
may be blamed, 432:11
miscall'd simplicity, 264:12
needs not many words, 432:12
never grows old, 432:13
put to the worse, who ever knew, 174:35
quench'd the open, 210:22
seeks no corners, 432:15
shall be thy warrant, 202:11
shall make you free, 337:47
sits upon the lips, 18:22
sole judge of, 195:39
sting of a reproach is, 422:30
tell, 414:17
that's brighter than gem, 40:19
the greater, 418:31
the poets sings, 293:33
this mournful, 130:9
time trieth, 427:55
to be a liar, doubt, 223:30
tongues can poison, 70:6
too near, follow not, 370:34
well known to most, 76:12
what is, 22:7
when he speaks, 352:17
which cunning times put on, 254:26
will paint it, as, 77:23
with Falsehood, strife of, 151:30
with gold she weighs, 194:12
Truth's sacred fort, 34:15
Truths are not to be told, all, 356:14
  fate of new, 128:8
  instruments of darkness tell us, 257:28
  that wake to perish never, 320:1
  to be self-evident, 129:29
Try before you trust, 432:16
  till you, 442:19
  try again, 121:19
Tub must stand on its own bottom, 369:49
Tubal Cain was a man of might, 154:17
Tuesday, born on, 363:54
  for health, 399:76
  sneeze on, 411:69
Tuesday's child, 399:77
Tug of war, then comes, 436:11
  of war, then was the, 147:25
Tugs in a different way, 52:33
Tully, said I, no, 39:36
Tumble down, must, 278:14
Tumbles and tosses, all night, 439:40

Tumult and the shouting dies, 140:25
Tun, drink of a, 349:5
Tune and harsh, out of, 224:12
  bring all things into, 350:27
  call, 382:31
  singeth a quiet, 69:34
  sweetly play'd in, 47:26
Tunes of Spain, slow old, 159:25
Turf, a green grassy, 26:16
  above thee, green be, 115:17
  that wraps their clay, 71:34
Turk, bear, like the, 198:2
  malignant and a turban'd, 262:16
  out-paramoured the, 241:32
  the unspeakable, 57:37
  work as hard as a, 342:21
Turkey, carps, hops, 432:19
Turkey, they always say in, 82:13
Turkey-cock, red as, 358:30
Turn again, pass and, 95:26
  cat in pan, 431:43
  deserves another, good, 404:43
  he that does you an ill, 378:16
  in his grave, 429:72
  it over once more, 310:30
  to him the other [cheek], 333:44
Turned, bees cannot be, 412:61
  him right and round, 47:27
  round, having once, 69:36
  up, in case anything, 84:3
Turning, lane that has no, 390:11
Turnip than his father, have, 131:20
Turnips cries, man who, 131:20
Turns, goes far that never, 375:60
Turpissimus, repente fuit, 135:26
Turret, the Sultan's, 375:60
Turtle [dove] is heard, voice of, 330:40
  love of the, 51:32
  to her mate, true as, 359:57
Turtle [sea-tortoise] eats, straight he, 38:15
  soup, I waved the, 104:17
Tuscany, even the ranks of, 154:6
Tutor, ill natures never want, 388:23
Twang, most melodious, 20:13
Tweedledum and Tweedledee, 49:34
Twelve good men into a box, 34:14
Twelve-month hence, appear, 132:17
Twenty, handsome at, 379:72
  kiss me, sweet and, 271:37
  not one among, 389:60
  per cent, clap on, 56:11
Twenty-four, we shall be, 126:19

Twice, he gives, 363:43
  he giveth, 375:58
  if things were to be, 387:38
Twig, bend while 'tis, 360:38
  is bent, as the, 196:15
Twilight and evening bell, 298:6
  dim with rose, 80:14
  grey had in her sober livery all things
    clad, 171:32
  of such day, 264:13
  sheds, disastrous, 169:22
  was falling, when, 296:12
Twilight's curtain spreading, 67:25
  last gleaming, 138:17
Twin Brethren, the great, 154:9
Twinkle, little star, 291:28
Twinkling of a bed-staff, in, 213:22
Twist ye, twine ye, 211:36
Two and one are three, 285:19
  are walking apart, 128:16
  attorneys can live, 432:22
  be away, if, 426:39
  birds with one stone, 429:55
  bites of a cherry, make, 430:3
  blacks do not make a white, 432:23
  can play at, game, 414:23
  cats and a mouse, 432:24
  contend against, 404:75
  daughters and a back door, 432:25
  ears, two eyes, 400:32
  eyes can see more, 432:29
  faces in one hood, 427:69
  fools in one house, 432:30
  for mirth, 404:41
  hares, run after, 387:61
  heads are better than one, 432:31
  hoards, he that has, 379:39
  [hours] after midnight, worth, 404:48
  in distress, 432:33
  is company, 432:35
  of a trade, 432:36
  or three are gathered, 324:35
  people happened to hit, 278:10
  places at once, in, 404:32
  roads diverged, 102:9
  she join'd the former, 90:18
  sorrows of one, make not, 398:2
  strings to one's bow, 429:46
  thereby, grows, 119:37
  to come and go, 59:31
  to make a quarrel, 392:30
  to one in all things, 433:41

too too will in, 431:63
voices are there, 285:19, 320:5
will, that which, 414:31
wives in one house, 32:24
wrongs don't make a right, 433:42
Two-and-twenty, sweet, 53:35
Two-legg'd thing, a son, 89:27
Twopence Coloured, 286:6
shall never want, 381:66
Tyburn and the rope, to, 298:25
Types, device of movable, 57:23

Tyranny begins, where law ends, 62:10
Tyrans, arrosé par le sang des, 24:1
Tyrant, impertinent, anonymous, 128:12
of his fields, little, 112:14
Tyrants, argument of, 191:16
from policy, 43:31
seem to kiss, when, 262:18
watered by blood of, 24:1
Tyrawley and I have been dead, 64:10
Tyre, which men still call, 99:28

U

Υδωρ, ριστον, 190:13
Uglification and derision, 58:11
Ugly as sin, 359:62
that makes me, 262:7
Ulpian at the best, 39:36
Ultima Thule, 305:25
Ultimate and sacred thing, 65:27
Ultra-poetical, super-aesthetical, 104:41
Ulysses, bend the bow of, 429:49
his naked, 62:3
Umble, not only humble but, 303:14
person, I'm a very, 84:6
Umbrella, unjust steals the just's, 32:6
Umpire, the pavilion cat, 145:24
Unadorned adorned the most, when 300:13
Unarm, Eros, 214:15
Unattempted yet, things, 168:2
Un-birthday present, for an, 59:29
Unborn, better, 362:23
Uncertainty, glorious, 155:22
nothing is certain but, 403:52
Uncharitableness, all, 340:34
Uncle, Prophetic soul! my, 222:14
Uncoffin'd and unknown, 51:29
Uncouth, unkissed, 433:47
Unction, lay not that flattering, 226:8
Underground, might well be, 106:11
Underlings, that we are, 228:11
Understand a good many things, 82:15
Understanding, but no tongue, give it,
220:32
find you an, 134:2

passeth all, 339:52
that have no, 341:46
will … extinguish pleasure, 126:23
Underwood and cover, green, 290:2
Undismayed, ruins would strike him,
125:31
Undone, done canot be, 426:12
we have left, 340:28
Undonne, to want, to be, 283:31
Unearned increment, 162:8
Uneasy lies the head, 234:21
Unexercised and unbreathed, 174:30
Unexpected always happens, 423:58
that always happens, 392:19
Unforeseen that always happens, 329:19
Unfortunate, if you are too, 387:47
one more, 124:8
Ungained, prize the thing, 270:14
Ungue leonem, ex, 369:59
Unguem factus homo, ad, 125:23
Unguess'd at, on earth, 18:16
Unhand me, gentlemen, 222:10
Unhanged, not three good men, 232:6
Unhappy in its own way, 302:4
Unheard are sweeter, 137:22
Unhouseled, disappointed, unaneled,
222:17
Un-idea'd girls, wretched, 132:7
Uniform 'e wore, 141:39
Union, dissolution of the, 200:30
in partition, an, 257:40
of hearts, the union of hands, 180:2

of lakes, the union of lands, 180:2
of States, 180:2
strong and great, 150:13
Unison with what we hear, in, 76:3
Unit, misses an, 39:29
Unite, love, friendship, respect, do not,
  64:3
United we stand, 180:2
Universe, born for the, 109:33
  into this, 98:7
  is his box of toys, 300:6
  to mingle with, 51:27
Universities, some to the studious, 272:24
  state of both, 302:9
University a collection of books, true,
  57:32
  his own Mother, 90:27
  should be, 85:34
Unjust fella, also on the, 32:6
Unkind, that are sodden and, 27:27
  thou art not so, 217:18
  unkissed, 433:46
  when I asked I was, 436:14
Unkindest cut of all, 230:2
Unkindness, tax you not with, 241:24
Unkissed, uncouth, 433:47
  unkind, 433:46
Unknowable, O world, 300:3
Unknown, argues yourselves, 172:4
  by what is still more unknown, 388:13
  is taken as marvellous, 290:7
  tread safely into, 117:26
  unkissed, 433:47
Unlearned, amaze the, 192:11
Unleaving, over Goldengrove, 124:17
Unlikely gets over, 396:1
Unlucky in love, 433:48
Unmannerly, better be, 361:62
Unminded, unmoaned, 433:49
Unmoved, cold, 265:18
Unnumbered laughter, waves', 16:12
Unparticular man, a nice, 115:23
Unpolluted in his beam, 291:29
Unpossessed, sweeter, 160:20
Unprofitable, flat and, 220:19
Unreasonable man, progress depends on,
  274:19
Unreprieved, unpitied, 169:35
Unrespited, unpitied, unreprieved, 69:35
Unrighteousness, mammon of, 336:28
Unseen, untalk'd of and, 267:41
  with a cheer, greet, 40:21

Unsound minds, 433:50
Unstable as water, 323:40
Untaught, better unborn than, 362:23
  than ill taught, better, 362:24
Untender, so young and so, 240:8
Unthankful, no worse than, 440:62
Unthrift, as bad as, 367:71
Unused, to fust in us, 226:15
Unutterable things, looked, 300:11
Unvalued persons do, as, 220:34
Unwashed, the great, 34:14
Unwept, unhonour'd, and unsung, 209:24
Up and doing, let us be, 149:29
  and not down, to look, 115:14
  before he is down, take, 430:29
  go we! hey! then, 200:25
  Guards, and at them, 310:14
  nor down, neither, 342:26
  only half-way, 342:26
  see me safe, 179:23
  up! my friend, 316:8
Ὑπείροχον εμμεναι αλλων, 123:28
Uphill all the way, wind, 206:11
Upper air, pass out to, 306:6
Upright, God hath made man, 330:22
  life, man of, 125:26
Upstairs and downstairs, 162:14
Upward, move, 296:7
Urania, govern thou my song, 172:22
Urbem fecisti, 208:2
Urchin found it yet, never, 57:39
Urn, bubbling and loud-hissing, 74:41
  drain not to its dregs, 277:26
  from her pictured, 113:27
  storied, 112:11
Usance, brings down the rate of, 253:38
Use and benefit of men, for, 302:1
  doth breed a habit, 272:31
  for it, you will find, 393:45
  for yourself, 364:27
  keener with constant, 129:21
  legs and have legs, 433:52
  more than we, 400:14
  strained from that fair, 267:31
  the means, 433:53
Useless each without the other, 150:15
Uses, to what base, 227:35
Ushant to Scilly, from, 342:30
Utter, lisps out in all they, 52:11
Utterance, how divine is, 160:34
Uttermost parts, dwell in, 328:12

V

upon veil behind, 18:12
Vein, in King Cambyses', 232:16
  this is Ercles', 257:27
Veins, sea itself floweth in your, 302:6
Velasquez, why drag in, 312:4
Velle atque idem nolle, idem, 208:7
Velvet, valiant in, 118:20
Veneres Cupidinesque, lugete, 60:12
Vengeance, do it with a, 387:43
  follows, 438:21
  is mine, 338:15
  noblest, 421:47
Veni, vidi, vici, 53:42
Venice, I stood in, 50:21
  sate in state, 50:22
Venison, all flesh is not, 355:71
Venom to that of the tongue, no, 425:48
Venture, drew a bow at a, 325:52
  not all in one, 433:60
  nothing, 403:59
Ventures, or lose our, 230:17
Venus, that's your, 39:25
  toute entière, 202:4
Venus's very self, 202:4
Ver, first-born child of, 100:7
Verboojuice, sesquippledan, 311:20
Verbosity, exuberance of, 85:37
  thread of his, 246:10
Verbum sat sapienti, 433:61
Vere de Vere, caste of, 292:15
Verfahren, niemals anders, 135:36
Verge of her confine, on, 261:31
Verger translated to me, 24:3
Verify your references, 207:21
Verisimilitude, artistic, 106:15
Veritas, in vino, 389:63
Vero, se non è, 409:73
Versate manu, nocturna, 126:4
Verse, a breeze mid blossoms, 71:21
  can gently steer, in, 91:31
  cursed be the, 198:3
  for the other's sake, one, 48:20
  hoarse, rough, 192:16
  join the varying, 198:11
  married to immortal, 164:9
  sail of his great, 264:14
  sisters, Voice and, 163:27
  softens toil, 104:13
  subject of all, 35:28
  will seem prose, 41:32
  you grave for me, 287:22
Verses, false gallop of, 217:24

rhyme the rudder is of, 48:16
  tear him for his bad, 230:8
Vesper's, 'st, there's, 37:32
Vessel, a goodly, 150:12
  as unto the weaker, 340:5
  goes, the gilded, 113:30
  grim and daring, 313:17
  strikes, till the, 281:6
  will ride, no, 438:16
Vessels, empty, 368:9
Vestal grace, her spirit's, 188:6
vestal's lot, blameless, 194:8
Veterans rewards, world its, 197:25
Vicar compelled him to walisbury, 344:12
  of Bray, I will be, 343:22
Vicar's skirts, by, 416:19
Vice, any taint of, 272:18
  by action dignified, 367:31
  he lash'd the, 288:13
  is a creature, 87:16
  is a monster, 195:40
  is, where, 438:21
  itself lost half its evil, 43:30
  makes virtue shine, 433:62
  parent of all, 385:61
  pays to virtue, homage, 384:24
  raptures and roses of, 298:36
  ruleth, 433:63
  so simple, no, 254:25
  that reverend, 232:17
Vices, bids others think of his, 381:64
  do appear, small, 242:5
  fight one another, 433:69
  of our pleasant, 242:11
Vicissitude of things, sad, 104:13
Vicisti, Galilaee, 135:22
Victim must be found, a, 106:11
Victims play, the little, 111:33
Victis, vae, 149:18
Victories, after a thousand, 263:34
Victorious cause was pleasing to the gods,
  152:2
  o'er a' the ills, 46:9
  send him, 243:23
Victors belong the spoils, to, 156:6
Victory Ball, fun of the, 184:13
  done, life's, 162:15
  fat, 361:42
  for humanity, till you have won some,
  156:4
  or to, 46:22
  'twas a famous, 282:5

Westminster Abbey or, 182:13
where is thy, 339:36
Victrix causa deis placuit, 152:2
Vieillesse pouvait, si, 95:31
quelle triste, 290:14
View, enchantment to the, 55:17
from every point of, 73:30
not fair to outward, 68:14
wide and luminous, 19:20
will landscape tire, 92:15
with extensive, 130:11
Vigilance, eternal, 78:15
Vigilant, be sober, be, 340:7
Vile, nought so, 267:31
seem vile, to the, 241:45
Villa, if one must have a, 179:31
Village of the plain, 108:12
which men still call Tyre, 99:28
Villages, in these peculiar, 129:20
Villain and he be many miles asunder, 268:4
condemns me for a, 245:28
determined to prove, 245:14
far be the, 291:18
hungry lean-faced, 218:19
smiling, damned, 222:21
still pursued her, 184:2
Villain's mind, fair terms and, 254:8
Villains by necessity, 240:11
Villainy, clothe my naked, 245:16
one piece of, 305:34
you teach me, 254:20
Vinchy, pronounce it, 303:27
Vine, and under his fig tree, under, 332:26
leaves in his hair, 332:26
monarch of the, 214:6
the gadding, 166:13
Vinegar aspect, of such, 253:26
of sweet wine, 412:74
sharpest, 412:59
Vines, foxes that spoil, 331:41
Vino veritas, in, 389:63
Vintage, trampling out, 127:25
Vintners buy, what the, 99:18
Violence, offer it the show of, 220:9
Violent delights have violent ends, 267:35
Violently if they must, 201:30
Violet by a mossy stone, 317:20
grows, nodding, 257:34
has and the camellia has not, what the, 78:3
here and there a, 26:16
the glowing, 167:22

throw a perfume on, 240:2
Violet-crowned, Athens, 190:14
Violets blue, 246:16
dim, 274:1
in the lane, finds, 439:39
it's raining, 151:27
plucked the sweetest rain makes not fresh, 100:3
purple, 263:20
sicken, when sweet, 276:19
spring, may, 227:37
upon a bank of, 271:24
were born, 40:16
wind-flowers and, 276:10
Vipers, generation of, 332:32
Virgil, not where Fancy, leads the way, where, 76:21
Virgin and the Scales, 346:3
thorn, withering on, 256:20
Virgin's sidelong looks, 108:14
Virginian, I am not a, 119:32
Virginity, power o'er true, 165:42
Virgo, plena gratiâ ave, 37:32
Virtue and a trade, 433:64
and happiness, 433:65
and vice, between, 132:20
and vice, to mingle, 133:30
could see to do what virtue would, 165:39
fall, some by, 252:5
feeble were, if, 166:7
fugitive and cloistered, 175:30
good my mouse of, 271:31
if there be any, 339:53
if you have it not, assume a, 226:9
in her shape how lovely, 172:5
is bold, 253:20
is its own reward, 433:66
is the sole and only nobility, 135:33
itself 'scapes not, 221:35
itself turns vice, 267:31
keep your, 142:15
let them look on, 190:2
lilies and languors of, 289:36
lovers of, 308:6
may unlock hell, 300:1
never grows old, 433:67
of necessity, make, 397:76
progressive, 300:10
reward of virtue is, 94:12
she alone is free, 166:7
she finds too painful, 197:23

Volcan, dansons sur un, 208:8
Volcano, dancing on a, 208:8
Volleyed and thunder'd, 295:28
Volo, sic jubeo, hoc, 135:29
Volontate, in la sua, 79:21
Volscians, flutter'd your, 219:29
Voltaire, mock on, 30:7
Volume, over my open, 145:17
  quaint and curious, 191:24
Volumes carry, all Earth's, 62:2
  in folio, whole, 246:3
  of stuff, written, 147:13
  that I prize, 268:21
Voluntas, sit pro ratione, 135:29
Volunteer is worth, one, 405:70
Voluptas, votum timor ira, 135:25
Vomit, turned to his own, 340:8
Vos non vobis, sic, 306:10
Votaress passed, imperial, 257:32
Votarist, like a sad, 165:34

Vote away, fortunes and lives, 34:11
  that shakes the turrets, 122:14
Voted at my party's call, 105:29
Voter, your every, 67:27
Vow and not pay, 330:16
  better that thou shouldest not, 330:16
Vowels tire, ear the open, 192:14
Vows forgotten in calms, 433:70
  made in storms, 433:70
  to the blackest devil, 226:23
Vox et praeterea nihil, 433:71
  populi vox Dei, 433:72
Voyage, goes a great, 375:59
Voyager at last, lands the, 94:2
Vulcan's stithy, foul as, 225:21
Vulgar boy, saw a little, 24:10
  throng, I hate the, 125:29
  [war] looked upon as, 314:6
Vulgus, odi profanum, 125:29
Vulture, rage of the, 51:32

W

Wabe, gyre and gimble in, 58:17
Wade no more, should I, 250:10
Wading, no safe, 402:29
Wage will get a page, 433:73
Wages and are dead, took their, 126:22
  if you pay not, 387:59
  need not be afraid to ask, 381:46
  of sin is death, 338:10
  ta'en thy, 220:1
Wagon to a star, hitch your, 95:18
Wagoner a small grey-coated gnat, 266:13
  as Phaethon, such, 267:41
Waist, bosom to thy slender, 200:8
  confin'd, slender, 307:22
Wait, all things come to those who, 356:13
  and see, 20:12
  for no man, time and tide, 427:48
  learn to labour and, 149:29
  upon, he come to, 49:32
Waite, to ride, to ronne, to, 283:31
Waiter roars it, the, 145:20
Waiting for Sir Richard Strachan, 344:4

Waiting-gentlewoman, like, 231:36
Wake not a sleeping lion, 433:74
  [sorrow] not, 436:25
  without owing, 411:58
Waked me too soon, you have, 309:34
Waking no such matter, 265:16
Wales England wed, 204:1
Walet lay biforn him, his, 63:36
Walk a mile, after supper, 355:57
  cat's, 350:4
  in fear and dread, doth, 69:36
  into my parlour, 127:28
  O why do you, 73:22
  on earth unguess'd at, 19:16
  over, for wise men to, 363:63
  over the western wave, 276:18
  where'er you, 192:3
  with God, closer, 76:15
Walking all alane, I was, 342:7
  I see them, 304:15
  up and down in it, 325:59
Walks between, echoing, 173:40

voices prophesying, 70:11
who preacheth, 439:55
whole art of, 310:16
will cease to be popular, 314:6
wither'd is the garland of, 214:17
War's alarms, used to, 123:35
Warbl'st at eve, 163:29
Ward has no heart, 205:18
Wardrobe (or from his straw valise), from his, 146:12
War-drum throbb'd no longer, 293:35
Ware [articles], brittle, 372:19
good, 373:59
in turn, deal in every, 54:8
is never cheap, ill, 388:25
pleasing, 406:33
Ware [aware] in time, that is, 376:29
Ware, I should dine at, 75:31
Wares, no keeping, 366:3
would not be sold, bad, 385:74
Warld, it's a weary, 25:25
to rest are gane, weary, 25:16
Warling, young man's, 361:52
Warm as toast, 359:63
can keep himself, 376:28
head and feet keep, 419:45
Warms himself for once, 377:73
too near that burns, 382:23
Warning, echoes the, 187:21
give little, 23:35
Warrant with them, carry, 389:68
Warrior dead, brought her, 294:19
painful, 263:34
taking his rest, 215:32
who is the happy, 319:24
Warriors, fierce fiery, 229:23
true, Clan-Alpine's, 211:27
Wars and rumours of war, 325:49
breed man's, 441:41
bring scars, 434:7
of old, thousand, 296:5
that make ambition virtue, 261:35
to try their fortune there, to the, 273:24
Was, nor is, what ne'er, 192:8
Wash a blackamoor white, 431:45
dirty linen in public, 431:46
your feet seldom, 434:8
your hands often, 434:8
your head never, 434:8
Washen louse, new, 403:57
Washeth the other, hand, 405:46
Washing ain't wanted, 345:19

and never getting finished, always, 116:1
his hands, seem'd, 124:2
never the whiter for, 365:70
Washing-day, being, 189:25
Wasp, stung in the arm by, 107:27
Waste, haste makes, 374:33
make no, 412:30
not, want not, 434:9
the hush'd Chorasmian, 19:23
wilful, 439:69
Wastes and withers there, 314:16
Watch and pray, 94:4, 325:58
one to, 16:9
out, ef you don't, 204:5
to babble, for the, 258:27
together, call the rest of, 258:26
whispers of each other's, 236:10
with more advised, 253:32
you can't make, 442:3
Watch-dog's honest bark, 52:15
voice that bay'd, 108:18
Watches, judgments as our, 192:4
Watchword recall, the, 180:2
Water, acid without any, 24:7
benison of hot, 34:6
[beware of] still, 362:34
bring in the clean, 364:6
cast not out the foul, 364:6
clear, watch the, 102:6
come down at Lodore, 282:3
complains it wants, 422:10
drawn wells have sweetest, 367:68
drink no longer, 339:60
famine, under, 433:45
fire, and soldiers, 434:10
goes by, much, 400:19
goes, don't care where, 64:20
honest, 270:6
I came like, 98:6
in a sieve, carry, 428:10
in an unknown, 402:29
in imperceptible, 124:2
in one's shoes, 359:66
in the deepest, 389:53
in the other [hand], 375:51
into the sea, cast, 428:11
is best, 190:13
is shallow, where, 438:16
like holy, 407:77
limns the, 22:23
little drops of, 57:41
name was written in, 138:5

it will be, good, 437:41
little we fear, 299:26
prepare for foul, 389:41
season of calm, 320:2
the cuckoo likes, 116:11
through cloudy, 23:35
'twill be winterly, 386:3
what dreadful hot, 21:30
will be cold and rough, 436:24
winter, 440:9
Weatherby George Dupree, 163:18
Weave the warp and weave the woof,
    113:29
with toil and care, 275:31
Web we weave, tangled, 210:12
Wed, December when they, 218:4
it, think to, 213:25
over the mixen, 362:26
over the moor, 362:26
the fair Ellen, was to, 210:9
where is hap is, will, 353:47
Wedding clothes, bought her, 16:4
day and death day, 354:32
day, barefoot on her, 268:12
day, it is my, 75:31
day, that earliest, 138:9
in the church, saw, 189:24
Wedding-ring wears, as, 359:71
Wedge, thin end of, 423:44
Wedlock hath oft compared been, 79:28
is a padlock, 434:35
tames man, age and, 355:59
Wednesday, born on, 363:54
sneeze on, 411:69
the best day of all, 399:76
Wednesday's child, 399:77
Weds with shame, 396:24
Wee, modest crimson-tippèd, 45:24
sleekit, cowrin', 44:11
Weed [plant], bites on every, 377:68
mars, one ill, 405:49
pernicious, 74:16
who art so lovely fair, 262:4
Weed [robe], rob Tellus of her, 263:20
Weeds [plants], garden full of, 353:50
grow apace, ill, 388:26
long live the, 124:18
no garden without, 402:4
reign o'er the land, 77:24
smell far worse than, 265:19
want no sowing, 434:36
Weeds [robes] outworn, her winter, 277:25

Week, days that's in the, 56:18
[happy], for, 394:39
is gone, 427:45
live well for, 388:5
see what can be accomplished in, 286:3
Weening is not measure, 434:37
Weep, and you weep alone, 313:29
but never see, may, 144:13
every house would, 385:73
for her, that he should, 223:46
for you, the Walrus said, I, 59:26
I saw my Lady, 343:16
no more, nor sigh, 100:3
not, my wanton, 114:1
or she will die, must, 294:19
out his eyes, may, 439:43
'tis that I may not, 53:26
who would not, 198:2
you no more, 343:17
Weeping and the laughter, 87:21
away, you'll come, 396:30
cross, comes home by, 378:33
may endure for a night, 326:27
there shall be, 324:8
Weigh right, 434:38
Weighed in the balances, 332:19
Weighs not, to whom it, 375:52
Weight and measure, 434:39
and measure, good, 373:60
he carries, 75:29
of another's burden, 402:38
Weird sisters, the, 247:22
we cannot shape, 434:16
Welcome as flowers in May, 359:65
as water in one's shoes, 359:66
bay deep-mouth'd, 52:15
both in bower and hall, 379:56
death, 435:40
ever smiles, 270:18
evil, 435:41
friend, 399:68
is the best cheer, 435:42
singing to, 96:5
such farewell, such, 412:51
to your gory bed, 46:22
Welcomest when they are gone, 237:26
Well [rightly], acts nobly, does, 322:5
all is well that ends, 355:79
all would be, 437:40
alone, let, 395:50
and fair, nothing but, 174:21
as the beggar knows his dish, 359:67

bed-time and all, 233:41
can't move her, looking, 288:1
done, 325:54
done, want a thing, 387:66
enough, knows when he is, 376:30
enough, soon enough if, 412:5
fast till he is, 278:21
he that would be, 382:11
it is not done, 132:21
laugh and be, 113:35
not how long but how, 392:10
oft we mar what's, 240:15
to make it, 291:21
'twill all be, 99:17
when I did, 436:13
when you are, 437:60
with him, all is, 355:80
with me, where it is, 438:6
with the child, is it, 325:53
Well [*hole*], at the bottom of, 432:10
goes so often to, 421:58
if you leap into, 387:57
not so deep as a, 267:40
runs dry, till, 434:23
Well-bred, sensible and, 74:15
very strange and, 72:11
Well-content, sweet, 79:30
Well-doing, weary in, 339:46
Well-favoured man, to be, 258:25
Wells are seldom dry, drawn, 367:67
have sweetest water, drawn, 367:68
Welshman keeps nothing, 423:66
Wen, the great, 68:6
Wenceslas, good King, 182:11
Wench [*needs*] no land, pretty, 351:56
Wept as I remembered, 73:26
when I was born, I, 385:43
with delight, 95:28
West begins, that's where, 61:30
bosom of the urgent, 33:17
Country, was in the, 80:15
down in the, 32:4
I dearly like the, 45:35
in her eyes, with the, 69:16
sailing away to the, 139:23
young man, go, 113:34
Westminster Abbey or victory, 182:13
Westminster for a wife, 439:41
Westward, stepping, 318:4
the course of empire, 28:13
Wet one's whistle, 431:50
wildness and, 124:18

Wether, give never the wolf, 372:16
Whale, sprat to catch, 431:38
very like a, 225:32
Whales, would talk like, 110:12
What has she, but, 392:14
he knew what's, 48:9
is she, it is not, 392:14
times ! what ways ! 67:18
why or which or, 147:21
will be, will be, 364:13
What-you-may-call-um, to, 59:36
Whaups are crying, 287:29
Wheamow, I am very, 384:25
Wheat, sorra take the, 185:21
two grains of, 253:31
Wheedling arts, taught the, 103:30
Wheel, beneath thy chariot, 124:13
broken at the cistern, 331:34
clicking of its, 87:18
had been in the midst of a wheel, 332:15
is come full circle, 242:12
is out of order, 56:5
put a spoke in, 430:8
put your shoulder to, 408:2
turn thy, 240:18
turns the giddy, 104:13
worst, 424:3
Wheelbarrow, drunk as, 357:79
Wheelbarrows tremble, twa, 45:30
Wheels, from the hindmost, 165:34
go wound, shee the, 114:11
of his chariots, 324:22
within wheels, 424:18
Wheeson week, Wednesday in, 234:12
Whelp his fill, give, 372:5
Whence and what art thou, 170:6
it cometh, tell, 337:41
Where, an Echo answers, 51:34
and when, fixed the, 117:28
did you come from, 154:4
I know not, 150:7
it is, as well as, 442:14
Wherefore, for every why he had a, 48:8
Whetstone, to deserve, 428:24
Whigs allow no force, 35:29
bathing, caught the, 85:31
Whim has seized me, strangest, 64:19
Whimper, not with a bang but, 93:33
whine, or sigh, 345:21
Whimpering to and fro, 140:15
Whip, in every honest hand, 262:5
of cricket's bone, 266:13

where there's a, 438:20
will have will, 439:71
woe win, though, 439:71
William replied, Father, 58:7
Willie died, since little, 16:7
there awa, wandering, 46:20
Willie Michie's banes, 45:31
Willie Winkie rins through the town,
162:14
Willin', Barkis is, 84:2
Willing horse, on the, 355:81
Willow tree, all under the, 62:14
wear the, 431:49
Willows are weak, 439:72
harps upon, 325:9
Wills, talk of, 243:39
when they live, have, 440:39
Willy-nilly blowing, 98:7
Wiltshire, born in, 440:33
Wimpled, whining, purblind, wayward
boy, 246:6
Win at first, 439:73
gold and wear gold, 439:75
heads I, 382:36
let them laugh that, 395:49
nothing, 403:59
yet wouldst wrongly, 247:34
Wince, galled horse, 431:64
let the galled jade, 225:26
Wind along the Waste, 98:7
and the rain, hey, ho, 272:21
as large a charter as, 216:14
away, to keep the, 227:36
bay'd the whisp'ring, 108:18
be still, if, 402:34
beat of the off-shore, 82:46
blow, thou winter, 217:18
bloweth where it listeth, 336:41
blows, a soft, 107:37
blows cold, how, 395:12
blows, dust which the, 241:44
blows it back again, 30:7
blows on you through a hole, if, 387:43
blows, which way, 412:45, 429:60
by the winnowing, 137:31
can blaw, a' the airts, 45:35
cold, 426:37
constancy in, 50:1
does move, the gentle, 30:6
ein sanfter, 107:37
fair stood the, 88:12
fill'd with a lusty, 62:1

God tempers, 285:27, 373:41
hear a voice in every, 111:32
hears Him in the, 195:30
hollow murmuring, 100:1
I go, like, 98:6
in that corner, sits, 258:19
is in the east, when, 437:48
is in the north, when, 437:49
is in the south, when, 437:50
is in the west, when, 437:51
it is an ill, 390:32
keeps not always in one quarter, 423:69
never so fast, blow, 363:52
of the western sea, 294:10
on the heath, 31:29
on the moors, blows, 287:29
out of one's sails, take, 431:36
pass by me as the idle, 230:14
passeth over it, 327:57
puff not against, 106:79
shorter in, 168:6
streaming to the, 168:17
streams . . . *against*, 51:25
swoln with, 166:20
that follows fast, 78:11
that grand old harper, 279:32
they have sown, 332:23
'twas but the, 50:12
upon the wings of, 326:20
warm western, 204:4
was a torrent of darkness, 184:11
was cold, 208:17
we shall not want, westerly, 437:46
wild West, 275:32
you need not fear, easterly, 437:45
Wind's soft song, in the, 147:26
Wind-flowers, pied, 276:10
Windmill, you cannot drive, 440:65
Window, love comes in at, 397:46
of the east, golden, 266:6
tirling at the, 162:14
where the sun came, 123:38
Window-blind, walloping, 60:6
Window-panes, upon the, 93:28
Windows, close, downy, 215:27
flare, crimson-blank, 142:7
I cleaned the, 104:28
not by eastern, 68:3
richly dight, storied, 165:25
that exclude the light, 113:22
Winds, and crack your cheeks, blow,
240:23

are breathing low, 275:35
are contrary, all, 427:57
blow, great, 374:3
come, come as the, 211:35
come to me, 319:33
courted by all the, 174:18
do blow, stormy, 55:23
do shake, rough, 263:32
fed it, young, 276:1
imprison'd in the viewless, 252:18
of heaven, beteem, 220:20
of March with beauty, take, 274:1
of the World, give answer, 140:15
rides on the posting, 219:34
shoreward blow, 18:17
speed with the light-foot, 114:4
Thy clarions, great, 65:34
visitation of the, 234:19
were love-sick with them, 214:2
Wine, and have the gout, drink, 367:73
and wenches, 439:75
ballast is old, 188:11
bin of, 286:20
bring me, 182:12
by the barrel, know, 440:68
doesn't get into the, 64:20
fetch to me a pint o', 45:41
Flask of, 97:30
gaming, women, and, 371:73
I'll not look for, 134:10
in old, 157:26
in the bottle, 423:71
in the stomach, in, 370:36
is a good familiar creature, 261:25
is a mocker, 329:45
is a turncoat, 439:76
[is] best, old, 404:6
is in, when, 436:1
is old men's milk, 439:77
it wasn't the, 82:8
Jug of, 97:31
look not thou upon, 329:52
makes all sorts of creatures, 440:1
mellow, like good, 190:9
needs no bush, good, 218:16, 373:62
of life is drawn, 249:28
sinks, when, 437:58
spill'd the, 188:4
sweetest, 412:59
that maketh glad, 327:58
the middle, of, 403:78
there is truth, in, 389:63

use a little, 339:60
vinegar of sweet, 412:74
when it is red, 329:52
wholesomest, old, 310:9
will taste of the cask, 423:71
Wine-cup glistens, taste not when, 211:39
Wing, flits by on leathern, 71:36
shadow of Thy, 310:24
Winged words, 123:24
Wings, eagle's, 419:62
girt with golden, 165:35
hear the beating of, 33:23
in vain, beating, 20:6
misfortunes come on, 399:72
O that I had, 327:41
on wide-waving, 79:26
shakes his dewy, 79:27
she clasps her, 152:10
spreads his light, 194:6
tail broader than, 398:1
that which hath, 330:27
under the shadow of thy, 326:19
you'll hear his, 414:6
Wink and choose, 440:2
and hold out mine iron, 235:46
at small faults, 440:3
I have not slept one, 219:35
nod is as good as, 353:61
Winketh with one eye, 382:7
Winner, good to leave off, 388:32
you'll see who's, 359:85
Winning, O the glory of, 160:16
worth the wear of, 27:30
Winter and rough weather, 216:4
comes, if, 275:34
eateth, 440:4
ending in July, 52:31
finds out, 440:5
frosty, but kindly, 215:42
green, 351:75
heel of limping, 266:8
in thy year, no, 40:22
in't, there was no, 214:19
is dreary, 123:37
is gone, 385:71
is past, lo, the, 330:40
it is a hard, 390:10
ling'ring chills, 108:4
never rots in the sky, 440:6
of our discontent, 244:10
ruler of th'inverted year, 76:1
sad tale's best for, 273:35

Spring, and Summer, 342:15
suddenly was changed to Spring, 276:9
weather, 440:9
when the dismal rain, 279:32
wild, it was the, 163:20
will have another flight, 385:71
Winter's day and a winter's way, 420:5
day, passeth, 380:30
pale, in, 273:40
rages, furious, 230:1
thunder, 440:7, 440:8
traces, on, 290:1
Winters cold, three, 265:21
Wisdom, all men's, 208:1
all, vain, 170:1
and goodness to the vile seem vile,
241:45
and Wit are little seen, 32:12
apply our hearts unto, 327:53
at one entrance quite shut out, 170:17
crieth without, 328:16
haste and, 374:30
is better than rubies, 328:22
is humble, 76:4
is justified, 324:17
learn, 394:21
less thy certainty, 285:21
like silence, no, 402:35
lingers, 293:36
of many, 208:1
shall die with you, 325:65
sometimes walks, 440:10
to let them alone, 392:23
with how little, 392:23
won with weariness, 42:6
Wise after the event, 391:42
all would be, 387:38
amazed, who can be, 249:29
and wonderful, things, 17:18
as a man of Gotham, 359:69
as serpents, 324:13
at all times, no man, 402:16
at fifty, 379:72
be not worldly, 200:23
before the deed, 419:64
before the hand, 354:6
better be happy than, 361:55
bread to the, 330:25
consider her ways, and be, 328:19
enough, he is, 376:28
erred not, if, 387:35
fair-spoken, and persuading, 239:25

few words to, 370:13
follies of the, 130:14
for himself, not, 376:23
good to be merry and, 391:49
he is, 376:29, 376:30
he is not, 376:23
healthy, wealthy and, 367:83
in his own conceit, 329:57
in the punishment, 379:67
in your own conceits, 338:14
least foolish is, 420:3
man better, makes, 431:70
man can answer, than a, 350:34
man changes his mind, 354:36
man does at the beginning, 435:68
man, he is not, 376:20
man on an errand, send, 410:15
man say, I heard a, 126:11
man, so well as, 402:10
man travels, 418:6
man, you may be, 442:3
man's son doth know, 271:36
men are caught with wiles, 440:11
men care not, 440:12
Men, Gotham's three, 188:11
men have their mouths in their hearts,
440:13
men learn by other men's mistakes,
440:14
men make proverbs, 440:15
men [marry] not at all, 383:71
men, plague of, 365:76
men play the fool, if, 387:43
men propose, 440:16
men to go over, for, 395:23
men's counters, 121:24
no man is born, 402:14
not rich, adversity makes, 355:53
one, nor ever did a, 204:8
so young, so, 245:19
some are, 411:76
strong, rich, or, 379:72
think with, 426:21
till to-morrow to be, 72:12
'tis folly to be, 111:34
to see't, man were, 100:4
to talk, leave the, 98:4
type of the, 320:11
we were very, very, 69:16
with speed, be, 322:7
word is enough to, 433:61
ye yourselves are, 339:41

Wisely but too well, not, 262:16
Wiser and better, grow, 199:28
 in their generation, 336:27
 man, sadder and a, 70:3
 men become, 307:27
 than a daw, no, 237:27
 than other people, be, 64:5
Wisest, brightest, meanest, 196:8
 fool in Christendom, 119:28
 man can answer, more than, 72:5
 men, not, 418:33
 to entrap the, 254:26
 virtuousest, discreetest, best, 173:29
Wish is father to the thought, 423:73
 was father to that thought, 234:31
Wishers and wolders, 440:17
Wishes, all made of, 218:10
 all their country's, 71:33
 can never fill a sack, 440:18
 exact to my, 345:19
 good meanings and, 383:48
 soon as granted, fly, 209:23
 were horses, if, 387:44
Wishing me like to one, 264:1
Wision's limited, my, 82:19
Wist, beware of Had I, 362:37
Wit a man has, less, 420:4
 a man, in, 199:19
 all thy Piety nor, 98:13
 among lords, only a, 132:8
 at will, he has, 375:71
 baiting-place of, 278:20
 brevity is the soul of, 222:27
 brightens, how·the, 193:18
 can fly, as metaphysic, 48:9
 degenerating into clenches, comic, 92:2
 devise, 246:3
 doth show her, 342:15
 highest reaches of, 156:12
 his weapon [was], 124:12
 in a jest, put his whole, 27:19
 in a poor man's breast, 440:44
 is best, bought, 363:58
 is in his fingers, 418:20
 is in other men, cause that, 234:1
 is nature, true, 192:9
 is out, when ale is in, 436:1
 is out, when the age is in, 258:32
 is worse, want of, 434:1
 mickle head, little, 399:66
 miracle instead of, 322:11
 more hair than, 400:9

 nor words, nor worth, 230:6
 of one, the, 208:1
 once bought, 440:19
 one man's, 208:1
 or arms, prize of, 164:7
 pleasant smooth, 20:14
 rust, makes, 385:62
 shoots his, 218:15
 skirmish of, 258:8
 staircase, 85:27
 that can creep, 198:7
 that doth harm to my, 271:27
 that's bought, 356:58
 the more, 420:37
 to boast his, 89:24
 to pick a lock, it is, 392:23
 too proud for a, 109:34
 was scant, born when, 442:27
 waver, wealth makes, 434:33
 whither wander you, 215:30
 will come, fancy, 199:23
 will shrine through, 90:14
 with dunces, a, 194:20
Wit's end, at their, 327:60
 in the wane, 437:42
Witch at fourscore, 354:39
 hath power to charm, nor, 220:12
 the world, 233:36
Witchcraft I have used, 260:6
Withered, fairest rose is, 417:58
Withers are unwrung, our, 225:26
Within, he never went, 74:5
 it hardens a', 45:25
 would fain go out, they that are, 79:28
Witness everywhere, there is, 424:26
Wits and Templars, 198:2
 are sure to madness near allied, great,
  89:25
 are wool-gathering, 383:65
 rash bavin, 233:31
Witty in myself, not only, 234:1
 weak men had need be, 434:29
Wive and thrive, hard to, 391:61
 thrive and then, 370:27
Wives at one time, married, 176:2
 bachelors', 360:2
 daidling, 360:4
 in one house, two, 432:24
 long-tongued, 395:29
 must be had, 440:24
 scold not, whose, 384:23
 sky changes when they are, 218:4

that deliberates, 15:13
that seduces, 'tis, 103:30
the Public is an old, 57:36
to manage a fool, needs a very clever, 143:26
to win, all your wish is, 298:28
to you, still be a, 187:24
was never yet fair, 241:26
wasteful, 188:4
weak and feeble, 93:35
weep, pity to see, 392:2
were little as she is good, if, 385:66
what is, 74:7
what mighty ills have not been done by, 186:3
which is without discretion, 328:26
whistling, 354:30
who can find a virtuous, 330:3
who is not dignified, 65:29
who tells one her real age, never trust, 314:11
will be the last thing civilised by Man, 160:26
will or won't, 121:20
with a brawling, 328:48
with a pretty, 133:40
with fair opportunities, 298:15
would be more charming, 29:17
yet think him an angel, 298:20
Woman's a whore, the, 133:30
at best a contradiction, 197:28
preaching, 132:21
tender care, can a, 76:18
whole existence, 52:17
work is never done, 355:45
Womanhood and childhood fleet, 150:2
heroic, 150:19
Womb, out of my mother's, 325:60
Women and bees cannot be turned, 412:61
and dogs, 440:27
and elephants, 187:21
and hens, 440:28
and music, 440:29
and their wills, 440:30
and wine, 440:31
and wine, gaming, 371:73
and wine undo men, 406:30
angels in the street, 440:35
apes in bed, 440:35
are always in extremes, 440:32
are angels, wooing, 270:14
are born in Wiltshire, 440:33

are necessary evils, 440:34
are saints in church, 440:35
bear, punishment that, 218:17
bevy of fair, 173:46
come out to cut up what remains, 141:41
could be fair, if, 186:12
dally not with, 365:79
devils in the kitchen, 440:38
discreet, 366:37
experience of, 87:25
false, framed to make, 260:13
from 'er, learned about, 141:47
gad, when, 419:59
[have become] men, my, 320:30
have I liked several, 269:35
have no history, happiest, 93:24
[have] only two [faults], 339:58
humours and flatters, 64:8
in state affairs, 440:36
laugh when they can, 440:37
look in their glass, 420:38
man of sense only trifles with, 64:8
Monstrous Regiment of, 143:34
more like each other, 64:9
must have the last word, 440:38
must have their wills, 440:39
must weep, 139:24
narrow the views of, 116:4
paradise of, 368:10
pass the time, how, 119:29
priests, and poultry, 440:40
to keep counsel, hard it is for, 229:26
weep when they will, 440:37
worst and best, as Heaven and Hell, 297:27
Woman's jars breed men's wars, 440:41
rougher, simpler, more upright judgment, 72:15
thoughts change oft, 440:9
weapons, water-drops, 240:22
Won are done, things, 270:14
glory of the winning were she, 160:16
her, until they, 297:35
not unsought be, 173:27
or lost, not that you, 204:2
therefore may be, 270:9
therefore to be, 237:28
woman in this humour, 245:15
Wonder and a wild desire, 40:9
at the least, one, 156:12
grew, still the, 109:27
is the daughter of ignorance, 440:42

so many, 295:3
Worm dieth not, where, 336:3
  early bird catches, 416:36
  I want to be a, 106:30
  I wish you joy o' the, 215:23
  i' the bud, like a, 272:4
  round little, 266:13
  sets foot upon a, 76:6
  that hath eat of a king, fish with, 226:14
  the canker, and the grief, 53:36
  will turn, 368:15
Worms, convocation of politic, 226:13
  forget, nor, 82:45
  have eaten them, 218:3
  of Nile, outvenoms, 219:34
  tasted two whole, 284:6
Worry, don't let me, 345:21
Worse appear the better reason, make,
    169:32
  for wearing, 369:53
  gives greater feeling to, 243:27
  I follow the, 186:7
  it might have been, 403:56
  one penny the, 24:5
  seven years, 404:71
  things happen at sea, 440:49
  when it comes late, 130:1
Worship is your furnaces, 32:1
  stated calls to, 132:1
  wealth makes, 434:34
Worst, good to fear, 391:52
  is better, his, 118:1
  is better than none, 134:5
  is not, the, 241:42
  is yet to come, the, 130:5
  of us, good in the, 121:27
  prepare for, 384:7
  provide for, 406:75
  so long as we can say, This is the, 241:42
  to come by, 415:53
  to himself, 350:14
  when things are at, 437:53
  will mend, at the, 426:11
Worth, conscience of her, 173:27
  doing badly, it is, 65:30
  doing well, 435:61
  doing, what is, 435:61
  doing, thing is, 65:30
  doth spend, more than he is, 439:34
  going to see, 133:46
  how much is he, 303:31
  know what you're, 406:17

makes the man, 196:4
  of a thing is best known, 424:4
  of a thing is what it will bring, 424:5
  prize not to the, 258:35
  slow rises, 130:9
Worthie to be fyled, 283:30
Worthily given, 363:54
Worthy to unloose, I am not, 336:39
  womman al hir lyve, 63:33
Wound did ever heal but by degrees, what,
    261:26
  is cured, ill, 356:39
  is soon healed, green, 351:76
  itself, did help to, 240:6
  take away the grief of, 233:42
  that never felt a, 267:19
  tongue in every, 230:7
  willing to, 198:2
Wounded and left, you're, 141:41
  in the house of my friends, 332:29
  to die, 55:30
Wounds, bind up the nation's, 148:11
  invisible, know the, 217:34
  look, sir, my, 218:21
  of a friend, 329:60
  wept o'er his, 108:20
Wrang, may gang a kennin, 44:21
Wrangle for religion, 72:3
Wranglers never want words, 440:50
Wrapt, all meanly, 163:20
Wrath, day of, 61:20, 209:26
  nursing her, 46:5
  sing, goddess, the, 123:21
  strong man in his, 36:2
  sun go down upon, 339:47
  to come, flee from, 332:32
  turneth away, 328:32
Wreck, with sunken, 235:42
Wrecks of matter, 16:1
  thousand fearful, 245:18
Wren goes to't, the, 242:2
  robin redbreast and, 310:10
Wrens, as sore fight, 358:42
Wretch, excellent, 261:27
  my wife, poor, 189:22
  needy, hollow-eyed, sharp-looking,
    218:19
Wretched he forsakes, 320:39
  I learn to aid, 305:31
  it is hard to be, 391:57
  to relieve the, 108:21
Wretchedness and want, convicted of,

281:27
Wretches, poor naked, 241:30
Wrinkle, time writes no, 51:30
Wrist, with gyves upon his, 123:40
Writ at first for filling, 288:10
  old odd ends stolen out of holy, 245:16
  over that same dore, 283:29
  proofs of holy, 261:32
Write and read comes by nature, to, 258:25
  any time, a man may, 132:6
  converse, and live with ease, 198:2
  down the advice, 440:51
  I never dare to, 122:12
  less, speak little, 426:17
  look in thy heart and, 278:18
  me as one, 127:38
  me down an ass, to, 258:40
  of me, 129:23
  one, though you cannot, 132:16
  so even, contrive to, 21:24
  well hereafter, hope to, 174:25
  with a goose-pen, 272:10
  with ease, 278:12
Writer, pen of a ready, 327:36
Writes, Moving Finger, 98:13
Writing, art of, 85:44
  itch for, 135:31
  [maketh] an exact man, 22:17
  true ease in, 192:16
Written down, never, 411:50
  to after times, leave something so, 170:5
  what I have, 337:36
Wrong, always in the, 89:34, 397:37, 414:33
  as dead as if he'd been, 345:20

brings on another, 422:34
  extreme, 369:62
  first blow makes, 412:67
  fler than no fler, better hang, 84:14
  for telling a man he was, 68:8
  he can't be, 196:1
  he done her, 344:2
  hopes, he that hath, 379:52
  how easily things go, 154:14
  in the teeth of a, 159:27
  king can do no, 29:26, 419:66
  ne'er pardon who have done, 91:38
  never comes right, 440:52
  no more, suffer, 154:1
  nothing goes, 106:8
  once, do, 367:60
  one, that is a, 133:23
  sow by the ear, have, 429:45
  submitting to one, 422:34
  that needs resistance, 23:33
  the oppressor's, 224:4
  to do a great right, do a little, 255:34
  to none, do, 213:24
  we do it, 220:9
Wrongs don't make a right, two, 433:42
  redressing human, 297:34
Wrote except for money, 133:37
  like an angel, 103:18
Wroth, soonest, 378:9
  with one we love, be, 70:6
Wrought, so distinctly, 86:12
  well made, well, 278:25
Wyn, wel dronken hadde the, 63:35
Wynken, Blynken, and Nod, 96:15

Y

Yarn, all I ask is a merry, 159:22
  of a mingled, 213:31
Yawp, I sound my barbaric, 312:15
Yes-forsooth knave, 234:2
Year, all in one, 432:19
  all the months in, 356:10
  at the gate of the, 117:26
  before the mellowing, 166:8

does not give you, 286:3
  doth betide a happy, 356:10
  [happy], for, 394:39
  [harvest], come every, 374:29
  in the ground, stand one, 390:15
  is going, let him go, 296:4
  of joy, one, 404:72
  old, book that is not, 94:19

rich, 354:14
ruler of th'inverted, 76:1
say no ill of, 409:60
snow, 354:14
sweet o' the, 273:40
three and twentieth, 163:30
wake year to sorrow, 276:12
wive and thrive in, 391:61
Year's at the spring, 37:19
Years a mortal man may live, how many,
 238:6
after long, 49:37
are, where all past, 86:7
down the arches of, 298:37
far back into other, 27:24
for the first seven, 372:15
glide away, 24:11
glide past, fleeting, 125:38
happens not in seven, 389:71
hence, same a hundred, 392:31
in thy sight, thousand, 327:50
into the vale of, 261:30
it ran a hundred, 122:15
keep a thing seven, 393:45
known him seven, 442:8
know more than books, 440:53
none would live past, 91:39
once in ten, 404:25
presage of his future, 145:25
return, golden, 277:25
shall roll, few more, 31:26
that are past, restore, 306:8
that bring the philosophic mind, 320:3
the days of our, 326:52
the fewer his, 417:63
the more thy, 420:36
thrice a thousand, 16:10
through the glorious, 28:10
to sever for, 49:36
we spend our, 327:51
were gone, knightly, 119:25
Yesterday's Sev'n Thousand, 98:3
Yeas, russet, 246:14
Yeeres, wait manie, 283:31
Yellow like ripe corn, 206:13
Yeoman's service, did me, 227:45
Yeomanry, head of, 361:61
'Yes' I answered you, 36:6
Yesterday and to-day, same, 340:1
call back, 243:38
not born, 385:42
the Rose of, 97:29

was it, 18:18
when it is past, 327:50
will not be called again, 440:55
Yesterday's pupil, To-day, 431:53
Yesterdays, all our, 251:37
man of cheerful, 320:7
Yestreen, late, 342:5
Yew, never a spray of, 19:24
stuck all with, 272:3
Yield, never to submit or, 168:6
to find and not to, 293:28
Yielding, valour is near, 433:55
Yo-ho-ho, and a bottle of rum, 286:9
Yoke, who beat bear his mild, 167:31
Yokel, waits for the river, 125:37
Yonder, 'tis not here, still, 57:39
Yonghy-Bonghy-Bò, lived, 147:18
Yorick, alas, poor, 227:33
York for a tit, 406:5
You, all too precious, 264:14
and me, between, 362:32
had been to her, told me, 58:14
Young and foolish, I was, 320:35
and so fair, 124:8
and so untender, so, 240:8
and tender, 404:4
blood must have its course, 139:28
both were, 52:6
I have been, 326:30
if he be caught, 133:28
lie upon roses when, 387:58
loved when all was, 139:29
man believes he shall ever die, no, 118:3
man, crime of being, 62:8
man expresses himself, 104:37
man, most intense, 104:31
man, never enriched, 406:23
man, ordinary, 160:8
man, out-of-the-way, 104:41
man should not marry yet, 355:50
man, where's the lost, 126:21
man who has brains enough, 285:34
man who said Damn, 116:12
man's warling, 361:52
men glittering and sparkling angels,
 302:7
men may die, 442:35
men shall see visions, 332:25
men think old men fools, 442:36
men's vision, 89:32
my lord, and true, so, 240:8
myself when, 98:5

Z